Alan Simpson's Windows® XP Bible

Second Edition

Alan Simpson's Windows® XP Bible

Second Edition

Alan Simpson

WILEY

Wiley Publishing, Inc.

Alan Simpson's Windows® XP Bible, Second Edition

Published by
Wiley Publishing, Inc.
10475 Crosspoint Boulevard
Indianapolis, IN 46256
www.wiley.com

Published simultaneously in Canada

ISBN: 0-7645-7815-4

Manufactured in the United States of America

10 9 8 7 6 5 4 3 2 1

2B/QT/QS/QV/IN

For general information on our other products and services or to obtain technical support, please contact our Customer Care Department within the U.S. at (800) 762-2974, outside the U.S. at (317) 572-3993 or fax (317) 572-4002.

Wiley also publishes its books in a variety of electronic formats. Some content that appears in print may not be available in electronic books.

Library of Congress Cataloging-in-Publication Data

Simpson, Alan, 1953-
  [Windows XP bible]
Alan Simpson's Windows XP bible / Alan Simpson.– 2nd ed.
    p. cm.
  Includes index.
  ISBN 0-7645-7815-4 (pbk.)
  1. Microsoft Windows (Computer file) 2. Operating systems (Computers) I. Title: Windows XP bible. II. Title.
  QA76.76.O63S559347 2005
  005.4'46–dc22   2004027091

About the Author

Alan Simpson is an award-wining computer book author with some 90 published books to his credit. His books are published in many languages throughout the world and have sold millions of copies. Alan is best known for his light, conversational writing style and clear jargon-free approach to dealing with technical topics. Prior to writing books full time, Alan taught introductory and advanced computer programming courses at San Diego State University and University of California, San Diego Extension. He also worked as a freelance programmer and computer consultant. He maintains the www.coolnerds.com Web site (when time permits) and can be reached via that Web site.

Credits

Acquisitions Editor
Katie Mohr

Project Editor
Pamela Hanley

Technical Editor
Todd Meister

Copy Editor
Foxxe Editorial Services

Editorial Manager
Mary Beth Wakefield

**Vice President & Executive
Group Publisher**
Richard Swadley

**Vice President and Executive
Publisher**
Joseph B. Wikert

Executive Editorial Director
Mary Bednarek

Project Coordinator
April Farling

Graphics and Production Specialists
Beth Brooks
Andrea Dahl
Kelly Emkow
Lauren Goddard
Heather Pope
Ron Terry

Quality Control Technicians
Jessica Kramer
Susan Moritz
Carl William Pierce

Proofreading and Indexing
TECHBOOKS Production Services

To Susan, Ashley, and Alec, as always.

Acknowledgments

While I take full responsibility for the written words and pictures (since that part of the job was my responsibility), there's a lot more to creating a book than typing the words and making the pictures. And for all the those other countless tasks, I hereby sincerely thank the following persons: Katie Mohr, acquisitions editor; Mary Beth Wakefield, managing editor; Kelly D. Henthorne, developmental editor; and Pamela Hanley, production editor.

Many thanks to Matt Wagner, Margot Maley, Maureen Maloney, and everybody else at Waterside Productions (my literary agency) for making everything work out.

And of course, all my love and thanks to Susan, Ashley, and Alec for tolerating weeks of neglect while Daddy, once again pounded furiously at the keyboard for weeks on end.

Contents at a Glance

Contents

Part VII: Using and Creating Digital Media 677

Part XI: Home and Small-Business Networking   1011

Introduction

Welcome to *Alan Simpson's Windows XP Bible,* Second Edition, the book with the verbose title written for Windows XP with Service Pack 2, Windows Media Player 10, and Windows Movie Maker 2.1.

Who This Book Is For

This book is definitely not for absolute beginners. Unlike the first edition of this book, which had a Beginner/Intermediate reader level, this edition has an Intermediate/Advanced reader level. That's not to say the book is for professional programmers or network administrators. I'm just assuming you already have some Windows experience, although not necessarily with Windows XP. Prior Windows 95, 98, ME, or 2000 experience is fine. You just need to be familiar with terms and concepts that haven't really changed in the last 15 or 20 years. For example:

+ You know the difference between a live mouse and the one you use to control your computer.

+ When you see a reference to something that's "on the screen" or "on the desktop," you know where to look.

+ You can point, click, double-click, and drag without specific how-to instructions.

+ You can press Ctrl+Esc or Ctrl+Alt+Del all by yourself.

+ You know what an icon looks like.

+ You can tell the difference between a program, a folder, and a document.

+ You have an Internet account and know your own e-mail address.

+ When you see a URL like www.microsoft.com, you know what it is and how to get there.

+ You can click on hyperlinks in Web pages.

+ You realize that neither clicking harder, or yelling at, a disabled (dimmed) option will make the option "wake up."

+ You've accepted the fact that your PC can't read your mind.

If you're thinking "Oh brother, who *doesn't* know that?", you've never read some of the e-mails I get.

Three editions

This is actually my third Windows XP book. The original *Alan Simpson's Windows XP Bible* that was written in 2001 when Windows XP was first released is being retired. So much has changed in the last three years, that book is already starting to read like a dinosaur.

The second book I wrote was *Alan Simpson's Windows XP Desktop Bible*, whose title is confusingly very similar to this book's title. (We authors don't always get to make up our own titles.) The Desktop Bible is the smaller, gentler version of this book with a reader level of Beginning/ Intermediate. As I write this book, that one hasn't been revised for SP2 yet. Although I imagine that revision will be next on my list of projects.

This book is much more of a "Let'er rip" book without the gentle hand-holding of the beginning book. Here, I lay it on the line and tell all the facts without watering things down. Still, it's not a book for professionals only, or even just Windows XP Professionals. This book covers the real core Windows stuff that everyone uses. It's also the same core Windows stuff that's identical in both the Home Edition and Professional Edition. So as far as this book is concerned, it doesn't matter whether you're using the Home Edition or Professional Edition, everything works as stated either way.

Who I am and what I used

I'm a firm believer in the expression "Write what you know," so naturally I actually did everything that I wrote about in this book. I used several different computers in the process. But I also figured that since I'm writing this book in 2004, I should use 2004 hardware. (One of the few fringe benefits to being an author of technology titles is that I can always justify buying cool new gadgets.) Before I got started I went out and bought the following components to build a new PC:

+ **Processor:** Intel Pentium IV, 3.0GHz with 800MHz Front Side Bus and Hyper-Threading

+ **Memory:** 1GB Dual-channel DDR at 400Mhz

+ **Hard disk:** 120GB SATA 150

+ **CD/DVD:** Sony DRU150A with write capabilities for CD-R, CD-RW, DVD-R, DVD-RW, DVD+R, and DVD+RW

+ **Display:** Matrox Millenium G400 DualHead

+ **Motherboard:** Biostar P4TCA Pro with the following features:

  • 800MHz Front Side Bus

  • Intel 875P Chipset (North Bridge)

  • Intel PAT (Performance Acceleration Technology)

  • Hyper-Threading Support

  • Two 128-bit Dual Channel DDR DIMM slots

  • USB 2.0

  • IEEE 1394

  • One AGP 8X, 1 CNR, 1 Wireless LAN, and 5 PCI slots

  • On-board SATA, Raid, and IDE ATA-100 slots

  • Gigabit Ethernet LAN Support

  • AC'97 sound board with SP/DIF connector.

After putting all the pieces together, I went to my local Comput-O-Rama and bought an off-the-shelf copy of Windows XP Professional. I have to confess that I had a twinge of anxiety when I realized I was about to install an operating system that was released before most of the hardware I had assembled was even invented. I was pleasantly surprised when the whole process went smooth as glass, and the computer was on the network, and online, by the time the installation finished.

I did have to contend with some random reboots when I first got the machine going. But by the time I got caught up on all my automatic updates and updated drivers from various hardware manufacturers, the random reboots were gone. Needless to say, the machine is a total screamer.

While writing the book I, of course, had to add some more stuff to actually experience what I was writing about. So I added the following:

+ A Western Digital 200GB SATA hard drive for additional storage

+ A Chaintec GEForce FX2500 PCI card to add a third monitor to my two-monitor system

+ A Sound Blaster Live! sound card to replace the onboard AC97 sound device

+ A NetGear Gigabit switch to support Gigabit Ethernet networking

+ A Microsoft 802.11g Network Access Point for wireless network and PC Card Wireless adapter to add a notebook to my existing LAN, which was initially a Linksys 80211b Wireless LAN

+ Some Bluetooth USB adapters to create a Bluetooth Personal Area Network (PAN)

Along the way I upgraded all six computers that I already had in my LAN to Service Pack 2, just to keep an eye out for any problems that might arise and warrant some discussion or troubleshooting advice. I used all six PCs to do various things in various ways. The book, as a whole, explains it all. But, as I think back through all I experienced along the way, some things in particular still stand out in my mind.

I wrote the better part of Chapter 9 just by talking, not by typing, using the speech recognition features of Microsoft Word and Windows XP. I laid in bed with some headphones on and listened while my notebook computer read aloud an e-book I had downloaded from the Web.

I ripped CDs, bought music online, burned my own audio CDs and backup CDs. I synched all kinds of songs to an MP3 player using both the manual method and the auto-sync method found in Media Player 10.

I copied movies from a digital video camera and IEEE 1394. I captured non-digital video tape using an ATI All-in Wonder graphics card and a Dazzle 150 USB video bridge with a USB 2.0 connection. I burned some movies to VCD, DVD, and High-Mat disks.

I replaced my Ethernet 10/100 network with a new Gigbabit LAN. I set up an 802.11b and an 802.11g wireless network. I even created a Bluetooth Personal Area Network between a notebook computer and another computer. I shared an Internet connection, printers, and moved and copied files between the computers within, and between, every type of LAN (including an existing PhoneLine network).

I even intentionally went online with my firewall down and anti-virus software disabled. I even clicked on some dumb pop-up ads and downloaded some cute freebies, which normally I wouldn't touch with the proverbial 10-foot pole. I did that to see what SP2 would block on its own, what kinds of warning I would get, and how much of a headache it would be to get rid of all the garbage I inherited.

One thing I learned from my defenseless browsing was that these days, if you want to turn your PC into a virtual epidemic of every type of slimeware known, you don't have to go online long with your defenses down. Pity the poor souls who think that dial-up accounts are somehow "safer" than always-on accounts. And thank goodness Microsoft decided to help batten down the security hatches in Service Pack 2.

How to Use This Book

This book is divided into eleven parts, each of which contains several chapters on a specific topic. There's no need to read the book cover-to-cover. If you have Windows XP experience already, you should be able to jump to any part, or any chapter, at your convenience. But if you're new to XP, you'll probably want to spend some time in Parts I and II to get a feel for the new interface.

Each part is followed by a troubleshooting chapter that focuses on troubleshooting techniques for tools and technologies covered within that part. Since I don't have an infinite number of pages to work with here, I've relied fairly heavily on links to appropriate Web pages in some of these troubleshooting chapters. Especially for the rare and obscure types of problems few people will probably ever face.

The Table of Contents lists all the chapters and such, so I won't repeat all of that here. Instead, I'll focus only on the parts.

Part I: Getting Started: This part provides a quick overview of what's new in Service Pack 2, as opposed to earlier versions of Windows XP. It might be of limited value to readers who are just now making the transition to XP from some earlier version of Windows. Chapters 2–4 are a must-read for people who don't have already have any experience with Windows XP.

Part II: Customizing Windows XP: This part covers all the things you can do to tweak XP to better suit your own work habits, needs, and hardware. That includes customizing the desktop, taskbar, and Start menu, setting up multiple user accounts, taking advantage of built-in accessibility features for motor and sensory impairments, and setting up multiple monitors.

Part III: Managing Files and Folders: Everything you need to know about getting organized and staying organized, so you can find what you want, when you want it. In this part, you'll learn to create folders, move and copy files, burn files to CDs, and use modern USB mass storage devices like thumb drives and memory cards. The all-important task of creating shortcuts to frequently-used resources, and backing up data and settings, are also covered in Part III.

Part IV: Printing and Faxing: Here we look at installing and using printers and faxes, printing and faxing documents, managing print jobs, and troubleshooting printing and faxing.

Part V: Securing Your System: Needless to say, this is an important part of the book that delves deeply into the new security features of Service Pack 2 and also goes well beyond that built-in security.

Part VI: Power Using the Internet: As the name implies, this is the place to go for all sorts of Internet services including browsing with Internet Explorer, doing e-mail and newsgroups with Outlook Express, instant messaging and transferring files with MSN Messenger, and uploading/downloading files with FTP.

Part VII: Using and Creating Digital Media: A nice break from some of the more technical stuff, this chapter is all about using your PC creatively. Pictures, photos, video, movies, and DVD are all covered here. Creating your own audio CDs, making your own movies and DVDs, and getting data from analog media like vinyl LPs, VHS, and Video 8 tape are important topics. Everything is written around the new Windows Media Player 10 and Windows Movie Maker 2.1 versions.

Part VIII: Installing and Removing Programs: Hot topics here include downloading programs, installing programs from CDs and floppies, getting older programs to run, controlling access to programs, getting rid of unwanted programs, and dealing with problem programs and processes.

Part IX: Installing, Using, and Troubleshooting Hardware: There was a time where we used to say "someday you'll only have to buy the hardware, and the software will all be free." But from the looks of things, it may be the other way around. Hardware just keeps getting smaller, better, faster, cheaper, and, well, just plain cooler. This part covers everything you need to know about adding and removing hardware, keeping your hardware drivers up to date, and troubleshooting problem hardware.

Part X: Performance and Maintenance Issues: We all want our PCs to run at tip-top speed so we can spend more time *doing* and less time *waiting*. Although the speed of your hardware largely dictates the speed of everything, there are plenty of things you can do to take full advantage of your hardware's capabilities and keep things running at maximum speeds. Part X explains how all that works.

Part XI: Home and Small Business Networking: Whether you have two PCs or 20, eventually you'll want them to let them share a single Internet account and printer, or perhaps several printers. And if you've been wasting time transferring files via floppies, CDs, or some other removable disk, you'll want to reduce all that to a simple drag-and-drop operation. This part explains it all and helps you set up a wired network, a wireless network, or even a mixed-mode network that uses both wired and wireless networking.

Contact Me

It's just not possible to cover everything there is to know about a program the size of Windows XP in a single book. Not even a big fat book like this one. The best we authors can do is define our audience (experienced users and power users in this case), choose our breadth (all the core features of both Windows XP Home and Professional Editions in this book), take a look at our allotted page count, and do the best we can with what we have to work with.

The first thing I'll do when I've finished writing this book is add a Windows XP SP2 section to my personal Web site at www.coolnerds.com. Feel free to stop by any time and look for the Windows XP link on the home page. If you need to get in touch with me, please do so via the Web site. Like most people, I get inundated with far too much junk mail and rarely even look to see what my spam filter dumped. If you contact me from the Web site, I'll be sure to get your message.

Thanks so much for buying (borrowing or stealing) this book. I hope it serves you well.

Getting Started

If you've been using Windows XP for a long time now, then getting situated is largely a matter of finding out what's new in Service Pack 2 (SP2). And Chapter 1 is the place for you. Chapter 1 quickly describes all the new stuff in SP2 and tells you where to look in the rest of the book to get up to speed on a new feature or program.

If you've just recently made the transition from Windows 98, ME, 2000, or some other earlier Windows version, Chapter 1 won't give you the big picture on everything that's new in Windows XP, but Chapters 2 through 4 will.

Chapter 5 will help experienced and new Windows XP users alike troubleshoot some common desktop and interface problems.

By the way, if you haven't quite gotten around to installing Windows XP, Appendix A will help you upgrade your existing Windows version to XP. Or, if you want to start off fresh, see Appendix B for doing a clean install of Windows XP.

What's New in Windows XP SP2?

Every year or so Microsoft releases a service pack (abbreviated SP) for Windows, and for some of their other major software products. A service pack includes all the improvements, hotfixes, security patches, and bug fixes released individually through individual Windows Updates prior to the release of the service pack.

Usually, the service pack includes some additional goodies of its own. This time, with the release the Service Pack 2, there are lots of extra goodies. This chapter is a quick overview of the most dramatic changes to Windows XP that you'll find in Service Pack 2. What's new in this chapter is only in relation to pre–Service Pack 2 Windows XP. If you're just now making the transition from Windows 98, ME, or 2000, just about everything will be new.

The New Security

If I had to summarize what's new in SP2 in two words, those words would be *Internet security*. Like the rest of us, I think Microsoft has had it with all the worms, viruses, adware, spyware, and every other type of *malware* (bad software). Not to mention the human slimedogs who are wasting all of our time and energy with this garbage for their own amusement or financial gain. So, Microsoft wisely decided to focus some major resources on that problem this time around and get everything rolled up into a single service pack that's easy to download and install.

It's difficult to miss the change. The once barely noticeable Internet Connection Firewall has been replaced by a much-improved Windows Firewall. The equally obscure Automatic Updates feature is now nearly impossible to miss. And even though Microsoft is still out of the antivirus software market, they don't make it easy for you to ignore the importance of protecting your computer against such threats.

The new firewall, automatic updates, and antivirus alerts and options have been brought together into a single Security Center window. The Security Center makes itself known automatically if there are any weaknesses in your PC's Internet defenses, through notification messages and a notification icon, as in the example shown in Figure 1-1.

Figure 1-1: New Security Center notification
and notification area icon

If there are no holes in your PC's defense, the Security Center stays out of your way. But you
can easily get to it through Control Panel, or by clicking the Start button and choosing All
Programs ⇨ Accessories ⇨ System Tools ⇨ Security Center. The Security Center, shown in
Figure 1-2, makes Internet security a much easier task, even for the helpless newbies and
casual users who are the most victimized group of users.

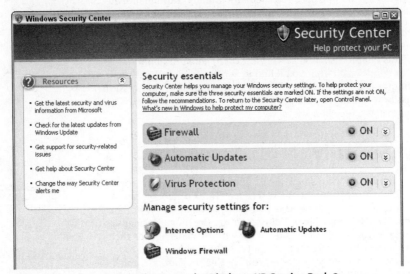

Figure 1-2: The new Security Center in Windows XP Service Pack 2

As you can see, the Security Center is divided into three main panes:

✦ **Resources:** Provides simple links explaining why security is important and tools for
battening down the security hatches on your own PC

✦ **Security essentials:** Three simple buttons for turning on (or off) your firewall, automatic updates, and virus protection

✦ **Manage security settings for:** Icons that provide easy access to your Internet Options,
Automatic Updates settings, and the new Windows Firewall

Part V of this book covers all the details on the new features of Service Pack 2. But goes
beyond the Security Center to cover issues such as pop-up ads, adware, spyware, and more.
If you already know your way around the Windows desktop, feel free to just go straight to that
section at any time.

Virus protection la DEP

The hardware folks have also had their fill of hacker invasions. The next-generation 64-bit processors have built-in antivirus security in the form of DEP (Data Execution Prevention), which makes it much tougher for rogue software to sneak bad code into executable memory—a favorite technique used by viruses and worms to gain unauthorized access to your PC.

Windows XP SP2 takes advantage of the new DEP capabilities of 64-bit processors. But you don't have to wait for those processors to reach mainstream computing. Service Pack 2 will let you use software-enforced DEP, right now on your existing PC. For details see "Using Data Execution Prevention (DEP)" in Chapter 28.

Outlook Express virus protection

Outlook Express now offers an option to leave pictures and other external HTML content on the e-mail server when you download your e-mail. This saves you time, because you don't have to wait for all the picture content in junk e-mail messages to download. It also makes your computer more secure by keeping bad code in attachments and malformed JPEGs off your computer.

When you do want to see a picture in an e-mail, you just click its placeholder in the e-mail message and that one picture downloads on the spot. For more information, see "Minimizing Virus Threats with Outlook Express" in Chapter 28.

Built-in pop-up blocker

Internet Explorer in Service Pack 2 comes with its own built-in pop-up blocker that's simple to configure and easy to use (see Figure 1-3). You can crank the up the blocker to stop virtually all site pop-ups, and then selectively choose the sites in which you need pop-ups for non-advertising purposes on a site-by-site basis. See "Blocking Pop-Ups with Internet Explorer" in Chapter 29 for the goods on the new pop-up blocker.

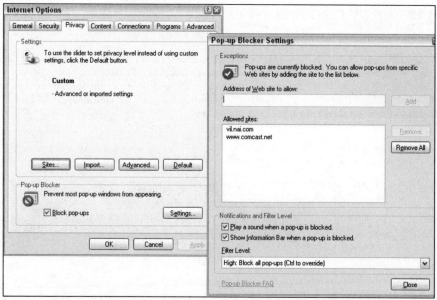

Figure 1-3: Internet Explorer's built-in pop-up blocker is easily configured in dialog boxes.

Stay in control with the Information bar

Not only does the new pop-up blocker prevent pop-up ads, but it also keeps you abreast of all content that wants to download. You don't have to worry about people sneaking unwanted programs or ActiveX controls into your computer and browser, because the Information bar (see Figure 1-4) will keep you informed and give you a choice. As discussed in Chapter 29, once you get the hang of it, you can streamline things by removing the message box and even the Information bar, without compromising your computer's security.

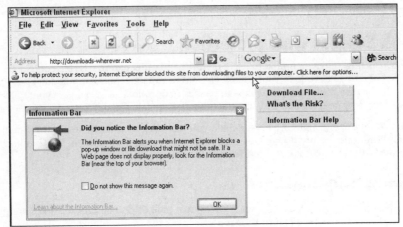

Figure 1-4: The pop-up blocker keeps an eye on downloads, too.

Regain control of your Web browser

Have you ever found your default home page suddenly changed without your knowing it? Or mistyped a URL and ended up at some new, previously unknown search site? Are you plagued by pop-ups that seem to come out of nowhere?

The new Manage Add-ons tool in Internet Explorer, shown in Figure 1-5, makes it easy to disable the intrusions into your Web browser that are hijacking its ability to work the way you want. "Disable Mysterious Add-ons" in Chapter 30 shows just how easy it is to turn off, and get rid of, most of these unwanted browser parasites. Choose Tools ➪ Manage Add-ons from Internet Explorer's menu bar to see the dialog box.

Figure 1-5: Get rid of ads and unwanted browser tools with Manage Add-Ons.

Wireless Network Setup Wizard

Setting a wireless network with new 802.11b and 802.11g standards has never been easier. Use either WEP or WPA to secure your wireless network. It's all Wi-Fi compatible, making it easy to access public Internet Wi-Fi hotspots found at many universities, airports, hotels, and other places. When you're on the road with your laptop, and within range of a public Internet access hotspot, you can just turn on your notebook, have it find the appropriate signal, and you're online without any cables or wires.

The new Wireless Network Setup Wizard makes (see Figure 1-6) it all so much easier than it's been in the past. "Setting Up a Wireless Network" in Chapter 61 tells the whole story.

Figure 1-6: The new Wireless Network Setup Wizard

Safe and Secure Home Networking

The new Windows Firewall makes it much easier to set up a secure home network with full Internet connection, printer, and file sharing. You no longer need to figure out where you have to enable the firewall, and not leave all the ports on some computers wide open. The new firewall just battens down the security on all your network connections, opening just enough ports to allow computers within your network to share files, printers, and Internet access without exposing other ports unnecessarily. Chapter 61 shows you exactly how it's done.

Bluetooth Is Really Here

If you've been wondering when all the hoopla about Bluetooth would turn into something you could get your hands on, wonder no more. Windows XP SP2 has complete Bluetooth support built right in. If you haven't heard about Bluetooth, you will now.

Bluetooth is a low-cost, efficient wireless connectivity technology that makes it easy for mobile phones, PDAs (personal digital assistants), PCs, printers, mice, keyboards, and other devices to communicate securely, wirelessly, and with very little effort on your part.

You can create a wireless Bluetooth network with all the Internet connection, printer, and file sharing capabilities of a TCP/IP network, without any of the headaches of TCP/IP. Just plug a device about the size of your thumb into a USB port, and you are most the way there. A single dialog box (see Figure 1-7) makes it easy to activate Bluetooth discovery and Bluetooth security. See "The World of Bluetooth" in Chapter 51 for the complete lowdown on Bluetooth.

Figure 1-7: The Bluetooth Settings dialog box simplifies Bluetooth connectivity.

UPnP, Too

Universal Plug-and-Play (UPnP) is a technology that promises to make virtually all networking nearly effortless. Just plug a UPnP device into any network port, and it's instantly installed for access to all device in the network. You'll even be able to do things like peek around the house from work, across the Internet, using wireless Bluetooth cameras placed throughout the house.

Unfortunately, there aren't too many devices to go along with the technology as I write this book. But that landscape is destined to change dramatically over the next couple of years. Windows XP SP2 is ready to take on whatever devices the hardware guys and dream up. As discussed in Chapter 63, you simply click one link in your My Network Places folder to gain instant access to whatever UPnP devices you make accessible to your computer or local network.

Windows Media Player 10

Though it is not officially a part of Service Pack 2, the timing was just about the same for Windows Media Player 10. The new Media Player 10, shown in Figure 1-8, offers a much-improved interface, built-in MP3 support, improved support for modern portable media players, High-MAT CD support, easier access to online media stores, and smarter automatic playlists. See Chapters 28 and 39 for the full scoop on Media Player 10.

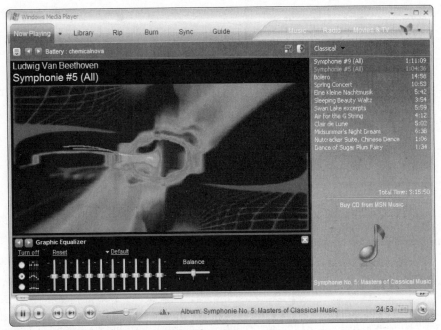

Figure 1-8: The new Windows Media Player 10

Windows Movie Maker 2.1

Windows Movie Maker 2 was a big improvement over the version 1 that originally shipped with Windows XP. Service Pack 2 takes things a step further by including Movie Maker 2.1, which adds the ability to burn movies straight to CDs. The CDs are automatically created in High-MAT format for the best playback quality.

If you have a digital video camera with pass through capabilities, you can use that as a bridge between your older analog video camera and Movie Maker 2.1. See Chapters 41 and 42 for the complete story on making movies with Windows Movie Maker 2.1.

Service Pack 2 Support Center

Whether you've already installed Service Pack 2 or have been holding off, you can find all the information you need at the Service Pack 2 Support Center. That includes top 10 reasons to download SP2, What to do before you download, how to download or order on CD, and what to do after you download. It's all at SP 2 Support Center at `http://support.microsoft.com/windowsxpsp2` (see Figure 1-9).

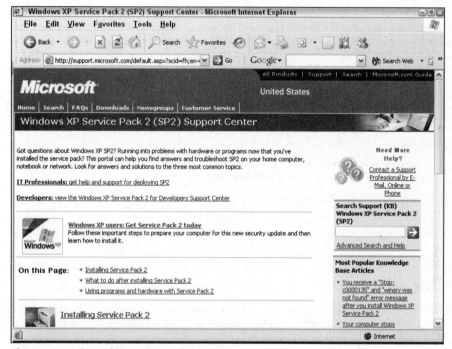

Figure 1-9: Microsoft's Service Pack 2 Support Center

And So Much More . . .

When I first started writing this book I assumed that it would be a revision of the first edition of my *XP Bible*. But I was wrong. The new features of Service Pack 2 pale in comparison to all the things that have changed and improved in the three years since I wrote the first edition. Cool new gadgets and better, faster, cheaper hardware have made it much easier to use out PCs as powerhouses of personal creativity and productivity.

Hard disk space is so inexpensive that there's almost no limit to the amount of stuff we can put in our PCs. Google searches have made it easier to find the information you need, when you need it, across the entire Web. Speech recognition in Word has improved to the point where dictating text to be typed is easy rather than a hassle. E-books make it easy to search an entire reference book in seconds, and you can even have the text read to you aloud.

It seemed that every time I reviewed an existing chapter to see what needed to be revised, I was faced with so many hardware and software improvements that had evolved in those three short years that there was nothing else to do but start all over from scratch. In short, I virtually rewrote the entire book rather than just plugging in a few sections on new SP2 features. It was a lot of work and took a lot of time, but I think you'll agree that it was time well spent!

Wrap Up

Like the rest of us, Microsoft finally got fed up with all the junk invading our computers, including unscrupulous Internet users who waste our time and energy for their own amusement or financial gain. Therefore, they used their formidable resources to really fight back in Service Pack 2, so we could fight back too. But Service Pack 2 alone doesn't tell the whole story of what's transpired since 2001 when XP was first released. Not by a long shot.

This book covers all the improvements to Windows XP, and personal computing in general, that all of us can use to boost our productivity and creativity in ways that one could only dream about in the twentieth century. In summary, the new Security Center in Service Pack 2 makes it much easier to:

✦ Protect your computer from viruses, worms, hackers, adware, spyware, and every other form malware flooding the Internet

✦ Block pop-ups and unwanted downloads with Internet Explorer's built-in pop-up blocker and security alerts

✦ Get rid of unwanted browser hijackers through the Internet Explorer's new Manage Add-Ons window

✦ Keep your entire home network secure with the new and improved Windows Firewall

✦ Easily setup a secure wireless network with the new Wireless Network Setup Wizard

✦ Start using modern Bluetooth devices to synchronize your mobile phone or PDA with your PC, or even to build a simple wireless network without all the usual networking hassles

✦ Be ready to take advantages of the new Universal Plug and Play (UPnP) devices

✦ Take advantage of all the cool new features of Windows Media Player 10 and the awesome new portable media devices that Media Player 10 supports

✦ Use new features of Windows Movie Maker 2.1 to transfer old videotapes to your computer, without the need for an expensive digital capture device, and burn your movies straight to the new High-MAT CDs.

And that's just the start!

✦   ✦   ✦

Getting Around in Windows XP

Even though I'm assuming that you have some computer experience under your belt, it might be worth stating some basic computer facts just to get things rolling. Personal computers (PCs) exist for one reason and one reason only: To enhance human productivity and creativity. The word "enhance" is key there and is not a synonym for "replace." Not by a long shot. Computers cannot produce, computers cannot create. Only people can do those things.

As productivity and creativity enhancers, PCs are fabulous tools. But there is a catch. And it's a doozy of a catch. Before a PC can help you do anything, you have to learn to *use* it. Clicking on the screen at random gets you nothing. As with most machines, you have to know how to work the darn thing before it will do you any good.

In and of itself, a computer does absolutely nothing. In fact, a computer needs a program called an operating system (OS) to even get started. Without an operating system, a computer is little more than an overpriced boat anchor. Turn it on, it does nothing (except display a little message that reads "OS not found").

In addition to making the computer function, the operating system determines how you, the human being in the mix, operates the computer. Learning to use a computer is largely a matter of learning to use the operating system that's installed in that computer. Windows XP is an operating system. Given this, the more you know about Windows XP, the better you can work your computer.

To make it possible for the computer to work, and for you to use the operating system, the operating system provides an *interface*. That interface is basically a set of tools represented by various symbols on the screen. You operate the computer by interacting with those tools via your mouse and keyboard.

What's on the Desktop

The interface that Windows XP provides is called the *Windows desktop*. The name "desktop" comes from the fact that it plays the same role as a real, wooden desktop. You work with programs on the Windows desktop in much the same way that you work with paper on a wooden desktop.

The desktop is on the screen from the moment you turn your computer on to the moment you turn it off. The desktop may get covered by program windows and other items. But the desktop is still under there no matter how much you clutter up the screen. It's the same as a real desk in that sense. Although your real desktop may be completely covered by random junk, like mine is right now, your desktop is still under there somewhere. You just have to dig through the mess to get to it.

The two main components of the Windows desktop are the desktop itself and the taskbar. The desktop is where everything that you open piles up. The taskbar's main role is to make it easy to switch from one open item to another. Everything you'll ever see on your screen has a name and a purpose. Virtually nothing on the screen is there purely for decoration. Figure 2-1 shows the main components of the Windows desktop and other items.

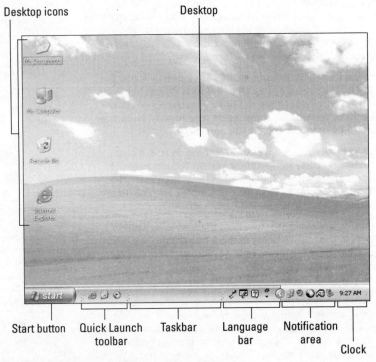

Figure 2-1: The Windows Desktop, uncluttered

It's unlikely that your Windows desktop will look exactly like the one shown in the figure. But it should have the same basic components. If not, don't worry about. As you'll learn in Chapter 6, you can customize the desktop to your liking at any time. Here's a quick overview of what each components represents. We'll look at each component in detail in the sections to that follow the list:

Tip Virtually everything you'll ever see on your screen, including the desktop, is an object that has properties. To customize any object, right-click that object and choose Properties.

✦ **Desktop:** The desktop itself is everything above the taskbar. Every program you open appears in a window on the desktop.

✦ **Desktop icons:** Icons on the desktop provide quick access to frequently used programs, folders, and documents. You can add and remove desktop icons as you see fit.

✦ **Start button:** Click the Start button to display the Start menu. The Start menu provides access to programs installed on your computer, as well as commonly used folders such as My Documents and My Pictures.

✦ **Quick Launch toolbar:** Provides easy one-click access to frequently used programs.

✦ **Taskbar:** A task is just the short, generic name for an open program window. The taskbar makes it easy to switch among all your open programs.

✦ **Language bar:** If your computer has built-in voice-recognition capabilities, you might see the Language bar to the right of the taskbar. You'll learn more about the Language bar in Chapter 9.

✦ **Notification area:** Displays icons for programs running in the background, often referred to as *processes* and *services*. Messages coming from those programs appear in speech balloons just above the Notification area.

✦ **Clock:** Shows the current time. Right-clicking the clock provides easy access to options for customizing the taskbar and organizing open program window.

That's the quick tour of items on and around the Windows XP desktop. We'll look at each major item in the sections that follow, starting with (what else?) the Start button.

Using the Start Button

Clicking the Start button displays the Start menu. The Start menu, in turn, provides access to every program that's currently installed on your program. When you first open the Start menu, you won't see an icon for every program on your computer, though. You'll see icons for only frequently used icons and frequently used folders like My Documents, as in the example shown in Figure 2-2.

Your Start menu probably won't look exactly like Figure 2-2. But like everything else in Windows, the Start menu is an object that has properties, meaning that you can customize it to your liking. We'll get into the details of that in Chapter 6. However, getting to those properties is a simple matter of right-clicking the Start button and choosing Properties.

Tip You can also open the Start menu by pressing Ctrl+Esc. On a Windows keyboard, you can also press the Windows key to open the Start menu. If you open the Start menu by accident, press Esc, tap the Windows key a second time, or click the Start button again to close it without making a selection.

The Start menu is divided into two columns. Icons for frequently used programs appear on the left. Icons for folders and other common items are on the right. To open any item, just click its icon. We'll look at each component of the menu in sections to follow.

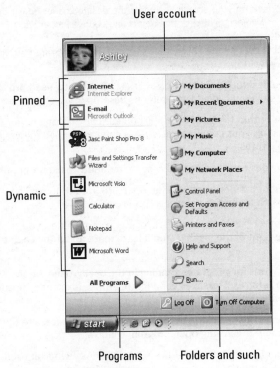

Figure 2-2: The Start menu

User account

The top of the Start menu always shows the name and picture associated with whatever user account you're currently logged into. Unlike twentieth-century versions of Windows, XP supports *user accounts*. The purpose of user accounts is to allow two or more people to share a single computer without stepping on each others' toes. Each user account has its own document folders, customization settings, and so forth. This means that each person can create and edit his or her own documents and set up the desktop as he or she sees fit, just as though the users were using two entirely separate PCs.

The user account name and picture at the top of the Start menu is for informational purposes only. Clicking on it doesn't do anything. If you have multiple user accounts on your computer and want to switch to another account, click the Log Off button at the bottom of the Start menu. Chapter 7 discusses user accounts in detail.

Program icons

The left side of the Start menu contains icons for frequently used programs. Those icons are divided into two groups. Pinned icons are at the top, above the horizontal gray line. Pinned items are permanent in the sense that they don't change automatically. They change only when you change them.

The first two pinned items represent your Web browser and e-mail client. In Figure 2-2 Internet Explorer is the Web browser and Microsoft Outlook is the e-mail client. Whether or not those icons are visible, and exactly which program icons appear, are determined by settings in the Properties dialog box of the Start menu. To get to those options:

1. Right-click the **Start** button and choose **Properties**.

2. Make sure that **Start menu** (not Classic Start menu) is selected and then click the **Customize** button to the right of that option. The Customize Start Menu dialog box shown in Figure 2-3 opens.

3. Use the **Show on Start menu** options near the bottom of the dialog box to choose what, if anything, you want to show for your Web browser and e-mail client.

Figure 2-3: The Customize Start Menu dialog box

For example, if you don't want to show an icon for your Web browser, clear the first checkbox under Show on Start menu. Likewise, if you don't want to show an icon for your e-mail client, clear the second checkbox.

If you do opt to display those items, you can use the first drop-down list to choose your Web browser. Likewise, if you do choose to display an icon for your e-mail client, you can also choose which program's icon you want to display from the E-mail drop-down list. After making your selections, click OK in both open dialog boxes.

Dynamic Start menu icons

Program icons on the Start menu that aren't pinned are dynamic, in the sense that they reflect the programs you use most often. On a new computer, the icons are just those that you're most likely to use on a new computer. But as you run and use programs, icons for rarely used icons will be replaced by icons for the programs you use most often.

The official name of that part of the Start menu is the Most Frequently Used Programs section. The optional TweakUI PowerToy includes an option to prevent unwanted programs from showing up in that part of the menu. See "PowerToys for Windows XP" at www.microsoft.com/windowsxp/downloads/powertoys for more information on the PowerToys.

Getting rid of dynamic icons

You're certainly not stuck with the status quo on the left side of the Start menu. If there's any dynamic icon you want to get rid of, just right-click that item and choose Remove From This List. Doing so will have no effect whatsoever on the program that the icon represents. Instead, that icon will just be removed from the left side of the Start menu. The icon for the next most frequently used program (if any) will then fill in the gap.

If you want to get rid of all the dynamic icons and start building a new set based on programs you use, click the Clear List button in the Customize Start Menu dialog box shown back in Figure 2-3. You'll have a clean slate, and new program icons will be added according to the programs you run from that moment on.

Pinning and unpinning icons

You can actually pin any program's icon to the top of the Start menu. The Web browser and e-mail client icons are special cases, in that you control them from the Customize Start Menu dialog box. But all other program icons can be pinned and unpinned right from the Start menu.

For example, let's say that you're using a particular program frequently for a particular job. You want to get that program's icon onto the left side of the Start menu and make sure that it stays there no matter what other programs you use, or how often. In that case, you can just right-click the desired program icon and choose Pin to Start Menu. The program's icon moves up toward the top of the Start menu, and stays there forever.

Well, not forever. It stays there until you don't want it to be there anymore. To get rid of the pinned icon, just right-click it and choose Unpin from Start menu. If it's a frequently used program, its icon will drop down to the lower half of the Start menu. If you want to get the icon off the Start menu altogether, then right-click the icon and choose Remove From This List.

The right side of the Start menu

The right side of the Start menu is different from the left side in a couple of ways. For one, the right side of the Start menu shows icons for frequently used folders, or other XP features that aren't application programs. For example, My Documents, My Pictures, and My Music are all folders for storing documents. Control Panel is a folder that contains icons for getting to all the Properties dialog boxes available on your computer.

Icons on the right side of the Start menu aren't dynamic. They never change by themselves, and right-clicking an icon on the right side of the menu won't give you options such as Pin, Unpin, and Remove. The only way to control which icons do and don't appear on the right side of the Start menu is through the Advanced tab of the Customize Start Menu dialog box shown in Figure 2-3.

As mentioned, we'll get into customization options in Chapter 6. Here, I only mention it so you don't waste time trying to get the right side of the menu to behave like the left side. The right side of the menu just doesn't work the same as the left side.

The All Programs menu

The small collection of program icons on the left side of the Start menu is by no means an indication of how many programs are actually installed on your computer. To see icons for all the programs at your disposal, click the (you guessed it) All Programs option on the Start menu. Doing so will show the much larger All Programs menu.

When you first click on All Programs, you'll see icons for specific programs, as well as icons for groups of programs. Icons for program groups all have a similar folder icon, and a

▶ to the right. To see what programs are available within a group, just point to or click on the icon. A group can contain still more groups. So, you can just work your way to a specific program's icon by clicking on, or pointing to, the appropriate program group icon.

To illustrate, Figure 2-4 shows the results of clicking the Start button and choosing All Programs ➪ Accessories ➪ Entertainment. All the programs in the Entertainment group — Sound Recorder, Volume Control, Windows Media Player, and Windows Movie Maker, all have to do with sound or video. Or, in other words, entertainment.

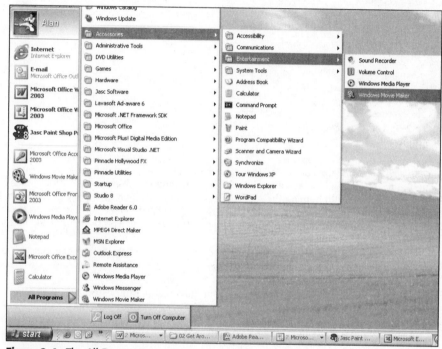

Figure 2-4: The All Programs menu

Note   Exactly how much stuff you can see on your screen, and whether or not your All Programs menu behaves as described in this chapter, depends on settings defined in the Display Properties and Customize Start Menu dialog boxes. See Chapter 6 for details.

Your All Programs menu won't look exactly like the example in Figure 2-4, for the simple reason that no two computers are likely to have the same programs installed. A computer is like a stereo or DVD player in that regard. Just because you own a stereo, that doesn't mean you have every CD ever created. Nor does it mean that your collection of CDs is identical to mine or you neighbor's.

Arranging menu items

When you first install and use Windows XP, icons on the All Programs menu are fairly tidy. There are a few fixed icons at the top of the menu. Below those are program groups listed in alphabetical order. Below the program groups are icons for individual programs, also listed in alphabetical order.

As time goes by, and you install programs on and remove programs from your computer, the arrangement of icons can get out of whack. If dragging and dropping is enabled on your All Programs menu, you can quickly whip the icons into the order by right-clicking any icon and choosing Sort By Name, as in Figure 2-5. The same technique works in any program group's icons.

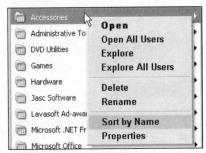

Figure 2-5: The Sort By Name option on a menu

You can also position icons on the All Programs menu by dragging them up or down on the menu. But again, that only works if the Enable Dragging and Dropping property for menus is active. If right-clicking an item on the All Programs menu gets you nothing but a brief flash, then the option is currently disabled. As you'll learn in Chapter 6, you can easily enable, or disable, dragging and dropping through the Advanced tab of the Customize Start Menu dialog box.

 Tip   There is no Sort By Name option for icons on the left side of the Start menu. But you can reposition icons by dragging them up or down.

There are plenty of other ways to customize your Start menu. But customizing isn't what this chapter is about. The main point here is that the Start menu gives you a means of starting every program that's currently installed on your computer. When you start a program, it opens into a window on the desktop—which brings us to the next major section of this chapter.

Using the Windows Desktop

As mentioned, the Windows desktop is the electronic equivalent of a real, wooden desktop. It's the place where you keep stuff you're working on right now. Every program that's currently open will be contained within some program window. When no programs are open, the desktop and all your desktop icons are plainly visible on the screen.

About desktop icons

Desktop icons are just like the icons on the Start menu. Each icon represents a closed object that you can open by double-clicking the icon. All desktop icons, except for Recycle Bin, are just shortcuts to files and folders. They're shortcuts in the sense that they duplicate icons available elsewhere. They just save you the extra clicks required to get to the same icon through the Start menu or All Programs menu.

There's always an exception to the rule. When it comes to desktop icons, Recycle Bin is the exception. The Recycle Bin icon exists only on the desktop, and you won't find it anywhere else. The role of the Recycle Bin is that of a safety net. Whenever you delete a file or folder from your hard drive, the item is actually just moved to the Recycle Bin. You can restore an accidentally deleted icon from the Recycle Bin back to its original location.

Caution   Deleting is risky business and never to be taken lightly. Never store files in the Recycle Bin unless you intend to delete them permanently. Never try to fix a problem by deleting icons you don't recognize. You'll only make matters worse. See Chapter 14 for more information on deleting and restoring files.

In addition to the Recycle Bin, there are four optional desktop icons that you can show or hide. Actually, three of them are folders, and the other is Internet Explorer. To choose which, of any, of those icons you want to show, follow these steps:

1. Right-click the Windows desktop and choose **Properties**.

2. In the Display Properties dialog box that opens, click the **Desktop** tab.

3. Click the **Customize Desktop** button at the bottom of the Desktop tab.

4. Under Desktop Icons, shown in Figure 2-6, choose which icons you want to show.

5. Click **OK** in each of the open dialog boxes.

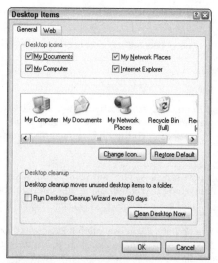

Figure 2-6: The Desktop Items dialog box

In addition to the five icons mentioned here, you can create a desktop shortcut to any program, folder, or document to which you need quick access. You don't want to clutter up your desktop with too many icons, though. Otherwise, you'll be looking all over the place for a specific icon, and that doesn't save you any time.

Chapter 16 will talk about creating, managing, and deleting shortcut icons in depth. But the technique for creating a desktop shortcut icon is so simple; it can be explained in a sentence: Right-click the icon to which you want to create a shortcut and choose Send To ⇨ Desktop (create shortcut). That's it.

Figure 2-7 shows a couple of examples of the steps involved. In the first example, I'm about to create a desktop shortcut to Calculator. To get to that point, I clicked the Start button, chose All Program ⇨ Accessories, and then right-clicked the icon for starting Calculator.

In the lower example, I'm about to create a shortcut to a folder named ClipArt on my D: drive (a second hard disk). To get to that icon, I clicked the Start button, clicked on My Computer, clicked the icon for my D: drive, and then right-clicked the ClipArt folder's icon on that drive.

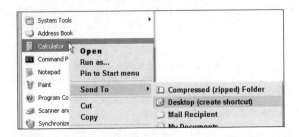

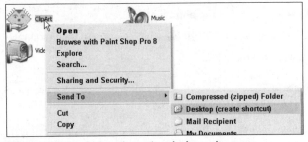

Figure 2-7: Examples of creating desktop shortcuts

Tip   The Pin to Start Menu option just above Send To on Calculator's icon in Figure 2-7 is universal. You can use it to add an icon for any program to the Start menu. Like a desktop shortcut, the Start menu icon saves you the trouble of going through the All Programs menu every time you want to start the program.

Both of the examples in Figure 2-7 are just arbitrary examples. The important point is that you can create a desktop shortcut to just about anything by right-clicking and choosing Send To ➪ Desktop (create shortcut).

Tip   I suppose it wouldn't hurt to throw in one more tip here. If you use Internet Explorer as your Web browser, you can just as easily create a desktop shortcut to the Web page you're currently viewing. Just choose File ➪ Send ➪ Shortcut to Desktop from Internet Explorer's menu bar.

Arranging desktop icons

Here are a few other mention-worthy factoids about desktop icons:

✦ If you have lots of overlapping icons spread randomly about your screen, you can right-click the desktop and choose Arrange Icons By ➪ Align to Grid to align them to an invisible grid so that they don't overlap.

✦ To put desktop icons into roughly alphabetical order, right-click the desktop and choose Arrange Icons By ➪ Name. Windows icons will always be listed first, with icons you created listed alphabetically after those.

✦ To force all icons to arrange themselves each time you create a new icon, right-click the desktop and choose Arrange Icons By ➪ Auto Arrange. If you change your mind, repeat that to turn off Auto Arrange.

✦ You can temporarily hide all desktop icons by right-clicking the desktop and choosing Arrange Icons By ➪ Show Desktop Icons. Do the same a second time to bring them out of hiding.

As I said, Chapter 16 covers shortcuts in detail. Let's get back to dealing with larger things on the desktop.

Running Programs

You can start any program that's installed on your computer by getting to the program's icon on the All Programs menu and then clicking that icon. There are other ways to start programs as well. For example, if there's an icon on the left side of the Start menu to start the program, just click that instead. If there's an icon for the program in the Quick Launch toolbar, you can click that. If there's a shortcut icon to the program on the desktop, you can click (or double-click) that icon to start the program.

Note   Whether you need to single-click or double-click a desktop icon to open it is up to you. See "To Click or Double-Click" in Chapter 3 for details.

Every time you start a program, an *instance* of that program opens in a program window. There's no rule that says you can have only one program open at a time. And there's no rule that says you can have only one copy of any given program open at a time. You can have as many programs as you can cram into your available memory (RAM) open all at the same time. And most programs will allow you to run multiple instances. The more memory your system has, the more stuff you can have open without any slow down in performance.

Note   When it comes to using programs, the terms *start, run, launch,* and *open* all mean the same thing—to load a copy of the program into memory (RAM) so it's visible on your screen. You can't use a program until it's open and visible.

Just about every program window will have a title bar, menu bar, and toolbar at the top. Every open program window will also have a corresponding button in the taskbar. The icon and name in the program's title bar match the icon and name in its taskbar button. That's how you know which taskbar button represents which program window.

As an example of that, Figure 2-8 shows a portion of the Windows desktop with Microsoft Word open. The title bar for Word shows Word's icon followed by the document name, Dear John.doc, then the name of the program, Microsoft Word. That window's taskbar button shows roughly the same thing. The taskbar button is usually smaller than the title bar, so part of the program's name is cut off in the taskbar button.

When you have multiple program windows open, they tend to stack up on the desktop just like multiple sheets of paper on your real desktop stack up. When you have multiple sheets of paper in a pile, you can't see what's on every page. You can only see what's on the top page, because all the other pages are covered by that page.

Titlebar

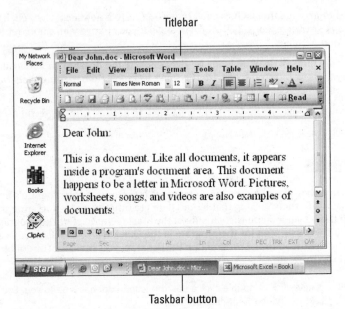

Taskbar button

Figure 2-8: Sample title bar and taskbar button

It works the same way with program windows. When you have multiple program windows open, you can only see the one that's on the top of the stack. We call the program that's on the top of the stack the *active window*. The concept of the active window is important enough to warrant its own section title. So here it is.

The active window

When two or more program windows are open on the desktop window, only one of them can be the active window. The active window has some unique characteristics:

✦ The active window is always on the top of the stack. Any other open windows will be under the active window so they don't cover any of its content.

✦ The taskbar button for the active window has a pushed-in appearance, and the taskbar buttons for all the inactive windows have a pushed-out appearance.

✦ Anything you do at the keyboard applies to the active window only. You can type in an inactive window.

You can easily make any open window the active window in a couple of ways:

✦ Click that window's taskbar button.

✦ Hold down the Alt key and press Tab until the program's icon is selected and then release the Alt key.

Nothing to it, really, after you get the hang of it. The same basic rule applies with multiple instances of the same program, although there's a bit of magic that occurs when you open lots of instances of the same program. Let's look at an example.

Suppose that you're browsing the Web with Internet Explorer, and you come across a link to a page you want to view. However, you don't want to "switch to" that page. Rather, you want to see that page, but also still be able to see the page you're currently viewing. In that case, you don't click the link to the other page. Instead, you right-click that link and choose Open in New Window. When you do, the page opens. However, it's in an entirely separate Internet Explorer window. Or, in other words, it's in a new instance of Internet Explorer.

Now suppose that you do the same thing for a few more links. Each time you do, another instance of Internet Explorer opens, and the taskbar gains another button for that instance. Each time another taskbar button appears in the taskbar, all the buttons in the taskbar need to shrink down to make room. If you keep opening instances, eventually all the tiny buttons will collapse into one button with an Internet Explorer icon, and a number indicating how many instances are open.

Suppose then that you want to get back to one of the pages you opened before. The page is still open, but it's buried under all the other instances you opened since. How do you make a specific instance of Internet Explorer the active window, to jumps to the top of the stack? Easy! You click the taskbar button. When you do, a list of all the specific pages that are open appears in a menu, as in the example shown in Figure 2-9. You just click on the name of the page you want to see. That page jumps to the top of the stack so you can see all of it.

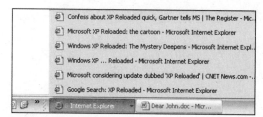

Figure 2-9: Multiple instances of Internet Explorer are open.

Here are some other handy things to know about a single taskbar button that represents multiple open instances of a program window. You can right-click the taskbar button that sports the number of open instances and then choose any of the following from the context menu that opens:

- ✦ **Cascade:** Stacks all the opens instances like sheets of paper, with just their title bars visible.

- ✦ **Tile Horizontally:** Sizes the windows equally and displays them like tiles. If only a few windows are open, each will be sized to the width of the screen.

- ✦ **Tile Vertically:** Same as above, but each window spans the height of the desktop. If only a few windows are open, each will be sized to the width of the screen.

- ✦ **Minimize Group:** Temporarily removes all open instances from the desktop. Use any option previously given to bring them back to the desktop.

- ✦ **Close Group:** Closes all the open instances in one click.

The main point to keep in mind here, however, is that program windows on the desktop stack up just like sheets of paper on a desk. It doesn't matter whether you're talking about a single instance of multiple programs, multiple instances of a single program, or multiple instances of multiple programs — they're all just program windows. Each program window is still like a sheet of paper on a real, wooden desktop — a very small wooden desktop at that (although it would be great to have a monitor that really is as big as a real desk!).

When you have multiple sheets of paper on a tiny desktop or multiple program windows on a computer screen, the sheet or window that's on the top of the stack is the only one you can actually see in full. With paper, you use your hands to shuffle sheets around. On the Windows desktop, you use the taskbar buttons (or Alt+Tab keys) to shuffle program windows around.

Arranging program windows

You can use four options on the context menu for the taskbar to quickly arrange all the program windows that are open on the desktop. To get to that context menu, you can right-click some empty spot on the taskbar, but the empty spot might be small, and getting the tip of the mouse pointer to exactly the right place can be tricky. As an alternative, you can right-click the clock, as in Figure 2-10, to get to the same options.

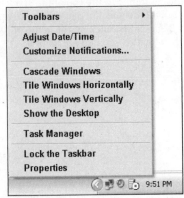

Figure 2-10: Context menu for the taskbar

The four options that apply to program windows on the desktop are:

✦ **Cascade Windows:** Stacks all the open windows like sheets of paper, fanned out so all or their title bars are visible, as in Figure 2-11.

✦ **Tile Windows Horizontally:** Resizes all open windows so they all fit on the screen and displays them like tiles. If only two or three windows are open, each window spans the width of the screen.

✦ **Tile Windows Vertically:** Same as preceding, but each open window spans the height of the desktop.

✦ **Show the Desktop:** Minimizes all open windows so only their taskbar buttons are visible. You can see the entire desktop at that point. To bring any window back onto the screen, click its taskbar button.

Tip   If your Quick Launch toolbar includes a Show Desktop button, you can click that to quickly minimize all open program windows.

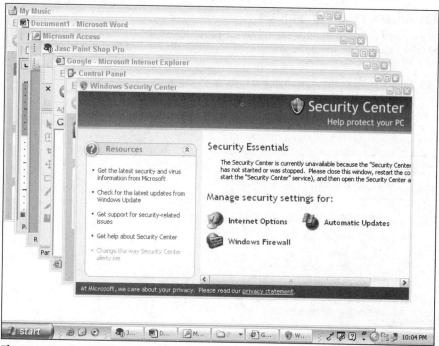

Figure 2-11: Cascaded program windows

The options just described are generally used for sizing and arranging multiple program windows. You can certainly work with one program window at a time, sizing and positioning it on the screen as best fits your needs at the moment. The next sections will look at techniques for dealing with any one open program windows that happens to be open on the desktop at the moment.

Sizing program windows

Most program windows can be any size you want them to be, but there are a few exceptions to the rule. For example, the tiny Calculator program can't be sized much. Some programs like Movie Maker, Media Player, and Solitaire will shrink down only so far. But in general, most open program windows can be three sizes:

✦ Maximized, in which the program fills the entire screen above the taskbar, covering the desktop.

✦ Minimized, in which only the program's taskbar button is visible, and the program window takes up no space on the desktop.

✦ Any size in between those two extremes.

Often you'll want to work with two or more program windows at a time. Knowing how to size program windows is a critical skill for doing that, because it's often difficult to work with multiple program windows if you can't see at least some portion of each one.

Maximize a program window

A maximized program window will fill all the space above the taskbar. This makes it easy to see everything inside the program window. If a program window isn't already maximized, you can maximize it in three ways:

✦ Click the Maximize button in the program's title bar.

✦ Double-click the program's title bar.

✦ Right-click the program's taskbar button and choose Maximize (see Figure 2-12).

Figure 2-12: Maximize an open program window.

Tip   Few buttons on the screen show their names. To see a button's name, point to the button (rest the tip of the mouse pointer on the button). The name appears in a ScreenTip near the mouse pointer, as in Figures 2-12 and 2-13. The same technique works for many menu options, icons, and items in dialog boxes.

Minimize a program window

If you want to get a program window off the screen temporarily, to better see something else on the screen, minimize the program window. When you minimize the program window, the program remains open. However, it takes up no space on the screen, and, therefore, can't cover anything else on the screen. When minimized, only the window's taskbar button remains visible. There are three ways to minimize a program window:

✦ Click the Minimize button in the program's title bar.

✦ Click the program's taskbar button once or twice (if the program isn't in the active window, the first click will just make it the active window. The second click will then minimize the active window).

✦ Right-click the program's taskbar button and choose Minimize (see Figure 2-13).

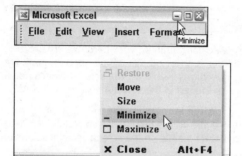

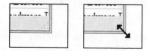

Figure 2-13: Minimize an open program window.

Sizing at will

Between the two extremes of maximized (hog up the entire desktop) and minimized (not even visible on the desktop), most program windows can be any size you want them to be. The first step to sizing a program window is to get it to an in-between size, so that it's neither maximized nor minimized. To do that:

✦ If the program window is currently minimized, click its taskbar button to make it visible on the screen.

✦ If the program window is currently maximized, double-click its title bar or click its Restore Down button to shrink it down a little. Figure 2-14 shows the tooltip that appears when you point to the Restore Down button. Optionally, use the Cascade Windows option described earlier to get all open program windows down to an in-between size.

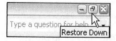

Figure 2-14: The Restore Down button in a maximized program window

After the program window is visible but not hogging up the entire screen, you can size it to your liking by dragging any edge or corner. You have to get the tip of the mouse pointer right on the border so that the pointer turns to a two-headed arrow, before you hold down the left mouse button and start dragging.

Many program windows have a little dragging handle—sunken dots that look like a nonskid surface—in the lower-right corner that you can drag. Figure 2-15 shows an example of such a handle, both without the mouse pointer in position and with the mouse pointer in position, ready to drag.

Figure 2-15: Sample program window dragging handle

Minimize versus Close

Everything that's "in your computer" so to speak is actually a file on your hard disk. The stuff on your hard disk is always there, whether the computer is on or off. When you open an item, two things happen. The most obvious is that the item becomes visible on the screen. What's not so obvious is the fact that a copy of the program is also loaded in the computer's memory (RAM).

When you minimize an open window, the program is still in memory. The only way you can tell that is by the fact that the program's taskbar button is still on the taskbar. When you want to view that program window, you just click its taskbar to make it visible on the screen again. It shows up looking exactly as it did before you minimized it.

When you close a program, its window and taskbar button both disappear, and the program is also removed from RAM (making room for other things you might want to work with). The only way to get back to the program is to restart it from its icon. However, this new program window will be an entirely new instance of the program, unrelated to how things looked before you closed the program.

Chapter 56 discusses how all that works in more detail.

Whether a program has a handle in its lower-right corner or not, you can always size the window by dragging any corner or edge. The handle just provides a large target on which to place the tip of the mouse pointer that saves you from having to get the tip of mouse pointer right on the skinny little border surrounding the program window.

You can also size a program window using the keyboard. Again, the program window has to be at some in-between size to start with. And you'll always begin the process from the program window's taskbar button. Here are the steps:

1. If the window is minimized or maximized, right-click its taskbar button and choose **Restore**. Otherwise, you can skip this step.

2. Right-click the program window's taskbar button and choose **Size**.

3. Press the navigation keys ($\leftarrow, \rightarrow, \uparrow, \downarrow$) until the window (or the border around the window) is the size you want.

4. Press the Enter key.

Moving a program window

You can easily move a program window about the screen just by dragging its title bar. However, you can't start with a maximized or minimized window. You have to get the program window to an in-between size before you even get started.

Dialog boxes work the same way. You can't size or minimize a dialog box, and dialog boxes don't have taskbar buttons. But you can easily drag a dialog box around the screen by its title bar.

If it were possible to do animations on paper, I'd show you. But since no such technology exists, you'll just have to try it for yourself. For example, if you right-click the Start button and choose Properties, the Taskbar and Start Menu Properties dialog box will open. Put the tip of the mouse pointer on the title bar at the top of that dialog box, hold down the left mouse button, drag the dialog box to wherever you want, and then release the mouse button.

Closing a Program

When you've finished using a program for the time being, that's the time to close it. Every open program and document consumes some resources, mostly in the form of using memory (RAM). When RAM is full, the computer has to start using *virtual memory*, which is basically space on the hard disk configured to look like RAM to the computer.

RAM has no moving parts and, thus, can feed stuff to the processor (where all the work takes place) at amazing speeds. A hard disk has moving parts and is much, much slower. As soon as Windows has to start using virtual memory, everything slows down. So, you really don't want to have a bunch of stuff you're not using anymore open and consuming resources.

There are lots of ways to close a program. Use whichever technique is most convenient for you because they all produce the same result: The program is removed from memory, and both its program window and taskbar button are removed from the screen:

✦ Click the Close (X) button in the program window's upper-right corner.

✦ Choose File ➪ Exit from the program's menu bar.

✦ Right-click the program's taskbar button and choose Close.

✦ If the program is in the active window, press Alt+F4.

If you were working on a document in the program and have made changes to that document since you last saved it, the program will (hopefully) ask if you want to save those changes in a message box like the example in Figure 2-16.

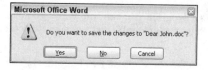

Figure 2-16: Last chance to save a document

Never take that dialog box lightly, because whichever option you choose is final, and there's no going back and changing your mind. Your options are:

✦ **Yes:** The document will be saved in its current state; both the document and the program will close.

✦ **No:** Any and all changes you made to the document since you last saved it will be lost forever. Both the document and the program will close.

✦ **Cancel:** The program and document will both remain open and on the screen. You can then continue work on the document and save it from the program's menu bar (choose File ➪ Save).

Using the Quick Launch Toolbar

The Quick Launch toolbar, pointed out in Figure 2-17, is an optional XP component that provides one-click access to frequently used programs. Exactly which programs you can start from there is entirely up to you. We'll talk about how you add and remove Quick Launch buttons in Chapter 16. For now, let's just talk about how you use the Quick Launch toolbar.

Like just about everything else in Windows, the Quick Launch toolbar is optional. The option to display, or hide, the Quick Launch toolbar is a simple toggle, meaning that it's an option you can turn on, or off, whenever you feel like it. To show or hide the Quick Launch toolbar, right-click the clock and choose Toolbars ➪ Quick Launch. When the Quick Launch toolbar is visible, its option is checked, as is also shown in Figure 2-17. When it's invisible, its option isn't checked. Like all toggles, clicking the option switches it to the opposite setting.

Tip   To leave a toggle option unchanged, press the Esc key or click outside the menu to close the menu without taking any action.

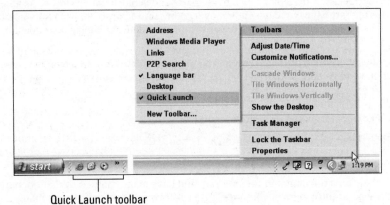

Quick Launch toolbar

Figure 2-17: Quick Launch toolbar and toggle

Each icon on the Quick Launch toolbar represents a program you can run. When you click the icon, the program starts. If you're not sure what an icon represents, just point to the icon for more information.

The number of icons visible in the Quick Launch toolbar depends on two factors: (1) The number of buttons it contains (I suppose that rates as a "duh now") and (2) the size of the Quick Launch toolbar. If there are more buttons in the Quick Launch toolbar than fit in the space allotted, you'll see a Show/Hide button (>>) at its right edge. Click that button to view any icons that are currently hidden, as in the example shown in Figure 2-18.

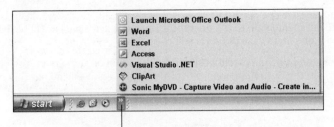

Show hidden icons

Figure 2-18: Viewing hidden Quick Launch buttons

There are many ways to size and position the Quick Launch toolbar. But that's a customization matter that's best left to Chapter 6. For now, just knowing how to work it is sufficient.

Using the Notification Area

Over on the right side of the taskbar is the Notification area. (That same area was called the *system tray* in earlier versions of Windows.) Like the Quick Launch, it contains icons. But clicking on one of those icons is unlikely to start a program. Instead, each icon in the Notification area represents a *service*, or a program that's running *in the background*. Basically, it's a thing that's active and running but doesn't have a program window and doesn't have a taskbar button.

To conserve space on the taskbar, Windows XP gives you the option of hiding inactive icons. When inactive icons are hidden, you'll see a button with a < symbol on it at the left side of the Notification area. Click the button to see icons that are currently hidden.

As with any icon or button, you can point to an icon in the Notification area to see the name of that icon. Right-clicking an icon usually provides a context menu of options for using the item. Clicking or double-clicking the icon usually opens whatever larger thing the icon represents.

For example, the Volume icon provides a simple service: it lets you control the volume of your speakers when sound is playing. To change the volume, you click the icon then drag the slider (shown in Figure 2-19) up or down. Optionally, you mute the speakers by choosing the Mute option. Double-clicking the Volume icon opens the larger Volume Control program that you'll learn about in Chapter 38.

Figure 2-19: Volume control in the Notification area

Unlike the Quick Launch toolbar, the icons in the Notification area don't represent programs that you *can* run. They represent programs that *are* running. The icon simply serves as a notification that the program is running. Although in most cases, the icon will also provide options to closing the program or changing how it runs. Different computers will have different Notification area icons. But some common examples include the following:

✦ **Network Connections:** When you're online or connected to some other network, you might see an icon that lets you disconnect from the network.

✦ **Instant Messaging Programs:** If you use Windows Messenger, AOL Instant Messenger, or a similar program, the icon will be visible while you're online.

✦ **Anti-Virus Programs:** If you have antivirus protection, it might show an icon in the Notification area.

✦ **Safely Remove Hardware:** If you have a USB device connected to your computer, the Safely Remove Hardware icon lets you disable the device before removing it, to make sure that it doesn't disconnect while the device is in use.

Showing/hiding notifications

You can choose for yourself which Notification area icons you do and don't want to see at any time. There's rarely any need to see them all, so you can hide some from yourself just to conserve the taskbar space they would otherwise take. To make choices about those icons, right-click the clock and choose Customize Notifications. When you do, two dialog boxes titled Customize Notifications and Taskbar and Start Menu Properties (see Figure 2-20) open.

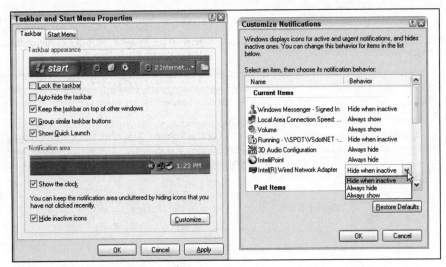

Figure 2-20: Notification area options

Near the bottom of the Taskbar and Start Menu Properties dialog box, you have two choices related to the Notification area:

✦ **Show the clock:** Choose this option to show the clock; clear its checkbox to hide the clock.

✦ **Hide inactive icons:** Choose this option to hide icons that aren't active. Clear it to make all Notification icons visible at all times.

The Customize Notifications dialog box lists items that are currently active, as well as inactive items that were active in the past. You can choose if and how you want to display an icon by clicking the Behavior icon to the right if the item's name. Your options are:

✦ **Hide when inactive:** The icon will be visible only when it's active and serving some purpose.

✦ **Always hide:** The item will always be hidden.

✦ **Always show:** The item will always be visible in the Notification area.

As always, what you choose to show or hide is entirely up to you. Just make your selections and click OK in each of the open dialog boxes.

Urban Myth: Notification Icons Are Bad

Each item in the Notification area represents a background process that's currently running and is, therefore, taking up some resources. Some people think that if they just get rid of all those Notification icons, their computer will run faster because there will be more memory available to other programs.

The problem with that reasoning has to do with the amount of resources consumed and the priority given those processes. As a rule, background processes consume very few resources and are given very low priority when other things are running. The fact of the matter is that getting rid of Notification area icons isn't likely to increase you computer performance one iota. You'll lean more about how that all works in Chapter 56.

Responding to notification messages

The Notification area mainly gets it name from the fact that it occasionally displays a notification message on the screen. These take the form of a speech balloon, like the example shown in Figure 2-21.

Figure 2-21: Sample notification

There are lots of different notifications, and most are self-explanatory. In most cases, you just click on the speech balloon to respond to the message. If you want to get rid of the message without responding, click the Close (X) button inside the speech balloon.

Using Show/Hide Buttons

Earlier in this chapter you saw examples of Show/Hide buttons, such as the >> symbol on the Quick Launch toolbar and the < button at the left side of the Notification area. Those two Show/Hide buttons aren't the only ones you'll ever see. In fact, you'll see them all over the place. Sometimes they're > or >> characters; sometimes they're solid triangles. They might point up, down, left, or right. Figure 2-22 shows six of them that I came across just by opening things up and looking around for some.

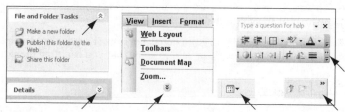

Figure 2-22: Some sample Show/Hide buttons

The whole trick to using Show/Hide buttons is just realizing what they are. They tend to be tiny, so you really have to keep an eye out for them. Pointing to such a button will usually display a name or other information. However, it can never hurt to click on one and see what comes out if hiding. Anything you take out of hiding you can put right back into hiding simply by clicking the same button a second time.

Using Dragging Handles

Dragging handles are like Show/Hide buttons in that you see them all over the place. The whole trick is realizing what they are when you see them. They tend to look like little nonskid areas — a vertical column of dots. Figure 2-23 shows some examples I found just by looking around at various programs on my system.

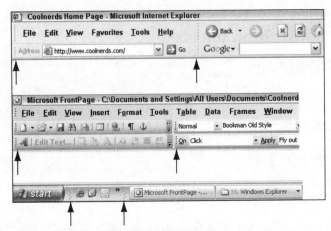

Figure 2-23: Examples of dragging handles

Pointing to a dragging handle rarely reveals any sort of explanatory text. Rather, the mouse pointer just changes to a four-headed arrow, meaning "hold down the left mouse button and drag in any direction."

One problem with dragging handles is that when you're whipping the mouse pointer about the screen, it's all too easy to sometimes drag an item by accident. All of a sudden, your toolbars are in disarray or your taskbar is three times its original height, just because you unwittingly dragged a handle.

Windows allows you to lock the taskbar, which makes the dragging handles go into hiding. You'll find that option on the context menu that appears when you right-click the clock (see Figure 2-24). The basic idea is to keep the taskbar locked so that you don't rearrange things by accident. When you do want to move things around, unlock the taskbar and make your changes. Then, relock the taskbar to avoid accidental dragging.

Chapter 6 discusses customizing the taskbar in more detail. For now, it's sufficient to be able to recognize dragging handles when you see them, and to know that you can drag them to move and size things.

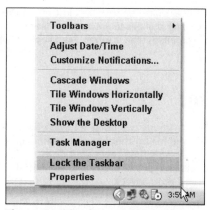

Figure 2-24: Lock the Taskbar option

The All-Important Undo

Many programs have an Undo command on their Edit menu that allows you to undo your most recent action. The universal shortcut key for Undo is Ctrl+Z. Windows also has an Undo command. But you wouldn't know it because in most cases, there is no Edit menu. In fact, there's no menu bar at all on the desktop. But the Undo capability is often there somewhere.

Figure 2-25 shows an example where just prior to shooting that screen, I moved an item from my My Documents folder to another folder. Right after the move, I right-clicked some empty space in my My Documents folder, and there, you can see the Undo Move option on the context menu. As you can see on the menu, Ctrl+Z is the shortcut key for undoing the move.

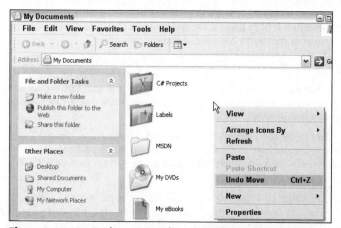

Figure 2-25: An Undo command on a Windows context menu

Although it's certainly good to know about Undo, you shouldn't use it as an excuse to try things out at random just to see what happens. That's because even though there are probably hundreds of actions you can undo, there are thousands of actions you can't undo.

Caution Never use System Restore as a substitute for Undo. Unlike Undo, which just undoes your most recent action, System Restore makes sweeping changes to your system files. If used incorrectly, System Restore can cause a lot more problems than it solves. See Chapter 55 for more information on System Restore.

Shutting Down Your Computer

Here's a question a lot of people ask: "Should I shut down my computer if I won't be using it for a while, or should I just leave it on?" Everybody and his brother has an opinion about this. So here's mine: It doesn't matter. Personally, about the only time I ever shut down my computers is when I need to, such as when installing certain types of hardware. Aside from that, all my computers are on, and online, 24 hours a day, 7 days a week.

I've built, worked the daylights out of, and then thrown away dozens of computers after they've served their purpose and better technology came along. Not a one ever "broke" before it had served its purpose. So, I'd have to say that not a one ever suffered from being left on too long, or shut down too often. So that's why my opinion on the leaving on or turning off debate is that it just flat out doesn't seem to matter.

If you do want to (or need to) shut down your computer, there are a few ways to do it. If you're shutting down to install some new hardware, your first step would be to close all open programs and save any work in progress, to get to a clean desktop. Then, click the Start button and choose Turn Off Computer ⇨ Turn Off. Give it a few seconds to get things in order before shutting down. If you see the message "It is now safe to turn off your computer," then go ahead and hit the main power button to complete the shut down. However, most modern computers will skip that message and just shut down on their own.

If you're shutting down your computer because you don't intend to use it for a while and don't want to hear the fan noise or whatever, then you have some other options to choose from. You can leave programs open on the desktop. But if you have any documents you're working on, you would be wise to save any work in progress before clicking the Start button and choosing Turn Off Computer. It only takes a second to press Ctrl+S to save your work, so there's no need to risk losing all that work because of a shutdown snafu.

Also, be aware that no matter how you shut down, you'll be disconnected from the Internet. So there's no point in leaving a Web page open on the screen with the hope of coming right back to that same page when you restart your computer. A computer can't be online unless it's on. Even a computer that's in Standby mode can't be online. Being "off" or in Standby mode, and being online, are just mutually exclusive things.

When you are ready to shut down the computer, click the Start button and choose Turn Off Computer. You'll be given a few options to choose from. Exactly which options depends on settings discussed in Chapter 57, but you'll likely see at least four of the five options described here:

- ◆ **Hibernate:** Copies an image of whatever is in memory at the moment to a file on the disk. When you restart the computer later, that image is reloaded into memory so that you're right back to where things were before you shut down.

- ◆ **Standby:** Keeps the contents of memory in tact by providing a tiny amount of power to the system while it's in Standby mode so that the computer restarts more quickly and you're taken right back to where you left off. However, if the computer loses power while in Standby mode, then the memory contents are lost and restarting will be the same as if you'd used the Turn Off option rather than the Standby option. In other words, this won't work if you plan on unplugging the system while it's turned off.

✦ **Turn Off:** Turns the computer all the way off. Nothing is saved, and no power is consumed while the computer is off. When you restart the computer, you return to a clean desktop with no programs open.

✦ **Restart:** Also known as a *warm boot* or *reboot*. A restart is required after installing certain types of software that need to be activated right at system startup, or when a software crash causes the system to hang (freeze up) and you need to get off to a clean start to get things working property again.

✦ **Cancel:** Abandons the shutdown procedure and leaves you right where you were before you clicked Start and chose Turn Off Computer.

If you chose Turn Off, you may see a message that reads "It is now safe to turn off your computer." At that point, you can press the power button on the system unit to finish the job and power down. Most modern computers, however, won't show the "It is now safe . . ." option. Instead, the computer will just shut itself down without any further action on your part.

Wrap Up

So that about wraps it up for the main Windows XP interface elements: the desktop, taskbar, and program windows. Knowing how all that works is critical to using Windows productively. To wrap things up and take a look at this chapter from 30,000 feet:

✦ The Windows desktop is where you'll do all your work.

✦ Most of your work will involve opening and using programs.

✦ You can start any program that's installed on your computer from the All Programs menu.

✦ Each open program will appear in its own program window on the desktop. Program windows stack up like sheets of paper.

✦ Each open program window has a corresponding taskbar button. The taskbar buttons help you switch from one open program window to another.

✦ You can move and size program windows to see exactly what you need to see, when you need to see it.

✦ Certain little design elements, like Show/Hide buttons and dragging handles, are sprinkled all through Windows and programs. You just need to recognize them when you see them.

That's enough for now about the desktop and programs. Time to get to the real reason you bought the machine in the first place: to make things. That brings us to documents, folders, and files in Chapter 3.

✦　　✦　　✦

Files, Folders, Documents, and Icons

You can use lots of different types of programs with a computer. Most of us spend most of our time working with *application programs* (often called *applications* or *apps* for short) that let us view, create, edit, print, and save documents. The program is the *toolbox* that allows us to work with documents. Your Web browser is one example. It's a program that allows you to view Web pages. Every Web page, in turn, is a document. A word processing program lets you create and edit your own documents.

Thousands of programs on the market allow you to create and edit documents. Although no two programs are exactly the same, most programs have a menu bar at top, followed by some toolbars, followed by a large document area. The menu bar provides access to all the commands that the program offers for viewing, editing, and saving documents. The toolbars provide simple one-click access to the most commonly used menu commands. All of those commands operate on whatever document is currently open in the program's document area. Figure 3-1 shows an example of this common organization.

Things have been this way since 1990 when Windows was first released, and little has changed. Given that this is not a book for computer beginners, we'll leave it at that, and turn our focus from programs to documents in this chapter. (Just making sure that we're on the same wavelength here.)

Document Icons

In the non-computer world, just about anything that's typed on a piece of paper is a document of some sort. We all deal with lots of documents, and most of us have plenty of documents stored in some file cabinet somewhere. In the computer world, just about anything that you could print on paper would also be considered a document. In fact, many of the documents in your filing cabinet probably originated on some computer somewhere.

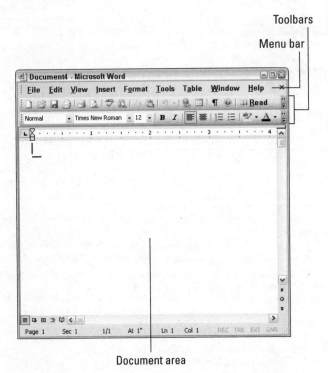

Figure 3-1: A typical program window and document area

In the computer world, virtually anything you can create or view in a program is a document. Certainly typed text qualifies, but pictures, songs, and videos are also examples of documents. Unlike programs, which you can open up on your screen at any time, a document can't just open on its own. A document, in the computer sense, is just *data* that's fed into a program. The program changes that data from a bunch of little dots stored on a disk somewhere into the meaningful information you see on the screen when you open the document.

Like a program, a document can be closed or open. A closed document is one that's stored on some disk somewhere. A closed document, like a closed program, is represented by an icon on the screen. Whereas the icon for a program is generally just a logo, an icon that represents a document generally has a little dog-eared sheet of paper as part of its icon, like the examples shown in Figure 3-2.

Figure 3-2: Examples of icons that represent documents

Plenty of exceptions exist to the dog-eared sheet of paper image for icons to represent documents. But let's just stick with what the examples shown in Figure 3-2. Every document is actually a file stored on a disk. And every file has a name. The name you see under each icon in Figure 3-2 is the filename of each document.

A document can't open by itself—it must open in some program. The logo on the dog-eared sheet of paper is the icon for the *default program* for opening that type of document. For example, the Dear John document is one that, when opened, will open in Microsoft Word. Hence the *W* icon for Word.

There are literally thousands of different types of documents. In a broad, general sense, a document can be a picture, text, music, or a video. But within any of those categories, the document can be any of many different types. For instance, a picture can be a bitmap, JPEG, GIF, TIF, or any of several dozen other files types. Another name for type is *format*. For example, a picture could be in *bitmap format* or *JPEG format*.

Windows has only one way of determining the format of the data inside a document file, and that's the filename's *extension*. The extension is a dot (.) followed by one or more letters. For instance, a picture stored in JPEG format will have a .JPEG or .JPG extension. A picture stored in bitmap format will have a .bmp extension. Because there are thousands of different document formats, there are thousands of different extensions.

Note   The most comprehensive collection of filename extensions of which I'm aware is at `http://filext.com/`. Currently, they claim to have 16,845 extensions in their database.

Whether or not filename extensions appear along with filenames is up to you. Most of the time I leave mine hidden, because I rarely need to know the exact extension of a filename. The logo on the document's icon tells me what program will open the file, and usually that tells me all I need to know. Plus, it's a lot easier to rename files with the extensions hidden and out of the way. (You never, ever, want to change a file's extension). Furthermore, the extensions just add that much more clutter to the screen, as you can see in Figure 3-3 where I've taken filename extensions out of hiding.

Figure 3-3: Icons from Figure 3-2 with filename extensions visible

Folder Icons

In the non-computer world, you probably keep your important paper documents in folders in some file cabinet somewhere. The obvious advantage to doing so is that the folders give you some means of organizing your documents so they're easy to find later.

You'll also store all your computer documents in folders for exactly the same reason that you store paper documents: to organize them so they're easy to find later. In the computer world, your hard disk is the file cabinet, and your folders are represented by icons. Unlike icons for programs and documents, icons that represent folders all tend to show a manila file folder as part of their icon, as in the examples shown in Figure 3-4.

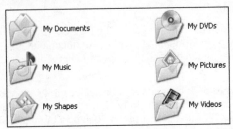

Figure 3-4: Sample icons that represent folders

To open a folder, you just click (or double-click) the folder's icon. When the folder opens, you'll see the documents contained within that folder. For example, if you click the Start button and choose My Documents from the Start menu, your My Documents folder will open, and you'll see its contents.

Note   The term *directory* means the same thing as *folder*. A folder is a directory and vice versa.

How folders are organized

In a file cabinet, your folders are arranged in a linear order. That is, when you open a file drawer, you see a row of file folders. On your hard disk, it's a different story, because folders can be organized hierarchically, which is to say, any folder can contain still more folders. We often refer to a folder that's contained within another folder as a *subfolder*. But a subfolder is no different from a folder. A folder is a folder is a folder, no matter where it's located.

For example, when you open your My Documents folder, you'll probably see at least two folders named My Music and My Pictures contained within it. They're just a couple of sample folders that Windows XP creates automatically, and the basic idea is simple. Pictures and music are just *categories* of documents. There are some differences between the two categories — the most obvious being that you look at pictures, but listen to music.

Parents and children

Two major buzzwords that are often used to describe relationships between folders are *parent* and *children*. That analogy comes from a family tree hierarchy. For example, My Documents is the parent to My Music and My Pictures, because the latter two folders are contained within My Pictures. My Music and My Pictures, in turn, are children of the My Documents folder.

If you put lots of songs in your My Music folder, you might want to organize those into still more subfolders. For example, you might have a separate folder for each artist whose music you've collected. You can create as many folders as you want, wherever you want. Exactly what folders you create and how you organize them is entirely up to you. Same as a file cabinet where you can add and label folders as you see fit.

If we extend the My Documents, My Music, My Pictures analogy with a few more folders, as in Figure 3-5, and show their relationship in a family tree format, you can see exactly how the terms parent and children make sense. You can also see how the hierarchical arrangement provides a much better means of organizing things than the file cabinet drawer does.

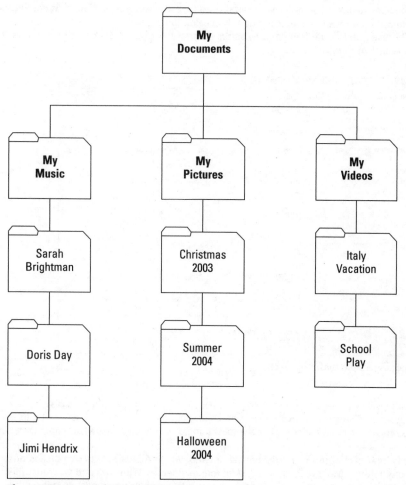

Figure 3-5: A sample folder hierarchy

So, looking at Figure 3-5, we see that My Documents is the parent to My Music, My Pictures, and My Videos. Those three folders, in turn, are children of My Documents. The My Music folder is parent to Sarah Brightman, Doris Day, and Jimi Hendrix. My Pictures is parent to Christmas 2003, Summer 2004, Halloween 2004. And My Videos is parent to Italy Vacation and School Play. Each of those folders can contain any number of documents, or still more folders.

Of course, you never actually *see* your folders as pictured in Figure 3-5. That's just a diagram of the logical relationship among the folders. But you can see why the hierarchical organization works just by thinking up an example. Suppose that you're looking for a Jimi Hendrix song you saved some months or years ago. You don't remember the exact filename, but you know it's a song, and you know all songs are documents. So you open My Documents, and then you open My Music. There, you see a folder named Jimi Hendrix.

By the time you get to the Jimi Hendrix folder, the rest should be easy. Maybe there are just a bunch of songs in that folder. Maybe there are still more folders. How you arrange things is up to you. But if you do open up the Jimi Hendrix folder and see something like Figure 3-6, finding the specific song you're looking for should be easy from there. Note that each folder in that example represents an album. Each document in that folder is one song from that album. There are also some documents (songs) in that folder that just don't belong to any of the albums shown as folders.

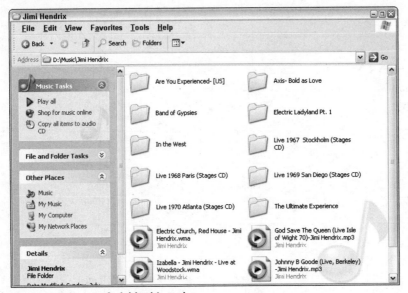

Figure 3-6: A sample folder hierarchy

Note   Just in case you weren't aware of this, there's probably room on your hard disk for tens of thousands of documents. No need to be chintzy about it and use floppies or CDs to store documents. Hard disk space is the cheapest thing on the planet — literally cheaper than dirt!

By the way, in this chapter we're discussing only *document folders*. Your hard disk is home to hundreds of folders. Most of them are *system folders* used by Windows and your installed programs. But there's no need to concern yourself with those right now because Windows takes care of those automatically. In this chapter, the focus is on folders you'll use to create the documents you create and download.

Document folders you already have

Right out of the box, Windows XP comes with at least eight document folders already made. By document folders, I mean folders that are specifically set up storing documents. Two of those folders, My Videos and Shared Videos, may not exist until you run Windows Movie Maker. But don't worry about that.

Of those eight folders, four have names that start with the word *My*, and four have names that start with *Shared*. The *My* folders are private to your computer and private to your user account, which means that if you share your computer with other users, or if your computer is on a network, other people can't see the documents in those *My* folders. To other users, your *My* folders don't even exist, so you don't have to worry about anyone else messing with them or even looking at them.

As mentioned, the other four document folders all have names that start with *Shared*. As the name implies, documents in those folders are available to all users. That includes people who share your computer, as well as people on other computers in your local network. Figure 3-7 shows the names of those eight folders and the relationships between them.

Note Shared or not shared, folders and documents on your computer aren't exposed to the Internet. That's because your PC is an Internet *client*, and clients can't expose files to the Internet. Only *servers* can do that. The only exception is when you join a Peer-2-Peer network and intentionally make folders available to other users.

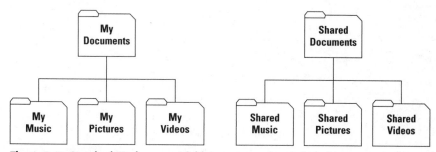

Figure 3-7: Standard XP document folders — personal and shared

We'll get into creating and organizing folders and documents in Part III of this book. In this chapter, we'll stay focused on using the folders you already have and on creating, saving, and opening documents. The main points to remember before we press on are:

✦ You use programs to create, download, view, edit, print, and save documents.

✦ Typed text, pictures, songs, and videos are all examples of documents.

✦ Like documents in a filing cabinet, you organize documents on your hard disk into folders.

✦ The folders you create can be arranged in a logical, hierarchical format, so it's easy to find things, even where there are tens of thousands of documents on the disk.

✦ In the folder hierarchy, a folder that contains still more folders is referred to as the *parent* of the folders it contains. Folders within the parent are its *children*.

Finally, if you're worried about how many of anything you can have, you can stop worrying. There are no limits to how many child folders or documents a given folder can contain.

Navigating Folders

The first step to using folders is knowing how to open them, view them, and get around from folder to folder. That's pretty easy to do because you use one program, Windows Explorer, to do it all. Windows Explorer is somewhat unique in that, unlike most programs, it doesn't show its own name in its own title bar. There is a Windows Explorer option on the All Programs menu, but you never actually need to click on that option to start the Windows Explorer because as soon as you open a folder — any folder — Windows Explorer opens automatically to show you that folder's contents.

For example, if you click the Start button and choose My Documents from the right side of the Start menu, Windows Explorer opens automatically to show you the contents of your My Documents folder. Although the exact contents of Windows Explorer's main pane vary from one folder to the next, the main tools in its menu bar and toolbar are always the same.

Like most programs, Windows Explorer has a title bar, menu bar, and toolbar at the top. Windows Explorer also has a thing called the Explorer bar at its left side. The main pane in Windows Explorer shows you the contents of whatever folder you happen to be viewing at the moment. Figure 3-8 points out the main components of Windows Explorer.

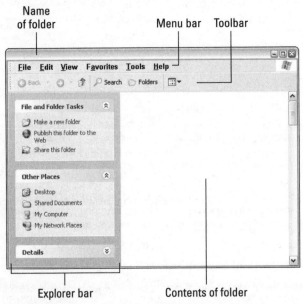

Figure 3-8: Main components of Windows Explorer

Like most programs, you can minimize and maximize Windows Explorer by using its Minimize, Maximize/Restore, and taskbar buttons. You can size Windows Explorer (when it's neither minimized nor maximized) by dragging its border. You can use its taskbar button to make it the active window if it gets covered by other windows. In short, even though Windows Explorer shows you the contents of folders, it's still a program and, thus, has all the same bells and whistles as any other program window.

The toolbar in Windows Explorer provides basic tools for navigating through folders. The first two buttons, Back and Forward, are disabled (dimmed) when you first open the program. That's because they don't do anything until you start viewing the contents of other folders. When you open a different folder from within Explorer, the Back button becomes enabled, and you can click on it to return to whatever folder you just navigated from. The Forward button will then be enabled. You can click that to return to the folder from which you just backed up.

Tip   As in any toolbar, you can point to any button in Explorer's toolbar to see the button's name.

Internet Explorer, Windows Explorer, and Explorer

Microsoft Internet Explorer is a Web browser. Basically, it's a program for exploring the Internet. Your computer needs to be online (connected to the Internet) for Internet Explorer to work. Windows Explorer often is referred to as simply Explorer in Windows help documentation. Because Windows Explorer lets you explore the contents of your own computer, you don't need to be online to use it.

Put in more technical terms, Internet Explorer is for exploring *remote* resources, things that are outside your computer on the Internet. Windows Explorer (or *Explorer* for short) is for exploring *local* resources—things that are inside your computer. There's no Internet involvement when you're looking at things in your own computer.

The Up button in the toolbar takes you to the current folder's parent, which is to say, if the folder you're currently viewing is contained within some other folder, clicking the Up button takes you straight to that folder's parent folder.

The Search and Folders buttons replace the standard Explorer bar with different bars, as we'll discuss later in this chapter. The last button, named Views, lets you specify how you want to view the contents of the current folder. We'll discuss that button a little later as well.

The Explorer bar provides easy one-click access to things you may want to do in the current folder. The options that appear in the Explorer bar at any given time depend on many factors, including which folder you happen to be in, whether or not you've selected icons in the current folder, and so forth. Notice the Show/Hide buttons in the headings in the Explorer bar. You can click that button to show, or hide, the options beneath the heading.

Opening folders

If the folder you're viewing at the moment contains any subfolders, you can open a subfolder just by clicking or double-clicking its icon. When you do, the title bar (and taskbar button) change to show the name of the folder you're currently viewing. The contents of that folder then appear in the main pane. Some of the options in the Explorer bar might change, too, to provide options that are more relevant to the kinds of files contained within the current folder.

For example, while viewing the contents of your My Documents folder, you'll see icons for the My Music and My Pictures folders that are contained within My Documents. If you click (or double-click) the icon for your My Music folder, the Explorer bar will change, showing a new set of options titled Music Tasks. Those options include things like Play All (to play all the songs in the folder) and Copy to Audio CD (to make a CD from the songs in the folder).

Clicking the Back button would then take you back to your My Documents folder. Opening your My Pictures folder from there would display the contents of your My Pictures folder. The Music Tasks options are replaced by Picture Tasks options such as "View as slide show," "Print this picture," and other things that are relevant only to pictures.

To click or double-click

I keep saying "click or double-click" to open an icon. Whether or not you have to double-click an icon in Explorer to open it is really up to you. In older versions of Windows, double-clicking was your only option. Now you have a choice. Here's how you make that choice:

1. From the menu bar in Windows Explorer choose **Tools ⇨ Folder Options**. The Folder Options dialog box opens.

2. Specify how you want to open icons by choosing options under **Click items as follows**, shown in Figure 3-9.

Tip   If your copy of Windows Explorer never shows the Explorer bar, make sure that "Show common tasks in folders" is selected near the top of the Folder Options dialog box.

3. Click **OK** after making your selection.

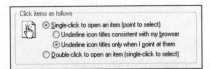

Figure 3-9: To click or double-click

Whichever option you chose will apply to all icons in all folders, as well as to any icons on the desktop. So, rather than saying "click or double-click" for the rest of this book, I'll just say "open" (the icon). Whether or not you have to click or double-click to do that depends on which option you chose in Figure 3-9.

About the Desktop folder

Speaking of the Desktop, you might have noticed under Other Places that you can go to the Desktop. If you click on that option, you really don't end up on the Windows desktop per se. Instead, you end up in a folder named desktop. You'll also end up in that desktop if you click the Up button in toolbar a few times, because the Desktop folder is at the very top of the folder hierarchy.

Even though the Desktop folder is different from the Windows desktop you learned about in Chapter 2, it's very similar in that it contains exactly the same icons as your desktop, as in the example shown in Figure 3-10. I suppose that fact might conjure up in some readers the profound question "What's up with that?" The rationale follows.

The desktop is the first thing you see when you start Windows. And it's also the easiest place to get to on your computer because it's always there, from the moment you turn on the computer until you turn it off. Therefore, the desktop is a great place to store icons for items you use all the time.

When you have a bunch of open program windows covering up the desktop, the icons on the desktop aren't so easy to get to. When you're in Windows Explorer and need to get to the desktop, you might have to minimize some program windows, do your thing at the desktop, then restore the windows you minimized just to get back to where you were. That's going to take a few mouse clicks.

Rather than make us burn any calories clicking our mice unnecessarily to get to our desktops, the programmers at Microsoft came up with an idea. Why don't we just make a folder named Desktop, and have it show exactly the same icons that are on the desktop? That way, the users don't have to go all the way back to the desktop to get to those icons. They can just navigate to the icons as they would any other folder.

Figure 3-10: The Desktop folder contains copies of desktop icons.

So they turned that idea into a reality, but then had to decide where to put the folders. Well, the desktop is its own separate thing in that it's not some normal folder contained within some other normal folder. So, they decided to put that special Desktop folder above all others. That's why there's a folder named Desktop that's a clone of the icons on your actual desktop. And that's why when you click Up a few times in the Explorer's toolbar, you'll eventually end up in that special Desktop folder.

Showing and hiding filename extensions

Earlier in this chapter I talked about file types and how a filename extension tells Windows how the data inside a document is formatted. I mentioned that you can make filename extensions either visible, or invisible. Sometimes it's useful to see them. But often they're just in the way. To decide whether or not you want filename extensions to be visible in Windows Explorer, follow these steps:

1. Choose **Tools ➪ Folder Options** from the menu bar in Windows Explorer.

2. In the Folder Options dialog box that opens, click the **View** tab.

3. If you want to hide filename extensions, select (check) the **Hide extensions for known file types**, option as shown in Figure 3-11. Or, to make the extensions visible, clear that checkbox.

4. Click **OK**.

By the way, folders aren't files and therefore don't have filename extensions. Adding an extension to a folder's name will have no effect.

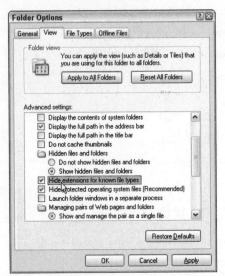

Figure 3-11: Hide extensions for known file types is selected.

Personally, I think Microsoft should make a shortcut key for showing/hiding filename extensions at will. When you're naming or renaming files, the extensions just get in the way because you have to edit around them. But obviously there are times when you really do need filename extensions. I've submitted a request for that feature to be added to the next version of Windows (code named Longhorn). If you agree, do the same, and maybe we'll get that in Windows 2006 (or whatever they end up calling it).

Lateral moves through the hierarchy

Have you ever heard the saying "You can't get there from here?" There's an ounce of truth to that when you're talking about moving up and down through folders using My Documents as your starting point. That's because not all folders are children of My Documents. To get to a folder other than Desktop, My Documents, or a child of My Documents, you may need to make a lateral move across to a *sibling* folder (a folder that's at the same level as My Documents). There are several ways to make a quick jump to a folder that can't be reached from the My Documents folder hierarchy.

Using other places

The Other Places portion of the Explorer bar gives you quick one-click access to other places you might need to look for a folder. The places listed there will vary, depending on which folder you're in at the moment. But typically you'll see links to the folders shown in Figure 3-12.

Urban Myth: Never Hide Filename Extensions

There are times when it's useful to see filename extensions and times when it's not. That's why you have the option of making them visible or invisible. Hiding the extensions reduces screen clutter and makes it a lot easier to rename files. Nonetheless, many an inexperienced computer user has told me I should never hide filename extensions. But I know better.

I think the justification for never hiding filename extensions has something to do with protecting your computer from malicious e-mail attachments. If your criterion for deciding on whether or not to open an e-mail attachment is the attachment's filename extension, then I can guarantee you that your computer will get infected by a virus. Seeing the filename extensions won't help at all.

You'll learn real ways to protect your computer from viruses and other bad things in Chapter 28. In the meantime, feel free to show or hide filename extensions whenever you please. Because filename extensions have absolutely nothing to do with making your computer more, or less, secure from Internet threats.

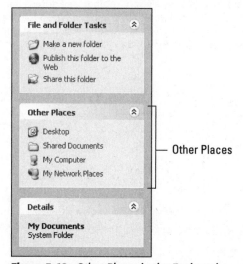

Figure 3-12: Other Places in the Explorer bar

Clicking on an option takes you directly to the folder. Note, however, that of the folders shown, only Shared Documents is an actual document folder. The other folders shown are special folders used to get to a specific disk drive, or perhaps to shortcuts you've stored on the desktop. Here's a quick overview of the folders you can jump to from the Other Places:

✦ **Desktop:** As mentioned, Desktop is a folder that contains a copy of all the icons on your desktop. The Desktop is a lousy place to *store* documents. But if it already contains shortcuts to document folders you use frequently, you can use that folder as an intermediate step to get to any folder that those shortcuts represent.

✦ **Shared Documents:** Shared Documents is a document folder, and is also the parent to Shared Music, Shared Pictures, and any other folder you create under Shared Documents. So you can use the Shared Document link under Other Places to get to any folder shared folders you create under Shared Documents.

✦ **My Computer:** Provides access to all of your computer's other disk drives including floppy, CD, DVD, and Zip drives, as well as Thumb drives and flash memory (such as memory sticks).

✦ **My Network Places:** If your computer is a member of a local network, this folder provides access to shared folders on other computers in that network. Use this folder to open, or copy documents from, those other remote drives.

Keep in mind that the items under Other Places do change. For example, if you go to Shared Documents, there won't be an option to jump there any more. After all, you're already there. You will, however, see an option to jump back to your My Documents folder.

Windows Explorer Address bar

Like Internet Explorer, Windows Explorer has an Address bar. You can turn it on and off at will, just as you can in any Windows program. Just choose View ➪ Toolbars ➪ Address Bar from Explorer's menu bar to show, or hide, the Address bar. While you *could* type a folders address into the Address box, it's never really necessary to do so. Rather, you can just open the drop-down list for the Address bar, as shown in Figure 3-13, then click the name of the folder or drive you want to jump to.

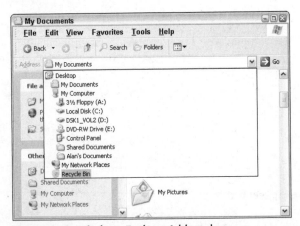

Figure 3-13: Windows Explorer Address bar

If you type a URL (a Web site address) into the Address bar, you will be taken to that Web site (provided that you're online). However, since Windows Explorer is for exploring your local computer, not the Internet, you'll no longer be in Windows Explorer. Instead, Windows Explorer will magically turn into Internet Explorer, and you'll be browsing the Web. When you click the Back button in Internet Explorer, Internet Explorer will magically turn back into Windows Explorer. (OK, so it's not really magic — just some clever programming on Microsoft's part. It seems kind of magical though).

When the toolbars in Explorer are unlocked, you can move and size any toolbar that's currently visible. If you put the Address bar to the right of the Standard Buttons toolbar, you could end up seeing just its label, as in Figure 3-14.

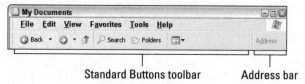

Standard Buttons toolbar   Address bar

Figure 3-14: Two Explorer toolbars

To make the Address bar usable, you'll need to resize and reposition the bar by dragging its handle, just to the left of the word "Address." If you don't see the dragging handle, that means the toolbars are locked. To unlock them (or relock them), choose View ⇨ Toolbars ⇨ Lock the Toolbars from Explorer's menu bar.

Using the Folders list

The Folders list is an optional temporary replacement for the Explorer bar that you can turn on and off at will. Just click the Folders button in the toolbar, or choose View ⇨ Explorer Bar ⇨ Folders from Explorer's menu bar. Either way, the Folders pane will appear. Unlike the Explorer bar, you can change the width of any optional bar by dragging its right edge left or right.

The Folders list provides access to all disk drives and folders on your system. Click on any name to see the contents of that drive or folder in the main pane to the right. You can get to most drives and document folders right from the list without expanding any items in the list. Though you can click the + or - key next to any name to show or hide resources available within that item.

For example, if you expand your hard drive's icon and the Documents and Settings folder, you'll see icons for all the top-level folders on your hard drive. If you click the + sign next to Documents and Settings, as shown in Figure 3-15, you'll see subfolders contained within that folder.

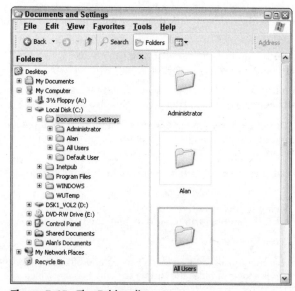

Figure 3-15: The Folders list

Research and Discussions

If you have Microsoft Office installed, you might also have Explorer bars named Research and Discuss. If your work involves research, the Research pane will give you quick access to online research services such as LexisNexis, Ovid, and many others. To learn move, visit http://office.microsoft.com/marketplace and click on Reference under "Browse Office Marketplace Services." Or search that same site for "Research services."

Web discussions allow you to participate in online discussions. These aren't random chats. Rather Web discussions are specifically about allowing people to collaborate on large projects. For more information, display the Discussion bar, and click the Help (blue circled question mark button) at the right side of the bar.

If you're new to XP and the whole concept of user accounts, the Folders list can be a bit confusing. Chapter 7 discusses how folders on your hard drive are organized in relation to user accounts. But basically each user account has a folder under Documents and Settings. Subfolders beneath a user's account name represent that specific user's My Documents, My Pictures, and other private folders. The All Users folder under Documents and Settings contains things like the Shared . . . folders, as well as other special folders that contain items that all user accounts share.

Also worth noting is that exactly what you see in the Folders list depends on whether you're currently logged into a user account with administrative privileges or limited privileges. Accounts with administrative privileges can get to any folder (except other administrator private folders). Limited accounts can't get to other users' folders at all. But again, I'm getting ahead of myself here, and these topics will make more sense in the Chapter 7.

Anyway, the Folders list gives you easy access to any and all storage media on your computer. For that matter, you can expand the My Network Places folder to get at any shared medium in your local network. In other words, the Folders list provides the easy way to get there from here no matter where "here" is. (I *think* that last sentence is a legitimate sentence. Correct me if I'm wrong.)

In addition to the standard Explorer bar and the Folders list, you can choose View ⇨ Explorer Bar from Explorer's menu bar to view any of the following optional bars:

✦ **Search:** Displays the Search Companion, which can search multiple hard drives for any file based on name, contents, date, and other criteria (see Chapter 17).

✦ **Favorites:** Displays your Internet Explorer Favorites. You can add local resources to your Favorites as well, using the Add button at the top of the Favorites list, or Favorites ⇨ Add to Favorites from Explorer's menu bar (see Chapter 32).

✦ **History:** Displays a list of Web sites you've visited recently with Internet Explorer (see Chapter 32).

To put an optional Explorer bar back into hiding and return to the default bar, click the Close (X) button in the bar's title. Or repeat the step(s) you took to display the bar in the first place.

Tip   As you'll see on the Explorer bar menu, you can turn some bars on and off using shortcut keys. For example, pressing Ctrl+H shows or hides the History bar.

When you choose View ➪ Explorer Bar from Explorer's menu bar, you'll also see a couple of extra options that aren't really bars.

✦ **Tip of the Day:** Opens a pane at the bottom of Explorer's window offering a daily tip.

Arranging icons in Explorer

A folder can contain any numbers of subfolders and documents. You can arrange those icons in a number of ways, making it easier to locate a specific file. You can arrange icons based on any of the following:

✦ **Name:** Folders are listed in alphabetical order, followed by files listed in alphabetical order.

✦ **Size:** Files are listed from smallest to largest size, after folders.

✦ **Type:** Files are listed in alphabetical order by type, after folders.

✦ **Modified:** Files are listed from oldest to newest, based on the date and time that you last saved the file.

You might see other options on the menu; it just depends on the particular folder you're in. For example, if you're in My Music, you'll see options for arrange icons by Artist or Album Title.

To choose a sort option, use whichever of these methods is most convenient at the moment:

✦ Choose **View** ➪ **Arrange Icons by** from Explorer's menu bar.

✦ Or right-click some empty space between icons and choose **View** ➪ **Arrange Icons By**.

Figure 3-16 shows an example where I've currently viewing a folder that contains mostly pictures. Notice that in addition to the standard options listed, the options allow sorting by criteria that are specific to pictures, such as the date the picture was taken, or the dimensions of the picture.

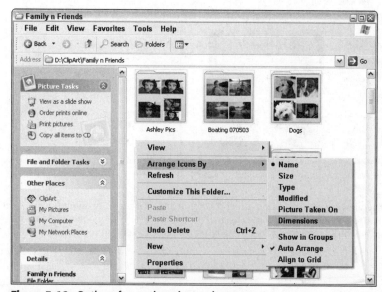

Figure 3-16: Options for sorting picture documents

The lower half of the Arrange Icons By menu offers some additional options. These all act as toggles, meaning that you can turn them on or off, as desired. Here's what the toggles offer:

✦ **Show in Groups:** If selected, icons are shown in groups with group headings (particularly useful when viewing many icons arranged by Type).

✦ **Auto Arrange:** If selected, icons will be sorted automatically, so they're always in order when you first open the folder.

✦ **Align to Grid:** If selected, icons align to an invisible grid as you add them to the folder. This keeps the icons neatly aligned, even when you move them yourself.

Some alert readers might have noticed that the icons in Figure 3-16 don't exactly look like normal icons — which brings us to our next Windows Explorer topic.

Umpteen ways to view icons

Icons aren't always the best way to view the information in a folder. For example, when viewing a folder that contains mostly pictures, it makes more sense to see the actual pictures than just an icon. When viewing a folder that contains hundreds or thousands of files, you're faced with a lot of icons to sift through. To help with such issues, Windows Explorer lets you choose exactly how you want to view the items in the current folder.

There are three ways to choose a view in Windows Explorer. As always, feel free to use whichever method is most convenient at the moment:

✦ Choose **View** from the menu bar.

✦ Or click the **Views** button in the toolbar (see Figure 3-17).

✦ Or right-click some empty space between icons, and choose **View**.

Figure 3-17: Views button near the mouse pointer

Keep in mind the viewing options don't affect *what* you see. Rather they affect *how* you see it. You'll see the entire contents of the folder no matter which view you choose. Picking one view or another is simply a matter of deciding what's most convenient for you at the moment.

Filmstrip view

The Filmstrip view is available only in folders that contain pictures, such as your My Pictures and Shared Pictures folders. A folder that contains anything other than pictures most likely won't offer a Filmstrip view. The Filmstrip view displays each picture in a strip along the bottom of the window. Use the horizontal scroll bar at the bottom of the window to look through all your icons.

To see an enlarged version of any picture, select that picture's icon. If you use double-clicking to open icons, click on a picture to select it. If you use single-clicking, just rest the mouse pointer on an icon for a moment to select it. The preview area up top will give you a better look at the selected picture, as in Figure 3-18.

Figure 3-18: Example of Filmstrip view

Keep in mind that the preview image isn't an icon. It's just a preview. You can right-click the preview to do a few things with it. But you can't open, edit, move, or copy the preview.

Caution   If your copy of Windows XP is set up to mimic the appearance of earlier versions of Windows, then you'll never see the Explorer bar, and you'll never be given a Filmstrip view option. To rectify that, choose Tools ⇨ Folders Options from Explorer's menu bar. Click on "Show common tasks in folders," and then click OK.

Thumbnails view

Like Filmstrip, the Thumbnails view works best when viewing icons that represent pictures. Rather than show some standard icon, Thumbnails shows a small thumbnail-sized image of the picture contained within the file. For folders that contain pictures, the Thumbnails view displays a manila file folder with tiny images of four pictures contained within the folder, as in the example shown in Figure 3-19.

Figure 3-19: Example of Thumbnails view

Tiles view

The Tiles view shows standard document and folder icons with the name of the folder or file to the right. For documents, the Tiles view also shows some additional information about the file. The exact information varies. For general documents, it will likely be the program associated with that document type and the size of the file. For music, you'll more likely see album title and artist name, as in Figure 3-20.

Figure 3-20: Sample icons shown in Tiles view

Icons and List views

The Icons and List views both show each item's icon and name only. No details. The only difference is the Icons view shows large icons, whereas the List view shows only tiny icons. The List view lets you see more of the items contained within the folder because each icon is small.

Details view

The Details view shows tiny icons and lots of information about each item. Figure 3-21 shows a small example. But you can choose exactly how much information you want to display for each file. If there are more columns of information than can fit into the window size, use the horizontal scroll bar at the bottom of the window to see columns currently scrolled out of view.

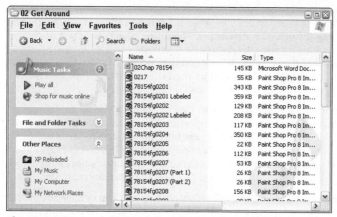

Figure 3-21: Sample icons shown in Details view

The Details view is unique in that all the information is presented in columns with headings at the top. The column headings are actually useful tools in themselves. For example, you can sort (or alphabetize) the list by clicking any column heading. The first time you click a heading, items are placed in ascending order. Clicking a second time reverses the order.

For example, you can click the Name column heading to put the files in alphabetical order by name. Click the Size column to list files from smallest to largest (or vice versa) size. To put the files in oldest to newest order (or vice versa), click the Date Modified column heading. You can click any column heading to sort all the files names by the contents of that column.

You can also move and size columns to your liking. To make a column wider or narrower, first place the tip of the mouse pointer on the bar just to the right of the column name, so you see the two-headed arrow mouse pointer. Then, drag left or right to whatever width you like. To move a column, put the mouse pointer right on the column name, and then drag left or right.

Choosing Details to view

You can even choose which columns you do, and don't, want to see in Details view. The settings you choose will be applied to the current folder only, so make sure that you get to the folder first. Also, keep in mind that your setting will be forgotten as soon as you leave the folder, unless you tell Windows to remember views as described in the next section.

To choose columns you want to see in Details view, choose View ➪ Choose Details from Explorer's menu bar, or right-click any column in the heading in Details view and choose More. The Choose Details dialog box opens. Select (check) the columns you want to see. Clear the checkmark next to any column you don't want to see.

Tip   To quickly add a single column to the Details view, right-click any column heading, and then click on the column you want to add. You may need to scroll to the right to find the column after adding it.

You can predefine a columns position and width while you're in the Choose Details dialog box. First, click on a column name to select it. Then, use the Move Up, Move Down, and Width. . . options in the dialog box to do as you please. Of course, you could also ignore the moving and sizing options in the dialog box. Then, move and size the columns in Details view after you click the OK button. When choosing columns to show, think about any you might want to include for sorting purposes. For example, The Date Created and Date Accessed columns are useful for looking for the oldest or newest version of a file. If "newest" means "most recently used," sorting that column into descending order lists files in a most recently viewed order down to the oldest files. Sorting the Created Date Sorting Date Created to descending order lists files from most recently created to oldest order.

The columns get the information they display from files' *properties*. The properties are part of the actual file, and Windows has access to the properties. Thus it can search for files based on any properties you use. In some cases, properties are filled automatically, such as when you copy music CD to your computer. As each song is copied from the CD, Media Player fills in the blanks on the properties with information such as the artist and album title, the title and duration of each song, and so on. Many digital cameras fill in properties relevant to pictures.

In Details view, you can see, and change, any file's properties. You can change the properties of several files at once by just selecting the items you want to change before you right-click and choose Properties. In any other view, you can right-click any item, or select multiple items and then right click. Choose Properties from the menu, and the file's Properties dialog box opens. Click the Summary tab to view a few properties. But if you really want to see what's going on, click the Advanced [n1] button. Anyway, I'm getting ahead of myself. You'll see more about that in Chapter 12.

Making view settings stick

Normally, Windows doesn't bother to keep track of the view you chose in a particular folder. If you just spent some time setting up a nice Details view for a folder, that's not necessarily a good thing. To make Windows remember and reuse your last view setting each time you open the folder in the future, follow these steps:

1. If the Choose Details dialog box is still open, click its **OK** button.

2. Choose **Tools** ➪ **Folder Options** from Explorer's menu bar.

3. In the Folder Options dialog box that opens, click on the **View** tab.

4. Scroll down to and select (check) the **Remember each folder's view settings** option, as shown in Figure 3-22.

5. Click **OK** in the Folder Options dialog box.

So, you can view anything you want in any order and lots of different ways. As long as the files are organized into folders, it should be easy to find anything you want. If worse comes to worse, you can use the Search Companion (see Chapter 17) to make Explorer find the file.

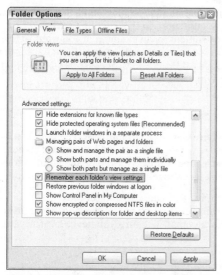

Figure 3-22: The Folder Options dialog box

Closing folders

Closing an open folder is just a matter of exiting the Windows Explorer program. You can exit any program using whatever method you prefer. Click the program's Close (X) button. Or if it's in the active window, press Alt+F4. If you have multiple folders open and want to close them all, right-click the Windows Explorer taskbar button and choose Close Group.

There is plenty more about folders coming up in Part III. Let's move on to documents. Quick Review: You use programs to create and save documents. You use folders to organize those documents. So what's the big fuss about documents? Well, they're why you probably bought the computer in the first place.

Get a Handle on Documents

We normally think of a document as something that's printed on paper. On a computer a document can be text, a picture, a song, a spreadsheet, a database, a Web page—just about anything. There are a few ways to create documents. Open a program and create a new document. Or get pictures from a camera or scanner. Or you could copy a CD to your hard disk. Each picture or song will be stored in a document file in whatever folder you specify.

Using programs to create documents

Many applications are written to allow us to create, download, open, and save documents. You keep track of your documents by organizing them into folders on your hard disk. Just as there are many different kinds of documents, there are many different kinds of programs. For example, you use a photo-editing or graphics program to work with pictures. You use a word processing program such as Microsoft Word, WordPerfect, or WordPad to type a document.

There are some techniques for working with documents that are universal, in the sense that they apply to all documents (or at least, most documents). In this section, we'll·cover those common techniques using a word processing document as an example. If you want to try some of these things yourself, you can open Microsoft Word or WordPad, if you have either one. Or, you can click the Start button and choose All Programs ➪ Accessories ➪ WordPad to start the free word processor that comes with Windows.

Typing and navigating text

Typing in a document, e-mail message, or anywhere else on a computer screen is similar to typing with a typewriter. The main difference is that when you type on a computer screen, you don't press Enter at the end of each line. You only press Enter after typing the entire paragraph. Pressing Enter a second time adds a blank like above the next paragraph you type.

After you've typed text, you can position the cursor anywhere within that text just by clicking the spot where you want to move the cursor. You can also use any of the keys listed in Table 3-1 to navigate through text. (I titled it "*Almost* Universal" because you never know where there will be some exception to the rule).

Table 3-1: (Almost) Universal Keys for Moving the Cursor through Text

Key	Where it moves the cursor
→	One character to the right
←	One character to the left
↑	Up one line
↓	Down one line
Home	Beginning of the line
End	End of Line
Ctrl+Home	Top of document
Ctrl+End	End of document
Page Up (PgUp)	Up a page (or screenful)
Page Down (PgDn)	Down a page (or screenful)
Ctrl+←	One word to the left
Ctrl+→	One word to the right
Ctrl+↑	Up one paragraph
Ctrl+↓	Down one paragraph
Ctrl+Page Up (PgUp)	To top of previous page
Ctrl+Page Down (PgDn)	To top of next page
Alt+Ctrl+Page Up (PgUp)	To top of visible text
Alt+Ctrl+Page Down (PgDn)	To bottom of visible text

Editing text

After you've typed text, you can easily insert and delete text to make changes. The first step is to get the cursor to where you want to make the change. When the cursor is in place you can:

✦ Press Backspace to delete the character to the left of the cursor

✦ Press Delete (Del) to delete the character to the right of the cursor

To insert text at the cursor position, just start typing. If you're in Insert mode, the new text will be inserted without replacing any existing text. If you're in Overwrite mode, the new text will replace (overwrite) existing text. To switch from Insert to Overwrite mode, or vice versa, press the Insert (Ins) key once.

Selecting text

If you want to work with larger chunks of text (as opposed to working with one character at a time), you first need to *select* the text with which you want to work. Selected text is highlighted. For example, in Figure 3-23, I selected the highlighted paragraph by triple-clicking that paragraph.

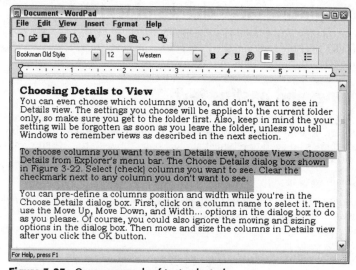

Figure 3-23: One paragraph of text selected

You can select text using either the mouse or keyboard. With the mouse, you can just drag the mouse pointer through any chunk of text you select. There are some optional mouse *shortcuts* you can use in most programs for selecting specific chunks of text as follows:

✦ **Select one word:** Double-click the word.

✦ **Select one sentence:** Hold down the Ctrl key, and click the sentence.

✦ **Select one line:** Move the cursor into the white space to the left of the line, and then click.

✦ **Select one paragraph:** Triple-click the paragraph.

✦ **Select multiple paragraphs:** Drag through all of them, or click where you want to start the selection. Then, hold down the Shift key and click the location you want to extend the selection to.

✦ **Select all text in the document:** Choose Edit ➪ Select All from the menu bar, or press Ctrl+A.

Keep in mind that the preceding selection methods aren't supported by all programs. If a particular method doesn't work in the program you're using at the moment, you can still select the text just by dragging the mouse pointer through that text.

To unselect selected text, just click anywhere outside the selected text. Or press the ↑, ↓, ←, or → key by itself (without holding down the Shift key).

Note   In Adobe Acrobat Reader, you need to click the Select Text button in the toolbar before you select. Otherwise, dragging will just cause the entire document to scroll. In Acrobat Reader 6.0 the toolbar button reads Select Text.

To select text using the keyboard rather than the mouse, just hold down the Shift key as you press any of the navigation keys listed in Table 3-1.

Deleting and replacing large chunks of text

To delete a large chunk of text, select the text you want to delete, and then press the Delete key. Optionally, you can select the text, and then just start typing new text. The selected text will disappear the moment you start typing, and only the new text you type will remain.

Copying, moving, and pasting text

Any place you can type text, you can also *paste* text. That boils down to this: If there's a chunk of text somewhere on your screen that you want to include in some document you're currently working on, there's no need to retype it all. Just copy the text from wherever it is and paste it into your document. Here are the steps:

1. Select the text you want to copy using any method cited earlier.

2. Copy the selected text to the Windows Clipboard, using whichever of the following methods is most convenient at the moment:

   • Press **Ctrl+C**.

   • Right-click the selected text and choose **Copy**.

   • Choose **Edit** ➪ **Copy** from that program's menu bar.

   Figure 3-24 shows an example where I've selected a chunk of text in a Web page, right-clicked that text, and am about to click on Copy. The program in the background is WordPad, currently showing a new, empty document. (Although it would be OK if that document already contained other text.)

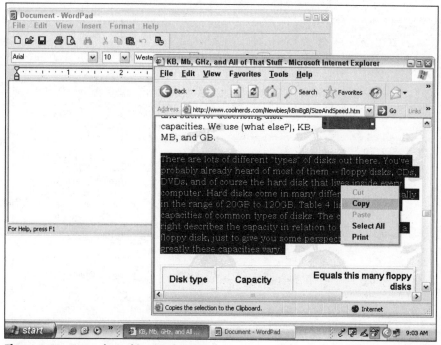

Figure 3-24: Text selected in a Web page

3. In the destination document (the one in which you want to place the copied text), move the cursor to the location where you want to put the selected text.

4. Paste the Clipboard contents using whichever technique is most convenient at the moment:

- Press **Ctrl+V**.

- Right-click near the cursor and choose **Paste**.

- Choose **Edit** ⇨ **Paste** from that program's menu bar.

Figure 3-25 shows an example where I pasted the selected text into the WordPad document. Remember, you can paste text wherever you can type text. So, the same technique will work with Microsoft Word, WordPerfect, and any other program that lets you type text.

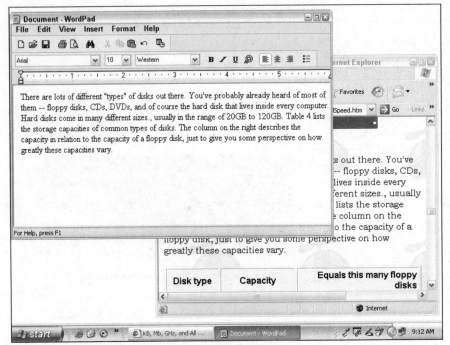

Figure 3-25: Copied text in the WordPad document.

Move text within a document

If you want to move a chunk of text within a document, the technique is basically the same. Though you'll want to Cut, rather than Copy, the text. When you cut text, a copy of the selected text is moved to the Clipboard, then removed (cut from) the original document. Here are the steps:

1. Select the text you want to move using any selection technique you like.

2. Cut the text using whichever method here is most convenient at the moment:

   - Press **Ctrl+X**.

   - Right-click the selected text and choose **Cut**.

   - Choose **Edit** ⇨ **Cut** from that program's menu bar.

3. Move the cursor to wherever you want to put the cut text.

4. Paste the text normally (press **Ctrl+V**, right-click and choose **Paste**, or choose **Edit** ⇨ **Paste** from the program's menu bar).

The methods given here work the same in small textboxes, not just word processing document. You could, for example, copy a URL (Web site address) from any page and then paste it into the Address bar of your Web browser to get to that page.

Adding special characters to text

Your keyboard has all the letters, numbers, and punctuation marks you need to type just about anything. Special characters such as copyright and trademark symbols can't be typed from the keyboard. Exactly how you type such a character into a document varies. For example, in Microsoft Word you can choose Insert ➪ Symbol from Word's menu bar to find and insert a character.

If the program you're using at the moment doesn't have its own capability for typing special characters, you can use the Windows Character Map to insert the character. Here's how:

1. In your document, position the cursor at the location where you want to insert the special character(s).

2. Click the Windows Start button and choose **All Programs** ➪ **Accessories** ➪ **System Tools** ➪ **Character Map**. The Character Map program opens, as shown in Figure 3-26

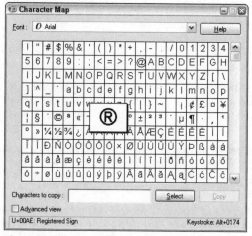

Figure 3-26: The Windows character map

3. If you don't see the character you want:

   - Use the scroll bar to the right of the characters to see additional characters.

   - Or choose a different font from the Font drop-down list.

Tip

If it's difficult to see a character in Character Map, click the character to magnify it.

4. To select a character to use, click it, and then click the **Select** button. You can repeat this step to select as many characters as you need.

5. Click the **Copy** button.

6. In your document, click where you want to place the special character(s).

7. Paste the character using any standard Paste method: **Press Ctrl+V**, or right-click near the cursor and choose **Paste**, or choose **Edit** ➪ **Paste** from that program's menu bar.

Note   Character Map is an optional Windows component. If it's not available on your System Tools menu, see "Installing and Removing Windows Components" in Chapter 45.

To close Character Map, click the Close (X) button in its upper-right corner.

Saving and Downloading Documents

A document on your screen isn't necessarily a document that's stored on your hard disk as a file. For example, a Web page you browsed to is a document, but it's not a file on your hard disk per se. (Well, it is a file in your Temporary Internet Files folder, but its life expectancy there is brief). A document you just created isn't a file on your hard disk until you save and name the document. In most programs, you can save a document by following these steps:

✦ Choose **File** ➪ **Save** from the Program's menu bar.

✦ Or, press **Ctrl+S**

✦ Or, click the **Save** button in the program's toolbar.

If this is the first time you've saved the document, the Save As dialog box will open. Use that dialog box to specify where you want to save the document, what you want to name the document, and the format in which you want to save the document. More on the Save As dialog box in a moment.

Note that once you've saved a document, future saves won't display the Save As dialog box. The program will assume that you just want to save changes you made to the document since the last save. So, it will just update the existing document to match what's currently open and on the screen.

If you do want to save the current document under a separate filename, choose File Save As rather than File Save. Doing so will force the Save As dialog box to open, so you can specify a different location, name, and/or format for the current document.

Downloading a document

When you download a document, you're actually saving a copy of that document to your own hard disk. Note that I'm talking strictly about downloading documents here. Downloading programs is a different matter, because you have to download and install a program before you can use it on your computer. But only programs need to be installed, not documents.

Note   See Chapter 45 for the full story on downloading and installing programs.

When you're using Microsoft Internet Explorer as your Web browser, you can download a Web page, a picture, or in some cases even videos and sound files, using any of the following techniques:

✦ To save the entire current Web page, choose **File ⇨ Save As** from Internet Explorer's menu bar.

✦ To download just a picture from the current Web page, right-click the picture and choose **Save Picture As**.

✦ To download a page, video, or music file, right-click the link that would otherwise take you to that item and choose **Save Target As**.

Note that the last method isn't always reliable, because the link might not point directly to the item that the link refers to. Rather, the link might point to a page that only displays the item. But, there's no harm in trying.

The Save As dialog box will open, so you can tell Windows where to store the file and what to name it, and perhaps choose a different format. In some cases the Save As dialog box will be titled File Download, Save Picture, or something else. But it's still the Save As dialog box— only the title in the title bar is different.

Using the Save As dialog box

The key to being able to find a document that you've saved is knowing where to look and what to look for. Windows will never force you to put a document in a particular folder or force you to use a particular filename. Where you put things and what you name them is entirely up to you.

If you don't already have a strategy for keeping your documents organized, now would be a good time to adopt one. The simplest strategy is to just use the built-in document folders. Choose a folder based on the item you're downloading as follows:

✦ If it's a picture, put it in your My Pictures or Shared Pictures folder.

✦ If it's sound or music, put it in your My Music or Shared Music folder.

✦ If it's a video, put it in your My Videos or Shared Videos folder.

✦ If it's anything else, put it in My Documents or Shared Documents.

The Save In option at the top of the dialog box is how you tell Windows where to save the document. Whatever name appears in that drop-down list is where the file will be saved. So your first step in the Save As dialog box is to get the appropriate folder name to show there. There are a few ways to do that, as discussed next.

Choosing a folder for the document

The Save As dialog box is actually sort of a mini–Windows Explorer, in the sense that you can navigate to any folder you wish using tools pointed out Figure 3-27. When you click the Save button in the dialog box, the document will be saved in whatever folder name appears in the Save In drop-down list. So, the first step is to make sure that name matches the name of the folder in which you want to store the document.

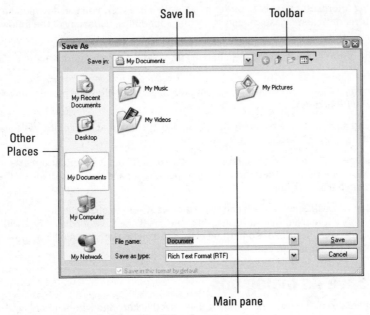

Figure 3-27: A typical Save As dialog box

To navigate through folders, use any combination of the following techniques:

✦ **Save in:** Choose a folder name (or disk drive) from the drop-down list. The main pane will show the contents of that folder, in case you need to choose a subfolder.

✦ **Other Places:** Not all Save As dialog boxes have this pane. But if yours does, click any icon to jump to that folder.

✦ **Main pane:** To choose a subfolder of the current folder as the location of your document, double-click the subfolder's icon in the main pane.

✦ **Toolbar:** Use toolbar buttons to help with folder navigation. Those buttons may vary from one dialog box to the next. The buttons shown in the figure, going left to right, are:

• **Back:** (return to the folder from which you just navigated).

• **Up:** Go to the current folder's parent folder.

• **New Folder:** Create a new subfolder within the current folder.

• **Views:** Change how icons look in the main pane, for example Thumbnails or Details view.

When the Save In option shows the name of the folder in which you want to save the document, you can move onto the next step, which is . . .

Naming a document

The File Name option under the main pane is where you specify the name of the document you're about to save. The rules on filenames are fairly straightforward. The maximum length is 254 characters (but in most cases you'll want to keep your filenames much shorter than that). The name can contain letters, numbers, spaces, and any characters except the following:

\ : / * ? " > < |

You can use any of the text editing techniques to change the name that currently appears in the File Name box. For example, select the entire current name and then type a new name.

Caution   Do not change the extension at the end of the filename. If filename extensions are hidden, it's not an issue because you won't even see the extension. But if filename extensions are visible, make sure that you change only the filename to the left of the dot and extension. Optionally, you can delete the suggested filename and extension, and type in a new filename without an extension. Windows will automatically add the appropriate extension for the format specified in the Save As Type option.

Choosing a document type

The Save As Type option at the bottom of the Save As dialog box allows you to chose a format for the saved files. The options available to you depend on many factors, including the current format of the document you're about to save and the programs you have installed on your computer.

The main pane is filtered to show only those documents in the current folder that match the format specified in the Save As Type box. So, if you choose a different Save As Type, the icons in the main pane will change.

Because the Save As Type option reflects the document's current format, there's no need to change it. However, there are situations where you may want to choose a different format. For example:

✦ If the item being saved is a picture in AOL's .ART format, choose .BMP, .JPEG, or .GIF, if possible. (Very few programs, other than AOL's Web browser, can handle .ART files.)

✦ If the item being saved is a bitmap picture and you want to create a smaller, more compact version, choose JPEG as the format.

✦ If the item being saved is a Web page, choosing **Web Archive, single file (*.mht)** will save it as a single file. Otherwise, you'll end up with two icons per downloaded Web page.

Note   When saving a Web page, the Save Web Page dialog box will include an Encoding option. There's no need to change that, because it already matches the encoding used by the page. But if you work in multiple languages and need to use a different encoding, you're free to choose one.

After you've chosen your folder and specified your filename, just click the Save button. Unless there's a conflict (as discussed below), the document will be saved and the dialog box will close.

Save Your Work Often!

When you save a document, you're saving a copy of that document as it exists in memory at that moment in time. Any changes you make after saving the document are *not* saved until you save the document again. It only takes a moment to save a document. It also only takes a moment to lose hours of hard work if you *don't* save your work often.

The smart thing to do is this: Every time you're happy with a change you made to the document, save the document. It only takes a moment to press Ctrl+S, click the Save toolbar button, or choose File ⇨ Save from the menu bar. That's a lot quicker and easier then redoing hours of work you lost simply because you didn't bother to save your work from time to time!

Do you want to replace it?

No two files in a given folder can have the same name. If you entered a filename that's identical to an existing filename, you'll see a message similar to the one in Figure 3-28. Your choices are as follows:

Yes: If you chose Yes, the current document will replace the existing document. The original document is permanently lost, so don't do thus unless you're sure you'll never need the original document again.

No: The existing file will remain intact, and you'll stay in the Save As dialog box. Change the document's File Name, then click Save to save the current document under a different name.

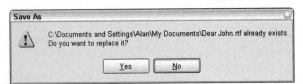

Figure 3-28: Do you want to replace it?

Closing a Document

To close a document, close the program you're using to view that document. If you've made any changes since your last save, the program will ask whether you want to save the changes. You should definitely choose Yes, unless you messed up the document since your last change and don't want to save those changes.

In some programs you can close the document without closing the program. That's especially true in programs that allow you to have multiple documents open at the same time. Typically, you just choose File ⇨ Close from the program's menu bar, or click the Close button in the upper-right corner of the document window. This brings us to the next major topic of working with documents.

Working with Multiple Document Windows

Some programs provide a multiple document interface (MDI), which allows you to have several documents open at the same time. Each document appears within its own document window inside the program's window. A document window is similar to a program window, except that it has no menu bar or toolbar. A document window doesn't need those things, because the program displaying the document already has all the menus and tools needed to edit the document.

Figure 3-29 shows an example, using a graphics-editing program named Jasc Paint Shop Pro (www.jasc.com). Each picture in the document area is a separate document. Having several documents open at once makes it easy to copy and paste content from one document to the other.

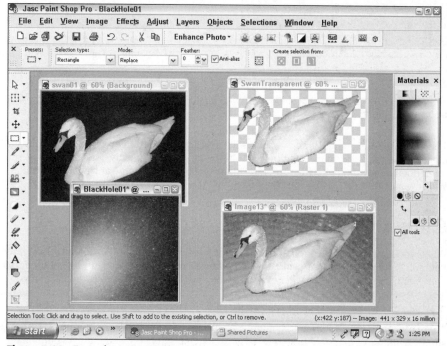

Figure 3-29: Four pictures open in a program

When you have multiple document windows open, each will have its own title bar with Minimize, Maximize/Restore, and Close buttons. Normally, you can size any document window as you would a program window—by dragging any corner or edge of the document window.

When you maximize a document window, it will fill the entire screen. The title bar for the document window is likely to disappear as well. The Minimize, Restore, and Close buttons will then be near the upper-right corner of the document area, as in the example shown in Figure 3-30. The program you're using will also likely have a Window option on the menu bar, like the example shown in Figure 3-30.

Buttons for maximized document window

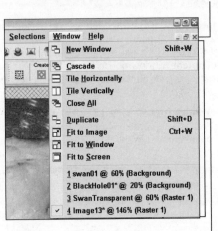

Window menu

Figure 3-30: Window menu and maximized document window buttons

The exact options on the Window menu will vary. But in general you can tile, cascade, or close all the open document windows within the program. Typically, you can also bring any open document window to the top of the stack by clicking its name at the bottom of the Window menu.

Opening Documents

When you save a document to a folder on your hard disk—whether it be one you created yourself or something you downloaded—it stays there forever. (Well, until you intentionally delete or move it.) Windows will never move or delete a document on its own. So, if you've lost a document, it's not the computer's fault. It's just that you've forgotten where you put it or what you named it.

There are many ways to open documents. As always, choosing one technique over another is simply a matter of personal preference. Here's a quick summary of the most common techniques, which will be discussed in the sections that follow:

   ✦ Click (or double-click) the document's icon.

   ✦ If you want to open the document in a specific program, right-click its icon and choose **Open With**.

   ✦ Click **Start**, choose **My Recent Documents**, and then click on the name of the document you want to open.

✦ Open the program you used to create the document and choose **File** from its menu bar. Click on the documents name at the bottom of the File menu.

✦ Open the program you used to create the document and choose **File ➪ Open** from its menu bar. Then, use the Open dialog box to navigate to the document's folder and double-click the document's icon in the main pane.

Opening a document from its icon

An easy way to open a document is to just open its icon by clicking, or double-clicking. For example, to open a document that's in your My Documents folder, first open your My Documents folder. Then, click or double-click the icon that represents the document you want to open.

When you use this method, the document will open in whatever program is set up as the default program for the type of document you're opening. For example, if you double-click the icon for a JPEG picture, the picture will open in whatever program is currently set as the default program for JPEG images.

To override the default program and choose some other program, don't click or double-click the document's icon. Instead, right-click the document's icon and choose Open With, as in the example shown in Figure 3-31.Then, click on the name of the program you want to use in the submenu that appears.

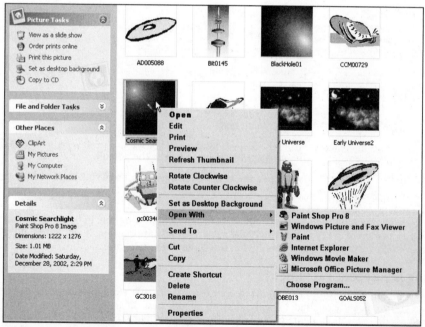

Figure 3-31: Sample Open With options after right-clicking a picture's icon

Changing the default program for a document type

The default program for opening a particular type of document isn't set in stone. You can change it at any time. If you find yourself right-clicking and choosing Open With often, you might want to change the default program to whatever it is you're choosing after you choose Open With. Here's how:

1. Right-click any document icon of the type for which you want to change the default program.

2. Choose **Open With** ⇨ **Choose Program**. The Open With dialog box shown in Figure 3-32 opens.

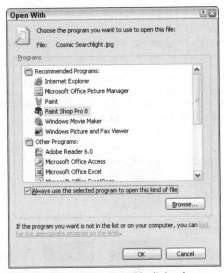

Figure 3-32: The Open With dialog box

3. Click on the name of the program you want to use as the default.

4. Choose (check) the **Always use the selected program to open this kind of file** option.

5. Click **OK**.

The document you right-clicked will open in the new default program. In the future, whenever you open an icon of the type for which you set a new default program, it will automatically open in whatever program you specified in the Open With dialog box.

Using My Recent Documents

Windows maintains a folder named My Recent Documents that contains shortcuts to documents you've recently opened. (The list doesn't include new documents you just created or downloaded—only documents you've recently edited.) While you *could* use the folder to open a recent document, it's much easier to use the My Recent Documents icon on the right side of the Start menu. With that you just have to:

1. Click the **Start** button.

2. Choose **My Recent Documents**, as shown in Figure 3-33.

3. Click on name of the document you want to open.

Figure 3-33: My Recent Documents on the Start menu

If you don't see a My Recent Documents icon on the right side of the Start menu, follow these steps to add it:

1. Right-click the **Start** button and choose **Properties**.

2. Click the **Customize** button. The Customize Start Menu dialog box opens.

3. Click the **Advanced** tab.

4. Choose (check) the **List my most recently opened documents** option at the bottom of the dialog box.

5. Click **OK** in each of the open dialog boxes.

If you ever need to clear the list of document names in the menu, repeat Steps 1 to 3. Click the Clear List button, and then click OK in each open dialog box.

Opening documents from programs

You can also open documents from within programs. The options for doing so will almost certainly be on the program's File menu. (I've never seen them anywhere else in any program). In most programs, when you first click the File menu, you'll see a list of recently saved documents. If the document you want to open is on that list, just click the document's name and you're done. The document opens right up.

If you don't see the document's name at the bottom of the File menu, then you'll need so click on the Open option. (That is, choose File ➪ Open from the program's menu bar). An Open dialog box will appear, looking (at least vaguely) similar to the example shown in Figure 3-34.

Figure 3-34: Example of an Open dialog box for opening documents

The Open dialog box is almost identical to the Save As dialog. Where the Save As dialog box shows Save In, the Open dialog box shows Look In. Your first step to opening a document is to get to the folder in which the document is stored. As with the Save In dialog box, you can navigate through folders using the icons at the left side of the dialog box, the Look In drop-down list, and the icons in the main pane.

Like the Save As dialog box, the main pane won't show all the files in the current folder. It will show only icons that match the type selected in the Files of Type drop-down list at the bottom of the dialog box. To see all the files in the main pane, you can generally choose All Files (*.*) or something similar from the Files of Type drop-down list.

Once you're in the folder that contains the document you want to open, and the icon that represents that document is visible, you can just double-click the icon, or click the icon once and then click the Open button in the dialog box. The document will open in the document area of the program.

Tip   Even when the program you intend to use is already open, you may find it easier to click the Start button, choose My Documents, and navigate to the document's icon in Explorer, just because it's a little easier to get around from Explorer than from the Open dialog box.

When Windows can't open a document

As you (hopefully) know, there are thousands of different types of documents in the world, and thousands of different programs. Nobody uses all the document types, and nobody owns every program ever published. Because of these basic facts, it's quite possible that you'll get documents for which you have no compatible program.

For example, suppose that someone sends you a document they created in WordPerfect. If you don't have WordPerfect (or a program that can import WordPerfect document), then you can't open the WordPerfect document. Likewise, if you download a PDF (Portable Document Format) document, you won't be able to open it unless you have Adobe Acrobat Reader (or a similar program) installed.

When you try to open a document that has no default program associated with it on your system, you'll get a message similar to the one shown in Figure 3-35. As you can see, you have three choices. The Cancel button is one choice, which just terminates the whole thing and leaves the document unopened. The other two choices are, frankly, longshots, unless you have enough computer experience to make an educated guess about which program might work. We'll look at each option in the sections that follow.

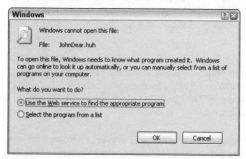

Figure 3-35: No default program is assigned to this document type.

Use the Web Service. . .

The Use the Web Service. . . option takes you to a Web page that provides some information about the document type. It doesn't actually "find the appropriate program" in any manner that could be considered easy. Rather, it tells you the name of one or more programs that can open that type of document and provides links to the program manufacturer's Web site.

Whether or not you can actually download the appropriate program from that Web site depends on many factors. But suffice it to say, if the program costs money, you're definitely not going to downloading a free copy from the Web.

On the bright side, though, sometimes you can download an appropriate program on the spot. For example, if the document in question is a .PDF file, then you can follow the link to Adobe's Web site. And from there you can download and install Adobe Acrobat Reader, for free. After you've downloaded that program, you'll be able to open any .PDF file you acquire.

Select the program from a list

The second option in the "cannot open . . ." dialog box lets you pick a program that's already on your computer. When you choose that option and then click OK, the Open With dialog box shown back in Figure 3-32 opens. If there's a recommended program, try that one. Otherwise, try some other program. It may take some trial-and-error guesswork to find a program that will work.

Then again, it's quite possible that no program on your computer will be able to open the document. If somebody sent you the document as an e-mail attachment, you could ask them to send it in some other format — a format that you can open.

If you can get the program open, you may want to change its document type to something more palatable to your system. Changing a document's format is the next (and thankfully, last) topic for this hefty chapter.

Changing a document's format (type)

The heading to this paragraph is a little white lie in that you can't actually change a document's type per se. But, if you can open the document, you can save another copy of the same document in a different format. There are several reasons why you might want, or need, to do this. Referring back to the previous section, let's say you manage to wrangle open a WordPerfect document in Microsoft Word. Once you get that document open, you'll want to save a copy in Word's standard .doc format.

Another example would be the inverse of the situation just described. Suppose that you make some changes to your copy of the document that you want to send back to the WordPerfect user. If you save a copy of your document in WordPerfect format, you can then send that copy of the document with your e-mail message. The recipient should have no problem opening that copy of the document in WordPerfect.

Caution   Simply renaming a document and changing the filename extension won't change the document's type. Rather, it will just change the extension to the wrong set of letters for the document's actual format — and possibly make it impossible to open the document at all (until you rename the document back to its original name).

Because we're talking about a general technique here that can be used in most Windows programs, I can't be too specific about any particular file type. But the general procedure goes like this:

1. Open the document you wish to convert.

2. From the menu bar of the program that opened the document, choose **File** ➪ **Save As**. The Save As dialog box opens.

3. Optionally, choose a folder for this copy of the document in the Save As dialog box.

4. Optionally, give this copy of the document a slightly different filename (so you can tell it apart from the original when filename extensions are hidden).

5. Click the Save As Type drop-down list button, and then click the file type you want to use for this copy of the document.

6. Click the Save button in the Save As dialog box.

Now you can close the program and open the folder in which you stored the converted document. If you made this conversion to send the document to someone else, make sure you send the converted copy of the document, not the original.

Wrap Up

That about wraps it up for file and folder basics. To recap from a big picture point of view:

✦ Many programs allow you to create and edit documents.

✦ A document can be a typed test, a picture, a song, a video, or even a spreadsheet or database.

✦ Every document you save is stored as a file in some folders.

✦ Folders on a computer play the same role as folders in a filing cabinet, in that they allow you to organize your documents so that they're easy to find in the future.

✦ Opening any folder automatically opens Windows Explorer, the program for navigating through all the folders on your hard drive.

✦ There are several ways to open documents, though the easiest is usually to just get to the folder in which the document is stored and then click (or double-click) the document's icon.

✦   ✦   ✦

Help and Support for Power Users

When it comes to computers, it's really not possible to know everything because there's just too much information for any one person to know. There are too many different hardware and software products on the market, not to mention new products that appear on the market daily. To further complicate things, no two computers are exactly alike. Problems and error messages can arise on your computer that only one in a million people will ever experience. That's because no two computers are exactly alike, and some problems occur just because of a specific combination of hardware and software on a system.

You can't expect a book to cover every conceivable problem and error message. There isn't a book in the world that's large enough — and there is no way for an author to test every conceivable combination of hardware and software to determine all the problems that could possible arise.

Furthermore, just because Windows displays an error message, that doesn't mean Windows is at fault. The problem could be in any program, or any piece of hardware on your system. Windows is just the messenger, and it never helps to shoot the messenger.

Knowing how to get exactly the information you need, when you need it, is a critical basic skill for all computer users. And the best place in the world to get specific information quickly is the Internet. After all, that's why the Internet exists. In this chapter, we'll look at all the different ways that you can get the information you need, when you need it.

Getting What You Need

I once took a creative writing course in which the professor walked into the room on the first day and described the course as follows: "In this course, you'll learn the top three rules of good writing. And those rules are (1) be specific, (2) be specific, (3) be specific." When it comes to searching for help with a specific problem, truer words were never spoken.

Some of what I'm going to say in this section will be patently obvious to some readers. If you're one of those readers, feel free to skip this section. But the first step to getting help is knowing where to look for it and what to look for. The "be specific" part applies to the "what to look for" part in a big way. Because if you search for something vague and general, you might get in return a zillion links to text that might, or might not, be useful to getting files from your hard disk to a CD.

Part of the problem stems from the simple fact that computers don't have brains. Computers don't get the concept of synonyms. For example, in your mind you might think "I want to *transfer* some files to a CD." So, you search for the word "transfer" and get a bunch of results. Chances are, however, that few of those results will be specific to the task you're trying to accomplish.

Another problem with searching for the word "transfer" is that it's simply not a term that's used much in programs. When you right-click an icon, or choose Edit from a program's menu bar, you'll often see words like "move" and "copy." But you won't see the word "transfer" too often. To a human being, "transfer" is just another word for "move" or "copy." But to a computer, the word "transfer" is no more similar to "move" or "copy" than "snorkel" or "wingnut."

Words don't have meaning to a computer. When you search for "transfer," you're just looking for pages that contain the word "transfer." The computer can't search on the general concept of *transfer*. The more specific you are when defining your search terms, the more specific the search results will be. If you can stick with words you see on the screen, in menus and such, rather than using synonyms, you'll be that much better off. For example, a search for *copy to CD* is far more likely to find the information you're looking for than a search for the vague, general synonym *transfer*.

Exactly *where* you search for information plays a big part in your likelihood of success, too. For example, when you search Windows built-in Help, you're specifically searching pages in that program's help text. You're not going to find information about your particular make and model of scanner, or how to make backups of your Quicken data. Those are not Windows topics, and won't appear in Windows' Help.

As an alternative, you can search Microsoft's Knowledge Base, which has far more information than the built-in help. But even so, you're searching text that has to do with Microsoft products, not every make and model of hardware and software ever created.

The next step up is to search the entire Web using a search engine such as Google. Now, you're searching more than four billion pages of text covering every topic imaginable. If you're not super-specific when you search that body of knowledge, you're likely to get links to more pages than you could possibly look at in a lifetime. So with all these basic facts in mind, let's look at the sources of help available to you, and when they're appropriate.

Using Windows Help and Support Center

The Windows Help and Support Center is the quickest and easiest way to get how-to information about Windows XP. That's because there's not much in Windows' built-in help that *isn't* specifically about Windows XP. To get to the Help and Support Center, click the Start button and choose Help and Support (or whatever option on your Start menu implies help or support). Optionally, you could press the Help key (F1). However, pressing F1 tends to bring up context-sensitive help. So if you happen to be in, say, Microsoft Word when you press F1, you'll end up in Word's Help, not Windows' Help.

Tip If you have a Windows keyboard, pressing ⊞+F1 will always bring up Windows XP's Help and Support Center.

If you have straight-out-of-the-box Windows XP, the Help and Support Center will open looking something like Figure 4-1. If Windows came preinstalled on your computer, your Help and Support Center might look a little different. That's because computer manufacturers such as Dell, HP, and Gateway who preinstall Windows XP on the computers they sell are allowed to tweak the Help and Support Center page to promote their own company rather than Microsoft.

Note If there is no Help or Support option on your Start menu, right-click the Start button and choose Properties. Click the Customize button, and then click the Advanced tab. Scroll through the list of Start Menu Items and make sure that Help and Support is selected (checked). Then, click OK in each open dialog box.

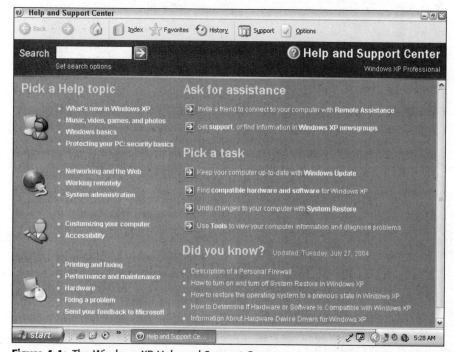

Figure 4-1: The Windows XP Help and Support Center

The Help and Support Center page you first see is just the tip of the proverbial iceberg. The actual help text beneath the Help and Support Center veneer is virtually the same on all computers. At least I assume that it is because I seriously doubt that any computer manufacturer would rewrite all the existing Windows help text. Doing so would just be too large and expensive an undertaking to justify—embellish, perhaps, but replace, doubtful.

Searching Windows help is the same no matter what your screen looks like when you first open the Help and Support Center. You want to type the key words that best describe what you want to do into the Search box. Then, press Enter or click the green Start Searching button. When you do, you'll get three categories of results, as in the example shown in Figure 4-2.

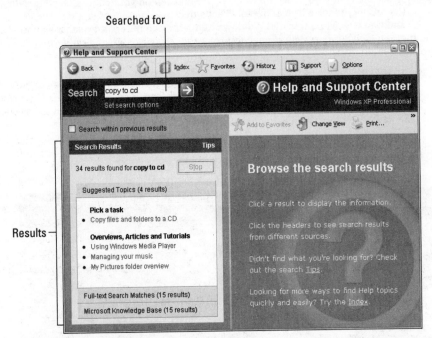

Figure 4-2: Results of searching for *copy to CD*

The search results will generally be divided into three major categories, indicated by the gray top headings in the Search Results pane. Click any heading to show or hide the topics within that category. The categories are as follows:

✦ **Suggested Topics:** These provide the most general help, mostly in the form of how-to, under Pick a Task, and more information under Overviews, Articles, and Tutorials.

✦ **Full-text Search Matches:** Contains links to help text that have the search term anywhere in the body of the page. Some topics are likely to be far removed from what you're looking for; others may be useful.

✦ **Microsoft Knowledge Base:** Microsoft's Knowledge Base is the biggest repository of information about Microsoft products. Here, you'll find more technical information as well as help with specific error messages, where appropriate.

Each item of blue text in the left pane is a link to a specific help page. Clicking on a link shows the help page in the pane to the right. At that moment, all the buttons above the Help text pane are enabled, and you can use them as follows:

✦ **Add to Favorites:** Adds the current help page to your personal collection of favorites help pages.

✦ **Change View:** Hides the left column so that only the Help text remains visible on the screen. Click the Change View button a second time (or click >> first if the button isn't visible) to get back to the two-pane view.

✦ **Print:** Prints the help page.

✦ **Locate in Contents:** Changes the left pane to a Table of Contents with the topic of the current Help text highlighted.

Tip   Any buttons missing from the toolbar are likely just hidden. Click the >> at the right side of that toolbar to see additional options. You can move and size the Help and Support Center program window like any other. It even has its own taskbar button.

As you view various Help pages, you'll occasionally come across some blue text and some green text. Green text represents a defined term. Just click the green text to see that definition. Blue text represents some other link that you can click on for more information, or to get to the specific dialog box the Help text supports.

You generally navigate through Help by clicking on blue links. Help acts similar to a Web browser in that regard. The Help Center toolbar has contains some buttons to help with that navigation. Those buttons, going left to right are as follows:

✦ **Back:** Takes you back to the page you just navigated from (if any).

✦ **Forward:** Returns you to the page you just backed out of (if any).

✦ **Home:** Returns you to the Help and Support Center home page.

✦ **Index:** Displays an index of topics in help. Use it as you would the index at the back of a book.

✦ **Favorites:** All the Help text topics that you've added to your Favorites. Click any item to jump to that page of Help text.

✦ **History:** Displays a list of topics you've visited recently. Click any item to jump to the page of Help text.

✦ **Support:** Presents alternative methods of getting help and support with Windows XP.

✦ **Options:** Provides a few options for customizing the look-and-feel, and behavior of the Help and Support Center.

All of those features of Help are self-explanatory and easy to use. It's just a matter of spending a little time in the Help and Support Center and trying them out. You can't do any harm from the Help pages. So, there's no reason to fear learning on your own by experience. Besides, because different computers have different Help and Support Centers, there's really no other way to master whatever Help Center appears when you choose Help and Support from the Start menu.

Quick help

You don't have to go digging through the Help and Support Center every time you need more information. At any given time, there's probably more help on your screen than you realize. It's just a matter of knowing how to look for it.

Often, you can get a brief description of what an object is, or what it's used for simply by pointing to the item. To point to an item, you just rest the tip of the mouse pointer on it for a moment. You won't get extensive help that way. But you'll often get a brief description of the role or purpose of the object in a ScreenTip (also called a ToolTip). Figure 4-3 shows an example of resting the mouse pointer on the desktop's Recycle Bin folder.

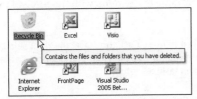

Figure 4-3: Example of a ScreenTip

Many programs offer Smart Tags. Although the tags don't usually provide helpful information, they do provide quick access to things people are likely to want to do at that moment in time. You have to click on the Smart Tag to see what it offers. As an example, Figure 4-4 shows the Smart Tag that appears when pasting text into Microsoft Word. The options let you choose how you want Word to treat that pasted text.

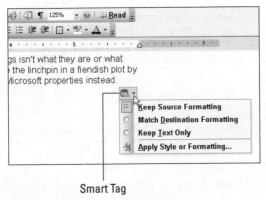

Figure 4-4: Example of a Smart Tag

Many dialog boxes have a question mark button in their upper-right corner. You can often use that for more details on an item in the dialog box. To use the button, first click on it. The mouse pointer gains a question mark. Then, click on the item with which you need help. You'll see some explanatory text right on the screen, as in Figure 4-5.

Help (?) button

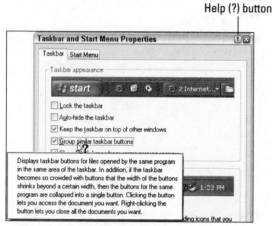

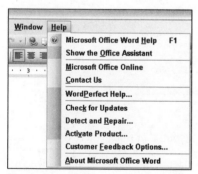

Figure 4-5: Dialog box Quick Help

Help in programs

The Windows XP Help and Support Center provides help for Windows XP only. There are tens of thousands of other programs on the market for which the Help and Support Center provide no information whatsoever. If you want help with some other program, you have to use the Help that's written for that program. Virtually all programs have a Help option in their menu bar, as in the example shown in Figure 4-6.

Figure 4-6: Most programs have a Help menu option.

Exactly how the Help works in any given program varies. It all depends on what the creators of that program thought would work best for that product. The best you can do it try things out until you get the hang of it.

But the main point is, there's plenty of information at your fingertips and right on the screen when you need it. You just need to know where to look for it.

Dealing with Error Messages

Whenever you ask your computer to do something it can't do, you get an error message describing the situation. As a somewhat obvious example, Figure 4-7 shows the error message I just got by intentionally trying to copy a file to an empty floppy disk drive.

Figure 4-7: Sample error message

That error message is fairly straightforward. You can't very well copy a file to an empty floppy disk drive. So, the message asks you to put a floppy into the drive.

To generate another error message, I tried to open an Excel worksheet in Windows Movie Maker. Trying to open a spreadsheet in Movie Maker makes about as much sense as trying brush your teeth with a Volvo. There's just no reason on earth why one should expect a program that's designed for making movies to open an Excel worksheet.

But, not everyone knows this. When I complete my bizarre request, the Movie Maker program has to respond *somehow*. Because the programmers who created Movie Maker didn't anticipate that specific problem, the program throws up a reasonable guess as to what the problem might be. That message is shown in Figure 4-8.

Figure 4-8: A second sample error message

It would be nice if the error message said "Excuse me but, that thing you're trying to open is an Excel worksheet, and Movie Maker is for making movies, not worksheets." You can't totally fault the programmers in this scenario. Because the fact of the matter is, in any given program there are thousands of things you can do correctly, but billions of things you can do incorrectly.

As a programmer myself, I know how impossible it is to anticipate every conceivable error and to write a clear, friendly error message to describe every possible scenario. There isn't nearly enough time, or space on a hard disk, to anticipate and handle all the billions of things a person might do wrong.

The best you can do is look at the things people are most likely to do wrong and cover those with clear, descriptive messages. But you also have to throw in some general error messages for the things people will do when just clicking around at random.

I often tell students "guessing doesn't work," partly because of this very scenario. If you have some clue as to what a program is, and does, then at least you can make reasonable guesses about what you can, and can't, do in that program. But if you just take wild guesses at random, you probably won't get too far, because even the error messages you see won't be particularly helpful.

Believe me, when it comes to the saying "if all else fails, read the instructions," I'm as guilty as the next person. Like everyone else, I want immediate gratification. The truth be told, I've probably learned more from the school of hard knocks than any official technical documentation. Well, maybe not. But I usually don't look for help until I've been knocked around a few times. The hard knocks forced me to read the directions.

The main point is that while guessing can be fun, it's not the only learning strategy available to you. Worse yet, really bad guessing can lead to really bad problems. I think one thing I've learned is to put a time limit on the guessing strategy. If guessing doesn't produce any meaningful results, don't keep trying. Use the program's Help feature to find out what you're supposed to do, before you do something you'll later regret.

Microsoft's Online Help

You might not always be satisfied with the help you get from the Help and Support Center. That's because the built-in Help is limited in size, mainly so that it doesn't eat up a ton of your available disk space. The really big repositories of information are online at Microsoft's Web site.

When the built-in help doesn't cut it, `http://search.microsoft.com` should be your next step. That page lets you search the entire Microsoft.com Web site, which has a whole lot more information than the built-in Help. Of course, because you're searching a huge body of information, you want to be very specific when typing your search phrase. Unlike the Help and Support Center, which covers only Windows XP, Microsoft.com has information on all of Microsoft's products. So it's worth it to include the letters XP in any search you perform, to narrow the search results to Windows XP.

For example, searching Microsoft.com for a general term such as *folder* will produce links to far more pages than you could realistically get through. That's because there are a lot of products that use folders and, hence, there are a lot of Help pages that contain the word "folder."

If you change that to *XP folder,* you'll narrow things down to pages that contain both the words "XP" and "folder." So, you won't get links to e-mail folders, FrontPage folders, and every other product that uses folders in one form or another.

The more you can narrow the search down, the better. For example, if you're looking to create a shortcut to a folder, a better search phrase would be *xp shortcut to folder*, which will produce pages that contain all four of those words. And you're far more likely to get pages that specifically describe how to create a shortcut to a folder in Windows XP.

Power users, tech heads, nerd brains, and other geek types might not even be satisfied with searching Microsoft.com. There are other places from which you can start your search. The page at `http://support.microsoft.com` provides access to all of Microsoft's support options. From there you can search the Knowledge Base, which is an enormous base of technical information about all of Microsoft's products. You can get to Microsoft's Public Newsgroups, where you can post questions.

For information on the latest security threats and how to avoid them, try starting at `http://support.microsoft.com/security`. For anything having to do with Microsoft Office products, `http://office.microsoft.com` is your best starting point. If you're a Media Player fan, try `www.microsoft.com/windowsmedia`. If making movies is your thing, try `www.microsoft.com/moviemaker`.

For the technologically fearless, there are TechNet and MSDN (Microsoft Developer Network). Some portions of those sites are for members only (read, "costs money"). But there's plenty of free information available to those of us who are too cheap to fork over subscription fees. To get to TechNet go to `http://technet.microsoft.com`. For MSDN see `http://msdn.microsoft.com`.

Searching the Web for Help

The PC industry is enormous, consisting of hundreds of companies producing thousands of products at an astonishing rate. When you look at the industry as a whole, all of Microsoft's products combined are but a drop of water in an Olympic-sized pool. Microsoft's Web site is about Microsoft's products, period. Microsoft doesn't make computers, printers, scanners, monitors, disk drives, digital cameras, or any other hardware (to speak of). Nor does their site contain much information about the products they don't make.

When looking for information on a particular product, you need to take into consideration who made that product—ditto for services, such as your Internet connection. If you need help with your AOL e-mail, you need to search AOL's Web site for information. If you need help with your Sony digital camera, you need to search Sony's site for information. If you don't know where to start, you might just have to search the Web.

Tip   You can often get to the home page for a company just by guessing. Try `www.companyname.com` where *companyname* is the company's name. More often than not, you'll end up at the right page. Some examples include `www.dell.com`, `www.hp.com`, `www.gateway.com`, `www.aol.com`, and `www.comcast.com`, just to name a few off the top of my head.

Searching the Web is a skill in and of itself. The Internet is by far the largest repository of information that has ever existed. Last time I checked, Google had about 4.2 billion pages in its search index. Most experts agree that that number probably represents about half the number of Web pages that are actually out there. Needless to say, 8 or 9 billion pages are more than enough to store virtually all human knowledge. Leaving plenty of room for random beliefs, ornery opinions, arbitrary attitudes, and plenty of other things that don't count as factual knowledge.

When it comes to searching the Web, the phrase "be specific" applies big time. If you're going to use a search engine such as Google (`www.google.com`) to search through billions of pages, you have to be very specific about what you want. Searching for general terms like *scan*, *print*, *copy*, and so forth will yield more links that you could view in a lifetime. Few of those links are likely to cover the specific information you're seeking.

If you're having a problem with your digital camera, searching the Web for *digital camera* won't help. There are probably millions of Web pages that contain the words "digital" and "camera." And your search will list them all. Specify the camera and program with which you're having trouble. For example, any of the following search phrases is bound to show up something more specific than *digital camera* would:

✦ Sony Digital Handycam Windows Movie Maker

✦ Windows XP Fuji Finepix

✦ Kodak Easyshare DX4350 XP Camera and Scanner Wizard

The idea isn't to form a meaningful question. There is no such thing as *meaningful* text in the computer world. Rather, the idea is to get as many specific terms as possible into your search phrase so you don't get millions of unrelated links in return. If you want specific information, you need to be specific about what you want.

Wrap Up

That's all I have to say about getting the information you need, when you need it. I'm sure most of it just sounds like common sense to many of you. But not everyone really understands the size and scale of the PC industry. Many people assume that one book, or one Web site, *should* contain everything they would ever want to know. But it just doesn't work that way. The industry is just too enormous for that to be a realistic expectation. To recap:

✦ When searching for information, be specific, be specific, be specific.

✦ For help with Windows XP, trying using the Help and Support Center.

✦ Be aware of quick, easy help, such as ScreenTips, Smart Tags, and the ? button in dialog boxes.

✦ For help with a specific program, choose Help from that program's menu bar.

✦ When the built-in Help doesn't work, try searching Microsoft's site at http://search. microsoft.com.

✦ Remember that Microsoft's Web site only covers Microsoft products; not every hardware and software product ever created.

✦ When all else fails, search the Web. But when you do, be extra specific about the information you're looking for, so you don't end up with millions of useless links.

✦   ✦   ✦

Troubleshooting Interface Problems

Each major part in this book ends with a troubleshooting chapter like this. The troubleshooting chapters provide quick solutions to common problems. That's about it. You won't catch me yammering on for paragraph after paragraph in these troubleshooting chapters! If you don't find what you're looking for in a troubleshooting chapter, be sure to check the Index at the back of the book for other possible resources.

Desktop Problems

My screen is too large/small; my screen colors look awful

For the best view of your desktop, your screen resolution should be set to at least 800x600 and color depth to at least 16 bits. To do so:

1. Right-click the Windows desktop and choose **Properties**.

2. Click the **Settings** tab.

3. Set the **Screen resolution** option to 800x600 or greater.

4. Set the **Color quality** to at least 16 bit, as in Figure 5-1.

5. Click **OK**.

Figure 5-1: Screen resolution and Color quality settings

If you're not happy with the results, you can repeat the steps to try other resolutions and color depths. If the desktop doesn't fit right on the screen after you change the resolution, see the next troubleshooting section.

When I right-click the Windows desktop, I don't get a Properties option

You're most likely right-clicking something that's covering the desktop, such as an icon or program window. Right-click the clock in the lower-right corner of the screen and chose Show the Desktop. Then, you'll see, and can right-click, the actual Windows desktop.

Parts of my screen are cut off or blank

When the desktop doesn't fill the screen correctly, you need to adjust settings on the monitor. You use knobs or buttons on the monitor to do that, not your mouse or keyboard. Exactly how you do it varies from one monitor to the next. But the typical scenario is to use the monitor's OSD (on screen display) options. In particular you need to adjust the Height, Vertical Centering, Width, and Horizontal Centering settings.

If you can't figure out how to use the monitor buttons, your only other recourse is to check the documentation that came with the monitor or notebook computer. Or, search the manufacturer's Web site for information on that specific model of monitor or notebook computer.

The picture on my desktop isn't right

You can use any picture that's on your computer as the background (also called a *wallpaper*) for your desktop. Any picture that's as large as, or larger than, your screen (as defined by the Screen Resolution setting in Display Properties) will automatically fill the screen. Smaller pictures can be centered, tiled, or stretched to fill the screen. To choose a picture and how you want it displayed:

1. Right-click the Windows desktop and choose **Properties**.

2. In the Display Properties dialog box that opens, click the **Desktop** tab.

3. Optionally, to choose a different picture, click a picture name in the **Background** list, or click the **Browse** button to find a different picture.

4. If the picture is smaller than the desktop, choose one of the following options from the Position drop-down list:

   • **Center:** The picture is shown at actual size centered on the screen.

   • **Tile:** The picture is shown at actual size, but tiled to fill the screen.

   • **Stretch:** The picture is stretched to fill the screen.

5. Click **OK**.

Icon names are too big or too small

In Chapter 6 you'll learn how to get your screen looking just the way you want. For now, if you just want to increase the size of the text on your screen, follow these steps:

1. Right-click the desktop and choose **Properties**.

2. Click the **Appearance** tab.

3. Optionally, under **Windows and buttons** choose a general style (Windows XP style is fine). The preview area above the controls gives you a sense of how things will look.

4. Optionally, choose an option from the **Color scheme** drop-down list. The preview area above the controls, once again, gives you a preview of how things will look.

5. From the **Font size** drop-down list, choose Large Fonts, as shown in Figure 5-2. Take a look at the text size in the preview area, and if those letters are large enough, go the next step. Otherwise, try the Extra Large Fonts setting.

6. Click **OK**.

Figure 5-2: Adjusting icon desktop font

That should be enough to make the text large enough to read. Chapter 6 will show you how to get things on your screen looking exactly the way you want.

I keep getting messages about unused desktop icons

The Desktop Cleanup Wizard is a program that Windows runs every 60 days to let you know when unused desktop icons are taking up space unnecessarily. But there's no rule that says you have to delete them. If you want the Desktop Cleanup Wizard to stop showing its message:

1. Right-click the desktop and choose **Properties**.

2. Click the **Desktop** tab.

3. Click the **Customize Desktop** button.

4. Clear the check mark next to **Run desktop Cleanup Wizard every 60 days**.

5. Click **OK** in each open dialog box.

The Desktop Cleanup Wizard removed icons

The Desktop Cleanup Wizard creates a folder named Unused Desktop Shortcuts on your desktop (you might only see a portion of that name). Double-click that folder to open it. You'll see a copy of each deleted icon. To restore an icon to the desktop, drag it from the folder back onto the desktop. Or, right-click the icon and choose Send To ⇨ Desktop (create shortcut).

There's a Web page stuck to my desktop

If your desktop looks more like a Web page than a picture, first right-click the clock and choose Show the Desktop to make sure that the page isn't in some program window. If the Web page still appears, follow these steps:

1. Right-click the desktop and choose **Properties**. If that doesn't work click the Start button and choose **Control Panel**. In Control Panel choose **Appearance and Themes** (if available). Open the **Display** icon.

2. In the Display Properties dialog box that opens, click the **Desktop** tab.

3. Click the **Customize Desktop** button.

4. Click the **Web** tab.

5. Clear the check mark from every checkbox in the dialog box.

6. Click **OK** in each of the open dialog boxes.

7. If you opened Control Panel in Step 1, click that now.

My Recycle Bin reads Norton Protected

If your Recycle Bin is named "Norton Protected" or "Norton Protected Recycle Bin," your computer has Norton AntiVirus or a similar Symantec program installed. Perhaps it was pre-installed by your computer manufacturer. You can replace that Recycle Bin with the original Windows version. However, be aware that any files currently in the Norton Recycle Bin will be permanently deleted in the process. If there are any files in the bin you intend to keep, you must unerase those files before proceeding.

Your best bet would be to learn to use the Norton product. You can do so from Symantec's Web site at www.symantec.com. But if you just want to take a shot at replacing the protected bin with the standard Windows Recycle Bin, the following steps should work:

1. Right-click the Norton Protected icon and choose **Properties**.

2. Click the **Global** tab.

3. Choose **Use One Setting for All Drives**.

4. Click the **Recycle Bin** tab.

5. Choose **Standard Recycle Bin**.

6. Change the Title to **Recycle Bin**.

7. Clear the **Show Norton Protection Status** if it's selected.

8. Click the **Norton Protection** tab.

9. Select a drive icon and clear the **Enable Protection** option. Repeat for each drive icon until no drives are protected.

10. Choose **Also Empty Protected Files**.

11. Click **OK** in each open dialog box.

12. Close all open program windows and restart the computer.

If the above doesn't help, refer to the manufacturer's, Symantec's Web site (`www.symantec.com`) for more information

Start Menu Problems

My Start menu shows one column, not two

1. Right-click the Start button and choose **Properties**.

2. Choose the **Start menu** option (not the Classic Start menu option).

3. Click **OK**.

Some items cannot be shown

If clicking the Start button displays *Some items cannot be shown*, you'll need to reduce the number of items on the desktop, or use small icons. Try reducing the number of items first by following these steps:

1. Right-click the Start button and choose **Properties**.

2. Click the **Customize** button next to Start menu.

3. Choose **Small icons**, or reduce the **Number of programs on Start menu** number.

4. Click **OK**.

See "Customizing your Start Menu" in Chapter 6 for more information.

The right side of my Start menu is missing some options

Chapter 6 explains how to customize your Start menu. If you're just looking for a quick fix right now, follow these steps:

1. Right-click the Start button and choose **Properties**.

2. Click the **Customize** button.

3. Click the **Advanced** tab.

4. Scroll through the list of **Start menu items**. Choose (check) any items you want on the menu, clear the check mark next to any items you don't want.

5. Click **OK** in each of the open dialog boxes.

I don't see the taskbar

Move the mouse pointer all the way to the bottom of the screen (as if you're trying to move it clear off the bottom of the screen). If the taskbar slides up into view, you just need to turn off its Auto-Hide option. Here's how:

1. Move the mouse pointer to the left edge of the screen, then off the bottom of the screen so that the taskbar slides up into view.

2. Right-click the Start button and choose **Properties**.

3. Click the **Auto-hide the taskbar** option to clear its check mark.

4. Click **OK**.

If the taskbar didn't slide up into view when you moved the mouse pointer off the bottom of the screen, move the mouse pointer to the bottom of the screen again. Hold down the left mouse button, and move the mouse pointer up slightly. When the taskbar is visible, release the mouse button.

My Taskbar is all messed up

There is no simple solution to this problem. You just have to make sure that the taskbar is unlocked, play around with it until you get things right, and then relock the taskbar. For details see "Customizing the Taskbar" in Chapter 6.

I don't have a Quick Launch toolbar

Right-click the clock in the lower-right corner of the screen, and choose Toolbars ⇨ Quick Launch from the menu that appears.

There is no Show Desktop button on my Quick Launch toolbar

First click the >> symbol at the right side of the Quick Launch toolbar (if any) to make sure that the button isn't just in a hidden part of the Quick Launch toolbar. If it's just not in the visible area, you can drag it to the visible area or make the Quick Launch toolbar larger as described under "Customizing the Taskbar" in Chapter 6.

If the Show Desktop button is nowhere to be found, follow these steps:

1. Click the Start button and choose **Search**.

2. In the Search companion, click on **All files and folders**.

3. Under **All or part of the file name**, type Show Desktop.

4. Click on **More advanced options**.

5. Make sure that **Search system folders**, **Search hidden files and folders,** and **Search subfolders** are all selected (checked). Leave the other two options unchecked.

6. Click the **Search** button.

7. Wait for the search to complete, and then click on **Yes, finished searching**.

8. Look at the blue-and-white icon named Show Desktop in the main pane to the right. (In Tiles View the description reads *Windows Explorer Command*). Right-click that icon and choose **Send To** ⇨ **Desktop** (create shortcut).

9. Close the Search Results window and go to the Windows desktop.

10. Drag the **Show Desktop** icon from the desktop onto the Quick Launch toolbar.

To remove the icon that's still on the desktop, right-click it and choose Delete ⇨ Yes. See Chapter 17 for more information on using the Search Companion.

Windows Explorer Problems

I don't have an Explorer bar

The Explorer bar is only visible when the Windows Explorer program window is large enough to display. So, first enlarge Explorer's window to make sure that the Explorer bar isn't just temporarily hidden.

The Explorer bar will only be visible when no other bar is taking its place. To make sure that the Explorer bar isn't just covered, choose View ⇨ Explorer Bar from Explorer's menu bar, and then click any bar name that has a check mark next to it. (If no name is checked, just press Esc to exit without making a selection).

If the Explorer bar still isn't visible, follow these steps:

1. Choose **Tools** ⇨ **Folder Options** from Explorer's menu bar.

2. Choose **Show common tasks in folders**.

3. Click **OK**.

I don't have a Filmstrip option

The filmstrip view is only available in folders that contain many photos, such as My Pictures or Shared Pictures. So, make sure that you're in your My Pictures folder before you attempt to fix the problem. If you still don't see a Filmstrip as an option in Windows Explorer, follow these steps:

1. From the menu bar in your My Pictures folder, choose **Tools** ⇨ **Folder Options**.

2. In the Folder Options dialog box choose **Show common tasks in folders**.

3. Click **OK**.

Filmstrip is missing in one folder

Make sure that you can see the Filmstrip view option in your My Pictures folder. If you can't, see and complete the section preceding this one. Then, return to the folder in which you can get a filmstrip view. If Filmstrip still isn't available as an option in the current folder, follow these steps:

1. Click the **Up** button in Explorer's toolbar to go to the current folder's parent.

2. Right-click the icon of the folder you just left, and choose **Properties**.

3. Click the **Customize** tab.

4. Under "What kind of folder to you want" choose **Pictures (best for many files)**.

5. If you want Filmstrip to be available in subfolders of the folder you're customizing, choose **Also apply this template to all subfolders**.

6. Click **OK**.

Reopen the folder you just customized. You should see Filmstrip as a View option on the View menu and Views button.

Built-in folder icons are messed up

While I've never experienced this myself, apparently icons for My Pictures, My Music, and other built-in folders can get out of whack. I'm guessing this is the case because the TweakUI PowerToy has an option to repair them. To download TweakUI, go to `www.microsoft.com/windowsxp/downloads/powertoys`, and click on **PowerToys for Windows XP**.

Troubleshooting Documents

You cannot save in the folder specified

The folder you've chosen in the Save In drop-down list can't be used to store files. Click OK to close the message box. Choose a different folder, such as My Documents, from the Save In drop-down list. Then, click the Save button again.

The file name is invalid

The filename you entered contains an invalid character. Try a different filename, make sure it doesn't contain any of the following characters:

```
\ : / * ? " > < |
```

Click the Save button to save the document with the new name.

Please insert a disk into drive A:

The error occurs when you attempt to save a document to an empty disk drive. Your best bet would be to click the Cancel button and choose a folder such as My Documents. However, if you really want to save the document to a floppy, you'll need to put a floppy disk with sufficient empty space on it into the floppy drive.

You have files waiting to be written to CD

When you save a document to your CD drive, nothing happens in the drive. Instead, you just see a Notification area message that reads *You have files waiting to be written to CD*. This isn't a problem needing troubleshooting. Rather, it's just the way CD burning works. See Chapter 15 for details.

My document isn't in the Open dialog box

Make sure the Look In option at the dialog box is showing the name of the folder in which the document is contained. If it doesn't, navigate to the appropriate folder. If the document still isn't visible in the main pane, change the Files of Type option at the bottom of the dialog box to All Files (*.*) or the type of file you're trying to open.

✦   ✦   ✦

Customizing Windows XP

When it comes to Windows XP, absolutely nothing is set in stone. The look, size, and position of virtually everything on your screen — the desktop, Start menu, taskbar, Quick Launch toolbar — can be just about anything you want it to be. Chapter 6 tells you how to make things look and work the way you want.

If you share a computer with other people, you can set up separate user accounts so that everyone can create their own custom desktops, Start menus, and other settings. Every user can also have their own private My Documents, My Pictures, My Music, and other document folders. Chapter 7 explains how that works.

Do you have any programs you would like to start automatically? Or, do you want to prevent a program from starting automatically? Chapter 8 will tell you how.

If a sensory or motor impairment makes it difficult to use your computer, or if you need to work in multiple spoken languages, Chapter 9 is for you. If you just can't type worth beans and want to dictate to Microsoft Word, or want your computer to read e-books aloud, Chapter 9 is still the place. If you need some more elbow room on which to work or an extra monitor, Chapter 10 is your guide to desktop real estate.

Setting Up Your Work Environment

The Windows desktop is where you work, and folders are where you store your documents. Programs are tools you use to create and edit documents. When you need to work on a document, you open its icon. This is basically the same as taking a paper document out of the filing cabinet and putting it on your desk. When you've finished working with a document, you close it, thereby putting it back into the filing cabinet and getting it off your desktop.

In a sense, your screen is your work environment — your virtual office. If you've ever been in a situation where you had to fill in for someone else and work in their work environment, you know how awkward it can feel. What that person thinks of as a good work environment might seem like a big disorganized mess to you. We all like to set up our own work environments for the kind of work we do and, in general, how we think and organize things in our own minds.

Windows XP offers lots of options for customizing your work environment. Most of the options available to you are located in the Display Properties and Taskbar and Start Menu Properties dialog boxes, which you can open by right-clicking the desktop or Start button, respectively, and choosing Properties. In this chapter, we'll focus on the tools and techniques for personalizing your own work environment.

Some General Tips on Customizing

Personalizing (or customizing) your screen involves changing settings in dialog boxes. Every setting is displayed in some type of control that allows you to change the setting. Windows has many dialog boxes. Although they're all different in some ways, they're also alike in some ways. Most of you are probably familiar with dialog boxes, because there are zillions of them. But just to make sure that we're all speaking the same language, Figure 6-1 points out some gizmos commonly found in dialog boxes.

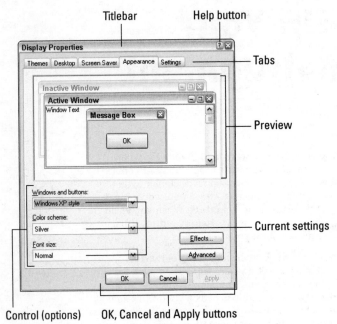

Figure 6-1: Examples of things you'll find in dialog boxes

✦ The name of the dialog box you're currently working in appears in the dialog box's title bar.

✦ As when moving a program window, you can move a dialog box by dragging its title bar. Unlike program windows, dialog boxes do not have taskbar buttons and cannot be sized, minimized, or maximized.

✦ Some dialog boxes contain tabs. You can click any tab to view the options on that tab.

✦ If the dialog box in which you're working has a preview area, the preview will provide an example of how the new setting will affect the actual screen if you decide to keep the new setting.

✦ Most dialog boxes contain some text that describes what its settings are about. If you see a Help (?) button in a dialog box, you can click that button, and then click any option for more information about that option. Or, press the Help key (F1) on your keyboard.

✦ If an option is dim, it's currently disabled, because it's not relevant at the moment. Don't bother clicking a dimmed option; it won't do any good.

✦ Do not play around with settings in dialog boxes or make changes just for the sake of making changes. Before you change a setting in a dialog box, you should know what you're changing and why.

✦ Before you change an option, notice what is currently selected in that option. That way, if you make a change but decide you don't like it, you can return it to the previous setting.

✦ Nothing you choose in a dialog box is a lifelong commitment. You can open a dialog box and change the settings within it at any time.

✦ Options you choose in a dialog box aren't actually applied to the computer until you click the OK or Apply button in the dialog box.

✦ To bail out of a dialog box without changing any settings, click its Cancel button or the Close button in its upper-right corner. (Settings you've already applied, by clicking the Apply button, won't be canceled.)

✦ If you have multiple user accounts on your computer, all the settings described in this chapter will apply only to the user account to which you're currently logged in. That's because each user gets to have a desktop, which is defined by the settings that user chooses.

✦ Dialog boxes for customizing Windows XP are in Control Panel, which you can get to by clicking the Start button and choosing Control Panel. In addition, you can often get to a dialog box by right-clicking the item you want to customize and choosing Properties from the shortcut menu that appears.

Customizing Your Desktop

To customize the appearance of your Windows desktop, you use the Display Properties dialog box. *Display* is a general term for what you see on your screen. There are two ways to get to the Display Properties dialog box. Use whichever is most convenient at the moment:

✦ Right-click the Windows desktop and choose Properties.

✦ Click the Start button and choose Control Panel. If Control Panel opens in Categories View, click Appearance and Themes. Double-click the Display icon.

The Display Properties dialog box will open, initially showing you options on the Themes tab, as in Figure 6-2.

Figure 6-2: Themes tab of the Display Properties dialog box

Creating your own theme

The Themes tab in Control Panel lets you choose a color scheme and overall look and feel for your desktop. When you choose an option from the Themes drop-down list, the preview (under the heading Sample) gives you a sneak peek at how that theme will look if you apply it to your desktop.

A good way to get started creating your own theme is to choose one of the sample themes as your starting point. The Windows XP theme is fine as a starting point, but you should choose whichever theme you like best. Once you've selected a theme, you should save a copy as your theme. That way, anything you do to further customize the theme will be yours, and yours alone. To create your own theme, you just need to save a copy of the currently selected theme under a name of your own choosing. Here's how:

1. On the Themes tab of the Display Properties dialog box, click **Save As**. The Save As dialog box opens.

2. Windows suggests putting the theme in your My Documents folder under the name My Favorite Theme (with .theme tacked on as the extension, if extensions are visible). You can change the My Favorite Theme part of the filename to anything you like.

3. Click the Save button.

Now you can customize to your heart's content. Your changes won't affect the original theme, so you'll always have that to fall back on. You'll know exactly which theme is your custom theme by the name you gave it in Step 2.

OK, let's look at all the different things you can do now to personalize the desktop so that it works well for you.

Changing the picture on your desktop

You can have your desktop display any picture in your My Pictures folder or no picture at all. To choose a picture, click the Desktop tab in Display Properties. The preview at the top of the dialog box shows the currently selected picture.

The list under Background provides more pictures, including all pictures you currently have in your My Pictures folder. Use the scroll bar at the right side of the list to scroll through all the picture names. Click any picture's name to see it in the preview.

Tip   Once you've clicked a picture name, you can use the ↑ and ↓ keys on the keyboard to go from picture to picture.

To use a picture not listed under Background, click the Browse button. Then, navigate to the folder in which the picture is contained, click its icon, and double-click the picture you want to use. If the picture you chose is smaller than your desktop, you can choose one of the following options from the Position dialog box to choose how you want the picture displayed:

✦ **Center:** The picture is centered on the desktop, surrounded by whatever color you choose from the Color drop-down list.

✦ **Tile:** The picture is repeated like tiles to fill the entire screen.

✦ **Stretch:** The picture is stretched to cover the entire desktop.

Note   If the picture you're displaying on your desktop is as large as, or larger than, the desktop, the Center and Tile options will have no effect.

The Color option lets you choose a color for the desktop. The color will only be visible, though, if you choose (None) as the background picture or if you center a small picture on the desktop.

Tip   The optional PowerToys Fun Pack download includes a Wallpaper Changer that lets you turn your desktop into a slide show of any pictures you want. Go to www.microsoft.com/windowsxp/downloads/powertoys, and click on PowerToys Fun Pack to get the Wallpaper Changer.

Choosing desktop icons

To choose some icons for your Windows desktop, click the Customize Desktop button on the Desktop tab in Display Properties. A new dialog box titled Desktop Items, shown in Figure 6-3, opens. Select (check) the name of any icons you want to place on your desktop. (As you'll learn in Chapter 16, you can put all sorts of other icons on your desktop).

Figure 6-3: The Desktop Items dialog box

If you want to change the emblem displayed by the My Computer, My Documents, My Network Places, or Recycle Bin icon, first click the icon you want to change just above the Change Icon button. In the Change Icon dialog box, click on the icon you want to use and then click the OK button.

Tip   So far I've found three sets of icon files that you can get to by using the Browse button in the Change Icon dialog box. Assuming that Windows is installed in C:\Windows on your computer, the icons should be in the files C:\Windows\system32\shell32.dll, C:\Windows\system32\moricons.dll, and C:\Windows\explorer.exe.

If you change your mind after customizing an icon, just click on that icon again in the Desktop Items dialog box, and then click the Restore Default button.

If your desktop is already cluttered with more icons than you need, you can click the Clean Desktop Now button. A Wizard will appear to help you move old icons you haven't used in the last 60 days, placing them in a folder named Unused Desktop Shortcuts. If you use this option and find that it has deleted too many icons, double-click the Unused Desktop Icons folder on your desktop. Within that folder, right-click any icon you want to redisplay on the desktop, and choose Restore.

Click OK after making your selections in the Desktop Items dialog box. You'll be returned to the Display Items dialog box.

Choosing a screen saver

A *screen saver* is a moving image that automatically appears on your screen after the computer has been sitting idle for a while. Originally, screen savers were created to prevent monitor *burn-in*, a condition caused by leaving an unchanging display on the screen for a long period of time (many hours). Burn-in isn't really a problem on modern monitors. But a screen saver can still be a fun thing to have and certainly can't hurt anything.

To choose a screen saver, first click the Screen Saver tab in the Display Properties dialog box. Then, choose any picture name from the Screen saver drop-down list. The preview at the top of the dialog box will show you how the selected screen saver will look when it actually appears on your screen.

The My Pictures Slideshow screen saver actually shows all the pictures in your My Picture folders in a slideshow fashion. If you want to display pictures from some other folder, first choose My Pictures Slideshow as your screen saver. Then, click the Settings button. In the dialog box that appears, use the Browse button to navigate to the folder that contains the pictures you want to display. Use other options in that dialog box to refine how the pictures are displayed, and then click OK.

To see what the screen saver will look like in real life, where it covers most or all of the screen, click the Preview button and let go of the mouse. After watching the screen saver, just move the mouse to return to the dialog box. After you've chosen a screen saver, you can click the Settings button to refine how the screen saver behaves.

The Wait option specifies how long the computer must sit idle (with no mouse or keyboard activity) before the screen saver kicks in. If you select the *On resume, display welcome screen* option, turning off the screen saver will take you to the Welcome screen described in Chapter 7, rather than to your desktop. When the actual screen saver does kick in on your computer, simply moving the mouse or pressing a key will turn the screen saver off and bring back your regular screen.

Caution   If the time delay for the Turn Off Monitor power option is less than the time delay for the screen saver, you'll never see the screen saver. That's because the monitor will turn off before the screen saver can appear!

The Power button on the Screen Saver tab provides a shortcut to the Power Options dialog box, used mainly to conserve battery power on laptop computers running on batteries. The Turn Off Monitor option in that dialog box specifies the amount of idle time required before the monitor shuts itself off. If you want your screen saver to play without the monitor going blank, set the Turn Off Monitor option to Never.

Tip The optional PowerToys for Windows XP and PowerToys Fun Pack downloads include a 3-D screensaver and a program to use any movies you create with Windows Movie Maker as a screen saver. See www.microsoft.com/windowsxp/downloads/powertoys for links to those downloads.

Fine-tuning your color scheme

As mentioned earlier in this chapter, you can choose an overall color scheme for your screen using the Themes tab in Display Properties. You can further refine the general appearance of program windows and buttons, colors, and the size of text on the screen using options in the Appearance tab.

That Appearance tab is fairly straightforward. You choose general look and feel from the Windows and Buttons drop-down list. Then, you can choose a color scheme and font size from the options with those names. The Preview area shows you how your selected options will look when you click OK or Apply.

The Effects and Advanced buttons on the Appearance tab give you superfine control over the colors and text sizes. Clicking the Advanced button opens the Advanced Appearance dialog box shown at left in Figure 6-4. The Effects button leads to the options shown in the right half of that same figure. (But you can only have one open at a time).

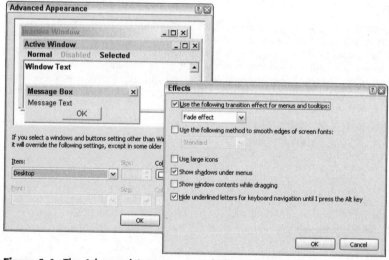

Figure 6-4: The Advanced Appearance and Effects dialog boxes

The top of the Advanced Appearance dialog is just another preview area. As you change items, it reflects how those items will look when you apply them. To change a specific item, first choose its name from the Item drop-down list. The Size, Font, and Color controls will then be enabled to reflect properties you can change for the selected item. For example, if you choose Active Title Bar, you can change the size of the item (in pixels). And you can change the font, font size (in points), and color of the text. When you choose something like Active Window Border, you'll have fewer options because borders don't contain any text. Any changes you make will be reflected in the preview area above the controls.

Tip   The Brightness and Contrast controls on your monitor work like those on a TV. You can't work those with the mouse or keyboard, though. You have to use controls that are right on the monitor, according to the instructions that came with your particular make and model of monitor or notebook computer.

The Effects dialog box offers options for controlling special effects. For example, you can choose transition effects, enable or disable drop-shadows under menus, and so forth. The option titled "Use the following method to smooth edges of screen fonts" is useful on some notebook and LCD monitors, because it helps get rid of the jagged edges on text that sometimes shows up on those monitors. If you choose that option, you can choose ClearType as your font-smoothing method, which should help reduce the "jaggies."

Tip   On an older computer that barely has enough "horsepower" to run XP, turning off special effects can help boost the computer's performance.

Choosing a screen resolution and color depth

While your screen looks like a smooth picture from where you're sitting, it's actually a collection of tiny lighted dots called *pixels*. The resolution of your screen determines how many pixels are visible, expressed as the number of pixels across the screen, and the number of pixels down. You can also choose a *color depth*, which determines the number of colors your screen can show.

To choose a screen resolution or color depth, click the Settings tab in the Display Properties dialog box. Use the Screen Resolution slider (see Figure 6-5) to adjust the resolution. With Windows XP, a minimum of 800 × 600 pixels is recommended, though you'll be able to get more stuff on the screen at a higher resolution, such as 1024 × 768. Be aware, however, that the higher the resolution, the smaller everything will look on your screen. Your best bet is to try both 800 × 600 and 1024 × 768 and to stick with whichever is most comfortable for your eyes.

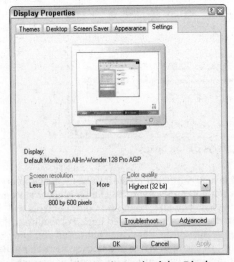

Figure 6-5: The Settings tab of the Display Properties dialog box

Resolution and Color Depth Affect Everyone

The Screen Resolution and Color Depth options on the Settings tab are settings that are applied directly to your graphics card. As such, they're not stored as part of your personal theme. Furthermore, if your computer is set up for multiple users, the resolution and color depth will be applied to everyone.

That's not to say that everyone is stuck using the same settings "forever." It just means that when you choose your own custom theme, it will never automatically change the resolution and color depth. You have to choose the theme you want to use. Then, change the resolution and color depth, if necessary, if you want those to be different.

Gotcha

Some notebook computers and flat monitors have their own separate dialog boxes for screen resolution and color depth. If changing those settings in the Display Properties dialog box has no effect on your screen, refer to the manual that came with your computer or monitor for instructions on changing its settings.

With color depth, bigger is generally better. The full range of options available to you depends on your computer's video card and monitor. As a rule, you want to choose Highest (32 bit) for the best display. However, 24 bit and 16 bit are also acceptable.

Using the bit number as an exponent of 2 tells you the number of different colors the screen can display. For example, 32 bits of color (2^{32}) gives you 4,294,967,296 different colors, ideal for viewing photographs and video. A lower resolution such as 2^{24} (16,777,216 colors) or 2^{16} (65,536 colors) can make photos look blotchy.

Hidden Display Properties

The options you see in the Display Properties dialog box aren't necessarily all the options available to you. Many graphics cards have additional settings tucked away elsewhere. Because there are about a zillion makes and models of graphics cards, I can't tell you anything about yours. But I can show you an example of what I mean. If I click the Advanced button on the Settings tab in Display Properties dialog box on one of my computers, I get to a dialog box of features that are unique to the ATI All In Wonder graphics card installed in that system, as shown in Figure 6-6.

When I click the Adapter tab in the dialog box, I find a button named List All Modes. Opening that gives me a wide choice of resolutions, color depths, and refresh rates, as shown in the right half of Figure 6-6. There, I can set the screen to 640x480, even though the Windows dialog box doesn't allow me to do that.

Caution

I've been told that changing the refresh rate can physically damage the monitor. I haven't tried it out to see if it's true or not (for obvious reasons). But to play it safe, you should check the current refresh rate in your dialog box, and stick with that number when choosing other options.

Of course, all these settings are unique to the graphics card in that computer. Different graphics cards will have different stetting. In many cases, you can get to the settings for a graphic card from the Start menu or Notification area. It all depends on what's installed in your computer.

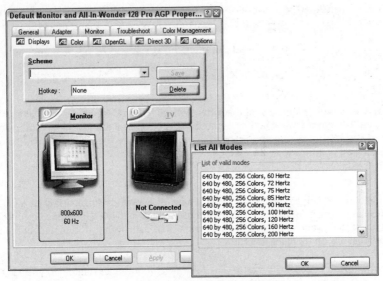

Figure 6-6: Hidden dialog boxes for a graphics display card

The only way to learn about your own graphics card is from the manual that came with the card or the computer or the card manufacturer's Web site. You'll need to know the make and model of the card to use the latter method. But you can generally get that information from System Information.

Note   To get System Information, click Start and choose All Programs ➪ Accessories ➪ System Tools ➪ System Information. Expand the Components category, and click on Display in the left column.

Getting the image right

The first time you switch from one screen resolution to another, the image on your monitor might be messed up. Perhaps there are big empty gaps on the screen, or the image is larger than the screen and you can't see the entire desktop. To fix those kinds of problems you need to adjust the Width, Height, Horizontal Center, and Vertical Center settings on your monitor.

I can't tell you, specifically, how to fix that because it's not something you do through Windows, the mouse, or the keyboard. It's something you do with buttons that are right on the monitor. Exactly where those buttons are and how they work varies from one monitor to the next. Once you find the right controls, you should have no problem sizing the desktop so that it fits the screen perfectly. But if you need help, your only resource is the documentation that came with the monitor or notebook computer.

Saving your theme

Keep in mind that any settings you might have changed (excluding Screen Resolution and Color Quality) are stored as part of the current theme. However, they're not saved immediately. To make sure that your new settings are stored as part of your theme, click on the

Themes tab in the Display Properties dialog box again. You should see your theme's name followed by *(Modified)*. That word tells you that the selections you made recently haven't actually been saved as part of the theme yet.

To save the settings and make them part of the theme, just click the Save As button. You'll be taken to the Save As dialog box, where you have the option of saving the current settings as yet another theme. But if you just want to make the newest settings part of your theme, click the Save button without changing anything else in the Save As dialog box. You'll see a message indicating that you're about to replace your existing theme. Click Yes to replace your original theme with the new theme you've created.

Arranging icons on your desktop

You can move icons around the desktop just by dragging them. You can delete any icon on your desktop by right-clicking the icon and choosing Delete. If your icons get all out of order and difficult to find, you can quickly rearrange them. Just right-click the Windows desktop and choose Arrange Icons By ⇨ Name as in Figure 6-7. Built-in icons such as My Documents, My Computer, and Recycle Bin are always listed first near the upper-left corner of the screen. Remaining icons will be listed in alphabetical order.

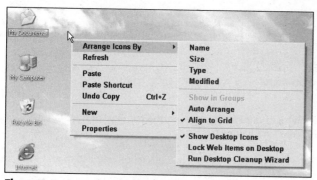

Figure 6-7: Arranging desktop icons

Personalizing Your Start Menu

The Start button, as you know, is the gateway to every program currently installed on your computer. The Start menu also provides easy access to commonly used folders such as My Documents, My Computer, Control Panel, and any others you care to add. As a rule, you want the Start menu to contain items you use frequently, so you can get to those items without navigating through too many submenus.

As you saw in Chapter 1, the Windows XP menu is split into two columns with icons for programs on the left and icons for folders and other places on the right. The left side of the menu is split into two groups. Icons above the horizontal line are *pinned* to the menu, meaning that they never change unless you change them. Beneath the horizontal line are icons that represent programs you use frequently. Those latter icons might change at any time to reflect programs you've been using frequently in the last few days. As a reminder, Figure 6-8 shows a sample Start menu.

Figure 6-8: A Windows XP Start menu

Tip   For information on pinning and unpinning items on the left side of the Start menu, see "Pinning and Unpinning Icons" in Chapter 1.

You can customize your Start menu in many ways. The dialog box you use to adjust those settings is named Taskbar and Start Menu Properties.

Controlling what you see on the Start menu

Earlier, I mentioned that you can usually get to an object's properties just by right-clicking the object and choosing Properties, or you can take the longer route through Control Panel. In this case though, you don't actually right-click the Start menu itself. Rather, you can use whichever of the following techniques is easiest for you:

   ✦ Right-click the Start button and choose Properties.

   ✦ Click the Start button and choose Control Panel. If Control Panel opens in Categories View, click Appearance and Themes. Then, open the Taskbar and Start Menu icon.

Options for customizing the taskbar and options for customizing the Start menu share the Taskbar and Start Menu Properties dialog box. Once you've opened that dialog box (using either of the preceding techniques), you need to click the Start Menu tab to get to options for personalizing your Start menu.

You'll initially be presented with two options: Start Menu (which displays the two-column Windows XP Start menu) and Classic Start Menu (which displays an old-fashioned Windows 98–style menu). To access the settings described here, select the first option, Start Menu. Then, click the Customize button just to the right of that option. The Customize Start Menu dialog box will open next. There are two tabs in the dialog box labeled General and Advanced, as shown in Figure 6-9.

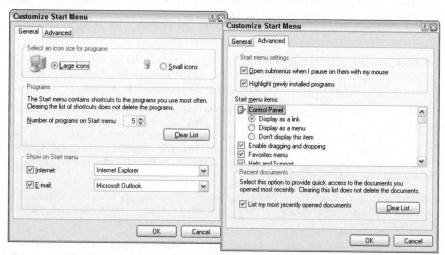

Figure 6-9: The two tabs of the Customize Start Menu dialog box

The General tab of the Customize Start Menu dialog box provides the following options:

✦ **Large icons/Small icons:** Choosing Large Icons displays icons at the size you've seen throughout this book. Choosing Small Icons displays smaller icons that are harder to see. But you can get more icons on the menu at the smaller size.

✦ **Number of items on Start menu:** Specifies the maximum number of items displayed on the left side of the menu. If you set this too high for your screen resolution and icon size, Windows will display a *Some items cannot be shown* message each time you open the Start menu. To get rid of that message, you need to decrease the number of items selected here. The Clear List button clears all of the unpinned icons from the left side of the Start menu.

✦ **Internet:** If you want to pin the icon for your Web browser to the top of the Start menu, choose this option. Then, choose your favorite Web browser from the drop-down list to the right.

✦ **E-mail:** If you want to pin the icon for your e-mail client to the Start menu, choose this option. Then, choose the name of your e-mail client or service from the drop-down list to the right.

The Advanced tab of the Customize Start Menu dialog box provides options that define the general behavior of the Start menu and the items visible on the right side of the menu. Items outside the list box are as follows:

Tip   If you're looking for advice, I suggest that you select (check) the following three options:

✦ **Open submenus when I pause on them with my mouse:** If you select this option, you can open any submenu simply by pointing to the option on the menu rather than clicking it. Items on the menu that have a ⇨ to the left or right, such as All Programs, My Recent Documents, and Favorites, all have submenus.

✦ **Highlight newly installed programs:** Selecting this option for starting any new program you install will be highlighted on the All Programs menu. That makes it much easier to find the appropriate icon after you've installed a new program.

✦ **List my most recently opened documents:** If selected, adds a My Recent Documents option to the right side of the Start menu. This makes it easy to open any document you've recently worked on. Rather than digging around for the document, you just click the Start button, choose My Recent Documents, and click the name of the document you want to open. The Clear List button empties the list of documents, allowing you to rebuild the menu from scratch.

The list of Start Menu Items in the center of the Advanced tab lets you choose which folder names you want to make available on the right side of the menu. For most items, you'll be given three options:

✦ **Display as a link:** Choosing this option tells Windows to open the corresponding folder when you click the menu option. This is the most natural method, once you're familiar with working in folders.

✦ **Display as a menu:** Choosing this option tells Windows to show items within the folder as options on a menu, without opening the folder. This option is a reasonable alternative for folders that contain few icons but is unwieldy for folders that contain many icons.

✦ **Don't display this item:** As it says, choosing this option will prevent the option from being displayed at all on the right side of the Start menu.

The Start Menu Items list contains mostly specific items you can choose to show, or hide, on the right side of the Start menu. But as you scroll through the list, you'll also find some options that define the overall behavior of the Start menu rather than specific items. Those items are summarized as follows:

✦ **Enable dragging and dropping:** If selected, this allows you to rearrange icons on the Start and All Programs menus simply by dragging them into position. You also need to select this option if you want to be able to create desktop shortcuts by right-clicking options on the Start and All Programs menus. I recommend that you select (check) this option.

✦ **Scroll Programs:** If you select this option, the All Programs menu won't fan out across the screen when you open it. Instead, you'll have to scroll through the menu using buttons at the top and bottom. I would recommend that you clear (not select) this option.

After making your selections from the Customize Start Menu dialog box, click its OK button, and click the OK button in the Taskbar and Start Menu Properties dialog box. Click the Start button to see the effects of your changes on the Start menu.

Renaming and removing Start menu items

The left side of the Start menu is very flexible. For example, if you pin an item to the Start menu, but later decide you don't need it there, you can unpin it. Just right-click the icon you want to unpin and choose Unpin From Start Menu. Or, if you don't see that option on the shortcut menu, choose Remove From This List instead. To get rid of an icon that isn't pinned to the Start menu, right-click the item and choose Remove From This List.

Caution   Removing a program's icon from the Start menu doesn't delete the actual underlying program. It only removes the program's icon from the menu. To uninstall a program, see Chapter 48.

If you want to change the name of an item on the Start menu, right-click the item and choose Rename. Then, edit the existing name or type a new name, and press Enter.

Rearranging Start and All Programs menu items

You can rearrange icons on the left side of the Start menu just by dragging any item up or down and dropping it wherever you want to place it. The same technique works on the All Programs menu as well. But on the All Programs menu, you can quickly whip icons into alphabetical order by following these steps:

Gotcha   If you can't move items around on the Start or All Programs menus, make sure that *Enable dragging and dropping* is selected in the Customize Start Menu dialog box is selected (checked), as described under "Controlling what you see on the Start menu" earlier in this chapter.

1. Click the **Start** button and choose **All Programs**.

2. Right-click any icon on the All Programs menu (or a submenu that you can get to from All Programs), and choose **Sort by Name** from the shortcut menu that opens (see Figure 6-10).

On the All Programs menu, program folders (groups) are always listed first. (Program groups all have a similar icon and a ⇨ to the right. Icons that represent programs have the program's logo as their icon and no ⇨ character to the right.)

Tip   Chapter 16 will show you how to add any shortcut icon to your Start menu.

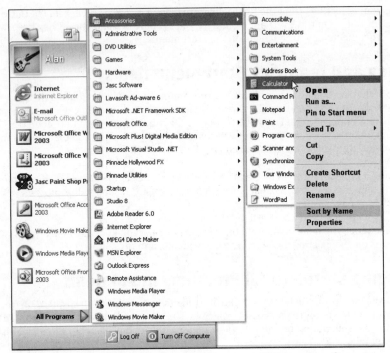

Figure 6-10: Use the Sort by Name option on any All Programs submenu to alphabetize its options.

Customizing the Taskbar

The taskbar at the bottom of your screen provides many useful items, including the Start button, the Quick Launch toolbar, the general taskbar area, which contains a button for each open program window, and the Notification area. Options for personalizing your taskbar are located in the Taskbar and Start Menu Properties dialog box, which you can get to by using whichever of the following techniques is most convenient:

✦ Right-click the Start button and choose Properties.

✦ Click the Start button and choose Control Panel. Then, click Appearance and Themes (if available), and open the Taskbar and Start Menu icon.

The Taskbar and Start Menu Properties dialog box opens on your screen. Click the Taskbar tab to reveal the options shown in Figure 6-11. The two preview taskbars let you see how the options you choose will affect the real taskbar. Your options are:

✦ **Lock the taskbar:** If you select this option, you'll lock the taskbar, which will prevent you from accidentally moving or resizing it. If you want to move or resize the taskbar, you first need to clear this option to unlock the taskbar.

✦ **Auto-hide the taskbar:** If you selected this icon, the taskbar will automatically slide out of view when you're not using it, to free up the little bit of screen space it takes up. After the taskbar hides itself, you can rest the tip of the mouse button on the thin line at the bottom of the screen to bring the taskbar out of hiding.

Figure 6-11: The Taskbar tab of the Taskbar and Start Menu Properties dialog box

✦ **Keep the taskbar on top of other windows:** Selecting this option ensures that the taskbar is always visible and can't be covered up by open program windows. To ensure that the taskbar is always visible, select (check) this option, and clear the *Auto-hide the taskbar* checkbox.

✦ **Group similar taskbar buttons:** Choosing this option allows the taskbar to combine multiple open documents or pages for a program into a single taskbar button. Taskbar buttons that represent multiple documents will display a number next to the program name on the button. You can open any document by clicking the taskbar button and clicking a document name. To close all open documents or pages in one fell swoop, right-click the button and choose Close Group.

✦ **Show Quick Launch:** Select this option to make the Quick Launch toolbar visible on the taskbar. Clear this option to hide the Quick Launch toolbar. (More on the Quick Launch toolbar later.)

✦ **Show the clock:** Choose this option to make the current time visible in the lower-right corner of the screen. Clear this option to hide the current time.

Tip   When the current time is visible, you can double-click the time to change the current time and date, or to get in sync with the official Internet time. Right-click the current time to see handy shortcuts for organizing open program windows.

✦ **Hide inactive icons:** If this is selected, Windows will hide inactive Notification area icons, thereby saving space on the taskbar. Clearing this option will make all notification icons visible. See Chapter 1 for more information.

Moving and sizing taskbar items

When the taskbar is unlocked, you can move and size the taskbar and size the Quick Launch toolbar as well. A quick way to lock or unlock the toolbar is to right-click the current time, and choose Lock the Taskbar. The option works as a toggle, locking the taskbar if it's unlocked or unlocking it when it's locked.

You can tell if the taskbar is currently unlocked by the dragging handles at the top of the bar and within the bar. When the taskbar is locked, no dragging handles are visible, and the Lock the Taskbar option on the shortcut menu has a check mark next to it.

The dragging handle for each component is at the left side of the component. For example, the handle to the left of the Quick Launch toolbar moves that toolbar. The handle to the left of the taskbar buttons moves that portion of the taskbar. You can stack portions of the taskbar as in the example shown in Figure 6-12. There, I've moved the buttons down to their own row and enlarged the Quick Launch toolbar.

Note Chapter 16 explains how to create shortcuts and add them to the Quick Launch toolbar.

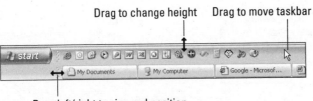

Figure 6-12: Customizing the taskbar

By the way, if you feel like a complete klutz when doing this stuff, join the club. It's awkward at first because if you move the mouse pointer ever so slightly up or down while dragging left or right, the bar will instantly stack or unstack. It all takes some patience. Just remember that when you put the mouse pointer on a handle, you're moving and sizing the item(s) just to the right of that handle. Here's how you work things:

✦ To move the entire taskbar, point to an empty portion of the bar and drag the entire bar to any edge of the screen.

✦ To size the taskbar, point to the thin bar at the top of the taskbar until the mouse pointer turns to a two-headed arrow. Then, hold down the left mouse button and drag that edge up or down.

✦ To change the width of a component (and at the same time, the width of the item to its left), drag the handle left or right. You can drag the handle right through another component to move to the left or right of that component.

✦ To stack or unstack items, drag the handle at the left of the item up or down (even through the mouse pointer only points left and right).

If you drag the top of the taskbar right off the bottom of the screen, the taskbar will seem to disappear. But if you look closely, you'll see that the thin gray bar is still visible along the bottom edge of the screen. If you rest the tip of the mouse pointer right on that bar, you'll see the two-headed arrow again, indicating that you can drag the top of the taskbar straight up to make the taskbar wider again.

Once you have the taskbar arranged the way you like, you'll be wise to lock it. That way, you don't have to worry about inadvertently rearranging it just by being a little klutzy with the mouse.

Optional taskbar toolbars

Windows XP comes with some optional toolbars you can add to the taskbar or allow to float freely on the desktop. To show or hide a toolbar, right-click the clock in the lower-right corner of your screen, choose Toolbars, and then click the name of the toolbar you want to show or hide. The toolbars that come with XP are listed here:

✦ **Address:** Displays an Address bar like the one in your Web browser. Typing a URL into the bar will open your Web browser and the page at the URL.

✦ **Windows Media Player:** Adds a set of Play Controls to the taskbar. But this toolbar will be visible only if you open, then minimize, Windows Media Player. Unlike the others, this one can't be dragged off the taskbar onto the desktop.

✦ **Links:** Displays the Links toolbar from Microsoft Internet Explorer.

✦ **Language bar:** Displays the optional language bar, but only if your computer has voice recognition or some similar software installed to activate voice recognition.

✦ **Desktop:** Shows all desktop shortcut icons from your Windows desktop in a condensed toolbar format.

✦ **Quick Launch:** Shows (or hides) the Quick Launch toolbar described earlier in this chapter.

When you first open one of these optional toolbars, you might see only its label in the taskbar. This is not a problem, because you can move and size most of the toolbars in lots of ways, including the following:

✦ On the taskbar, drag the toolbar's dragging handle left or right to size and position, or up and down to stack.

✦ To show or hid a toolbar's title, right-click its handle and choose Show Title.

✦ To show or hide icon names, right-click its handle and choose Show Text.

Note   The Media Player and Language Bar toolbars are the exceptions, because they're not "normal" customizable toolbars.

As an example, Figure 6-13 shows the taskbar with lots of toolbars on it. The obvious disadvantage here is that the tall taskbar does take up quite a bit of valuable screen real estate. Though if you enable Auto-hide for the taskbar, the whole thing will slide out of view when you're not using it. It will slide back into view when you move the mouse pointer to the bottom of the screen.

Figure 6-13: Several toolbars on the taskbar

As an alternative to piling the toolbars onto the taskbar, you can put them on the desktop. To move a toolbar from the taskbar to the desktop, just drag its handle to the desktop. Once the toolbar is on the desktop, you can do any of the following:

✦ Move the toolbar by dragging its title bar

✦ Size the toolbar by dragging any corner or edge

✦ Dock the toolbar to any edge of the screen by dragging it to that edge (so the mouse pointer is actually touching the very edge of the screen)

✦ Change the width of a docked toolbar by dragging its inner edge left or right

✦ Undock a docked toolbar by dragging it by the handle toward the center of the screen

✦ Put a floating desktop toolbar back on the taskbar by dragging the toolbar back to the taskbar

Figure 6-14 shows a different toolbar arrangement. There, I've moved the Quick Launch, Links, Address, and Language Bar toolbars onto the desktop. The Quick Launch and Links toolbars are anchored to the right side of the screen. The other two are floating.

The taskbar is back to its one-row height. The center bar is the Desktop toolbar with its title and text (icon names) hidden. The Media Player toolbar is to the right of the Desktop toolbar.

Figure 6-14: Another way to arrange toolbars

Tip Chapter 16 explains how to add your own shortcuts to the Quick Launch and Links toolbars, but the basic idea is simple — drag the shortcut onto the toolbar, and drop it there.

Having the toolbars on the desktop isn't quite as convenient as having them on the taskbar. But when the desktop is covered, you can get to them quickly by minimizing all the open program windows (click Show Desktop in the Quick Launch toolbar, or right-click the clock and choose Show the Desktop). The open program windows will be minimized, but the toolbars will stay put.

Tip After you minimize all open windows, you can bring them back one at a time from their taskbar buttons. To bring them all back at once, click the Show Desktop button again, or right-click the clock and choose Show Open Windows.

To close a taskbar toolbar, right-click the clock, choose Toolbars, and click on the name of the toolbar. Optionally, you can right-click the toolbar's handle and choose Close Toolbar. To close a toolbar that's on the desktop, click its Close (X) button. On a docked toolbar, right-click its handle, or any empty portion of the bar, and choose Close Toolbar.

As I've said, you'll probably feel like a total klutz when you first get started. The distances you have to drag are usually so short that you'll probably end up dragging things all over the place. But it gets easier with practice. Still, once you get things arranged you'll want to lock the taskbar so that you don't mess things up by accident.

Introducing Control Panel

So far in this book we're taken shortcuts to the Display Properties and Taskbar and Start Menu Properties. Mainly because that's the easy way to get to an object's properties — right-click the object and choose Properties. However, things that you see on the screen aren't the only things that have properties. For example, your mouse and keyboard are devices that have properties. But you can't very well right-click your mouse or keyboard!

Note A *device* (or *hardware device*) is any piece of hardware that's in or attached to the computer.

In Windows XP, all the properties for all the objects and devices are in Control Panel. That special folder gets its name from the fact that it's the place from which you control things. The dashboard in your car is the control panel for your car. The cockpit of an airplane is the control panel for the airplane. The Windows Control Panel is where you get to all the options of for controlling object and device properties.

To open the Control Panel, click the Start button and choose Control Panel. On Control Panel's home page you can choose how you want to view icons using the Switch to Classic View or Switch to Category View option under Control Panel in the Explorer bar at left. Figure 6-15 shows each view. The difference between the two views is:

✦ **Category View:** Shows categories of Control Panel icons. To see the icons in any category, click the category name.

✦ **Classic View:** Shows all icons at once, as in previous versions of Windows.

Figure 6-15: Two views of Control Panel

Note   Category View might not provide access to all your Control Panel icons. To see any that don't' fit within a category, click on Other Control Panel Options under See Also in the Explorer bar.

Control Panel is actually a special folder, so its menu bar and toolbar have Windows Explorer options in them. You can move, size, minimize, maximize, and close Control Panel as you would any other program window. Control Panel also has its own taskbar button when open.

Each icon in Control Panel represents a dialog box (or a window that's sort of like a dialog box, but let's not confuse matters). The dialog box, in turn, contains controls that allow you to change properties of objects and devices. Different computers have different icons in their Control Panel, because some dialog boxes allow you to control the properties of specific devices. You'll see examples of most of the dialog boxes as appropriate in upcoming chapters. For now, let's focus on the Mouse and Keyboard dialog boxes, because they definitely have some say in configuring your work environment.

Personalizing Your Mouse

Mice have properties. (There's a sentence you could interpret a couple of ways). Different mice have different properties. But whatever properties your mouse offers should be in the Mouse Properties dialog box. To get to it:

1. Click the **Start** button and choose **Control Panel**.

2. If you're in Category View choose **Printers and Other Hardware**. Otherwise, skip this step.

3. Open the **Mouse** icon.

The Mouse Properties dialog box opens. I can't say exactly what yours will look like, but Figure 6-16 shows an example. I can't say what settings you'll find. Though if you have any trouble interpreting your settings you can click the ? button in the upper-right corner of your dialog box, and then click any option for more information. Pressing Help (F1) or clicking the Help button in the dialog box (if there is one) should also give you more information.

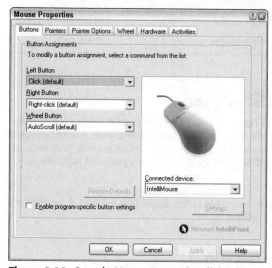

Figure 6-16: Sample Mouse Properties dialog box

Even though I can't say, specifically, what's in your Mouse Properties dialog box, I can give you some examples of "typical" settings.

Mice for lefties

If you're left-handed and you want the main mouse button to be below your left index finger, you need to reverse the normal functioning of the buttons. Generally, the left mouse button is the primary button, and the right mouse button is the secondary button. In some dialog boxes, you can just choose "Switch primary and secondary buttons" to reverse the buttons. In the example shown back in Figure 6-16, you'd need to set the Left Button to Right-click and the Right button to Click.

If you do reverse your mouse buttons, you'll have to adjust all the standard mouse terminology accordingly. Table 6-1 shows how the various mouse terms apply to right-handed mouse settings and to left-handed settings.

Table 6-1: Mouse Terminology for Righties and Lefties

Standard Terminology	Righties	Lefties
Primary button	Left	Right
Secondary button	Right	Left
Click	Left button	Right button
Double-click	Left button	Right button
Drag	Left button	Right button
Right-click	Right button	Left button
Right-drag	Right button	Left button

Adjusting the double-click speed

To double-click, you generally have to tap the primary mouse button twice very quickly. Otherwise, it counts as two single clicks. If it's difficult to tap the button quickly enough, or if you're so fast than two single clicks are being interpreted as a double-click, look around for a Double-click speed option. That will allow you to adjust the delay needed between two clicks to count as a double-click.

Tip   If double-clicking is a pain, consider switching to the single-click method of opening icons. See "To click or double-click" in Chapter 3.

Controlling the mouse motion

Many mice have a Motion property that defines the relationship between how far you move the mouse and how far the pointer moves on the screen. For example, if you find it difficult to get the tip of the mouse pointer on small screen objects, then you may want to slow down the mouse motion so that it's not so touchy. Or, if you feel you have to move your mouse too far to move the pointer a small distance on the screen, you can increase the motion speed.

Some mice have an Enhance pointer precision option that lets you have the best of both worlds. When that option is enabled, it's easier to drag things within small distances, such as when you're trying to size and position taskbar items.

Tip   The Accessibility options described in Chapter 9 also let you control the behavior of your mouse.

Making the mouse pointer more visible

If you keep losing sight of the mouse pointer on your screen, there are some things you can do to make it more visible. Some typical options are listed below:

✦ **Display pointer trails:** If selected, this causes the mouse pointer to leave a brief trail when you move it, making it easier to see the pointer.

✦ **Snap to:** If selected, this causes the mouse pointer to jump to the default button (typically OK) automatically as soon as the dialog box opens.

✦ **Show location of pointer when I press the Ctrl key:** If you selected this option and lose sight of your mouse pointer, hold down the Ctrl key. The mouse pointer will send out waves making it easy to see.

Tip

When you use a projector to give a demonstration on-screen, turn on the pointer trails to make following the mouse across the screen easier for your audience.

Yet another way to make your mouse pointer more visible is to use a large or animated mouse pointer.

Changing mouse pointers

If you're tired of the same old mouse pointer, or need to make your mouse pointer easier to see, you can (probably) change your mouse pointers. Typically, you just click on the Pointers tab in the Mouse Properties dialog box to see your options. On the Pointers tab, the first step is to choose a general scheme from the Scheme drop-down list. All the mouse pointers from the currently selected scheme will appear in the Customize list, as in the example shown in Figure 6-17.

Figure 6-17: Pointers tab in Mouse Properties dialog box

Once you've chosen a scheme, you can scroll through the list under Customize to see how various mouse pointers will look on your screen. If you like, you can change any mouse pointer by double-clicking its name. You'll be taken to a folder named Cursors where you can choose a different pointer if you like.

Selecting "Enable pointer shadow" displays a small drop-shadow under the mouse pointer, giving it a slightly raised appearance. If you change any pointers for a scheme, click the Save As button to give your new collection a new name.

Using ClickLock

If you find it difficult to select multiple items by dragging the mouse pointer through them, you may want to try activating the ClickLock feature. Enabling that feature lets you select multiple items without holding down the mouse button. First you need to choose the Turn on the ClickLock option. Then, use the Settings button to specify how long you need to hold down the primary mouse button before the key is "locked."

For example, let's say that you turn on ClickLock and set the required delay to about one second. To drag the mouse pointer through some items, you position the mouse pointer to where you plan to start selecting and hold down the mouse pointer for one second. Then, you can release the mouse button and move the mouse pointer through the items you want to select. Those items will be selected as though you were actually holding down the left mouse button.

When you've finished selecting, just click some area outside the selection. The mouse pointer returns to its normal function, and the items you selected remain selected.

Mouse wheel and AutoScroll

Many mice have a wheel between the two mouse buttons. The wheel plays several roles, mostly as an alternative to using scroll bars. If there's a vertical scroll bar (or both vertical and horizontal scroll bars) in the current program window, spinning the mouse wheel scrolls up and down (so you don't have to bother with the scroll bar). If there's a horizontal scroll bar (only) in the current window, spinning the mouse wheel scrolls left and right

In many graphics programs and Print Preview screens, you can use the wheel as an alternative to options on the View menu to zoom in and out. For example, let's say you're editing a photograph with a red-eye problem. You could spin the mouse wheel to where the pupil is huge, and then recolor the red pixels black. Spin the mouse wheel in the opposite direction to zoom back out and see the effects of your change.

The mouse wheel also acts as a third, middle mouse button when you press it. Typically, tapping the mouse wheel once goes into AutoScroll mode. Many (though not all) programs support autoscrolling if it's activated on your mouse. Internet Explorer, Word, and Excel all support it for sure. Here's how it works:

1. Move the mouse pointer to a location within the document you want to scroll through, and then tap the mouse wheel. A symbol like the example shown in Figure 6-18 appears.

2. To start autosrolling up, move the mouse away from yourself slightly. To scroll down, pull the mouse toward you slightly. The farther you move the mouse in either direction, the more quickly the page scrolls.

3. To turn off autoscrolling, click anywhere in the document.

If your mouse has a wheel, chances are your Mouse Properties dialog box will have a tab for determining its sensitivity. Also, you'll probably find an option for specifying what you want the mouse wheel to do when you press it.

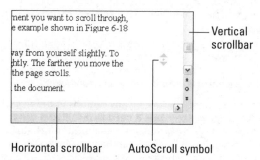

— Vertical scrollbar

Horizontal scrollbar   AutoScroll symbol

Figure 6-18: AutoScroll symbol

Personalizing the Keyboard

Most keyboards have a Properties dialog box in Control Panel as well. As with the mouse, however, the options in that dialog box will vary from one keyboard to the next. To get to the Keyboard Properties dialog box:

1. Click the **Start** button and choose **Control Panel**.

2. If you're in Category view choose **Printers and Other Hardware**. Otherwise, skip this step.

3. Open the **Keyboard** icon.

Figure 6-19 shows an example of a Keyboard Properties dialog box. The settings in that dialog box are as follows:

Figure 6-19: Sample Keyboard Properties dialog box

✦ **Repeat delay:** Determines how long you have to hold down a key before it starts auto-typing (repeating itself automatically).

✦ **Repeat rate:** Determines how fast the key types automatically while you're holding it down.

✦ **Cursor blink rate:** Determines how quickly the cursor blinks in a document.

If your keyboard offers programmable buttons, there may not be any options in the Keyboard Properties dialog box for defining those keys. More likely, you'll need to install and use the program that came with the keyboard to do that. There is no "one rule fits all" for that sort of thing. The only places to get the information you need will be from the instructions that came with the keyboard and the keyboard manufacturer's Web site.

Wrap Up

In this chapter, we've looked at the main customization settings for setting up your work environment. The idea is to get your desktop, mouse, and keyboard all working in a way that's easy for you. To recap the main points:

✦ The collection of settings that define the look and feel of your Windows desktop is called a theme.

✦ The Display Properties dialog box provides options for controlling the appearance of your desktop, and saving those settings as a theme.

✦ The quick and easy way to get to the Display Properties dialog box is to right-click the desktop and choose Properties, though you can also get to it through Control Panel (choose Appearance and Themes in the Category view).

✦ Options for customizing your Start menu and taskbar are located in the Taskbar and Start Menu Properties dialog box.

✦ The quick route to Taskbar and Start Menu Properties is to right-click the Start button or an empty portion of the taskbar and choose Properties, though like all dialog boxes you can also get to it through Control Panel (the Appearance and Themes category).

✦ When the taskbar is unlocked, you can move and position the entire bar or portions of the entire bar.

✦ Optional toolbars that you can add to the taskbar or put on the desktop are located on the Toolbars menu, available when you right-click the time in the lower-right corner of the screen.

✦ Control Panel is the name of a special folder that gives you access to all the properties for all the objects and devices that make up your computer system.

✦ Most mice also have customizable properties, which you can change via the Mouse Properties dialog box (the Mouse icon in Control Panel).

✦ Most keyboards have properties as well, which you can get to via the Keyboard icon in Control Panel.

✦   ✦   ✦

Sharing a Computer with User Accounts

Imagine that one day you leave the office for lunch. When you return, you discover that someone has done a major remodel of your office. They've changed all the furniture, and reorganized all your files for you. Only problem is, you hate the décor, you can't find anything in this new organizational scheme, and the decorator has left a bunch of her irrelevant junk scattered all over your office.

That sort of thing can happen all the time when two or more people share a single PC. If you've ever been in that situation, you know it doesn't take long before tempers start to flare. The solution to the problem is *user accounts*. With user accounts, every person has their own desktop, their own Start menu, their own My Documents, My Music, and other folders.

When someone makes wild and crazy changes to his or her desktop or downloads a bunch of junk from the Internet, it affects only that person's account. When you sign into your user account, everything is exactly as you left it. No unpleasant surprises. It's the next best thing to each person having his or her own separate PC, because what other people do in their user accounts has no bearing on your user account.

What's a User Account?

Even if you've never set up user accounts, you've actually been using your computer under some generic user account since day one. The name of the user account appears at the top of the Start menu whenever you click the Start button. If Windows came preinstalled on your computer, it may be something like Owner or Administrator. But it's a user account nonetheless.

If you want to keep other people from messing with your stuff, you'll need to give each of those other people their own user account. You can password-protect your own account, if you like, to make sure other people stay out. Once you have two or more user accounts, the computer will no longer start by going straight to your desktop. Instead, the first stop will be the Welcome screen, which displays an icon for each user account you've created, as in the example shown in Figure 7-1.

Figure 7-1: The Welcome screen for a computer with multiple user accounts

Each user account is like a separate PC. For example, when Wilbur clicks on his user account in Figure 7-1, he's take to his own desktop, settings, My Documents, My Music and other My . . . folders. Whatever Wilbur does in his account has no bearing on the other accounts.

Every user (including Wilbur) has access to all the customization settings described in Chapter 6. However, the settings a user chooses apply only to that user's desktop, start menu, and taskbar. All users also have access to the same programs. You don't need to reinstall any programs just because you've created a user account. The programs on the All Programs menu are the same for everyone.

When Wilbur is finished with the computer for the time being and logs off, any other user can log into his or her user account. Whatever Wilbur did while in his user account has no effect on other people's accounts. So, if you're that other user, everything on your desktop, menus, and document folders will be exactly as you left them, no matter what Wilbur did while in his account. It's as though Wilbur were using his own separate PC.

Creating and managing user accounts in Windows XP is easy. It only takes a couple of minutes to create a new user account. And the time spent doing do so is well worth it. It'll save you a lot of aggravation, and keep those tempers from flaring. Before you launch into it though, you'll need to make some decisions about how much power you want to give other users.

Administrators versus limited users

When two or more people share a computer, and each person has a user account, one or more persons usually play the role of *administrator*. The administrator has limitless power over the computer in that she can look at other people's stuff (as in spying on what kinds of things the kids are up to), create (and take away) user accounts, install new hardware and software, make systemwide changes (things that affect all user accounts), and so forth.

A *limited* user can still use the computer normally. However, a limited user can't do certain things. For example, a limited user can't see other people's documents and can't make big changes to the computer that might affect other users. Only the administrator can do the big things. That's because the administrator is (presumably) the most knowledgeable user and, therefore, gets to be the person in control. Table 7-1 summarizes the differences between administrator and limited-user capabilities.

Table 7-1: Differences between Administrators and Limited Users

Capability	Administrator	Limited User
Install programs and hardware	Yes	No
Create and delete user accounts	Yes	No
Change other people's user accounts	Yes	No
Change your own user account type	Yes	No
Change your own user account picture	Yes	Yes
Create, change, or remove your own password	Yes	Yes
See other people's documents	Maybe	No

The typical scenario in a corporate environment is that only certain people with sufficient computer knowledge have Administrator accounts. All other users have Limited accounts, which give them just enough computer access to do their jobs, but not enough power to make any changes to the computing environment that would compromise the system or allow them to look at other people's work. The same general idea can be applied to a family computing environment, where the parent (or child, as the case may be) with the most computer knowledge has the only Administrator account on the computer. All other family members have Limited accounts to keep them from messing things up for other family members.

Private documents versus shared documents

Back in Table 7-1 I wrote *maybe* as to whether or not an administrator can see other people's documents. That's because there's no rule that says there can be only one administrator user account on the computer. You can have any number of administrator accounts and/or limited accounts. How you set up your user accounts is entirely up to you.

An administrator can always look at the documents created and stored by limited users. That is, there's no way that limited users can keep an administrator from peeking at their files. So, what about two different administrator accounts? If you create and administrator account for yourself, you can make its documents *private*, which means that nobody else on the computer can see your documents — not even other administrators.

You'll see the prompt for making an administrator account private when you create a user account. Though as we'll discuss a little later in the chapter, you can make any folder private or public at any time. The term "public" in this sense only means "visible to other user accounts on the same computer, and other computers in a local network." As mentioned, shared files and folders aren't made public to the Internet.

The Guest account

Windows XP has a built-in *Guest account*, which you can activate while you're setting up accounts. That account isn't ascribed to any one person. Rather, it's a catch-all account for anyone who doesn't have a user account.

Limited Accounts Are More Secure

This is no urban myth. Using a Limited account provides better computer security than an Administrator account. That's because most viruses and other malicious programs need administrative privileges to do their dirty work. But a program doesn't have its own privileges. Rather, it gets its privileges from the current user account. If you're logged into a Limited account, the malicious program won't have sufficient power to do its job. Hence, no infection.

Most computer administrators create two accounts for themselves, an Administrator account and a Limited account. They use the Limited account for day-to-day work such as creating and saving documents, browsing the Web, and so forth. They use the Administrator account only to do things that require administrative privileges, such as installing new programs, or modifying other people's user accounts.

For example, let's say that you're having a houseguest who wants to be able to use the computer once in a while. You don't want to create a user account for your guest, so you just let the person use the Guest account. Like a limited user, a guest won't be able to make any substantial changes to the overall computer system but will be able to do the day-to-day things that a regular computer user needs to do. As described under "Activating/deactivating the Guest account" later in this chapter, whether or not you even have a Guest account is entirely up to you.

How to Create a User Account

Creating a user account is simple—a wizard will take you through the whole procedure. Think of the name you want to give the account first (just the person's first name will do), and think about whether or not you want make this person an administrator or limited user. Then, follow these steps:

1. Click the **Start** button and choose **Control Panel**.

2. In Control Panel, open the **User Accounts** icon. If Control Panel initially opened in Category view, click the **User Accounts** icon under *or pick a Control Panel icon*. You should be at the main User Accounts window, shown in Figure 7-2.

Tip   Note the links under "Learn about" in the Explorer bar at the left side of the User Accounts window. You can click any such link in any User Account window for more information.

3. Click **Create a new account**.

4. As instructed, type the new user's name. Keep the name short and simple, just a first name will do. The maximum length is 20 characters. Then, click the **Next** button.

5. On the next page, choose either Computer administrator or Limited, depending on how much power you want to grant this user. Then, click **Create Account**.

Tip   While you're in the User Accounts window, you can use the Back and Home buttons in its toolbar to navigate through screens. Use options under *Learn about* in the Explorer bar to get more information on any page.

You're taken to a new Users Accounts window that shows your account, the new account, and perhaps one or two others, which you'll learn about later in this chapter. For now, you might want to take the new user account for a spin, because doing so will help you gain a better understanding of how it all works.

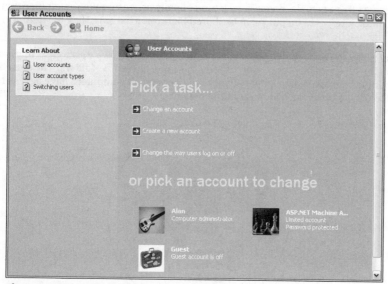

Figure 7-2: The main User Accounts window

Logging on to a new account

When you first create a new user account, it's really little more than a placeholder. Windows doesn't actually create that user's My. . . folders until the user (or you) logs into the account. To really get the job done and to make it easier to configure the account, you should log in to the account. Here's a quick and easy way to do that:

1. Click the **Start** button and choose **Log Off** from the bottom of the Start menu.

2. Click the **Switch User** button.

3. Click the name or picture of the new user account you just created, and then wait.

It takes a minute or two to get a new account all squared away. You don't have to do anything except be patient. Eventually, you'll be taken to the Windows desktop. Right off the bat, you'll notice something about this desktop—it the desktop looks a lot like the desktop on a brand-new PC. There's a reason for that. A new user account is like a brand-new PC, because each user account is like a separate computer.

There is one major difference, though, between a new user account and a new PC. The new PC has access to all the programs on the current computer. You can see that for yourself by clicking the Start button and choosing All Programs. The All Programs menu should provide access to the same programs that your account did.

If you open the My Documents, My Music, or My Pictures folder in this new account, you won't find any of your documents there. That's because each user has their own My . . . folders. What you put in your My . . . folders has no bearing on others' folders. Likewise, whatever junk they stick in their My . . . folders won't show up in your folders.

About the shared folders

All users have access to the built-in Shared Documents, Shared Music, and other folders contained within the Shared Documents parent folder. This is handy because it means that you don't have to ask permission, or go digging around through other people's accounts, to get at shared documents. For example, if you have a ton of family photos on your computer that everyone might be interested in, put them in Shared Pictures. That way, they're within everyone's immediate reach.

Figure 7-3 illustrates the concept, where each user account has its own desktop settings and My. . . folders. But all users have access to exactly the same Shared . . . folders. The same idea applies to multiple computers in a local network. All users on all computers have access to the shared documents on every computer in the network.

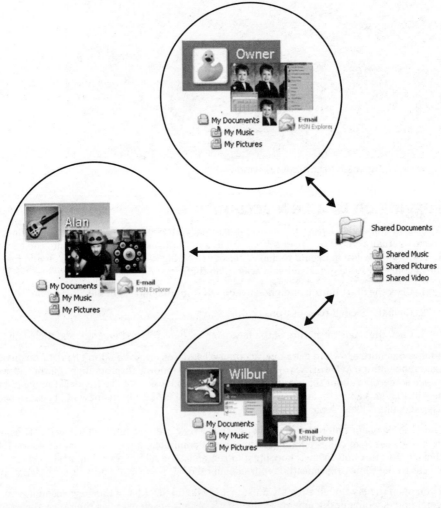

Figure 7-3: All users have access to shared documents.

Getting back to your own user account

If you've been following along, you're currently logged into two accounts, the one you started with and the one you just switched to. To log out of the current account and get back to your own account, follow these steps:

1. Click the **Start** button; click **Log Off**.

2. Click the **Log Off** button.

3. On the Welcome screen that opens, click on your own user account name or picture.

You're taken back to your own user account, where things will be just as you left them. From there you can create more user accounts, change accounts, or just do whatever it is you normally do at the computer.

Managing User Accounts

Like everything else in Windows, when it comes to user accounts nothing is set in stone. You can add new accounts, change existing accounts, and delete accounts at will. Though deleting an account is serious business, so you shouldn't do it until you've read the section on that in this chapter. To manage user accounts, just get back to the User Accounts window. The steps are the same as before:

1. Click the **Start** button and choose **Control Panel**.

2. If Control Panel opens in Category view, click **Users Accounts**.

3. Open the **User Accounts** icon.

The main pane for managing user accounts opens, showing an icon for each user account you've created. Figure 7-4 shows an example where there's now one Administrator account, two Limited accounts (one oddly named ASP.Net Machine. . . . which you might or might not see in your own window), and a Guest account that is currently off.

The options in the main User Accounts window are largely self-explanatory. Options under Pick a Task let you change any existing account, create a new account, or change some settings that I'll describe in a moment. Items under "or pick an account to change" represent existing user accounts.

If you click on an account name or picture, you'll come to options for changing that specific account. For example, to get to the page shown in Figure 7-5, I clicked on the Ashley account picture near the bottom of Figure 7-4. Note the options to change or delete the account, also the standard Back and Home navigation buttons and links under Related Tasks. There are plenty of ways to get around, so you don't ever have to worry about getting stuck or lost when working with user accounts.

Other options that an administrator can change for any user account include:

✦ **Change the name:** Change the user's name.

✦ **Create a password:** Password-protect the user account.

✦ **Change the account type:** Change the account from administrator to limited, or vice versa.

✦ **Delete the account:** Delete the user account.

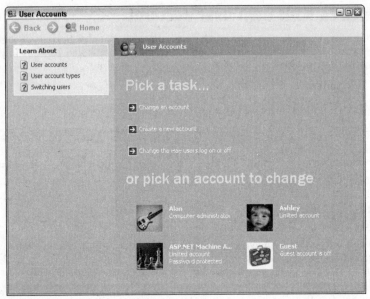

Figure 7-4: Page for managing user accounts

Figure 7-5: Options for changing an existing user account

Caution Deleting a user account is serious business that will permanently delete many folders and files. Be sure to read the section on deleting user accounts, later in this chapter, before you choose this option.

The "Change the name" option is self-explanatory. You just click the option and give the user account a different name. The only tricky thing is that the folder for the user account will retain the original name. That's a topic I'll address under "Renaming a user account" later in this chapter.

Creating and managing passwords

If you create a user account and don't apply a password to it, that means anyone who sits down at the computer can log in to the account and do as they please. If you want to keep other people out of your user account, you'll need to create a password, and keep it to yourself. The number one rule is, *don't forget the password.*

Newbies forget passwords all the time. When prompted to enter a password for a new account, they just think one up on the fly, type it in, and go about their business. A few hours or days later, when they want to get back to the account, they have no clue what the password is. And there's nobody to ask because nobody else knows the password either. So, here's a warning:

Caution   Never take passwords lightly. Forgetting your own password could leave you locked out of your own account. Your best bet is to write down the password on a piece of paper and store it in a secure place so that if you ever forget the password, you can find it.

Password-protect an account

Passwords for XP user accounts can be up to 14 characters in length, with no blank spaces. Passwords are always case-sensitive, so your best bet is to use all lowercase letters. You won't be able to see your password when you type it. So, using a mixture of uppercase and lowercase letters could make things difficult. To password-protect your user account:

1. If you're at the Windows desktop, click **Start**, choose **Control Panel**, and work your way to the **User Accounts** window.

2. Choose **Change an account** when you get to the appropriate screen, then click on your own user account.

3. Click on **Create a password**.

4. Type in the password in the two places indicated. Each character you type will appear as a dot (this to prevent shoulder surfing, where someone learns your password just by watching what you type on the screen).

5. Type a hint for yourself in case you forget the password. The hint will be visible to all users, so don't make it too obvious. Figure 7-6 shows an example of a competed password page.

> Create a password for your account
>
> Type a new password:
> `••••••••`
>
> Type the new password again to confirm:
> `••••••••`
>
> If your password contains capital letters, be sure to type them the same way every time you log on.
>
> Type a word or phrase to use as a password hint:
> `My usual casual password without numbers`
>
> The password hint will be visible to everyone who uses this computer.
>
> [Create Password] [Cancel]

Figure 7-6: Password-protecting your account

6. Click the **Create Password** button.

7. If you're password-protecting an administrator account, the next page will ask if you want to make your account private. Choosing **Yes, Make Private** will make your folders and files invisible to all other user accounts. Choosing No will allow people to see the contents of your folders from their user accounts.

The account will be password-protected and you'll be returned to the User Accounts window. If you want to try it out, close the User Accounts window and Control Panel. Then click Start and choose Log Off. You're taken back to the Welcome screen.

To log back into your account, click your account picture or name. You won't be taken to the desktop. Instead, you'll be prompted to enter you password, as shown in Figure 7-7. You need to type in the correct password and press Enter or click the green Go button before you'll be taken to your user account and desktop.

Figure 7-7: Password prompt for logging in to an XP user account

Changing and removing passwords

Any user can manage (create, change, or delete) his or her own password. Administrators can manage their own passwords as well as passwords on Limited accounts. However, to change or delete a password, you need to know the current password. To change or remove a password, click on any password-protected account, and then do the following:

✦ To change a password, click on **Change my password** (or **Change the password**).

✦ To remove a password, click on **Remove my password** (or **Remove the password**).

Follow the instructions on the screen. In both cases, you'll need to type in the existing password to show that you know the password you're about to change or delete. This is to prevent users from changing each other's passwords at will.

Changing the account picture

Changing the picture associated with a user account is easy. Just get to the User Accounts screen and choose an account to change. Then, choose Change my picture (or Change the picture for someone else's account). You're taken to a page offering several generic pictures to choose from, as shown in Figure 7-8. If you want to use one of those generic pictures, just click on the picture you want to use, and then click the Change Picture button.

Beneath the generic pictures you'll see an option to browse for more pictures. Clicking that option opens an Open dialog box, initially showing bitmap (.bmp), GIF, JPEG, and Portable Network Graphics (.png) files in your MY Pictures folder. You can choose any picture you like by clicking its icon, and then clicking the Open button. Or, navigate to any other folder that contains pictures.

If you have a camera or scanner connected to the computer, you'll also see an option to get a picture from the camera or scanner. Choosing that option, though, isn't too likely to produce very satisfying results because the account picture will be perfectly square at a tiny height and width of 48 pixels.

Figure 7-8: Page for changing user account picture

To use a custom picture, your best bet would be to open an existing picture in a graphics program that you already know how to use. Then, crop out a perfect square and size it to 48x48 pixels. Save that small cropped picture as its own file, perhaps as a JPEG. Then, use that small cropped picture as the user account picture.

Note   Chapter 37 discusses types of pictures and photo editing in some detail.

Deleting a user account

As you'll see under "User Accounts behind the Scenes" in this chapter, a user account is much more than a name and picture. It's a complete collection of files and folders. When you delete a user account, you have the option of deleting all the folders and files that go with that account, which means that any documents you stored in that account's My . . . folders will be lost forever. This is not good if you were planning on using any of those documents in the future, because once you delete those files, you won't be able to use them again in the future.

It may be very tempting to delete any user accounts you didn't create yourself. For example, if your computer came with an Administrator or Owner account already defined, you might be tempted to delete that account and create one with your own name. Likewise, the mysterious ASP.NET account you might see, or the built-in Guest account, might seem like obvious candidates for deletion. But those accounts serve a purpose and are best left alone.

Rather than delete an existing Owner or Administrator account, you can create a second user account for yourself   perhaps a Limited account that you use for day-to-date computing when you don't need to do administrative tasks. As mentioned in the "Limited Accounts Are More Secure" sidebar, the restricted permissions of a Limited account provide a degree of security against malicious programs that need administrative permissions to do their dirty work.

You can create a Limited account and move all your documents from the My . . . folders in the Administrative account to the folders in your new Limited account. You'll see how to move and copy files from one account to another under "User Accounts behind the Scenes" later in this chapter.

About the ASP.NET User Account

If you've downloaded and installed .NET Framework Version 1.1 or later, you'll see a Limited user account named ASP.NET in the main User Accounts window. The account usually won't show up on the Welcome screen, because it's not an account for people to use. It's a special account used to run certain types of Web applications that are based on Microsoft's ASP (Active Server Pages) .NET technology.

If you don't see a user account named ASP.NET, that's OK too. The account is really only relevant to people who develop and use certain types of Web applications. So, the bottom line is this. If you see an ASP.NET user account on your computer, the best thing to do is leave it alone. If you see no such account, don't worry about it. It's not the sort of thing that's required, or even relevant to, all Windows XP users.

But, if you actually do create a new user account and then decide to get rid of it, you certainly do have that option. First of all, you can't delete the account that you're currently logged into. So if you're currently logged into the account you want to delete, the first step is to log out (Click the Start button and choose Log Off > Log Off). Then, click on an Administrator account so that you have permission to delete user accounts.

Once you're in the Administer account, get to the User Accounts window through Control Panel as you normally would. Click to Change an account, and then click on the account you want to delete. At the bottom of the list of options, you'll see the option to Delete the account. Clicking that option presents a prompt asking if you want to delete the files for that account. This is where you're making a big commitment from which there's no turning back. If you choose the Delete Files option on that page, all the documents, Internet Favorites, e-mail messages, settings — everything about that user account — will be permanently wiped from the hard disk.

If you choose Keep Files when prompted, then all of the documents for that user account will be placed in a folder on your desktop. The folder's name will be the same as the name of the account you deleted. When you open the folder it will contain all of the My . . . folders and files from that user account. From there, you can then move the files to the Shared . . . folders, or any other user account's My. . . folders as you see fit.

Renaming a user account

If you're planning on deleting an account to replace it with a new account with a different user name, you could just rename the existing account instead. In the User Accounts window, click on the account you want to rename and choose Change the name.

As an alternative to deleting an account and creating a new account with a different name, you can always rename the account instead. To do so, get to the User Account window and choose the account you want to change. Then, choose Change the Name and enter the new name.

The user name will change in the User Accounts window and also on the Welcome screen where you log in. However, the folders for that account will retain their original names. That's not a problem, because everything will still work fine. It's just a little confusing when you go look at the actual folders for the account and still see the original account name.

You don't want to change the folder names to match the account name, because there may be other files on the system that still refer to the original name. And there's really no way to ferret out all those files and change the account name within them. (That's why Windows itself doesn't change the folder name.)

The only alternative would be to create a brand-new account with the user name you desire. Then, move all the documents from the original account to the new account. Then, delete the original account. Whether or not it's worth all the trouble is something you have to decide for yourself.

Activating/deactivating the Guest account

The Guest user account is an optional account for guests, people who want to borrow the computer for a short time. Allowing such people to use the Guest account prevents them doing anything that would significantly change the computer or anyone else's documents.

The Guest account is built into Windows XP, so you don't need to create it. Instead, you can just activate it, thereby making it an option on the Welcome screen, or deactivate it so that it's not accessible at all. To activate or deactivate the Guest account:

1. Click the **Start** button and choose **Control Panel**.

2. Open the **User Accounts** icon. (From Category view, click the second User Accounts icon that appears after you click on User Accounts the first time).

3. Click the picture that represents the Guest account.

4. To activate the Guest account, click the **Turn On the Guest Account** button. Or, if the Guest account is already active, click the **Turn off the guest account** option that appears on the screen.

You won't see any major changes on your screen. But next time you see the Welcome screen, an icon for the Guest account will be available.

I've mentioned the folders and files that make up a user account name several times in this chapter. So, it's time we take a look behind the scenes now and see what's really going on when you create user accounts.

User Accounts behind the Scenes

A brand-new installation of Windows XP generally starts off with three folders in the root (highest-level) folder of you hard disk, drive C:. The typical folder names, and the purpose of each, are summarized here:

✦ **Documents and Settings:** Contains a subfolder for each user account on the system. Within each user account folder are subfolders for one user's My Document, My Pictures, My Music, and other folders. Various customization settings that are unique to each user are also contained in subfolders for each user account.

✦ **Program Files:** Most programs you installed (other than Windows) are stored in subfolders in the Program Files folder. Basically, there's nothing in those folders for human beings — only programs use those files.

✦ **Windows:** Windows XP itself stored all of its system files in a folder named Windows. As with program files, there may be thousands of files in the subfolders under Windows, but few are documents that you'd ever want to work with directly. Instead, they're all files that Windows uses to do its many jobs.

You're not likely to stumble onto any of those folders by accident. In fact, they're all some-what hidden because there's really not much in those folders for normal people (other than programmers, whom I guess don't qualify as "normal") to be messing with. But since the Folders list in Windows Explorer must give you access to all your drives and folders, you can always take a look at what's really going on via the Folders list.

You can open the Folders list from any folder, just by clicking on the Folder button in the Windows Explorer toolbar. If you're starting from the desktop, you can just follow these sim-ple steps:

1. Click the **Start** button and choose **My Computer** to open your My Computer folder opens in Windows Explorer.

2. Click the **Folders** toolbar button, or choose **View** ➪ **Explorer Bar** ➪ **Folders** from Explorer's menu bar.

Either way, the Folders list opens at the left side of the Explorer window, as in the example shown in Figure 7-9.

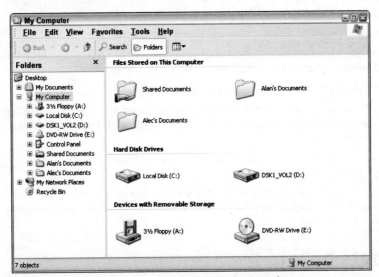

Figure 7-9: Folders list at the left side of Windows Explorer

The Folders list consists of numerous icons representing disk drives and folders that make up your computer system. Any item that has a plus sign to the left of the subfolders beneath it are currently hidden from view. Clicking any + sign expands the list so you can see icons for subfolders within, and the + sign changes to a - sign. Clicking a - sign collapses the list again to put subfolder icons back into hiding.

As with any pane, you can narrow or widen the Folders list by dragging its inner border to the left or right. When you click on a drive or folder icon in the Folders list, the contents of the drive or folder appear in the main pane to the right. To close the Folders list at any time, click the Close (X) button in its title, or click the Folders button in the toolbar again, or choose View ➪ Explorer Bar ➪ Folders from the menu again.

The Documents and Settings folder

The Documents and Settings folder where user account folders are stored is on your hard drive. Typically that drive is named Local Disk (C:), though the "Local Disk" part could be any name. If you click the + sign next to the icon for drive C: you'll see the Documents and Settings folders, as well as the folders used for storing program files and Windows files.

Clicking the + sign next to Documents and Settings will expand that folder to show the subfolder for each user account on the system. (Remember though that a new user account's folders aren't created until you actually log in to the user account. So don't expect a brand-new user account's name to appear under the Document and Settings folder.)

Note　In all of these examples I'm assuming that you're logged in to an account with administrative privileges. Limited user accounts don't have as much power as Administrator accounts. When exploring from a Limited account, some folders will be hidden from view. Also, private Administrator folders are hidden from all users except the administrator who owns those folders.

Figure 7-10 shows an example from a computer with four user accounts, named Administrator, Alan, Alec, and Ashley. The subfolder named All Users is the place where all the Shared . . . folders reside, and everyone has that folder. The Default User folder is for the Guest account, and it exists only if you enable the Guest account.

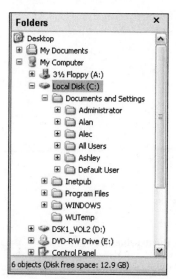

Figure 7-10: Subfolders under Documents and Settings on drive C

Not that it's relevant to the topic at hand, but in case you're wondering, the Inetpub folder is sort of a virtual Web server used with programs like Microsoft FrontPage to test locally authored Web pages. WUTemp is a folder for storing temporary files from Windows Update.

User Account subfolders

Each user's My . . . folders are actually subfolders within the main user account folder. The exact subfolders in any user account depend on many factors, including which programs that user has already run, what subfolders within My . . . folders that user has created, and so forth. But since each user has their own My . . . folder, their own custom desktop and Start menu and so forth, there are some folders that appear automatically within every user account you create.

As an example, Figure 7-11 shows the same thing as Figure 7-10, but with the Alec folder expanded. As a rule, you would never need to work directly in any of those folders, because their contents are handled automatically by other programs. But here's a quick overview of what each subfolder contains:

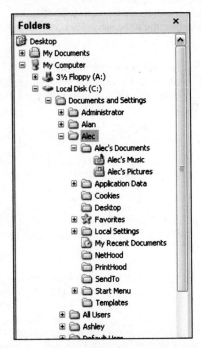

Figure 7-11: Subfolders contained within one user account named Alec

✦ **Alec's Documents:** The My Documents folder for the user named Alec

✦ **Alec's Music:** The My Music folder for the user named Alec

✦ **Alec's Pictures:** The My Pictures folder for the user named Alec

✦ **Application Data:** General information about Alec used by application programs like Internet Explorer and Outlook Express

✦ **Cookies:** Internet cookies stored by Web sites that user Alec has visited

✦ **Desktop:** Unique desktop icons that Alec has created

✦ **Favorites:** Favorite Web sites that Alec has created while Web browsing with Internet Explorer

✦ **Local Settings:** Miscellaneous settings that Alec's programs have created automatically, such as Alec's history of recently visited Web sites, files waiting to be written to CD, and security credentials

✦ **My Recent Documents:** Alec's list of recently opened documents, the same items that are listed when clicking Start and choosing My Recent Documents while logged into Alec's user account

✦ **NetHood:** Unique icons for Alec's Network Neighborhood folder (assuming that the computer is on a local network and Alec has created custom shortcuts to favorite network resources)

✦ **PrintHood:** Printers in the local network to which the user Alec has access

✦ **SendTo:** Options that appear on the submenu when the user Alec has right-clicked an icon and chosen Send To

✦ **Start Menu:** Custom or other specialized icons that are unique to user Alec's Start menu

✦ **Templates:** Any custom templates that user Alec has created, including templates from the Microsoft Office

The document folder names Alec's Documents, Alec's Music, and Alec's Pictures aren't really named as shown. They're actually just named Documents, Music, and Pictures. But since every user account has those folders, Windows precedes each folder's name with the possessive from of the user name (e.g., Alec's folders). When logged into the account named Alec, those names automatically change to My Documents, My Music, and My Pictures.

Keep in mind that just because you *can* get to all those user account files from the Folders list, that doesn't mean you *must* manage files through those files. All of the folders excluding Documents, Music, and Pictures, really exist for other programs to store information that's unique to that user.

Tip If you're logged into a user account with Administrator privileges, you can get to any user's My Documents folders using icons that appear right at the top of the My Computer folder, without even opening the Folders list.

Don't be alarmed if you open a subfolder under a user account and some icons seem to be missing There are some items — such as icons on the Start menu and items desktop icons — that are the same for all users. Those items won't appear under any one user's folder. Instead, the items that are the same for all users are stored in subfolders under the All Users account name. And there are items that aren't stored in folders at all, but rather in specific settings files.

The one time when it is handy to get to all those user account folders is when you need to move or copy information from one user account to another, as we'll discuss in the section after next. But first we need to talk about private folders, which may not be accessible from the Folders list, even by an Administrator.

Keeping your documents private

As mentioned earlier in this chapter, Limited account users can see only their own documents and shared documents. A Limited account user can certainly get to the Folders list and expand the Documents and Settings folder to see some folders beneath it. However, when a Limited account user tries to open another user's document folder, he gets only the classic Access is Denied message rather than access to the folder.

Access is different from Administrator accounts, because they have free reign over the entire system. Simply put, an Administrator account has no restrictions at all. If two or more people on the computer have Administrator accounts, they can usually get to each other's document folders as well, via the Folders list, and see what each other is up to.

That's where the whole concept of making one's files private comes into play. When you first create a new Administrator account, you're given the choice of making its files private. But whatever option you choose there isn't set in stone. The fact is, an Administrator can make his or her own files or folders either private or public at any time. When an Administrator privatizes his or her folders, not even other Administrators can see what's in those private folders.

As an Administrator, you can make your folders private at any time by first logging into your own account. You must be in your own Administrator account for this to work. Once you're logged into your account, follow these steps:

1. Click the **Start** button and choose **My Computer**.

2. Click the **Folders** button in the toolbar.

3. Expand the hard drive (**Local Disk C:**) and **Documents and Settings** folders.

4. Right-click the folder icon whose name matches the name of your own user account and choose Sharing and Security. Figure 7-12 shows an example where I've right-clicked the folder named Alan.

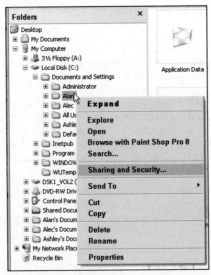

Figure 7-12: About to make a user account named Alan private

5. On the Sharing tab that opens automatically, do either of the following:

- Choose (check) the **Make this folder private option** to make the folder and all of its files private.

- Or, if the folder was already private, and you want to make it public, clear that same checkbox.

6. Click **OK** in the dialog box.

Wait as Windows privatizes all the subfolders and files. If the account you just privatized has no password protection, you'll be asked if you want to password-protect the account now. You should choose Yes to prevent other users from gaining access to your folders by simply logging in to your account. Choosing Yes will take you through the steps necessary to password-protect your account.

When all is said and done, you won't notice any visible change to your account. But all other users, both Limited users and other Administrator account users, who attempt to open any of your folders and snoop through your documents will be greeted with the "Access is Denied" message. Nobody, not even other administrators, will be able to see, change, or delete the documents you have stored in your own My . . . folders.

Hidden Administrator accounts

On some computers, you might see a folder named Administrator under Documents and Settings. Yet, when you're at the Welcome screen, you see no icon for logging into the Administrator account. There are two things that could account for that. Once would be if you renamed the Administrator account, the icon for the account would show the new name but the Administrator account files would still show the original folder name Administrator.

If you never renamed a user account, then the second reason would apply, that reason being that the all-powerful Administrator account is intentionally hidden. This is actually quite common in corporate settings. Though if you bought your computer with Windows XP preinstalled, your computer manufacturer may have set things up that way at the factory. Your best bet, in that case, would probably be to leave things as they are, and create a new, separate Limited account for yourself.

Once you've created a new Limited account for yourself and logged into that account at least once, you can move any documents that you previously stored in the Administrator account's My . . . folders to that new account. I'll present an example of how that's done in the next section. However, be aware that even after you create a new user account for yourself, you still may not see the hidden Administrator account on the Welcome screen when you log in.

There are a couple of ways to log in to a hidden Administrator account. One is to simple press Alt+Tab right at the Welcome screen to bring up the hidden login for the hidden Administrator account. If the account requires a password, yet you've never created a password for yourself, use the password *password* (one word, all lowercase letters) to get into the account.

Yet another way to deal with a hidden user account named Administrator is to use the more traditional Windows login window rather than the Welcome screen to log in. More on that topic under "Controlling how users log on" later in this chapter.

Yet a third option would be to change your new Limited account to an Administrator account, and then log into that account. From there, you should be able to get to the My . . . folders for the Administrator account so that you can move its documents to your new account. When you've finished moving the documents, change your new account back to the Limited account.

Moving files between user accounts

As mentioned briefly earlier in this chapter, corporate network administrators often create two user accounts for themselves. For their day-to-day work with documents, Web browsing, and e-mail, they use their own Limited account. Doing so provides an all-around safer environment that can thwart any malicious code that may have snuck onto the system from doing any damage. When the administrator needs to install a program or manage other user accounts, she logs into her Administrator account, does what needs to be done, logs out, and returns to her Limited account for the day-to-day stuff.

The same idea can work just as well on a home or small office computer. But, if you've been using only an Administrator account for a while, you probably already have documents in its My Documents, My Music, My Pictures, and perhaps other folders. So the question is, if you create a Limited account for yourself, how do you get the documents from your Administrator account to the new Limited account?

The answers to that is, the same you way you move any other files from any other folder to another folder. If you're new to all of that, then you'll probably want to learn the general techniques for creating folders, selecting icons, and moving files soon, as discussed in Chapter 14. But the general idea is fairly simple, so I'll just go ahead and explain it now.

I'll need to use a slightly different example here than the ones you've been seeing. In this example I'll be Wilbur. The computer is a notebook that came with an Administrator account named Owner. I've been using the Owner account for a while and have documents in its My Documents, My Music, and My Pictures folders. I've just created a new Limited account, named Wilbur, for myself, and logged into that account to make sure all its folders are created.

Next, I want to move all the documents from the Owner account's My . . . folders to the My folders for the new Wilbur account. First, I need to log out of the Wilbur account and back into the Owner account to get Administrator privileges. Next, I open My Computer and the folders list. I expand the C: drive, Documents and Settings, Owner, Wilbur, and Documents folders so that I can see the icons both accounts' My . . . folders. Then, I click on the My Pictures folder for the Owner account to see icons all the pictures in that folder in the main pane.

Next, I select all the icons in the My Pictures folder (press Ctrl+A or choose Edit ⇨ Select All from the menu bar). Then, to move them all into the My Pictures folder, I just drag any selected icon to the Wilbur's Pictures folder in the Folders list, and drop them there (see Figure 7-13).

Then, I can do the same for the My Music folder — select all its icons and then drag any selected icon to the Wilbur's Music folder. Finally, I go to My Documents for the Owner account and select all icons except My Pictures and My Music (because I don't want to move the actual folders). Then, I drag all the selected icons from My Documents to Wilbur's documents.

Dragging to Wilbur's folders in the Folders list is just one way to do it. You could accomplish the same goal by opening My Computer from the Administrator account. At the top of the My Computer window you'll see a Documents folder for each user. If you hold down the Shift key and double-click on the folder for the Limited account, that folder will open in a separate Explorer window. (Right-click the clock and choose Cascade Windows if you can't see both folders on the screen.) Back in the My Computer window, click on My Documents under Other Places.

Now you have two folders open — one for the Administrator account My Documents folder and one for the Limited account's My Documents folder. From there you can select and drag files from one account to the other. But it's best not to drag the entire My Music or My Pictures icon from one folder to the other, because those are built-in folders that shouldn't be moved from their original locations. Better to open each folder, and drag the *contents* of one My . . . folder to the other account's folder.

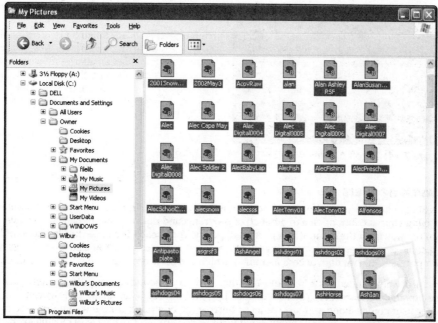

Figure 7-13: Move pictures from Owner's Pictures to Wilbur's Pictures.

But the real point is that, as an Administrator, you can open your own folders as well as any Limited user's folders. And if you can open a folder, you can freely move or copy any files to/from that folder to any other folder, using any of the techniques described in Chapter 14.

Logging In, Logging Out

As mentioned near the start of this chapter, after you've defined two or more user accounts on your system, you'll see the Welcome screen each time you start your computer. You just have to click your own user-account picture. If you password-protected the account, you'll have to enter your own password as well. Then, you'll be taken to the desktop.

When a user has finished using the computer for the time being, she should close all open programs, save any work in progress, then log out of her account. Doing so ensures that other users won't mess with her account and also frees up computer resources so other users get the best performance from the computer when they log in. To log out of your user account, follow these simple steps:

1. Remember to close all open windows so you're back to a clean desktop.

2. Click the **Start** button, and choose **Log Off**.

3. In the next box that appears (see Figure 7-14), click the **Log Off** button.

It will take Windows a few seconds to get everything closed and squared away. Then, your desktop will disappear, and you'll be taken to the Welcome screen. At that point, anybody else who has an account on this computer can click his or her user account picture and log in.

Figure 7-14: Logoff options

Switching users

It's always best to log off from your account if you won't be using the computer for a while. Leaving your account open and a bunch of programs and documents on the screen while you're away from the computer is just a bad policy. You greatly increase the likelihood of losing some work when you leave things lying around on the desktop. You also leave things in the computers RAM (random access memory), which can slow down the computer considerably.

You probably noticed back in Figure 7-14 that there is a second option titled Switch User in the box that appears after you first choose Log Off from the Start menu. If, however, some other user comes along and just wants to borrow the computer for a few minutes—to check e-mail or whatever—you probably won't want to go through the hassle of closing everything, logging out, and logging back in when the other user is done. In that case, you can click Switch User in the Log Off Windows box. Clicking the Switch User button will take you back to the Welcome screen, where the other user can sign in and do whatever needs to be done.

When that person is done using the computer, he or she should log off, using the Log Off button (not Switch User) in the Log Off Windows box. When he or she does, the Welcome screen will appear, and you can click your own account picture to get back to where you were before you switched user accounts.

You really don't want to use Switch User for any situation other than the preceding one, where you'll be leaving your account only for a few minutes, then coming right back. There are several reasons for this:

✦ Each open user account needs to store data in RAM. The more stuff you cram into RAM, the slower your computer runs.

✦ Leaving user accounts open by using Switch User rather than Log Off complicates things immensely for the computer. The more complicated things are at any given moment, the more likely the computer is to hang (freeze up) or to generate some *fatal error* (a problem that requires restarting the computer without even getting a chance to save any unsaved work you left behind).

So, the bottom line is: If you want to keep things running fast, and running safely, don't use the Switch User button. Always log off from your account (or shut down the computer) whenever you plan to be away from your account for more than a few minutes.

Controlling how users log on

It's somewhat unfortunate that Microsoft put the Switch User button where they did. When most people see it, they'll assume that it's the best button to push to get to some other user account. It's not. The Switch User button should be used only for those brief, temporary user account switches described previously.

As the administrator of the computer, you might seriously consider disabling the Switch User button if other computer users insist on leaving their user accounts open. The last thing you need, as an administrator, is more headaches, and Switch User is one of the leading causes of administrator headaches.

Also worth mentioning is that there are two ways to control how users log on. One is to use the Welcome screen you've seen earlier in this chapter. The other is to use the more traditional Windows Logon window. The latter method is generally used in corporate domain networks. As an Administrator, you can control both the logon method and the Switch User option by following these steps:

1. Click the **Start** button and choose **Control Panel**.

2. Get to the main **User Accounts** window. (If you're using Category view, click on User Accounts, then click on the User Accounts icon that appears on the second page).

3. Under Pick a Task on the main User Accounts page (see Figure 7-15), click **Change the way users log on or off**. Then, make your choices as follows:

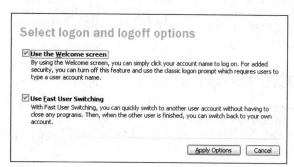

Figure 7-15: Logon and logoff options in User Accounts

- To use the Welcome screen for logons, select (check) the **Use the Welcome screen** checkbox.

- To use the traditional Login window, clear that **Use the Welcome screen** check box.

- To allow users to see and use the Switch User option, select (check) the **Use Fast User Switching** check box.

- To prevent users from seeing the Switch User option, clear the **Use Fast User Switching** checkbox.

4. Click the **Apply Options** button.

Keeping E-Mail Separate

Exactly how you do your e-mail has nothing to do with Windows XP. E-mail is a service provided by your ISP (Internet service provider), and how you do your e-mail is up to them. So, I can't tell you anything too specific about dealing with e-mail and multiple user accounts. But I can give you some useful tips.

Some ISPs will allow you to set up multiple e-mail accounts, which you then handle by creating multiple identities in your e-mail client (be it Outlook Express, Microsoft Outlook, or some other program). Personally, I find the whole "identities" thing to be a big pain—one for which an ISP might even charge you extra money.

My solution to the multiple e-mail accounts problem is that I'm the only person on my network who uses the e-mail provided by my ISP, and the only person who uses Outlook as an e-mail client Everyone else has a free Hotmail account that they use for all their own e-mail. They use their Web browsers for e-mail. This keeps all our e-mail entirely separate—and bypasses the identities problem altogether.

If users are likely to want to use an Instant Messenger service along with e-mail, your best bet might be to go to www.passport.com and set up a new .NET Passport, each with a unique e-mail address, for each user. You can get a Kid's Passport for minors. You'll learn more about the whole .NET Passport thing in Chapter 34 of this book.

If you prefer not to go the .NET Passport route, you can set up a free e-mail account through some other provider, such as Yahoo (www.yahoo.com). Exactly how you go about it us up to you. But if you want to keep things simple, and keep everyone's e-mail separate, you should seriously consider setting up a unique e-mail account and e-mail address for each person who uses the computer.

Preventing Forgotten Passwords

If you plan to password-protect your user account, you would do well to create a password reset disk. You can use that disk to get into the system should you ever forget the password. To create a password reset disk, you'll need a blank, formatted 3.5-inch floppy disk. To create a password reset disk:

1. Click the **Start** button and choose **Control Panel**.

2. If Control Panel opens in Category view, click on the **User Accounts** category.

3. Open the **User Accounts** icon.

4. If you're in an Administrator account, click on the icon of the account for which you want to create a password reset disk. If you're in a Limited account, ignore this step.

5. Under Related Tasks on the left side of the window, click on **Prevent a forgotten password**.

The Forgotten Password Wizard opens. Just read and follow the instructions on each page of the wizard. Be sure to store the disk in a safe place, because anybody can use that disk to sign in to your user account without knowing your password. Even if you change your password, the password reset disk will still work even if you didn't update it after changing your password!

Caution   You cannot create a password reset disk *after* you've forgotten your password. You need to create the password reset disk *before* that problem occurs!

If you forget your password, you can use the password reset disk that you already created to get into your account. Here's how:

1. Get to the Welcome screen as usual and click on your account name or picture.

2. Type anything into the password prompt, and press Enter. You'll see a prompt like the one in Figure 7-16.

Figure 7-16: Results of entering an invalid password

3. Click the **use your password** reset disk link.

4. Follow the instructions in the wizard that opens on your screen.

Wrap Up

If your previous computer experience is limited to single-user versions of Windows, like 95, 98, or ME, the whole concept of user accounts will be foreign to you. But after you understand the basic concepts, you'll find that user accounts are worth their weight in diamonds if you share your PC with other users.

The main thing to remember about user accounts is that everything you need to know, and do, to create and manage user accounts, is in one place: The User Accounts window in Control Panel. The only time you would ever really need to fiddle with folders in the Documents and Settings folder would be if you want to move some documents from one user account's My . . . folders to another user accounts. To summarize:

✦ Windows XP user accounts allow multiple users to share a single PC without stepping on each other's toes.

✦ Each person who has a user account has his or her own desktop, Start menu, My . . . folders, Internet Explorer favorites, and so forth. What one user does in his or her account has no bearing on other people's user accounts.

✦ As a rule, all users have access to all programs that are installed on the computer, so you rarely need to reinstall any programs to make them available to other user accounts.

✦ Administrator accounts have free reign over the entire computer. Limited accounts can use the computer but can't make the sort of changes that would affect the entire computing environment or other people's accounts.

✦ All options for creating and managing user accounts are located in the User Accounts window, accessible from Control Panel. Help topics in the User Accounts window Explorer bar provide useful information as you go.

✦ Each user account is defined by a subfolder within the Documents and Settings folder on the root folder of the primary hard drive (C:).

✦ An administrator can move and copy files from one user account's My . . . folders to another user's My . . . folders using standard techniques for moving and copying files.

✦   ✦   ✦

Customizing Startup Options

When you first start (or log into) Windows XP, you get to the Windows desktop. After the desktop first appears, some other programs might start as well. Many of those other programs are "services" whose icons appear in the Notification area down near the lower-right corner of the screen, although any program can actually start automatically as soon as Windows starts.

This chapter is about controlling exactly what programs and services do, and don't, start automatically along with Windows. It's as simple as that really. The only thing that confuses matters is that there are several different ways, and several different places, from which you can control auto-starting programs. Some examples include the following:

◆ Small Notification Area services such as Volume Control and the networking icon are controlled via dialog boxes in Control Panel.

◆ Some programs that run automatically in the Notification area are controlled by settings within those programs.

◆ There's a folder named Startup in each user's account that can start any program on the All Programs menu automatically.

◆ The (somewhat hidden) Services.msc snap-in controls some things that don't appear on the screen at all.

First steps first — you want to get a good look at what's in your Notification area right now.

First Things First

To keep Notification area icons from hogging most of your taskbar, Windows XP lets you choose which icons you want to be visible all the time and which you prefer to keep hidden. If you skipped the section titled "Using the Notification Area" in Chapter 2, you might want to read that now. But the main issue at the moment is to make all your Notification area icons. Otherwise, you'll have to keep clicking the ◷ button to bring hidden icons into view. To keep Notification icons from hiding, follow these steps:

1. Right-click the Start button and choose **Properties**.

2. In the dialog box that opens, click the **Taskbar** tab.

3. Clear the check mark next to **Hide inactive icons**.

4. Click **OK**.

You should now see all active icons in the Notification area. When you've finished with this chapter and want to reduce the size of the Notification area, repeat those steps, but choose (check) the Hide inactive icons option in Step 3.

Built-in Icons

Some of the icons in the Notification area come straight from Windows and hardware devices in your computer. For example, in Figure 8-1 the network icon on the left (the one showing the speech balloon message) is from my network card.

Figure 8-1: Notification area icons and a Notification message

Whether or not you have a similar icon depends on three things:

✦ If your computer has no network card, you'll never see the icon.

✦ If your computer has a network card that's not in use (because there's no cable connecting it to a network hub or router), then you might see the icon with a red X through it.

✦ If your computer has, and is using, a network card, you won't see that icon if certain options aren't set.

To show or hide the network icon, follow these steps:

1. Click the **Start** button and choose **Control Panel**.

2. If Control Panel opens in Category view, click the **Network and Internet Connections** category.

3. Open the **Network Connections** icon.

The Network Connections folder opens. You may see several icons in that folder. The one labeled Local Area Connection is the one most likely to have the ability to show its icon in the Notification area. To choose whether or not the card shows a Notification icon, right-click its icon and choose Properties. Then choose, or clear, the "Show icon in notification area when connected option," depending on whether or not you want the icon to appear in the Notification area. Figure 8-2 shows an example of such an icon and its Properties dialog box.

The sample notification message back in Figure 8-1 appears only briefly, and only right after a connection is made. So, don't expect to see that message often. In fact, you may never see the message at all because often the connection is made as the computer is starting and by the time you get to the desktop, the message has come and gone. However, if the card is disconnected, then the icon will appear with a red X through it.

Note If the network card is set to Always Hide or Hide When Inactive in the Customize Notifications dialog box, then the icon won't appear when Notification icons are hidden.

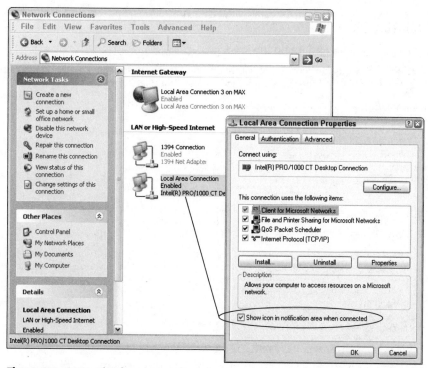

Figure 8-2: Properties for a network card

The Volume Control icon

The Volume Control icon appears as a little speaker in the Notification area. If you click on it once, a slider appears so that you can adjust the volume of your speakers, as shown in Figure 8-3. The Mute checkbox allows you to mute the speakers. When you select that icon, the speaker icon will show a red X.

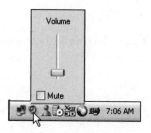

Figure 8-3: Properties for a network card

Whether or not the speaker icon appears at all depends on a setting in your sound card's Properties dialog box. To get to those settings, follow these steps:

1. Click the **Start** button and choose **Control Panel**.

2. If Control Panel opens in Category view, click the **Sounds, Speech, and Audio Devices** category.

3. Open the **Sounds and Audio Devices** icon.

4. To show the speaker icon, choose (check) the **Place volume icon in the taskbar** option as in Figure 8-4. To hide the speaker icon, clear that checkbox.

5. Click **OK**.

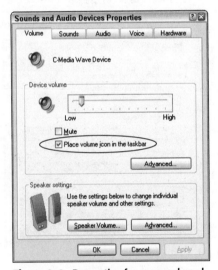

Figure 8-4: Properties for a sound card

Showing/hiding the clock

Whether or not the current time appears at the right side of the Notification area depends on a setting in the Taskbar and Start Menu Properties dialog box. To show or hide the clock:

1. Right-click the **Start** button and choose **Properties**.

2. Click the **Taskbar** tab in the dialog box that opens.

3. To show the time, choose (check) the **Show the clock** option. To hide the time, clear that checkbox.

4. Click **OK**.

If your clock is wrong, you can get it in sync with Internet time. If you have a dial-up Internet account, you need to get online first. Then, double-click the clock to open the Date and Time Properties dialog box. In the dialog box that opens, click the Internet Time tab. Click the Update Now button, and then click OK.

Note I assume that the other options in the Date and Time Properties dialog box are self-explanatory, so I won't get into those in this book.

Program Icons in the Notification Area

Some icons in the Notification area represent running programs. The ones that appear automatically represent programs or services that start automatically when you start your computer. There are hundreds (perhaps thousands) of programs that can display icons in the Notification area, and there's no "one rule fits all" that applies to all those different programs. So, the best I can do here is show you an example of one. The example I'll use is the Windows Messenger icon shown in Figure 8-5.

Figure 8-5: Windows Messenger icon in the Notification area

Note To get Windows Messenger to work at all, you need a .NET Passport. See Chapter 34 for more information.

If you have a Windows Messenger icon in your Notification Area already, you can open that program just by double-clicking that icon. Otherwise, you have to click the Start button and choose All Programs ➪ Windows Messenger. Once the Windows Messenger program window is open, choose Tools > Options from its menu bar. In the Options dialog box that opens, click the Preferences tab. You'll see the options shown in Figure 8-6.

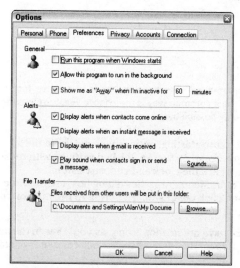

Figure 8-6: Preferences tab in the Windows Messenger Options dialog box

Even though this is just an example, it's fairly representative of how many programs are run automatically. The two options that are relevant to auto-starting and the Notification area are listed below:

◆ **Run this program when Windows starts:** If selected, Windows Messenger starts automatically when you start your computer. If cleared, Windows Messenger doesn't start automatically.

◆ **Allow this program to run in the background:** If selected, this option allows the Notification area icon to appear even when the main Windows Messenger program window is closed. If you clear this option, there won't be a Notification area icon when the main program window is closed.

Let me emphasize that the Windows Messenger example is *just* an example. Not all programs have the same, or even similar, options. However, if a program has a built-in capability to auto-start, and if the program has the ability to run in the background, then the options for those capabilities are likely to be in that program's Options (or Preferences) dialog box.

For specific information on any given program, your best bet would be to search that program's Help for "start" or "Options" or "Preferences." You can get to just about any program's Help by choosing Help from that program's menu bar, or by pressing Help (F1) when the program is open and in the active window on your desktop.

Often, you can get to options for programs that are already in the Notification area just by right-clicking the icon and choosing Properties, as in the example shown in Figure 8-7. In other cases, you may need to double-click the notification area icon to open the program first, then look for an Options or Preferences option in that program's menu bar.

Figure 8-7: Right-clicking a Notification area icon

Tip   The most common way to get to a program's Options dialog box is to choose Tools ⇨ Options from its menu bar. The second most common way is the choose File ⇨ Preferences from its menu bar. But those aren't the only possibilities.

Keep in mind that no matter how you handle auto-starting, options you choose in the Customize Notifications dialog box still apply. So, when you've finished working with those notification icons, you may still want to right-click the clock and choose Customize Notifications. Or, get back the Taskbar and Start Menu Properties dialog box, choose Hide inactive icons from the Taskbar tab, and then click the Customize button to the right of that checkbox to further refine your notifications.

Finally, not all programs that auto-start even have notification icons. As you'll see in the next section, you can configure just about any program that's installed on your computer to start automatically when Windows starts.

Starting Programs Automatically

If you always use a certain program when you start your computer, you can configure Windows to start the program automatically as soon as you get to the desktop. It can be any program—it doesn't have to be one that has an icon in the Notification area. For example, you could auto-start your Web browser, e-mail client, a word processing program—any program that you'd otherwise start from the Start menu or All Programs menu.

A good first step is to create a desktop shortcut for starting the program. That's easy to do, and is almost the same as starting the program. Here are the steps:

1. Click the **Start** button and choose **All Programs**.

2. If necessary, choose the appropriate program groups to get the icon you normally click to start the program. But don't click that icon. Instead . . .

3. Right-click the program's icon and choose **Send To ➪ Desktop (create shortcut)**.

 Tip   To automatically open a folder at startup, get to that folder's parent folder so you can see the folder's icon. Then, right-click that icon and choose Send To ➪ Desktop ➪ Create Shortcut. The same process works with documents.

A shortcut icon for the program appears on the desktop. The icon will be the usual icon for the program, though it will sport a little curved shortcut arrow. For example, Figure 8-8 shows the shortcut icons for Calculator (available from the Accessories menu) and Microsoft Excel (one of the programs that come with Microsoft Office).

Figure 8-8: Examples of desktop shortcut icons

If you've configured Windows with multiple user accounts, the next step is to decide for which users the program should auto-start. You can make the program start automatically for all users. Or, you can make it auto-start for just yourself, or only some users. The procedure is basically the same. It's more a matter of where you place the shortcut icon. We'll start with the example of making a program auto-start for all users.

Auto-starting a program for all users

To make a program open automatically as soon as any user logs into his or her user account, you need to put a copy of the program's shortcut icon into the C:\Documents and Settings\All Users\Start Menu\Programs\Startup folder. The quick-and-easy way to get to that folder is:

1. Right-click the Start button and choose Open All Users (or Explore All Users), the only difference being that if you choose the Explore option, the Folders list opens automatically when the folder opens.

2. In the Start Menu folder that opens, open the Programs icon.

3. In the Programs folder that opens, open the Startup folder.

When the Startup folder opens, you may find that there are already some shortcut icons in that folder. Those icons represent programs that are already configured to start automatically. If you want to prevent a program from auto-starting for all users, you just have to delete its shortcut icon from the Startup folder.

To make some new program start automatically, follow these steps:

1. Get back to the desktop, right-click the shortcut icon you created for the program, and choose **Copy**. Optionally, you can select multiple icons, right-click any one of them, and then choose **Copy** to copy them all.

2. Right-click any empty space within the Startup folder and choose **Paste**. The icon(s) should appear in the Startup folder. Figure 8-9 shows an example where I already had one icon in the Startup folder and have just pasted in copies of the shortcut icons for Excel and Calculator.

Figure 8-9: Shortcut icons in the All User's Startup folder

3. Close the Startup folder.

The programs won't start immediately. You'll just be taken back to the Windows desktop. To test the changes you've made, you'll need to log out (click the Start button and choose Log Off), and then log back in to any user account. Or, if you don't have multiple user accounts, you'll need to restart the computer (Click Start and choose Turn Off Computer ➪ Restart.)

Auto-starting a program for one user

If you just want to auto-start a program for your own user account, or a particular user account, don't put the desktop icons in the All Users Startup folder. Instead, put the shortcut icons in C:\Documents and Settings*UserName*\Start Menu\Programs\Startup, where *UserName* is the name of the user account.

Whenever you see a long path like the one above, there are a couple of ways to get to the folder or file at the end of the path. One is to Open My Computer and then click the icon for the drive letter at the start of the path (C: in this example). From there, open each folder name in succession. That is, open the Documents and Setting folder, then the *UserName* folder, then the Start Menu Folder, and so forth, until you've opened the Startup folder. The other method is to use the Folders list to navigate down to the last folder name.

For example, let's say I want to start Excel and Calculator in my own User Account. The name of the User Account is Alan. So in the Folders list I'd just need to navigate down to that folder as in Figure 8-10. If you break out your electron microscope and look closely at the figure, you can see how I expanded icons in the order necessary. First I expanded My Computer, then Local Disk C:. Then I expanded the folders Documents and Settings, Alan, Start Menu, Programs, and then finally clicked on the Startup folder. The title bar verifies that the main pane is showing the contents of a folder named Startup. The path in the Address bar verifies that I'm in C:\Documents and Settings\Alan\Start Menu\Programs\Startup.

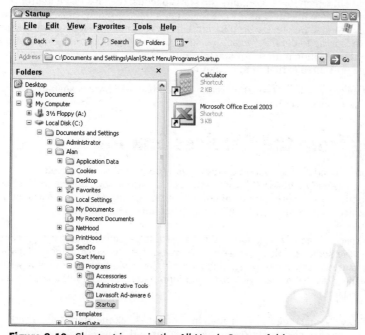

Figure 8-10: Shortcut icons in the All User's Startup folder.

Tip To make the full path to the current folder visible in the Address bar, as in Figures 8-9 and 8-10, first make sure that the Address bar is visible. If it isn't, choose View ➪ Toolbars ➪ Address Bar from Explorer's menu bar. Then, choose Tools ➪ Folder Options and click the View tab. Choose "Display the full path in the address bar" and click OK. If you can only see the title of the Address bar, drag its handle down a row. See "Windows Explorer Address bar" in Chapter 3 for more information.

Once you're in the appropriate user's Startup folder, just copy the icon(s) for the programs you want to auto-start into that folder (the main pane). For example, in Figure 8-10 I've already copied the shortcut icons for Excel and Calculator into the Startup folder for my user account.

Preventing auto-start

If you have some programs that auto-start, and you don't want them to auto-start anymore, first you have to figure out which Startup folder contains the shortcut icons. If the programs start in all user accounts, then the shortcut icons are in `C:\Documents and Settings\ All Users\Start Menu\Programs\Startup`. If the programs start in only one user account, then the icons are in the `C:\Documents and Settings\`*UserName*`\Start Menu\Programs\ Startup`.

Once you've figured out which folder contains the startup icons, then it's just a matter of opening that folder and deleting the appropriate shortcut icon(s). To delete a shortcut icon, just right-click it and choose Delete. Do keep in mind, however, that not all auto-starting programs have icons in Startup folders. For example, some of the programs in the Notification area will have their own built-in options for starting automatically, as in the Windows Messenger example presented earlier in this chapter.

Last, but not least, in the whole auto-starting realm is the obscure Services snap-in, which you'll learn about in the next section.

Auto-Starting from the Services Snap-In

Windows XP includes an advanced system configuration tool called the Microsoft Management Console (MMC). The MMC provides access to various *snap-ins*, where each snap-in provides options for different types of configuration options. Once of those snap-ins is named Services.msc. Before we get into that snap-in, an important warning.

Caution   The Services snap-in is an advanced tool and not a place to be experimenting with options. Don't try to solve some "problem" by taking wild guesses about which items in Services might be the causes. Even a minor typographical error in the Services snap-in can have wide-ranging consequences that prevent your computer form starting at all, or from working correctly once it's started.

There are several ways to start the Services snap-in. One is to click the Start button and choose Run. Then, type services.msc into the Open textbox and press Enter or click OK.

Note   If you don't see a Run option on your Start menu, but want that option, right-click the Start button and choose Properties. Click the Customize button and then click the Advanced tab in the Customize Start Menu dialog box. Choose Run command from the Start Menu Items list and then click OK in each open dialog box.

Another way to get to the Services snap-in is to first start the Computer Administration tool. To do so, click the Start button and choose Control Panel. If Control Panel opens in Category view, click the Performance and Maintenance category. Finally, open the Administrative Tools icon, and then open the Component Services icon. Finally, click on Services in the left pane of the Component Services window that opens.

Note   You can start the Administrative Tools from the Start menu if System Administrative Tools is selected in the Start Menu Items list mentioned in the previous note.

Once the Services snap-in is open, you can choose how to view services by clicking the Extended or Standard tab at the bottom of the main pane to the right. You can also choose options from the View menu to determine how you want icons to be displayed. You can widen or narrow the tree in the left column by dragging its inner border left or right. Or, you can show or hide, the column using the Show/Hide Console Tree in the toolbar. More information on using the program is available by choosing Help ➪ Help Topics from its menu bar.

When you're in the Extended view, as shown in Figure 8-11, you can click the name of any service in the left column to see a description of that service to the left. For example, in Figure 8-11 I've clicked on Automatic Updates. The Help text explains how that's the service that enables automatic updates (described in Chapter 27). However, as you'll see in that chapter, you can also control automatic updating without even opening the Services snap-in. The Services snap-in is just a general tool for controlling all different types of auto-starting programs and services.

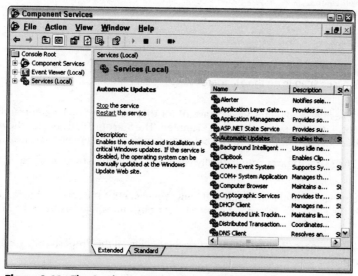

Figure 8-11: The Services snap-in, in the Extended View

To see all the columns in the MMC, you can click on the Standard tab, as shown in Figure 8-12. To show or hide columns, choose View ➪ Add/Remove Columns from the menu bar. You can size columns using the standard methods of dragging the bar to the right of a column heading left or right. Move columns by dragging the entire column heading left or right. Pointing to any text in the Description column displays the full description in the ToolTip at the mouse pointer.

If you scroll through the list of Services, you'll probably see there are quite a few. Exactly which services are listed will vary from one computer to the next. Few, if any, of the services will have any meaning to the average computer user. These things are really only of use to professional programmers, network administrators, or other experienced professionals. What follows is really for those folks. I won't bother to summarize what each service does, because doing so would eat up several pages and only repeat the information that's already in the Description column.

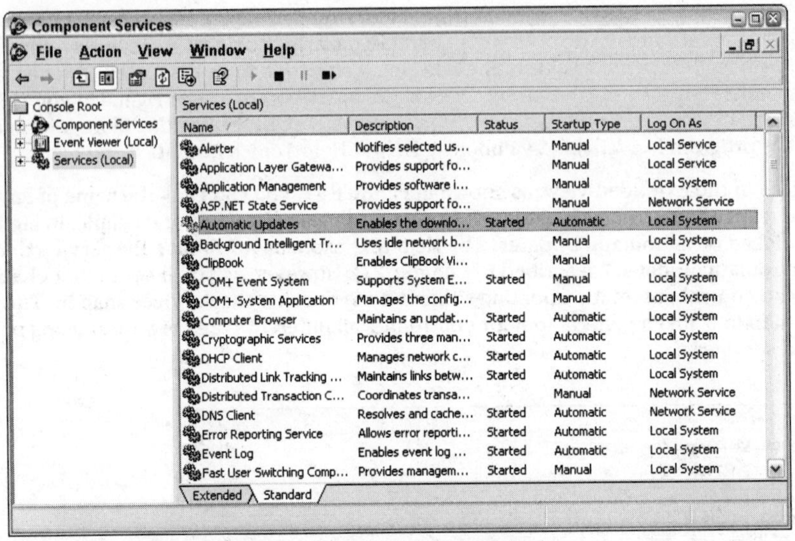

Figure 8-12: The Services snap-in, in the Standard View

In general, though, the Status column shows "Started" for those services that are currently running. It shows nothing for services that aren't running. The Startup Type column shows whether or not the service is configured to run automatically, if at all. Common settings are:

✦ **Automatic:** The service starts automatically when the computer starts or when a user logs in.

✦ **Manual:** The service doesn't start automatically. You can start the service, however, by right-clicking the service name and choosing Start or by choosing Start from the Action menu.

✦ **Disabled:** The service is disabled and must be enabled from the Properties dialog box before it can be started.

To get more information about a service, or change its Startup Type, right-click the service name and choose Properties. For example, Figure 8-13 shows the Properties dialog box for the DNS (Domain Name System) Client service.

The DNS client service is critical for networking because it converts textual names to 32-bit IP addresses such as 11001111100101101101101011011100. When you type a URL such as www.coolnerds.com into your Web browser and press Enter, the DNS service changes that name to the 32-bit address, because the name has no meaning to the Internet. Only the number has meaning to the Internet. Of course, you can browse the Web for the rest of your life without knowing anything about DNS or IP addresses. But, you couldn't browse the Web without a DNS service running. So, again, the Services snap-in is not a place to play around.

Anyway, the options you see in Figure 8-13 are typical of the items listed in the Services snap-in. The Description textbox provides a description of the services and also tells what will happen if you disable or stop the service. The Path to Executable textbox shows the location and name of the program that provides the service. The Startup Type option provides the Automatic, Manual, and Disabled options.

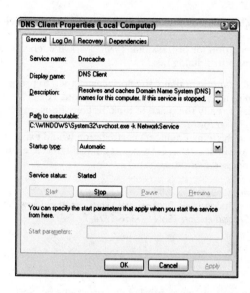

Figure 8-13: Properties for the Domain Name System (DNS) Client service

The buttons let you stop, pause, resume, or start the service. Some programs will accept parameters, which you can add to the Start parameters textbox.

The Log On tab provides options for granting rights to services that need permissions to run. The Recovery tab provides options for dealing with problems when a service fails to start.

The Dependencies tab is one of the most important of the bunch, because it specifies which services the current service depends on (if any), and which services depend on the current service. For example, DNS is a TCP/IP thing (which is the protocol used by the Internet and most modern local networks). If you click the Dependencies tab while viewing the DNS client properties, you'll see that the DNS client can only run if the TCP/IP service is running, as shown in Figure 8-14. This can be useful information when trying to debug a service startup problem, because the problem could well be that the prerequisite service isn't running.

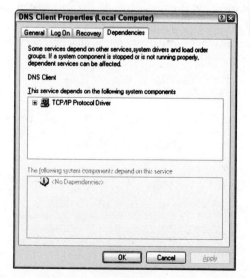

Figure 8-14: Dependencies tab for the DNS client service

The Properties dialog box also shows which services, if any, depend on the current service. That lets you see, in advance, what other services you might be preventing if you stop or disable the current service. It's all useful information for professionals who work at such a technical level. And it's all right there in the Properties dialog box.

In Chapter 28 you'll actually see a practical example of using the Services snap-in to prevent certain types of Internet pop-up ads. If you're interested in learning more about TCP/IP and how the Internet works, a Windows book isn't really the place to look. But any book on TCP/IP, or any book or course that prepares you for MCSA (Microsoft Certified Systems Administrator) or MCSE (Microsoft Certified Systems Engineer) certification would explain all that in depth. For broader technical coverage of services, consult a technical reference such as the *Microsoft Windows XP Resource Kit, Second Edition.*

Note   For more information on Microsoft Certifications, see www.microsoft.com/learning/mcp. For detailed technical information on Windows XP Professional, consider the *Microsoft Windows XP Professional Resource Kit, Second Edition,* ISBN 0-7356-1974-3.

Wrap Up

This chapter has covered all the different ways you can control which programs do, and don't, automatically start when Windows first starts up or when you first log into your Windows user account. In summary:

✦ Icons that automatically appear in the Notification area represent programs and services that start automatically when you log into Windows.

✦ Some of those icons, such as the Volume Control and Network icon, are controlled via settings in Control Panel dialog boxes.

✦ Still other programs have their own built-in options for choosing whether or not the program starts automatically and appears in the Notification area.

✦ You can start any program automatically, even one that has no Notification area icon, by adding a shortcut to the program to the Startup folder.

✦ The full set of services that can be started and stopped automatically are listed in the Services.msc snap-in.

✦ The Services.msc snap-in is an advanced tool designed for professional programmers and network engineers. As such, it contains very little information that would be useful to the average computer user.

✦   ✦   ✦

Using Speech, Language, and Accessibility Features

◆ ◆ ◆ ◆

In This Chapter

Use Accessibility features to overcome motor and sensory impairments

Talk, don't type, documents with speech recognition

Use Text-to-Speech to have documents and e-books read aloud

Switch among multiple languages without changing keyboards

◆ ◆ ◆ ◆

This chapter is all about XP's Accessibility, Speech Recognition, Text-to-Speech, Handwriting Recognition, and Language options. Though somewhat separate features, all offer alternatives to standard read, type, and click interaction with the computer. Some features are designed for people with specific sensory, motor, cognitive, or seizure-related disabilities. Others aren't for any specific disability, but rather just an alternative way of doing things.

For example, if you just can't type worth beans, speech recognition lets you talk to Microsoft Word, having your spoken text translated to typed text automatically. Text-to-Speech reads text aloud from the screen, which is good for any preschooler or any 40-something adult whose eyesight just ain't what it used to be. In short, this isn't just a chapter for people with impairments or disabilities. There's something for just about everyone here.

Considering Multiple Users

We'll start with Accessibility options for specific sensory and motor impairments. Before you launch into the Accessibility features of Windows XP, consider everyone who is using the computer. If only one of several users is impaired, some accessibility options might make it more difficult, rather than easier, for the unimpaired users. Because of this, a good starting point might be to set up a separate user account for the impaired user. Then log in to that user account and choose accessibility options there. Limited account users can set accessibility options within their own accounts.

Note   See Chapter 7 for the goods on creating and managing user accounts.

If all users need access to specific documents, be sure to store those documents in the Shared Documents folder, or one of its subfolders. Doing so will ensure that all users will have easy access to the same documents, regardless of whether or not their user accounts provide accessibility features.

Quick-and-Easy Accessibility Setup

The easiest way to get started with Accessibility options is to run the Accessibility Wizard. Once the Wizard starts, answer each question as it appears on the screen, followed by a click on the Next button. To start the Accessibility Wizard:

1. Click the **Start** button and choose **All Programs** ➪ Accessories ➪ Accessibility Wizard.

2. Read the first Wizard page, click **Next**, then follow the instructions on each page of the Wizard.

The Wizard is self-explanatory, so I won't hand-hold you through each page. Besides, you can change your mind, or fine-tune any settings you select along the way in the Wizard. So, you can consider the Accessibility Wizard to just be a means of getting your accessibility options in the ballpark of where you'll finally end up placing them.

When you get to the last Wizard page, click the Finish button. All your selections will be activated. Figure 9-1 shows an example in which I've selected several options for visual impairments, including large text and icons and a high-contrast color scheme.

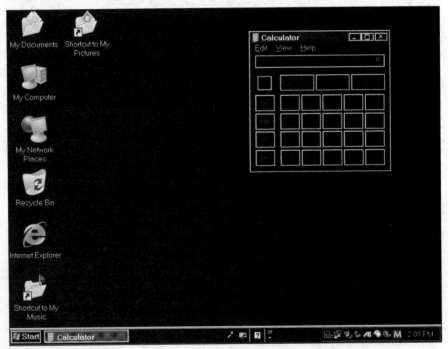

Figure 9-1: Accessibility options for visual impairments are applied

In the sections to follow we'll look at specific accessibility options so that you can enable, fine-tune, or disable any settings you chose while in the Accessibility Wizard.

Administering Accessibility Options

Many options for controlling accessibility options are in the Accessibility Options dialog box in Control Panel. To get to that dialog box:

1. Click the **Start** button and choose **Control Panel**.

2. If Control Panel opens in Category view, click the **Accessibility Options** category.

3. Open the **Accessibility Options** icon.

Accessibility options are divided into five groups, each represented by a tab near the top of the dialog box. For example, the Keyboard tab offers options for controlling how the keyboard works. The Sound tab controls how sound plays, and so forth. Each of the sections to follow describes the options on a specific tab.

Keyboard accessibility options

The Keyboard tab of the Accessibility Options dialog box provides options that are related to motor and visual impairments that might make using the keyboard difficult (Figure 9-2).

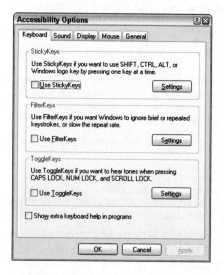

Figure 9-2: Accessibility Options Keyboard tab

Using StickyKeys

StickyKeys overrides the need to hold down two keys simultaneously to press shortcut keys, such as Ctrl+Esc. When StickyKeys is active, you need only tap the *modifier key* (the first key in the key + key sequence) once or twice (not hold it down) and then tap the second key separately. For example, to press Ctrl+Esc with StickyKeys active, tap the Ctrl key once or twice, and then tap the Esc key.

Caution   The options you choose in the Accessibility Options dialog box (or any other dialog box, for that matter) aren't actually applied until you click the OK or Apply button in the dialog box.

To activate StickyKeys, choose (check) the Use StickyKeys checkbox. Then, to determine exactly how StickyKeys work, select from the following options in the Settings for StickyKeys dialog box that opens:

✦ **Use shortcut:** If selected, you can activate/deactivate StickyKeys at any time by tapping the Shift key five times. If you clear this option, you can only activate or deactivate StickyKeys from the Utility Options dialog box, not from the keyboard.

✦ **Press modified key twice to lock:** Use this option is you want to make sure that you can press the second key multiple times after pressing the first key. For example, with this option activated you can select text in a document by pressing the shift key twice and then pressing navigation keys multiple times. If you turn this option off, pressing the second key will work only on the first press. The second keystroke will unlock the modifier key.

✦ **Turn StickyKeys off if two keys are pressed at once:** Selecting this option allows you to disable StickyKeys by pressing any two keys simultaneously.

✦ **Make sounds when modifier key is pressed:** If this is selected, the computer will emit a small beep when a modifier key is locked or unlocked, to provide some auditory feedback.

✦ **Show StickeyKeys status on screen:** If selected, this provides visual feedback in the form a Notification icon when a modifier key is locked. The icon disappears when the modifier key is unlocked.

Using FilterKeys

The FilterKeys option disables autotyping (repeated typing of the character) when a key is held down too long or when multiple rapid keystrokes occur. This is to aid those with muscular impairments that cause slow or uneven typing. If you choose FilterKeys, you can fine-tune its behavior by clicking its Settings buttons and choosing options as follows:

✦ **Use shortcut:** When this is selected, you can activate or deactivate FilterKeys by holding down the Shift key for five seconds.

✦ **Ignore repeated keystrokes:** If selected, this ensures that repeat keystrokes are ignored. The Settings button for this option lets you define and test the threshold beyond which key presses are assumed to be intentional rather than caused by involuntary muscular movements of the hands.

✦ **Ignore quick keystrokes and slow down the repeat rate:** If selected, this instructs Windows to ignore brief keystrokes, such as those that might be caused by involuntary muscular movement. The Settings button allows you to define specific time thresholds for voluntary and involuntary keystrokes.

✦ **Click and type here to test FilterKey settings:** Click within the textbox and hold down keys to test the settings you chose for the *Ignore quick keystrokes* option.

✦ **Beep when keys pressed or accepted:** If selected, provides auditory feedback whenever a keystroke is typed and accepted by the computer.

✦ **Show FilterKeys status on screen:** If selected, this shows a Notification area icon whenever the FilterKeys option is active.

Using ToggleKeys

The ToggleKeys feature, when activated, provides auditory feedback as to the status of the Caps Lock, Num Lock, and Scroll Lock keys. When you press a key and its lock is activated, the speaker emits a high-pitched tone. Pressing the key a second time to unlock it causes it to emit a low-pitched tone.

The Settings dialog box for this feature provides only the option to turn ToggleKeys on and off by pressing the Num Lock key five times.

The "Show extra keyboard help in programs" option, when selected, ensures that any extra information about keyboard accessibility features that programs can provide is visible in the Help for those programs.

Auditory feedback accessibility options

The Sound tab in the Accessibility Options dialog box, shown in Figure 9-3, provides visual alerts in conjunction with the usual sound alerts that accompany warning messages. These options are particularly useful for the hearing-impaired who might not otherwise hear the beeps.

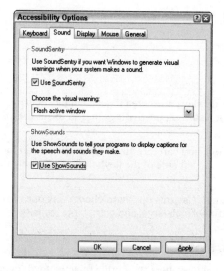

Figure 9-3: Accessibility Options Sound tab

Using SoundSentry

Choosing Use SoundSentry tells Windows to provide additional visual feedback whenever it emits a warning sound, or any other sound designed to get the user's attention. If you choose this option, you can choose the extent of the visual feedback from the "Choose the visual warning" drop-down list.

Using ShowSounds

Selecting the Use ShowSounds option ensures that any accessibility-enabled programs that present information through sound or speech also display that information visually through icons or text captions.

Using visual accessibility options

The Display tab of the Accessibility Options dialog box, shown in Figure 9-4, provides options for activating and deactivating options for certain types of visual impairments, as described below:

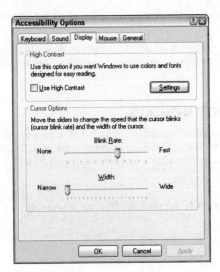

Figure 9-4: Accessibility Options Display tab

✦ **Use High Contrast:** If selected, Windows displays all screen items in highly contrasted colors. If you choose this option, you can also click the Settings button to set the following two options:

- **Use Shortcut:** If you select the option, you can turn High Contrast on or off by holding down the Alt+Shift keys on the left side of the keyboard and tapping the Print Screen (PrtScrn) key once.

- **Your current high contrast scheme is**: Use this option to choose any one of several different contrast schemes with normal, large, and extra large icons.

Using mouse accessibility options

The Mouse tab of the Accessibility Options dialog box offers the option to activate, or deactivate, MouseKeys. When activated, MouseKeys allows the user to move the mouse pointer freely about the screen using the numeric keypad rather than the mouse. This is useful for those with motor impairments that make it difficult to operate a mouse smoothly.

If you enable MouseKeys, you can also click its Settings button to get to the options shown in Figure 9-5. Those options determine how MouseKeys operates:

✦ **Use shortcut:** Selecting this option allows you to turn MouseKeys on and off by holding down the left Alt+Shift keys and tapping the Num Lock key.

✦ **Top speed:** This sets the maximum speed at which the mouse pointer moves as you hold down an arrow key on the numeric keypad.

✦ **Acceleration:** This sets how quickly the mouse pointer accelerates relative to how long you hold down an arrow key.

✦ **Hold down Ctrl to speed up and Shift to slow down:** This allows you to control mouse pointer acceleration by holding down the Ctrl or Shift key while holding down an arrow key button.

✦ **Use MouseKeys when NumLock is:** on. This allows you to choose whether MouseKeys is active only when the Num Lock key is in the On, or Off, position.

✦ **Show MouseKey status on screen:** If this is selected, a mouse icon will appear in the Notification area. When MouseKeys is inactive; the mouse icon will have an international "No" symbol over it.

Figure 9-5: Settings for MouseKeys dialog box

To work move the mouse pointer while MouseKeys is active:

✦ Use the ↑, and ↓ keys on the numeric keypad to move the mouse pointer vertically.

✦ Use the ← and → keys to move the mouse pointer horizontally.

✦ Use the Home, PgDn, PgUp, and End keys to move the mouse pointer diagonally.

✦ To click the item under the mouse pointer, press the 5 key on the numeric keypad.

✦ To double-click, press the + key on the numeric keypad.

✦ To right-click, press the - key on the numeric keypad.

✦ To drag, press the Insert (Ins) key on the numeric keypad, and then move the mouse pointer with the keys previously described.

✦ To stop dragging (release the mouse button), press the Delete (Del) key on the numeric keypad.

General accessibility options

The General tab of the Accessibility Options dialog box, shown in Figure 9-6, provides options that apply to all, or some, of the Accessibility options, as described in the following list.

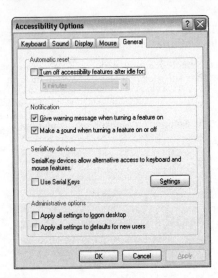

Figure 9-6: Accessibility Options General tab

Note   The first two options that follow are really designed for multiple users sharing a single computer without user accounts. If each user has his or her own account, it's not really necessary to deactivate accessibility features in the account that uses those features.

✦ **Turn off accessibility features after idle for:** If you choose this option, you can set a time limit after which all accessibility features deactivate when the computer is idle.

✦ **Give warning message when turning a feature on:** If selected, this option displays a message on the screen before activating an accessibility feature.

✦ **Make a sound when turning a feature on or off:** If this is selected, Windows emits an audible sound whenever you activate or deactivate an accessibility feature.

✦ **Use SerialKeys:** Enable this feature only if you've purchased and installed special hardware replacements for the mouse or keyboard. After you choose this option, use the Settings button to specify the port and baud rate (speed) of the device you've connected to the computer.

Tip   For more information on assistive input devices for motor and sensory impairments, see www.microsoft.com/enable.

✦ **Apply all settings to the logon desktop:** If this is selected, accessibility options will be applied to the Welcome screen to help impaired users log on. You must be logged in to a user account with Administrator privileges to set this option.

✦ **Apply all settings to defaults for new users:** If this is selected, any new user accounts you create will have accessibility features enabled automatically. You must be logged in to a user account with an Administrator account to activate this option.

Don't forget that you must click the OK button in the Accessibility Options dialog box to activate all settings and return to the desktop.

Using Microsoft Magnifier

Microsoft Magnifier is an assistive tool for those with visual impairments who require magnification of items on the screen. When activated, a portion of the screen shows the area around the mouse pointer magnified along the top of the screen. To illustrate, in Figure 9-7 I turned on the magnifier after typing the preceding sentence. The actual text I typed is visible near the bottom of the screen. The top of the screen shows the text magnified 2× in Microsoft Magnifier.

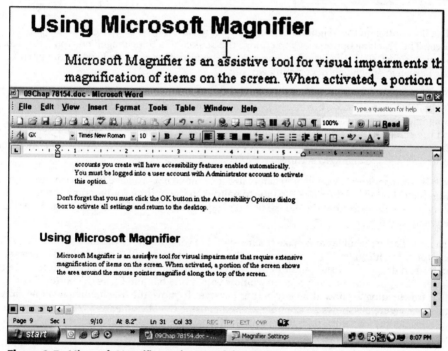

Figure 9-7: Microsoft Magnifier at the top of the screen

To turn on Microsoft Magnifier, click the Start button, and choose All Programs ➪ Accessories ➪ Accessibility ➪ Magnifier. You'll see a dialog box describing magnifier. Click OK to close that dialog box. A second dialog box titled Magnifier Settings, shown in Figure 9-8, also appears.

Figure 9-8: Microsoft Magnifier Settings dialog box

The first option in the Magnifier Settings dialog box allows you to choose the magnification level. The Tracking options let you choose the screen area to be magnified. You'll probably want to select all three options to ensure that the magnifier stays focused on the portion of the screen in which you're currently working.

The Presentation options allow you to invert colors in the magnifier, start Magnifier with the Magnifier Settings dialog box minimized, and show or hide the magnifier. If you close the Magnifier Settings dialog box, you'll also close the magnifier window. So to get the dialog box off the screen without losing the magnification window, minimize the Magnifier Settings dialog box. Once minimized, the dialog box will have a taskbar button that you can click whenever you need to change a setting.

While the magnifier is visible, you can resize it or move it as you see fit. To size the magnification pane, first move the tip of the mouse pointer to the bottom (or innermost) edge of the magnifier window so that the mouse pointer turns to a two-headed arrow. Then, drag that edge up and down.

To undock the magnifier and make it a free-floating window, move the mouse pointer to the center of the magnifier. Then, hold down the mouse button until the magnifier turns a solid color and drag toward the center of the screen. When you release the mouse button, the magnifier will appear in its own program window with a title bar and Close (X) button. To size that free-floating window, drag any corner or edge. To move the free-floating window, drag its title bar. Figure 9-9 shows an example where I'm using the Magnifier as a free-floating window in conjunction with a graphics program. The Magnifier shows the portion of the photo I'm working on, magnified 4×.

To change Magnifier settings at any time, just click the Magnifier Settings taskbar button to bring back the dialog box. From there, you can clear the Show Magnifier checkbox to temporarily hide the magnification window. If you want to close the Magnifier window and dialog box:

✦ Click the **Exit** button in the Magnifier Settings dialog box.

✦ Or, click the **Close** (X) button in the upper-right corner of the free-floating Magnifier window.

Figure 9-9: Magnifier in a free-floating window

Using Microsoft Narrator

Microsoft Narrator is an assistive technology that reads aloud text on the screen. To start Narrator, click the Start button and choose All Programs ➪ Accessories ➪ Accessibility ➪ Narrator. A message box, shown at the left side of Figure 9-10 opens, explaining the purpose of Narrator. Click OK in the message box to see the Narrator dialog box, shown at right in that same figure.

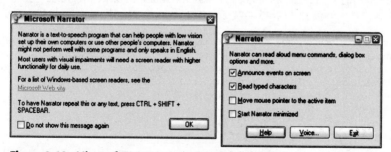

Figure 9-10: Microsoft Narrator message and dialog box

Use Narrator to Read Web Pages

The multicolumn formats used by many pages make it difficult to use Narrator as a tool for reading Web pages. To get around that, you can drag the mouse pointer through just the text you want read, press Ctrl+C to copy that text, and then open Notepad (Click Start and choose All Program ⇨ Accessories ⇨ Notepad) and press Ctrl+V to paste the text into Notepad.

Finally, make sure that Narrator is enabled and Notepad is in the active window. Press Ctrl+Shift+Spacebar to have Narrator read the text in the document. Narrator may stop reading after the first 72 words. Pressing Ctrl+Shift+Enter will resume reading in most cases. If not, press the ↓ to read aloud one line at a time.

The options in the Narrator dialog box let you control Narrator's behavior as follows:

✦ **Announce events on screen:** If this is selected, Narrator announces program events as they occur on the screen and reads items from menus.

✦ **Read typed characters:** If this is selected, Narrator announces each character you type at the keyboard.

✦ **Move mouse pointer to the active item:** If this is selected, the mouse pointer automatically jumps to whichever active item the Narrator has just announced.

✦ **Start Narrator minimized:** If this is selected, Narrator starts with the options dialog box initially minimized (so it's not in the way).

✦ **Voice:** This allows you to choose an alternative voice for Narrator (if any are available) as well as a speed, volume, and pitch for the voice.

Once you've made your selections, you can minimize the Narrator dialog box to get it out of the way. Narrator will continue to read aloud, while the dialog box remains available as a taskbar button.

To change Narrator options, or stop Narrator, click the Narrator taskbar button. To stop Narrator, click the Exit button in that Narrator dialog box.

Narrator works best with the Windows desktop, Microsoft Internet Explorer, WordPad, Notepad, and Control Panel windows. It doesn't work too well with other programs. You'll see other techniques for reading text aloud under "Reading Documents Aloud" later in this chapter.

Note   Narrator provides only minimal functionality. Users with low vision or blindness will likely need more powerful software for extensive computer use. To review such products, see www.microsoft.com/enable. Optionally, for information on having Microsoft Word and e-books read aloud, see "Reading Documents Aloud" later in this chapter

Using the On-Screen Keyboard

The On-Screen Keyboard is just what its name implies — it's a keyboard that appears on the screen, so you can type by clicking on keys with the mouse pointer rather than by typing. This is useful for those with a variety of motor impairments, but not too bad for one-fingered hunt-and-peck typists either. To open the On-Screen Keyboard, click the Start button and choose All Programs ⇨ Accessories ⇨ Accessibility ⇨ On-Screen Keyboard.

The keyboard appears in a free-floating widow on the screen (see Figure 9-11). You work it as you would a normal keyboard. First, on the screen, click the spot where you intend to type text. That space can be anyplace that accepts text, from the Address bar in your Web browser to a full Microsoft Word document. Then, just start typing one character at a time by clicking on the appropriate key on the On-Screen Keyboard.

Figure 9-11: The on-screen keyboard

Use the Backspace (bksp) and Delete (del) keys to delete text. To type an uppercase letter, type click the Shift key, then type the letter you want to type in uppercase. To press a *key+key* combination, such as Ctrl+Esc, click the first key, then the second key.

When you've finished with the On-Screen Keyboard, click the Close (X) button in its upper-right corner.

Using the Accessibility Utility Manager

Utility Manager is a program for controlling how and when Magnifier, Narrator, and the On-Screen Keyboard start. The main idea is to allow visually impaired users to be able to start any of those programs just by pressing ⊞+U (hold down the Windows logo key and tap the letter U). The shortcut keys work at any time, even in the Welcome screen.

If you don't have a Windows keyboard, you can start the Utility Manager by clicking the Start button and choosing All Programs ➪ Accessories ➪ Accessibility ➪ Utility Manager. However, that approach doesn't always allow Utility Manager to function within a specific program that's running, so the keyboard method is generally preferred.

When Utility Manager first opens, it looks like Figure 9-12. The list at the top of the window shows which programs are running and which aren't. By default, Narrator starts as soon as Utility Manager starts, although you can change that, as discussed in a moment.

Figure 9-12: Utility Manager for some Accessibility programs

To start or stop a program listed in Utility Manager, click the program's name and then click the Start or Stop button. To choose which programs start or stop automatically when Utility Manager opens, first click on the name of a program in the list. To make that program start automatically when Utility Manager opens, choose the "Start automatically when Utility Manager starts" checkbox. To prevent the program from starting automatically with Utility Manager, clear that checkbox.

You can use a similar technique to decide which programs start automatically when the user logs in. The settings will be applied to whatever user account you're logged into at the moment. To make one of the programs start automatically at login, click its name in the list and choose the "Start automatically when I log in" checkbox. To prevent the program from starting automatically at login, clear that checkbox.

The "Start automatically when I lock my desktop" option is available only on domain networks, where users can lock and unlock their desktops by pressing ⊞+L On a computer that's not part of a domain, pressing ⊞+L takes you straight to the Welcome page without logging you out of the current user account.

When Utility Manager starts a program, it also displays the descriptive message for that program. When you no longer need to see that descriptive message, you can choose the "Do not show this message again" checkbox in the message box to prevent the message from appearing in the future. That way, only the dialog box that lets you control the program's behavior will open when the program starts.

When you click OK in the Utility Manager, the dialog box closes but any programs that started remain open. You can leave any program running without its Settings dialog box on the screen by minimizing that Settings dialog box. When you do, the Settings dialog box becomes a taskbar button, which you can click at any time to reopen the dialog box.

To end one of the programs, return to its Settings dialog box and click its Exit button. Optionally, you can bring up Utility Manager again, click the name of the program you want to stop, and then click the Stop button.

Using the Language Bar

The Language bar is a tool for managing three main features used in a variety of programs. Those are:

✦ **Speech Recognition:** Allows you to dictate text and commands to the computer by voice. In other words, you talk, it types what you say.

✦ **Text-to-Speech:** This feature tells the computer to read aloud text that's typed on the screen.

✦ **Handwriting Recognition:** Converts handwritten text to typed text on the screen.

Whether or not you can use these features depends on several factors, including the hardware available to you, and the program you happen to be using at the moment. You use Windows XP to install and manage these services, though you actually use the services within specific program such as Microsoft Internet Explorer, Microsoft Word, Excel, Outlook, or any third-party program that supports the feature.

The Language bar, which you initially saw way back in Chapter 2, is the main tool for using these features. When you use a program that supports speech recognition, the Language bar usually appears automatically. However, it is one of the optional taskbar toolbars. So, it might appear as a free-floating toolbar, as in the top of Figure 9-13, or it might be anchored to the taskbar, as in the bottom of that same figure.

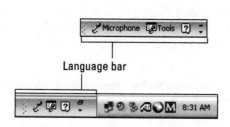

Figure 9-13: The Language bar, free-floating and docked

A third possibility is that the Language bar doesn't appear at all. If the Language bar isn't visible on your screen, right-click the clock and choose Toolbars ➪ Language bar. If that works, then there's no need to go looking around for the Language bar. But if you can't find the Language bar anywhere, not even as an option on that Toolbars menu, you'll need to do some exploring to find out why, and to make it visible if appropriate for your system. The most likely scenario is that the Language bar is disabled at some deeper level.

If you can't find the Language bar or Language bar option anywhere, here's how you can dig a little deeper to find out what's up:

1. Click the **Start** button and choose **Control Panel**.

2. If Control Panel opens in Category view, click **Date, Time, Language, and Regional Options**.

3. Open the **Regional and Language Options** icon.

4. Click the **Languages** tab, and then click the **Details** button. The Text Services dialog box, shown in Figure 9-14, opens.

Figure 9-14: Text Services and Input Languages dialog box

5. Click the **Language Bar** button.

Note If the Language Bar button is disabled, click the Advanced tab and clear the Turn off advanced text services checkbox. Then, click the Apply button, and click the Settings tab again. If the Language Bar button is still disabled, click OK, restart your computer, and start over at Step 1.

6. Make sure that at least the first and third checkboxes, **Show the Language bar on the desktop** and **Show additional Language bar icons** in the taskbar are selected (checked), as in Figure 9-15. The other options aren't as important and may be disabled. But you can choose those too, if they're enabled.

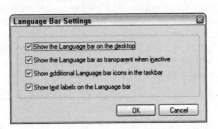

Figure 9-15: The Language bar Settings dialog box

7. Click **OK** in all open dialog boxes. You can close Control Panel as well.

By now, you should see the Language bar somewhere on your screen. If not, right-click the clock in the lower-right corner of your screen and choose Toolbars ➪ Language bar. And open Microsoft Internet Explorer as well. If the Language bar is nowhere to be seen, be patient. You may have to install some services first, as described in sections that follow. But the most likely scenario is that you can see the Language bar somewhere on your screen now.

If you can only see a small portion of the Language bar on your taskbar, you may want to drag it up onto the desktop to make it larger. You'll need to unlock the taskbar first, if it's locked, by right-clicking the clock and choosing Lock the Taskbar. Once the Language bar is free-floating, you'll be able to see more of it, especially if you open a speech-enabled program like Microsoft Internet Explorer or Microsoft Word. Figure 9-16 shows the Language bar as it might appear and points out the roles played by various optional buttons.

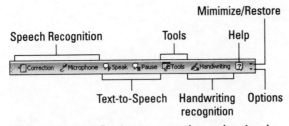

Figure 9-16: Free-floating Language bar and optional buttons

Choosing Language bar buttons

The buttons available to you will vary depending on the tools available to you in whatever program you happen to be using at the moment. However, some buttons may be hidden even when a feature is available, just because of selections on the Options menu in the Language bar. To ensure that you can see all the buttons representing options that are available to you, click the Options as in Figure 9-17.

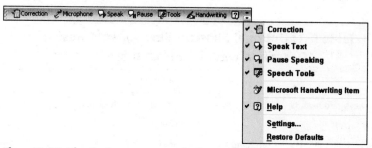

Figure 9-17: The Options menu on the Language bar

The toolbar you'll be seeing in this chapter is showing all of the buttons that have check marks next to their names in Figure 9-17. I suggest that you click on any buttons names that aren't checked on your own Options menu if you want to have your toolbar look the ones you'll be seeing here. Again, some features might not be available to you just yet. But as you progress through the chapter, many of those features may come to life for you.

Finally, as I write this chapter I'm using certain settings available through the Speech Input Settings dialog box shown in Figure 9-18. To get to that dialog box yourself, and get your settings in sync with mine, click the Tools button on the Language bar and choose Options. Some items may be disabled if speech recognition isn't installed. But if you can select options, make sure that the items checked in Figure 9-18 are also checked in your dialog box. Then, click OK to save those settings and close the dialog box.

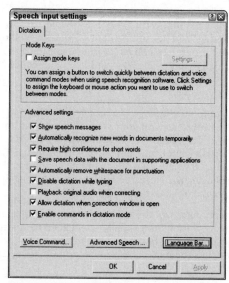

Figure 9-18: The Speech Input Settings dialog box

Many of the buttons on the Language bar can also be activated through shortcut keys. Some require a Windows keyboard, which has an extra ⊞ key. For future reference, Table 9-1 lists those optional shortcut keys.

Table 9-1: Optional Shortcut Keys for Features Described Later in this Chapter

Desired action	Shortcut key
Switch between keyboard layouts	Ctrl+Shift or left Alt+Shift
Turn microphone on/off	⊞+V
Switch between Dictation and Voice Command	⊞+T
Correct a dictated word	⊞+C
Turn handwriting on/off	⊞+H
Turn Japanese keyboard on/off	Alt+~
Turn Korean keyboard on/off	Right Alt
Turn Chinese keyboard on/off	Ctrl+Spacebar

With the Language bar (reasonably) under control, we can move onto specific tools to which the Language bar provides access. We'll start with speech recognition.

Using Speech Recognition

Speech recognition is one of those Windows XP capabilities that very few people are aware even exists. Perhaps this is because speech recognition doesn't actually work with Windows XP per se. Rather, it works with speech-enabled programs such as Internet Explorer (version 5.0 or later) and the programs that come with Microsoft Office 2003 and Microsoft Office XP (a.k.a. Microsoft Office 2002). You *manage* speech recognition from Windows XP, but you *use* speech recognition with speech-enabled programs only.

Despite the fancy name, current speech recognition technology is a far cry from the kind you see in the movies. While you can control some programs with your voice through speech recognition, you won't be barking orders at your computer like Captain Kirk on *Star Trek*. You'll need to use specific words, not plain-English sentences. And while speech recognition can type what you say, it can't format text to match what you're envisioning in your mind. So, dictation usually involves a combination of speaking the words you want typed and using your mouse and keyboard to make corrections and apply formatting to your text.

Still, if you can't type worth beans, and your computer has the right stuff for doing speech recognition, it might be worth taking speech recognition for a spin. You will need to invest some time into the endeavor, because you have to train it to recognize your voice. Not everyone can use speech recognition, because there are some minimal requirements that need to be met first.

What you need for speech recognition

For speech recognition to work at all, you need at least three things:

✦ A computer with at least a 400 Mhz processor and at least 128 MB of RAM.

Tip

To find out your own computers speed and RAM, right-click the My Computer icon on the desktop or Start menu, then choose Properties. The speed and RAM are listed under Computer on the General tab. Note that 1 Ghz is about 1,000 Mhz. So any speed at or over 1 Ghz is more than enough.

✦ A microphone, preferably a high-quality headset microphone.

✦ A speech recognition engine and speech-enabled programs.

Most computers manufactured after the year 2000 will meet the hardware requirements. The USB headset you can pick up at just about any store that sells computer components. For example, CompUSA, Staples, and Office Max will carry them. You can also buy them online at www.staples.com, www.amazon.com, www.walmart.com, and so forth. The buzzwords to search for are *USB headset*. Just make sure that you don't get a phone or video game headset. Ideally, you want a PC headset with a USB connection and built-in noise cancellation, which keeps background noise from interfering with your spoken words.

The speech engine is a program that comes with certain speech-enabled programs. The first step to using the speech recognition engine is to find out if it's already installed and, if it isn't, to install it. We'll deal with that step first.

Seeing if speech recognition is installed

The speech recognition engine is the trickiest part of the whole process. If Windows XP or Microsoft Office came preinstalled on your computer, there's a good chance the speech recognition is already installed and you're ready to go. If you installed Microsoft Office XP (a.k.a. Microsoft Office 2002), or Microsoft Office 2003 yourself, you have speech recognition. But it may not be installed yet. So, the first step to using speech recognition is to see if it's already installed and, if not, to install it. To do that, you need to get to the get to the Speech Properties dialog box by following these steps:

1. Click the **Start** button and choose **Control Panel**.

2. If Control Panel opens in Category click on the **Sounds, Speech, and Audio Devices** category.

3. Open the **Speech** icon.

The Speech Properties dialog box opens. If you see the Speech Recognition tab shown in Figure 9-19, your speech recognition engine is installed. You can click OK to close the dialog box and skip the next section on installing the recognition engine.

If you don't see a Speech Recognition tab in your Speech Properties dialog box, then you'll need to install an engine before you can use that feature. In which case, you can't skip the next section.

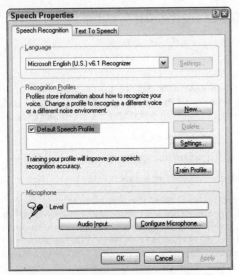

Figure 9-19: Speech recognition is already installed on this computer.

Installing speech recognition

As mentioned in the preceding paragraph, you should only install speech recognition is it's *not* already installed. Oddly, you can't install it from the Windows XP CD. You need to own Microsoft Office XP (a.k.a. Microsoft Office 2002) or Microsoft Office 2003. This is because speech recognition works in all the Office programs, but doesn't work in Windows XP per se.

If you installed Microsoft Office yourself, you'll need to have the original Microsoft Office CD handy. If Office came preinstalled, you might not need that CD. But you should find it and have it at the ready, just in case. Then, follow these steps:

1. Click the **Start** button and choose **Control Panel**.

2. Open the **Add or Remove Programs** icon.

3. Click on the **Microsoft Office *whatever* Edition** (where *whatever* is any edition name).

4. Click the **Change** button that appeared after you completed the previous step.

5. In the Setup Wizard that opens, choose **Add or Remove Features,** and then click **Next>**.

6. Click the + sign next to **Office Shared Features**.

7. Click the + sign next to **Alternative User Input**.

8. Click the icon next to **Speech** and choose **Run from My Computer**.

Tip   If you plan to install handwriting recognition, you can do so right now. Just click the icon next to Handwriting icon and choose Run from My Computer.

9. Click the **Update** button and follow the instructions on the screen.

10. When you've completed all the steps, close any remaining open windows, including Add or Remove Programs and Control Panel.

By now, you should have your speech engine installed. You can verify this by opening the Speech Properties dialog box, as discussed under "Seeing if speech recognition is installed" earlier in this chapter.

Once the speech engine is installed, you need to spend some time training it to recognize your voice. If several people will be using speech recognition, each user should create his or her own speech profile.

Creating a speech profile

Everyone's voice is a little different, and everyone has his or her own unique way of pronouncing certain words. The differences are subtle, and it's easy for us human beings to understand what someone else is saying, so long as the person is speaking the same language we speak. Computers, however, don't have brains and can't recognize human speech at all.

The process of training speech recognition is called "creating a speech profile." Each person who uses speech recognition can create, and use, his or her own speech profile, which helps speech recognition adapt to different users. Before you start your training session, make sure that you can spend at least 15 minutes at the computer without interruption, and without a lot of background noise. Don your headset, and get the microphone to where it's about an inch from your mouth. Then, follow these steps:

1. Click the **Start** button and choose **Control Panel**.

2. If Control Panel opens in Category View, click the **Sounds, Speech, and Audio Devices category**.

3. Open the **Speech** icon. The Speech Properties dialog box opens.

4. On the Speech Profile tab, click the **New** button. The Profile Wizard opens.

5. You should see your user account name under Profile. If not, type your first name in the textbox beneath the Profile heading.

6. Read the first Wizard page, and then click the **Next** button.

From here on out, it's a simple matter of reading and following the instructions on the next Wizard page that appears. Read and follow the instructions on each page carefully.

There's no need for me to describe what's going on in the Wizard, because each page is self-explanatory. When you've finished with the Wizard, you'll be returned to the Speech Properties dialog box. There, you'll see a new speech profile with the name you provided. For example, in Figure 9-20 I've created a speech profile named Alan.

Figure 9-20: Speech recognition profile named Alan is selected.

Using speech recognition

Windows XP's role in the whole speech recognition scenario is largely over at this point. You only use Windows to install and manage speech recognition engines, and to manage the Language bar. You actually *use* speech recognition in speech-enabled programs like those that come with Microsoft Office. Microsoft Internet Explorer also provides some minimal speech recognition, in the form of allowing you to fill in forms (textboxes) on pages that allow you to "fill in the blanks."

When you start a program that supports speech recognition and move the cursor to some-place you can type within that program, the Language bar appears automatically. If the language bar is free-floating, you can drag it by the handle at left into any place within the program window. To actually use speech recognition, you'll need to put on your headset and choose Tools ➪ Speech from Word's menu bar.

Tip   You'll choose Tools ➪ Speech from any Office program's menu bar to use speech recognition within that program.

The Language bar should expand to show two additional buttons named Dictation and Voice Command. To the right of the Voice Command button you'll see a small button-shaped speech balloon. That balloon provides feedback as you speak, and you'll want to keep an eye on it as you use speech recognition. The Dictation and Voice Command buttons allow you to use the program in two different ways:

✦ **Dictation:** Use Dictation when you want the computer to type your spoken words into a document. To use dictation, click the "Dictation" button in the Language bar.

✦ **Voice Command:** To choose options from menu bars, toolbars, and dialog boxes, click on the Voice Command button in the Language bar.

For example, if you have Word and are following along right now, you should see "Listening..." or "Dictation Paused" in the speech balloon, as in Figure 9-21. Note that you can turn the microphone on or off at any time by clicking the Microphone button in the Language bar. So, if you don't see the Dictation and Voice Command buttons, just click the Microphone button to turn on the microphone.

The first time you use speech recognition in a program, you'll be prompted to do some training. Again, the instructions for doing so will appear in a Wizard. Just follow the instructions on each Wizard page and click Next. When you finish the training session, click the Finish button. Then, with the cursor in your Word document at a place you can type, you're ready to start dictating.

Taking speech recognition for a spin

If you've been following along here and have Microsoft Word at the ready, your headset on, and the Language bar showing the Dictation and Voice Command buttons, you can create your first speech document by following the steps below. But don't expect it to be easy on the first try. Speech recognition is one of those things you really need to practice for a while before it feels natural. But you have to start somewhere, so here goes:

First, make sure that the microphone is on and you can see the Dictation and Voice Command buttons in the Language bar. Click the Dictation button. You should see Listening... in the Language bar speech balloon as in Figure 9-21. Then, follow the next set of steps. When you see words in italic, say exactly those words.

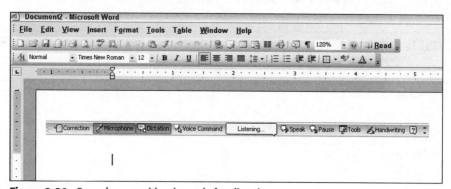

Figure 9-21: Speech recognition is ready for dictation.

1. Read the text below, say the words comma and period where shown in italics:

   Speech recognition feels strange at first *period*. We don't normally talk to machines *comma* and machines sure don't respond like humans do *period* But I know if I practice and train *comma* it will get easier and start to feel more natural *period*.

2. After you speak three or four sentences, say *voice command* or click on Voice Command in the Language bar. Make sure that the yellow box turns gray and shows the words "Voice Command."

3. Say the following (but not too quickly), and watch the screen: *Go Left Go Left Select Paragraph Format Font Arial Bold 16 OK end.*

4. Say *dictation* (or click on Dictation in the Language bar) then say *new paragraph the end period.*

It will feel strange at first, and many of your words won't translate correctly. That's because it takes practice and training to master speech recognition. But if you were able to follow along, at least you now get a sense of how it works. Notice how some spoken text was spoken as dictation, while other text was spoken as commands. You said the word *voice command* to switch to Voice Command mode, and said the word *Dictation* to switch to dictation mode. If you watched the Language bar while doing so, you could actually see the buttons push in as you spoke.

If you really made a mess of things, you can delete all the text from your first try, or create a new blank document and try again. Keep an eye on the Language bar, and if you see something like *What as that?*, say the word again.

Caution   If you create multiple speech profiles, make sure that you choose your own profile before you start dictation or training. To do so, choose Tools ➪ Current User from the Language bar and then your own name from the menu that opens.

Dictating special characters

When dictating in Microsoft Word, you can type special characters by saying their names, as listed in Table 9-2. Notice that I've spelled some double words, such as *OpenParen*, as one word, because you want to say the name as though it were one word. So, I intentionally spelled each word exactly as you should speak it. You must be in Dictation mode, not Voice Command mode, for the special characters to be typed correctly.

Table 9-2: Words for Characters in Speech Recognition Dictation Mode

Say. . .	to type a(n) . . .
Ampersand	&
Apostrophe	'
Asterisk	*
AtSign	@
Backslash	\
Caret	^
CloseParen	)
CloseQuote	"
CloseSingleQuote	'
Colon	:
Comma	,
DollarSign	$
DoubleDash	--
Ellipses	...
Equals	=
ExclamationPoint	!
GreaterThan	>

Say. . .	to type a(n) . . .
LeftBrace	{
LeftBracket	[
LeftParen	(
LessThan	<
OpenParen	(
OpenQuote	"
OpenSingleQuote	'
Percent	%
Period	.
PoundSign	#
QuestionMark	?
RightBrace	}
RightBracket	]
RightParen	)
Semicolon	;
Slash	/
Space	(Inserts a space)
VerticalBar		

Moving the cursor in Dictation mode

Don't forget that the mouse and keyboard still work during speech recognition. And realistically, you'll probably use your view, mouse, and keyboard to type, format, make corrections, and dictate all at the same time. You can, however, make minor changes and corrections with your voice while in Dictation mode by speaking the words listed in Table 9-3.

Table 9-3: Special Words That You Can Use in Dictation Mode

Spoken Word (Dictation Mode)	Effect
Backspace	Deletes character to left of cursor
SelectWord	Selects the word at the cursor
Delete	Deletes character or selected text
NewLine	Moves cursor down one line (presses Enter once)
NewParagraph	Ends paragraph, moves cursor down (presses Enter twice)

For most formatting and cursor positioning, you'll probably want to switch to Voice Command mode.

Barking orders in Voice Command mode

In Voice Command mode, you can say the name of any option on the menu bar to open that menu. Then, say the name of the command on the open menu to select it. As you saw in the previous example, you can also select options from a dialog box, just by saying the name of the item you want to choose.

In addition, you can use toolbar buttons by saying their names. Use the exact name of the button, as shown when you rest the mouse pointer on the button. In Voice Command mode it's important to keep an eye on the yellow speech balloon in the Language bar, because it provides feedback as to how your speech is being recognized.

In addition to speaking the names of menu commands and buttons, you can speak any of the words from Table 9-4 to move the cursor and make changes while in Voce Command mode.

Table 9-4: Some Words You Can Speak in Voice Command Mode

Spoken Word	Effect
Bold	Applies boldface to selected text
Center	Centers the text on the line
Down or GoDown	Moves the cursor down a line
End or GoEnd	Moves cursor to end of line
Escape	Same as pressing the Esc key (for example, to close the right-click menu)
Home or GoHome	Moves cursor to start of line
Italic	Italicizes selected text
Left or GoLeft	Moves the cursor back one character
NewLine	Moves the cursor down a line
NewParagraph	Ends the paragraph and moves the cursor down two lines.
NextPage	Moves to the next page
PageDown	Same as pressing Page Down (PgDn)
PageUp	Same as pressing Page Up (PgUp)
PreviousPage	Moves to the previous page
Right or GoRight	Moves the cursor to next character
RightClick	Shows the context menu at cursor
SelectLastLine	Selects the previous line in the paragraph
SelectLastWord	Selects the previous word in the sentence
SelectLine	Selects the current line
SelectNextLine	Selects the next line in the paragraph
SelectNextWord	Selects the next word in the sentence
SelectParagraph	Selects the current paragraph
SelectWord	Selects the word at the cursor

Spoken Word	Effect
Undo	Undoes the previous command
Unselect	Unselects the selected text
Up or GoUp	Moves the cursor up a line

I'm not saying it's easy to do all that. Remember, we're not talking *Star Trek* speech recognition here. This is the twenty-first century, not the twenty-fourth. It takes time, practice, training, and learning. But I'm not talking months and years of practice, as when learning a musical instrument. I'm talking about minutes and hours, which is a small price to pay if you want to dictate text to your computer.

There are plenty of things you can do to improve the accuracy of dictated text, as we'll discuss in the following sections.

Making corrections to dictated text

The Correction button on the Language bar is useful for making corrections to spoken text, while at the same time helping speech recognition to better understand your voice. You need to be in Dictation mode to use Correction, and you can only use it on dictated words. Here's how:

1. In your document, click on the word that speech recognition misinterpreted.

2. Click the Correction button in the Language bar, or press ⊞+C. A menu of options, including possible other words appears, as in the example shown in Figure 9-22. You have three options at that point:

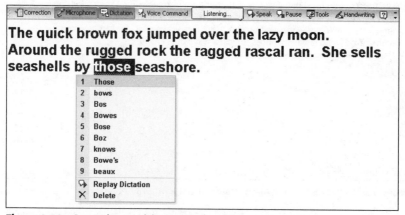

Figure 9-22: Correcting a misinterpreted word

- If the correct word appears in the menu, click that word.

- To hear what speech recognition heard, click Replay Dictation.

- To delete the word, click Delete.

Stopping speech recognition

Keep in mind that your microphone picks up every word you say, even casual remarks spoken to passersby. If you're going to speak words that you don't want the computer to hear, click the Microphone button in the Language bar to temporarily turn off speech recognition. To resume, just click the Microphone button a second time.

Increasing dictation accuracy

The more you train speech recognition to recognize your voice, the more accurately it will dictate your spoken words. It helps to understand that speech recognition contains a dictionary of spoken words. As it interprets your text, it relies on words from the dictionary, as well as the order of words you've spoken. Thus, it's much better at recognizing dictionary words than it is at recognizing proper names like Guinevere and Magillicuddy.

Adding words to the dictionary

If you often use nondictionary terms in your documents, and speech recognition keeps misinterpreting them, you can add those words to the speech dictionary. Doing so will greatly help speech recognition to recognize those words. There are a couple of ways to add words to the dictionary.

If you've already dictated a document and corrected all the mistakes, you can choose Tools ⇨ Learn from Document from the Language bar. When you do, Windows will create the list of all unrecognized terms from the document and display them in a dialog box, like the one shown in Figure 9-23.

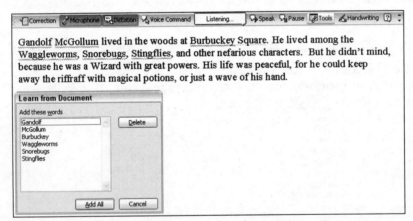

Figure 9-23: Finding unrecognized words in a document

You won't actually do anything with the words at this point. You'll just be saving them to the dictionary. You can then pronounce those words, later, to train speech recognition to understand them when you say them. If you see any words in the list that you don't want to train, click that word and then click the Delete button. When the list contains only the words you want to dictate, click Add All. Then, at your leisure, you can pronounce those words for the speech dictionary using the feature described next.

Pronouncing new words for the dictionary

To make new words for the speech dictionary recognizable, you'll need to pronounce them for the dictionary. It's not necessary to use the Learn from Document option first. You can add and pronounce any word at any time. Again, the purpose of all off this is to increase speech recognition's accuracy in translating your spoken text to words.

To pronounce words, you'll need to don your headset. Then, open a speech-enabled program such as Microsoft Word and turn on the microphone (click the Microphone button in the Language bar). The Add/Delete Words dialog box shown in Figure 9-24 opens.

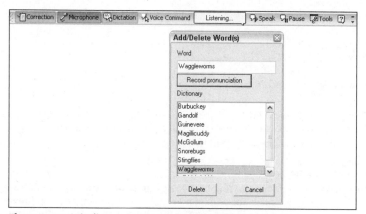

Figure 9-24: Finding unrecognized words in a document

To add a new word to the speech dictionary, click on the word you want to pronounce in the list of words. Or, if the word you want to pronounce isn't in the list, just type the word you want to add into the Word text box. Finally, click the Record Pronunciation button and say the word. If there are any words in the list that you want to remove, just click that word and click the Delete button.

You can add and pronounce as many, or as few, words as you wish. When you're done, just click the Close button at the bottom of the Add/Delete Words dialog box. To try out the new words, get the cursor into a Word document, click the Dictation button in the Language bar, and say the word.

Then, click on any listed word to put it in the Word textbox. Or, if the word isn't listed, type the word into the Word textbox. Next, click the Record Pronunciation button and say the word. Hopefully, the speech dictionary will correctly translate the word from now on.

Doing more training sessions

Speech recognition training is a two way street. The more you teach it to recognize your voice, the more it trains you to use speech recognition. The more time you spend training, the less time you'll have to spend correcting dictation errors. To can do extra speech training at any time. Just put on your headset, turn on the microphone, and choose Tools ⇨ Training from the Language bar. You'll see the dialog box shown in Figure 9-25.

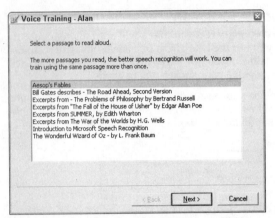

Figure 9-25: Extra training for speech recognition

Click on any passage to read aloud—it doesn't matter which. The more you do, the better. Then click the Next button and follow the instructions on the screen. Each session will take five or ten minutes. Every minute you spend will lead to easier, more accurate speech recognition.

Getting more information

Different programs support speech recognition in slightly different ways. For example, every program will have its own unique words for commands and cursor movements. To fully take advantage of speech recognition in the program you're currently using, search that program's help for *speech recognition*.

For example, if you want to use speech recognition in Microsoft Excel 2003, start Excel and choose Help ➪ Microsoft Excel Help from its menu bar. Type speech recognition as the text to search for, and then press Enter or click the Go button. You'll probably get links to lots of Help pages. The more of those you read, the better off you'll be.

And don't forget about the Microsoft Office Web site. There's always plenty of useful assistance and training there. To get to the site, just choose Help ➪ Microsoft Office Online from any Office program's menu bar. Or browse to http://office.microsoft.com. Search the Web site for speech recognition, and read whatever pages look interesting. The more you know about speech recognition, the better it will work for you.

Reading Documents Aloud

Text-to-Speech (TTS) is a text service that allows your computer to read text aloud from Microsoft Office documents. This is obviously of great value to anyone with visual impairments. It's also a good tool for preschool children who haven't yet learned to read. For a writer, it's a good way to review your own text without actually reading it. Because as every writer knows, when you try to edit your own text, you tend to read what you *think* you said, which may not be what you actually *did* say.

Text-to-Speech works from a *TTS engine*, which is a program containing a synthesized voice and lots of words. Windows XP comes with a basic TTS engine, which is probably already installed on your computer. In addition to the freebie engine that comes with XP, you can buy third-party engines with different voices, different spoken languages, and even engines that contain jargon from specific professions such as law, medicine, and computer science.

Tip   Microsoft's main Web page for speech, in general, is located at www.microsoft.com/ speech. Third-party engines are listed at www.microsoft.com/speech/evaluation/ thirdparty/engines.asp.

Despite all that technical-sounding stuff, Text-to-Speech is usually simple to use. First, you'll need some text on the screen to read, within a speech-enabled program. You can open up any Microsoft Word document that already contains text for starters.

Then, make sure that you can see the Language bar and the Text-to-Speech buttons, as shown back in Figure 9-16, and described under "Choosing Language bar buttons." Finally, click the Speak button in the Language bar. You should hear the text being read aloud starting at the cursor position.

To pause Text-to-Speech, click the Pause button in the Language bar. To resume reading, click the Resume button. To stop reading, click the Stop button. That's about all there is to it.

If it doesn't work, check for the obvious problems. For example, does your computer have a sound card installed and speakers connected? Are the speakers turned on? Is the volume set high enough to hear the spoken text? Is the voice being played in headphones that aren't on your head?

Note   For more information on sound and volume control, see Chapter 38. For sound troubleshooting, see Chapter 43.

Reading E-Books Aloud

E-books (electronic books, also called *digital books*), are the computer versions of their printed counterparts. Most bibliophiles, who love a good old-fashioned book, will scoff at the idea of downloading a book, or having it delivered on a CD. However, e-books do have certain advantages, such as:

✦ E-books generally cost less than their printed counterparts.

✦ You can buy and download an e-book on the spot, without leaving your chair.

✦ E-books don't take up any space on your bookshelf.

✦ You can search the entire book for any word or phrase in two seconds flat (great for reference books).

✦ A computer can read the book aloud to you.

The last part may take a little extra software. But the software is free, and you can download that right on the spot as well. The program I'm referring to is called Microsoft Reader, and there are versions of it available for standard desktop and laptops PCs, Pocket PCs, and tablet PCs. You can learn about the different readers from www.microsoft.com/reader.

The last time I checked, Microsoft actually recommended a couple of free downloads for Reader on desktop and laptop PCs. The first is the basic reader without Text-to-Speech capabilities, which I found at www.microsoft.com/reader/info/pc.asp. You need to download and install that one first. Complete instructions are available at the bottom of the page.

The second component is the Text-to-Speech Package for Reader, which I found at www.microsoft.com/reader/developers/downloads/tts.asp. Again, complete instructions for downloading and installing are at the bottom of the page.

URLs do change. If you don't find the free readers at the Web pages mentioned here, just go to the www.microsoft.com/reader Web site and start from there. Or, go to http://search.microsoft.com and search for XP download microsoft reader.

Once you've downloaded and installed both programs, the rest is easy:

1. Click the **Start** button, and choose **All Programs ➪ Microsoft Reader**.

2. To try it out, click on the **Microsoft Reader Help** book at the top of the page.

3. Click on **Go To** and choose **Begin Reading**.

With the Text-to-Speech component installed, you'll get some simple tools for at the bottom of each page for reading aloud, flipping through pages, and annotating the text, as shown in Figure 9-26.

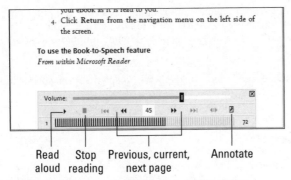

Figure 9-26: Extra training for speech recognition

With or without the Text-to-Speech component, you can still easily search a book, jump to section of the book, choose a text size, and add notes, highlights, and bookmarks. You can even shop for, and download, e-books right from the Reader window. It's so easy to use, you'll have it working like a champ in minutes.

You can also purchase and download books from all the usual booksellers, including www.amazon.com. But make sure that you download books specifically for Microsoft Reader.

Using Handwriting Recognition

Handwriting recognition lets you enter text by writing, rather than by typing. It can also be used to convert handwritten notes from a handheld or pocket PC into Microsoft Word as typed text. As with speech recognition, handwriting recognition isn't a feature of Windows XP per se. Rather, you install a handwriting recognition engine in Windows. Then, you can use that in any programs that support handwritten input.

Here I'm talking about handwriting recognition with a Windows XP Home Edition or Profession Edition on a standard desktop or notebook PC. A tablet PC, of course, basically *is* a tablet, and no extra hardware is required.

You can actually do handwriting with your mouse, by holding down the primary mouse button as you move the mouse to write the characters you want. It isn't easy, but it is possible. More realistically, you'll probably want to use some kind of handwriting input tool, such as a pen stylus and tablet. You can also use more advanced 3-D drawing and CAD tablets. In case you've never seen such devices, Figure 9-27 shows a couple of examples from Wacom Technology Corp. (www.wacom.com). On the left is the Wacom Graphire tablet. On the right, Wacom's fancier PL 500 LCD tablet.

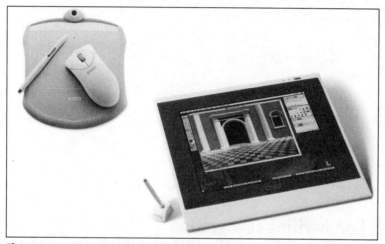

Figure 9-27: Wacom Inc.'s Graphire (left) and PL 500 LCD (right) tablets

Handwriting recognition requirements

Handwriting recognition doesn't require extensive processor speed or memory. So, it will work in any computer that's capable of running Windows XP. You will, however, need a *handwriting recognition engine*. Windows XP doesn't provide such an engine. However, many modern computers come with such an engine already built in. Microsoft Office XP (a.k.a. Office 2002) and Office 2003 come with a handwriting recognition engine that you can install. To see if you already have an engine installed:

1. Click the **Start** button and choose **Control Panel**.

2. If Control Panel opens in Category View, click on **Date, Time, and Regional Options**.

3. Open the **Regional and Language Options** icon.

4. Click on the **Languages** tab.

5. Click on the **Details** button.

If handwriting recognition is already installed, you'll see it listed under Installed Services, as in Figure 9-28. In that case, skip the section on installing handwriting recognition, which follows.

Before you install, or use, handwriting recognition, click Cancel in both open dialog boxes. Then, close Control Panel.

Figure 9-28: Text Services and Input
Languages dialog box

Installing handwriting recognition

Even though you install and manage handwriting recognition in Windows XP, you actually use it in handwriting-enabled programs, such as those that come with Microsoft Office. In fact, you need Microsoft Office or some other enabled program to install the capability. If you installed Microsoft Office yourself, you'll need your original Office CD to complete the installation. If Office came preinstalled on your computer, you may not need the original CD. But you should keep it handy, just in case. To install handwriting recognition, follow these steps:

1. Click the **Start** button and choose **Control Panel**.

2. Open the **Add or Remove Programs** icon.

3. Click on **Microsoft Office** *whatever* (where *whatever* is XP, 2003, Standard, Professional, or some combination thereof).

4. Click the **Change** button that appears.

5. Choose **Add or Remove Features**, and then click **Next**.

6. Click the + signs next to **Office Shared Features** and **Alternative User Input**.

7. Click the icon to the left of **Handwriting**, and choose **Run from My Computer**.

8. Click the **Update** button, and follow any instructions that appear on the screen.

9. Close the Add or Remove Programs window and Control Panel.

When the engine is installed, follow these steps to activate handwriting recognition:

1. Click the **Start** button and choose **Control Panel.**

2. If Control Panel opens in Category View, click on **Date, Time, and Regional Options.**

3. Open the **Regional and Language Options** icon.

4. Click on the **Languages** tab.

5. Click on the **Details** button.

6. Click the **Add** button.

7. Choose (check) the **Handwriting recognition** checkbox.

8. Click the **OK** button in each open dialog box, and then close Control Panel.

Windows is out of the picture from this point on. Programs that support handwriting will be able to use handwriting recognition. If you're using a tablet, you'll probably be able to use the pen instead of a mouse to click, drag, and so forth. But exactly how things play out from here depends on the hardware you're using and the handwriting-enabled program that you're using at the moment. The best I can do is provide some general guidelines and present an example.

Using handwriting recognition

When you start a program that supports handwriting recognition, the Language bar will appear on the screen. (If you have any problems getting the Language bar to appear, see "Using the Language Bar" section in this chapter.) To use handwriting recognition, click on the Handwriting button, and then choose an option from the menu shown in Figure 9-29. The options available to you depend on many factors, including the hardware connected to your computer and the program you're using at the moment. Some possibilities are listed below:

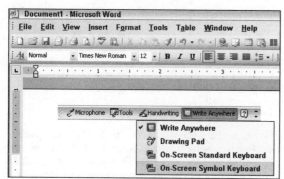

Figure 9-29: Sample drop-down menu under Handwriting on the Language bar

✦ **Writing Pad:** Opens a window that accepts handwriting separate from the program you're using at the moment. Clicking the Recognize Now button converts the handwriting to typed text and places it within the program or document you're working with.

✦ **Write Anywhere:** Accepts handwritten input anywhere within the document, rather than in a separate pad.

✦ **Drawing Pad:** Opens a pad in which you can draw, rather than write, using your tablet or mouse.

✦ **On-Screen Standard Keyboard:** Places an image of a standard keyboard on the screen, so that you can tap keys with your pen and tablet to type.

✦ **On-Screen Symbol Keyboard:** Same as the previous option, but the keyboard displays special characters rather than standard text.

As a brief example, I will demonstrate using a tablet and writing pad for handwriting recognition in Microsoft Word. Though I must confess, my tablet handwriting is so bad that it's a miracle that any program in the world can recognize it. (I suspect it has something to do with the fact that my drawing abilities fall somewhere between "stick man" and "none.") So, it's not with any great pride that I expose by dreadful tablet writing to you here. This isn't so much an example of "how to do it" as it is a demonstration of how it works.

For the example I connected a tablet to my computer's USB port, started Microsoft Word, and then clicked the Handwriting button on the Language bar and chose Writing Pad. Doing so opened the writing pad shown in Figure 9-30 (but without the handwritten text showing yet).

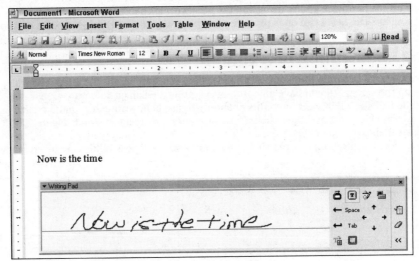

Figure 9-30: Handwritten text converted to typed text

Next came the task of handwriting. I scratched out the words *Now is the time*, as you can see in the figure (yes, that supposedly reads *Now is the time*). Miraculously, handwriting recognition instantly placed those very words right into the document, just above the writing pad. And that, in a nutshell, if how handwriting recognition works: You write; it types what you write.

But again, that's really just a small, simple example. Once you've installed handwriting recognition in Windows XP, exactly how and when you use it depends on many factors. Your best resource for information on that is the documentation for the tablet you're using, as well as the Help in the handwriting-enabled program you're using at the moment.

Multiple-Language Keyboarding

For people who work in multiple languages, Windows XP offers some handy options for adjusting your keyboard to work in a specific language. These features are especially useful for translators who need to switch from one language to another quickly, using a single PC and keyboard.

Multiple-language keyboard features also offer rapid font substitution when switching among different languages. Also, sorting and comparison rules can easily be adopted for different locales and cultures

The options for controlling language-related keyboard options are in the Text Services dialog box. To get to it from the Language bar, click the Tools button and choose Settings. Then, click the Language Bar option in the dialog box that opens. If the Language bar isn't available, you can take the long route:

1. Click the **Start** button and choose **Control Panel**.

2. If Control Panel opens in Category view, then click the **Date, Time, Language, and Regional Options** category name.

3. Open the **Regional and Language Options** icon.

4. Click the **Languages** tab, and then click the **Details** button.

Whichever method you use to get to the dialog box, you should see a language abbreviation and name near the top of the Installed Services list. Also, you should see the word *Keyboard* listed with an abbreviation beneath that. For example, in Figure 9-31 the top line shows *EN English (United States)*, and the letters *US* appear under the Keyboard heading.

Figure 9-31: Text Services and Input Languages dialog box

Notice the Add button to the right of Installed Services. That's the tool you'll use to add alternative keyboard layouts for other languages to your system.

Setting keyboard languages and layouts

To add another language to your list of installed services, follow these steps from the dialog box shown in Figure 9-31:

1. Close all open program windows, saving any work in progress (but don't close the Text Services dialog box).

2. Grab your original Microsoft Windows XP CD-ROM.

3. Click the **Add** button.

4. In the Add Input Language dialog box that opens, click the **Input Language** drop-down list, shown in Figure 9-32, and choose the language you want to install.

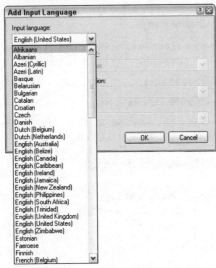

Figure 9-32: The Add Input Language
dialog box

5. Choose a keyboard layout for the currently selected language, and choose **OK**.

6. Repeat Steps 2 and 3 to add as many languages as you want.

7. If you want to use a shortcut key for switching languages, click the **Key Settings** button. Then, choose the options you prefer.

8. If you want to switch languages by clicking an icon on the taskbar, click the Language Bar button and choose your preferred options.

9. Choose **OK** in each open dialog box when you finish making your selections.

If any additional instructions appear onscreen, be certain to read and follow them.

Switching among languages and layouts

After you install languages and keyboard layouts, switching among them is easy. If you selected "Enable indicator on taskbar" while you chose layouts, you see a two-letter abbreviation at the right end of the taskbar indicating which language is currently in use—for example, En if you're working in English.

To switch to another language and keyboard layout, do either of the following:

✦ Click the language indicator in the taskbar and then click the language you want to use (see Figure 9-33).

✦ Press the shortcut key you specified in Step 7 to cycle through installed languages.

Figure 9-33: Language name at the left of the Language bar

Now you can fire up your word processing program and type with the currently selected language and keyboard layout. In fact, you can switch to another language and layout on the spot. Anything new you type will use the language, layout, and (if applicable) font for that language. In a true multilingually aware program, you can even select existing text and change it to whatever language and font you're currently using.

Removing languages

If ever you decide to eliminate a foreign language keyboard layout, return to the Text Services dialog box. Click any language option you want to eliminate, and click the Remove button. Then, click the OK button to save your changes and close the dialog box.

Wrap Up

Needless to say, Windows XP offers many alternatives to the mouse, monitor, and keyboard for getting information into, and out of, a PC. I don't know about you, but I got to have some fun, kicked back with my feet up on the desk, dictating parts of this chapter into Microsoft Word. To summarize the many topics covered here:

✦ The Accessibility options in Control Panel and on the Accessories menu offer mouse, keyboard, and monitor adjustments as aids for those with specific sensory and motor impairments.

✦ Microsoft Magnifier acts as a magnifying glass for any portion of the screen.

✦ MouseKeys lets you use your keyboard as mouse, while On-Screen Keyboard lets you use your mouse as keyboard.

✦ The Language bar acts as the gateway to speech recognition, Text-to-Speech, and handwriting recognition.

✦ Speech recognition lets you dictate text into Microsoft Word and other programs in the Microsoft Office Suite.

✦ Text-to-Speech can read text aloud from Microsoft Word documents.

✦ For reading e-books aloud, Microsoft offers the free Microsoft Reader and Reader Text-to-Speech downloads from its Web site.

✦ Handwriting recognition provides a means of converting handwritten text to typed text, and it works with a variety of PC tablets.

✦ Mutliple-language keyboarding lets you adapt your keyboard to different languages and keyboard layouts on the fly.

✦ ✦ ✦

Setting Up Multiple Monitors

Your Windows desktop is a lot smaller that your real, wooden desktop. So when you're working in multiple programs, you usually have to stack program windows one atop the other. Although it's easy to switch among those open windows using taskbar buttons or the Alt+Tab keys, it's often nice to be able to see more than one thing at a time. One way to get more desktop real estate is to increase your screen resolution. But there's a limit to how far you can take that, because the higher you set your screen resolution, the smaller everything looks on the screen.

The alternative is to add more monitors, which you can do in several ways. Some computers, particularly laptops, often come with a second monitor plug already installed. If your computer has one only one monitor port (plug), you can always add more ports and more monitors. As you've probably figured out by now, different ways of expanding your desktop real estate and adding monitors is what this chapter is all about.

Using DualView

DualView is the generic term for two-monitor systems based on a single graphics card. However, it's also the general term used for the setup used on many laptops that have an extra VGA, DVI, or TV Out port on the back for connecting an external monitor or TV. In the laptop scenario, the fold-up LCD monitor is the primary monitor that always works. The extra external port is optional, and the primary monitor works fine with or without a TV or monitor plugged into that second port.

Having two standard monitors allows you to treat the two monitors as one large desktop. This is often handy for using programs like Microsoft Excel, in which you need a lot of width or height to see all the cells in a worksheet. You can stretch Excel across the two monitors, doubling its normal width, as shown in Figure 10-1.

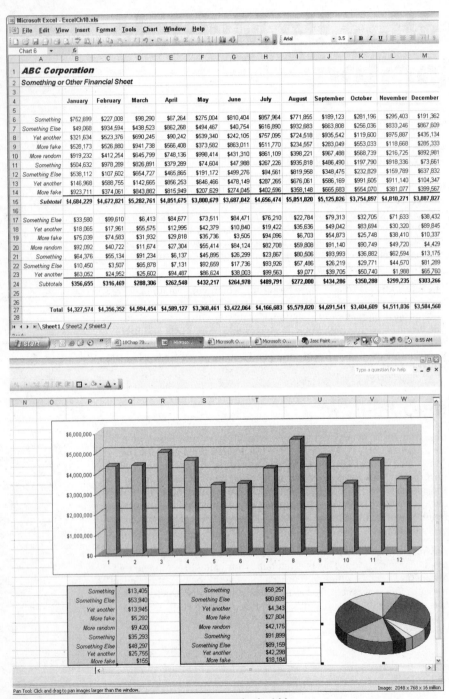

Figure 10-1: Excel worksheet at twice the standard width

Because there are two monitors involved, half the worksheet will be on one monitor, and the other half on the other monitor, as in Figure 10-2. But the two monitors act as one. For example, when you move the mouse pointer of the right edge of the left monitor, it instantly appears on the right monitor. You can move the mouse pointer and drag things about on the two monitors as though they were just a single extra-wide monitor. It's as easy as it could possibly be, and it doesn't take long to feel as though you're just using a single superwide monitor.

Figure 10-2: Single worksheet split across two monitors

You're certainly not limited to having a single program window stretched across two monitors. You can have as many program windows open as you wish and arrange them however you want on the giant desktop. For example, Figure 10-3 shows a two-monitor desktop with Microsoft Access open at left, the VBA Editor for Access on the right, and Media Player in a skin between the two. You can also see some desktop icons above the Start button.

Of course, the desktop in Figure 10-3 would be split across two monitors, with about half of Media Player on one monitor and the other half on the other monitor. But it doesn't take long before you stop "seeing" the desktop as two separate monitors. Because they work as one desktop, you tend to see things as shown in Figures 10-1 and 10-3. And you also use them as one large desktop, because that's how they work.

Activating the second monitor

With DualView, you can set the resolution and color depth of each monitor independently. You use the Settings tab in Display Properties just as you would with a single monitor. But there will be two monitor icons rather than one on the tab. You get to the Display Properties dialog box in the usual way. The quick route is to right-click the desktop and choose Properties. However, you can also open the Display Properties dialog box from the Display icon in Control Panel. (If Control Panel opens in Category view, you have to click the Appearance and Themes category name first). Then, click the Settings tab in the dialog box. You'll see a box for each monitor, as shown in Figure 10-4.

On the Settings tab, you work with each monitor independently. You choose which monitor you want to work with by clicking its "box image," or by choosing its name from the Display drop-down list. For example, In Figure 10-4, I'm working with the second monitor, as indicated by the larger border around that image.

If you have two monitors connected and one is blank, the first thing you need to do is click that monitor's box and choose Extend my Windows desktop onto this monitor. If you don't, that monitor will remain blank, which doesn't do you any good at all.

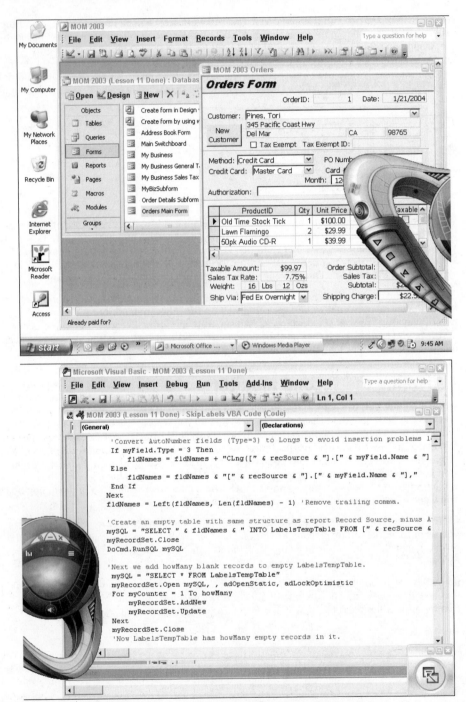

Figure 10-3: Multiple program windows on a double-wide desktop

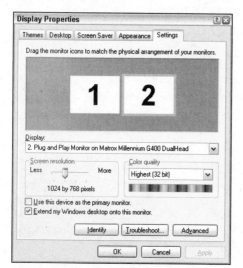

Figure 10-4: Settings tab of the Display Properties dialog box

Arranging the monitors

You can choose which monitor will act as the *primary monitor*. The primary monitor is the one that shows the Welcome screen at startup and also the desktop icons. (If you're really into desktop icons, you can fill up both monitors with icons.) The taskbar tends to stick to the primary monitor as well. But, once the taskbar is unlocked, you can drag it and position wherever you like, on either monitor.

Note   The Settings tab is strictly for choosing the resolution, color quality, and basic arrangement of the monitors. To decide what windows will appear where, you just work straight from the desktop, moving and sizing things exactly as you would on a single monitor. See the "Arranging items on the desktop" section that follows.

The arrangement of the boxes at the top of the Settings dialog box needs to match the actual arrangement of your monitors, otherwise things can get confusing. For example, if monitor 2 in Figure 10-4 were actually to the left of monitor 1, then everything would seem out of whack. You'd either need to switch the plugs from the monitors so the boxes really do match the physical arrangement of the monitors or drag box number 2 over to the left of box number 1.

To see which box represents which physical monitor, click the Identity button. Each monitor will display an enormous number 1 or 2 to let you know which box number represents which monitor. You can also place the mouse pointer on either numbered box and hold down the left mouse button to see the giant 1 or 2 on that monitor. The main idea here is to get those boxes to reflect how the monitors are actually arranged on your desk.

For example, if you have the monitors arranged vertically on shelves, rather than side by side, then you want to arrange the boxes to match that. This is a simple matter of placing the mouse pointer right on the box and dragging it into position. For example, if monitor 1 is actually above monitor 2 on the shelf, then you want to drag the 1 box so that it's above the 2 box, as in Figure 10-5.

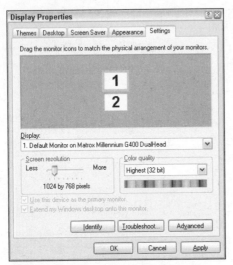

Figure 10-5: Box arrangement for two monitors arranged vertically

Setting monitor resolution and color quality

Each monitor has its own screen resolution and color quality settings. To set a monitor's resolution and color quality, first click on that monitor's box. Then, adjust the Screen resolution and Color quality settings for that one monitor. Click the other box and do the same for that monitor.

If you're going for the standard extra-wide desktop look, then you'll probably want to make each monitor's resolution and color depth the same. For example, in Figures 10-1 and 10-3, I have each monitor set to 1024×768 with a color 32-bit color depth. But there's no rule that says you have to make the two monitors the same. And of course, you're not making any bog commitment when you set a monitor's resolution and color depth. You can go into the Display Properties dialog box and change things around whenever you want.

If you're a Web page or software developer and want to know how things will look at both 1024×768 and 800×600 resolutions, just set the two monitors accordingly. For example, in Figure 10-6 I've reduced the screen resolution of monitor 2 to 800×600.

Tip

As is always the case in dialog boxes, any changes you make on the Settings tab won't actually be applied until you click the Apply or OK button. The only difference between the two buttons is that OK also closes the dialog box, while Apply leaves the dialog box open.

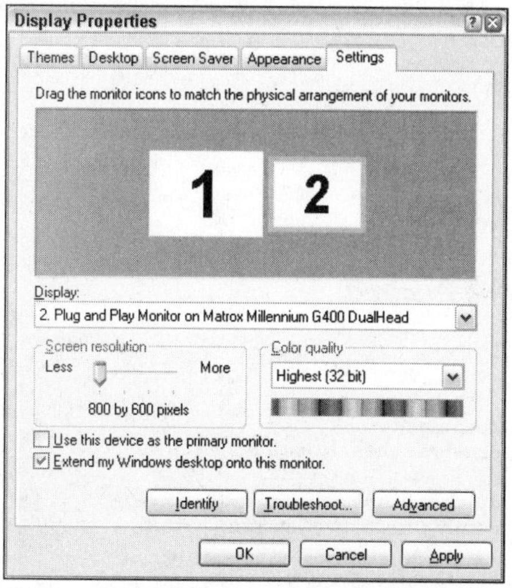

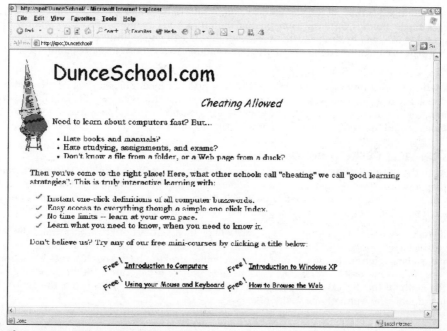

Figure 10-6: Monitor 2 reduced to 800 × 600

When you're done, just open two instances of the Web page (or whatever you're creating). Put one on the 1024 × 768 monitor and the other on the 800 × 600 monitor, and maximize each program window. You'll be able to see, at once, how it looks at both resolutions. I can't really show much of an example here, because the figures have to be reduced to fit in the book. But just to give you the general idea, Figure 10-7 shows a hypothetical Web page at 1024 × 768. Figure 10-8 shows the same Web page at 800 × 600. (The page doesn't actually exist on the Web either—I just threw it together to create the example.)

Figure 10-7: Web page at 1024 × 768

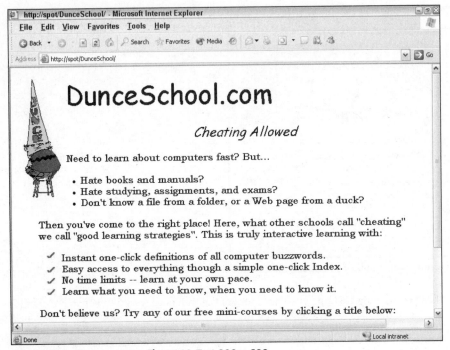

Figure 10-8: Same page as Figure 10-7 at 800 × 600

Arranging items on the desktop

As mentioned earlier, all the standard techniques for moving and sizing programs windows on a single monitor work the same on dual monitors. You can move a program window wherever you like, just by dragging its title bar off the edge of one monitor and onto the other. You can also size most (though not all) program windows to span two or more monitors.

As always, you can't move or size a maximized program window. You'll have to shrink the window down a bit first by clicking its Restore button or by double-clicking its title bar. If you do maximize a program window that spans two monitors, the window will likely fill just one monitor. If it doesn't fill the monitor you intended, shrink it down, move it over to the other monitor, and then maximize the window on that monitor.

DualView desktop background

As to the desktop itself, you can choose a picture for the desktop from the Desktop tab of the Display Properties dialog box, as usual. Exactly how that picture appears depends on several things. If you choose the Stretch or Center Position option, the picture will appear once on each monitor. In other words, you'll see two copies of the same picture, one on each monitor.

If you choose the Tile position, the picture will be tiled across both monitors. But if the picture is large enough, it will appear as a single picture spread across both monitors. If you have a large picture that you want to use as a single desktop background across both monitors, and you want it to fit exactly, you'll need to presize the picture to fit the desktop. Doing the math for that is fairly simple. If the monitors are side by side, the width of the desktop is just double the width of one desktop.

TV Displays

Some graphics cards and computers come with a standard VGA port for connecting a monitor and a second port for connecting a television. Analog TVs make for lousy computer monitors. The intent of the TV Out plug is for actually watching TV, because the graphics card has a TV tuner built in. In most cases, you can also use the connected TV to display video from the computer. For example, if you're creating a movie in Windows Movie Maker that you intend to copy to DVD or VHS tape, you can use the TV to preview how your movie will look when played on TV.

There's really nothing in Windows XP that deals with the TV Out option directly. And there's no "one rule fits all" that applies to the dozens (or hundreds) of different products that offer that capability. The only place to get information on that is from the manual that came with the product or the product manufacturer's Web site. The only thing I can tell you with any confidence is that trying to figure out how it works by guessing may not be productive or fun.

For example, if each monitor is set to 1024×768, then the size of the desktop is 2048×768. If each monitor is set to 800×600, then the size of the desktop is 1600×600. If you start with a small picture and try to enlarge it to such a large size, you'll get a lot of pixilation and the picture might not look so good. But if you start with a large picture, such as something from a 5-megapixel camera or a full-resolution photo from the Hubble space telescope (http://hubble.gsfc.nasa.gov), you should have no problem sizing the picture.

Note

In the preceding paragraph, I'm assuming that you have a decent graphics program and know how to use it. You'll need to crop the picture to the rectangular shape of the desktop, as well as size it, if you want a perfect fit.

Figure 10-9 shows an example where I cropped and sized a large high-resolution Hubble picture to 1600×800 to fit two 800×600 monitors. After I created the image, it was a simple matter of choosing it as the image from the Desktop tab in Display Properties and setting the Position option to Tile. (The icons are standard desktop icons. The two open programs on the desktop are Windows Media Player in a skin, and Calculator.)

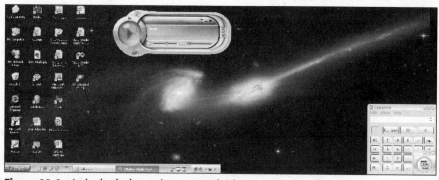

Figure 10-9: A single desktop picture stretched across two monitors

DualView screen captures

Screen captures with DualView are similar to normal single-monitor screen captures. Pressing Print Screen (Prnt Scrn) captures the entire desktop as one large image. For example, to create Figures 10-1, 10-3, and 10-9, I just pressed Print Screen, opened up my trusty graphics editor (Jasc Paint Shop Pro), and pressed Ctrl+V to paste the screenshot into an editable image. The size of the image matches the size of the desktop; 2048 × 768 for the 1024 × 768 resolutions, and 1600 × 600 for the 800 × 600 resolutions.

Regardless of how many monitors you have, only one program will be in the active window at a time. The keyboard still applies only to the active window. So to capture a single program window, as in Figures 10-7 and 10-8, I pressed Alt+Print Screen (which always captures the active window only).

Adding More Monitors

Regardless of how many graphics ports and monitors you have right now, if it's a desktop computer, you can always add more. Theoretically, you can have up to 10 monitors per PC. Personally, however, I've never had more than four going at a time. Each monitor will need a graphics card, except in the case where you're using a dual-head, triple-head, or quad-head video card. The generic buzzword (on Microsoft's site) for multiple video cards is *multiple monitors* rather than DualView.

Tip   Matrox (www.matrox.com) makes several models of multihead graphics card. All the screenshots earlier in this chapter are from a Matrox Millenium G400 DualHead graphics card. As I write this, Microsoft has some additional XP-compatible multihead cards listed at http://support.microsoft.com/default.aspx?scid=kb;en-us;307397. The page is already dated, however, as many newer-model cards aren't listed on the page.

Adding more monitors by using a multihead graphics card is relatively simple. You just install the card and software per the manufacturer's instructions. Then, you can manage the monitors using the Settings tab in the Display Properties dialog box, exactly as described in the preceding sections.

Things get a bit more complicated, however, when you start adding multiple video cards to a computer. Often it's as easy as installing the card and activating it in the Settings tab in the Display Properties dialog box, as described previously in this chapter. But sometimes getting the cards to work is a real nightmare. That's especially true if one of the monitors is connected to an on-board graphics device rather than a video card.

You can tell whether or not your computer has an on-board graphics device or card just by looking at the back of the computer. If the VGA or DVI port that the monitor plugs into isn't on an expansion card, then it's an on-board graphics device. If the VGA port is in with the expansion slots, then it's a graphics card, most likely an AGP or PCI card.

On most motherboards, the innermost slot is an AGP (Accelerated Graphics Port) slot. So if your VGA plug is in that first slot, your computer most likely has an AGP graphics card installed. The remaining slots are usually PCI (Peripheral Component Interconnect slots). PCI graphics cards are becoming rare, so it's unlikely that a newer computer would use a PCI graphics card. The most likely scenario is either an on-board VGA port or a VGA port on an AGP card. The computer in Figure 10-10 has an on-board graphics device. The AGP port and six PCI slots on that computer are currently empty.

VGA versus DVI

I tend to refer to the plug that the monitor plugs into as the VGA port here. (VGA stands for Video Graphics Array and is the most widely used standard in the PC industry.) There are plenty of graphics cards that offer a DVI port in place of, or in addition to, a VGA port. The main difference is that the VGA port is the one for used for standard CRT (cathode ray tube) monitors.

The DVI (Digital Video Interface) port is used with digital flat panel monitors. But everything I say about VGA ports in this chapter should apply to DVI ports as well. Matrox (www.matrox.com) makes several graphics cards with multiple DVI ports. Cyberguys (www.cyberguys.com) sells some really cool stands for holding two, three, or four digital monitors Search their site for *LCD mount* to see some examples.

You can use an on-board graphics card for one monitor in a multiple-monitor scenario, provided that on-board card is set to function as VGA. Because that's almost universally the case, it shouldn't be a problem. My laptop uses an on-board Intel Extreme Graphics device for the external monitor, and I know that's not a traditional AGP or PCI card.

Because there's no way for me to test all of the thousands of different makes and models of motherboards with on-board graphics, I couldn't bet my life on whether or not your particular on-board graphics device would work in a multimonitor setting. All you can do is try it. If the additional card doesn't work, you might have to disable the on-board graphics device in Device Manager.

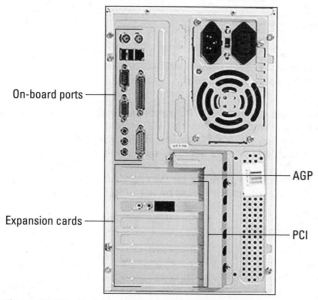

Figure 10-10: On-board versus expansion card ports

It never hurts to gather all the information you can about your current graphics device. You can use XP's System Information applet to get that information. Click the Start button and choose All Programs ➪ Accessories ➪ System Tools ➪ System Information. Click the + sign next to Components, and then click on Display. The brand name and model of the device is listed first next to *Name*. Figure 10-11 shows an example where the computer has a Matrox Millennium G400 DualHead card installed. (I happen to know it's an AGP card because I installed it myself.)

Finally, you should know how to get to, and use, the BIOS setup for your computer. There's a good chance that you'll have to make some changes there if you use both AGP and PCI graphics cards. And there's not much I can tell you about your BIOS, because it varies a lot from one computer to the next. Typically, you get to the BIOS setting by pressing F2 or Delete shortly after turning on the computer, but before Windows starts loading. It can be a narrow window of opportunity on computers that boot up rapidly. Once you're in the BIOS setup, you'll need to use your keyboard to get around.

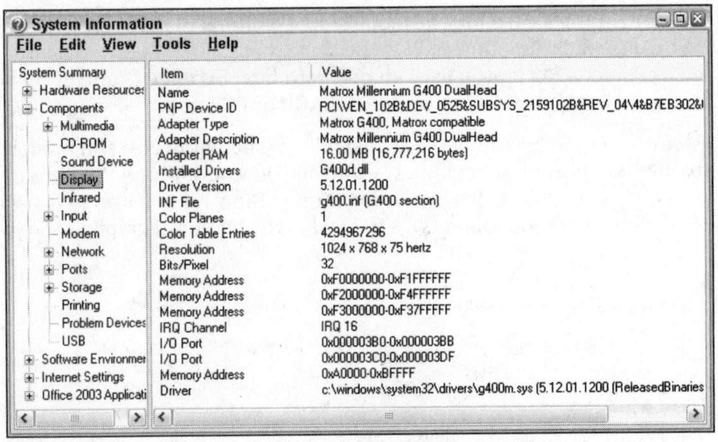

Figure 10-11: System Information on a graphics card

You can combine an AGP card with any number of PCI cards up to a maximum of nine VGA slots and monitors. For example, if you already have an AGP graphics card with one, two, three, or four heads (VGA ports), you can add PCI graphics cards until you've reached the maximum on nine VGA ports. But (and this is a big "but," no pun intended), according to the Microsoft's documentation at http://support.microsoft.com/default.aspx?scid=kb; en-us;296538, you must use Microsoft's XP driver for the every card. Although you can mix brands and models of cards, each card must be based on one of these chipsets:

3DFxVoodoo3 2000 AGP

3DFxVoodoo3 2000

3DFxVoodoo3 3000 AGP

3DFxVoodoo3 3000

3DFxVoodoo3 3500 TV

3DFxVoodoo4 4500 AGP

3DFxVoodoo4 4500

3DFxVoodoo5 5500 AGP

3DFxVoodoo5 5500

3DLabs Permedia2 Compatible Graphics Adapter

3DLabs Permedia2 Compatible Graphics Adapter

3DLabs Oxygen VX1 AGP

3DLabs Oxygen VX1 PCI

3DLabs Oxygen VX1 1600SW

3DLabs Permedia3 Create!

Accel Graphics AccelStar II AGP

Accel Graphics AccelStar II

Appian Graphics Jeronimo Pro

ATI RADEON DDR

ATI RADEON SDR

ATI All-in-Wonder Radeon AGP

ATI All-in-Wonder Radeon SDR AGP

ATI All-in-Wonder Radeon PCI

ATI RADEON VE

ATI RADEON M6

ATI RAGE 128 AIW AGP

ATI RAGE 128 AIW PCI

ATI RAGE 128 GL AGP

ATI RAGE 128 GL PCI

ATI RAGE 128 VR AGP

ATI RAGE 128 VR PCI

ATI RAGE 128 4X AGP

ATI RAGE 128 4X PCI

ATI RAGE 128 PRO PCI

ATI RAGE 128 PRO AGP 2X

ATI RAGE 128 PRO AGP 4X

Creative Labs Graphics Blaster Extreme

Creative Labs Graphics Blaster Extreme

Diamond Multimedia Fire GL1000 Pro AGP

Diamond Multimedia Fire GL1000 Pro

Digital Comet

Elsa GLoria Synergy AGP

Elsa WINNER 2000/Office AGP

Elsa GLoria Synergy

Elsa WINNER 2000/Office

Leadtek Winfast 3D L2300 AGP

Leadtek Winfast 3D L2300

Matrox Millennium G200 SD PCI

Matrox Marvel G200 PCI

Matrox MGA-G200 AGP

Matrox Mystique G200 AGP

Matrox Millennium G200 AGP

Matrox Marvel G200 AGP

Matrox Mystique G200 VIDEO AGP

Matrox Millennium G200 SG AGP

Matrox Millennium G200 SG LE AGP

Matrox Mystique G200 SD AGP

Matrox Millennium G200 SD AGP

Matrox Millennium G250 AGP

Matrox Millennium G250 LE AGP

Matrox G400 AGP

Matrox Marvel G400 AGP

Matrox Millennium G400 DualHead Max

Matrox Millennium G400 DualHead

Matrox Millennium G450 DualHead

Matrox Millennium G450 DualHead LE

Matrox Millennium G450 DualHead PCI

NVidia Riva TNT

NVidia Riva TNT2

NVidia Vanta

NVidia Riva TNT2 Ultra

NVidia Aladin TNT2

NVidia Riva TNT2 Model 64

NVidia GeForce 256

NVidia GeForce DDR

NVidia Quadro

NVidia GeForce2 GTS

NVidia GeForce2 Pro

NVidia GeForce2 Ultra

NVidia Quadro2 Pro

NVidia GeForce2 MX

NVidia GeForce2 Go

NVidia Quadro2 MXR

NVidia Geforce3

The only problem with this list is that it is not exhaustive, mainly because it was posted in July 2002. Many other compatible chipsets have been released since then, and many of them work. If you're thinking of buying an additional graphics card, you might want to check to manufacturer's Web site to see whether the card will be compatible with your existing cards.

Caution   Apparently Adobe Type Manager prevents you from using multiple monitors at all. So, if you have Adobe Type Manager, your only choices are to either forget about multiple monitors or uninstall Adobe Type Manager through Add/Remove Programs.

Adding a PCI graphics card

Whether or not you follow all the advice and specs, adding more monitors can still be a challenge. Case in point, after writing everything up to this point in this chapter, I set about adding a Chaintech GeForce FX5200 PCI graphics card to my system with the Matrox DualHead AGP card, to get a total of three monitors. The new card uses NVidia's GeForce FX Series chipset, which isn't in the list, so perhaps I was asking for trouble right there.

Things did not go well, but I want to tell you how I solved the problem because you may encounter a similar situation, and the solution might work for you. After installing the new card and driver and rebooting, the new third monitor showed only black with a big purple stripe down one side. When I tried to go into the Settings tab of Display Properties, I got an error message about the driver being outdated.

I downloaded and installed a new driver from Chaintech's Web site to no avail. I scanned Windows Update for new drivers, to no avail either. I downloaded the most recent driver from NVidia's Web site, and that didn't seem to help matters either. The NVidia driver had the most recent date on it, so I stuck with that one. Still, I encountered some weird stuff with only two of the three monitors lighting, usually just monitors 1 and 3.

Eventually I went for the slightly more extreme measure of disabling the Matrox card altogether via Device Manager (hoping I wouldn't end up with zero monitors working, which would make further progress a bit difficult). With the Matrox card disabled, Windows would have no choice but to try to boot up from the new PCI card. That worked, in that the new PCI card was working fine at that point. It's just that I was now down to one monitor.

At that point, I went back into Device Manager and enabled the Matrox DualHead card again. Then, I went back into Display Manager, choose the Matrox card and the "Extend my Windows desktop onto this monitor" option. That worked, only I found that I couldn't change the primary monitor. I could only keep all three monitors going if I left the PCI card selected as the primary monitor.

Even so, a later reboot got the whole problem going again. So, I finally broke down and started digging around that computer's BIOS setup. Under Advanced Chipset Features there, I changed the Init Display First option from AGP to PCI Slot. After saving the BIOS settings and rebooting, the weird things that were going on subsided, and things have remained stable and working.

So, I guess the moral of the story is that even if you read all the documentation, sometimes it's not enough. I think what really did it here was temporarily disabling the AGP card and rebooting with only the PCI card enabled That, and allowing the PCI card to be the primary display after reenabling the AGP card is what cinched the deal. To get the desktop icons onto the leftmost monitor, I just rearranged the plugs on the back of the computer to connect the leftmost monitor to the PCI card. So, now I have three monitors, each set to 1024 × 768, which means that my desktop is 3072 pixels wide and 768 pixels tall, as shown in Figure 10-12.

Figure 10-12: Desktop extending across three monitors

Using multiple monitors

As far as setting screen resolutions and color depths go, working with multiple monitors is the same as DualView. Each monitor is represented by a box on the Settings tab. You can choose any monitor to work with by clicking its box number, or by choosing its name from the Display drop-down list as shown in Figure 10-13.

Remember, you must choose each monitor and select "Extend my Windows desktop onto this monitor" for each monitor in the list. Any monitor that has that setting turned off will be black. Then, you can set the screen resolution and color quality of the selected monitor. The Advanced button at the bottom of the Settings tab displays options for the currently-selected graphics card only. For example, when I choose NVidia card from the Display drop-down list in Figure 10-13 I get settings that are unique to that card, as shown in Figure 10-14. If I choose the Matrox card, then click on Advanced, I get options for the Matrox card.

Tip   The Troubleshoot button on the Settings tab includes some help for solving DualView and multiple monitor problems. If you have a problem, consider using the Troubleshoot button as your first recourse.

In System Information, all cards will be listed on the Display option under Components. When you first click on Display, you'll probably see the specs for only one of the cards. Use the scroll bar on the right side of the window to see the specs on any additional installed cards.

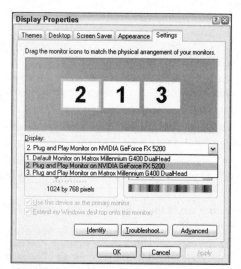

Figure 10-13: Settings tab in Display
Properties with three monitors

Once you have all the monitors arranged and working, everything I said about DualView
applies to multiple monitors as well. You just drag things about the desktop, and they'll automatically move from monitor to monitor. If you want to stretch a single desktop picture
across all of the monitors, you'll need to size that picture to the desktop, and choose the Tile
from the Position option.

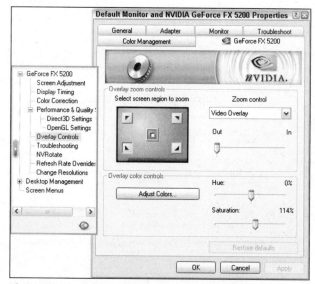

Figure 10-14: Advanced settings for my NVidia card

Wrap Up

If your workspace feels cramped on a single monitor, you can gain considerable elbow room by adding one or more additional monitors. All the action for enabling and configuring multiple monitors takes place in the Settings tab of the Display Properties dialog box. Moving and sizing things on the giant desktop is no different from doing so on a single monitor. To recap the main points:

✦ *DualView* is the general term for two monitors, usually in reference to a laptop with a built-in external monitor port or a single graphics card with two monitor ports.

✦ Simply connecting a second monitor isn't enough. You also have to go into the Settings tab in Display Properties and choose the "Extend my Windows desktop onto this monitor" option to get the second monitor to light up.

✦ On the Settings tab, you need to arrange the boxes that represent each monitor to match the physical arrangement of the monitors.

✦ Screen captures on multiple monitors are the same as with a single monitor. Pressing the Print Screen key captures a snapshot of the entire desktop to the Windows clipboard.

✦ The term *multiple monitors* is generally used when you're talking about using multiple graphics cards to support multiple monitors.

✦ Getting multiple monitors graphics cards to work can be tricky business, sometimes requiring some educated guesswork.

✦ Once you have multiple graphics cards installed and working, they'll work exactly the same as two monitors in a DualView scenario.

✦   ✦   ✦

Troubleshooting Customization Problems

Troubleshooting Desktop Customization

Some desktop troubleshooting really is a matter of knowing where to look for options that control the desktop appearance. If you've recently upgraded from an older version of Windows, you should know about many options. Here, we'll look at those options from a troubleshooting perspective.

Can't get taskbar back to one row

When you resize the taskbar, you can get into a situation where it seems as if you can't get the taskbar back to being just one row tall. It's "double or nothing" (either hidden or showing two rows). First, you need to make sure that the taskbar is unlocked so that you can see the dragging handles as in Figure 11-1.

Tip   To lock or unlock the taskbar, right-click the clock and choose Lock the Taskbar.

It might also help to temporarily remove any optional toolbars that you really don't need, just to give yourself some more elbow room. To hide an optional toolbar, right-click the clock, choose Toolbars, and click any selected (checked) toolbar that you don't really need at the moment.

Finally, drag the leftmost dragging handle on the bottom row to the right and then up into or to the right of Quick Launch buttons (or whatever is on the top row), as in the middle of Figure 11-1. From there, you should be able to drag the top of the toolbar down slightly to make the taskbar one row tall again, as in the bottom of Figure 11-1.

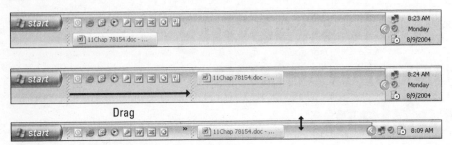

Figure 11-1: Get the taskbar down to one row.

Once you get things the way you want, consider locking the taskbar to avoid accidentally changing the taskbar.

Control Panel option on the Start Menu missing or wrong

If you don't see a Control Panel option on the right side of the Start menu, or if clicking the Control Panel option won't open Control Panel, do this:

1. Right-click the **Start** button and choose **Properties**.

2. Choose **Start Menu** (not Classic Start Menu), and then click the **Customize** button.

3. Click the **Advanced** tab in the Customize Start Menu dialog box that opens.

4. Choose **Display as Link** under **Control Panel**.

5. Click **OK** in each open dialog box.

Note   See also "Desktop Problems" in Chapter 5 for additional desktop troubleshooting techniques.

Can't drag items on the Start menu

Items on the right side of the Start menu can never be dragged up and down the menu. Icons on the All Programs menu and submenus can only be dragged if Start menu dragging is enabled. To enable dragging:

1. Right-click the **Start** button and choose **Properties**.

2. Choose **Start Menu** (not Classic Start Menu), and then click the **Customize** button.

3. Click the **Advanced** tab in the next dialog box that opens.

4. Choose (check) **Enable dragging and dropping**.

5. Click **OK** in each open dialog box.

Troubleshooting User Account Problems

Creating and managing user accounts is generally simple and straightforward in Windows XP. The User Accounts icon in Control Panel provides all the tools you need. But once in a while, things don't work out as planned. The sections that follow talk about ways to deal with those unforeseen problems.

Can't log in, even with the correct password

Passwords are case-sensitive, meaning you have to type each character using the same uppercase/lowercase letters you used when defining the password. If you created the password using all lowercase letters, make sure the Caps Lock key isn't on when you're trying to enter the password at the Welcome screen.

Deleting a shortcut icon from one desktop deletes it from all desktops

When you create a desktop shortcut in your own user account by right-clicking an icon and choosing Send To ➪ Desktop (create shortcut), that icon is unique to your desktop. So, when you delete the icon, it should disappear from your desktop only. That's because the icon is stored in the Desktop folder for your user account only. That folder's name is C:\Documents and Settings*Username*\Desktop, where *Username* is the name of your user account.

Sometimes when you install a new program, that setup procedure automatically creates a new desktop shortcut icon on every user's desktop. That icon is stored in the All Users desktop folder at C:\Documents and Settings\All Users\Desktop. So, when you delete that icon from your desktop, you actually delete it from the folder and all other users' desktops.

If you just want to get the icon back, so that other users have it again, open the Recycle Bin and restore the icon from there. If you're a patient administrator, you can then copy the shortcut from the All Users Desktop folder to every other user's Desktop folder except your own. If you're not that patient, you can just remind other users that they can create any shortcut they want in two seconds flat by right-clicking any icon and choosing Send To ➪ Desktop (create shortcut) to make any shortcut they want.

Program reconfigures itself on first use in new user account

When you log into a new user account and start a program, or open a document, some programs will self-configure on the first run. Sometimes the process goes smoothly; sometimes it doesn't. One of the most common problems is that the configuration procedure tries to read files from the original program CD, even though the CD isn't in the drive.

Sometimes you can just click through the error messages and get to the program anyway. But really your best bet would be to close the program (if it opens) or cancel the installation (if possible) and get back to a clean desktop within the new user account. Hold down the Shift key and put the original program CD into the drive. (Holding down the Shift key while inserting a CD prevents the CD from auto-starting.)

Wait a few seconds to see of the program tries to install from scratch. If it does, or if you see a message asking for administrator information, cancel out of all that again. Leave the CD in the drive, but get back to a clean desktop. Finally, try running the same program again or opening the same document again. This time, the configuration should go smoothly. Once the program is running, you can remove the CD from the drive and put it back to wherever you keep your original program CDs.

Program won't run in a Limited user account

Some programs won't run in Limited accounts because they're designed to be used only by people with Administrator accounts. If you're logged into a Limited account and try to run such a program, you'll see a message indicating that you don't have appropriate permissions to use that program.

If you also have a password-protected administrator account, you can run the program as an administrator. Instead of clicking the program's start icon, right-click it and choose Run As, as in the example shown at the left of Figure 11-2. In the Run As dialog box that opens, also shown in Figure 11-2, choose "The following user," choose an administrator account, and type in the password for that account. Click OK and the program will run.

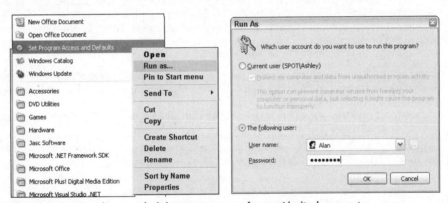

Figure 11-2: Running an administrator program from a Limited account

Some older programs won't run at all from a Limited account, simply because they were created for some older version of Windows that didn't have Limited accounts. Those programs assume that everyone who uses the computer has administrative rights, because in the olden days, every user did have administrative rights. There are three possible solutions to that problem:

- ✦ If you have access to an administrative account, try using Run As, as described previously, to open the program with administrative privileges.

- ✦ Or, use the Program Compatibility Wizard discussed in Chapter 47 to get the program to run.

- ✦ Or, upgrade to a more recent version of the same program.

"The System Could Not Log you On" message

If you see an error message "The System Could Not Log you On" when you try to log into an Administrator account, there may be an incorrect setting in the Windows registry. This is listed as a known problem in Microsoft's Knowledge Base, which means that it's something they might fix through an automatic update. I'm skittish about publishing registry modifications for problems that might be fixed, because anything I say here might change after the book is printed.

Caution   Editing the registry is risky business with zero margin for error. If you've never done it before, see Chapter 58 for general information and precautions.

Welcome screen appears even with only one user account defined

If you download and install the .NET Framework Version 1.1, it will create a hidden Limited user account named ASP.NET Machine A. That account appears only in the User Accounts window, never on the Welcome screen because it's used only to give .NET Web applications a limited environment in which to execute. But the addition of that new account will cause the Welcome screen to appear, even though the ASP.NET account icon doesn't appear on the Welcome screen.

Note   If the account is password-protected, then there is nothing to fix here. The Welcome screen must appear with a password-protected account. You'll be prompted for the password after you click the account picture or name.

You have two choices here. One is to just live with the extra click it takes to get to the desktop. The other is the change the Windows registry to prevent the Welcome screen from appearing. As discussed in Chapter 58, editing the registry is serious stuff with no margin for error. To fix this problem you need to change the following subkey:

```
HKEY_LOCAL_MACHINE\SOFTWARE\Microsoft\Windows
NT\CurrentVersion\Winlogon\SpecialAccounts\UserList
```

For that subkey create a new DWORD value. Change NewValue #'1. Change that to ASPNET. Then, close the registry Editor and restart the computer. See the following Web page below for more specific information:

```
http://support.microsoft.com/default.aspx?scid=kb;en-us;827072
```

User accounts have unknown passwords

After you first install or upgrade to Windows XP, setup may create temporary passwords to user accounts it creates automatically. To find those temporary passwords, follow these steps:

1. Click the **Start** button and choose **Search**.

2. In the Search Companion, choose **All files and folders**.

3. Type SetupAct.log as the file to search for.

4. Under **More advanced options** make sure the first three options are selected (checked), and then click the **Search** button.

5. When the search companion finds the file, double-click its icon.

6. Look through the file for the line that reads **Random password for *Username* is** where *Username* is the name of the account for which you're trying to locate a password.

7. Jot down the password(s) and close the SetupAct.log file and Search Results window.

Restart the computer and enter the random passwords when prompted. Then, you can go into the User Accounts window and remove or change the password(s).

If the above steps don't work for you, see the page at http://support.microsoft.com/default.aspx?scid=kb;en-us;318026 for other possibilities and techniques.

Troubleshooting Startup Problems

There's nothing more exasperating than a computer that won't start normally. After all, you can't very well troubleshoot a problem if you can't even get the darn machine started. We'll look at some common problems and their solutions.

Computer won't start at all

Check the most obvious problems first. For example, make sure that the power, monitor, keyboard, and mouse are all plugged into the appropriate ports on the back of the computer. Make sure that the monitor is turned on.

If there are any disks in the floppy drive or CD drives, remove them, because Windows may try to boot from those drives if they contain a disk.

Computer starts in Safe Mode

If there's a problem in the system BIOS, or some other setting that's activated before Windows loads, Windows may open in Safe Mode. Once you're in Safe Mode, there are a couple of ways to try to resolve the problem. One is to use the Startup and Shutdown Troubleshooter by following these steps:

1. Click the **Start** button and choose **Help and Support**.

2. If possible, click on **Fixing a problem**, and then click on **Startup and Shutdown Problems**. Finally, click **Startup and shutdown Troubleshooter**, and follow the onscreen instructions.

If you don't see "Fixing a problem" on the Help and Support screen that first opens, try searching Help for startup troubleshooter. Then, click on "Startup and shutdown Troubleshooter" under Suggested Topics.

If you see a message that reads "Please select the operating system to start" before Windows loads, press the F8 key. Use the arrow keys to highlight "Last Known Good Configuration," then press Enter.

If the problem began after installing new hardware or software, consider using System Restore to revert to previous system files. In that scenario, when you see the "Please select the operating system to start," press F8 and choose Safe Mode to start Windows with minimal capabilities. Then, use System Restore to revert to the most recent good restore point. To get to System Restore from Safe mode:

1. At the Windows desktop, press Help (**F1**) to open the Help and Support Center.

2. Type `system restore` in the Help center's Search box, and then press **Enter**.

3. If the mouse is working, click on **Run the System Restore Wizard**. If the mouse isn't working, press the **Tab** key until Run the System Restore Wizard is framed by dots, and then press **Enter**.

See Chapter 55 for more information on restoring your computer to an earlier time, and using System Restore in general.

Caution

Do not use System Restore as a general "undo" for every little problem. System Restore makes extensive changes to your system and should only be used as described in Chapter 55.

I get a STOP . . . error

A STOP error (also called the *blue screen of death*) is also caused by hardware or configurations errors that prevent Windows from starting or continuing to run smoothly. Each Stop error is followed by a lengthy error number such as 0x00020151. You might also see a symbolic name with the message, such as KERNEL_STACK_INPAGE_ERROR. Unfortunately, there are so many possible error numbers and names that it would probably take more pages than are in this book to cover them all.

Your best bet would be to go to `http://search.microsoft.com` and type in the exact error number or symbolic name you received. That should get you to the exact description and fix you need.

If the first search doesn't work, or if the information is too brief or too technical to make sense of, go to the online XP Resource Kit at `www.microsoft.com/resources/documentation/Windows/XP/all/reskit/en-us`. Once you're on that page, click on "Part VI: System Troubleshooting." Then, click on Troubleshooting Startup and take a look at options in the Table of Contents at the left side of the page.

Troubleshooting Accessibility, Speech, and Language Problems

When speech recognition doesn't work, diagnosing and fixing the problem can be difficult. Likewise for text to speech. The sections that follow discuss some ways of dealing with these tough nuts to crack.

Troubleshoot speech in Microsoft Word

Even though you install and manage speech recognition through Windows, you use it in other programs such as Microsoft Word. If you are having problems using speech recognition in a Microsoft Office program, your best bet is to diagnose and troubleshoot from that program, not Windows. For specific information on troubleshooting speech recognition in Microsoft Word see one of the following articles, depending on whether you're using Word 2002 (from Office XP) or Word 2003:

✦ **Word 2002:** `http://support.microsoft.com/default.aspx?scid=kb;en-us;295947`

✦ **Word 2003:** `http://support.microsoft.com/default.aspx?scid=kb;en-us;826323`.

Microsoft Reader won't read an e-book

The bad news is that Microsoft Reader can't read all e-books. It can only read e-books specifically designed to work with Microsoft Reader. Some e-books don't work with all readers; some work with Adobe Reader only. The good news is that if you have a book that can be read aloud by Adobe Reader, you can download that reader for free from `www.adobe.com/products/acrobat/readstep2.html`. If that URL doesn't work, go to Adobe's home page at `www.adobe.com`, click on Search at the top of the page, and search for `download reader`.

Troubleshooting Multiple Monitor Problems

Setting up multiple monitors can be a major technical challenge. Often, the only solution is to get to the system BIOS and change the settings that load AGP prior to PCI card graphics.

Multiple monitors don't work when one graphics card is PCI

This is a common problem when using an AGP slot for one or more monitors and a PCI slot for an additional monitor. The solution is generally to go into the computer's BIOS Setup program and choose whatever options are necessary to initialize PCI graphics before AGP graphics. I wish I could tell you something more specific, but there are a lot of different BIOS setup programs in the world, and they don't all offer the same options.

 Caution   Legacy EISA and ISA graphics cards cannot be used for multiple monitors.

Changing BIOS settings

Every computer has a basic input/output system (BIOS) that provides connections between the processor, which does all the work, and all the devices that can input data to, and get data from, the processor. This includes the keyboard, some basic video capability for the monitor (the ability to view and type in text, no graphics), all disk drives, and all installed PCI cards.

Those connections are (and need to be) made as soon as you turn on the computer. For example, the BIOS provides access to the hard disk shortly after you turn the computer, so that the operating system (Windows) can be loaded and executed. Like just about everything else, there are different ways that the BIOS can access the hardware. And those different ways of doing things are all settings in the computer's BIOS.

Because the BIOS kicks in before the operating system loads, there is only a narrow window of opportunity to get to it. You have to press a specific key, usually F2 or Delete, during the Power-On Self Test (POST), which begins almost immediately after you turn on the computer's main power switch or after you reboot.

If you can't see the POST during startup, you'll need to tap the F2 or Delete key a few times right after starting the computer. Once you're in the computer's BIOS, you'll need to use the keyboard to interact. That's because the mouse driver and operating system aren't loaded yet.

The settings in the BIOS vary depending on the BIOS on your system's motherboard. There's nothing I can tell you that would apply to all BIOS setup programs, except that typically there's enough information on the screen to tell you how to get around and choose settings. For specifics, you'll need to refer to the documentation for your system's motherboard (if you even have such documentation). Or, go to your computer manufacturer's Web site and find the specs for your specific computer.

Note In case you're wondering why this isn't a chapter about BIOS setup in this book, it's partly because the BIOS isn't a Windows thing. Furthermore, there's really nothing I can say on the matter that would apply to all computers.

Don't play around with options in the BIOS just to see what happens. Don't try to solve problems by changing options that look as if they might be relevant. However, if things get ugly, you can generally choose the "Load setup defaults" or "Load optimized defaults" or something like that from the BIOS Setup screen. Then, save and exit the BIOS, and (hopefully) the computer will start normally.

✦   ✦   ✦

Managing Files and Folders

Things you type, pages you download, songs you copy, pictures you take, movies you capture—all these things are documents. And there's probably room on your hard disk for many thousands of them. The only way to keep track of all these things is by getting organized and staying organized. That's what Part III is all about.

Windows Explorer (Chapter 12) is the tool of choice for managing all your documents, and the folders into which you organize them. Need to make some new folders or move some things around in existing folders? Chapters 13 and 14 will tell you how.

If you need to mail copies of things to someone or just want to make extra backup copies of important documents, Chapter 15 will help you do that using blank CDs and DVDs.

Are you tired of navigating through a bunch of icons to get to a favorite program or folder? Want to reduce that to a single click on the desktop, Quick Launch toolbar, or Start menu? Then, Chapter 16 is the place to go.

Ever wonder why everyone warns you to back up your hard disk but never tells you how? Wonder no more, because Chapter 18 covers all the issues and methods of backing up files and settings in Windows XP.

Industrial-Strength File Management

Hard disk space is cheap these days, and just about everyone has plenty of it. If you envision your hard disk as a file cabinet, it's a really big file cabinet, with room for thousands of folders and tens of thousands of documents. As discussed back in Chapter 3, the main program you use for getting around through all those folders and files is Windows Explorer. Any time you open any folder, Windows Explorer is the program that opens to display the contents of that folder.

In this part of the book we'll be looking at Windows Explorer in depth, and how you use it to create and manage folders, find documents, burn files to CD-R and CD-RW disks, move, copy, rename, and delete folders and files, and more. We'll start off in this chapter by looking at the many ways you can customize Windows Explorer to best suit your needs.

Windows Explorer Redux

At first glance, Windows Explorer doesn't look like much. It's just a program with a title bar, menu bar, toolbar, and status bar. The left pane shows the Explorer bar or any optional bar you choose, as discussed back in Chapter 3. The title bar shows the name of the folder whose contents you're viewing. The contents of the folder appear in the main pane. When open, Windows Explorer has a taskbar button like any other program. Figure 12-1 points out the main components of Windows Explorer.

Main pane

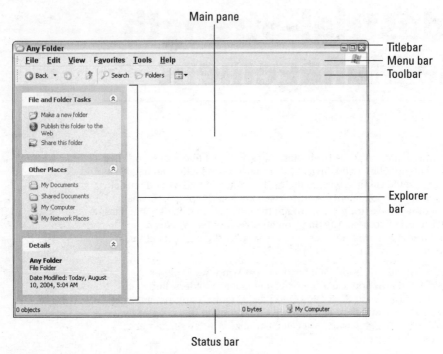

Titlebar
Menu bar
Toolbar

Explorer
bar

Status bar

Figure 12-1: Main components of Windows Explorer

Note   In this chapter and the chapters to follow, I assume that you're already familiar with the concepts and buzzwords covered in Chapter 3, "Files, Folders, Documents, and Icons."

Choosing Folder Options

As discussed in Chapter 3, any time you open a folder, you also open Explorer (also called Windows Explorer). That's because Explorer is the general program for navigating through the many thousands of folders on your hard disk. Windows Explorer is also the program you use to view the contents of external disks such as CDs and floppies. You use the My Computer folder to get to icons that represent those external disk drives.

Any time you're in Explorer, you can choose Tools ➪ Folder Options from its menu bar, as shown at the top of Figure 12-2. Doing so opens the Folder Options dialog box shown at the bottom of that same figure. The options in the Folder Options dialog box determine how Windows Explorer looks and works. In the sections that follow, we'll look at the various options available to you.

You can also open the Folder Options dialog box from Control Panel. If Control Panel opens in Category view, click on Appearance and Themes to get to the Folder Options icon. In Classic view, it will be included with all the other icons.

Figure 12-2: The General tab of the Folder Options dialog box

Showing/hiding the Explorer Bar

Options on the General tab in the Folder options dialog box let you choose how you want folders to look and behave. Choosing "Show common tasks in folders" allows the Explorer bar to appear at the left side of every folder you open. Choosing "Use Windows classic folders" prevents the Explorer bar from appearing.

Whether you chose "Show common tasks in folders" or not, the Explorer bar won't be visible in certain circumstances. For example, if you size the Explorer window down to where there's not enough room for the Explorer bar and icons, then the Explorer bar will vanish to make room for the icons. Enlarging the window will automatically bring the Explorer bar back into view.

Any alternative bar you choose will replace the Explorer bar. For example, clicking the Search or Folders button in the toolbar will cover the Explorer bar with the bar you specified. Clicking that same button again will bring the Explorer bar back into view.

Note   See "Using the Folders list" in Chapter 3 for more information on alternative Windows Explorer bars.

Opening multiple instances of Explorer

The second option on the General tab of the Folder Options dialog box, Browse Folders, offers two options. If you choose "Open each folder in the same window," then every time you double-click a subfolder's icon in Explorer, the contents of that folder will appear in the same Explorer window, replacing the previous contents. This prevents a lot of Explorer windows stacking up on the screen as you browse through folders.

If you choose "Open each folder in its own window," then Explorer behaves differently. Each time you double-click a folder name, or click on a folder name under Other Places in the Explorer bar, that new folder opens in a new instance of Explorer. So, you could arrange the folders in such a way as to see the contents of both folders at the same time.

 Tip   Choosing "Open each folder in its own window" causes Explorer to open a new instance every time you open a subfolder, which you might find extreme. You can leave that option turned off and open any subfolder in a new instance on the fly by holding down the Shift key and double-clicking the subfolder's icon.

If you do open many instances of Explorer, you can neatly stack them on the desktop, as shown in Figure 12-3, by right-clicking the clock and choose Cascade Windows. Or, if you open enough instances that all of their taskbar buttons collapse into a single button titled Windows Explorer, you can right-click that Windows Explorer button and choose Cascade to cascade only the Explorer windows.

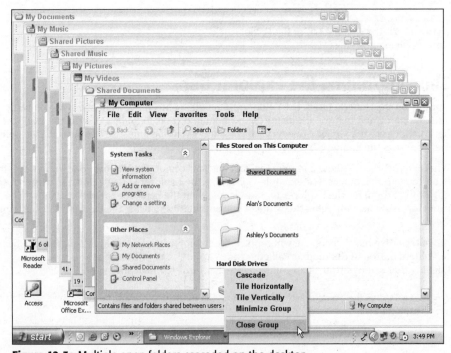

Figure 12-3: Multiple open folders cascaded on the desktop

Each folder you open will have its own taskbar button. So, you can bring any folder to the top of the stack just by clicking its taskbar button. If the folders collapse into a single Windows Explorer button, then you can click that button and click any folder's name to bring it to the top of the stack. To close all open folders in one fell swoop, right-click the Windows Explorer button and choose Close Group, as shown at the bottom of Figure 12-3.

The last option on the General tab of the Folder Options dialog box determines whether or not you need to double-click icons in Explorer, and on the desktop, to open them. See "To click or double-click" in Chapter 3 if you missed that discussion.

Folder Options View tab

The View tab in the Folder Options dialog box, shown in Figure 12-4, offers a long list of advanced settings. All the checkboxes under Advanced Settings apply to Windows Explorer, the program, and hence to all folders. Here, we'll look at what each option offers.

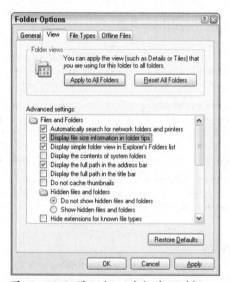

Figure 12-4: The View tab in the Folder Options dialog box

Tip   Double-clicking any folder icon in the Advanced Settings list shows/hides options beneath that icon.

Automatically search for network folders and printers

This option applies to the My Network Places folder only. If selected, Windows will periodically scan the network for new shared printers and folders and add them to My Network Places automatically. Clearing this option prevents Windows from periodically scanning the network.

Note   Chapter 63 discusses My Network Places in depth.

Display file size information in folder tips

Choosing this option ensures that when you point to a folder icon in Explorer, the ScreenTip that appears shows the size of the folder, as in Figure 12-5. Clearing this option prevents the entire tip from appearing (not just the size). This option has no effect on the information that appears when you point to a file icon.

Figure 12-5: The mouse pointer resting on a folder icon

Display simple folder view in Explorer's Folders list

This option applies to the Folders list that appears when you click the Folders button in the toolbar, choose View ➪ Explorer Bar ➪ Folders, or choose an Explore . . . option from a context menu. (For example, if you right-click the Start button and choose Explore All Users). The purpose of this option, when selected, is simply to make it easier to use the Folders list.

For example, clicking a folder name in the Folders list always displays the contents of that folder in the main pane. When the simple folder view is enabled, clicking another subfolder name in the same parent folder does two things: It displays the contents of the folder you just clicked, as usual, but it also collapses the details under the folder you just left. The idea is to prevent the Folders list from becoming so lengthy that it becomes difficult to get around.

If you clear this option, then the Folders list acts as it did in older versions of Windows, which means that the details under a particular folder will never close automatically. If you want to shorten the Folders list, you'll need to click the - button next to any expanded folder to hide its details.

Display the contents of system folders

Normally when you try to open a system folder, such as the folder in which Windows XP is stored, you'll see a message like the one in Figure 12-6. The idea is to prevent naïve computer users from messing around in folders where they shouldn't be messing around. (Though, you can just click on "Show the contents of this folder" to open the folder.)

If you choose the "Display the contents of system folders" option, then that warning message won't appear. The folder will open without showing any warnings.

Display the full path in the address bar

If selected the Address bar in Explorer will show the full path the folder whose contents you're currently viewing. If you clear this option, the Address bar shows only the folder name.

Tip   Choose View ➪ Toolbars ➪ Address Bar from Explorer's menu bar to show or hide the Address bar. See " Windows Explorer Address bar" in Chapter 3 for more information on using the Address bar.

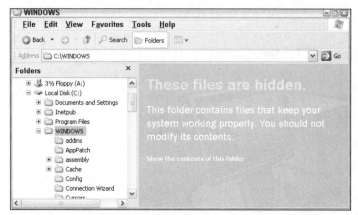

Figure 12-6: Warning that precedes displaying contents of system folders

Display the full path in the title bar

By default, this option is not selected, so Explorer's title bar shows only the name of the folder whose contents it's currently showing. The top of Figure 12-7 shows an example. If you chose this option, the title bar will display the full path in the title bar, as in the example at the bottom of that same figure.

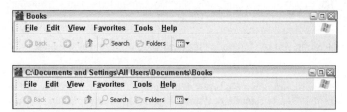

Figure 12-7: Full path to folder in lower title bar

Personally, I find it irritating to see the full path of every file and folder in the title bar. I prefer to leave this option turned off and use the Address bar to display the full path on an as-needed basis. But of course, that's just my opinion and you're welcome to choose options as you see fit.

Do not cache thumbnails

Here's a bizarre-sounding option that has to do with pictures shown in the Thumbnails view in folders. Normally this option is disabled, so that copies of thumbnail images in a folder are stored in memory. The advantage to that approach is that the thumbnail images appear quickly when you're switching among open folders.

The only downside to caching the thumbnails is that it eats up a little memory. There's also a slight chance that if you change an image, the cached thumbnail image may not accurately reflect the actual image that the thumbnail represents. If your computer has very limited memory, and you're trying to conserve all you can, you can choose "Do not cache thumbnails" to prevent the thumbnails from taking up any space in memory and to keep thumbnails current at all times.

Show hidden files and folders

You can hide a file or folder by right-clicking its icon, choosing Properties, and selecting Hidden, as shown in Figure 12-8. The "Show hidden files and folder" option applies only to items for which you've chosen that option, as below:

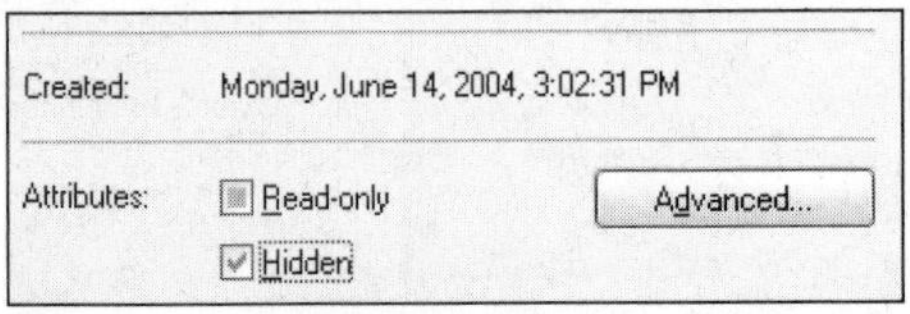

Created:	Monday, June 14, 2004, 3:02:31 PM	
Attributes:	☐ Read-only	Advanced...
	☑ Hidden	

Figure 12-8: The Hidden option in a folder or file Properties dialog box

✦ **Do not show hidden files and folders:** Items that you've marked Hidden are invisible.

✦ **Show hidden files and folders:** Items that you've marked Hidden are visible, but dimmed to distinguish then from nonhidden items.

Hide extensions for known file types

Determines whether or not filename extensions are visible on names of known file types. A "known" file type is any file that Windows can open. See "Document Icons" and "Showing and hiding filename extensions" in Chapter 3 for more information.

Tip   Even if you hide extensions, you can force some extensions to be visible all the time.

Extensions are always visible on unknown file types. For example, let's download a .pdf file. If you don't have Adobe Acrobat Reader installed, Windows can't open any .pdf file. So the .pdf extension will be visible, whether or not you hide extensions on known file types. The .pdf extension won't go away until you download and install Adobe Acrobat reader. Once you've done that, .pdf files will be a "known" file type, and the extension will be hidden if you've chosen the Hide extensions . . . option.

Hide protected operating system files (recommended)

This option is selected by default and, as you can see, Microsoft recommends that you keep it that way. Doing so prevents you from seeing icons folders flagged as System files by Windows. There are thousands of those files. Though the ones you're most likely to notice are Thumbs.db (a collection of thumbnail pictures) and Index.dat (used by the indexing service for rapid file searching).

If you clear this option, icons for system files will be visible. Making them visible also makes it possible to delete them, which can have disastrous effects if you delete a critical system file. Thumbs.db and Index.dat aren't critical, so deleting those won't have any disastrous consequences. But, it can be confusing having these files show up in folders and reappear at some time in the future after you do delete them.

Launch folder windows in a separate process

This oddly named option really has nothing to do with processes listed in Task Manager. Normally, Windows Explorer sets aside a little bit of memory to store the contents of the currently selected folder. As you go from one folder to the next, it overwrites that portion of memory with the current folder's contents.

If you choose this option, each folder's contents are stored in a separate area in memory. I suppose that choosing this option might make the Back and Forward buttons in Windows Explorer move a little quicker, although I doubt the speed difference would be noticeable. The more likely reason you'd use this would be if Windows crashed often when navigating through folders. Choosing this option might make the whole process more reliable.

Managing pairs of Web pages and folders

If you have Office 2003 installed, you'll see this option in your advanced settings list. Here's how it works. When you save a Web page using File ➪ Save As in Internet Explorer, you usually get two icons per page, one document icon and one folder icon. The document icon contains the actual HTML page, which means that it's all text. The folder contains every picture that is shown within the page when you open the page with a Web browser.

Tip If you have Microsoft Office, you can download Web pages to a single Web Archive file. To do so, choose File ➪ Save As from Internet Explorer's menu bar, as usual. Then, choose Web Archive, single file (*.mht) from the Save As Type option, before you click the Save button.

The "Managing pairs . . ." option gives you three choices for handling those paired icons:

✦ **Show and manage the pair as a single file:** Oddly, this option never seems to *show* the pair as a single file (unless you choose the aforementioned .mht format). But it does ensure that anything you do to one icon gets carried out on the other. For example, if you move, copy, or delete one of the icons, the other icon gets moved, copied, or deleted with it.

✦ **Show both parts and manage them individually:** Choosing this option breaks the bond between the folder and the document, so you can move, copy, and delete them independently.

✦ **Show both parts but manage them as a single file:** This option is the same as the first. However, it is applied to pages you've downloaded in the past as well as pages you download in the future.

Remember each folder's view settings

When you choose a view, such as Thumbnails or Details, in Windows Explorer, that view usually lasts only while the folder is open. When you revisit the folder in the future, its contents are displayed in the default view for that folder.

Note For more information on Explorer views, see "Umpteen ways to view icons" in Chapter 3.

Choosing "Remember each folder's view settings" overrides the automatic return to the default view when you leave a folder so that when you come back to the folder in the future, it displays icons in whatever view you had chosen when you left the folder.

Restore previous folder windows at logon

In older versions of Windows, when you first logged on, Windows automatically reopened folders that were open when you last logged off. Whether or not that was a good idea is debatable, but now it doesn't matter, because the choice is yours. Normally, Windows doesn't restore those previous folders when you log on. But if you choose this option, it will, just as in the older Windows versions.

Show Control Panel in My Computer

Normally, your My Computer folder only shows icons for document folders and drives on your system. Choosing this option adds a Control Panel icon to My Computer.

Show encrypted or compressed NTFS files in color

NTFS is a file system that didn't exist in older 16-bit versions of Windows like '98 and ME. It does exist in XP, and two of its advantages are the ability to encrypt files so that they can't be read by prying eyes, and the ability to compress files without going through a big compression procedure.

Choosing this option ensures that the names of encrypted and compressed files appear in color. Filenames of compressed files are shown in blue, encrypted files in a different color.

Note   To compress or encrypt a file, right-click its icon and choose Properties. Then, click the Advanced button in the Properties dialog box that opens.

Show pop-up description for folder and desktop items

Choosing this option allows ToolTips to appear when you point to folder icons and desktop icons, as in the example shown in Figure 12-9. If you don't like those little descriptions, clear this option.

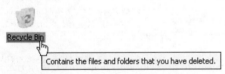

Figure 12-9: Pop-up description for a desktop icon

Use simple file sharing (recommended)

Available in Windows XP Professional (only), this option applies to how items are shared on the network, a topic addressed in Part XI of this book. Choosing this option makes the Sharing tab in a file or folder Properties dialog show simple options for sharing the item, as in the left side of Figure 12-10. Clearing this option shows the somewhat more complex view showed at the right side of that same figure.

Restore defaults

The Restore Defaults button does what its name implies — it sets all the checkboxes back to their original settings, as defined when you first installed Windows XP.

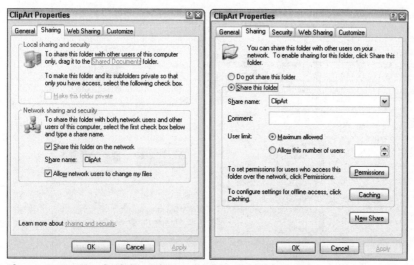

Figure 12-10: Simple (left) and more traditional (right) Sharing tabs

Changing file associations

For every document type you can open, there's one *default program*. The default program is the program that opens automatically when you open a document icon. For example, when you open a .doc file, the program that opens automatically to display the document is the default program for the .doc document type.

The default program for opening a document type may not be the only program on your computer that's capable of opening that type of document. If you have more than one program that's capable of opening a file type, you can always bypass the default program by right-clicking a document's icon, choosing Open With, and then choosing the name of any program that appears on the submenu. Figure 12-11 shows an example.

You can change the default program for opening any document type at any time. Just right-click any document icon of the type you want to change, choose Open With, then click the Choose Program option. In the dialog box that opens, click on the name of the program you want to use as the default for that document type, and choose the "Always use the selected program to open this kind of file" option. If any of this is news to you, take a look at "Opening a document from its icon" in Chapter 3.

The File Types tab of the Folder Options dialog box, shown in Figure 12-12, offers an alternative technique for changing the association between document types and default programs. The File Types tab offers a centralized place for managing all document types, and even media types like CD and DVD. The File Types tab also has some more advanced options for defining extra properties associated with specific document types.

Under Registered File Types you'll see all "known" disk types and file types. A "registered" or "known" disk or file type is one that Windows can open. Disks and URLs (Uniform Resource Locators, a.k.a. *addresses*, of Internet resources) are shown with NONE as the extension. Clicking on such an item offers little information about the item. There are easier ways to change most of those options. For example, you can change how audio CDs and DVDs open by right-clicking the drive's icon, choosing Properties, and then clicking the AutoPlay tab.

Figure 12-11: Example of choosing Open With

Figure 12-12: The File Types tab in Folder Options

Note   See "Setting Defaults for CDs and DVDs" in Chapter 15 for information on choosing how you want your computer to react when you insert a CD or DVD into your disk drive.

Clicking a document file extension shows the name of the default program for opening that file type, and the icon currently used to display those documents. For example, in Figure 12-12 I've click on the GIF extension. The lower part of the dialog box shows that the default program for opening GIF files is currently Paint Shop Pro 8, and you can see the icon just to the left of that program name.

To change the default program for opening the currently selected file type, click the Change button. The Open With dialog box will open. Click on the name of the program you wish to make the default for that file type, and then click OK. After you change a file type, the Advanced button will change to a Restore button. You can click that Restore button to revert to the previous association.

Caution   Don't assign file types to programs at random. Before you change the default program for a file type, make sure that the program you intend to use actually can open that type of file!

The Advanced button in the dialog box opens the Edit File Type dialog box for that file type, as in the example shown in Figure 12-13. We'll look at the options that dialog box offers in the sections to follow.

Figure 12-13: A sample Edit File Type dialog box

Changing the icon and description

The first option in the Edit File Type dialog box lets you change the icon and description of the file type, as they appear in Explorer. Whatever icon and description you specify, though, will be applied to all files that open in the specified program.

For example, in Figure 12-13 the default program for opening GIF images is Paint Shop Pro. If I were to change the icon, or the description, of GIF files, the same icon and description would be applied to other file types that open in Paint Shop Pro by default, such as JPEGs. Paint Shop Pro would still be the default program for opening GIF images as well.

Changing the icon and description has no effect on which program actually opens the document. You choose the default program for opening a document type using the Open With dialog box described earlier in this chapter. Changing the icon affects only the icon that's displayed for the default program (in all views except Thumbnails and Filmstrip). Changing the Description changes only the descriptive text that appears under the filename in Tiles View, and in the Type column of the Details View.

Confirm Open after download

The "Confirm open after download" checkbox determines what happens when you download a file of that type. If you choose the "Confirm open after download" option, then any time you download a file of that type, the downloaded file will open automatically. If you clear that checkbox, downloaded files won't open immediately after downloading.

Caution   Some file types can contain malicious code that's executed when you open the downloaded file. If you select the "Confirm open after download" option, you won't have time to scan downloaded files for viruses before the file opens.

Always show the filename extension

The "Always show filename extension" checkbox does what its name implies. Files that have the extension will always show their extension, whether or not you've selected "Hide extensions for known file types." Clearing the Always show . . . option reverts to the normal behavior where the extension is shown only if "Hide extensions for known file types" isn't activated.

The "Browse in same folder" option applies to very few document types and so is often disabled. When available and selected, it causes a document to open in a new instance of a program window rather than the current instance of that window.

Customize the shortcut menu

The Actions area provides a means of adding items to the shortcut menu (also called the *context menu*) when you right-click the icon for a document of the selected type. For example, Figure 12-14 shows the shortcut menu that appears when you right-click a GIF image's icon.

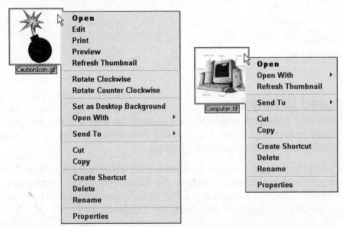

Figure 12-14: Shortcut (Context) menu for GIF (left) and TIFF (right) images

If you click on an existing action, then click the Edit button, you'll see how the action is currently defined. Figure 12-15 shows an example using the Open action for GIF images. The first option, Action, specifies how the option appears in the right-click menu. The second option specifies the path- and filename of the default program for opening that file type.

Figure 12-15: Editing a shortcut menu action

The remaining options apply only to programs that use DDE (Dynamic Data Exchange). Change these only if you know the DDE capabilities of the default program. If you choose Use DDE, you can then specify a DDE message. Use %1 in the message as a placeholder for the filename. For example, in Figure 12-15 Paint Shop Pro gets a DDE message that tells it to open the file.

The Application option under Use DDE lets you specify the DDE application string used to initiation a DDE conversation with the program. The DDE Application Not Running option allows you to specify an alternative action to choose if the program isn't already running. If you leave this blank, the DDE Message is always used. The Topic option is DDE-specific as well. If you leave this blank, Windows uses the default System DDE topic.

Clicking the New button next to the Actions list that opens lets you add a new action to the shortcut menu. You get a New Action dialog box that offers the same options as those shown in Figure 12-15, only all of the textboxes are empty. In the Action box, you type the word that you want to appear on the menu. Then, you need to fill in the correct application path and, if appropriate, DDE conversation data.

If you look back at Figure 12-16, you can see that the shortcut menu for TIFF images provides fewer options than the menu for GIF images. Suppose that you want to add a Preview option to the shortcut menu for TIFF options, so you can just quickly open such a file for a quick peek using the Windows Picture and Fax View.

Obviously, you won't know the exact application path or DDE images offhand. But if you find or make a document type that opens in that program, you can take a peek at how the Open option for that item is already defined, and copy and paste that information into Notepad or whatever. In the case of Windows Picture and Fax Viewer the Application path and Application message are defined as shown here:

```
rundll32.exe C:\WINDOWS\System32\shimgvw.dll,ImageView_Fullscreen %1shimgvw
```

To add a Preview option to TIFF images shortcut menu, you first need to click on TIFF in the Registered File Types list. Then click the Advanced button, and then click the New button. Type in your action name, such as Preview or View (or whatever you want to appear on the menu). For the "Application used to perform action" option you need to paste in that `rundll32.exe C:\WINDOWS\System32\shimgvw.dll,ImageView_Fullscreen %1` path. Then, choose Use DDE and enter `shimgvw` under Application. Clicking OK then takes you back to the Action list, and you can see the new action in the Actions list.

When you have two or more items in the Actions list, you can make any one of them the default action that occurs when you double-click the icon (or click the icon once, if you're using single-click). The default action appears in boldface both in the Actions list and on the shortcut menu. (You can also delete any action in the list by clicking its name and clicking the Remove option).

For example, Figure 12-16 shows a Preview option added to the shortcut menu for TIFF images (after filling in and closing the New Action dialog box). The default action is still Open.as you can tell by the boldface on the shortcut menu. I've just added Preview as an alternative action. The right side of the figure shows the results. Right-clicking a TIFF Image now shows a Preview option, which was absent back in Figure 12-14.

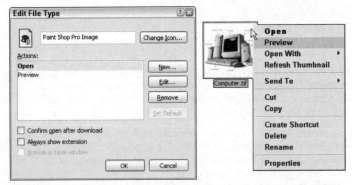

Figure 12-16: Preview option added to the shortcut menu for TIFF images

Note   Obviously, not all the options on a shortcut menu are listed under Actions in the Edit File Type dialog box. Most of those options are defined in the registry under HKEY_CLASSES_ROOT. Chapter 58 discusses the registry in general. But the specifics of shortcut menu actions in the registry are beyond the scope of this book. You'll need to use Microsoft's Knowledge Base, or a technical registry reference, to get to the specifics on working with shortcut menu items.

Whether or not you even want to mess with options in the File Types tab depends on your experience level. There certainly isn't any situation where you would need to mess around there. You can choose the default program for any file type right from the Open With dialog box, and there's rarely any need to do more than that. But if you're into tinkering with the fine details, the File Types tab provides the options to do that.

Using offline files

The Offline Files tab in the Folder Options dialog box applies only to the Professional edition, networks, and situations where you can work with network files even when you're offline. Offline files aren't supported at all if Fast User Switching is enabled in User Accounts. If you click on the Offline Files tab with Fast User Switching enabled, you'll see a message to that effect. The options shown in Figure 12-17 won't be available until you disable Fast User Switching.

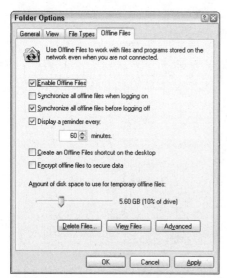

Figure 12-17: The Offline Files tab in Folder Options

The Offline Files feature stores a local copy of shared documents from a network on your computer so that you can work with those files even when you're disconnected from the network. It's mainly used for network computers that are frequently offline, such as laptop computers for working on the road, or remote computers that dial-in infrequently or only in short, temporary bursts.

On the server side (that is, the computer on which the original documents are stored), it's up to an administrator to determine which files will be available offline. On the client side (where I'm assuming you're working here), you need to choose the Enable Offline Files option on the Offline Files tab, as shown in Figure 12-17, to activate that feature.

Once you've enabled Offline Files, the rest of the options on the tab will be enabled. As you can see, the options are self-explanatory in that they specify when your local copies of network files are synchronized with the originals on the network. For more information on any option, click the ? button in the dialog box, and then click the option for which you need more info. Optionally, you can open Windows Help and search for Offline Files.

Viewing the Explorer Status Bar

The Status bar at the bottom of Windows Explorer, shown in Figure 12-18, displays a little information about the current folder that varies from time to time. When you first open a folder, the Status bar shows how many objects (folders and files) are contained within that folder and their combined sizes. (Note, however, that the counts and totals don't include files in subfolders.) The indicator at the right shows the general source of the folder, for example, My Computer if the folder is on your own computer or Local Intranet if the folder is on another computer in your local network.

Status bar

Figure 12-18: Windows Explorer Status bar

Note   You'll learn about selecting files, and getting their exact combined sizes, in Chapter 14.

When you select icons, the status bar shows you how many items are currently selected. You can show, or hide, the status bar by choosing View ➪ Status Bar from Explorer's menu bar.

Customizing Explorer's Toolbar

As with many programs, you can customize Windows Explorer's Standard Buttons toolbar to provide one-click access to frequently used menu commands. To do so, just choose View ➪ Toolbars ➪ Customize from Explorer's menu bar. The Customize Toolbar dialog box, shown in Figure 12-19, opens.

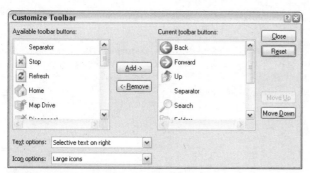

Figure 12-19: Customize Toolbar dialog box from Explorer's Standard Buttons toolbar

The Available Toolbar Buttons column lists all the different buttons you can add to the toolbar. The Separator option there puts a separator line between buttons on the toolbar. To add a separator or button to the toolbar, just click its name, and then click the Add button. The button moves over to the Current Toolbar Buttons column to indicate that it will be visible on the toolbar.

To move or remove an item on the toolbar, click the button or separator you wish to change in the Current Toolbar Buttons column. To remove the currently selected button, just click the Remove button. To move a button or separator line, clicks its name, and then use the Move Up or Move Down button to position the item in the list.

Tip To show, or hide, the Standard Buttons toolbar in Explorer, choose View ⇨ Toolbars ⇨ Standard Buttons from Explorer's menu bar.

The Text Options drop-down list lets you choose whether or not you want text labels to appear on selected buttons. Your options are:

✦ **Show text labels:** Each button will have its name displayed beneath it.

✦ **Selective text on right:** Certain buttons, such as Back, Search, and Folders, will have descriptive labels to their right.

✦ **No text labels:** No buttons will show labels, but you can still point to any toolbar button to see its name.

The Icon Options drop-down list lets you choose between large icons and small icons in the toolbar. To revert to the original Standard Toolbar buttons and settings at any time, click the Reset button in the dialog box. To save your changes and close the dialog box, click the Close button.

Figure 12-20 shows an example of customizing where I've added a separator and buttons for Undo, Stop, Refresh, and Folder Options to the toolbar. I've turned off text labels and used large icons. You can see buttons I've added both in the Current Toolbar Buttons column and in the toolbar itself, just above the Customize Toolbar dialog box.

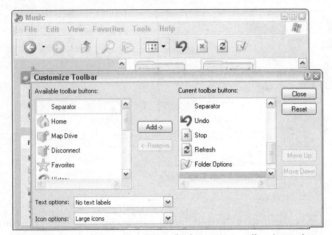

Figure 12-20: A customized Standard Buttons toolbar in Explorer

In case you're wondering, here's what each of the buttons I've added does when clicked:

✦ **Undo:** Undoes your most recent action. For example, if you delete or move a folder or file from the current folder, clicking Undo brings it back.

✦ **Refresh:** Mostly used for shared network folders, where things can get out of sync.

✦ **Stop:** Used to stop attempts to connect to shared drives that aren't available. (It tends to take a while for Windows to do this on its own.)

✦ **Folder Options:** Provides quick one-click access to the Folder Options dialog box.

So the basic idea here on customizing the toolbar is this: If you find yourself using a menu command often and want to reduce your effort to a single click, add a button for that command to the Standard Toolbars button.

Wrap Up

Needless to say, there are a lot of ways you can customize how Windows Explorer looks and behaves. Whether or not you want to is something you have to decide for yourself. In the next few chapters, you'll be learning how to actually *use* Windows Explorer to accomplish many tasks. First, a quick wrap up of this chapter's main points:

✦ Windows Explorer is the program you use to explore the contents of your computers disk drives and folders. It opens automatically whenever you open a folder.

✦ The Folder Options dialog box provides many optional settings for tweaking the appearance and behavior of Windows Explorer.

✦ To get to the Folder Options dialog box, choose Tools ⇨ Folder Options from Explorer's menu bar.

✦ To show or hide Status Bar in Explorer, choose View ⇨ Status bar from its menu bar.

✦ To customize the Standard Buttons toolbar in Explorer, choose View ⇨ Toolbars ⇨ Customize from its menu bar.

Creating and Managing Folders

Hard disk space is dirt cheap these days. Because of that, even an average-sized hard disk has room to store many thousands of documents. Any time you're talking about managing that many documents, be they paper documents in file cabinets or electronic documents on a computer hard disk, you need to have some means of organizing things. If you don't organize, you'll never be able to find anything when you need it.

Organizing documents in Windows is different from organizing paper documents, because Windows allows you to organize things hierarchically. The idea behind hierarchical organization is that you have the most general level of organization at the top. From the top, you "drill down" through more specific levels of organization until you get to the file you're looking for. Let's start off with an example.

An Example of Organizing Files

A lot of computer users spend more time looking for files they've created and downloaded than they do actually using those files. In some cases, it's just from not realizing that they can choose where they put every file they create or download. In other cases it's just because they haven't really organized things to make them easy to find. When it comes to being able to find the file you need, when you need it, organization is everything.

I run into the problem of needing to find older files all the time — files that I have no idea where I put, or what I named them. In this part I'll just explain how I solved the problem, using an example from my own work as a freelance author. Obviously, I don't assume that everyone reading this book is an author. But the basic idea of how I solved the problem should be applicable to anyone who needs to store, and have access to, lots of files. So, here's the typical scenario I run into.

A foreign publisher sends me an e-mail telling me that they're translating a book I wrote maybe six months or a year ago. For the sake of example, let's say that they need Figure 7-2 from my *VBA For Dummies* book. Of course, I have no idea what I named that file, or where I put it, because it's been so long and I've created and saved a zillion other documents since that time. So, how the heck am I going to find that specific file among the tens of thousands of other files on my hard disk?

Actually, it's not a problem at all, because I have a simple rule. I have a folder named Books. Every time I start a new book the first thing I do is open that folder and create a new folder for the new book. The first thing I did with the *VBA For Dummies* book was create a folder named, appropriately, VBA Dummies.

Within any given book's folder, I create a subfolder for each chapter in the book. For example a book's folder will contain subfolders named 01Chap, 02Chap, 03Chap, and so forth. When I write a chapter, all the files that make up that chapter go into the appropriate chapter subfolder. Typically that means one file for the text of the chapter, then another file for each picture.

I name the files within a chapter according to what each contains. For example, the text for Chapter 7 would be 07ChapText. Each figure in that chapter would be named something like 0701fig.tif, 0702fig.tif, 0703fig.tif, and so forth.

So, when the foreign publisher asks me for Figure 7-2 from the *VBA For Dummies* book, finding that file is a no-brainer for me. I open the Books folder, open the VBA Dummies folder, open the 07Chap folder, and look for 0702fg.tif. Then, I open that to make sure my copy is OK. Assuming that it is, it's a simple matter of attaching to a reply e-mail. Problem solved and out of my life in under 30 seconds.

Notice that I didn't need to remember exactly where I put that file, or what I named it; I only have to remember one thing — every book I write is in a folder named Books. Finding any file from any chapter in any book is simple. I just drill down through Books ➪ the book's folder ➪ and the Chapter's folder. Once that folder is open, the filenames in that folder tell exactly which file is which.

Again, that's just an example. The same idea works for any types of files. Pictures, songs, and videos are no exception. If you have lots of any kind of file, there's got to be a way to organize them into folder so that it's easy to find whatever you need at any time in the future.

Downloading and Saving Files

As discussed back in Chapter 3, any time you save anything, whether it's something you're downloading or something you created yourself, Windows displays a Save As dialog box like the example shown in Figure 13-1. Your main jobs in that dialog box are to tell Windows where to put the file and what to name it.

Initially, Windows XP provides a few predefined folders for storing documents. The simple rule of thumb for using those folders is that you choose whatever folder best describes the thing you're about to save:

✦ If it's a picture, put it in your My Pictures folder.

✦ If it's music, put it in your My Music folder.

✦ If it's a video, put it in your My Videos folder.

✦ If it's anything else, put it in your My Documents folder.

Where to save it

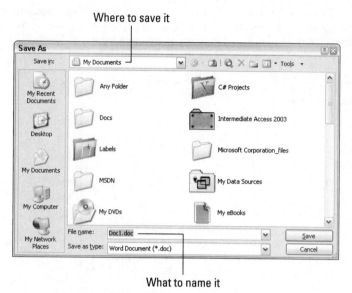

What to name it

Figure 13-1: A Save As dialog box

Not exactly quantum mechanics on the "intellectually challenging" scale. But you'd be amazed at how some people ignore even those most obvious folder selections, putting things in weird places like program folders, the root folder of drive C:, or floppy disks (perish the thought). Before I go any further here, a few important points:

✦ I'm talking strictly about documents here. Programs are an altogether different matter, as discussed in Chapter 44.

✦ The built-in My Videos folder doesn't actually appear until the first time you use Windows Movie Maker (see Chapter 40).

✦ For more information on the above-mentioned folders, see "Folder Icons" in Chapter 3.

✦ For information on using the Save As dialog box, see "Saving and Downloading Documents" in Chapter 3.

Those built-in folders are really just enough to get you started. For example, if you have 10,000 pictures to worry about, you probably don't want to be faced with 10,000 icons every time you open your My Pictures folder. More likely, you'll want to create subfolders to organize the photos into smaller groups.

Creating those new subfolders is really what this chapter is about. I should point out, however, that the same ideas apply to the built-in Shared Documents, Shared Music, Shared Pictures, and Shared Videos folders. The only difference between the My . . . and Shared . . . folders is that all users have access to the Shared . . . folders, while documents in your My . . . folders are private to your user account.

Furthermore, if you have more than one hard disk drive, you can certainly start create folders on those drives as well. For example, if you have 5,000 songs in your music collection, and you have a drive D:, you might prefer to put all those songs on drive D:. A good starting point, though, would be to create a folder on drive D:, perhaps named Music, in which to store those files.

Speaking of music, the way in which Media Player automatically organizes songs you copy is a good example of organizing files hierarchically from the general to the specific. Within the parent folder (be it My Music, Shared Music, or some folder you created yourself), Media Player automatically creates a new folder for each artist, as in the example shown in Figure 13-2.

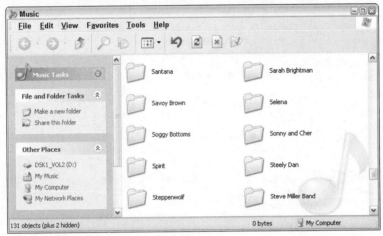

Figure 13-2: Artists in a music folder

When you open an artist's folder, you see all the albums by that artist that you've copied to your hard disk. For example, in Figure 13-3 you can see where I've copied several albums by Santana.

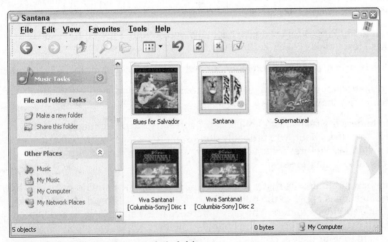

Figure 13-3: Albums in an artist's folder

Other Folders You May Already Have

My Documents, My Music, and My Pictures, along with their Shared . . . counterparts, are folders that everyone with XP has automatically. My Videos and Shared Videos are created the first time you run Windows Movie Maker.

You might also have a folder named My Received Files, which is created automatically when you use Windows Messenger or MSN Messenger to transfer files over the Internet. If you install Microsoft Reader, it may create a folder named My Library for storing all e-books that you download. In your Shared Music folder you may find a folder named Sample Music that contains some sample digital music. Typically there's a shortcut to that folder in My Music.

Some programs may create folders automatically. For example, if you have software for burning DVDs, you might find a folder named My DVDs in your My Documents folder. But regardless of what folders you already have, you can always create more.

When you open the folder for a specific album, you see the songs that are on that album. For example, Figure 13-4 shows the contents of the Supernatural folder which, of course, contains an icon for each song on the *Supernatural* album.

Figure 13-4: Songs in an album's folders

How to Create a Folder from Explorer

The first thing to understand about creating folders is that every folder you create is created within whatever folder you're in when you create it. So Step 1 is always to open the folder that will contain the folder you're about to create. For example, if you want to create a subfolder for storing a certain category of pictures, then the first thing you want to do is open your My Pictures folder and create the folder there. If you want to create a subfolder for a certain type of document such as "Financial Worksheet," go to your My Documents folder first and create the folder there. If you want to create a folder on your second hard disk (perhaps D:), open My Computer then open the icon for that drive first.

As discussed in Chapter 3, the folder that houses a subfolder is referred to as the subfolder's *parent*. So, the short way to say what I said I the above paragraph is "Open the parent to the new folder that you're about to create." OK, so here are the steps to create a new folder:

1. Open the parent folder. Then, do whichever of the following is most convenient for you at the moment (see Figure 13-5):

   • Right-click any empty space in the current folder and choose **New** ⇨ **Folder** (see Figure 13-5).

   • Or, Choose **File** ⇨ **New** ⇨ **Folder** from Explorer's menu bar.

   • Or, click on **Make a new folder** under File and Folder Tasks in the Explorer bar (also pointed out in Figure 13-5).

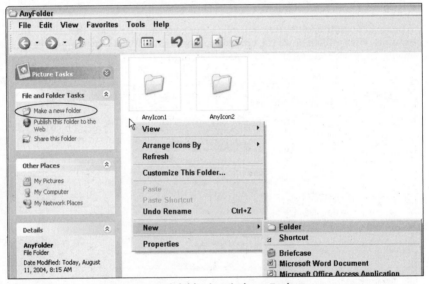

Figure 13-5: Two ways to create a folder in Windows Explorer

2. A new folder named New Folder appears. Type in a name of your choosing for the folder.

3. Press **Enter** or click outside the folder you just created.

That's it, the folder is created. A couple of quick things to know that might be useful:

   ✦ To quickly whip all icons into shape, right-click any space between icons, and choose **Arrange Icons By** ⇨ **Name**. (Or choose **View** ⇨ **Arrange Icons By** ⇨ **Name** from Explorer's menu bar.)

   ✦ If you forget to name the new folder, or change your mind about it after the fact, right-click the folder, choose **Rename**, and type in the new name.

If you want to quickly move an icon from the current folder into the new folder, just drag the icon so that it's right on top of the new folder's icon, and then release the mouse button. You can also select multiple files first, and then drop any one of them onto the new folder to move them all into the subfolder in one fell swoop. To open the new folder, just double-click (or click) its icon as you would any other folder.

Tip   You can move, copy, delete, and rename folders using the techniques described in Chapter 14. Techniques for selecting icons are also covered in Chapter 14.

Aside from the total capacity of your hard drive, there's no limit to the number of folders you can create, so don't worry about running out. There's no limit to how deep you can go in creating folders. And any folder can contain still more folders.

Saving Files to the New Folder

Saving files to the new folder is the same as saving a file to an existing file. When you're in the Save As dialog box, use the Save In drop-down list (Figure 13-6) or the folder names at the side of the dialog box if available) to get to the parent of the new folder (or as close as you can get). Then double-click the folder in which you want to store the file, so that folder opens and its name appears in the Save In drop-down list. Then click the Save button.

Save in drop-down list

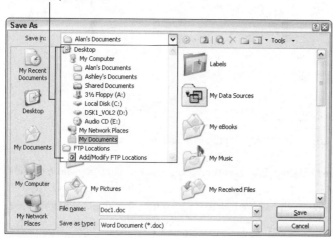

Figure 13-6: The Save In drop-down list

Whenever you save a file, you should think to yourself, "Where would I look for this, and what would I look for, six months or a year from now?" That will give you a sense of how you might go about organizing folders and naming files so that you can easily find things in the future. Remember, it's really not so different from grabbing an empty manila file folder, writing some name on its label, and sticking it in your filing cabinet. It's just that in Windows, you can organize things hierarchically so that you can always drill down from a general topic to a specific file without knowing specific names.

You can create a shortcut to any folder so that you can get right to it from the Desktop or My Documents folder without a lot of navigating through folders. See Chapter 16 for more information on creating shortcuts.

Creating a Folder on the Fly

Sometimes you might already be in the process of saving or downloading a file, when you suddenly realize that creating a new folder might be a good idea. That's no problem, because you can also create a new folder right from the Save As dialog box. You still need to get to the parent of the new folder first. But the steps are very similar to those used in Windows Explorer:

1. In the Save As dialog box, navigate to the folder that will be the parent of the new folder you're about to create.

2. Click the **Create New Folder** button, shown near the mouse pointer in Figure 13-7. Or right-click any empty space between existing icons in the folder and choose **New ⇨ Folder**.

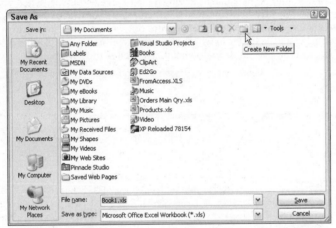

Figure 13-7: The Create New Folder button in a Save As dialog box

3. Type in a new name for the folder, and then press Enter or click anywhere outside its icon.

4. To put the file you're about to save into that new folder, first double-click the new folder's icon.

5. Click the **Save** button in the Save As dialog box.

That's about all you need to know about creating new folders. The most common mistake people make is forgetting the first step of getting to the folder that will be the new parent's folder. But even that's not a big deal, because you can easily move the new folder wherever you want after you create it. But again, moving and copying things is a topic for Chapter 14. For the rest of this chapter, I'll cover optional ways of personalizing and protecting folders.

Personalizing Your Folders

Every folder is based on a *folder template* that defines things like:

✦ Options that appear in the Explorer bar (such as Picture Tasks and Music Tasks).

✦ The background image used in the folder's main pane.

✦ How the folder's icon looks in Thumbnails View (for example, whether it shows four small pictures or one large picture).

✦ To some extent, the view that's used when you first option the folder (such as Thumbnails or Filmstrip).

That two items are easily overridden via other options. For example, if you've selected "Remember each folder's view settings" in Folder Options (see Chapter 12) then the folder will always open in whatever view you left it in. There are also ways to override how pictures look on folders in Thumbnails View. So, I guess it would be accurate to say that the template mainly determines the options that are visible in the Explorer bar, and whether or not the Filmstrip view is available on the Views button and View menu.

Note   See "Umpteen ways to view icons" in Chapter 3 for more information on different ways you can view icons.

The built-in folders already have folder templates applied to them. For example, when you open your My Pictures folder, you see Pictures Tasks in the Explorer bar, you have a Filmstrip option on the Views button and View menu, and you see a faint photo image in the background, behind the icons.

When you create a folder yourself, and it's not contained within My Pictures, My Music, or some other specialized folder, then no special template is applied to the folder. So, for example, you might not see Picture Tasks in that folder's Explorer bar, and you might not see Filmstrip as an option in its View menu. But you can apply any folder template listed below to change that:

✦ **Documents (for any file type):** No special options in the Explorer bar, no Filmstrip View.

✦ **Pictures (best for many files):** Folder opens in Thumbnails view. Picture Tasks and Filmstrip View are available.

✦ **Photo Album (best for fewer files):** Folder opens in Filmstrip view. Picture Tasks and Filmstrip View are available.

✦ **Music (best for audio files and playlists):** Folder opens in Tiles View (or maybe Thumbnails View). Music Tasks available in the Explorer bar.

✦ **Music Artist (best for works by one artist):** Folder opens in Tiles View. Music tasks available in the Explorer bar.

✦ **Music Album (best for tracks from one album):** Folder opens in Tiles View. Music Tasks available in the Explorer bar.

✦ **Videos:** Folder opens in Thumbnails View. Video Tasks available in the Explorer bar.

You can apply a template to any folder you create yourself by following these steps:

1. Open the folder's parent, so you can see the icon of the folder you wish to customize.

2. Right-click the icon of the folder you want to customize, and choose **Properties**.

3. In the Properties dialog box that opens, click the **Customize** tab to see the options shown in Figure 13-8.

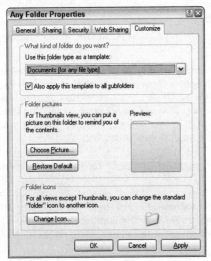

Figure 13-8: Customize tab of a folder's Properties dialog box

4. Choose a folder template from the **Use this folder type as a template** drop-down list.

5. If you want to apply the same template to subfolders within the folder (and you probably will want to do that), choose **Also apply this template to all subfolders**.

6. Click **OK**.

That's all there is to it. When you open the folder, you'll mainly notice the background image and the top set of options in the Explorer bar. If you chose one of the picture templates, you'll be able to choose the Filmstrip View from the Views button or View menu at any time.

Changing folder pictures

When you're looking at the contents of a folder in Thumbnails or Filmstrip Views, icons for subfolders within that folder are shown in any of four possible ways:

✦ **Standard icon:** If the folder that the icon represents does contain any pictures, music, or video, and you haven't assigned a custom icon to the folder, then a standard folder icon is shown, as is the case with the Not Organized Yet folder in Figure 13-9.

✦ **Four small pictures:** If the folder contains pictures or albums, then the folder icon shows small four pictures from the folder, as is the case with the Clip Art folder in Figure 13-9.

✦ **One large picture:** You can replace the four small pictures, or even a standard icon, with any picture you like. For example, the Peter, Paul, and Mary folder in Figure 13-9 shows a single large picture.

✦ **Custom icon:** Optionally, you can choose a custom icon for the folder, like the Databases example in Figure 13-9. Unlike pictures, which are only visible in Thumbnails and Filmstrip Views, custom icons appear in all views.

Figure 13-9: Four different folder icons in Thumbnails or Filmstrip View

The template that you apply to a folder plays some role in how the folder's icon looks. But you can also override the template's choice for icons that show pictures by using the Folder Pictures option on the Customize tab.

To choose between the four-pictures or one-picture view in a folder that contains pictures, video, or music albums, you need to get to the folder's Customize tab as described in Steps 1 to 6 at the start of this section. Then, if you want to show a single picture on the folder, click on the Choose Picture button. In the Browse dialog box that opens, navigate to any folder that contains pictures, click on the picture you want to use, and click the open button.

Once you've chosen a single picture, the dialog box shows you an example of what the folder will look like in Thumbnails and Filmstrip views. If you change your mind about showing a single picture on a folder, just click the Restore Default button to revert to the default method of showing the folder's icon.

Choosing a custom icon for folders

Unlike pictures that appear on folders in Thumbnails and Filmstrip View (only), a custom icon for a folder appears in all views. This is a very handy thing, because you can use custom icons to make certain folders stand out from the crowd. For example, let's say that you have a folder full of subfolders, and all the folder icons look alike. If there's a particular "hot" folder you use more often then others, you can change its icon to make it stand out from the crowd, like the checked folder in Figure 13-10.

When the folder with the check mark is no longer the "hot" folder, you can change it back to the original icon. Then, use the check mark folder icon for whatever folder is "hot" this week, or this month, or whatever. Anything you can do to make the hot folder stand out from the crowd will make it easier to spot on the screen.

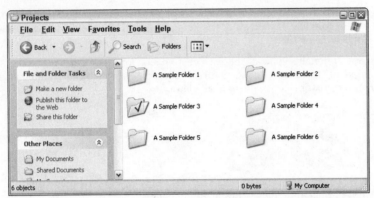

Figure 13-10: Four different folder icons in Thumbnails or Filmstrip View

The Change Icon button on the Customize tab of the folder's Properties dialog box, visible back in Figure 13-8, is the tool you use for choosing a custom icon for the folder. When you click that button you're taken to the Change Icon dialog box shown in Figure 13-11.

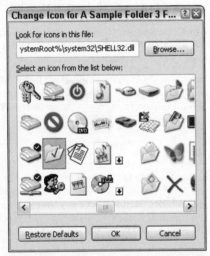

Figure 13-11: The Change Icon dialog box

The icons shown in Figure 13-11 are from the %SystemRoot%\system32\SHELL32.dll icon collection, which is usually the first collection that opens. But you can use the Browse button to navigate to any folder that contains icons in .ico format, or any file type (such as a .dll or .exe file) that contains icons images. Once you've found the icon you want, click on it and then click OK.

Note SystemRoot is a placeholder for the folder in which Windows is stored. Typically that's C:\Windows, but it could be C:\WINNT, or just about any other name.

To remove a custom icon and revert to the original, click the Change Icon button. But when you get to the Change Icon dialog box, don't choose a new icon. Instead, click the Restore Defaults button and then click OK.

Finding custom icons

You can buy custom icon collections or even find some free ones to download from the Web. If you have some artistic talent and an appropriate program, you can also create your own custom icons. You can find icons and programs for creating icons at many shareware sites, such as TUCOWS (www.tucows.com). Search for something like "Create Windows XP Icons" at the site. No doubt you'll get some irrelevant links. But I've found some great custom icon collections, and programs for creating icons, at TUCOWS in the past.

Many of the free icon collections I've found download as .zip files (also called *compressed folders*). You'll need to extract the icons from the .zip file before you can use them. More on that topic under "Using Compressed Folders (.zip Files)" later in this chapter.

If you keep all your icons in a folder named Icons (or whatever), within your My Documents or My Pictures folder, it will be easy to navigate to that folder and find all your icons from the Change Icon dialog box. Just click the Browse button in the Change Icon dialog box, and then navigate to the Icons folder. You can use the Views button to choose how you want to see the icons in the folder. For example, Figure 13-12 shows a folder of custom icons in Icons view.

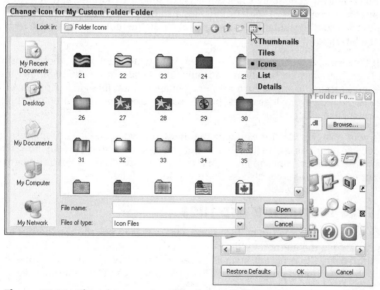

Figure 13-12: Choosing a custom icon from a folder.

Hiding (and Unhiding) Folders

You can hide and unhide folders just as you can files. First, get to the parent folder so that you can see the folder you want to hide. Then, right-click that folder's icon, choose Hidden, and then click OK. Whether or not the folder disappears altogether, or just goes dim, depends on the "Show hidden files and folders" option in the Folder Options dialog box discussed in Chapter 12.

If you've already hidden a folder and want to take it out of hiding, you'll first need to choose "Show hidden files and folders" from the aforementioned Folder Options dialog box so that you can see the dimmed icon. Then, right-click that icon, choose Properties, clear the Hidden checkbox, and then click OK.

.zip Files, Zip Disks, Compressed Folders

.zip files and Zip disks are two totally unrelated things whose names are similar only by coincidence. The files on a Zip disk are not compressed in any way (unless you intentionally put compressed files on the disk). So, don't confuse any of the material in this chapter with Zip disks.

Microsoft uses the name *compressed folders* rather than .zip file. But the name *compressed folder* is a little misleading too. The .zip file truly is a file, not a folder. For example, when you arrange icons in a folder, subfolders are listed first, followed by files. The *compressed folder* won't be listed with the *real folders*, though. The icon for the .zip file will be mixed with the other regular files.

Using Compressed Folders (.zip Files)

Many people use .zip files to transfer files over the Internet. A .zip file, also called a compressed folder in Windows, is actually a file. But it's also similar to a folder in that any one .zip file can contain multiple files or folders. .zip files also have the advantage of compressing certain file types to make them smaller. The smaller a file is, the more quickly it can be transferred across the Internet.

Most ISPs limit the size of attachments you can send. With dial-up accounts, that varies from about 1 to 3 MB per message. On broadband accounts it's usually more like 10 MB per message. Compressing certain file types, such as bitmap images (.bmp files) in a .zip file can reduce the size of the image considerably. (Though, compression has almost no effect on pre-compressed formats like .GIF and .JPEG).

You can create your own .zip files for e-mailing to others. And you can also decompress .zip files that you receive either as e-mail attachments or that you download. Exactly how you create .zip files, and extract files from .zip files you receive, depends on the programs you have installed on your computer, as we'll discuss in the sections to follow.

Programs for managing .zip files

There are basically two ways to work with .zip files. One way is to use the capabilities built into Windows XP. That is the method we'll be describing in this chapter. As an alternative, you can use a third-party Zip program, such as the ever-popular WinZip. If you're already familiar with such a third-party program and are happy with it, you can continue using that program.

If you have a third-party Zip program installed, the .zip file capabilities built into Windows may be inaccessible to you. The options to create and extract from .zip files, as described in this section, may not even be available to you. You may have to uninstall the third-party program to get the built-in capabilities to work at all. Though, as discussed under "Using third-party Zip programs" later in this chapter, you may be able to use both the built-in capabilities and the third-party program on the same computer.

Making .zip files in Windows XP

The Windows method of creating .zip files is fairly simple and straightforward. You'll need to know how to select icons first, as discussed in Chapter 14. But once you've selected one or more files to compress, it's just a simple matter of right-clicking any selected icon. Here are the exact steps:

1. Open the folder that contains the files that you want to compress into a single .zip file.

Tip To select files from multiple folders, use the Search Companion (see Chapter 17) to locate the files you want to copy. Then, select the appropriate files in the Search Results window.

2. Select the file(s) you want to compress using any of the selection methods described in Chapter 14.

3. Right-click any selected icon and choose **Send To** ⇨ **Compressed (zipped) Folder**, as shown in Figure 13-13.

Figure 13-13: Several files selected and about to be zipped

4. After a brief delay, an icon representing the .zip file will appear in the folder (usually below the existing filenames).

The icon for a .zip file looks like a manila file folder with a zipper on it. The file name of the .zip file will be the same as the name of the file you right-clicked in Step 3. If you don't see the icon immediately, scroll down through the current folder. There's a good change the new icon will be the last one in the folder.

If you don't like the name that was automatically given to the .zip file, just right-click its icon, choose Rename, and type in a name you prefer. To see the size of the .zip file, first select the icon by pointing to it or by clicking on it. The Details area and status bar in Explorer will show the file's size. Also, just pointing to the file may display the file's size in a ToolTip, as shown in Figure 13-14.

The original uncompressed files will remain unchanged. Windows never moves files into a .zip file; it simply puts compressed copies of the selected files into the .zip file. It works this way because the assumption is that you're creating the .zip file to send someone copies of files you have, not to send them your original files.

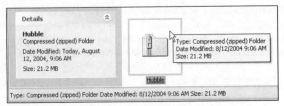

Figure 13-14: Example of a Windows compressed folder (.zip file)

E-mailing .zip files

Zipping files provides no guarantee that the resulting file will be small enough to send as an e-mail attachment. For example, the .zip files in Figure 13-14 is still 21.2 MB, which is too big to use as an e-mail attachment with most ISPs. The reason is because I intentionally selected enormous bitmap images for this example. If you ended up with a similar situation, you'd probably want to make .JPEG copies of the original bitmaps, since the JPEGs would be much smaller that the bitmaps. Also, you could create several .zip files, each of which is small enough to send as an e-mail attachment, and then attach each .zip file to a separate e-mail message.

Exactly how you e-mail a .zip file depends on what program you use as your e-mail client. Chapter 33 covers that in depth. But if you're using Outlook Express or Outlook as your e-mail client, you could just right-click the compressed folder and choose Send To ➪ Mail Recipient.

Tip   To learn more about your e-mail accounts' attachments and limitations, check your ISP's Web site. Most of the time, though, when you're typing an e-mail message, you'll see a simple Attach or Attach Files option somewhere near the subject line, which will allow you to attach any file to the message.

Using .zip files you've received

When someone sends you a .zip file as an e-mail attachment, or you download a .zip file from the Internet, you first need to save the file to your hard disk. Then, you need to *extract* the compressed files from within the .zip file to normal, uncompressed files. Exactly how you extract the files depends, once again, on the software installed on your computer. If you have a third-party Zip program installed, then you'll use that program. In this section, I'll show you how it's done in Windows when you have no third-party Zip program installed.

Caution   Don't open or decompress any e-mail attachment unless you know exactly what it is, who it's from, and what it contains. The same goes for files you download. See Chapter 25 before you download anything or open any e-mail attachments.

Without a third-party Zip program installed, the icon for a .zip file will always have the zippered-folder appearance. (If you have a third-party Zip program installed, the .zip file will most likely show that program's logo in its icon.) If someone sent you a .zip file as a file attachment, you'll see the attachment's file name in the Attach line or box of the e-mail message.

If the .zip file came as an e-mail attachment, the first step is to save it to some folder on your hard disk. Your My Documents folder will do. Though you could create a new folder called Zip Files, or whatever, to store all your .zip files. That way, you'll always be able to find them. To save an attached .zip file, open the e-mail message, right-click the attachment's icon, and choose Save As, as in Figure 13-15. Then, navigate to the folder in which you want to put the .zip file, and click the Save button.

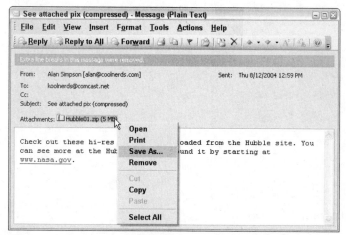

Figure 13-15: A compressed folder sent as an e-mail attachment

If you're downloading a .zip file straight from the Internet, then it's just a matter of choosing the Save option when given the choice to Save or Open the file. After you choose Save, navigate to the folder in which you want to put the .zip file and click the Save button.

Once you have the .zip file in a folder, just get to that file's parent folder so that you can see the icon for the .zip file. Then, right-click that icon and choose Extract All, as shown in Figure 13-16.

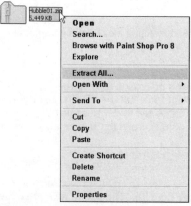

Figure 13-16: Extracting files from a compressed folder (.zip file)

The Windows Extraction Wizard will open. Click Next on the first page to get to the second page shown in Figure 13-17. The page asks where you want to put the extracted files. If you accept the suggested destination, the uncompressed files will be put in a folder within the current folder. The compressed folder will be the same as the .zip file. However, it will be a normal file with no filename extension and a normal-looking folder icon.

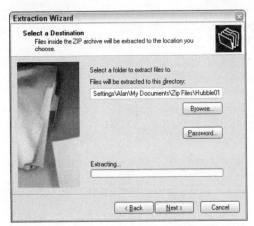

Figure 13-17: Second page of the Extraction Wizard

Click Next after accepting the suggested destination or choosing a different destination. The last Wizard page will ask if you want to see the extracted files immediately. If you select that check box, the folder containing the uncompressed files will open automatically. If you clear that option, you'll be taken to the parent folder, which shows the icon for the uncompressed folder. Either way, click Finish to complete the process and close the wizard.

Figure 13-18 shows an example where I extracted files from the Hubble01.zip file without changing the suggested destination. Also, I cleared the "Show extracted files" option on the last wizard screen. The icon on the right is the uncompressed copy of the original .zip file, whose icon is shown at left.

Figure 13-18: Extracting files from a compressed folder (.zip file)

Once you have the uncompressed files in hand, there's no reason to keep the compressed .zip file, unless you want to keep it as a backup. If you want to delete the .zip file, just right-click its icon and choose Delete. If you need to move the extracted folder to some other folder, just use any normal method of moving files and folders, as discussed in Chapter 14.

Using self-extracting .zip files

Some third-party Zip programs, such as WinZip, allow users to create self-extracting .zip files. Those files have a .exe (executable) extension rather than .zip. Though be aware that not all .exe files are self-extracting .zip files. An .exe file could be any kind of executable code, even a virus. So, don't assume that every .exe file you see is a compressed .zip file, or even a safe file at all.

An example of when you might get a safe, self-extracting .zip file is when you download custom icons or cursors from a safe site like www.tucows.com mentioned earlier in this chapter. When you double-click a self-extracting .zip file to open it, you'll likely get a small dialog box like the one shown in Figure 13-19.

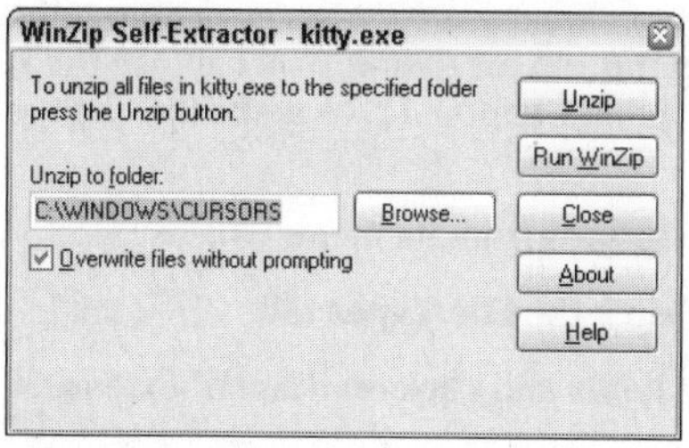

Figure 13-19: Sample dialog box for a self-extracting .zip file

The first step is to click the Browse button in the dialog box and navigate to the folder in which you want to place the extracted files. Then, just click the Unzip button and wait for the feedback message. Click OK in that message, and then click the Close button in the dialog box. You'll find the extracted files in whatever folder you chose after you clicked the Browse button.

Using third-party Zip programs

As mentioned, if you have a third-party Zip program installed, the icons for your .zip files may not have the zippered folder look. For example, if that third-party program is WinZip, your icons will have the WinZip logo, like the example shown in Figure 13-20. When you right-click such an icon, you probably won't see the Extract All option. But you should see some options that are relevant to your Zip program like the example shown in the figure. Just choose the option you want form the submenu and follow the instructions on the screen.

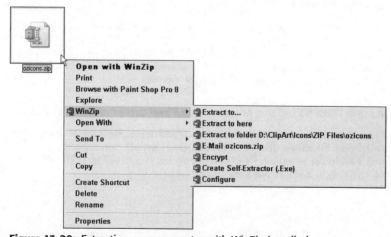

Figure 13-20: Extracting on a computer with WinZip installed

Caution   I've only used the procedure below with WinZip Version 9.0. I can't guarantee it will work with all third-party Zip programs. If you don't really know much about the third-party Zip program you have, it might be better to uninstall that program and use only the Windows methods of creating and using .zip files.

With many Zip programs, you can still keep the built-in Windows XP Zip capabilities alive by changing the default program for opening files with the .zip extension. You can use the File Types tab of the Folder Options dialog box, discussed in Chapter 12, to make the change. Here are the steps:

1. Open any folder and choose **Tools ➪ Folder Options** from its menu bar.

2. In the Folder Options dialog box that opens, click the **File Types** tab.

3. Scroll down through the list of registered file types and click on the **.ZIP** extension, as in the left side of Figure 13-21.

4. Click the **Change** button, then click on **Compressed (zipped) folders** in the Open With dialog box, as in the right side of Figure 13-21.

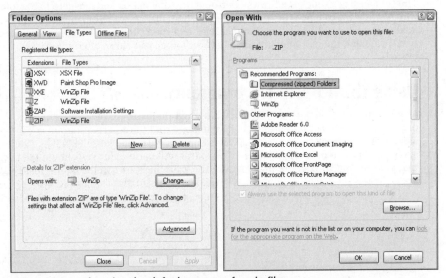

Figure 13-21: Changing the default program for .zip files

5. Click **OK** in the Open With dialog box, then click **Close** in the Folder Options dialog box.

Icons for your .zip files will have the zippered folder appearance. Right-clicking any such icon will provide the Extract All option described previously. However, you should also see options for using WinZip (or whatever third-party program you're using) in the shortcut menu when you right click. You can use either to extract the files.

Using NTFS Compression

Whereas .zip files are mainly about combining and compressing files for e-mailing as attachments, NTFS compression is about conserving hard disk space. You can only use NTFS compression if your hard disk is formatted as NTFS (as opposed to FAT).

You can easily tell which edition of Windows you're using by looking at the screen while Windows is starting up. Or, right-click your My Computer icon and choose Properties. To find out if you're using NTFS, open your My Computer folder, right-click the icon for your hard drive, C:, and choose Properties. If you're using NTFS, you'll see that next to File System as in Figure 13-22.

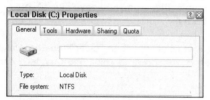

Figure 13-22: This drive is using the NTFS file system.

While compressing a folder does save disk space, you pay a price in performance. Windows automatically decompresses any file you open from that folder and automatically compresses every file you put into that folder. That takes time. So, before you start compressing folders just to conserve disk space, make sure that you know how much disk space you have. There's not much point to taking a performance hit if you have tens of gigabytes of free hard disk space left.

If you do want to compress a folder using NTFS, the procedure is quite simple. First, you need to get to the folder's parent so that you can see the folder's icon. Then, right-click that folder's icon and choose Properties. On the General tab of the folder's Properties dialog box, click the Advanced button. You'll be taken to the Advanced Attributes dialog box shown in Figure 13-23.

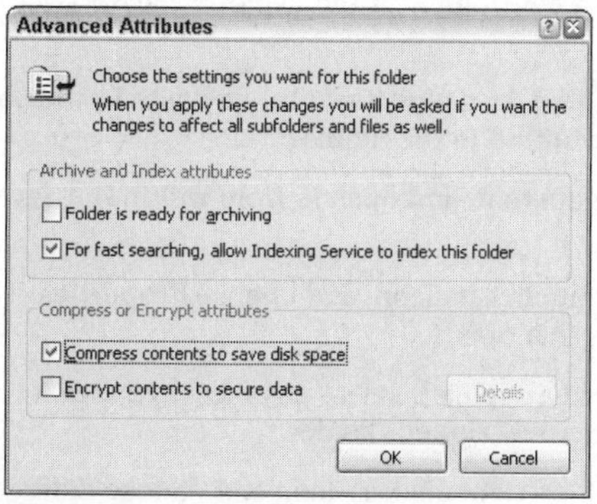

Figure 13-23: The Advanced Attributes dialog box

In the Advanced Attributes dialog box, choose "Compress contents to save disk space," and then click OK. Click OK in the Properties dialog box, and you'll see a prompt asking if you want to apply the changes to the current folder only, or the folder, subfolder, and files. Most likely you'll want to choose the second option to compress everything within the folder to get the maximum savings on hard disk space. Then, click OK and wait.

Exactly how long you have to wait depends on what's in the folder. The Properties dialog box will remain open until the folder is compressed, and then it will close automatically.

Once the compression is done, the folder won't look any different, except that its name may be shown in blue letters. Using the compressed folder is no different from using any other folder. There's no separate .zip file involved, no extra copies of the items within the folder. The original folder and its contents are compressed, but are automatically decompressed and recompressed on an as-needed basis. So, you can open files from, and save files to, the compressed folder just as you would with any other folder.

 The "Show encrypted or compressed NTFS files in color" option in Folder Properties determines whether or not compressed folder names are shown in color. See Chapter 12 for details.

Should you ever change your mind and decide to uncompress the folder, just repeat the procedure you used to compress it, but clear the "Compress contents to save disk space" checkbox in the Advanced Attributes dialog box when you get there.

Wrap Up

As in a filing cabinet, folders on your hard disk are the key to keeping files organized so that you can find them when you need them. You can create as many folders as you wish, name them as you wish, and organize them in any way that makes sense to you. To recap the main points of this chapter:

✦ Before you create a new folder, make sure that you open the new folder's parent and create the new folder within that parent folder.

✦ To create a new folder, right-click some empty space in Explorer's main pane and choose New ➪ Folder. Or, click on "Make a new folder" in the Explorer bar, or choose File ➪ New ➪ Folder from the menu bar.

✦ To create a folder on the fly while in the Save As dialog box, first navigate to the parent folder. Then, click the Create New Folder button in the toolbar.

✦ To save a file in the new folder, just navigate to it, and open it, from within the Save As dialog box.

✦ To change the appearance of a folder, right-click its icon, and choose Properties. Then, click the Customize tab in the dialog box that opens.

✦ To create a compressed folder (also called a .zip file), select any file(s) you want to compress, and choose Send To ➪ Compressed (zipped) Folder.

✦ To extract all files from a compressed folder, right-click its icon and choose Extract All.

✦   ✦   ✦

Managing Disks, Folders, and Files

Getting organized and staying organized requires managing your files and folders. That often means renaming files, deleting them, and moving them from one folder to another. The program you use to manage files is, of course, Windows Explorer, because that's the program that gives you access to all your disk drives and folders.

If you have experience with any version of Windows, then you may already know at least some techniques for selecting, deleting, renaming, moving, and copying files, because not much has changed in those areas since 1990 when Windows 3.0 was first released. You can accomplish just about any file management technique by selecting, right-clicking, and/or dragging icons.

Accessing Removable Disks and Memory Cards

All of your My . . . and Shared . . . folders are on your computer's hard disk, drive C:. But your computer may have several disk drives that support *removable media*. Unlike your hard drive, which you never actually see and can't take out of the computer, removable media are disks (or cards) that you can insert and remove from their disks drives. Common examples include floppy disks, CDs, and DVDs. But there are others. Here's a quick rundown of the most common types of drives that use (or *are*) removable media:

- ✦ **Floppy disks:** Most desktop computers, and some laptops, have a floppy drive for using 3.5-inch floppy disks. The floppy drive is typically drive A:. Each floppy disk holds about 1.4 MB of data (which isn't much).

- ✦ **CD/DVD drives:** These common drives play CDs and DVDs. Most of the techniques described in this chapter *don't* apply to CDs and DVDs, so those types of disks get their own chapter (see Chapter 15).

- ✦ **Zip disks:** A Zip disk is similar to a floppy disk and works just like a floppy disk. But a single Zip disk can generally hold as much as hundreds of floppy disks. To use Zip disks, you need a Zip drive.

✦ **Thumb drive:** Also called a *jump drive* or *flash drive*, these are tiny thumb-sized hard disks that you can put on your key chain. Some are actually hidden inside pens or a Swiss Army knife. The disk itself isn't removable from the drive. To use the drive you just plug it into a USB port on your computer.

✦ **Memory Cards:** Memory cards are typically used in digital cameras to store pictures. To read data from a memory card, you need a *card reader*. When you insert a card into the reader, the card appears as a disk drive in My Computer. Synonyms and specific product types include *flash card, flash memory, SmartMedia, CompactFlash, Memory Stick, SD/MMC, and USB mass storage device.*

Tip

To see examples of any of the preceding, go to any Web site that sells computer hardware and search for the type of product in which you're interested. For example, you can go to `www.TigerDirect.com` and search for `thumb drive`, `card reader`, `flash memory`, `DVD drive`, `floppy drive`, `hard drive`, or whatever.

Excluding CDs and DVDs, the techniques described work with any of the preceding types of media. For example, you can copy data to and from any disk or card using techniques described in this chapter. You can also rename and delete folders and files on those media using techniques described in this chapter.

They're all in your My Computer folder

All of the drives that are currently installed in your computer are accessible from your My Computer folder. You can open that folder from the Start menu, or its desktop icon, if you have one. For example, Figure 14-1 shows the My Computer folder for a computer to which I've attached lots of different removable media.

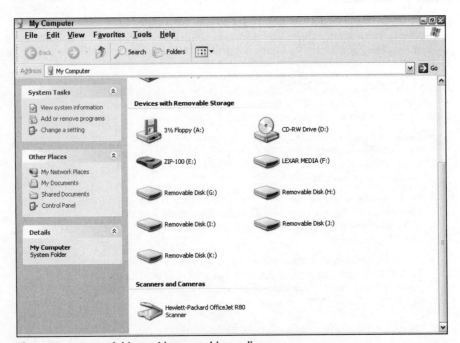

Figure 14-1: Lots of drives with removable media

USB Mass Storage Devices

Many digital cameras, MP3 players, and thumb drives use memory cards to store data. Most also connect to the computer through a USB port. Windows initially "sees" each of these things as a USB mass storage device. The name stems from the fact the device can store data, and you can move and copy data to and from the device via the USB port.

A USB mass storage device will always have an icon in My Computer. You can use any of the techniques described in this chapter to manage folders and files on the device. Though in many cases, you'll have other methods to choose from as well. For example, you can use Windows Media Player (see Chapter 38) to copy songs to MP3 players. You can use the Camera and Scanner Wizard (see Chapter 37) to get pictures from digital cameras.

In the example, drive A: is a floppy drive, D: is a CD-RW drive, E: is a Zip drive, F: is a thumb drive, and drives G: through K: are slots on a card reader that can read all different types of memory cards. If you plug a digital camera directly into a computer, and that camera stores pictures on a memory card, its icon would look like one of those icons.

Tip   To view the contents of your My Computer folders grouped and with heading, as in Figure 14-1, choose View ➪ Tiles from My Computer's menu bar. Then choose View ➪ Arrange Icons by Type. If you still don't see headings, choose View ➪ Arrange Icons By ➪ Show in Groups.

Each hard drive in your computer is also indicated by an icon in My Computer. Most computers only have one, drive C:. But a computer can contain several hard drives. You'll see icons for hard drives under the Hard Disk Drives heading, as in Figure 14-2.

Figure 14-2: My Computer icons for folders and hard disk drives

The folders at the top of My Computer represent folders on your hard drive, C:. The folder icons do not represent separate disk drives. Each, instead, represents a single folder on your hard drive, C:. Those icons are provided merely as quick shortcuts to your Shared Documents and My Documents folders. If you're an administrator, you'll also see icons for other users' My Documents folders.

Aside from your My Computer folder, the Save As and Open dialog boxes will also provide access to any removable disks on the drive. You'd rarely want to save a document to a removable disk. Better to keep all your documents in your My . . . or Shared . . . folders. Use removable disks for backups, or for copying files to a computer to which you don't have network access, or to send someone copies of files by snail mail.

Note   Different programs offer different Open and Save As dialog boxes, so yours may not always look like the examples shown in this chapter. But they all work the same way, allowing you to choose where to save a file, or where to look for a file you want to open.

As you can see in Figure 14-3, the Look In drop-down list in the Open dialog box does provide easy access to all drives. The Save In drop-down list in the Save As dialog box will offer the same list.

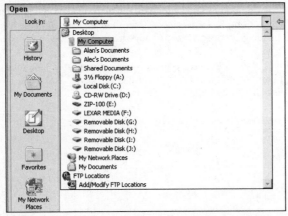

Figure 14-3: The Open dialog box provides access to all drives.

The Open and Save As dialog boxes also offer a My Computer icon. You can choose that to see all of your My Computer icons within the main pane, as shown in Figure 14-4, and then double-click any drive's icon to see the contents of the disk that's in that drive.

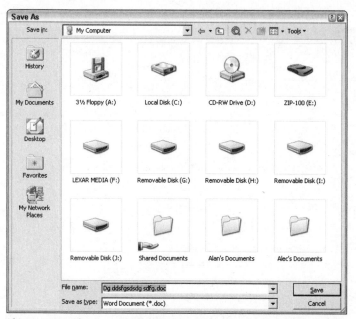

Figure 14-4: The Save As dialog box after navigating to My Computer

Viewing the contents of a removable disk

To see the contents of a disk, insert the disk into the drive. Or, to copy data to a disk, insert a blank disk into the drive. In the case of the thumb drive, plug the drive into a USB port. For a memory card, slide the card into the appropriate slot on your card reader. Or, in many cases, you can just connect the camera to the computer and turn on the camera.

Once the disk to which you want to copy data to, or from, is in the drive, just double-click (or click, if you're using single-clicking) the My Computer icon that represents the drive. The contents of the disk will appear in Windows Explorer. If there are any folders on the disk, you can navigate through them using the same techniques you use to navigate through folders on your hard drive.

As mentioned, all the techniques to follow generally work with any type of drive, the only exceptions being CD and DVD, which are covered in the next chapter.

Managing files on a network

If your computer is part of a network, you can use the techniques described in this chapter to move and copy files between shared drives, and to rename and delete files on shared drives. Use your My Network Places folder to get to shared drives, folders, and files on other computers in the network. You can also use these techniques to manage files on certain types of Internet resources, such as a Web site you own or an FTP site. Figure 14-5 shows an example of a My Network Places folder.

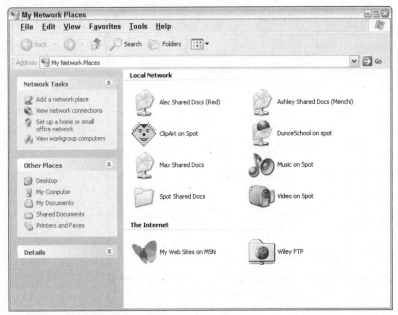

Figure 14-5: Sample My Network Places folder

The Open and Save As dialog boxes also offer access to your My Network Places folder, so you can save files to, and open files from, other computers in the network. For more information on networking and My Network Places, see Part XI in this book.

Note   If you're using a wireless network, the Explorer bar in My Network Places will offer options related to wireless networking.

Sizes and capacities (KB, MB, GB)

Every disk and every card has a *capacity* that specifies how much data it can hold. Every file has a size that specifies how much space the file consumes. We measure sizes and capacities in *bytes*, where 1 byte is the amount of space it takes to hold a single character, like the letter "a."

Most of the time you're dealing in thousands, millions, or billions of bytes. The numbers are too big to worry about the details, so we tend to round things off using some abbreviations and buzzwords. Those words, and their approximate meanings, are listed in Table 14-1. (The actual numbers are a little higher than what I've listed in the table, but the numbers in the table are close enough.)

A floppy disk holds about 1.4 MB (1,400,000 bytes) of data. A memory card, Zip disk, or thumb drive might hold anywhere from 64 MB (64 million bytes) to 1 GB (a billion bytes, or a thousand megabytes). Your hard disk holds anywhere from 20 GB to 200 GB, which is a lot more than any single removable disk or card can hold. If we liken disk capacities to water containers, a floppy disk is a shot glass, a Zip disk, memory card, or thumb drives is anywhere from a bucket to a bathtub, and your hard disk is a swimming pool.

Table 14-1: Buzzwords for Disk Capacities and File Sizes

Letter	Word	Approximate Amount	Approximate (word)	Actual
K	Kilo	1,000	Thousand	2^{10} or 1,024
M	Mega	1,000,000	Million	2^{20} or 1,048,576
G	Giga	1,000,000,000	Billion	2^{30} or 1,073,741,824
T	Tera	1,000,000,000,000	Trillion	2^{40} or 1,099,511,627,776

To see how much space is available on a disk or card, insert the disk or card into its drive or slot. Then, open My Computer, right-click the icon that represents the disk drive or card slot, and choose Properties. The dialog box that opens will show the total capacity of the item, how much space is used, and how much space is available. For example, in Figure 14-6 I'm looking at the capacity of a thumb drive that's plugged into a USB port.

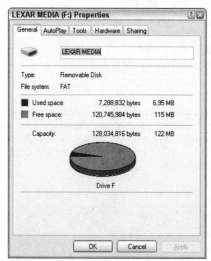

Figure 14-6: Capacity and available space on a removable disk

As you can see in the figure, the thumb drive has a total capacity of 122 MB. Currently, 6.95 MB is in use by files already stored on the drive, leaving 115 MB of free space in which you could store more files. Optionally, you could move the existing files on the thumb drive and onto the hard drive, or delete them, to regain the other 6.95 MB of space.

Tip   To see the capacity and available space on your hard drive, right-click its icon in My Computer and choose Properties, just as you would with a removable disk.

But the important point is, when you're copying files *to* a removable disk, you can only copy what will fit. To see the size of any single file, just point to the file. The Details area in the Explorer bar, and perhaps the ToolTip, will show the size of the file, as in Figure 14-7. In both the ToolTip and the Details area of the Explorer bar you can see that the file that the mouse pointer is resting on is 311 KB in size. That's about a third of a megabyte, since 1 megabyte equals roughly 1,000 kilobytes.

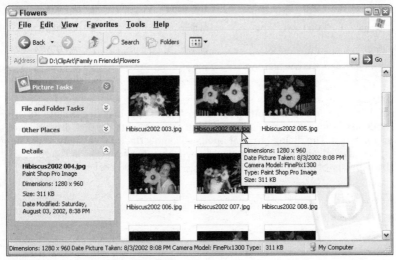

Figure 14-7: The size of a single file

Folders are a different story in that the size of the folder isn't readily apparent when you point to the folder. If you plan on copying an entire folder to a removable medium, you need to know the combined sizes of all the items in the folder. To get that information, right-click the folder's icon and choose Properties. You'll get two sizes, one titled Size and the other titled Size on Disk, as in the example shown in Figure 14-8.

Figure 14-8: Size on Disk shows the size of all files in a folder.

The Size measurement doesn't take into consideration the overhead that accompanies files stored on disk. The Size on Disk measurement, 613 MB in Figure 14-8, is the more accurate one that you'd use if you were planning to copy the folder to a disk or card. At 613 MB, it would take about 600 floppies to hold that folder, or roughly one CD. It would take about two and a half 256-MB thumb drives or memory cards to hold all the files in that folder.

If you wanted to copy that entire folder to 256-MB memory cards, you'd need three cards. You'd have to open the folder, select 256 MB or less worth of files, copy them to one card, and then, remove that card, put in another card, select a different 256 MB worth of files, and copy them to the second card, and finally replace the second card with a third and copy the rest of the files to that card.

Obviously, selecting the icons plays a big role here, so let's talk about how that works.

Selecting Files and Folders

Anything you do to one file or folder, you can do to multiple files and folders in one fell swoop. You just have to *select* the icons of the files and folders you want to work with first. The term "select" in this context has a very specific meaning. It means to point to, or click on, the icon so that it's highlighted, usually in the reverse colors of the unselected items.

There are lots of ways to select icons in Windows Explorer. Choosing one method or another is simply a matter of personal preference, and deciding which would be the most convenient method at the moment. It often helps, though, to choose a view, like Details or List first, if you need to select a lot of icons.

You might also find it helpful to arrange the icons by name, date, or some other criterion before you select. That way, the icons you plan to select might already be bunched together, making it easy to select them just by dragging the mouse pointer through them. As discussed back in Chapter 3, to arrange icons in a folder, right-click some empty space between icons and choose Arrange Icons By. Or, choose View ⇨ Arrange Icons By from Explorer's menu bar. In Details view, you can arrange icons just by clicking on any column heading.

Caution   You can't delete, rename, move, or copy an open file. So you'll want to make sure that you close any file you plan on managing before you start selecting icons.

Selecting multiple icons by dragging

If the icons you want to select are adjacent to one another within the folder, perhaps the easiest way to select them will be to drag the mouse pointer through them. The main trick to selecting by dragging is to make sure the tip of the mouse pointer isn't touching an icon or filename. Otherwise, you'll only succeed in dragging the file. If you want to select multiple icons by dragging, you need to start with the tip of the mouse pointer just outside the first item you want to select. Here are the steps:

1. Position the mouse pointer so it's near the first icon you want to select, but not actually touching an icon for filename.

2. Hold down the left mouse button, and drag the mouse pointer through the name or icon of each item you want to select.

3. When all the items you want to select are highlighted, release the mouse button.

Figure 14-9 illustrates the basic idea using the List view as an example. But the technique works the same way in any view.

Point just outside the first item to select...

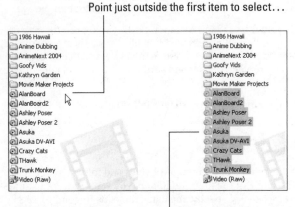

...then drag through the icons and release the mouse button.

Figure 14-9: Select icons by dragging.

The selected items are highlighted. If you need to unselect one or more selected items, hold down the Ctrl key and click the items you want to unselect. Or, to start over, just click some empty space between or outside the selected icons, or press Esc, to unselect the items.

If you use single-clicking, rather than double-clicking, be aware that simply pointing to an icon will select it. If you select a bunch of icons, then leave the mouse pointer resting on an icon, you unselect all the selected icons and end up with only the current icon selected. So, if you use single-clicking, be careful where you leave the mouse pointer after you drag and release the mouse button.

Selecting all icons in a folder

If you want to select all the icons within the current folder, that's easy. You can use whichever of the following methods is most convenient at the moment:

✦ Choose Edit ➪ Select All from Explorer's menu bar.

✦ Or, press Ctrl+A.

All the icons will be selected. You can unselect individual icons using Ctrl+*Select* or Shift+*Select*, described in the next section. To unselect all icons, click any empty space between icons or press Esc. If you're using single-click to open icons, then *Select* (in italics) means *point*. If you're using double-click to open icons, then *Select* (in italics) means *click*. Though if you're using single-click to open icons, you can actually point or click while holding down the Ctrl or Shift key.

Selecting most of the icons in a folder

If you need to select most, but not all the icons in a folder, first select the few icons that you *don't* want to select. Then, choose Edit ➪ Invert Selection from Explorer's menu bar to select all but the currently selected icons.

Selecting multiple icons using Ctrl and Shift keys

If you want to select multiple icons that aren't near each other, you can use the Ctrl and Shift keys in combination with the mouse. You have to select one icon first. And how you do that depends on whether you're using single-click or double-click to open icons, as follows:

✦ If you're using double-click, you need to click on an icon to select it.

✦ If you're using single-click, point to (don't click on) the first icon you want to select.

Note   See "To click or double-click" in Chapter 3 for details on choosing between using single-click-ing or double-clicking to open icons.

Once you've selected a single icon, you can then use the Ctrl and Shift keys to select more icons.

Selecting multiple icons with Ctrl+Click

After you've selected one icon, you can select additional icons by holding down the Ctrl key as you select more icons. If you're using double-click to open files, then you have to Ctrl+Click each additional icon. That is, you need to hold down the Ctrl key as you click on each additional icon.

If you're using single-click to open icons, then you can use either Ctrl+Click or Ctrl+Point to select additional icons. To use Ctrl+Point, just hold down the Ctrl key as you point to each icon you want to select. You'll need to rest the tip of the mouse pointer right on the item for about a second, maybe a little less.

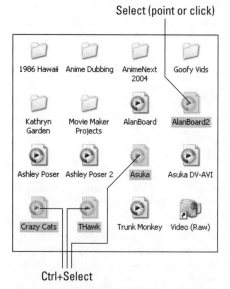

Figure 14-10: Using Ctrl+*Select* to select multiple icons

To unselect any selected icon without unselected them all, Ctrl+*Select* that one icon.

Selecting a range of icons with Shift+Click

Once you've selected a single icon, you can also select any range of adjacent icons by holding down the Shift key as you click or point. Unlike the Ctrl key, which selects one icon at a time, the Shift key selects the current icon plus all icons between that and the first selected icon.

As with the Ctrl key, the term Shift+*Select* always means Shift+Click. But if you're using single-click to open icons, then Shift+*Select* means either Shift+Click or Shift+Point. Whether you click or point, in that case, is just a matter of personal preference. To select a range of icons using Shift+*Select*:

1. Select the first icon without holding down any keys.

2. Shift+*Select* the last icon you want to select.

3. Release the Shift key.

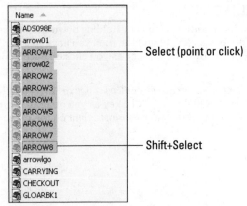

Figure 14-11: Selecting multiple icons with Shift+*Select*

If you need to unselect a few of the selected icons, Ctrl+*Select* those you want to unselect. To unselect all selected files and start over, click any empty space between icons.

Selecting across multiple folders

If you want to select multiple icons that aren't in the same folder, your best bet is to use the Search Companion to search for some characteristic that all the files have in common. For example, if you wanted to dig up all the .zip files on your hard drive, use the Search Companion to search for all files and folder with the name *.zip.

In the Search Results, you can select icons just as you would in any other folder. The fact that the icons are all in different folders is irrelevant at that point. You can delete, move, or copy all of the selected items using any of the techniques described in the following sections.

Note   For more information on the Search Companion, see Chapter 17.

How much stuff have I selected?

There will be times when you'll want to know how much stuff you've selected. For example, if you plan to copy all the files you've selected to a 256-MB thumb drive, their combined sizes must be no more than 256 MB.

If there are no folders, only files, in the selection, then you can see how much space all the selected files take just by looking at the Details area in the Explorer bar or the status bar. For example, the 10 selected files in Figure 14-12 have a combined size of 507 KB, or roughly half a megabyte (about half of a floppy disk). You can see that size both in the Details area and down in the Status bar.

Figure 14-12: The total size of 10 selected files is 507 KB.

However, if there are any folders in the selection, neither the Details area nor the status bar will give you an accurate measure of all the files involved, because it doesn't add up the sizes of all the files in the subfolder. You have to right-click any selected icon and choose Properties to see the true size.

For example, in Figure 14-13 I've selected four icons. Three of them are folders, one is a file. The Details bar says that I have four items selected (which is true). But the Total File Size of 15.8 KB is for the selected file only, which doesn't take into the sizes of all the files in the sub-folders. The Size on Disk measurement in the Properties dialog box, 50.9 MB, is the accurate measurement. So in other words, if you wanted to copy, in one fell swoop, all the selected items to a removable disk or card, that disk or card would need at least 50.9 MB of available space on it.

Figure 14-13: The total size of all files, including files in selected subfolders

Renaming Files and Folders

You can rename just about any file or folder at any time. But, you'll definitely want to stick to renaming files and folders you've created yourself. Changing the names of built-in folders and files is definitely not a good idea, because Windows "expects" those built-in items to always have the names it has given them. Also, you can't rename folders and files on CD-ROMs and DVDs, because the contents of those disks can't be changed in any way.

Also, be careful not to change a file's extension, because doing so will make the file unusable—that is, unusable until you rename the file's extension back to its original name. If filename extensions are hidden when you rename files, then you don't have to worry about changing the extension. The extension won't even be visible, so you couldn't rename it if you tried.

Note See "Showing and hiding filename extensions" in Chapter 3 for more information on file-name extensions.

If you just want to rename a single file or folder, use whichever method below is most convenient at the moment:

✦ Right-click the item and choose **Rename**.

✦ Or, select the icon and choose **File ➪ Rename** from the menu bar.

✦ Or, select the item and click on **Rename this file** or **Rename this folder** under File and Folder Tasks in the Explorer bar.

The folder or filename will be highlighted and will contain the blinking cursor. Anything you type will immediately replace the original name. You can use most of the standard navigation keys and editing techniques, summarized in the following list, to edit, rather than replace, the existing name:

- ✦ **Home:** Press the Home key to move the cursor to the start of the name.
- ✦ **End:** Press the End key to move the cursor to the end of the name.
- ✦ **Delete:** Delete the character at (to the right of) the cursor.
- ✦ **Backspace:** Delete the character to the left of the cursor.
- ✦ **Shift+*Navigation Key*:** Hold down the Shift key while pressing the ←, →, Home, or End keys to select text. Any new text you type replaces the selected text.
- ✦ **Drag:** Drag the mouse pointer though the part of the name you want to change. For example, if filename extensions are visible, drag the mouse pointer through every character to the left of the dot to replace the filename without changing the extension.

After you've made your changes, press Enter or click some empty space outside the icon. In the unlikely event that the new name doesn't show up right away, choose View ➪ Refresh from Explorer's menu bar. To get things into alphabetical order, right-click any empty space between icons and choose Arrange Icons By ➪ Name.

If you do change the extension . . .

There are cases where it's perfectly fine to change a filename extension. For example, if you use Notepad to create a file that contains text and HTML tags, then save it as `MyPage.txt`, no problem. You can just rename the file `MyPage.htm` or `MyPage.html`, and it will work fine in any Web browser. That works because .txt files and .htm files are both plain-text files. Once you've made that change, the file will open in your Web browser, rather than Notepad, when you double-click its icon. (Though you can still right-click and choose Open With to open the file in any program that can read text files).

Tip   You cannot change a file's extension when the extensions are hidden. You must disable the *Hide extensions for known file types* option in Folder Options first. See "Showing and hiding filename extensions" in Chapter 3 for details.

But, if you think that changing a filename's extension will change its file type, that's a big mistake. It doesn't work that way. Changing a file's extension changes only the extension, not the format of the file inside the file. If filename extension no longer accurately reflects the actual format of the data inside the file, then most likely the file won't work at all.

Tip   If you want to rename a file to some lengthy name that's similar to other files in the folder, you don't need to type out the entire name. Instead, right-click the icon of the file that already has the name you want, choose Rename, press Ctrl+C to copy that name, and then click outside the icon so that you don't actually rename that file. Next, right-click the icon on the file you do want to rename, choose Rename, press Ctrl+V to paste in the copied name, and then use standard editing techniques to change that pasted name.

If you do change a filename's extension you'll see the message shown in Figure 14-14. Unless you know what you're doing, your best bet is to choose No, to cancel the whole process and keep the existing filename and extension.

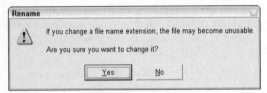

Figure 14-14: Message that tells you when you've changed a file's extension

Renaming multiple files

You can also rename multiple files, though you don't have much control over how the icons are named. You'll always end up with the first file having whatever name you gave it. Other icons will have that same name followed by (1), (2), (3), and so forth. That's not such a bad thing, though, if all the files have something in common, and you want them to have similar names.

To rename multiple files, just select all the files you want to rename first. Then, right-click any one of them, choose Rename, and enter the new name. For example, Figure 14-15 shows a group of icons that I copied from the Pictures folder on a Kodak Photo CD. The names of the files are the original names from the CD. In the figure, I've already selected all the icons, right-clicked on of them, and am about to choose Rename.

Figure 14-15: About to rename multiple selected files

Why Two Filename Extensions?

If you rename a file with filename extensions hidden, the extension you add won't be an extension at all. Rather, it will just be part of the filename. With extensions hidden, it will look like a filename with an extension. But when you open the file, it will still open as the original document type. That's because the filename still has the original extension. You just can't see that extension when extensions are hidden.

For example, suppose that you see a file named MyText. You rename it to MyText.txt. Even with extensions hidden, the .txt is still visible, because the .txt isn't the extension. Rather, it's part of the filename. That's because Windows XP allows you to put dots in filenames.

When you take extensions out of hiding, you'll see what's really going on. The file might be named something like MyText.txt.doc when extensions are visible. In this example, the filename is MyText.txt and the extension is .doc. The filename extension is .doc whether extensions are visible or not.

After choosing Rename, I renamed the first selected icon to 2005, Jan 15.JPG (being careful not to change the extension). After pressing Enter, the new names are as shown in Figure 14-16.

Figure 14-16: Renamed files from Figure 14-15

If the one icon without a number after its name bugs you, you can rename that one to match the format of the others. Just add (x) to the existing filename, where x is 0 or the next number in the sequence of filenames.

Undoing a rename

If you rename a folder or file and then change your mind (before you do anything else), you can undo the rename by pressing Ctrl+Z or by choosing Edit ➪ Undo Rename from Explorer's menu bar. If you renamed a bunch of files, you'll only be able to un-rename 10 of them that way. And you'll have to press Ctrl+Z 10 times to do so.

Deleting Files and Folders

Deleting files and folders is easy—perhaps too easy in some ways, because deleting can be dicey business. Experienced users know this and know better than to run around deleting things at random. Newbies, however, often delete things at random, hoping that doing so will solve some problem. This is unfortunate, because deleting things at random is far more likely to cause major new problems than solve any existing problem.

The basic rule of thumb on deleting is this: Never delete *anything* unless you know exactly what it is, and you know you'll never need it again for the rest of your life. Or, at the very least, make sure that you know how to get another copy of the thing you're about to delete, just in case.

Caution
When you delete a folder, you delete all of the files and subfolders inside that folder! That means one small delete can lead to many lost files. Never delete a folder unless you're absolutely sure that the folder and its subfolders contain only files that you'll never need again.

That said, deleting is a simple process. If you want to delete a single icon, just select that icon first. To delete multiple icons, select all the icons you want to delete first. Then, do whichever of the following is most convenient for you:

✦ Right-click the icon (or any selected icon), and choose **Delete**.

✦ Or, Press the **Delete** (Del) key.

✦ Or, choose **File** ➪ **Delete** from Explorer's menu bar.

✦ Or, choose **Delete this file** or **Delete this folder** under File and Folder Tasks in the Explorer bar.

✦ Or, drag the selected item(s) to the Recycle Bin and drop them right on top of the Recycle Bin icon.

You'll see a message asking for confirmation, like one of the examples shown in Figure 14-17. There's a big difference between the two messages. The top message with the Recycle Bin icon tells you that if you choose Yes, then the file will be moved to the Recycle Bin. That's not so bad, because if you change your mind you can restore the file from the Recycle Bin.

If you send a file to the Recycle Bin, and then realize your mistake, you can undo that action by pressing Ctrl+Z, or by choosing Edit ➪ Undo, or by right-clicking the empty space left behind and choosing Undo. The icon will return, though not in the empty spot. More likely it will be the last icon in the folder.

Figure 14-17: About to delete a file

The bottom message, which shows the more serious "delete" icon with an exclamation point, tells you that if you choose Yes, the file will be permanently deleted on the spot. And by "permanent," I do mean "forever." The file won't be placed in the Recycle Bin, and Undo won't work! So, there will probably be no way to get it back.

There's a slim chance that you might be able to get it back with some third-party "undelete" utility. But you'd have to do so soon, because the space that was used by the deleted file will be overwritten as you save new files.

> **Tip**
>
> To bypass the Recycle Bin and delete the selected file(s) permanently, hold down the Shift key before you press Delete or before you choose Delete from the shortcut menu.

Using the Recycle Bin

The Recycle Bin, whose icon lives on your desktop, acts as a safety net for files and folders you delete from your hard disk. Most of the time, when you delete a file or folder from your hard disk, the item just gets moved into the Recycle Bin. However, extremely large files and folders are generally deleted on the spot, without going to the Recycle Bin.

Also, the Recycle Bin *only* keeps copies of files you delete from your hard disk. When you delete an item from a floppy, CD-RW, or Zip disk, the item is permanently deleted on the spot, and there is no changing your mind. So, the moral of that story is, never assume that deleting is safe just because there's a Recycle Bin. Always know exactly what you're deleting, and assume that there will be no turning back, before you delete anything.

> **Caution**
>
> Never use the Recycle Bin as temporary storage for a file or folder you don't plan to delete. That would be like storing important paper documents in your trash can. Risky, to say the least!

Of course, moving a file to the Recycle Bin has one strange side effect. The file in the Recycle Bin takes up just as much disk space as the original file. So, if you thought you were regaining some empty disk space by deleting, you might be surprised when there's no change to your available disk space after you delete some files.

So, there are basically two ways to use the Recycle Bin:

✦ *Restore* files that you've accidentally deleted, so they go back to their original folders.

✦ *Empty* the Recycle Bin, thereby permanently deleting the files within it to reclaim the disk space they were using.

The *empty* part is a one-way street. Once you empty the Recycle Bin, there's no way to get back any files that were in it before. Again, there are some third-party utilities that might be able to reclaim files that you've emptied from the Recycle Bin. But "might be able to" is not the same as "will be able to." But let's start with restoring files.

Recovering accidentally deleted files

If you accidentally deleted some files or folders from your hard disk, and if they were sent to the Recycle Bin, you can get them back, provided that you don't empty the Recycle Bin first. Here's how:

1. Open the Recycle Bin icon on the desktop. It will open looking something like Figure 14-18.

Figure 14-18: The Windows XP Recycle Bin

2. Optionally, you can choose a view and arrange icons in the Recycle Bin, using the same techniques you use in any other folder, so you can see what's in the bin. Then:

   • To restore all items in the bin back to their original locations, click on **Restore all items** under Recycle Bin Tasks in the Explorer bar.

   • To restore a single item, right-click it and choose **Restore**, or click **Restore this item** in the Explorer bar, or choose **File** ➪ **Restore** from the menu bar.

   • To restore multiple items, select the items you want to restore. Then, right-click any one of them and choose **Restore**, or choose **Restore the selected items** from the Explorer bar, or choose **File** ➪ **Restore** from the menu bar.

Each file and folder you restore will be returned to its original location. You can then close the Recycle Bin by clicking the Close (X) button in its upper-right corner.

Undeleting Files and Folders

Even though there's no way to recover a permanently deleted file in Windows XP, that doesn't mean it's entirely impossible. You can purchase and install a third-party undelete program that provides one last, slim hope of restoring deleted files from removable media and even files that have been emptied from the Recycle Bin. But those deleted files won't hang around forever. Eventually, new files you save will replace the deleted ones. And once that happens, the deleted files no longer exist and nothing can bring them back.

Still, if you can jump on the problem shortly after an accidental deletion, there's a good chance you'll be able to undelete. For an example of a third-party undelete program, check out the RecoverMyFiles program at www.recovermyfiles.com. Or, try out the free trial version by going to www.tucows.com and searching for RecoverMyFiles.

Permanently deleting Recycle Bin files

When you feel confident that the Recycle Bin contains only folders and files that you'll never need again, you can empty the Recycle Bin. To do so, first open the Recycle Bin. Then, use whichever of the following techniques is most convenient:

✦ Click **Empty the Recycle Bin** under Recycle Bin Tasks in the Explorer bar.

✦ Or choose **File ⇨ Empty Recycle Bin** from Recycle Bin's menu bar.

Tip   You can empty the Recycle Bin without opening it first. Just right-click the Recycle Bin's icon, and choose Empty Recycle Bin.

When you've finished with the Recycle Bin, you can close it as you would any other window — by clicking the Close (X) button in its upper-right corner.

Moving and Copying Files

Keeping files organized often requires moving and copying files. Whenever you move or copy a file, there's a *source* and a *destination* involved. The difference is as follows:

✦ **Source:** The drive and/or folder that contains the files you want to move or copy (the "*from*" drive and/or folder).

✦ **Destination:** The drive and/or folder to which you want to move or copy files (the "*to*" drive and/or folder).

The source can be any folder on your hard disk, a floppy disk, a Zip disk, a thumb drive, a memory card, even a CD. The same is true for the destination in most cases. Though copying files to CDs and DVDs requires methods that are different from those described in this chapter. As mentioned, Chapter 15 will provide all the goods on working with CDs and DVDs.

Move versus copy

The terms *move* and *copy* in the computer sense have the same meanings that they do in regular English. For example, when you *move* a file from one location to another, you remove it from its current location and place it in a new location. For example, if you move a file from your My Documents folder to your My Pictures folder, you still have only one copy of that photo — the one now in your My Pictures folder.

When you *copy* a file, you end up with two exact clones of the file. For example, if you copy a file from your My Documents folder to a floppy disk, you'll have two copies of the file: the one still in your My Documents folder and the one on the floppy. We can say that the copy on the floppy is a *backup* of the one in the My Documents folder. If you somehow mess up the copy in your My Documents folder, it's no big deal. You can just grab a copy of the original from the floppy disk.

There are lots of ways to move and copy files. As usual, there's isn't a right way or a wrong way. The result is always the same. Choosing one method over another is simply a matter of deciding what's most convenient at the moment or what's easiest for you to remember.

Moving files to a subfolder

One of the most common reasons to move files is when you create a new, empty subfolder within some existing folder. Then, you want to move some files into that new subfolder. That's easy to do:

✦ Drag any item onto the subfolder's icon, and release the mouse button.

✦ Or, select the items you want to move, and drag any one of the selected items to the subfolder's icon, and then release the mouse button.

The main trick is making sure that you get the mouse pointer right on the subfolder's icon. The subfolder's icon will be highlighted when the cursor is in the right place, as in the example shown in Figure 14-19.

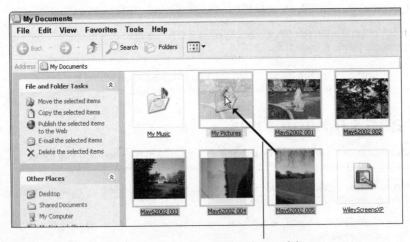

Select, drag and drop

Figure 14-19: About to drop selected icons onto a subfolder's icon

If you change your mind partway through the drag-and-drop operation, just tap the Esc key, and then release the mouse button.

Tip To copy a folder to a subfolder, hold down the Ctrl key as you drag the icon. Or, drag using the right mouse button then choose Copy Here after you drop the icon on the subfolder's icon.

If you want to copy files, or move them to someplace other than a subfolder within the current folder, use one of the other techniques described in the sections that follow.

Moving and copying by dragging

When you can't see both the source folders and destination folders at the same time, you can just open both folders. Then, select and drag files from one folder to the other. If you're planning on copying files to or from a removable disk, such as a floppy, Zip, or thumb drive, or a memory card, make sure that you insert the appropriate disk or card first. Then, open the drive's icon from My Computer.

For example, suppose that you want to copy some pictures from a memory card to your My Pictures folder. You'll need one Explorer instance for the memory card, which you can get to by opening My Computer, and then opening the icon for the drive. Then, you'll need a second instance of Explorer to show the contents of the My Pictures folder. To quickly size and position the two windows so that you can see both, right-click the clock and choose Cascade Windows. Then, drag one of the windows down and the right a little, as in the example shown in Figure 14-20..

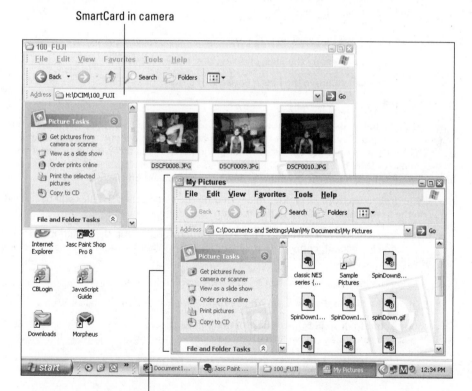

Figure 14-20: Two Explorer windows open for drag-and-drop moving/copying

Figure 14-20 is just an example. Each open window can be any folder on your hard drive, any removable disk (other than CD or DVD), or any shared folder on your network. The techniques work the same no matter what's showing in each window.

You can copy files *from* a CD using the technique described here. You can copy files *to* a CD using these methods as well. But you'll also need to perform the additional step of "burning" the files to the CD, as discussed in Chapter 15.

Tip   To open a subfolder in a new window, hold down the Shift key and double-click the folder's icon.

Once you have the two Explorer windows open, you can move or copy files from one to the other by following these general steps:

1. In the source folder, select the icon(s) of the item(s) you want to move or copy.

2. Use the right mouse button to drag the icon (or any selected icon) to an empty area in the destination folder.

Tip   If you get part way through a drag-and-drop operation then change your mind, press the Esc key, and then release the mouse button.

3. Release the mouse button. Then . . .

   • If you want to copy the files, choose **Copy Here**.

   • If you want to move the files, choose **Move Here**.

That's all there is to it.

Right-dragging (that is, using the right mouse button) to drag from one folder to the other, is optional. It's just a handy way to do it because you can get choose if you want to move or copy right after you drop. But you can drag using the left mouse button if you prefer. If you use the mouse button, the files will either be moved, or copied, without your being able to choose. Windows will make the decision to move or copy based on the following:

✦ If you drag icons from one folder to another on the same drive, the files will be moved (on the assumption that you're just reorganizing your documents).

✦ If you drag icons to a separate drive, the files will be copied (on the assumption that you're making backup copies, or copies to transfer to another computer via the removable disk).

✦ To copy the files, hold down the **Ctrl** key before you release the mouse button.

✦ To move the files, hold down the **Alt** key before you release the mouse button.

When you're about to drop files into a destination folder, the mouse pointer will sport a little + sign. When you're about to move files to the destination, the mouse pointer will show a minus sign (-).

Move or copy using the Folders list

Yet another way to move or copy files is to open the Folders list. Make the source folder visible in the main pane. Then, just select the items you want to move or copy and drag them to the destination drive or folder's icon in the Folders list. Here are the specific steps:

1. Open My Documents, My Computer, or any other folder.

2. Navigate to the source folder, so you can see the items you want to move or copy.

3. Click the **Folders** button in the toolbar to make the Folders list visible.

4. Expand drives and folders in the Folders list, as necessary so that you can see the icon for the destination drive and/or folder.

5. In the main pane, select the icons you want to move or copy.

6. Right-drag the selected items to the icon that represents the drive or folder to which you want to copy the items.

7. Release the mouse button and choose Copy Here or Move Here, depending on which you want to do.

Figure 14-21 shows an example where I've selected a few icons in a folder named Banking. To move or copy those files, I would just right-drag them to any drive or folder icon in the Folders list.

Figure 14-21: Right-drag selected icons to any folder or drive in the Folders list.

If you use the left mouse button to drag, the same rules that apply to dragging with two open windows will apply. And, you can use the Ctrl key to copy, or Alt key to move, while holding down the left mouse button.

Using cut and paste to move or copy files

You can also copy and paste files to copy them, or use cut and paste to move files. The procedure goes like this:

1. Open My Computer, My Documents, or any other folder.

2. Navigate to the source folder that contains the items you want to move or copy.

3. Select the items you want to move or copy. Then:

   • If you want to move the items, right-click any selected item and choose **Cut** (or press **Ctrl+X**).

   • If you want to copy the items, right-click any selected item and choose **Copy** (or press **Ctrl+C**).

4. Navigate to the drive or folder in which you want to place the items.

5. Paste the items using whichever method is most convenient at the moment:

   • Press **Ctrl+V.**

   • Or, right-click some empty space between icons and choose **Paste**.

   • Or, choose **Edit ⇨ Paste** form Explorer's menu bar.

That's all there is to it.

Move/copy files using the Explorer bar

The File and Folder Tasks category in the Explorer bar offers options for moving and copying files as well. The starting technique is the same as most the others. Open the icon of the source drive or folder that contains the items you want to move or copy. In the main pane of the folder, select the icons for the items you want to move or copy. Then, do one of the following:

✦ To move the selected items, click on **Move the selected items** under File and Folder Tasks in the Explorer bar.

✦ To copy the selected items, click on **Copy the selected items** under File and Folder Tasks in the Explorer bar.

In the Move Items or Copy Items dialog box that opens, expand drive and folder icons, as necessary, until you find the icon that represents the destination drive and/or folder. Click on the destination drive or folder's icon so that it's highlighted. For example, in Figure 14-22 I've selected a Zip drive as the destination.

Click the Copy or Move button at the bottom of the dialog box, and you're done.

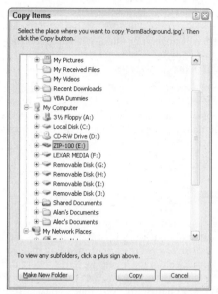

Figure 14-22: The Copy Items dialog box

Making a copy in the same folder

There are situations where you might want two copies of the same file in a single folder. For example, if you're about to tear into some document you've already spent hours on, and don't want to risk messing up that one, you can make a copy of the document and use the copy for your upcoming edits. There's no problem with having two or more copies of a document in a folder, provided their names are different.

You can use either the copy-and-paste or dragging method to copy the file. To use copy and paste, just select the icon(s) for the file(s) you want to copy. Next, press Ctrl+C (Copy), and then Ctrl+V (paste). Or, right-click the icon of the file you want to copy and choose Copy. Then, right-click some empty space between icons and choose Paste.

To use the drag method, point to the item you want to copy, and then hold down the Ctrl key. Drag the icon to where the mouse pointer is touching some empty space between icons and release the mouse button. You can release the Ctrl key too, after you've released the mouse button.

The copied file will have the same name as the original, preceded by the words "Copy of..." For example, if you copy a file named *Faded Bliss*, the copied file will be named *Copy of Faded Bliss*. If you don't see the new icon right away, scroll to the end of the folders list. It should be there.

Undoing a move or copy

If you complete a move or copy operation and then change your mind, you can undo the action as long as you don't do any more moving or copying (you can only undo one move/copy operation—the one you performed most recently).

To undo a move or copy, just press the universal Undo key, Ctrl+Z. Or, right-click within the source folder or destination folder (or Desktop, if that was your source or destination), and choose Undo Move or Undo Copy. Or choose Edit ➪ Undo from the source or destination window's menu bar. You may see a prompt asking if it's OK to delete the files. Choosing *Yes* will delete only the copied file(s), which is OK, since that's what's actually required to undo the copy.

Dealing with Read-Only Files

A read-only file is one that can be opened and viewed, but not changed. A file that's not read-only is considered a read-write file, because you can open it, view it, and change it. Files on read-only disks, such as CD-ROMs and DVD-ROMs, are always read-only, meaning that you can view the contents of the file, but you cannot change the file in any way, nor delete it from the disk. You can copy the file to a folder on your hard drive, or any other drive. There, you can do whatever you wish with the file. You just can't change the copy that's on the CD-ROM.

On normal read-write drives like your hard disk, floppies, and so forth, most documents are read-write by default, though you can easily make a read-write file into a read-only file. You might want to do that to avoid accidentally changing the file. Sometimes, files you copy from CDs still retain their read-only status, even on your hard drive. When you try to move or copy a read-only file, you're always asked for confirmation by a message box like one of those at the top of Figure 14-23.

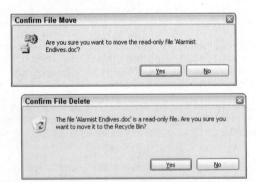

Figure 14-23: Confirmation messages for moving/deleting a Read-Only file

Neither confirmation box prevents you from moving or deleting the file. You can click Yes to proceed, or No to cancel the operation.

If you open and edit a read-only file and then try to save it, you see a message box similar to the one in Figure 14-24. There's no getting around that message box. All you can do is click OK, and then save this copy of the file with a different filename so that you don't lose any work. If necessary, you can choose File ⇨ Save As from the program's menu bar to save the edited copy of the file under a new filename.

Figure 14-24: Error message when trying to save an edited read-only file

To make a file read-only, or read-write, first make sure that the file isn't on a CD-ROM, as there's no point in even trying to change a file's status on that kind of drive. Then, follow these simple steps:

1. If you want to change the status of several files, select their icons first.

2. Right-click the file's icon (or any selected icon), and choose **Properties**. Then:

   • To make the file read-only, select the Read-only checkbox as shown in Figure 14-25.

   • To make the file read-write, clear the Read-only checkbox.

3. Click OK.

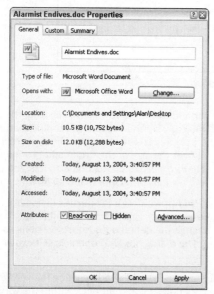

Figure 14-25: This file is flagged as read-only.

Easy!

Managing Files with DOS Commands

This section is for people who were around in the DOS days and remember commands like CD (change directory), Copy (to copy files), and so forth. All those old DOS commands still work, even though there is no DOS in Windows XP. There are some instances where using DOS commands is useful, such as when you want to print a list of filenames or paste them into a file. So, we'll look at how all that works in this section.

Getting to a command prompt

The first step to using DOS commands is to get to the Command Prompt window. To do so, click the Start button and choose All Programs ➪ Accessories ➪ Command Prompt. A window reminiscent of ye olde DOS days opens, complete with the standard prompt that displays the folder (er, I mean, *directory*) that you're currently in (or "on," or whatever the terminology was back then). Figure 14-26 shows an example.

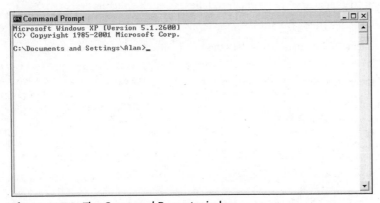

Figure 14-26: The Command Prompt window

The Command Prompt window has a title bar and taskbar button. You can drag the window around by its title bar. To a limited extent, you can size the Command Prompt window by dragging any corner or edge. But the height is limited to the number of lines currently displayed within the window. To get full control over the size of the Command Prompt window, you need to use its Properties dialog box. That Properties dialog box also lets you choose a cursor size, a Full Screen View, a font, text and background colors, and so forth.

There are two ways to get to the Command Prompt window's Properties dialog box, If you want to change properties for the current session only, right-click the Command Prompt title bar and choose Properties. If you want to change the defaults for future sessions as well, right-click the title bar and choose Defaults. The dialog box that opens is self-explanatory and a normal Windows dialog box.

You can scroll up and down through the Command Prompt window using the vertical scroll bar at its right. The navigation keys don't work unless you right-click within the window and choose Scroll. You can't type normal characters in the scroll mode, just navigate up and down. To get out of scroll mode and back to normal typing, press Enter.

To exit a command prompt session, type `exit` and press Enter. Or close the Command Prompt program window by clicking its Close (X) button or by right-clicking its taskbar button and choosing Close.

Using the command prompt

The Command Prompt window works just like the screen did in DOS. You type a command and press Enter (assuming that you're not in the aforementioned "scroll mode," wherein typing normal characters just sounds a beep). After you press Enter, you see the results of the command and another command prompt appears. For example, if you enter `Help` (that is, type the word `help` and press Enter), you see a list of all the supported DOS commands.

To get help with a command, type its name followed by a slash and question mark. For example, entering the command `dir /?` shows help for the dir command. The Doskey feature is enabled automatically (again assuming that you're not in the bizarre scroll mode). So, you can use the ↑ and ↓ to retrieve previous commands from the current session. Press → and ← keys to bring back and remove the previous command one character at a time.

> **Note**   If the characters you type result only in a beep, and nothing on the screen, right-click in the Command Prompt window and choose Scroll to get back to normal typing.

The mouse doesn't do much in the Command Prompt window. As mentioned, you can right-click the title bar (or its taskbar button) to get to the Properties sheet. You can right-click and choose Scroll to enter the (disturbing) scroll mode where navigation keys move through the window and normal characters do nothing but beep at you. (Though pressing Enter terminates the disturbing scroll mode).

Copy and paste in the Command Prompt window

Right-clicking in the Command Prompt window provides some options that allow you to use copy and paste. It's a bit tricky, but handy when you want to copy a lengthy list of filenames into a Word, WordPad, or Notepad document. If you'll be using the keyboard to select only a portion of the text, you first want to use the scroll bar to get up to where you can see where you want to start selecting text. If you'll be using the mouse to select a portion of text, or will be selecting all the text in the window, it's not so important where you start.

To select the entire window, right-click within the window and choose Select All. To select only a portion of the window's contents, right-click within the Command Prompt window and choose Mark. You'll see a square cursor. To select with the keyboard, hold down the Shift key and use the →, ←, ↑, ↓, PgUp, and PgDn keys to extend the selection through the text you want to select. With the mouse, move the mouse pointer to the far-right edge of the window, hold down the left mouse button, and then drag diagonally through the text you want to select.

Once you've selected some text, press Enter to copy the selected text and also clear the selection. From there, you can paste the copied text into any document that accepts pasted text.

You can paste a command into the window, but it has to be a valid DOS command. Just right-click near the command prompt and choose Paste.

Searching the Command Prompt window

Unlike DOS, the Command Prompt has a Find capability, so you can search for any word or phrase within the window. To use it, right-click within the Command Prompt window and choose Find. Type in the word or phrase you're looking for, choose a direction to search, Up or Down, and then click Find Next. You can keep clicking Find Next until you find what you're looking for, and then click Cancel to close the Find dialog box.

Navigating from the command prompt

Navigating to a particular drive at the command prompt is easy. Just type the drive letter followed by a colon and press Enter. For example, entering `d:` takes you to drive D:. Entering `c:` takes you to drive C:.

Use the `cd` (Change Directory) command, just as you did in DOS, to go to a folder on the current drive. Two short cd commands you can use are:

✦ `cd\`   Takes you to the root folder of the current drive

✦ `cd..`   Takes you to the parent of the current folder

Unlike DOS where names were limited to eight characters, file and folder names in Windows can be quite lengthy. For example, if you wanted to navigate to the Shared Music folder, and were forced to type the entire command, you'd have to enter `cd C:\Documents and Settings\All Users\Documents\My Music`. That's a lot of characters to type.

Fortunately, there are a couple of ways to avoid typing out the length pathnames. The simplest method is to use Windows Explorer to navigate to the folder of interest. Make sure that the Address bar is visible and is set to show the full path. Then, you can just select that full pathname and press Ctrl+C to copy it.

Note   See Chapter 6 for information on displaying the full path in the title bar.

Next, go back to the Command Prompt window, type `cd` followed by a space, and then right-click there next to the cursor and choose Paste. Figure 14-27 shows an example. Press Enter to complete the command and get to the folder of interest.

The other alternative to typing lengthy pathnames is to use the short name to drill down one folder at a time. The short name for a folder is the first six nonblank characters followed by a tilde (~) and a number. For example, the short name for the *Documents and Settings* folder is *docume~1*. The short name for the *All Users* folder is *AllUse~1*.

You can see the short name of any folder within the current folder by entering `dir /x` at the command prompt. The full name appears in the last column, the short name just to the left of that, as in the example shown in Figure 14-28. Though I think you'll probably find it easiest to copy and paste pathnames from Explorer's Address bar.

So for example, let's say you're on drive C: and enter the command `cd\` to go to its root folder, `C:\`. To see short names of folders in the root, enter `dir /x`. If you want to go to the Documents and Settings folder, type `cd docume~1` and press Enter. To see subfolders in the Documents and Settings folder, enter `dir /x` again (or press ↑ twice), and then press Enter. If a given folder has a short name already, such as Ashley, you can just enter `dir ashley` and press Enter. If the subfolder name is lengthy or contains a space, such as All Users, use the short name in the cd command. That is, type `cd alluse~1` and press Enter to go to the All Users folder.

Select and copy path…

Shared Music
File Edit View Favorites Tools Help
Back
Search
Folders
Address C:\Documents and Settings\All Users\Documents\My Music
Go
Music Tasks
Command Prompt
C:\Documents and Settings\Alan>cd\
C:\>cd C:\Documents and Settings\All Users\Documents\My Music

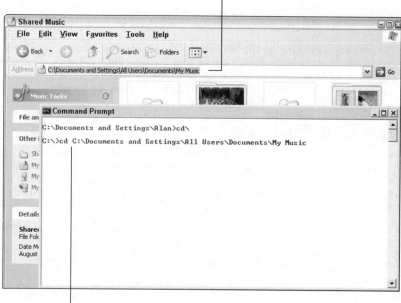

…type **cd** and a space, then right-click and choose Paste.

Figure 14-27: Copying a path from Explorer to the Command Prompt

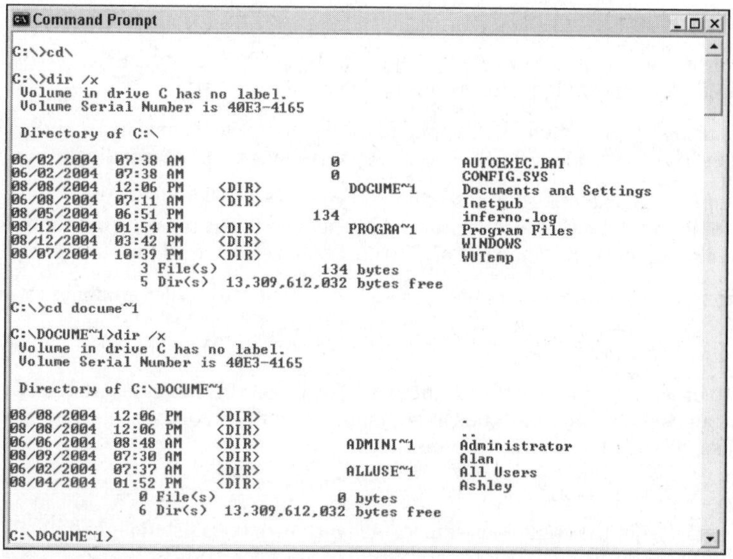

Command Prompt
C:\>cd\
C:\>dir /x
Volume in drive C has no label.
Volume Serial Number is 40E3-4165
Directory of C:\
06/02/2004 07:38 AM 0 AUTOEXEC.BAT
06/02/2004 07:38 AM 0 CONFIG.SYS
08/08/2004 12:06 PM <DIR> DOCUME~1 Documents and Settings
06/08/2004 07:11 AM <DIR> Inetpub
08/05/2004 06:51 PM 134 inferno.log
08/12/2004 01:54 PM <DIR> PROGRA~1 Program Files
08/12/2004 03:42 PM <DIR> WINDOWS
08/07/2004 10:39 PM <DIR> WUTemp
3 File(s) 134 bytes
5 Dir(s) 13,309,612,032 bytes free
C:\>cd docume~1
C:\DOCUME~1>dir /x
Volume in drive C has no label.
Volume Serial Number is 40E3-4165
Directory of C:\DOCUME~1
08/08/2004 12:06 PM <DIR> .
08/08/2004 12:06 PM <DIR> ..
06/06/2004 08:48 AM <DIR> ADMINI~1 Administrator
08/09/2004 07:30 AM <DIR> Alan
06/02/2004 07:37 AM <DIR> ALLUSE~1 All Users
08/04/2004 01:52 PM <DIR> Ashley
0 File(s) 0 bytes
6 Dir(s) 13,309,612,032 bytes free
C:\DOCUME~1>

Figure 14-28: Short filename and full filename in the last two columns

Tip   Remember, to go up one folder (the current folder's parent), type `cd..` and press Enter.

Tip   You can get away with typing the first few letters of the folder name, followed by an asterisk (*) when using the cd command. You'll see an error message, but it will work nonetheless. For example, if you're at `C:\` and enter `cd doc*` you'll be taken to `C:\Documents` and `Settings` (after the error message tells you the command syntax is incorrect).

Printing a list of filenames

Perhaps the one thing that the DOS command has the Explorer doesn't is the ability to easily print a list of filenames from any folder, or even a parent folder and all its subfolders. While you can print directly by following any command with a >prn character, I'm sure most people would prefer to get that list into a Word or WordPad document. From there you can edit and sort the filename list to your liking, and then print it.

You'll use the `dir` command to list the filenames. You may find some of the following optional switches useful for controlling how dir displays its output:

/s Include filenames from subfolders

/b Display filenames in bare format (not headings or summary)

/w Show in wide format

/d Same as wide, but sorted by columns

/n Use long list format with filenames to the far right.

/l Use lowercase letters

/o Sort output by column as follows: N (by name), S (by size), E (by extension) D (by date), - (prefix for descending sort), G (group folder names first)

As an example is using the /o switch, the command `dir /on` lists filenames in ascending alphabetical order. The command `dir /o-s` lists filenames by size, in descending order.

So, let's look at a practical example, Suppose that you've use Windows Media Player to copy lots of CDs to a folder, such as My Music or Shared Music. The songs are organized into folders by artist and album. But you want a list of all song filenames, from all the subfolders.

Step 1 is to get to the parent folder of all the files you want to list. The DOS command would be cd followed by the full path to that folder. For example, `cd C:\Documents and Settings\All Users\Documents\My Music` to get to the Shared Music folder.

Next, you need to enter a dir command with the /s switch to list the filenames from all the subfolders. You can use any other switches in combination with /s. For example, here's a dir command that lists all the filenames in bare format:

```
dir /b /s
```

Here's one that lists files in the columnar wide format with filenames listed alphabetically by name:

```
dir /d /on /s
```

You can try out various DOS commands to see which presents the most reasonable list of filenames. Then, when you get a decent list, enter that command again, but follow it with >*filename*.txt where filename is any name of your choosing. The file will be stored in whatever folder you're currently in. For this example, I'll use SongList.txt as the filename. So, you might enter a command like this at the command prompt:

```
dir /d /on /s >SongList.txt
```

You won't get any feedback on the screen after you pipe the output to a file. But no matter. You can just exit the Command Prompt window. Then use Windows Explorer to navigate to the folder from which you ran the dir command—Shared Documents in this example. You'll find you SongList.txt file there. Right-click it and choose Open With ⇨ Microsoft Word (or whatever program you want to use to edit the file).

The list will look exactly like DOS output ⇨ which might not be ideal. Figure 14-29 shows a small portion of the output from the aforementioned dir /d /on /s >SongList.txt command. But if you know how to use the program, it shouldn't be too tough to select and delete anything you don't want in the document. Then, save it, print it, and keep it for future reference.

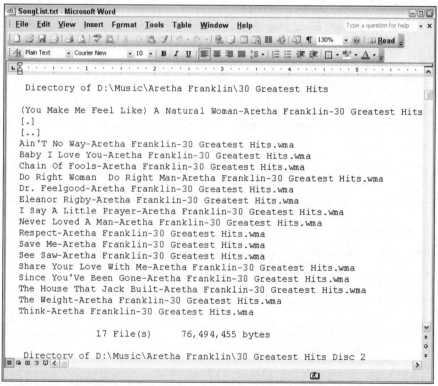

Figure 14-29: Exported filename list in a Word document

Tip
If you're a Microsoft Office guru, you could create a macro to clean up the output from a DOS command, maybe even convert it to a list of comma-separated values. Then, you could save *that* file as a text file, and import it into an Access table or Excel spreadsheet.

Whether or not this example of exporting filenames is of any value to you, I couldn't say. But it is just an example. If you know DOS, you may be able to come up with more useful applications of your own. You can do anything at the Command Prompt window that you could do in DOS, even copy and delete files. Remember, for a quick overview of all the DOS commands available in the Command Prompt window, just type help and the command prompt and press Enter.

Wrap Up

Managing files and folders in Windows XP is a lot like it was in earlier versions of Windows. You just have more ways of doing things and more kinds of media to deal with in the twenty-first century. Here's a quick wrap up of the main topics covered in this chapter:

✦ To get to all the disk drives and card slots your computer has, open your My Computer folder.

✦ To select multiple icons, drag the mouse pointer through them. Or, hold down the Ctrl or Shift keys while clicking on icons.

✦ To rename a file, or selected files, right-click and choose Rename.

✦ To delete a file or selected files, right-click and choose Delete.

✦ Small items you delete from your hard drive are just moved to the Recycle Bin.

✦ Large files, and files you delete from removable media, are not sent to the Recycle Bin.

✦ To recover a file from the Recycle Bin, right-click its icon and choose Restore.

✦ To permanently delete all the files in the Recycle Bin and reclaim the disk space they're using, empty the Recycle Bin.

✦ To move or copy selected files and folders, drag them to some new location, or use copy and paste, or use the Copy or Move options under File and Folder tasks in the Explorer bar.

✦ If you're a DOS guru, you can still use DOS commands to manage files. Just click Start and choose All Programs ➪ Accessories ➪ Command Prompt to get to a virtual DOS command prompt.

✦   ✦   ✦

Using CDs and DVDs

CD (compact disc) and DVD (digital versatile disc) are media for storing information. In that regard, they're just like any other type of disk, like floppies, Zip disks, and hard disks. The big difference is that CDs and DVDs use a laser as the means of reading and writing to the disc, whereas most other media use magnetism. The laser makes a big difference because you don't just "copy" data to those discs. You actually "burn" the information to the disk. Well, sort of . . .

It's actually a bit more complicated than that because there are different kinds of CDs and DVDs and drives. For example, there are CD-ROMs and CD Rom drives, CD-Rs and drives, and CD-RW discs and drives. There are even more different types in the DVD world. It can all be very confusing, especially if you start out assuming that all disks are alike. As you'll see in this chapter, they're not at all alike. The laser media, CD and DVD, are definitely in a class of their own.

Understanding CDs

CDs are everywhere. You buy albums that are stored on CD. Many programs you buy are also stored on CDs. If you go to the store to buy blank CDs, you're faced with data CDs, audio CDs, CD-Rs, and CD-RWs. The first thing you need to understand is the difference between CD-ROM, CD-R, and CD-RW. So, we'll address those differences first.

CD-ROM discs

The ROM in CD-ROM stands for read-only memory, and that's exactly what a CD-ROM is. It's a disc from which you can read or copy information. However, you cannot change the contents of the disc in any way, shape, or form. For example, you can't add files to the disc, nor can you delete files from the disc.

You can't change the contents of a file that's on a CD-ROM. Though you can copy any file from a CD-ROM to a folder on your hard disk and then open it, edit it, and save the changes to your hard disk. But there's no way to get that edited version of the file back onto the CD-ROM.

CD-ROMs are what we call *distribution media*. The whole idea is to allow record companies and software companies to sell their music and software on discs that cannot be changed. If you could change the contents of those discs, the record and software companies would be up to their eyebrows with peoples calling in saying, "I erased all the files on my CD. Help! What can I do to get them back?" It would probably cost those companies millions of dollars a year just to have people answer the phone and say, "You can't get them back."

So, CD-ROMs are read-only discs, and they're that way for a reason. The people who sell their wares on those discs don't want you changing or deleting the contents of the disc. You can play CD-ROMs in any computer that has a CD drive, as well as in most stereos that play music (provided that the CD has songs on it).

CD-Rs

The R in CD-R stands for *recordable*, though a more accurate acronym would be WORM. (I suppose people would be less likely to buy a CD-WORM disc than a CD-R, so they stuck with the shorter acronym.) WORM stands for write once, read many, and that's exactly how a CD-R works. You write (copy) some files to it once, and only once. At that point, it becomes a CD-ROM, and you cannot change the contents of the disc in any way, shape, or form.

In other words, a CD-R is a blank *distribution medium*, because once burned, it becomes a CD-ROM. When a record company wants to make a few thousand copies of some album they're about to sell, they need to first buy a few thousand CD-Rs. Then, they load those up into special machines that stamp out CDs by the thousands, which are eventually distributed to music stores for consumers to buy.

Your computer can't stamp out thousands of CD-Rs a day. But you can certainly burn CD-Rs. (Which is to say, you can copy files to CD-Rs.) But, you only get one shot per disc. If you copy a couple of files to a CD-R and still have plenty of empty space left over, that empty space is wasted. You can't add any more files to the disc or delete files from the disc because once you've burned a CD-R, it's a CD-ROM, and there's no going back. You can *read* the contents of the disc as many times as you want, and that includes copying files from the disc. Hence, the write once, read many moniker. But you get one shot, and one shot only, at burning the disc.

Note   There is a tiny little white lie in the preceding paragraph. There are some programs that support multisession burning, where you can add more files to a CD-R. However, the CD-R isn't usable outside that program until you *close* the disc. And Windows XP doesn't offer multisession CD recording.

To copy files to a CD-R, your computer needs a CD-R drive. Most CD-RW drives can handle both CD-Rs and CD-RWs. But a CD-ROM drive can't write files to CD-Rs or CD-RWs. CD-ROM drives can only read CD-ROMs. (When you burn a CD-R, it becomes a CD-ROM. So, any CD-ROM drive can read any CD-R you burn yourself.)

CD-RWs

The RW in CD-RW stands for *read/write*. As the name implies, you can read data from, and write data to, the disc at will. Instead of write once, read many, it's write many, read many. CD-RWs are often referred to a *backup media* or *archive media*, because you can periodically reuse the same disc to make updated backup copies of files on your hard disk.

Burning versus Phase Transition

The phrase "burn a CD" comes from the fact that when you copy files to a CD-R, the laser literally "burns" the information onto the disc. You can't "unburn" a CD any more than you can "unburn" a log. Burning things is a one-way street. (Actually it's a bit more like "pitting" than "burning," but that's not important.)

We do use the term "burn" with CD-RWs, but there really isn't any burning involved. CD-RW works, instead, by the principle of *phase transition*. An everyday example of phase transition would be water in a cup. If you leave a half cup of water sitting on the counter all day, it stays liquid. If you put it in the freezer, it turns solid. The change from liquid to solid is a phase transition.

If you take the cup out of the freezer and leave it on the counter all day, it goes back to being a liquid. There's no permanent change to the water during the phase transition. It's the same water whether it's frozen or not. The same basic idea holds true when the laser in a CD-RW drive changes data on the surface of a CD-RW disc. The change can be undone.

Both the laser used in CD-RW and the material on the surface of a CD-RW are different from those of CD-ROM and CD-R. Thus, you can only create, and use, CD-RWs if you have a CD-RW drive in your computer. You can't use CD-RWs in CD-ROM or CD-R drives. Very few stereos can recognize and play music from CD-RWs.

So to summarize, you don't buy blank CD-ROMs at all, because you can't do anything with a CD-ROM except read its contents. If you want to distribute software or make music CDs to play in a stereo, you use CD-Rs (because few stereos can read CD-RWs). If you have a CD-RW drive, then you can use CD-RWs to make backup copies of important files. You can also reuse those discs, so you don't have to start with a brand new blank disc every time you want to make backup copies of files.

Data CD versus audio CD

CDs come in two capacities, commonly referred to as data CDs and audio CDs. A data CD has a capacity of 650 MB, or enough space to store about 74 minutes worth of music. An audio CD has a capacity of 700 MB, or enough space to store about 80 minutes worth of music. And that's really the main difference between the two types of CDs.

Of course, the manufacturers will all tell you that their products are "the best" for music and "the best" for data. But the truth of the matter is you can store music on either type of disc or data (computer files) on either type of disc. There are definitely some brand and quality differences between CDs though. In fact, you can run into a situation where one brand of blank CD doesn't work at all with your drive, while another brand works just fine.

Unfortunately, there's no way to tell in advance which brand will or won't work. I've had situations where a brand of CD works in one drive, but not another. But that's extremely rare. Most of the time, everything works fine. I've used many different brands of CDs to make audio CDs and have never noticed any difference in sound quality between one brand and another. (Though maybe I'm tone deaf. Perhaps an audiophile with good stereo equipment could tell the difference.)

12 Hours of Music on One CD

The 74-minute and 80-minute limits on music CDs apply only to music stored in CDA (Compact Disc Audio) format. That's the format used by the recording industry and on all commercial music CDs you buy for stereos. If you plan to create an audio CD and play it in a standard stereo, then you have to use CDA format as well.

However, computers can store and play music in a variety of compressed formats, such as MP3 and WMA. Some stereos can play music stored in those formats as well. If you copy songs stored in MP3 or WMA format to a CD, you can get between 10 and 12 hours onto one single CD. How you do this is a topic for Chapter 39.

X marks the speed

CDs that you play in a stereo always play at a certain speed, conveniently referred to as simply × or 1×. If the CD played any faster than 1×, it would sound like The Chipmunks. Played any slower and, well, you get the picture.

When you're copying files to or from a CD, you're not *playing* music or anything else. You're just copying, so there's nothing to hear. Hence, there's no need for the CD to spin at 1×. Which is a good thing, because 1× is slow as molasses when compared to the speed of a other types of disk drives.

As an example, suppose you were going to create an 80-minute CD by copying 80 minutes worth of music from your computer to a blank CD-R. If you did that at 1×, it would take 80 minutes to burn the CD. But if you spin the CD twice as fast, 2×, then it takes half the time, or 40 minutes. Spin the CD at 4×, and it takes one-quarter the time, or 20 minutes.

Every CD drive has a maximum speed at which it can spin a disc. A fast drive might be 48× or higher, which means that you can create an 80-minute CD in about two minutes instead of 80 minutes. There is a catch though. The blank CD-R or CD-RW disc to which (or from which) you're copying must be rated to handle that speed.

So, when you're out buying blank CDs, you want to take a look at the top speed rating. Most blank CDs there days are rated for 48×, so you shouldn't have any difficulty finding CDs that can handle that high spin rate. The rating on the CD is the maximum recommended speed for writing files to the CD. So it's OK to get CDs that are rated higher than your CD drive's speed.

Using CDs

Using (or playing) CDs is generally pretty easy. When you buy a program that's delivered to you on a CD, it's usually a simple matter of putting the CD into your CD drive, closing the drive door, and waiting a few seconds. After a while, an installation program will start, and you just follow the on-screen instructions to install the program. When the installation is done, you remove the CD and store it away for safekeeping as a backup. Once the program is installed, you should be able to start and run it from the All Programs menu without using the CD.

To play an audio CD (the kind you normally play in a stereo), you put the CD into your CD drive, close the drive door, and wait a few seconds. Most likely, some program will open and play the music for you. I'll get into the details of all that in Chapter 38.

Both of the preceding scenarios are "likely" scenarios, but certainly not guaranteed. Like everything else in Windows, you can choose exactly how you want Windows to respond when you insert an audio CD. You do so by setting *defaults* (automatic behaviors) for different types of CDs, as discussed next. I'll cover DVDs in that section too.

Setting Defaults for CDs and DVDs

When you insert a CD or DVD into your CD or DVD drive, just about anything can happen. Exactly what happens depends on what kinds of files are on the disc and how Windows is configured to deal with those files. Windows divides CDs and DVDs into categories bases on *content type*, as follows:

✦ **Music Files:** The disc contains mostly music files in .MP3 or .WMA format (as opposed to commercial music CDs, which store each song in .CDA format).

✦ **Pictures:** The disc contains mostly pictures.

✦ **Video Files:** The disc contains video files just as .WMV or .MPEGs (not the same as a DVD movie, which contains .VOB and other file types).

✦ **Mixed Content:** The disc contains a mixture of file types.

✦ **Music CD:** A commercial music CD, or one you create yourself using a program like Windows Media Player.

✦ **DVD Movie:** A standard DVD movie like the kind you buy or rent, or create using a third-party program.

✦ **Blank CD:** A blank CD-R or CD-RW.

Note   CD drives can't play DVDs. Only DVD drives, or DVD/CD combo drives, can play DVDs.

You can specify a default action to take for each content type. You can do so at any time; there's nothing set in stone here. Also, you can override the default setting and have Windows do absolutely nothing after you insert a CD, just by holding down the Shift key as you close the CD drive door. To define default behaviors for different kinds of CD content, follow these steps:

1. Open your My Computer folder (you can click the **Start** button and choose **My Computer**).

2. Right-click the icon that represents a CD or DVD drive, as at left of Figure 15-1, and choose **Properties**.

3. In the Properties dialog box that opens, click the **AutoPlay** tab. You'll see options similar to this shown in the right side of Figure 15-1.

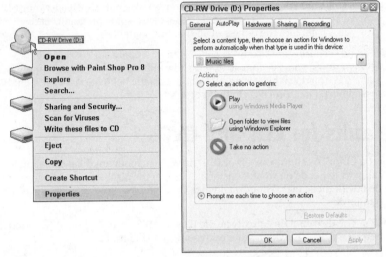

Figure 15-1: AutoPlay options for a CD and/or DVD drive

The first step on the AutoPlay tab is to choose the content type for which you want to set a new default behavior. For example, if you want to control what happens automatically after you put a blank CD in the drive, choose Blank CD from the drop-down list. If you want to control what happens after you insert a commercial audio CD into the CD drive, choose Music CD. The options under Actions in the center of the dialog box will change to reflect the things you can do with that type of content. First, you have two major options to choose from:

✦ **Select an action to perform:** If you choose this option, you can then click on any action listed under the item to make that default action. For example, if you're setting a default for music CDs, you might want to choose Play using Windows Media Player so that Media Player opens and starts playing the music automatically.

✦ **Prompt me each time to choose an action:** If you choose this option, then no specific action will be taken when you insert a disc that reflects the currently selected content type. Instead, after you insert a CD or DVD (and wait a few seconds), you'll see a message asking what you want to do with the disc. I'll show you an example in a moment.

So the idea here in the CD drive's Properties dialog box is to set different defaults for different types of CD content. For example, if you want commercial music CDs to automatically play in Windows Media Player, set the Music CD content types to "Select an action to perform" and "Play using Windows Media Player."

If you don't have a particular preference for a certain type of CD, set its option to "Prompt me each time . . ." For example, let's say that you create different kinds of CDs, some for music and some for backups of important documents. In that case, you might choose Blank CD from the drop-down list, and then set its action to "Prompt me each time to choose an action," as shown in Figure 15-2.

After making your selections, click OK in the dialog box. You can also close the My Computer folder.

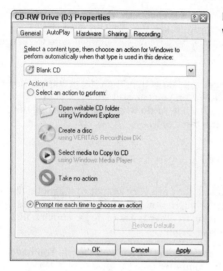

Figure 15-2: Blank CDs will display a prompt when inserted.

To test your changes, insert a CD and wait a few seconds. Referring back to the previous example, if you choose "Play using Windows Media Player" for music CDs, insert a commercial music CD (or one you created yourself using Windows Media Player) and wait a few seconds. Window Media Player should open and start playing the CD.

If you set the action for blank CDs to "Prompt me each time to choose an action," insert a blank CD into the drive and wait a few seconds. You should see a prompt offering options similar to those shown in Figure 15-3 (though again, the exact options available to you will vary, depending on the programs installed on your computer).

Figure 15-3: Prompt that appears after inserting a blank CD

The prompt dialog box offers options similar to those in the Properties dialog box. Click on whichever action you want to perform, and then click OK. The action you choose will apply to the current CD only. However, if you also choose "Always do the selected action" checkbox before you click OK, then the action you chose will apply to all future CDs of that type that you insert. To undo that change you'd need to go back to the drive's Properties dialog box and reset the content type action to "Prompt me each time . . ."

Caution   Some programs, especially promotional freebies, surreptitiously change drive defaults to open themselves, as a marketing ploy to get you to use the program often. Personally, I always banish such programs from my computer, because it's just outright rude to change my personal preferences behind my back!

If you are prompted, as in Figure 15-3, and choose Take no action, then the prompt dialog box will close, and no further action will be taken. However, you can still view the contents of the CD (assuming that it's not a blank CD), copy files from it, or do whatever by opening the drive's icon in My Computer. This brings us to the topic of . . .

Copying Files from a CD

Even though CDs aren't exactly like magnetic discs, they are very similar to magnetic disks in one big way: every CD contains files that might (or might not) be organized into folders. And while copying files *to* a CD isn't the same as copying to other types of disks, copying files *from* a CD is the same. However, a few caveats before we begin:

✦ Copying files from a CD that contains a commercial program won't work. You have to *install* a program before it will run on your computer (see Chapter 45).

✦ While you *can* copy songs from commercial CDs using this technique, you'd be better off using a program like Windows Media Player (see Chapter 38).

✦ If some program starts automatically after you insert a CD, and you just want to view or copy the contents of that CD, close or Cancel that program before you open My Computer.

✦ If you get the prompt that asks what you want to do with the CD currently in the drive, choose Take No Action to close the prompt box.

With all the caveats aside and the CD in the drive, you can copy the files from that CD to any folder on your hard drive using whatever technique described in Chapter 14 is most convenient. First, you need to open the CD drive's icon. To do that, open your My Computer folder (click the Start button and choose My Computer). Then, right-click the icon for the CD drive and choose Open, as in the example shown in Figure 15-4.

Figure 15-4: Right-click the icon for a CD drive that contains a CD.

You'll see the contents of the CD in a standard Windows Explorer window. You can choose a view or arrange icons however you wish. If you don't see the files you want to copy, look through any folders on the CD for the files you want to copy. For example, if you open a Kodak Photo CD you'll see several folder and file icons at first, but no pictures. To get to the actual photos, you need to open the folder named Pictures on the CD.

If you want to use the drag-and-drop method to copy the files to your hard disk, open another instance of Explorer. For example, if you're copying pictures, you can click the Start button and choose My Pictures. Optionally, you can create a new subfolder the files you're about to copy, and then open that new folder. Finally, size and position the two Explorer windows so that you can see at least some portion of both, as in the example shown in Figure 15-5.

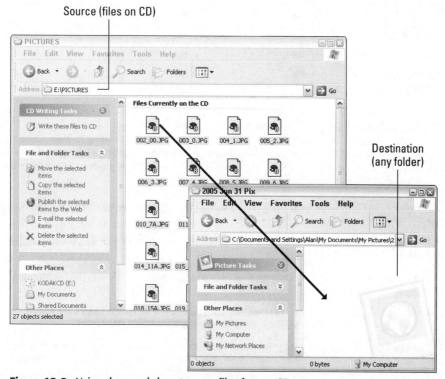

Figure 15-5: Using drag-and-drop to copy files from a CD

In the CD's folder, select the icons of the files you want to copy. If you want to copy them all, just press Ctrl+A or choose Edit ➪ Select All from the menu bar in the CD's folder. Then, just drag any selected icon to the destination folder and wait while the files are copied. (CDs are rather slow compared to other types of disks, so don't expect the job to be too speedy.)

After all the files have copied, remove the CD from the drive. Store the CD away for safekeeping as a backup. Open the folder to which you copied the files, and you should be able to open and edit them normally. If the copied files are all read-only, select all their icons, choose Properties, clear the Read-only checkbox, and click OK. (Remember, you can't clear the Read-only checkbox for files on the CD, but you certainly can clear that checkbox on the files you copied from the CD.)

Copying Files to CDs

Windows XP includes some basic capabilities for burning CDs (that is, for copying files to CDs). But it can only do so if you have a *CD burner* in your computer. The CD burner can be either a CD-R or CD-RW drive. Table 15-1 summarizes the different kinds of CD drives and the types of CD each can read (play) and write (burn).

Table 15-1: CD Drive and Disc Compatibilities

Drive Type	CD-ROM Drive	CD-R Drive	CD-RW Drive
Can read CD-ROM	Yes	Yes	Yes
Can write CD-R	No	Yes	Yes
Can read CD-RW	No	No	Yes
Can write CD-RW	No	No	Yes

Note At first glance it might look like something is missing from Table 15-1, such as "read CD-R" or "write CD-ROM." But nothing is missing. A CD-R disc contains nothing to read. Once you copy files to a CD-R, it becomes a CD-ROM and you can't put anything else on it because it's not possible to write to a CD-ROM. On the other hand, a CD-RW is always a CD-RW, whether it's empty, full, or somewhere in between.

So, assuming that you have a CD burner and some blank CDs, there are basically three ways in which you can copy files to a CD:

✦ To make an audio CD to play in a stereo, ignore this chapter and use Windows Media Player, discussed in Chapter 38.

✦ To copy pictures or any other type of files to a CD-R or CD-RW, use the techniques described here, unless . . .

✦ You have some third-party CD-burning software, such as Roxio Easy CD Creator or Nero Burn, in which case the techniques described below might not work.

That last bullet item is a real doozy for folks who haven't yet figured out exactly what programs they do/don't have on their computers. But here I'm just going to forge ahead with the assumption that you have no such software installed. After all, this is a book about Windows XP so it behooves me to talk about how you copy files to CDs using Windows XP.

If you're not sure what programs you have, you can go ahead and try the next method. There's no harm in trying. I'll talk about third-party programs later in this chapter. Also, there are lots of troubleshooting tips in Chapter 19. So, here are that steps for copying files to a blank CD-R or CD-RW using Windows XP:

1. Insert a blank CD-R, or a CD-RW, into your CD burner.

2. If some unexpected program or prompt appears, close it. Then, open My Computer or any other folder to get into Windows Explorer.

3. Navigate to a folder that contains the files you want to copy to the CD.

Tip

If you want to copy all files of a certain type, such as all pictures, from multiple folders to a CD, use the Search Companion (see Chapter 17) to locate the files. Then, select all and right-click from within the Search Results main pane.

4. Select the files(s) you want to copy to the CD using any technique from Chapter 14.

5. Right-click any selected icon and choose **Send To**, then click on the menu option that represents your CD drive. It may read something like CD Drive (D:) as in the example shown in Figure 15-6.

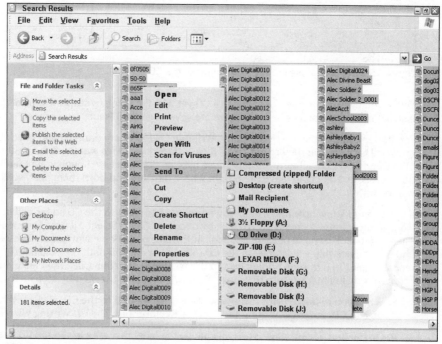

Figure 15-6: Sending selected icons to a CD burner

Tip

Don't worry if a little reminder keeps popping up telling you that you have files waiting to be written to CD. There's no hurry on that; you can ignore the message. And don't worry if the Copying . . . message says it's going to take umpteen hours to complete the copy. That number will start decreasing very rapidly.

6. Optionally, if you want to select more files from other folders, repeat steps 3 through 5 for as many different folders as you wish.

7. When you're ready to burn, click on the **You have files waiting to be written to the CD** message, if it's visible. Otherwise, open your My Computer folder, right-click the icon for your CD drive, and choose **Open**. The Writable CD folder opens, looking something like Figure 15-7.

Figure 15-7: Folder of files ready to be burned to a CD

You haven't actually copied any files to a CD yet. But I'm going to stop with the step-by-step instructions for a moment because there are several general issues to discuss.

For starters, notice that the icons in the Writable CD folder are dimmed and have little down arrows. That tells you they're not "real" files — they're just files waiting to be written to a CD. There's no hurry on actually burning those files, so don't feel as though you're under any time pressure. You could leave them right where they are and burn them next week, if you wanted to.

If you want to know how much stuff you've selected to burn to the CD so far, select all the icons in the folder by pressing Ctrl+A or by choosing Edit ➪ Select All from the menu bar. Then, right-click any one of them and look at the Size on Disk measurement. If you're well under the space that's available on the CD (650-MB or 700-MB limit on a blank CD), you can repeat Steps 3 to 7 to keep adding files to the Writable CD folder. Click the Cancel in the Properties dialog box to close that box. OK, now I'll resume the step-by-step instructions.

8. When you're happy with the files waiting to be written to the CD, click on **Write these files to CD** under CD Writing Tasks in the Explorer bar. The CD Writing Wizard opens.

9. On the first Wizard page, you can change the label that appears to the CD to something other than the date, but doing so is optional. The tiny label appears only next to the CD drive's icon in My Computer when the CD is in the CD drive. Click Next after reading the first Wizard page.

10. Wait for all the files to be copied and the last Wizard page.

11. If you want to copy the same files to another CD, insert another blank CD into the drive, choose the checkbox that lets you copy the same files to another CD, and then click **Finish**. If you don't want to copy the same files to another CD, don't select the checkbox. Just click the **Finish** button.

You're (finally) done. The CD should eject automatically after the files have been written. But if it doesn't you can just right-click the CD drive's icon and choose Eject, or press the little button on the front of the CD drive. You can store the CD away for safekeeping, or send it off through the mail, or stick it in any CD drive to verify its contents.

You don't want to delete the original copies of the files you copied to the CD. You always want to save your files, and keep those files, on your hard drive. Use removable discs only to make backup copies of files, or to copy files to a different computer when a network or e-mail isn't an option.

If at some point you start seeing the "You are running low on disk space" message (meaning you have less than a gigabyte of hard disk space), *then* you can start thinking about archiving some old files you rarely use any more to CDs or other external media. But don't bother to move files you use often to external media. You're just making life difficult for yourself and increasing the chances of losing some important files.

Another way to copy files to CDs

The technique of selecting icons, right-clicking, and choosing Send To to copy files to a CD is just one of several ways to do it. You can actually use any method described in Chapter 14 to copy files to a CD. For example, you can put a blank CD or partially filled CD-RW into a CD drive. Then, open My Computer and the icon that represents your CD drive.

If the disc is empty, the folder that opens will be empty. If the disc is a partially filled CD-RW, you'll see icons for all the files on the CD-RW. You can size and position that window so it doesn't take up much space on the screen. Then, you can add files to its window by dragging them from other open Explorer windows or by using copy and paste.

Tip   To see how much free space is available on a partially filled CD-RW, put the disc into the CD-RW drive, open My Computer, and point to the drive's icon. If the available space doesn't show in a ToolTip, right-click the drive's icon and choose Properties.

Regardless of the method you use to get icons into the CD's folder, keep in mind that any dimmed icons with down-pointing arrows are files that are "in limbo" so to speak. They haven't actually been written to the CD yet; they're just waiting to be written.

For example, in Figure 15-8 the four icons at the bottom of the list are folders I just dragged into the CD folder from the ClipArt folder shown in the same figure. Those four items haven't actually been burned to the CD yet. All the icons above those four are already on the CD-RW.

But getting back to this general method, once the files to be written to the CD are in that CD folder, the rest of the process is exactly the same. When you're ready to go, just click "Write these files to CD" under CD Writing Tasks in the Explorer bar, and follow the instructions presented by the CD Writing Wizard.

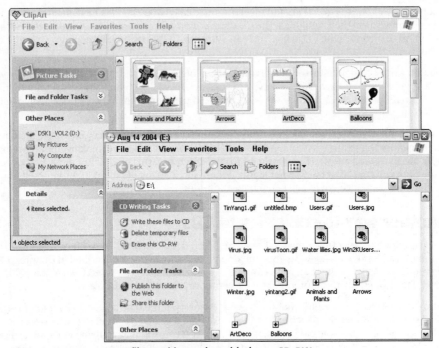

Figure 15-8: Some new files waiting to be added to a CD-RW

Deleting temporary files

If ever you copy a bunch of files to the CD folder and then change your mind about writing them to a CD, that's no problem. Just open the folder and click on "Delete temporary files" under CD Writing tasks, visible in Figure 15-9. Answer Yes when prompted for confirmation, and all the temporary files will disappear.

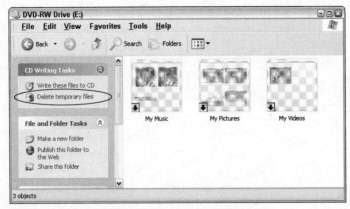

Figure 15-9: Deleted files waiting to be written to CD

Erasing CD-RWs

Because CD-RWs are read-write, you can add files to them, as described in the preceding section. You can also erase a CD-RW. But unless you have special software installed, you can't delete individual files. You either have to delete all of them, or none.

 Tip See "About CD-Burning Software" later in this chapter for more information on deleting files individually from CD-RWs.

If you do want to erase all the files on a CD-RW, that's simple. Just insert the CD-RW into the drive, and open the My Computer icon that represents the CD drive (if it doesn't open automatically). Then, click on "Erase this CD-RW" under CD Writing Tasks, and follow the wizard instructions that appear on the screen.

Duplicating a CD

If you want to make an exact duplicate of a CD, create a folder, perhaps named CDTemp, in your My Documents folder. Open that folder, size and position it so that it's not taking up a lot of space on the screen.

Put the CD you want to copy into the CD drive and close the drive door. If a program or dialog box opens automatically, close it. Then, open your My Computer folder, right-click the CD drive's icon, and choose Open. You can now see the contents of the CD. Size and position that window so that you can see it as well as the open CDTemp folder. Select all the icons in on the CD, and drag them to the CDTemp folder. Doing so will copy all the files and folders from the CD to the CDTemp folder.

When the copying is finished, remove the CD from the drive and replace it with a blank CD. The CD's Explorer window should go blank automatically. Select all the icons in the CDTemp folder, right-drag them to the CD's folder, and choose Copy Here after you release the right mouse button. When the copying is done, the CD folder should contain a temporary icon for each item in the CDTemp folder.

Figure 15-10 shows an example where the Explorer window is the CDTemp folder. It contains a set of files I copied from a CD. The lower-right folder is the folder for the blank CD. It contains a temporary icon for each actual icon in the CDTemp folder.

Now you just have to click "Write these files to CD" under CD Writing tasks in the Explorer bar, and wait. Make as many copies as you care to. When you're done, just delete the CDTemp folder. To permanently delete it so that it doesn't take up space in the Recycle Bin, hold down the Shift key, right-click the CDTemp folder's icon, and choose Delete.

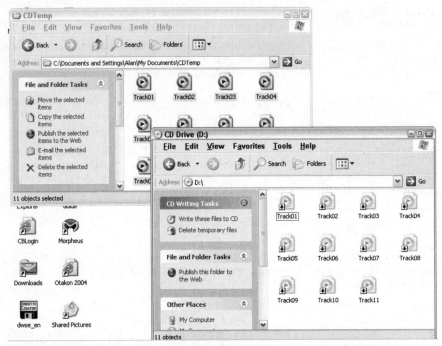

Figure 15-10: Files copied from one CD waiting to be written to another CD

About CD-Burning Software

Windows XP, by itself, allows you to copy folders and files to CD-R and CD-RW discs using the techniques described in this chapter. As you've seen, it's basically the same process as copying files to any other type of disk. The only difference is at the end, where you have to click on "Write these files" to CD to "burn" the temporary icons from CD folder onto the CD.

As you'll learn in Chapter 38, Windows Media Player has some great capabilities for creating music CDs that you can listed to in any stereo. For most people, that about covers anything you'd ever want to do with CDs. However, there are many third-party CD-burning programs out in the world that can do more. The two products that come to mind first are Roxio Easy CD Creator and Ahead Software's Nero Burn, both of which are often bundled with many computers that come with CD burners.

If you have any difficulty burning CDs using the techniques described in this chapter, it might be because you have one of those third-party programs installed. As far as burning CD-Rs goes, those third-party programs shouldn't create any problems. If you do have problems burning CDs, you may want to check the "Troubleshooting CDs and DVDs" section in Chapter 19 first.

Formatting blank CDs

When it comes to writing files to CD-RWs, third-party programs can make things radically different though their inclusion of *packet-writing* utilities that allow you to treat CD-RWs like floppies and other magnetic disks. Some of the more widely used products in that category include DirectCD, DLA (Drive Letter Access), InCD, FileCD, Drag-To-Disc, and Clip.

The main difference you'll notice with packet-writing software is that you're generally prompted to *format* a CD-RW before you can write files to it. Formatting the CD-RW makes it look and act like a magnetic disk to Windows. Once the CD-RW is formatted, you can copy files to and from the CD-RW just as you would a magnetic disk. Furthermore, you can individually delete and rename files on the CD-RW, just as you would on a floppy or hard disk. For more information on all that, see the documentation, Help, or Web site for your Roxio or Nero product.

Note   Personally, I see no advantage to formatting CD-Rs, even if the option presents itself. You'd be better off choosing No if asked about formatting a CD-R, especially if you plan to use that disc in a stereo or another computer.

The only problem is that Windows itself won't be able to access the formatted CD-RW. You'll need to use your third-party program for all your CD-RW burning. If your third-party program also interferes with CD-R burning, check the Roxio Web site (www.roxio.com) or Nero (www.nero.com) Web site for upgrades.

Some other features you'll find in third-party CD-burning programs that you won't find in Windows XP are:

✦ **MultiSession:** You can copy files to a CD-R in multiple sessions, burning a few files each time. However, the CD won't be usable in other sessions until you close the CD, at which point you won't be able to add any more files to the CD.

✦ **Backup CD:** If you have two CD drives, and one is a burner, you can copy from one CD drive to the other without copying all files to a folder on the hard drive first.

✦ **Disk-at-Once:** Copy music to CDs without the two-second gap normally found between songs. This is especially useful for making CDs of classical music without gaps between movements.

✦ **Burn DVDs:** Some third-party programs offer both CD and DVD burning. Windows XP doesn't have any built-in capabilities for copying files to DVDs.

So that about covers the basics of CDs, Chapters 38 and 39 will talk about ways to create custom music CDs to play in any stereo or computer. For the rest of this chapter, we'll focus on the world of DVDs.

Understanding DVDs

DVDs are a laser medium like CDs. If you hold a CD in one hand and a DVD in the other, you can't tell the two apart just by looking. But there are some major differences. The biggest difference is in capacity. While a CD stores about 650 to 700 MB of data; a DVD stores 4.7 GB worth of data. That's 4,700 MB — roughly the equivalent of 6.7 CDs, or 4,700 floppies, per DVD. Movies are distributed on DVDs because there's simply not enough room on a CD to store a full-length motion picture.

You can't play a DVD in a CD drive. Your computer needs to have a DVD drive. There are plenty of DVD drives in the world that can handle all sorts of DVDs and CDs though. So, even if your computer has only a DVDs, you may be able to use that drive to read CD-ROMs, copy to CD-R and CD-RWs, as well as to watch DVDs and copy files to DVDs.

There is one catch though. Windows XP doesn't have any built-in capabilities for copying files to DVDs. Nor can it copy DVDs that contain movies or other media. About all you can do with DVDs in Windows is watch DVD movies in Windows Media Player. However, most DVD burners come with software that will allow you to write files to DVD.

As with CDs, there are DVD-ROMs, recordable discs, and read/write discs. When you rent or buy a DVD movie, you're getting a DVD-ROM that you can watch as many times as you wish. However, you cannot change the contents of the disc in any way.

DVD burners have × ratings like CD drives. However, as I write this chapter the maximum copy speed for DVD is about 4×. So, for instance, at 4× it would take about half an hour to burn two hours of video to a DVD.

DVD-R and DVD+R

In the recordable write once, read many category, there are two types of DVDs: DVD-R and DVD+R. Both are write once, read many distribution media, the same blank CDs that the movie industry uses to create the DVD movies you buy or rent at stores. As with a CD-R, you get one shot, and one shot only, at burning a DVD-R or DVD+R.

You need a DVD burner, and special software, to copy files to DVD-Rs and DVD+Rs. A CD burner won't do, nor will a DVD-ROM drive that can only read DVDs.

Most of the differences between -R and +R have to do with esoteric technical things that are more in the realm of video engineers than computer users. For computer users, the main difference is that a burned DVD-R will play in about 96 percent if standard set-top DVD players, while burned DVD+Rs work in about 87 percent of those players. (By "set-top" DVD player I mean one that's connected to a television as opposed to a computer.)

Note   Specs for the -R and -RW discs are defined by a group called the DVD Forum (www.dvd forum.com). The +R and +RW discs are defined by another group called the DVD Alliance at www.dvdrw.com.

DVD-RWs and DVD+RWs

As the RW implies, both these disc formats are backup media in the sense that you can write to a disc more than once. You need a DVD drive that's capable of handling DVD-RWs and DVD+RWs. There are some burners out there that can only write to DVD-R and DVD+R.

Exactly how compatible DVD-RWs and DVD+RWs are with set-top boxes varies with the set-top box. Unlike the stereo world, where the ability to read from a CD-RW disc is rare, the ability to read from, and even record, to DVD-RWs and DVD+RWs is fairly common in DVD players. But, you have to know the capabilities of your own DVD player, and it's something to take into consideration when you're thinking of buying a DVD player.

DVD-RAMs and DVD DLs

In addition to the more common types of DVDs described previously, there are DVD-RAMs and DVD DLs. Both are relatively rare in the CD industry and so far seem to have found niches only in production video studios. Though like all technologies, both of these will no doubt find their way into the mainstream PC world eventually.

The DVD-RAM requires a DVD-RAM drive. Its basic advantage is speed and flexibility. A DVD-RAM acts much like a hard disk in that you can quickly read data from and write data to the disc without going through an elaborate "burning" procedure.

The DVD DLs (double layer) can store about 8.5 GB of data each, about double the capacity of a standard DVD. While a DL disc can be played in any standard DVD player, you need a DL-capable burner in order to be able to write to DL discs.

At this point, there's really nothing more to tell about DVDs, because there's really nothing in Windows XP that can copy files to DVDs, or from media DVDs. But as I said, we'll look at examples of using third-party programs to backup data to DVD in Chapter 18. And in Chapter 42 we'll look at using third-party programs to make your DVD movies.

Wrap Up

CDs and DVDs are both examples of laser media and therefore differ substantially from the more familiar magnetic media. Copying data from a CD isn't really different from copying data from any other medium. But copying data to a CD requires the extra step of "burning" the CD. Windows XP doesn't have any built-in capability for copying to, or from, a DVD. But you can watch DVD movies if your computer has a DVD drive. As far as a details go, here's a quick summary of the facts:

✦ Music CDs and programs you purchase are stored on CD-ROM, meaning that you can read (or play) the CD all you want, but you can't change the contents of a CD.

✦ CD-R is a recordable distribution medium. You can copy to a CD-R once only. Once you've done so, it becomes a CD-ROM whose contents can't be changed in any way.

✦ CD-RWs can be written to and read from indefinitely. These are often referred to as backup media because they're useful for making backup copies of important documents on your hard disk.

✦ How Windows reacts when you insert a CD depends on settings in the CD drive icon's Properties dialog box.

✦ To copy files from a CD, right-click the CD drive's icon and choose Open. Then, use any technique from Chapter 14 to select and copy files to a folder on your hard drive.

✦ You can copy files to a CD using any technique discussed in Chapter 14 to get icons to the CD drive's Writable CD folder. But the process isn't finished until you click on "Write these files to CD" in the Explorer bar.

✦ DVD-Rs and DVD+Rs are recordable distribution media like CD-Rs. You need a DVD burner and special software to copy files to either type of disc.

✦ DVD-RWs and DVD+RWs are backup media like CD+RWs that you can write to more than once. You need a DVD RW burner and special software to copy files to DVDs.

✦　　✦　　✦

Creating Shortcuts to Favorite Places

In This Chapter

Saving time with shortcuts

Creating desktop shortcuts to Web pages

Customizing shortcut icons

Creating custom shortcut keys for opening programs and documents

Handy places for extra shortcuts

Just about everyone has certain things on their computers that they use frequently and things they use infrequently. Things change over time. What are hot projects and documents this week or this month may go to the back burner next. One of the best ways stay productive is to create shortcuts to things you use frequently or things that are hot right now.

You can put shortcuts anywhere. One of the most obvious places is the desktop, because the desktop is always there, even though it may be covered by program windows. The Quick Launch toolbar is a good place to put shortcuts as well. In this chapter, you'll learn how to create shortcuts, and good places to keep them.

Creating Desktop Shortcuts

You can create a desktop shortcut to any program, folder, or document that you use frequently. It only takes two or three mouse clicks to create a desktop shortcut:

✦ Right-click the item to which you want to create a shortcut and choose **Send To** ➪ **Desktop (create shortcut)**.

For example, suppose that there's a program buried deep in your All Programs menu, and you're tired of clicking through all the options every time you want to start that program. Just create a desktop shortcut by getting to the icon you normally click to start that program. Then, right-click the icon and choose Send To ➪ Desktop (create shortcut). Figure 16-1 shows an example of creating a shortcut to Calculator.

If you're working on a project that's in a folder, and you want to be able to get to that folder from the desktop, just go to that folder's icon, but don't open the folder. Instead, right-click the folder and choose Send To ➪ Desktop (create shortcut). Figure 16-2 shows an example. You can use the same technique to create a shortcut to any document.

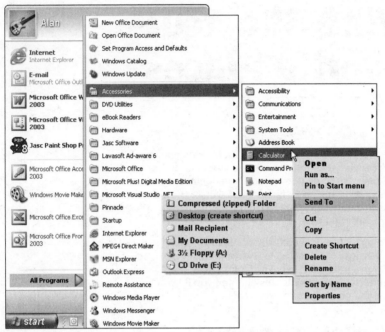

Figure 16-1: Creating a desktop shortcut to a program

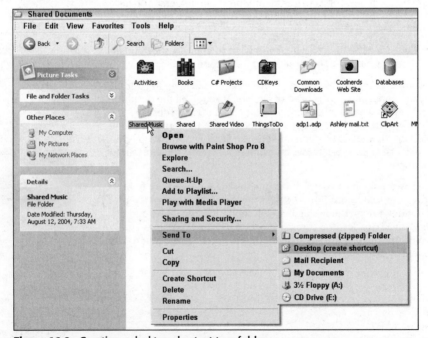

Figure 16-2: Creating a desktop shortcut to a folder

Shortcuts to Web pages

If you use Internet Explorer as your Web browser and want to create a quick desktop shortcut to a frequently visited Web page:

✦ While you're viewing the page to which you want to create a shortcut, choose **File** ⇨ **Send** ⇨ **Shortcut to Desktop** from Internet Explorer's menu bar.

Figure 16-3 shows an example.

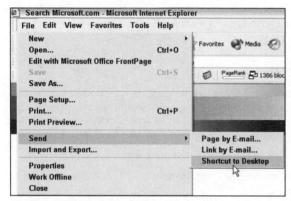

Figure 16-3: Creating a desktop shortcut to a Web page

Shortcut icons

It's easy to tell a shortcut icon from a regular icon. A shortcut icon always displays a little curved arrow, like the examples along the bottom of Figure 16-4. Also, if filename extensions are visible, a shortcut icon will have a .lnk (for *link*) extension.

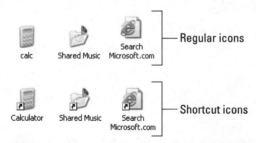

Figure 16-4: Regular icons compared to shortcut icons

No matter how large the file that the shortcut refers to, the shortcut itself will always have a tiny size of about 1.4 KB. That's because the shortcut isn't a copy of the program, folder, or document. It's just a reference to the larger item, telling Windows where to find the item. For example, a shortcut icon to your Shared Music folder wouldn't contain any music at all. It would contain only the path `C:\Documents and Settings\All Users\Documents\My Music`. That takes so little disk space as to be inconsequential. So feel free to create all the shortcuts you want.

Because a shortcut isn't the actual file, but merely a reference to that file, there are three important facts about icons that make them all more useful:

✦ You can delete a shortcut icon at any time without losing the program, folder, or file to which it refers.

✦ You can rename any shortcut at any time without harming or changing the program, folder, or file to which the shortcut refers.

✦ You can move and copy shortcuts at will, without messing up anything at all.

So, shortcuts are as convenient as you can get, because you can create, rename, move, and copy them at will with no adverse consequences whatsoever. We'll look at other good places for shortcuts in a moment.

Using desktop shortcuts

Using desktop icons is simple, you just click (or double-click, depending on your settings) the icon on the desktop. Of course, the desktop isn't always visible, because you can pile up a lot of windows on it. But the desktop is never more than one or two clicks away because you can always get to the desktop using either of these methods, illustrated in Figure 16-5:

✦ Click the **Show Desktop** button in the Quick Launch toolbar.

✦ Or, right-click the clock and choose **Show the Desktop**.

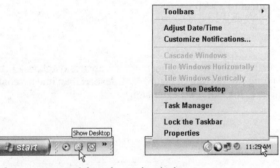

Figure 16-5: Quick paths to the desktop

Note   The Quick Launch toolbar is optional. To show or hide it, right-click the clock on the lower-right corner of the screen, and choose Toolbars ⇨ Quick Launch.

When you want to bring all the open program windows back onto the desktop, just click the Show Desktop button a second time, or right-click the clock and choose Show Open Windows.

When you're in the Open or Save As dialog box, all your desktop icons are also only one click away. This provides a handy means of opening any folders to which you've created a desktop shortcut. To get to your desktop shortcut icons from the Open or Save As dialog box, choose Desktop from the Look In or Save In drop-down list, as in Figure 16-6. Then double-click the folder's desktop icon to open the folder.

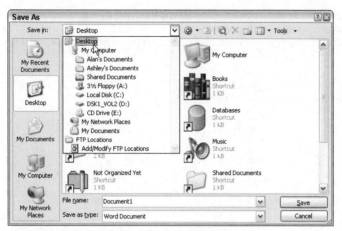

Figure 16-6: Quick path to desktop shortcut icons

Right-clicking an icon and choosing Send To ➪ Desktop (Create Shortcut) isn't the only way to create shortcuts. It's just a handy way to get a shortcut onto the desktop. But you can also use any of the following methods to create a shortcut to most icons:

✦ Right-click the icon and choose **Copy**. Then right-click where you want to put a shortcut and choose **Paste Shortcut**.

✦ Right-drag an icon to where you want to place an icon, release the mouse button, and choose **Create Shortcuts Here**.

✦ Right-click an icon, and choose **Create Shortcut**. The new shortcut will be in the same folder (which is a strange place to put an icon). But you can then right-click the new shortcut and choose Cut. Then, go to wherever you want to place the icon, and choose Paste.

Customizing Shortcuts

Having too many similar icons on the desktop forces you to read through a bunch of icons' names to figure out which is which. Many shortcuts you create will automatically be named Shortcut to . . ., which doesn't help a whole lot when you alphabetize the desktop icons (by right-clicking the desktop and choose Arrange Icons By ➪ Name).

Fortunately, you can rename any shortcut to any name you like. The more meaningful the name is to you, the better. Renaming a shortcut icon is simple, and has no adverse affects on the item to which the shortcut refers. To rename a shortcut icon, just right-click it, edit or replace the existing name, and then press Enter or click outside the icon.

Changing a shortcut's icon

Having too many similar looking icons on the desktop forces you to read through the shortcut names to find the one you're looking for. This is mainly a problem with shortcuts to folder's you've created yourself, because they all tend to use the generic manila file folder icon.

You can make it easier to find specific shortcuts by giving them easily recognizable icons that stand out from the crowd. Changing a shortcut's icon is no different from changing any other icon. You just right-click the shortcut icon and choose Properties. The Properties dialog box for the shortcut opens, looking something like Figure 16-7.

Figure 16-7: Properties for a shortcut icon

To change the icon for the shortcut, click the Change Icon button and choose your icon. You can use any icon .ico file you like. Also, there's no rule that says a shortcut to a folder *must* look like a folder. If you know that the item to which the shortcut refers is a folder, then there's no need to use a folder icon to constantly remind yourself of that fact.

Note   The techniques described under "Choosing a custom icon for folders" in Chapter 13 apply to shortcut icons as well.

Shortcut keys for shortcuts

If you create a desktop shortcut, you can also assign a custom shortcut key to that icon. The shortcut will being with Ctrl+Alt, but you can chose the third keystroke yourself. That third keystroke can be any letter or number — really any key other than Esc, Enter, Tab, Spacebar, Backspace, Delete, or Print Screen. That means you can make keyboard shortcuts like Ctrl+Alt+W to start Microsoft Word, or Ctrl+Alt+V to open your Shared Videos folder — whatever makes sense to you.

There are a couple simple rules to remember about shortcut keys though. If a program is open and in the active window, and that program also uses the shortcut key for something, then the shortcut key will play out in the program. This means that the desktop icon won't work in that instance. But you can always shift the keyboard focus to the desktop just by clicking the desktop before you press the shortcut key combo. Furthermore, not may programs have built-in Ctrl+Alt shortcut keys. So, those problems are trivial.

For obvious reasons, no two shortcut icons can share the same shortcut key. After all, how would Windows know which item to open if two or more shortcuts shared the same shortcut key? So, aside from those minor caveats, shortcut keys for shortcut icons are very handy things. Especially if your work requires that your hands be on the keyboard more often than on the mouse.

To create a shortcut key for a shortcut icon, right-click the shortcut icon and choose Properties. Then, click in the Shortcut Key textbox and press the key that you want to use as the shortcut key. You need not press the Ctrl and Alt keys at that point. For example, in Figure 16-7 I typed the letter m to make Ctrl+Alt+M the shortcut key for opening a folder named Music on my D: drive (a second hard drive). As you can see in the figure, I previously assigned a custom icon to that shortcut as well — a musical note and speaker.

Figure 16-8: Pressing Ctrl+Alt+M will open a folder named Music on drive D:.

Controlling how an item opens

Shortcuts to local resources (folders, programs, documents) have additional options that you can customize. Shortcuts to Web pages don't have these additional options. But that's a minor inconvenience. One thing you can do is control how the item to which a shortcut refers will open. Your options are:

✦ **Normal window:** The program, folder, or document will open at whatever size it was when you closed it.

✦ **Minimized:** The item will open with only its taskbar button visible, nothing on the desktop.

✦ **Maximized:** The item will open full-screen.

The option for choosing how the item to which a shortcut refers will open is right there in the Properties dialog box next to Run, as shown in Figure 16-9.

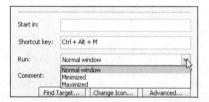

Figure 16-9: Options for defining how an item opens

Make your own ToolTip

The Comment box lets you create a ToolTip that appears whenever you point to the shortcut icon. This is particularly handy for shortcuts you put on toolbars without labels, because you can just point to the icon as a reminder. If you created a shortcut for the desktop shortcut, you can give yourself a reminder about its shortcut key as well.

For example, in Figure 16-10 I added the comment *Music Archive (Ctrl+Alt+M)* to my custom Music shortcut. That same picture shows the Desktop toolbar on the desktop. The mouse pointer is resting on the Music icon in the toolbar and, as you can see, the ToolTip displayed is exactly the Comment text in the shortcut's Properties. (I'll talk about the Desktop toolbar more in a moment).

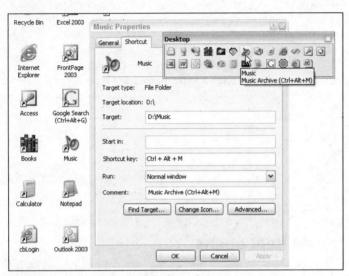

Figure 16-10: A custom ToolTip for a shortcut icon

Unfortunately, the optional Comment isn't available in shortcuts to Web pages. But you can assign a shortcut key to a Web page shortcut. As an alternative to using a comment, you can just put the shortcut key right in the icon's name. For example, the shortcut to Google in Figure 16-10 is named *Google Search (Ctrl+Alt+G).lnk*. So, you can see the shortcut key combo right on the desktop.

Actually, when you're first creating shortcut icons, it might not be a bad idea to include the shortcut key combo in all of their names. Doing so lets you see, at a glance, which combo keys you've already used. With time, you'll memorize the combo keys. At that point, you can just rename any shortcut icon whose combo key you've memorized, so you don't have to see that reminder on your desktop all the time.

Where is this thing anyway?

Just about every icon on the Start menu is a shortcut icon. That's why deleting icons from the Start menu and All Programs menu has no effect on the underlying program. If you're ever curious as to the name and location of a program (or anything else that a shortcut opens), right-click the icon and choose Properties. The path to the item is in the Target textbox. To open the folder in which the program's startup file is stored, just click the Find Target button in that same dialog box.

Programs that are part of Windows XP are generally stored in the same folder as Windows itself. Typically that's C:\Windows, but can vary. Because of the potential variation, the path to the Windows folder is expressed as %SystemRoot% rather than literally, as in C:\Windows or C:\WINNT. '

Caution   Deleting the file to which a program icon refers is not a good way to delete a program. There may be dozens or hundreds of other files that are part of that same program. The only safe way to delete a program is to uninstall it, as discussed in Chapter 48.

If the path in Target textbox is too lengthy to see, you can click in the textbox and use the Home, End, → and ← keys to scroll through it. To copy the path to the clipboard, click the path text in the textbox, and then press the Home key to move the cursor to the start of the text. Press Shift+End to select all the text in the textbox; then press Ctrl+C to copy the selected text to the clipboard. Then, go to any program (or other textbox) that accepts pasted text and press Ctrl+V to paste the entire path.

Tip   The Home, Shift+End, Ctrl+C combo works for copying the contents of any textbox that the cursor is currently in. For example, it works in the Address bar of Windows Explorer and your Web browser too — any box of text.

Normally, there'd be no need to change the target. Unless by some peculiar circumstance you happened to know the exact location of the target file and wanted to change it. Though, even then, it would probably be much easier to just navigate to the file's icon, right-click it, and choose Send To ➪ Desktop (create shortcut). After all, you can't make any typographical errors using that method.

The Start In option

The Start In option in a shortcut icon's Properties is similar to the Target property, in that's it's generally not something you want to mess with. It's often blank by default, because few shortcut items even need that option. In other cases, it's just the name of the folder in which the actual file resides — though in rare cases it might be a reference to a folder that contains other files the program needs to run.

One thing is for sure, you don't want to take any wild guesses at filling in the Start In textbox. Doing so is unlikely to solve anything; it is far more likely to cause problems.

Running a shortcut's program as another user

The Advanced button in a shortcut's properties provides advanced options related to security and memory usage. Figure 16-11 shows those options. As in that example, options that aren't relevant to the shortcut at hand will be disabled. Both options apply only to shortcut icons for programs. And not all programs support both options.

Figure 16-11: Advanced properties for a shortcut icon

If you choose "Run with different credentials," the program won't start normally when you click its icon. Instead, clicking the program's icon will open a Run As dialog box. To start the program you have to sign into the program as a specific user who has a user account on the system.

The "Run in separate memory space" applies only to ancient 16-bit Windows 3.1–era programs that can get out of control in the 32-bit protected mode memory space of today's programs. You rarely get to change that option, and would do so only if an older program crashed, or caused other programs to crash, whenever you ran the program.

General properties for a shortcut icon

The General tab for a shortcut icon's properties, shown in Figure 16-12, is mostly for information rather than customization. You can rename the icon by typing a new name in the top textbox (which has the same result as right-clicking the icon and choosing Rename).

The Read-Only and Hidden attributes on the General tab are the same as for any other icon, though not terribly relevant to shortcut icons. See "Hiding (and Unhiding) Folders" in Chapter 13, and "Dealing with Read-Only Files" in Chapter 14. The Advanced button takes you to options for backup, indexing, compression, and encryption, also shown in the figure. Those topics aren't terribly relevant to shortcut icons either and are discussed elsewhere.

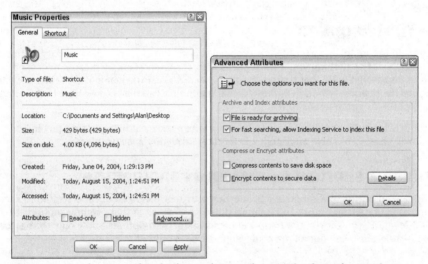

Figure 16-12: The General and Advanced General properties for a shortcut icon

Moving and Copying Shortcut Icons

When you take the time to create a custom desktop shortcut with a custom icon, shortcut key, ToolTip, or whatever, you'll want any copies of that shortcut you create to have the same characteristics. If you just create new shortcuts from scratch in other locations, those new shortcuts won't have all the custom features you created in that desktop shortcut.

A simple way to copy a custom shortcut is to just right-click it and choose Copy. Then, you can paste copies of that shortcut anyplace you like. (The next section will talk about other places you might want to place custom shortcuts). Optionally, you can right-drag the short-cut icon to a new location and choose Copy Here.

Caution　Simply dragging an icon off a menu or even the desktop is no guarantee that you'll create a shortcut. You may end up moving or copying the entire item. Always use the right mouse button to drag. If the thing you dragged wasn't a shortcut, choose Create Shortcuts Here after you release the right mouse button, to ensure that you don't move or copy the original item.

But the important thing to remember is that if you create new shortcuts at other locations, those new shortcuts won't have your desktop icon's custom features. If you're going to take the time to create a fancy desktop shortcut, you'll want to make sure that you move or copy *that* shortcut to the other locations I'll describe in subsequent sections.

Handy Places for Shortcuts

Besides the desktop, there are lots of handy places you can put shortcuts. For example, you may want to move or copy a desktop shortcut to the Quick Launch toolbar or Start Menu.

If the shortcut is one to a frequently used folder, you may want to add the shortcut to your My Documents, My Pictures, or some other folder that is easy to get to. The My . . . folders are especially useful places because when you choose File ⇨ Open or File ⇨ Save As from a program's File menu, the first folder to appear in the Open or Save As dialog box is often one of the My . . . folders. That way, you can just double-click the folder's shortcut in the Open or Save As dialog box main pane to get to the folder without navigating.

Toolbars are another handy place to put shortcuts. Let's start by looking at how you can add shortcuts for programs, folders, Web pages, and so forth to the Quick Launch toolbar, or even a custom toolbar you create yourself.

Putting shortcuts on the Quick Launch toolbar

The Quick Launch toolbar has one advantage over the desktop as a repository for shortcuts: The Quick Launch toolbar is always visible, even when the desktop is covered with program windows. There's no rule that says you can launch only programs from the Quick Launch toolbar. It can contain shortcuts to folders, documents, and Web pages too.

Your best bet, before adding an icon to the Quick Launch toolbar, is to create a desktop short-cut first. Customize that icon to your liking before you start putting copies of it elsewhere. Once you've done that, adding the icon to the Quick Launch toolbar is simple. Just right-drag the icon right onto the Quick Launch toolbar. You'll see a dark I-beam, as in Figure 16-13, when the cursor is in position.

Figure 16-13: Putting a shortcut on the Quick Launch toolbar

The I-beam shows you where the icon will be placed. Release the right mouse button, then choose Move Here or Copy Here, depending on which you want to do. Once the icon is on the Quick Launch toolbar, you can drag it left or right (with the left mouse button) to change its position.

Using the Desktop toolbar

It's not necessary to put a lot of shortcuts on the Quick Launch toolbar though, because all of your desktop icons appear on the Desktop toolbar automatically. To make the Desktop toolbar visible, just right-click the clock and choose View ➪ Toolbars ➪ Desktop. Initially the toolbar will likely be crammed into the right edge of the toolbar. But when the taskbar is unlocked, you can size and position the toolbar to your liking.

Note See "Customizing the Taskbar" in Chapter 6 for the full scoop on showing, hiding, sizing, and positioning the Desktop toolbars and other optional toolbars.

If you move the Desktop toolbar off the taskbar and anchor it to an edge of the screen, or make it free-floating, you can decide for yourself whether or not you want it to always be visible. Just right-click its title bar, or an empty space within the toolbar, and choose Always On Top. To hide, or show, the icon labels, as in the example shown in Figure 16-10, right-click some empty space within the Desktop toolbar and choose Show Text.

Keep in mind that the Desktop toolbar is an exact clone of your actual desktop icons. If you delete an icon from the toolbar, you'll delete it from the desktop as well. You can arrange buttons in the Desktop toolbar independently of the desktop arrangement though. Just drag any icon to wherever you want it to appear in the toolbar. It's a little tricky though. As you drag, look for a little sideways I-beam near the mouse pointer. When you drop, the icon will go right under (not over) that I-beam.

Creating a Custom Shortcuts toolbar

As an alternative to using the Desktop folder, you can create a custom folder of shortcut icons, and display that as a toolbar. Doing so breaks the tie between the Desktop toolbar and the Windows Desktop. So, the custom toolbar can contain any shortcuts you like.

To create a custom shortcuts toolbar, first create a new folder, perhaps named *My Shortcuts* or something. It doesn't matter where you create the folder, your My Documents folder will do just fine. Then, open that folder and drag any custom icons you like from your desktop into the folder. Though, you create any shortcut you like within the folder using any of the shortcut methods described earlier in this chapter. Figure 16-14 shows an example where I've put several shortcut desktop icons into a folder named My Shortcuts.

Next, click the Up button in the toolbar to get to the folder's parent. Then, drag the My Shortcuts folder to the very top edge of the screen, as though you're trying to drag it right off the screen, and release the mouse button. A toolbar of the folder will be anchored to the top edge of the screen. To make it free-floating, like the example shown in Figure 16-15, drag the handle (column of vertical dots) at the left edge of the toolbar down and to the right a little, away from any screen edge.

Tip You can display any folder's contents in a toolbar — even a program group on the All Programs menu — by dragging its icon to any edge of the screen.

Figure 16-14: Folder named My Shortcuts with custom shortcut icons

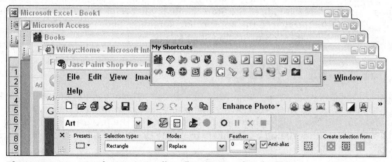

Figure 16-15: My Shortcuts toolbar floating on the desktop

Unlike the Desktop toolbar, the custom toolbar isn't tied to the desktop. So, you can delete icons from the desktop, or the toolbar, without one affecting the other. You can still arrange icons in the toolbar by dragging them left and right, show or hide text labels, and choose the Always On Top option on the toolbar's shortcut menu. To add a new icon to the toolbar, right-drag any icon onto the toolbar, release the mouse button, and choose Create Shortcuts Here. To close the custom toolbar, just click its Close (X) button. Or, right-click the toolbar and choose Close Toolbar.

When the toolbar is closed, you can reopen it from the Toolbars menu and place it on the taskbar. Here's how:

1. Right-click the clock and choose **Toolbars** ➪ **New Toolbar**.

2. In the New Toolbar dialog box that opens, expand the My Documents folder, and click on the shortcut folder's name, as shown in Figure 16-16.

3. Click **OK**.

Figure 16-16: The New Toolbar dialog box

Adding shortcuts to the Start menu

You can put a copy of any desktop on the Start menu simply by dragging the icon from the desktop to the Start button and dropping there. When you click the Start button, you'll see the shortcut is pinned to the left side of the Start menu. If you prefer to put the icon on the All Programs or elsewhere, just drag it to the appropriate subfolder. See "Personalizing Your Start Menu" for more information on managing Start Menu icons.

Putting shortcuts in folders

The Save As dialog opens whenever you download a document, save a document for the first time, or choose File ⇨ Save from a program's menu bar. When you choose File ⇨ Open from a program's menu bar, the Open dialog box opens. Depending on the program you're using, the first folder to appear in either dialog box is likely to be My Documents, My Pictures, or some other commonly used folder.

You can make navigating within the Open and Save As dialog boxes easier by adding shortcut icons for your frequently used folders to those common folders. For example, suppose that you often save pictures to your Shared Pictures folder, rather than your My Pictures folder. Or, perhaps you have a folder on a second disk drive named Photos in which you regularly store photos. If you put shortcuts to those folders in your My Pictures folder, the icons will be available on the main pane of the Open and Save As dialog boxes whenever you're viewing the contents of My Pictures. Figure 16-17 shows an example.

Keep in mind, too, that you can easily get to all your desktop shortcuts from the Open and Save As dialog boxes. If the dialog box you're using has a Documents icon at left, just click that icon. Otherwise, choose Desktop from the Look In or Save In drop-down list.

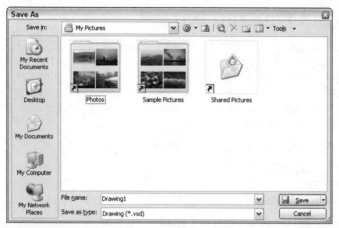

Figure 16-17: Shortcuts from My Pictures folder are visible in the Save As dialog box.

Who Gets What Desktop Icons?

Any desktop shortcut icons you add to your own desktop appear only in your user account. Other user's desktops aren't affected by anything you do to your desktop. But desktop icons that program installations create automatically generally appear on all users' desktops.

You can also create icons that appear on all users' desktops just by putting those icons in the `C:\Documents and Settings\All Users\Desktop`. You can easily navigate to that folder from the Folders list, as shown in Figure 16-18.

Figure 16-18: The C:\Documents and Settings\All Users\Desktop folder

The All Users Desktop folder is a two-way street in that if any user deletes one of its icons from their desktop, it disappears from all users' desktops. But any user can easily create a new icon on his or her own desktop using any of the techniques described earlier in the chapter.

Using the Desktop Cleanup Wizard

Windows XP comes with a Desktop Cleanup Wizard, which is a handy tool if you tend to let your desktop get too cluttered with icons. The Wizard lists every desktop icon that you're never used, or haven't used in the last 60 days, and lets you choose whether or not you want to keep the icon on the desktop.

The Wizard is simple to use, and you can configure to run automatically every 60 days, if you like. To start the Desktop Cleanup Wizard:

1. Right-click the desktop and choose Properties. The Display Properties dialog box opens.

2. Click the **Desktop** tab.

3. Click the **Customize Desktop** button.

4. Choose, or clear, the **Run Desktop Cleanup Wizard every 60 days** option, depending on whether or not you want the Wizard to run automatically every 60 days.

5. To start the wizard immediately, click the **Clean Desktop Now** button.

6. Follow the instructions presented by the wizard, then click Finish on the last wizard page.

7. When the wizard closes, click **OK** in each open dialog box.

When you get back to the desktop, the icons you specified will be gone. They'll all be in a new folder named Unused Desktop Shortcuts on the desktop. If you change your mind about any icon you deleted, just open the Unused Desktop Shortcuts folder. Then, drag any icons you want to keep out of that folder on onto the desktop.

Wrap Up

Shortcuts make it easy to get to frequently used programs, folders, and documents. Creating a desktop shortcut is easy. Just right-click any icon to which you want to create a shortcut and choose Send To ➪ Desktop (create shortcut). But there's more, as summarized below:

✦ You can create shortcuts to programs, folders, and documents by right-clicking, by using copy-and-paste, or by right-dragging.

✦ To create a desktop shortcut to a Web page from Internet Explorer, choose File ➪ Send ➪ Shortcut to Desktop from Internet Explorer's menu bar.

✦ To customize a shortcut icon, right-click the icon and choose Properties. Customization options appear in the icon's Properties dialog box.

✦ To make a shortcut key for opening a shortcut icon's target from the keyboard, click the Shortcut Key option in its Properties dialog box, then type the character you want to use for the shortcut.

✦ To create a custom ToolTip for a shortcut to a program or folder, fill in the Comment box in the shortcut's Properties dialog box.

✦ You can move or copy any shortcut icon to the Quick Launch toolbar, a custom toolbar, and the Start menu

✦ Placing shortcuts to your frequently used folders in My Documents and other My . . . folders can make it easier to get to those folders from the Open and Save As dialog boxes.

✦ Icons you create yourself are unique to your user account. Icons in the `C:\Documents and Settings\All Users\Desktop` folder appear on all users' desktops.

✦ The Desktop Cleanup Wizard is a tool to help you get rid of infrequently used desktop shortcuts.

✦　　✦　　✦

Searching for Files and Folders

Noo matter how well you organize your files and folders, you're going to lose track of some. We all do. Also, there will be times where you want to take inventory of all files that have some characteristic in common, regardless of where those files are stored.

Whenever you need to hunt for a lost file, or take inventory, the tool of choice will be the Search Companion. As its name implies, the Search Companion is your pal whenever it comes time to search an entire folder or disk drive for specific information or document type.

Using the Search Companion

The Search Companion is a tool offered by Windows Explorer to help you find lost files, or all the files of a certain types across folders, or all files that contain a particular word or phrase. To find a file or folder, you need to know something about it. You don't necessarily need to know its exact name. But any of the following information about the file will certainly help with the search:

✦ Approximately when you created, saved, or downloaded the file

✦ All or part of the filename, or the filename extension

✦ Some word or phrase in the document or the document's properties

✦ The approximate size of the file

The Search Companion can search all your hard disks, one hard disk, a folder and its subfolders, or just a single folder. If your computer is on a local network, the Search Companion can search any shared folder on any computer to which you have access.

The broader your search, the longer it will take to complete the search. So, if you can narrow the search down to a particular parent folder, the search will go more quickly. There are three ways to use the Search Companion:

✦ Click the **Start** button, and choose **Search**. By default, this will search all your hard drives.

✦ Or, navigate to the folder you want to search, and then click the **Search** button in Explorer's toolbar. You may start from My Network Places and choose a folder on any computer to search. This method this will narrow the search to the current folder and all of its subfolder.

✦ Or, press the **F3** key at the desktop, or in Windows Explorer or Internet Explorer.

Regardless of where you start the search, you can change the scope of the search, as you'll see in a moment. The Search Companion opens in the left side of Explorer, covering the standard Explorer bar. Most likely, the bar will look like the example shown in Figure 17-1. But you can customize the Search Companion, as you'll learn later, so yours might look different.

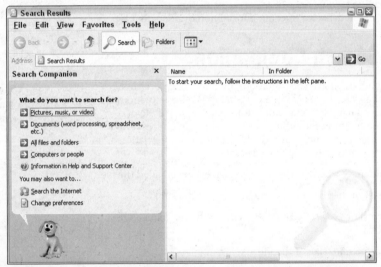

Figure 17-1: The Search Companion open in the left side of Windows Explorer

Narrowing down your search to the fewest possible matching files is an important part of performing a search. Too broad a search will result in hundreds, if not thousands, of files, which doesn't do you much good when you're trying to locate a particular file or folder. So, the first step is to try to narrow things down to one of the following types of file:

✦ **Pictures, music, or video:** If you know for certain that the file you're looking for is a picture, a song (music), or video, choose this option. On the next page, choose the exact type of file to search for, either Pictures and Photos, or Music or Video. This type of search will search file properties as well as filenames. See "Showing hidden properties" later in this chapter for more information on that.

✦ **Documents (word processing, spreadsheet, and so on):** If the file you're looking for is some other type of document, such as a file that contains text, an Excel worksheet, or a database, choose this option. This type of search examines only known file types — that is, documents that are associated with a program that's installed on your computer.

✦ **All files and folders:** If you're looking for a folder, or a file that doesn't qualify as either of the above, choose this option. The search will look at all file and folder names.

Depending on which of the preceding options you chose, you'll get a series of additional options. Some won't appear unless you click on *Use advanced search options* in the Search Companion. In many cases, you'll only see the option heading at first, like "When was it modified?" or "What size is it?" Click that heading, or the Show/Hide button to its right, to see, or hide, the options beneath that heading.

When there are more items than will fit in the Search Companion pane, use the vertical scroll bar at the right side of the pane to scroll up and down. As with most bars and columns, you can size the Search Companion pane by dragging its inner border left and right.

Caution E-mail messages aren't files or folders. They're *messages*, which are in a class all their own. The Search Companion can't help you find messages. Only your e-mail client can search for e-mail messages.

Specifying the filename, properties, or contents

The next option that the Search Companion presents, shown in Figure 17-2, asks for *All or part of the file name*. If you know the exact name of the file you're looking for, go ahead and type it in. Optionally, you can just type in part of the filename. For example, if you think the filename contains the word `vacation` or `Christmas` go ahead and type that in.

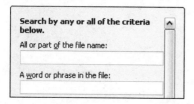

Figure 17-2: Search filenames, file content, or hidden properties.

If you're looking for files that have a particular extension, such as .gif or .jpeg, type an asterisk followed by a period and the extension. For example, a search for `*.gif` will search for all files that have the .gif extension. A search for `*.zip` will locate all files that have the .zip extension. If you don't know anything abut the filename, it's okay to leave that first option blank.

As an alternative to looking at just the filename, you can look at the file's contents or properties. Use the *A word or phrase in the file* option to specify a search on the contents of the file. For example, suppose that you wrote a letter to someone named Hank Haney. All you remember about the file is that it contained a phrase with his name, such as Dear Mr. Haney. If you're searching for Documents, or All Files and Folders, typing Haney under *A word or phrase in the file* will locate all documents that contain Haney somewhere within the document.

When you're searching for pictures, music, or video, the *A word or phrase in the file* plays a slightly different role. That's because pictures, music, and videos don't contain typed words. In fact, the *A word or phrase in the file* won't even appear initially when you're searching those types of files. You have to click *Use advanced search options* to even get to that option. But once that option is visible, you can include a word to search the file's hidden properties. For example, if you're searching music files and specify Franklin as the word or phrase in the file, you'll get songs that have that name in their title or artist hidden property, such as all songs by Aretha Franklin.

Note Some hidden properties are filled in automatically, as you'll see in Chapter 38. You can also fill in or change any file's hidden properties. Right-click the file's icon, and choose Properties. Then, click on the Summary tab, and click on the Advanced button, if it appears.

Telling Companion where to look

The Look In drop-down list tells the Search Companion how large an area to search. The broadest search on your own computer would be Local Hard Drives followed by the drive letter of each hard drive. For example, if your computer has two hard drives, it will be Local Hard Drives (C:;D:). To search drive C: only, choose Local Disk (C:).

Clicking the Look In option's drop-down button displays a list of all your hard drives and the document folders on your hard drive, as in the example shown in Figure 17-3. To search a removable disk or card, choose its drive letter. To search a particular folder, choose its name.

Figure 17-3: Places to look for files

If you don't see the drive or folder you want to search, click the Browse option at the bottom of the drop-down menu. A Browse for Folder dialog box will open, allowing you to choose any folder you want to search. That dialog box will include a My Network Places option that you can use to search shared folders on other computers in your local network, or even your entire network. Once you've made a selection from the Browse for Folder dialog box, click OK to return to the Search Companion.

Tip If at any time in the Search Companion you change your mind about a previous selection, just click the Back button near the bottom of the Search Companion to return to the previous page and change your selection.

Telling Companion when you last used the file

If the file is one you saved or downloaded recently, you can greatly increase your chances of finding it by giving the Search Companion some clue as to the age of the file. If you have no idea how the file might be dated, you can skip this option by choosing Don't Remember, as in the left side of Figure 17-4. Or, if you have a general idea about when you last saved the file, you can choose a general frame, such as "Within the last week" or "Past month."

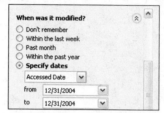

Figure 17-4: Searching based on the date you last saved the file

If you know the exact date, or the approximate date, that you created, last opened, or last saved the file, choose Specify Dates. Then, choose one of the following options from its drop-down list:

✦ **Modified Date:** The date you last changed and saved the document

✦ **Created Date:** The date you originally created or downloaded the file

✦ **Accessed Date:** The date you last opened or used the file

Tip   When you download a file, its Created, Modified, and Accessed dates are all set to the date on which you downloaded the file.

After you've chosen one of the preceding date types, use the From and To options to specify a range of dates. For example, if today as 12/31/2004 and you downloaded or created the file today, choose Created Date and set both the From and To dates to 12/31/2004. If you viewed the file within the last three days, you would choose Accessed Date, set the From date to 12/29/2004 and the To date to 12/31/2004.

Telling Companion the size of the file

The *What size is it?* option, shown in Figure 17-5, lets you narrow the search to files meeting a certain size criterion. If you haven't a clue as to the file's size, choose *Don't remember*. But, if you happen to know the approximate size of the file, choose the Small, Medium, or Large option. However, those options are a bit misleading because a file that's more than 1 MB in size isn't a particularly large file. A single song or picture is likely to be larger than 1 MB.

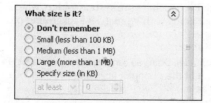

Figure 17-5: Searching based on a file size

A more practical use of the size option would be a situation where you're seeing the "You are running low on disk space" notification because you have less than 800 MB of hard disk space left. To make room, you might want to move some of your larger documents to another hard disk, or perhaps to CDs. In that case, you could start the Search Companion by searching for Pictures, Music, *and* Video files (all three types) as in the top of Figure 17-6.

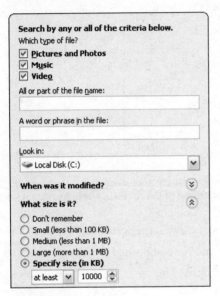

Figure 17-6: Searching for pictures, songs, and video files greater than 10 MB

If you don't find any files quite that large, you can work your way back to the search options and use a smaller size. For example, a search for files of at least 3,000 KB will find all files that are 3 MB or greater in size.

Using the more advanced options

The *More advanced options* shown in Figure 17-7 allow you to expand or narrow the search to certain files and folders, as described in the following list:

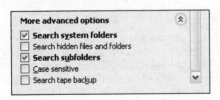

Figure 17-7: Choosing additional search criteria

✦ **Search system folders:** If selected, the search will include the system folders where Windows XP and some of the documents that come with it (such as background pictures) are stored.

Caution

Never delete, move, or rename a file in a system folder. Doing so can wreak serious havoc on your computer to a point where you can't even start the computer anymore!

✦ **Search hidden files and folders:** If selected, the search will include files and folders whose Hidden property is turned on. If not selected, hidden files and folders are excluded form the search.

✦ **Search subfolders:** If selected, the search will include all subfolders of the current folder. Normally, you want to choose this option.

✦ **Case sensitive:** If selected, only files that contain the same letters in the same case (uppercase or lowercase) will be found by the search.

✦ **Search tape backup:** If you have a tape drive for backups, and use NT Backup to backup up files to that drive, select this option to search tapes for the files.

Once you've specified all your search criteria, you're ready to begin your search.

Starting the search

To make the Search Companion find whatever it is you're looking for, click the Search button. Text in the pane and a visual bar will let you know that the search is ongoing and keep you apprised of that's being searched at the moment. How long the search takes depends on many factors. For example, searching all your hard drives for all documents that contain a particular word or phrase will take a lot longer than searching for a specific filename in your My Documents folder.

When the search is complete, the main pane to the right will show all files that match the search criterion. The left pane will tell you how many files were found and provide options for changing the search or the search results, as in the example shown in Figure 17-8.

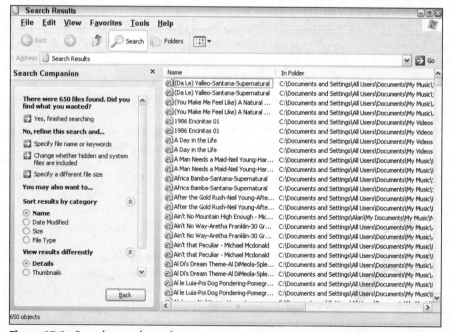

Figure 17-8: Sample search results

Using the search results

The Search Results window is actually Windows Explorer. So, all the options for arranging and viewing icons are in its menu bar and toolbar. If you choose *Yes, finished searching*, the Search Companion bar will close and the standard Explorer bar will appear in its place. Optionally, you can choose other options that appear in the Search pane. The options available to you will depend on how you conducted the search. But they're all self-explanatory. For example, if you choose *File Type* under *Sort Results by Category* the filenames will be regrouped by their general type.

The Details view provides the most information about the found files. If the Search Results pane isn't shown in Details view automatically, you can choose Details form the left column, or click the View button in the toolbar and choose Details, or choose View ➪ Details from the menu bar. In Details view you can use the horizontal scroll bar at the bottom of the window to scroll left and right through the visible columns. All the standard methods for moving and sizing columns, and sorting items in the list apply to the Search Results window.

Note   For more information on the Details View, see "Details view" in Chapter 3. Note, however, that the Show in Groups option is not available in a Search Results window.

Opening a file's folder

You can open any file right from the Search Results pane by clicking (or double-clicking) its icon. You can select, move, copy, rename, and delete files from the Search Results pane as well, using any of the techniques described in Chapter 14. For example, if you searched for *.zip and are now looking at all your .zip files, you could choose Edit ➪ Select All (or press Ctrl+A) to select all the files in the Search Results folder. Then, move them to some new folder, perhaps named Zip Files, in your My Documents or Shared Documents folder.

In Details view, the In Folder column tells you where each file is located. But it's not necessary to use that if you want to get to a file's containing folder. Instead, you can open the folder in which any file is contained using either of these methods:

✦ Right-click the filename, and choose **Open Containing Folder**, as shown in Figure 17-9.

✦ Or, select the folder name, and choose **File ➪ Open Containing Folder** from the menu bar.

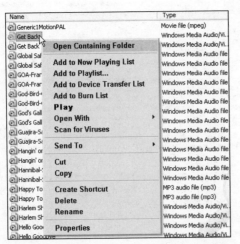

Figure 17-9: The quick route to a file's containing folder

The folder in which the file is contained will open in a separate Explorer instance. So, you'll still have the Search Results window open in case you want to continue to work in that pane as well.

Showing hidden properties

In Details view, you can also make columns for hidden properties visible by following these steps:

1. Choose **View** ➪ **Choose Details** from Explorer's menu bar.

2. In the Choose Details dialog box (see Figure 17-10), select the properties you wish to view.

3. Click **OK**.

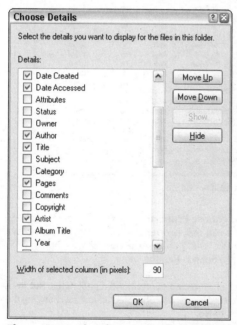

Figure 17-10: The Choose Details dialog box

The new columns will probably be off to the right, so you'll have to use the horizontal scroll bar to get to them. But once you can see them, you can move and size them by dragging their column headings or the lines that separate the column headings.

> **Note**   The technical term for hidden properties is *metadata*. Every document is a file of data. Metadata is "data about data," or information about the data contained within the file.

You can also sort and group the files by any property in the Details view. For example, suppose that you searched for all music files and are now viewing every song on your hard disk. In Details view, you could then make the Artist column visible. Then, click the Artist column heading to sort all the songs by artist name.

Suppose that you do that, and find all the songs by The Beatles. You could change the Genre or Artist property for all the songs at once right in the Search Results window (assuming that the songs aren't protected content). In the Name column, select the names of the files you want to change. For example, in Figure 17-11 I've selected all the files that have "The Beatles" in the Artist column.

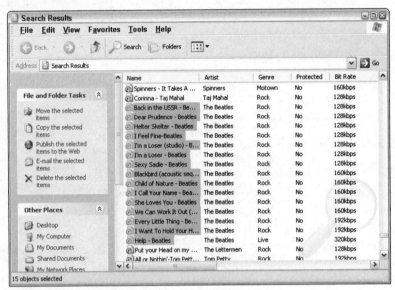

Figure 17-11: Selecting all songs by The Beatles

Next, right-click any selected file, and choose Properties. Next, click the Summary tab, and click the Advanced button so that you can edit properties. Then, type in a new artist name (perhaps just `Beatles` to get right of the "the") and/or the new genre. Finally, click OK. The change will take place right there in the Search Results pane.

Note   Chapter 38 discussed the concept of protected content and digital rights. But in case you're wondering, you can't change protected content to unprotected just by changing the contents of the Protected property from Yes to No.

In short, anything you can do in a normal folder and Explorer window you can do in the Search Results pane. Things might seem a little sluggish in the Search Results pane, depending on how many files are listed. You may need to be more patient than usual.

So, the Search Companion isn't just about finding lost files. It's also good for finding files that have some characteristic in common, even when those files are spread across many folders and disk drives. Plus, once you've found the files, you can manage them as you would files that are in a single folder, using any of the techniques described in Chapter 14.

Saving and reusing search criteria

All the selections you make in the Search Companion combine to define a single search criterion. If you often need to search for the same types of files, you can save your search criteria as follows:

1. After the search completes and you're sure it works, choose **File** ➪ **Save Search** from the Search Results menu bar.

2. Choose, or create, a folder for the search criteria.

3. Optionally, change the suggested filename, then click the **Save** button.

The file will be saved with an .fnd extension and the icon shown in Figure 17-12. To reuse a previous search, go to the folder in which you saved the search criteria. Then, double-click (or click) the icon.

Figure 17-12: Icon for a saved Search Companion search

Customizing the Search Companion

The Search Companion is usually displayed along with a little animated character who, I guess, is supposed to be the companion or something. You can customize the Search Companion in several ways, including changing the character or getting rid of it altogether, as the case may be. Options for customizing the Search Companion are available when you first open the Companion. Look for the Change Preferences option right after you click Start and choose Search, or right after you click the Search button in Explorer's toolbar. You'll see the options shown in Figure 17-13.

Figure 17-13: The Search Companion preferences options

The Search Companion animated character

The first option(s) are simple enough. If the animated character is enabled, you can change to a different character or turn off the character. If the animated character is disabled, you can turn it back on.

Searching with or without the Indexing Service

You can search with or without the Indexing Service. Searching with the Indexing Service is faster and provides for more powerful searches. Searching without the service is slower. The section titled "Industrial-Strength Document Searching" later in this chapter explains what that's all about.

Changing file and folder search behavior

The search behavior option determines how you use the options in the Search Companion. The method described earlier in this chapter is the standard method, where you're prompted for search criteria one step at a time. For example, the companion starts by asking if you want to search for pictures, music, or video; search through all files and folders; and so forth.

The alternative behavior is the Advanced option. With the Advanced option, there is no step-by-step process involved. Instead, the Search Companion opens with all the optional search criteria displayed. But you can still click on the headings to choose date, size, and other advanced options. Or, click on Other search options to use the standard search method.

Changing the Internet search behavior

As the name of this option suggests, you can use the Search Companion to search the Internet as well as your own computer. The section titled "Searching the Internet with the Search Companion" later in this chapter discusses that preference in detail. But here's a quick overview of the options available to you when you click on Change Internet search behavior:

✦ **With Search Companion:** Choosing this option takes you step by step through the process of searching the Internet and allows you to submit your search to multiple search engines.

✦ **With Classic Internet search:** Choosing this option causes the Search Companion to take you straight to a prompt for searching the engine of your choice without prompting.

In the long run, there's very little difference between the two preferences, because you have access to the same set of options either way. The difference is in the manner in which the options appear as opposed to what's available to you. You may want to try each one just to see which you prefer.

Show/don't show balloon tips

Balloon tips are little blinking messages that help you with Internet searches. The Refinement Suggestions box in Figure 17-14 is an example. If balloon tips are currently enabled, you'll see an option titled *Don't show balloon tips* that you can click to turn those tips off. If balloon tips are currently enabled, you see a *Show balloon tips* option that you can click to turn them back on.

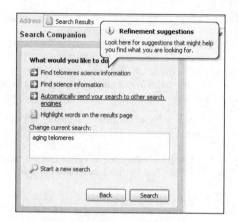

Figure 17-14: Sample balloon tip in an Internet search

Turn AutoComplete on or off

AutoComplete is the feature that automatically displays items you've typed in the past that match what you're typing right now. When AutoComplete is on and you type a question under *What are you looking for?* during an Internet search, a drop-down list of similar text you've typed in the past appears. If an item in the drop-down list matches what you intend to type at the moment, you can just click on that text to select it without manually typing the rest of it.

When AutoComplete is turned off, there is no drop-down list of previous searches. In Change Preferences, the *Turn AutoComplete on* option appears only if AutoComplete is turned off. Just click on that option to enable AutoComplete. When AutoComplete is on, the option reads *Turn AutoComplete off*, and you can click that option to disable the feature.

Searching the Internet with the Search Companion

In many ways, Windows Explorer and Internet Explorer are two entirely separate programs with two separate functions. Windows Explorer is a tool for navigating your own computer. Internet Explorer, on the other hand, is a tool for browsing the Internet, which, of course, exists outside of your computer. Even though they're two different programs, they're very similar. So, similar, in fact, that either one can change into the other.

This close relationship between the two programs allows you to use the Search Companion as a tool for searching the Internet, provided that your computer is online at the time. As mentioned previously, you can use the Search Companion, or Classic Internet Search for searching outside your computer. Here, I'll use the Search Companion method to illustrate how it works.

Taking it all from the top, let's say you're at the Windows desktop (not in a Web browser) and your computer is online. You want to search the Internet for some information, so you click the Start button and choose Search.

Near the bottom of the Search Companion pane, click on Search the Internet. Assuming that someone has changed the default options (or something you didn't even know you were downloading changed them for you), you'll see the prompt *What are you looking for?* You can type a question in plain English, or just type the keyword or words you're looking for. The Sample Question provides an example of a plain-English question. You can even click on the sample question just to see what results you get. For the sake of example, let's say you type the question *Do telomeres cause aging?* and click the Search button.

The results of your search appear in the main pane, and some additional questions appear in the Search Companion pane, as in the example shown in Figure 17-15. If you look closely at the title bar, menu bar, toolbar, Address bar, and taskbar button, you'll see something else has happened. Even through you're still in the same program window, you're in the Internet Explorer program, rather than Windows Explorer. (You can tell by the lowercase "e" icon.)

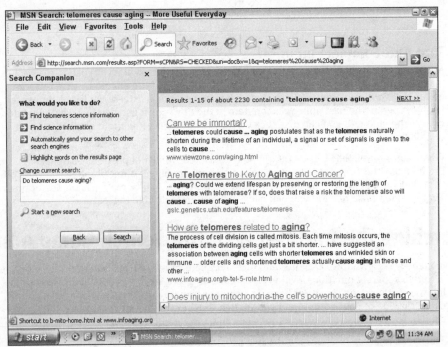

Figure 17-15: Results of a Search Companion Internet search

Each title in the main pane to the right is a link to a specific Web page that you can click. That's standard operating procedure for search engines. The Search Companion is still open as well, and it provides some options that allow you to refine and expand your search. The exact options available to you will vary, depending on what you searched for. So, I can only provide a general example. The options for the sample search are:

✦ **Find telomere science information:** Choosing this option displays specific references, such as online encyclopedias and specialized search directories, for the question you submitted.

✦ **Find science information:** Similar to the above, but allows you to rephrase your question to specific words that represent the general topic of interest.

✦ **Automatically send your search to other search engines:** This option displays a list of general search engines, as in Figure 17-16. To search any listed engine, just click its option button.

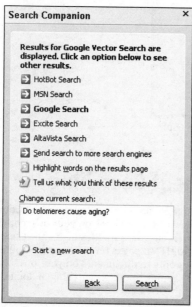

Figure 17-16: Search Companion lets you quickly search multiple engines

If you have experience searching the Web, you can see the advantage that using the Search Companion offers. You need only type your search question once. Then, you can quickly scour many different Internet resources for specific information.

Searching for Computers or People

When you first open the Search Companion, you'll also see an option that allows you to search for computers or people. Choosing that option leads to the two options:

✦ **A computer on the network:** If your computer is a member of a local network, this option allows you to locate a specific computer by name.

✦ **People in your address book:** This option allows you to search Windows Address Book, or an online directory service, for a person based on their name, e-mail address, or other criteria.

If you're using anything other than Windows Address Book (discussed in Chapter 33), the second option really won't help you find anyone in your own address book. However, after you choose this option, you'll be taken to the Find People dialog box. From there, you can use the Look In drop-down list, shown in Figure 17-17, to specify a different resource for finding people. Then, enter your search criteria and click OK.

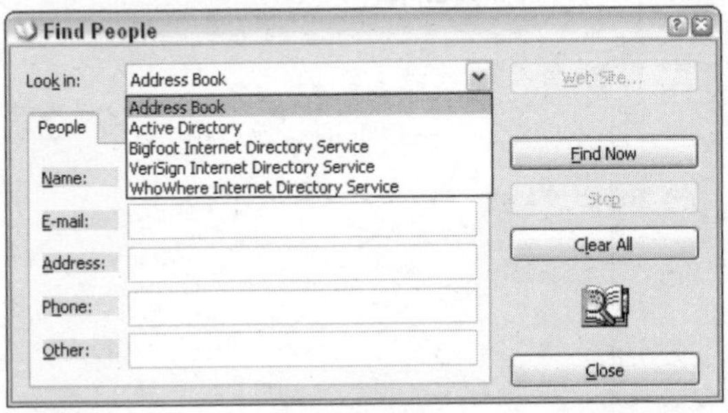

Figure 17-17: The Look In option in the Find People dialog box

Industrial-Strength Document Searching

As mentioned earlier in this chapter, the Change Preferences option in Search Companion allows you to use (or not use) the Indexing Service for searches on your own computer. The Indexing Service is an optional Windows component that provides high-speed searching capabilities for Microsoft Word documents and HTML pages on your own computer. It has nothing to do with Internet searches. It applies only to documents on your own computer. But like an Internet search engine, it allows for rapid, complex searching of documents on your own computer.

Originally, the Indexing Service was a component of IIS (Internet Information Services), a Microsoft product for Web developers. It allowed a Web author to create an index, much like the index at the back of a book, of keywords in documents, to allow users to quickly search the Web site for information.

If you've ever developed Web pages and worked directly with HTML, you know that in the document heading for any page you can include tags that define *metadata*, text about the document that doesn't actually appear in the document. Here's an example of what those tags might look like:

```
<head>
<title>What is Computer Hardware?</title>
<meta name="title" content="What is Computer Hardware?">
<meta name="description" content="Computer Hardware for beginners">
<meta name="keywords" content="PC Hardware monitor system unit hard
disk drive floppy CD speakers microphone">
<meta name="author" content="Alan Simpson">
</head>
```

Microsoft has extended the Indexing Service to include words and properties from all Microsoft Office documents. The information about all those documents is maintained in a *catalog*. When you perform a search with the Indexing Service, it quickly searches the catalog first for appropriate Office documents, providing almost instant search results for those documents.

Properties for Office documents aren't stored in HTML tags. Rather, they're stored as part of the file. You can see the properties for any Office document by right-clicking its icon and choosing Properties. Also, in most Office documents you can set documents properties the first time you save a document. Exactly how you do it depends on the specific application you're using. Search that program's help for *properties* to get the details.

Figure 17-18 shows a couple of examples. The one on the left shows summary properties for a Microsoft Word document, the one on the right for a Visio document. When cataloging Office documents, the Indexing Service includes all properties, as well as words from the document itself.

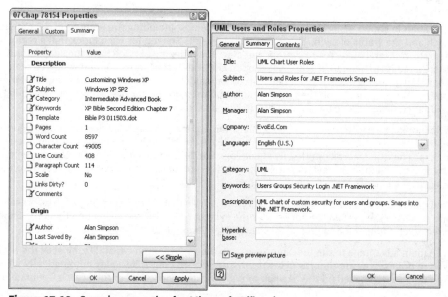

Figure 17-18: Sample properties for Microsoft Office documents

How the Indexing Service works

The catalogs that the Indexing Service creates and uses aren't text document you can open and manipulate. Rather, they're binary files that the Search Companion can use for rapid document searching. Windows builds and maintains the catalogs during computer idle time, when the computer is on but not doing anything else.

To determine whether or not the Indexing Service is already active, open the Search Companion and click on Change Preferences. If you see *Without Indexing Service* as a preference option, that means the Indexing Service is currently working. On the other hand, if you see *With Indexing Service (for faster local searches)*, then the service isn't running.

When you click either preference for the Indexing Service, you're taken to a pane where you can choose whether you do, or don't, want to use the Indexing Service. On that pane you'll also see a *Change Indexing Service settings (Advanced)* option. Clicking that option takes you to an MMC snap-in for managing the service. Figure 17-19 shows an example of what that snap-in looks like.

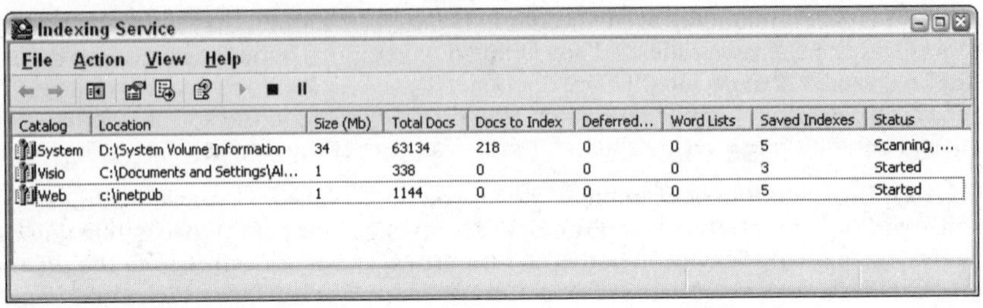

Figure 17-19: The Indexing Service snap-in

The snap-in shows general information about catalogs, including the number of documents in each and the status of each. The Status column reads Started for each index that's ready to search. You can pause, resume, stop, and start the Indexing Service from the snap-in, but there's really no need to. If you leave it open and watch the Status column while it's scanning (building a catalog), you'll see it pause automatically the moment you start using the computer. Take your hands off the mouse and keyboard, and the service will resume scanning and building indexes. Close the snap-in by clicking its Close (X) button.

The Indexing Service organizes the catalogs for maximum search efficiently. Thus, it ignores *noise words* like "a," "the," and so forth, which are contained in virtually all written documents. The exact words omitted from catalogs are defined in a file named noise.*xxx*, where *xxx* is a three-letter abbreviation for a language. For example, noise words excluded from English documents are listed in the file named `noise.eng`.

You can open and edit the noise file using any simple text editor like Notepad. The noise files are stored in the System32 folder under the system root. You can easily find them by using the Search Companion to find all files and folders named `noise.*`.

The main advantage to the Indexing Service is the rapid search capability. Most of the time, you're not even aware that it's being used. The service comes into play automatically when you do a search based on the "*A word or phrase in the document*" in the Search Companion.

In addition to speed, the Indexing Service offers a *query language*. The query language allows you to use special tags and symbols to do complex searched that include things like Boolean logic ("and" and "or" searches), searches for "meaning" as opposed to exact words, and more. Like all computer languages, the query language has a very rigid *syntax*, the rules that dictate exactly how the query must be phrased.

Using the Indexing Service query language

An Indexing Service query can be as simple as a single word or sentence, or a complex expression involving logic, properties, patterns, and relations. You type your search word or query into the *A word or phrase in the document* textbox that appears on the second page of the Search Companion. I'll show an example later in this chapter. For now, I'll focus on the many different types of queries you can perform.

Typing a single word such as *volcano* into the *A word or phrase in the document* textbox returns a list of all Office documents that contain the word "volcano." A more complex query might look something like this:

```
@access >= 2004/01/01 and @access <= 2004/12/31
```

That sample query searches documents for documents that were last opened and viewed in the year 2004. The @access part is a *property name*. The >= and <= parts are examples of *relational operators*.

Most components of the query language offer a *long form* and a *short form*. You can use either form when writing your own queries. Next, we'll look at types of queries and the main components or the query language.

Free-text and phrase queries

A free-text query is one that locates documents that closely match the meaning of a query phrase, rather than the exact words in the phrase. A free-text query looks at the contents, and properties, of each document. The order of words in the free-text query aren't important. Rather, a free-text query is more a search for "meaning" and "relevance" than it is a search for a specific set of words.

Any time you do a search for a single word or group of words and don't use any special query language syntax or quotation marks, the Search Companion automatically performs a free-text search. Optionally, you can specify a free-text query using the long form syntax below:

```
{freetext} {prop name=contents} search phrase
```

where *search phrase* is the word or phrase you're searching for. There's also a short form of the free-text search that uses this syntax:

```
$contents search phrase
```

A *phrase query* is different from a free-text query in that the exact words, and the order of those words is taken into consideration when looking for documents. The long form of a phrase query is:

```
{phrase} search phrase {/phrase}
```

The short form is to simply enclose the phrase in quotation marks:

```
"search phrase"
```

For example, a search for `"run marathon"` or `{phrase} run marathon {/phrase}` returns only documents that contain exactly the words `run marathon`, in that order.

Searching properties and contents

Whenever you perform a basic search such as *red wagon*, the assumption is that you want to include documents that have those words either in the document only. You can use property names in queries to narrow things down so that you're looking only at specific properties.

The query language offers both long forms and short forms for specifying properties. The long form is:

```
{prop name = "property name"}
```

where *property name* is the name of the property you want to search. The quotation marks are only required if the property name contains spaces. For example the quotation marks in `{prop name = "Word count"}` because the property name `Word count"` contains a blank space. However, `{prop name = Title}` is acceptable because the property name `Title` contains no blank spaces.

The short form for specifying a property is `@"property name"`. For single-word properties, you can use #*propname* where *propname* is a one-word property name such as `title`.

Note Property names are not case-sensitive. The text you're searching for is never case-sensitive either. The Indexing Service is strictly a non-case-sensitive search engine.

Indexing properties that all Office documents support are listed in Table 17-1.

Table 17-1: Property Names Included in All Microsoft Office Documents

Property name	Description
All	Document contents and all properties
Contents	Words and phrases contained within the document only, no properties
Filename	The document's filename
Size	The size of the document in bytes
Write	The date and time that the document was last modified and saved

Other widely supported properties are listed in Table 17-2. The exact properties offered by a document will vary, depending on the document type. When you right-click an Office document and choose Properties, you'll see some of these properties on tabs within the Properties dialog box. The names used in the Properties sheet, however, may be slightly different. For example, the DocAuthor property refers to the document's Author property.

Table 17-2: Indexing Service Search Properties for Office Documents

Property name	Description
Access	Last time the document was opened
Created	Date and time the document was created
Directory	Path to the document excluding the filename
DocAppName	Application used to create the document
DocAuthor	Document's author
DocCharCount	Number of characters in document
DocComments	Comments about the document
DocEditTime	Total time spent editing document
DocKeywords	Document keywords
DocLastAuthor	Person who last edited document
DocLastPrinted	Time document was last printed
DocLastSavedTm	Time document was last saved
DocLineCount	Number of lines contained in a document
DocManager	Name of the manager of the document's author
DocPageCount	Number of pages in document
DocParaCount	Number of paragraphs in a document
DocRevNumber	Current version number of document
DocSubject	Subject of document

Property name	Description
DocTemplate	Name of template for document
DocTitle	Title of document
DocWordCount	Number of words in document
Path	Path to document, including the filename
Write	Last time document was modified and saved

The CONTAINS and EQUALS operators

The CONTAINS and EQUALS (=) operators let you search document properties for either an exact match or a partial match. If you don't use either operator, the CONTAINS operator is assumed. For example, either query below will find documents that have the words *blue sky* in their titles:

```
@doctitle "blue sky"

@doctitle Contains "blue sky"
```

Either of these searches would find a document titled "Flying High the Blue Sky," because the title contains the words "blue sky."

The queries that follow, which use the equal operator, will find only documents whose title is exactly *blue sky*. A document titled "Flying High the Blue Sky" wouldn't match the criterion, because that title has more words than "blue sky":

```
@doctitle = "blue sky"

@doctitle Equals "blue sky"
```

Relational operators

Relational operators are useful for searching numeric and date properties. For example, you can search for documents whose size if greater than, or equal to, some number. The relational operators are listed in Table 17-3.

Table 17-3: Query Language Relational Operators

Relational Operator	Description
<	Less than
<=	Less than or equal to
=	Equal to
>=	Greater than or equal to
>	Greater than
!=	Not equal to

For example, a query for `@DocPageCount>=20` locates all documents that contain 20 or more pages.

Logical operators

Logical operators (also called *Boolean operators*) are listed in Table 17-4. These allow you to combine search criteria using "and" and "or" logic, to omit certain documents, and to find documents that have words near each other in the document, but not necessarily side by side.

Table 17-4: Query Language Relational Operators

Operator	Long form	Short form
AND	AND	&
OR	OR	|
NOT	AND NOT	&!
NEAR	NEAR	~

As an example, the query below locates documents whose page count is greater than or equal to 10 and less than or equal to 15.

```
@DocPageCount>=10 AND @DocPageCount<=15
```

The query below finds all documents that have the name Smith or Jones in the Author property:

```
@DocAuthor"Jones" OR @DocAuthor"Smith"
```

The query below also finds documents authored by Smith or Jones, but omits documents whose size is under 1,000 bytes:

```
@DocAuthor"Jones" OR @DocAuthor"Smith" AND NOT @Size<1000
```

The query below finds documents that contain the words *red wagon*. The words need not be right next to each other, just near each other. For example, the query that follows would find a document that contains the sentence "Gee, you some kinda math whiz or something?" Because no property name is specified, the search looks at document contents only:

```
gee ~ whiz
```

Alternate word form queries

Alternate word forms include prefixes and inflected versions of words. A prefix would be something like `cani*` that matches any words that begin with the letters *cani*—for example, canine, canis, and Canidae.

Inflected word forms include the past tense, the future tense, and gerunds. For example, inflected forms of the word "dream" include "dreamed," "dreamt," and "dreaming." Table 17-5 lists alternate word form operators.

Table 17-5: Alternate Word Form Operators

Form	Long form	Short form
Prefix	{Generate method=prefix} *word* {/Generate}	*word**
Inflected	{Generate method=inflect} *word* {/Generate}	*word***

Date and time queries

When searching document properties for dates and times, use the form *yyyy/mm/dd hh:mm:ss* or *yyyy-mm-dd hh:mm:ss*. You can omit the first two characters of the year for dates between 1930 and 2029. You can omit the entire time specification if you're interested only in the date. For example, the query below finds documents last viewed in the year 2004:

```
@access >= 2004/01/01 and @access <= 2004/12/31
```

Submitting Index Service queries

To submit index queries to the Search Companion, type your query statement into the *A word or phrase in the file* textbox. If your Search Companion preferences are set to Standard (step by step), choose *Documents (word processing, spreadsheet, and so forth)* on the first page, and then choose *Use advanced search options* on the second page so that you can see the *A word or phrase in the document* option.

If you change your Search Companion preferences to use the Advanced form (not step by step), the Search Companion will display the *A word or phrase in the file* option as soon as it opens. Then, type your query into the text box and click the Search button. For example, Figure 17-20 shows an Indexing Service query for documents that were last viewed in the year 2004.

Search by any or all of the criteria below.

All or part of the file name:

A word or phrase in the file:

@access >= 2004/01/01 and @access <= 2004/12/31

Look in:

Local Hard Drives (C:;D:)

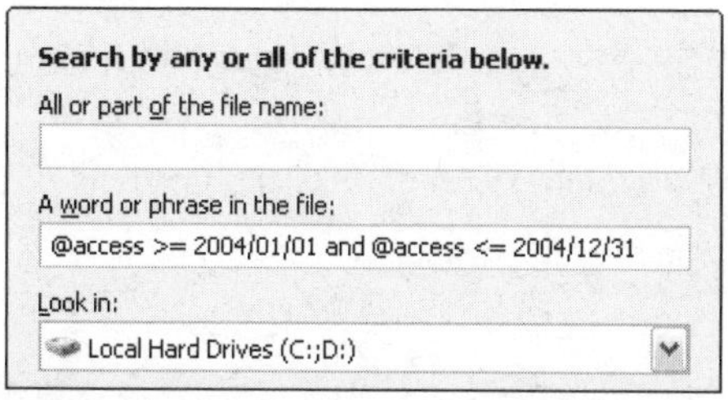

Figure 17-20: A sample Indexing Service query

For more information on using the Indexing Service, and more advanced forms of the query language, open the Search Companion, and click on Change Preferences. Next, click on the option to change the Indexing Service, and then click the *Learn more about indexing service* link at the bottom of the column.

Wrap Up

The Search Companion is your best friend when it comes time to find a lost file or take inventory of files spread across multiple folders. To recap the high points:

✦ To search your entire hard drive (or all hard drives), click the Start button and choose Search.

✦ To search a specific folder and its subfolder, open the folder, and then click the Search button in Explorer's toolbar.

✦ Optionally, use the Search Companion's *Look In* option to search a specific disk drive or folder.

✦ To search for files based on their names, fill in the *All or part of the filename* option in the Search Companion.

✦ To search for files based on their extensions, enter *.ext* into the *All or part of the file name* text box, where *ext* is the extension you're looking for.

✦ To search the contents of documents, or document properties, fill n the *A word or phrase in the file* text box in the Search Companion.

✦ Use the *advanced options* in the Search Companion to search for files based on date or size.

✦ To customize the Search Companion, click its *Change preferences* option.

✦   ✦   ✦

Realistic Backup Strategies

Have you ever noticed warnings on Web sites telling you to back up your hard disk before doing some risky stunt? Have you ever noticed that nobody ever tells you *how* to back up your hard disk? If so, you're probably in the same boat as a lot of other people, wondering just how you're supposed to go about backing up your hard disk.

The truth of the matter is that people who own personal computers generally don't back up their hard disks. The reason for that is simple — normal PC users don't have expensive backup hardware that the big corporations use to back up their mission-critical data.

In this chapter we'll look at realistic strategies for backing up your hard drive. As you'll see, it's really not so much a matter of backing up the entire hard disk. Rather, it's more a matter of backing up things like documents, messages, contacts, and favorites. And you don't need anything special to back up those things.

The Problem with Backups

There are two fundamental problems that make backing up your entire hard disk a difficult endeavor. The first is the sheer quantity of data. If you open your My Computer folder, right-click the icon for your hard drive (typically Local Disk C:), and choose Properties, you'll see how much "stuff" there is on your hard disk right now. For example, the hard drive in Figure 18-1 currently has 23.2 GB of files on it.

To back up that 23.2 GB worth of files you'd need about 46 CDs, or about 7 DVDs, or a walloping 23,000 floppies. Or, a second hard drive that's equal in size to the first (which is actually the most cost-effective and time-efficient approach, if you want to bother with that). But no matter what type of disks you copy to, it's going to take a long time to back up your hard disk. And as soon as you're done and start saving new files, the backup is already out of date.

Even if you did take the time to back up your entire hard disk, the backup disks wouldn't do you any good unless you had some means of recovering all the files from those disks in the event of a disaster. You would really need to purchase, and learn to use, a third-party backup utility.

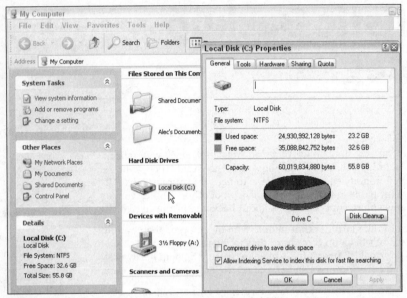

Figure 18-1: Used space and free space on a hard drive

Last time I checked, there were about 65 backup utility programs listed in the Windows Catalog. To see them, go to www.WindowsCatalog.com. On the home page, click the Software tab. Then, click Utilities in the left column. Finally, click the Backup option.

But the fact of the matter is, outside the corporate world hardly anyone bothers to back up their entire hard disk. Doing so is time-consuming and not terribly practical. Large corporations handle the backups with specialized hardware and people with job titles like "backup administrator." But those of us with limited budgets and no staff of administrators aren't likely to make that sort of an investment. And in truth, there's really no need to.

Backing Up Windows XP and Programs

Most of the files are system files and program files — those files that make up Windows XP and all your programs. Backing up all those system and program files takes a lot of time and a lot of disks. Fortunately, there's no need to back up your system and program files over and over again, because most of them never change.

Whether or not you even want to bother making backups of those files is debatable, because of the very nature of programs and system files. Unlike documents, which you can just copy to your hard disk and use, programs (that is, system files and program files) need to be *installed* on your computer to work properly. The installation process configures the program to run properly in your particular hardware and software environment. You can't take a program installed on one computer and just copy it to another computer and expect it to work. It won't.

So, consider this. Let's say that you have copies of all your installed programs on CDs or some other medium. Your hard disk crashes, and you have to replace it. How are you going to get all those programs that were installed on the old hard disk to the new hard disk? And how are you going to be sure that they'll work on the new hard disk without ever having been installed on that disk? (Remember, you can't just copy an installed program to another computer; you have to install the program.) They *might* work. But there's a big difference between *might* and *will*.

Here's a strategy that can avoid the whole business of backing up all those tens of thousands of system and program files and living with the anxiety of really not knowing if they'll do you any good. When you buy a program, it's usually delivered on a CD. When you buy a computer with software already installed, you usually get an extra copy of all the system files and program files on one or more CDs.

In a sense, those CDs are better than backups, because the copies on the CDs contain the actual installation files needed to install the program. In other words, they're the very files you need to *install* the program. So, in a sense, you already have backups of all those tens of thousands of program and system files that are on your hard disk. If you lose Windows and all your programs, you can just reinstall them from the original CDs.

Caution   Many programs require a serial number or product key to install. You should store all your original CDs, and any serial numbers/product keys, in a safe place. A fireproof safe would be your best bet, because many insurance companies won't cover software, no matter how you lose it.

Then, of course, there are programs you download for which you don't have any original CD. Probably the best solution to backing those up is to just remember where you got them. In the unlikely event of a serious disk crash, you could always go back to the Web site and get the latest-and-greatest version of that program. Once again, you're installing from scratch, which is the proper way to do it.

Backing Up Documents

Documents are files you create or download. Reports and letters you type, spreadsheets, pictures, songs, and videos are all examples of documents. You're free to open and change documents at any time. Thus, unlike system files and program files, documents can, and do, change.

You can easily back up any given document or set of documents just by copying them to a CD or some other removable disk. There's no need to use fancy backup software there. Just use the built-in copying capabilities discussed in Chapter 14. CDs are good candidates because each one holds 650 to 700 MB worth of data. If you use CD-RWs you can reuse the same disc each time you make a backup.

DVDs are even better, because a DVD holds 4.7 GB worth of data, about seven times as much as a CD. But Windows XP has no built-in capabilities for copying files to DVDs. You have to use the backup software (if any) that came with the DVD burner. Or, purchase a backup utility program that can backup to DVDs for you. Again, using DVD-RWs or DVD+RWs would be your best bet, because you can reuse the same disc each time you make a backup.

Note   See Chapter 15 for more information on different types of CDs and DVDs.

If you keep all your documents in your My Documents and Shared Documents folders, making backups of all those files is relatively easy. Just copy each folder to a CD or DVD (if it will fit) and be done with it. If all the files won't fit on a single disc, you may need to back up individual folders. For example, you might copy your My Pictures and Shared Pictures folders to one disc, your My Music and Shared Music folders to another disc, and so forth. That way, if you ever lose your hard drive and need to replace it, you can reinstall Windows XP and all your programs from their original discs. Then, copy all your documents from the CDs or DVDs into the appropriate folders on the new hard drive, and you're back in business. Almost, anyway. Chances are, you will have lost all your e-mail messages, favorites, and settings. However, there are ways to back up those things as well.

Caution   Account information, such as that needed to get to your Internet account and e-mail, should really be backed up on paper. Keep that information on file in a safe place, so you can set your account back up, from scratch, should you ever lose any Internet account information on your hard disk.

Backing Up Settings

Settings files store things such as all the options you've selected in all those dialog boxes that Windows offers. The files are tiny. Usually, you can fit them all on two or three blank floppy disks. (Finally, you have a use for that floppy drive!) The problem is that the settings files are scattered about your hard drive and not particularly easy to find. But there's a tool in Windows that can find them for you. It's called the Files and Settings Transfer Wizard.

The Files and Settings Transfer Wizard is actually a tool designed to help you transfer documents and settings from an old computer to a new computer that already has Windows and other programs installed on it. But there's no rule that says you can't use it to make backup copies of files on your hard disk. The program is easy to use, and you can use it to back up documents as well as settings. But as mentioned in the preceding section, there are other ways to back up documents, so here we'll just look at backing up settings. Here's how you do that:

1. Click the **Start** button and choose **All Programs** ➪ **Accessories** ➪ **System Tools** ➪ **Files and Settings Transfer Wizard**.

2. On the first page of the wizard that opens, click **Next**.

3. Choose **Old Computer** from the second page of the wizard, and click **Next**.

4. On the third wizard page, choose where you want to save the settings file. You have two options here:

   • If you want to back up your settings to a magnetic removable disk such as a Zip disk, or thumb drive, choose **Floppy drive or other removable media**, and then choose the drive from the drop-down list beneath that option.

Caution   I doubt that even a backup of your Settings file would fit on a floppy disk. Though it would fit on a thumb drive or Zip disk. (CDs and DVDs are not magnetic media, and so won't appear as options when you're choosing where you want to store the Settings file.)

   • If you want to copy the settings to your My Documents folder, and back them up along with everything else you back up from My Documents, choose **Other . . .**, and then click the **Browse** button and choose **My Documents**.

5. Click the **Next** button. On the next page choose **Settings Only**, as in Figure 18-2.

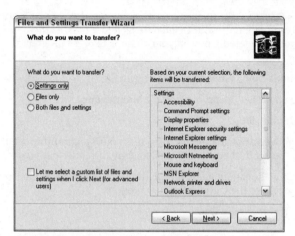

Figure 18-2: Choosing Settings Only in the Files and Settings Transfer Wizard

6. Follow any remaining instructions that appear on the screen, and then click the **Finish** button in the last wizard page.

If you copied the settings to you My Documents folder, you'll see a new subfolder named USMT2.UNC as in the left side of Figure 18-3. The next time you make a backup copy of your My Documents folder, that folder will be included in the backup. If you chose to save the settings to a removable disk, you'll just see a file icon named USMT2IMG (or USMT2IMG.DAT), as in the right side of Figure 18-3.

Figure 18-3: Backup of settings as created by the File and Settings Transfer Wizard

Should you ever need to recover those settings, install Windows and all your programs to the hard disk first. Then, run the Files and Settings Transfer Wizard again. This time, choose New Computer when the wizard asks, and follow the on-screen instructions to bring those settings files to your new hard disk.

Backing Up E-Mail Messages and Contacts

E-mail messages and contacts in your address book are neither documents nor settings. So, unless you make an extra effort to back those items up, they won't be included with a document or settings backup. Unfortunately, there are so many different e-mail services and e-mail clients out there in the world, there's nothing I can say that will apply to all readers of this book. The best I can do is talk about backing up messages and contacts in Outlook Express, which is the e-mail client that comes with Windows XP.

Backing up Outlook Express messages

If you use Outlook Express 6 as your e-mail client, backing up your messages is a little weird, but not difficult. You may want to empty your Deleted Items folder first, as there's no need to backup all the messages you've deleted. Then, in your Outlook Express program window, follow these steps:

1. Choose **Tools** ➪ **Options** from Outlook Express's menu bar.

2. In the Options dialog box that opens, click on the **Maintenance** tab.

3. Click the **Store Folder** button.

4. In the Store Location dialog box that opens, drag the mouse pointer through the entire path that appears to select it, then press **Ctrl+C** to copy the entire path name.

5. Click **Cancel** in the Store Location dialog box, and then click **Cancel** in the Options dialog box. You may then close the Outlook Express program.

6. Click the **Start** button and choose **Run**.

Note   If you don't have a Run option on your Start menu, see "Personalizing Your Start Menu" in Chapter 6.

7. In the Run box, press **Ctrl+V** to paste in the path you copied, and then click **OK**. Each icon you see represents a mail or newsgroup folder. However, the data is stored in binary, so don't even attempt to open any of those icons.

8. Click the **Up** button in Explorer's toolbar to go to the parent folder. You should see a folder icon named Outlook Express.

9. Right-click the Outlook Express folder icon, and choose **Copy**.

10. Navigate to the folder in which you want to place the backup copy (such as your My Documents folder, or an external magnetic disk).

11. Right-click any empty space between icons, and choose **Paste**.

12. Right-click the folder you just pasted, choose **Rename**, and give this folder a more meaningful name such as Mail Backup or OE Mail Backup. Then, press **Enter**.

If you pasted the Outlook Express folder into your My Documents folder, it will be backed up the next time you back up your My Documents file. If, instead, you backed up to a removable disk, that removable disk is your backup.

Backing up Windows Address Book

Names and addresses from Outlook Express are actually stored in a separate program named Windows Address Book (WAB for short). The steps for backing up the address book are also a little strange, and separate from backing up messages:

1. From Outlook Express's menu bar choose **File** ➪ **Export** ➪ **Address Book**.

2. Click on **Text File (Comma Separated Values)**, and then click **Export**.

3. Click the **Browse** button, and navigate to the folder or drive to which you want to back up. Again, if you back up your My Documents folder, you can choose My Documents.

Backing Up Microsoft Outlook Data

If you use Microsoft Outlook as your e-mail client, you can easily back up your messages and contacts by choosing File ➪ Import and Export from Outlook's menu bar. Choose Export to a File, and then click Next. Choose Personal Folder File (.pst), and click Next once again. When asked what to export, you can choose any folder you like. If you want to back up all your messages, contacts, and calendar, click on Personal Folders at the top of the list. Choose the Include Subfolders option, and click Next.

When asked where you want to store the exported file, you can choose a common folder like My Documents. That way, when you back up that folder later, you'll automatically back up everything that's in Outlook as well. Optionally, you can choose an external magnetic disk, like a Zip disk or thumb drive. Click the Finish button, and you'll see some options for encrypting the data. Personally, I wouldn't recommend password-protecting the file, unless you're certain that you won't forget the password should you ever need to recover the data from the .pst file.

For more information, choose Help ➪ Microsoft Office Outlook Help from Outlook's menu bar. Search for the word export, and take a look at the "About importing and exporting," and anything else that looks relevant, in the links that appear.

4. Type a filename such as **WAB Backup**, click the **Save** button, and then click **Next**.

5. Optionally, choose the fields you want to export, or just make sure that you check all the checkboxes, and then click **Finish**.

6. Click **OK** in the feedback message, and then click **Close** in the Export dialog box.

A copy of all your names and addresses will be in the WAB Backup file (or whatever file name you provided in Step 4).

Backing up Outlook Express mail account data

If you use Outlook Express for e-mail, information like your e-mail address, ISP's mail server names, and so forth is stored in its Accounts dialog box. You can back up that account information. Here's how:

1. From Outlook Express's menu bar, choose **Tools** ➪ **Accounts**.

2. In the Internet Accounts dialog box that opens, click on the **Mail** tab.

3. Click on the mail account name, and then click the **Export** button.

4. In the Export Internet Account dialog box, choose the drive or folder to which you want to back up your data. Again, your My Documents folder is fine. Then, click the **Save** button.

5. If you have multiple e-mail accounts, repeat Steps 3 and 4 for each account.

6. Click the **Close** button.

Recovering lost Outlook Express data

In the unlikely event that you ever lose all, or some, of your Outlook Express data, you can recover it from whatever backup files you created in the preceding sections. You can recover any single component or all components.

Recovering lost messages

To recover e-mail messages from the backup folder you make:

1. Choose **File** ➪ **Import** ➪ **Messages** from Outlook Express's menu bar.

2. In the Select Program list, click on **Microsoft Outlook Express 6**, and then click **Next**.

3. Choose **Import mail from an OE6 store directory**, and then click **OK**.

4. Click the **Browse** button, navigate to the drive or folder in which you placed the backup folder, and then click on the backup folder's icon and click **OK**.

5. Click **Next**.

6. Choose **All Folders**, and then click **Next**.

7. Click the **Finish** button.

To verify that you have your mail messages back, click on your Inbox or any other folder under Local Folders.

Recovering lost contacts

To recover names and addresses from your exported Windows Address Book file, follow these steps:

1. Choose **File** ➪ **Import** ➪ **Other Address Book** from Outlook Express's menu bar.

2. Click **Text File (Comma Separated Values)**, and then click **Import**.

3. Click the **Browse** button and navigate to the drive or folder in which you stored the exported Windows Address Book data.

4. Click the name of the Windows Address Book file, and then click **Open**.

5. Click **Next**, and then click **Finish**.

6. Click **OK**, and then click **Close**.

Recovering mail account information

To restore lost mail account information to Outlook Express:

1. Choose **Tools** ➪ **Accounts** from Outlook Express's menu bar.

2. Click on the **Mail** tab, and then click the **Import** button.

3. Navigate to the drive or folder in which you stored the mail account backup file, click the file's name, and then click the **Open** button.

4. If you exported multiple mail information files, repeat Steps 2 and 3 for each account you need to recover.

5. Click the **Close** button in the Internet Accounts dialog box.

Backing Up Your Favorites

You can back up all your Internet Explorer favorites to a file. The file that's created is usually small enough to fit even on a floppy disk. But if you back up to My Documents or some other normal folder, and then back that folder up to a CD or whatever, you'll have that backup along with all your others. To back up your favorites in Internet Explorer:

1. Start Internet Explorer and choose **File ➪ Import and Export** from its menu bar.

2. Click **Next** on the first wizard page, choose **Export Favorites**, then click **Next**.

3. To export all of your favorites, click on the top **Favorites** folder, and then click **Next**.

4. Choose **Export to a File or Address**.

5. Click the **Browse** button, and then navigate to the drive or folder in which you want to store the backup.

6. Optionally, rename the folder from Bookmark or bookmark.htm to a name of your own choosing, such as **IEFavorites**.

7. Click **Save**, click **Next**, click **Finish**, and then click **OK**.

The backup file is actually a Web page that you can open and use directly. Double-click that file to see the names of all your favorite Web sites. Click any Web site name to go to that site.

Should you ever need to recover all your favorites from the backup file:

1. Choose **File ➪ Import and Export** from Internet Explorer's menu bar.

2. Click **Next** on the first wizard page, choose **Import Favorites**, and click **Next**.

3. Choose **Import from a File or Address**.

4. Click the **Browse** button, and then navigate to the drive or folder in which you want to store the backup.

5. Click on the name of the backup file you created (e.g., bookmark or IEFavorites), and then click **Save**. (Yes, that option in the dialog box should read Open, not Save. But it works nonetheless.)

6. Click **Next**, click on **Favorites** at the top of the list, and then click **Next.**

7. Click **Finish**, and then click **OK**.

Using NT Backup

After all that I've said about backing up individual items, using third-party programs and such, you might be surprised when I tell you that Windows XP actually comes with a built-in backup program named NT Backup. I suppose lately it's been retitled to just Backup or Backup Utility for Windows, but it's still the old NT Backup program that's been hanging around in Windows for years. The only reason I didn't mention it until now is because, personally, I'm a little skeptical on just how "realistic" a backup tool it is for most PC users.

Installing NT Backup on XP Home Edition

NT Backup comes with both the Home Edition and Professional Editions of XP. However, you wouldn't know it's available in Home Edition because you can't find it in any of the usual haunts, not even the Add/Remove Windows Components dialog box. To install NT Backup in XP Home Edition:

1. Insert your original Windows XP Home Edition CD into your CD drive.

2. When the autostart options appear in the screen, click on **Exit**.

3. Open your My Computer folder.

4. Right-click the icon for your CD drive and choose **Open**.

5. Open the folder named **VALUEADD**.

6. Open the **MSFT** folder.

7. Open the **NTBACKUP** folder.

8. Double-click the **NTBACKUP** (or **NTBACKUP.MSI**) icon, and follow the instructions on the screen.

When you've completed the wizard and clicked the Finish button, you should be able to click Start and choose All Programs ➪ Accessories ➪ System Tools ➪ Backup to start the NT Backup program.

NT Backup stores all the files you tell it to back up in a single, large .bkf file. Personally, I prefer to have my backups look and act like the original files so that I can poke around through the file and pick and choose what I want to restore from backups. But, not everyone feels that way so feel free to ignore my dumb personal opinion there.

The .bkf file that NT Backup creates is likely to be too large to fit on a CD   maybe even too large to fit on a DVD. Furthermore, there's no way to back up directly to CD or DVD with NT Backup. So, you have to write the large .bkf file to your hard disk first, and then hope it will fit on a CD or DVD.

On the other hand, if you do have a large extra drive, such as a second hard drive, an external hard drive, or network drive, then NT Backup might not be such a bad choice. It's not the speediest program in the world. Chances are, you'll want to start your backups just before you're about to leave the computer unattended for a while. But it does work, so I suppose I'd be remiss in my duties if I just ignored it altogether in this book.

NT Backup isn't installed by default in Windows XP Home Edition. To install it in that edition, see the sidebar on that topic in this chapter. If you find that NT Backup isn't available on the System Tools menu in XP Professional Edition, then you can install it yourself from your original XP disk. In Professional Edition, you can install NT Backup as you would any other Windows component.

Note

See "Installing and Removing Windows Components" in Chapter 45 for information on Add/Remove Windows Components.

Assuming that NT Backup is installed, here's how you run it in Wizard mode to back up files from your hard disk:

1. Click the **Start** button, and choose **All Programs** ➪ **Accessories** ➪ **System Tools** ➪ **Backup**.

2. Click **Next** on the first wizard page.

3. On the second wizard page, choose **Back up files and settings**, and then click **Next**.

4. On the third wizard page, shown in Figure 18-4, choose how much data you want to back up, and then click **Next**.

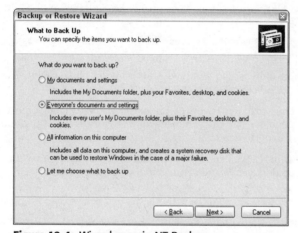

Figure 18-4: Wizard page in NT Backup

5. On the third wizard page, click the Browse button and navigate to the drive or folder to which you want to back up your files, and then click **Save**. Optionally, type a name for your backup file, or just accept the suggested named *backup*.

6. Click **Next**, and review the settings shown on the next wizard page.

7. Then, click **Finish**, and wait while NT backup creates the backup file.

In the event of a major hard-disk crash that loses all your documents and settings, you can repeat the basic steps just given. But, when you get to Step 3 choose Restore files and settings, and follow the wizard instructions from there.

Wrap Up

There are many ways to make backup copies of files on your hard disk. As a rule, you don't have to worry about backing up Windows XP or any of your programs. Chances are, they wouldn't reinstall properly even if you did back them up. You do, however, want to back up your documents, and possibly other important information such as e-mail messages, names and addresses, and so forth. In this chapter, we looked at ways to back up specific types of files. To wit:

✦ The best way to back up Windows XP and all your programs is to keep the original CDs and product keys (if any) in a safe place where you can find them if you ever need them.

✦ One way to make a backup of all your documents is to simply copy everything in your My Documents folder to a CD or DVD.

✦ You can use the Files and Settings Transfer Wizard to back up only your settings, or documents and settings.

✦ To back up Outlook Express e-mail messages, choose File ➪ Export ➪ Messages from Outlook Express's menu bar.

✦ To back up names and addresses in Windows Address Book, choose File ➪ Export ➪ Address Book from Outlook Express's menu bar.

✦ To back up your Internet Explorer Favorites, choose File ➪ Import and Export from Internet Explorer's menu bar, and then choose Export Favorites from the options presented by the Import/Export Wizard.

✦ Windows XP comes with NT Backup, which you can use as an alternative to the above techniques to back up documents and settings to a single large .bkf file.

Troubleshooting File and Folder Problems

Here are some common problems and their solutions for working with files and folders in Windows Explorer. Remember, Windows Explorer is the program that opens whenever you open any folder. You don't need to specifically open Windows Explorer from the All Programs menu.

Explorer bar is missing

The Explorer bar disappears if you size the Windows Explorer window so small that there's not enough room for icons and the Explorer bar to fit. If the Explorer bar is covered by some other bar, click the X button at the top of that other bar, or choose View ⇨ Explorer Bar, and click whichever bar name has a check mark to the left.

If the Explorer bar is never visible, choose Tools ⇨ Folder Options from the menu bar. Choose "Show common tasks in folders" (not the classic folders option), and then Click OK.

Files and Folders Tasks not available in Explorer bar

Make sure that you're in a document folder. For example, Control Panel and My Network Places are not folders for storing documents. If the window is small, use the scroll bar at the right side of the Explorer bar to scroll through options. Click any heading in the Explorer bar to show or hide the items beneath that heading.

Can't open source/destination folder in a separate window

You can't open a second instance of Windows Explorer from the Other Places section of the Explorer bar. You need to open a new instance by clicking the Start button and choosing My Documents, or My Computer, or whatever folder gets you closest to the source/destination folder you're trying to open.

When I try to select by dragging, the icons move, and nothing is selected

To *move* an item, you put the mouse pointer *on* the item you want to move, and then drag. To *select* items by dragging, start with the mouse pointer *near* the first item you want to select, but not at a point where it's actually touching an icon.

Error message "Cannot delete/rename/move file: The file is in use by . . ."

Whenever you see this message, it means that the file you're trying to delete, rename, or move is currently open. Close the open document on the desktop (or from the taskbar, if it's minimized). Then, try again.

Error message "Source and Destination are the same"

You've tried to move or copy a file or folder to itself, which doesn't make sense. Double-check your source and destination folders.

Error message "If you change a file name extension, the file may become unstable."

You've attempted to rename both the filename and the extension. Changing a filename extension can be bad news because the extension will no longer accurately reflect the format of the data in the file. Choose No, and then rename the file. This time, don't change the file extension. To avoid this problem in the future, enable the "Hide extensions for known file types" option in Folder Options (See "Choosing Folder Options" in Chapter 12).

Error message "This folder already contains a file named . . ."

No two files in a folder can have the same name. Here, you're trying to move or copy a file to a folder that already contains a file with the name of the one you're trying to move or copy. Your best bet would be to choose No. Next, rename the file or folder you're trying to move or copy, and then move or copy the renamed file.

Optionally, if you choose Yes, the file that's already in the folder will be replaced by the one you're trying to move or copy, which means that the original file will be lost forever.

"Problem with Shortcut" dialog box opens

When a shortcut stops working, that means the folder, file, or Web page to which the shortcut refers no longer exists. In the case of a file or folder, you've either deleted, moved, or renamed the original item since creating the shortcut. In the case of a Web page, either you're not online, or the Web page no longer exists at that location.

Deleting a shortcut from my desktop deletes it from all users' desktops

See the description of this problem under "Troubleshooting User Account Problems" in Chapter 11.

Note See also Chapter 5 for related Windows Explorer and document icon problems.

Troubleshooting CDs and DVDs

CDs and DVDs pose some unique problems because unlike most computer storage media, they use laser technology rather than magnetism. You can't read from and write to CDs and DVDs as you can other types of disks. And, CDs and DVDs are likely to generate some unique error messages, described and addressed in the sections that follow.

Error message "Invalid function" when attempting to write files to a CD

You can only write files with CD-R and CD-RW drives, not a CD-ROM drive. Also, the recording capabilities of your CD-R or CD-ROM drive must be enabled as follows:

1. Click the **Start** button, and choose **My Computer**.

2. Right-click the icon for your CD drive, and choose **Properties**.

3. In the Properties dialog box that opens, click the **Recording** tab,

4. Make sure **Enable CD recording on this drive** is selected (checked).

5. Click **OK**.

If the problem persists, repeat the preceding steps and try a slower speed on the Recording tab.

An invalid or outdated CD driver can also cause the problem. See Chapter 53 for the goods on finding an updated driver.

Finally, a conflict with third-party CD-burning software can generate this message. Try using that third-party program to copy files to a CD. For general information about Roxio CD-burning products, see www.roxio.com. See www.nero.com for general information on Nero Burn products.

Writing files to a CD often fails

Try setting a slower recording speed on the Recording tab of the Properties dialog box. See the steps in the preceding section on Invalid Function messages.

Partially filled CD shows "0 bytes free"

A CD-ROM always shows "zero bytes free" because once you've created a CD-ROM, you cannot change its contents in any way. Copying files to a CD-R always creates a CD-ROM. You only get one shot at copying files to a CD-R disk.

Confirmation message "The file Thumbs.db has extra information attached . . ."

The `Thumbs.db` file is used by Windows to rapidly display thumbnail icons from the current folder. There's no need to copy `Thumbs.db` to a CD or DVD. So, you can choose "Repeat my answer each time this occurs," and then click Skip.

Error message "Windows encountered a problem when trying to copy this file."

If the first character of the filename that couldn't be copied is a tilde (~), it's just a temporary file that need not be copied. Click the Skip button. Also, you can't copy an open document to a CD. Close and save the document, and then click Retry.

Message "Cannot complete the CD Writing Wizard"

Specifics of the problem that caused this error are described beneath the message. The most common cause is choosing more files to copy than can fit on the CD. Click Finish, and check the combined sizes of files waiting to be written to the CD, plus any files already on a CD-RW. To do so, select all the icons in the CD Writing folder, right-click, and choose Properties. The Size on Disk setting must be less than the total capacity of the CD. Click Cancel after checking the combined file sizes.

To reduce the amount of data to be written to the CD, delete some of the items waiting to be written to the CD, and check their combined sizes. Keep trying until only as much data as will fit on the CD is waiting to be written to the CD.

Icons remain in CD Writing Tasks folder after CD has been burned

You chose to leave the icons in the folder from the last wizard page. If you've changed your mind and want to clear out those icons, click on "Delete temporary files" in the Explorer bar at the left side of the CD Writing folder.

The original files and folders that those icons represent will remain on your hard disk. That, too, is intentional because there's rarely any reason to move files from your hard disk to a CD. If you're certain you're running low on hard disk space (because of a message to that effect in the Notification area), you can delete the original files from your hard disk after copying them from the CD. But you can't do so from the CD Writing folder. You'll need to go back and delete the original files using any technique described in Chapter 14.

Can't delete/rename files from CD-RW

When you right-click the icon for a file that's already on a CD and choose Delete or Rename, you receive a message stating that files on the CD are read-only. In Windows XP, you cannot individually rename or delete items on a CD-RW. Your only option is to erase all the items on the CD-RW using the *Erase this CD-RW* link under CD Writing Tasks in the Explorer bar.

To manage files individually on a CD-RW, or to move and copy files using drag and drop, you'll need to install third-party packet writing software such as DirectCD or DLA. Some third-party

CD-burning programs such as Roxio Easy CD and Nero Burn have packet-writing capabilities installed.

Cannot copy files to/from a DVD

Windows has no built-in capabilities for copying files to or from a DVD. You must use the third-party software that came with your DVD burner or computer. If you bought your computer with a DVD burner preinstalled, your computer manufacturer probably preinstalled DVD burning software as well.

Microsoft Knowledge Base Articles

Microsoft's Knowledge Base offers several articles for more advanced CD and DVD troubleshooting. Go to `http://support.microsoft.com/default.aspx?scid=kb;` `en-us;321641&Product=winxp` or go to `http://support.microsoft.com` and search for `321641`. Look at the bottom of the page that opens for more links to specific problems with CD and DVD drives.

Troubleshooting Searches

The Search Companion usually runs without a hitch. Here are a few problems you might encounter and their solutions. If you encounter a problem not covered here, consider searching `http://support.microsoft.com` for your specific problem.

Search Companion didn't find my file

If you're searching for a file based on the filename, you must know the exact spelling of that filename. If you're only sure of a few letters within the filename, search for only those letters. To make sure that you get the broadest search possible, conduct the search as follows:

1. Choose **Tools** ⇨ **Folder Options** from the Search Results menu bar. Click the **View** tab, choose **Show hidden files and folders**, and then click **OK**.

2. Under *What do you want to search for?* choose **All files and folders**.

3. If you're not sure of the exact spelling of the filename, enter the part of the name you do know under *All or part of the file name*.

4. From the **Look in** drop-down list choose **Local Hard Drives** (. . .) to select all of your local hard drives.

5. Click on **More advanced options**.

6. Select **Search system folders**, **Search hidden files and folders**, and **Search subfolders**. Do not choose the other two checkboxes.

7. Click the **Search** button, and wait for the search to complete.

If the search is still unsuccessful you (or someone else) may have already deleted the file and removed it from the Recycle Bin. Or, perhaps someone moved the file to a removable disk, or renamed the file. Or, you've misspelled the name of the file you're looking for.

Search Companion or Search Results pane opens unexpectedly

If your Search Companion or Search Results appear when you don't expect it, such as when you just double-click a drive's icon or a folder's icon such as My Pictures or My Documents, the problem could be a flaw in the registry. If you're comfortable editing the registry, here's how to correct it:

Caution   Editing the registry is serious business with no margin for error or sloppiness. Always back up your registry before making a change. See Chapter 58 for more information.

1. Click the **Start** button and choose **Run** (or press ⊞+R).

2. Type regedit and click **OK**.

3. Click on **My Computer** at the top of the left column and make your backup using **File ➪ Export**.

    • If the problem occurs when opening a drive icon, click on the **HKEY_CLASSES_ROOT\Drive\Shell** folder icon.

    • If the problem occurs when opening a folder icon, click on the **HKEY_CLASSES_ROOT\Directory\Shell** folder icon.

4. Right-click **(Default)** in the right pane and chose **Modify**.

5. Under Value data type the word none, and then click **OK**.

6. Close the Registry Editor.

No Search option on the Start menu

To add the Search option to your Start menu, follow these steps:

1. Right-click the **Start** button, and choose **Properties**.

2. Click the **Customize** button next to Start menu.

3. Click the **Advanced** tab in the Customize Start Menu dialog box that opens.

4. In the Search Menu Items list, scroll down to and select (check) the **Search** option.

5. Click **OK** in each open dialog box.

Search Companion won't open

If starting the Search Companion only gets you a warning dialog box (yellow triangle with exclamation mark), your system is missing the Search Results folder. There's a registry fix for that. As always, editing the registry is risky business. Back up the registry before making your change, as described in Chapter 58. That way, if you make matters worse rather than better, you can restore from the exported backup registry.

To fix the problem with the Search Companion, follow these steps:

1. Click the **Start** button and choose **Run**, or press ⊞+R.

2. Type regedit in the Run dialog box and press Enter.

3. Locate, and click on, the following registry key:

   HKEY_LOCAL_MACHINE\SOFTWARE\Microsoft\Windows\CurrentVersion\
   Explorer\Desktop\NameSpace

4. Choose **Edit** ➪ **New** ➪ **Key** from the menu bar.

5. Rename the new key to *exactly* the sequence of the following characters (no margin for error here!): {e17d4fc0-5564-11d1-83f2-00a0c90dc849}

6. Right-click **Default** in the right pane, and choose **Modify**.

7. In the Value Data box type *exactly* the three words Search Results Folder, and then click **OK**.

8. Close the Registry Editor.

Restart the computer before trying the Search Companion again.

✦　　✦　　✦

Printing and Faxing

The truly paperless office doesn't exist. Sometimes you just have to get a document onto paper, no two ways about it. Chapters 20 and 21 tell you all about installing printers and printing documents. Printing applies not only to documents you type but to pictures and photos as well.

If you print lots of documents, Chapter 22 will help you manage those print jobs efficiently. If you want to install some new fonts to add some flair to your written documents, Chapter 21 will help with that task as well.

When you need to send a document to someone who doesn't have an e-mail address or when you receive a document that exists only on paper, fax may be your best bet. Chapter 23 tells you all about the fax capabilities of Windows XP.

Installing and Managing Printers

Installing a printer is usually an easy job. There's one rule that applies to installing any hardware, and it certainly applies to printers. The rule is: Read the instructions that came with the printer first. Trying to save time by ignoring the instructions and winging it is likely to cost you more time in getting the thing to work.

In many cases, you'll have the option to connect the printer to a USB port or a printer port. If your computer is a member of a network, you might want to install a shared printer that's physically connected to some other computer. In this chapter, we'll look at different ways of installing printers, as well as techniques for managing installed printers.

Installing a New Printer

Before you can use a new printer, you need to connect it to the computer and install it. Many printers give you the choice of using the "easy" USB port to connect the printer, or a standard printer port. Personally, I think the USB port is a bad idea, because you can run into a lot of problems when you disconnect the printer to plug some other item, such as a digital camera, into the port. In the long run, it's best to use the USB ports for devices you connect and disconnect often. You're better off using other ports, whenever possible, for devices that are connected to the computer all the time.

As mentioned at the top of this chapter, the main rule on installing a printer is to follow the instructions that came with the printer. Sometimes you need to install drivers first, sometimes you don't. There is no "one rule fits all" when it comes to installing printers, or any other hardware device for that matter. But in a pinch, where there are no instructions, the techniques in the following sections will be your best first guess.

Installing printers with parallel and serial port connections

If your printer is a typical plug-and-play printer that connects to the computer via an LPT port or COM port, the best approach is:

1. Save any unsaved work, close all open programs, shut down Windows, and turn off your computer.

2. Plug the printer into the wall; connect the printer to the computer's LPT or serial port, turn on the printer, and turn on the computer.

3. When Windows restarts, look for the *Found new hardware* notification message to appear.

It's tough to say what will happen next. If you see a notification message indicating that the printer is installed and ready to use, you're probably done.

Installing printers with USB and infrared connections

If your only option is to connect the printer through a USB port, or by infrared, the installation procedure should go like this:

1. Close all open programs on your Windows desktop, so that you're at the Windows desktop with nothing else showing.

2. Plug the printer into the wall; connect the printer to the computer with its USB connection, or configure the infrared as instructed by the printer manufacturer.

3. Turn on the printer, and wait a few seconds.

You should see a message in the Notification area that tells you the device is connected and ready to use. You're done. The printer is installed and ready to go.

Regardless of which of these methods you used, you'll want to test the printer, and perhaps make it the default printer, as discussed later in this chapter.

Installing a shared network printer on a home network

If your computer is a member of a home or small-business network, and you know of a shared printer on another computer in that network, you can use the technique described here to install that printer on your own computer. However, it may not be necessary to do so, because Windows XP often detects network printers and makes them available automatically.

Note   For information on sharing a printer, see Chapter 62. Also, make sure that you run the Network Setup Wizard as described in Chapter 61 before following the steps given here.

Before you go through the steps that follow, make sure that both the printer and the computer to which the printer is physically connected are turned on. Then, go back to the computer from which you want to access the printer, and take a look at the Printers and Faxes folder. To do that, follow these steps:

1. Click the **Start** button. If you see **Printers and Faxes** on the Start menu, click it, and skip the next two steps.

2. Choose **Control Panel** on the Start menu.

3. If Control Panel opens in Category view, click the **Printers and Other Hardware** category.

4. Open the **Printers and Faxes** icon.

At this point you'll be in the Printers and Faxes folder. If the shared printer's name appears in the folder, you need not install it. Though, if you want to make it the default printer, right-click its icon and choose Set as Default Printer. Then, close the Printers and Faxes folder and Control Panel. You'll be able to use the printer as described in Chapter 21.

If there's no sign of the printer in your Printers and Faxes folder, first choose View ➪ Refresh from the menu bar in the Printers and Faxes folder to make sure that it's up to date. Then, follow these steps to install the printer:

1. Under Printer Tasks in the Explorer bar, choose **Add a printer**.

2. Click **Next** on the first wizard page.

3. Choose the second option, **A network printer, or a printer attached to another computer**, and then click **Next**.

4. Choose **Browse for printer** on the next wizard page, and then click **Next**.

5. Look for the name of the computer and printer in the list of shared printers that opens. If you don't see the printer, double-click the name of the computer to which the printer is attached, and then click on the printer's name, as shown in Figure 20-1.

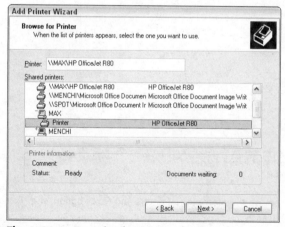

Figure 20-1: Browsing for a network printer

6. Click **Next**. Follow any additional instructions that appear on the screen until you get to the last wizard page, and then click **Finish**.

The printer should appear in the Printers and Faxes folder. You can test it and make it the default printer, if you like, as discussed in the next sections.

Opening the Printers and Faxes Folder

Aside from actually printing documents, just about everything you do with printers will take place in the Printers and Faxes folder. The quick way to that folder is to click the Start button and choose Printers and Faxes from the right side of the Start menu. If you don't see a Printers and Faxes option on the Start menu, you can add it. There are other ways to get to the folder, though. Whether or not you want to add Printers and Faxes to your Start menu depends on how often you need to get to that folder. First, I'll show you how to get to the folder via Control Panel:

1. Click the **Start** button, and choose **Control Panel**.

2. If Control Panel opens in Category View, click the **Printers and Other Hardware** category.

3. Open the **Printers and Faxes** icon.

The Printers and Faxes folder shows an icon for each installed printer. If you have fax capabilities, and fax services are installed, you'll see some icons for that service as well. Figure 20-2 shows an example of the Printers and Faxes folder with a single printer installed, and no fax service.

Figure 20-2: Sample Printers and Faxes folder

Note   If you want to add or remove the Start menu Printers and Faxes option, see "Personalizing Your Start Menu" in Chapter 3.

Setting the default printer

If your Printers and Faxes folder contains more than one icon, only one of them will be the default device for printing. By "default" I mean the printer that's used automatically if you don't specify something else. For example, many programs allow you to print a document to the default printer by pressing Ctrl+P. The program may not ask what printer you want to use. Instead, it just sends the document to the default printer.

In the Printers and Faxes folder, the default printer is indicated by a check mark. If you want to change the default printer, right-click the printer's icon and choose Set As Default Printer. For example, in Figure 20-3 I'm about to make an HP OfficeJet printer on my network the default printer.

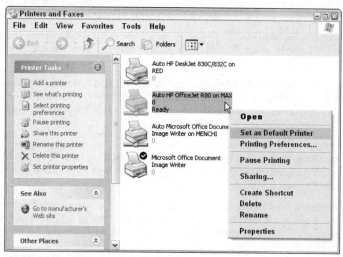

Figure 20-3: Choosing a default printer

That printer's icon will now be the only one in the folder that shows a check mark.

Testing a printer

If you've just installed a printer and want to test it out, follow these steps. (Here, I'm assuming that you're already in the Printers and Faxes folder.):

1. Right-click the printer's icon and choose **Properties**.

2. At the bottom of the Properties dialog box that opens, click the **Print Test Page** button.

Wait a minute or so before answering the question that appears on the screen. If the printer prints a page, click OK in the message box, and then click OK in the Properties dialog box. If nothing prints, make sure that the printer is on, has paper, and isn't out of ink (or toner). Click the Troubleshoot button in the message box for additional troubleshooting tips.

Note

The Windows Print Troubleshooter provides a step-by-step means of troubleshooting common printing problems. Chapter 24 in this book also offers some troubleshooting advice. But there are thousands of makes and models of printers out there. So, don't overlook the documentation that came with your printer, or the printer manufacturer's Web site, which may provide troubleshooting advice.

Managing Print Drivers

Virtually all hardware devices, including printers, come with special programs called *device drivers*, or just *drivers* for short. The driver provides the interface between the device and a specific operating system, such as Windows XP or Windows 98. You need to have the correct and current print driver installed on your computer to get your printer to work correctly.

Many printers come with the drivers on a CD or floppy disk. How you install a driver from the disk depends on the printer you're using. But an older printer may not even have a Windows XP driver to offer. In that case, you'll need to look for a current driver online.

Many printer manufacturers post current drivers on the Microsoft Windows Update Web site. To get to that Web site, click the Start button and choose All Programs ➪ Windows Update. If you don't see a Windows Update option on your All Programs menu, point your Web browser to www.WindowsUpdate.com.

The Windows Update site went through a major facelift just before I wrote this chapter. Exactly how things look and act when you get there depends on how up to date you are with your updates. The most likely scenario is that when you get to the first page of the site, you'll be given the option to do Express Install or Custom Install.

Driver updates are considered noncritical, so you'll want to click on Custom Install to view available driver updates. If any such updates are available, click on *Select optional hardware updates* in the left column. If you see a printer driver in the list of driver updates, be sure to download and install it as instructed on the page.

If you're using an older version of Windows Update, click on *Scan for updates* on the first Windows Update page. When the scan is complete, click *Driver updates* under *Pick updates to install* in the left column. Then, download and install any printer drivers that appear in the list.

As an alternative to the Windows Update site, you can check your printer manufacturer's Web site. Driver updates are usually distributed from the Support Web page at the manufacturer's Web site. There's definitely no one rule that fits all that I can tell you for acquiring printer drivers. Only your printer manufacturer can help with this issue.

Setting Default Printer Properties

Like objects on your screen, many devices have properties that you can customize. Most printers have such properties. You can make selections from those properties to define defaults for the printer. Those default settings for properties won't be set in stone. As you'll see in Chapter 21, you can override the defaults any time you print a document. The defaults are just a way of choosing a specific option every time you print a document.

As with other objects, a printer's properties are accessible from its icons. To view the properties for an installed printer, first open the Printers and Faxes folder if you haven't already done so. Then, right-click the printer's icon and choose Properties. The options available to you will vary depending on the make and model of your printer. The options shown in Figure 20-4 are from an HP OfficeJet R80 printer.

Most printers offer options, as in the Printer Preferences dialog box shown at the right side of Figure 20-4. On my HP printer, I clicked the Printer Preferences button in the Properties dialog box, shown at the left side of that same figure, to view the preferences. Since those options are so common, and they are the ones you're most likely to want to change on your own printer, we'll look at those preferences in the sections that follow.

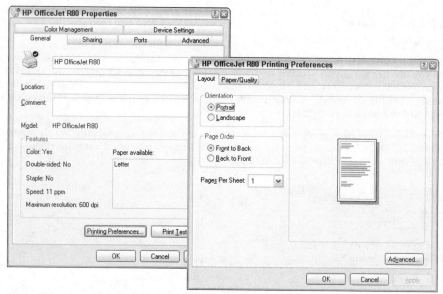

Figure 20-4: Printer properties and Printer Preferences dialog boxes

Making pages print in the right order

When you print a multiple-page document, the last thing you want to have to do is shuffle the pages around to get them in the correct order. You want the pages to come out of the printer in the right order. The Page Order property, which you can see in Figure 20-4, is the option that determines whether or not the pages are printed in the right order. The rules are as follows:

✦ If the pages come out of the printer face down, use Front to Back order.

✦ If the pages come out of the printer face up, use Back to Front order.

Said another way, if you have to reshuffle printed pages, choose whichever of those options currently *isn't* selected.

Normal versus sideways printing

Unless your printing needs are very unusual, you'll probably want to print most of your documents in a portrait orientation. That's the orientation that normal letters and other documents use, so you'll almost want to choose the Portrait as your default Orientation, as in Figure 20-4.

You can always override that default and print the occasional document in Landscape orientation (sideways, to the page is wider than it is tall). Chapter 21 talks about choosing Landscape orientation for a document on the fly.

Saving time and money

Printers, as a rule, are just plain slow. That's because they're clunky mechanical devices, and it takes time to move a page through a printer and get the ink or toner onto the paper. If you want a really fast printer, you're going to pay really big bucks for it. But, no matter what the cost or general speed of your printer, one general rule will apply: The higher the print quality of the document you're printing at the moment, the longer it will take to print.

Here's another fact about printers in general. Printers are cheap, but ink cartridges cost an arm and a leg. Sort of like the shaving industry where they give you the razor for free, and then drive you to bankruptcy when you buy blades.

The printer property that most determines how quickly your documents print and how much ink you use per document is called *print quality*. The higher the print quality, the longer it takes to print a document, and the more ink you use in the process. You can save time and money by doing all your day-to-day printing in Draft quality, perhaps even without color if you want to conserve color ink.

On my OfficeJet printer, quality and color settings are on the Paper/Quality tab shown in Figure 20-5. To get to those options, I clicked on the Paper/Quality tab shown in Figure 20-4. Your printer will likely have similar options.

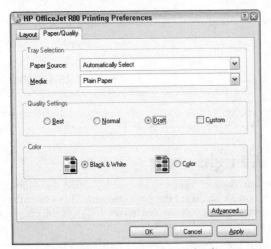

Figure 20-5: Sample print quality and color properties

As with other printer properties, setting the printer defaults to low-quality and black-and-white settings won't prevent you from printing the occasional fancy color document. As you'll learn in Chapter 21, you can override those defaults any time you print a document. When you want to print a professional-looking report or a fine photo, just increase the print quality and activate color for the one print job.

Those three properties that I've just mentioned are the ones that most printers have. Beyond those, the properties vary greatly from one printer to the next. The only resource for learning all the details of your particular make and model of printer is the documentation that came with that printer. Or, the printer manufacturer's Web site.

Wrap Up

That about wraps it up for installing and testing printers, and setting defaults. In the next chapter, you'll learn how to print documents, how to choose color and quality settings on the fly, and so forth. The main points from this chapter are:

✦ There are many makes and models of printers. Your best resource for your specific printer is the documentation that came with that printer.

✦ If you have a choice between using USB or a printer port to connect your printer, seriously consider using the printer port to keep your USB ports free for other devices.

✦ The typical scenario for installing a printer that connects to a printer port is to shut down the computer, connect the printer and turn it on, and then restart the computer.

✦ To connect a printer by USB, don't shut down the computer. Instead, leave the computer on, connect the printer to the computer, and then turn the printer on.

✦ All installed printers are represented by icons in your Printers and Faxes folder.

✦ If you have access to multiple printers, right-click the icon for the printer you want to use on a day-to-day basis and choose Set as Default Printer.

✦ To test a printer, right-click its icon, and choose Properties. Then, click the Print Test Page button.

✦ To ensure that your printer driver is appropriate for your operating system, check the Windows Update site and the printer manufacturer's Web site.

✦ To set default properties for day-to-day printing, right-click the printer's icon and choose Properties.

✦   ✦   ✦

Printing Documents and Screenshots

Windows XP, in and of itself, doesn't print documents. The main
reason for that being that Windows XP can't even open documents. You use programs, not Windows, to print documents.
Typically, you open the document first by clicking or double-clicking
its icon. Then, you print the document from the program that opens.

This chapter looks at different ways to print documents. As everyone
knows, printer ink, toner, and paper are expensive. For that reason,
I'll be sure to present some techniques to help you get the most for
your printing buck.

Printing a Document

If you have a printer, using it should be easy. First, you want to make
sure that the printer is turned on, has paper, and is ready to go. Then,
if the document you want to print is open and on the screen, do
whichever of the following is most convenient:

✦ Choose **File ➪ Print** from the program's menu bar.

✦ Or, click the **Print** button in the program's toolbar.

✦ Or, press **Ctrl+P**.

✦ Or, right-click the any page of the document and choose **Print**.

Tip   Web pages are documents, so you should be able to use any of
the preceding methods to print whatever Web page you're viewing at the moment.

In many cases, you can print a document, or several documents,
without first opening the document. To print a single document that
way, right-click its icon and choose Print. To print multiple documents, select the icons first, using any technique from Chapter 14.
Then, right-click any selected icon and choose Print, as shown in
Figure 21-1.

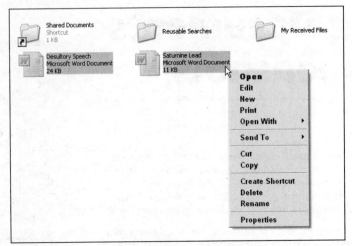

Figure 21-1: Printing multiple closed documents

Yet another option for printing closed documents is to open the Printer and Faxes folder. Select the icons for any documents you want to print, drag them into the Printers and Faxes folder, and drop them right onto the printer's icon.

What happens next depends on what program you're using, and which method you used. Often, right-clicking a closed document or pressing Ctrl+P starts the print job automatically. So, no further input is required.

Tip　　Don't expect the document to start printing immediately. There's always some prep work that needs to be done, and that will take a few seconds.

In most cases, printing a document will first take you to the Print dialog box. Exactly how the Print dialog box looks will vary from one program to the next. Figure 21-2 shows examples of Print dialog boxes from two different programs.

In the Print dialog box, click the Print or OK button to print to whatever printer is currently selected near the top of the dialog box. That's the simple approach, if you want to print the entire document immediately. But as you can see in the sample Print dialog boxes, you may also have quite a few options to choose from before you click the Print or OK button.

Common printing options

Because different programs offer different Print dialog boxes, I can't really say exactly what you'll see when you print a document. However, the options shown in the sample dialog box are fairly common. Those common options include:

✦ **Select Printer:** If you have access to multiple printers (for example, when you're connected to a network), choose the printer you want to use.

✦ **Page Range:** Choose which pages you want to print, ranging from *All* (the entire document), the *current page* (the page visible on your screen), *Selection* (only the text and pictures you selected in the document prior to getting here), or *Pages* (define a specific page, such as 1, or a range of pages, such as 2-5, to print only pages 2, 3, 4, and 5).

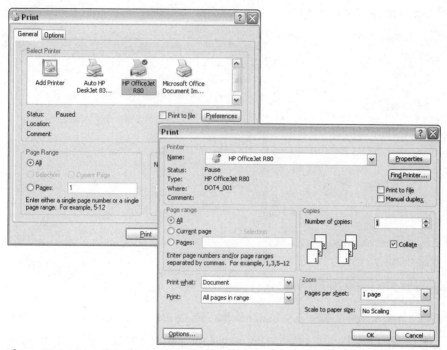

Figure 21-2: Examples of Print dialog boxes

✦ **Manual Duplex:** Print pages back to back on printers that don't have the capability to do that automatically. (*Duplex* is nerd word for *back to back*.) When you choose this option, odd-numbered pages will be printed first. You'll then be prompted to reinsert those pages, so the remaining pages can be printed on their backs.

✦ **Number of Copies:** Specify the number of copies to print.

✦ **Collate:** If this is selected, and you print multiple copies, pages are collated. If you print multiple copies, and clear the Collate option, you'll get multiple page 1s, followed by multiple page 2s, and so forth.

Choosing a print quality and other options

The general options that appear in the Print dialog box are almost universal. Depending on the make and model of your printer, you might have some other options to choose from. For example, you might be able to control the print quality of a document, opting for a quick draft or a time-consuming but better-quality job.

In most cases, you'll click the Properties button in the Print dialog box to get to those options. Figure 21-3 shows an example from an HP R80 OfficeJet printer. The figure shows options on both of the tabs in that dialog box.

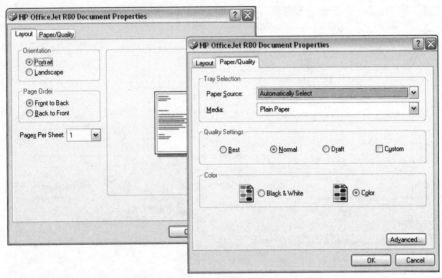

Figure 21-3: Sample Printer Properties dialog box

Here's a description of what each option in the sample dialog box offers:

✦ **Orientation:** Portrait prints in the normal vertical orientation; Landscape prints horizontally across the page.

✦ **Page Order:** Front to Back prints pages from lowest page number to highest. It keeps printed pages in correct order if those printed pages come out of the printer face up. Back to Front prints pages from last to first, which keeps them in order if the printed pages come out face up.

✦ **Pages per Sheet:** If you specify a number greater than one, multiple pages are reduced to fit on the page. For example, choosing **2** prints two document pages on each piece of paper, making each document half its actual size.

✦ **Paper Source:** If your printer has more than one paper feeder, use this option to choose which one you want to use. For example, if you can keep regular paper in one printer bin and envelopes in a second bin, choose the second bin whenever you want to print envelopes.

✦ **Media:** Lets you specify the type or quality of paper you're printing on, such as Plain Paper or Premium Photo Paper.

✦ **Quality Settings:** To conserve ink, consider choosing this option and using a low-quality setting, such as Draft, and perhaps Black and White or Grayscale printing, for day-to-day printing. Use higher-quality settings and color for more professional-looking documents and photos.

✦ **Color:** Lets you print a color document in black and white, to conserve color ink.

Tip   If you have to change print options often, consider setting the printer's default properties to the options you select often. See "Setting Default Printer Properties" in Chapter 20 for details.

After you've made your selections in the Printer Properties dialog box, click OK to return to the Print dialog box. There, you can choose additional options. Or, click the OK or Print dialog button in the Print dialog box to start printing.

If you change your mind after starting the print job, there's no simple "undo" that can stop the print job. You'll have to open the printer's icon in the Printers and Faxes folder, and then right-click on the document job and choose Cancel.

 Note   See Chapter 22 for information on canceling a print job.

Printing the Screen

If you were around in the olden days of computers with text screens, you might remember a time when you could print whatever was on the screen just by pressing the Print Screen key (perhaps abbreviated PrtScn, Prnt Scrn, or something like that). This was a so-called *screen dump*. It doesn't work that way in Windows. You can print the screen directly to the printer. But you can *capture* the screen, paste it into a program, and print it from there. Here are the steps:

1. Get the screen to look the way you want.

2. To capture the entire screen, press the **Print Screen** key. To capture only the active window, dialog box, or message, press **Alt+Print Screen**.

3. Open your favorite graphics program.

 Tip   If you don't have a favorite graphics program, you can use the simple Paint program that comes with Windows. Click the Start button and choose All Programs ➪ Accessories ➪ Paint.)

4. Press **Ctrl+V** or choose **Edit ➪ Paste** from the graphics program's menu bar.

A snapshot of the screen or program window opens in your graphics program. If you view it at 100 percent magnification, it might look like a hole through your graphics program or something hovering over it. If your graphics program allows it, zoom out to get a more complete view. For example, Figure 21-4 shows a screenshot in Jasc Paint Shop Pro, a third-party program that I use for most of my graphics and photo editing.

 Tip   In some graphics programs, you can spin your mouse wheel to change the image's magnification. In others, you have to choose some option from the program's View menu, such as View ➪ Zoom.

Once the screenshot is in a graphics program, print it as you would any other open document, using any technique described earlier in this chapter. If you plan to use the screenshot as a picture in a Web page, save it as a JPEG or Portable Network Graphics (PNG) file (if possible), using the Save As Type option in the Save As dialog box.

Figure 21-4: Screenshot in a graphics program

Using Print Preview

Many programs offer a Print Preview feature that lets you see how a document will look on paper before you actually print it. That way, you'll know what to expect, and avoid unpleasant surprises and wasted paper. To use Print Preview, you'll need to open the document first. Then, choose File ➪ Print Preview from the program's menu bar (assuming that the program you're using has a Print Preview feature). See Figure 21-5.

For example, suppose that you're considering printing a Web page that you're currently viewing. Before you start printing, you'd like to know how many pages will print and how things will look on paper. Choosing File ➪ Print Preview form Internet Explorer's menu bar will take you to the Print Preview window. Options along the top of the window tell you how many pages are in the document.

The toolbar shows you which page, out of how many total pages, you're currently viewing. The arrows allow you to look through the document page by page. The magnifying glass buttons and drop-down list allow you to change the magnification of the document. For example, the document in the figure is currently displayed at 25 percent. Reducing that to 10 percent would show more pages, albeit tiny ones!

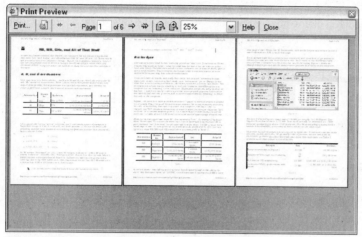

Figure 21-5: Internet Explorer's Print Preview window

If you're looking to get the most bang for your printer buck, click the Page Setup button near the left side of the toolbar. In the Page Setup dialog box that opens (see Figure 21-6), set the margins to the smallest allowable size on your printer. If you're not sure what those sizes are, set all the margins to 0 (zero). The margins should automatically adjust to the smallest allowable size for you printer.

Figure 21-6: Page Setup dialog box for printing a Web page

If you want to print a black-and-white draft of the page, to save time and ink, click the Printer button in the Page Setup dialog box. From there you should be able to set a "cheap" print quality, such as Draft, and turn of color printing as well. Figure 21-7 shows how those options might look.

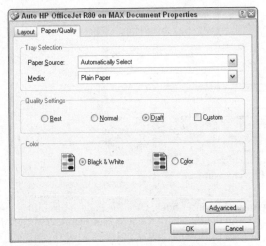

Figure 21-7: Page Setup dialog box for printing a Web page

When you've finished previewing the document, click the Close button in the Print Preview window's toolbar to return to Internet Explorer (or whatever program you're using at the moment).

Wrap Up

Printing should be a simple matter of choosing File ➪ Print from a program's menu bar. Or, right-click a document's icon to open and print it in one fell swoop. Here's a quick recap of the main points of this chapter:

✦ To print the document you're currently viewing, choose File from that program's menu bar. Or, click the Print button in its toolbar, or press Ctrl+P.

✦ To print a closed document from its icon, right-click that icon and choose Print.

✦ When the Print dialog box opens, you can choose a printer, a print quality, and other settings before you print.

✦ To print the screen, first capture the entire screen by pressing the Print Screen key. Or, press Alt+Print Screen to capture just the current window. Then, open any graphics program and press Ctrl+V. Finally, print the screenshot from that program.

✦ To see what an open document will look like before you print it, choose File ➪ Print Preview from the program's menu bar.

✦   ✦   ✦

Managing Print Jobs

When you print a document, there's more going on than you might expect. The printer doesn't immediately start printing. Instead, the computer needs to convert your document to a set of instructions that tells the printer what to do. Then, those printer instructions have to be sent to the printer in small chunks, because the printer is a slow mechanical device compared to a computer, which is much faster.

When you print multiple documents, each has to wait its turn. Each document you print becomes a *print job* that has to wait its turn in line if there are other documents already printing, or waiting to be printed. Most of this activity takes place in the background, meaning that you don't have to do anything to make it happen. In fact, you can just go about using your computer normally. There's no need to sit there and wait for the document to finish printing.

How Printing Works

When you print a document, quite a bit of work takes place invisibly in the background before the printer even "knows" there's a document to print. First, a program called a *print spooler* (or *spooler* for short) makes a special copy of the document that contains instructions that tell the printer exactly what to do. Those instructions don't look anything like the document you're printing. They're just codes that tell the printer what to do so that the document its spits out ends up looking like the document that you printed.

After the spooler creates the special printer file, it can't just hand the whole thing off to the printer as one giant set of instructions. A printer is a slow mechanical device that can hold only a small amount of information at a time in a *buffer*. The buffer is a small storage area within the printer that contains instructions for printing perhaps a page or two of text. Perhaps even less than a page if the document is a large photograph.

Furthermore, when the spooler has finished created the special printer file, there may be another document already printing. There may even be several documents waiting to be printed. So, the spooler has to put all the print jobs into a *queue* (line). All of this activity takes computer time (not *your* time, per se). And since each document has to be spoon fed to the printer in small chunks, there's often time for you to do things like cancel documents you've told Windows to print but that haven't yet been fully printed.

To manage those print jobs, you use the *print queue*. To get to the print queue, you open the printer's icon in the Printers and Faxes folder. Though, if you create a shortcut to the printer's icon, you don't even have to open the Printers and Faxes folder first. So, let's start out by looking at how you could create a shortcut to a printer's queue.

Making a Printer Shortcut

The print queue for managing print jobs appears when you double-click (or click) the printer's icon in the Printers and Faxes folder. You can also get to the print-queue by double-clicking the little printer icon in the Notification area, shown in Figure 22-1. But that icon might appear only briefly. So, double-clicking that icon isn't always an option.

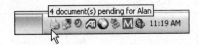

Figure 22-1: Printer icon in the Notification area

Chapter 20 covered a couple of ways to get to the Printers and Faxes folder where printer icons live. If you like, you can create a desktop shortcut to a printer's icon. Doing so is entirely optional, but will make it easier to get to the icon when you want to.

A printer's icon is one of the few that doesn't offer a Send To option on its shortcut menu. If you want to create a shortcut to a printer's icon, you need to drag that icon onto the desktop. Here are the exact steps:

1. Click the **Start** button and, if you see a Printers and Faxes option on the right side of the menu, click that option and go straight to Step 5. Otherwise, continue with Step 2.

2. Choose **Control Panel** from the Start menu.

3. If Control Panel opens in Category View, click the **Printers and Other Hardware** category.

4. Open the **Printers and Faxes** icon.

5. Drag the icon for the printer to which you want to create a shortcut out to the desktop and drop it there.

The shortcut icon will have the same name and icon as the original icon, but will sport the usual shortcut arrow. You can rename the shortcut icon if you like. As always, you can arrange your desktop icons by right-clicking the desktop and choosing Arrange Icons By ➪ Name.

Tip   You can print closed documents by selecting their icons and dragging them to the printer's shortcut icon.

Managing Print Jobs

Before I get into the specifics on managing print jobs, let me point out that in this section I'll be referring to a *local printer*—one that's directly connected to your computer by a cable. On a network, the print queue will be on the *print server*—the computer to which the printer is physically connected by cable. So on a network, you have to go to the printer server and open the print queue there to manage print jobs. But, assuming that your printer is connected to your computer, everything described here will work as stated right from your PC.

Once you've opened the print queue, you'll see the name of the document that's printing as well as any documents that are waiting to be printed (if any). Figure 22-2 shows an example where one document is printing and two are waiting in line.

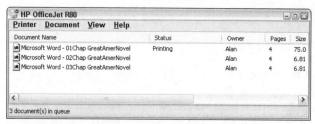

Figure 22-2: Sample documents in a print queue

Managing a single document

To pause or cancel a specific print job, right-click its line in the print queue and choose one of the following options from the shortcut menu that appears:

✦ **Pause:** Stops printing the document until you restart it.

✦ **Restart:** Restarts the paused print job.

✦ **Cancel:** Cancels the print job so that it doesn't print and removes the job from the print queue.

✦ **Properties:** Provides detailed information about the print job. You can also set the document's priority. The higher the priority, the more likely the print job is to butt in line ahead of other documents waiting to be printed.

Managing several documents

To pause, restart, or cancel several documents in the queue, select their icons. For example, click on the first job you want to change. Then, hold down the Shift key and select the last one. Optionally, you can select (or deselect) icons by holding down the Ctrl key as you click. Then, right-click any selected item, or choose Document from the menu bar, and choose an action. The action will be applied to all selected icons.

Managing all documents

You can use commands on the print queue's Printer menu, shown in Figure 22-3, to manage all the documents in the queue without selecting any items first. The options that apply to all documents are:

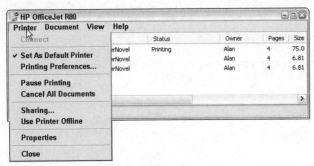

Figure 22-3: Printer menu in the print queue

✦ **Pause Printing:** Pauses the current print job and all those waiting in line. See "Printing Offline" later in this chapter for an example of when this would be useful.

✦ **Cancel All Documents:** You guessed it — this cancels the current print job and all those waiting to be printed.

Butting in line

In the print queue, you can change the order in which documents in the queue will print. For example, if you need a print out right now, and there's a long line of documents waiting ahead of yours, you can give your document a higher priority so it prints sooner. In other words, your print job gets to butt in line ahead of others.

To change an item in the print queue's priority, right-click the item in the queue and choose Properties. On the General tab of the dialog box that opens, drag the Priority slider, shown in Figure 22-4, to the right. The farther you drag, the higher your document's priority. Click OK. Your document won't stop the document that's currently printing, but it may well be the next one to print.

Figure 22-4: Priority slider in a print queue item's Properties dialog box

You can close the print queue as you would any other window — by clicking the Close button in its upper-right corner or by choosing Printer ➪ Close from its menu bar. To get help with the print queue while it's open, choose Help from its menu bar.

How Do I Stop This Thing?

Don't expect a paused or canceled print job to stop right away. Several more pages may print, even after you've canceled a print job. That's because the print queue sends chunks of a document to the printer's *buffer*. That buffer, in turn, holds information waiting to be printed. Canceling a print job prevents any more data from being sent to the buffer. But the printer won't stop printing until its buffer is empty (unless, of course, you just turn the printer off).

Solving Common Printer Problems

When Windows can't print a document, it alerts you through a Notification area message like the example shown in Figure 22-5. Before you assume the worst and delve into any major troubleshooting, check for some of the more common problems that cause such errors, as listed next.

Figure 22-5: Notification message for a printing problem

- ✦ Is the printer turned on and ready to go?

- ✦ Are both ends of the printer cable plugged in securely?

- ✦ Is there paper in the printer, and is it inserted properly?

- ✦ Does the printer still have ink or toner?

Tip   To make Windows show the error message in Figure 22-4, I just loosened the printer cable at the back of my computer slightly. To fix the problem, I pushed the cable back in securely.

More often than not, you'll find that the printer problem is something as simple as the printer being out of paper or out of ink.

Printing Offline

Printing is a means of going through the process of creating the spool file for the printer without actually printing the document. There are times when this is useful, such as when you're working on a notebook computer with no printer attached, but intend to print later when you can attach the computer to a printer or network.

To make this work, right-click the printer's icon or shortcut icon, as shown in Figure 22-6, and choose Pause Printing. Or in the print queue, choose Printer ➪ Pause Printing. Either way, you won't see any change on the screen. If there's a document printing at the moment, it won't stop. The only visible change is likely to be the word Paused in the print queue's title bar.

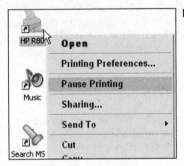

Figure 22-6: The Pause Printing option

But when you print documents using your notebook computer, you won't get an error message. Instead, each document will be sent to the print queue where it will just sit and wait. When you get back to your printer or network and connect the notebook, you can start printing immediately. Just choose Resume Printing using any of the techniques described previously.

Printing to a File

You can print a document to a special print file, rather than directly to paper. This offers yet another means of deferring printing until later. But the result is a little different from using the Pause Printing method because the file you create can be printed on someone else's printer. Better yet, it works even if the computer that's connected to that printer doesn't have the program that you used to create your document.

This method is often used to print documents on high-end typesetting equipment at print shops and service bureaus that specialize in that sort of thing. They might even be able to convert a favorite photo into a bus-sized poster, if that's your desire.

The first thing you'll need is a printer driver for the fancy printing equipment, unless the service bureau tells you otherwise. You may be able to get by just by saving a copy of the document as a PostScript file, or Encapsulated Postscript (.eps file). But again, that's entirely up to the service bureau.

The next step is to print your document to a file, using the appropriate printer driver. That part is much the same as printing normally. Here's how it goes:

1. Open, just as you normally would, the document you intend to print to a file.

2. Choose **File** ➪ **Print** from the program's menu bar to get to its Print dialog box.

3. Choose the **Print to file** option in the Print dialog box. Figure 22-7 shows an example of a Print dialog box with the Print to file option selected.

4. Choose any other settings, such as a high print quality and size, from the Print dialog box.

5. Click the **Print** (or **OK**) button.

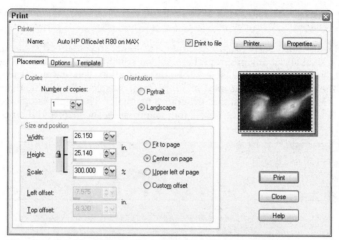

Figure 22-7: The Print to file option is selected in this Print dialog box.

6. A Save As (or similar) dialog box will open asking where to put the file and what to name it. Choose My Documents (or any convenient folder).

7. Enter a filename. You may need to use a DOS command to print the file, so use a short filename (eight or fewer characters) and a .prn or .ps extension, as required by the service provider.

8. Click the **Save** button.

The resulting .prn file is ready to go. If you're sending it to a service bureau, and the file is small enough, you may be able to e-mail it as an attachment, or upload it to their FTP server (if they have one). Otherwise, you can copy the file to a CD, thumb drive, or some other medium. Then, mail or deliver the disk to whoever will print it.

Note   If you open the .prn file in Notepad, you'll see the printer codes, not the document. Don't change those. In fact, don't even save the file if you open it, because doing so might ruin the file.

If you need to print the file yourself, you'll need to put the disk to which you copied the file into the disk drive. Next, click the Start button and choose All Programs ➪ Accessories ➪ Command Prompt. Then, enter a Copy command at the prompt using this syntax:

```
copy path\file lptx /b
```

where `path\file` is the name of the file to print, and `x` is the port to which the printer is attached, typically 1. For example, if the file to print is named `MyPoto.prn` in the root folder of drive D:, and the printer is attached to LPT1, enter the command:

```
copy d:\myphoto.prn lpt1 /b
```

The `/b` option at the end of the Copy command indicates that the file to be printed is a *binary* file, meaning that it already contains all the necessary special codes needed to format the document properly.

Managing Fonts

Windows XP and many third-party programs come with fonts, so you already have quite a few fonts to work with. Just about any program that lets you compose text will also let you apply fonts to that text. It's usually a simple "select then do" operation. You first drag the mouse pointer through the text to which you want to apply a font, to select (highlight) that text. Then, you choose Format ➪ Font from that program's menu bar. The Font dialog box opens, as in the example shown in Figure 22-8. Choose a font name, style, and size, and then click OK.

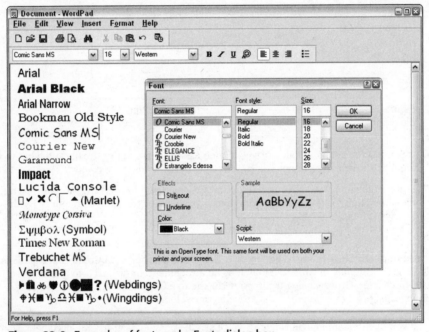

Figure 22-8: Examples of fonts and a Fonts dialog box

Each font that's available to you is stored in a file in your Fonts folder. To open that folder:

1. Click the **Start** button, and choose **Control Panel**.

2. If Control Panel opens in Category View, click **Switch to Classic View** under Control Panel in the Explorer bar.

3. Open the **Fonts** icon.

Each font that's installed on your system is represented by an icon in the Fonts folder that opens. There are some special buttons for choosing views in the toolbar at the top of the folder. Figure 22-9 shows an example using the Large Icons View.

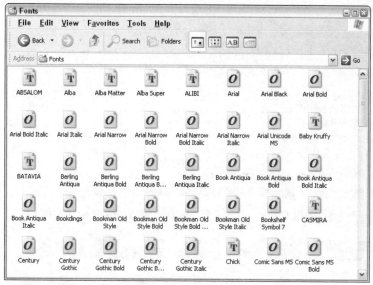

Figure 22-9: A sample Fonts folder

Font technologies and types

Windows supports three font technologies as summarized here:

✦ **Outline fonts:** These fonts can be scaled and rotated to look good at any size. TrueType, OpenType, and Adobe Type1 (PostScript) fonts are all examples of Outline fonts.

✦ **Vector fonts:** These fonts are rarely used these days, except in specialized equipment such as plotters.

✦ **Raster fonts:** Each character in these fonts is a small bitmap of dots displayed on the screen and paper. This, too, is an older technology.

Icons in the Fonts folder indicate the types of fonts. For example, a TT icon represents a TrueType font, an O represents an OpenType font, and an A represents a vector or raster font.

When you open a font icon, you'll see a description of the font and examples of it displayed at various sizes, as in Figure 22-10. To print a copy of the font example, click the Print button in the upper-right corner. To close the sample, click the Done button.

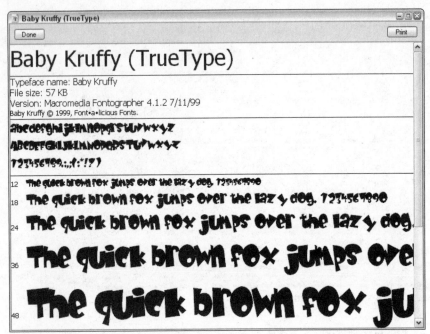

Figure 22-10: Example of opening a font icon

Installing fonts

You can purchase Outline fonts and programs to create your own fonts. When you download fonts, they'll likely come in a .zip file. You'll want to save that .zip file to your My Documents folder, or some other folder. Then, extract all the files from the folder before you attempt to install the fonts in the .zip file.

Note See "Using Compressed Folders (.zip Files)" in Chapter 13 for the goods on extracting files from .zip files (also known as compressed folders in Windows XP).

Once you have font files in hand (such as TrueType .ttf files), installing them is easy. You need to start out in the Fonts folder shown back in Figure 22-9. Then, follow these steps:

1. Choose **File ➪ Install New Font** from the Font folder's menu bar. The Add Fonts dialog box opens.

2. If the fonts are on a floppy disk, CD, or other drive, select that drive from the **Drives** drop-down list.

3. If the fonts are in a folder, navigate to the appropriate folder in the **Folders** list.

Caution Don't clear the *Copy fonts to Fonts folder* option unless you're installing fonts from another computer on the network and don't want to copy the actual font files. Be forewarned that if you clear that checkbox, you won't be able to use the fonts on the networked computer when the computer is turned off.

4. Wait for the *Retrieving font names* indicator to reach 100 percent. Then, choose the fonts you want to install from the **List of Fonts**. You can:

- Click any single font to select it

- **Ctrl**+Click additional fonts

- Click the **Select All** button to select all the listed font names, as shown in Figure 22-11

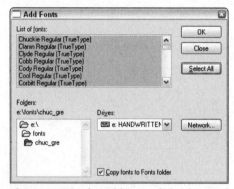

Figure 22-11: The Add Fonts dialog box and selected fonts

5. Click **OK**.

The fonts will be copied to the Fonts folder and ready for use. They should be available in the Fonts dialog box and Fonts menus in all your programs that support the use of fonts.

Wrap Up

The typical printing scenario is that you choose File ➪ Print from a program's menu bar, or press Ctrl+P, to print whatever document you're viewing at the moment. But as you've seen in this chapter, there's more going on behind the scenes, and things you can do to manage your print jobs. To whit:

✦ Every document you print is a print job, temporarily stored in a print queue.

✦ To open the print queue, double-click the printer icon in the Notification area, or the printer's icon in the Printers and Faxes folder.

✦ To manage print jobs in the queue, right-click any job and choose an option from the shortcut menu.

✦ To cancel all documents that are waiting to be printed, choose Printer ➪ Cancel All Documents from the print queue's menu bar.

✦ To install new fonts for your screen and printed documents, choose File ➪ Install New Fonts from the menu bar in the Fonts folder.

✦ ✦ ✦

Sending and Receiving Faxes

If you need to send documents to fax machines (because the recipient doesn't have a computer), you can fax files directly from your computer to a fax machine. Likewise, if someone needs to send you a fax, you can accept the fax from a PC. But there is one major catch to it all. You need a computer with a faxmodem installed.

There's a second catch too. Exactly how you send and receive faxes depends on the faxing hardware in your computer. In this chapter, you'll learn the general faxing techniques for 100 percent XP-compatible fax hardware that's been properly installed. But you may need to spend some time reading up on your particular faxmodem or multifunction printer to get things to work as stated in this chapter.

Installing the Fax Service

The Windows XP Fax Service provides tools for sending and receiving faxes. The service can't work alone. You need to have a faxmodem installed in your computer, and that modem needs to be connected to a phone line. Assuming that those criteria are met, you also have to install the Fax Service (if you haven't already done so). You may need your original Windows XP CD for this, especially if you installed XP yourself.

With your faxmodem ready to go, and perhaps your Windows XP CD on hand, here's how you install the Fax Service:

1. Click the **Start** button, and choose **Control Panel.**

2. Open the **Add or Remove Programs** category or icon.

3. Click **Add/Remove Windows Components** in the left pane of the window that opens.

4. When the Windows Components Wizard opens, choose (check) **Fax Services**, and then click **Next**.

5. Follow any additional instructions that appear on the screen, and then click the **Finish** and **Close** buttons.

You can close the Add or Remove Programs window and Control Panel as well.

Configuring the Fax Service

Before you use Fax Services for the first time, you'll need to fill it in on some facts about your system. You're going to be filling in a lot of blanks along the way. So make sure that you have a few minutes so that you can complete the whole process. Here's the whole shebang:

1. Click the **Start** button, and choose **All Programs** ➪ **Accessories** ➪ **Communications** ➪ **Fax** ➪ **Fax Console**.

2. On the first page of the Fax Configuration Wizard that opens, click the **Next** button.

3. On the Sender Information page that opens, fill in the blanks to describe yourself. What you type will appear as your return address on all your fax cover pages. Then, click **Next**.

4. On the Select Device . . . page that opens next, click your faxmodem. Also:

   - If you want to be able to send faxes from this computer, make sure that the **Enable Send** checkbox is selected (checked).

   - If you also want this computer to receive faxes, make sure that the **Enable Receive** checkbox is selected (checked).

   - If you chose Enable Receive in the previous step, you may also choose **Manual answer**, if you want to manually answer incoming fax calls. Or choose **Automatically answer after** to have the computer receive faxes automatically. Then, specify the number of rings to wait before answering.

5. Click the **Next** button.

6. If you have a TSID (see the "TSID, CSID, Huh?" sidebar), enter that information on the next page. If you don't have a TSID, type your business name and fax number. Then, click Next.

7. If you have a CSID, enter that information on the CSID page. If you don't have a CSID, type your business name and fax number. Then, click Next.

8. Depending on the options you chose, you may be taken to the last wizard page. If so, click **Finish** and skip the remaining pages. Otherwise, on the Routing Options page that opens:

   - Choose **Print it on** if you want to print each incoming fax as soon as it arrives. Then, choose the name of the printer to use.

   - Every fax you receive will be stored in the Inbox of your Fax Console. If you want to create and store an additional copy of each fax you receive, choose the **Store a copy in a folder option**, and then choose an easily accessed folder such as My Documents or perhaps a new subfolder within My Documents named My Faxes.

9. Click the **Next** button. On the last Wizard page, you can review the options you selected. Click Back if you discover any mistakes. Otherwise, click the **Finish** button, and you're done.

You won't need to go through that ritual ever again. The Fax Console, described next, is ready for use.

TSID, CSID, Huh?

If you're as clueless about TSID and CSID as I was the first time I saw them, here's what you need to know. A TSID (Transmitting Subscriber Identification) is required only on special complex routing software, such as when using the Internet or a large corporate network for faxing. A CSID (Called Subscriber Identification) is similar but is displayed on the receiving fax machine. This allows the recipient to verify that the fax was sent from your computer and isn't a forgery sent from some other computer. The bottom line is that, if nobody ever hands you a TSID or CSID to use for faxing, you probably don't need one.

Using the Fax Console

With the Fax Service installed and configured, you can fire up the Fax Console at any time using either of the following methods:

✦ Click the **Start** button, and choose **All Programs** ➪ **Accessories** ➪ **Communications** ➪ **Fax** ➪ **Fax Console**.

✦ Or click the Start button, choose **Printers and Faxes**, and double-click the **Fax** icon in that folder.

Tip　　If you don't have a Printers and Faxes on your Start menu, you can add one. See "Personalizing Your Start Menu" in Chapter 6. To create a desktop shortcut to Fax Console, right-click the Fax Console icon on the Fax menu, and choose Send To ➪ Desktop (create shortcut).

When the Fax Console opens (see Figure 23-1), you'll see several folders down the left pane. Click any folder name to see its contents. If you haven't sent or received any faxes yet, all the folders will be empty, as in Figure 23-1. But once you get going with faxes, here's what each folder will contain:

✦ **Incoming:** Contains faxes currently being received

✦ **Inbox:** Contains faxes that have been received

✦ **Outbox:** Contains faxes waiting to be sent

✦ **Sent Items:** Contains faxes that have been successfully sent

The Fax Console is "Faxes Central," in the sense that every fax you send and receive will end up there (unless you opt to print incoming faxes but not have them sent to the console). So, any time you need to look at a received fax, review faxes you've sent in the past, and so forth, the Fax Console is the place to go. As in any program, there are plenty of options in the menu bar and toolbar that you can use to manage faxes.

Like most programs, the Fax Console has its own Help, which you can get to by pressing F1 while Fax Console is the active window or by choosing Help from the Fax Console's menu bar. To close the Fax Console, click its Close button or choose File ➪ Exit from its menu bar.

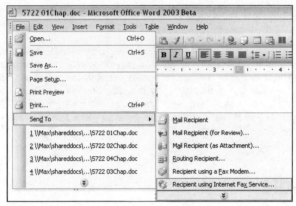

Figure 23-1: The Fax Console

Sending a fax

The easiest way to send a fax from your computer is to use the Send Fax Wizard. There are lots of ways to start that wizard. Use whichever method here is most convenient at the moment:

✦ If you're in the Fax Console, click **New Fax** in its toolbar, or choose **File** ➪ **Send a Fax** from its menu bar.

✦ From the Windows desktop, click the **Start** button and choose **All Programs** ➪ **Accessories** ➪ **Communications** ➪ **Fax** ➪ **Send a Fax**.

Tip   To create a desktop shortcut to the Send a Fax option on the menu, right-click that option on the menu and choose Send To ➪ Desktop (create shortcut).

✦ If you want to fax the document you're currently creating in a program that supports faxing, choose **File** ➪ **Send To** ➪ **Recipient Using a Fax Mode**. If that option isn't available, choose **File** ➪ **Print** from that program's menu bar. In the Print dialog box that opens, choose **Fax** as the "printer" to use, and then click OK.

✦ From Control Panel's Category view, click **Printers and Faxes**, and then click **Send a Fax** under Printer Tasks.

The first page of the Send Fax Wizard opens. The rest is largely self-explanatory. When you click Next on the first wizard page, the Recipient Information page opens, as in Figure 23-2. Fill in the blanks to describe to whom you're sending the fax, and then click Next.

Tip   The Address Book referred to in the wizard might be Windows Address Book (WAB). If you use Microsoft Outlook to manage contacts, the wizard will use the Outlook's Contacts folder as your address book.

The second wizard page, titled Preparing the Cover Page, lets you create a cover page. If you select the checkbox, you can choose a cover-page template for the page (Confident, FYI, Generic, or Urgent styles), and then you can fill in a brief subject line and note. After that, click Next.

The third wizard page, titled Schedule, lets you choose when you want to send the fax and with what priority. Make your selections, and click Next.

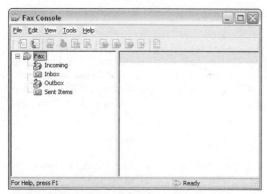

Figure 23-2: The Recipient Information page

The last wizard page lets you review your options and preview the fax. If you want to make any changes to the fax, use the Back button in the wizard. If you're ready to send the fax, click the Finish button. The fax will be sent. Or, if you opted to send the fax at a later time, the fax will be sent to your Outbox in the Fax Console and sent at whatever time you specified.

Receiving faxes

Exactly what happens when you receive a fax depends on how you configured Fax Services, as described earlier in this chapter. If you opted to receive faxes automatically, the fax program will answer the phone after the specified number of rings. If you opted for Manual answer, you can use whichever of the following methods is most convenient:

✦ From the Fax Monitor that appears on your screen when the fax arrives, click **Answer now**.

✦ From the Fax Console, click the **Receive Now** button on the toolbar. Or choose **File** ➪ **Receive Fax Now** from its menu bar.

Can't Edit a Faxed Document

Fax is short for facsimile, because it works by sending a "facsimile copy" (a photocopy) of the document though the phone lines. When you send that photocopy to another computer, the recipient gets, quite literally, a photograph of the original document.

For example, let's say you fax a WordPad document or Microsoft Word document to some other computer user. What you're sending is a *photo* of that document. When the recipient opens the document, it will be in a graphics program, which, in turn, makes it impossible to edit the document using Microsoft Word, WordPad, or any other word processing program.

If e-mail isn't an option, then the only other choice is to use optical character recognition (OCR) software to convert the photocopy to some sort of editable text. Many scanners and faxmodems come with OCR software as part of the package. You can also check out XP-compatible software at the Windows Catalog site at www.WindowsCatalog.com.

Faxing without a Faxmodem

You can bypass the whole faxmodem/phone-line business and use the Internet to send and receive faxes. This isn't really a Windows XP thing *per se*. It's a service you subscribe to on the Internet. But once you've established an account, you can certainly use Windows XP to send and receive faxes with that account. Exactly how you do that depends on which service you use. To learn more about these services, visit either of the following Web sites:

eFax: www.efax.com

Venali: www.venali.com

If you use Microsoft Office, you may be able to sign up for a fax service right from an Office application. For example, if you open a document in Microsoft Word and choose File ➪ Send To ➪ Recipient Using Internet Fax Service (see Figure 23-3), you can work your way to the Office Marketplace, which may provide more offerings by the time you read this.

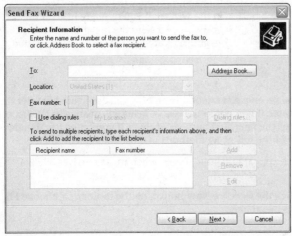

Figure 23-3: Information about Internet fax services from Word 2003

More on Faxing

Faxing with a computer is actually a large topic — one that could fill a small book as opposed to part of a chapter in a book. To supplement the basics you've learned here, use the Help menu in the Fax Console. Or, take a look at the fax articles at Microsoft's Knowledge Base by following these steps:

1. Point your Web browser to http://support.microsoft.com.

2. In the Search the Knowledge Base box that appears on the Web page, type 306550, and press **Enter** or click the green **Go** button.

3. Click the **View Results Only** tab. Then, click whichever article title best describes the task you're trying to accomplish.

Remember that most of the articles in the Knowledge Base are specifically about faxing with a faxmodem. To learn more about a given Internet fax service, you'll need to use the Web site for that service, not Microsoft's Web site.

Wrap Up

A computer can mimic a fax machine, and even send and receive faxes without any paper involved. The main points about faxing with Windows XP are:

✦ A fax is a photograph of a document that cannot be edited like a normal word processing document.

✦ Install Fax Services via Add/Remove Windows Components in Add or Remove Programs.

✦ You need to configure the Fax Console (once) before you can send a receive faxes.

✦ To send a fax from the Fax Console, click on New Fax in the Fax Console.

✦ To receive an incoming fax from the Fax Console, click the Answer Now button.

✦   ✦   ✦

Troubleshooting Printing and Faxing

Troubleshooting Printing

Since no two printers are exactly alike, printing is more a matter of knowing your printer rather than knowing your computer or Windows. The best I can do here is provide some general pointers that apply to most printers. But for specifics on your printer, the manual that came with the printer, or the main Web page for the product, will be your best bet.

First aid for printing problems

Before you start digging around the computer for solutions to a printing problem, check all the things outside the printer:

+ Make sure that the printer is plugged in and turned on.

+ If the printer has an Online/Offline switch, make sure that it's online.

+ Make sure that the printer cable is connected snugly at both the printer and computer ends.

+ Make sure that the printer has paper.

+ Make sure that the printer has ink or toner.

+ Check for, and clear, a paper jam.

If none of the above help, take a look at the Help topics for printing, as described next.

Viewing printer help

The Windows Help and Support Center and Microsoft Knowledge Base offer many printer-related help topic pages. To view those:

1. Click the **Start** button and choose **Help and Support**.

2. Type `Print Troubleshoot`print in the Search box, and press **Enter**.

3. Scroll through all the links under Suggested Topics, Full-text Search Matches, and Microsoft Knowledge Base.

Click on any topic that describes the problem you're experiencing for help in the main pane to the right.

Problems printing after installing Service Pack 2

If your computer is a member of a network, and your printing problems start right after installing Service Pack 2, the most likely problem is that the firewall has blocked communication with the printer. Follow these steps on each computer involved:

1. Open your **Network Connections** folder. (Click the **Start** button, and choose **Control Panel**. If Control Panel opens in Category View, click on **Network and Internet Connections**. Open the **Network Connections** icon.)

2. Right-click the icon that represents your local network connection, and choose **Properties**.

3. In the Properties dialog box, click the **Advanced** tab.

4. Click the **Settings** button under Windows Firewall.

5. Click the Exceptions tab, and make sure that **File and Printer Sharing** is selected (checked) as shown in Figure 24-1.

6. Click **OK** in each open dialog box, and close Control Panel.

Figure 24-1: File and Printer Sharing enabled in Windows Firewall

Printer prints garbage

If the printer used to print properly, turn off the printer. Then, close all open program windows and turn off the computer (click **Start** and choose **Turn Off Computer** ➪ **Turn Off**). Make sure that there is no paper jam in the printer, turn the printer back on, and wait a few seconds. Then, restart the computer normally.

If the trouble persists, delete all documents in the print queue and repeat the preceding procedure.

If the problem is persistent, make sure that you have the most current printer drivers installed. For details see Chapter 53. Also, check the manual that came with the printer to determine what type of printer port is required (for example, ECP). Then, go to your computer's BIOS Setup program and set the printer port (also called the parallel port or LPT1 port) to the appropriate setting. See "Changing BIOS settings" in Chapter 11 for more information.

Printing from Print Preview produces nothing

On some Epson printers you might see a *Printing . . .* message after starting a print job, but nothing actually prints. To resolve the problem:

1. Open your **Printers and Faxes** folder. (From Control Panel choose **Printers and Other Hardware** in Category View. Open the Printers and Faxes icon.

2. Right-click the icon that represents the printer, and choose **Properties**.

3. On the General tab of the Properties dialog box, click on **Printing Preferences**.

4. On the Main tab, clear the **Print Preview** checkbox.

5. Click **OK**.

Advanced printing features are disabled

To use all the capabilities of a printer, you need to make sure that you have the most current printer drivers installed. Also, make sure that the printer's advanced features are enabled by following these steps:

1. Open your **Printers and Faxes** folder.

2. Right-click the icon for the printer, and choose **Properties**.

3. On the General tab, click the **Printing Preferences** button.

4. Click the **Advanced** button.

5. If you see Disabled next to Advanced Printing Features, click on that word, and choose **Enabled**, as shown in Figure 24-2.

6. Click **OK** in all open dialog boxes.

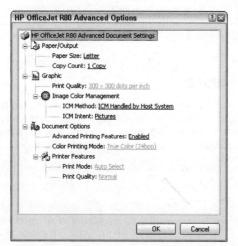

Figure 24-2: Advanced Options dialog box for a sample printer

Printed colors don't match screen colors

On some Hewlett Packard and Cannon BubbleJet printers, ICM (Image Color Management) may incorrectly color the printed page. To fix the problem, go to the Advanced Options shown in Figure 24-2, and choose Disable ICM.

Error message "Problem communicating with printer"

This error occurs on some Lexmark printers that connect through a USB port. Getting the latest driver for the printer should resolve the problem. Optionally, you can turn off the USB hub's ability to turn off the device as follows:

1. Right-click your **My Computer** icon, and choose **Properties**.

2. In the System Properties dialog box, click the **Hardware** tab.

3. Click the **Device Manager** button.

4. Click the + sign next to **Universal Serial Bus controllers**.

5. Right-click **USB Root Hub**, and choose **Properties**.

6. Click the **Power Management** tab.

7. Clear the **Allow the computer to turn off this device to save power** checkbox.

8. Click **OK** in the Properties dialog box.

Note   If you have multiple USB root hubs, you'll need to repeat Steps 7 and 8 for each one.

9. Close Device Manager.

10. Click **OK** in the System Properties dialog box.

Troubleshooting Faxing

Like printing and scanning, faxing is more a matter of knowing your specific faxing hardware than it is about knowing your computer or Windows. Your best bet is to learn to use your fax hardware as described in the manual that came with the hardware device before you try to fax directly from Windows or a program. Again, the best I can do here is provide some general troubleshooting tips.

First aid for faxing problems

Windows XP only provides access to your faxing hardware. To learn to use the fax that's part of an all-in-one printer, refer to the manual that came with the printer, or the manual that came with your faxmodem or computer. If the fax device came with its own software, you may be better off using that software as opposed to the generic Windows Fax Services.

Also, make sure that the fax phone port on your computer or printer is attached to a phone jack on the wall.

Tip   Remember, if you're trying to send a document that's already on your hard disk (as opposed to on paper only), you'll get better results by e-mailing the document as an attachment.

Using the Fax Services Troubleshooter

The Troubleshooter that comes with Fax Services will be your next best bet for troubleshooting a fax problem. Follow these steps to get to that troubleshooter:

1. Click the **Start** button, and choose **All Programs** ➪ **Accessories** ➪ **Communications** ➪ **Fax** ➪ **Fax Console**.

2. Choose **Help** ➪ **Help Topics** from the Fax Console menu bar.

3. In the Help window that opens, click the + sign next to **Troubleshooting and Additional Resources**.

4. Click the **Troubleshooting** page icon, and then click whichever icon best describes the problem you're experiencing.

✦   ✦   ✦

Securing Your System

Just when you thought it might be safe to go online again, some-body somewhere has thought up some new virus, worm, or other unpleasantry destined to make your Internet time less rewarding. This part covers all the threats and how to prevent and deal with them in Windows XP SP2.

I assume that most of you already have Internet accounts. But just in case you don't or are thinking of changing to a different kind of account, Chapter 25 covers all the details. Chapter 26 talks about protecting your computer from hackers and worms using the new Windows Firewall. Chapter 27 covers keeping your security patches up-to-date with Windows Update.

You can block most pop-up adds with the Internet Explorer pop-up blocker. Chapter 28 talks about that, plus ways of blocking other types of pop-ups. Chapter 29 covers adware and spyware, how tough they can be to seek and destroy, and tools and techniques for pro-tecting yourself from these ruthless invaders.

Getting Online

As just about everyone knows, the Internet is an enormous collection of computers connected by cables. The two most widely used services that the Internet provides are e-mail and the World Wide Web. Plenty of other lesser-known services are available, however, such as instant messaging, file transfer, and P2P (peer-to-peer) file sharing.

No one company owns and runs the Internet. The American taxpayers, who paid for the Internet during the Cold War, are the owners. Because of this, the Internet is protected by American constitutional law, which includes freedom of speech and freedom of press. Hence, there is no censorship, no governing editorial policy. It's the Wild, Wild West out there, and to some extent everyone needs to take responsibility for protecting their own computers.

I assume that most readers already have an Internet connection and will skip this chapter. As far as protecting your computer goes, that all starts in the next chapter. This chapter will cover more basic Internet concepts and techniques for getting your computer online, just in case you haven't done that yet, or are considering dumping your ISP for something better.

What Is the Internet?

The Internet consists of millions of computers throughout the world, all connected by cables. In networking diagrams, the Internet is always displayed as a cloud, as in Figure 25-1. The cloud is a good symbol for the Internet; just as a cloud is made up of millions of tiny water droplets, the Internet is made up of millions of computers.

You connect to the Internet through an ISP (Internet service provider). The ISP is a company that has a very high-speed connection to the Internet. It makes money by renting small "chunks" of that bandwidth to individuals like you and me. Your chunk of bandwidth is basically your Internet account.

You computer alone can't connect to your ISP. You need a device to make that connection either a *modem* or a *router* (also called a *residential gateway*). That device might be *internal* (inside your computer), such as a modem where you connect the computer to a phone line via a jack on the back of the computer. Or the device might be *external* (outside your computer), with a cable that connects the computer to the device. A second cable connects the device to a phone line or cable-TV jack.

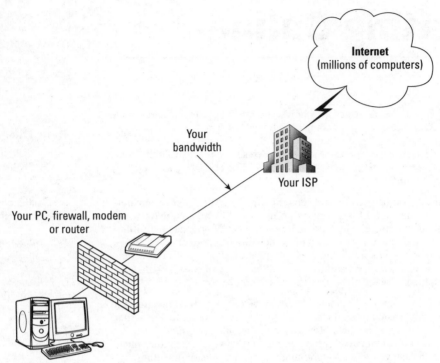

Figure 25-1: A modem and ISP provide your computer's connection to the Internet.

For security reasons, you also want a firewall, which keeps uninvited Internet traffic from getting into your computer. If you have a router, the firewall might be built right into the device. Or, the firewall could be a separate device connected to your computer and the modem by a couple more cables. The firewall can also be *software*, meaning that there is no hardware device at all. It's a program that sits between your modem and computer to block unwanted traffic.

Note   As you'll learn in Chapter 26, Windows XP comes with its own built-in software firewall.

When you request information from the Internet, be it a Web page, an e-mail message, or whatever, that request gets shipped out through your modem or router to your ISP. Your ISP then forwards the request to the Internet. The Internet sends the appropriate information back to your ISP. Your ISP, in turn, passes it on to you. There are no human beings involved in any of that, just computers.

It takes almost no time at all for the requested information to get from the Internet to your ISP. That's because your ISP has an expensive high-speed connection to the Internet. How long it takes for that information to get from your ISP to your computer depends on the speed, or *bandwidth*, of your Internet account. The higher your bandwidth, the less time it takes.

Urban Myth: Dial-up Accounts Are Safer Than Always-on Accounts

Some people believe that using a slow dial-up account will protect them from Internet threats. The rationale being that the less time you spend online, and the slower the connection, the less likely you are to encounter "bad things." That's similar to the notion that it's safer to run, rather than walk, across a freeway because you're exposed to the freeway for less time if you run. Statistically, there's some truth to that. The problem is, whether you run or walk across a freeway, there's a good chance you're gonna get killed.

In and of itself, a slow dial-up account provides absolutely no protection from Internet threats. Even if you go online for only 2 minutes a day using a dial-up account, bad things *will* happen if your computer isn't secure. For example, the vast majority of viruses are spread by e-mail attachments, which naïve users download and open voluntarily without realizing what they're doing. They get tricked into opening the attachment because it appears to be something valid, like a returned e-mail message or something that Microsoft sent out to all of its customers. That particular threat is the same regardless of the speed of your connection and how much time you spend online.

As we'll discuss in upcoming chapters, the bottom line is that your computer is either secure, or it isn't. If your connection isn't secure, limiting your bandwidth and the time you spend online won't help one bit. But if your connection is secure, you can leave your computer on and online 24/7 at any bandwidth and still sleep like a baby at night.

What is bandwidth?

Bandwidth, measured in kilobytes per second (Kbps or Kb), is a measure of how much information at a time can be sent through the line that connects your computer to your ISP. For example, a dial-up account tops out at about 48 to 50 Kbps. That's roughly 48,000 to 50,000 bits per second (bps). That sounds like a lot. Because any given file can contain millions of bits, however, it's really not that fast.

The lower the bandwidth, the longer the wait for things you've requested from the Internet. For consumers, accounts generally cost anywhere from $10.00 to $20.00 a month for a 56K dial-up account, to maybe $30.00 or $40.00 a month for a broadband connection. Here's the difference:

✦ **Dial-up:** Connection to your ISP goes through a standard modem and traditional telephone lines. (Your phone line is busy if anyone tries to call while you're online, provided you just have one phone line.) The maximum speed of a dial-up account is usually in the 48 to 50 Kbps range. Even though your modem may be rated at 56K, the phone lines can't move traffic quite that quickly.

✦ **Broadband:** Connection to your ISP is through cable (the type used by cable TV companies), or special Digital Subscriber Lines (DSL), owned by the phone companies, that can carry more data at faster than 50 Kbps. You connect to a broadband account using a modem or *router*. You can get just about any connection speed you want.

A typical broadband cable account moves data at about 750 to 2,000 Kbps. So, wait times are brief. What might take several minutes to accomplish with a dial-up account takes only a few seconds with a broadband account.

Upstream versus downstream bandwidth

Some accounts will have two bandwidth ratings, often referred to as *upstream* (or *upload*) and *downstream* (or *download*). The difference is as the names imply:

✦ **Upstream:** The speed at which data can be transferred *from* your computer *to* your ISP

✦ **Downstream:** The speed at which data can be transferred *to* your computer *from* your ISP

Of the two, the downstream bandwidth is the most important, because it determines how long it takes for Web pages, e-mail messages, and the like to reach your computer. When you send a request for such information, that request travels upstream. But that request is just a tiny packet of information that moves quickly even with severely limited upstream bandwidth.

On the other hand, if you're a Web author, or if you upload large files to FTP sites, or whatever, the upstream bandwidth will be more noticeable. For example, if you need to upload a bunch of pictures, video, or other large files to a remote site on the Web, the faster your upstream bandwidth, the less time it will take to upload those files.

Only your ISP can tell you your upstream and downstream bandwidth. However, there are some Web sites out there that will test your bandwidth for you. The results of the test will be approximate, most likely a little lower than your actual bandwidth. That's because there's bound to be some unpredictable overhead during the test that adds time to the actual speed measurements. So, don't take the results of any such test as being 100 percent accurate.

You may want to try a few different sites, just to see what kinds of rating you get. If you search any engine, such as www.Google.com, for bandwidth speed test you should find links to sites that offer such tests for free. If you're testing a broadband account, keep in mind that 1 Mbps (1 megabit per second) equals a million bits per second, or 1,024 Kbps (about a thousand kilobits per second).

Clients and servers

Most of the computers on the Internet at any given time are *clients*. That is, they are consumers of what the Internet has to offer. Your computer is most definitely a client.

Other computers on the Internet are *servers*. Servers provide the services that clients are using. Generally, nobody sits at a server and does work. Rather, the server just sits online and answers requests coming from clients. For example, a *Web server* is a computer that holds a Web site people visit. All day and night, the Web server sends its Web pages to whoever happens to request those pages. That's the Web server's only job.

IP addresses and URLs

Every computer on the Internet has a unique *IP address*, just as every house has a unique mailing address, and every telephone has a unique "phone number" address. Each address must be unique, otherwise there'd be no way to tell all the different computers, homes, and phone numbers apart. And at any given moment in time, there's a good 30 to 40 million computers connected to the Internet all exchanging information at the same time.

Every IP address is a unique 32-bit number, meaning that it's a unique pattern of ones and zeroes. For example one, and only one, computer on the Internet has the address 01101011001100110001100001100110. Because such numbers are difficult for human beings to read, they tend to be expressed in *dotted quad* format rather than a string of ones and zeroes. Dotted quad addresses are expressed as *xxx.xxx.xxx.xxx* where each *xxx* is a number between 0 and 255. Right now my IP address is 64.68.82.168. However, that's subject to change because my computer is a client, not a server.

Tip   To find out what your IP address is right now, visit www.WhatIsMyIP.com or www.What IsMyIPaddress.com.

Server computers have *static* IP addresses, meaning that their IP addresses don't change. But even dotted quad IP addresses are tough for people to remember, so most servers also have a URL (Uniform Resource Locator). The URL is an address that expressed in words rather than numbers. For example, Microsoft's main Web server is at the URL www.Microsoft.com. Google's URL is www.Google.com.

Your computer has neither a static IP address nor a URL, because your computer is a client. People can't request information from your computer, because your computer isn't a server. Each time you log on to the Internet, your ISP creates a *dynamic* IP address for your computer from a pool of currently unused addresses. Your ISP uses that address to forward information you've requested from the Internet to your computer. When you log off, someone else may get that IP address. When you log back on, you'll likely get a different dynamic IP address from whatever IP addresses are available at that moment.

Online, offline, local, and remote

The term *online* means *connected to the Internet and ready to use its services*. When you're online, you have an IP address and can communicate with the Internet. The term *offline* means *not connected to the Internet*.

When you're offline, you have access to only *local* resources. Local resources are the things that are "in your computer," such as your hard disk and all your other drives. When you're online, you have access to both local resources and *remote* Internet resources. In other words, when you're online, you have access to all those millions of servers sitting out there on the Internet.

Note   The terms local and remote apply to a small local network as well. But for the sake of simplicity in this chapter, we'll assume that your PC isn't part of a local network.

A *resource* is anything that's useful. Local resources are things like the programs and documents stored on your own hard disk. Remote resources are things like Web pages. Each Web page is actually a document—a file on some computer on the Internet.

Downloading and uploading

One thing people do a lot of on the Internet is *download* stuff. The term *download* means to copy something from some other computer to your own computer. The term *upload* means the opposite: to copy something from your computer to some other computer on the Internet.

If you envision the Internet as a cloud, it's easy to keep the terms straight. *Download* means to copy something down from the cloud onto your computer. *Upload* means to copy something from your computer up to the cloud. You can't upload things to other computers unless you have permission to do so. That generally means that you have some sort of account (involving a user name and password) that gives you the right to upload files from your computer to a specific computer on the Internet.

Getting an Internet Account

Most people who buy a computer just sort of stumble into their first Internet account by double-clicking some icon on their screen. AOL and MSN sell lots of Internet accounts through that method. If you want to be more choosey, you need to do a little homework. If you look up Internet service provider in your local yellow pages, you'll probably find you have lots of companies and account types from which to choose.

For broadband accounts, many people go through their local phone company or cable TV provider. Although some tools in Windows XP are designed to help you set up an Internet account, the truth is that people rarely need them or use them. The typical scenario is you choose an ISP, and you set up an account with them, and then one of three things happens:

✦ Your ISP sends a representative to your house and sets everything up for you (that's ideal).

✦ Your ISP sends you some sort of instructions, and you follow those instructions to set up your account.

✦ Your ISP sends you some program that you run on your computer, and the program sets up your account.

Because there are thousands of ISPs doing business in the world, there isn't a single set of instructions I can give you to set up an Internet account. Only your ISP can tell you how to set up the account you've purchased from them. If your ISP doesn't provides a disk or set of instructions for setting up your account, you can try using the New Connection Wizard, described next, to get the account working.

Using the New Connection Wizard

The New Connection Wizard, which comes with Windows XP, tends to kick in automatically whenever you try to access the Internet when you're not connected. If you already have an Internet connection and the wizard kicks in, you should just cancel the wizard and close the program that caused the wizard to start. Then, get online, and restart the program that made the wizard pop up.

The only time you really want to use the New Connection Wizard is when you've already signed up for an account and have received your account information from your ISP. Again, you should definitely do whatever the ISP tells you to do to set up your account. But, if that doesn't work, or if your ISP tells you to use the Internet Connection Wizard or New Connection Wizard, here's how you can pursue that course of action:

1. Click the **Start** button, and choose **All Programs** ➪ **Accessories** ➪ **Communications** ➪ **New Connection Wizard**.

2. From the first wizard screen, click the **Next** button.

3. Choose **Connect to the Internet** from the second wizard screen, and then click the **Next** button.

4. The third wizard screen asks how you want to set up your account. Choose whichever option best describes what you want to do. For clarification, here's what they mean:

   - **Choose from a list of Internet service providers (ISPs):** Select this option only if you've never contacted an ISP or set up an account, and you want to purchase an account right now.

   - **Set up my connection manually:** If you've set up an account with an ISP and have a user name and password, choose this option.

   - **Use the CD I got from an ISP:** If you have purchased an account already and your ISP has provided you with a CD, choose this option.

5. After making your choice, click the **Next** button and follow the instructions on the screen.

If you chose the first or third option, it's all just a matter of doing what the wizard tells you to do. I cannot take you step by step through those options because how you progress through the wizard depends on how you answer the questions. It's important, however, to pay attention to the following warning.

Caution

Passwords are case-sensitive. Any time the New Connection Wizard asks you to type a password, make sure that you type it using the *exact* upper/lowercase letters provided by your ISP.

If you chose the second option, Set up my connection manually, the wizard will present the options shown in Figure 25-2. You'll need to know which type of account you're setting up to proceed. Again, only your ISP can tell you the specifics. For the sake of example, I'll show the options that appear when setting up a dial-up account. If you're setting up a broadband account that required you to sign in (also called a PPPoE connection), you'll see similar options.

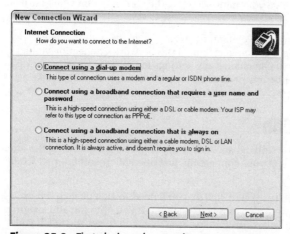

Figure 25-2: First choice when setting up an Internet connection manually

Choosing the third option in Figure 25-2 will end the wizard, because there's nothing more the wizard can do. If you have an always-on broadband connection and it's not working, you'll need to troubleshoot through your ISP.

After you choose an option from those shown in Figure 25-2, the rest will be self-explanatory. The questions you're likely to see, and how you should respond, are summarized below:

✦ **ISP Name:** You don't have to provide an exact name here. This is actually just the name that appears under the connection's icon in your Network Connections folder. So, you'll want to keep the name brief.

✦ **Phone number:** If you're setting up a dial-up account, type in the toll-free number for getting online as provided by your ISP.

✦ **User Name:** This will be the user name provided by your ISP. It has nothing to do with the user name of your Windows XP user account.

✦ **Password:** This is the password provided by your ISP and again has nothing to do with the password for your Windows XP user account, nor the password you use for e-mail. (Though your password for logging in, and your password for retrieving e-mail *could* be the same.)

✦ **Use this account name and password when anyone connects to the Internet from this computer:** Choose this option if two or more people will use this same account to connect to the Internet. If you plan to set up multiple Internet accounts for multiple users, clear this option.

✦ **Make this the default Internet connection:** If you're offline when you open an Internet program such Internet Explorer, that program will automatically connect to the Internet through the default Internet connection. Choose this option if you plan to have only one Internet account.

✦ **Add a shortcut to this connection to my desktop:** Choose this option to add a desktop shortcut for the connection to your Windows desktop. Doing so will allow you to get online right from the desktop, without going through your Network Connections folder, or anything else. If you change your mind, deleting the shortcut icon won't harm your connection in any way.

Be aware that you're not making any big commitments as you go through the New Connection Wizard. Mainly what you're doing is creating an icon in the Network Connections folder. As discussed later in this chapter, you can change any settings in that icon by right-clicking and choosing Properties. There won't be any need to rerun the Wizard, even if you make a mistake as you go through the process.

Making the connection

If you have set up an always-on broadband account, you should be connected to the Internet and ready to go at this point. To test your connection, just open Microsoft Internet Explorer and browse to any Web page.

If you set up an account that requires you to sign in, you'll need to sign in each time you want to go online. There are many ways to sign into your account. If you opted to add a shortcut icon to your desktop, you can just click (or double-click) that icon to get started. If you didn't

Adding Network Connections to Your Start Menu

You can add a Network Connections option to your Start menu, so that you don't have to dig through All Programs⇨Accessories to get there. Right-click the Start button and choose Properties. Then, click on the Customize button and click on the Advanced tab. Under Start Menu Items, scroll down to the Network Connections option. You'll have two choices for displaying that option.

If you choose "Display as Connect to menu," the Start menu will gain an option titled Connect To. Clicking that option will display a submenu of all available Internet connections. If you select Link to Network Connections Folder instead, your Start menu will gain a Network Connections option. Clicking that option will take you to the Network Connections folder.

set up a desktop shortcut, you'll need to get to the connection's icon (sometimes called a *connectoid*) in your Network Connections folder. To open that window, follow these steps:

1. Click the **Start** button.

2. Choose **All Programs** ⇨ **Accessories** ⇨ **Communications** ⇨ **Network Connections**.

3. Click (or double-click) the icon for your Internet account. For example, the My ISP icon under Dial-Up in Figure 25-3 represents a dial-up account for the Internet.

Figure 25-3: Sample icon for a dial-up account in Network Connections

Once you've opened the icon that represents your Internet account, you'll see a Connect To dialog box like the example shown in Figure 25-4. If you filled out all the questions correctly in the New Connection Wizard, all the information you need to log on will already be filled in. Otherwise, you'll need to fill in the user name, password, and local access number provided by your ISP. Then, click the Dial button to make your connection. You'll see a dialog box that keeps you informed of what's going on (dialing, connecting, and so forth). Once you're connected, you can do anything you wish online.

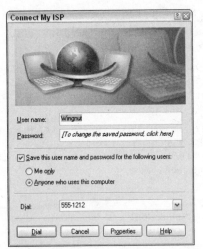

Figure 25-4: The Connect To dialog box

When you're ready to go offline, use any technique described in the next section.

Ending the connection

If you have a dial-up account, remember that you're connected until you specifically disconnect, which means if you use the same telephone line for both voice and Internet connectivity, anybody who calls will get a busy signal. To disconnect, usw whichever of the following
methods is most convenient for you:

✦ Right-click the little two-monitor icon in the Notification area and choose **Disconnect**.

✦ Or, open Network Connections as described earlier, right-click the connectoid's icon,
and choose **Disconnect**.

Configuring an Internet Connection

As mentioned, the options you choose in the New Network Connection Wizard aren't set in
stone. You can change any Internet connection option that's relevant to your account at any
time from the connection's icon in your Network Connections folder. Just open the folder,
right-click the icon, and choose Properties. You'll first see the General tab, as in the example
shown in Figure 25-5 (I'm using a dial-up account icon as the example here).

Caution   If you use Internet Connection sharing on a local network, these settings only apply to the
Internet Connection Sharing Host. Don't bother trying to change any of these settings on PCs
that just use that shared Internet connection.

We'll look at the General tab's options in the sections that follow.

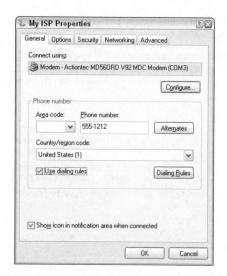

Figure 25-5: The General tab on an Internet connection's Properties dialog box

General Internet connection options

Most of the options on the General tab shown in Figure 25-5 are self-explanatory. If you have only one modem, that modem is selected automatically under *Connect using*. If you have multiple modems, you can choose which one you want to use for this connection.

Choosing the *Show icon in notification area . . .* option just ensures that whenever you're online, an icon will appear in the Notification area. That's a handy little icon to have, because you can right-click it and choose Disconnect any time you want to end your current dial-up session.

Configuring a modem

Clicking the Configure button on the General tab takes you to the obscure Modem Configuration dialog box shown in Figure 25-6. The Maximum speed option should be cranked up to at least the 115200 number shown in the figure — even higher for a DSL modem. Note that the number is expressed in bits per second (bps). You need to divide that number by 1,024 to translate it to Kbps.

Figure 25-6: The Modem Configuration dialog box

If you don't want to listen to your modem squeal every time you log on, clear the Enable modem speaker option to turn off the modem's speaker.

The options under Hardware features are best left alone, unless your ISP specifically tells you to change some setting. Likewise, you probably won't want to show a terminal window for an Internet connection. However, that option might prove necessary for connecting to bulletin boards or directly to other PCs.

Alternate dialing numbers

Clicking the Alternates button takes you to the Alternate Phone Numbers dialog box shown in Figure 25-7. If your ISP has provided several numbers, you can list all those numbers in the order in which you want Windows to try them. Just make sure that all the numbers you enter are within your toll-free dialing region. Otherwise, you could end up spending a lot of time online on a connection that's costing you money, which can lead to some ghastly phone bills.

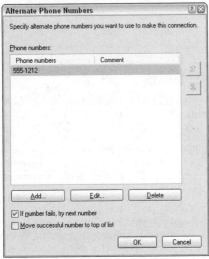

Figure 25-7: The Alternate Phone Numbers dialog box

To add an alternate phone number, click the Add button and fill in the blanks. You can add as many alternate phone numbers as your ISP provides. To change or delete an alternate number you've previously entered, click on that number in the list, and then click the Edit or Delete button below the list.

To ensure that the modem tries to alternate numbers automatically, choose the *If number fails, try next number* option. Over time, Windows can also arrange the numbers for you, behind the scenes, based on how often the number succeeds in making a connection. Choose the *Move successful number to top of list* option to let Windows rearrange numbers automatically.

Caution   I'm not kidding about the ghastly phone bill that might ensue if you dial-up to the Internet using a number that's not toll-free. If you spend a lot of time online, you may be in for a real shocker from Ma Bell. Make sure that *all* the numbers your modem might dial are within in toll-free dialing region.

Defining dialing rules

The Dialing Rules option is an important one and is the cause for many faulty Internet connections. Dialing rules vary from one location to the next, so you want to make sure that you set the rules properly for your area. Click the Dialing Rules button to get to the Phone and Modem Options dialog box shown in Figure 25-8.

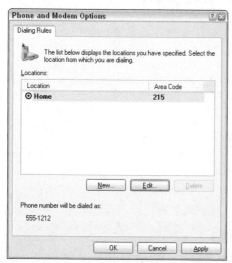

Figure 25-8: Dialog Rules tab of the Phone and Modem Options dialog box

If you're working from a desktop computer, you'll have only one location listed in the dialog box. Click that location, and choose Edit to change the dialog rules for that location. Optionally, you can create a new connection by clicking the New button. Either way, you'll come to the options shown in Figure 25-9.

Tip   The Location is the place *from* which you're dialing. If you use a notebook computer and dial-up from multiple locations, you can define settings for each location from which you dial.

The options on the tabs are straightforward and self-explanatory. Perhaps the most important one is the option to disable call waiting. The call-waiting service in some areas will cause you to lose your Internet connection. So, if that's a problem, choose the option to disable call waiting while you're online.

The Area Code Rules tab lets you specify whether or not you need to dial an area code even for local numbers. There are quite a few regions throughout the country where such 10-digit dialing is required, even for local calls.

The Calling Card tab lets you put any phone charges that you acquire onto your calling card. (This assumes that you have a calling card, of course. Unfortunately, you can't put the charges on someone else's calling card.)

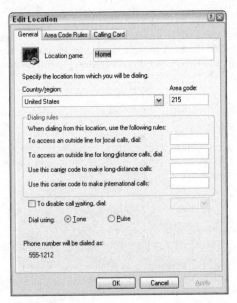

Figure 25-9: Dialing Rules for a location from which you dial in to the Internet

Dial and Auto-Redial options

The Options tab for a connectoid's properties, shown in Figure 25-10, enables you to choose how to dial. If you always dial into the same account, for example, you can clear the two Prompt checkboxes, as in Figure 25-10, to have the connectoid dial without displaying the Connect dialog box. If your ISP's line is often busy, you can set the Redialing options to have Windows keep trying the number until a successful connection is made.

Figure 25-10: The Options tab of a connectoid Properties dialog box

Hanging up automatically

If you're concerned that you might leave your Internet connection on by mistake long after you've stopped using it, set the Idle time before hanging up option to any duration you want. You also can have Windows automatically redial the connection in the event that the connection is dropped accidentally.

X.25 accounts

If your account uses the X.25 protocol, and you have an X.121 address, click the X.25 button on the Options tab. If you have no idea what I'm talking about, then you probably don't have an X.25 account. If you have an X.25 account, click the X.25 button on the Options tab to set it up. Just fill in the blanks, according to your ISP's instructions, in the dialog box that opens, and then click OK.

Security options

The Security tab in the Properties dialog box lets you turn on your Windows Internet Connection Firewall, which is something you almost certainly want to do. Chapter 26 covers the firewall in depth.

The Security tab also allows you to share an Internet connection, which is a topic addressed in Part XI of this book.

TCP/IP, DHCP, and DNS options

The Networking tab of a connectoid's properties, shown in Figure 25-11, provides a lot of uber-nerdy options related to TCP/IP networking. The Internet is a one gigantic TCP/IP network. Most local Windows networks are also TCP/IP. That acronym, by the way, stands for *Transmission Control Protocol/Internet Protocol*, but that's not terribly important right now.

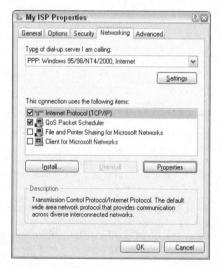

Figure 25-11: Networking tab of a connectoid's properties

The first option on the Networking tab is important, because it defines the general configuration of your Internet account. Most dial-up accounts will use the PPP (Point-to-Point Protocol) option selected in Figure 25-11. You should choose a different option only if instructed to do so by your ISP. The Settings button beneath that lets you change some PPP-related options. But again, that's not something you want to mess with unless specifically instructed by your ISP.

The list of items that the connection uses gets into things that aren't strictly related to the Internet. The QoS (Quality of Service) Packet Scheduler is Internet-related, and is a means of maximizing the quality of your Internet connection through prioritization and traffic control. That option has no properties. As a rule, you just want to select it unless your ISP tells you otherwise.

The Internet Protocol (TCP/IP) item is a biggie for Internet accounts, but again it's not something you need to mess with on an Internet connection unless you have a DHCP (Dynamic Host Configuration Protocol) or DNS (Domain Name Service) problem, such as an error message that refers to one of those services when you try to use the Internet. To get to DHCP and DNS options, click on Internet Protocol (TCP/IP) in the list of items, and then click the Properties button. You'll come to the options shown in Figure 25-12.

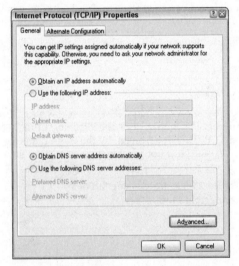

Figure 25-12: Internet Protocol (TCP/IP) Properties dialog box

Configuring DHCP

DHCP is an acronym for Dynamic Host Configuration Protocol. It is the service that provides for the dynamic IP addresses I mentioned at the top of this chapter. A *host* is any single computer or other device that connects to a computer. A *protocol* is a set of rules that define how things are done. The entire Internet is basically a bunch of cables and protocols that define how things get transmitted across those cables.

If you're like most people, then you want to choose the first option to obtain an IP address automatically. However, if your ISP gave you a static IP address, subnet mask, and default gateway address, choose *Use the following IP address*, and fill in blanks with the information provided by your ISP. Then, click OK to return to the previous dialog box.

Configuring DNS

As mentioned at the top of this chapter, server computers on the Internet have static numeric IP addresses. But numbers like 123.198.05.128 are difficult to remember, so most sites also have a URL like `www.microsoft.com` or `www.nasa.gov`. When you type a URL into your Web browser's Address bar and press Enter, that URL needs to be translated to a numeric IP address so the Internet can find the Web server.

The act of getting a numeric IP address from a URL is called *name resolution* and is handled by DNS, which stands for Domain Name Service. The service is almost identical to a telephone directory in that each domain name is listed alphabetically, followed by its IP address. Just like each person's name in the phone book is listed, followed by their phone number.

Only there's no paper copy of the DNS service; it's all done by computers called *DNS servers* or *name servers* on the Internet. Each ISP maintains its own DNS server to provide name resolution for its customers. When you type a URL and press Enter, there's a brief moment of time where that URL is sent to your ISP's DNS Server, which looks up the URL then spits back the IP address for that URL. Once that step is complete, *then* your Web browser sends the page request to the Web server using its IP address.

Actually, the looking up and spitting back only happens the first time you visit a site. Your browser also keeps track of the IP addresses of the URLs whose names have already been resolved. It will always check that local file of known URLs and IP addresses before it bothers to send out a name resolution request to the ISP's name server. But that's getting a bit more technical than we really need to get right here.

As you can see in Figure 25-12, there are two main options for configuring DNS. The first option, and the one most people use, is to obtain the address of your ISP's DNS server automatically. When you dial into your account, your ISP sends back those addresses as soon as you log in, so you don't need to know the address of your ISP's name server.

The second option, *Use the following DNS server addresses,* should only be used in situations where your ISP has provided you with those addresses. In most cases you'll be given two addresses, a preferred or primary address and an alternate, or secondary, address. As always, there is zero margin for error when typing those addresses into the dialog box. So, make sure you know the exact addresses and type them carefully. Click OK to return to the previous dialog box when you've finished.

Configuring Your PC to Connect Automatically

With an always-on Internet account, you should be able to open Internet Explorer and go to any Web site without any further ado. If you have any other type of account, Internet Explorer should dial-in automatically when you open it. But if it doesn't, you can make it do so by following these steps:

1. Click the **Start** button, and choose **Control Panel**. If Control Panel opens in Category View, click the **Network and Internet Connections** category.

2. Open the **Internet Options** icon.

3. Click the **Connections** tab to see the options shown in Figure 25-13.

Figure 25-13: Connections tab of the Internet Options dialog box

4. If you have more than one dial-up account, click the one that you'll use as the default, and then click the **Set Default** button. What you do next depends on your configuration:

- If you only have a dial-up connection, choose **Always dial my default connection**.

- If you have a notebook computer that uses a fast connection while connected to a local network and a dial-up modem on the road, choose **Dial whenever a network connection is not present**.

5. Click **OK**.

Remember, if you have any problems with your Internet connection, your best resource for getting help is your ISP. After all, they're the ones providing the connection, and they know more about the service they provide than anyone else.

Wrap Up

Getting your computer connected to the Internet is largely a matter of setting up an account with an Internet service provider (ISP) and doing whatever they tell you to do to make the connection work. The main points made in this chapter include:

✦ The Internet is a collection of millions of computers throughout the world, all connected by cables.

✦ Some computers on the Internet act as *servers*, in that they provide the very services the Internet offers.

✦ Other computers, like yours and mine, are *clients*, in that they use those services as consumers.

✦ Bandwidth is a measure of how quickly information can get from your ISP to your computer. Low (or *narrow*) bandwidth means slower traffic and more wait time. Broadband offers higher speeds and less wait time.

✦ Your Network Connections folder holds the icon that represents the modem (or router) you use to connect to the Internet.

✦ The Network Connections folder also provides access to the Network Troubleshooter, which can help with a problematic Internet connection.

✦ When it comes to troubleshooting a network connection, your ISP is your best resource, because only they know the specifics of the service they provide.

✦   ✦   ✦

Blocking Hackers with Windows Firewall

The Internet today is like the Wild Wild West of early America.
There are plenty of good guys, but quite a few bad guys, too. It's
too late to start all over on the Internet and turn it into something
where the bad guys can't do anything. And there's no way to create a
computer or operating system that can isolate you from all the bad
things. So, the bottom line is that to some extent, each and every one
of us has to take some responsibility in securing our own computers
against Internet threats.

One of the most common threats these days are *worms,* which are
tiny programs that sneak into your computer from the Internet
through open ports in your Internet connection. In this chapter, you'll
learn how to block those worms, and other forms of "hacking," using
the new Windows Firewall that comes with Windows XP and Service
Pack 2.

How Firewalls Work

To understand what a firewall is, you need to first understand what a
network connection is. Even though you have only one skinny wire
connecting your computer to the Internet (through a phone line or
cable outlet), that connection actually consists of 65,535 *ports.* Each
port can simultaneously carry on its own "conversation" with the
outside world. So, theoretically, you could have 65,535 things going
on at a time. But of course, nobody ever has that much going on all at
once. One, or maybe a few ports, is more like it.

The ports are divided into two categories: TCP (Transmission Control
Protocol) and UDP (User Datagram Protocol). TCP is generally used
to send text and pictures (Web pages and e-mail), and includes some
error checking to make sure all the information that's received by a
computer matches what the sending computer sent. UDP works more
like broadcast TV or radio, where the information is just sent out and
there is no error checking. UDP is generally used for real-time communications, such as voice conversations and radio broadcasts sent
over the Net.

Without a firewall, all those ports are *open*, meaning other computers can send information into any port on your computer. With a firewall, the ports are closed and guarded against unauthorized entry. Another way to state this is that the closed ports aren't "listening" for incoming data. So, any data that comes knocking at the port door will be wasting its time, and eventually will just be dropped.

Here's how it works, in a nutshell, using the example of browsing the Web. When you type a URL into your browser's Address bar and press Enter, the computer sends out a little packet of information requesting the page from some Web server on the Internet. It then immediately forgets all about that request. A few seconds later, when the Web page start streaming in to an Ethernet port, your computer just *assumes* that it's the page you requested and lets it in.

When you send out a request for a Web page from your Web browser with a firewall, the firewall "remembers" the request. When data comes knocking at some port from the Internet, the firewall compares the return address of each incoming packet to make sure that it's something you requested. If that address doesn't match what it remembers as something you've requested, then the incoming data is killed right on the spot. If the return address does, however, match something you requested, then the firewall lets it in, and then erases its "memory" of the request.

In short, a firewall works by blocking unsolicited traffic — anything that you didn't specifically request.

Hackers and hacking

Sneaking something into a computer without the owner knowing it, through an unguarded port, is called *hacking* (or *cracking*). People who do that sort of thing are called *hackers*. Contrary to popular belief, very few hackers are human beings. The vast majority of "hackers" are programs running on computers. Hackers create the programs. But they don't use them in the way most people envision, to "break into your computer" and steal stuff. That sort of hacking is virtually impossible with PCs.

The nonhuman hackers that affect PCs don't target a specific computer. They just send out millions of "hack attempts" in an attempt to plant some program (usually a *worm*) in whatever unprotected computer ports they can get into. Neither the program, nor the human being who created it, knows (or cares) which specific computers got hacked. They're just trying to hack into as many computers as possible to plant some sort of spyware, adware, or some other unpleasant worm program.

As a network security friend once told me, it's kind of like finding a pack of raccoons living in the trunk of your car. The raccoons don't care that it's *your* car they're living in. To them it's just a comfy place to hang out. Nothing personal. Likewise, hackers and worms don't care that it's *your* computer they've hacked into, and they have no intent of taking anything away from that computer. They just see it as another place to post ads or do some other sort of unpleasant task. Nothing personal, but unpleasant nonetheless.

These days, going online without a firewall is asking for trouble. There are so many nonhuman hackers out there sending out so many worms and such that you're sure to start picking up all kinds or pleasant things the moment you go online. Using a dial-up account for 5 minutes a day, as opposed to an always-on account, won't help one bit. Never leaving your computer online while you're away from the keyboard won't help either. It only takes a fraction of a second for a worm to infect your computer, and there's absolutely nothing on the screen that would alert you to the fact that you've just been hacked or allow you to stop the intrusion.

What a firewall doesn't protect against

A firewall will protect you against unsolicited network traffic, some of which might contain worms. But there are quite a few bad Internet things that a firewall will not protect against. For example:

✦ The firewall will not disable viruses or worms that are already on your computer. You need to scan your computer with antivirus software to get rid of those (see Chapter 29).

✦ The firewall does not protect you from viruses or in programs you download or e-mail attachments that you open. You need antivirus software for that.

✦ The firewall will not block pop-up ads. Chapter 29 discusses techniques for blocking pop-ups.

✦ The firewall does not block junk e-mail. You need some sort of antispam software for that, or learn to use the junk mail protection built into your e-mail client.

Well-known ports

Some Web services always use specific ports. These commonly used ports go by the high-tech name of *well-known ports*. There are also some not-so-well-known ports that do useful things, such as ports for voice conversations and file transfers in MSN Messenger. Table 26-1 shows some examples of the well-known ports and other useful Windows ports.

Table 26-1 Examples of Well-Known and Commonly Used Ports

Port number	Primary Protocol	Acronym/ Name	Service
20-21	TCP	FTP	File Transfer Protocol
25	TCP	SMTP	Simple Mail Transfer Protocol (e-mail)
53	TCP	DNS	Domain Name Server
80	TCP	HTTP	Hypertext Transfer Protocol (World Wide Web)
88	TCP	Kerberos	Secure authentication protocol
110	TCP	POP3	Post Office Protocol Version 3 (e-mail)
119	TCP	NNTP	Network News Transfer Protocol (newsgroups)
443	TCP	HTTPS	Secure Sockets Layer (secure Web transactions)
445	TCP	Microsoft-DS	Active Directory, Windows shares (also Sasser Worm)
563	TCP	AIM	AOL Instant Messenger file transfers
1027	UDP	ICQ	Instant messaging

Continued

Table 26-1 *(continued)*

Port number	Primary Protocol	Acronym/ Name	Service
3074	TCP and UDP	Xbox	Xbox Music Mixer PC Tool
3306	TCP	MySQL	MySQL database
5000	TCP	UPnP	Universal Plug-and-Play
5000-5001	TCP	Yahoo	Yahoo Messenger chat
5190	TCP	AOL, AIM	America Online and AOL Instant Messenger
5055	UDP	Yahoo	Yahoo Messenger Phone
5631-5632	TCP	PCAnywhere	Symantec's PCAnywhere program
6667	TCP	IRC	Internet Relay Chat
6891-6900	TCP	Microsoft	MSN Messenger file transfer
6901	TCP and UDP	Microsoft	MSN Messenger voice conversations
8080	TCP	HTTP (Secondary)	Alternate World Wide Web port
28800-28809	TCP	MSN	MSN Game Zone[1]
31337	TCP	RAS	Remote Administration Services

[1]The page at www.practicallynetworked.com/sharing/app_port_list.htm maintains a list of ports for popular games, messaging, multimedia, remote control, and other Internet services.

Note   Port assignments are managed by the Internet Assigned Numbers Authority (IANA). If you're interested, you can visit their Web site at www.iana.org for more information.

As a rule, you don't have to mess with ports manually. Your Web browser, e-mail client, and other common Internet programs will work just fine if you just leave the firewall alone. Those programs already know how to work through the firewall. In most cases, all you have to do is make sure that the firewall is on, and forget about it.

Introducing Windows Firewall

Prior to the release of Service Pack 2, Windows XP came with a built-in Internet Connection Firewall (ICF). It worked pretty well, but hardly anybody knew it was there. Most people went online without the firewall turned on. As a result, most people got eaten alive by virtually everything "bad" that could come sneaking in through one of the 65,535 wide-open ports on their Internet connection.

That's all changed in Service Pack 2. The new firewall, called Windows Firewall, is enabled by default and is very much "in your face" from the get-go. If you turn off your firewall, you'll know about it immediately. And unlike the old ICF, which did its thing silently in the background and never provided any feedback, even when it was functioning, the new Windows Firewall does pop up an occasional message to let you know when it has blocked a hack attempt. In short, it's almost impossible to be unaware of the new Windows Firewall.

Using Windows Firewall

You can get to your Windows Firewall through the Security Center or directly through Control Panel. The Security Center tells you if your firewall is on or off. You can get to the Security Center using whichever of the follow methods is most convenient:

✦ Click the **Start** button and choose **All Programs** ➪ **Accessories** ➪ **System Tools** ➪ **Security Center**.

✦ Or, click the **Start** button, and choose **Control Panel**. Then, click on the **Security Center** category (or open the Security Center icon in Classic View).

✦ Or, click on **Change Windows Firewall Settings** under Network Tasks in your Network Connections folder.

✦ Or, if you see a small red Security Center shield in the Notification area, double-click that icon.

Figure 26-1 shows how the Security Center looks when you first open it. If your firewall is on, you'll see the word On to its right, as in Figure 26-1. If your firewall is Off, click on the word Off to see more information. Then, click the Recommendations button. Click the Enable Now button, and then click Close and OK.

Figure 26-1: Windows Security Center

Caution   One firewall is sufficient. Multiple firewalls won't make your computer more secure and will likely cause problems. If you have a third-party firewall that you prefer to the Windows Firewall, you can use that third-party firewall and leave the Windows Firewall turned off.

Responding to Firewall messages

When Windows Firewall is turned on and running, you don't really have to do anything to use it. There will be times, though, when it's not so apparent how to handle a specific program, in which case it will display a message similar to the one shown in Figure 26-2.

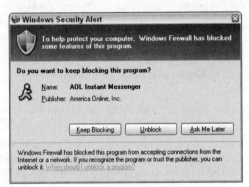

Figure 26-2: Message when running some programs for the first time

The message doesn't mean the program is "bad." It just means that to use the program, the Firewall has to open a port. If you want to use the program, go ahead and click Unblock. If you don't recognize the program name and publisher shown, choose Keep Blocking. If you're not sure what you want to do and want to look into the program some more, click Ask Me Later.

Configuring Windows Firewall

As mentioned earlier, you don't need to configure Windows Firewall to do common tasks such as browse the Web or send and receive e-mail. But some programs, such as Internet games, file-sharing clients, and other special services, may require that you open up some ports manually through Windows Firewall.

To configure Windows Firewall, click the Windows Firewall icon under *Manage security settings for* in the Security Center shown in Figure 26-1. Optionally, you can click the Start button, choose Control Panel, switch to Classic View, and open the Windows Firewall icon in Control Panel. Whichever method you use, you'll end up in the Windows Firewall dialog box shown in Figure 26-3.

First and foremost, you want to make sure that the On (Recommended) setting is selected, unless you're using some third-party firewall instead of the Windows Firewall. (If Windows Firewall is Off, then there's no point in doing any of the things described in this section.)

To use any program other than your Web browser and e-mail client, you'll need to clear the *Don't allow exceptions* checkbox. Once you've done that, you can define which programs are allowed to communicate through the firewall.

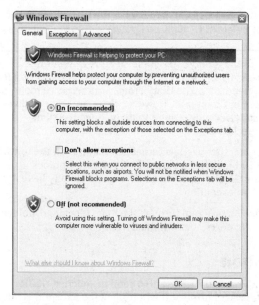

Figure 26-3: Windows Firewall dialog box

Allowing programs to work through the firewall

By default, Windows Firewall blocks just about everything but basic Web browsing and e-mail. The Exceptions tab in the Windows Firewall dialog box lets you define other Internet programs that you want to use. When you first click the Exceptions tab, you'll see a list of programs and services, beyond your browser and e-mail, that are allowed to communicate through your firewall, as in the example shown in Figure 26-4.

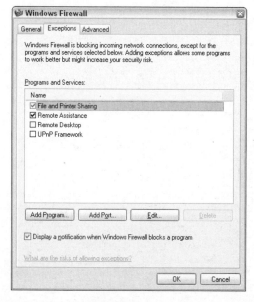

Figure 26-4: Exceptions tab of the Windows Firewall dialog box

The File and Printer Sharing option only applies to local networks of the type described in Part XI of this book. That option must be selected to allow computers within your network to communicate with one another.

The Remote Assistance option works with the Remote Assistance feature of Windows Messenger (see Chapter 34). Remote Desktop refers to the Remote Desktop Connection feature of Windows XP Professional (see Appendix C). The UPnP Framework refers to modern Universal Plug-and-Play devices discussed in Chapter 63. However, there are some online services that work through the same port and they may require that you open the UPnP Framework by selecting (checking) its checkbox.

Recall that the first time you start a program that needs Internet access through the firewall, you get the options to Keep Blocking or Unblock the program. Had I chosen Unblock in response to that message, the Exceptions tab shown in Figure 26-4 would already have AOL Instant Messenger listed and checked as an exception.

In the unlikely event that you can't unblock a program through the Keep Blocking/Unblock options, you can add a program, or specific ports, through the Exceptions tab.

Adding a program exception

When you specify an exception, you're allowing the program to send unsolicited traffic through the firewall. Clicking the Add Program button at the bottom of the Exceptions tab is the easiest way to add a program to the exceptions list. When you click that button, a list of all your installed programs appears, as in Figure 26-5. Since it lists all of your installed programs, including those that have nothing to do with the Internet, you don't need to deal with all of them. You just need to click on the name of the program that's currently being blocked by the firewall.

Figure 26-5: Add Program dialog box for firewall exceptions

Choosing a scope

After you click on a program's name, you can choose a scope for that program. The scope defines the addresses from which the unsolicited traffic is expected to originate. For example, if you're using a program that provides communications among programs within your local network only, you wouldn't want to accept unsolicited traffic coming to that port from the Internet. You'd only want to accept unsolicited traffic coming from computers within your own network. Click the Change Scope button to see the options shown in Figure 26-6. Your options are as follows:

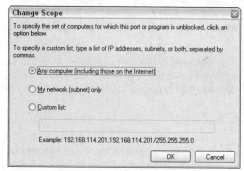

Figure 26-6: The Change Scope dialog box

✦ **Any computer (including those on the Internet):** If you want to use the Internet program normally (so your computer has access to the Internet), choose this option.

✦ **My network (subnet) only:** If the program in question has nothing to do with the Internet, and is for your home or small business only, choose this option to block Internet access but allow programs within your own network to communicate with each other through the program.

Tip   The term subnet is another term for a home or small-office network.

✦ **Custom list:** If you want only certain computers in your local network, as opposed to all programs in that network, to use the program, you can specify their IP addresses individually.

If you choose the Custom List option, you need to type all the IP addresses that can use the program. Separate each IP address by a comma. Follow the last IP address with a slash and the subnet mask for the entire network. For example, the following allows hosts 1, 2, and 160 in a local network to communicate with one another through a firewall via whichever program you chose in the list of exceptions:

```
192.168.0.1,192.168.0.2,192.168.0.106/255.255.255.0
```

IP Addresses on Home/Office Networks

When you set up a network using the Network Setup Wizard described in Part XI of this book, each computer is automatically assigned a 192.168.0.*x* IP address, where *x* is unique to each computer. For example, if the computers are sharing a single Internet connection, the first computer will be 192.168.0.1, the second computer you add will be 192.168.0.2, and so forth (although that last number could vary).

All computers will have the same subnet mask of 255.255.255.0. The subnet mask just tells the computer that the first three numbers are part of the *network address* (the address of your network as a whole), and the last number refers to a specific *host* (computer) on that network. The 192.168 . . . addresses are called *private addresses* because they cannot be accessed directly from the Internet.

To see the IP address of a computer on your local network, go to that computer, click the Start button, and choose All Programs ⇨ Accessories ⇨ Command Prompt. At the command prompt, type `ipconfig /all`, and press Enter. You'll see the computers IP address and subnet mask listed along with other Internet Protocol data.

Click OK after choosing your program. You'll see its name added to the list of exceptions. For example, Figure 26-7 shows my list of exceptions after clicking the Unblock button for AOL Instant Messenger and after manually adding LimeWire Pro through the Add Program button.

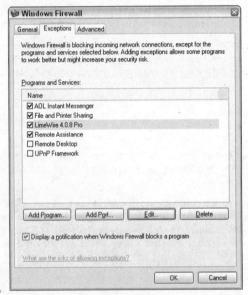

Figure 26-7: AOL and LimeWire programs added to list of exceptions

Adding a port

If you know the exact port and protocol needed to use a specific program, you can use the Add Port button to add the port or a range of ports. When you click the Add Port button, you're taken to the Add a Port dialog box shown in Figure 26-8. Fill in the blanks as summarized below:

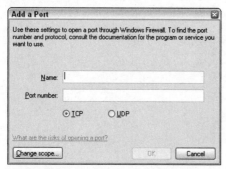

Figure 26-8: The Add a Port dialog box

- ✦ **Name:** This is the name that appears in the exceptions list, and can be any name you like.
- ✦ **Port:** This is the port number through which you're willing to accept traffic.
- ✦ **TCP/UDP:** Choose either TCP or UDP, depending on which type of traffic you're willing to accept.

Note   Only the Help or documentation for the program in question can provide the port numbers and protocol you need to open. Guessing sure won't work.

To define the range of addresses from which you're willing to accept traffic on the port, click the Change Scope button. You'll be given the same options described under "Choosing a scope" earlier in this chapter.

Disabling, changing, and deleting exceptions

The checkboxes in the Exceptions list indicate whether the exception is enabled or disabled. When you clear a checkbox, the exception is disabled and traffic through the port is rejected. This makes it relatively easy to enable and disable the port on an as-needed basic, because the program name always remains in the list of exceptions.

To change the scope of an exception in your exceptions list, click the exception name, and click the Edit button. Then, click the Change Scope button and choose your new scope. To remove a program from the exceptions list, and stop accepting unsolicited traffic through its port, click the exception name, and then click the Delete button.

Advanced firewall settings

The Advanced tab of the Windows Firewall dialog box, shown in Figure 26-9, lets you configure specific network connections. If you have an IEEE 1394 port and a mixed-mode network, the 1394 device may be used as a network bridge between the two different types of networks (for example, to connect a wireless computer or network to a wired network). This is normal and need not be changed unless it causes problems with devices you plug into the port externally.

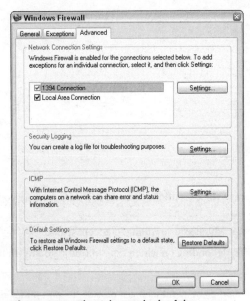

Figure 26-9: The Advanced tab of the Windows Firewall dialog box

The exceptions you define on the Exceptions tab are applied to all of the selected (checked) connections listed in the first box. If you clear a check mark, that device will reject traffic, and the program won't work as expected. So, don't clear any check marks unless you're certain that the device need not accept traffic.

If you use a dial-up modem and custom dialer provided by your ISP to connect to the Internet, that connection may not show up under Network Connection Settings. You'll need to contact your ISP to determine what, if any, steps you need to take to configure firewall protection and exceptions for that custom connection.

The Settings button to the right of the Network Connections Settings list allows you to define settings for a single connection. First, you click on the connection for which you want to define settings individually, so its name is highlighted in the list. Then, click the Settings button. The settings for that one connection are split into two tabs, as in Figure 26-10.

At first glance, the fact that none of the services is selected might seem a mystery, especially if you've already been using some of the services such as FTP, e-mail, and the Web. But you have to keep in mind that all these checkboxes refer to that one connection and services available on your own network, not necessarily to Internet services.

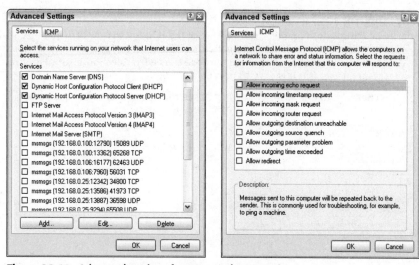

Figure 26-10: Advanced settings for a network connection

The left side of Figure 26-10 shows settings on a network card that acts as an Internet Connection Sharing Host (ICS Host) on a network where all computers share a single Internet connection. The DNS and DHCP services are enabled because that computer will get requests for domain name resolution (needed for browsing the Web), which DNS provides. That ICS host will also get requests for IP addresses from other computers in the local network, and DHCP (Dynamic Host Configuration Protocol) provides that service. The Network Setup Wizard (described in Part XI) sets that up automatically, so you don't really need to worry about all the details.

On the left side of Figure 26-10 you'll notice that many standard Internet services like FTP, e-mail, and Windows Messenger (`msmsgs`) aren't selected. That's because the computer won't get requests for FTP, e-mail, or Windows Messenger services from other computers in the local network. Those requests will be sent out to the Internet where the services reside. So, it's not necessary to open those ports on the ICS Host computer.

Note   ICMP stands for Internet Control Message Protocol and is generally used as a means of testing connections between computers. Common network testing commands such as ping and traceroute both use features of ICMP.

The ICMP options are all related to ports used by network engineers for testing networks. If you're not a network engineer who designs, builds, and tests networks, there's really no need to enable those ports. Better to leave them unchecked so that they can't be tested for connectivity by unauthorized persons.

Caution   As the saying goes, "If it ain't broken, don't fix it." If you're fretting over what ports to open or not to open, don't do anything. The various wizards and setup programs you use to install things will take care of firewall settings for you. If your Internet connection is working, there's no need to start opening ports at random.

Security logging

The Security Logging option on the Advanced tab of the Windows Firewall dialog box, shown in Figure 26-9, allows you to track inbound network traffic. Like all logs, it's not the most user-friendly document you'll ever read. Its main purpose is as a troubleshooting tool for professional network engineers. But it is easy to turn on and off:

1. Click on **Settings** under Security Logging to see the options show in Figure 26-11.

Figure 26-11: Log settings for Windows Firewall

2. To keep track of dropped packets (information that was rejected by the firewall), choose the first checkbox, **Log dropped packets**.

3. To keep track of accepted packets (information that made it through the firewall), choose the second checkbox, **Log successful connections**.

4. To specify a folder and filename for the log, click the **Save As** button and use the Save As dialog box to navigate to the folder in which you want to store the log, and give it a filename. (I chose my My Documents folder in the figure, though part of the path is cut off.)

5. To limit the size of the log, type a size, or use the spin buttons, next to **Size limit (KB)**.

6. Click **OK**.

When you want to check the log, just navigate to the folder in which you put it and double-click the icon for the log. Or, right-click the log's icon and choose Open With and the program you want to use. The log contains a lot of text and numbers. Headings across the top of the log describe what's in each column as follows:

✦ **Date:** The date that the packet was received.

✦ **Time:** The time that the packet was received.

✦ **Action:** Indicates the action taken by the firewall such as OPEN or CLOSE the port, or DROP (reject) the packet.

✦ **Protocol:** TCP, UDP, or ICMP for most packets, a number for packets that don't follow any of those protocols.

✦ **Source address (src-ip):** The address from which the packet was sent (that is, the return address).

✦ **Destination address (dst-ip):** The address to which the packet was sent.

✦ **Source port (src-port):** The port from which the packet was sent on the sending computer (a number between 1 and 65,535).

✦ **Destination port (dst-port):** The port to which the packet was sent.

✦ **Size:** The packet size in bytes.

✦ **Flags (tcpflags):** TCP control flags in the TCP header of the packet, such as Ack (Acknowledgment), Fin (No more data from sender).

✦ **Sequence number (tcpsyn):** The sequence number of the packet.

✦ **tcpack:** Packet acknowledgement number.

✦ **tcpwin:** Size of the TCP window in bytes.

✦ **icmptype:** Type of field in an ICMP message.

✦ **icmpcode:** Code field of an ICMP packet.

✦ **info:** Type of action that occurred, such as RECEIVE for received packet.

Any information that isn't relevant to a specific packet is indicated by a hyphen in the log. Figure 26-12 shows an example of the first few columns of a firewall log.

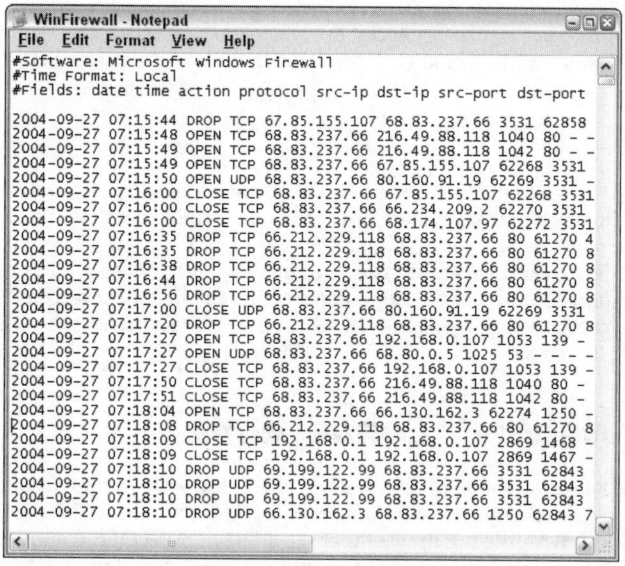
WinFirewall - Notepad

File Edit Format View Help

```
#Software: Microsoft Windows Firewall
#Time Format: Local
#Fields: date time action protocol src-ip dst-ip src-port dst-port

2004-09-27 07:15:44 DROP TCP 67.85.155.107 68.83.237.66 3531 62858
2004-09-27 07:15:48 OPEN TCP 68.83.237.66 216.49.88.118 1040 80 - -
2004-09-27 07:15:49 OPEN TCP 68.83.237.66 216.49.88.118 1042 80 - -
2004-09-27 07:15:49 OPEN TCP 68.83.237.66 67.85.155.107 62268 3531
2004-09-27 07:15:50 OPEN UDP 68.83.237.66 80.160.91.19 62269 3531 -
2004-09-27 07:16:00 CLOSE TCP 68.83.237.66 67.85.155.107 62268 3531
2004-09-27 07:16:00 CLOSE TCP 68.83.237.66 66.234.209.2 62270 3531
2004-09-27 07:16:00 CLOSE TCP 68.83.237.66 68.174.107.97 62272 3531
2004-09-27 07:16:35 DROP TCP 66.212.229.118 68.83.237.66 80 61270 4
2004-09-27 07:16:35 DROP TCP 66.212.229.118 68.83.237.66 80 61270 8
2004-09-27 07:16:38 DROP TCP 66.212.229.118 68.83.237.66 80 61270 8
2004-09-27 07:16:44 DROP TCP 66.212.229.118 68.83.237.66 80 61270 8
2004-09-27 07:16:56 DROP TCP 66.212.229.118 68.83.237.66 80 61270 8
2004-09-27 07:17:00 CLOSE UDP 68.83.237.66 80.160.91.19 62269 3531
2004-09-27 07:17:20 DROP TCP 66.212.229.118 68.83.237.66 80 61270 8
2004-09-27 07:17:27 OPEN TCP 68.83.237.66 192.168.0.107 1053 139 -
2004-09-27 07:17:27 OPEN UDP 68.83.237.66 68.80.0.5 1025 53 - - - -
2004-09-27 07:17:27 CLOSE TCP 68.83.237.66 192.168.0.107 1053 139 -
2004-09-27 07:17:50 CLOSE TCP 68.83.237.66 216.49.88.118 1040 80 -
2004-09-27 07:17:51 CLOSE TCP 68.83.237.66 216.49.88.118 1042 80 -
2004-09-27 07:18:04 OPEN TCP 68.83.237.66 66.130.162.3 62274 1250 -
2004-09-27 07:18:08 DROP TCP 66.212.229.118 68.83.237.66 80 61270 8
2004-09-27 07:18:09 CLOSE TCP 192.168.0.1 192.168.0.107 2869 1468 -
2004-09-27 07:18:09 CLOSE TCP 192.168.0.1 192.168.0.107 2869 1467 -
2004-09-27 07:18:10 DROP UDP 69.199.122.99 68.83.237.66 3531 62843
2004-09-27 07:18:10 DROP UDP 69.199.122.99 68.83.237.66 3531 62843
2004-09-27 07:18:10 DROP UDP 69.199.122.99 68.83.237.66 3531 62843
2004-09-27 07:18:10 DROP UDP 66.130.162.3 68.83.237.66 1250 62843 7
```

Figure 26-12: Sample Windows Firewall log

Most of the information is useful only to a network engineer, which gets into topics that go beyond the scope of a Windows book like this. But it's often interesting to look at the source IP address, which tells you where the packet was sent from. If you type `http://` followed by the source IP address, and there's a Web page at that address, you'll be taken to that Web page.

For example, some dropped packets came from 66.212.229.118. Typing http://66.212.229.118 into Internet Explorer's Address bar and pressing Enter takes you to the Web site that owns that IP address. The destination address will be whatever your IP address is at the moment. You can find that address by browsing to www.WhatIsMyIP.com. If you're working from a home or small office network, computers within your local network will have addresses starting with 192.168.0.

The port number to which the packet was sent will usually match one of the port numbers listed in Table 26-1. For example, packets sent to your Web browser will have a destination port of 80. It's not terribly useful information, but a good way to spy on who is trying to spy on you.

Not all dropped packets are "bad" packets. Some may be from perfectly legitimate Web sites where the packet was dropped because of a perfectly legitimate pop-up. Also, not all addresses correspond to Web sites. If you get a *Page not found* error when trying the http://IPaddress trick, this just means that the place that sent the packet isn't a Web site.

ICMP settings

As mentioned earlier, ICMP (Internet Control Message Protocol) is generally used by network engineers for testing and debugging purposes. The Windows Firewall typically blocks those packets, except perhaps for incoming echo requests that just respond to a ping text. The ICMP Settings button takes you to a dialog box where you can specify error and status requests to which the computer will respond. If you enable TCP port 445, the computer will respond to all ICMP requests.

Caution   Logging eats up a little bit of computer resources. So, when you've finished checking out your security logs, you should go back and clear the checkboxes in the log settings dialog boxes to stop logging.

Restore defaults

As its name implies, the Restore Defaults button sets the Windows Firewall back to its default configuration. If you're losing track of what's good and not good on the Exceptions tab, click this button to get back to ground zero. If your computer is part of a local network, you'll want to enable File and Printer Sharing on the Exceptions tab right away. Otherwise, your computer won't be able to communicate with the other computers on the network. You can then start unblocking other programs on case-by-case basis as the security alerts (like the example shown back in Figure 26-2) arise.

The Firewall and Network Connections

If you're familiar with the ICF firewall from earlier versions of Windows XP, you might be surprised to see that all connections in your Network Connections folder are firewalled, as in the example shown in Figure 26-13. With the ICF firewall that would have prevented computers within your own network from communicating with each other. But it doesn't work that way with the new Windows Firewall.

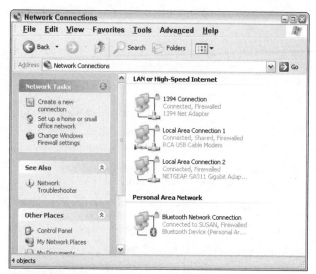

Figure 26-13: Every connection icon in Network Connections is firewalled.

With the Windows Firewall in SP2, every connection is purposely firewalled, and you can keep things that way. If you find that you're unable to connect to another computer in your own network, you just have to enable file and printer sharing on that connection. As you can see in the figure, the Network Tasks panel in the Explorer bar provides a quick shortcut to firewall settings. Optionally, you can:

1. Right-click any connection, and choose **Properties**.

2. In the Properties dialog box that opens, click the **Advanced** tab.

3. Click the **Settings** button on the Advanced tab to open the Windows Firewall dialog box.

4. Click the **Exceptions** button, and select (Check) **File and Printer Sharing** to allow the connection to communicate with other computers in your network.

5. Click **OK** in both open dialog boxes.

As you can see in the figure, even Bluetooth Personal Area Network connections are firewalled. You need to enable File and Printer Sharing on Bluetooth just as you would any other network connection. Just follow Steps 1 to 5 as you would on any other network connection.

Wrap Up

Windows Firewall is a much improved version of the Internet Connection Firewall that originally shipped with Windows XP. Unlike the original firewall, the new Windows Firewall is enabled by default and hard to miss. The new firewall is also much easier to configure than the original one. In summary:

✦ A firewall protects your computer from unsolicited network traffic, which is a major cause of worms and other hack attempts.

✦ A firewall will not protect you from e-mail viruses, pop-up ads, or junk e-mail.

✦ You don't need to configure the firewall to use standard Internet services like the Web and e-mail. Those will work, and use the firewall, automatically.

✦ When you start an Internet program that needs access to the Internet through a closed (protected) port, you'll be given a security alert with options to Unblock, or Keep Blocking, the port. You must choose Unblock to use that program.

✦ To get to the Windows Firewall, click Start and choose All Programs ➪ Accessories ➪ System Tools ➪ Security Center, and then click the Windows Firewall icon.

✦ Optionally, you can get to the firewall through the Security Center icon in Control Panel's Category View or the Windows Firewall icon in the Classic View.

✦ To ensure that you can use local network file and printer sharing, and Internet programs beyond your Web browser and e-mail client, make sure that the *Don't allow exceptions* option on the General tab of Windows Firewall's dialog box is *not* selected.

✦ The Exceptions tab in the Windows Firewall dialog box allows you to open ports based on program name or port. You can also change or delete an exception from the Exceptions tab.

✦ The Advanced tab lets you configure settings for individual network connections, enable logging, and restore default firewall settings.

✦ Unlike the original ICF, Window Firewall protects all network connections. To share files and printers in a local network, you just have to enable File Printer Sharing on the Exceptions tab in the Windows Firewall dialog box.

✦   ✦   ✦

Keeping Current with Security Patches

Internet security is a never-ending cat-and-mouse game between the security experts and the hackers who seem to have endless amounts of time to search for new ways to exploit the basic programmability of PC. It seems that every time the good guys find a way to patch some security hole the bad guys have learned to exploit, the bad guys find two more holes to exploit.

Maybe someday that cat-and-mouse game will end. Maybe someday there will be PCs and an Internet that can discriminate between good software and *malware* (bad software). But that someday isn't likely to come soon. So in the meantime, the best you can do is keep up with the security patches as they become available. And that's what Windows Update and this chapter are all about.

Understanding Automatic Updates

Many people are afraid of Windows Update. They're afraid that the changes to their system that the update makes will break something that they can't fix. It's certainly true that any change to your system could create a problem. But it's unlikely that keeping up with updates is likely to cause any significant problems — ertainly nowhere near as many problems to which you expose yourself by *not* keeping up with updates.

Others fear that Microsoft will somehow exploit them through automatic updates. No offense, but Microsoft doesn't care about you, or me, or what files we have on our hard disks. Microsoft has tens of millions of customers, and they don't need to exploit *any* of them. Desperate people (and companies) do desperate, exploitive things. Microsoft is as far from desperate as you can possibly get.

If anything, you should fear the things that updates are intended to protect you against. Just this week I learned of a new exploit, dubbed JPGDown or JPGDownloader, that allows even unskilled programmers (namely, teenagers) to create JPEG images that can punch a hole through your firewall and download whatever the hacker wants from a Web site to your computer.

Note   See www.internetweek.com/allStories/showArticle.jhtml?articleID=47902912 (if the story is still there by the time you read this) for more info on this nasty piece of software.

So, you casually open some JPEG image that's attached to some e-mail message, and without your having the slightest clue, your computer will be infected in an eyeblink's time. Not good. The longer you put off keeping up on your security patches, the more you expose yourself to these kinds of threats. And if you think fixing some problem caused by an automatic update is difficult, just wait until you try to get rid of some of the stuff these exploits put on your machine.

Tip   All updates from Windows Updates are free of charge. You won't be asked to for credit card information or asked to provide personally identifiable information.

Enabling Automatic Updates

Automatic updates are probably the best way to keep up with security patches. Enabling automatic updates is simple:

1. Right-click the **My Computer** icon on your desktop or **Start menu** and choose Properties. The System Properties dialog box opens.

2. Click the **Automatic Updates** tab.

3. To automatically download and install updates as they become available, choose **Automatic (recommended)**, as shown in Figure 27-1. Choose a time when your computer is likely to be on and online to check for updates. Optionally, you can choose from among the other options listed here:

   - You can choose to have the updates downloaded automatically, but not installed.

   - You can choose to just be notified of updates as they become available, and then download and install them at your leisure.

   - You can choose to turn off automatic updates. If you choose this option, you'll need to check www.WindowsUpdate.com to know see what updates are available, and then download and install them from that site.

4. Click **OK**.

What Are Exploits?

The term *exploit*, when used as a noun in computer science, refers to any piece of software that can take advantage of some vulnerability in a program in order to gain unauthorized access to a computer. Some hackers actually publish, on the Internet, exploits they discover, which is both a good thing and a bad thing. The bad thing is that other hackers can use the exploit to conjure up their own malware, causing a whole slew of new security threats. The good thing is that the good guys can quickly create security patches to prevent the exploits from doing their nefarious deeds.

The hacking world is replete with its own terminology. A *zero day exploit* is one that becomes available before a software product is even released to the public. A *blackhat hacker* is a hacker who doesn't share his exploits by publishing them on the Internet. A *script kiddie* is an inexperienced programmer who doesn't have enough skill to create or discover his own exploits, but instead has only enough skill to take advantage of published exploits.

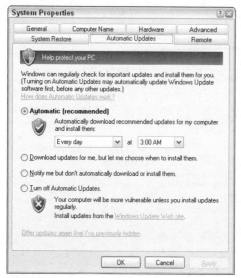

Figure 27-1: Automatic Updates tab of System Properties

If you choose to have updates downloaded automatically, but not installed, you'll see a notification message like the one in Figure 27-2. Just do as the message states — click the balloon or the tiny globe icon in the Notification area and follow the instructions on the screen.

Figure 27-2: New updates ready to install notification

Using Express Install

Some updates are large and will take a long time to download if you have a slow Internet connection. So, you might prefer to handle updates manually so that you can start the process at a time where you can leave the computer on and online for a while — preferably at a time when you're not using the computer to surf the Internet because the download will eat up some bandwidth and slow down normal Internet operations.

Even if you do use automatic updates, you should check in at the Windows Update site occasionally for optional updates to Windows, programs, or hardware drivers in your system. On most systems, you can get to that site by clicking the Start button and choosing All Programs ➪ Windows Update. Optionally, you can just get online, open Internet Explorer, and go to www.WindowsUpdate.com.

Windows Update is a Web site, so it could change by the time you read this. But here's how it works, in general. When you get to the home page, you're given two main types of updates to choose from, Express Install and Custom Install, as in the example shown in Figure 27-3.

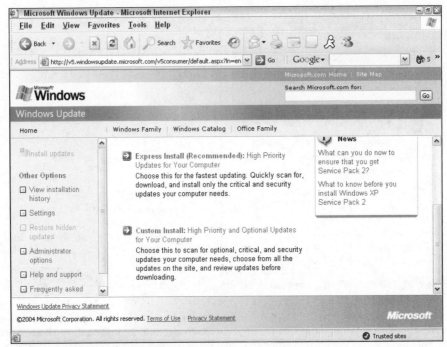

Figure 27-3: First page of www.WindowsUpdate.com

To get just the security patches and other critical updates, click the Express Install (Recommended) option. Wait a few seconds for Windows Update to scan your system to determine which updates you've already downloaded, and then click the Install button.

From that point on, it's just a matter of following the on-screen instructions. You may be prompted to restart your computer when the job is complete.

Using Custom Install

The Custom Install option lets you pick and choose from among all available updates, including optional program upgrades and driver updates. (Again, these cost no money so don't be worried about bills magically appearing in the mail a few weeks later.) Custom install will list high-priority updates first (if any). The left column will show categories of all available updates, as shown in Figure 27-4 and described next:

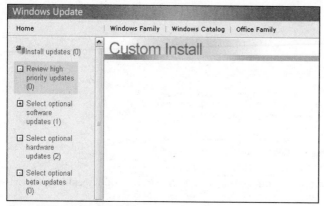

Figure 27-4: Types of updates in the left column

The number in parentheses at the end of each category name indicates how many updates are available within that category. The categories are:

✦ **Review high priority updates:** These are security patches and bug fixes that you should always download.

✦ **Select optional software updates:** These are optional (and free) upgrades to existing XP programs or other software. When you click this category name, you may see subcategories, such as Windows XP Family, beneath the category name. Click each category to see what's available within that category.

✦ **Select optional hardware updates:** These are optional hardware driver updates. These are important, because they ensure that all your installed hardware works properly with Windows XP.

✦ **Select optional beta updates:** Beta software consists of programs that are currently being tested and are not available to the general public. Recommended only for experienced users who can deal with the problems that untested software might cause.

Tip Beta updates are optional. To add or remove that category, click on Settings under Other Options in the left pane. Then, select (or clear) the *Show beta products and related updates* option on the next page that opens.

As you click on each category, you'll see the name and a description of each available update. You'll also see two checkboxes, one to the left of the update name and one next to Hide this update, as in the example shown in Figure 27-5. Here is how they work:

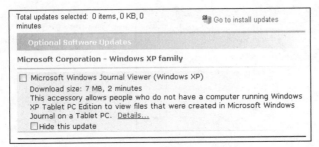

Figure 27-5: Sample available software update

✦ If you want to download an update now, select (check) the top checkbox next to the update's name.

✦ If you don't want to download the update right now, but want to keep it available for the future, leave both checkboxes empty.

✦ If you don't think that you'll ever want to download this update, leave the top checkbox empty and select (check) the Hide this update option.

Note   You can unhide hidden updates, as discussed a little later in this chapter. So, you're not making any big commitment when you choose to hide an available update.

As you select items to download the Total updates selected section will display the number of updates you've selected, their combined file sizes, and the amount of time the download is likely to take. You can select as many or as few updates, as you wish.

When you've finished making your selections, click on *Go to install updates* (visible in Figure 27-5). Or, click on Install Updates at the top of the left column. On the Install Updates page that opens, you'll see the total number of updates you've selected, their combined size, and the approximate download time in minutes, as in Figure 27-6.

Install Updates

This page provides a summary of the updates that are selected to be installed.

To install the following optional updates, click Install.

Total updates selected: 3 items, 9.8 MB, 3 minutes   [Install...]

Optional Updates

Microsoft Corporation - Windows XP family

☑ Microsoft Windows Journal Viewer (Windows XP)
  Download size: 7 MB, 2 minutes
  This accessory allows people who do not have a computer running Windows XP Tablet PC Edition to view files that were created in Microsoft Windows Journal on a Tablet PC. Details...
  ☐ Hide this update

C-media - C-Media AC97 Audio Device

☑ C Media Electronics Incorporation - Sound - C-Media AC97 Audio Device

Realtek - Realtek RTL8180 Wireless LAN (Mini-)PCI NIC

☑ Realtek Semiconductor Corp - Networking - Realtek RTL8180 Wireless LAN (Mini-)PCI NIC

Figure 27-6: Three updates selected and ready to install

If you change your mind about any of the items you chose to download, just clear the checkbox to the left of the update's name. When only the updates you want to download and install immediately are listed, click the Install button and follow the instructions on the screen.

What happens next depends on what you download. For optional software you may need to agree to the standard EULA (End User License Agreement), which is a bunch of legalese stating that you won't sell or give away copies of the software. You may need to restart the computer when all is said and done. But all you have to do is follow the instructions presented on the screen.

More Windows Update Options

The left column of the Windows Update home page offers the general topics shown in Figure 27-7 and summarized next.

Figure 27-7: Other Options section of the Windows Update Web site

✦ **View installation history:** Provides a list of all the updates you've installed in the past, their status (for example, Successful or Canceled), the date, and the source. Click the Print All button at the top of the list to print the page.

✦ **Settings:** Click this button to choose your language (such as English, Danish, German, or whatever), and also to choose whether or not you want beta products to be included in your list of available updates.

✦ **Restore hidden updates:** Choose this option to view updates for which you previously chose *Hide this update*.

✦ **Administrator options:** Provides options for network administrators, security experts, and other power users.

✦ **Help and support:** Provides many options for dealing with Windows Update problems, including a Windows Update Troubleshooter.

✦ **Frequently asked questions:** Provides answers to the questions most often asked by people who are unsure of how to use Windows Update.

If you have any problems using Windows Update, be sure to click the Help and Support link, and try the Windows Update Troubleshooter. Likewise, if you have any questions at all about Windows Update, you should really check out the Frequently Asked Questions page.

First Aid for Windows Update Failures

If you can't get your PC to automatically keep up with Windows updates, or if your manual updates consistently fail, I have a solution that just might take care of the problem. I found that I had to do this on all the computers except the ICS host in my own home network. Here are the steps:

1. Start Microsoft Internet Explorer, and choose **Tools ⇨ Internet Options** from its menu bar.

2. Click the **Security** tab in the Internet Options dialog box.

3. Click on the **Trusted Sites** icon.

4. Click the **Sites** button.

5. Clear the **Require sever verification (https:) for all sites in this zone** checkbox.

6. Type one of the following URLs under **Add this Web site to the zone:** box, and then click the **Add** button. Repeat this step for each of the three URLs:

Caution   You must type each URL exactly as shown here. There is no margin for error.

```
https://*.windowsupdate.microsoft.com
http://*.windowsupdate.microsoft.com
http://download.microsoft.com
```

7. After you've added all three URLs as shown in Figure 27-8, click the **OK** button in the Trusted Sites dialog box. Then, click **OK** in the Internet Options dialog box.

Tip   If you want to download Sun's Java Virtual Machine, but find that it's blocked, add `http://java.sun.com` to your list of trusted sites, and download the Java VM from the page at that URL.

Figure 27-8: Adding Microsoft download sites to your list of Trusted Sites

Microsoft Office Updates

If you own Microsoft Office or any Office program, such as Microsoft Word or Microsoft Office, be aware that Windows Update doesn't include updates for those programs. Like any program, Office applications can be vulnerable to attack. So, you'll want to keep up to date on those programs as well.

But even if there aren't any current security holes that need patching, there are lots of cool things you can download from the Office Update site, such as free clip art a media, templates, and worksheets and databases, and much more. You can also get assistance and take free online courses for using all the Office products.

You can get to the Office Update site using any of the following techniques:

✦ Click on **Office Family** in the toolbar at the top of the `www.WindowsUpdate.com` home page.

✦ Or, browse to `http://office.microsoft.com`.

✦ Or, choose **Help** ⇨ **Microsoft Office Online** from any Office program's menu bar.

Once you get to the home page, click the Check for Updates link near the top of the page, as shown in Figure 27-9. Or click on Downloads in the left column of any Office Online page, and then click on Check for Updates under Office Update on the Downloads page.

Figure 27-9: Sample home page from http://Office.Microsoft.com

Wrap Up

Not everybody who uses the Internet is nice. There are plenty of hackers out there who spend a lot of time finding new ways to gain unauthorized access to other PCs on the Internet. They use that unauthorized access to plant worms, download stuff you really don't want to your computer, and more. You really need to learn to separate the good guys from the bad guys, choose your allies wisely, and take some action to protect yourself from

Internet threats. One way to keep your computer safe and secure is to keep abreast of critical downloads from the Windows Update Web site. To summarize:

✦ To keep your security patches up to date automatically, right-click your My Computer icon, choose Properties, click the Automatic Updates tab, and choose Automatic (recommended).

✦ To manually download critical updates, or to download optional software updates and hard drivers, click the Start button and choose All Programs ➪ Windows Update. Or browse to www.WindowsUpdate.com with Microsoft Internet Explorer.

✦ At the Windows Update Web site, use the Express Install option to download critical security patches only.

✦ Use the Custom Install option to review, choose, and download optional software and hardware driver updates.

✦ While you're at the Windows Update Web site, click on Help and Support or Frequently Asked Questions in the left column for general information and current news about the site.

✦　　✦　　✦

Blocking Viruses and Worms

Despite the cute TV commercials, computer viruses aren't microbiological organisms that infect your computer and give it a cold. A computer virus is a computer program designed to do bad things to your computer. These viruses don't just happen. They are written by human programmers with some sort of mental health problem that makes them want to ruin everyone else's fun.

Most viruses are spread by people unwittingly downloading and installing them on their own computers. The virus may be disguised as a legitimate e-mail message attachment, or some cool program you can download for free from some cute pop-up ad.

This chapter is about preventing, and getting rid of, viruses and worms. But it's going to be a short chapter because there's not enough stuff built into Windows XP to prevent virus attacks. You really need to purchase and install antivirus software to handle the problem. Either that or exercise extremely good judgment when it comes to downloading things and opening e-mail attachments.

Viruses, Worms, Trojans, and Such

Computer viruses get their names from the fact that they spread by replicating themselves. In fact, one of the reasons they can spread quickly and infect a lot of machines is because they replicate like bacteria. First there's one; that splits into two. Those two each split into four, and then 8, 16, 32, 64, 128, 256, 512, and 1,024. If you keep counting like that, doubling the previous number each time, it doesn't take long before you're counting like 2 million, 4 million, 8 million, 16 million. . . .

The most popular method of spreading viruses is through e-mail attachments. You open an e-mail attachment that's presumably from a legitimate software company or Web site such as Microsoft, eBay, Amazon, or your ISP (a fake bounce-back message). As soon as you open the attachment, you install the virus (without realizing it). The virus then starts e-mailing copies of itself, from your computer, to people in your address book. Before long, millions of people are sending copies of the virus to each other without even realizing it.

A worm is similar to a virus. The only difference is that a worm can act independently of other files, and can spread without being embedded in e-mail attachments or programs. For example, a worm can work its way into your computer through on open port in your Internet connection, which is why it's important to keep a firewall up at all times when you're online.

Viruses and worms are examples of a larger class of software called *malware*, for "bad software." Trojans (also called Trojan horses) are also malware. Unlike viruses and worms, Trojans don't replicate themselves. Most appear to be normal programs that do their dirty work behind the scenes. Some Trojans are even perfectly legitimate programs that could be used to do bad things. For example, a program that can recover lost passwords from documents might be considered a Trojan, because someone could use it to break into other people's files.

Whatever you call it, virus, worm, Trojan horse, adware, spyware, scumware, or whatever, it's all stuff you don't want on your computer. This chapter focuses on viruses, worms, and Trojans because there are ways to deal specifically with those types of malware. Unfortunately, Windows XP alone doesn't have what it takes to really protect yourself from all the threats. As discussed later in this chapter, you'll probably want to purchase and install some third-party antivirus software to deal with these kinds of threats.

Using Data Execution Prevention (DEP)

Data Execution Prevention (DEP) is a new feature of Windows XP Service Pack 2 designed to minimize the damage that a virus can do. Exactly how DEP works is a bit technical. But I'll just throw it out there for the more sophisticated readers. Nontechnical readers can just think of DEP as a feature you can activate to keep the bad effects of viruses to a minimum.

There are two types of DEP, hardware-enforced and software-enforced. Hardware-enforced DEP requires an AMD Operton 32/64 or Athlon64 processor with No-Execute Page-Protection (NX), or an Intel Itanium processor with Execute Disable Bit (XD). The processor must be running in Physical Address Extension (PAE) mode for these features to work.

Hardware-enforced DEP marks all memory addresses within a process as nonexecutable unless the memory location specifically contains executable code. When code from nonexecutable data memory attempts to inject code into executable memory locations (a common trick used in worms and viruses), DEP raises an exception, preventing the code's execution.

Since few of us are running 64-bit processors, we'll be most likely be using software-enforced DEP, which is available on any processor that can run Windows XP Service Pack 2. This method prevents malicious code from overrunning a data buffer with code and then executing that code—the most common technique of executing worms and viruses. You can use software-enforced DEP independently or in conjunction with hardware-enforced DEP on an NX or DX processor.

So much for the technical stuff. Turning on DEP is a relatively simply thing to do. Here are the steps:

1. Right-click your **My Computer** icon, and choose **Properties**. Or, open the **System** icon in Control Panel's Classic View. (This is also available under Performance and Maintenance in the Category View.)

2. In the System Properties dialog box that opens, click the **Advanced** tab.

3. Under the **Performance** heading, click **Settings**.

4. In the Performance Options dialog box, click the **Data Execution Prevention** tab to see the options shown in Figure 28-1.

Note Professionals and other uber-gurus, see Microsoft Knowledge Base article 875352 for details on configuring DEP through the `boot.ini` file.

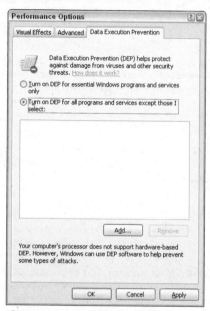

Figure 28-1: The DEP tab of the Performance Options dialog box

You have two options in the dialog box. The first, which is selected by default, is to enable DEP for Windows programs and services only. This is the easy approach to using DEP, because it rarely causes problems with legitimate programs.

The second option, which enables DEP for all programs and services, provides better protection. However, it can lead to some misleading error messages because some perfectly legitimate hardware drivers and programs will trigger error messages when this option is selected. If you're not familiar with all your installed programs and the companies that created them, you might not be able to tell the difference between a legitimate DEP error and a false alarm.

When a driver for a hardware device triggers a DEP error, you'll get an error message that takes this form:

```
0x000000FC (ATTEMPTED_EXECUTE_OF_NOEXECUTE_MEMORY)
```

The only thing you can do about that sort of error is to try to track down the latest version of the driver. If you can find a driver that's digitally signed by Microsoft to work with Windows XP SP2, that should solve the problem. Optionally, you'll need to check the hardware manufacturer's Web site for updated drivers.

Note See Chapter 53 for more information on updating drivers.

BIOS Virus Warning and Intrusion Detection

Your system BIOS might support Virus Warning and Intrusion Detection. In most cases Virus Warning, when enabled, sends up a warning whenever code attempts to change the boot sector on your hard drive. Intrusion Detection works by detecting code logic commonly found in worms and other Internet threats.

If your system BIOS supports these features, you'll find them somewhere in your BIOS Setup program. If you know your BIOS manufacturer's name (which usually appears on the screen briefly right after you start your computer), you can check their Web site for details. Here are Web sites for the main BIOS manufacturers include www.phoenix.com for Phoenix BIOS and Award BIOS, and www.ami.com for AMIBIOS (American Megatrends, Inc.).

If you enable DEP for all programs, and a program triggers a DEP error, Windows will close the program and display an error message with wording along these lines:

```
Data Execution Prevention
A Windows security feature has detected a problem and closed this program.
Name: Program name here
Publisher: Publisher name here
```

If the program is some junkie freebie you downloaded from a pop-up add or something, your best bet would be to uninstall the program immediately. On the other hand, if you're familiar with, and trust, the program and the software company that created it (displayed where *Program name here* and *Publisher name here* are shown in this example), then it's reasonable to assume that the error is a false alarm.

If you feel confident that the DEP error was just a false alarm, you can add that program to the list of exceptions on the DEP tab. You'll need to know the location and name of the program's main executable file. Often you can get that info by following these steps:

1. Click the **Start** button, choose **All Programs**, and work your way to the startup icon for the program (but don't click that icon).

2. Right-click the program's startup icon, and choose **Properties**.

3. In the Properties dialog box that opens, click on the **Shortcut** tab.

4. If the **Target** textbox is enabled, drag the mouse pointer through the entire string of text in that textbox. Or, click inside the textbox, press **Home** to move the cursor to the start of the text, and press **Shift+End** to select the entire string. Figure 28-2 shows an example.

5. Press **Ctrl+C** to copy the entire string in the Target textbox.

6. Open Notepad (Click the **Start** button and choose **All Programs** ➪ **Accessories** ➪ **Notepad**) and press **Ctrl+V**.

Select and copy all text in Target text box.

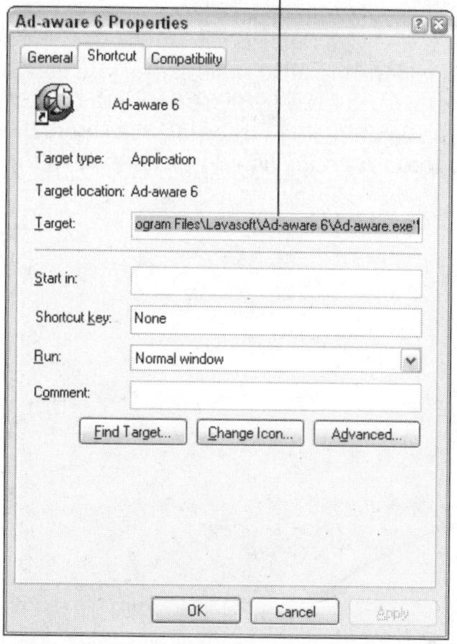

Figure 28-2: Copying a program path
from the Target textbox

If you were able to do that, you should see the entire path to the program enclosed in quotation marks, as follows. You'll know the path includes the program name if the path ends with a filename extension, such as the .exe example here:

```
"C:\Program Files\Lavasoft\Ad-aware 6\Ad-aware.exe"
```

If the Target dialog box is disabled, or if the path doesn't end with a specific filename, you there's not enough information there for your current needs. But the Start In textbox should contain the path to the program's folder, as in the following example:

```
"C:\Program Files\Jasc Software Inc\Paint Shop Pro 8\"
```

Once you know the path, you can work your way to the specified folder using the Folders list in Explorer. (Or just page that path, without the quotation marks, into Internet Explorer's Address bar and click Go.) Once you're viewing that folder, you should be able to identify the appropriate file by its icon (which matches the icon on the All Programs menu) and .exe extension (if filename extensions are visible). Once you know the filename, you can tack it onto the path. For example, the startup program for Paint Shop Pro 8 is Paint Shop Pro.exe. So the entire path is:

```
"C:\Program Files\Jasc Software Inc\Paint Shop Pro 8\Paint Shop Pro.exe"
```

To test the path, click Start and choose Run. Copy and paste the entire path, without the quotation marks, into the Run textbox and click OK. If the path is correct, the program will start normally.

Caution   Don't add either of the sample paths above to your DEP exceptions. The programs I'm using here are just examples of finding paths, and have never generated a DEP error on my computer. In fact, none of my installed programs has ever generated a DEP error.

Once you have the full path to the program that's generating false DEP errors, you can add it to the list of exceptions on the DEP tab. Just click the Add button, paste the path (without the quotation marks) into the File Name textbox on the Open dialog box, and click Open. If you do everything correctly, you should see the excepted programs listed by name, as in the example shown in Figure 28-3.

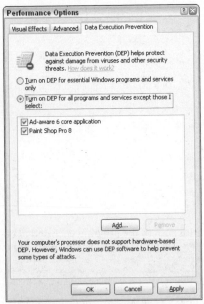

Figure 28-3: Two (hypothetical) programs added to DEP exceptions

If using the *Turn on DEP for all program . . .* option turns out to be too much of a hassle to manage, it's perfectly OK to choose *Turn on DEP for essential Windows programs and services only*. As we'll discuss a little later in this chapter, you'll want to install antivirus software either way.

Virus-Infected E-Mail Attachments

The majority of viruses are spread through e-mail attachments. I see them go by all the time. For example, Figure 28-4 shows a bunch of e-mails I've received, all of which probably contain viruses. Note that just because they're sitting in my e-mail Inbox doesn't mean that my computer is infected by the virus. For the virus to take effect, I would have to open one of the infected attachments.

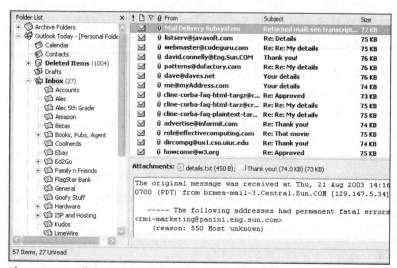

Figure 28-4: All these e-mail messages have viruses attached.

Admittedly, I don't know for a fact that all those attachments are viruses. But I'm not about to open them up to find out. I'm pretty sure they're viruses though because I don't recognize any of the senders. Furthermore, I can tell that the currently selected e-mail is a fake bounce-back message, because I've never sent an e-mail to the address that the message supposedly bounced back from.

The e-mail messages listed in Figure 28-5, all supposedly from `support@microsoft.com`, I received while the Blaster worm was making its rounds. Again, I didn't open any of them to find out, because I knew the messages were fakes and not really from Microsoft. I knew this because legitimate software companies like Microsoft, don't send out e-mail with attachments.

Figure 28-5: None of these messages is really from support@microsoft.com.

When it comes to e-mail attachments, you should consider them all "lethal," no matter who they're (supposedly) from. Be especially suspicious of e-mails from Mail Delivery Subsystem. There's no need to open the attachments from those. Even if you recognize the e-mail address from which the message bounced back, there's still no need to open any attachments. Just delete the message and attachment, and send another copy of the e-mail to the recipient, asking if he or she got the original message.

Minimizing virus threats with Outlook Express

If you use Microsoft Outlook Express to send and receive e-mail, there are a couple of things you can do to minimize your exposure to virus-infected e-mail attachments, and prevent the spread of any viruses you do pick up. Here are the steps:

1. Open **Outlook Express** from the All Programs menu.

2. Choose **Tools** ⇨ **Options** from the Outlook Express menu bar.

3. In the Options dialog box, click on the **Security** tab.

4. Choose **Restricted sites zone (more secure)**.

5. Choose **Warn me when other applications try to send mail as me**.

6. Choose **Do not allow attachments to be saved or opened that could potentially be a virus**.

7. Choose the third option, **Block images and other external content in HTML e-mail**.

8. Click **OK**.

The *Warn me . . .* selection will cause Outlook Express to display a warning whenever a virus tries to send a copy of itself to someone in your address book. If you see such a warning, you should stop the e-mail and scan your system for viruses.

The second option, *Do not allow attachments to be saved or opened . . .* will prevent you from opening any attachment that *could* contain a virus. Unfortunately, this is a bit of overkill, because it will prevent you from opening attachments that don't contain a virus. If you have third-party antivirus protection or an e-mail account that scans all e-mail attachments for viruses, you can skip this selection. When you choose it, some attachments in some e-mails will be disabled, like the .reg file in Figure 28-6.

Figure 28-6: One blocked e-mail attachment in this e-mail message

You won't be able to open or save such an attachment right away. Instead you'll need to choose Tools ⇨ Options, clear that option on the Security tab, click OK, click on some other e-mail message header, click on the message header again, and then save the attachment. But do so only if you're confident that the attachment is safe. (Then go back and turn the security feature back on.)

The *Block images and other external content in HTML e-mail* option takes things a step further by blocking some embedded and attached pictures. As I write this chapter a new JPEG exploit is making the rounds through the hacking underworld, so blocking images is probably a good idea. But again, innocent pictures will be blocked along with bad ones. So, a third-party antivirus program might be preferable to blocking all images.

Scanning e-mail attachments and downloaded files

Another way to play it safe with attachments, as well as downloads, is to save, rather than Open or Run them. If you have a third-party antivirus program that supports the scanning of individual files, you can then right-click the file's icon and choose Scan for Viruses, as shown in Figure 28-7, before you open the file.

Figure 28-7: Scanning a saved e-mail attachment or downloaded file

Note　In case you're wondering, I use McAfee VirusScan, and any examples from this chapter will be from that program.

About Third-Party Antivirus Software

The Security Center in Windows XP SP2 makes a loud-and-clear announcement if you don't have antivirus software installed or if your antivirus software is currently disabled. Figure 28-8 shows an example where I've disabled my antivirus software.

Figure 28-8: Security Center antivirus alert

Clicking the message or the Security Center icon in the Notification area opens the Security Center. You can also open the Security Center at any time using either of these methods:

✦ Click the Start button and choose Control Panel, and then click on Security Center.

✦ Or, click the Start button and choose **All Programs** ➪ **Accessories** ➪ **System Tools** ➪ **Security Center**.

Who Is the Third Party?

In the computer biz, a third-party is any company that didn't create your microprocessor or operating system. On your PC, Intel or AMD — whichever company created your computer's central processing unit — is the first party. The second party is whoever created the operating system for your computer. In this book, your operating system is (presumably) Windows XP. Thus, Microsoft is the second party because they created all versions of Windows.

Any company that wants their hardware or software to work with a Windows-based PC must play by the rules imposed by the processor and the operating system. So, they're third parties in the sense that they design their products to work with the products produced by the first two parties.

Once you've opened the Security Center, as shown in Figure 28-9, you'll see more details and options relevant to third-party antivirus software. Click the Recommendations button for more information. Optionally, you can click on any link under Resources in the left column for more information and options.

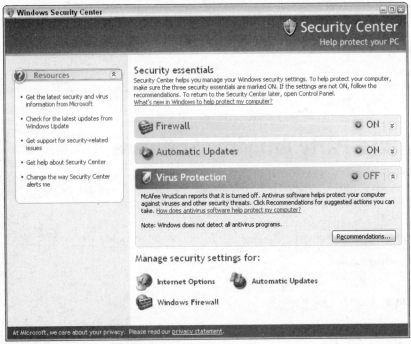

Figure 28-9: Third-party antivirus software

If you don't have antivirus software yet, you should get some. After you click the Recommendations button in the Security Center, you can click the How? link in the Recommendations dialog box to look review available products. Most offer free trial periods so you can try them out before you buy.

If your computer came with antivirus software installed, but you haven't learned to use it yet, you should learn to use it. See the documentation that came with that program, the Help within that program, or the program manufacturer's Web site for more information. Table 28-1 lists some popular antivirus programs, along with their main Web page and Support Web page.

Table 28-1: Popular Antivirus Software Web Sites

Product	Home Page	Support Page
Norton AntiVirus	www.symantec.com	www.symantec.com/techsupp/consumer.html
eTrust EZArmor	www.my-etrust.com	www.my-etrust.com/services
F-Secure	www.f-secure.com/protectyourpc/	http://support.f-secure.com
McAfee VirusScan	www.mcafee.com	http://ts.mcafeehelp.com
PC-cillian	www.trendmicro.com	http://kb.trendmicro.com/solutions/search
Panda Anti-Virus	www.pandasoftware.com	www.pandasoftware.com/support/
VirusBuster	www.virus-buster.com	www.virus-buster.com/en/support/

Using antivirus software

Unfortunately, I can't teach you how to use your antivirus program. There are just too many of them out there to even make an attempt. But as with any programs, you can learn to use your antivirus software from its built-in help, the program manufacturer's Web site, or the printed documentation that comes with the software. Specific things you want to learn about are as follows:

Make sure the antivirus software scans all incoming e-mail attachments and all files you download. Also, be aware that new viruses and worms hit the Net all the time, some able to sneak past your antivirus software. Your best protection there is to make sure that your antivirus software is always up to date. Most antivirus programs keep themselves up to date automatically. But you should learn to use that feature so that you know that your program is up to date at all times.

Finding free virus removal tools

Once your computer gets a virus, worm, or Trojan horse, your antivirus software should be able to delete it for you. But there are some viruses and worms that are more difficult to get rid of and require special software. For a complete list of viruses, worms, Trojans, adware, and spyware along with removal instructions and free removal tools, see McAfee's Virus Information Library at http://vil.nai.com/vil/.

Wrap Up

Viruses, worms, and Trojan horses are all examples of malware — software that designed to invade your privacy or do compromise your system. Your best bet in keeping these things away is to purchase, install, and learn to use a third-party antivirus program and service. The main points covered in this chapter include:

✦ Data Encryption Protection (DEP) is a new feature of Windows XP SP 2 designed to prevent worms and viruses from executing.

✦ Never trust an e-mail attachment, and never open one unless you know who it's from and what it contains.

✦ If you use Outlook Express as your e-mail client, use settings on the Security tab in its Options dialog box to secure your system against viruses and worms spread through e-mail attachments.

✦ Your best bet is to purchase, install, and learn to use a third-party antivirus program.

✦ Rather than open e-mail attachments and downloads, consider saving them first, and scanning them prior to opening them.

✦ ✦ ✦

Conquering Pop-Up Ads

I hate ads. Especially ads that pop up on my computer screen. My computer days started long before there was even such a thing as an ad on a computer screen. I intend to keep my screen ad-free forever. But I've had to fight my share of pop-up battles to keep it that way.

Windows XP SP2 adds a new pop-up blocker to Internet Explorer that does a pretty good job of keeping some ads away, while allowing legitimate pop-ups to come through. In this chapter we'll look at that new pop-up blocker, plus some additional weapons you can use in your own pop-up battles.

Blocking Pop-Ups with Internet Explorer

A pop-up ad is any advertisement that appears on your screen in a window. But not all pop-ups are advertisements. Some pop-ups are actually useful. For example, when you come to a Web page that shows a small picture of an item and an option to see a larger view, the larger view might be displayed in a pop-up window.

Some Web page links are intentionally written to bring up an entire service in a new, separate browser window. For example, I can check my e-mail through Outlook or through my Web browser. When I go through my Web browser and click on e-mail on the home page, the whole e-mail portion of the site comes up in a separate window, which would be blocked as a pop-up.

So, you often have to deal with pop-ups on a case-by-case basis. The new pop-up blocker in Internet Explorer and XP Service Pack 2 lets you do just that. You can block pop-ups in general, but allow a site to temporarily display pop-ups. Or, you can add a site to a list of excepts so that pop-ups from it are always allowed.

To get started with the Internet Explorer pop-up blocker, you need to make sure that it's turned on, and make some decisions as to how you want it to behave. Here's how:

1. Start Internet Explorer as you normally would.

2. Choose **Tools** ⇨ **Internet Options** from Internet Explorer's menu bar.

3. Click the **Privacy** tab in the Internet Options dialog box.

4. Select (check) the **Block pop-ups** checkbox as shown in Figure 29-1.

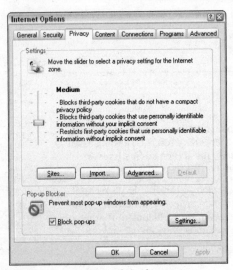

Figure 29-1: Privacy tab in the Internet
Options dialog box

5. Optionally, click the **Settings** button to see the Pop-up Blocker Settings dialog box
shown in Figure 29-2.

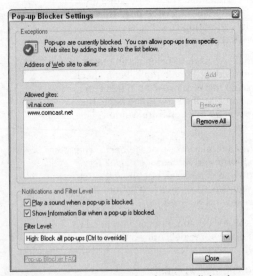

Figure 29-2: Pop-up Blocker Settings dialog box

The Exceptions area near the top of the dialog box is where you list sites from which you will allow pop-up ads. But it's not necessary to manually add sites to the list right there. You can add them automatically on a case-by-case basis while you're browsing, as I'll discuss in upcoming paragraphs.

The Notifications and Filter Level options near the bottom of the dialog box are self-explanatory. The first option, if selected, plays a tiny chirping sound whenever Internet Explorer blocks a pop-up window, just to call your attention to the fact that something has been blocked. The second option, if selected, ensures that the Information bar, which you'll see shortly, appears whenever a pop-up is blocked.

The Filter Level option determines how aggressively the pop-up blocker does its things. Your options are:

✦ **Low: Allow pop-ups from secure sites:** Allows pop-up windows from any secure (`https:///`) site.

✦ **Medium: Block most automatic pop-ups:** Allows pop-ups triggered by a link you clicked, but stops pop-ups triggered by code within a Web page.

✦ **High: Block all pop-ups (Ctrl to override):** Blocks all pop-ups from all sites, unless you hold down the Ctrl key while the page is opening. However, it's not even necessary to hold down the Ctrl key if you choose *Show Information Bar when pop-up is blocked*, because that bar will allow you to temporarily allow pop-ups from the page.

Given my own zero-tolerance attitude toward ads, I went straight for the High setting. But you, of course, can choose any setting you want. Click the Pop-up Blocker FAQ links at the bottom of the dialog box for more information on how the settings work. After choosing your settings, click OK in each of the open dialog boxes.

Letting good pop-ups through

If you chose settings similar to those shown back in Figures 29-1 and 29-2, this is how the pop-up blocker works. When you're at a Web page and click a link, and a pop-up window tries to open, you see the dialog box and Information bar (just under the Address bar) in Figure 29-3.

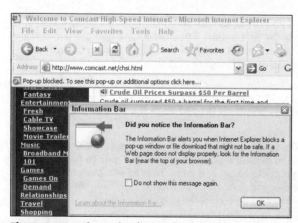

Figure 29-3: Information bar under the Address bar

The dialog box is just there to call your attention to the fact that the Information bar is there. Once you get the hang of how it all works, you can choose the *Don't show this message again* option in the dialog box to make that message stop appearing. Microsoft only put that dialog box there because in testing, not many people noticed the Information bar when it first appeared and didn't know what to do.

When you click OK in the dialog box, the Information bar remains visible. If you don't want to do anything, just leave the pop-up blocked; you can ignore the Information bar and just go about your business. But if the pop-up was something good, such as a larger image of a picture or a valid Web page opening in a separate browser window, then you can click the Information bar to see the options shown in Figure 29-4 and summarized next.

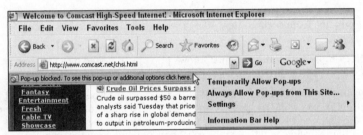

Figure 29-4: Clicking the Information bar

- ✦ **Temporarily Allow Pop-ups:** Choose this option if you want to see pop-ups for this page visit only. You can test the waters in this manner to see if the pop-up really is something you need to see before you choose the next option.

- ✦ **Always Allow Pop-Ups from This Site:** Choose this option if you've determined that pop-ups from this site are always acceptable to you. You'll be asked for confirmation. Just click Yes. Doing so will add the site to the list of exceptions in the Pop-up Blocker Settings dialog box shown earlier.

- ✦ **Settings and Information Bar Help:** Provides another route to the options and FAQs shown in the Pop-up Blocker Settings dialog box.

So, the bottom line here is that if you're not so sure about the pop-ups being blocked, and just want take a peek, you choose the first option. If you determine that the pop-ups are just a normal part of the site's operation, and not a bunch of dumb ads, then you can choose Always Allow Pop-Ups from this site on some future visit.

Even if you choose *Always Allow Pop-Ups . . .*, you're not making any big commitment. You can always go back to the Pop-up Blocker Settings dialog box, click the name of the site, and then click Remove to remove it from the exceptions list and make it a normal pop-up blocked site again.

After you've made your selection, you'll likely need to click the sample link that triggered the Information bar in the first place to make the pop-up appear. That gets to be a bit of a pain after a while because it takes four clicks to get to a page. That is, you have to click the original link, then click the OK in the *Did you notice the Information Bar?* box, then click the Information bar and make a choice, and then click the original link again.

But as I said earlier, once you get the hang of it you can choose the *Do not show this message again* option to get the dialog box out of the way, and just work from the Information bar. Once you've chosen to Always Allow Pop-ups from This Site, the site will work normally and you won't have do to any extra clicks to see the page to which the link refers.

Streamlining the pop-up blocker

Once you've really gotten a feel for how the Internet Explorer pop-up blocker works, you may want to get rid of the little chirping sound and the Information bar. After you've done so, the only hint you'll get when something has been blocked is a page with a No symbol through it in Internet Explorer's status bar.

Tip If there is no status bar at the bottom of your Internet Explorer browser window, choose View ➪ Status Bar from the menu bar in Internet Explorer.

You can still click that little icon for options, just as you would the Information bar, as shown in Figure 29-5. This is really the way to go after you've determined which sites you're willing to accept pop-ups from, because it really keeps the pop-ups out of your attention sphere altogether: No chirps, no dialog box, no Information bar.

Figure 29-5: Status bar indicator when a pop-up has been blocked

You just have to remember that when you click a link at some new site and nothing opens, the tiny status bar icon is the place to go to decide what you want to do about it.

Using other pop-up blockers

You might have noticed that I have the Google toolbar showing next to the Address bar in some of the above figures. I mainly use that for quick Google searches right from the toolbar. But I have its pop-up blocker turned on as well. I haven't noticed any problems at all with having both the Internet Explorer and Google pop-up blockers working at the same time.

Note To get a copy of the Google toolbar, or learn more about, visit `http://toolbar.google.com`.

Blocking Flash and Multimedia Ads

Internet Explorer's pop-up blocker can't block multimedia or Macromedia Flash pop-ups, which are some of the most irritating pop-ups going. You can recognize them by the fact that some play music, some are animated, and some have transparent backgrounds that almost make them look like they're right on the page you're viewing. You really have to look around for the tiny Close button to close these dreadful things.

Supposedly you can right-click these ads and block them by clicking the button at the bottom left of the Macromedia Flash Player Settings dialog box that opens, and choosing Deny, as in Figure 29-6. But, every time you block one a new one seems to come along, and that method just wasn't supporting my zero-tolerance attitude toward these things.

Figure 29-6: Lame settings for disabling Macromedia Flash ads

As I was investigating better ways to deal with a problem, I came across a free program that seemed to solve the problem for me. It's called No Flash, and it just sits in your Notification area and minds its own business most the time. I was so impressed I paid the $9.95 registration fee to get the extended features. (It blocks many types of adware and shareware too.) You can download No Flash from `http://noflash.bbshare.com`. If you hate ads as much as I do, you won't mind parting with the 10 bucks.

Blocking Messenger Pop-Ups

When Microsoft first released Windows XP, they left the Alerter service open. That service is normally used to send message between computers in a local network. But of course someone found a way to exploit it from the Internet and use it to display pop-up ads. That service has since been turned off in Service Pack 2. But it's possible that some new work or virus could reach in and turn it back on.

You can recognize those types of ads by their text-only appearance (no fonts or pictures) and the words Messenger Service or Windows Messenger in the title bar, like the example shown in Figure 29-7.

Caution The Messenger Service Ads have nothing to do with .NET Passport, Windows Messenger, or MSN Messenger. Terminating your .NET Passport will not stop the Messenger Service ads.

By the way, every single word in that ad is a complete lie. Any time you see a threatening pop-up ad like that, you should ignore it and close it. Your computer is not exposing personal information to the Internet, it is not broadcasting its IP address to the world so that people can break into your computer, or doing anything else in these bogus ads that these companies try to scare you into believing. Never believe anything you read in an ad. Never buy anything from any ad, under any circumstances.

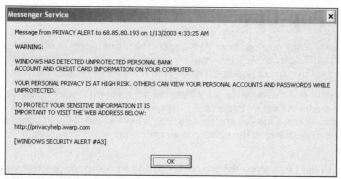

Figure 29-7: Sample Messenger Service ad (every word in this ad is a lie)

To stop the Messenger Service ads, carefully follow the steps below (you can't be sloppy here; be sure to follow the instructions to a tee):

1. Click the **Start** button and choose **Run** or press ⊞+R.

2. Type services.msc and click **OK**. The Services window opens.

3. In the Services program that opens, scroll down to **Messenger**.

4. Right-click on **Messenger** as shown in Figure 29-8, and choose **Stop**.

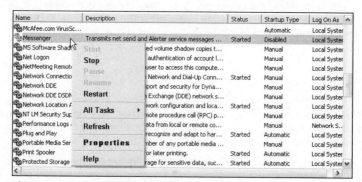

Figure 29-8: Stopping the Messenger service

5. Double-click the word **Messenger** to open the Messenger Properties dialog box.

6. In that dialog box, choose **Disabled** from the Startup type: drop-down list.

7. Click the **OK** button to close the dialog box.

8. Close the Services window by clicking its **Close** button or by choosing **File** ➪ **Exit** from its menu bar.

And that will be the end of those Messenger pop-ups.

Blocking Other Pop-Ups

Internet Explorer can only block pop-ups from Web pages. There are plenty of other sources from which pop-up ads can originate. Any time you download any free *ad-supported* software, you're opening yourself up to a ton of pop-ups that no Web browser or toolbar can block.

The best thing to do would be to remove the ad-supported program from your PC altogether, using Add/Remove Programs in Control Panel (see Chapter 48). Then, see if you can find an equivalent program with no ads. Chances are, though, you'll have to pay for that version. So, really, it's up to you to decide between the lesser of two evils. Part with the money, or put up with the ads.

The only other choice would be to scour the Web to try to find a pop-up blocker that works with that ad-supported software. But since most pop-up blockers work with specific Web browsers such as Internet Explorer or Mozilla (Netscape Navigator), it may take a while to find something that actually does the job.

If your ISP is sending the pop-ups (the kind with the microscopically small No Thanks button comes to mind), the best thing you can do is terminate your account with them and get a real ISP. Any ISP that has the audacity to charge money for their service *and* force pop-up ads on you doesn't deserve your business anyway. So, it would serve them right.

There are lots of cute freebies, including toolbars, that you can download from the Internet. And they seem innocent enough while sitting on your screen or in some program window. But they may be bring in pop-up ads that normal Web browser pop-up blockers can't prevent. Your best bet would be to get rid of those through Add/Remove Programs in Control Panel.

Last, but not least, are hidden adware programs. For these, there is nothing on the screen nor anything in Add/Remove Programs to delete to get rid of the pop-up ads. For those, you'll need some adware and spyware removal tools discussed in the next chapter.

Wrap Up

If you like ads, you're gonna love the Internet. If you don't like ads, you're gonna have to take some action to keep them away. This chapter has focused primary on blocking pop-up ads from the Web and Microsoft Internet Explorer, the Web browser that comes with Windows XP. Major points covered include:

✦ Windows XP Service Pack 2 added a new pop-up blocker to Internet Explorer.

✦ To configure the Internet Explorer pop-up blocker, choose Tools ➪ Internet Options from Internet Explorer's menu bar, and click the Privacy tab.

✦ As you grow accustomed to the Internet Explorer pop-up blocker, you can do away with the dialog box, Information bar, and sound effects to streamline your Web browsing while still blocking pop-ups.

✦ Internet Explorer's pop-up blocker won't block Flash or multimedia ads. You'll need some other product to get rid of those.

✦ Messenger Service pop-ups have nothing to do with MSN Messenger. Those you can disable through the Windows XP Services snap-in tool.

✦ Browser pop-up blockers can't block pop-ups from ad-supported software. With those programs, you either have to put up with the ads, buy the non-ad-supported version of the product, or try to find a pop-up blocker that will work with that product.

✦ Some programs and toolbars you download for free will put pop-ups on your screen. To get rid of those, you may have to uninstall the program or toolbar through Add/Remove Programs in Control Panel.

✦ Still other ads may be controlled by adware, which you can only get rid of with appropriate adware and spyware removal tools.

✦　　✦　　✦

Dealing with Adware and Spyware

Adware and spyware are more forms of malware that can infect your computer. Adware consists of programs that display pop-ups on your screen and other forms of advertising. Spyware is software that gathers information about your browsing habits, and perhaps information about your computer, and sends it to some company without your knowing about it.

Subcategories of adware and sypware include *hijackers*, which redirect your Web browser to some unexpected Web site when you mistype a URL. *Dialers* are programs that dial you're phone when you don't expect it. *Keyloggers* are programs that record your keystrokes. This chapter is about finding and destroying such things.

Avoiding Adware and Spyware with Internet Explorer

Adware and spyware are forms of malware that can be difficult to detect, and difficult to remove. All of the protection and removal tools described in Chapters 26 through 29 — firewalls, security patches, antivirus software, and pop-up blockers — can help keep these things to a minimum. But there are some tools and techniques you can use to further reduce their invasions and to get rid of them after the fact.

Adjusting your cookie settings

Cookies can play a role in adware and spyware infections. Deleting all of your cookies occasionally through the Internet Options dialog box (choose Tools ⇨ Internet Options from Internet Explorer's menu bar) can help. You can also reduce spyware by disallowing third-party cookies by following these steps:

1. From Internet Explorer's menu bar, choose **Tools ⇨ Internet Options**.

2. Click on the **Privacy** tab.

3. Click on the **Advanced** button.

4. Choose **Override automatic cookie handling**.

5. Under **First-party cookies** choose **Accept**.

6. Under **Third-party cookies** choose **Block**.

7. Select the **Always allow session cookies** option as shown in Figure 30-1.

8. Click **OK**.

Figure 30-1: Advanced Privacy Settings dialog box

Disable mysterious add-ons

The Programs tab in the Internet Options dialog box includes a Manage Add-ons button that you can click to see what items are currently enabled and disabled as in Figure 30-2. The Show option at the top of the dialog box lets you choose between two categories of Add-ons, Add-ons that currently loaded in Internet Explorer, and a more complete list of add-ons.

Figure 30-2: Manage Add-ons dialog box

Unfortunately, you can't enlarge the Manage Add-ons window to make all the columns wider, but you can widen or narrow any column by dragging the bar at the right edge of the column heading. Many (but not all) adware add-ons give themselves away in the Publisher column by showing the word "ad" or "advertising" in the Publisher column. As always, you can click any column heading to sort by that column.

Caution   Some add-ins are good, and even required. If you have trouble reaching a specific Web site after disabling an add-in, go back and reenable that add-in by clicking its name and choosing Enable. Always close and reopen Internet Explorer after enabling an add-in.

To disable a suspicious add-in, click its name and choose Disable from the Settings area down below in the dialog box. For example, in Figure 30-2 you can see where I've disabled some eXact Advertising add-ons to prevent them from working in Internet Explorer. Click OK after making any changes. Then, close and restart Internet Explorer to make the settings take effect.

Unfortunately, some of these adware things have remarkable self-preservation capabilities and will soon reenable themselves. But if the item has an icon in Add or Remove Icons, you can remove it after you click OK and close Internet Explorer, but before you restart Internet Explorer. More on that in the next section.

Delete undesired toolbars and the like

Some optional toolbars, especially ones that seem to have appeared on their own with no effort on your part, double as adware and spyware tools behind the scenes. To see a quick list of all your installed toolbars, choose View ⇨ Toolbars from Internet Explorer's menu bar.

Obviously, you don't want to get rid of any built-in toolbars such as the Address bar Standard Buttons. Nor do you want to get rid of any toolbars you've intentionally downloaded and trust, such as the Google toolbar. But chances are that any "mystery" toolbars you never intended to download are best taken off your computer.

Fortunately, most toolbars have entries in Add or Remove Programs. So, you can just delete the toolbar as you would any other program. See Chapter 48 for details.

Caution   Don't delete things at random in Add or Remove Programs. If you're a newbie and not yet familiar with the names of all the programs on your computer, don't delete a program just because you don't recognize its name.

Rerouting adware

Here's a little trick that you can use to frustrate any pop-ups you can't block through the pop-up blocker or easily get rid of through some other means. If you see the URL in the title bar of any pop-up ad, you can reroute that URL to refer to your own computer. You may still get a pop-up ad window from time to time. But rather than an ad you'll see a *Page not found* error in the window. Not great, but at least it prevents the server at the other end from getting any information from your PC.

The trick is to locate your HOSTS file, which is typically stored in C:\WINDOWS\System32\ drivers\etc. But it could be under C:\WINNT or just about any folder really. You have to make sure you locate the HOSTS file (with no filename extension). Disable the *Hide extensions for known file types* option in Folder Options to make sure you don't get the wrong HOSTS file.

Note   See "Folder Options View tab" in Chapter 12 for more information on changing settings on the View tab in Folder options. If you have trouble finding your HOSTS file, try the Search Companion described in Chapter 17. Use the *All Files and Folders* option, and the *Search system folders*, *Search hidden files and folders*, and *Search subfolders* advanced search options.

When you locate the icon for the folder, right-click it and choose Open. Because it doesn't have an extension, you'll get an Open With dialog box. Choose Notepad (not WordPad or anything else—it most be Notepad) and click OK.

Caution   There is zero margin for error when you're messing with things at this level. If you're not the technical type, don't do this. Don't guess, experiment, play around, or anything else here.

When the HOSTS file is open, you'll see many comments (lines that start with a # symbol), probably followed by a single line that reads:

```
127.0.0.1 localhost
```

That's called the *loopback address* because it makes the IP address 127.0.0.1 refer to your own computer. To make an advertiser's URL loop back to your own computer, add another line that reads:

```
127.0.0.1 <tab>    URL
```

where *<tab>* indicates that you press the Tab key, and *URL* is the advertiser's URL. Figure 30-3 shows a file where I've added a bunch of examples.

```
hosts - Notepad
File  Edit  Format  View  Help
# Copyright (c) 1993-1999 Microsoft Corp.
#
# This is a sample HOSTS file used by Microsoft TCP/IP for windows.
#
# This file contains the mappings of IP addresses to host names. Each
# entry should be kept on an individual line. The IP address should
# be placed in the first column followed by the corresponding host name.
# The IP address and the host name should be separated by at least one
# space.
#
# Additionally, comments (such as these) may be inserted on individual
# lines or following the machine name denoted by a '#' symbol.
#
# For example:
#
#      102.54.94.97     rhino.acme.com          # source server
#       38.25.63.10     x.acme.com              # x client host

127.0.0.1       localhost
127.0.0.1       www.igetnet.com
127.0.0.1       code.ignphrases.com
127.0.0.1       clear-search.com
127.0.0.1       r1.clrsch.com
127.0.0.1       sds.clrsch.com
127.0.0.1       status.clrsch.com
127.0.0.1       www.clrsch.com
127.0.0.1       sds-qckads.com
127.0.0.1       status.qckads.com
127.0.0.1       ads.flashtrack.net
```

Figure 30-3: Sample HOSTS file with extra advertiser's URLs looped back

If you end up with any unexpected, unpleasant side effects after you close and save the file and reboot, you may have to go back and remove or comment out the offending line (another reason why newbies should avoid trying this trick). Hopefully, you won't have to take this

Let's Sue 'em

Personally, I find it outrageous that I should have to spend 1 minute of my time finding, and getting rid of, any adware or spyware. My PC and hard drive are my personal private property. I'm no lawyer, but I don't see where anybody, anywhere has the right to change, compromise, or damage my personal property without my consent.

If there are any lawyers out there who want to sue these jerks for invading our privacy, messing with our personal property, and wasting our time, I'll be more than happy to contribute as an expert witness. And bring a small army of other experts with me. After all, I don't have the right to spray paint their furniture or carve my initials in their cars. So, I don't see where they get off doing *anything* to my hard drive, or taking time away from my work by forcing me to ferret out their useless junk and idiotic ads.

Make sure that you contact me through my Web site at `www.coolnerds.com` so my spam filter doesn't trash your e-mail message.

measure, especially if you can get one of the third-party removal tools described later in this chapter to remove the offending *parasite* (another generic term for adware and spyware).

Using Third-Party Tools

There are many third-party tools you can use to eliminate, and perhaps block, adware and spyware. Some are free; some aren't. Some are relatively easy to learn and use; some are for experts only. Here, I'll describe three of the more popular products. Unfortunately, the people putting these dreadful things out on the Internet seem to come up with ever-better ways to add *stealth* and *self-preservation* to their wares (meaning that they're difficult to find, and difficult to get rid of), so even the third-part tools don't always work. But you should at least be aware that such products exist.

Lavasoft Ad-Aware

One of the most popular adware removal tools out there is Lavasoft's Ad-Aware. You can download and install the SE version for free from popular download sites such as `www.download.com`, `www.tucows.com`, or the manufacturer's site at `www.lavasoft.de`. Ad-Aware is easy for anyone to use, and never seems to have any unpleasant side effects that need to be tweaked later.

Using the program is easy. After you've downloaded and installed it, you start it from the All Programs menu. The program is like a wizard in that you read the instructions on each page and click Next to move on to the next page. After it scans your drive, you'll see a list of tracking cookies and other unpleasant things, each with a checkbox to the left.

You have quite a few options as to how you can handle these things. I always right-click and choose Select All Objects (see Figure 30-4). Then, click Next and let Ad-Aware delete them all. It may be somewhat risky to do that without taking a close look at all the found objects. However, I've never had any problems using that approach, so I think it's safe to say the risks are minimal.

Lavasoft has more advanced products, including adware blockers you can purchase and install. Whether or not you want to pursue those is a decision you have to make for yourself. Given that the free version is so easy to use and that I've never had any unpleasant side effects from letting Ad-Aware delete everything it finds, I'd think everyone should at least get the free version and run it once in a while to get rid of the more common and more easily removed adware parasites.

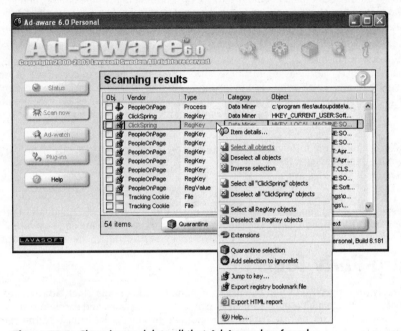

Figure 30-4: Choosing to delete all that Ad-Aware has found

Aluria Spyware Eliminator

Aluria Spyware Eliminator is another popular product. As the name suggests, its focus is on spyware. The program is remarkably thorough, though not exactly a tool for newbies. It's so aggressive in its removal of spyware that sometimes you end up with unpleasant side effects that only a more experienced user can deal with.

There is no "free" version of Aluria Spyware Eliminator to download, other than a version that scans your drive and lists what it has found. But unlike the freebie Ad-Aware program, Aluria's freebie version won't actually eliminate the items it has found. For more information, visit Aulria's Web site at www.aluriaSoftware.com.

Hijack This

Hijkack This is a free program that will seek and destroy browser hijackers — programs that redirect your Web browser to search engines when you enter an invalid URL and so forth. It'll find other malware along the way, including Browser Helper Object (HBOs), which can also be forms of malware.

There is a catch, though. It's very much a tool for experts. Hijack This won't discriminate between "good things" and "bad things" for you. So, you have to be able to make that distinction yourself. But it sure is a quick way to find out what files (and registry keys) you have.

To learn more about Hijack This (and download it, if you feel qualified) and lots of other anti-adware and anti-spyware products, check out www.spywareinfo.com. The Software button (if it's still there by the time you read this) lists a bunch of software recommendations, including Hijack This.

Manually Removing Adware and Spyware

As briefly mentioned earlier in this chapter, many adware and spyware products have truly remarkable stealth and self-preservation capabilities. Once you know the filename of an adware or spyware parasite, you can often do a Google search on that name to find removal instructions. But even the removal instructions don't always work, because the people putting these things out there can always change their strategy to compromise published removal instructions.

Note   The people who put these things out there *should* post removal instructions on their own sites, but rarely do. Personally, I think that should be considered some sort of crime.

Deleting from Safe mode

If you're an experienced power user, and you know the location and filename of the parasite, you can often get rid it by clearing out all related registry keys and removing the file and folder in Safe mode. For example, a while ago someone asked me to get rid of a parasite named tvm.exe that their antivirus program found but could not remove. I was able to ascertain that the offending file was C:\Program Files\TV Media\tvm.exe, but couldn't delete it through the normal means.

Caution   All the material from this point on is definitely "power-user-only" stuff. Newbies should not attempt any of this under any circumstances. Be aware that if you choose not to heed this warning, and get yourself in a pickle, it's unlikely that anybody anywhere (including me) will be able to help via the phone or e-mail.

So using tvm.exe as an example, you'd open and backup (export) the registry, and then search the entire registry for all references to *tvm*. This part takes some judgment, and that's why newbies don't want to attempt this approach. But as it turned out in my example, there wasn't anything in the registry containing "tvm" that was useful, so I ended up deleting every key that contained those letters.

The next step is to close regedit and restart the computer in Safe mode, which is to say, you restart the computer and tap the F8 key before Windows starts so that you can get to the alternative startup options. I generally choose Safe Mode with Command Prompt, and log in as Administrator.

At the command prompt, use the cd, rd, and del commands to remove the parasite and its folder. For example to get rid of all the files in C:\Program Files\TV Media and the entire folder, I entered the following series of commands:

```
cd \progra~1\tvmedi~1
del *.* /f
cd..
rd tvmedi~1
exit
```

That gets rid of the files and folder and gets you to a point where you can press Ctrl+Alt+Del to pop open Task Manager. From Task Manager's menu bar, choose Shut Down ⇨ Turn off, and shut down the computer. Then, restart and pray.

Amazingly, some parasites will resist even this all-out counterattack, preventing you from deleting all the files in the folder with "Access denied" messages. I've occasionally had to boot to the Recovery Console from the Windows XP CD and delete from its command prompt, as discussed next.

Deleting from Recovery Console

Recovery Console is a feature of the original Windows XP CD. To use it, you need to be able to boot from the Windows XP CD. Doing so may require adjusting your BIOS settings to make sure that the CD drive is listed before the hard drive as a boot device. Then, put your original Windows XP CD into the CD drive, restart the system, and tap the spacebar as soon as you see the *Press any key to boot from CD* prompt.

Windows Setup will go through an elaborate process of loading files. However, it's not making any changes to your system at that time. It's just booting up. Eventually, you're taken to a screen where the second option is:

```
  To repair a Windows XP installation using Recovery Console, press R.
```

You tap the R key, and the next prompt asks which Windows installation you want to log on to. You must type a number here (typically 1) and press Enter. The next prompt asks for the administrator password. If you don't have one, just press Enter. Finally, you come to a C:\WINDOWS> prompt.

Next, you need to use the cd command to get to the folder that contains the file(s) you need to get rid of. For example, let's say that the file is in C:\Windows\System32. You type the following command and press Enter:

```
cd \windows\systeme32
```

The prompt changes to match the current folder. Next, you have to make sure that the file isn't read-only. Use the attrib command with the -R switch for that. For example, let's say that the name of the file is BackDoor.dll. You would enter the command:

```
attrib -r backdoor.dll
```

You don't get any feedback from that one — just a brief delay before the command prompt reappears. Finally, you can delete the file using the Erase or Del command. In this example, you would type the following and then press Enter:

```
del backdoor.dll
```

That should get rid of the file. To finish up, type the following command and press Enter:

```
exit
```

You can remove the CD from the drive after the machine starts booting up and boot into Windows normally.

For more information on using Recovery Console, search Microsoft's Support site (http://support.microsoft.com) for XP Recovery Console or search the Knowledge Base for article Q314058.

Wrap Up

Just when you thought it was safe to go online, there's still a lot of bad stuff out there that's not easy to find, and not easy to get rid of. To summarize the things that can help:

✦ Blocking third-party cookies in Internet Explorer can help prevent many unacceptable cookies from being placed in your Cookies folder.

✦ Many adware products are add-ons that you can disable through the Internet Explorer's Manage Add-ons dialog box.

✦ Some items, which work through optional toolbars, can be removed through Add or Remove Programs in Control Panel.

✦ You can loop some URLs back to your own PC via the HOSTS file.

✦ Third-party adware and spyware tools are probably your best bet for eliminating most adware, spyware, and browser hijackers.

✦ Advanced power users can disable most products via registry settings and by deleting files and folders in Safe mode.

✦   ✦   ✦

Troubleshooting Security

Troubleshooting Your Internet Connection

Getting your Internet connection to work usually involves following the instructions provided by your ISP. Likewise, you might need to contact them for troubleshooting help with their service. But here are a couple of general techniques you can try first to see if either will provide a quick fix.

First aid for Internet connection problems

As a first step to troubleshooting an Internet connection, try the Modem Troubleshooter by following these steps:

1. Click the **Start** button, and choose **Help and Support**.

2. In the Search box type troubleshooters, and press Enter.

3. Under Suggested Topics, click on **Modem Troubleshooter**.

The troubleshooter will take you step by step through the troubleshooting process. Answer any questions that appear and click Next> at the bottom of the page.

Keep in mind that neither the Internet nor your Internet connection is a Windows XP thing, per se. There are hundreds (if not thousands) of ISPs in the world, each providing its own service. Your best bet for troubleshooting an Internet connection will always be your ISP, because they know their own system better than anyone.

Can't connect with Internet Explorer

If you can get online, in general, but can't get online to browse the Web with Microsoft Internet Explorer, first try getting online in the usual manner, and leave your Web browser open on the desktop.

Then, click Start, choose All Programs ⇨ Internet Explorer, and see if Internet Explorer can get online while your other Web browser is still online.

1. Click **Start**, and choose **All Programs ⇨ Internet Explorer**. Ignore the *Page not found* message, or whatever else, appears in the main pane for now.

2. Choose **Tools ⇨ Internet Options** from the Internet Explorer menu bar.

3. In the Internet Options dialog box, click the **Connections** tab.

4. If the options under *Choose Settings if you need to configure a proxy server for a connection* are enabled, choose options as follows:

   • **Never dial a connection:** Choose this option only if you connect without a dial-up modem and don't even have a dial-up modem.

   • **Dial whenever a network connection is not present:** Choose this option if you have a dial-up account only, or if you have both a broadband account and a dial-up account you use as a backup.

   • **Always dial my default connection:** Choose this option only if you have set up a default account for dialing into the Internet, and the name of that account appears next to Current below this option.

   • **Set Default:** Click this button, and then click the name of the ISP you always use to connect to the Internet.

5. Click **OK**.

Troubleshooting Firewall Problems

The Windows Firewall that comes with Service Pack 2 really battens down the hatches on ports. So, you may experience a few problems when you first make the switch to Windows Firewall. Here are some common problems and solutions to those problems.

Some Internet programs stop working after installing Service Pack 2

The tighter security imposed by Windows Firewall may prevent some online games and other Internet programs from working correctly. Microsoft maintains a list of such programs and ways to correct the problem in Knowledge Base article 842242. To get to that page, browse to http://support.microsoft.com and search for 842242. Optionally, you can browse directly to: http://support.microsoft.com/default.aspx?scid=kb;en-us;842242&Product=windowsxpsp2

Error message "Windows Firewall has blocked this program from accepting connections"

The message is actually just an alert. Assuming that you're familiar with the FTP site and trust its owners, you can choose Unblock and proceed with uploading the file(s).

Can't adjust Windows Firewall for AOL dial-up connection

AOL doesn't follow the same standard that other ISPs do, so you may have to disable the firewall to access America Online. (That's risky business, and you may want to consider contacting AOL about a better workaround, or consider switching to a different ISP.) To get to Windows Firewall without going through the standard means:

1. If you're currently online, disconnect from the Internet.

2. Click the **Start** button and choose **Run**, or press ⊞+R.

3. In the Run dialog box type `firewall.cpl` and press Enter or click **OK**.

4. If you need to disable the Windows Firewall, choose **Off (not recommended)**, and then click **OK**.

Phone dialer stops working after installing SP2

Windows Firewall blocks TCP port 1720, which is used by many phone-dialing programs. It does so to prevent unauthorized dialing programs from connecting to a network without your knowledge. To get your phone dialer to work, you'll need to open that port as follows:

1. Click the **Start** button, and choose **All Programs** ➪ **Accessories** ➪ **System Tools** ➪ **Security Center**.

2. Under Manage security settings for: click on **Windows Firewall**.

3. If the *Don't allow exceptions* option is checked, clear that check mark.

4. Click on the **Exceptions** tab.

5. Click the **Add Port** button.

6. Type any name you like in the Name box. Type 1720 as the port number, and choose **TCP**.

7. Click **OK** in each open dialog box.

8. Close the Security Center.

Caution   Opening port 1720 allows all dialers to dial out through that connection, even unauthorized programs you might pick up accidentally from the Internet. To block that port, return to the Exceptions tab of the dialog box and clear the check mark to the left of the name you provided in Step 6 of the preceding set of steps.

Troubleshooting Automatic Updates

Automatic Updates have changed several times since Windows XP was first released, and there are quite a few things that can go wrong. This section covers some of the more common problems and resources for dealing with specific problems online.

Can't get to, or download from, Windows Update

See "First Aid for Windows Update Failures" in Chapter 27.

Clients in home network don't keep up with automatic updates

See "First Aid for Windows Update Failures" in Chapter 27.

You get an error message with an 0x80 . . . number

Microsoft maintains a list of Windows Update problems and solutions in the Windows Update Web site. To get to the Troubleshooter:

1. Browse to www.windowsupdate.com.

2. In the left column of the page that opens, click on **Help and support**.

3. Click on **Try the Windows Update Troubleshooter**.

4. Scroll down through the list of problems to see if you find your error number. Note that there may be multiple pages of problems by the time you read this. Use the Next> button at the bottom of each page to move to the next page.

When you locate a matching description, click the link and follow the instructions it provides.

Troubleshooting ActiveX Control Downloads

The new Windows Firewall will block ActiveX control downloads. If clicking a link doesn't provide the results you expected, look to Internet Explorer's Information bar for more information. Assuming that you consider the ActiveX control safe, click the bar and choose Install ActiveX control as in Figure 31-1.

Caution   Accept ActiveX controls only from legitimate companies with which you've done business in the past and can trust.

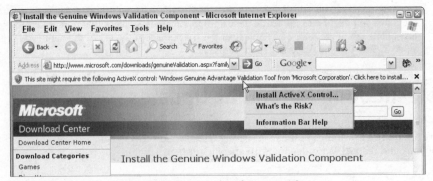

Figure 31-1 Sample blocked ActiveX control and menu options

✦   ✦   ✦

Power Using the Internet

This part is about using the Internet. Chapters 32 and 33 talk about the ever-popular Web and e-mail services, using the Web browser (Internet Explorer) and e-mail client (Outlook Express) that come with Windows XP.

Chapter 34 moves on to real-time communications using .NET Passport and MSN Messenger. Real-time messaging includes typing messages back and forth, talking (like on the phone), and using Web cams so you and the person you're talking to can see each other while talking. You can also use MSN Messenger to transfer files that are too large to attach to e-mail messages.

Chapter 35 discusses the FTP (File Transfer Protocol), which allows you to upload and download files with Internet FTP servers and Internet Explorer. This chapter also describes how to use Outlook Express to participate in Usenet newsgroups.

Browsing the Web with Internet Explorer

Virtually all human knowledge is on the World Wide Web. No matter what the question, the answer is out there on one of the eight or nine billion Web pages available 24/7. My kids take this for granted. When they need to know something, they fire up a Web browser and go find out whatever it is they need to know.

It doesn't matter if the question is, "What's playing at the local movie theater and what are the show times?" or "What microorganism was responsible for the Black Plague and what are its genetic characteristics?" My kids know where the answer lies, and they know how to get it. To them, that's just the way it is and the way it has always has been. No biggie.

Those of us who grew up in pre-Internet days don't think that way. We still find it difficult to believe that *all* factual answers to *all* factual questions are out there on the Web. But over the years I've come to accept that my kids are right. When you have a question, the answer is out there, somewhere, on the Web. You just have to know where to look, how to look, and what to look for.

How the Web Works

As mentioned in the previous chapter, the Internet consists of tens of millions computers throughout the world connected by cables. A few million of those computers are *Web servers*, computers that store, and dish out, copies to Web pages to anyone who asks for a copy.

All Web pages use the Hypertext Transfer Protocol, abbreviated HTTP. For that reason, the "official" URL for every Web page starts with http://. But because so many Web sites use www (for World Wide Web) as their *host name*, the http:// part is often omitted and assumed. Often you see the URL for Web site expressed without the http:// part, as in www.microsoft.com. The part of the URL after the http:// is expressed in the format

hostname.domain.tld

The *hostname* corresponds to a specific computer in a *domain* (group) of computers. The *TLD* is the *top-level domain.* The top level domain describes the "type" of site. The most common TLDs are listed in Table 32-1.

Table 32-1: Examples of Top-Level Domains and URLs of Web Sites

Top-Level Domain (TLD)	Type	Example URL
.com	Commercial	www.amazon.com
.edu	Education	www.ucla.edu
.gov	Government	www.fbi.gov
.org	Nonprofit organization	www.redcross.org
.net	Network	www.comcast.net
.mil	Military	www.army.mil

For example, the URL www.microsoft.com refers to a *host* (computer) named www at the domain (computers) owned by Microsoft Corporation. Microsoft is a commercial business, hence the .com TLD.

No two domains can have the same domain, for the same reason that no two telephones can have the same phone number. But anybody, including you, can own a domain name. You just have to find one that's available at a service like www.networksolutions.com, pay your fees, and the domain name is yours.

To use the Web, you need two things: an Internet connection and a Web browser. The latter is a program that lets you access the World Wide Web. There are lots of Web browsers out there, the most common being Microsoft Internet Explorer, America Online, Netscape Navigator, and MSN Explorer. If you've already been browsing the Web, you've probably been using one of those Web browsers.

All Web browsers work the same way. You type a URL into the Address bar and press Enter or click Go. Through a bit of magic known as *name resolution*, that name is translated into a numeric IP address. Your computer then sends out a little packet of information, addressed to the Web server, that says something to the effect of "Please send a copy of your Web page to me at" followed by your IP address.

That packet leaves your computer, goes to your ISP, and your ISP hands it off to the Internet. A fraction of a second later, the Web server gets that packet and hands a copy of the requested Web page off to the Internet, addressed to your ISP. Your ISP's computer gets the Web page a fraction of a second later, and then forwards it to your computer.

How long the page takes to get from your ISP to your computer depends on your bandwidth—the speed of your Internet connection. But eventually, the page does get to your computer where it's stored as a file in your temporary Internet folder and displayed as a document in your Web browser.

 Note   Actually, the Web server sends its Web page out in a zillion tiny little packets, each packet addressed to you. The packets arrive in some random order. But your browser puts them in the right order, so by the time you see the page, it looks like "one thing."

Anyway, as I said, all Web browsers do the same thing. Windows XP comes with two Web browsers. One is Microsoft Internet Explorer, often abbreviated MSIE or IE. The other is MSN Explorer, a watered-down version of IE specifically geared for folks who use MSN (the Microsoft Network) as their ISP. Since IE is the more generic (and powerful) of the two, that will be the focus of this chapter.

Using Microsoft Internet Explorer

As with any program, you have to open (start) Microsoft Internet Explorer to use it. You also have to be online (connected to the Internet), unless Internet Explorer is configured to connect you automatically when it opens. The icon for Internet Explorer is a blue lowercase "e." Figure 32-1 points out the locations where you're likely to find an Internet Explorer icon.

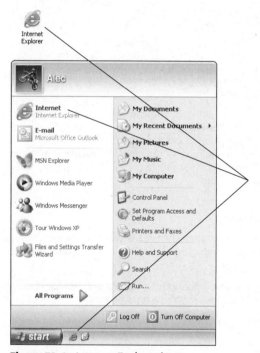

Figure 32-1: Internet Explorer icons

You can start Internet Explorer using whichever of the following techniques work, and are convenient, for you.

✦ Click the **Launch Internet Explorer Browser** button in the Quick Launch toolbar.

✦ Click the **Start** button, and choose **Internet Explorer** from the left side of the Start menu.

✦ Click the **Start** button, and choose **All Programs ⇨ Internet Explorer**.

✦ Double-click (or click) the **Internet Explorer** icon on your desktop.

When Internet Explorer opens, you'll be taken to your *default home page*. That's just the fancy name for the first Web page you see when you open your Web browser. As we'll discuss later in this chapter, you can choose any page you like as your default home page.

Tip

You can move and size Internet Explorer's program window as you would any other. When open, Internet Explorer will also have a taskbar button.

Getting to a Web Site

To get to a Web site, you type its URL into Internet Explorer's Address bar. When you click the URL that's already in the Address bar, that URL is automatically *selected* (highlighted), as in the example shown in Figure 32-2.

Figure 32-2: URL selected in Internet Explorer's menu bar

Any new text you type will automatically replace the selected text. So it's not necessary to press Backspace or Delete before typing a new URL.

It's also not necessary to retype each URL from scratch. You can use all the standard text editing technique to change only a portion of the current URL. For example, if the current URL is `http://www.microsoft.com` and you want to change that to `http://www.google.com`, you can just select (drag the mouse pointer through) the word *microsoft* so only that portion of the URL is selected. Then type `google` to change just that part. Then press Enter or click the Go button to go to the site.

Using AutoComplete

Internet Explorer will remember URLs you've typed in the past. When the URL you're typing now matches ones you've typed in the past, a *history menu* will drop down, showing those previous URLs. When that happens, you can:

✦ Ignore the menu and keep typing. Each new character you type will reduce the number of items in the menu to those that match what you've typed so far.

✦ Click any URL in the history menu to put it into the Address bar.

✦ Point to an item in the history menu and press Delete (Del) to delete that item.

You can empty the history menu at any time by clicking the Clear History button in Internet Explorer's Internet Options dialog box, as discussed later in this chapter.

The AutoComplete feature is optional. To turn it on or off, choose Tools ➪ Internet Options from Internet Explorer's menu bar. Click the Advanced tab. Under the Browsing category in the list that appears, you can click the checkbox next to Use Inline AutoComplete to turn this feature on (checked) or off (not checked).

Copy and paste a text URL

When somebody sends you a URL via some sort of text message, like certain e-mail messages and discussion boards, the text won't be a hyperlink. That is, it won't be colored or under-lined, and clicking it will do nothing. When that happens, it's not necessary to retype the URL into your browser's Address bar. You can use standard copy and paste to copy it. Here's how:

1. Start with the mouse pointer just outside the URL to copy, and then drag the mouse pointer through the whole URL, and nothing but the URL, as in Figure 32-3.

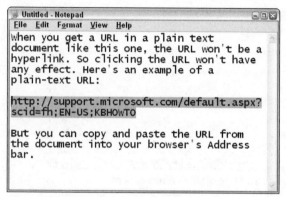

Figure 32-3: Selected URL in a text document

2. Press **Ctrl+C** or right-click the selected text, and choose Copy.

3. In Internet Explorer's Address bar, click to the right of the URL currently in the bar so that the entire URL is selected.

4. Press **Ctrl+V** to paste it. The URL you copied replaces the selected text in the Address bar.

5. Press **Enter** or click the green **Go** button.

You can copy and paste from your Address bar as well. For example, to copy the URL that's currently in your Address bar to an e-mail message, or any other document, click the URL so that the whole URL is selected, and then press Ctrl+C. Click where you want to paste the URL, and then press Ctrl+V or right-click the spot and choose Paste.

Shortcuts to the Web

There are a couple of other ways to get to a Web site besides using Internet Explorer's menu bar. If the Address bar is visible in Windows Explorer, as in the My Documents folder shown in Figure 32-4, you can use it to get to a site. Just replace whatever name currently shows in that Address bar with the site's URL, and then press Enter or click the Go button. To make the Address bar visible in Windows Explorer, choose View ➪ Toolbars ➪ Address Bar from Explorer's menu bar.

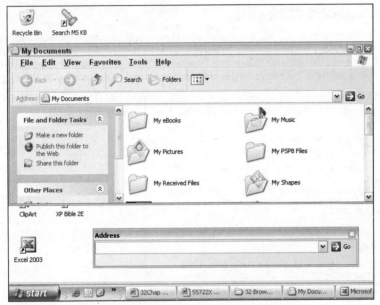

Figure 32-4: Windows Explorer and free-floating Address bars

You can also place an Address bar in your taskbar or let it float freely on the desktop as in Figure 32-4. You can type or paste a URL into that Address bar, and then press Enter or click Go, to get to any Web page.

To create a desktop shortcut to the Web page you're currently viewing, choose File ➪ Send ➪ Shortcut to Desktop from Internet Explorer's menu bar. To revisit the site in the future, click (or double-click) its shortcut icon on the desktop.

Note   See "Optional taskbar toolbars" in Chapter 6 for details on the optional Address bar. See Chanter 16 for more information on shortcuts.

Using Hyperlinks

When you're at a Web site, you may not have to do much more typing of URLs. After you're at a page, you can click any *hyperlink* (also called a *link*) to go to whatever page the link represents. Hyperlink text can be anything—it need not be a URL. But it will most likely be underlined and either blue or magenta. Blue indicates a link to a Web page you've never visited. Magenta identifies pages you've already visited.

A picture, or even a portion of a picture, can be a hyperlink too. You can't tell just by looking whether a picture is a hyperlink or not. You have to point to it. If the mouse pointer changes to a hand, as in any of the examples shown in Figure 32-5, it's a hyperlink. The hand means *click here to go*. If the status bar in your Web browser is turned on, the URL that the hyperlink will take you to appears in the lower-left corner of your browser window, as shown in the same figure.

Mouse pointer on hyperlinks   Status bar

Figure 32-5: Mouse pointer turns to hand on clickable links

When you know that the mouse pointer is touching a hyperlink, you just click (tap the left mouse button) to follow the hyperlink (that is, to go wherever the hyperlink points you). When you get to the new page, you can click the Back button in your Web browser to return to the page you just left. More on the Back button a little later in this chapter.

Internet Explorer's new built-in pop-up blocker will display its Information bar if a link attempts to open its page in a new window. See "Blocking Pop-Ups with Internet Explorer" in Chapter 29 for more information.

Opening a page in a new window

If you want to keep the Web page you're viewing at the moment visible on the screen and also go to a linked page, don't click the hyperlink. Right-click it instead, and choose Open in New Window from the shortcut menu that opens (see Figure 32-6). The Web page will open in a new Internet Explorer browser window, which you can move and size independently of the first.

Figure 32-6: Shortcut menu for a hyperlink

If you open lots of separate Internet Explorer program windows, their taskbar buttons may combine into one button. You can click that one large taskbar button to see a menu of all open Web pages. Click any page in the menu to bring that Web page to the top of the stack.

Other hyperlink tricks

There are quite a few items on the shortcut that opens when you right-click a hyperlink. First, let me point out that in the menu, the word *page* means the Web page you're currently looking at. The word *target* refers to whatever the hyperlink points to.

For example, if clicking the hyperlink displays a video, *target* refers to that video. If clicking the hyperlink takes you to a Web page, *target* refers to the Web page that you'd land at. So, with that in mind, here's what various options in the shortcut menu for a link will offer:

✦ **Open:** Opens the resource that the link refers to. (It's usually another Web page, but it could be a movie, song, picture, or file you download — anything.)

✦ **Save Target As:** Rather than showing you the resource, this option opens the Save As dialog box so that you can download the resource to your own hard disk. (That is, you can download the resource. More on downloading later in this chapter.)

✦ **Print Target:** If the link points to a Web page, clicking this option will print that target page.

✦ **Copy Shortcut:** Creates a shortcut icon to the target resource, which you can then paste to the Windows desktop or into any folder.

✦ **Add to Favorites:** Creates a *favorite* to the target resource. See "Tracking Favorite Web Sites" later in this chapter.

✦ **Properties:** Shows general information about the link, including the URL that the hyperlink points to.

Navigation tools

The Standard toolbar in Internet Explorer, shown in Figure 32-7, provides some handy tools to help with your browsing. Many of the same options are available when you right-click on text (not a link or picture) on the page. Looking at the first few buttons, going from left to right, you have:

Figure 32-7: Standard toolbar in Internet Explorer

✦ **Back:** After you've navigated from one page to another, click the Back button to return to the previous page.

✦ **Forward:** After you've clicked the Back button at least once, click the Forward button to return to the page you just backed out of.

✦ **Stop:** If a page is taking too long to load, or if you think you clicked the wrong link, clicking the Stop button will stop the download and make it easier to navigate to the preceding page or another page.

✦ **Refresh:** Redownloads the current page from the Web server so that you can see recent changes to that page.

✦ **Home:** Takes you to your default home page.

Tip   If the standard buttons aren't visible, choose View ⇨ Toolbars ⇨ Standard Buttons from Internet Explorer's menu bar.

The Back and Forward toolbar buttons each maintain a small drop-down list of pages you've navigated through recently. Click the down-pointing triangle to see that list. To revisit a page, click its name in the list.

The Back and Forward buttons are *session-specific*. A session begins when you first open your Web browser and ends when you close the browser. So, when you first open your browser, both Back and Forward will be disabled, because you haven't been to any other pages yet in this session. But as you navigate around, the Back and Forward buttons will let you easily move among those pages you've visited during the current session.

Clever Bar Tricks

Like most program windows, Internet Explorer offers toolbars, an Explorer bar, a status bar, and a main document window. Here are some optional things you can do to work with those various components:

✦ To display or hide one of the toolbars, choose **View ⇨ Toolbars**, and then either **Standard Buttons**, **Address Bar**, or **Links**.

✦ To display or hide text labels on the Standard Buttons toolbar, choose **View ⇨ Toolbars ⇨ Customize**, and select **Show text labels** from the Text Options drop-down list. Then, click the **Close** button.

✦ To display or hide the status bar, choose **View ⇨ Status Bar**.

✦ To display or hide an Explorer bar, choose **View ⇨ Explorer Bar**, and then choose the Explorer bar you want. (You also can click the **Search**, **Favorites**, or **History** buttons on the Standard Buttons toolbar.)

✦ To display or hide a toolbar quickly, right-click in any visible toolbar, and then click the name of the toolbar you want to show or hide.

✦ To narrow or widen an Explorer bar, move your mouse pointer to the border on the right side of the bar until the pointer changes to a two-headed arrow. Then, drag the border to the left or to the right.

Moving and sizing toolbars

You can reposition the toolbars if you want. To reposition a toolbar, move your mouse to the dotted line at the left side of the toolbar. (If you don't see the dotted line, choose View ⇨ Toolbars, and select Lock the Toolbars to clear its check mark and unlock the bars.) Then, drag the bar up, down, left, or right. (As you drag, the mouse pointer changes to a four-headed arrow.) When the bar pops into place, release the mouse button.

Tip   To prevent the toolbars from being moved accidentally, you can choose View ⇨ Toolbars ⇨ Lock the Toolbars to Reselect that option.

When the toolbars are unlocked, you can also resize them, making them narrower (to show fewer buttons) or wider (to show more buttons). To resize a toolbar, drag the dotted vertical line at the left of the toolbar to the left or to the right. (This line won't appear if the toolbars are locked.) The mouse pointer changes to a two-headed arrow when it's safe to drag. If you want to shrink or expand the toolbar quickly, double-click the vertical line instead.

Using full-screen view

To display a full-screen version of Windows Explorer with no menu bar or title bar, as in Figure 32-8, press the F11 key. There, I've also right-clicked an empty portion of the Standard Buttons toolbar to show the customization options summarized next:

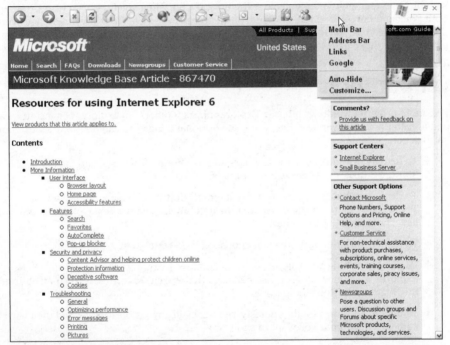

Figure 32-8: IE in full-screen view

> ✦ If you don't see the Standards Button toolbar in full-screen view, move the mouse pointer to the top of the screen to bring it into view.
>
> ✦ To lock the Standard Buttons toolbar into place (or unlock it), right-click an empty area of the bar and choose **Auto-Hide**.
>
> ✦ To show or hide the menu bar or Address bar, right-click a toolbar and choose the bar's name.
>
> ✦ To customize the Standard Buttons toolbar, right-click an empty portion of the toolbar and choose **Customize**.

When you're in full-screen view, you can click the Restore button in the upper-right corner, or press F11, or right-click Internet Explorer's taskbar button and choose Restore to return to the standard program window view.

Printing Web Pages

To print the Web page you're currently viewing, use any of the standard techniques for printing documents. That is, press Ctrl+P, or click the Print button in Internet Explorer's toolbar, or choose File ➪ Print from Internet Explorer's menu bar.

Some Web pages are divided into frames — multiple sections that you can scroll through independently. Some frames might contain ads or a table of contents, or something else you don't particularly want to print. If you want to print the contents of just a single frame within a page, anywhere in the text within that frame first, you can press Ctrl+P or choose File ➪ Print, or right-click the text and choose *Print* to bring up the Print dialog box. When the Print dialog box opens, click its Options tab to reveal the options shown in Figure 32-9.

Figure 32-9: Printing options for frames

To print only the frame you clicked in, choose the Only selected frame option. You could also choose *All frames individually* to ensure that each frame's contents are printed on a separate page.

Be careful of the Print all linked documents option. It prints the current Web page, plus all the Web pages that this page provides links to. It could end up being a heck of a lot of pages if the current page contains a lot of links. As an alternative, you can choose the Print table of links option, which will print just the hyperlinks in the page without printing the actual pages to which those links refer.

Tip

If some text is cut off at the right margin, even after printing individual frames, try narrowing the margins by choosing File ➪ Page Setup from Internet Explorer's menu bar. Set the left and right margins to some small number, such as 0.5.

Revisiting Previous Sites

Internet Explorer keeps track of all the sites you've visited in the current session and previous sessions. As mentioned, when you type a URL into the Address bar, URLs of sites you're recently visited appear in the drop-down menu. You can also view a history of recently visited sites using any method that follows:

✦ Click the **History** button in the toolbar.

✦ Press **Ctrl+H**.

✦ Choose **View** ➪ **Explorer Bar** ➪ **History** from Internet Explorer's menu bar.

Using the History bar

Using the History bar is simple. Links are organized by day. Click any day to show or hide sites (and local folders). Click any day heading to expand or hide the list of sites visited that day. Each folder icon in the list represents a Web site. Click any site's folder icon to see pages you visited at that site. Pointing to a site will display the page's title and URL, as in Figure 32-10. Click a page icon to revisit that page.

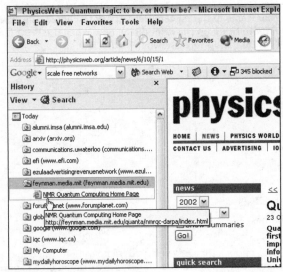

Figure 32-10: History bar

> **Tip**   To delete an item in the history list, right-click it and choose Delete.

Notice the little toolbar near the top of the History bar. If you want to rearrange the list, click the View button. On the menu that appears, click a new sort order, such as By order visited today.

To search through your history list for Web pages that contain some keyword, click the Search button. Under Search For in the box that opens, type any word or phrase; and then click Search Now. The resulting list of pages will contain your search text. You can use the View button to rearrange those results. To get back to seeing all items in the history, click the View button and choose any view.

Closing the History bar

To close the History bar, do any of the following:

✦ Click the **X** in the upper-right corner of the History bar.

✦ Click the **History** button in Internet Explorer's toolbar.

✦ Press **Ctrl+H**.

Closing the History bar doesn't change its contents in any way. It just gets the History bar off the screen and out of your way. You can reopen the History bar at any time.

Clearing and controlling history

You can delete any single item from the history list by right-clicking and choosing Delete. Optionally, you can delete the entire history. This works best if you leave have the History bar open when you start. If you don't, you may end up clearing only items prior to today's list. Here are the steps:

1. Choose **Tools ➪ Internet Options** from Explorer's menu bar.

2. Click the **Clear History** button on the General tab (see Figure 32-11).

3. Optionally, use the **Days to keep pages in history** option to change how long history items are maintained.

4. Click **OK**.

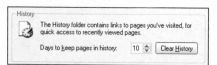

Figure 32-11: History options in the Internet Options dialog box

Changing Your Default Home Page

As you may recall, the first Web page you come to when you open Internet Explorer is referred to as your default home page. Most likely, you're going to want to change your default home page to something you really do need to visit often. For example, if you search the Web a lot using Google, you might want to make Google your default home page. To define a new default home page:

1. In Internet Explorer, go to the page you want to make the new default (for example, www.Google.com).

2. Once you're at the page, choose **Tools ➪ Internet Options** from Internet Explorer's menu bar.

3. On the General tab, click the **Use Current** button shown in Figure 32-12.

4. Click **OK**.

Figure 32-12: Default home page option in the Internet Options dialog box

In the Internet Options dialog box, you can also type the URL of the page you want to use as your default home page into the Address textbox. Choosing Use Default reverts to the default home page (usually MSN). Choosing Use Blank allows you to open Internet Explorer with no page showing, which means that you can open Internet Explorer offline without getting an error message.

Tracking Favorite Web Sites

As you follow links and explore the Web, you're sure to find sites you'll want to revisit. You can make the return trip easier by adding the site to your Favorites while you're there. Here's how:

1. While viewing the page you want to add, choose **Favorites** ⇨ **Add to Favorites** from Internet Explorer's menu bar, or right-click any empty area or text in the page and choose **Add to Favorites**. The Add Favorite dialog box, shown in Figure 32-13, opens.

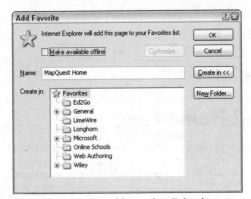

Figure 32-13: The Add Favorite dialog box

2. Optionally, in the Add Favorite dialog box you can:

   - Type a new name for the page in the Name textbox.

   - Click the **Create in** button, then choose (click on) a folder in which to place the favorite.

   - Click the **New Folder** button to create a new folder for this favorite and others like it.

   - Make the page available offline by choosing the **Make available offline** checkbox.

3. Click **OK**.

Note   The section titled "Avoiding the Wait with Offline Browsing" later in this chapter explains what the *Make available offline* option is all about.

As a shortcut, you can go to the page you want to add to Favorites and then press Ctrl+D. Internet Explorer adds the page to your Favorites list without displaying the Add Favorite dialog box.

Revisiting favorite sites

To return to a favorite site, you need not retype its URL. Instead, you can just use any of the following techniques to view your collection of favorites, and then click the site you wish to visit:

✦ Click the **Favorites** button in the Standard Buttons toolbar.

✦ Or, press **Ctrl+I**.

✦ Or, choose **View** ⇨ **Explorer bar** ⇨ **Favorites** from Internet Explorer's menu bar.

✦ Or, click **Favorites** in the menu bar, and then click the name of the site you wish to visit.

✦ Or, click the **Start** button and choose **Favorites** from the right side of the Start menu.

Note   If your Start menu doesn't offer a Favorites option, see "Personalizing Your Start Menu" in Chapter 6.

If you use one of the first three options, the left side of Internet Explorer's program window will display your favorites, as in Figure 32-14. To expand any folder you've already created, click the folder's name. Each item that shows an Internet Explorer icon is a Web page.

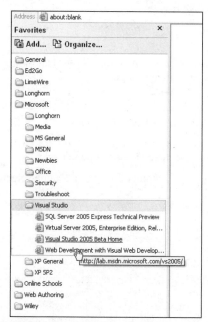

Figure 32-14: The Favorites bar on the left side of Internet Explorer

To move an item in the favorites list, just drag it to some location. That is, point to the item you want to move, hold down the left mouse button, drag the item to its new position, and release the mouse button.

Organizing your favorites

As your collection of favorites grows, you might want to organize it into folders. That way, you won't be faced with a huge list of favorites each time you open your Favorites bar. To organize your favorites, click the Organize button at the top of the Favorites bar. Or choose Favorites ➪ Organize Favorites from Internet Explorer's menu bar. Either way, you'll be taken to the Organize Favorites window shown in Figure 32-15.

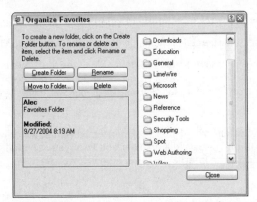

Figure 32-15: The Organize Favorites window

The left side of the dialog box provides instructions, buttons, and information. The right side shows you your current folders (all with folder icons) and favorites.

Creating a favorites subfolder

Creating folders in the Organize Favorites dialog box is easy. Here are the steps:

1. If you want to create a subfolder within a folder, open that the parent folder first. Otherwise, make sure that the highlighter is on a closed folder or page icon.

2. Click the **Create Folder** button. A folder named New Folder appears, its name selected and ready to be edited.

3. Type a name for the folder, and press **Enter**.

That's all there is to it.

Moving, changing, and deleting favorites

To move a favorite or folder icon in Organize Favorites, you can just drag it and drop it wherever you want to place it. If you want to move an item into a folder you've created, you can just drag the item and drop it right onto the folder's icon. Or, you can click the item you want to move and click the Move to Folder button. In the Browse for Folder dialog box that opens, click the name of the folder to move the favorite to. If you're trying to pull the favorite out of a folder back up to the first list, click Favorites at the top of the folder list. Click the Close button.

To change the name of a favorite or folder, click the item, and then click the Rename button. Or, right-click the item and choose Rename. The name will be selected (highlighted). Type the new name, or edit the existing name using any of the standard text-editing techniques. To edit it, you'll need to position the cursor by clicking the spot where you want to put the cursor or by pressing the ← or Home key to move the cursor to the left. Press Enter when you're done.

Starting Your Favorites Collection

If you're new to the Web and want to visit some useful Web sites that you might want to add to your favorites, here are a few to help you get started. Not everyone will want to add all of these to his or her favorites, of course. But you're likely to find some sites you'll want to revisit:

- www.Dictionary.com: **Look up a word in a dictionary or thesaurus, or translate text from one language to another.**

- www.eBay.com: **The ever-popular buy-and-sell-anything-and-everything site.**

- www.fandango.com: **Find out what movies are playing in your local theaters, their start times, and so forth.**

- www.FirstGov.gov: **The U.S. Government's official Web site.**

- www.Google.com: **A popular site for searching the World Wide Web.**

- www.MapQuest.com: **A great resource for maps and driving directions.**

- http://search.Microsoft.com: **Search Microsoft's Web site for technical support.**

- www.OnlineConversion.com: **Convert all types of measurements, such as feet to meters or gallons to ounces.**

- www.USPS.com: **The United States Postal Service site, including a Calculate Postage option to figure out the cost of shipping an item.**

- www.WindowsCatalog.com: **A catalog of hardware and software products for Windows XP.**

To delete a favorite or folder, click its name, and then click the Delete button, or press the Delete (Del) key on your keyboard. Optionally, you can right-click the item and choose Delete. If asked "Are you sure . . .?" choose Yes.

Tip   If you delete a favorite or favorite folder by accident, you can get it back by restoring it from the Recycle Bin. See Chapter 19 for details.

Closing up favorites

To close the Organize Favorites window, just click its Close button. To close the Favorites bar, click the Close (X) button in its upper-right corner. Or, click the Favorites button in Internet Explorer's toolbar, or press Ctrl+I.

Tip   The Favorites option on the XP Start menu provides a handy shortcut for getting to favorite places without even opening Internet Explorer first. See "Personalizing Your Start Menu" in Chapter 6 for details.

General Browsing versus Secure Browsing

Browsing the Web is usually a very anonymous endeavor. When you visit a Web page, the Web server that sent you a page has no idea who you are, where you are, what type of computer you have, or anything else. All the Web server can do is hand the Web page off to the Internet and assume that it will get to you. You are completely anonymous to the Web site.

When you shop online, you need to enter some personally identifiable information, such as your name, address, e-mail address, and maybe even credit-card information. In other words, you need to enter some information that you don't necessarily want to make public. While it's extremely unlikely that any information you transfer over the Internet would ever become public, a highly knowledgeable Internet nerd could grab some information off the Internet and dig around it looking for credit-card information and the like.

To be absolutely sure that it's impossible (not just remotely possible) for your credit-card information to be lifted off the Internet, legitimate businesses use a technology know as Secure Sockets Layer (SSL) to encrypt sensitive information as it crosses the Internet. In the unlikely event that someone does get a hold of that encrypted information, it won't do that person any good. He or she will only see a bunch of meaningless gobbledygook, and there's no way to decipher that information into anything useful. Only the Web site that you're dealing with can make sense of the encrypted information.

To alert you to when you are entering, or leaving, a secure site, Internet Explorer displays a couple of little messages on your screen. First, let me point out that the URL for a general, anonymous Web site usually begins with the letters `http://`, where `http` stands for Hypertext Transfer Protocol. The URL of a secure site, where it's safe to send sensitive information, starts with the letters `https://`, where the `s` stands for *secure*.

When you leave a general `http://` site and are about to enter a secure `https://` site, Internet Explorer shows the Security Alert message at the left side of Figure 32-16. What the message is really saying is, "You're about to enter a secure site, so if they ask you for sensitive information, such as a credit card number, it's safe for you to provide that." When you leave a secure (`https://`) site and are about to go to a regular `http://` site, the Security Alert on the right of that same figure appears. The purpose of the second message is really just to tell you, "You're not on a secure Web site anymore. So, if you're asked for sensitive information such as a credit-card number, there's a remote possibility that someone could intercept and use that information."

Figure 32-16: Entering, and leaving, a secure site

When you start shopping online, setting up special accounts, and so forth, you'll see the two security alerts often, because there are lots of unsecured, general-information type pages (`http://`) on the Web and lots of secured ones (`https://`) too. If you get sick and tired of seeing these same two messages over and over again, just click the In the future, do not show this warning option before you click the OK or Yes button.

When you start downloading files from the Web, you're likely to come across other types of security warnings. We'll discuss those in the downloading section later in this chapter.

Searching the Web

The World Wide Web contains just about all public knowledge. You can find anything on the Web; you just need to know how to look for it. Internet Explorer offers you several ways to search for information on the Internet. Perhaps the handiest is the built-in Search Companion. To use it, click the Search button on the Standard Buttons toolbar, or press Ctrl+E, or choose View ⇨ Explorer Bar ⇨ Search from the menu bar. (You can use all of the same techniques to close the Search bar.)

It's difficult to say exactly what your Search bar will look like. The default in Internet Explorer is called the Search Companion and is shown in Figure 32-17. But your Search bar might look completely different. For example, you may have already configured Google as your default search engine, in which case a bar for searching Google will appear in place of the Search Companion.

Figure 32-17: Internet Explorer's Search Companion

The more specific you are when entering your search text, the better off you'll be. For example, if you search for just the word Mustang, you'll get links to about a zillion Web pages that have the word mustang in them, including Web pages about the horse breed, the car, and any other page that happens to contain that word. However, if you search for Ford Mustang, that will narrow it down considerably. If you search for 1966 Ford Mustang convertible, that will narrow it down even more. The more specific your request, the better results you'll get.

Once you've typed the word or phrase you want to search for, click the Search button. After a brief delay, you should see some links in the main pane to the right, and some new options in the Search Companion, as in Figure 32-18. However, I can't say exactly what you'll see on your screen because it depends on what you searched for and many other factors. But, regardless of how the details play out, you should be able to scroll through links in the main pane to the right to see what's available. Click any hyperlink in the right page to visit a page. Click Internet Explorer's Back button to return to the Search results.

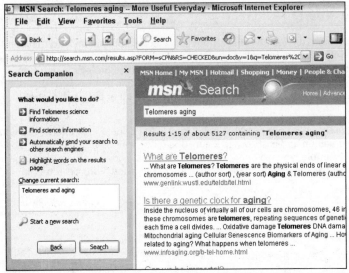

Figure 32-18: Results of a search using the Search Assistant

Caution   Spelling counts big time in searches. The search is based on exactly the characters you type into the Find a Web page containing textbox. If a search results in nothing, click the New button and check your spelling.

If you don't find what you're looking for, you can click the New button at the top of the Search bar and try a different search. If you don't find anything, check to make sure that your spelling is correct.

Searching without the Search bar

The World Wide Web is home to many *search engines*. These are Web sites that regularly scan the entire World Wide Web for new pages and then create an index to those pages, similar to the index in the back of a book. Because the Web contains billions of pages, the index is enormous — somewhere along the lines of an index for a million different books. There are lots of search engines to choose from, including www.google.com, www.altavista.com, www.yahoo.com, www.infoseek.com, www.lycos.com, and www.hotbot.com, just to name a few.

Tip   You can also search the Internet from the Windows Explorer Search Companion, as discussed in Chapter 17.

Quite a few search engines actually use Google as their index source. Google is one of the more popular search engines on the Internet. People often use its name as a verb, as in "I googled *<some word or phrase>*." In English, that translates to "I went to www.google.com and searched for *<some word or phrase>*." To get to Google, just type its URL (www.google.com) into your Web browser's Address bar and press Enter.

Once you get to Google's home page, type the word or phrase you're looking for into the Search box, and then click the Google Search button. After a few seconds, you'll see the results of your search, as in the Example shown in Figure 32-19, where my search resulted in 86,900 matching Web pages. Each underlined title is a hyperlink that you can click to visit the

Changing the Default Search Bar

If you can't get the Search Companion to appear when you click the Search button in Internet Explorer, close Internet Explorer. Then, open Windows Explorer by opening a local folder, such as My Documents. In that folder, click the Search button in the toolbar, and then click Change Preferences in the Search Companion bar. Next, click *Change Internet search behavior*, choose the first option, "With Search Companion," and click OK. Then, open Internet Explorer and click the Search button in its toolbar again.

If you find that your Internet Explorer search bar has been hijacked by some unknown third party, try using the Manage Add-ons tool in Internet Explorer to disable that unwanted bar. See "Disable mysterious add-ons" in Chapter 30 for details.

referenced page. If there are multiple results, you'll find links for accessing other pages at the bottom of the current page.

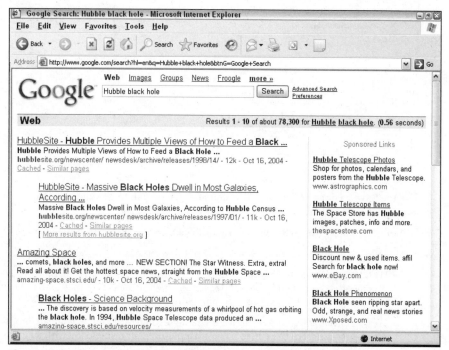

Figure 32-19: Results of searching the Web using Google's search engine

In Google's search results, you can use the tabs above the links to narrow the search results to certain types of results. For example, clicking the Images tab takes you to pictures that relate to the search text. Clicking the News tab displays news articles that relate to the search text.

If your searches keep producing thousands, or millions, of pages, and you want to try to get things narrowed down, you can use Google's Advanced Search. Just return to Google's home page at www.google.com, click the Advanced Search link near the top of the page, and fill in the blanks on the form that appears.

Saving Web Content

Web pages don't generally go away, so there's rarely any need to save an entire Web page. However, if you're using a Web site where you need to sign in to gain access, and your account is limited to several weeks or months of access time, then saving a local copy of a page would make sense. To save a copy of the Web page you're currently viewing, follow these steps:

1. Choose **File** ➪ **Save As** from Internet Explorer's menu bar. A Save As dialog box (titled Save Web Page) opens, as shown in Figure 32-20.

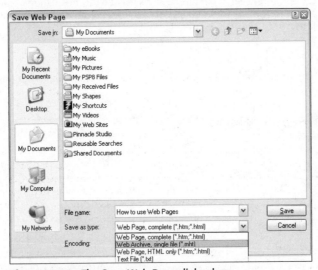

Figure 32-20: The Save Web Page dialog box

2. Use the **Save in** drop-down list and main pane to navigate to the folder in which you want to change the page.

3. Optionally, change the page's name using the **File name** option.

4. Optionally, choose a **Save as type** from one of these options:

   - **Web Page, complete (*.htm,*.html):** The entire Web page with all pictures is downloaded. You'll end up with two icons, one for the HTML page and the other a folder containing pictures and perhaps other miscellaneous code files.

   - **Web Archive, single file (*.mht):** If you have Microsoft Office, you can choose this option to store the entire page, with pictures, in a single file with a single icon.

   - **Web Page, HTML only (*htm,*.html):** Saves all the text and HTML of the page, but no pictures.

   - **Text File (*.txt):** Saves only the text of the page, no pictures or HTML tags.

5. Optionally, change the **Encoding** option, but only if you have a good reason, such as when saving non-English pages.

6. Click the **Save** button.

Figure 32-21 shows examples of how the icon(s) for a saved page will look, depending on which Save As Type option you selected.

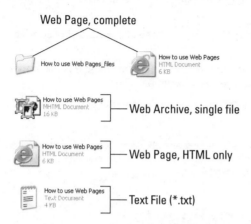

Web Page, complete

How to use Web Pages_files

How to use Web Pages
HTML Document
6 KB

How to use Web Pages
MHTML Document
16 KB
——— Web Archive, single file

How to use Web Pages
HTML Document
6 KB
——— Web Page, HTML only

How to use Web Pages
Text Document
4 KB
——— Text File (*.txt)

Figure 32-21: Icons for saved Web pages

For those of you who aren't familiar with Web authoring, HTML (Hypertext Markup Language) is a set of *tags* that all Web pages use to define certain page elements. For example, text enclosed on <b> and </b> tags is displayed in boldface. Pictures, which are never actually stored within a Web page (.htm) are indicated by <IMG SRC="*path*"> tags. Hyperlinks are defined by <A HREF="*url*">visible text</A> tags. The HTML specifications are published at www.w3c.org.

When you're viewing a Web page in Internet Explorer, you can take a peek at its underlying HTML by choose View ➪ Source form Internet Explorer's menu bar. You can view and edit any .htm or .html page that's on your own computer by right-clicking the file's icon and choosing Open With ➪ Notepad. However, few authors actually create Web pages that way. Most use a more powerful Web-editing application like Microsoft FrontPage, or perhaps a shareware HTML editor.

Tip

To find, and optionally download, a shareware Web-authoring program, go to www.tucows.com and search for HTML editor. The CoffeeCup HTML Editor is a popular one.

If you download a Web archive (.mht file), double-click its icon; the page will most likely open in a Web browser. If you want to convert that page to an editable Microsoft Word document, right-click the .mht file's icon and choose Open With ➪ Microsoft Word. To create a Word document from the open page, choose File ➪ Save As from Word's menu bar. In the Save As dialog box, choose a folder, enter a filename, and choose Word Document from the Save As Type option.

Copying text from Web pages

If you want to save a chunk of text from a Web page to a document on your computer, open a word processing program such as WordPad or Microsoft Word. In the Web page, select (drag the mouse pointer through) any portion of the page you want to copy, then press Ctrl+C, or right-click the selection and choose Copy.

In your WordPad or Word document, click at the place where you want to paste the copied content. Then, press Ctrl+V or right-click near the cursor and choose Paste.

Downloading pictures and videos

You can often (though not always) download multimedia items from Web pages as independent files on your own computer.

✦ To copy a picture you see on a Web page, right-click the picture and choose **Save Picture As**.

✦ To download a video or sound, you'll first need to get to the link that leads to that object. Right-click that link, and choose **Save Target As**.

The Save As dialog box will open, as usual, so you can choose a folder and specify a filename for the item you're copying.

Tip   If you're unable to copy a picture by right-clicking and choosing Copy, you can also take a picture of the entire screen with the picture visible. Then, paste the screenshot into a graphics program and crop out whatever you don't want.

Playing Music and Video Online

The Internet is home to some *streaming media*: sound and video that you can watch in real time. By real time I mean that the content plays as it would on a radio or TV. There is no file to download first, the content just plays as it arrives. When you click a link to streaming media, you may see the dialog box shown in Figure 32-22.

Figure 32-22: Options for playing music or video from the Web

What happens next depends on a lot of things. But here are the most common scenarios:

✦ If you choose Yes, the song or video will play in the Media bar at the left side of Internet Explorer's program window.

✦ If you choose No, the song or video will play in some other player, either one provided by the Web site itself or Windows Media Player (discussed in Chapter 38).

✦ In some cases, the music or video will play in some other player no matter which option you choose, because the Web site you're viewing always uses its own player.

You can show or hide the Media bar at any time by clicking the Media button in Internet Explorer's menu bar. Or choose View ➪ Explorer Bar ➪ Media from Internet Explorer's menu bar.

Exactly how the bar looks depends on what you're viewing at the moment. In the example shown in Figure 32-23, the Media bar is currently playing a movie trailer from www. windowsmedia.com/Mediaguide/Movies.

Media bar on/off

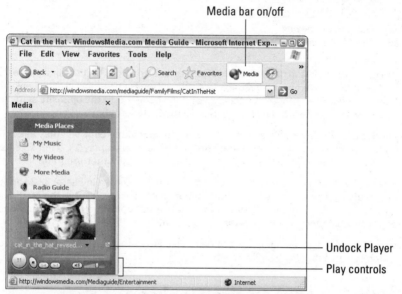

Undock Player

Play controls

Figure 32-23: Video playing in Internet Explorer's Media bar

Click the tiny Unlock Player to the right of the video title to undock the player from the Media bar and make it free-floating. Click it a second time to dock the player to the bar. The play controls below the video work just like the controls on a VCR, as follows:

✦ **Play/Pause:** When a song or video is playing, shows two vertical bars (‖), which stand for Pause. After clicking the button, a right-pointing triangle replaces the bars, and clicking that button resumes playback.

✦ **Stop:** Stops the song or video currently playing and rewinds it to the beginning.

✦ **Next Track/Previous Track:** When playing a CD, allows you to go to the next or previous song on the CD.

✦ **Mute:** Click to mute all sound. Click a second time to turn sound back on.

✦ **Volume:** Drag the slider left to decrease volume. Drag it right to increase volume.

To change how Internet Explorer plays music or video, click the Media Options drop-down list and point to Settings, as shown in Figure 32-24. Clicking the More Media option takes you to the WindowsMedia.com Web site, where you can find music and video clips to play. Clicking the Radio Guide option takes you to a Web site where you can find radio stations that broadcast over the Internet.

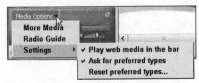

Figure 32-24: Options for playing music or video from the Web

The Settings submenu offers the options summarized as follows. Note that the first two options are *toggles*. If the option has a check mark next to it, the option is currently On. No check mark means that the option is currently Off. Clicking an option changes it to the opposite state: from On to Off, or vice versa. Here's what all the options on the Settings submenu do:

✦ **Play web media in the bar:** If selected (On), music and video clips will play in the Media bar (if the Web site you're visiting doesn't have its own player). If not selected, music and video will play in Windows Media Player or some other program.

✦ **Ask for preferred types:** If selected (On), the dialog box shown in Figure 32-23 appears when you play a new media type, asking whether you want to play it in the Media bar or elsewhere. If this option is Off, the dialog box doesn't open and the song or video just plays in whatever player you chose in the past.

✦ **Reset preferred types:** Clicking this option erases any selections you've made concerning which types of media files play where.

Adding Web Content to the Desktop

You can place live Web content, such as a stock ticker, weather alerts, and sports scores on your Windows desktop. These small Web components are called *active desktop items*. They display live data from the Web whenever you're online. Options for adding and removing desktop items are located on the Web tab of the Desktop Items dialog box. Here's how you get there:

1. Right-click the desktop, and choose **Properties**.

2. Click the **Desktop** tab.

3. Click the **Customize Desktop** button.

4. Click the **Web** tab to get to the options shown in Figure 32-25.

To add a new desktop item to your desktop, click the **New** button. If you know the URL of a specific active desktop item you want to add, enter its URL into the Location box in the New Desktop Item dialog box that opens. Otherwise, click the **Visit Gallery** button to choose from among several free items available from Microsoft. When you find a component you like, click the **Add to Active Desktop** button near that item.

Next, you'll most likely be taken through some options relevant to whatever item you chose. When you've finished, the item will be on your desktop and also listed on the Web tab. Figure 32-25 shows an example with the Microsoft Investor Active Desktop Ticker shown on the desktop, above the Web tab of the Desktop Items dialog box.

Note   You can actually put an entire Web page on the desktop. But doing so can make your desktop a busy and confusing place.

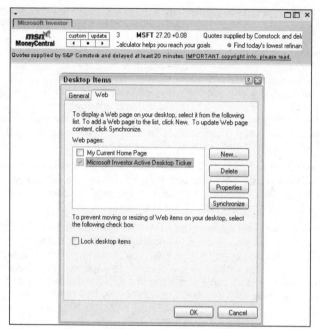

Figure 32-25: The Web tab in Customize Desktop and a sample item

Although there may be some differences among desktop items, most items can be positioned on the desktop by pointing to them to display a title bar. Drag that title bar to place the item anywhere on your desktop. The investment ticker offers a tiny Custom button that you can click to further customize that desktop item. For example, you can choose specific stocks to watch in the investment ticker.

To hide a desktop item without removing it from your computer, clear its check mark on the Web tab. To permanently remove a desktop item from your desktop, click on the item's name, and then click the Delete button on the Web tab.

Note   Desktop item synchronization options work the same as those described in the next section.

Avoiding the Wait with Offline Browsing

Offline browsing offers a way to control when time-consuming downloads take place so that you can make the time you spend on the Web more productive. Essentially, offline browsing enables you to update your favorite Web content during off-hours (such as when you're asleep) so that when you do come back to review your favorite Web pages, they will have already been downloaded to your computer, and so will appear instantly as you go through their links. In fact, because you don't even need to be online to view the pages, you could review them on a laptop on your way to work or whatever (assuming that you're not driving a car at the time!).

A Simple Way to Avoid the Wait

Here's a simple way to avoid waiting some of the time involved in downloading Web pages. It works during normal, everyday browsing, and doesn't involve offline browsing at all. Here's how it works. Suppose that you come to a Web page that has several interesting links. Before you start reading the current page, you can right-click any link that looks interesting and choose Open in New Window. The new page will start to appear in a separate browser window. You can minimize that window by clicking its Minimize button to get it out of the way during the download. You can do that for as many links as you want. Then, just continue reading the page that's still open on your desktop. Or, do any other work that needs to be done on your computer.

It still may take a while for the download to complete. The more links you open in new windows, the longer it takes to download all the pages. After you have finished viewing the current page, click any Internet Explorer icon in the taskbar to open the minimized page. If the download was completed while the window was minimized, you won't have to wait to view its full content.

You will end up with several copies of Internet Explorer open, each in its own window. You can close any window by clicking its Close button, as usual. Alternatively, right-click the window's taskbar button and choose Close. The taskbar button for the page you're viewing at the moment will have the "pushed-in" appearance on the taskbar. If you open more windows than there is room for on the taskbar, the buttons are joined into a single Internet Explorer button. Click that button to display a menu of all open pages. Click any menu option to view that open page.

Pages that can be downloaded during off-hours are called *offline favorites* in Internet Explorer jargon. Creating an offline favorite is simple and works with any Web site. While you're in Internet Explorer and viewing a page that you want to add to your offline favorites, just follow these steps:

1. Choose **Favorites** ⇨ **Add to Favorites** from the Internet Explorer menu bar. The dialog box shown in Figure 32-26 opens.

Figure 32-26: Add Favorites dialog box

2. Choose **Make available offline**.

3. Optionally, you can click the Customize button to get to the Offline Favorite Wizard, discussed under the section with that title later in this chapter.

4. Click **OK**.

If you have already built up a list of favorite Web sites and want to convert some of those to offline favorites, follow these steps:

1. In Internet Explorer, click the **Favorites** button in the toolbar, or choose **View** ➪ **Explorer Bar** ➪ **Favorites**, to open your list of favorites.

2. Right-click any Web item that you want to convert to an offline favorite, and choose **Make available offline**.

The Offline Favorite Wizard, discussed next, will start automatically.

The Offline Favorite Wizard

The Offline Favorite Wizard provides an easy way to specify how much material, and how often, you want an offline favorite page to update. The second wizard page, shown in Figure 32-27, lets you specify how many linked pages you want to download automatically. A linked page is any page that you can get to by clicking a link on the page you've defined as an offline favorite.

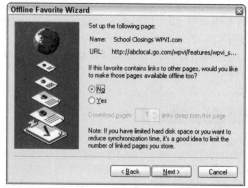

Figure 32-27: A page from the Offline Favorite Wizard

On the third wizard page, you can choose between manual updating of all offline pages, and downloading while you're away. If you choose *Only when I choose Synchronize . . .*, then Windows will never attempt to update the page automatically. If you do want Windows to update pages automatically while you're away from the computer, choose the second option, and then click Next. The page shown in Figure 32-28 opens so that you can define a schedule.

As you can see on the wizard page, you can choose how often, and at what time, you want to update pages. You can give the schedule a name as well. This is handy if you need to create multiple schedules for different types of pages, such as sites you update in the morning and sites you update in the evening. If you have a dial-up account that requires logging on, choose the checkbox that logs on automatically while you're away from the computer. Then, click Next.

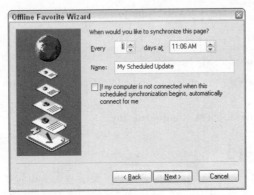

Figure 32-28: Define a frequency and update time on this page

The next wizard page asks if you need to log in to the Web site. That might be true if your offline favorite is, say, a news service that charges money and requires you to log in on each visit. If you do need to log in to the site on each visit, fill in the user name and password you use to log into that site, and then click Next.

When you've completed the wizard, click the Finish button. The copy of the page on your computer will be synchronized with the page on the Web server according to whatever schedule you defined.

Allowing for the automatic download

Keep in mind one important point regarding these automatic downloads. Your computer needs to be on when the scheduled time arrives. Likewise, if you access the Internet through an external modem, the modem needs to be turned on as well. You can turn off the monitor, however, because it is not needed for automatic downloads.

Tip   Some network cards support a Wake On LAN capability, which automatically wakes up a hibernating computer when the request to access the Internet arises. See your computer documentation to see whether it has this capability.

Browsing offline

Whenever you want to view the downloaded pages on your PC, open Internet Explorer in the usual manner. Then, choose File ➪ Work Offline from the menu bar. Doing so prevents Internet Explorer from attempting to download the offline favorite from the Internet. Then, open your Favorites bar and click any favorite that you've designated as an offline favorite. Internet Explorer shows you the copy of the page that has already been downloaded, so there's no need to wait.

While working offline, you won't have access to pages that require you to be online. If you click a link that requires that you to be connected to the Internet, you'll see a message explaining that with the options to Connect or Stay Offline.

Updating pages manually

If you ever want to update all your offline favorites on the spur of the moment, get online and choose Tools ⇨ Synchronize from the Internet Explorer menu bar. Then, click Offline Web Pages at the top of the list of pages, and click the Synchronize button. You must wait for the downloads, of course (which is why you usually want pages to be synchronized while you're away from the computer, such as when you're asleep). After the downloading has been completed, the pages in your Internet cache will indeed be in sync with the latest pages on those favorite Web sites.

Managing downloading schedules

You can change how often or at what time Windows downloads your offline favorites. In Internet Explorer, choose Tools ⇨ Synchronize. Then, click Offline Web Pages and click the Setup button. The Synchronization Settings dialog box shown in Figure 32-29 opens.

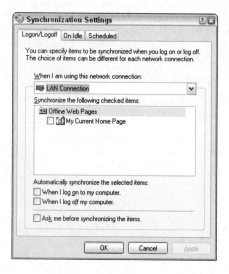

Figure 32-29: Synchronization Settings dialog box

The three tabs across the top of the Synchronization Settings dialog box provide many different ways to control how and when offline favorites are synchronized, as follows:

✦ **Logon/Logoff:** Enables you to synchronize selected items automatically when you log on or log off of the computer.

✦ **On Idle:** Enables you to synchronize selected items while the computer is idle but still connected to the Internet.

✦ **Scheduled:** Enables you to create your own schedules for synchronizing offline favorites.

On the Scheduled tab, you can click the Add button to create a schedule based on time. For example, you could create a schedule that updates offline favorites every day at 6 A.M. Note that regardless of the type of schedule you create, you will always see a list of offline favorites with checkboxes next to them. Only pages that you select (by filling their checkboxes) will be updated according to the schedule you create.

Removing offline favorites

To convert an offline favorite to a regular favorite, open the Favorites bar again in Internet Explorer. Right-click any listed page in the bar and choose Make Available Offline again to clear the check mark next to that menu option. You are asked for confirmation. Just click the Yes button.

Dealing with Cookies and Temporary Files

Every Web page you view is stored in a folder named `Local Settings\Temporary` Internet Files in your user account. That folder is also called your Internet *cache* (pronounced *cash*). The cache stores copies of recently visited pages mainly so that when you're navigating through recent pages with the Back and Forward buttons, your browser doesn't have to redownload the page every time you view it.

Of course, the temporary files don't just pile up forever. The folder has a maximum size, usually under 2 MB in size (which is a very small amount on a hard disk). So as new pages get added to the folder, older pages are automatically deleted to make room for the newer ones. But you can work directly with temporary Internet files and change some settings via the Internet Options dialog box. To get to that dialog box:

1. Open Internet Explorer (if it isn't already open).

2. Choose **Tools** ⇨ **Internet Options** from Internet Explorer's menu bar. The Internet Options dialog box shown in Figure 32-30 opens.

Figure 32-30: The General tab of the Internet Options dialog box

Right off the bat, you can see there's a button for deleting all cookies, and all temporary Internet files. There's no harm in doing either, so you needn't be worried about using those buttons. The only side effect will be that some pages you visit after the site might take a little longer to download because you won't have any temporary copies of pages in your cache.

Managing temporary Internet files

As you can see in Figure 32-30, there's a third button labeled Settings in the Temporary Internet files section of the Internet Options dialog box. Clicking that button takes you to the settings shown in Figure 32-31.

Figure 32-31: Settings dialog box for temporary Internet files

The temporary copy of each Web page you visit doesn't stay in your Temporary Internet Files folder forever. Even if there is a copy of a given page in your temporary folder, Internet Explorer will automatically *refresh* (redownload) the page periodically. For example, it might give you the local copy all day Monday. But when you return to the site on Tuesday, it might refresh the page, just because many Web sites change daily.

Tip You can make Internet Explorer redownload any page at any time. Just click the Refresh button in its toolbar, or press F5, or choose View ➪ Refresh from its menu bar.

The first set of options let you change how often pages are refreshed. For example, if you visit sites that change frequently, such as news sites, and you have a fast Internet connection, you may want to increase the refresh rate so that you get a fresh copy every time. On the other hand, if you have a slow Internet connection and mostly visit sites that don't change much, you may want to refresh less often so you don't have to wait for pages to download on revisits.

Changing the refresh rate

By default, Internet Explorer makes decisions on when to refresh based on settings at the Web site and by comparing the date and time that you downloaded the page to the date and time of the page on the Web server. It only takes a second for the Web browser to change the date and time that a page was posted, even if you have a slow Internet connection, because it doesn't take long to transmit that tiny bit of information across the Internet. Downloading the whole page, especially pictures, is the part that takes time. But anyway, the Settings dialog box lets you choose, for yourself, how often Internet Explorer refreshes pages:

✦ **Every visit to the page:** Ensures that every visit to a Web site is fresh, but can make browsing very slow indeed.

✦ **Every time you start Internet Explorer:** Faster than the preceding option, this option checks only for updates if you've closed Internet Explorer since your last visit. Definitely speeds up browsing through pages you've visited in your current Internet Explorer session.

✦ **Automatically:** Windows handles updates and downloading for you, to maximize your productivity while browsing the Web.

✦ **Never:** Always takes material from the Internet cache (if possible). The only way to ensure that you're getting fresh material is to click the Refresh button when you get to a page.

Setting the cache size

Use the slider bar to decide how much disk space you want to sacrifice to the Internet cache. The larger the cache, the more pages can be stored and the faster your browsing goes. A small cache saves disk space but doesn't allow for many temporary Internet files to be stored locally. This, in turn, may slow down your browsing because only enough room exists to store information from, say, the last two or three sites you visited.

Moving the temporary files folder

The default folder used for the Internet cache is `C:\Documents and Settings\`*your user name*`\Temporary Internet Files` (where *your user name* is the user name you log on with). If, for whatever reason, you want to move that, click the Move folder button and browse to a new location. This might be useful if you have a second hard disk drive on which you want to place your temporary files (thereby freeing up the disk space the folder takes up on your C: drive).

Covering Your Tracks

The fact that Internet Explorer stores temporary Internet files on your hard disk means that anyone who can access the folder can browse around and see where you've been on the Internet. If you're concerned about privacy, you may want to delete those files. To do so, click the Delete Files button under Temporary Internet Files in the Internet Options dialog box. For reasons described a little later, I don't recommend deleting cookies! However, you may want to delete *some* cookies, as discussed under "Managing cookies" in this chapter.

Don't forget that the History bar also keeps track of where you've been. You can clear out your History bar by clicking the Clear History button in the Internet Options dialog box. Finally, be aware that some sites will automatically add themselves to your list of favorites. To get rid of any of those, choose Favorites from Internet Explorer's menu bar. Right-click any item on the menu that you want to get rid of, and choose Delete.

Viewing downloaded objects

The Settings dialog box also offers a button labeled View Objects. An object, in this context, is a program that's used in conjunction with Web pages. Some objects, such as the ones by Microsoft, won't be things you specifically downloaded, but rather are ones installed automatically by Microsoft Office or Windows Update. Your antivirus software will likely have objects in there as well, to help with virus protection.

Clicking the View Objects button shows you current objects, as in the example shown in Figure 32-32. Clicking on any object's name displays more information about the object. As a rule, you don't want to delete objects that appear in that list. Better to leave the list intact and see if you can delete the object from Add/Remove Programs in Control panel.

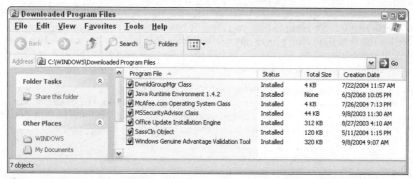

Figure 32-32: Sample results of clicking on the View Objects button

Managing cookies

Cookies that you acquire while browsing the Web are stored in a folder named Cookies in your user account. A cookie is a tiny file, less than 1 KB, that contains a little text data used to pass information one page to another within a site. For example, when you log in to a site that requires a sign-in, your sign-in information is stored in a cookie. When you go from one page to the next within the site, your sign-in information is pulled from the cookie so that you don't have to sign in again.

There are two types of cookies. Most are *session cookies*, which exist for only the duration of your current browsing session. A session begins when you open Internet Explorer and ends when you close Internet Explorer. There are also *persistent cookies*, which, as the name implies, last longer — indefinitely, in fact, unless you go in and delete them yourself.

Some cookies, which go by the highly technical name of *unsatisfactory cookies*, are put on your computer by third-party Web sites as *spyware*. Such cookies keep track of which pages you visit so that advertisers can better target their ads to your browsing preferences. This is very unsatisfactory indeed, because the only good ad is an ad that doesn't exist. At least, for those of use who have a zero-tolerance attitude toward any form of Internet advertising.

Why "Cookies"?

The name *cookies* comes from an old story where some kids decide to explore some spooky forest. But they're afraid they'll get lost. So, they leave a trail of cookie crumbs behind so that they can find their way back. This turns out to be a bad idea though because forest animals eat the crumbs. There's probably some moral to that story. But computers don't eat cookies, so whatever the moral might be, it's not relevant to Internet cookies.

There are anti-adware programs on the market, such as Lavasoft's Ad-Aware (discussed in Chapter 30) that can clean out unwanted adware and spyware cookies for you. Though, there's no hardship in deleting cookies yourself because they're never required to use a Web site. A Web site really can't assume that you already have a given cookie, because people visiting a site for the first time won't have any cookies from that site. So, if you delete a site cookie, you just get treated as a first-time visitor the next time you visit the site. No big deal. To delete all cookies, just click the Delete Cookies button shown in Figure 30-30.

As mentioned, cookies are stored in the folder `C:\Documents and Settings\`*user name*`\Cookies` where *user name* is folder name for your user account. For example, Figure 32-33 shows the Cookies for a user account named Alec. The `index.dat` file in that example is one that Windows creates and shouldn't be deleted because it's not a cookie.

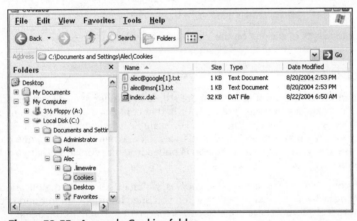

Figure 32-33: A sample Cookies folder

You can delete cookies individually by right-clicking any cookie's name and choosing Delete. But it's not easy to tell the good cookies from the bad cookies just by looking. Part V of this book is "security central" for all types of Internet threats. See Chapter 30 for more information on the types of threats cookies might pose and ways of protecting yourself from bad cookies.

Wrap Up

The World Wide Web consists of many billions of Web pages, encompassing virtually the whole of human knowledge (plus a lot of worthless junk). The program you use to browse the Web is called your *Web browser*. There are several brands of Web browsers, such as AOL, Netscape Navigator, MSN Explorer, and Microsoft Internet Explorer. This chapter has focused on Internet Explorer, because that's the main Web browser that comes with Windows XP. High points include:

✦ Web site addresses are called URLs (for Uniform Resource Locators).

✦ One way to visit a Web site is to typed its URL into your Web browser's Address bar and press Enter.

✦ Hyperlinks provide easy one-click access to Web sites.

✦ Internet Explorer's History bar lists all sites you've visited recently and is also used for the Address bar's AutoCompete drop-down list.

✦ To clear out your history list, choose Tools ➪ Internet Options from IE's menu bar. Then, click the Clear History and OK buttons.

✦ To make it easy to return to a favorite Web page, choose Favorites ➪ Add to Favorites, or press Ctrl+D, while you are visiting that page.

✦ To return to a Favorite site, click in Favorites in the menu bar, and then click the site you want to visit. Optionally, you can click the Folders button in IE's toolbar to see all your favorite sites in an Explorer bar.

✦ For expediency in loading, copies of Web pages you visit are stored in your Internet cache, which is actually a folder named Temporary Internet Files in your user account.

✦ Cookies are generally used to pass small bits of information about you from one page to the next within a site, so you don't have to sign in repeatedly.

✦ To delete and manage temporary Internet files and cookies, choose Tools ➪ Internet Options from Internet Explorer's menu bar.

✦ ✦ ✦

Doing E-Mail with Outlook Express

It seems that just about everyone knows what e-mail is these days. The *e* stands for *electronic*. With e-mail, you type a letter or message on your computer, you send it to the recipient's e-mail address, and it ends up in the recipient's e-mail Inbox a few seconds later. You can attach things like pictures and other files to the message so that the recipient gets those too. It's a lot faster than the postal service (called *snail mail* by computer jocks), and it doesn't cost a cent.

To use e-mail, you need an Internet connection, an e-mail address, and an e-mail client. All e-mail addresses follow the format *someone@somewhere.tld*, where *someone* is your username and *somewhere.tld* is a domain name. The e-mail client is the program you use to send and receive e-mail. This chapter focuses on Outlook Express, the e-mail client that comes Windows XP.

How E-Mail Works

Every person who has Internet access has an account with an Internet service provider (ISP). Each ISP has its own unique domain name. For example, America Online's domain name is `AOL.com`. MSN's domain name is `MSN.com`. Comcast's domain name is `Comcast.net`. Those are just a few examples. There are thousands of ISPs in the world.

Every person who has an account with an ISP has a unique *user name* (called a *screen name* by AOL). No two people who share the same ISP can have the same user name. If they did, there would be no way to tell them apart. Each person who has an account with an ISP also has an e-mail address that's expressed in the format *username@domain.name*. To send an e-mail to someone, you just need to address the e-mail message to his or her e-mail address. The Internet and ISP take care of making sure that your message gets to the right person.

Each ISP has two main computers for handling e-mail. One is called the *outgoing mail server*, or *SMTP (Simple Mail Transfer Protocol) server*. That server handles all mail being sent by the ISP's customers or users. The second e-mail server is called an *incoming mail server*, or *POP (Post Office Protocol) mail server*. That server handles all incoming mail. Figure 33-1 shows an example using two ISPs named abc.com and xyz.com.

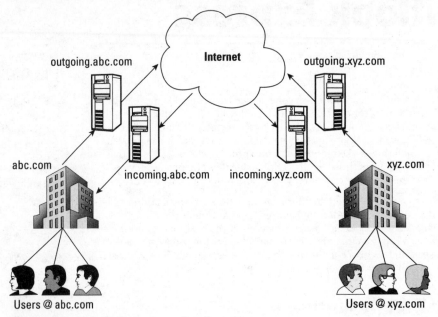

Figure 33-1: Each ISP has users and mail servers.

Let's say that you're mary@abc.com, and you send an e-mail to hank@xyz.com. When you click the Send button, the message travels to abc.com's outgoing mail sever, and then gets handed to the Internet. The Internet doesn't know exactly where hank@xyz.com is located. But it knows where xyz.com's incoming mail server is, so it hands the message to that server. xyz.com's mail server then stores a copy of the message. When Hank logs in and checks his e-mail, he sees only e-mail messages addressed to hank@xyz.com. He doesn't see, and can't download, other people's messages.

When hank@xyz.com sends a message to mary@abc.com, the same process happens in reverse. Hank's message gets handed to his ISP's outgoing mail server, which in turns hands it off to the Internet. The Internet hands it of to abc.com's incoming mail server, where the message sits until mary@abc.com checks her e-mail. It's pretty simple, really.

The program you use on your computer to send and receive e-mail is called your *e-mail client*. There are many e-mail clients on the market. The one that comes with Windows XP is called Outlook Express. The one that comes with Microsoft Office is called Outlook. In many cases, you use your Web browser as your e-mail client. For example, AOL users don't have an e-mail client separate from their Web browser. The same is true for people with MSN accounts. You can do e-mail from MSN Explorer or Internet Explorer.

Some ISPs give you the choice of using your Web browser or an e-mail client. Some don't give you that choice. Since there are thousands of ISPs, I can't tell you exactly what your choices are. Only your ISP can tell you that. In fact, only your ISP can tell you how to *do* e-mail, because each ISP is free to set up its e-mail service as it sees fit.

Introducing Outlook Express

Windows XP comes with an e-mail client named Outlook Express. If you're already sending and receiving e-mail without using Outlook Express, you can ignore this entire chapter and keep doing e-mail the way you always have. Whether or not you need Outlook Express, or can even use Outlook Express, depends on how you do your ISP or e-mail service.

Previously, I implied that how you do e-mail depends entirely on your ISP. But I told a little white lie there because you can do e-mail independently of your ISP by setting up a free e-mail account with a service such as Hotmail (www.hotmail.com) or Yahoo! (http://mail.yahoo.com). Doing that is often handy when several people in the same household share a single Internet account, because it keeps everyone's e-mail separate. But both Hotmail and Yahoo! let you do e-mail with your Web browser. So, Outlook Express isn't required for doing e-mail with those free services.

Who needs Outlook Express?

There is only one group of people in the world that actually needs Outlook Express. Those are people who have no other e-mail client that works with their service. Again, I can't tell you what your ISP requires or offers; only your ISP or e-mail service provider can tell you that.

If you're already using some other e-mail client, there may not be much reason to switch to Outlook Express. For example, if you have Microsoft Office and Microsoft Outlook, you'd be better off using Outlook. Using Outlook Express would be sort of a downgrade rather than an upgrade, because Outlook has more features and meshes better with other programs in the Microsoft Office suite of programs.

Who can use Outlook Express?

If your ISP or e-mail provider allows you to use Outlook Express, you might want to read this chapter to see if there's something in Outlook Express that you like better than whatever e-mail client you're using right now. But there's certainly no rule that says you *must* use Outlook Express if your ISP gives you a choice. So, the choice is up to you.

What you need to know to get started

To use Outlook Express, you must configure it to work with your e-mail service. Exactly how you do that depends on your mail service. But for "traditional" Internet e-mail accounts (also called POP3 accounts, for Post Office Protocol version 3), you'll need the six pieces of information shown in Table 33-1:

✦ **E-mail address:** You must know your own e-mail address, the one that people use to send you e-mail messages.

✦ **Account type:** Typically this would be either POP or HTTP (Hypertext Transfer Protocol).

✦ **User account name:** The name you use to sign into your ISP's service.

✦ **E-mail password:** You should be able to define your own password. But if your ISP has set up a temporary password, you'll need to know what that is to set up your account.

✦ **Outgoing (SMTP) mail server:** You will need to know the exact name of your ISP's outgoing mail server.

✦ **Incoming (POP3) mail server:** You will need to know the exact name of your ISP's incoming mail server.

Table 33-1: Information You Need to Set Up Outlook Express

Information Needed	Example	Write Your Information Here
Your e-mail address	somebody@somewhere.com	
Your e-mail username	Somebody	
Your e-mail password	********	
E-mail account type	POP3, IMAP, or HTTP	
Outgoing (SMTP) mail server	smtp.somewhere.com	
Incoming (POP3) mail server	mail.somewhere.com	

There is no point in trying to guess what any of the preceding might be. There is no point in trying the examples form the middle column. You need exact information, and only your ISP or mail service can provide that. You can either look around their Web site for information or call on the phone. I mention this because I've seen *a lot* of people try to set up their e-mail accounts through sheer guesswork, which rarely works.

Setting up your e-mail account

If you've decided you're going to use, or at least try out, Outlook Express, and you feel confident that you have the information you need from your ISP, you can set up your e-mail account in several ways:

1. Click the **Start** button, and choose **All Programs ➪ Outlook Express**.

Tip   As a shortcut, you may be able to click the Start button and choose E-mail from the top left side of the Start menu.

2. If you see a message asking if you want to make Outlook Express your default e-mail client, you can choose **Yes** if you think that Outlook Express will be the only program you'll use for e-mail. Otherwise, click No.

3. If you've never used Outlook Express, the Internet Connection Wizard may open automatically to help you set up an account. If you see the Internet Connection Wizard, skip to Step 5.

4. When Outlook Express opens, you can set up a new account by choosing **Tools ➪ Accounts** from its menu bar. In the Internet Accounts dialog box that opens, click the **Add** button and choose **Mail**.

5. Answer all question presented by the wizard, clicking the Next button at the bottom of each page, until you get to the page with the Finish button.

Be sure to read the information on each wizard page carefully, and type your answers accurately. Any misinformation or simple typographical errors will start to haunt you the minute you try to send or receive any e-mail messages. When it comes to setting up your e-mail account, there is no margin for even minor typographical errors.

Once you've set up your e-mail account, the Folders pane will display a set of folders for your account. The exact folders that appear will vary with different types of accounts, as in the example shown in Figure 33-2. The most common, and most useful, folders are:

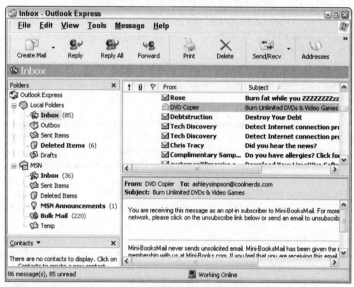

Figure 33-2: The Outlook Express program window

✦ **Inbox:** Every e-mail message that you receive initially appears in your Inbox. If messages don't arrive automatically, click the Send/Recv button in Outlook Express's toolbar to bring your Inbox up to date.

✦ **Outbox:** On some e-mail accounts, the Outbox gathers up e-mail messages waiting to be sent. To send messages waiting in the Outbox, click the Send/Recv button.

✦ **Sent Items:** Maintains a history of all e-mail messages you've sent.

✦ **Deleted Items:** Contains messages you've deleted from your Inbox (or any other folder), but haven't completely removed from your hard disk yet.

Writing E-Mail with Outlook Express

Once Outlook Express is open, you can use any of the following techniques to compose a new e-mail message to send to anybody who has an e-mail address:

✦ Click the **Create Mail** button on the Outlook Express toolbar.

Tip   To add a fancy background to your message, click the ↓ on the Create Mail button, and then click a stationery name.

✦ Or, choose **Message** ⇨ **New Message** from the Outlook Express menu bar.

✦ Or, press **Ctrl+N** when a mail folder is open.

A New Message window for composing your e-mail message appears on-screen. To compose your message, fill in the address portion of the window as explained in the following steps.

1. Type the recipient's e-mail address next to To:. If you want to send the message to several people, you can type several addresses separated by semicolons (;).

   - Optionally, to send carbon copies of the message to other recipients, put their e-mail addresses in the Cc: box. Again, you can separate multiple e-mail addresses by semicolons.

   - Optionally, to send blind carbon copies of the message to other recipients, type their e-mail addresses into the Bcc: box, again separating multiple addresses with semicolons.

Tip   A blind carbon copy sends the e-mail message to the recipient with all other recipients' names hidden. This protects the privacy of other recipients and makes the e-mail look as though it were sent to the recipient directly. If you don't see a Bcc: box at the top of the New Mail Message window, choose View ⇨ > All Headers from Outlook Express's menu bar.

2. In the Subject: box, type a brief description of the subject of the message. This part of the message appears in the recipient's Inbox and is visible prior to the recipient's opening the message.

3. Type your message in the large editing window below the address portion of the e-mail. You can use all the techniques described under "Typing and navigating text" in Chapter 3 to make changes and corrections.

Figure 33-3 shows an example of a simple text message typed in the New Message window.

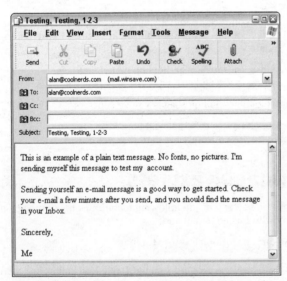

Figure 33-3: A plain-text e-mail message addressed and ready to send

If you want to add any fonts, pictures, or hyperlinks to your e-mail message, read the following section. Otherwise, you can skip to the "Sending the message" section.

Composing fancier e-mail messages

E-mail messages can be *plain text* or *rich text* (also called HTML [Hypertext Markup Language]). Plain-text messages contain only plain text. Rich-text messages can include fonts, pictures, and hyperlinks, as in the example shown in Figure 33-4.

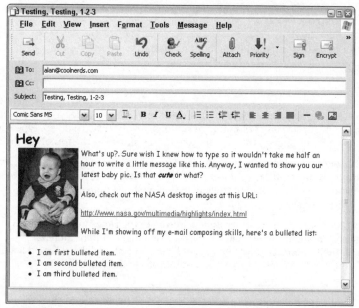

Figure 33-4: A sample rich-text (HTML) e-mail message with a picture and fonts

To compose a rich text e-mail message, use formatting buttons in the toolbar, just above the message text. If you don't see a formatting toolbar, choose Format ⇨ Rich Text (HTML) from the New Message window's menu bar. You can type your text normally. Then, select (drag the mouse pointer through) any text you want to format, and choose your formatting options as described in the sections that follow.

Tip If you've installed Microsoft Word, Microsoft Excel, or Microsoft PowerPoint on your computer, you can use the Spelling button in Outlook Express's toolbar to correct misspellings in your e-mail message.

Using fonts and alignments

As an example of using fonts and alignments in an e-mail message, suppose that you want to put a large, centered heading at the top of your message (or anywhere in your message). Type the line of text, and press Enter. Then, select the same line of text using any of the text-selection techniques described in Chapter 7 (for example, just drag the mouse pointer through the text you want to format). Then, choose your font, size, color, and click the Center button in the toolbar, as illustrated in Figure 33-5.

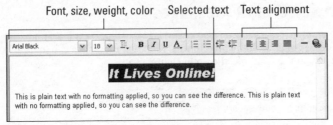

Figure 33-5: Text selected and formatted using buttons on the toolbar

Typing a list

Numbered and bulleted lists are useful ways of organizing text. For example, you might want to show some numbered steps or a list of points or options in your text. To do so, type each item in the list, pressing Enter once at the end of each line, as shown at the top of Figure 33-6.

Next, select all the lines of text (and only those lines) as in the center of Figure 33-6. An easy way to do this is to simply start with the mouse pointer just outside the last item in the list, and then drag the mouse pointer up and to the left so that all items (and only the items) you want to put into list form are selected (highlighted).

Click the Formatting Numbers or Formatting Bullets button in the New Message toolbar. Optionally, to indent or unindent the list, click the Decrease Indentation or Increase Indentation button in the toolbar. The bottom part of Figure 33-6 shows the selected list after clicking the Formatting Numbers and Increase Indent buttons in the toolbar.

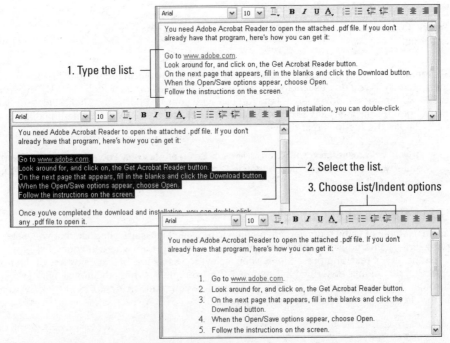

Figure 33-6: Typing a numbered or bulleted list

Inserting a picture

You can insert a small photo or picture into the body of your e-mail message, like the baby picture shown back in Figure 33-4. You'll have to make sure that you're using the Rich Text (HTML) format. Then:

Tip

Use Insert ⇨ Picture to insert small pictures only. As described later in this chapter, you can *attach* large pictures and photos to messages.

1. Move the mouse pointer to about where you want to place the picture.

2. Then:

   - Click the **Insert Picture** button in the New Message toolbar.

   - Or, choose **Insert** ⇨ **Picture** from the New Message menu bar.

3. In the Picture dialog box that opens, click the **Browse** button and navigate to the folder that contains the pictures you want to insert. Then, double-click the picture's icon or click the picture's icon, and click the **Open** button.

4. If you want the picture to appear to the left of text (like the baby picture in Figure 33-4), choose Left from the Alignment drop-down list. Or, choose Right to make the picture align to the right of adjacent text.

5. If you want to put a border around a picture, enter a thickness (in pixels) in the Border Thickness option (the number **1** will put a nice thin border around the picture).

6. If you chose the Left or Right alignment option, use the Horizontal and Vertical options to put some space between the text and the picture (a setting of **5** is usually plenty).

7. Click the **OK** button.

The picture lands in your e-mail message. If you want to change any of the options you initially chose, right-click the picture and choose Properties. If you change your mind and want to delete the picture, click the picture and press Delete (Del).

Inserting a Hyperlink

A hyperlink is a clickable URL. If you simply type a URL into a message, Outlook Express will automatically make it into a hyperlink. Optionally, you can copy a URL from your Web browser's address bar or a Web page and paste it into your e-mail message. (The latter method saves a lot of time and eliminates possible typographical errors).

If you want to create a "Click here" type of link, where plain-English words rather than a URL are visible in your message, follow these steps instead:

1. Type the text you plan to use as a URL (for example, the words Click here).

2. Select the text that will act as a hyperlink.

3. Click the **Create a Hyperlink** button in the New Message toolbar, or choose **Insert** ⇨ **Hyperlink** from the New Message menu bar.

4. In the Hyperlink dialog box that opens, type (or paste) the URL of the Web site into the URL textbox, as in Figure 33-7.

5. Click **OK** in the Hyperlink dialog box.

The text you selected in Step 1 will be colored and underlined as a hyperlink. The recipient of your e-mail message need only click that link to visit the site.

Selected text

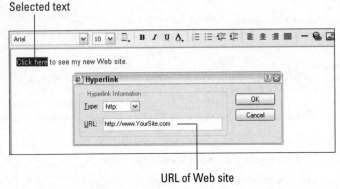

URL of Web site

Figure 33-7: Making selected text a hyperlink

Attaching files to e-mail messages

An e-mail message isn't a document — it's, well, a *message*. The main difference is that unlike documents, which are stored in regular document folders such as My Documents and Shared Documents, e-mail messages are stored in your e-mail client's folders.

If you want to send someone a document via e-mail, attach the document to the message. The document can be anything: something you've typed, a photograph, a song, a video, and so on. But there is one big catch: Most ISPs won't let you attach any more that 1 or 1.5 MB worth of files to a single message. (One MB equals roughly 1,000 KB.) Songs and videos tend to be larger than that, so they're not always good candidates for e-mail.

Tip

Many people use .zip files (see Chapter 13) to compress one or more large files into a single, smaller file that's easier to e-mail. You can also use the Send a File or Photo option in Windows Messenger or MSN Messenger (see Chapter 34) to send someone a file of any size.

Attached documents don't appear in the body of the e-mail message. They just follow the message along on the Internet to the recipient's e-mail Inbox. The filenames and sizes of the attachments will appear just above the text, as in Figure 33-8.

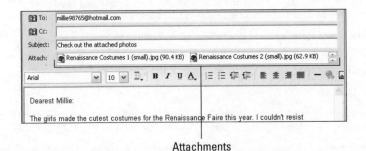

Attachments

Figure 33-8: Two photos attached to an e-mail message

A Shortcut for E-Mailing Photos

Here's a handy shortcut for e-mailing pictures that will automatically shrink large photos to a more manageable size for your recipients. The shortcut method works with Outlook Express, Outlook, and a few other e-mail clients. But it doesn't work with all e-mail accounts. So, whether or not this option will work for you depends on the program you use as your e-mail client.

Here's how the shortcut works. Let's say that you're browsing around your folders and haven't even opened your e-mail client. You come across a document file you want to e-mail (we'll use a photo as an example, but the method works with any type of document file). Rather than opening your e-mail client, just right-click the file's icon and choose Send To ➪ Mail Recipient.

To attach multiple files to an e-mail message using the shortcut method, select the files you want to send, and then right-click any one of them and choose Send To ➪ Mail Recipient. If the attachment is a large picture (or pictures), you'll be given the option to make your picture(s) smaller. Click OK and choose any size (640 × 480 is plenty big). If no sizing options appear, this just means that all photos you've attached are already smaller than 640 pixels wide and 480 pixels tall.

Sending the message

Once your message is addressed, composed, and ready to go, just click the Send button in the upper-left corner of the New Message window to send the e-mail. If Outlook Express is configured to send mail immediately, and you're online, the message will be sent to recipient, and a copy will be added to your Sent Items folder.

Cross-Reference   See "Customizing and Configuring Outlook Express," later in this chapter, for details on configuration.

If you're not online, or Outlook Express isn't configured to send messages immediately, the message will be placed in your Outbox. Click the Send/Recv button in Outlook Express's toolbar to send the message from your Outbox to the recipient.

Tip   To set options in Outlook Express, choose Tools ➪ Options from its menu bar. The option to send messages immediately when you click the Send button is located on the Send tab. If you clear, rather than select, that option, all newly sent messages will be sent to your Outbox and remain there until you click the Send/Recv button in Outlook Express's toolbar.

Reading Your E-Mail with Outlook Express

E-mail messages that people send to you are initially stored on your ISP's mail server computer. To see them, you need to get them from that server to your own computer. Depending on how Outlook Express is configured, you might, or might not, have to click the Send/Recv button to retrieve your mail. Either way, all new messages will be added to your Inbox. So, you need to click the Inbox folder (see Figure 33-9) to see your messages.

Cross-Reference   See "Customizing and Configuring Outlook Express," later in this chapter, for details on configuration.

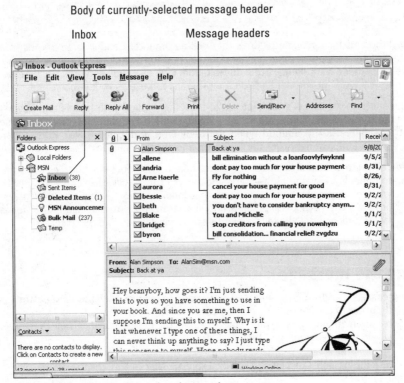

Figure 33-9: Inbox, message headers, and one message

Outlook Express's program window and taskbar button are no different from any other program's. So, you can:

✦ Move, size, minimize, and maximize Outlook Express's program window using all the standard techniques.

✦ Sort (alphabetized) items in either ascending or descending order by clicking the column heading.

✦ Change the width of any column by dragging, left or right, the bar to the right of the column name.

✦ Move any column by dragging its column name left or right.

✦ Choose **Help** ➪ **Contents and Index** from Outlook Express's menu bar, or just press **F1**, to get help with the program.

The Inbox is split into two panes. The top pane shows *message headers* — who sent the message, the subject, and the date and time that you received the message. Headers for new messages you haven't read yet are in boldface. Click any message (once) to see its contents in the lower *preview* pane.

To see the contents of a message in more detail, double-click the message header. The message opens in a new window, as in the example shown in Figure 33-10. Items in the toolbar provide quick access to the most commonly used menu commands, summarized as follows.

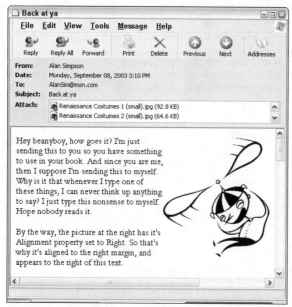

Figure 33-10: Viewing an open e-mail message in its own window

+ **Reply:** Click this to send a reply to the sender (only). Then, type your reply and click **Send**.

+ **Reply All:** Click this to reply to everyone who received this message. Type your reply, and click the **Send** button.

+ **Forward:** If you think that a friend should see an e-mail, click the **Forward** button, type the new recipient's e-mail address, and click **Send** to pass the message along.

+ **Print:** To print the message, click the **Print** button.

+ **Delete:** If you never want to see the message again, click the **Delete** button. The message is moved to the Deleted Items folder.

+ **Previous:** This displays the previous message from the header list.

+ **Next:** This displays the next message in the header list.

To close the open message and get back to your Outlook Express window, click its Close (x) button at the right side of its title bar. Or, you can size and arrange the preview window and Outlook Express so that you can see both on the screen at the same time.

Tip To reply to or forward a message that isn't open, right-click the message header and choose one of the Reply or Forward options on the shortcut menu that appears.

Opening attachments

Before I tell you how to open an attachment, be advised that e-mail attachments are how the vast majority of viruses and worms are spread. You should open an attachment only if you know whom it's from and what it is. So, please don't practice what you learn here with the first e-mail attachment that comes along. Send an e-mail and attachment to yourself, and practice with that. Also, see Chapter 28 for tips on blocking virus-infected e-mail attachments.

Caution   Don't assume that an e-mail from a large company such as Microsoft or eBay really *is* from that company. Spoofers can fake the return e-mail address on the messages they send out. For more information, see the Security at Home Web site at www.microsoft.com/athome/ security/spam/default.mspx.

Checking your attachment security

Outlook Express had some serious virus protection built into it, in the form of *you can't open this attachment because it's the type of file that could contain a virus*. That's different from the kind of virus protection discussed in Chapter 28, which is a little more choosey. Virus-protection programs usually only block attachments that *do* contain a virus.

Before you try to open any attachments, you'll want to check, and possibly change, Outlook Express's security settings. Here's how:

1. From the menu bar in Outlook Express, choose **Tools** ⇨ **Options**.

2. In the Options dialog box that opens, click the **Security** tab.

3. To be warned when some program attempts to send e-mail through Outlook Express, choose **Warn me when other applications try to send mail as me**.

4. To block all potentially unsafe e-mail attachments, choose **Do not allow attachments to be saved or opened that could potentially be a virus** (see Figure 33-11).

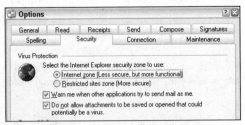

Figure 33-11: Virus-protection options in Outlook Express's Options dialog box

5. Click the **OK** button.

Viewing (opening) an attachment

Recall that all new incoming e-mail messages are stored in your Inbox. While viewing your e-mails, you can tell which ones have attachments by the little paper-clip icon that appears next to message headers. When you click such a message, a large paper clip will also appear above the message text, as in Figure 33-12.

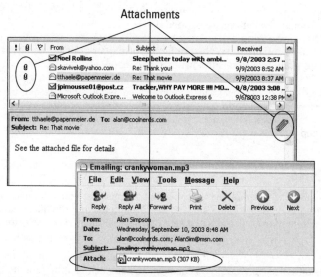

Figure 33-12: Paper clips indicate e-mail attachments.

Let's assume that you've clicked on the message header for a message that has a file attached. You know who sent you this attachment, the message looks legitimate, and you feel it's safe to open the attachment. You can use any of the following techniques to open an e-mail attachment in Outlook Express:

✦ Click the message header, and then double-click the paper-clip icon to the left of that message header.

✦ Click the message header, and then click the large paper clip in the lower preview pane.

✦ Double-click the message header, and then double-click the attachment filename just above the body of the message that opens.

Windows will attempt to open the attachment as a regular document. If you have a program that can open the attached document, the document will open. If you'd like to print the attachment, choose File ➪ Print from that program's menu bar. If you'd like to save the attachment as a document on your own hard disk, choose File ➪ Save As from that program's menu bar. When the Save As dialog box opens, make sure that you navigate to My Documents or some other folder before clicking the Save button.

Note Sometimes when you open an attachment, all you get is a blank message with another attachment. So, you have to double-click the attachment there to open its attachment. You may have to repeat this several times — it all depends on how many AOL users forwarded it to each other before you got it.

If the attachment is a .zip file, it will have a .zip extension. A .zip file is actually one or more files compressed into a single file for fast transport across to the Internet. If you receive a .zip file, you're probably better off saving it (as discussed in a moment) than trying to open it. After you've saved the .zip file, you can extract its contents, as discussed under "Using Compressed Folders (.zip Files)" in Chapter 13.

If you don't have an appropriate program for the document you're trying to open, you'll see that Windows cannot open this file dialog box, described under "When Windows can't open a document" in Chapter 3. There are a couple of solutions to the problem. You can reply to the sender, asking him or her to send the file to you in a different format, or ask the sender if he or she knows of a suitable program that you can download and install for free.

Tip   To view .pdf files, you'll need to download and install Adobe Acrobat Reader from www.adobe.com. To view .ppt files, go to www.microsoft.com/downloads and search for the keyword PowerPoint viewer. Then, download and install PowerPoint Viewer 97 for PowerPoint 97, 2000, and 2002 Users.

Saving attachments

Attachments are generally saved with e-mail messages, which means that you can't use them as freely as documents stored in regular folders such as My Documents and the like. If you want to keep an e-mail attachment around and use it as a normal document, you need to *save* the attachment.

Saving an attachment isn't the same as opening it. That is, saving an attachment won't trigger any viruses. So, if you have antivirus software, you can save any suspicious attachments first. Then, scan them for viruses *before* you open them. (If the scanning program finds a virus, just delete the infected file; do not open it!) To save an attachment:

1. In Outlook Express, click the e-mail message header to which the file is attached.

2. Click the large paper-clip icon in the preview area. Then, click **Save Attachments** (see Figure 33-13).

3. In the Save Attachments dialog box that opens, only attachments whose names are selected (highlighted) will be saved. You can select and unselect attachments to save using **Ctrl+Click**.

4. When the names of attachments you want to save are selected, click the **Browse** button, then navigate to the folder in which you want to save the attachments and click **OK**.

5. Click the **Save** button in the dialog box.

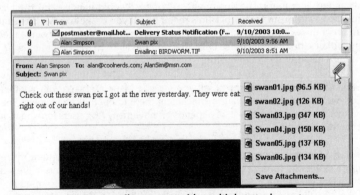

Figure 33-13: An e-mail message with multiple attachments

I Can't Save or Open Any Attachments!

As mentioned, Outlook Express's built-in virus protection blocks any file that *could* contain a virus, not just files that *do* contain viruses. Therefore, you may not be able to open some perfectly innocent files, such as photos.

When Outlook Express blocks an attachment, clicking the large paper-clip icon in the preview area reveals only disabled (dimmed) options. If you open the e-mail message, you won't see the usual filenames above the body of the message. Instead, you'll see a bar that reads *OE removed access to the following unsafe attachments in your e-mail* (where OE stands for Outlook Express).

If you're sure that the attachment is safe, and you do want to open it, you can repeat Steps 1-4 under "Checking Your Attachment Security," earlier in this chapter. But clear, rather than select, the *Do not allow attachments to be saved or opened . . .* option in Step 4 to turn off virus protection. Don't forget to turn that option back on if you want to continue to use it in the future.

Once you've saved the attachment, it will be just like any document you have created yourself. So, you can use Windows Explorer to navigate to the folder in which you placed the attachment(s). Then, double-click any attachment's name to open it. You can also delete the original e-mail message and attachment if you wish. The copy on your hard disk is its own separate file and won't be affected by anything you do in Outlook Express anymore.

Managing E-Mail Messages

As time goes by, your collection of e-mail messages will grow. To manage those messages, you can organize them into folders, delete the junk mail or any messages you don't need any more, and so forth. You do most of these managerial tasks in the list of message headers in Outlook Express's program window.

Selecting messages

In the list of message headers, you can work with individual messages or groups of messages. To work with multiple messages, you first need to *select* the messages you want to work with. You can use the same techniques you use to select multiple icons (described in more depth under "Selecting Files and Folders" in Chapter 14). For example, you can:

1. First, click any message header to select only that message. Then:

   - To select more message headers, hold down the **Ctrl** key while clicking additional messages you want to select.

   - To extend the selection through a group of messages, hold down the **Shift** key and click the header to which you want to extend the selection.

   - To select from the currently selected message to the end of the list, press **Shift+End**.

   - To select from the currently selected message to the top of the list, press **Ctrl+Home**.

   - To select all message headers, press **Ctrl+A** or choose **Edit ➪ Select All** from Outlook Express's menu bar.

You can also use Ctrl+Click to unselect selected messages. For example, suppose that most of the messages in your Inbox are junk mail, and you just want to get rid of them without even opening them up. You can click the first message header, then press Ctrl+A to select all the message headers. Next, hold down the Ctrl key and click the messages you *don't* want to delete, as in Figure 33-14. Pressing the Delete key in that figure would delete all the selected messages.

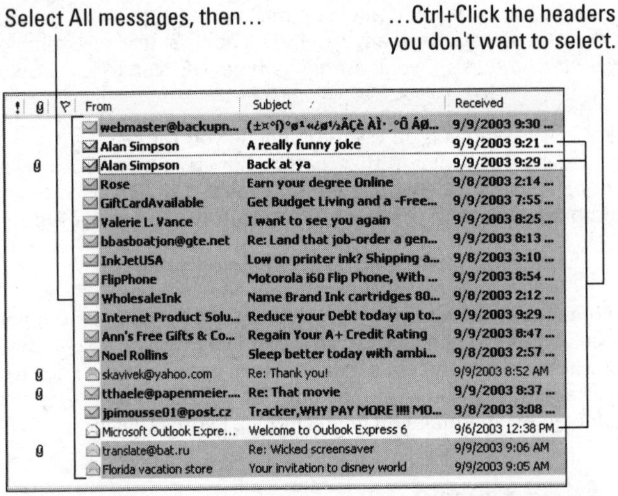

Select All messages, then...   ...Ctrl+Click the headers
                                                  you don't want to select.

Figure 33-14: A quick way to select most (but not all) messages

Deleting messages

Deleting messages is simple. If you want to delete a single message, you can just right-click its message header and choose Delete. Optionally, you can select the headers of the messages you want to select, as in the example shown in Figure 33-14. Then, use whichever of the following techniques is most convenient to delete the selected messages:

✦ On your keyboard, press the **Delete (Del)** key, or **Crl+D**.

✦ Click the **Delete** button in Outlook Express's toolbar.

✦ Choose **Edit** ➪ **Delete** from Outlook Express's menu bar.

✦ Right-click any selected message, and choose **Delete**.

The message isn't permanently deleted from your hard disk. It's just moved into your Deleted Items folder. So, if you ever delete an e-mail message by accident, here's how you can get it back:

1. Click the **Deleted Items** folder.

2. If you want to undelete several messages, you may select them all first.

3. Right-click the message (or any selected message), and choose **Move to Folder** ➪ **Inbox**.

There are a couple of disadvantages to using the Deleted Items folder. For one, the messages in that folder are still on your hard disk, taking up space. Each message is a trivial amount of disk space. But when you have thousands of them stored in there, it adds up. So once in a while, it would be good to empty the Deleted Items folder. Once you do, there will be no way to recover any messages that where there. So, you want to make sure that there's nothing important in the Deleted Items folder. To empty the folder:

✦ Choose **Edit** ➪ **Empty 'Deleted Items' Folder** from Outlook Express's menu bar.

✦ Or, right-click the **Deleted Items** folder and choose **Empty 'Deleted Items' Folder** (see Figure 33-15).

Caution   The term *permanently delete* always means just that — to forever remove the item from your hard disk. There's no changing your mind after you've permanently deleted an item.

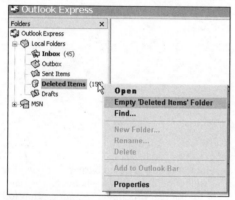

Figure 33-15: Shortcut menu when you right-click the Deleted Items folder

If you opted to delete all messages in the Deleted Items folder, you'll have one last chance to change your mind, in the form of a dialog box that asks *Are you sure you want to permanently delete the contents of the Deleted Items folder?* Click Yes only if you're certain you're willing to part with the selected messages forever.

Grouping messages into folders

You're not limited to using the folders that first appear when you open Outlook Express. You can create as many folders as you wish. For example, I keep a number of subfolders under Inbox to store messages that I might need to refer to later, as in Figure 33-16. When I get an order-confirmation message from a Web site where I've purchased something, that message goes into my Orders folder until the package arrives. You can also organize your messages by the person or company that sent you the message, by project if you work online — whatever makes sense for your situation.

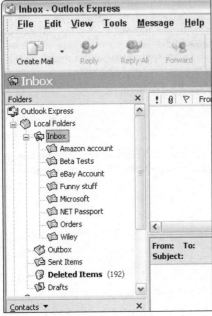

Figure 33-16: Custom subfolders beneath the Inbox folder

Before you create a folder, you need to decide which folder will be its parent. For example, if you want to create subfolders for your Inbox, as in Figure 33-16, Inbox will act as the new folder's parent. Once you've decided on a parent folder, use whichever technique that follows is most convenient to create a new folder:

1. If you're not already in Outlook Express, go ahead and start that program. Then, do whichever of the following is easiest for you:

   • Right-click the folder that will act as the parent and choose **New Folder**.

   • Choose **File** ➪ **Folder** ➪ **New** (or press **Ctrl+Shift+E**). In the Create Folder dialog box that opens, click the folder that will act as parent to the new folder.

2. Type the name of the new folder, and then press **Enter** or click the **OK** button (if you're in the Create Folder dialog box).

If you change your mind about a folder's name, right-click that folder, choose Rename, type your new name, and press Enter. You can also delete a folder. But be aware that if there are any messages in that folder, you'll delete those as well. Aside from that, deleting a folder is pretty much the same as deleting anything else: right-click the folder you want to delete, and choose Delete.

Moving messages into folders

An easy way to move a message from your Inbox to one of your subfolders is to simply drag the message header so that the mouse pointer is sitting right on top of the folder in which you want to put the message. Then, release the mouse button.

Keep Your Messages to Yourself

If you have one computer in a household with several users, having one e-mail address for every-one can get very old, very fast. It's not necessary to pay extra to your ISP to set up extra e-mail accounts. Nor is it necessary to try to set up and manage multiple e-mail identities. You'd likely find it easier to set up a separate user account and e-mail account for each family member (see Chapter 7).

Once you've set up a user account for a family member, you can then set up a free MSN or Hotmail e-mail account for each member and a separate .NET Passport for each user (see Chapter 34). That way, each family member has his or her own e-mail account, My Documents folder, personal settings, and so forth. And best of all, it keeps everybody's e-mail entirely separate. (If you're the administrator, however, you can always spy on people and see what they're up to.)

Optionally, you can right-click any message and choose Move to Folder. Or, to move a bunch of messages into a subfolder, select their message headers first. Then, right-click any selected message and choose Move to Folder. In the Move dialog box that opens, click the folder in which you want to put the selected message(s), and then click OK.

Marking messages as read or unread

As mentioned, headers for any new messages you receive will be shown in boldface. When you click a message header to view its contents in the preview pane, or double-click a message to open it, the bold text turns to regular text, indicating that you've read the message. (Actually, you have to leave the highlighter on the message header for a few seconds before the boldface goes away.)

You can manually mark a message header as "read" or "not read" by right-clicking the message header and choosing Mark as Read or Mark as Unread. Or, select a group of messages first; then, right-click any one of them, and choose a Mark As . . . option.

Tip A boldface folder name with a number to the right contains unread messages. The number indicates how many unread messages are in the folder.

For example, suppose that you read an important message but can't deal with it right away. You want to make its header bold again to call attention to it next time you open Outlook Express. To make the read message look like an unread message, just right-click its header and choose Mark as Unread.

Using Windows Address Book

Windows XP provides the handy Windows Address Book (WAB), a program that lets you store and manage people's names and addresses. You also can use the Address Book to fill in the e-mail addresses of your recipients automatically when you compose a new message or when you reply to or forward a message. Before we look at the Address Book, let's look at a couple of ways you can add *contacts* (people's names and addresses) automatically from Outlook Express.

Tracking names and addresses automatically

It's not entirely necessary to manually add names and addresses to your Address Book. You can automatically add people's names and addresses using any of the following techniques. You can have Outlook Express automatically add the name and e-mail address of anybody you reply to in an e-mail message by following these steps:

1. Make sure you're in Outlook Express's program window.

2. Choose **Tools** ➪ **Options** from Outlook Express's menu bar.

3. In the Options dialog box that opens, click the **Send** tab.

4. Select (check) **Automatically put people I reply to in my Address Book**.

5. Click the **OK** button in the Options dialog box.

A slightly less automated technique (but one that still saves you some typing) is to add the e-mail address of the person who sent you a message. There are a couple of ways to do that. In Outlook Express's list of message headers, right-click the message header, and choose Add Sender to Address Book, as shown near the top of Figure 33-17. Or, if the message is already open and you're reading it, right-click the name next to From and choose Add to Address Book from that submenu, as in the lower half of the same figure.

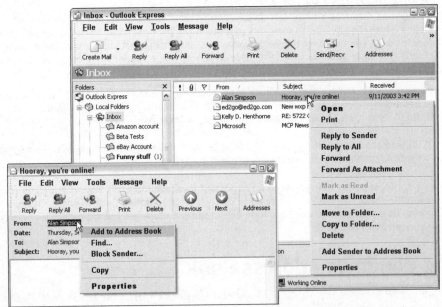

Figure 33-17: Two ways to add a contact to Windows Address Book without typing

If a Properties dialog box opens, just click its OK button. Later, you can go back and add information if you like, as discussed in a moment.

Opening Windows Address Book

You can open Windows Address Book at any time to view, change, delete, or print information. From Outlook Express, you just have to click the Addresses button in Outlook Express toolbars or press Ctrl+Shift+B. Optionally, you can start Windows Address Book without going through Outlook Express. Just click the Start button and choose All Programs ➪ Accessories ➪ Address Book. Either way, your Address Book will open, looking something like Figure 33-18. In that example, I've already added one contact whose name, e-mail address, and phone numbers appear across the top of the main pane.

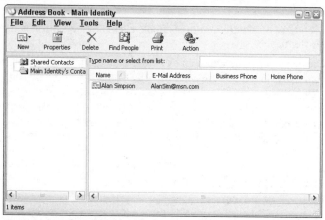

Figure 33-18: Windows Address Book is open.

The Shared Contacts folder at the left side of the window contains names and addresses accessible to all users of your computer. The Main Identity's Contacts folder contains names and addresses added by the current user or identity only. Unless someone has already set up an identity for you, you want to click consider yourself Main Identity and use that folder exclusively.

Creating and Managing Identities

Identities are optional in Outlook Express. And if you ask me, they're too complicated a solution to having multiple e-mail accounts on your computer. If you really want to create Outlook Express identities, you'll have to look to your ISP for specific instructions. They're the only ones who can tell you exactly how to set up identities for the e-mail service they provide.

I'm not a big fan of the identities approach to handling multiple e-mail accounts. I prefer the alternative described in the sidebar titled "Keep Your Messages to Yourself," earlier in this chapter. It would be no big loss to just dispense with the view of the folders either. To do so, choose View ➪ Folders and Groups from the Address Book menu bar.

Managing contacts

Your address book will grow. Keeping it up to date and organized is going to take some management on your part: things like adding contacts, changing and deleting contacts, putting together groups of people so that you can send them all an e-mail, such as a family newsletter. Let's start with adding and changing contacts.

Adding and changing contacts

You may (or may not) have already added some contacts to your Address Book from Outlook Express. You can add contacts at any time. And you can change contact information at any time. It's simple:

✦ If you want to add a contact to Windows Address Book, click the New button in its toolbar, and choose New Contact.

✦ If you want to change or add information to an existing contact (such as one that was added automatically), right-click the contact's line in the main pane of the Address Book and choose Properties.

If you add a contact, you'll come to a Properties dialog box similar to the one in Figure 33-19, but all the textboxes will be empty. If you right-click an existing contact and choose Properties, you'll come to the same dialog box. But you have to click the Name tab to see the options shown in Figure 33-19.

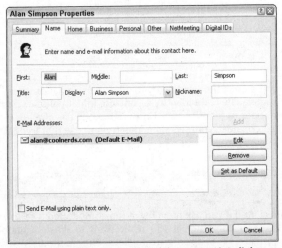

Figure 33-19: The Name tab of the Properties dialog box for a contact

The rest is easy. Fill in the blanks with whatever information you want. For example, click the Home tab, and type the home address and telephone number. Or click the Business tab, and type a business address and phone number. (You can do both.) You can fill in additional information, if appropriate, on the other tabs. Then, click OK.

Tip   If you click the Home or Business tab, you can then fill in street addresses and telephone numbers. Amazingly, after you fill in a street address, you can click the View Map button on either of those tabs to see an instant map of the address and some surrounding area. You can zoom in and out from the map, print, save, or e-mail the map, and see a map of nearby motels. Very handy!

Deleting contacts

Deleting a contact permanently removes that contact's information from your Address Book and your hard disk. There's no changing your mind after you delete a contact. So be careful with what you delete. Other than that, deleting a contact is pretty much the same as deleting anything else. Use whichever method is most convenient at the moment:

✦ In Address Book's main pane, right-click the contact you want to delete and choose **Delete**.

✦ Click the contact you want to delete and click the **Delete** button in Address Book's toolbar, or press the **Delete** key.

Optionally, you can select multiple contacts using any of the techniques you'd use for selecting multiple icons in Windows Explorer. Then, delete them all in one fell swoop by clicking the Delete button in the toolbar or by pressing the Delete key.

Cross-Reference

See "Selecting Files and Folders" in Chapter 14 for all the different ways you can select multiple icons.

Printing contacts

You can print the contents of your Address Book in a variety of formats. If you want to print information for just one contact, click that contact's line in the Address Book's main window. If you want to print information for all contacts, you can click any contact in the list. If you want to print information for several contacts, select those contacts first. You can select multiple contacts using any of the standard techniques for selecting icons in Explorer.

Next, click the Print button in Address Book's toolbar or choose File ➪ Print from Address Book's menu bar. A Print dialog box opens. To print all contacts, choose All. Otherwise, choose Selection to print only the currently selected contacts. Next, choose a print style, Memo, Business Card, or Phone List. Then, click the Print button and wait a few seconds.

Creating groups and mailing lists

There may be times when you want to send sort of a form letter to a group of people. They might be people in your family, coworkers on a project, or members of a group. When it comes time to send a message to all these folks, you probably won't want to type all their e-mail addresses individually. It's easier to just send the message to the group as a whole, especially if you have to do it often.

To send a message to a group, you have to define who is in the group. To do so, click the New toolbar button in Address Book and choose New Group. Or, choose File ➪ New Group from Address Book's menu bar. A Properties dialog box opens. On the Group tab, give the group a name of your own choosing. For example, in Figure 33-20, I named my group My Mailing List, though you're welcome to think up something better than that.

Next, click the Select Members button. In the Select Group Members dialog box that opens, click any name in the left column; then, click the Select ➪ button to add that person to the group. You can select any number of names in the left column first, using any standard technique for selecting multiple icons. Then, click the Select ➪ button to add them all to the right column. If you change your mind about an address in the right column, right-click that name and choose Remove. Once the right column contains the names of everyone you want in your mailing list, click the OK button. The contact names appear under Group Members, as in the example shown in Figure 33-20.

Figure 33-20: A new group named My Mailing List

Click the OK button in the Select Members dialog box; then, click the OK button in the Properties dialog box for the group. You'll be returned to the Address book, where you'll see the group name added with all the individual names. If you ever want to change the group, just right-click its name in the Address Book and choose Properties.

Using the Address Book to send e-mail

You can send an e-mail message to anyone in your address book, including all members of a group. Start your e-mail message in the normal manner, but don't type anything in the To: portion of the mail. Use the Address Book button instead. Here are the specific steps:

1. If you haven't already done so, start Outlook Express.

2. Click the **Create Mail** button in Outlook Express's menu bar to create a new, blank e-mail message.

3. Click the Address Book button to the left of To: The Select Recipients window opens.

4. To add a group or contact name to the To: portion of the e-mail message, click the person name or group name; then, click the **To: ⇨** button. You can use the same technique to add names or groups to the Cc: and Bcc: portions of the message. In Figure 33-21, I've opted to send the message to people in the My Mailing List group only.

5. Click the **OK** button to return to your message. The recipient addresses (or group name) appear above the subject line.

6. Type the Subject and main body of the message; then, click the **Send** button.

That's it. The e-mail message will be sent to all intended recipients.

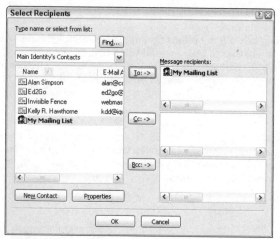

Figure 33-21: About to send an e-mail message to all members of the My Mailing List group

Customizing and Configuring Outlook Express

Outlook Express has a ton of optional settings, all accessible via its Options dialog box. To get to the dialog box, choose Tools ➪ Options from Outlook Express's menu bar. As you can see in Figure 33-22, the dialog box offers many tabs and many options. I think most are self-explanatory. If not, you can always press F1 or use Outlook Express's Help to get more information. In the sections that follow, we'll look at some of the main options available to you.

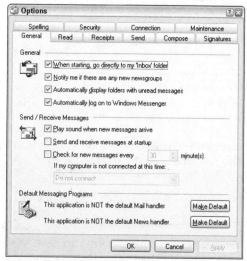

Figure 33-22: The General tab of Outlook Express's Options dialog box

General options

The General tab of the Options dialog box offers options that apply to Outlook Express as a whole. For example, you can choose whether to play a sound when new messages arrive, whether to check for new messages automatically and how often to check, and whether to put e-mail addresses of people you reply to in your Address Book automatically.

Read options

The Read tab in Options, shown on the left side of Figure 33-23, contains options for that let you control how Outlook Express handles e-mail messages you've received. You can choose whether to mark previewed messages as read and how long to wait before marking them. You also can choose the font used to display your messages.

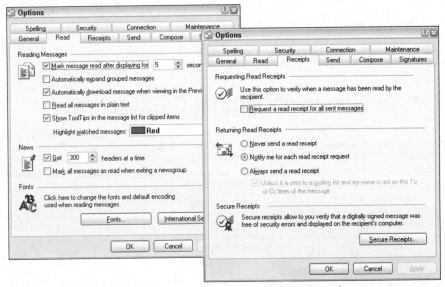

Figure 33-23: The Read and Receipts tabs of Outlook Express's Options

Receipt options

A "read receipt" is a message that you get, automatically, as soon as someone opens an e-mail message you've sent. Use read receipts when you need to know that your recipient has received your message. Secure receipts require a digital signature, described later in this chapter.

Send options

The Send tab offers options that control how the messages that you write are sent. As you can see in the left side of Figure 33-24, you can choose whether or not to save copies of sent messages to your Sent Items folder, to send messages immediately when you click the Send button (as opposed to just putting them in your Outbox). The Mail Sending Format option defines the format of each new e-mail message you create. If you want to be able to use fonts and pictures in your e-mail messages, choose HTML as your Mail Sending Format.

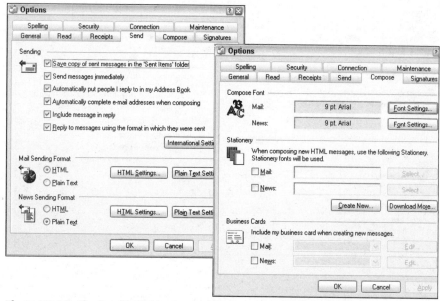

Figure 33-24: The Send and Compose tab's of Outlook Express's Options

Compose options

The Compose tab in Outlook Express's Options dialog box, shown on the right in Figure 33-24, lets you choose options for formatting e-mail messages. For example, you can choose a default Compose Font for all new messages. You can choose a custom stationery to use as a background for your messages. And finally, you can choose whether or not to include your business card with each message you send. (You'll need to add yourself to your Address Book for this option to work.)

Automatic signature options

Outlook Express can automatically insert a signature at the bottom of every e-mail message you send, saving you the time and trouble of doing so. To create an automatic signature, click the Signatures tab in Outlook Express's Options dialog box, shown in the left side of Figure 33-25.

Click the New button to create a signature. Initially, the signature is named Signature #1. You can change that name to My Signature or whatever you want, using the Rename button. Once you've created a new, empty signature, the Edit Signature options are enabled, and you can type a signature in the textbox. It can be as simple or as complex as you want, but it can contain only text (no pictures or fonts).

As an alternative to typing a signature, you can choose the File option, and then use the Browse button to specify the file that contains the signature information. The file must either be a text (.txt) file or an HTML file. A text file is one you create and save using a text-only editor like Notepad (which comes with Windows XP). And an HTML file is one you create using HTML and may contain fonts, pictures, hyperlinks, and so on.

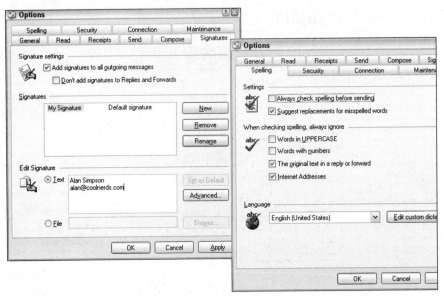

Figure 33-25: The Signatures and Spelling tab's of Outlook Express's Options

Note HTML is a large topic and is beyond the scope of this book. You can learn what HTML is about from the World Wide Web Consortium (W3C) Web site at www.w3C.org. A brief introduction to the topic is available at http://www.w3.org/MarkUp/Guide.

Once you've defined a signature, you need to choose *Add signatures to all outgoing messages* under Signature Settings near the top of the dialog box to add the signature to all your messages. You can choose whether or not you want that signature added to your replies and forwarded messages as well.

If you don't opt to add the signature to all outgoing messages, you can manually insert the signature anytime you're in the New Message window or when you're typing a reply or forwarding a message. Just move the cursor to where you want to insert the signature. Then, choose Insert ➪ Signature from the menu bar above the message.

About Virtual Business Cards (vCards)

A vCard is a virtual (electronic) business card. To create one, you need to add yourself to your own Address Book. Then, click your own address information in Address Book's main pane, and choose File ➪ Export ➪ Business Card (vCard) from Address Book's menu bar. In the Export dialog box that opens, choose a folder in which to store the card (My Documents will do fine), and click Save. When writing a message in the New Message window, or replying to a message, you can add your vCard to the message by choosing Insert ➪ My Business Card.

If you receive a message with a vCard attached, the vCard appears in your message as a Rolodex card icon with a big *V* on it. You can then click or right-click the vCard icon and choose Open or Delete from the shortcut menu that appears. For more information, choose Help ➪ Contents and Index from Outlook Express's menu bar. Then, search for vCard.

E-mail spelling options

Outlook Express's Spelling options, shown in the right side of Figure 33-25, let you choose how to handle spell-checking in your messages. Outlook Express doesn't have its own built-in spell checker. Instead, it uses the Microsoft Office spell-checker, if available, on your computer. If you don't have Microsoft Office (or at least Microsoft Word, Microsoft Excel, or Microsoft PowerPoint), spell-checking won't be available to you as an option in Outlook Express.

E-mail security options

The Security tab in Outlook Express's Options dialog box, shown at left in Figure 33-26, offers the Virus Protection options described earlier in this chapter, as well as more advanced features. The Internet Explorer security zone options define what's acceptable in e-mail messages. Your options are:

✦ **Internet zone (Less secure, but more functional):** Allows objects that are generally secure, such as Java applets and signed ActiveX controls, to be opened and executed in e-mail messages.

✦ **Restricted sites zone (More secure):** Severely restricts allowable e-mail content by preventing access even to objects whose security risk is minimal.

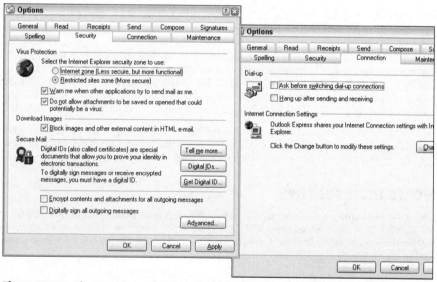

Figure 33-26: The Security and Connection tabs from Outlook Express's Options dialog box

Tip　For more information on Internet security zones, choose Help ⇨ Contents and Index from Internet Explorer's menu bar. In the Help window, click the Search tab, and search for the word `zone`.

Beneath the zone options are three other security options as described next.

Warn me . . .

The *Warn me when other applications try to send mail as me* option provides an alert when some program (not you) attempts to send e-mail without your knowing it. That's exactly how most viruses spread themselves from computer to computer — by e-mailing copies of themselves to people in your Address Book, using your e-mail client as the sending program. Selecting this option won't prevent you from picking up a virus. But it will prevent you from spreading the virus to other people.

Do not allow attachments . . .

As mentioned under "Checking your attachment security," earlier in this chapter, the *Do not allow attachments . . .* option on the Security tab puts extremely tight controls on the types of attachments you can open. If you select this option, Outlook Express will block access to any attachment that *could* contain a worm or virus. But unlike an antivirus program, this option can't discriminate between those files that actually *do* contain a virus and those that don't.

Block images . . .

If selected, the *Block images and other external content* in HTML e-mail option does exactly that — when you download your e-mail messages, you get all the text, but not the pictures or anything else that might be included in the message. Where the picture should be you'll see a red X and a message that reads something like *Some pictures have been blocked to help prevent the sender from identifying your computer. Click here to download pictures.*

Note   The Block images . . . option described below is part of Windows Service Pack 2 (SP2). See Chapter 27 for information on Windows Update.

A big advantage to choosing this option, especially for dial-up users, is that messages download much more quickly. Pictures and other nontext message content take the longest to download. More often than not, you're waiting for pictures from junk e-mail messages that you'll probably never read (or at least, *shouldn't* read) anyway. This option also adds some security against malicious JPEG images sometimes used to send information to Web sites.

The only minor disadvantage to choosing this option occurs when you get a legitimate e-mail from a friend that contains a picture. Initially, you won't see the picture in the e-mail message. No big deal though, since you just have to click on the placeholder to download and view the image.

Secure mail settings

The Secure Mail options all concern digital signatures, a technology that allows you to verify your identity in e-mail transactions. Click the Tell me more button to learn more about digital IDs. Use the Get Digital ID button to create a digital ID. Use the Digital IDs button to manage existing digital IDs (if any).

Connection options

The Connection tab of Outlook Express's Options dialog box, shown at the right in Figure 33-26, provides options for automatically connecting to your ISP when you request mail. If you don't have a dial-up Internet account, the Dial-Up options will be disabled. That's because the Dial-Up options make no sense with broadband accounts, which don't use traditional phone lines to provide your connection.

Maintenance options

The Maintenance tab in Outlook Express's Options dialog box provides a few options for automatically managing e-mail message. The first option, *Empty messages from the Deleted Items folder on exit*, keeps your Deleted Items folder from becoming huge. If you select that option, all messages in your Deleted Items folder will be deleted automatically as soon as you close Outlook Express. The disadvantage to choosing that option is that it limits your ability to undelete an accidentally deleted message. Once a message has been removed from your Deleted Items folder, it no longer exists on your hard disk and hence cannot be retrieved.

The second option, *Purge deleted messages when leaving IMAP folders*, only applies to IMAP e-mail accounts. If selected, this option permanently deletes any messages you marked for deletion as soon as you leave the folder.

The options under *When compacting messages* apply to newsgroup messages rather than e-mail messages. The first option, if selected, automatically deletes newsgroup messages that you've read. The second option puts a time limit, in days, on how long newsgroup messages are maintained in Outlook Express.

Cross-Reference

For more information on newsgroups, see "About Newsgroups" in Chapter 35.

Quick Outlook Express Troubleshooting

Troubleshooting e-mail can be a tricky proposition, because there are so many players involved. But, far and away, the best resource for fixing e-mail problems is your ISP; they're the only ones who know the specifics of the e-mail service you're using. You can either call them for advice or visit the Support page they provide on their Web site.

There's also an e-mail troubleshooter built into Windows XP, which can help with problems at your end. To get to the e-mail troubleshooter:

1. Click the **Start** button, and choose **Help and Support**.

2. Click **Fixing a problem**.

3. Click **E-mail and messaging problems**.

4. Click **E-mail Troubleshooter**.

Note

If your computer manufacturer has removed the Fixing a Problem option from your Help and Support Center, type **e-mail troubleshooter** in the Search box in Help and Support. Then, click the Go button or press Enter. Under Suggested Topics, click E-mail Troubleshooter.

On the first page of the troubleshooter that opens, click whichever option best describes the problem you're having; then, click the Next button. Follow this procedure to work your way through the problem.

If the Troubleshooter can't help, take a look at the section on troubleshooting e-mail in Chapter 36. But don't forget that e-mail is a service provided by your ISP, and it's not the same for everyone. The people who can best help you with e-mail are the people who are providing you with that service.

For more general information on using Outlook Express, see the following resources:

✦ Choose **Help** ⇨ **Contents and Index** from Outlook Express's menu bar. Then, use the **Contents**, **Index**, and **Search** tabs in the Help window to look up the information you need.

✦ Use your Web browser to visit the main Outlook Express Web site at `http://www.microsoft.com/windows/oe`.

✦ For information on backing up messages and addresses, see `http://support.microsoft.com/default.aspx?scid=kb;en-us;270670&Product=oex`.

Wrap Up

I could spend another 100 pages rambling on about Outlook Express. It's that big a topic. But as I mentioned at the start of this chapter, I don't want to dedicate too many pages in this book to that topic. One reason is that e-mail isn't really a Windows XP thing. It's an Internet thing and a service provided to you by your ISP. Exactly how you do your e-mail is entirely up to your ISP. Windows XP plays almost no role. Outlook Express is just one of many possible e-mail clients. Whether or not it's required, or even an option, with your particular e-mail address is entirely up to your ISP. Here's a quick recap of what you've learned in this chapter:

✦ E-mail is a service of the Internet and is provided by your ISP. Different ISPs offer different types of services.

✦ Outlook Express is an e-mail client — a program for sending and receiving e-mail messages. Outlook Express is optional and isn't even supported by all ISPs.

✦ Regardless of the program you use for e-mail, all new e-mail messages you receive end up in your e-mail Inbox.

✦ If you use Outlook Express as your e-mail client, you use the Create Mail button in its menu bar to write new e-mail messages.

✦ Windows Address Book (WAB) is a handy program for storing contact information (people's names and addresses). It's integrated with Outlook Express, so you can use it to create mailing lists and address new messages.

✦ All options for configuring and customizing Outlook Express are located in its Options dialog box, which you can get to by choosing Tools ⇨ Options from Outlook Express's menu bar.

✦ When it comes to troubleshooting e-mail problems, your best bet is to go straight to your ISP. Only they know the specifics of the e-mail service they provide.

✦   ✦   ✦

Communicating Online with .NET Passport

If you've been using XP for a while, you may have noticed a small message popping up in the Notification area, inviting you to set up a .NET Passport. Some of you may have already followed through on that and created your passport. Others may have totally ignored the message. It really doesn't matter, because you can set up a .NET Passport at any time. I suppose the real question for many is "What is a .NET Passport, and why would I want one?" This chapter aims to resolve those questions.

For starters, a .NET Passport is basically a type of Internet account that provides access to services that go beyond what an ISP can provide. These added services include things such as live toll-free voice and video conversations with anyone anywhere in the world, the ability to transfer files of any size, and Remote Assistance, where you can give a trusted expert access to your computer to fix some problem. That's just a start.

What Is a .NET Passport?

Everyone who has a .NET Passport has a unique user name. Rather than force everyone to make up some name, .NET Passport lets everyone use his or her e-mail address as a user name. The two advantages to that approach are (1) it's easy to remember your own user name, because it's the same as your e-mail address, and 2) no two people have the same e-mail address. So by using e-mail addresses, the uniqueness of each person's user name is guaranteed.

In order to set up a .NET Passport, you need to know your own e-mail address, and you need to know how to send and receive e-mail using that e-mail address. Using your e-mail address as your .NET Passport user name will not affect the way you do e-mail. Even after you've set up your .NET Passport, you'll continue to do e-mail exactly as you always have in the past.

Note   Don't be afraid to use your existing e-mail address as your .NET Passport user name, even if your e-mail address ends in @aol.com, @earthlink.com, or anything else. Your .NET Passport won't change or interfere with your e-mail account in any way.

You'll also have to think up a password. The password has to be at least six characters and should not contain any blank spaces. Also, passwords are case-sensitive, meaning that upper-case and lowercase letters are not treated the same. So when you create your password, use all lowercase letters so that you don't have to remember the case of each letter.

If you have a favorite password you use for all your accounts, you can use that one, which is easier than trying to remember a bunch of different passwords for a bunch of different accounts. Before you even get started, I suggest that you write down your e-mail address and password. It might sound a little goofy at first, but you'd be amazed at how many people set up their .NET Passports and two days later can't get into their own accounts because they've forgotten their user name, password, or both.

Creating a .NET Passport

Creating a .NET Passport for yourself is fairly easy. Your best bet will be to start right off by associating your .NET Passport account with your Windows XP user account. If you're an administrator, you can make up a separate Hotmail or Yahoo! account for each user and give each user his or her own passport. You need to log into a user account to associate a .NET Passport with that account. Here are the steps:

Caution   You need only set up your .NET Passport once, not each time you intend to sign in to your account. If you've already created a .NET Passport, skip the steps presented here and go to the section titled "Opening Windows Messenger, Signing In," later in this chapter.

1. If you're setting up a .NET Passport for another user account, log out of your user account and log into the other person's.

2. Click the **Start** button and choose **Control Panel**. If Control Panel opens in Category view, click the **User Accounts** category. Open the User Accounts icon.

3. Click the icon that represents the account to which you're currently logged in.

4. In the next window that opens, click **Set up my account to use a .NET Passport**.

Note   If you see *Change my .NET Passport* rather than *Set up my account to use a .NET Passport*, you have (or somebody else has) already set up the user account to have a .NET Passport. You can close all open windows and go to "Opening Windows Messenger," see "Signing In," later in this chapter. If you don't see any options for .NET Passport, you've clicked someone else's user account, not your own. Click the Back button, and go back to Step 3.

5. Read the first page of the .NET Passport Wizard that opens; then, click the **Next** button.

6. The next wizard page asks whether you already have an e-mail address. Assuming that you do, choose **Yes**, and click **Next**.

7. The next wizard page asks if you've already registered your e-mail address with a .NET Passport. Assuming that you haven't, click **No, I want to register my e-mail address with Passport now**, and click **Next**.

8. The next wizard page informs you that you'll be taken to a Web page where you'll be guided through the rest of the steps required to set up your .NET Passport. Click **Next**.

9. On the Web page that opens, shown in Figure 34-1, type your e-mail address and password exactly as you wrote them in this book earlier in this chapter. Follow all the instructions on the page carefully. Scroll down and click the **I Agree** button.

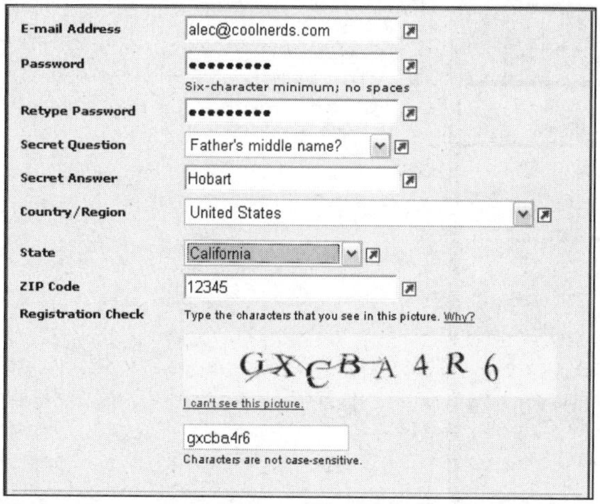

Figure 34-1: .NET Passport Wizard page for entering your .NET Passport account information

Assuming that you did everything correctly, you'll come to a Registration is Complete page. There you can click the Continue button to return to the .NET Passport Wizard. In the wizard, make sure that the *Associate my Passport with my Windows user account* option is checked, and then click Next. On the last Wizard page, click the Finish button, and you'll be returned to the User Accounts window. You can close the User Accounts window and close Control Panel as well.

If there were any problems along the way, you won't get to the *Registration is Complete* page. Instead, you'll see a description of the problem and be given some choices as to how to proceed. But once you've set up your .NET Passport, you'll be able to sign in to your .NET Passport account at any time, as described in the sections that follow.

Opening Windows Messenger, Signing In

Probably the main reason that most people set up a .NET Passport is so they can use the Windows Messenger program that comes with Windows XP. As you'll learn in this chapter, Windows Messenger provides access to all sorts of .NET Passport services. To start Windows Messenger, use whichever technique is available and most convenient at the moment:

✦ Click the **Start** button and choose **All Programs ➪ Windows Messenger**.

✦ Double-click the little **Windows Messenger** icon in the Notification area.

If you're not already signed in to your account, you'll see your .NET Passport account user name, which is the same as your e-mail address. Click the *Click here to sign in* option beneath that and follow any instructions that you see on the screen. Eventually, you'll be taken to the Windows Messenger program. The main window of that program, as it's often called, will look something like the example shown in Figure 34-2.

Windows Messenger is similar to other programs in that it has its own title bar, menu bar, and taskbar button (when open). Before you get started using Windows Messenger, there may be a couple more things to attend to.

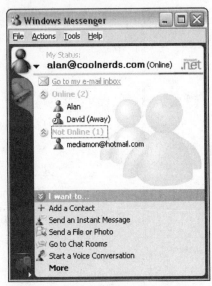

Figure 34-2: Windows Messenger's main window

E-mail address not verified

When you first start using Windows Messenger, you're likely to see the *E-mail Address Not Verified* message near the top of the program window. E-mail verification involves guaranteeing that you do, indeed, own the e-mail address you specified. How do you verify such a thing? It's easier than you might think. .NET Passport sends an e-mail message to the e-mail address you gave as your user name.

Your job is to keep an eye out for that e-mail message every time you check your e-mail. All you have to do is check your e-mail as you always do (ignore the *Go to my e-mail inbox* option in Windows Messenger for now). Eventually, you should get an e-mail message from Microsoft Passport with *Please verify your e-mail address* in the Subject line. When you get that message, open it and follow the instructions it provides. Once you do that, you'll have verified that you are, indeed, the owner of the e-mail address, and the *E-mail Address Not Verified* message in Windows Messenger will disappear.

Sign Me in Automatically

In some situations, you'll see an option that reads *Sign me in automatically* at a .NET Passport prompt. If you choose that option, you'll be able to sign in to your account without typing your user name and password. This is perfectly safe if you're the only person who uses this computer. But on a public computer, or a computer you share with other people, choosing that option will allow other people to sign in to your .NET Passport. As a rule, that isn't a good idea.

Unblocking Windows Messenger

If you have any trouble using Windows Messenger, make sure that it's listed as an exception in Windows Firewall. To do so, click the Start button and choose All Programs ⇨ Accessories ⇨ System Tools ⇨ Security Center. Click on the Windows Firewall icon, and then click the Exceptions tab in the dialog box that opens. Select (check) Windows Messenger to unblock Windows Messenger. For more information on using the Windows Firewall, see Chapter 26.

A new version of Windows Messenger is available

Windows Messenger has gone through quite a few revisions since it was initially packaged into Windows XP. So, there's a good chance that when you open Windows Messenger for the first time, you'll see a message that reads *A new version of Windows Messenger is available. Click here for more information.* You'll be given the option to update (for free) your current copy of Windows Messenger. Choose Yes and click OK.

Tip   Microsoft has recently blurred the distinction between MSN Messenger and Windows Messenger. By the time you read this, there may be only one: MSN Messenger. But don't worry, you can download and install it anyway. It will work as described in this chapter.

Next, you'll get the standard security warning that appears whenever you download and install any program. Just click Yes, and follow the instructions on the screen until the update is complete. After you've finished this whole hullabaloo with e-mail verification and updates, everything will be ready to go, and you can forget all about setting up your account and verifying your e-mail address. From here on out, you can just sign in and use Windows Messenger as described in the sections that follow.

Instant Messaging with Windows Messenger

Instant messaging is a lot like a telephone call in that your conversation takes place in *real time*. Unlike the phone, which costs money, all communications via Windows Messenger are free. It doesn't matter where in the world the other person is located. Also, with the phone, you're limited to voice communications. With Windows Messenger, you can type messages back and forth or use voice. Throw in a *Web cam*, and you can see each other during the conversation as well.

There are some limitations to instant messaging, however. The person you want to communicate with also needs to have a computer, an Internet connection, a .NET Passport, and either the Windows Messenger program or MSN Messenger. Windows Messenger comes with Windows XP and is only for Windows XP. People using other versions of Windows, or a Macintosh computer, will need to download and install MSN Messenger from `http://messenger.msn.com`.

Setting up your list of contacts

A *contact* in Windows Messenger is any person with whom you plan to do instant messaging. To create a contact, you just need to know that person's .NET Passport user account name (which is the same as his or her e-mail address). Then, follow these steps:

1. Choose **Tools** ⇨ **Add a Contact** from Windows Messengers' menu bar (or click **Add A Contact** in the lower half of the window). The Add a Contact Wizard starts.

2. Choose **By e-mail address or sign-in name**, and click the **Next >** button.

3. Type the complete e-mail address of the person you plan to communicate with, and click the **Next>** button.

4. What happens next depends on whether the person you added already has a .NET Passport. The wizard will present your options. Just follow the instructions on the screen.

5. Click the **Finish** button on the last wizard page.

You can repeat Steps 1 to 5 to add as many contacts as you wish. Each contact you create will appear in the main pane beneath the menu bar. For example, in Figure 34-2, I set up three contacts: Alan, David, and one whose name still appears as an e-mail address.

Tip   The first time you have a conversation with someone, his or her e-mail address in Windows Messenger is replaced by his or her *display name*. You need to make contact before that name will show on your screen though, because that name comes from the other person's computer.

Starting a conversation

Windows Messenger lists your contacts in two groups: those currently online (and therefore available for instant messaging) and those not online. For example, in Figure 34-2, my contacts named Alan and David were both online. (Click the Online or Not Online heading to show/hide items under each heading.)

Tip   If your contacts are shown in groups other than Online/Not Online, choose Tools ▷ Sort Contacts By ▷ Online/Offline from Windows Messenger's menu bar.

You can start a conversation with anybody who is currently online by sending an instant message. Just double-click the online contact's name, or right-click the name and choose *Send An Instant Message* to get started.

A Conversation window opens, like the example shown in Figure 34-3. The Conversation window is separate from Windows Messenger's main window and has its own separate taskbar button. You can move and size the Conversation window like any other program window and independently of the main window.

To send a message to someone, type in the lower portion of the window near the Send button. Type your message; then, press Enter or click the Send button. Whatever you typed moves up into the Conversation area and also appears in the Conversation area of whomever you're talking to. Figure 34-3 shows the Conversation window with a conversation between two people just getting started.

While typing in the Conversation window, you can use all the standard text-editing techniques described in Chapter 3. But one difference in the Conversation window is that when you press Enter, you don't start a new paragraph. Instead, you send the message (the same as clicking the Send button). If you want to start a new line or paragraph without sending the message, press Shift+Enter or Ctrl+Enter (once or twice).

Conversation

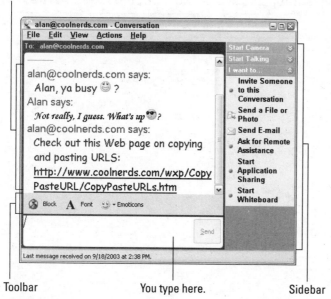

Toolbar　　　　　You type here.　　　　Sidebar

Figure 34-3: The Conversation window, with a conversation in progress

Adding emoticons

Emoticons (emotion icons) are little symbols you can use to express emotions in your typed messages. To add an emoticon to your message, just make sure that the cursor is positioned where you want to place the icon in your text. Click the Emoticons button; then, click the icon you want to insert. You can edit emoticons like text. For example, to delete an emoticon from your message, move the cursor just to the right of that icon, and press the Backspace key.

Note　If you don't have an Emoticons button just above where you type your text, choose View ⇨ Show Toolbar from the Conversation window's menu bar.

You can also type emoticons using special combinations of keystrokes. For example, typing :D or :d displays the happy-face emoticon. Typing :-(or :(types the sad-face emoticon and so forth. Table 34-1 lists the emoticons and the optional keys you can use to type them.

Tip　To see the complete set of emoticons, including animated ones, go to http://messenger.msn.com/Resource/Emoticons.aspx. To see all other add-ons and some more freebies, go to http://messenger.msn.com.

Table 34-1: Conversation Emoticons and Optional Keys to Type Them

Emoticon	Name	To type
	Happy	**:-D** or **:d**
	Sad	**:-(** or **:(**
	Wink	**;-)** or **;)**
	Angel	**(A)** or **(a)**
	Angry	**:-@** or **:@**
	Cool	**(H)** or **(h)**
	Confused	**:-S** or **:s**
	Crying	**:'(**
	Embarrassed	**:$** or **:-$**
	Surprised	**:-O** or **:o**
	Tongue out	**:-P** or **:p**
	WatchuTalkingAbout?	**:-|** or **:|**
	Smile	**:-)** or **:)**
	Crying (animated)	**:'(**
	Sick	**+o(**
	Secret	**:-***
	Lips sealed	**:-#**
	Nerdy	**8-|**
	Doubtful (animated)	**:^)**
	Boring (animated)	**|-)**

Emoticon	Name	To type
	Eye roll (animated)	**8-)**
	Star	**(*)**
	Thumbs down	**(N)** or **(n)**
	Thumbs up	**(Y)** or **(y)**
	Rose	**(F)** or **(f)**
	Wilted rose	**(W)** or **(w)**
	Kiss	**(K)** or **(k)**
	Love	**(L)** or **(l)**
	Broken heart	**(U)** or **(u)**
	Bat	**:-[** or **:[**
	Dog	**(&)**
	Cat	**(@)**
	Dude hug	**({)**
	Girl hug	**(})**
	Hands across (girl)	**(X)** or **(x)**
	Hands across (guy)	**(Z)** or **(z)**
	Messenger	**(M)** or **(m)**
	Bright idea	**(I)** or **(i)**
	Coffee	**(C)** or **(c)**
	Time	**(O)** or **(o)**

Continued

Table 34-1: *(continued)*

Emoticon	Name	To type
	Birthday	**(^)**
	Party	**<:o)**
	Gift	**(G)** or **(g)**
	Music	**(8)**
	Telephone	**(T)** or **(t)**
	Picture	**(P)** or **(p)**
	Movie	**(~)**
	Mail	**(E)** or **(e)**
	Beer	**(B)** or **(b)**
	Martini	**(D)** or **(d)**
	Moon	**(S)**

Choosing a message font

You can choose a font, size, and color for the text you type. Just click the Font button above where you type your message. In the *Change My Message Font* dialog box that opens, choose the Font, Style, and Size you want to use. Use the Effects options to choose Strikeout font, underline, and/or a color, and then click OK.

Tip   In Figure 34-3, the line that starts with *Alan* is Comic Sans MS, Regular, 14 point size. The *Not really* message is in Monotype Corsiva, Regular, 14 point size.

Pasting to the Conversation window

As you know, anywhere you can type, you can also paste. The typing area of the Conversation window is no different. For example, you can select (drag the mouse pointer through) any chunk of text from a document, Web page, e-mail message or whatever, and press Ctrl+C to copy it. Then, either right-click in the typing area of the Conversation and choose Paste, or click the exact spot in the typing area where you want to paste the copied text and press Ctrl+V.

Note   You can't paste a picture to the typing area — only text. If you try to paste a picture, Paste will be disabled on the shortcut menu, and pressing Ctrl+V will do nothing. But you can always send a picture as a file, as described later in this chapter.

If you use Microsoft Internet Explorer as your Web browser, you can copy and paste a hyperlink from a Web page into your message. In Internet Explorer, right-click the hyperlink you want to copy and choose Copy Shortcut. Then, right-click in the typing area of your Conversation and choose Paste. The actual URL will show. But it will be *hot* (meaning that the recipient can get to the site just by clicking the link in the message you send).

When someone contacts you

Just as you can add contacts to your copy of Windows Messenger, your friends can add you to their list of contacts. If you're online and signed in to your .NET Passport when someone else adds you to his or her list of contacts, you'll see the dialog box shown in Figure 34-4. If the person is someone you're interested in conversing with, choose the first option. If it's some knucklehead you can do without, choose the second option. Then, you can decide whether or not you want to add that person to your own list of contacts and click OK.

Figure 34-4: Someone is adding you as a contact in his or her copy of Windows Messenger.

Once you've allowed someone to contact you via Windows Messenger, you'll be alerted when that person sends you an instant message, via the Notification area message shown in Figure 34-5. The taskbar button for the conversation window will also change color and blink. Click that taskbar button to open the Conversation window and have your conversation.

Figure 34-5: Yoo-hoo — someone wants to have an instant message conversation.

Inviting others to join in

Up to five people can join in on an instant message, provided that you're typing messages back and forth (only two people when you get voice or video involved, however). To invite someone to join your conversation, click *Invite Someone to this Conversation* under *I want to . . .* in the sidebar. Or choose Actions ⇨ Invite Someone to this Conversation from the Conversation Window's menu bar. In the Add Someone . . . dialog box that opens, click the name of the person you want to add. Or click the Other tab, and enter the new person's .NET Passport user name (usually the same as the person's e-mail address). Click OK.

Inviting others to get lost

If anyone starts being a pain in a conversation, you can prevent that person from sending you more messages. To block anyone in the current conversation, click the Block button in the toolbar; then, click the name of the person you want to block. There are other ways to block people, as you'll learn under "Managing Your Contacts," later in this chapter. But the Block button on the toolbar is a quick and easy way to kick someone out of the current conversation.

Ending a conversation

To end a conversation, just close the Conversation window. The Windows Messenger window will remain open, so you can still start or accept other conversations. To go offline entirely, so nobody can reach you, choose File ⇨ Sign Out from the menu bar in Windows Messenger.

Your *do not disturb* options

If you stay online, but don't actually use your computer for about 10 minutes, Windows Messenger will automatically change your status to *Away*, like David's status back in Figure 34-2. You can set your own status message at any time. Whatever you choose will appear next to your name in all the Windows Messenger programs that have you as a contact.

To change your status:

✦ Choose **File** ⇨ **My Status** from Windows Messenger's main window, as in the top part of Figure 34-6. Then, click the status message you want to display next to your name.

✦ Or right-click the little **Windows Messenger** icon in the Notification area and choose My Status, as in the bottom part of Figure 34-6; then, click the status message you want to display.

If you find that Messenger has changed your status to *Away* automatically and you want to change that, just use either of the preceding techniques to change your status to Online (or to whatever you want). If you want Windows Messenger to stop showing you as *Away* after 10 minutes of inactivity, you can disable or change that setting using its Options dialog box, described under "Configuring Windows Messenger," later in this chapter.

Tip   If you want to see (who is online) without being seen, set your status to Appear Offline. You'll be able to see who is online. But everyone else will think you're offline.

Regardless of your status, you can still see who is online at the moment by opening Windows Messenger. If you want to disconnect altogether, right-click the same Windows Messenger icon in your Notification area and choose Sign Out. You won't be logged in to your .NET Passport anymore. All your contacts will see you as Not Online.

To get back online to communicate with your contacts, you'll need to right-click the Windows Messenger icon in your Notification area and choose Sign In . . . from the menu that appears.

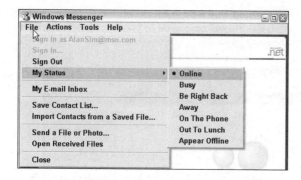

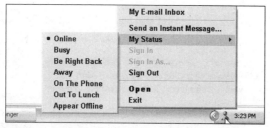

Figure 34-6: Change your status from Windows Messenger's File menu or its Notification Area icon.

Transferring Files and Photos

While you're in a conversation with someone, you can send files to each other. Unlike e-mail, which tends to put a limit on the size of the file you can attach to a message, there really is no size limit on transferring files in a conversation. Of course, the larger the file, the longer it will take to transfer, especially if either party in the conversation is using a dial-up connection.

1. If you haven't already done so, start a conversation with the person to whom you want to send a file.

2. Click **Send a File or Photo** under *I want to . . .* in the Conversation window's sidebar.

3. The Send a File . . . dialog box that opens is the same as an Open dialog box, in the sense that you first have to get to the folder that contains the file(s) you want to send. For example, to send a picture from your My Pictures folder, choose **My Documents** from the Look In drop-down list; then, double-click **My Pictures** in the main pane.

4. Double-click the file you want to send.

5. The recipient gets an invitation to accept the file. If the recipient clicks **Accept**, the file will be transferred.

Assuming that you're the sender of the file, there's nothing left to do. The file is transferred and that's the end of it. If it doesn't work, you or the other party might need to open a firewall port. See the sidebar titled "File Transfers, Talking, and Security" for more information.

If someone sends you a file using this method, you'll be given the option to Accept or Decline the transfer. When you choose Accept, the file will be copied to your computer; then, you'll see a message like the one shown in Figure 34-7.

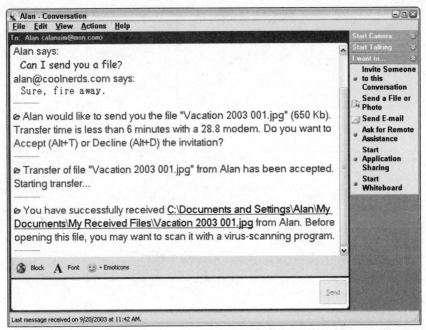

Figure 34-7: This person has received a file transferred by someone in a conversation.

The big chunk of underlined text is the path to the transferred file. The `C:\Documents and Settings\Alan\My Documents\My Received Files` is the *path* to the My Received Files folder in Alan's My Documents folder. Vacation 2003 001.jpg is the name of the file. The whole path is a hyperlink. So, if you just click that, the file will open in whatever program is appropriate for that file type.

Tip   If you miss the opportunity to click the link in the message, choose File ⇨ Open Received Files from Windows Messenger's menu bar to open the folder where all your received files are stored.

If you don't have a program capable of opening the file you've received, you'll get the *Windows Cannot Open This File* message described under "When Windows can't open a document," in Chapter 3. You'll either need to get to send the file in a format you can open or to download and install (if possible) a program capable of opening that file type.

You can also get to your My Received Files folder at any time (even when you're not using Windows Messenger) by opening your My Documents folder and double-clicking the My

File Transfers, Talking, and Security

File transfers, voice conversations, and some other features of Windows Messenger might fail due to firewall settings that block the ports needed for those features to work. Voice conversations in Windows Messenger require that TCP and UDP ports 6901 be open. File transfers require open TCP ports 6891 through 6900. Although you need to open all 10 ports if you want to be able to transfer up to 10 files at a time. For example, you could just open port 6891 and transfer one file at a time. See Chapter 26 for information on opening ports in Windows Firewall.

Even with the appropriate ports open, Messenger file transfers and voice conversations can fail just because of the different ways in which different ISPs handle the service they provide. If opening the appropriate firewall ports doesn't help with Messenger voice conversations and file transfers, check your ISP's support page or service for more information. For more technical information, see Knowledge Base article 324214 at `http://support.microsoft.com/default.aspx?scid=kb;en-us;324214` and the TechNet article at `www.microsoft.com/technet/prodtechnol/winxppro/deploy/worki01.mspx` if you use Windows Firewall from Service Pack 2.

Received Files icon in My Documents. When you open (double-click) the My Received Files folder's icon, you'll see all files you've received through Windows Messenger file transfers. You can then move those files to more appropriate folders, using any of the techniques described in Chapter 14.

Toll-Free Talking

If you're not a big fan of typing messages, you can communicate with other Windows Messenger users by voice. But you'll need one extra piece of computer hardware to do that — a microphone (and speakers, to hear what the other person is saying). If you don't have a microphone for your computer, you can buy one at any computer store. Microphones that you wear on your head are generally better than the ones you just set on your desktop, because having the microphone close to your mouth helps cancel out all the background sound in the room.

Telex Communications makes several USB microphone headsets that you might want to check out next time you're shopping online or at a computer store. USB is good, because it means you just have to plug it into your computer to use it. There's no complicated installation to go through. The first time you use your microphone, you'll need to run the Audio Tuning Wizard to get the best performance from Windows Messenger. Here's how:

1. Open Windows Messenger, if it isn't already open, by double-clicking the **Windows Messenger** icon in the Notification area or by clicking the **Start** button and choosing **All Programs ➪ Windows Messenger**.

2. From the menu bar in the Windows Messenger window, choose **Tools ➪ Audio Tuning Wizard**.

3. Follow the instructions that appear on each page of the wizard. Click the **Next** button after completing each page.

4. When you get to the wizard page that asks which microphone and speakers you want to use, you probably won't need to change the Speakers option. But you should definitely click the drop-down list for the Microphone option and choose whichever microphone description best describes the microphone you'll be using. For example, in Figure 34-8, I selected Telex USB microphone as my Microphone; that's the type of microphone I have plugged in to my computer.

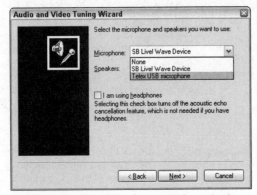

Figure 34-8: Choosing your microphone in the Audio Tuning Wizard

After you've installed a microphone and have run the Audio Tuning Wizard, you're ready to talk online. This is easy to do:

✦ If you're already having a conversation with someone in the Conversation window and want to switch to voice, click **Start Talking** in the Conversation window.

✦ If you're not already in a typing conversation with someone, open Windows Messenger normally. Then, right-click the name of the Online contact you want to talk to and choose Start a voice conversation. The contact will receive a message that you're ready to talk and will reply if ready.

The recipient will get a text message that shows your name followed by . . . *would like to have a voice conversation with you. Do you want to Accept (Alt+T) or Decline (Alt+D) the invitation?* You'll then get some feedback as to whether the recipient accepted or declined. Assuming that the person accepted, you can just start talking.

To adjust the volume of the other person's voice, drag the Speakers slider left or right under the Stop Talking heading (see Figure 34-9). If the other person has trouble hearing you, try increasing the volume of your microphone by using the Microphone volume control slider. (That person could, however, turn up his or her speakers.)

When you're ready to end a voice conversation, click Stop Talking in the Conversation window. It's easy! If you can't get it to work, see the sidebar titled "File Transfers, Talking, and Security" in this chapter.

Figure 34-9: Volume controls under Stop Talking appear in a voice conversation.

Twenty-First Century Toll-Free Videophone

You can update your toll-free Windows Messenger voice communications to voice plus live video, provided that you have a Web cam. A Web cam is a small, inexpensive digital video camera that doesn't record video. Rather, it just sits on top of your computer monitor and shows your face live to the person with whom you're conversing in Windows Messenger.

Video communications work best with broadband Internet connections, such as cable or DSL. You can still use a Web cam with a dial-up account and modem, but the picture won't be as smooth as, say, regular TV. The video will look a little jerky, like pictures sent from astronauts in the early days of the space program. But not a big deal—you can still see and hear each other.

If you've never seen or heard of a Web cam, you can check out some available products at any computer store or large office-supply store. Optionally, you can go to any online store that sells computer stuff and search for Web Cam. You don't need anything particularly fancy, though. Any USB Web cam compatible with Windows XP will do. A few models have built-n microphones, which saves you from having to install both a microphone and the camera.

Once you've installed a Web cam, you can start a video conversation with someone in the same way that you start a voice conversation. That is, if you're already in a typing conversation with someone, you can just click Start Video to turn on your Web cam. If you're not already in a conversation with someone, open Windows Messenger, right-click any contact who is online, and choose Start a Video Conversation. The recipient will get an invitation that he or she can accept or decline. If the recipient accepts, you'll automatically get both voice and video once the connection is made.

Once you're in a voice and/or video conversation, as in Figure 34-10, you can use the Speakers and Microphone sliders to adjust the volume of your conversation. If you're having a bad-hair day, and don't particularly want to be showing it off on your Web cam, you can click the Stop Camera button on the right side of the Conversation window to keep talking without sending your video image.

Figure 34-10: Having a video conversation in Windows Messenger

Using Remote Assistance

Remote Assistance is a special feature of Windows Messenger where you can have a typing, voice, and/or video conversation going on. But you can also turn control over to a trusted expert. The expert can then see your screen on her screen. And she can work your computer using her own keyboard or mouse. This is why we use the term *trusted expert*. You wouldn't want to turn your computer over to a crook or knucklehead.

Unblocking Remote Assistance

If you have any trouble using Remote Assistance, make sure that it's listed as an exception in Windows Firewall. To do so, click the Start button and choose All Programs ➪ Accessories ➪ System Tools ➪ Security Center. Click on the Windows Firewall icon, and then click the Exceptions tab in the dialog box that opens. Select (check) Remote Assistance to unblock that service, and then click OK. For more information on using the Windows Firewall, see Chapter 26.

Unfortunately, there aren't any free experts floating around, helping people with they're computers. The only trusted expert you're going to be able to get is someone you know and who (you can hope) knows a lot about computers. It could be your son or daughter, your brother-in-law, or the computer guy at the office—anyone with a Windows XP computer and an Internet account.

Caution   Remote Assistance is definitely slow if either party has a dial-up account. Leave the video off, and maybe even the voice up, to free up bandwidth for all the other activity involved in controlling your computer from afar.

Starting a Remote Assistance session

Starting a Remote Assistance session is a lot like starting any other conversation. First, your trusted expert needs to be online. If you're already in a Conversation window with the person, click *Ask for Remote Assistance* in the sidebar of the Conversation window. Otherwise, in Windows Messenger's main window, right-click the online contact who'll be your trusted expert, and choose Ask for Remote Assistance. Either way, a Conversation window opens, and an invitation is sent to the recipient.

If the recipient accepts the invitation, you'll get some feedback to that effect. Then, it will take a while to get your screen over to the expert's screen. Eventually, you'll get a dialog box confirming the invitation. Click Yes to chat with the expert. When the expert attempts to take control of your screen (by clicking Take Control), you'll see the dialog box shown in Figure 34-11.

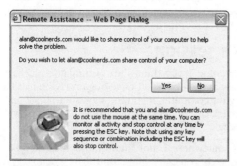

Figure 34-11: Are you ready to turn control of your computer over to this trusted expert?

Assuming that you click Yes to give control to your expert, you won't notice too much change on your screen. There will be a large chat area for Remote Assistance, as on the right edge of Figure 34-12. And you can use that to converse by typing, voice, and/or video while the expert has control. The other change will be that Casper the Ghost will be working your screen. Well, it might seem like a ghost. It's actually your trusted expert working your computer with her mouse and keyboard.

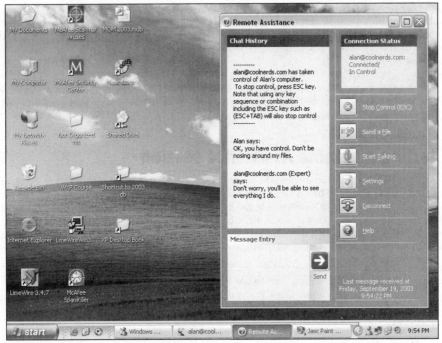

Figure 34-12: What you see while getting Remote Assistance from a trusted expert

Ending a Remote Assistance session

You'll be able to see everything the expert is doing. If you think she's getting into places you don't want her to be, tap the Escape (Esc) key at the upper-left edge of your keyboard. That will instantly cut off the expert's control of your computer. If you totally want to disconnect from the expert (not even be able to chat), click Disconnect in the Remote Assistance window. Or, close that Remote Assistance window.

You'll be lucky to find such a trusted expert somewhere. Unfortunately, there are no businesses out there that provide free trusted experts you can contact on the fly when you have a question or problem. And truthfully, very few people have any compu-nerdy friends or relatives to call upon. But if you have someone in mind, Remote Assistance is the way to go for fixing problems without taking the computer anywhere.

Working in Teams

Windows Messenger's Application Sharing is a feature that allows two people to view the same program, and same document, on their screens at the same time, even if they're thousands of miles apart. Application Sharing is another one of those high-bandwidth applications that really work best if all parties are using broadband accounts. Using Application Sharing with a dial-up modem will require some patience, because things will be very slow indeed.

Tip Many programs in Microsoft Office have a Collaborate option on their tools menu, which you can use to schedule and start online meetings right on the spot.

To use Application Sharing, get into a conversation with the person (or persons) you want to team up with as described under "Starting a conversation," earlier in this chapter. Then, open the document you want to share. The appropriate program will open as well.

In your Conversation window, click *Start Application Sharing* under *I want to . . .* in the sidebar, or choose Actions ➪ Start Application Sharing from the menu bar in the Conversation window. The recipient receives an invitation to share the application. If she clicks Accept, both of you will see a little Sharing Session window, like the example shown in the upper-left side of Figure 34-13. It may take a few seconds for the Connected message to show and the buttons to be enabled. So, you may need to be patient there.

Figure 34-13: Application Sharing dialog boxes

If you're the person who started Application Sharing, you'll also see the Sharing window, shown in the lower right of Figure 34-13. That window might be covering the small one. But you can move it around by dragging its title bar. Either person in the conversation can open the Sharing window by clicking the App Sharing button in the smaller Sharing Session window.

Tip The word *application* is synonymous with *program. App* is slang for *application*.

The next step is to choose the document (or program) you want to share. If you forgot to open that document first, you can do so right now. If the document you plan to share is a photo, and you both have high-speed Internet connections, you can choose *Share in True Color*. But choosing that option does slow things down. If it's not really necessary for the other person to see the entire document in photographic-quality color, you can leave that option unselected to speed up the sharing.

Next, click the name of the document (or program) you want to share with the other person; then, click the Share button. The document and program open up on your screen and also open up on the recipient's screen. You can both see the same program and same document on your screens at the same time.

At first, the other person will be able only to see the document (not to make and changes to it). If you want to allow the other person to make changes to the document, click the Allow Control button. The other person can then request control of the program by choosing Control ⇨ Request Control from a window that appears only on his or her side of the conversation. When that person requests control, you'll see a message on your screen informing you of the request. You have to click its Accept button to allow the other person to take control.

If both of you are working on the document, and you get sick of the other person's requests for control, choose either, or both, options beneath the Prevent Control button that now appears. If you choose the *Automatically accept requests for control* option, you're basically allowing the other person to take control whenever desired, so you don't have to be bothered clicking Accept anymore. The *Do not disturb* . . . option is the same idea. But if you don't select *Automatically accept* . . ., all requests for control will just automatically be denied, and only you will have control of the program.

Tip   While you're in an Application Sharing session, things will really slow down if you both try to work the mouse pointer at the same time. If you can resist the temptation to touch the mouse while the other person has control of the program, you'll save time.

To stop sharing a document or program, click its name in the Share Programs list; then, click the Unshare button. If you're sharing several programs, click the Unshare All button to stop sharing all of them. To close the Sharing dialog box, click its Close button. (To reopen it, click the App Sharing button in the Sharing Session dialog box.) To terminate the Application Sharing session altogether, either member of the conversation window can click the Close button in the Sharing Session dialog box.

Caution   Remember that any changes made to the document during your sharing session will be saved only on your computer and only if you save the document.

Using the Whiteboard

I guess everyone knows what a blackboard is. A whiteboard is the same idea. But on a whiteboard you write with Dry-Erase markers rather than chalk. The Whiteboard in Windows Messenger is similar to a whiteboard in a classroom. But you draw on this Whiteboard with your mouse. You can also paste pictures to your virtual Whiteboard. To use the Whiteboard in a Windows Messenger conversation, first start the conversation as described earlier in this chapter. You can have up to five people in the conversation.

Then, click *Start Whiteboard* under *I want to* . . . in the Conversation window's sidebar, or choose Actions ⇨ Start Whiteboard from the Conversation window's title bar. The Sharing Session window described in the previous section will open. A few seconds later, the Whiteboard will pop up on your screen, as well as on the screens of everyone else in the conversation. (Not immediately though, so be patient.)

Tip   If you're already in an Application Sharing session, you can just click the Whiteboard button in the Sharing Session dialog box to open the Whiteboard.

The Whiteboard is its own program window, with its own title bar, menu bar, and taskbar button. It also offers several tools around its border, pointed out in Figure 34-14 and summarized in the following list.

Drawing tools

Line Widths   Colors   Pages

Figure 34-14: Playing around on the Whiteboard

✦ **Drawing tools:** Point to any tool to see its name. Click any tool to use it. Going from left to right, top to bottom, the tools are:

- **Selector:** The normal mouse pointer. Use it to move (drag) items on the Whiteboard or to change/delete an item by right-clicking it.

- **Eraser:** Click this tool; then drag a rectangle around anything you want to erase in the Whiteboard. (Careful, there is no *undo* in Whiteboard!)

- **Text:** To type text on the Whiteboard, click this tool; then, click the Font Options button that appears in the program window. Choose a font, style, size, and color, and then click OK. On the Whiteboard, click where you want to place the text, and type your text. When you're done, click the Selector tool in the Drawing tools to get back to a normal cursor. To change or delete a chunk of text, use the normal Selector tool to right-click the text. Then, choose an option from the shortcut menu that appears.

- **Highlighter:** To highlight something on the Whiteboard, click this tool, click a line width, and click a color. Then, drag the mouse pointer through whatever you want to highlight.

- **Pen:** To draw freehand, click this tool, click a line width, and click a color. To draw, drag the mouse pointer around on the Whiteboard.

- **Line:** To draw a straight line, click this tool, click a line width, and click a color. In the Whiteboard, point to where you want to start the line, and drag the mouse pointer in the direction you want to extend the line. Release the mouse button when the line is the desired length and angle.

- **Unfilled Rectangle:** To draw an empty rectangle, click this tool, click a line width, and click a color for the line. Drag out your rectangle on the Whiteboard.

- **Filled Rectangle:** Same technique as previously, but no need to select a line width, because the rectangle you draw will be a solid shape.

- **Unfilled Ellipse:** To draw an empty circle or ellipse, click this tool, click a line width, and click a color for the line. Then, drag out your ellipse on the Whiteboard.

- **Filled Ellipse:** Same technique as previously, but no need to select a line width, because the ellipse you draw will be a solid shape.

- **Zoom:** To zoom in on the Whiteboard, click this tool. Click it again to zoom out.

- **Remote Pointer On:** Kind of the same idea as a laser pointer on a real whiteboard. All viewers should click this button to make the remote pointer visible. Then, anyone can drag the pointer to call attention to any item. Click the same button again to turn the Remote Pointer off.

- **Lock Contents:** To prevent other people in the Conversation window from messing with your beautiful artwork, click this button. The drawing tools on all their Whiteboards will be disabled (dimmed), so they can't change the drawing. Click this button a second time to unlock the Whiteboard.

- **Unsynchronize:** Any conversation member can use the Pages buttons to insert new pages and scroll through existing pages. Normally, if one member scrolls to a new page, everyone's Whiteboard scrolls to the same page. Click the Unsynchronize button to prevent that so you can create and scroll through pages independently. Click this button a second time to get back in sync with other conversation members.

- **Select Area:** To paste a snapshot of some portion of your screen into the Whiteboard, click this button. The mouse pointer turns to crosshairs, and the Whiteboard temporarily disappears. Drag a rectangle around the portion of the screen that you want to copy to the Whiteboard. When you release the mouse button, the Whiteboard will reappear, containing a snapshot of the area you lassoed.

Tip   To move a pasted snapshot, click the Selector tool in the Drawing tools area, and drag the item to its new location. To change or delete one, click the Selector tool in the Drawing tools, and click the item to select it. Then, right-click the item to see your options for changing or deleting it.

- **Select Window:** To paste a snapshot of an entire program window into the Whiteboard, size and position that window on your desktop so that it will fit. Then, click the Select Window button. The mouse pointer changes to crosshairs in a rectangle. To take a snapshot, click the title bar of the subject window.

✦ **Line widths:** Available after clicking any tool that draws lines. Click any line width to select it.

✦ **Colors:** The large square at left shows the currently selected color. Click any color square to the right to draw in that color.

✦ **Pages:** Use these buttons to scroll through multiple-page Whiteboards. Click the rightmost button to create a new Whiteboard page.

Pasting into the Whiteboard

You can use the Select Area tools described previously to paste a copy of anything currently visible on your screen into the Whiteboard. For example, if your My Pictures folder is showing pictures in Filmstrip or Thumbnails view, you can use the Select Area tool in the Whiteboard to drag a frame around an image to paste it into the Whiteboard.

To copy a picture that's in some open document, like a Web page, you can right-click the picture and choose Copy. Then, choose Edit ⇨ Paste from the Whiteboard's menu bar. To copy a snapshot of text from some document to the clipboard, first select that text in its current program window by dragging the mouse pointer through the text. Next, press Ctrl+C or right-click the selected text and choose Copy. Then, choose Edit ⇨ Paste from the Whiteboard's menu bar.

To move or change a pasted picture or chunk of text, first click the Selector tool in the Drawing tools area. Then, drag the item to some new location on the Whiteboard, or right-click the picture to see your other options. Note that the text will be a snapshot of the original text, treated as a unit. You can't edit the pasted text, because it will be treated as a single unit — like a picture — in the Whiteboard.

Erasing from the Whiteboard

You can erase material from the Whiteboard in a few ways:

✦ To erase the entire Whiteboard at once, choose **Edit** ⇨ **Clear Page** from the Whiteboard menu bar or press **Ctrl+Delete**. Then, choose Yes when asked for confirmation.

✦ To delete an object from the Whiteboard (such as a chunk of text or picture), click the **Selector** tool in the Drawing tools. Then, right-click the item you want to delete and choose **Delete**.

✦ To erase a drawn object or block of text, click the **Eraser** tool in the Drawing tools. Then, drag a rectangle around the items you want to erase. (To undo the deletion, choose **Edit** ⇨ **Undelete** from the menus or press **Ctrl+Z**.)

✦ To delete individual letters that you typed using the Text tool, click the **Text** tool in the Drawing tools. On the Whiteboard, select the letters that you want to erase, and press the **Delete (Del)** key.

Saving a Whiteboard

To save a Whiteboard, choose **File** ⇨ **Save** from the Whiteboard's menu bar. Navigate to the folder in which you want to place the board (My Documents will do just fine), type a filename, and click **OK**. To reopen that Whiteboard in a future Whiteboard session, choose **File** ⇨ **Open** from the Whiteboard's menu bar. Navigate to the folder in which you saved the Whiteboard and double-click its icon.

Closing a Whiteboard session

To close a Whiteboard session, just close the Whiteboard's program window by clicking its **Close** button or by choosing **File** ⇨ **Exit** from the Whiteboard's menu bar. If you haven't already saved the Whiteboard, you'll be given one last chance to do so. The Sharing Session dialog box will remain open. To fully end the Whiteboard session, click its **Close** button.

Managing Your Contacts

Windows Messenger's main window shows all the contacts you've added through the **Add a Contact** option. There are two ways to view those contacts: You can group them simply as either Online or Offline, as in the example shown in Figure 34-2, or you can choose **Tools** ➪ **Sort Contacts By** ➪ **Groups** to see contacts organized into groups such as Coworkers, Family, Friends, or any other group name you wish, as in the example shown in Figure 34-15. You can still easily tell which contacts are online and offline by the colors of their icons and the statuses to the right of their names.

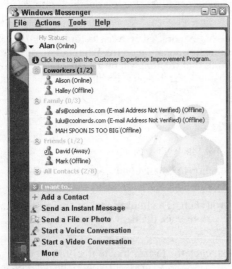

Figure 34-15: Displayed and sorted into groups

Grouping contacts

When viewing contacts by groups, you can click any group name to show, or hide, the contacts within that group. Initially, all your contacts will be in the All Contacts group at the bottom of the list. To group your contacts, follow these steps:

In the All Contacts list, right-click the contact you want to group and choose Copy Contact To and the name of the group to which you want to add the contact. The contact is copied to that group.

> **Tip** The All Contacts list always contains all your contacts. There's no way to move a contact out of the All Contacts list and into a group.

If you copy a contact to a group, but later change your mind, there are a couple of ways to deal with the problem. First, make sure that you can see all members of the group in which the contact is currently stored. Then, right-click the contact's icon within the group. Because you're not in the All Contacts list, you'll see a couple of other options that aren't availing in that list:

✦ **Move Contact To:** To move the contact from the current group to another, click this option, and click the group to which you want to move the contact.

✦ **Remove Contact from Group:** To remove the contact from the current group, click this option. The contact will remain in All Contacts and in any other groups to which the contact is a member.

Creating groups

You're not limited to the few sample groups that first appear in Windows Messenger. You can create whatever groups you wish. To create a new group, click *Add a Group* under *I want to . . .*, or choose Tools ➪ Manage Groups ➪ Add a Group from Windows Messenger's menu bar. A group named New Group appears, with its name selected. Type a new name, and press Enter.

If you make a mistake, right-click the group name and choose Rename Group. Edit the name, or type a new name. Then, press Enter.

Once you've created a group, you can use the *Copy Contact To* and *Move Contact To* options described previously to add contacts to your new group.

Deleting groups

To delete a group, first remove all contacts from the group. To remove a contact, right-click its icon within the group. Then, move the contact to a different group, or delete it from the current group. After the group is empty, right-click its name and choose Delete Group.

Deleting a contact

To delete a contact from all groups, first open your All Contacts group. Within the All Contacts list, right-click the contact you wish to delete. (Or, click the contact name and press the Delete key.) You'll see a dialog box asking if you're sure you want to complete the deletion. If you choose Yes, you'll permanently delete the contact from all groups. If that isn't your intention, choose No.

Configuring Windows Messenger

Like most programs, Windows Messenger has an Options dialog box that you can use to control how the program behaves. You get to that Options dialog box the same way you do in many other programs — by choosing Tools ➪ Options from Windows Messenger's menu bar. In the sections that follow, we'll look at how you can use those options to control how Windows Messenger starts, your degree of privacy, and more.

Choosing your display name and font

Even though you add contacts to Windows Messenger via your contacts' e-mail addresses, your contacts' names usually appear in your list of contacts. Each user gets to choose a Display Name. When you choose Tools ➪ Options from the Windows Messenger menu bar, the first choice you come to (on the Personal tab) is your Display Name, as shown in Figure 34-16.

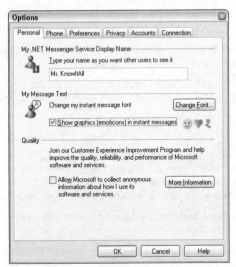

Figure 34-16: The Preferences tab of Windows Messenger's Options dialog box

The My Message Text options on the Personal tab let you choose a general font for all your instant messages. To ensure that emoticons are visible in your messages, choose the Show graphics . . . checkbox. The last option lets you choose whether or not you want to partici-pate in Microsoft's quality-control and improvement program. Click More Information if you want to learn what that's about.

To autostart or not to autostart

After choosing Tools ➪ Options to get to Windows Messenger's Options dialog box, click the Preferences tab to see the options shown in Figure 34-17. Your general options are:

✦ **Run Windows Messenger when Windows starts:** If selected, this ensures that the Windows Messenger icon appears in the Notification area when you first start your computer. If you disable this option, Windows Messenger won't start automatically and won't appear in the Notification area. You'll need to click Start and choose All Programs ➪ Windows Messenger when you want to run the program.

✦ **Allow Windows Messenger to run in the background:** Generally, you want to choose this option to allow Windows Messenger to run as a background process, using mini-mal resources while idle but ready for action at a moment's notice.

✦ **Show me as "Away" when inactive for _x_ minutes:** Select this option if you want Windows Messenger to automatically change your status to *Away* after a period of inac-tivity. If you choose this option, you can then specify how long a period of inactivity is required to change your status to *Away*.

✦ **Allows Windows Messenger to receive ink:** If selected, this option allows people with Web-enabled mobile devices to send you handwritten messages, often referred to as ink.

Figure 34-17: The Preferences tab of Windows Messenger's Options dialog box

Showing/hiding message alerts

Also on the Preferences tab of Windows Messenger's Options dialog box are some options for controlling how you receive alerts. Your options are:

✦ **Display alerts when contacts come online:** If this is selected, you'll see a little message in the Notification area each time one of your contacts signs in to his or her .NET Passport. (You must also be signed in yourself.) Clearing this option prevents the Notification area message from being displayed.

✦ **Display alerts when an instant message is received:** If this is selected, you'll see a message in the Notification area whenever someone invites you to join an instant-messaging session. If you clear this option, the Notification area message won't be displayed.

✦ **Block alerts and set status to "Busy" when running full-screen programs:** If you use your computer to watch DVDs or other movies in full-screen, you may not want to be disturbed by message requests at that time. Choosing this option will show your status as *Busy* to other contacts whenever you're watching something in full-screen mode.

✦ **Play sound when contacts sign in or send a message:** If you select this option, you'll hear a little sound whenever a contact signs in or sends you a message. You can then click the Sounds button to get to the Sounds and Audio Devices dialog box. From that dialog box, you can click the Sounds tab. Then, scroll down to Windows Messenger in the Program Events list, and choose your own sound effects for various events (Contact Online, New Alert, New Mail, and New Message).

Choosing where to put received files

Any time someone sends a file during a Windows Messenger conversation, that file is stored in a folder named My Received Files folder in your My Documents folder. You can change that default folder to anything you want. To change where Windows Messenger stores your received files, click the Browse button under File Transfer on the Options dialog box. In Figure 34-18, I chose my Recent Downloads folder. It's listed under Alan's Documents in that figure, because I'm currently signed in to the user account named Alan.

Figure 34-18: Browsing to a folder named Recent Downloads within My Documents

Maintaining your privacy

People vary a lot in how they use instant messaging. Some people use it in a very public manner, chatting with strangers in chat rooms, making information about themselves available to other people, and so forth. Other people don't want any public exposure at all. They want to use instant messaging to converse with people they know, and that's it. You can have it either way. It's all a matter of knowing which settings to choose. The Privacy tab in Windows Messenger's Options dialog box, shown in Figure 34-19, provides your privacy options.

Blocking known and unknown contacts

When you first open the Privacy tab, you'll see two lists: the My Allow List and the My Block List. People in the My Allow List can see when you're online and can send you instant messages. People on the My Block List can't see when you're online and cannot send you messages. To move a contact from one list to the other, click the contact name. Then, click the << Allow or Block>> button to move the contact to the opposite list.

The boldfaced item *Other .NET Messenger Users* refers to umpteen million people in the world who have a .NET Passport and are not your contacts. When *Other .NET Service Users* is in your Allow List, anyone can add you to his or her list of contacts and send you messages. If you move *Other .NET Service Users* to your Block List, only the people in your My Allow List can see when you're online and can contact you.

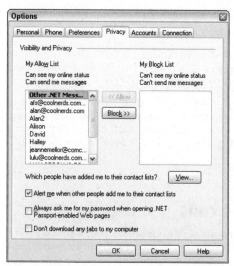

Figure 34-19: The Privacy tab in Windows Messenger's Options dialog box

Note If you send an instant message to someone, but they don't receive it, ask that person to add you, or *All other users*, to his or her My Allow List. If you can't receive a message from someone, check your own My Allow List.

See who has you as a contact

If you're curious who has you listed as a contact in Windows Messenger programs, click the View button next to *Which people have added me to their contact lists?* option on the Privacy tab. In the dialog box that opens, you can right-click any person and choose Properties to see his or her e-mail address.

If you want to be alerted anytime someone adds you as a contact, choose the *Alert me when other people add me to their contacts lists* option. Choosing the *Always ask me for my password when opening .NET Passport-enabled Web pages* disables the ability to sign in automatically.

Selecting the last option, *Don't download any tabs to my computer*, prevents Web sites from adding tabs to your Windows Messenger contacts. See "Using an Alternative to Sign-ins and .NET Alerts," later in this chapter, for information on tabs.

Showing/hiding your phone number

When you right-click a contact in your Windows Messenger list and choose Properties, you see some basic information about that person in a Properties dialog box. That information might, or might not, include the contact's phone number. You can choose whether or not to make your own phone number visible to your contacts by clicking the Phone tab in Windows Messenger's dialog box. To make phone numbers visible to your contacts, choose a Country/Region Code from the drop-down list. Then, type any phone numbers you want to make visible. To prevent contacts from seeing your phone numbers, leave all the options empty.

Voice Conversations versus Telephone Calls

Anyone with a computer, sound card, speakers, and a microphone can have voice conversations using the techniques described under "Toll-Free Talking," earlier in this chapter. Those voice conversations always involve two or more computers (no telephones) and are always free of charge.

Telephone conversations are different in several ways. For one thing, there's a standard telephone, a cell phone, or some other noncomputer communications device involved in the conversation. For another, telephone calls are never free of charge. In fact, you can't even use Windows Messenger to make phone calls unless you sign up with a Serial Information Protocol (SIP) Communications Service.

Windows Messenger phone calls

The Phones tab in Windows Messenger's Options dialog box allows you to set up alternative communications services that can work with Windows Messenger. There are two types of services you can add, though neither is free, nor simple:

✦ **SIP Communications Service:** Session Initiative Protocol (SIP) is a technology used by some corporations to allow employees to place telephone calls over the Internet. If your company has this capability, your network administrator can configure your copy of Windows Messenger to work with SIP.

✦ **Exchange Instant Messaging:** Companies that have Microsoft Exchange 2000 or 2003 installed can configure instant messaging so that members of a local network can communicate with another with Windows Messenger.

Both services require products and expertise that go beyond Windows XP and the scope of this book. To learn more about SIP and making telephone calls through Windows Messenger, choose Help ➪ Help Topics from Windows Messenger's menu bar. Then, click the Search tab and search for SIP or Exchange. However, network administrators need to be aware that the options for configuring SIP, Exchange, and other basic information about your Internet connection are on the Accounts and Connection tabs in Windows Messenger's Options dialog box.

Using an Alternative to Sign-ins and .NET Alerts

You can use your .NET Passport as an alternative sign-in for Web sites that require signing in. For example, let's say you have an account with eBay (www.ebay.com). Each time you visit that site, you have to go through the whole sign-in rigmarole. As an alternative to constantly signing in, you can use your .NET Passport to sign you in automatically.

To do so, first go to www.ebay.com and click the Sign In option. At the Sign-in page, scroll down to where you can see the alternative sign-ins, as in the upper-left corner of Figure 34-20. After you click the button, you're taken to the .NET Passport sign-in sheet shown in the lower portion of that figure. Type your .NET Passport name and password, and optionally choose the *Sign me in automatically* option to automate your sign-in for future sessions.

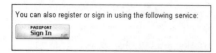

Figure 34-20: Sample alternative sign-in prompts

You want to use only automatic sign-in on your own personal computer, though. If you're using a public computer, or anyone else's computer, you won't want to enable that automatic sign-in, because doing so allows people who don't know your password to sign in as you.

Some Web sites (eBay isn't one of them) will add a tab to the left side of your Windows Messenger window when you set up your alternative sign in. When you add such a site to Windows Messenger, you'll be able to take a quick shortcut to the Web site, and sign in, just by clicking the site's tab in Windows Messenger.

Note   Web sites can only add tabs if you've disabled the *Don't download any tabs to my computer* option on the Privacy tab shown in Figure 34-19.

You can also use Windows Messenger to receive .NET Passport Alerts. Like alternative sign-ins, alerts are actually provided by third-party companies. Using eBay as an example once again, you can set up eBay alerts such that you receive a message as soon as someone outbids you on an item you're gunning for.

To enable .NET Alerts, click the Bell tab at the left side of Windows Messenger's program window. (If you don't see the tabs down the side of the window, choose Tools ➪ Show Tabs ➪ Microsoft Alerts from Windows Messenger's program window.) The first time you click the Bell tab, you'll see the option to sign up for your free alerts. Just click the Sign Up Now button and follow the instructions on the screen. From there, you'll see a list of companies offering .NET Alerts. Click any company name to learn more about the types of alerts they offer and to choose the types of alerts you'd like to receive.

Signing Off, Closing, and Terminating

Closing Windows Messenger doesn't automatically take you out of your .NET Passport account. Instead, the program window just closes, but the Notification Area icon remains. To sign out altogether, so that nobody can send you messages or alerts, do either of the following:

✦ Choose **File** ➪ **Sign Out** from Windows Messenger's menu bar.

✦ Right-click that little messenger icon in the Notification area (see Figure 34-21) and choose **Sign Out**.

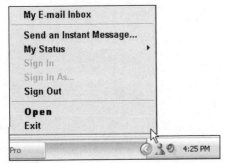

Figure 34-21: Signing out of your .NET Passport

Once you're signed out, you cannot use any .NET Passport features. To sign back in, double-click the Windows Messenger icon in the Notification area. Or right-click that icon and choose Sign In.

Caution   The gray pop-up ads that you might get, which show *Messenger Service* in their title bars, aren't related to your .NET Passport or Windows Messenger. To get rid of those, see "Blocking Messenger Pop-Ups" in Chapter 29. Terminating your .NET Passport won't disable those pop-ups.

Still More .NET Passport Stuff

There's even more to .NET Passport than you've learned in this chapter. But these other features take place through the Internet or your Web browser and aren't directly related to Windows Messenger. Here are more resources you can visit and take advantage of using your .NET Passport:

✦ **Create your own Web site:** Your .NET Passport entitles you to create an MSN Group, which is much like a Web site where you can post text, pictures, and the like. For more information, visit http://groups.msn.com.

✦ **Meet people:** Stop by a chat room, where you can meet new people and debate hot topics. Visit http://chat.msn.com to get started.

✦ **Play games online:** Want to show off your gaming skills online? Stop by http://zone.msn.com to get started.

✦ **Free extras:** Add some style to your instant messages using the Cool Extras available from `http://messenger.msn.com/Resource`.

✦ **MSN on your cell phone or PDA:** For information on extending Windows Messenger's reach to your cell phone, PDA (personal digital assistant), or wristwatch, take at look at `http://mobile.msn.com`.

✦ **.NET Passport help and support:** For general information, troubleshooting, and other .NET Passport support, swing by `http://messenger.msn.com/Help`.

Wrap Up

Windows Messenger (a.k.a. MSN Messenger) is a tool for setting up a connection between two or more computers on the Internet. That connection allows for real-time communications much like that offered by the phone. Though unlike the telephone, where you can only talk to the other person by voice, Messenger allows you to type messages back and forth, use video-phone, transfer files between computers, collaborate on projects, and more. Plus, unlike the phone company, the connection is always free of charge. To summarize the main points in this chapter:

✦ A .NET Passport is a free account that provides Internet services that go beyond basic e-mail and Web browsing.

✦ Windows Messenger is a program that allows you to communicate with other people in real time, by typing, talking, or videophone.

✦ You can also send and receive files of any size using Windows Messenger.

✦ Remote Assistance is a Windows Messenger feature that allows you to turn control of your computer over to a trusted expert on the Internet.

✦ To personalize Windows Messenger, choose **Tools** ⇨ **Options** from its menu bar.

✦ To sign out of your .NET Passport, right-click the little Windows Messenger icon in the Notification area and click **Sign Out**.

✦   ✦   ✦

Using FTP and Newsgroups

Usenet is a popular service on the Internet that enables people who share a similar interest to post messages to one another. The "rooms" where people post their messages are called newsgroups. That name is a little strange, however, because few of the rooms have anything to do with what most of us consider "news." Instead, each newsgroup just focuses on a particular subject. They can be a great resource for getting information or just a place to sound your opinion.

File Transfer Protocol (FTP) is an Internet service used for transferring files from one computer to another across the Internet. Unlike sending files as e-mail attachments, FTP puts no limitations on file size and doesn't require an e-mail message, attaching, or anything else. You just drag and drop, or use any method you like, really, to move or copy any number of files and folders from one computer to another.

About Newsgroups

Millions of people on the Internet communicate through newsgroups every day. You can find newsgroups that discuss just about any subject imaginable. The newsgroup game is replete with jargon. The buzzwords you're likely to encounter as you enter this realm are defined here:

+ Each message in a newsgroup is officially called an *article*, although I'll stick with the term *message* in this book. An article or message might also be called a *post*.

+ A series of messages that originate from a single post is called a *thread*. For example, if I post a question, and 9 people answer with messages of their own, those 10 messages constitute a thread.

+ Many newsgroups are *moderated* by people who screen messages for suitability to the newsgroup. Others are *unmoderated*, and messages pass through to the newsgroup unscreened and uncensored.

+ *Lurking* is hanging around a newsgroup to see what's being said without actually contributing anything. When you're new to a newsgroup, lurking for a while is a good idea, just to get an idea of what subject matter the group thinks is appropriate.

✦ *Flaming* is sending nasty messages to people in the group. If you post irrelevant messages to a group, you might get flamed! Anything that smacks of advertising in a newsgroup will surely result in flame mail directed at you!

✦ *Spamming* is sending blatant advertisements or sneaky ads disguised as newsgroup messages to a newsgroup. Highly unacceptable, and sure to get you flamed!

✦ *Netiquette* is observing proper newsgroup etiquette by not sending irrelevant comments and not spamming the group. A good *netizen* (network citizen) follows proper netiquette.

✦ While there are many ways to communicate online, in this chapter I'll mainly be focused on *UseNet Newsgroups*. A *UseNet Newsgroup* exists on a *news server* or *NNTP server* (Network News Transfer Protocol).

✦ Every news server has an *address*. Most ISPs offer free access to a news server as part of their service. To learn the address of your ISP's news server, contact your ISP.

On any given news server, you're likely to find hundreds, if not thousands, of newsgroups. Each newsgroup discusses specific topics, and the name of the newsgroup provides a strong clue as to its topic of discussion.

On any given news server, the names of newsgroups are arranged hierarchically. The name consists of several parts separated by periods. The least specific portion of the name is always listed first. Each name to the right of that first name narrows things down to a more specific category or topic. Table 35-1 lists examples of major category names and specific newsgroup names within the category.

Table 35-1: Some Newsgroup Main Categories, Descriptions, and Names

Main Category	Description	Sample Newsgroup Names
Alt	Alternative topics	alt.humor.puns, alt.pets.rabbits, alt.test
Bionet	Biology	bionet.microbiology, bionet.mycology
Biz	Business	biz.comp.hardware, biz.comp.software
Comp	Computers	comp.human-factors, comp.jobs
Humanities	Arts and humanities	humanities.classics, humanities.music
Misc	Miscellaneous	misc.books.technical, misc.computers.forsale
News	Usenet news network	news.announce.newusers, news.answers
Rec	Recreation, arts, and hobbies	rec.food.drink.coffee, rec.food.chocolate
Sci	Science	sci.agriculture.beekeeping, sci.bio.food-science
Soc	Social topics	soc.culture.punjab, soc.geneology.surnames
Talk	Debates, opinions	talk.environment, talk.politics

There are a couple of ways to use newsgroups. By far, the easiest is to use a Web browser such as Microsoft Internet Explorer. The other, more traditional, method is to use a *newsreader*. As discussed later in this chapter, you can use Outlook Express, which comes with Windows XP, as a newsreader. Though doing so is quite a bit more complicated than using Internet Explorer. So, let's start with the quick-and-easy approach here.

Doing Newsgroups with Internet Explorer

Many newsgroups now make their homes on the Web. Sometimes they're called *message boards*, *discussion groups*, or *communities*. But regardless of what you call them, all the groups work on the same basic principal of posting messages to a server so that people can "converse" online. The main difference is that Web-based newsgroups don't require access to a news server, or even a newsreader such as Outlook Express. You can do everything you need to do right from Microsoft Internet Explorer.

As an example, Figure 35-1 shows the list of communities available at `www.microsoft.com/communities`. Not all are newsgroups, but they're all a means of sharing information. To get to that Microsoft Communities page, get online, open Internet Explorer, type the URL into the Address bar, and press Enter. The home page won't look exactly like the figure, of course, because it's a Web site. But as you scroll around you'll see there are newsgroups, technical chats, user groups, blogs, and other ways of sharing information available.

Figure 35-1: Home page for Microsoft Technical Communities

Like many newsgroups, Microsoft's are easily accessible from Internet Explorer. In newsgroups they tend to refer to a Web browser as a *Web-based newsreader*. But it's still just a Web browser. When you click on the Newsgroups link on the Communities home page, you're taken to a page where you can search newsgroups based on your topic of interest. When the search is complete, your browser will be divided into three panes, as in the example shown in Figure 35-2. The panes (which are squished down because of the 800 × 600 resolution of my screenshot) are:

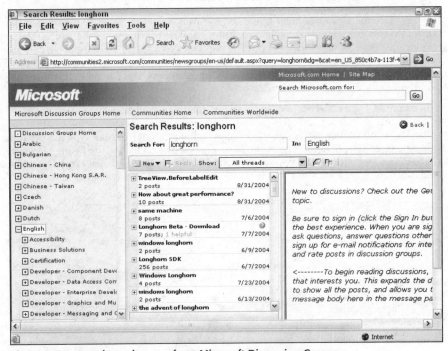

Figure 35-2: Search results page from Microsoft Discussion Groups

✦ **TOC pane:** The left pane is a table of contents that lists available newsgroups (called discussion groups) by language.

✦ **Thread pane:** The center pane is a list of threads. The subject of each thread is shown in boldface, the number of posts and the date of the thread appear beneath the subject. Clicking the + sign next to a subject displays the name of each person who contributed to the thread.

✦ **Message pane:** The message pane on the right shows the content of a single post. Click on any entry beneath the expanded subject line to read the text of the post. To get a better look at the post, double-click it. The thread will open in a separate browser window without all the accouterments that crowd the search results page.

Note You need a .NET Passport to post to most Microsoft newsgroups. If you don't want a .NET Passport, you can find plenty of non-Microsoft newsgroups on the Web. Just search Google (www.google.com) for newsgroups, and you'll find tons of them.

What's a Blog?

The term *blog* is short for *Web log* and is a form of personal, open-ended publishing on the Internet. In some ways, a blog is like a public diary. As you browse through Web pages, you keep track of your thoughts, opinions, and recommendations. Then, you publish the log where anyone who is interested can take a look. Blogs are relatively new, but have really caught on, and some people estimate that there are over a million people publishing blogs to the Web.

Many blogs are available on the Web right from a Web browser. Though if you are really serious about keeping up with blogs, you'll want an *RSS feed* or *RSS Reader*. (RSS stands for Really Simple Syndication). You can download an RSS Reader for free from many blog sites on the Web.

To publish a blog, you need to find a site that will allow you to publish it. That's generally easy and free. If you search Google (or any other engine) for `publish blog`, you'll find tons of links to sites that publish Web logs.

To ask a question in a discussion group, click the New button and choose Question, as shown in Figure 35-3. In that same toolbar, you'll find buttons to Reply to a post, print a post, copy the URL of a post to the Windows clipboard, and request automatic notifications of replies of your questions.

Figure 35-3: Toolbar from Microsoft's discussion groups

Admittedly, I'm talking about a sample Web-based newsgroup here. There are thousands of such newsgroups in the Web, and not all will look exactly like the example shown here. But every newsgroup offers help and instructions to new members. So, you shouldn't have any trouble getting the hang of any newsgroup you find.

Tip   Microsoft offers many free support newsgroups at `http://support.microsoft.com/newsgroups`. To check them out, just type that URL into Internet Explorer's Address bar and press Enter.

Using Outlook Express as a Newsreader

As discussed in Chapter 33, Outlook Express is an e-mail client that you can use to send and receive e-mail with certain types of e-mail services. Outlook Express can also double as a newsreader for subscribing to newsgroups, reading messages, and posting messages of your own.

Before you set up a newsgroup account in Outlook Express, you'll need to know the name of the news server to which you want to connect. For example, if your ISP has a news server, you'll need to contact them, or search their site, for the address of their news server. Also, if the news server requires that you log in, you'll need to know your user name and password,

which again comes from your ISP. With that information in hand, here's how you set up
Outlook Express to access newsgroups:

1. If you don't have an always-on Internet account, get online.

2. Click the **Start** button, and choose **All Programs**⇨**Outlook Express**.

3. Choose **Tools**⇨**Accounts** from the Outlook Express menu bar.

4. In the Internet Accounts dialog box that opens, click the **News** tab.

5. Click the **Add** button, and choose **News**.

6. As instructed on the screen, fill in your display name and e-mail address, clicking **Next>**
   at the bottom of each wizard page.

7. When you get to the page that asks about your news server (shown in Figure 35-4),
   make sure that you type the server name exactly as specified by your ISP. Typically, it
   will consist of three parts, such as `news.yourisp.com` or `nntp.yourisp.com`.

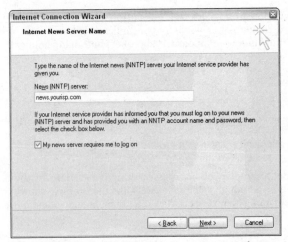

Figure 35-4: Enter facts about your news server here.

8. If your news server requires that you log on, choose the **My news server requires me**
   to log on checkbox.

9. Click **Next>**.

10. If you chose the log on option, enter your user name and password as specified by your
    ISP, and then click **Next>**.

11. Follow any remaining wizard instructions to completion, and then click **Finish**.

Most likely you'll see the message shown in Figure 35-5. Choosing Yes will download the
names of newsgroups from the news server. If you miss that prompt, don't worry about it.
You can download that information at any time.

Figure 35-5: Message for downloading newsgroup names

Subscribing to newsgroups

After you've added a newsgroup server to your Internet accounts, Outlook Express will display its name in the list of folders at the left edge of the window. (If you don't see that list, choose View ⇨ Layout from the Outlook Express menu bar. Then, choose the Folder List icon and click the OK button.)

In Figure 35-6, for example, news.comcast.giganews.net is the name of a news server provided to Comcast.net customers. If you didn't download newsgroup names the first time around, clicking that name will ask again if you want to download the newsgroup names. You'll want to choose Yes, eventually, because you need to see the names of all the newsgroups before you can subscribe to a newsgroup.

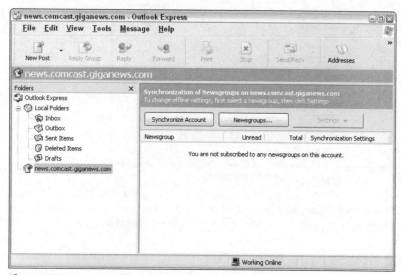

Figure 35-6: Message for downloading newsgroup names

> **Tip** If you also use Outlook Express for e-mail, you can instantly get to your Inbox just by clicking on Inbox near the top of the Folders list in the left pane.

To interact with a newsgroup, you need to subscribe to it. This is nothing like a magazine subscription. It won't cost you anything, you won't be bombarded with renewal notices, and you can unsubscribe at any time. Subscribing to a newsgroup just places a quick link to the newsgroup beneath the news server name in the left column of Outlook Express, and also downloads messages from the newsgroup to your computer so that you can start interacting.

To see what kinds of newsgroups are available on your news server, first make sure that you've clicked your newsgroup server's name in the Folders list. Then, click the Newsgroups button in the pane on the right. The Newsgroups Subscriptions dialog box opens, displaying a list of all the newsgroups available to you. You can scroll through the list if you like. It is probably going to be quite lengthy. Optionally, you can type any word (or words) that describe the subject matter you're interested in. The list changes to include only newsgroups whose names contain that word (or words).

You can broaden your search by having Internet Explorer search both the newsgroup names and their descriptions. Just choose the Search Descriptions checkbox. If you've never downloaded the descriptions, you may have to wait a few minutes for the download to be completed.

Figure 35-7 shows an example where I've searched for the term *new user*. The list now contains only newsgroups that have that phrase as part of their name. The group named news.newusers, highlighted in the list, is a good first group to join if you're a beginner.

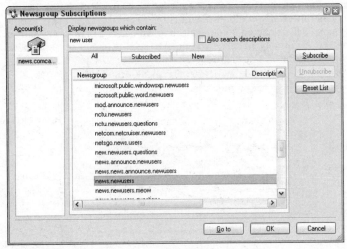

Figure 35-7: Search for groups that contain *new user*

You can subscribe to as many newsgroups as you want. When you've finished, just click the OK button near the bottom of the Newsgroup Subscriptions dialog box.

Viewing newsgroup messages

To see what's happening in a newsgroup, just click its name in the Folders list. Any new messages since your last visit (if any) will be downloaded to your computer and displayed in the pane on the right. (That may take a couple of minutes, depending on the speed of your connection). In Figure 35-8, for example, I've clicked the news.newusers newsgroup in the Folders list.

The top pane on the right shows *message headers*, where the header for each message is just its subject line, who sent the message, when the message was sent, and the size of the message. Notice that some message headers have a plus sign (+) next to them. Each such message is the beginning of a thread—perhaps a question that was asked by one of the newsgroup members. Clicking that plus sign reveals the rest of the messages in the thread—typically answers to the question posed by whomever sent the initial message.

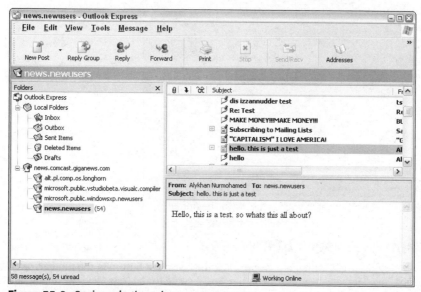

Figure 35-8: Seeing what's up in news.newusers

Messages that you've never read will be shown in boldface. Clicking a message header reveals the body of the message in the lower pane. Within a few seconds after you've clicked, the boldface in the message header will fade.

Tip   To arrange message headers into chronological order, click the Sent column heading. Each time you click a particular heading, the sort order is reversed. Hence, if the first click puts the headers in oldest-to-newest order, the next click will put them in newest-to-oldest order.

You can search through existing messages to see whether anybody has already brought up whatever's on your mind. If you're thinking of asking a question, for example, the answer might already be posted somewhere in the current messages. To find out, you can search through existing messages by clicking the Find button on the toolbar, or by choosing Edit ➪ Find ➪ Message from the menu bar. The Find Message dialog box opens, as shown in Figure 35-9.

The dialog box offers many ways to search (although that's largely because it's the same dialog box you can use to search for e-mail messages). In a newsgroup, you will probably want to search through subject lines and messages. In Figure 35-9, for example, I've opted to search message subjects for the word *beginner*. Click the Find Now button when you're ready to begin your search. The Find Message dialog box will expand to list messages (if any) that match your search criteria.

When the search is complete, double-click any message header to view the body of the message. To close the Find Message dialog box, click its Close (X) button.

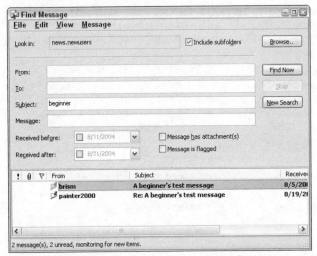

Figure 35-9: Result of searching for the word "beginner"

Posting a newsgroup message

If you have a question for the newsgroup, click the New Post button in the toolbar, or choose Message ⇨ New Message from the menu bar. You'll come to the New Message dialog box shown in Figure 35-10. Be sure to type a meaningful subject into the subject line, because this is what appears as the message header. Most other newsgroup members will read the subject before deciding whether to open the message. Then, type in your message, just as you would type an e-mail message.

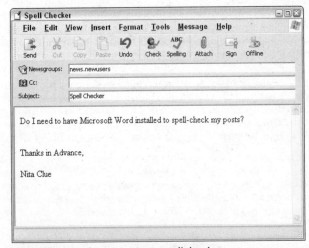

Figure 35-10: The New Message dialog box

When you've finished composing your message, just click the Send button. A message will display, telling you how the message will be handled. If Outlook Express isn't set up to send messages immediately, you'll see a dialog box telling you that the message will be placed in your Outbox and won't be sent until you click the Send and Receive (Send/Recv) button. You'll need to click the OK button, and then click the Send and Receive button in Outlook Express to actually send the message. (Alternatively, you can click the little arrow on the button and choose Send All if you want to just send without receiving.)

If Outlook Express is set up to send messages immediately, you'll see a dialog box telling you that the message is being sent; remember, however, that it might not be visible right away. If the message doesn't appear soon, however, you might want to synchronize your PC with the news server, as discussed later in the section "Getting the latest messages."

Replying to newsgroup messages

If you read a message and decide to post a reply, you can do so in a couple of ways:

✦ **Reply to Group:** Your message is sent to the news server, and all newsgroup members can see it.

✦ **Reply:** Your message is sent to the poster's e-mail address, where only he or she will see your response.

To choose a reply option, click the Reply to Group or Reply button on the toolbar. Alternatively, right-click the message to which you want to reply and choose Reply to Group or Reply to Sender. You'll be taken to the standard dialog box for composing messages. Just type in your message, and click the Send button. Replies are handled in the same way as new posts are. After all, replies are messages as well. Therefore, when you click the Send button, you'll see a dialog box telling you how the message will be handled. If you don't see your reply for a while after sending it, you might want to synchronize your computer with the server, as discussed in the next section.

Getting the latest messages

When you post a message or a reply, you may not see your message right away in the newsgroups messages. There are several reasons for this—some of them on the server side where the messages are located. Those, you can do nothing about. You can ensure that you can download new messages at any time, however, just to make sure you have what's on the server. More often than not, your posts will be visible as soon as the new messages have been downloaded. To bring messages from the current newsgroup up to date, follow these steps:

1. In the Folders list, click the name of the newsgroup you want to bring up to date.

2. Choose **Tools ⇨ Synchronize Newsgroup** from the Outlook Express menu bar.

3. In the Synchronize Newsgroup dialog box that appears, choose **Get the following items**. Then, choose one of the following options:

   • **All messages:** Gets all messages from the server. This can take a long time.

   • **New messages only:** Gets only those messages that aren't yet visible on your screen.

   • **Headers only:** Downloads message headers only, which is quick. Remember, however, that clicking a message header does not reveal the body of the message. Instead, it only marks it for downloading. You need to repeat Steps 1 and 2, and then choose **Get messages marked for download** to see the bodies of the messages whose headers you click.

4. Click the **OK** button.

To update messages for all your subscribed newsgroups, click the newsgroup server name in the Folders list, and then click the Synchronize Account button.

You can adjust some additional settings to choose how all your messages — both e-mail messages and newsgroup messages — are handled. They're all available in the Options dialog box for Outlook Express, shown in Figure 35-11. To open that dialog box, choose Tools ➪ Options from the Outlook Express menu bar.

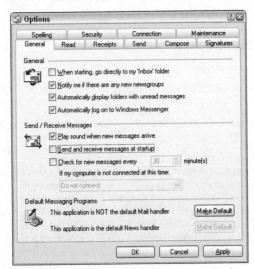

Figure 35-11: The General tab of the Outlook Express Options dialog box

The Options dialog box provides the following newsgroup-related options:

✦ If you want messages to be updated automatically each time you start, choose the **Send and receive messages at startup** option on the General tab.

✦ If you want Outlook Express to update messages automatically, choose the **Check for new messages every . . .** option, and then specify how often you want Outlook Express to check. If you don't have an always-on Internet connection, you also can choose whether you want the computer to dial in to your ISP when it's time to check for new messages.

✦ If you want your messages to be sent as soon as you click the Send button, choose the **Send messages immediately** option from the Send tab. If you don't choose this option, messages will be placed in your outbox until you click the Send and Receive button, or until you choose Tools ➪ Send and Receive from the menu bar.

Caution   The options discussed in this section apply to your e-mail messages as well. So if you don't want to change your current e-mail settings, don't make any changes to the settings described here.

Unsubscribing

If you find there are newsgroups that you're not using much and want to stop downloading their messages, just unsubscribe from the group. To do so, right-click the newsgroup's name in the Folders list and choose Unsubscribe. Alternatively, click the name of the newsgroup server, and then click the Newsgroups button that appears. Click the Subscribed button, click the name of the newsgroup that you want to leave, and then click the Unsubscribe button.

Using FTP

FTP stands for File Transfer Protocol and is a standardized method of transferring files from one computer to another on the Internet. FTP is not the same as peer-to-peer (P2P) file sharing where you can download files from any computer that's in the network. Nor is it like the transferring files with Windows Messenger, where you can send and receive files with whomever you're having a conversation. Rather, FTP allows you to copy files from, and perhaps to, a computer called an FTP server.

In FTP, the words "upload" and "download" have very specific meaning:

✦ **Download:** To copy files from the FTP server to your own computer.

✦ **Upload:** To copy files from your computer to the FTP server.

Every Web server has a URL (address) that takes the general form:

ftp://*host.domain.tld*

where *host* is a specific computer's name,. *domain* is the name of the company or site that owns the server, and *tld* is one of the common top-level domain names such as .com or .net.

Anonymous FTP versus FTP accounts

There are two basic ways to do FTP. *Anonymous FTP* allows you to download files from the FTP server without having an account name and password. Often, you can download files using anonymous FTP. However, the ability to upload to an FTP server using anonymous FTP is rare, because the owner of the FTP site doesn't want millions of people uploading files at random.

To upload files to an FTP server, you generally need an account, which includes a user name and password. As an example, let's say that your ISP provides some empty space on a Web server on which you're allowed to publish your own Web pages. Or, maybe you've rented space on a Web server somewhere to publish your Web pages. Either way, the service provider may give you the URL of the Web server, a user account name, and a password that allows you to upload Web pages from your computer to the Web server. Once the pages are on the Web server, anyone with an Internet account and Web browser can view those pages.

To upload and download files with FTP, you may need an *FTP client*. As the name implies, the FTP client is a program, stored on your computer, that lets you transfer files between your computer and FTP server to which you have access. However, like so many Internet things these days, many FTP sites will allow you to use Microsoft Internet Explorer, and perhaps other Web browsers, to upload and download files.

Using Internet Explorer as an FTP client

Using Microsoft Internet Explorer as an FTP client is quite easy, because you copy files to and from the Web server using exactly the same techniques you use to copy files between folders and drives on your own computer. In fact, the FTP looks and acts just like any folder on your own hard drive, and you can use any technique described in Chapter 14 to copy, move, rename, and delete files. (Though, you can't rename, delete, or move files off of the FTP server unless your account provides permission for that sort of thing.)

Getting to an anonymous FTP server in Internet Explorer is no different from getting to a Web site. You just type the FTP server's URL into Internet Explorer's Address bar, and then press Enter or click Go. When you get to the site, you may be prompted to enter a user name or password, as in Figure 35-12. If you get an error message instead of the Log On As dialog box shown in the figure, choose File ➪ Login As from Internet Explorer's menu bar to get to that same dialog box.

Figure 35-12: The Log On As dialog box for an FTP site

If the site you're trying to open allows anonymous access, just choose the Log on anonymously checkbox, and then click the Log On button. You may need to provide an e-mail address; you may not. It all depends on the FTP server.

As you can see in Figure 35-12, the sample FTP site that I'm trying to access does not allow anonymous access. So, choosing the *Log on anonymously* option won't work there. Instead, you need to enter the user name and password granted to you by the owners of the FTP server. Optionally, you can choose Save Password so that you don't have to enter the password every time you log in to the site.

Once you've connected to the FTP server, the rest will be very much like using a folder on your own hard disk.

Transferring files with FTP and Internet Explorer

Once you've connected to an FTP site with Internet Explorer, the rest should be easy. Though, things won't be quite a speedy as when you're working with folders and files on your own computer, especially if you're using a dial-up account. But you can, for example, use the View option on the menu bar, or the Views toolbar button as shown in Figure 35-13 to choose how you want to view icons on the FTP server.

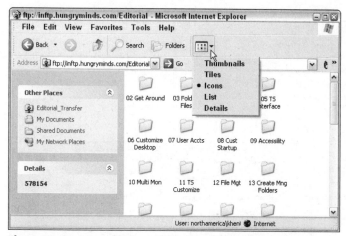

Figure 35-13: Logged in to an FTP site with Internet Explorer

The sample FTP site shown in the figure is actually one provided by Wiley, the publishers of this book. It's not an anonymous FTP site, and the URL you see isn't the full URL of the site. So, don't bother trying to go there are download files. I used that site as an example, though, because I have an account that gives me total access to one folder on that site—the folder for submitting this book to the publisher. Each folder you see in Figure 35-13 contains all the files (text and pictures) from one chapter of this book.

On my own computer here at home, I created a folder for this whole book. Within that folder I have a subfolder for each chapter. Each chapter folder, in turn, contains the text and all the figures for that chapter. When I finish a group of chapters and am ready to submit them to the publisher, I log in to their FTP site. Then, I just drag and drop each completed chapter's folder from my computer to theirs. (I never see anything on paper until I get the completed bound book from the publisher several weeks later.)

But anyway, that's basically how FTP works when you use Internet Explorer as your FTP client. Figure 35-14 shows a better example. The window in the upper-left corner is a folder on my computer with its contents being displayed by Windows Explorer. The window in the lower-right corner is the publisher's FTP site, being displayed by Internet Explorer.

With my local folder and the FTP site displayed as in Figure 35-14, I can easily copy stuff from my computer to theirs. I just select the folders I want to submit, drag them into Internet Explorer's document window, and release the mouse button. This is exactly the same as I'd do if I were moving or copying files between folders on my own computer. As you can see in the figure, I've already copied quite a few folders from my computer to theirs.

If you have upload permissions for the FTP server, you can manage folders on the FTP server just as you do on your own computer. For example, you can right-click any file or folder's icon to see the usual Cut, Copy, Delete, and Rename options, as in Figure 35-15.

So that, in a nutshell, is what FTP is all about: You can copy files from any computer in the world that's connected to the Internet using the same techniques you use to copy files on your own computer. If you have an account with appropriate permissions on the FTP server, then you can copy files to the server, and move, delete, and rename files on the server using standard Windows techniques described in Chapter 14 of this book.

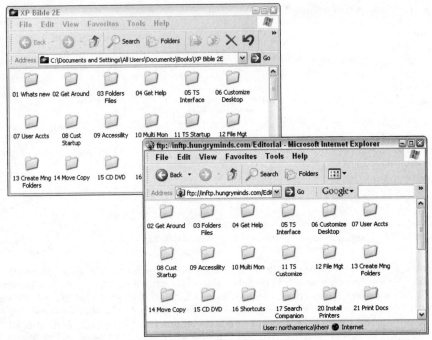

Figure 35-14: Folder on my computer (upper left) and on an FTP site (lower right)

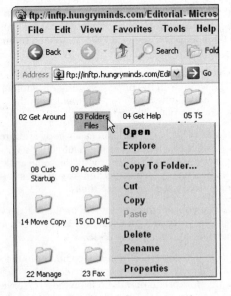

Figure 35-15: Managing folders on an FTP server

Using an FTP client

If, for whatever reason, a particular FTP site won't work with Internet Explorer, you'll have to use a dedicated FTP client to move and transfer files. There is no graphical FTP program built into Windows XP. But there are plenty of them around that you can download. For example, if you go to www.tucows.com and search for FTP client, you'll be able to download shareware versions of the popular WS-FTP Pro client, published by IPSwitch (www.ipswitch.com), among others.

If at first you don't succeed in connecting to an FTP site with Internet Explorer, don't assume that it can't be done. If at all possible, contact the owners of the FTP site for specifics on using Internet Explorer with their site. Getting it to work might be a simple matter of changing a setting or two in the Internet Options dialog box.

To try a possible quick fix, choose Tools ⇨ Internet Options from Internet Explorer's toolbar. Click the Advanced tab, and make sure *Enable folder view for FTP sites* is selected. You might also try selecting, or clearing, the *Use Passive FTP (for firewall and DSL modem compatibility)* option to see if that helps. As always, click OK after making your selections in the dialog box.

Wrap Up

Like e-mail and the Web, newsgroups and FTP are Internet services that everyone can use. Newsgroups provide a virtual meeting place for like-minded people to discuss topics, get and give help, or just to hang out. FTP provides a simple means of transferring files of any size between an FTP server computer and your local computer. Key points of this chapter are:

✦ Newsgroups allow people to communicate online by posting, and replying to, messages.

✦ You can access and use many modern newsgroups using Internet Explorer.

✦ To subscribe to traditional UseNet Newsgroups that don't support Internet Explorer, use Outlook Express.

✦ FTP (File Transfer Protocol) is a technology for transferring files from one computer to another over the Internet.

✦ The easiest way to do FTP is with Microsoft Internet Explorer, because it allows you to manage files using the same techniques you use on your own computer.

✦   ✦   ✦

Troubleshooting Internet Problems

Troubleshooting Internet Explorer

Internet problems can be caused by your connection, a problem with the page you're viewing, or a problem with your Web browser. Here, we'll focus on problems that are related to Microsoft Internet Explorer. If the problem began shortly after installing Service Pack 2, you may want to take some time to familiarize yourself with the new built-in pop-up blocker (see Chapter 29) and the new Manage Add-ons window discussed under "Disable mysterious add-ons" in Chapter 30.

Clicking a hyperlink has no effect

The link you clicked may open in a new window, which is being blocked as a pop-up. Click the Information bar to allow pop-ups, or click the No symbol in the status bar (see Figure 36-1) and choose an option to allow pop-ups.

Note   Everything described in Chapter 29 applies to Web pages that open in new browser windows as well.

Can't download program or ActiveX Control

Service Pack 2 adds extra security, preventing downloads from occurring without your permission. When an expected download doesn't start, click the Information bar (see Figure 36-2) and choose Download File to star the download.

Caution   Do not accept unsolicited downloads. Download only programs from sites you know and trust.

Figure 36-1: Choose an option to allow a secondary Web page.

Figure 36-2: Use the Information bar to download programs.

Security warning about trusted sites

When you click a link to go to a Web site that you've added to your list of trusted sites, Internet Explorer displays a security warning like the example in Figure 36-3. If you weren't intending to download a program or visit the trusted site, the page listed next to Trusted Site might be trying to sneak something past your security settings.

Figure 36-3: Warning about entering a trusted site

In the example shown in Figure 36-3, I intentionally opted to go to Microsoft's download page, and so would click Yes to proceed to that page. Remember, a Security Warning doesn't always mean something bad is about to happen. In most cases (such as this example), it's just a heads up so that you can see if, and when, something fishy is going on.

To get to Internet Explorer's Security Zones settings, choose Tools ➪ Internet Options from Internet Explorer's menu bar. Then, click the Security tab in the Internet Options dialog box. For more information on Internet Explorer Security Zones and changes in Service Pack 2, visit the Internet Explorer Web site at www.microsoft.com/ie.

Error message "This page cannot be displayed"

The two most common causes of this problem are trying to browse to a Web page when you're offline, and mistyping a URL. If you have a dial-up account, first make sure that you're online. (If you can check your e-mail, then you know you're online).

Keep in mind that there is no margin for typographical errors when typing a URL. Even a minor misspelling, such as typing `www.windowscatalogue.com` rather than `www.windowscatalog.com` will cause this error. Putting a blank space in a URL will almost always cause the same problem. (The blank space is changed to %20 after you press Enter).

For additional causes of frequent Page not found errors and solutions, go to `http://support.microsoft.com` and search for `Page Cannot Be Displayed`.

Can't change the default home page

Normally, you can change your default home page (the page that opens automatically when you first open Internet Explorer) at any time. You just browse to whatever Web page you want to make your home page, choose Tools ⇨ Internet Options from Internet Explorer's menu bar, and then click Use Current and click OK.

Note   In a corporate environment an administrator can also control your home page by using the Internet Explorer Administration Kit. In that case, you can't override the change without the administrator's consent.

If you find that your default home page keeps being reset to something else, look in Add or Remove Programs for programs that know how to do this, such as SecondPower Multimedia Speedbar, GoHip! Browser Enhancement, and Xupiter toolbar, and uninstall those products. Similarly, you can choose Tools ⇨ Manage Add-Ons and disable any Add-ons that include those names.

If the options to change your default home page are disabled (dimmed), your computer has probably been infected with a virus or worm such as the IRC.Becky.A worm or the Trojan.JS.Clid.gen virus. Use your antivirus software to scan your entire system for viruses, and delete everything that the scan finds.

If the problem persists even after deleting all known viruses, you'll need to perform a clean boot and manually edit the registry. Refer to Knowledge Base article 320159 for complete instructions on performing a clean boot and the specific registry keys to change. To get to that article, search `http://support.microsoft.com` for `320159` or browse to `http://support.microsoft.com/default.aspx?kbid=320159&product=ie`.

Saved pictures stored as bitmaps (.bmp files)

When you right-click a picture on a Web page, it normally saves as a JPEG or GIF file with whatever filename you provide. If all of your images are saved as bitmaps instead, follow these steps:

1. Choose **Tools ⇨ Internet Options** from Internet Explorer's menu bar.

2. Click the **Delete Files** button and wait for all the temporary Internet files to be deleted (don't worry; you won't lose any programs, documents, or anything else worth keeping).

3. When the deletion is complete and the mouse pointer works normally, click the **Advanced** tab in the Internet Options dialog box.

4. Scroll down to the **Security** heading in the advanced Settings list and clear the check mark (if any) next to *Do not save encrypted pages to disk.*

5. Click **OK** to close the dialog box.

6. Click the **Refresh** button in Internet Explorer's toolbar or choose **View** ➪ **Refresh** from its menu bar (or press **F5**).

Content Advisor dialog box or message opens

Content Advisor is an optional feature of Internet Explorer designed to allow parents to limit kids' access to Web sites. To use Content Advisor the parent must think up a password. As always, *Do not forget the password!* To activate or deactivate Content Advisor, choose Tools ➪ Internet Options from Internet Explorer's menu bar and click the Content tab. The rest is self-explanatory.

If you get error messages relating to Content Advisor, go to http://support.microsoft. com, and chose Internet Explorer 6 from the *Select a Microsoft Product* drop-down list. Type content advisor as the Search For text, and then click Go.

All other Internet Explorer problems/features

Internet Explorer is a large program that has more to do with the Internet than Windows XP per se. So, it's not something I can cover in depth in a general Windows book like this. But there's plenty of information available to you. I suggest that you start with the Help that's built into Internet Explorer, as follows:

1. Choose **Help** ➪ **Contents and Index** from Internet Explorer's menu bar.

2. In the Help window that opens, click the **Contents** tab. Then:

   • Click any item that sports a book icon to see topics within that category.

   • Click any icon that shows a page or open book icon to view that information in the pane on the right.

The Index tab in the Help window works just like the index at the back of a book. The Search tab allows you to search Help for any word or phrase.

For current news, downloads, and more information about Microsoft Internet Explorer, visit the IE home page at www.microsoft.com/ie. For specific features that are new in Service Pack 2, see www.microsoft.com/windowsxp/sp2/ieoeoverview.mspx.

Troubleshooting Outlook Express

If you're having problems with e-mail, and use Outlook Express as your e-mail client, the troubleshooting tips that follow may help solve the problem. Microsoft occasionally adds more security to Outlook Express through automatic updates. If you can't find the solution here, check out the main Web site for Outlook Express at www.microsoft.com/windows/oe/.

Error message "The host *name* could not be found . . ."

This error message occurs when the host name for your ISP or e-mail server is specified incorrectly for your service. To use Outlook Express as an e-mail client you must (1) make sure that your e-mail provider supports the use of Outlook Express, and (2) use the name, e-mail address, password, incoming mail server name, and outgoing mail server name specified by your ISP. If you have the correct information from your e-mail provider, here's how you can correct the entries for your account:

1. Click **Start** and choose **All Programs** ➪ **Outlook Express**.

2. Choose **Tools** ➪ **Accounts** from the Outlook Express menu bar.

3. In the Internet Accounts dialog box that opens, click the **Mail** tab.

4. Click the name of the account you wish to correct, and then click the **Properties** button.

5. In the account Properties dialog box, click the **Servers** tab to get to the options shown in Figure 36-4.

Figure 36-4: The Servers tab of an e-mail account's Properties sheet

6. Fill in the blanks using exactly the information provided by your ISP or e-mail service provider.

Caution Attempting to "figure out" appropriate entries on the Servers tab by guessing is like trying to guess a total stranger's phone number — futile. (The sample data shown in the figure is hypothetical, and also won't work).

7. Follow any other instructions provided by your ISP to fill in information on other tabs.

8. When you've finished entering all of your account information, click **OK** in the Properties dialog box.

9. Click the **Close** button in the Internet Accounts dialog box.

Click the Send/Recv button in the Outlook Express toolbar to test the new settings.

Pictures are missing from e-mail messages

Outlook Express intentionally replaces the pictures in some e-mail messages with a box containing a red X. Doing this protects you from *Web beacon* software, which alerts an online server when you click the picture, and also protects you from JPEG images that could be hiding malicious code. It also saves you from having to wait for all the pictures in your junk e-mail to download.

When you get a legitimate e-mail with pictures you do want to see, just click the Information bar (see Figure 36-5) to download a view images for that message only.

Blocked image   Information bar

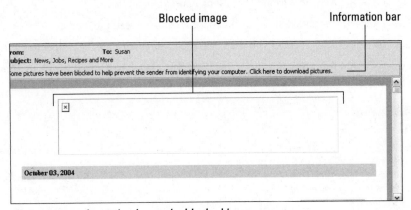

Figure 36-5: Information bar and a blocked image

Can't open or save e-mail attachment

Outlook Express blocks access to potentially unsafe e-mail attachments. When it blocks such an attachment you should see a message like *OE removed access to the following unsafe attachments* in the Information bar. See "Minimizing virus threats with Outlook Express" in Chapter 28 for details.

Caution   Don't trust the extension you see on an e-mail attachment, because there may be another hidden behind the one you see. For example, the ILOVEYOU virus was spread an e-mail attachment named `Love-letter-for-you.txt.vbs`, and *a lot* of people fell for it. Never open any attachment unless you know exactly what it is and whom it's from.

Message "Your current security settings prohibit running ActiveX controls . . ."

This is usually a good thing because an ActiveX control in an e-mail message is likely to be spyware or some other malicious code that you don't want. Click OK and delete the message.

All other Outlook Express problems/features

Windows XP provides Outlook Express as an optional e-mail and newsgroup client for people who use ISPs that support that program. As such, it's not directly relevant to Windows XP, the operating system, which is the main topic of this book. I don't have room in this book to cover Internet programs in great depth. But you can get plenty of information from the Help in the program. To do so:

1. Open Outlook Express in the usual manner.

2. Choose **Help** ➪ **Contents and Index** from the Outlook Express menu bar.

3. In the Help window that opens, click the **Contents** tab. Use the tab like the table of contents in a book:

   • Click any book icon to see a list of topics within that category.

   • Click any page marked with a question mark or open book to view Help information in the pane on the right.

Optionally, use the Index tab in the left pane of the Help window just as you'd use the index at the back of a book. Or click the Search tab to search the help for any word or phrase of your choosing.

Also, take advantage of the Outlook Express home page at `www.microsoft.com/windows/oe/`. On that page, click the Outlook Express Support Center page for highlights, step-by-step instructions, how-to articles, and more. To focus specifically on Outlook Express features that are new in Service Pack 2, see `www.microsoft.com/windowsxp/sp2/ieoeoverview.mspx`.

But keep in mind that when it comes to e-mail, the only people who can really help with your account are the people who have provided you with that account—either your ISP or the e-mail service with whom you created the account.

Troubleshooting Windows Messenger

Here are some general troubleshooting tips and techniques you can use with Windows Messenger. If Windows Messenger worked prior to installing Service Pack 2, fixing the problem may be a simple matter of opening appropriate ports in the new Windows Firewall.

Can't start Windows Messenger or Remote Assistance after installing Service Pack 2

If you see a security alert when you try to start Windows Messenger, just click the Unblock button in the message. Optionally, to enable Windows Messenger and Remote Assistance, open the Security Center (Start ➪ All Programs ➪ Accessories ➪ System Tools ➪ Security Center), and click the Windows Firewall icon.

In the Windows Firewall dialog box, click the Exceptions tab. Select (check) Remote Assistance and Windows Messenger, as shown in Figure 36-6. If you don't see Windows Messenger listed as a program, click the Add Program button and choose Windows Messenger.

For more information on using Windows Firewall, refer to Chapter 26.

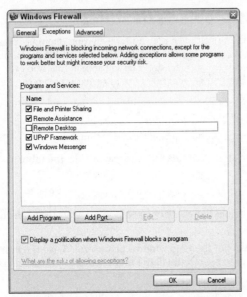

Figure 36-6: Windows Messenger and Remote Assistance enabled

Cannot establish a voice conversation

If you try to establish a voice conversation with someone through Windows Messenger, make sure that you're using the latest version of the program. Both you and the other party should go to http://messenger.microsoft.com, download, and install the most recent version of the program.

If you still can't establish a voice connection, both you and the other party need to open TCP 6901 and UDP port 6901 in Windows Firewall. For information on opening ports in Windows Firewall see "Adding a port" in Chapter 26.

Cannot transfer files

If you're unable to send and receive files using Windows Messenger, make sure that both you and the other party are using the latest version of the program, available from http://messenger.microsoft.com. If the problem persists, both you and the other party may need to open TCP port 6891 in Windows Firewall. See "Adding a port" in Chapter 26 for more information.

Tip
Opening just port 6891 will allow you to transfer one file at a time. You can open up to ten ports, TCP 6891 through TCP 6900, to transfer up to ten files at a time.

Getting rid of Messenger Service pop-ups

Pop-up ads that show Messenger Service in the title bar are not related to .NET Passport or Windows Messenger. These should be blocked by default in Service Pack 2. If you receive such messages, see "Blocking Messenger Pop-Ups" in Chapter 29 to prevent them.

All other Messenger issues

For more information and troubleshooting tips regarding .NET Passport and Windows Messenger, see the following Web sties:

✦ www.microsoft.com/windows/messenger/helphome.asp

✦ http://memberservices.passport.net

✦   ✦   ✦

Using and Creating Digital Media

Time for some fun and creativity here in Part VII. Chapter 37 starts off with pictures, both clip art and photos from your own digital camera. Chapters 38 and 39 move on to the new Windows Media Player 10. Chapter 38 covers music, including ripping CDs, burning your own custom CDs, and copying music to portable MP3 players. Then, we move on to watching DVDs and videos.

Chapters 40 through 42 are all about making movies with Windows Movie Maker 2.1. You'll learn to copy video from digital and analog video cameras, arrange scenes into a well-edited movie, and add special effects and sound tracks. You'll even learn how to burn your video productions to DVD and other media.

Playing with Pictures

The terms *graphic image, digital image*, and *picture* all mean the same thing, which is anything you might think of as a picture, including photographs and hand-drawn illustrations. On a more technical level, a picture is a collection of tiny dots called *pixels*. Each tiny pixel has a color and brightness that's expressed as a number. You never see the numbers, however, or even the individual pictures. You just see the picture.

You can edit pictures using a *graphics editor* or *graphics program*. Windows doesn't come with any fancy graphics programs built into it. If you want to get serious about working with pictures, you'll want to buy and learn to use a serious graphics program like Adobe PhotoShop, PhotoShop Elements (www.adobe.com), or Jasc Paint Shop Pro (www.jasc.com).

About Pictures

If you held a powerful magnifying glass to your computer monitor, or even a printed picture, you might be able to see that the whole thing is composed of tiny individual lighted dots. Each of those lighted dots has a specific color and brightness. But because the dots are so tiny, you don't see dots when you look at the screen. Rather, you see the icons, desktop, program windows, title bars, and so forth that the current combination of pixels provides. Every time something on your screen changes, it's because certain pixels on the screen have changed color and brightness.

Anything that's on the screen is actually a pattern of pixels. For example, when you're looking at a picture on a computer screen, you're really seeing a pattern of pixels lit and colored to show whatever the picture is showing. In other words, a picture, in the computer sense, is nothing more than data that tells a program which pixels to light up and in what colors to show that picture.

Picture dimensions

Like a printed photo, every digital image has *dimensions*. For example, the prints you get from a developed roll of film are usually 3½ inches by 5 inches, generally expressed as *3½× 5*. Digital images stored on a disk also have dimensions. But we measure their dimensions in *pixels*. Each pixel in the picture corresponds to one tiny lighted dot on the screen. For example, a 640 × 480 (640 by 480) picture is 640 pixels by 480 pixels.

Exactly how large a picture looks on your screen depends on your screen resolution and the magnification of the picture. For example, the picture of the first shot in Figure 37-1 is 640 × 480 pixels. The top image shows how large that picture looks at 100 percent size (no reduction or magnification) on a desktop at 800 × 600 resolution. The bottom of that same figure shows how the same picture looks on a desktop set to 1024 × 768 resolution.

640x480 picture on an 800x600 desktop

640x480 picture on an 1024x768 desktop

Figure 37-1: A 640 × 480 picture shown full size at two different screen resolutions

Note   See "Choosing a screen resolution and color depth" in Chapter 6 for the lowdown on your screen resolution.

The pixel size of a picture doesn't define the only size at which you can view the picture. If you have a good graphics program, you can view the picture at any size. For example, Figure 37-2 shows two copies of one picture in Jasc Paint Shop Pro. The picture at the left is zoomed to 400 percent. Only a tiny portion of the picture fits in the document window at the high magnification. But that large magnification allows me to do touch-up work on the photo — get rid of red eye, blemishes, stray hair, that sort for thing. The picture on the left is exactly the same picture shown at 20 percent magnification.

Figure 37-2: A 640 × 480 shown at 400 percent and 20 percent magnifications in Paint Shop Pro

You might wonder why dimensions matter at all if you can just zoom in and out to any size you want. However, dimensions do matter because they define the number of pixels in the photo. When it comes to photo quality in terms of clarity, depth, realism, and detail, the more pixels the better.

For example, let's say that you start with a tiny original that's only 1 × 1.25 inches in size. When you print an 8 × 10 of that picture, the printed copy won't look too good, because it's a stretched-out version of the original. But if you print a picture that's already 8 × 10 or bigger, then the printed photo will look fine.

Exactly how pixel size translates to printed size, in inches, is a bit thorny because the concept of *dots per inch* comes into play. The next chapter will deal with that issue. For now, keep in mind that when it comes to overall picture quality, bigger is better. That's because you can always make a smaller copy of a large picture without losing quality. But the opposite isn't true. Going from small to large reduces picture quality.

Picture file size

Besides dimensions, every picture also has a *file size* that defines the amount of space it takes to store the picture on a disk. Figure 37-3 shows an example where the Size column shows the size of each picture in a folder. Notice how the sizes range from 151 KB to 901 KB.

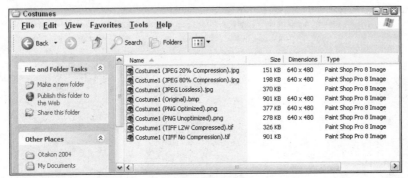

Figure 37-3: Several copies of a 640 × 480 picture

The pictures whose filenames appear in Figure 37-3 are all copies of a single picture. Each is 640 × 480 pixels in size. The Dimensions column proves that, except in cases where that column is empty. Unfortunately, not all file types have a Dimensions property. Those file types show nothing in the Dimensions columns. So, you'll just have to take my word for it that they're all the same picture, and each is 640 × 480 pixels in size. So, why the differences between the file size? That brings us to the concept of picture compression.

Uncompressed picture files

It takes a lot of bits to store all the information for a picture. It takes at least 24 bits of data to store the information needed to properly light a single pixel in a color photo. A 640 × 480 containing 307,200 pixels is composed of 7,372,800 bits. Divide that by 8 (for bytes), and then divide that result by 1,024 (for kilobytes), and you end up with a file size of about 900 KB.

If you want every single one of those bits preserved so that you get the best possible photo to work with, you store the file in an *uncompressed* format. This most likely means that you save it as a Windows/OS2 Bitmap (.bmp file) or an uncompressed TIFF (Tagged Image Format File). The 901-KB files in Figure 37-2 are both uncompressed copies of the same 640 × 480 picture.

Compressed picture files

The 901-KB file size is trivial when you're talking about storing the picture on a hard disk or CD. Heck, it would even fit on a floppy. There's probably room for tens of thousands of pictures that size on your hard disk. You could store about 700 of them on a CD. But if you plan on transmitting the picture across a wire, then the size of a file, in bytes, matters, because the number of bytes determines how long it takes for the picture to traverse the wire.

For example, if you want to use the picture in a Web page you've created, you want the picture to be transferred quickly to the visitor's Web browser. Otherwise, he or she might not stick around long enough to see it. Likewise, if you're planning to e-mail a picture, you need it to be within the attachment size limitations imposed by your ISP.

So, if your plans for the picture include using it on the Internet somehow, then you you'll want to store a copy of the original in a *compressed* format. You can use any of the formats shown in Figure 32-2 including JPEG, PNG, and TIFF with compression. Actually, there are a lot more formats to choose from, but let's stick with those for a moment.

When you store a picture in a compressed format, you don't change the dimensions of the picture. The compressed picture is still the same size as the original in terms of width and height. But some of the bits are removed to make the byte size of the file smaller. The loss of bits causes some loss of quality in terms of picture clarity and detail. How much quality you lose depends on how much you compress the file.

The program you happen to be using when you save a copy of a picture determines how much control over compression you'll have. Earlier I mentioned Jasc Paint Shop Pro, which is the program I use for graphics editing. In that program, when you save a picture, you can choose a file type from the Save As Type dialog box that opens, and then click the Options button to choose options for the file type you've chosen. Figure 37-4 shows an example where I've chosen JPEG as the file format for saving the picture and I am viewing the options for JPEGs.

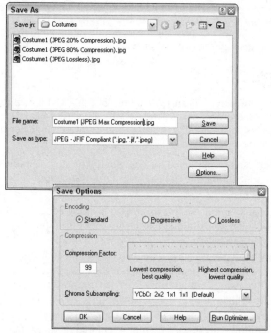

Figure 37-4: Options for saving a JPEG image

I realize that not everyone reading this book owns, or is familiar with, Jasc Paint Shop Pro. But there's nothing built into Windows XP that gives you that kind of control over picture compression. So, I'm forced to use a third-party program to illustrate how it works. The main point is that you can use compressed file types to save a picture at a smaller file size without reducing the dimensions of the picture.

The catch is this. The more you compress a file, the more quality you lose. In this sense, quality refers to overall detail and clarity of the picture. The compressed picture's file contains fewer bits of information than the uncompressed file, and hence there's some loss of detail in the picture.

Picture quality

Picture quality boils down to the amount of data that's used to store information about the picture. In a large, uncompressed file format, all the information is there, so you have perfect quality. In a compressed format, some of the details have been omitted to reduce the file size of the picture. So, the picture isn't as accurate or as detailed as the original.

The most important thing to understand about picture quality is that it's a one-way street. You can always take a high-quality uncompressed image and maker a lower-quality version of it. But you can't take a compressed version of a file and make an accurate higher-quality picture from it.

It's like working with wood or cloth. If you need it a certain size, but cut it too big, no big deal. You can cut it shorter. However, if you cut it to short you're in trouble, because you can't make it longer.

Getting back to pictures, suppose that you have a nice big uncompressed original photo. If you change that photo to a compressed format, then you'll lose the option to go back to your big uncompressed original. Because no matter what you do to the compressed file, it will never be quite as good as the original, simply because the file doesn't contain enough bits — enough information — to accurately redisplay the original picture.

BMP, TIFF, JPEG, and GIF

There are many different file formats in which you can store pictures. Table 37-1 lists most of them. But the most widely used formats are Windows Bitmap (BMP), Tagged Image File Format (TIFF), Joint Photographic Experts Group (JPEG), and Graphics Interchange Format (GIF). Each plays a slightly different role:

✦ **Windows Bitmap:** An uncompressed format used for high-quality photos. Suitable for just about any computer use and printing, though too large for Internet applications. These files have a .bmp extension.

✦ **TIFF:** Most book and magazine publishers use this format for printing because it's a high-quality format that works well with printing presses and other printing devices. Files of this type have a .tif or .tiff extension.

✦ **JPEG:** The industry-standard for displaying photos on Web pages and in e-mail messages. The file size is reduced through compression, but the loss of quality is minimized due to the fact that the Joint Photographic Experts Group who defined the file format knew what they were doing. This type of file has a .jpeg or .jpg extension.

✦ **GIF:** Also called *CompuServe GIF*, this is the industry-standard for displaying nonphoto-graphic illustrations and animations. GIF allows a picture to contain no more than 256 unique colors (including "transparent"), which makes for very small files. This type of file has a .gif extension.

Table 37-1: Examples of File Formats for Pictures

Filename Extension	Format
.iff	Amiga
.art	AOL Art file
.dxf	Autodesk Drawing Interchange
.gif	CompuServe Graphics Interchange
.cgm	Computer Graphics Metafile
.cmx	Corel Clipart
.cdr	CorelDraw Drawing
.lbm	Deluxe Paint
.cut	Dr. Halo

Filename Extension	Format
.eps, .ai, .ps	Encapsulated PostScript
.fpx	FlashPix
.img	GEM Paint
.hgl	HP Graphics Language
.jpg, .jif, .jpeg	Joint Photographic Experts Group
.kdc	Kodak Digital Camera
.pcd	Kodak Photo CD
.pic	Lotus PIC
.pct	Macintosh PICT
.mac	MacPaint
.drw	Micrografx Draw
.msp	Microsoft Paint
.psp	Paint Shop Pro
.pic	PC Paint
.psd	Photoshop
.pbm	Portable Bitmap
.pgm	Portable Greymap
.png	Portable Network Graphics
.ppm	Portable Pixelmap
.raw	Raw File Format
.sct, .ct	SciTex Continuous Tone
.ras	Sun RasterImage
.tif, .tiff	Tagged Image File Format
.tga	Truevision Targa
.gem	Ventura/GEM Drawing
.clp	Windows Clipboard
.emf	Windows Enhanced Metafile
.wmf	Windows Meta File
.rle	Windows or CompuServe RLE
.bmp	Windows Bitmap
.dib	Windows Device Independent Bitmap
.wpg	WordPerfect Bitmap or Vector
.dcx	Zsoft Multipage Paintbrush
.pcx	Zsoft Paintbrush

What about PNG?

I didn't include a GIF version of the picture back in Figure 37-3, because GIF isn't a very good format for pictures. The 256-color limit can make the photo look blotchy. I did include a couple of files in PNG (Portable Network Graphics) format though. That format is slowly gaining popularity as an Internet format, because it allows for high compression with little or no loss or quality.

The only reason that PNG hasn't caught on is because there are a lot of Web browsers out there that can't display PNG files. Where the picture should be, the viewer sees only the red X placeholder. Whether or not PNG ever becomes a "mainstream" Internet format depends on how much support it gets from the people who create the Web browsers and e-mail clients. Currently, two other newer formats, JPEG 2000 and SVG (Scalable Vector Graphics), are competing to become the new mainstream standards. Like PNG, these formats provide better compression with little or no loss of picture quality.

Clip art

Clip art is ready-drawn art often used to decorate Web pages, newsletters, and other printed matter. Unlike a photograph, which usually contains millions of colors, a clip art image might contain only a few colors. Because of this, many clip art images are stored in GIF format. However, there are other formats with minimal colors that can also be used for storing clip art.

I imagine many readers already know what clip art is all about. For example, if you have Microsoft Word, open a document, and choose Insert ➪ Picture ➪ Clip Art, you see a task pane that lets you search through the clip art collection that comes with Microsoft Office. If you search for a specific word or phrase, such as *sign*, you get a list of relevant clip art images, like the example in Figure 37-5. To add a clip art image to the document you're writing, you just click on its picture.

You can also find lots of extra free clip art online. For example, Microsoft maintains a large clip art collection at `http://office.microsoft.com/clipart`. If you search Google for something like `free clip art` you'll find other resources. You can also purchase clip art collections online and in many computer stores.

Tip   Don't forget that you can also save a copy of any picture you see on a Web page. Just right-click the picture and choose Save Picture As. To search for pictures on a given topic, go to `www.google.com` and click on the Images link. Type your search text and press Enter. The links you get will all be to pictures rather than to entire Web pages.

For now, the main thing to understand is that both photographs and clip art illustrations are digital images. That is, they're just two different kinds of pictures. How you use, edit, and print them is exactly the same.

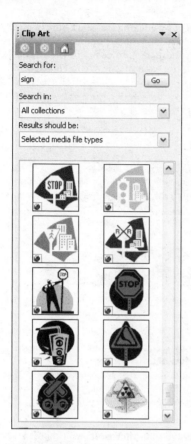

Figure 37-5: Sample Microsoft Office clip art images

Where to Store Pictures

Every picture is a document file and should be stored in a document folder on your hard disk. Windows XP comes with two predefined folders that are especially well suited for storing pictures:

✦ **My Pictures:** Contained within My Documents, this folder includes options for working with pictures. You can use both the Thumbnails and Filmstrip Views, where each picture appears as a tiny copy of itself rather than as a generic icon.

✦ **Shared Pictures:** Same as My Pictures, but on a network or computer with multiple user accounts, everyone has access to the pictures in the Shared Pictures folder. Only you have access to pictures in your My Pictures folder, however.

Any subfolders contained within My Pictures or Shared Pictures will offer the same tools and options that the parent does. Thus, you can organize pictures into folders within My Pictures or Shared Pictures without losing the special capabilities of those folders.

You should be able to open your My Pictures folder just by clicking the Start button and choosing My Pictures form the right side of the menu bar. Or, you can open My Pictures, and then double-click the icon for your My Pictures folder there. Regardless of how you get there, you should see Picture Tasks in the Explorer bar, as in the example shown in Figure 37-6.

Figure 37-6: A sample My Pictures folder

Note   If you're not so sure what's up with the Thumbnails and Filmstrip Views, see "Umpteen ways to view icons" in Chapter 3.

The options available under Picture Tasks vary. If no picture is selected (highlighted) in the folder, then Picture Tasks contains options for working with all the pictures. If you select one picture, then Picture Tasks reflects options for working with a singe picture. If you select multiple pictures, Picture Tasks offers options for working with just the selected pictures.

Tip   You can use any of the techniques described under "Selecting Files and Folders" in Chapter 14 to select icons in any document folder, including My Pictures and Shared Pictures.

You won't find any great options for editing photos under Picture Tasks, because Windows has no built-in graphics-editing capabilities. By itself, Windows can only do the things described in the sections that follow.

Tip   You can make any folder show Picture Tasks in its Explorer bar. See "Personalizing your folders" for specifics on how that works.

Viewing pictures as a slide show

Clicking on the View as a Slide Show under Picture Tasks in the Explorer bar presents the pictures in the folder on-screen for a few seconds each in a slide show. While the slide show is playing, move the cursor anywhere on the screen to view the toolbar shown in Figure 37-7. The buttons in the toolbar, from left to right, do the following:

Figure 37-7: Toolbar for a slide show

✦ **Play:** Plays the slide show (if it isn't already playing)

✦ **Pause:** Pauses the slide show at the current picture

✦ **Previous Picture:** Displays the previous picture in the show

✦ **Next Picture:** Displays the next picture in the show

✦ **Close:** Ends the slide show and returns to the desktop

If you want the slide show to kick in automatically as a screen saver whenever the computer has been idle for a while, follow these steps:

1. Right-click the Windows desktop, and choose **Properties** to open the Display Properties dialog box.

2. Click the **Screen Saver** tab.

3. Choose **My Pictures Slideshow** from the Screen Saver drop-down list shown in the left side of Figure 37-8.

4. Optionally, click the **Settings** buttons and choose options to define how long each picture appears, how big each picture should be, the folder from which pictures should be taken, and so forth, as shown on the right side of Figure 37-8.

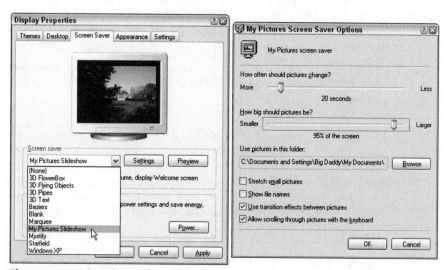

Figure 37-8: Using pictures for a slide show

Making Custom Slide Shows and More

Microsoft Plus! Digital Media Edition comes with a program named Photo Story 2 that makes it very easy to create picture slide shows you can send to friends via e-mail or CD. The program is simple to use, and you can add your own special effects and music soundtrack. You can learn more about, or buy, Plus! Digital Media Edition at www.microsoft.com/plus.

To learn more about digital photography and Windows XP, be sure to check out the Digital Photography home page at www.microsoft.com/windowsxp/using/digitalphotography. And be sure to check out all the free PowerToys and Fun Packs at www.microsoft.com/windowsxp/downloads/powertoys.

5. On the Screen Saver tab, use the **Wait** option to specify how long the computer must sit idly (no mouse or keyboard activity) before the slide show starts.

Tip

Use the Power button on the Screen Saver tab to specify how long the computer can sit idly before the monitor shuts off. If you want your slide show to play indefinitely, set the Turn off monitor option in the Power Options Properties dialog box to Never.

6. Click **OK** in all open dialog boxes.

The slide show won't start until the computer has sat idly for the amount of time you specified in Step 5. Once the slide show starts, simply tapping a key or clicking on the screen will end the slide show.

Printing pictures

You can print any picture, or group of pictures, right from the Explorer bar, provided that you're in My Pictures, Shared Pictures, or a subfolder of either of those. First, get to the folder that contains the pictures you want to print and perform these steps:

1. Open your My Pictures folder, or navigate to the folder that contains the pictures you want to print.

2. Optionally, if you want to print one, or a few pictures, select their icons using any technique described under "Selecting Files and Folders" in Chapter 14.

3. In the Explorer bar, under Picture Tasks, click **Print pictures**. The first page of the Photo Printing Wizard opens. Click the **Next** button.

4. The Picture Selection page of the wizard opens, with all pictures selected (checked) to be printed. If there are any pictures in the folder that you don't want to print, clear their check marks. Then, click **Next**.

5. On the next wizard page, choose the printer you want to use (if you have multiple printers). If you're looking for high quality, click the **Printing Preferences** button and choose a good paper and quality setting, as in Figure 37-9. Then, click **OK**.

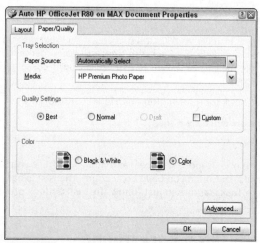

Figure 37-9: Printing high-quality pictures on photo paper

6. Click **Next** to get to the Layout Selection page shown in Figure 37-10. Scroll through the list of available layouts and choose how you want to print each picture. Then, click **Next**.

Figure 37-10: The Layout Selection page of the Photo Printing Wizard

7. Click **Next**, and your pictures will print.

Ordering prints online

If you don't have a printer, or prefer to have your digital pictures developed as you would a roll of film, you can order prints online. This service is not free, and you must be connected to the Internet before you begin. Most likely, you'll want to explore the services available to you. To do so, take a look at these Web sites:

✦ `http://photos.msn.com` (Look for information on Print@FUJIColor).

✦ `www.ofoto.com` (A service provided by Kodak)

✦ `www.shutterfly.com`

You should set up an account with one or more services, and make sure that you understand the pricing, before you order prints. But once you have an account, the rest is easy. Click on Order Prints Online under Picture Tasks, and then just follow the instructions presented by the Online Print Orders Wizard that opens.

Using a picture as a desktop background

If you want to use one of the pictures from the current folder as your desktop background, first select the icon of the picture you want to use so that only its icon is highlighted. When you do, Picture Tasks will gain a *Set as desktop background* option. Click that option to instantly make that picture your background.

If you change your mind, or need to change how the picture is displayed, right-click the Windows desktop and choose Properties. In the Display Properties dialog box that opens, choose a different picture or a Position option for the current picture, as described under "Changing the picture on your desktop" in Chapter 6.

Tip   Microsoft's PowerToys Fun Pack includes a Wallpaper Changer that can convert your desktop background to a slide show, and use videos as your screensaver. Download the Fun Pack free of charge from `www.microsoft.com/windowsxp/downloads`.

Copying pictures from a CD

If you get pictures developed onto a CD, you'll be able to view and print them right from the CD. But if you want to be able to change them in any way, you'll need to copy them to your hard disk first. You can use any of the techniques described in Chapter 14 to copy the pictures. For example, you could just select all the picture icons from the CD and drag them to your My Pictures folder. Optionally, you can use a wizard to help you through the process. Here's how:

1. Put the photo CD into your CD drive and wait a few seconds. Then:

   • If it's a Kodak Picture CD, you'll most likely see a slideshow of your pictures or of the Kodak Photo CD program, or the Kodak Picture CD program will open. If either happens, skip the remaining steps and go to the sidebar titled "Using a Kodak Picture CD."

   • If you see the dialog box asking what you want to do with the CD, click **Copy pictures to a folder on my computer. . . .** Then, go to Step 2.

2. The Scanner and Camera Wizard opens. Click the **Next** button on the first page of the wizard. The Choose Pictures to Copy page opens. Initially, all pictures are selected for copying, as shown in Figure 37-11. If there are any pictures that you don't want to copy, clear their check marks. Then, click **Next**.

Figure 37-11: Choosing pictures to copy from a CD or camera

3. The next page asks what you want to name the group of pictures and where you want to put them. Type a brief, descriptive name of your own choosing, such as 2003 Christmas or Mandy's New Do. The name you enter will be the name of the folder in which the pictures are stored. Click **Next**.

4. The next wizard page shows you the program's progress. Nothing to do there but wait. When all the pictures have been copied, the Other Options page opens.

5. On the Other Options page, choose **Nothing**, and then click **Next**. On the last wizard page that opens, click **Finish**.

The folder on your hard drive will open. You can remove the CD now and put it someplace for safekeeping. From now on, you'll do all your work on the copies in the folder on your hard disk. The CD will just be a backup of your original photos, in case you ever want to recopy an original photo to your hard disk.

The folder that the pictures are in is a subfolder of your My Pictures folder. So, if you click the Up button in Explorer's toolbar to go to this folder's parent, you'll end up in My Pictures. To return to the photos, double-click the new folder's icon.

Using a Kodak Picture CD

When you insert a Kodak Picture CD into your CD drive, you'll most likely see a slide show of the pictures on the CD. Clear the check mark next to *Show Opening Slideshow*, or press the Spacebar on your keyboard. You should come to the main program for managing a Kodak Photo CD. Here's how to proceed:

1. Click the first option, **My Pictures**, on the main menu.

2. Click the **Save As** option on the next page that appears.

3. Click the **Select All** button near the upper-left corner of Kodak's program window.

4. Under *Choose picture size*, I recommend that you choose **Large** (for printing), because this will give you the best originals to work with.

5. Click the **Save** button in the Kodak program.

In the Save As dialog box that opens, navigate to the folder in which you want to store the pictures. For example, to put the pictures in your My Pictures folder, click the large My Documents icon at the left side of the Save As dialog box; then, double-click the icon for your My Pictures folder.

Change the filename to whatever you want to name this group of pictures. Click the Save button in the Save As dialog box. When copying is done, you'll see a dialog box telling you how many pictures were copied. Click its OK button. Then, you can close the Kodak program (click the large X near its upper-right corner) and remove the CD. Keep the CD in a safe place as a backup of your original photos. From now on, you can work with the copies of the photos in a subfolder within your My Pictures folder.

Getting Pictures from a Digital Camera

If your digital camera is a recent model supported by Windows XP, and that camera connects to your computer with a USB or FireWire cable, you can use the Scanner and Camera Wizard to get pictures from your camera to your hard disk. Here's the basic procedure:

1. Connect the camera to the computer via the USB or FireWire cable.

2. Turn on the camera, and wait a few seconds. Little messages in the notification area will appear as Windows gets ready to copy from the camera. Then, you might see a dialog box asking what you want to do. Click **Copy pictures to a folder on my computer . . .**, and click **OK**.

3. The first page of the Scanner and Camera Wizard opens. Click the **Next** button.

4. On the next wizard page, choose which pictures you want to copy (most likely all of them), then click **Next**.

5. The Picture Name and Destination page appears next. Under option 1, give the pictures a meaningful name—something that describes the whole group of pictures. Something like Vacation 2004 or Christmas 2004 might be good. In Figure 37-12, I named my pictures 2004 Wildflowers Tour as an example.

6. Under *Choose a Place*, you can leave that setting unchanged to place all the pictures in a subfolder within your My Pictures folder.

Tip The backslash (\) separates a folder's name from its parent folder's name. For example, *My Pictures\2004 Wildflowers Tour* means *A folder named 2004 Wildflowers Tour contained within the My Pictures folder.*

7. If you want to have Windows remove the pictures from the camera when it has finished copying them, choose the **Delete pictures from my device after copying them** option, as shown in Figure 37-12. Then, click **Next**.

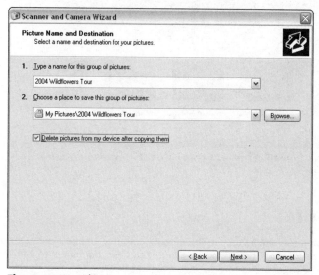

Figure 37-12: What to name the group of pictures and where to put them

8. The next wizard page just keeps you informed of how the copying is going. When all the photos have been copied, the Other Options page appears. Choose **Nothing**; then, click the **Next** button (you can publish photos to the Web or order prints online at any time).

9. On the last wizard page, click the **Finish** button.

Tip You don't have to buy a digital camera to take digital photos. You can have your regular film developed and delivered to you on CD or use a disposable camera such as the Kodak PLUSDigital.

A folder will open, showing you all the copied images in Filmstrip View, as in the example shown in Figure 37-13. You can turn off and disconnect the camera now. All of its pictures are now safely stored on your computer's hard disk. If you didn't tell Windows to delete all the pictures from the camera, you can do so using the controls on the camera.

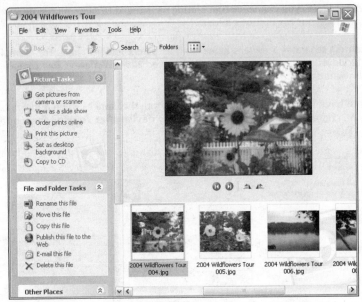

Figure 37-13: Pictures from the camera are now in a folder named 2004 Wildflowers Tour.

Scanning Pictures

A scanner is like a photocopy machine attached to a computer. Unlike a photocopy machine, which copies a document directly to paper, a scanner copies a document to a file on your hard disk. Most modern scanners work through a printer or are a separate device that connects to the computer through a USB port. Exactly how you install and use a scanner varies from one model to the next. Only the instructions that came with the scanner can help you there.

Once the scanner is installed and working, you may have to use the software that came with the scanner to scan pictures. However, if the scanner is XP-compatible you can also use this method:

1. Put the picture that you want to scan face down in the scanner, or into the appropriate feeder on your printer.

2. Open your **My Pictures** folder. Wait a few seconds.

3. Under Picture Tasks in the Explorer bar, click **Get pictures from scanner or camera**.

Note If you don't see *Get pictures from scanner or camera*, make sure that your camera or scanner is connected and turned on. If it is, the scanner may not be fully compatible with Windows XP, or it may need an updated driver from Windows Update or the scanner's manufacturer.

An Alternative to the Scanner and Camera Wizard

If the Scanner and Camera Wizard doesn't detect your camera, but the camera stores pictures on a Smart Card, you should be able to copy pictures from the camera just using basic drag-and-drop techniques. After you connect the camera to the computer and turn it on, open your My Computer folder. The icon for the camera should appear as a disk drive in My Computer. Double-clicking that icon will open the Smart Card as though it were a disk drive.

At first, you may just see a folder, or several folders for the Smart Card's contents. You may have to open folders until you find the one that contains the actual pictures. But once you've found the pictures, you can just select them then drag them, or copy and paste them, to your My Pictures folder, or any other folder of your choosing. See Chapter 14 for more information.

4. After a brief delay, the Camera and Scanner Wizard opens. Click the **Next** button on the first page of the wizard.

5. The second page of the Wizard, titled Choose Scanning Preferences, opens. Choose whichever option best describes how you want the scanned image to look, as follows:

   - **Color picture:** All colors, identical to the original.

   - **Grayscale:** Black, white, and shades of gray only. No color.

   - **Black and White picture or text:** Black and white only, no color or grays. Useful when original is only black text on white paper.

   - **Custom:** Lets you choose from among the options shown in Figure 37-14. The higher you set the resolution (dots per inch, or dpi) the bigger and better quality the scanned image will be, which is good for prized photos you intend to edit and print at a high quality.

Figure 37-14: Custom settings for a sample scanner

6. If you loaded multiple pages into the scanner's document feeder, choose **Document Feeder** from the Paper Source drop-down list. Then, choose a page size, if necessary. If you'll just be scanning one item, choose **Flatbed**. Click **Next**.

7. Click the **Preview** button. Wait as your scanner scans the image. If the scanned image doesn't fill the preview area, or if you want to scan only a portion of the image, drag the sizing handles so that only the area you want to scan is framed, as shown in Figure 37-15. After you've framed the area, you may click the **Stretch** button (shown at left) to hide everything outside the framed area.

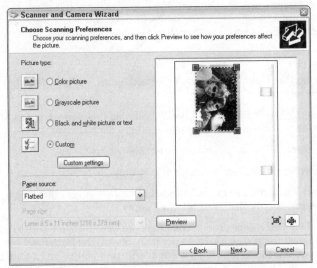

Figure 37-15: An image scanned to, and framed within, the Preview area

8. Click the **Next** button to get to the Picture Name and Destination page of the wizard. Type the name of your choosing to identify the picture (or group of pictures).

9. Choose a format from the *Select a file format* drop-down list. Your options will be the BMP, JPEG, TIFF, and PNG options described earlier in this chapter.

10. Click the **Next** button, and wait as the image is scanned. When the Other Options page appears, choose **Nothing**, and click the **Finish** button in the wizard.

The scanned image is now a file in whatever folder you place it in. You can open, edit, move, copy, rename, or do whatever you like with the file.

Installing Troublesome Cameras and Scanners

If you tried getting pictures from a camera or scanner using the preceding techniques and couldn't get it to work, there are a few possibilities. First, eliminate the obvious ones: Is the camera/scanner turned on? Is the camera/scanner connected to the computer? If those things are OK, the most likely scenario is that the device does not connect to the computer through a USB or FireWire cable and hence needs to be installed.

Adjusting Resolution (dpi)

On most scanners, the Custom Settings option lets you adjust the resolution of the scan. Resolution is measured in dots per inch (dpi). The original printed picture has a height and width expressed in inches, such as 31/2 by 5. The dpi setting is really pixels per inch, or ppi. For example, if you scan a picture at 100 dpi, the scanned image will be 350 by 500 pixels. If you scan it at 600 dpi, the scanned image will be 2,100 × 3,000 pixels.

A 2,100 × 3,000 picture is huge. If you save the photo as a bitmap (.bmp) the file itself will be huge. But remember, huge is good when you're looking for high-quality originals to work from. You can always create smaller, lower-quality copies of photos from large photos. So, you're not committed to using the large bitmap image for everything.

The first step in installing *any* device on your computer is this: Follow the instructions that came with the camera or scanner. There are hundreds of makes and models of these things on the market, and they're not all the same. Although the general techniques described here and in Windows Help and Support might help, there's no substitute for following specific instructions for your specific device.

If you've been through that procedure and still can't get things to work, or for some reason you were unable to complete the installation procedure by following the manufacturer's instructions, the next step is to grab a software disk that came with your camera or scanner and put it into the appropriate drive. Then, follow these steps:

1. Click the **Start** button, and choose **Control Panel**.

2. If Control Panel opens in Category View, click **Printers and Other Hardware**. Otherwise, skip this step.

3. Open the **Scanners and Cameras** icon. The Scanners and Cameras folder opens. If you have a scanner or camera installed on your computer, each will be represented by an icon, something like the example shown in Figure 37-16.

Figure 37-16: The Scanners and Cameras folder

Caution   A device that connects through a USB or FireWire port won't appear in Scanners and Cameras, even when it's working perfectly. That's because such devices are installed and uninstalled on the fly and hence don't need a permanent icon in Scanners and Cameras.

4. Under Imaging Tasks in the Explorer bar, click **Add an imaging device**. The first page of the Scanner and Camera Wizard opens. Read the first page; then, click **Next**.

5. The next wizard page asks what device you want to install. Here's how that works:

- If you inserted a disk from your camera or scanner already, click the **Have Disk** button.

- If you don't have a disk for your device, click your device manufacturer's name in the left column, and then (if possible) click your specific make and model of printer in the right column. Click **Next**.

From this point on, you have to read and follow the instructions that appear on the screen as you go through the wizard. If you still can't get your device installed, you'll probably have to use the software that came with the device to get pictures from that device. Only the instructions that came with your camera or scanner can tell you how to install and use that software.

Opening a Picture

Every picture is a document, and so you can open it as such. For example, double-clicking (or clicking) the icon for a picture opens that picture in whatever program is currently set as the default program for opening that type of image. To open a picture in a specific program, right-click its icon and choose Open With, as in the example shown in Figure 37-17.

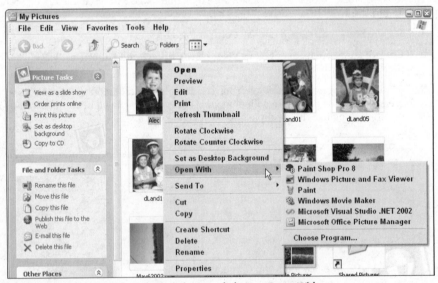

Figure 37-17: Right-click a picture's icon and choose Open With.

Using Windows Picture and Fax Viewer

Windows XP comes with a program named Windows Picture and Fax Viewer. As its name implies, you can use it to view any picture. Figure 37-18 shows an example of the program displaying a picture. Buttons along the bottom of the viewer provide some simple options for working with pictures. You can point to any button to see its name. Here's what each button does:

Figure 37-18: A picture open in Windows Picture and Fax Viewer

✦ **Previous Image/ Next Image:** If several pictures are in the folder, this option lets you view the next or previous image.

✦ **Best Fit:** Displays the picture at the largest size possible within the window.

✦ **Actual Size:** Shows the picture at its actual size.

✦ **Start slide show:** Starts a slide show of pictures in the folder. (Optionally, press F11.) Move the mouse or press the **Spacebar** to bring the slide show toolbar to the screen. Click the **Close** button in that toolbar to end the slide show and return to your program.

✦ **Zoom In:** Clicking this button magnifies the picture. To zoom in on a particular part of the picture, click the **Zoom In** button; then, click the part of the picture that you want to magnify. Each click increases the magnification slightly.

✦ **Zoom Out:** Does the opposite of Zoom In.

✦ **Rotate Clockwise:** Rotates the picture 90 degrees to the right.

✦ **Rotate Counterclockwise:** Rotates the picture 90 degrees to the left.

✦ **Delete:** Deletes the image file from your disk.

✦ **Print:** Starts the Photo Printing Wizard so that you can print the picture.

✦ **Edit:** Closes the picture and the viewer and opens the picture in a program that allows you to edit the picture.

✦ **Help:** Brings up the Help for Windows Picture and Fax Viewer (also called Image Preview), where you can learn more about the program.

As with any program window, you can close Windows Picture and Fax Viewer by clicking the Close (X) button in its upper-right corner.

Recording Details about Your Photos

If you're a serious camera buff, you can record details about each photo as part of the file's properties. Right-click any single photo's icon and choose Properties. Or, if you want to assign the same properties to several photos, select the appropriate icons first. Then, right-click any selected photo and choose Properties. Either way, the Properties dialog box for the picture(s) will open.

Note   See "Selecting Files and Folders" in Chapter 14 for more information.

In the Properties dialog box, click the Summary tab. I can't say exactly what properties you'll see; that depends on the type of file(s) you're working with. But if you're working with a JPEG image, you'll probably see the items shown in Figure 37-19. If the properties don't appear in a list, as shown in the figure, click the Advanced >> button in the dialog box to switch to that view.

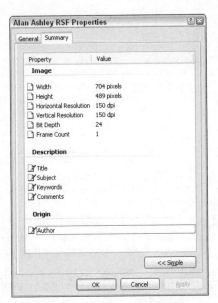

Figure 37-19: The Properties for a JPEG image (Advanced view)

The properties listed under Image are facts about the picture that you can't change. But you're welcome to fill in the blanks on other items, such as Title, Subject, Keywords (for searching), and so forth. Later, when looking through pictures, or after performing a search for all pictures on your hard drive, you can display that information in Details View.

For example, let's suppose that you do a search for all pictures. When the search is completed, you can switch to Details View, choose the details you want to see, and arrange columns as suits your needs. You can click any column heading to sort the pictures on that column. Figure 37-20 shows an example, with the Title, Dimensions, Subject, and Author properties visible.

Cross-Reference   See "Details view" in Chapter 3 for information on using columns in Windows Explorer. See Chapter 17 for information on searching for files.

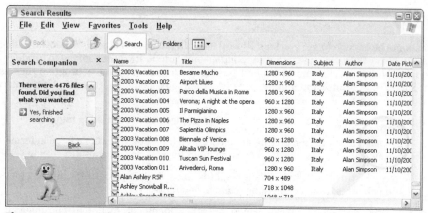

Figure 37-20: Icons for pictures in Details view

Making a Working Copy of a Picture

On your hard disk, you're free to make changes to your pictures. But before you do, understand that it's always a good idea to keep a copy of the original picture on disk. This is handy even if you just plan to rotate a picture, as described in the next section. You can use any technique described in Chapter 14 to move and copy pictures (because each picture is a file). But if you just want to make a quick copy of one picture:

1. Right-click the icon for the picture you want to copy, and choose **Copy**.

2. Right-click some empty space near the icon you just right-clicked, and choose **Paste**.

Optionally, you can point to the picture, hold down the Ctrl key, drag the picture a slight distance so that the mouse pointer is touching some empty space between icons, and release the mouse button. Either way, you'll end up with a new copy of the image named Copy of . . . followed by the original picture name. To rename the copy, right-click it and choose Rename.

Rotating a picture

If you hold a camera sideways when you take a picture, that picture will likely show up sideways on your screen. If the picture is in your My Pictures folder (or any other folder on your hard disk, for that matter), you can rotate it. It's better to rotate a copy of the original picture rather than the original itself. So, if you haven't already done so, you can make a copy. To rotate the copy:

1. Right click the icon of the picture you want to copy.

2. Choose **Rotate Clockwise** to rotate the picture 90 degrees to the right or **Rotate Counter Clockwise** to rotate it 90 degrees to the left.

Note The rotate options will be available on GIF, JPEG, BMP, and some other picture types, but not all picture files. A good graphics program will allow you to rotate pictures of any type.

3. You might see a message recommending that you work with copies. Assuming that you are working with a copy, click **Yes** to proceed.

That's it. If you rotate a picture in the wrong direction, just rotate it in the opposite direction twice to straighten things out.

Wrap Up

That should be enough to get you started working with pictures. As I said, Windows XP doesn't have any heavy-duty picture-editing capabilities built into it. If you're looking to produce art-quality photos, you'll want to but and learn to use a good third-party program such as Paint Shop Pro or PhotoShop. But, as you've learned in this chapter, there is plenty you can do with Windows XP alone, as summarized here:

✦ Every picture is a document file. Like all files, pictures are stored in folders.

✦ The quality and size of a picture are closely related. A picture that's large in terms of dimensions and bytes is a good starting point for any kind of graphics editing.

✦ Your My Pictures and Shared Pictures folder have built-in options for printing pictures, getting pictures from a camera or scanner, and more.

✦ You can open a picture as you would any other document, by double-clicking its icon, or by right-clicking the icon and choosing Open With.

✦ Most picture files contain hidden properties, such as Date Picture Taken, Subject, and Keywords, that you can use to record extra information about each picture.

✦   ✦   ✦

Making Music with Windows Media Player 10

Windows Media Player 10 is the latest and greatest version of Windows Media Player. Released to public shortly after the release of Windows XP Service Pack 2, the new Media Player offers extensive support for purchasing music online, better music library management, and more.

This chapter focuses on the music aspects of Media Player 10. For example, here you'll learn to create and manage a music library from music CDs you already own, and new content you purchase online. You'll learn how to burn your own custom music CDs to play in any stereo CD player, and how to copy music to a portable MP3 player. And that's just the tip of the proverbial iceberg. But the main idea here is to have fun, and enjoy music in new ways.

Before You Get Started

Before we get into Windows Media Player, there are a few things you need to know up front about music and video. In particular, you want to get your sound working and under control, so you can listen to whatever you like, without blasting your eardrums out!

Controlling sound volume

Before you get started, make sure that you can control the volume of your speakers. At any given time, you're likely to have at least three volume controls available to you. Whichever control is set the lowest wins, in the sense that it puts a upper limit on the other volume controls.

If you have powered speakers, you need to make sure that the speakers are plugged in and turned on, and connected to the Speaker output jack on your computer. If the speakers have a Mute button, that needs to be turned off. If the speakers have a volume control button, that needs to be turned up.

The Windows Volume Control, shown in Figure 38-1, controls the relative volumes of various sound devices that are connected to your computer. To get to the Volume Control, double-click the speaker icon in the Notification area. Or, click the Start button and choose All Programs ➪ Accessories ➪ Entertainment ➪ Volume Control. Make sure that only devices that you don't want to hear are muted.

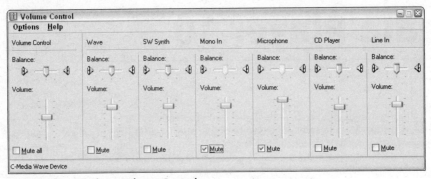

Figure 38-1: Windows Volume Control

The leftmost slider in Volume Control controls the overall volume of sound. If that one is turned down too low, you won't hear sound from any of the other devices for which you have volume control sliders. When you've finished adjusting settings in Volume Control, click its Close (X) button.

Tip   To choose which devices on your computer do and don't show volume control sliders, choose Options ➪ Properties from the Volume Control menu.

The speaker icon in the Notification area links directly to the leftmost slider in Volume Control. So, it controls overall sound volume. You can also mute (and unmute) the speakers from the Notification area speaker icon, as shown in Figure 38-2.

Figure 38-2: Controlling volume from the Notification area

Once you get into Windows Media Player (as you'll do in a moment), you'll have yet another slider in its playback controls to control the sound or music that's currently playing in Media Player.

Understanding protected content

You'll come across the term "protected content" throughout your work with digital media (music and video). The term "protected" in this context has nothing to do with "safe" or "secure" in the sense that "nothing bad will happen to the file." Rather, the song itself is

What Speaker Icon?

If you don't see a speaker icon in your Notification area, it may be hidden, or it may be turned off. If it's only hidden, clicking the < button at the left side of the Notification area will reveal it. To ensure that the speaker icon is always visible in the Notification area, right-click the clock and choose Customize Notifications. Then, set the Volume icon to Always Show. See "Using the Notification Area" in Chapter 2 if you need help with that.

If the little speaker icon is nowhere to be found, click the Start button and choose Control Panel. If Control Panel opens in Category View, click on "Sounds, Speech, and Audio Devices." Open the "Sounds and Audio Devices" icon and choose (check) *Place volume icon in the taskbar*. Then click OK, and close Control Panel.

protected against copyright infringement. It basically boils down to the fact that once you put a protected song on your computer, that song will play only on that computer. If you try to play the same song on another computer, it won't work.

Note   There are exceptions to this. For example, some licensed songs can be played on three computers, or five computers. It all depends on the online store from which you purchase the song.

Most protected songs can be burned to CDs and copied to portable MP3 players. But, there's a limit to how many times, usually somewhere between 5 and 10, that you can copy the song to a CD. Sometimes it's difficult or impossible, to change information about songs, which in turn makes it difficult to organize songs the way you want. Also, you usually can't convert a protected song to another format, say from WMA to MP3. Nor can you import a protected song into a program like Movie Maker to use as background music in a movie you create.

All the restrictions are part of a hidden license that comes with the song. You need to manage your licenses and make backups from time to time. If you lose the license, you lose the ability to play the song.

A song that's not protected is just a normal file on you hard drive. As such, you can move it, rename it, changes its properties (for example Artist name, genre, title, and so forth). You can convert an unprotected song to WMA or MP3 format. You can import it into Movie Maker to use as background music in a movie you create.

Protection all boils down to the concept of *digital rights management*, abbreviated DRM. The purpose is to give the companies that record and distribute the songs a means of protecting the song against copyright infringement. If you're interested in learning more about digital rights management in Windows Media Player, see www.microsoft.com/windows/windowsmedia/drm.

Getting Windows Media Player 10

In this chapter, I'll be discussing Windows Media Player 10 (abbreviated WMP 10), which was released shortly after Service Pack 2. Media Player 10 isn't part of the service pack. You have to download it separately. You should be able to find a link for the download at www.WindowsMedia.com. You don't need to uninstall your existing copy of Windows Media Player first. Just go to the site, click the link, and follow the on-screen instructions.

If you choose Run (or Open) during the download, the program will install automatically and be ready to go as soon as you complete the download. If you choose Save, you'll need to open the downloaded file and follow the on-screen instructions to install the Windows Media Player.

Starting Windows Media Player

It's difficult to say exactly how you'll start Windows Media Player, because it all depends on whether or not Windows XP came preinstalled on your computer and if so, how the manufacturer configures things. But at least one of the following methods should be available to you:

✦ Click the **Windows Media Player** button in the Quick Launch toolbar.

✦ Or, click the **Start** button and choose **All Programs** ➪ **Windows Media Player**.

✦ Or, click the **Start** button and choose **All Programs** ➪ **Accessories** ➪ **Entertainment** ➪ **Windows Media Player**.

Exactly how Media Player will look when it first starts varies. But once the program is open, you can click on the large Now Playing button to see the components pointed out in Figure 38-3.

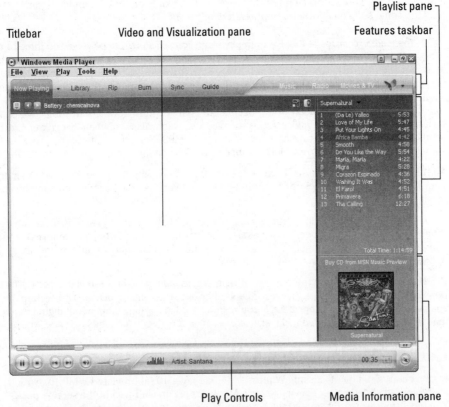

Figure 38-3: Main components of the Now Playing tab in Windows Media Player 10.

As in most programs, you can control the width of any pane by dragging its innermost border left or right. Size any horizontal pane by dragging its innermost border up or down.

Changing your view

The View menu in WMP 10 offers many options for choosing how you want to view things—too many to describe at length right now. But they're all simple toggles that you can choose to show, or hide, some component. So, you certainly can't do any harm by experimenting with them.

You have a lot of control over exactly what is, and isn't visible in Windows Media Player. As in most programs, many of the options for changing how Media Player looks on your screen are on the View menu in its menu. But there's a lot more to it, because you can change the whole interface using *skins*. Chapter 39 will cover skins. Right now you should be aware that even the standard title bar and menu are optional.

Media Player title bar and menu bar

When the standard title bar and menu bar are visible, you can click the button to the left of the Minimize, Maximize/Restore, and Close buttons, shown at left in Figure 38-4, to hide them. When the standard title bar and menu bar are hidden, the custom title bar at the top of the window still functions like a normal title bar, in the sense that you can move the window by dragging that title bar, or maximize/restore the window by double-clicking.

When the standard title bar and menu bar are hidden, you can still get to menu options by clicking the *Access application menus* button near the Minimize, Maximize/Restore, and Close buttons in the special title bar, as shown at right in Figure 38-4. Choosing the last item on that menu brings the standard title bar and menu bar back into view.

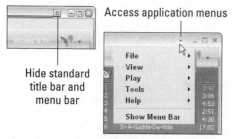

Figure 38-4: Showing and hiding the standard title bar and menu bar

You can move and size Windows Media Player as you would any other program window. When the standard title bar is hidden, you can still drag, or double-click, the title bar at the top of the window to move, maximize, or restore the window. Whenever you maximize Media Player's program menu, the standard title bar and menu bar come out of hiding automatically.

About the Features Taskbar

The Features taskbar across the top of Windows Media Player provides quick access to major features of the program as summarized below:

✦ **Now Playing:** Displays a visualization of the song you're playing, or the video output of the video or DVD you're currently watching.

✦ **Library:** Takes you to your Media Library (collection of songs, videos, and pictures).

✦ **Rip:** Provides options for copying songs from commercial audio CDs (CDs you buy at a music store) into your Media Library.

✦ **Burn:** Provides options from copying songs from your Media Library to a music CD that you can play in any stereo or CD player.

✦ **Sync:** Provides options for copying songs from your Media Library to a portable media device, such as an MP3 Player.

✦ **Guide:** Takes you to the WindowsMedia.com Web site where you can find information about artists, watch movie trailers, and more.

✦ **Music:** Takes you to the currently selected online music store. The icon of that start appears to the far right of the Features taskbar.

✦ **Radio:** If the online store you've currently selected offers radio broadcasts, clicking this button takes you to their radio offerings.

✦ **Movies & TV:** If the currently selected online store offers movies and/or TV, you'll see Movies or Movies &TV. Clicking this button takes you to that store's offerings.

✦ *Icon*: Provides easy access to several online music and video stores including Napster, CinemaNow, MusicNow, MSN Music, and Wal-Mart.

Playback controls

The playback controls (also called the *play controls*) are at the bottom of Media Player's program window (see Figure 38-5). They work only when you're playing a song or video, or have at least selected something to play. They work much like the controls on a VCR, stereo, or DVD player. The exact role of each button varies slightly with the type of content you're viewing. But the buttons always work the same way.

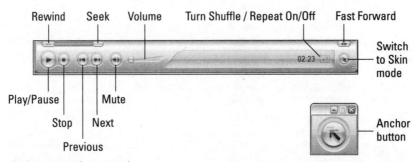

Figure 38-5: Play controls

For example, when you click the Play button the content starts playing and the button turns to a Pause button with two vertical bars. Clicking the Pause button stops playback without rewinding, and the button turns then shows the Play symbol (⇨) again. Clicking the Play button then resumes playback from the current position.

The Seek button moves along the Seek bar as the content in playing. You can jump ahead, or back, by clicking any spot along the bar. You can also drag the moving Seek button left or right to move forward or backward quickly.

When you switch to Skin mode, the player radically changes in appearance (depending on what skin you're using) and an anchor button appears in the lower-right corner of the screen. To go from skin mode back to the normal view, click the Anchor button and choose Switch to Full Mode (or press Ctrl+1).

Closing/minimizing Windows Media Player

You can close Windows Media Player as you would any other program:

✦ Click the **Close** (X) button in the upper-right corer of Media Player's program window.

✦ Or, choose **File** ➪ **Exit** from Media Player's menu.

✦ Or, right-click Media Player's taskbar button and choose **Close**.

✦ Or if Media Player is in the active window, press **Alt+F4**.

When you close Media Player, it stops playing whatever it was playing. If you simply want to hide Media Player and continue listening to music, minimize its program window. When you minimize it, may see a message about Media Player still being open and in the taskbar. If you turn on the Media Player toolbar, you'll still be able to control playback right from the taskbar.

Tip   To enable or disable the Media Player toolbar, right-click the time in the lower-right corner of the screen and choose Toolbar ➪ Windows Media Player.

Listening to a CD

A *music CD* (also called an *audio CD*) is a CD on which each song is stored as a separate file in .cda (Compact Disk Audio) format. They're not files in the traditional sense, because they don't have normal sizes, and can't be copied using standard drag-and-drop techniques. This has to do with the fact that music CDs use CDFS (Compact Disk File System), which is just fundamentally different from the NTFS and FAT file systems used on PCs. But you can still play the CD on your computer, just as you would on a stereo.

To listen to a music CD, just put it in your CD drive, label side up, of course, and close the drive door. Then wait a few seconds. Windows Media Player might open and start playing the CD automatically. However, there are other things that could happen:

✦ **A dialog box asks what you want to do:** If you see a dialog box like the example in Figure 38-6, click the **Play audio CD using Windows Media Player**, then click **OK**.

Figure 38-6: Windows has detected a music CD in the drive.

Tip   To choose how your computer reacts when you insert a music CD, see "Setting Defaults for CDs and DVDs" in Chapter 15 to choose what happens when you insert a CD on your own computer.

✦ **A program other than Media Player opens and plays the CD:** If a program other than Windows Media Player opens to play the CD, close that program. Then, do as indicated under the next item, "Nothing happens."

✦ **Nothing happens:** If absolutely nothing happens after you insert an audio CD, or if some other program opened and you closed it, start Windows Media Player. From Windows Media Player's menu choose **Play ⇨ DVD, VCD, or CD Audio**.

Once the CD starts playing, you'll (probably) be taken to the Now Playing tab in Media Player. If not, just click on Now Playing in the Features taskbar. Use the playback controls to control volume and playback.

Using the Playlist pane

The Playlist pane will attempt to show the title and length of each track (song) on the CD, as in the example shown in Figure 38-7. Most CDs don't store song titles, so Media Player has to look up the CD in the CDDB (CD Database) on the Internet to get those titles. Media Player can only do so if you're online. Furthermore, while the CDDB contains songs titles for a lot of CDs, it doesn't contain titles for every CD ever produced.

Figure 38-7: Playlist pane for a sample music CD

If, for whatever reason, Media Player can't find the song titles, each song will be titled simply Track 1, Track 2, and so forth. Either way, if you want to listen to a specific song, just double-click its title or track number in the Playlist pane.

To play songs in random order, click the ▼ next to the album title at the top of the Playlist pane and choose Shuffle List Now (to visually shuffle the titles), or Play Shuffled (to play in random order without rearranging the titles visually).

Tip   The Playlist pane is often referred to as the *list* in Media Player. For example, when you click on Library in the Features taskbar, and click the Library Options button in its toolbar, the Show List option hides, or displays, the Playlist pane.

Choosing visualization options

As added entertainment, Windows Media Player displays a *visualization* that changes in response to the music you're playing. There are many visualizations to choose from; feel free to try them out. Or for that matter, you can turn off the visualization altogether. Buttons above the visualization, shown in Figure 38-8 let you choose a visualization, maximize the visualization to fill Media Player's program window, and fill the entire screen with the visualization.

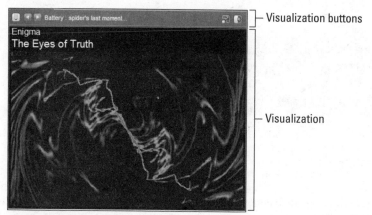

Figure 38-8: Visualization buttons

The View Full Screen and Maximize the Video And Visualization buttons at the right side of the toolbar above the visualization also let you control the size of the visualization. After you switch to full-screen view, move the mouse or press any key to bring back the normal view. To end full-screen view, press Alt+F11 or right-click and choose Exit Visualization.

Tip To prevent your screen saver from kicking in while watching a visualization, choose Tools ⇨ Option from Media Player's menu. Clear the check mark from the *Allow screen saver during playback* option, and click OK.

Choosing enhancements

If you're an audiophile who likes to fine-tune sound using a graphic equalizer, SRS WOW effects, and so forth, click the Select Now Playing Options button, shown near the mouse pointer in Figure 38-9, and click Enhancements to view optional tools to display beneath the visualization. At the bottom of Figure 38-9, you can see the Graphic Equalizer.

Once you've chosen an enhancement, use the buttons in the upper-left corner of the enhancements pane to cycle through the enhancements. Drag the upper border of the pane vertically to size it. Click the Close (X) button in the upper-right corner of the pane to close it.

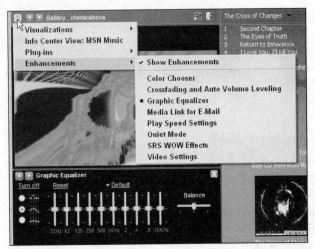

Figure 38-9: Optional Enhancements menu

Stopping a CD

When you've finished listening to a CD, click the Stop button in the play controls. To eject the CD, choose Play ➪ Eject from Media Player's menu, or press Ctrl+E, or push the Eject button on your CD drive.

Ripping (Copying) Music CDs

Media Player isn't just about playing CDs. The real idea is to build up a library of digital media on your hard drive, from which you can create custom playlists and music CDs. If you already own some music CDs, ripping a few CDs will be a great way to start creating your personal media library. Though the term "rip" might sound like something bad, it's not. It simply means to "copy," and no harm will come to the CD when you rip songs from it to your media library.

When you rip a CD, you store a copy of each song from the CD on your hard drive. Once they're on your hard drive, you can play the music at any time without the CD. You can also create custom playlists of favorite songs to play, or to copy to your custom music CD or MP3 player.

Options for ripping CDs

Before you start ripping CDs, you'll need to make some decisions, such as where to put the songs, what format to use, how you want filenames to appear, and so forth. You specify your settings in Media Player's Options dialog box. To get to those options:

1. Open Windows Media Player (if it isn't already open).

2. Choose **Tools** ➪ **Options** from Media Player's menu.

3. Click the **Rip Music** tab to see the options shown in Figure 38-10.

The sections that follow describe what each option offers.

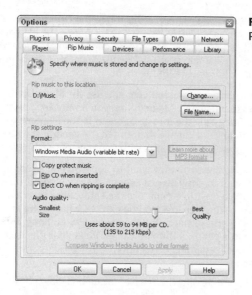

Figure 38-10: Rip Music tab in Media Player's Options

Choosing where to put songs

By default, all songs you copy from CD will be placed in your My Documents folder. But there's no rule that says you have to put them there. If you want all users of this computer to have access to the same songs, you can put them in Shared Music instead. Or, if you have a second hard drive, you can create a folder named Music or Music Library or whatever on that drive, and copy all your CDs to that new folder. It makes no difference to Media Player — it's simply a matter of choosing how you prefer to organize your files.

Caution

It's not necessary, nor helpful, to choose a new folder for each CD you copy. The folder you create will be the parent folder to all ripped songs. CDs within the folder will automatically be organized into subfolders by artist and album title.

To tell Media Player where to put your songs, click the Change button under *Rip music to this location*. Navigate to the folder in which you want to store the songs. If you haven't already created a folder, navigate to the disk drive and use the Make New Folder to create a new folder on the spot. Click the name of the folder to use, and then click OK.

The full path to the folder you chose appears under *Rip music to this location*. For example, if you chose Shared Music, the location will be expressed as `C:\Documents and Settings\ All Users\Documents\My Music`.

Choosing how to name files

You're free to choose how you want song files named. Whatever you choose has no bearing on song information displayed in Windows Media Player. Media Player always shows the title, artist, album title, bit rate, and other information for every song. Media Player gets that information from hidden properties in each song, not from the filename, the folder location, or anything else that you normally see in Windows Explorer. The filenaming convention you choose shows up only when viewing song files *outside* of Windows Media via Windows Explorer.

To choose your filenaming convention, click the File Names . . . button in the Options dialog box. The File Name Options dialog box opens, as shown in Figure 38-11. Choose the elements you want to use in each song's filename. At the very least you should choose Song Title and Artist, because those are certainly useful pieces of information. Use the Separator drop-down list to choose which character will separate each portion of the name.

To change the order of item in the file name, click any selected item and use the Move Up or Move Down button to change its position in the filename. Chances are, you'll want to view songs in alphabetical order by title. Making Song Title the first component in the filename will allow you to do that. As you choose components and change their order, the generic song name under Preview gives you a sense of how each song title will look with your current settings.

Depending on how you plan to use your music files, you may want to copy certain songs at multiple bit rates. For example, you might want to copy favorite songs at very high bit rates to get the maximum quality. If you plan to make multiple copies of the same song at different bit rates, be sure to include Bit Rate as part of the filename, so you can tell which song is which while in Windows Explorer. I'll be using the settings shown in Figure 38-11; Song Title - Artist - Bit Rate, in the sample CDs I rip for this chapter. But you can arrange your filenames however you like. Click OK after defining your filenaming convention.

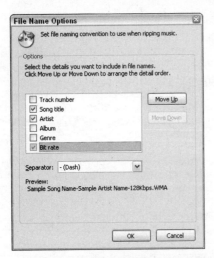

Figure 38-11: The File Name Options dialog box

Choosing a file format and audio quality

Under Rip Settings on the Rip Music tab, the Format drop-down list lets you choose a format in which to store songs you copy. You have four primary choices:

✦ **Windows Media Audio:** Songs are copied to Windows Media Audio (.wma) format files and compressed to conserve disk space. You can choose the amount of compression using the Audio Quality slider in the same dialog box.

✦ **Windows Media Audio (variable bit rate):** Same as the preceding format, but the amount of compression varies with the complexity of the information being stored. As a rule, you get better quality with smaller file sizes using a variable bit rate.

✦ **Windows Media Audio Lossless:** Same as the preceding format, but files are not compressed at all. The sound quality is excellent, but the files are huge. Still, if you're a true audiophile, or are interested in creating HighMAT CDs (High-Performance Media Access Technology), this is an excellent choice.

✦ **mp3:** MP3 is the most widely used format for digital music. It's been around the longest and, unlike the .wma formats listed previously, you're not limited to playing the songs on Windows-based computers.

After you choose a Format option, use the Audio Quality slider to choose a bit rate (sound quality) for copied songs. The rule here is simple — the higher the quality the better the music sounds, and the larger the file. Given that hard disk space is cheap these days, there's really no reason to be chintzy on sound quality. Most of you could copy hundreds of songs and barely put a dent in your available hard disk space.

Tip   To see how much hard disk space you have available right now, open your My Computer folder, then point to the icon for your hard drive. Or right-click your hard drive's icon and choose Properties.

Choosing a high quality does not, in any way, limit how many songs you can put on a custom audio CD you create. An audio CD always store x minutes worth of music, where x is either 74 or 80, depending on whether you use a blank data CD or a blank audio CD. So, there's no reason to settle for a low-quality setting in hopes of putting more songs on custom audio CDs you create.

To illustrate how format and audio quality relate to disk space consumption, I ripped a 3-minute song at various sound qualities. I had to deduce the size of the original .cda file on the commercial CD, since the CDFS file system on commercial CDs centers around minutes rather than size in bytes. But you wouldn't want to copy songs in .cda format to a hard drive anyway. I've included the .cda format in the table just for comparison purposes.

Tip   These days, hard disk space costs anywhere from $1.00 to $2.00 a gigabyte. If you figure about a buck eighty a gigabyte, you'll be pretty close.

The exact sizes involved depend on many factors. So, if you copy a 3-minute song at various bit rates, you won't get exactly the same numbers. Nonetheless, the table provides some general guidelines on how audio quality relates to hard disk space consumption, and provides some fairly accurate numbers in terms of how many songs you can expect to store per gigabyte of hard disk space.

Table 38-1: A 3-Minute Song at Various Bit Rates

Format/Quality	Bit Rate	Size	Songs per GB
CDA (baseline)	128 Kbps	8,545 KB	123
Windows Media Audio (Medium)	128 Kbps	2,872 KB	365
Windows Media Audio (Best)	192 Kbps	4,305 KB	244
WMA Variable Bit Rate (Medium)	185 Kbps	3,980 KB	263
WMA Variable Bit Rate (Best)	480 Kbps	10,507 KB	100
MP3 Medium	192 Kbps	4,248 KB	247
MP3 Best	320 Kbps	7,082 KB	148
WMA Lossless	927 Kbps	18,768 KB	56

Tip   An uppercase "B," as in KB, MB, GB, stands for "bytes" and is a measure of size. A lowercase "b," as in Kb or Kbps, stands for "bits" and is generally used to measure speed. In reference to music, the higher the bit rate in Kbps (thousands of bits per second), the better the sound quality in terms of detail, clarity, and realism.

Copy protecting music

If you choose the Copy Protect Music option, all the songs you rip will be copy protected in the same way that content you purchase online is copy protected. You'll place limitations on your own music. The only justification for doing this that I can think of would be to prevent yourself from accidentally sharing your ripped songs and infringing on the copyright.

But the chances of "accidentally" sharing your songs seem to fall somewhere between slim and none. To share your songs, you'd first need to download and install a P2P client such as Limewire (www.limewire.com), Morpheus (www.morpheus.com) or Kazaa (www.kazaa.com). Then, you'd need to intentionally configure that program to share your ripped songs, or copy your ripped songs to the default shared folder for that program. To me, it seems like far too many specific steps to ever do by accident.

Rip CD when inserted

If selected, this option tells Windows Media Player to copy all the songs from a CD as soon as you insert the audio CD. Choosing this option, along with the Eject CD option, described next, makes it easy to rip a whole collection of CDs in assembly-line fashion. For example, if you have a few dozen CDs you want to rip, you can just insert a CD, wait for it to be copied and ejected, then insert the next CD.

When you've finished ripping your CD collection, you can then clear this option so that you have more flexibility in deciding what you want to do with each CD you insert into your hard drive.

Eject CD when ripping is completed

If selected, this option just tells Media Player to eject the CD from the drive when it's finished copying the CD. As mentioned, choosing this option along with the *Rip CD when inserted* option is a great way to copy multiple CDs in a quick, assembly-line manner.

Digital or analog?

Some CD drives and sound cards let you copy and create digital music CDs, while others support only analog. What your particular computer offers depends on your computer's CD drive, sound card, and a couple of little cables that connect the two inside your computer. Quality-wise, it really doesn't seem to matter much if you use digital or analog; it'll probably sound the same either way. But if you at least want to know what your options are, follow these steps:

1. If you're still in Media Player's Options dialog box, click the **Devices** tab. Otherwise, choose **Tools** ⇨ **Options** from Media Player's menu; then, click the Devices tab.

2. Click the icon that represents the CD drive you use to copy music; then, click the **Properties** button. The Properties dialog box for that drive opens, as in the example shown in Figure 38-12.

3. To copy in digital, select **Digital** under the Rip option. You can also choose **Error Correction**, which allows Media Player to correct any flaws in the CDs (such as crackles and pops caused by scratches).

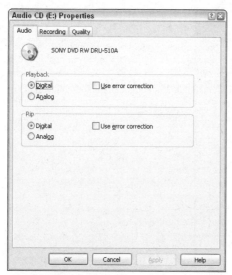

Figure 38-12: The Audio tab in the Audio CD Properties dialog box

4. Click **OK** after making your selections.

All the settings we've described up to now need only be set once. They will then be applied to all CDs you copy in the future. Just make sure that you click OK in any open dialog boxes to save your settings and close the dialog boxes before copying your first CD.

Choosing columns to display

Before you rip a CD, you'll be able to view song titles and other information about each song. You can also change any information that appears before you copy. This is handy for defining categorizing songs into your own genres, changing the album artist name that appears in you Media Library, and so forth. To choose the columns you want to see, follow these steps:

1. Click on the **Rip** tab in Media Player's Feature's taskbar.

2. Choose **View** ➪ **Choose Columns** from Media Player's menu.

3. Choose the columns you want to see, clear the check marks of columns you don't want to see. (Dimmed column names cannot be selected or cleared).

4. Use the **Move Up** and **Move Down** button to move the currently selected column name up or down in the list. Figure 38-13 shows an example.

5. Click **OK**.

Figure 38-13: The Choose Columns dialog box for ripping CDs

As an alternative to the preceding steps, you can right-click any column heading, and then click the name of any column you want to add or remove to the display. To move a column, drag its column heading left or right. To size a column, drag the right border of the column heading left or right.

Now you're ready to start ripping CDs. Remember, all the settings you've chosen up to this point will apply to every CD you copy. So feel free to do as many CDs as you wish in assembly-line fashion.

Ripping a music CD

Ripping a CD is easy. Here are the steps:

1. If your Internet account requires logging in, get online so that you're connected to the Internet and Media Player can download sound titles and such.

2. If you haven't already done so, open Windows Media Player. Then, click the **Rip** tab in the Features taskbar.

3. Insert the CD you want to rip (copy) into your CD drive and close the drive door.

4. If you chose the Copy CD when inserted option described earlier in this chapter, skip down to Step 10 now.

5. If the CD starts playing, click the **Stop** button down in the Play controls. While it's OK to copy and play songs at the same time, copying will be faster and more reliable if Media Player doesn't have to play and copy the CD at the same time.

6. Wait for song titles to appear. If song titles don't appear within 30 seconds or so, the CD might not be in the CDDB. In that case, you can go ahead and rip the CD, and then fill in the details later in your media library.

7. Clear the check mark to the left of any songs that you don't want to copy.

8. Optionally, if you want to change any information before you copy the CD:

   • To change a single item of information, such as a song title, right-click the title, choose **Edit**, type the corrected information, and press **Enter**.

Note Some columns, such as Album Artist, apply to the whole CD and can't be changed individually. But, after you rip the CD, you can change the album artist for any individual song in the Library.

   • To change an entry for all items on the CD, select (click) the first song title then press **Shift+End** to select all the listed songs. Right-click the column you want to change (for example, Artist, Album Artist, or Genre), choose **Edit**, type in the new text, and press **Enter**. If asked for confirmation, click **Yes**.

Tip The Artist column in the Rip pane defines contributing artists to a song. To list multiple artists, separate their names with a semicolon. For example, entering `Yardbirds;Eric Clapton` in the Artist column of a song will categorize that song under Yardbirds, and also under Eric Clapton.

9. Click the **Rip Music** button.

10. Wait until the Rip Status column shows *Ripped to Library* for all songs you've opted to copy, as in Figure 38-14. If the CD isn't ejected automatically, go ahead and eject it.

11. Put the CD back to wherever you normally keep your CDs. You won't need it any more to play songs from your computer, or to copy files to custom audio CDs or an MP3 player.

That's it for ripping one CD. To rip more CDs, just repeat Steps 3 to 11 for each CD. Optionally, you can see how things are shaping up in your Media Library at any time, as discussed next.

What to Do If titles Are Wrong or Missing

Sometimes when you insert a CD to rip, no titles, or the wrong titles show up in Media Player. If no titles show up, make sure that you're online, because it's not possible to download song titles if you're offline. It's also possible that the CD you're trying doesn't even exist in the CDDB. But it's worth taking a look to see if you can find the right information.

Before you click the Rip Music button, click on the Find Album Info button above the columns. A Web page will open in the lower portion of Media Player's program window. Read and follow the instructions in the "If this information is incorrect, click Search . . ." information box. The page will act like a wizard, with Search, Next>, Cancel, and similar buttons at the bottom of the page.

If you're lucky, you'll find the exact album and Media Player will fill in the titles and other information for you when you click Finish. If you're not so lucky, you can still fill in the information manually using the technique described under Step 8 under the "Ripping a music CD" heading. Or, you can rip the CD without the media information, and then go back and correct it later in Media Library.

Figure 38-14: All songs have been ripped to Media Player's media library.

Buying Music Online

In addition to ripping CDs you already own, you can purchase music online. The exact procedure varies from one online store to the next. But in general you pay anywhere from 88 cents to a buck or so for an individual song. The song you download is protected content that comes with a license. As mentioned at the top of this chapter, there are limits to what you can do with protected content.

Purchasing protected content

Allowing Media Player to remind you to back up your licenses periodically is a good idea. At least until you get the hang of how it works. To choose whether or not reminders appear on your screen, choose Tools ➪ Options from Media Player's menu. On the Player tab in the Options dialog box, choose (check) the *Prompt me to back up my licenses* option if you want Media Player to provide reminders.

On the Privacy tab of the Options dialog box, you'll find an option labeled *Acquire licenses automatically for protected content*. If you choose that option, then you don't get any feedback when downloading a license. Personally, I wouldn't recommend choosing that option because occasionally you might download licensed content without realizing that it's protected. In those cases, you'll want to know, beforehand, that you're about to download a license. Leaving that option unselected gives you a heads-up, and the option to cancel the license, before you open the licensed file.

Anyway, here I'll go through a quick example of purchasing protected content, using Wal-Mart as the vendor. Most sites, including Wal-Mart, will require that you set up an account and download some software. I won't get into that here because it has nothing to do with Windows, and you can easily just follow the instructions on the screen to set up an account and get what you need. You don't need to worry about viruses and the like from legitimate vendors such as Wal-Mart. Legitimate businesses don't spread that stuff.

After you've set up an account, click the down-pointing triangle on the far-right side of the Features Taskbar and choose an online store. That store's logo appears where the MSN Butterfly logo usually appears by default, as shown in Figure 38-15.

Figure 38-15: About to purchase music online from Wal-Mart

I pay my 88 cents and see a little progress meter at the bottom of Media Player's window as the song downloads. When the progress meter reaches 100%, I click on Library in Media Player's Features taskbar, click the + sign next to Purchased music, and then click on WalMart. The song I purchased appears in the Details pane to the right, as in Figure 38-16.

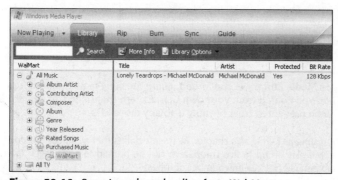

Figure 38-16: Song I purchased online from Wal-Mart

In the figure, I clicked on Library Options above the Contents pane and selected the Choose Columns option to add the Protected and Bit Rate columns to the Detail pane. I positioned those columns so that you can see them in the figure. Notice that the Protected column shows Yes, indicating that this downloaded song is protected content. (I'll talk more about the library in a moment).

Viewing license information

For information about the license, right-click the song title in the Contents pane on the right, and choose Properties. Then, click the License tab in the Properties dialog box. The license details, shown in Figure 38-17, show me that I can burn the song to a custom CD up to 10 times. I can copy the song to MP3 an unlimited number of times (that's what the *This file can be synchronized an unlimited number of times* detail means).

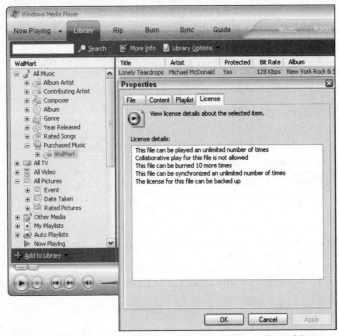

Figure 38-17: License details for protected song purchased from Wal-Mart online

As far as using the song in Media Library is concerned, using the song is no different from using an unprotected song you copied from your own CDs. Except that once you've burned it to 10 different CDs, you'll be prevented from burning it to any more CDs.

Tip   Though still in beta testing as I write this chapter, Microsoft claims that all songs you download from their site will play on up to five computers, can be burned to a CD seven times, and copied to portable music devices any number of times.

Backing up and restoring licenses

If you chose the option to be reminded periodically about backing up your licenses, you'll see a reminder to backup your licenses within two weeks of acquiring the song and license. You can view and manage your licenses at any time. To do so, choose Tools ➪ Manage Licenses from Media Player's menu. The Manage Licenses dialog box shown in Figure 38-18 opens.

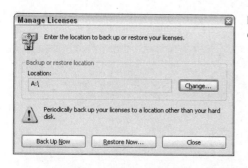

Figure 38-18: The Manage Licenses dialog box

Ideally, you'll want to back up licenses to a removable disk, and store that disk for safekeeping. Each license is a tiny file. So, you can use floppy or Zip disk for the backups. You could also use a thumb drive or memory card. If all else fails, you can copy the licenses to a folder in your My Music folder. Then, when you back up your entire My Documents folder, you'll back up your licenses as well.

In the Manage Licenses dialog box, click the Change button to choose where you want to backup your licenses, and then click the Back Up Now button. Click OK when the transfer is complete, and you're done.

Should you ever accidentally delete your licenses, you can follow the same basic procedure to restore them. Choose Tools ⇨ Manage Licenses from Media Player's menu, click the Restore Now button, and just follow the on-screen instructions.

 Tip   If you have any difficulty using protected content that you downloaded using an earlier version of Windows or Media Player, see www.microsoft.com/windows/windowsmedia/ windowsxp/movetoxp.aspx for information on moving digital content to XP.

Music in Your Media Library

The whole point of a program like Windows Media Player is to build and manage a library of digital media. To see and manage your Media Player library, click on the Library tab in the Media Player's Features taskbar, as shown in Figure 38-19. The left column, called the *Contents pane*, displays major categories of media, including All Music, All TV, All Video, and others. Every category name will have a + or - sign to the left so you can visually expand or collapse subcategories to see as much, or as little, detail as you want.

For example, when you click on All Music, the Details pane to the right lists all the music in your media library. You can instantly sort the music by clicking on any column heading once or twice. Each click reverses the sort order from ascending to descending, and vice versa. So, you could, for instance, see all song titles in alphabetical order by clicking on the Title heading once or twice. Or, to see songs grouped by artist or genre, click the Artist, Album Artist, or Genre heading.

When you click on a major subcategory heading, you'll only see items within that category list. For example, if you click on Album Artist, you'll see all the Album Artists in the Details pane to the right. If you click the + sign next to Album Artist, you'll see all artist names listed beneath the heading. If you click on an individual artist's name, you'll see all songs by that artist in the Details pane. In short, you can see your music grouped and sorted however you like, just by clicking on items in the left pane.

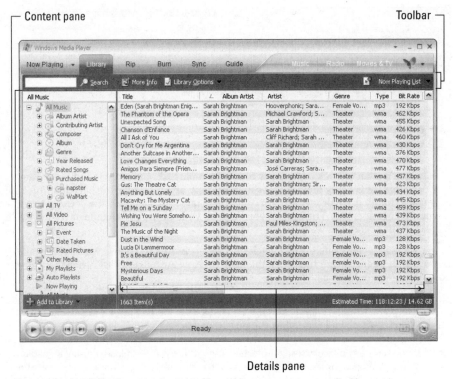

Content pane   Toolbar

Details pane

Figure 38-19: Click Library in the Features taskbar to see your media library.

The whole trick to getting the hang of Media Library is just to play around with it. It's easy, once you get the hang of it. Click on the + sign next to all Music to see all categories under that heading. Then, click the + sign next to any subcategory name, such as Contributing Artist. In the Details pane to the right, you'll see all songs by that artist.

Want to see all songs in a genre? Click the - sign next to Contributing Artist, just to collapse that list and get it out of the way. Then, click the + sign next to Genre. Click on a Genre name, and the Details pane to the right shows all songs in that genre. It works the same way for all the categories.

Want to play a specific song in the Details pane? Just double-click the song title, or right-click the song title and choose Play. Want to play all the songs by a specific artist, or all the songs in a genre? Just double-click the genre name or artist name in the Contents pane at left, or right-click the name and choose Play. Want to show or hide the Playlist pane on the right? Click the Library Options button in the toolbar above the panes, and choose Show List.

Choosing columns for Media Library

You're free to choose which columns you want to see in the Details pane. First, click on All Music at the top of the Contents pane. Then, click on Library Options in the toolbar and click on the Choose Columns option. Select (check) the name of any column you do want to see, clear the check mark next to any column heading you don't want to see. To control the left-to-right order of columns, click any column name and use the Move Up or Move Down to position the column within the list, as in the example shown in Figure 38-20.

Figure 38-20: Choose Columns for All Music.

You can choose different column arrangements for different types of media. For example, to choose columns for displaying information about videos in Media Library, click on All Video in the left column, and then click on Library Options and click the Choose Columns options. Then, choose and arrange columns to your liking for viewing video files. Use the horizontal scroll bar at the bottom of the Details pane to scroll left and right through columns.

Tip   You can also add or remove a column by right-clicking any column heading and clicking a column name.

Of course, none of the selections you make in the Choose Columns dialog box are set in stone. When that dialog box is closed, you can size any column by dragging the border at the right edge of the column heading left or right. To move a column, drag the entire column heading left or right.

Tip   Custom 1 and Custom 2 are extra fields in which you can add any information you like.

Controlling Media Library behavior and appearance

When you click on the All Music category name in the left column and then click on Library Options, you'll see the options shown in Figure 38-21. The "double-click" options define what happens when you double-click in category name in the Contents pane. Other options define visual aspects of Media Library as summarized in the following list:

Figure 38-21: Library Options for the All Music category

✦ **Show List:** Choose this option to show or hide the Playlist pane at the right side of the program window.

✦ **Add to List on Double-click:** Choosing this option copies all items from the selected artist, album, or genre to the Playlist pane.

✦ **Play all Items on Double-click:** Choosing this option plays all the items in whatever category name you double-click in the Contents pane.

✦ **Play selected Item on Double-click:** Limits double-clicking to playing just the item that's currently selected in the main pane.

✦ **Group by Sorted Field:** If selected, this option shades like items in the Details pane by whatever column you sort on. For example, if you sort All Music by Genre, each genre will be shaded for easier viewing.

Chapter 39 discusses the library in more detail. For now, that should be enough to get you started playing around with it. But basically, you can double-click and song title or subcategory name to play it. Right-click any item to see other things you can do with the item.

Manually Editing Media Information

All the information you see in the Library view is *media information*. As in any large collection, organization and accurate media information are the keys to being able to what you want, when you want it. The CDDB that contains information about song titles isn't always 100 percent accurate, and you may come across CDs that aren't in the CDDB at all. Any missing media information often is filled in with the word "Unknown." Sometimes, you have to fill in the correct information yourself.

The first step is to click on Library in the Features taskbar. Use the Contents pane on the left to locate the song(s) you want to change. For example, if you have "Unknown" artists to change, click the + sign next to Contributing Artist in the Contents pane. Then, click on Unknown under Contributing Artists. The idea is to choose whatever is necessary in the Contents pane so that the songs you need to change are visible in the Details pane to the right.

To change a single item of information in the Details pane, right-click the text you want to change and choose Edit. Optionally, you can click one, wait a second, and then click again. The field turns white and shows the cursor. Type in the new text, and press Enter.

If you want to make the same change to several items, first select all the items you want to change. To select songs in the Details pane, use the same general techniques you use to select icons in Windows Explorer:

✦ To select on item, click it once.

✦ To extend the selection through multiple rows, **Shift+click** the row to which you want to extend the selection.

✦ To select or unselect individual rows, **Ctrl+click** individual items.

✦ To select all items, press **Ctrl+A**.

✦ To select all items from the current item to the last item, press **Shift+End**.

✦ To select from the current item to the top, press **Shift+Home**.

✦ To select by dragging, start with the mouse pointer in a blank portion of the Title column (not touching any text). Then, drag the mouse pointer through the items you want to select.

Note Some of the information in the library, such as the size or type of an item, is purely factual and can't be changed.

To select songs by dragging the mouse pointer, start with the mouse pointer in the Title column, but not touching any text within the column. You may need to first widen Title column so that there's blank space to the right of some titles. Then, drag the mouse pointer to the left and up or down through the song titles you want to select.

Once you've selected two or more songs, right-click the column where you want to make the change and choose Edit. For example, in Figure 38-22 I've selected several songs that have Unknown in the Artist category and am about to change them all to the artist's name. Type in the new information, and press Enter. The change you made in the one selected song will spread to all of the selected songs.

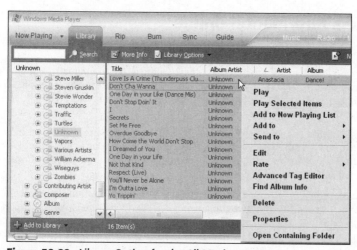

Figure 38-22: Library Option for the All Music category

Using the Advanced Tag Editor

As an alternative to working directly in the columns, you can make changes using the Advanced Tag Editor. Again, the first step is to select the song, or songs, to which you want to make the change. Then, right-click any selected item and choose Advanced Tag Editor. The dialog box shown in Figure 38-23 opens. Notice that there are several tabs, each representing media information fields that you can change. To change a field for all selected items, click the empty checkbox next to the field name to make the field editable, and then type in your text.

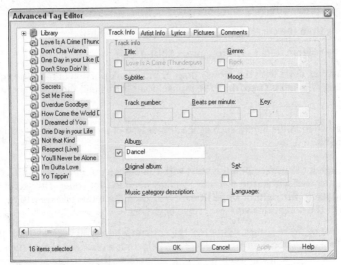

Figure 38-23: The Advanced Tag Editor for changing media information

Finding media information online

If you copied a CD while offline, the song titles will be missing. Sometimes when you copy a CD while online, you still end up with the wrong media information. That second problem often occurs when copying CDs from two-CD sets. As an alternative to manually filling in the information, you may be able to find the appropriate album online. Ideally, you should fill in the Album Title first (if you know it). Or fill in the Album Artist if you know it (though, the Album Artist might not help if it's a "various artists" compilation CD).

The top half of the Contents pane in Figure 38-24 shows an example where I've clicked on an album under Byrds in the Album Artist category. The Title for each song is just Track1, Track2, and so forth. To look for the album online, right-click the album title in the Contents pane and choose Find Album Info.

If Media Player can find the album (or a close match) the Media Information pane will show whatever information it has. If the album is the correct one, just click the Finish button at the bottom of the Media Information pane, and all the missing information will be filled in for you. If the wrong album shows up, follow the instructions in the information box. That is, click the Search button at the bottom of the pane, and follow the instructions on the pages to follow.

You may still have to fill in some information manually, it all depends on the CD you're working with. To put the Media Information pane back into hiding, click the More Info button in the toolbar above the Contents pane.

Figure 38-24: Note the Search, Edit, Finish, and Cancel buttons below the album.

Adding lyrics

You can find lyrics to just about any song somewhere on the Web. Or, if you know the lyrics already, you can type them yourself. There are two ways to show lyrics:

✦ **Static lyrics:** All the lyrics appear in a pane beneath the Now Playing visualization, with a scroll bar to scroll through the lyrics manually.

✦ **Synchronized lyrics:** Lyrics are shown in the same pane mentioned, but one line at a time in sync with the song.

To get started adding lyrics, click on Library in the Features taskbar, and choose whatever options are necessary in the Contents pane so that you can see the song for which you want to add lyrics in the Contents pane. Then, right-click the song title and choose Advanced Tag Editor. Click on the Lyrics tab in the dialog box that opens. Choose a language from the Language drop-down list.

If you want to type in the lyrics yourself, click Add, and then type the lyrics into either textbox, pressing Enter at the end of each line. If you want to try to find the lyrics online, open up your Web browser and go to a Web site such as www.lyrics.com. Optionally, go to a general search engine like www.google.com and search for the song lyrics. Make sure you provide enough words to zero-in on the song lyrics. For example, if you're looking for the lyrics to the song "Buenos Aires" from *Evita*, your search text should be Lyrics Buenos Aires Evita. When you find the lyrics, copy and paste them into the top textbox.

Tip 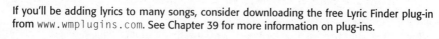   If you'll be adding lyrics to many songs, consider downloading the free Lyric Finder plug-in from www.wmplugins.com. See Chapter 39 for more information on plug-ins.

To synchronize the lyrics to the song, click the Synchronized Lyrics button. Lyrics from the top textbox will move to the lower textbox. Scroll up to the first lyric and click the Play button. To test out the lyrics, click the OK button in the open dialog box(es). In the library, right-click the song and choose Play. Then, click on Now Playing in the Features taskbar. If you don't see lyrics at the bottom of the visualization pane, click the Select Now Playing Options in the toolbar above the visualization and choose any visualization except Info Center View.

If you tried to synchronize the lyrics, and they're out of sync with the song, you've got your work cut out for you. Rewind the song to the beginning and watch the timer near the lower-right corner of the screen as the song is playing. Note the point time at which the first lyric starts. Stop the playback, go back to the Library View, get back to the Synchronized Lyrics dialog box.

Click the first lyric in the list and figure out the time difference between what's shown and when the lyric actually starts. For example, if the first lyric doesn't start until 33 seconds into the song, but the first lyric is set to start at 0:000:03:00 (3 seconds), you're off by 30 seconds. You need to click each time in the list, click Edit, add 30 seconds to whatever time is currently shown, and press OK. You'll need the patience of a saint. You can click the Play button to hear the sound and see a red indicator showing where each lyric kicks in. But even so, it's probably going to take some time and practice to get everything synched up just right.

Deleting songs

You can delete any single song from the library just by right-clicking the song title and choosing Delete. Or, you can select multiple songs, right-click any one of them, and choose Delete. If you want to delete an entire album (which means, all the songs on that album), you can expand the Album category in the Contents pane, right-click the album you want to delete, and choose Delete.

Caution   While it's OK to delete unrecognized files from your media library, you don't want to delete them from the computer. They unrecognized sound files may be sound effects or other files that other programs use. Deleting them from your computer will affect those other programs in negative ways!

Regardless of what you delete, you'll see a dialog box like the one in Figure 38-25 (assuming that you haven't previously chosen the *Don't show this message again* option. Pay careful attention to what you choose here, because it makes a big difference. Here's the effect of each choice:

Figure 38-25: Windows Media Player Delete options

✦ **Delete from library only:** Removes the item(s) from your media library so they don't show up there any more, but keeps the files on the disk. You might use this to get rid of small sound effects or other undesirable sound files in your media library without ruining other programs' abilities to play the sound effects.

✦ **Select from library and my computer:** Choose this option to delete the item(s) from your media library and your hard disk. For example, if you plan to rerip an album with new settings, you would choose this to get rid of the current media library entries for that album, and the songs you intend to replace.

To minimize the likelihood of accidentally deleting songs, choose Tools ⇨ Options from Media Player's menu. Click the Library tab and clear the check mark next to *Delete files from my computer when deleted from library*. It will still be possible for you to delete files so that you'll still need to exercise caution. But with that option turned off, the default setting will be to delete items from the library only.

Creating Custom Playlists

Once you've built up a collection of songs, you can start creating custom *playlists*. As the name implies, a playlist is a group of songs that somehow go together. For example, you can make a playlist of dinner music, another playlist of party music, another of favorite Motown tunes, whatever suits your fancy.

Playlists are also a good first step to creating your own custom CDs, because you can see exactly how many minutes the combined songs take to play. If you use blank 80-minute audio CDs, you can create playlists that have a little less than 80 minutes, and then burn them to CDs. You can keep the playlist so that if a CD gets scratched up, you can just throw it in the trash and create another from your playlist.

Tip   Blank CDs are cheap if you buy them in large spindles without the plastic jewel cases. I think the jewel cases cost more than the CDs. You can store your CDs in a CD wallet, binder, or inexpensive paper sleeves instead of plastic jewel cases.

Creating playlists is easy, and there are several ways to do it. Perhaps the easiest is as follows:

1. In Windows Media Player, click the **Library** tab in the Features taskbar.

2. In the Contents pane, scroll or collapse categories as necessary so that you can see the My Playlists category name. Then, right-click **My Playlists** and choose **New**. An empty Playlist pane opens on the right side of the window as shown in Figure 38-26.

Tip   If the Media Information pane takes up too much space at the bottom of the Details pane, click the More Info button in the toolbar (near the Library Options button) to hide that pane.

3. To save the playlist, click on New Playlist at the top of the Playlist pane and choose Save Playlist As. In the Save As dialog box that opens, type a filename of your choosing (something that describes the playlist), and then click the Save button.

Tip   You can create playlists of any length, for any occasion. To make it easy to identify your CD-burning playlists, consider putting "CD" somewhere in the playlist name.

4. Drag any songs you want to add to the playlist from the Details pane into the playlist (see paragraph that follows these steps for tips).

Figure 38-26: Creating a new, empty playlist

Don't forget that you can view songs however you wish in the Media Library. For example, if you plan on putting songs by a single artist in the playlist, click expand the Album Artist category, and then click the click the name of the artist to see songs by that artist in the Details pane. Or, if you plan to use songs from a specific genre, expand the Genre category and click a genre name. In the Details pane, click the Title column heading to alphabetize songs by title, or click the Album Artist or Artist heading to alphabetize songs by artist.

It's not necessary to drag songs one at a time. You can select multiple song titles in the Details pane using the Ctrl+click and Shift+click methods described earlier in this chapter. Then, drag any one selected song title to the Playlist pane to add them all.

Tip   The Auto Playlists beneath My Playlists automatically create playlists based on content protection, high and low bit rates, how often and when you listen to songs, and other factors.

As you add songs to the list, the Total Time indicator at the bottom of the Playlist pane will show the total time for the selected songs, expressed as *hours:minutes:seconds*. If you're creating the playlist to burn to a CD, keep in mind that there might be a little overhead on the CD. So, you might not be able to get exactly 80 minutes worth of music on an 80-minute CD. You may be limited to 1:19:30 (1 hour, 19 minutes, and 30 seconds) or so. On a data CD that holds 74 minutes with of music, a realistic upper limit might be more along the lines of 1:13:30.

After you've added some songs to the playlist, you can arrange and remove songs in the Playlist pane as follows:

✦ To move a song, drag it up or down within the list.

✦ To remove a song, right-click it and choose **Remove from List**.

✦ To start over, click the playlist name at the top of the playlist and choose **Clear List**.

✦ To select multiple items in the list, use the standard **Ctrl+Click** or **Shift+Click** methods. Optionally, you can put the mouse pointer just beneath the last song in the list and drag upward.

Optionally, you can click on the playlist name and choose Edit using Playlist Editor to work with the playlist in an easy-to-use alternative editor. Figure 38-27 shows a sample playlist named Doris containing 1:18:24 (78 minutes, 24 seconds) worth of Doris Day songs.

Figure 38-27: A custom playlist named Doris CD

Tip

To add a song to a custom playlist on the fly (when the playlist isn't even visible on the screen), right-click the song title and choose Add To. Then, click the playlist name to which you want to add the song, or choose Additional Playlists to find the name of the playlist to which you want to add the song. You can even create a new playlist on the fly after choosing Add To ➪ Additional Playlists.

When you're happy with your custom playlist, click the playlist name at the top of the Playlist pane and choose Save or Save Playlist As. You can create as many playlists as you wish. To create a new playlist at any time, repeat Steps 1-4. To view your playlists, expand the My Playlist category in the media library's Contents pane, as shown in Figure 38-28. To play a playlist, right-click its name and choose Play.

Figure 38-28: Names of several custom playlists in the Contents pane

Viewing and editing playlists

After you've created a playlist, clicking its name under My Playlists in the Details pane shows the contents of the list in the Contents pane. The Contents pane works a little differently from the Playlist pane. You can still right-click any song within the Contents pane and choose "Remove from List" to remove a song from the playlist.

But you can't rearrange songs by dragging them up and down in the Contents pane. You have to right-click and choose Move Up or Move Down to move a song. Or, redisplay the custom playlist in the Playlist pane and drag up and down there. To do that, right-click the custom playlist name under My Playlists in the Contents pane and choose Play. If the Playlist pane isn't open, click on Library Options above the Contents pane and choose Show List.

To rename or delete an entire playlist, right-click its name under My Playlists in the contents page and choose Rename or Delete.

Using and creating auto-playlists

In addition to the drag-and-drop style playlists described earlier, you can create auto-playlists based on criteria if your own choosing. When you expand the Auto Playlists group beneath My Playlists, you'll see examples of auto-playlists that come with Media Player 10. Click on any play list name to see the current contents of that playlist.

Some of the auto-playlists are based on your listening habits, and won't contain any songs until you've been using Media Player for a while. But some, like *Music tracks with content protection*, you may find useful right off the bat. The real beauty of auto-playlists, though, isn't in that handful of examples, but rather in how you create your own auto-playlists.

To create a custom auto-playlist, right-click the Auto Playlists category name in the Contents pane and choose New. A dialog box with areas to give the playlist a name and define criteria opens as in Figure 38-29. Type any name you like in the Auto Playlist Name box, and then follow the instructions in the larger pane to define your criteria.

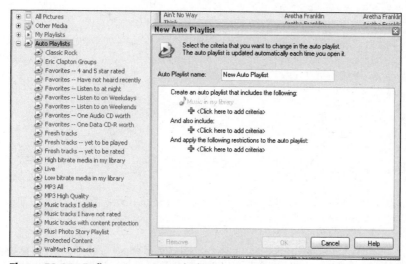

Figure 38-29: Define a new Auto-playlist.

For example, suppose that you want to create a playlist containing only your high-quality MP3 files. You might name it High-Quality MP3s or whatever. Then, click the first green + sign and choose File type. You'll see the underlined words Contains" and <click to set>. Click Contains and choose Is. Then, click <click to set> and choose mp3.

A second + sign appears immediately under the first so that you can add another criterion. Choose Bit rate as the criterion field, *Is at least* as the comparison, and 300 as the value. So, you end up with criteria that look like this:

```
Music in my library
    File type Is mp3
    Bit rate (in Kbps) Is At Least 300
```

The criteria always combine in "and" fashion. So, the preceding auto-playlist will automatically display all .MP3 songs that have 300 Kbps or better bit rates.

The optional + sign under *And also include* allows you to extend the playlist to include video, pictures, and TV shows in the playlist. The optional + sign under *And apply the following restrictions to the auto playlist* lets you limit the playlist to a specific number of songs, time limit, or total file size.

Media information fields and other data on which you can base criteria includes (but is not limited to) things like Composer, Conductor, Contributing Artist (the Artist column in media library), Date Added, File name, File Size, Keywords, Length, and My Rating. Since you can use the Custom 1 and Custom 2 fields for anything, you can base auto-playlists on any data you store in those fields. It's a very handy thing, once you get the hang of it. Examples of custom auto-playlist names and criteria you might want to create are:

```
Eric Clapton Groups
    Contributing Artist Contains Eric Clapton

Flamenco Headset
    Genre Is Flamenco
    Limit total size to 512 Megabytes
Jimi Live
    Contributing Artist Contains Jimi Hendrix
    Title Contains Live

MP3 High Quality
    File type Is mp3
    Bit rate (in Kbps) Is At Least 300
Protected Content
    Protection Is Present

Wal-Mart Purchases
    Content Provider Is WalMart

WMA Lossless
    File type Is wma
    Bit rate (in Kbps) Is At Least 750
```

The beauty of every auto-playlist is that it generates its list of songs each time you open the playlist. So the playlist you see is always current with whatever is in your media library at the moment. You can use any auto-playlist as the basis for generating a custom playlist from which you burn CDs, or copy songs to a portable music device. You manage auto-playlists like most other objects in Windows:

✦ To rename an auto-playlist, right-click it and choose **Rename**.

✦ To change an auto-playlist, right-click it and choose **Edit**

✦ To delete an auto-playlist, right-click it and choose **Delete**.

Burning Your Own CDs

If your CD or DVD drive is capable of burning CD-Rs, you can create your own custom audio CDs to play in any car stereo or CD player. If you know for a fact that your stereo can read CD-RWs, and your drive can burn them, you can use CD-RWs instead. But, the vast majority of stereos are only capable of playing CD-ROMs, which means that you have to start by burning a blank CD-R.

Caution   You only get one shot at burning a CD-R. So don't try to burn a few songs now and a few songs later. See "Understanding CDs" in Chapter 15 for details.

Choosing burn options

Before you burn your first custom music CD, take a moment to configure your options. Here's how:

1. From Media Player's menu choose **Tools ➪ Options**.

2. In the Options dialog box that opens, click the **Devices** tab.

3. Click the icon that represents your CD drive, and choose **Properties**.

4. In the drive's Properties dialog box, click the **Recording** tab to see the options on the left side of Figure 38-30.

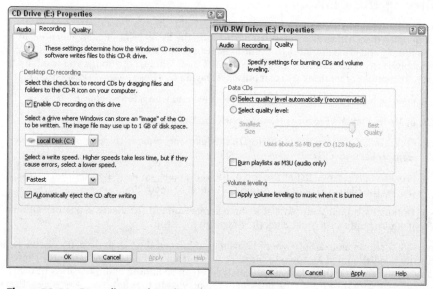

Figure 38-30: Recording and Quality tabs

5. Make sure that **Enable CD recording on this drive** is selected (checked); otherwise, you won't be able to burn any CDs.

6. Choosing a drive for the image file that's created before burning a CD isn't terribly important, it just has to be a hard drive

7. Feel free to choose **Fastest** as the write speed. However, if you have any problems recording to a particular brand of CD, reducing that value may solve the problem.

8. Choose **Automatically eject CD after writing** to have the drive tray open when the CD is finished and ready to play.

On the Recording tab, shown on the right side of Figure 38-30, choose options as follows:

✦ **Select quality level:** The first, recommended, option, will burn songs at the best quality based on the quality settings of the songs being burned. Choosing the second option lets you specify a quality, but might also force Media Player to change quality settings during the burn, which slows things down.

✦ **Burn playlists as M3U (audio only):** Choosing this option makes Media Player use settings found in MP3 playlists, as opposed to Windows Media Player playlists, which are unique to Media Player.

✦ **Apply volume leveling to music when it is burned:** Choosing this option equalizes the volume of songs burned to the CDs so that you don't end up with some songs playing much more loudly than others.

As always, click OK in the Options dialog box after making your selections.

Burning the disk

There are several ways to burn a CD. For example, right after you've created a playlist you can click on burn disc. Or, you can create a burn list on the fly by right-clicking any song in your media library and choosing Add To ⇨ Burn List. But probably the easiest way, as mentioned previously, is to create and save a custom playlist that contains the songs you want, up to the maximum number of minutes you can put on a single CD. These steps describe that method:

1. Insert a blank CD-R disk into your CD-R drive and wait a few seconds.

2. In Media Player's Features taskbar, click the **Burn** option.

3. From the drop-down list at the top of the left pane, choose the custom playlist you want to burn to a CD.

4. From the drop-down list at the top of the right pane, choose the CD drive in which you placed the blank CD, and the Audio CD option beneath that.

5. Optionally, adjust your playlist if some songs won't fit (as discussed later). Otherwise, if you're ready to go, just click the **Start Burn** button.

Figure 38-31 shows an example where I haven't yet burned the CD. In the left column, I chose a custom playlist named Motown to burn. At the bottom of the list, you see Total Time: 78 minutes, meaning that this playlist will easily fit on an 80-minute audio CD. In your own playlist, make sure to scroll to the bottom of the playlist in that left pane. Because if there are any songs that won't fit on the CD, their checkmarks will be cleared and their Status column will read Will not fit. If that happens, you can clear the check mark next to your least-favorite song(s) in your playlist until all the selected (checked) songs show *Ready to burn*.

The right pane shows that an audio CD in CD drive E: is about to be burned. The *There are no items on the CD* and *80 minutes free* indicators let you know that the CD is empty and ready to burn.

The burning will start when you click the Start Burn button above the left column. Media Player will make two passes through the songs. On the first pass, it will convert each song to .cda format, as is required for standard music CDs. Those .cda files will be stored, temporarily, on your hard drive. On the second pass, it will copy each .cda song to the CD. When all the songs have been copied and the CD is ready to be removed, the Status column for each song will read *Ripped to Library*.

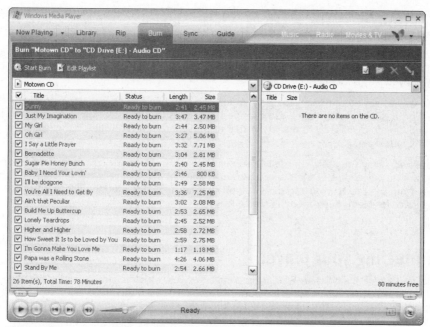

Figure 38-31: Custom playlist (left pane) and blank CD (right pane)

Copying Music to Portable Music Players

Portable music devices come in many shapes and sizes. Most people call them *MP3 players*. But in truth many can play songs in MP3 or WMA format. Some devices can play movies in WMV and MPEG formats. Some devices can hold a few songs. Others have built-in hard drives that can store thousands of songs as well as several feature-length movies. It all depends on what you buy.

Tip

For the latest in Media Player–compatible portable players, see www.microsoft.com/windows/windowsmedia/devices. If the page is no longer there by the time you read this, go to www.microsoft.com/windows/windowsmedia and click on (or search for) cool devices.

Whereas copying music to a blank CD is called *burning* a CD, we use the term *sync* when talking about copying media files to portable players. Not all players are the same. Some newer devices are 100 percent compatible with Windows Media Player, and can use its *autosync* feature. Some players are semicompatible, meaning you can sync files to them manually only. Some older players won't work with Media Player at all. Those you have to use the software that came with the player.

Removing Gaps between Tracks

Just as there are gaps between tracks (songs) when you play a CD, there are gaps between songs on a CD you create. Even classical CDs will put gaps between tracks, which may seem out of place when you play back the CD.

The best way to get rid of those gaps is to import the songs into Windows Movie Maker. Each track will be a clip in Movie Maker. You can then drag clips to the Audio/Movie track in Movie Maker, and drag tracks slightly to the left so that they overlap. You can listen to the overlap and tweak it to your liking.

When the tracks play smoothly, choose File > Save Movie from Movie Maker's menu bar. As long as there are no video clips in the project, Movie Maker will automatically create a single large .wma file from the project. You can them import that finished clip into Media Player using the Tools ⇨ Search for Media Files option in Media Player.

Connecting your player

Most modern MP3 players are *USB mass storage* devices, which means you stick the player into a USB port, and you're done. In your My Computer folder, the player is represented by an icon and drive letter. In the example shown in Figure 38-32, Removable Disk (G:) is actually a Creative Muvo portable music device. Opening that icon displays the songs currently on device as normal files in a normal folder.

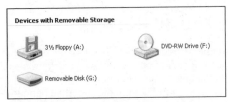

Figure 38-32: Removable disk (G:) is a portable music player.

The really isn't any need to use Media Player to copy unprotected songs to such devices. You can just open the icon for the device and treat the songs on it as normal files, using any technique descried in Chapter 14 to delete files from the device and copy songs to the device. You do need to use Media Player, however, to copy protected content to the player. With Media Player, you can also copy any custom playlist you create to the player with just a few mouse clicks.

Tip   You can also view the contents of a portable media player from Control Panel. In Category View, click on Sounds, Speech, and Audio Devices. Then, open the Portable Media Devices icon.

To use Media Player to sync songs to a portable player, just plug in the device while Media Player is open. Or, open Media Player after you plugged in the device. It really doesn't matter which. Everything you need is on the Sync tab, which you get to by clicking the Sync button in Media Player's Features taskbar.

When you click on sync in the feature taskbar, the main display area splits into two panes, just as when you burn CDs. The pane on the right shows songs that are already on the portable device (is any). You'll use the left pane to lists the songs you want to copy. Figure 38-33 shows an example where currently there's only a demo song named Create PDE Experience Demo.wma. The left pane is empty at the moment, so you can see the instructions that will appear to help you choose songs to sync to the device.

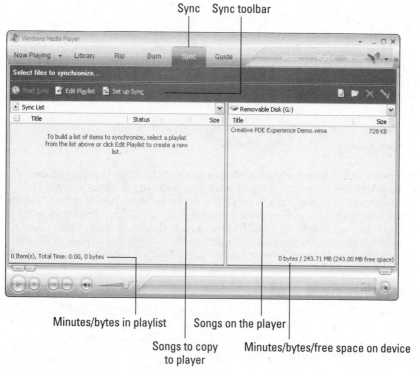

Figure 38-33: Sync tab in Features taskbar with portable music player connected

Autosync and manual sync

Players that support Windows Media Player 10 provide the option using autosync or manual sync. With autosync, songs are automatically copied to the device as you as you insert the device into a USB port. With manual sync, nothing is copied to the player automatically when you plug it into the computer. Instead, you can copy songs individually, or copy any custom playlist you've previously created. Both methods are really easy, so don't fret if your player doesn't support auto sync.

You can choose autosync or manual sync at any time, you're never committed to one method or the other. Just click Set Up Sync button in the Sync toolbar. The Synchronization Settings dialog box, shown in Figure 38-34 opens. If you want to use autosync, just select (check) the Synchronize device automatically checkbox. If you want to use manual sync, clear that checkbox.

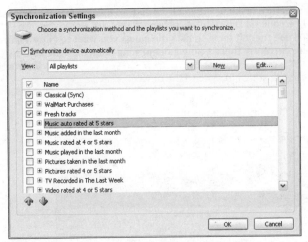

Figure 38-34: Synchronization Settings dialog box

If you do choose to use autosync, the playlist names and checkboxes will be enabled. You can scroll through the list of playlist names, and select (check) any playlists you want to autosync. Then, you can prioritize the playlists by ordering them. The first-listed selected playlist gets copied first. If there's still room on the player after that, the next selected playlist is copied next, and so on down the list. To move a playlist up or down in the list, just drag its name up or down. Optionally, click on a playlist's name to select it, and then use the up or down arrow buttons in the Synchronization Settings dialog box to move the selected playlist.

Player properties and settings

To get to properties and settings for your player, click the Display Properties and Settings button in the Sync toolbar. The Properties dialog box for the player opens (though it may just look like properties for a removable disk). Figure 38-35 shows the Synchronize (left) and Quality (right) tabs of that properties dialog box.

Some of the options, particularly those concerning putting folders on the device, are mainly for portable media players with large hard disks that can store and play video, recorded TV shows, and pictures. On a portable music player, you'll want to ignore those options unless you're certain your player can use folders. Going through the options on the Synchronize tab gives you:

✦ **Device name:** You can change this option to have the device name, rather than the generic Removable Drive, appear in the drop-down list above the right pane in Media Player.

✦ **Create folder hierarchy on device:** Choosing this option automatically creates a folder hierarchy of media files on larger portable media players.

✦ **Start synch when device connects:** Activates the autosync feature described earlier in this chapter so that content is copied to the player automatically on connection.

✦ **Settings:** Opens the Synchronization Settings dialog box shown in Figure 38-34.

✦ **Details:** Takes you to the Cool Devices page at the Windows Media Web site. There, you can learn about the latest players and technologies that Media Player 10 supports.

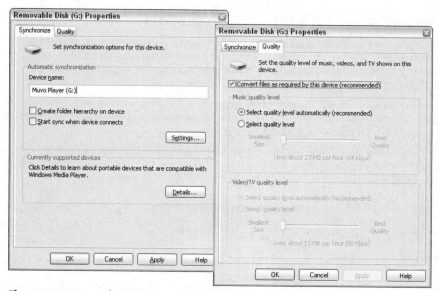

Figure 38-35: Sample Properties dialog box for a portable music player

There's always a trade-off between the quality (detail) of music and the number of bytes stored per song. On a portable player, you're limited to the storage capacity of the player. So, if you want to store lots of music on the device, you may have to settle for lower-quality settings. However, there's no objective way to say exactly where you'll even be able to hear a detectable difference. It all depends on your player, your headphones, and your own musical ear.

The Quality tab is the place to go to choose your settings. Your best bet would be to start with the recommended settings. If you can't get as much music as you'd like to on your player, or if the quality isn't what you'd hoped for, you can experiment with other settings. Here's what the various settings on the Quality tab mean:

✦ **Convert files as required by this device (recommended):** You should choose this option unless you're very familiar with all the details of your device. If you don't choose this option, and your player requires conversion, you may not be able to hear the music that you synched to the player.

✦ **Select quality level automatically (recommended):** Again, this is the best choice when you're first learning to use your player.

✦ **Select quality level:** Choosing this option enables the Smallest Size-Best Quality slider, so you can choose between putting lots of music at a low quality setting on the device or less music at a very high quality.

The Video/TV Quality Level options are disabled on a music device, because there is no screen on which you can watch video. But if have a portable media that supports video and recorded TV playback, you can adjust quality exactly as you would for music.

Creating playlists for portable players

Just as you can create custom playlists for CDs, you can create custom playlists for your portable player (see "Creating Custom Playlists" earlier in this chapter). Creating your own playlists is certainly a handy way to copy music to your device, because you can create all the playlists you want and copy any playlist to the device with just a couple of mouse clicks.

To choose a custom playlist you've previously created and named, just select the playlist's name from the drop-down list at the top of the left pane. All the songs from that playlist will be listed in the left pane, ready to copy to the device.

As an alternative to creating and saving custom playlists, you can click the Edit Playlist button in the Sync toolbar to create a playlist on the fly. When you click that button, the Edit Playlist dialog box shown in Figure 38-36 opens.

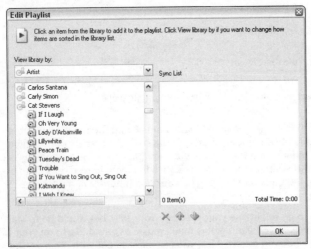

Figure 38-36: Edit Playlist dialog box for a Sync playlist

From the *View library by* drop-down list, choose how you want to organize music from your library in the left pane. For example, in Figure 38-36 I chose Artist, so the left pane shows an alphabetical list of artists' names. To view songs by any artist, click the artist's name. To add a song to the Sync list, just click the song title. Click OK after choosing all the songs you want to sync.

Deleting songs from the device

To delete a song from your portable device, just right-click its name and choose Delete from Device, as shown in Figure 38-37. You can select multiple items using any of the usual methods, such as Shift+Click, or click the first song and press Shift+End. Then, press the Delete (Del) key, or click the Delete (X) button in the Sync toolbar to delete all the selected songs.

It the player is a USB mass storage device, you can also delete the songs from the player's folder in My Computer.

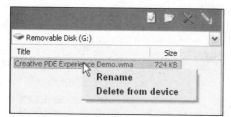

Figure 38-37: Right-click any song, and choose Delete from Device.

Synching the songs

Regardless of how you choose the songs you want to sync to your portable device, the song titles will be visible in the left pane, each with a checkbox to the left and the words *Ready to synchronize* in the Start column as in the example shown in Figure 38-38. When you're ready to copy, just click the Start Sync button in the Sync toolbar.

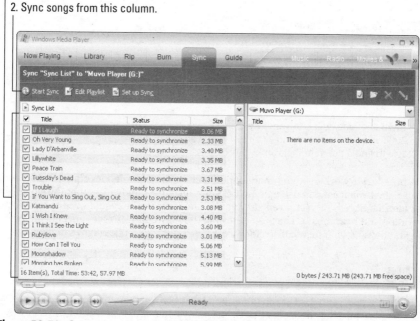

Figure 38-38: Songs to copy to portable player in the left column

When you're ready to start copying songs to your device, just click the Start Sync button in the Sync toolbar. It may take a few minutes to copy all the songs. Even longer with a large portable media player that can handle video and music.

After all the songs have been synched, take a look at the *MB free space* number near the lower-right corner of Media Player's program window. That tells you how much space you have left on the player to copy more songs. If you want to add a new more songs, choose any category name from the drop down list above the left column, and clear the check marks next to any songs that you don't want to copy. Then, click Start Sync to add those songs to the player.

When the right column lists the songs you want on the device, you can close Media Player and unplug the device from the computer. Plug your headphones into your portable device, and you're ready to go.

Listening to the Radio

Some of the online stores offer free radio content. Unlike traditional radio, where you're limited to radio stations within your broadcast range, radio stations that broadcast over the Internet have a global presence. So, you can listen to radio stations from all over the world.

Not all radio stations broadcast over the Internet. So, you won't know if your favorite radio station is available online until you look for it. To see if a an online store offers radio, use the *Choose online store* drop-down list to choose a store. If the store offers radio, you'll see a Radio button (see Figure 38-39) that you can click to see what the store offers.

Figure 38-39: Some online stores offer a Radio button

Note There's nothing built into Windows Media Player 10 that can capture content from the radio. But if you go to a site like www.tucows.com and search for capture radio, you may be able to find a program that can help with that.

Radio broadcasts work best on broadband DSL and cable Internet accounts. On a dial-up account, the broadcast will use up much of your available bandwidth, thereby slowing all other Internet access. In fact, even after you're chosen a station you'll need to wait to make a connection and hear music. The Stop button in the play controls disconnects you from a radio station. The volume control slider works as it does with other types of media.

Wrap Up

In this chapter, we've looked at the Windows Media Player 10 main music capabilities. As you've seen in this chapter, Media Player has many capabilities, and you have many options. The main points from this chapter include:

✦ Controlling sound volume on your computer is a necessary first step to playing music.

✦ The Features taskbar along the top of Media Player's program window provides easy access to all of its main components.

✦ The Now Playing tab shows a visualization of music that's playing or the visual content of the playing video or DVD.

✦ The Library button on the Features taskbar gives you access to all songs and other media you've downloaded or copied from CDs.

✦ The Rip button in the features button lets you copy songs from music CDs to your media library.

✦ The Burn button in the Features taskbar lets you burn your own custom music CDs.

✦ The Sync button in the Features taskbar lets you copy music to portable media devices.

✦   ✦   ✦

Watching DVD, Video, and More

There's much more to Windows Media Player than ripping and burning CDs. Media Player can play digital media stored on DVD, VCD, and HiMat disks. It can play media files (songs, videos, and Media Center recorded TV shows).

You can add music and video files you created or downloaded using programs to your Media Player library. You can even add pictures to your media library to make it easier to find specific pictures based on keywords and such. This chapter is about all those aspects of Media Player that go beyond using and creating music CDs.

Watching DVDs

As most of you probably know, DVD is a storage medium similar to CD, the main difference being that a single DVD holds about 4.7 GB while a CD holds between 650 and 700 MB. This means that a single DVD stores the equivalent of about seven CDs. That's why music is distributed on CD, and movies are distributed on DVD. There's isn't enough room on a CD to store a feature-length movie at a decent quality.

To watch DVDs on your computer, you need a DVD drive and a DVD decoder that's compatible with Windows Media Player. If your computer came with a DVD drive already installed, the computer manufacturer has probably installed a decoder already. Whether or not that decoder is compatible with Media Player 10 is something you'll find out the moment you try to watch a DVD.

Playing a DVD

To play a DVD, put the disk into the drive and wait a few seconds. If the disk doesn't start playing automatically, start Windows Media Player. Likewise, if some program other than Windows Media Player opens, close that program. Then, start Windows Media Player. Once you're in Windows Media Player, and the VCD or DVD is in the drive, choose Play ⇨ DVD, VCD, or CD Audio from the menu.

If you see the message shown in Figure 39-1, you don't have an appropriate decoder. You can buy and download a Media Player 10 compatible decoder as discussed next. If the DVD does start playing, you can skip the next section and go straight to "Controlling DVD Play" after that section.

Figure 39-1: You need a decoder to play DVDs.

Getting a DVD decoder

If you need to purchase and install a DVD decoder, choose Tools ➪ Plug Ins ➪ Download Plug Ins from Media Player's menu. You'll come to a Web page that sells several different kinds of plug-ins for Media Player. Here you're only interested in DVD Decoder Plug-ins.

Unfortunately, there are no freebies available for download. When choosing a decoder, make sure that you don't pick one that's incompatible with Windows Media Player 10. By the time you read this, they may all be compatible with version 10. I only mention it because when I went to get one, only two of the three products offered were compatible with Media Player 10.

After you choose your product, just follow the on-screen instructions to pay your dues and install the decoder.

Note   Windows has no built-in capabilities for copying from DVDs. Some third-party products that offered that capability have already been outlawed.

Controlling DVD play

To see the DVD movie, first click the Now Playing tab in the features taskbar to see the video playback. The playlist panel will show titles and chapters on the disk. Each title refers to a major section of the disk. Some titles will be further divided into chapters.

To start playing the movie, click whichever option on the movie's main menu starts the movie. This part can be a little tricky because sometime clicking on the wording of a menu option isn't sufficient. You may have to click on the little highlighter that appears next to the menu option after you click the option. Watch for the mouse pointer to change from an arrow to a pointing hand to know when the mouse pointer is on the hotspot.

The play controls at the bottom of Media Player's program window work like the controls on a standard DVD player or VCR. For example, you can click the Pause button to pause playback, click the Play button to resume playback. Use the volume slider to adjust the sound of the movie.

Choosing the screen size

As your movie is playing or paused, right-click on the movie image. You'll see a shortcut menu titled Show Video as in the example shown in Figure 39-2. Like a picture, every video has certain predefined dimensions, such as 640×480. The first two options on the shortcut menu let you set defaults for how Media Player reacts when you change the dimensions of the playback or when you resize the program window as follows:

Figure 39-2: A DVD movie playing and the shortcut menu

✦ **Fit Video to Player on Resize:** If selected, this option prevents Media Player from cropping the movie when the size of the video is larger than the program window. When you resize the program window to smaller than the dimensions of the video, the movie is resized as well.

✦ **Fit Player to Video on Start:** If selected, Windows Media Player automatically resizes its own program window to avoid cropping out a portion of the movie when you first start playing a DVD movie or video.

The recommended setting for the preceding options is to leave both on (checked). Options lower on the menu size the visible video image as a percentage of the movies actual dimensions:

✦ **50%:** Plays the movie at half its actual size.

✦ **100%:** Plays the movie at actual size.

✦ **200%:** Doubles the size of the movie. You'd more likely use this option for small video clips than a DVD movie.

✦ **Full Screen:** Expands the movie to full-screen size. Player controls will appear briefly, then fade away.

To quickly switch between full screen mode and the player window, press Alt+Enter.

Using DVD features

At the bottom of the Show Video shortcut menu, the DVD Features option provides easy access to features that are unique to DVD movies. The options available to you depend on the capabilities of your DVD drive. Options that aren't relevant to your drive will be disabled (dimmed). In general, though, you'll find the following options:

✦ **Root Menu:** Choosing this option takes you to the highest-level menu that the current DVD offers.

✦ **Title Menu:** This option takes you to what's typically considered a DVD movie's main menu.

✦ **Close Menu (Resume):** If you got to the root or title menu from either of the preceding options, choosing this option will take you right back to where you left off.

Tip   The Menu and Close Menu (Resume) options in the toolbar just above the playing movie play the same roles as the Root Menu and Close Menu options on the DVD Features menu.

✦ **Back:** If the DVD you're watching contains Internet links, and you click one of those links, choosing Back will take you back to where you were prior to clicking the link.

✦ **Camera Angle:** Though rare, this option allows you to change the camera angle on the DVD movie you're currently watching.

✦ **Update DVD Information:** If the DVD you're viewing has media information on the Internet, clicking this option will update current media information with media information form the Web.

Using captions and subtitles

Some (but not all) DVD movies offer captions and subtitles. You can turn these options on or off from the DVD's main menu or from the Play menu in Media Player. If the menu is visible, choose Play from the menu bar. Otherwise, click the Access Application Menus button, choose Play, and point to Captions and Subtitles as in Figure 39-3.

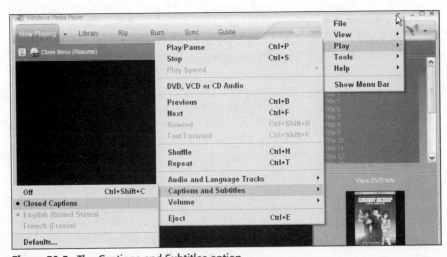

Figure 39-3: The Captions and Subtitles option

You can choose either captions or subtitles (if the DVD you're watching supports both), but you cannot display both at the same time. The difference is that subtitles appear right on the video, as in traditional subtitled movies. Captions appear in a line beneath the playing video.

Choosing DVD audio and language tracks

Some DVDs offer multiple audio and language tracks, so you can listen to the movie in any of several languages. If the DVD you're watching offers this feature, choose Audio and Language Tracks from the Play menu shown in Figure 39-3. Then, click on the language of your choice.

Setting language defaults

Most DVDs are set up to play in a specific language by default. You can change the default language for any DVD you insert into your DVD drive by following these steps:

1. Choose **Tools** ➪ **Options** from Media Player's menu.

2. In the Options dialog box, click the **DVD** tab.

3. Click the **Defaults** button.

4. Choose a default language for audio, captions and subtitles, and the DVD menus from the Default Language Settings dialog box shown in Figure 39-4.

5. Click **OK** in each open dialog box.

Figure 39-4: The Default Language Options dialog box

When you've finished watching a DVD, click the Stop button in the play controls. To eject the CD from the drive, choose Play ➪ Eject, or press Ctrl+E, or press the Eject button on your DVD drive.

Tip   To prevent your screen saver from clicking in while watching a video, choose Tools ➪ Options from Media Player's menu. Make sure the *Allow screen saver during playback* option is disabled (unchecked), and click OK.

Playing VCDs

A VCD (Video CD) is a CD-ROM disk that contains video in much the same way a DVD does. However, you don't need a DVD drive to play a VCD, and CD-ROM drive will do. A CD can only hold about ½ the amount of information that a DVD can, so you're not likely to find any feature-length movies stored on VCDs. The amount of compression required would make for a low-quality presentation.

Most VCDs are home-made, and few even have menus. Typically, when you insert a VCD into your CD drive, Windows Media Player opens automatically and plays the whole video through. You can also play a VCD by putting it in your CD drive and choosing Play ⇨ DVD, VCD, or CD Audio from Media Player's menu. If the VCD contains multiple tracks, you'll see each track represented in the playlist pane, as in the example shown in Figure 39-5. To play a single track from a VCD, double-click the track's name or right-click it and choose Play.

Figure 39-5: Playing a VCD in Media Player 10

Creating VCDs

Windows Movie Maker lets you copy movies you create to CDs. But the resulting disk isn't a VCD — it's a High-MAT CD, which is different. If you want to create your own VCDs, you'll need to use a third-party program such as Sonic's My DVD (www.sonic.com).

Copying VCDs

Like commercial audio CDs and DVDs, VCDs aren't like computer disks with data organized into normal files. When you view the contents of a VCD in Windows Explorer, you'll probably just see folders named CDI, EXT, MPEGAV, SEGMENT, VCD, and perhaps others. None of the files within those folders is a video file that you can copy to your hard disk and use in a normal manner. But, you can usually make additional CD copies of any VCD by following the steps below:

1. In your My Documents folder (or any folder you like), create a new folder and name it whatever you like (for example Copied VCD).

2. Open the new folder and size it to about ⅓ the screen (right-click the clock and choose Cascade Windows).

3. Insert the VCD you want to copy into your CD drive. If a program opens to play the VCD, close that program.

4. Open your My Computer folder, right-click the icon for your CD drive, and choose Open.

5. Select all the folders and files from the VCD and drag them to the Copied VCD folder so that the folder contains exactly the same contents as the VCD.

6. Remove the VCD disk from the CD drive, and insert a blank CD-R or CD-RW.

Note Any computer with a CD drive can play a VCD that you burned to a CD-R. But only computers with CD-RW drives can play VCDs stored on CD-RWs.

7. Select all the files and folders in the Copied VCD folder and drag them to the empty folder for the CD drive.

8. Click on **Write these files to CD** under CD Writing Tasks, and follow the wizard instructions to copy all the files to the blank CD.

To make more copies, repeat Steps 6 to 8. When you've finished making your copies, you can delete the Copied VCD folder.

Tip Options for sizing the video on the screen, as discussed in the section on DVD at the top of this chapter, apply to all forms of video: DVD, VCD, HighMAT, and video files.

Playing HighMAT CDs

HighMAT (High Performance Media Access Technology) is a new technology designed to extend the relationships among the PC and consumer electronic devices such as car stereos, DVD players, and CD players. The consumer electronics industry is still playing catch-up in this arena. But Windows Media Player 10 and Movie Maker 2 both offer considerable support for High-MAT.

For example, when you save a Movie Maker 2.1 movie to a CD-R or CD-RW, you automatically create a HighMAT CD. Anyone who owns Media Player 10 can watch that CD on their computer. The steps are the same for other media discussed in this chapter. Put the HighMAT CD into the drive. If it doesn't start playing automatically, open Windows Media Player and choose Play ⇨ DVD, VCD, or CD Audio.

Tip See www.microsoft.com/windows/windowsmedia/consumerelectronics for more information on HighMAT.

Playing Media files

CD and DVD aren't the only media for storing audio and video. Not by a long shot. There are lots of PC file types that can store audio and video on your hard disk. Some of those file types such as Apple Quicktime (.qt, .mov), RealAudio and RealVideo (.ra, .ram, .rm, .rmm) can only be played by the producer's players. Windows Media Player 10 can play most of the nonproprietary formats. Table 39-1 lists the supported file types and the filename extensions commonly used to identify each type of file.

Table 39-1: Music and Video File Formats Supported by Media Player 10

File Format	Extensions
Audio formats	
AIIF audio (Audio Interchange File Format)	.aif, .aifc, .aiff
AU (audio)	.au, .snd
Compact disk audio	.cda
MIDI (Musical Instrument Digital Interface)	.mid, .midi, .rmi
MP3	.mp3, .m3u
Windows audio file	.wav
Windows Media Audio	.wma, .wax
Video formats	
Audio-Video Interleave	.avi*
Microsoft Recorded TV	.dvr-ms
MPEG (Moving Picture Experts Group)	.mpa, .mpe, .mpeg, .mpg, .m1v, .mp2, .mpv2, .mp2v**
Windows Media File and Advanced Streaming Format	.asf, asx, .wm, .wmd, wmx, .wmz. .wpl
Windows Media Video	.wmv, .wmx

* DivX-compressed .avi files require a DivX codec, which won't download automatically. See www.divx.com for details and the codec.

**MPEG2 files require a DVD decoder. See "Getting a DVD decoder" earlier in this chapter.

Even if Windows Media Player is closed, you can play any of the file types right from Windows Explorer. If Media Player is the default program for the file type, just double-click (or click) the file's icon, as you would any other document's icon. If some other program is the default program for that file type, right-click the document icon and choose Open With ➪ Windows Media Player.

Making Media Player the default for media files

Any time you double-click (or click) a document icon, the document opens in whatever is currently defined as the default program for that file type. You can always override the default program by right-clicking the document icon and choosing Open With. To make Windows Media Player the default program for any or all of the file types it supports, follow these steps:

1. Open Windows Media Player if it's not already open.

2. Choose **Tools** > **Options** from Media Player's menu.

3. In the Options dialog box that opens, click the **File Types** tab, as in Figure 39-6.

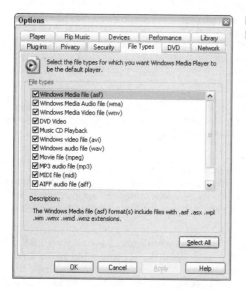

Figure 39-6: File Types tab in the Media Player Options dialog box

4. Make your choices as follows:

   • Choose (check) the file types for which you want to make Media Player the default program.

   • Or, click **Select All** to make Media Player the default for all of its supported file types.

   • Clear the check mark for any file type for which you don't want Media Player to be the default.

5. Click **OK**.

Don't forget that once you open a file, you need to click the Now Playing tab in the features taskbar to view video or a visualization of music.

Note   The File Types dialog box applies on to situations where you actually double-click a media file's document icon. What happens after you insert a CD or DVD into a drive is determined by the AutoPlay properties of the drive, as discussed under "Setting Defaults for CDs and DVDs" in Chapter 15.

Why Defaults Get "Unset"

Occasionally, you'll come across a program that makes itself the default player for certain types of files. Freebie versions of program that come preinstalled on some computers are the usual culprits here. It's very irritating and, in my book (no pun intended), grounds for immediate removal from my system. If you like the program that's causing the problem and don't want to remove it, upgrading to the non-freebie version should solve the problem.

Bringing Media Library up to date

If you copied or downloaded music or videos to your computer prior to running Media Player, there's a good chance that none of those titles will show up in Media Library. The includes songs you download using Peer-2-Peer (P2P) a program like LimeWire, Morpheus, or Kazaa.

Likewise, if you add more media files to your hard disk using other programs, these may not show up in Media Player either. You can make Media Player scan your hard drive(s), or just selected folders, to create links to other media files that are already on a hard drive in your system.

The reason I say "links" is because Media Player is a program, and every media file — including every song you rip from a CD — is a document. Programs never "store" documents. Documents are stored in folders. Media Player only contains *metadata* — a fancy term form that textual media information you see when you click on Library in Media Player's features taskbar.

But anyway, to add music, video files, and pictures that you already have on your hard drive to Media Player's library, you just have to tell it scan the disk for compatible media files. You can limit the scan to specific folders if you like, so you don't end up with every single little sound effect file in your media library. Or, you can scan an entire hard drive. The choice is up to you. Either way, the steps are the same:

1. Open Windows Media Player (if it isn't open already).

2. Choose **Tools ➪ Search for Media Files** from its menu, or press the F3 key on your keyboard. The Add to Library by Searching Computer dialog box, shown in Figure 39-7, opens.

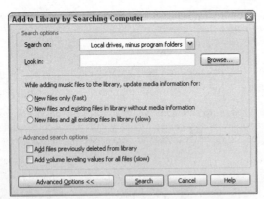

Figure 39-7: Add to Library by Searching Computer dialog box

3. From the Search on drop-down list, choose how broad an area you want to search.

The default setting shown in the figure searches all your hard drives, but ignores program folders which might contain little sound effects files and the like that you probably don't want in your library anyway. You can extend that to all folders in all drives, narrow it to a specific drive or folder, or choose <User-selected search path> to narrow the search down to a single folder of your own choosing.

4. If you chose <User-selected search path>, use the **Browse** button to choose the folder you want to search. All subfolders within that folder will be included in the search.

5. Choose from one of the following options (note that these options apply only to music files, not videos or pictures):

   - **New files only (fast):** Ignores any file that's already in your media library, which helps speed things along.

   - **New files and existing files in library without media information:** Ignores files that are already in your media library, unless that existing file is missing information. In that case, the search will try to fill in missing media information for you.

   - **New files and all existing files in library (slow):** Ignores no files and updates media information in all files, even those that are already in your media library.

6. Optionally, choose from the following Advanced Options:

   - **Add files previously deleted from library:** If you've already deleted some files form your library, but didn't opt to remove them from your hard disk at the time, choosing this option will put those deleted files back in. This is useful if you have previously deleted the files from your library, then moved the files to another drive or folder, and now want to readd them from their new location.

   - **Add volume leveling values for all files (slow):** Volume leveling helps all sound files play at a consistent volume. However, you can do that on the fly when you burn CDs. Doing it at this stage will take a lot of time!

7. Click the **Search** button, wait for the search to complete, and then click **Close**.

Now you can go see what your search uncovered. Click the Library button in the Features taskbar. Check out any major category or subcategory. For example, if you picked up any video files, their names will be listed in the contents pane when you click on All Video. If you picked up any pictures, their names will show when you click on All Pictures. Any new songs you picked up will be categorized under My Music.

When you expand a major category or subcategory, there may items in "Unknown" categories, especially for pictures and videos. That's because there is no online resource for media information about your own videos and pictures. I'll talk about ways to update that information under "Organizing Media Files" later in this chapter.

Watching videos in your library

Videos added to your library will all be listed in the details pane when you click on All Videos in the library contents pane, as in the example shown in Figure 39-8. The videos will include supported file types that you've captured from a home video camera, movies you've created with Windows Movie Maker or other video-editing software, Photo Story slide shows created Plus! Digital Media Edition, and videos you've downloaded from the Web.

To watch a video, double-click its title in the details pane. You'll be taken to Now Playing automatically. There, you can use the play controls at the bottom of the program window to stop, rewind, pause, play, rewind, and fast forward the video, as well as to control the volume.

To size the video image, right-click the playing video and choose a size from the shortcut menu that opens. To stop a video and return to the library, click the Stop button in the play controls. Then, click the Library button in the features taskbar again. In the library, you can change or fill in missing Actors and Genre media information using any of the techniques described under "Manually Editing Media Information" in Chapter 38.

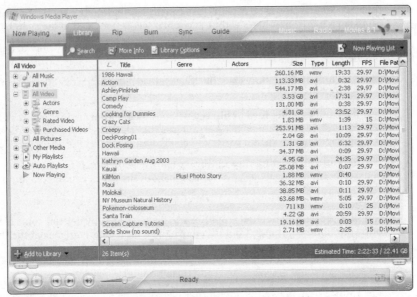

Figure 39-8: Some videos added to All Videos in my media library

Viewing recorded TV shows

If you have Windows Media Center and use it to record TV, you can also import the recorded TV shows (.dvr-ms files) into your media library. Since this is a book about XP, not Media Center, I won't get into how all that works. Suffice it to say that recorded TV shows will be in the All TV category, categorized by Series, Genre, and other attributes. Double-clicking the name of any recorded TV show will play the show in Windows Media Player.

Viewing pictures in your library

You can add all your still photos to you media library. Of course, you don't need a program like Media Player to work with pictures, since there are plenty of other ways to work with pictures. For example, the Thumbnails and Filmstrip Views, and Picture Tasks options in Windows Explorer provide lots of ways to work with pictures. To edit pictures, you need some sort of graphics editing program—Media Player won't help with any of that.

Pictures in Media Library don't behave like digital media. The different summary properties offered by different picture file types can make things really confusing, unless all the pictures come from a single digital camera. The whole experience of working with still pictures in Media Player can drive you batty if you're expecting pictures to be treated the same as music and video.

There are a few advantages to importing pictures into Media Player though. For one thing, you can create playlists of pictures. Then, you can watch any playlist as a slide show. If you have a portable media player that can store pictures, you can copy selected pictures to that device as well.

Tip   If you want to create slideshows of photos, to which you can add background music and narration, consider purchasing a program like Microsoft Plus! Digital Media Edition. Slide shows you create using its Photo Story feature can be viewed on any Windows PC.

Media Center, Portable Media Players, and Synching

Portable Media Players are similar to MP3 players, except that they have a screen on which you can watch video. They also have a hard drive capable of storing 20 GB to 40 GB of data, which is about what you need to store video. For more information on portable media players, see the Cool Devices page at the Windows Media Web (www.microsoft.com/windows/windowsmedia/devices/).

Windows XP Media Center Edition is a version of Windows with added support for managing multimedia, including the ability to record TV shows. For more information on Media Center, see www.microsoft.com/windowsxp/mediacenter. For details on synching Media Player content to portable media players, see the Try It! videos at www.microsoft.com/windows/windowsmedia/knowledgecenter/videos.aspx.

Pictures you add to your media library will be in the All Pictures category. To see an individual picture, click on More Info, and then click on the picture you want to view. Figure 39-9 shows an example with All Pictures category selected in the contents pane, and a single picture selected in the details pane.

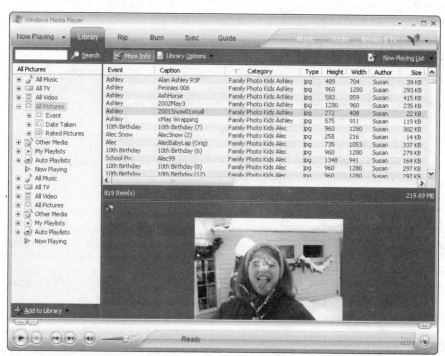

Figure 39-9: All Pictures category lists all pictures; the selected picture is visible in bottom pane.

Tip   If you don't see All Pictures as a category in Media Player, choose Tools ➪ Options form Media Player's menu. Select (check) the "Enable picture support for devices" option, and click OK. If you still don't see an All Pictures category, close and reopen Media Player.

Subcategories under the All Pictures category include Event, Date Taken, and Rates Pictures. The Event subcategories reflect the names of the folders in which the pictures are stored. The Date Taken subcategory breaks down into years and months. Column headings act as they do for other media. Right-click any column heading to choose columns. Click any column heading to sort on that column.

To see a slide show of all the pictures in your library, right-click the All Pictures category name and choose Play. You'll be taken to Now Playing, where each picture will appear in the video and visualization pane for a few seconds. You can size the screen as you would with video, by right-clicking on the picture you're currently viewing and choosing a size from the shortcut menu that appears. To stop the slide show, click the Stop button in the play controls. Click in the Features taskbar in the Library to return to the library.

You can create playlists of pictures in the same way you create playlists of songs. You can also create auto-playlists using the same techniques as for songs. You just have to choose *Pictures in my library* under *And also include* in the Edit Auto Playlist dialog box. After you do, you'll see *Click here to add criteria* under *Pictures in my library*. Clicking that option will allow you to specify criteria that are unique to pictures, such as Date Taken and Year Taken.

To open the folder in which a picture is stored, right-click the picture's row in the details pane and choose Open Containing Folder. Once you're in the folder, you can select pictures and change summary properties for pictures. Most of the media information for pictures comes from the picture summary properties. The Organizing Media Files section later in this chapter explains how to get to, and change, file summary properties.

Searching your library

The Search box in the toolbar above the contents pane in the library searches the library for any word or phrase you enter. Just type any word or phrase into the search box and click the Search button. All media items that have the word or phrase in their media information will be listed in a temporary playlist named Search Results.

To create a new playlist from the search results, follow the usual procedure as described in Chapter 38. Right-click My Playlists, and choose New. Then, click on Search Results in the contents pane, and drag any or all songs from the details pane to the new playlist.

Organizing Media Files

Windows Media Player is a program, not a folder. Every song, video, and picture that shows up in you Media Player library is a document. As such, none of the items you see in your media library are actually "stored in" Media Player. Each item that you see in your library is a file stored in a folder. When you're in the library, the File Path column shows the full path to every file in the library. Right-clicking an item in the library and choosing Open Containing Folder opens the folder in which the item is contained.

Much of the media information you see in Media Player's library comes from the files' summary properties. When you're in Windows Explorer, rather than Media Player, you can see a file's summary properties by following these steps:

1. Right-click the document's icon, and choose **Properties**.

2. Click the **Summary** tab.

Wacky Picture Properties

The correlation between media information for pictures in Media Player and file summary properties is often wacky. For example, on my camera the Caption column gets its information from the Title summary property, the Category column from the Keywords summary property. But the Author and Subject columns are as one would expect.

Also, when you change summary properties for pictures, that change isn't automatically reflected in Media Player. You have to delete the items from the library (without deleting them from your hard disk). Then, you need to add the pictures again with the *Add files previously deleted from library"* option selected in the Add to Library by Searching Computer dialog box.

There are two ways to view summary properties. The Simple View shows only a few of the summary properties. The Advanced View shows all of the properties, and also lets you edit those properties. Summary properties vary widely among the different document file types. For example, songs have summary properties such as Artist and Title. Pictures have properties like Keywords and Date Picture Taken. A .avi video file might have only a Duration property. A .wma video file might have, into addition to Duration, summary properties named Width, Height, Title, Comments, and Protected, among others.

You can use the Simple View, shown at the left of Figure 3-10, or the Advanced view, shown in the right side of the same figure. The Simple View shows only the most basic information. The Advanced View shows all the summary properties, and also lets you change those properties.

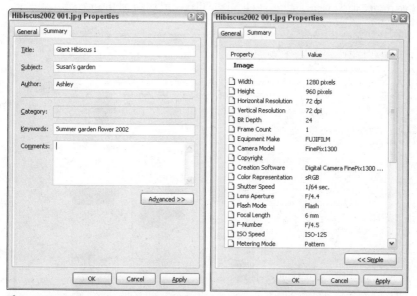

Figure 39-10: Sample summary properties in Simple and Advanced Views

You can change the summary properties for multiple files by selecting the icons of those files first, using any technique described in Chapter 14. But be aware that if you select multiple file types, the summary properties available to you will only be those that all the files have in common. For example, if you select multiple video files@mdsome of which are .wmv, some MPEGs, and some AVI—you might not get any summary properties because those file types don't offer any similar summary properties. You'd need to select just the .wmv files, change their summary properties, and then select just the MPEGs and change their properties.

Also, you need to understand that many summary properties are purely factual information that cannot be changed. For example, the Height, Width, Bit Depth, and many other numeric properties are facts about the picture that cannot be changed through summary properties.

Most of the information you see in Media Player's library comes from the summary properties. If you change the summary properties for files that are already in the library, that change carries over to the media information in the library. The reverse isn't true though. Changes you make to media information in Media Player don't carry over to the file's summary properties.

Viewing and changing summary properties

As you know, when you rip a CD, Media Player gets song titles and some other information about the CD from the Internet. It actually stores that information in each song's summary properties. Media Player, in turn, picks up that information from the summary properties. You can see how it works by opening the folder (in Windows Explorer) in which you've ripped your CD and drilling down to specific songs.

As an example, I set my Media Player Rip options to store all ripped CDs in my D:\Music folder. When I navigate to the folder in Windows Explorer, I see a folder for each artist for whom I've ripped a CD, as in Figure 39-11. Media Player created all the folders.

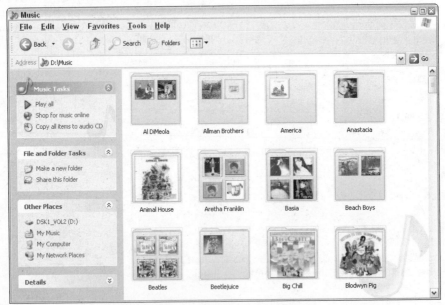

Figure 39-11: Contents of my D:\Music folder to which I rip CDs

When you open a folder for an artist, you'll see that the folder contains a subfolder for each CD by that artist that you've previously ripped. For example, Figure 39-12 shows the contents of my Basia folder. It contains four subfolders — one for each Basia CD I've ripped. The album cover pictures are called *album art* and are downloaded along with song titles when you rip a CD. Those are visible only in Thumbnails View.

Basia
File Edit View Favorites Tools Help
Back
Search
Folders
Address D:\Music\Basia
Go
Music Tasks
Play all
Shop for music online
Copy all items to audio CD
File and Folder Tasks
Make a new folder
Share this folder
Other Places
Music
Time & Tide
Sweetest Illusion
London Warsaw New York
Brave New Hope

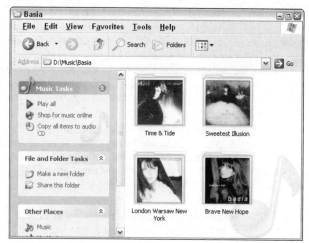

Figure 39-12: Contents of my D:\Music\Basia folder

Opening the folder for an album displays a document icon for each song on that album. For example, in Figure 39-13 I've opened the folder for the `D:\Basia\Time and & Tide` folder. Each icon there represents a song from Basia's Time & Tide CD. There I've switched to Details view and have chosen to view the Title, Genre, Protected, and other columns you see there using the Choose Columns capabilities of Details view.

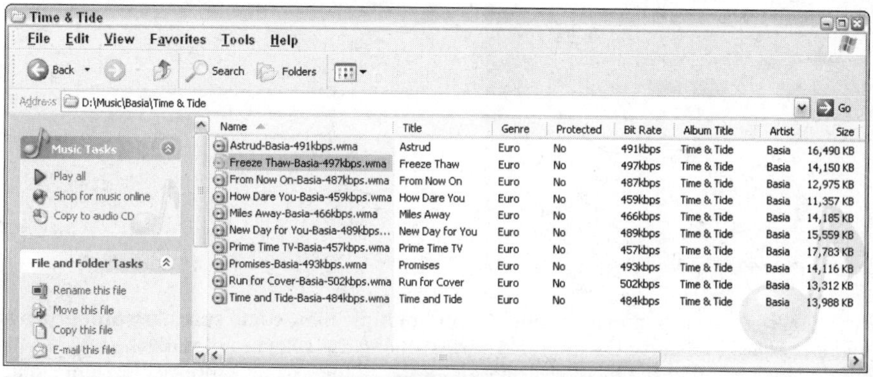

Time & Tide
File Edit View Favorites Tools Help
Back
Search
Folders
Address D:\Music\Basia\Time & Tide
Go
Music Tasks
Play all
Shop for music online
Copy to audio CD
File and Folder Tasks
Rename this file
Move this file
Copy this file
E-mail this file
Name Title Genre Protected Bit Rate Album Title Artist Size
Astrud-Basia-491kbps.wma Astrud Euro No 491kbps Time & Tide Basia 16,490 KB
Freeze Thaw-Basia-497kbps.wma Freeze Thaw Euro No 497kbps Time & Tide Basia 14,150 KB
From Now On-Basia-487kbps.wma From Now On Euro No 487kbps Time & Tide Basia 12,975 KB
How Dare You-Basia-459kbps.wma How Dare You Euro No 459kbps Time & Tide Basia 11,357 KB
Miles Away-Basia-466kbps.wma Miles Away Euro No 466kbps Time & Tide Basia 14,185 KB
New Day for You-Basia-489kbps... New Day for You Euro No 489kbps Time & Tide Basia 15,559 KB
Prime Time TV-Basia-457kbps.wma Prime Time TV Euro No 457kbps Time & Tide Basia 17,783 KB
Promises-Basia-493kbps.wma Promises Euro No 493kbps Time & Tide Basia 14,116 KB
Run for Cover-Basia-502kbps.wma Run for Cover Euro No 502kbps Time & Tide Basia 13,312 KB
Time and Tide-Basia-484kbps.wma Time and Tide Euro No 484kbps Time & Tide Basia 13,988 KB

Figure 39-13: Contents of my D:\Music\Basia\Time & Tide folder

Details View and Folder Templates

In this section, I'm (obviously) assuming that you're familiar with Windows Explorer. If I lost you in this passage, see "Umpteen ways to view icons" in Chapter 3 for the scoop on Explorer views and choosing columns for Details View. Remember, in this passage I'm talking about Windows Explorer. Windows Media Player is out of the picture in this section of the chapter.

The reason that Music Tasks shows up in the Explorer bar is that I right-clicked my `D:\Music` folder's icon and set its folder template to *Music (best for audio files and playlists)*. Before clicking OK on that step, I chose the *Also apply this template to all subfolders* option before clicking OK there too. The section titled "Personalizing Your Folders" in Chapter 13 explains how all that folder template stuff works.

Now, suppose I wanted to change summary properties for all the songs in the `D:\Basia\ Time & Tide` folder. They're all the same file type, so it would be easy. Just select all the file-names in the folder (press Ctrl+A), right-click any selected filename, and choose Properties. Click the Summary tab, click the <<Advanced button if necessary, and there are all the properties for all the songs in that Time & Tide folder, as in Figure 39-14.

Figure 39-14: Summary properties of all files in my D:\Music\Basia\Time & Tide folder

When you're viewing summary properties for multiple files, some summary properties show *(multiple values)* because the contents varies among the selected files. Each song has its own unique Track Number, Title, and Duration. But the Album Artist, Album Title, Genre, and Protected properties are all the same. Changing any of those properties here will change the properties in all of the selected files, and in Media Player as well.

So, the point is the songs, videos, and pictures you see listed in Media Player aren't actually "in" Media Player. They're just normal document files. The Media Player library isn't a collection of "files" per se, but rather a collection of information *about* files. Sort of like the index at the back of a book. The index at the back of a book lists words, followed by the page number where that topic can be found. Media Player's library also shows words, but refers to specific documents by their paths. Media Player doesn't build the index every time it opens. Instead, it t creates, stores, and reuses its own index.

Changing summary properties across folders

In Media Player, if you wanted to see all songs by an artist, you would just click the artist's name under Contributing Artists. In Windows Explorer it's not so easy. But it's not terribly difficult either. Here are the steps, using my own D:\Music folder as an example:

1. In Windows Explorer, go to the parent folder of the folders whose contents you want to view. For example, if I want to see all the songs in my D:\Music Folder, I open my D:\Music Folder as in Figure 39-11.

2. Click the **Search** button in Explorer's toolbar to open the Search Companion.

3. In the Search Companion, click on **Pictures, music, or video**.

4. On the next page of the Search Companion, choose the type of files you want to view, for example **Music** to view songs or **Video** to view video files.

5. Click on **Use advanced search options**. The Look In option should already be set to the name of the current folder, so there's no need to change anything there.

6. Click on **More advanced options**.

7. Choose only **Search subfolders** and leave the other options unchecked, as in Figure 39-15.

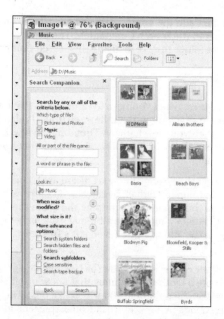

Figure 39-15: About to search all of D:\Music for music files

8. Click the **Search** button, and wait for the search to complete.

When the search is finished click *Yes, finished searching*. Now you can treat the Search Results folder as you would any other. Switch views using the View menu or Views button. Figure 39-16 shows all the files from all the subfolders in my D:\Music folder, just as a general example.

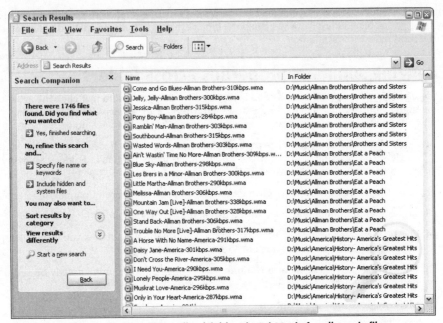

Figure 39-16: Result of searching all subfolders in D:\Music for all music files

If you wanted to further limit the search, just add the appropriate criterion. For example, add *.mp3 to the *All or part of filename* text box in the Search Companion. The point is, you can get to any group of files, regardless of what folder they're in, using the Search Companion.

Finding missing album art

As you saw in a couple of the preceding figures, when you rip a CD and Media Player downloads media information from the Internet, it grabs more than the song titles. It also grabs a copy of the album art, and displays that when you view icons in Thumbnails View. But, the Internet doesn't have every picture for every album ever published, so sometimes you get a generic cover art picture, or no picture at all.

If you don't get the album art for a CD, or get the wrong album art, there are a couple of ways you may be able to fix that problem. One is to open Media Player, click on Library, expand the All Music and Album categories, and locate the album that's missing the art in the list of album titles. Or, expand the Album Artist category, locate the album artist's name, and expand that subcategory, and then click on the album's title (even if it's Unknown) under the Artist name.

Either way, once you have the mouse pointer on the album title (or Unknown), right-click that album title and choose Find Media Info. Take a look at the albums that show up (if any). Then, just click the appropriate album cover, or whichever album cover you like best. Go back to the folder where the album art is missing, choose View ➪ Refresh from Explorer's menu, and you should see the album art when in Thumbnails View.

If that doesn't work, you may be able to find the album art through a more general Internet search. First, close Media Player because it's out of the picture at this point. In Windows Explorer, navigate to the folder that's missing the album art, and then open that folder.

Choose the Thumbnails View, and leave the folder open because you're going to find a picture to use for album art and put it in that folder.

Tip The Plus! MP3 Audio Converter LE plug-in has some tools that can make it a bit easier to find album art. See the section on plug-ins later in this chapter for more information.

Open up your Web browser, and try to find a picture of the album cover. You might start by going to www.gracenote.com and searching the CDDB for the artist name. In the search results, click on the album name, or any album name by that artist. look for a picture of the album anywhere on the page. Or, you might try searching Amazon.com or even Google. Any Web site that might have a picture of the album cover.

When you find a small picture of the album cover (or at least some album cover you like), right-click that picture and choose Copy. Then, right-click some empty space near a song within the folder that's missing the album art and choose Paste. The file will probably have a weird filename. You need to rename the file to folder.jpg. Click the Up button in Explorer's toolbar so that you can see the folder's icon again. It should now show whatever picture you pasted into the folder.

Caution The picture you download must be a JPEG and must be named folder.jpg. If filename extensions are hidden, you may want to unhide them to make sure that you get the right picture type.

Making MP3 and .wma CDs

Now that we've been outside of Media Player for a while and in Windows Explorer, I suppose this would be a good time to talk about creating a .wma or MP3 CD. First, you need to understand that standard commercial CDs that play in normal stereos all store music in .cda format. The same is true of custom CDs you create in Media Player, because if it weren't, the custom CDs wouldn't play in normal stereos and CD players.

But there are many CD players that can play songs stored in MP3 or .wma (or both) formats. Of course, any computer can play CDs that have songs stored in MP3 and .wma format too. If you want to create a CD with songs stored in .wma or MP3 format, you don't use Media Player to burn the CD. Instead, you use the technique described under "Copying Files to CDs" in Chapter 15 to burn the CD as a regular data CD.

Tip If you burned songs as .wma files, and your CD player only plays MP3 files, you can convert from .wma to MP3. The www.wmplugins.com site offers several tools to help with that. See the section on plug-ins at the end of this chapter for more information.

When you burn and MP3 or .wma CD, you're not limited to 74 or 80 minutes worth of music. In fact, minutes don't matter at all, only bytes matter. If you're using a 650-MB data CD, then you can put up to 650 MB worth of songs on the CD. Likewise, the limit will be 700 MB if you're burning to 700-MB audio CDs. If the device on which you'll be playing the CD supports CD-RW, then you can use either CD-R or CD-RW to burn the music.

Step 1 is to put a blank CD into your CD drive. If some program opens, close that program. Then, open My Computer and double-click the icon for your CD drive. An empty folder will open (unless you're using a CD-RW that already contains data, in which case you'll see an icon for each song that's already on the disk). Leave that folder open, because it will be a temporary holding store for songs to be copied the CD.

Next, open the folder in which all your songs are stored. You can use the Search Companion as described earlier to find all the songs in all the subfolders, or all .MP3 songs, or whatever files you want. To see the combined sizes of all the songs in the folder, select all the icons (press Ctrl+A or choose Edit ➪ Select All). Right-click any selected song, and choose Properties. The Size on Disk measurement provides the most accurate measure.

Now it's just a matter of choosing a little under 650 or 700 MB's, depending on the capacity of the CD in the drive, worth of songs and dragging them to the folder for the CD. Optionally, you can right-click any song or group of selected songs and choose Send To ➪ CD Drive. As you add songs to the CD folder, you can select all the icons in that folder, right-click, and choose Properties to see the combined sizes of the files waiting to be written to the CD. Remember, the limit is the capacity of the disk, either 650 MB or 700 MB.

Figure 39-17 shows an example where I've added songs from the Search Result folder in the upper-left corner to the CD folder on the lower right. Though you can't tell by looking at the figure, the CD folder has a little less than 700 MB's worth of files in it. If you want to organize the files on the CD by Artist or some other property, switch to Details view in the CD folder, choose the column by which you want to sort, and click that column heading.

Figure 39-17: Some selected songs (left) and CD Writing folder (right)

Note   If you have to delete songs from the CD folder, don't be alarmed by the *Are you sure that you want to send these files to the Recycle Bin?* message. They're just temporary files at that point, so deleting them won't delete the actual song from your hard drive.

When you have all the songs you want in the CD folder, and you're sure you're not over the limit on their combined sizes, just click on Write these files to CD under CD Writing Tasks in the Explorer bar. If you get a prompt asking whether you want to make an audio CD or data

CD, make sure you choose data CD. Otherwise, you'll end up with a standard music CD with songs in .cda format. Follow the CD Writing Wizard instructions, and wait for the burning of the CD to finish. That's all there is to it.

Fun with Skins

Whenever you're using a program, the part that you see on the screen is just one snowflake on the tip of the proverbial program. The real "guts" are in memory, and invisible. That part you see on the screen is called the *user interface*, abbreviated UI, and often referred to as simple the *interface* or *skin*. Some programs, including Windows Media Player, allow you to change the interface without changing the functionality of the program.

Windows Media Player comes with several skins for you to try out. To see them, choose View ⇨ Skin Chooser. Click each skin's name in the left column to get a preview of how Media Player will look if you apply the skin. To download additional free skins, click the More Skins button above the left column. When you find a skin you like, click the Apply Skin button.

Once you've applied a skin, you'll need to figure out how to work it by pointing to buttons to see their names. You'll also see an *anchor window* in the lower-right corner of the screen. It's actually just a large round button, as in the example shown in Figure 39-18. In that figure, I've put Media Player in its Ducky skin (which I downloaded from the Web).

Figure 39-18: Media Player in Ducky skin, with anchor window at lower right

When you need to get out of the skin and back to the normal Media Player view, do any of the following:

✦ Press **Ctrl+1**.

✦ Or, click the large button in the anchor window and choose **Return to Full Mode**.

✦ Or, point to buttons on the skin until you find one that returns to full mode, and click that button.

Extending Media Player with Plug-ins

Plug-ins are optional add-on capabilities that you can purchase or, in some cases, download for free. A plug-in might be as simple as a new visualization or skin. Or, it could be an audio or DVD driver or enhancer that extends the capabilities of Media Player. Some plug-ins add capabilities to Media Player. It all depends on what you download and install.

About Microsoft Plus! Digital Media Edition

Before I get into specific plug-ins, I should mention Microsoft Plus! Digital Media Edition. That program itself is a set of plug-ins that work with Media Player and Windows Movie Maker. Some of the downloadable plug-ins are actually enhancement to the Plus! program itself.

Plus offers some very handy features right off the bat. For example, Plus will let you can print CD jewel labels of songs from playlists you burn to CDs. You can create Photo Stories with Plus!—photo slides shows with music and narration. It also contains a programs to help with capturing music from analog devices such as cassette recorders and vinyl LPs. Its Audio Converter can convert .wma songs to MP3, and MP3 songs to .wma. There's even more to it than that, so it's well worth the $20 it costs to purchase and download.

You can learn more about Plus! Digital Media Edition from `www.microsoft.com/windows/plus`. You can also purchase and download the program from that site. Though can also find it at any store that sells software. Once installed, the main features of Plus! will be available from your All Programs menu. Additional Media Player skins that come with Plus! will be available in Media Player when you chose View ➪ Skin Chooser from Media Player's menu.

Other plug-ins

There are plenty of other plug-ins available, even if you don't spring for Plus! Digital Media Edition. I just thought I better discuss that product first, because you'll see many references to that product at the plug-ins site. There are three ways to get to the plug-ins site, and each offers a slightly different interface. Use any of the following methods to check out currently available plug-ins:

✦ Choose **Tools** ➪ **Plug-ins** ➪ **Download Plug-ins** from Media Player's menu.

✦ Or, browse to `www.wmplugins.com`.

✦ Or, browse to `www.microsoft.com/windows/windowsmedia/download`.

From there, you can look around and choose your downloads. Once you start a download, choose Run or Open from the security warning boxes. When the download is complete, you'll probably see a ReadMe file describing how to use the product. You may want to print or save that so that you can figure out how to use whatever you've downloaded.

Managing plug-ins

There isn't anything specific I can tell you that would apply to all plug-ins. But some general guidelines that should apply are:

✦ To access visualizations, click **View** ➪ **Visualizations** or click the **Visualizations** button on the Now Playing toolbar.

✦ To access skins, choose **View** ➪ **Skin** from the Media Player's menu.

✦ To get to plug-ins that are part of Media Player, choose **View** ➪ **Plug-Ins or Tools** ➪ **Plug-Ins** from Media Player's menu.

If you install Micosoft Plus! Digital Media Edition, you can start many of its programs right from the All Programs menu. You'll also find Plus! skins in Media Player, and Movie Maker add-ins in Movie Maker.

Choosing Tools ⇨ Plug-Ins ⇨ Plug-Ins ⇨ from Media Player's menu will take you to the Plug-ins tab of Media Player's Options dialog box, shown in Figure 39-19. Click any category in the left pane to see plug-ins within that category.

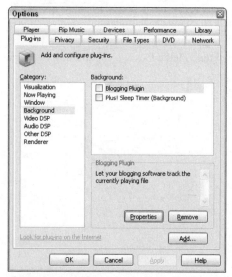

Figure 39-19: Plug-ins tab of Media Player's Options dialog box

Some plug-ins have properties that you can configure within the dialog box. When you click on the name of a plug-in that offers properties, the Properties button will be enabled. Click the Properties button to see what's offered.

To uninstall a plug-in, click its name, and then click the Remove button. Optionally, you can choose the checkbox next to several plug-in names, then click Remove to remove them all.

Wrap Up

Windows Media Player 10 is a large program in its own right. These last two chapters have covered most of what's available. As with any program, you can choose Help ⇨ Windows Media Player Help from Media Player's menu for more information about any Media Player feature. The main points covered in this chapter include:

✦ To play a DVD, VCD, or HighMAT CD in Windows Media Player, insert the disc into your drive and choose Play ⇨ DVD, VCD, or CD Audio from Media Player's menu.

✦ You can access many of the special features of DVDs from the menus on the DVD title menu, or from Media Player's Play menu.

✦ To size a video that's playing, right-click the video pane in Now Playing and choose a size.

✦ All of the content in your Media Library is metadata, information about documents stored on your hard disk. Each media file is a normal document that you can manage through Windows Explorer.

✦ Most of the media information you see in Media Player's library comes from summary properties stored with each file in the library.

✦ You can manage your library either from the Library tab in Media Player, or directly form the files using Windows Explorer.

✦ Skins are optional interfaces you can use to change the appearance of Media Player without changing its functionality.

✦ Plug-ins are optional components that extend Media Player's capabilities, available from www.wmplugins.com.

✦　　✦　　✦

Getting Started with Windows Movie Maker 2

Every movie or TV show you've ever seen is a collection of *scenes* organized into a story. Windows Movie Maker is a program that lets you create professional-grade videos in a similar manner — by combining your favorite scenes from home movies or even video you download from the Web. Your can add background music, narration, still photos, and special effects to your movies. In short, you get to be cameraman, director, and producer all wrapped into one.

The movies you create are stored in Windows Movie (.wmv extension) files. Just about anybody who has a Windows PC will be able to play them. Theoretically, you could even e-mail movies to people. However, movie files tend to be large, so it's more likely you'd be sending out copies on CD or DVD to people.

Introducing Windows Movie Maker 2.1

Windows XP originally shipped with a program named Windows Movie Maker, which has since been updated to Windows Movie Maker 2. I'll be writing about Windows Movie Maker 2.1 in this chapter. Actually, there's a version 2 and a version 2.1, the latter being part of Service Pack 2. But the two versions are virtually identical, so if you're using Version 2 there's no need to rush out and update to 2.1 right now. Anyway, here's how to check which version of Movie Maker you're currently using:

1. Click the Start button and choose **All Programs ⇨ Windows Movie Maker**.

Note

If you don't see Windows Movie Maker on the All Programs menu, point to Accessories to see whether it's on that submenu. If not, point to Entertainment and see whether it's on that submenu.

2. From the menu bar in Windows Movie Maker, choose **Help ⇨ About Windows Movie Maker**. Then, take a look at the About Windows Movie Maker dialog box that opens and:

✦ If you're using Version 1, as shown at the left of Figure 40-1, click **OK** and go to the section titled "Upgrading to Movie Maker 2" later in this chapter.

✦ If you're already using Movie Maker 2 or 2.1, as on the right side of Figure 40-1, click **OK** and go to the section titled "Taking Control of Movie Maker 2" later in this chapter.

Figure 40-1: The About dialog box for the original Movie Maker (left) and Movie Maker 2 (right)

Gotcha

If you see a message indicating that your screen resolution is set to 800 × 600 or lower, you'll probably want to increase that resolution to 1024 × 768.

Upgrading to Movie Maker 2.1

If you're reading here, you've started Windows Movie Maker, discovered you have Version 1, and have clicked OK to close the About . . . dialog box. Upgrading to Version 2 will get you a lot of cool stuff, and it won't cost you a penny, just a little time to download and install the program. To get to the download Web page, choose Help ➪ Windows Movie Maker on the Web from Movie Maker's menu bar. Or, use your Web browser to go to www.microsoft.com/windowsxp/MovieMaker.

On Movie Maker's home page, look around for, and click, *Windows Movie Maker 2 Download*. You'll be taken to a page that describes Movie Maker 2. As you scroll down the page, you'll come to the Download Instructions. Or, under Download at the right side of that page, choose your language and click the Go button. When the File Download dialog box opens, click its Open button; then, follow the instructions on the screen.

Getting around in Movie Maker

Producing a movie is very much a step-by-step process. More accurately, it is a task-by-task project. For example, the first task is to *get* some video to work with. Then, the video needs to be organized into scenes (clips). You need to be able to watch clips, edit out junk you don't want, and maybe add narration or background music. Then, the scenes need to be arranged into a movie and so on.

Like most program windows, Movie Maker 2 has its own title bar, menu bar, and toolbar at the top, as well as it's own taskbar button. So, you can move and size its window like any other. There's a limit, however, to how small you can make the window.

Movie Maker also works best at a minimum resolution of 1024 × 768. If you open Movie Maker at a smaller resolution, you'll see some advice along those lines in a message. You can skip the message and open Movie Maker anyway. But in the long run, you'd be better of increasing your resolution as described under "Choosing a screen resolution and color depth" in Chapter 6.

Making a movie is very much a step-by-step process. First, you need some raw material to work with. Next, you need to pick what you do and don't want from that material. Then, you need to assemble what you want into a movie. Perhaps add special effects, and so forth. To help with all of that, Movie Maker offers a couple of *panes*, described in the next section

Windows Movie Maker panes

When the Movie Tasks pane is open in Movie Maker, the program might look something like the example shown in Figure 40-2. The panes pointed out in that figure are described in the following sections.

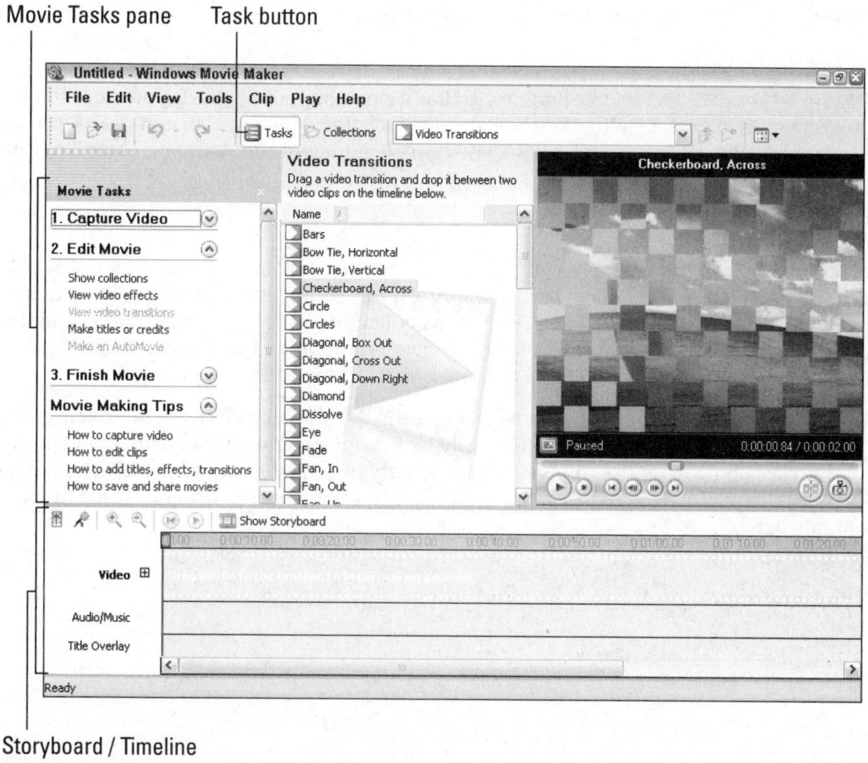

Figure 40-2: Windows Movie Maker 2, with its Movie Tasks pane open

Movie Tasks pane

Options in the Movie Tasks pane provide quick access to all the tools and dialog boxes you need to make a movie. To show or hide the task pane, click the Tasks button in the toolbar, or choose View ➪ Task Pane from Movie Maker's menu bar.

When the Movie Tasks pane is open, it shows a list of numbered tasks, such as 1. Capture video, 2. Edit Movie, and so forth. They allow you to step through the process of producing your movie in a task-by-task manner. You can click any of those headings to show or hide tasks beneath the heading. Use the scroll bar at the right edge of the pane, when it's visible, to scroll up and down through the list. To get started with a task, just click the task name.

To hide the Movie Tasks pane, click the Close (X) button near its upper-right corner.

Storyboard/Timeline

The Storyboard/Timeline, also called the work area, is where you create your movie. You lay out your scenes (clips) in the order you want them played along the Storyboard/Timeline. Only the clips you place in the Storyboard/Timeline will be part of the final movie you create.

You'll also use the Storyboard/Time to add titles and credits, special effects, background music, narrations, and other enhancements. The movie that you're currently creating in the Storyboard/Timeline is called a *project*. You'll see exactly how to take full advantage of the Storyboard/Timeline a little later in this chapter.

Collections pane

A Movie Maker *collection* is like a folder, in that it's a container in which you store things. But you don't store files in a collection. You store video clips. You can also edit the clips there, doing things such as getting rid of junk you don't want in your movies and compiling small clips into individual panes.

Contents pane

The contents pane, also shown in Figure 40-3, shows the contents of whatever collection is currently selected in the Collections pane or the Collections drop-down list. For example, in Figure 40-3, I've selected the Video Transitions collection in the Collections pane and the Collections drop-down list in the Collections pane. Each of the large icons in the Contents pane represents one transition from the Video Transitions collection.

The Contents pane in Figure 40-3 shows its icons in Thumbnails view. If you prefer, you can show those icons in Details view, where only textual information about each item appears. Use the Views button on the toolbar to choose Details or Thumbnails View for the Contents pane. Use the Arrange Icons By on the Views button to change the order of icons in the Contents pane.

Collections button   Collections drop-down list   Views button

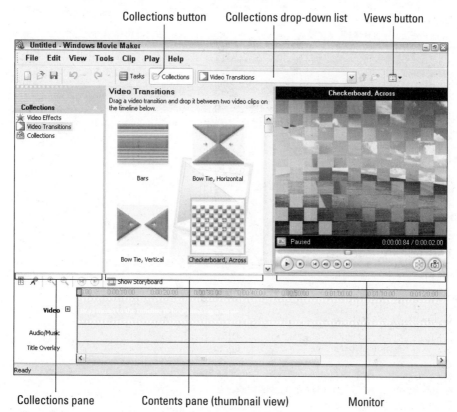

Collections pane   Contents pane (thumbnail view)   Monitor

Figure 40-3: Windows Movie Maker, with the Collections pane open

Monitor

The monitor is where you can watch clips, transitions, or your entire movie so far as a work in progress. The first frame of the currently selected clip (if any) appears in the Monitor. To select a clip, click its name in the Contents pane. Once you've selected a clip, you use the Play controls shown in Figure 40-4 and summarized as follows to watch the clip, split it, or to take a snapshot of the current frame.

Tip The Video Transitions and Effects are really just special effects, not pictures. When you play a transition, you see it played out on generic photos. But when you actually *use* a transition in your movie, those generic pictures aren't included.

Name of this clip

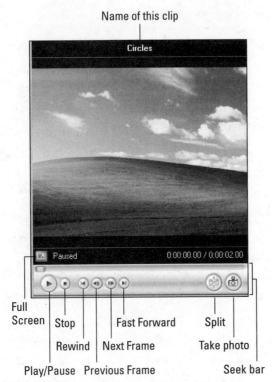

Full
Screen | Stop   Fast Forward   Split

Rewind   Next Frame   Take photo

Play/Pause   Previous Frame   Seek bar

Figure 40-4: The Play controls in Movie Maker 2

✦ **Name of this clip:** Shows the name of the clip you're currently viewing in the monitor. Matches the name of the clip selected in the Contents pane.

✦ **Full screen:** Expands the monitor to full-screen while a clip is playing. Click anywhere on the full-screen view to return to Movie Maker.

✦ **Seek bar:** The handle moves along this bar as the clip is playing. You can drag that handle to the left or right to zoom to a particular spot in the video. This works best if you click Play, then Pause, and then drag the handle while the clip is paused.

✦ **Play/Pause:** When the clip is paused or not playing, click this button to play the clip. When the clip is playing, click this button to pause it at the current position without rewinding.

✦ **Stop:** While the clip is playing, you can click this button to stop playback and rewind the clip to the beginning.

✦ **Previous frame:** When the clip is paused, click this button to move one frame at a time to the left.

Tip   A video is actually a collection of still images, in the same way that movie film is a series of tiny pictures. Each picture in the video is a *frame*.

✦ **Next frame:** When the clip is paused, click this button to move one frame at a time to the right.

✦ **Fast Forward:** Moves the seek bar to the end of the clip.

✦ **Split:** When a clip is paused, click this button to break it into two clips at the current frame.

✦ **Take photo:** When a clip is paused, click this button to copy the current frame to a still photograph.

You'll have plenty of chances to try out the tools as we progress through this chapter. But before you can make a movie, you really need to have some *content* (video, pictures, or music) to work with.

Gearing Up for Movie Making

Every video you capture and create is a document. As such, it's stored in a folder on your hard drive. Movie Maker automatically creates folders named My Videos and Shared Videos the first time you start it. It uses My Videos as the default folder for storing captured video. But the files you capture are likely to be huge, so if you have multiple hard drives, you want to use whichever one has the most space available.

One thing is for sure: You don't want to move the captured raw video after you've started creating your movies, because Movie Maker "expects" the raw footage to be in one location. So, choosing exactly where you want to keep your raw footage is an important first step.

If you don't have a second hard drive, then you can capture to the My Videos or Shared Video folder that Movie Maker created. You might also consider creating a subfolder, perhaps named something like Raw Footage, within that folder, just to help you keep track of what's where.

If you have a second hard drive such as D:, and want to use that for your captured video, you should open that drive via My Computer and create a folder for your captured video. For example, I use a second hard drive for video. On that drive I have a folder named Video. Within that folder I have a subfolder named DV Raw Footage for video I capture from a digital video camera.

Note   See Chapter 13 for info on creating folders.

Movie Maker doesn't care where you put the video files. The choice is entirely up to you. But it's really to your advantage to make a decision up front, and stick with it, so you don't create any complications by moving things around after the fact.

Choosing Your Defaults

The last preparatory step in creating movies is to choose some default settings. These are settings that Movie Maker will use unless you specify otherwise later. To set your defaults, open Windows Movie Maker from the All Programs menu (or wherever its startup icon might be). Then, choose Tools ⇨ Options from Movie Maker's menu bar. You'll see options shown in Figure 40-5. Those options are:

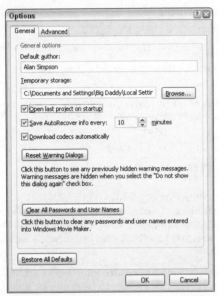

Figure 40-5: General tab of Movie Maker's Options dialog box

✦ **Default author:** Whatever you enter here will be entered as the Author property in all movies you create. You can just type your own name into this dialog box.

✦ **Temporary storage:** Movie Maker creates some temporary files (which it also deletes when it no longer needs them). You'd only change this if your C: drive is nearly full, and you have a second hard drive with much more space.

✦ **Open last project on startup:** Each movie you create is a *project*. Choosing this option ensures that Movie Maker always displays the project you're currently working on as soon as you open Movie Maker.

✦ **Save AutoRecover info every:** Movie Maker occasionally saves everything so that, in the event of a program crash, it can get back some of the material that might have gotten lost. A setting of 5 or 10 minutes is sufficient here.

✦ **Download codecs automatically:** Some video and audio files require a codec (compressor/decompressor) to run correctly. Choose this option to make sure any codecs you need get downloaded to your computer automatically.

✦ **Reset Warning Dialogs:** Clicking this button just brings back warning messages in which you previously chose *Do not show this dialog again*.

✦ **Clear All Passwords and User Names:** This is used only in conjunction with sending movies to online hosting services. Clicking this button just clears out any user names and passwords you may have defined while using that feature.

✦ **Restore All Defaults:** Clicking this button resets all the options on the General tab to their original settings, as defined the first time you start Movie Maker.

The Advanced tab in the Options dialog box, shown in Figure 40-6, also offers some default settings, as discussed in the list that follows.

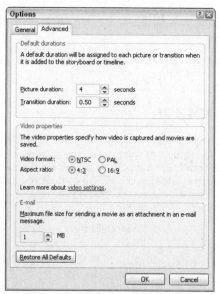

Figure 40-6: Advanced tab of Movie Maker's Options dialog box

✦ **Picture duration:** If you plan on incorporating still photos into your video, consider how long you want each to appear and enter that value here. The default of 5 seconds is reasonable, though you can change it.

✦ **Transition duration:** Movie Maker makes transitions from video to still photos smoothly. Use this option to define how long you want that transition to be. Anything from 0.5 to about 1.5 seconds is sufficient.

✦ **Video format:** NTSC is the most widely used video format in the United States. In Europe and Asia, PAL is the more widely used format. Stick with NTSC unless you know for certain that you'll be using PAL.

✦ **Aspect ratio:** This has to do with the shape of TV screens. If you plan to (eventually) watch movies on a standard TV, choose 4:3. If you have a wide-screen TV (HDTV), and want all your saved movies to play on such a TV, choose 16:9. Note, however, that if you choose 16:9 the movie will look distorted when played on a traditional 4:3 TV screen.

✦ **E-mail:** Sets the maximum size of e-mail attachments. For example, if you have a broad-band account with a 10-MB limit on attachments, set this to 10. However, keep in mind that all recipients have their limits too. The smaller of the two limits is the one that counts. So, if you plan on e-mailing movies to someone whose limit is 1 MB, you should leave this set to 1.

Note   Sending movies by e-mail isn't very realistic, because the files are just inherently large. You can only e-mail a very short, small, low-quality videos because "real" movies are just too large for e-mail.

The Restore All Defaults button in the Advanced tab resets all the options on that tab to their original settings. Click OK after making your selections.

At this point, you have all your ducks in a row, and you're ready to start being a movie mogul. The first thing you need is some raw footage to work with.

Stage 1: Getting the Raw Footage

The first step to creating a movie is to get some raw footage into the computer, From the standpoint of Hollywood movie moguls, this stage it the equivalent of all the camera crews bringing the scenes they've shot on film into the editing studio. Those scenes are the raw footage from which the editors and producers can create the movie. The content you capture from your videotapes will be your raw footage from which you can create your movies. There are basically three ways to get your raw footage:

✦ If you have a digital video camera, you can *capture* video straight from any tape you're previously recorded.

✦ If you've previously captured video to your computer using some program other than Movie Maker, you can *import* that footage into Movie Maker.

✦ You can also capture content from an analog video camera, VCR, or TV. Though the latter requires some extra hardware, and I'll reserve that whole discussion for Chapter 41.

Note   Capturing content from an analog camcorder, VCR, or TV is covered in Chapter 41.

Capturing content from a digital video camera

Windows Movie Maker works best with digital video cameras that connect to the computer through an IEEE 1394 port. That same port is called iLink by Sony, and FireWire by Apple, but it's all the same thing. It's a high-speed connection method suitable for transferring digital video. To use this method, you need a digital video camera with an iLink, FireWire, DV, or 1394 connection. You also need an IEEE 1394 port on your computer. The symbol and general shape of the port is shown in Figure 40-7. You also need a cable to connect those two ports.

Figure 40-7: Symbol and shape of an IEEE 1394 port

I suggest that you start by closing all open program windows so that you're just at the Windows desktop. Load a tape that you've already shot some footage on into the video camera, turn the camera on in VCR mode (not Camera mode), and rewind the tape to the beginning.

Caution   When capturing content from your camera to the computer, you'll always use the camera's VCR mode, never its Camera or Record mode.

Then turn the camera off. Connect the 1394 port on the camera to the 1394 port on the computer using the appropriate cable (which most likely came with your camera, not your computer). Then turn on the camera. Wait a few seconds, and one of three things will happen:

Tip   If you have a digital video camera with a 1394, iLink, or FireWire port, but no corresponding port on your computer, don't fret. Adding an IEEE 1394 port to a computer is a relatively simple and inexpensive procedure. To see examples of products you can use for this purpose, go to any online distributor, such as www.tigerdirect.com and search for 1394 port.

✦ Windows Movie Maker opens automatically: If this happens, go to the next section, "Using the Video Capture Wizard."

✦ If a dialog box appears, asking what you want to do with the camera, choose Capture Video using Windows Movie Maker (if possible), click OK, and go to the next section, "Using the Video Capture Wizard." Otherwise, choose Do Nothing, click OK, and continue with the next item.

✦ If nothing happened, or you chose Do Nothing, start Windows Movie Maker from the All Programs menu (or wherever its icon is). Then, choose File ⇨ Capture Video from Movie Maker's menu bar.

Using the Video Capture Wizard

The Video Capture Wizard helps you capture video from tape to a file in your computer. The video will play on your computer screen at normal speed. Movie Maker will make a copy of the video as it's playing. It all happens in real time; meaning if you're going to copy an entire 30-minute tape, it will take 30 minutes to capture it.

Assuming that you're at the first page of the Video Capture Wizard now, your first choices will be as follows:

✦ **Enter a file name for your captured video:** Type a short, meaningful name that describes the tape, such as *Summer 2004 Raw* or *Fiji Vacation Raw* or whatever. Adding "Raw" to the filename helps to distinguish this raw, captured video from any movies you create using a similar filename.

✦ **Choose a place to save your captured video:** This will be the folder you decided up earlier. For example, your My Videos folder, or another folder on a second hard drive. Use the Browse button to navigate to the folder of your choosing.

Click the Next button to get to the Video Setting page of the Video Capture Wizard. Your options are:

✦ **Best quality for playback on my computer (recommended):** This option will choose a video format based on the capabilities of your computer. The actual settings appear under Setting Details lower in the dialog box. Use this setting only if you don't plan to copy movies to DVD or VHS tape.

✦ **Digital device format (DV-AVI):** This format will create enormous files at the 720:480 pixel size needed for playback on a standard TV. (If you chose 16:9 as your default aspect ratio, the pixel size will be different). This option creates enormous files. So, you needn't choose it if you don't plan on playing your finished movie on a television screen.

✦ **Other Settings:** This lets you choose settings for everything from a pocket PC to DVD quality, and everything in between (see Figure 40-8). More on this option later.

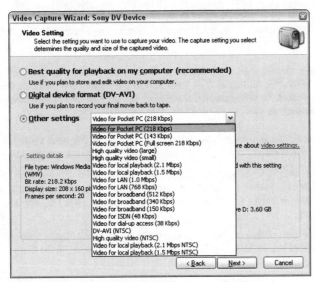

Figure 40-8: Choosing a setting for captured video

You can choose any setting you want from the Other Settings drop-down list shown in Figure 40-8. The most important thing to remember, though, is that whatever setting you choose will be the maximum quality you can get from the content. Quality, in this case, can be estimated from the speed (bps, or bits per second) of the setting you choose.

Tip   1 Mbps (one megabit per second) is equal to 1,024 Kbps (over a thousand kilobits per second)

You can always create smaller, lower-quality movies from high-quality content. For example, even if you choose the ultra-high-quality DV-AVI (NTSC) format, your raw footage files will be enormous. But you can make all kinds of lower-quality movies from that, such as things you'd e-mail or display on a Web page. The opposite isn't true though. For example, if you choose the tiny *Video for pocket PC (143 Kbps)* setting, then you cannot make movies that are any better quality than that without recapturing the video at a better quality.

As always, the better the quality of the raw material you have to work with, the more flexibility you have in working with it. If you're sure you'll eventually be watching your movies on TV, you should choose one of the NTSC settings from the bottom of the menu. Otherwise, of you'll only be producing movies for computers, the Web, and so forth, you can choose a high-quality non-NTSC setting such as *Video for local playback (2.1 Mbps)* or *High Quality Video (large)*.

Note

The *Video for local playback (2.1 Mbps)* stores captured video in .wmv format at a display size of 640 × 480 pixels and 30 frames per second. The *High Quality Video (large)* uses the same display size and frame rate, but uses a variable bit rate to keep the file size to a minimum.

The Setting Details section of the Video Setting page tells you how the setting you chose will play out. The Bit Rate is the overall quality of the video, and the higher the number, the better the quality. The Display Size is the dimensions of the video. The largest size is 640 × 480. The Frames Per Second defines how smoothly the video plays. The lower the frames per second, the more "jerky" the movie will look.

The Video File Size pane tells you how much disk space each minute of video will consume at the current setting. For example, each minute of captured video at the highest quality setting of DV-AVI NTSC will gobble up about 178 MB of disk space. Or, in other words, each 6 minutes of captured video will devour about a gigabyte of disk space. (Which is the perfect excuse for adding a second 200-GB or 300-GB hard drive!).

Once you've made your Settings selections, click Next. The Capture Method page will ask if you want to capture the entire tape automatically, or capture parts manually. Again, that choice is up to you. It's easiest to just let Movie Maker capture the whole thing. You can always get rid of any junk you don't want after the fact. If you choose that option, there's nothing left to do but wait for the wizard to tell you when the capture is finished. But then again, if you only want small segments of the tape that's in the camera, you could conserve quite a bit of disk space by choosing the second option.

The option *Capture parts of the tape manually* lets you pick and choose which parts of the tape you want to capture. With this method, you can choose specific parts to capture from the tape that's currently in the camera. This is a good choice if there's a lot of content on the tape that you don't intend to use in any of your movies. If you choose this option, you'll be taken to the Capture Video Wizard page I'll describe in the paragraph after next.

Keep the *Show preview during capture* checkbox selected, because that's the only way to see what's happening on the screen. If you'll be capturing parts of the tape manually, you really need to keep this option selected (checked). The only reason to clear that checkbox is that your computer isn't quite fast enough to handle the job and your videos were coming out "jerky." Also, it's not really necessary to preview the tape is you opted to capture the entire tape automatically.

Capturing parts of the tape manually

If you opted to capture parts of a tape manually, you'll come to the options shown in Figure 40-9. Before you do anything else, take a look at the checkboxes near the bottom of the dialog box. Your choices there are:

✦ **Create clips when wizard finishes:** Choose this option to have Movie Maker automatically divide the video into smaller scenes (clips). Doing so will make it easier to edit your movie.

✦ **Mute speakers:** Choose this option if you don't want your computer speakers to play the video while it's being captured.

✦ **Capture time limit (hh:mm):** If you want to capture a fixed amount of video (for example, exactly 30 minutes), choose this option and set your time limit.

You're finally ready to capture the video; click Start Capture in the dialog box. The video in the camera will start playing in the preview pane. If you're capturing chunks of the tape, click the Stop Capture button to stop capturing at any time. After you click the Stop Capture button, you can use the DV Camera Controls under the preview screen to wind the tape forward or backward. Note that those controls actually operate the camera.

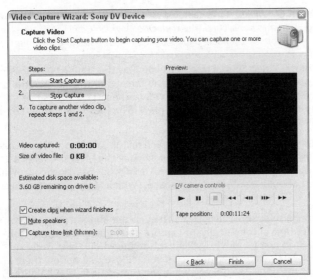

Figure 40-9: The Capture Video page for a digital video camera.

For example, after clicking Stop Capture, you can click the Fast Forward button to get to the next part you want to capture. Click the Pause button when you get to where you want to start capturing again. Use the Previous Frame and Next Frame buttons to move through the tape one frame at a time until you get to the exact frame where you want to start capturing again. Then, click the Start Capture button. The tape will play, and be captured, at normal speed.

You can start capturing, stop capturing, fast forward, pause, and resume capturing all you want. The Video captured and Size of video file headings keep you apprised of how much content you've captured, and how much disk space the captured file will consume. When you've finished capturing the tape that's in the camera, click the Finish button. Movie Maker will then break the captured video into clips, which you'll see in the content pane.

The next section isn't relevant to capturing content from a digital video camera. So, feel free to skip down to "Step 2: Creating and Organizing Scenes" later in this chapter if you're ready to forge ahead with your movie.

Importing video from files

If you already have video stored in files on your hard disk, there's no need to capture that video. For example, if you've already captured some video using a program other than Movie Maker, you can import that video into Movie Maker, and use that as your raw footage. You can also import video you've acquired from other sources such as the Web or an MPEG file that someone sent you on CD.

Note   You *capture* video from tape only. You *import* video that's already in a file on your hard disk.

In addition to importing video from files on your disk, you can import music and still pictures. But you can't import every conceivable type of file, only the file types listed here:

Note   You cannot import protected content (digitally licensed) into Movie Maker.

✦ **Video:** .asf, .avi, .m1v, .mp2, .mp2v, .mpe, .mpeg, .mpg, .mpv2, .wm, and .wmv.

✦ **Still pictures:** .bmp, .dib, .emf, .gif, .jfif, .jpe, .jpeg, .jpg, .png, .tif, .tiff, and .wmf.

✦ **Audio:** .aif, .aifc, .aiff .asf, .au, .mp2, .mp3, .mpa, .snd, .wav, and .wmv.

If the content you intend to import isn't already on your hard disk, you must copy it to your hard disk first. Trying to import content from a CD, a floppy, a scanner, or a camera simply won't work. All of your raw, unedited content must be in some folder on a hard drive. Assuming that you know where that content is located, importing it is easy:

1. From Movie Maker's menu bar, choose **File ➪ Import into Collections**. (Optionally, you can click Import Video under *1. Capture Video* in the Tasks pane.) The Import File dialog box opens.

2. In the Import File dialog box, navigate to the folder that contains the content you want to import.

Tip   Use these same steps to import still photos or music into a movie project. Details are covered in Chapter 41.

3. If you're importing video and want Movie Maker to create clips automatically, make sure that *Create clips for video files* is selected near the bottom of the Import File dialog box.

4. In the main pane, select the item(s) you want to import. Use the **Views** button in that dialog box to choose how you want to see icons. If you want to import all the files in the folder, click within the main pane and press **Ctrl+A (Select All)**.

5. Click the **Import** button and wait.

Once the file is imported, it will be stored in its own collection with the same name as the file you imported. If the imported name isn't descriptive enough for you, just right-click the collection name, choose Rename, and type in a better name. Figure 40-10 shows an example where I've captured a videotape and named the collection Hawaii Tape 2. Its name is selected in the Collections pane, so the clips in the content pane to the right are from that one tape.

Remember, you can capture as much content as you have space for on your hard disk. You can't completely fill the hard disk though, because you need some space to store the movies you're about to create. If you have an idea for a movie in mind, you should at the very least capture all the content needed for that one movie.

You now have some raw material to work with. It doesn't matter if you captured it or imported that content. It's all the same to Movie Maker. Your next step is the editorial phase, where you go into the "cutting room" and start separating the wheat from the chaff.

Stage 2: Creating and Organizing Scenes

At this stage of the game, you have some raw footage to work with. Each captured or imported movie will be stored in a collection. When you click on a collection's name, you'll see the clips within that collection in the content pane. If you don't see the Collections pane at all, click the Collections button in the toolbar, which is visible at the top of Figure 40-10. In that example, you can see that I've selected the Hawaii Tape 2 collection. The clips in the main pane to the right are all from that collection.

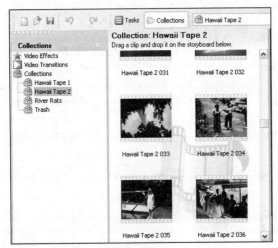

Figure 40-10: A collection of clips

The clips in a collection roughly correspond to scenes in a movie. It's a very rough approximation, because Movie Maker can't see, hear, or understand the video that it's dividing into clips. Like everything else, the video is just a stream of ones and zeroes screaming through the processor, and the machine is as oblivious to what's going on as a rock would be.

The decision on whether or not to make a given frame the start of a new clip is based solely on the color of the upper-left pixel in the frame. If there's a significant difference between the color of that pixel on the current frame as compared to the preceding frame, then Movie Maker starts a new clip at that frame. The trick works fairly well, but don't expect your clips to be exactly the scenes you had in mind for your movie.

Getting Organized

Before I go on, let me point out there you've reached another place where being organized can really help. As time goes by, you're likely to build up more and more collections, and each of those collections will contain any number of clips. Eventually, you have collections and clips all over the place, and it's easy to lose track of what's where.

You can create your own, empty collections and use them as folders. For example, if you have a movie title in mind, you can create a collection that has the movie title as its name. You might create another collection named Trash (or Cutting Room Floor) for truly bad clips you'd never use in any movie. (Though, you could also just delete those clips if you prefer).

To create a new collection, right-click the parent collection and choose New ⇨ Collection. For example, to create a new collection at the same level as other collections, right-click Collections at the top of the list and choose New Collection, as shown in Figure 40-11. A new collection named New Collection appears. Type in a new name for the collection and press Enter. To rename an existing collection, right-click it and choose Rename.

Figure 40-11: Creating a new collection

You can create subcollections much the same way that you create subfolders. Just right-click the parent collection name, and choose New ⇨ Collection. For example, every movie has a beginning, middle, and end. As you review your clips, you might decide some would be best used at the start of the movie, others might be best for the middle of the movie. Still other clips you may want to reserve for the end of the movie.

Creating a separate subfolder for each movie section gives you yet another way to start organizing your scenes. For example, in Figure 40-12 I created a new, empty collection named My Hawaii Movie. Within that collection I created subcollections named Beginning, Middle, and End. To create each subfolder, I just right-clicked the parent folder, My Hawaii Movie, and choose New Folder. Then, I named each folder as I created it.

Figure 40-12: My Hawaii Vacation collection contains three subcollections

There's no rule that says you must create new empty folders for a movie you're making. But I've found that when you have a ton of clips to work with, things are less confusing if you get organized and stay organized while reviewing your clips. In this scenario, as I watch clips from Hawaii Tape 1 and Hawaii Tape 2, I can move or copy clips I intend to use in my movie to one of the subfolders in My Hawaii Movie.

Watching a clip

When you click on a collection name in the Collections pane, all the clips within that collection appear in the Contents pane. In Thumbnails View, you see the first frame of each clip. In Details View, you just see information about each clip. You won't know what's really in a clip until you watch it. To watch a clip, click on its icon in the contents pane. The first frame of the clip appears in the monitor. To watch the whole clip, click the Play button under the monitor.

After you watch a clip, you can decide what you want with it. For example, you can:

✦ You can rename the clip to something more descriptive, if you like.

✦ Delete the clip if you think you'll never use it in any movie you create.

✦ Move or copy the clip to some other collection.

✦ Split the clip into two.

✦ Combine the clip with one or more clips that follow it.

✦ Add the clip to the Storyboard/Timeline if you intend to use it in the movie you're creating right now.

As you go through your clips, the goal is to start coming up with scenes that you can use in a movie. You're not actually building the movie at this point. You're just better organizing your raw material — your clips — into scenes that you can drop into your movie.

Tip To enlarge or shrink the monitor, drag its inner border left or right.

Splitting a clip

Suppose that you play a clip, and it has some content you want to use in your movie. But you don't want the whole clip, just a portion of the clip. In that case, you can split the clip into two. That part you want to keep becomes one clip; the part you don't want becomes a separate clip.

The clip needs to be in the monitor for this to work. Presumably, it's already there because you just watched it, and now you want to split it. Remember, you use the buttons under the monitor, pointed out back in Figure 40-4, to play, and control the clip that's currently in the monitor.

To split a clip, drag the Seek bar to about the point where you want to divide the clip in two. Once you're near the point where you want to split the clip, you can use the Previous Frame and Next Frame buttons to move frame by frame through the clip. When you split the clip, the frame that's showing in the monitor will be the first frame of the new clip. The frame preceding that clip will be the last frame of the original clip.

Figure 40-13 shows an example where I'm near the center of a clip named Hawaii Tape2 008 (notice where the handle is in the Seek bar). The mouse pointer is resting on the Split button; clicking that button splits the clip into two clips. After splitting the clip, the original Hawaii Tape 2 008 clip contains only frames before that split point. A new clip named Hawaii Tape 2 008 (1) appears, containing the frame shown in the monitor and all the frames that follow.

Figure 40-13: About to split a clip in the monitor

At this point, you can do whatever you want with either clip—rename it, move or copy it to another folder, delete it, or just leave it as is.

Tip   If you change your mind after splitting a clip, choose Edit ➪ Undo Split from the menu bar, or press Ctrl+Z.

Combining clips

Sometimes when you import video, Movie Maker creates clips in a manner that doesn't reflect how you intend to use the clips. For example, Movie Maker might create three separate clips that you would prefer to use as a single scene in your movie. Rather than try to keep track of the three separate clips, you can combine them into a single clip.

Caution   Combining clips isn't necessary to create a movie. You combine clips only to help organize a group of clips into one scene for your movie. The scenes will all come together later when you drag them to the Storyboard/Timeline.

You can only combine clips that are adjacent to one another in the Contents pane. In a sense combining clips is really a matter of unsplitting them. For example, Movie Maker divided a sunset scene from Hawaii Tape 2 into several clips, as shown in Figure 40-14. This has to do with the fact that Movie Maker uses the color of one pixel to decide when to split a clip. In this case, it was a bad decision on Movie Maker's part. To my thinking, they should all be one clip named Sunset.

To combine clips, select the icons of the clips you want to combine. You can use the standard Ctrl+Click or Shift+Click, or mouse-dragging method to select the clips. Once all of the clips you want to combine are selected, choose Clip ➪ Combine. Once the clips are combined, you can rename the resulting clip if you like. For example, I'd rename the combined clips Sunset. I'd probably copy that clip to the End subcollection under My Hawaii Movie, just because a sunset seems like it goes at or near the end of the movie.

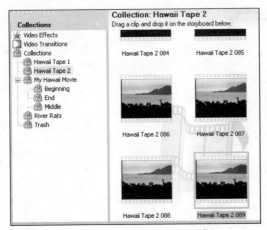

Figure 40-14: A sunset split into several separate clips

Renaming and deleting clips and collections

The collection and clip names that appear in Movie Maker aren't set in stone. You can change the name of any clip, or any collection, to something more meaningful. To do so, just right-click the collection or clip name you want to change and choose Rename. Type the new name and press Enter.

If you have any junk clips that you wouldn't use in any movie and therefore just want to get rid of, you can do that. I usually create a collection named Trash and move unwanted clips to that collection. That way, I can always rummage through the trash later in case I change my mind about something. But you can delete a clip, if you want, just by right-clicking and choosing delete. Just be aware that there's no way to get the clip back should you change your mind in the future.

Tip   If you delete a clip and realize your mistake right away, choose Edit ➪ Undo Remove Clip, or press Ctrl+Z, to undo that action and bring the clip back.

Moving and copy clips

Keeping track of clips can be a challenge in itself. For example, my Hawaii Tape 2 collection contains over 80 clips. As mentioned, organizing your clips can help a lot. You can move or copy a clip from its current collection to any other collection in the Collections pane. The advantage to moving a clip is that it gets it out of the current collection and into some other collection. For example, if I move the Sunset clip to the End subcollection for My Hawaii Movie, I won't see Sunset in the Hawaii Tape 2 collection anymore. So, I don't have to try to remember if I've already used that clip in a movie or not.

To move a clip, just drag its icon to the name of the collection into which you want to move it, and drop it there. The collection icons are small targets, so you have to be careful. You might find it easiest to drag the top-left corner of the clip, so you can easily see the tip of the mouse pointer and what's under the mouse pointer. When the tip of the mouse pointer is on the collection to which you want to move the clip, and the collection name is highlighted, then you can release the mouse button to drop the clip into that collection.

If you think you might use a clip in several movies, then you may want to copy rather than move clips. To copy, follow the same procedure you use to move a clip, but hold down the Ctrl key as you drag. You'll see a little + sign near the mouse pointer as you drag. That + sign is the indicator that lets you know you're about to copy, rather than move, the clip.

By the way, don't worry about copies of clips eating up lots of disk space. Even though video files are real disk-space hogs, clips are not. That's because a clip doesn't actually contain any video at all. It *looks as if* it contains video. After all, you can play a clip in the monitor at any time. But that's something of an illusion. All the clip really contains is a tiny amount of data that looks something like this:

```
Source: D:\Video Raw Footage\Hawaii Tape 2
Start Time: 19:12.65
End Time: 19:12.65
```

The source tells where the actual video file is located. The Start Time and End Time indicate points within that video file at which the clip begins and ends. So, when you play the preceding clip, what you're really seeing is that portion of the larger Hawaii Tape 2 video that starts at 19:12.65 and ends at 19:12.65. The clip itself doesn't need to contain any video.

There's a tiny bit more information than that in the clip, as you can see by right-clicking any clip and choosing Properties. But there's no actual video in the clip, and so each clip consumes an insignificant amount of disk space.

It will take some time to go through all your clips and make decisions about how you want to use them. Making movies is a creative, artistic thing that just takes some time. But once you've reviewed all your clips and made decisions about which ones you want to use, you're ready to move onto stage 3, where you produce your movie.

Convert a video frame to a photo

You can take a snapshot of any frame in any video clip or movie, thereby converting it to a photo. This step is entirely optional and really has nothing to do with making a movie. And it won't have any effect on your movie either. It's just a means of making still photos from frames in your clips or movie. The process is pretty simple:

1. Play the clip that contains the content from which you'd like to create a photo.

2. When you get to the place where you want to make a photo, click the Pause button to pause playback.

3. Use the Previous Frame and Next Frame buttons, as needed, to get to the exact frame from which you want to make a photo.

4. Click the **Take Picture** button at the far right of the play controls, shown near the mouse pointer in Figure 40-15.

A Save Picture As dialog box will open. Navigate to the folder in which you want to store the photo, (for example, My Pictures). Enter a filename and click OK. Later, when you open that saved picture, you'll see it's just a still photo, no different from a photo you copied from a digital camera.

Figure 40-15: Take a picture of a video frame

Stage 3: Producing Your Movie

Like every movie you see in a theater or on TV, the movie you create will be a series of scenes. To make the movie interesting, you want to avoid having the scenes played out in some random order. Rather, you want to try to organized scenes to give the movie a sense of having a beginning, middle, and end. Like a story. You organize your scenes into a movie by adding them to the Storyboard/Timeline (also called the *workspace*). The Storyboard/Timeline determines exactly which clips will be part of the movie, as well as the order in which they'll be played.

There are three ways to view the contents of the Storyboard/Timeline. When you're in the Storyboard View, click Show Timeline to switch to the Timeline View. When you're in the Timeline View, click Show Storyboard to switch to that view. Figure 40-16 shows an example of each view, with some sample clips already in place. Here are the features of each view:

✦ **Storyboard:** Shows only the first frame of each clip, with a small space in between for adding special transition effects.

✦ **Timeline:** Shows the first frame of each clip along a timeline so that you can see the moment at which each clip starts. The size of the clip is proportional to its duration, where long scenes are wide and short scenes are narrow. Use the + and – magnifying glass buttons to extend, or shrink the timeline to whatever size is most convenient at the moment.

✦ **Extended Timeline:** In Timeline View, the Video label has a + sign next to it. Clicking that + sign expands the view to include Transition, Audio, Audio/Music, and Title Overlay timelines. You can use those to add special effects, background music, narration, and titles to your movie.

Tip   To change the height of the Storyboard/Timeline, drag its upper border up or down.

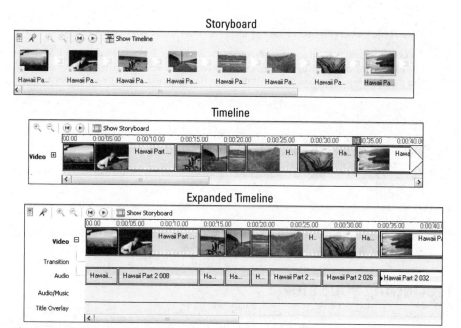

Figure 40-16: Storyboard, Timeline, and Expanded Timeline Views

Arranging your scenes

You create a movie by copying clips from the Contents pane into the Storyboard/Timeline, in the order you want them played in your final movie. You can add any clip from any collection, they don't all have to come from the same collection. There are several ways to add a clip to the Storyboard/Timeline, and you can use whichever is most convenient for you:

✦ Drag the clip from the Contents pane to where you want it to appear in the Storyboard/Timeline and drop it there.

✦ Right-click the clip that you want to add to the movie and choose Add to Storyboard or Add to Timeline.

✦ Click the clip you want to add to the movie and choose **Clip ➪ Add to Storyboard** or **Add to Timeline** from Movie Maker's menu bar.

✦ Click the clip you want to add and press **Ctrl+D**.

✦ Select several clips using **Ctrl+Click**, **Shift+Click**, or **Edit ➪ Select All (Ctrl+A)**. Then, drag any selected clip to the Storyboard/Timeline.

If you change your mind about a clip after adding it to the Storyboard/Timeline, you can do any of the following to back up:

✦ In the Storyboard/Timeline, right-click the clip you want to remove, and choose Delete. Doing so only removes the clip from the workspace, not the collection or contents pane.

✦ In the Storyboard/Timeline, click a clip to select it. Then, drag it left or right to move it within the movie. Or, right-click the clip, and press Ctrl+X to cut it. Then, right-click the frame to the right of where you want to place the clip, and press Ctrl+V.

✦ To select multiple clips to move or delete, click one clip in the Storyboard/Timeline. Then, hold down the Ctrl key while clicking other clips you want to select.

✦ To select a range of adjacent clips, click the first one; then, hold down the Shift key, and click the last one you want to select. Or move the mouse pointer past the last clip in the movie; then, drag the mouse pointer to the left through clips you want to select.

✦ To select all clips in the movie, right-click any click in the Storyboard/Timeline, and choose Select All.

✦ To clear the Storyboard/Movie, choose **Edit** ➪ **Clear Storyboard** or **Edit** ➪ **Clear Timeline** from the menu bar, or press **Ctrl+Delete (Del)**.

✦ To undo your most recent action, choose **Edit** ➪ **Undo** from Movie Maker's menu bar, or press **Ctrl+Z**.

You can add as many, or as few, clips to the Storyboard/Timeline as you wish.

Tip   When dragging video clips to the Timeline, make sure that you drag them to the bar titled *Video*, not the bar titled *Audio/Music or Title Overlay*.

Previewing your movie

Once you've dragged one or more clips to the Storyboard/Timeline, you can preview the entire movie at any time. If you use the Timeline view, you'll be able to see the Play Indicator (Figure 40-17) move through the movie as the movie is playing in the Monitor. You can drag the Play Indicator left or right to any place in the movie. You can also use the seek bar and buttons under the preview monitor to control playback. The duration of the entire movie is visible at the lower-right corner of the monitor.

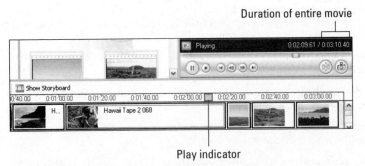

Figure 40-17: Play Indicator in Timeline View

Saving your project

It may take some time to pick and choose all your clips and arrange them in the Storyboard/Timeline. If it's a sizable movie, it might take several days. You can save all the work you've done so far in the Storyboard/Timeline at any time. That's called saving the *project*, and is different from actually creating a movie file. A project can only be used in Movie Maker's Storyboard/Timeline, whereas a finished movie file can be played on any computer that has any program capable of playing .wmv files.

To save your work so far, choose File ➪ Save Project. The Save Project As dialog box opens. Choose the folder in which you want to store the project, and enter a filename. The extension of the file you save will be .MSWMM (for Microsoft Windows Movie Maker). It's icon will look like the example shown in Figure 40-18. If filename extensions are hidden, you won't see the extension, as in the lower half of Figure 40-18. But the icon has a unique look that makes it easy to identify the project. Later, when you create your actual movie, you'll see how the finished movie file's icon looks different from the project's icon.

My Hawaii Movie.MSWMM
Windows Movie Maker Project
193 KB

My Hawaii Movie
Windows Movie Maker Project
193 KB

Figure 40-18: Icon for a movie project (work in progress)

Note   The file for the project is tiny compared to the file for the actual movie. That's because the project doesn't contain any actual video, only the information needed to create the movie.

To resume work on a movie you've saved as a project, just double-click (or click) the project's icon. Or, open Windows Movie Maker and choose File ➪ Open Project from Movie Maker's menu bar, navigate to the folder in which you saved the project, and double-click the project's icon.

Stage 4: Creating the Final Product

There are all kinds of fancy things you can do to embellish your movie, such as add special effects, background music, titles, and so on. But those things are all optional. Once you've organized all the clips you want on the Storyboard/Timeline, you've completed the minimal number of steps necessary to create a movie. To create the final movie from the clips currently in the Storyboard/Timeline, follow these steps:

1. Choose **File ➪ Save Movie File** from Movie Maker's menu bar. The Save Movie Wizard shown in Figure 40-19 opens.

2. To save the movie as a file on your hard disk, click on **My Computer** at the top of the list, and then click **Next**.

3. On the second wizard page, type in a filename of your own choosing for you movie, and use the **Browse** button to choose the folder in which you want to store the movie. Then click **Next**.

Figure 40-19: First page of the Save Movie Wizard

4. On the next Wizard page, shown in Figure 40-20, choose how you want to save the movie. Your options are:

- **Best quality for playback on my computer:** Choosing this option tells Movie Maker to choose the maximum quality that can be played on your computer, and also fit within your available disk space. If this is the only choice, click on *Show more choices. . . .*

- **Best fit to file size:** If you're shooting for a specific file size, such as just under 700 MB to fit on a CD, choose this second option, and then specify a size using the options to the right.

- **Other settings:** Choose the quality yourself using the drop-down list visible in Figure 40-20.

5. Click the **Next** button and wait.

6. When Movie Maker finishes creating the final movie file, you'll have the option of watching the movie right on the spot (it's not necessary to do so though). Click **Finish**.

You're done. However, you might want to repeat the steps above a few times, each time saving the movie with a slightly different filename and a different quality setting. That way, you can see how the movie looks at different quality settings, and get a better feel for how video quality relates to file size and what you see on the screen.

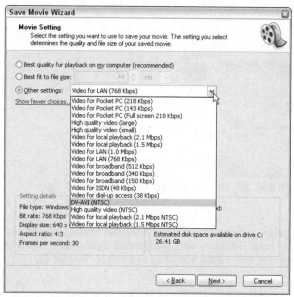

Figure 40-20: Choose a quality for your finished movie.

Closing Windows Movie Maker

You can close Windows Movie Maker using the same techniques you use to close any other program window. That is, click the Close button in its upper-right corner, or choose File ⇨ Exit from Movie Maker's menu bar. If you made any changes to the current project, you'll be asked if you want to save those changes. Chances are, once you see the completed movie, you're going to get a lot of ideas for improving it. So, I suggest that you choose Yes so that you can easily get back to the same movie and make your changes.

Once Movie Maker has closed, open the folder in which you stored your finished movie (or movies). The finished movie will have Windows Media Player's icon. (Assuming that Windows Media Player is the default player for .wmv files). Figure 40-21 shows an example where I've saved several copies of the same move at various quality settings.

The first four icons in the folder are different copies of the same movie at various quality settings. The range in size from about 8 MB for the small, 218-Kbps Pocket PC version of the movie to a walloping 1 GB for the DV-AVI version of the movie. The last icon in the folder is the Movie Maker project. It's a tiny 401 KB in size because it doesn't contain any video. Rather, it contains only the clips —the basic information—that Movie Maker needs to create the movie.

To play any movie double-click (or click) its icon. If Media Player isn't the default player for .wmv files, you can right-click a movie icon and choose Open With ⇨ Windows Movie Maker.

Figure 40-21: Four movies (.wmv and .avi) and one project (.MSWMM) in this My Videos folder

That about wraps it up for the basics of creating movies in Windows Movie Maker. If you have a hankering to spice up your cinematic creations with background music, special effects, still photos, titles, or narration, you'll find everything you need to know in Chapter 41.

Wrap Up

Making movies is largely a four-step process. You need to acquire some video, organize it into scenes, layout the scenes in the order you want them shown in the movie, then finally create the video file. To whit:

✦ To get video from a videotape into the computer, use Movie Maker to *capture* the video as it's playing on your computer screen.

✦ To get video, music, or photos from files already on your hard disk, choose File ➪ Import into Collections from Movie Maker's menu bar.

✦ To view the clips in a collection, choose the collection's name from the drop-down list, or click the collection name in the Collections pane. Clips within that collection appear in the Contents pane.

✦ To watch a clip, click its icon in the Contents pane; then, click the **Play** button in the Monitor.

✦ To add a clip to your movie, drag the clip to the Storyboard or Timeline.

✦ After you've placed your desired clips into the Storyboard/Timeline, Choose **File** ➪ **Save Movie File** from Movie Maker's menu bar to create your final movie file.

✦   ✦   ✦

Power Users Guide to Movie Maker 2

Getting all your clips arranged into a movie is always the first step. Once you're happy with how the entire movie plays out, you can start adding special effects and additional audio, in the form of custom background music and narration, to your movie.

When it comes to adding any kind of sound to the movie, you always want to do that last. Otherwise, if you start chopping up clips or moving them around, you'll be chopping up and moving the audio along with it.

This chapter discusses the ways in which you can add professional polish to your movies using fade transitions, special effects, titles, credits, and finally custom sound tracks. Here, I assume that you've already assembled all your clips into a movie and are happy with the order of the scenes in your movie.

Using Pictures and Photos in Movies

Your movie can contain still pictures and photographs. When you take a snapshot of a video frame, as discussed in Chapter 38, the snapshot becomes a clip in your collections automatically. To use pictures and photos, you didn't create from video frames, you first have to import the pictures into Movie Maker.

Each picture you import will have a default duration, which defines how long the still image is on the screen in the final movie. As discussed under "Choosing Your Defaults" in Chapter 40, you can change the default duration at any time using the Picture Duration in Move Maker's Options dialog box. But the new setting only applies to picture you import after changing the setting. Pictures you've already imported will retain their original durations. But that's no biggie, because you can change the duration of any picture at any time.

Here's how you import photos and other still pictures into Movie Maker:

1. Choose (click on) the collection name in the Collections pane in which you want to import the pictures. Optionally, you can create a new folder, perhaps named Photos. Then, select that folder to put the photos in that folder.

2. Choose **File ⇨ Import into Collections** from Movie Maker's menu bar.

3. In the Import Folder dialog box, navigate to the folder that contains the pictures you want to import.

4. In the main pane of Import Folder dialog box, select the pictures you want to import. Use the **Views** button to choose a view, Use any of the section techniques discussed in Chapter 14 to select the icons of the pictures you want to import.

5. Click the **Import** button.

The pictures will be imported into the current collection folder. When you click on that collection, each picture will appear as a clip. Use the **Views** button in the toolbar to view them as thumbnails. Click on a picture to see it in the monitor. Figure 41-1 shows an example where I've imported some still pictures into a collection named Still Images.

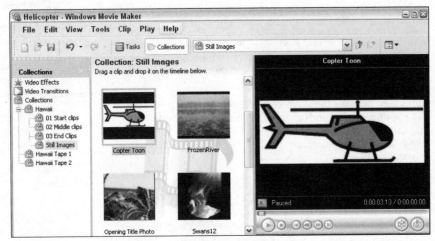

Figure 41-1: Pictures added to a Still Images collection

To add a photo to a movie, just drag its clip into the storyboard/timeline, same as you would a video clip.

Adding Titles and Credits

Titles and credits are textual information you can place anywhere in your movie. Typically, you'll want to add these before you add any special effects or sound, as you might want to include titles and credits as part of an effect or sound track. A title can be its own unique scene with a plain background. Or you can superimpose the title onto a scene or a still image in the movie. Make sure that you put the clip or photo that the title will precede, or be superimposed upon, in your movie first. Then, follow these steps:

1. In the storyboard/timeline, click the scene that the title will precede, or the scene on which you want the title to appear. That scene is now the *selected clip*.

2. Choose **Tools ⇨ Titles and Credits** from the menu bar.

3. Choose whichever option best describes where you want to place the title. The options are self-explanatory, though I've added a few comments to the list below:

- **title at the beginning of the movie** (selected clip doesn't matter with this option)

- **title before the selected clip**

- **title on the selected clip** (title is superimposed on the selected clip [video scene or still photo])

- **title after the selected clip**.

- **credits at the end** (the selected clip doesn't apply here either, since credits will be placed at the end of the movie)

4. On the next page, enter the main title text in the top box. You can add a subtitle in the lower textbox if you wish. Optionally, you can choose from among the following two options beneath the textboxes:

- Click **Change the title animation** to change how the title is animated. As you scroll through the list of options, notice that there are effects for one-line titles (only), and a separate set of options for two-line titles. Click any animation name, and then click the **Play** button in the monitor to see an example of the animation.

- Click **Change the text color and font** to choose a font, weight, color, transparency, size, and position for the text.

5. When you're happy with your title, click **Done, add title to movie**.

To see how your title looks, click the title scene in the storyboard/timeline, or the scene on which you placed the title. Then, click the **Play** button under the monitor window.

How the title looks in the storyboard timeline depends on where you placed the title. If you didn't place the clip on a scene, and then the title will be its own scene. Figure 41-2 shows an example with a title in the Storyboard View (top) and the same title in the Timeline View (bottom).

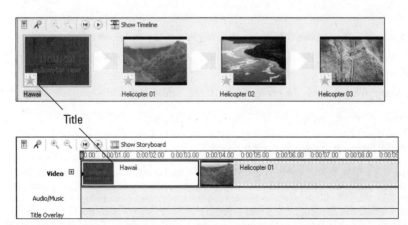

Figure 41-2: Title as its own scene in Storyboard and Timeline Views

If you place the title on a scene, it may not show up at all in the storyboard, or on the video track of the timeline. Instead, it will show up in the Title Overlay track of the timeline, as in Figure 41-3.

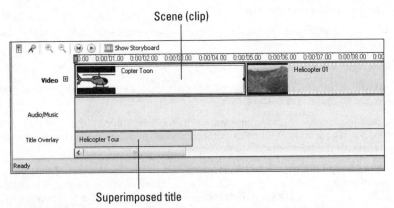

Figure 41-3: Superimposed title in Title Overlay track (Timeline View)

Adding credits

Credits always play at the end of a movie. To add credits to the movie currently showing in the Storyboard or Timeline View, follow these steps:

1. Choose **Tools ➪ Titles and Credits** from Movie Maker's menu bar.

2. In the page that opens, choose **Add credits at the end of the movie**.

3. Type an opening line at the top of the table that appears.

3. The roles and names are in the two columns beneath, as in Figure 41-4. Optionally:

   • Choose **Change the title animation** to change how titles scroll.

   • Choose **Change the text font and color** to change how the text looks (and to make sure it all fits).

4. When you're happy with the credits, click **Done, add title to movie**.

Credits will be the last scene in the movie in both the Storyboard and Timeline Views.

Edit or delete a title or credits

To edit or delete a title, right-click it in the Storyboard or Timeline View, and choose Edit Title. If it's a superimposed title, right-click its bar in the Title Overlay track in the timeline and choose Edit title. You'll be taken to the textboxes where you can change the text. You'll also see the *Change the title animation* and *Change the text font and color* options down below, which you can click to change other aspects of the title. Click the Done link when you've finished making your changes.

To delete the title altogether, right-click it in the storyboard/timeline, or right-click the bar in the Title Overlay track, and choose Delete.

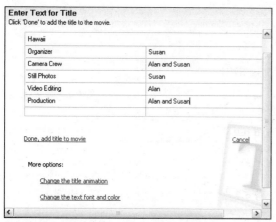

Figure 41-4: Writing the credits

Changing Scene Durations

You can lengthen or shorten the duration of any picture or title in the storyboard/timeline. You can also shorten any video or audio clip, though you can't make those run any longer than the original clip. To trim a scene (or lengthen a title/photo):

Tip

When it comes to trimming scenes, you'll probably find it easiest to work with a wide timeline. Click the + magnifying glass icon, if necessary, to get some width to work in.

1. If you're in the Storyboard View, click on **Show Timeline**.

2. Select (click on) the scene you want to shorten or lengthen. It can be any clip in the Video, Audio/Music, or Title Overlay track.

3. Move the tip of the mouse pointer to the right edge of the scene you want to trim or lengthen. When the mouse pointer is positioned correctly, it will turn to a red two-headed arrow and maybe show a ToolTip as in the top of Figure 41-5.

4. Drag left to shorten, or right to lengthen, the duration of the scene. The ToolTip shows the duration, in seconds, as you drag. For example, in the bottom of Figure 41-5 I lengthened a title overlay to 5.00 seconds to match the duration of the Copter Toon still picture.

5. Release the mouse button when you're done.

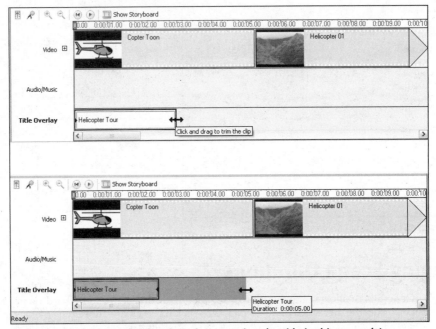

Figure 41-5: Changing the duration of a scene (overlay title in this example)

Overlapping Scenes

You can overlap scenes in the Video, Audio/Music, or Title Overlay tracks. Doing so creates a *fade transition* between them. During that transition, the first scene in the pair fades out at the second scene fades in. The duration of the transition matches the width of the overlapping scenes. To overlap two scenes:

1. If you're in the Storyboard View, click **Show Timeline**.

2. Select (click on) the second of the two scenes you intend to overlap.

3. Place the mouse near the center of that second scene. The mouse pointer changes to a hand, as shown at the top of Figure 41-6.

4. Hold down the left mouse button and drag left. The sloping left edge of the blue bar that appears indicates the amount of overlap with the preceding scene, as in the middle of Figure 41-6.

5. Release the mouse button when you're happy with the amount of overlap. The overlap in the timeline reflects the duration of the overlapping between the scenes, as shown in the bottom of Figure 41-6.

To watch the results, click the first of the two overlapping scenes and click the Play button in the monitor. When playback reaches the point of overlap the first scene will slowly fade out as the second scene slowly fades in. Remember, you can overlap video, titles, or audio in this manner.

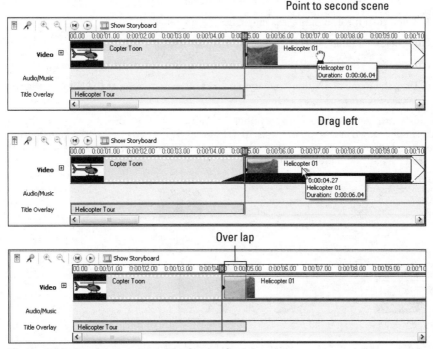

Figure 41-6: Overlapping scenes in the timeline

If you need to increase or decrease the overlap only slightly, stay in the Timeline View and click on the second scene in the transition. Then, choose Clip ⇨ Nudge Left or Clip ⇨ Nudge Right. Each nudge equates to about three-fourths of a second in duration.

Adding Video Transitions

Video transitions use special effects to transition from one scene to the next. Windows Movie Maker comes with several predesigned transition effects. To see their names, click on Video Transitions in the Collections pane. To see an example of how the transition looks in a movie, double-click its name or click its name, and then click the Play button under the monitor. The sample will use a couple of generic pictures from Windows, not content from your movie. But you'll still see how the transition works.

Before you add any video transition effects, you can set a default transition duration that will apply to all video transitions you add to the move from that point on. To set a default video transition duration, choose Tools ⇨ Options from the Movie Maker's menu bar. Click the Advanced tab, and set the Transition Duration option. Then click OK.

To add a video transition to your movie, follow these steps:

1. If you're in the Timeline View, click **Show Storyboard**.

2. In the Collections pane, click on **Video Transitions**.

3. In the Storyboard, click the second of the two clips you're be transitioning between.

4. Drag the name of a Video Transition name to the empty box at the left of the second scene.

The box between the clips shows a symbol that represents the transition type, as shown in the example shown at the top of Figure 41-7. Pointing to that box shows the name of the transition in a ToolTip. To watch the transition, click the first scene in the Storyboard, and then click the Play button under the monitor.

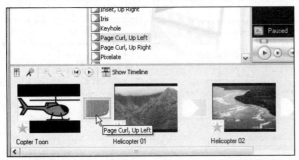

Figure 41-7: Page Curl, Up Left video transition added between two scenes

Tip   Microsoft Digital Media Edition adds several new video effects and video transitions. When you install that product, the Plus! transitions will be listed automatically. See `www.microsoft.com/plus` for more information on Plus! Digital Media Edition.

In the Timeline View, video transitions appear along the Transition track. If you see the + sign next to the Video track title, click that to make the Transition track visible, as in Figure 41-8. There, you can see the Page Curl, Up Left transition that I added between the Copter Toon and Helicopter 01 scenes in the Transition track.

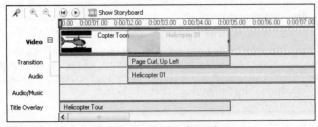

Figure 41-8: Video transition in Timeline View

Adding Video Effects

Unlike transitions, a video effect is applied to a single scene, not to a transition between scenes. Windows Movie Maker 2 comes with several built-in special effects. To see their names, click on Video Effects in the Collections pane. To see what an effect looks like, click its name, and then click the Play button under the monitor. Adding a video effect is easy:

1. If you're in the Timeline View, click on **Show Storyboard** to switch to the Storyboard View.

2. Click on **Video Effects** at the top of the collections pane.

3. To see an example of an effect applied to a generic scene, double-click the effect name, or click the effect name and click the **Play** button in the Monitor.

4. When you find an effect you like, drag its name to the clip to which you want to apply the effect and release the mouse button. The star in the lower-left corner of the scene turns blue. Pointing to that star shows the name of the video effect you applied to the scene.

Figure 41-9 shows an example where I've applied the Film Age, Older video effect to the first scene in the movie. To change the effect, remove the effect, or add more effects to the same scene, right-click the star and choose Video Effects. A dialog box titled Add or Remove Video Effects opens. You'll see in the dialog box how easy it is to add or remove effects. Click OK in that dialog box after making your changes.

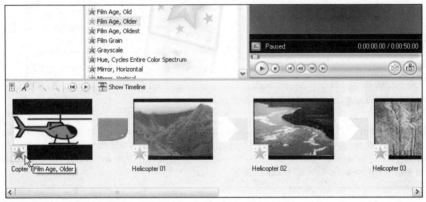

Figure 41-9: Video effect added to first scene in the movie

Tip   Be sure to check out Microsoft's free PowerToys and Fun Packs at www.microsoft.com/windowsxp/downloads/powertoys for creative extras you can add to your movies. Be sure to visit www.microsoft.com/moviemaker often, because there's always something new to learn or download from that site.

Setting Trim Points

As a rule, the easiest way to control the duration of video scenes is by splitting and combining clips before you start adding them to the storyboard/timeline. But that's not the only way to do it. If you already have a scene in your movie, and you want to trim a little off the front, back, or both, you can set trim points within the scene. The trim points won't affect the original clip. Instead, the trim points determine which frames from the clip play in the movie you're currently creating. You can set a Start trim point, End trim point, or both.

✦ **Start Trim Point:** Deteremines where the clip will start to play. Content to the left of the start trim point, within the clip, won't play in the final movie.

✦ **End Trim Point:** Determines where the clip will stop playing. Content to the right of the end trim point won't play in the final movie.

To set a trim point, go to the Timeline View and click on the scene you want to trim. To play the scene from the beginning, click the Back button in the play controls, or drag the top of the blue play indicator in the timeline to the start of the scene, as in Figure 41-10.

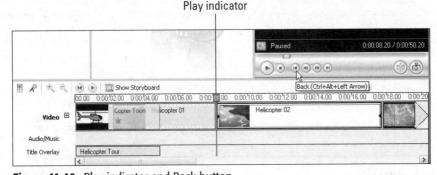

Figure 41-10: Play indicator and Back button

Click the Play button in the monitor to watch the scene. When you get to the point where you want to trim out scenes before, or after, the current scene, click the Pause button. Use the Previous Frame and Next Frame buttons under the monitor to zero in on the specific frame at which you want to set the trim point. Then:

✦ To remove all frames to the left of the current frame, choose **Clip ⇨ Set Start Trim Point**.

✦ Or, to remove all frames to the right of the current frame, choose **Clip ⇨ Set End Trim Point**.

Scenes to the left of the start trim point, or to the right of the end trim point, disappear as though not even part of the current clip. If you change your mind and want to remove trim points, click on the scene once again in the timeline. Then, choose **Clip ⇨ Clear Trim Points** from Movie Maker's menu bar.

Adding Audio to Movies

Any video you capture from a video camera, VCR, or TV will already have a sound track associated with it. You can overlay, or replace, that sound with music or voice narration of your own. The first step is to be aware of how audio looks in the timeline:

1. If you're in Storyboard View, click **View Timeline**.

2. If you see a + sign next to the Video track title, click it to expand the Transition and Audio tracks.

The audio that accompanies each clip appears in the Audio track beneath each clip. When you right-click the audio track for a video scene, you'll see some audio options on the shortcut menu, as in the example shown in Figure 41-11.

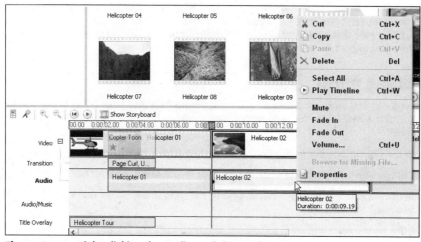

Figure 41-11: Right-clicking the Audio track for a video scene

If you plan to add your own audio to the movie, you may want to mute or lower the volume of the clip's sound track. To mute the sound, choose Mute from the shortcut menu. To reduce the volume of the selected audio clip, choose Volume. The Audio Clip Volume dialog box opens. There, you can adjust the volume by dragging the slider left or right. You can also mute or unmute sound from the same dialog box. Click OK after choosing your options.

The Fade In and Fade Out options apply only to the sound, not the video. The Fade In option causes the sound to fade in gradually. The Fade Out option causes the sound to fade out gradually.

If you want to mute, or unmute, multiple video sound tracks, first select the tracks you want to change using any combination of the methods below:

✦ To select all the sound tracks, right-click any one of them and choose Select All.

✦ To select multiple adjacent sound tracks, click the first one you want to select. Then:

✦ Hold down the **Shift** key and press ↓ to select clips to the right.

    ✦ Press **Shift+End** to select all clips to the end of the movie.

    ✦ Press **Shift +Home** to select all clips to the start of the movie.

    ✦ Hold down the **Shift** key and click the last video clip you want to select.

    ✦ Select and deselect individual clips using **Ctrl+Click**.

Once you've selected all the clips you want to mute or make quieter, right-click any one of them and choose the Mute option. All of the selected clips will be muted (or unmuted if you previously muted them).

Adding music to a movie

You can add music to your movie, provided that you already have the music file in a folder on your hard disk. For example, if you want to add a favorite CD song to a movie, you first need to rip the CD (or at least that specific song) using Windows Media Player. The main catch here is that you can't import protected content. So, if you do plan to use music from a CD that you rip, make sure that you clear the Copy Protect option in Media Player's Options dialog box before you import the song.

Importing music

Before you can add music to a movie, you need to import it into your collections. You might want to create a new folder for holding the music, just to keep things organized. Then, follow these steps:

1. In the Collections pane click on the folder into which you want to import music.

2. Choose **File ➪ Import into Collections** from Movie Maker's menu bar.

3. In the Import Files dialog box that opens, navigate to the folder that contains the music you want to import.

4. Click on the song you want to import, and then click the **Import** button.

Each music clip will be represented by a generic music icon. Figure 41-12 shows an example of a single song, titled Rainbow Connection, imported into a folder named Imported Music. To listen to an audio clip, click its icon, and then click the Play button in the Preview. You won't see anything in the preview screen, because the clip is purely audio. But you will hear the music play.

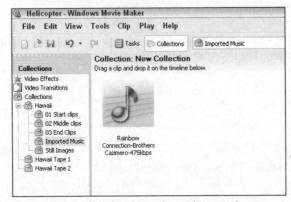

Figure 41-12: Thumbnail icon for an imported song

Editing music

You can split a lengthy song into smaller music clips using the same technique you use to split lengthy video clips into smaller clips:

1. Click on the clip's icon, and click the **Play** button in the preview.

2. When you get to a point where you want to split the clip, click the **Pause** button. Optionally, use the **Previous Frame** and **Next Frame** buttons in the monitor to zero in at exactly the time point at which you want to split the clip.

3. Click the **Split Clip** button in the monitor or choose **Clip** ➪ **Split** from the menu bar.

The song will split into two clips. As usual, you can rename either clip to any name that's meaningful to you. Click either clip and click Play in the monitor to listen to the clip. If you split at the wrong place, press Ctrl+Z or choose Edit ➪ Undo Split. Or, if it's too late for that, select both clips and choose Clip ➪ Combine from the menu bar.

Placing your custom music track

To add a music clip to your movie:

1. If you're in the Storyboard View, click **Show Timeline**.

2. Drag the audio clip into the Audio/Music track with its left edge at about the point where you want the music to start playing.

If the music clip runs longer than the video, drag its rightmost edge, as discussed under "Changing Scene Durations" earlier in this chapter, to where you want the music to stop playing. The reposition the music clip within the Audio/Music track, drag left or right from the center of the clip.

Figure 41-13 shows an example where I've added the "Rainbow Connection" song as a sound track that runs the length of the movie. As you can see, the song is in the Audio/Music track, which the original audio from the video is still in the Audio track.

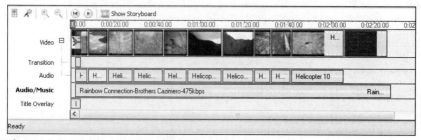

Figure 41-13: Imported song added as a sound track for the movie

To adjust the relative volumes of the imported song and the audio that's already in the videotape, choose Tools ➪ Audio Levels. The Audio Levels dialog box shown in Figure 41-14 opens. To increase the relative volume of the original audio from the videotape, drag the slider to the left. To make the music louder than the original sound from the videotape, drag the slider to the right. Close the dialog box by clicking its Close (X) button.

Figure 41-14: Audio Levels dialog box

To hear how the music will play in your final move, just click any scene within the timeline and click the Player button in the monitor. If you're not happy with the results, open the Audio Levels dialog box again and try a different setting.

Adding narration to a movie

If you have a microphone or headset that works with your computer, you can record your own voice narration and add it to your movie. To get started, you'll probably want save your project, close Movie Maker, and then plug in your microphone. If it's a USB microphone, wait until the notification area message tells you that the device is ready to use. Then, restart Movie Maker and open your project.

Note If you've already added music to the Audio/Music track, you cannot narrate over that track. See "Adding multiple sound tracks" later in this chapter to get around that problem.

Narrating is a lot harder than most people realize, so you may want to practice a bit first. Just play the movie and narrate out loud as it plays. (You family will think you're talking to yourself, but don't worry about them). If you find it difficult to remember everything and speak smoothly and clearly, you may want to write a script to read from as you're narrating the movie.

When you're ready to record your narration, make sure that your microphone is plugged in and ready to go. Play your movie in the preview until it gets to a point where you want to start narrating. Or, in the Timeline View, drag the top of the play indicator to where you intend to start your narration. Then:

Choose ⇨ Narrate Timeline. You'll see some of the options shown in Figure 41-15. Click on Show more options . . . if you don't see the items in the lower portion of that figure.

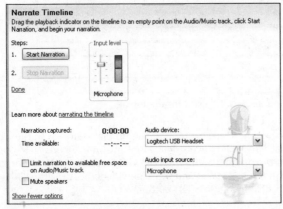

Figure 41-15: Narrate timeline options

Adjust the Input Level slider until your speaking voice reaches into the yellow portion of the bar without crossing over into the red. If your voice doesn't register at all, make sure that you've selected the microphone you're using under Audio device, and select Microphone under Audio input source. Optionally, you can:

✦ Choose the **Limit narration . . .** option if you want to make sure that your narration doesn't extend beyond the available space in the Audio/Music track.

✦ Choose **Mute speakers** if your spoken voice is being played through the speakers as you speak.

When you're ready to start narrating, click the Start Narration button, and start talking. The movie will play as you're narrating, so you can time your spoken words to events that play out in the movie. To stop narrating, click the Stop Narration button.

When you click the Stop Narration button, a Save Windows Media File dialog box will open. If you're not to thrilled with your narration, click Cancel in that dialog box, reposition the play indicator at your starting point, and try again. When you're happy with your narration, you can save it. The dialog box will suggest a folder named Narration and a filename. Click Save to accept those suggestions unless you want to place the narration file elsewhere.

The narration will appear in the Audio Music track. For example, in Figure 41-16 I narrated a small portion near the front of the movie. The mouse pointer is resting on that narration clip so you can see its name and duration.

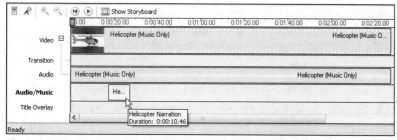

Figure 41-16: Narration sound clip in the Audio/Music track

Feel free to move the play indicator to any other part of the movie you want to narrate. Then repeat the process. That is, click Start Narration, speak for as long as you want, and then click Stop Narration. Each narration will be stored as a separate file, and will appear as a clip within the Audio/Movie track. When you save this copy of the movie as a file, the finished movie will include your voice narrations.

When you've finished, you can save your completed movie as described under "Saving Multiple Copies of Movies" later in this chapter.

Adding multiple sound tracks

Movie Maker offers only one Audio/Music track. You can't add more audio on top of a section of the track that already contains audio. However, you can add multiple sound tracks in a roundabout way. First, you save your movie with the custom sound track in place. Then, you import that movie back into Movie Maker as your starting point. The Audio/Music track in the imported copy of the movie will be empty, because the previous sound tracks are all combined on the Audio track of the newly imported movie. Here are the steps:

1. Save your current project by choosing **File ➪ Save Project**.

2. Make a movie of the current project by choosing **File ➪ Save Movie File**.

3. In the Save Movie Wizard, choose **My Computer** and click Next.

4. Give this movie a recognizable name such as "My Movie, Music Only" so that you know it's the one that doesn't yet contain narration. Choose your folder, and click Next.

5. Choose a very high-quality setting, because you can always make lower-quality movies later. First, choose Show more choices . . . if that option is visible. If you don't already have a preference, I suggest that you do the following:

   • If the movie will eventually be played on TV, choose a high-quality NTSC setting such as **DV-AVI (NTSC)** or **High quality video (NTSC).**

   • If the movie will only be played on computers, choose **High quality video (large).**

6. Click **Next**, and wait for the Movie Maker to create the movie. Then, click **Finish** on the last page of the Save Movie Wizard.

The movie you just created will have both the original audio track from the video camera, plus any custom music track you've added. To add narration, reimport that finished movie without splitting it into clips. Here's how:

1. Choose **File ➪ Import into Collections** from Movie Maker's menu bar.

2. In the Import File dialog box that opens, clear the check mark next to *Create clips for video files* so that the imported movie won't be divided into clips.

3. Navigate to whatever folder you saved the movie in Step 4.

4. Click the icon of the movie you just saved, and then click the **Import** button.

5. Again, make sure you save your current project (choose **File ➪ Save Project**). Then, clear the storyboard/timeline by right-clicking just beyond the last scene in the move and choosing **Clear Timeline**.

6. Drag the movie you just imported into the storyboard/timeline.

When you play the movie, you'll see that it has all the titles, effects, and sound track you've already added. They're all part of the movie now, so those things won't show up in any of the tracks below the timeline. In other words, the movie you just imported is now your new "raw footage," your new starting point for whatever else you want to do to the movie. The Audio/Music track will be empty, as in Figure 41-17. So, you're free to add additional sound or narration as you see fit.

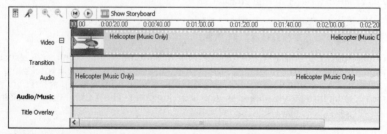

Figure 41-17: Imported movie has a clear Audio/Music track.

To save the project you just created independently of the original project, choose File ➪ Save Project As. And give this project another name.

Saving Multiple Copies of Movies

There's no rule that says you can only create one movie from your project. In fact, you may want to create several different copies at various quality settings, just to get a sense how the quality setting you choose affects the file size and the size and quality of video quality. You should always save at least one high-quality copy of your movie, in case you ever want to reimport it and use it as the raw footage for creating a new-and-improved version of the movie.

If the movie will ever be played on a television set, you should definitely save at least one copy in one of the NTSC quality settings. The NTSC settings all size the final movie to 720 × 480 pixels, which is the appropriate size for a TV set. Any smaller size will be stretched to fit the TV screen, which causes the quality of the video image to deteriorate.

Recall that to save your movie, you choose File ➪ Save Movie File from Media Player's menu bar. In the Save Movie Wizard that opens, first choose My Computer as the location for your local copy of the movie. Then click Next>. On the second wizard screen, give the movie a name that reflects the quality you intend to choose, such as "My Movie (DV-AVI)" or "My Movie (NTSC High Quality)" or "My Movie (Pocket PC Full Screen)". Then on the third wizard page, click Show more options.

The exact file size of a movie will vary, depending on the movie's content. But just to give you an idea of what to expect, Table 41-1 lists several different qualities. The video size is the visual size of the video on the screen when you play the movie in Windows Media Player or a similar program. The Size Per Minute column shows how much disk space is consumed per 1 minute of movie content.

Table 41-1: Video Size and File Size Comparisons for a 1-Minute Movie

Quality	Video Size (pixels)	Size Per Minute
Pocket PC 218 Kbps	208 × 160	1.7 MB
Pocket PC Full Screen	320 × 240	1.7 MB
High quality (large)*	640 × 480	11.7 MB
High quality (small)*	320 × 240	4.9 MB
Local Playback (2.1 Mbps)	640 × 480	15.7 MB
Broadband (512 Kbps)	320 × 240	3.97 MB
High Quality NTSC*	720 × 480	12.4 MB
Local Playback (2.1 Mbps NTSC)	720 × 480	15.7 MB
DV-AVI	720 × 480	228.78 MB

*Variable bit rate formats

Viewing icons for movies

When you save a project, you're not saving a finished movie. Instead, you're saving the arrangement of tracks in the storyboard/timeline, so you can resume work on the project at any time in the future. The filename extension for the project will be .MSWMM. Filename extensions for movies will be .WMV unless you chose the DV-AVI format, in which cast the extension is .AVI.

But even if extensions are hidden, it shouldn't be difficult to discriminate between movie and project icons. The Project files have a Movie Maker document icon. The finished movies will have a Media Player icon. Or, in Thumbnails View, the movie icon will display the first frame of the movie. Figure 41-18 shows examples.

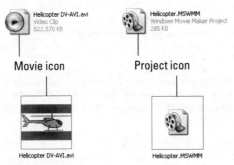

Movie icon   Project icon

Figure 41-18: Icons for movies (left) and projects (right)

If you intend to send your finished movie to someone, don't bother to sent the project file. It won't do them any good. But if you send the finished .WMV or .AVI file to someone on CD, that person will be able to watch the movie on any Windows computer that has a CD drive and Windows Media Player installed.

Other destinations for movies

The first page of the Save Movie Wizard asks where you want to store your finished movie. After you choose one of the options summarized in the following list and click Next, the wizard will take you through the process of saving the movie to the location you specified:

✦ **Recordable CD:** If you have a CD burner on your computer, put a blank CD into the drive and choose this option to burn the movie straight to a CD. The resulting CD will be in HighMAT format, which can be played by anyone with Windows XP and Windows Media Player 10, as well as any other device that supports HighMAT CDs.

✦ **E-mail:** If you have a standard POP3 mail account, choosing this option will create the movie and attach it to a blank e-mail message that you can address to whomever you want. Note, however, that the movie cannot exceed the maximize attachment size allowed by your, or the recipient's, ISP.

E-Mailing Movies

The e-mail attachment size limit varies from one ISP to the next. For dial-up accounts, the limit is usually between 1 and 3 MB. For broadband accounts it's usually in the 10 MB range. Neither size, though, allows for very large movies. In fact, you'll be lucky if you can send a single short, low-quality clip.

If you don't have a POP3 mail account, choosing the E-mail option in the Save Movie Wizard isn't likely to work. However, you can save the movie to your hard disk, and then attach the movie to an e-mail message you create within your standard e-mail client for your account.

✦ **The Web:** If you have an account with a video hosting service that supports direct uploading of movies from Windows Movie Maker, choose this option to upload the movie to your site. See www.microsoft.com/windowsxp/using/moviemaker/ partners.mspx for a list of potential providers.

✦ **DV camera:** If you have a digital video camera and a blank tape, choose this option to copy the finished movie to a blank videotape. From the tape, you'll able to watch the movie on TV, and copy it to standard VHS tape, provided that you know how to use those capabilities of your digital video camera.

Wrap Up

That chapter has looked at more advanced techniques for creating movies with Windows Movie Maker 2.1. The next chapter addresses still more Movie Maker issues, such as getting content from analog devices (TVs and VCRs) and ways to burn movies to DVDs. The main points covered in this chapter include:

✦ To add pictures and photos to a movie, first import them into a collection. Then, drag any picture or photo to the storyboard/timeline.

✦ To add text titles and credits to a movie, choose Tools ➪ Titles and Credits from Movie Maker's menu bar.

✦ To change the duration of a scene, including a photo or audio track, go to the Timeline View and drag the rightmost border of the track left or right.

✦ To overlap scenes in a movie, drag the left border of the second scene toward the left so that it overlaps with the scene that precedes it.

✦ The Video Effects and Video Transitions collections offer cool special effects that you can easily add to any movie.

✦ To add custom background music to a movie, import a song into a collection, and then drag it to the Audio/Music track in the timeline.

✦ To narrate a movie, connect your microphone and choose Tools ➪ Narrate Timeline from the menu bar.

✦   ✦   ✦

Using VHS, LPs, DVD, and More

As you saw in preceding chapters, capturing music from CDs and capturing video from digital video cameras are fairly easy. Things aren't quite so easy when you want to capture *analog* content. Analog sources include things like vinyl phonograph LPs, cassette tapes, VHS movie tapes, Video 8, and other tapes used in analog (nondigital) video cameras.

You can capture content from all of these analog media, but there are some hurdles. For one thing, you have to know your hardware fairly well. For example, you need to know what kind of connectors are on the device and on your computer. You need get a cable to connect the device to the computer. You'll see examples of the various connectors in this chapter.

Capturing Analog Video

Analog video is any nondigital video coming from a television, VCR playing VHS tape, or an nondigital video camera. Just about any device that can play analog video will have connectors on the back to sending the video and audio signals out to another device. The most common are RCA Video and Audio plugs, usually with two audio plugs. Some devices may have an optional S-Video port, which carries video at a higher quality than the regular video plug. Figure 42-1 shows an example of S-Video and RCA Video and Audio jacks often found on televisions, VCRs, and analog digital cameras.

Figure 42-1: S-Video (left) and RCA Video and Audio jacks

Some devices will have an A/V plug rather than the S-Video or RCA-style plugs. The A/V plug doesn't look like much, just a hole about ⅛ inch in diameter, usually labeled A/V.

Unfortunately, I can't tell you exactly how to connect your TV, VCR, or analog video camera to your computer because there are so many makes and models of those devices. We're all on our own when it comes to learning how to use a specific make and model of product we buy. But I can give you some guidelines to get you started in the right direction.

You need cables and corresponding ports on your computer to make the connection. Whether or not your computer already has the appropriate connectors depends on whether or not you computer already has a *video capture device* built in. Most off-the-shelf computers don't come with video capture capabilities built in. That's something you usually have to add on your own. There are two ways to do that.

One way to add video capture capabilities is to add an internal video capture card to the computer. That requires some internal hardware installation. The other approach is to use a bridge, which connects to the computer through a USB port. With a bridge, you don't have to install any internal hardware.

Tip To see makes and models of XP-compatible video capture devices, go to www. WindowsCatalog.com, click the Hardware tab, and then click on Cameras and Video ⇨ Video Capture Cards in the left column.

If you have a digital video camera that connects to the computer through an IEEE 1394 port, and also a 1394 port on your computer, you may be able to use your digital video camera as a bridge. You must be using Windows Movie Maker 2.1 (the version that comes with the Service Pack 2 download) for this to work. Also, you'll need to learn how to use the DV Pass-Through feature of your camera.

The main point here, though, whether you're using a bridge or a capture card is this: Since you want to capture content *from* the external device to the computer, you must connect the Out ports on the external device to the *In* ports on the computer. If you have a choice between using either S-Video or the standard RCA video plugs, you should go with S-Video, because it transfers higher-quality video. But be aware that both RCA and S-Video connectors carry only the video signal. You still have to connect audio ports with either type of connection.

Tip If you don't have appropriate cables for your hardware, you can probably find the cables you need at any Radio Shack

Figure 42-2 shows some examples. There, I show an analog video camera on the left as the external device. But that external device could just as easily be a standard VCR or television. Also the figure shows a bridge between the computer and device. If your computer has a built-in video capture card, you won't need the bridge in the middle. Instead, you'll connect the Out ports on the device to the In ports right on the computer.

USB-Connected Video

Personally, I've never had any luck getting Movie Maker to capture video from a USB port. I have a Dazzle DVC 150 bridge that connect and analog device to a USB 2.0 port, but couldn't capture directly to Movie Maker with that. Instead, I had to use the Pinnacle Studio 8 software that came with the device to capture the video. Then I was able to import the captured video into Movie Maker.

Some video cameras may offer a direct USB connection to the computer. If your camera has such a connector, and Movie Maker can't capture from it, look take a look at the software that came with the camera. Chances are, you'll be able to capture video using that software and then import the captured content into Movie Maker.

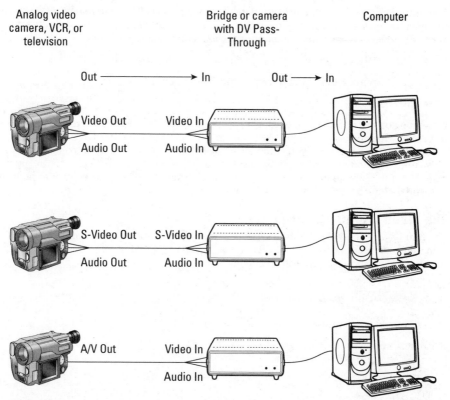

Figure 42-2: Connect Out ports on external device to In ports on bridge or computer.

Using the Video Capture Wizard

You get video from a video camera, TV, or VCR by *capturing* it. The video actually plays on your computer screen at normal speed, and your computer also captures a copy in a file as it's going by. It all happens in real time; if you're going to copy an entire 30-minute tape, it will take 30 minutes to copy it.

Once you've connected the device to the computer, or through a bridge to the computer, you need to turn the device on. If you're capturing form an analog video camera, make sure that you turn on the camera in VCR mode, not in Camera or Record mode. You want the camera to play, not record, video here.

Next, insert the tape from which you'll be capturing content (obviously no tape is required if you're capturing straight from a TV). Rewind the tape to the beginning, or to the point where you want to start capturing content. If you're not capturing from the start of the tape, rewind a few seconds back from the starting point. Better to capture too much rather than too little, because you can always edit out anything you don't want later.

If Windows can detect your camera, Windows Movie Maker might start automatically. Or, you might be given the option to start Movie Maker. Either method is OK. If Windows Movie Maker doesn't start within a minute or so, automatically, go ahead and start it yourself. Click the Start button and choose All Programs ➪ Windows Movie Maker (or All Programs ➪ Accessories ➪ Windows Movie Maker).

The Video Capture Wizard might automatically open as well. If so, you're ready to start capturing video as described in a moment. If the wizard doesn't open automatically, just go ahead and open it using whatever method is most convenient:

✦ Choose **File ➪ Capture Video** from Windows Movie Maker's menu bar.

✦ Click **Capture from video device** in the Tasks pane.

✦ Press **Ctrl+R**.

Depending on the camera you're using, the Video Capture Wizard might present anywhere from one to four pages of options. We'll look at each page of the wizard in the sections that follow. Remember that after you complete a page of the wizard, you need to click Next to move onto the next page. If you click Next too soon, just click Back to return to the precious page. Don't be alarmed if some pages don't appear. The wizard is smart enough to present only the options needed for your particular camera.

The Video Capture Device page

The first page of the Video Capture Wizard is titled Video Capture Device and might look something like Figure 42-3, when it first opens. This page is asking where the video and audio feed that you plan to capture will be coming from.

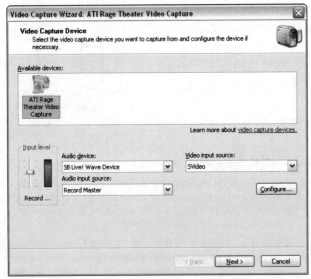

Figure 42-3: The Video Capture Device page of the Video Capture Wizard

The options available to you will depend on your computer and camera. Under Available Devices, you need to click the icon that represents your camera or the plug to which the camera is connected. Click whichever icon represents your device. As a rule, once you click an icon under Available Devices, you can leave all other settings as they are and click the Next button. However, if you don't see the video and hear the sound when you get to the Capture Video page, you may need to try other options in the Audio Device, Audio Input Source, and Video Input Source dialog boxes.

The Captured Video File page

The second page of the wizard, titled Captured Video File, asks what you want to name the video you're about to capture and where you want to put it. Think up a brief but descriptive name, and type it under *Enter a filename for your captured video*. Under *Choose a place to save your captured video*, choose My Videos (unless, for whatever reason, you want to put the video in some other folder). Then click Next.

The Video Setting page

The third page of the wizard lets you choose a quality for your captured video. The general rule of thumb is, the better the quality, the better the video looks and sounds, but the larger the resulting file. You always want the best quality that your machine can handle. The simple solution is to choose *Best quality for playback on my computer (recommended)*. Click Next to get to the fourth and final wizard page.

The Capture Video page

The fourth wizard page, titled Capture Video (see Figure 42-4), is where the actual capture takes place. Before you do anything else, take a look at the checkboxes near the bottom of the dialog box, and make selections as appropriate for your goals:

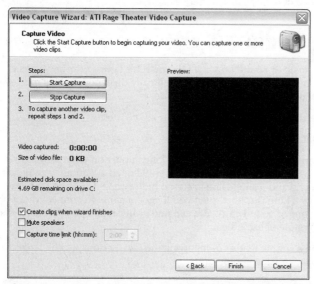

Figure 42-4: The Capture Video page of the Video Capture Wizard

✦ **Create clips when wizard finishes:** Choose this option to have Movie Maker automatically divide the video into smaller scenes. Doing so will make it easier to edit your movie.

✦ **Mute speakers:** Choose this option if you don't want your computer speakers to play the video while it's being captured.

✦ **Capture time limit (hh:mm):** If you want to capture a fixed amount of video (for example, exactly 30 minutes), choose this option and set your time limit.

You're finally ready to capture. Press the Play button on your video camera to get the tape going, and click Start Capture in the dialog box. Whatever video plays in the monitor on your screen will also be captured in Movie Maker.

When you've finished capturing video, just click the Stop Capture button in the dialog box, and then stop the playback on the camera as well. Click the Finish button to complete the Wizard, and wait for the file to be split into clips (if you chose the *Create clips . . .* option in the Caption Video page of the Wizard).

The video you captured will be added to your Collections under whatever filename you gave the movie near the start of this process. When you click the collection's name in the Collections pane, or choose the collection's name from the drop-down list on the toolbar, you'll see an icon or icons that represent the captured video. To play a captured video or clip from the video, click its icon in the Contents pane, and click the Play button under the Monitor.

Once you've captured the video and you can see the clips in Movie Maker, you've finished capturing. You can disconnect the analog video device. Create your movie using your captured clips and the techniques described in Chapters 41 and 42.

Capturing Analog Audio

Analog audio refers to any music or sound on vinyl LPs, cassette tapes, or other types of tape. You best bet here will be to purchase software specifically designed for this purpose. Two very popular products for this type of capture include:

✦ **PolderbitS Sound Recorder and Editor:** www.PolderbitS.com

✦ **Microsoft Plus! Digital Media Edition:** www.Microsoft.com/Plus

You need to connect the stereo or cassette player to the Line In port on your computer's sound card. If your stereo has two RCA Audio Out ports, you'll need a Y-adapter cable with two male RCA plugs on one end and a single line-in stereo mini-connector on the other end. If your cassette player has only a Line Out port, then you'll need a cable to connect that port to the Line In port on your computer sound card. You can find either type of cable at any Radio Shack. Figure 42-5 shows a couple of examples.

From that point on, it will be a simple matter of following the instructions in whichever program you purchased to capture analog audio.

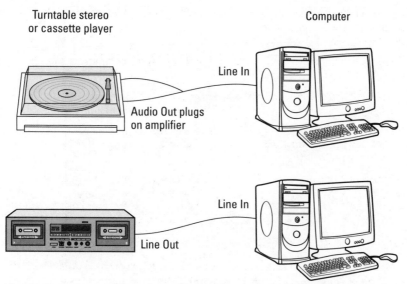

Figure 42-5: Connecting analog audio devices to a computer Line In jack.

Copying Windows Movie Maker Movies to DVD

Windows XP has no built-in capabilities to copy files to DVDs. But, if your computer has a DVD burner in it, chances are you already have software that can copy data to blank DVD disks. For example, I added a Sony DVD burner to one of my computers a few months back. That drive came with Sonic MyDVD, an easy tool for authoring DVDs from video on your computer.

With MyDVD, you create a main menu for your DVD as in the example shown in Figure 42-6. Each frame in the main menu represents a video that can be played. Adding the buttons to the main menu is easy. You just click the Get Movies button in the left column, navigate to the folder where your WMV or AVI movies are stored, select your movies, and click Open.

When it comes time to actually burn the blank DVD, be aware that most standard set-top DVD players (the kind you connect to a TV) can handle either DVD-Rs or DVD+Rs. Some, but not all, can handle DVD-RWs and DVD+RWs. But once you've inserted a blank DVD into the DVD burner on your computer, you just need to click the Burn button in MyDVD, and wait for it to burn the DVD.

The MyDVD example is just an example. Again, that's not a program that everyone has. If you have a DVD burner, it may have come with some other DVD-burning software. Chances are, you can use that software to copy your movies to DVDs. If not, you might consider purchases the MyDVD product, because it handles Movie Maker .wmv file nicely. See www.sonic.com for more information on MyDVD.

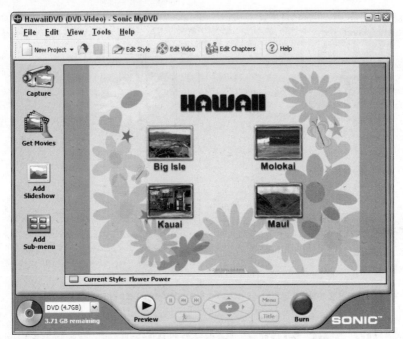

Figure 42-6: Using a third-party product to burn movies to a DVD

Copying Movie Maker Movies to Tape

If you have a digital video camera, copying Movie Maker Movies to digital tape is easy. Just put a blank DVD tape into the camera. Open your project, choose Save Movie to File, then choose DV Camera in the Save Movie Wizard. Once you've copied the movie to DVD tape, you should be able to copy it to VHS tape by connecting to the camera to a VCR and copying the DV movie to a blank VHS tape.

If you don't have a digital video camera, you need a video card or bridge that can send audio and video out of the computer through analog ports such as S-Video, RCA Video and Audio Out, or A/V Out ports. You then need to connect those Out ports on the computer or bridge to the corresponding ports on the VCR or analog video camera, as illustrated in Figure 42-7.

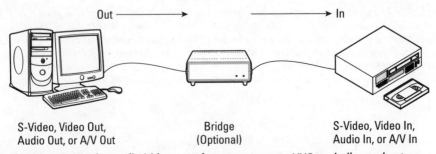

Figure 42-7: Getting audio/video out of a computer onto VHS or similar analog tape

This type of connection is likely to be the most difficult to make. You really have to know the hardware you're using and set everything up by following the manufacturer's instructions to a T. Guessing in this arena is almost guaranteed to lead to hours of hair-pulling frustration.

But, once you have the Video and Audio Out plugs on the computer connected to Video and Audio In plugs on the VCR or analog camera, the next step is to put a blank tape into the VCR or video camera. (If you're copying to an analog video camera, make sure that you turn the camera on in VCR more, not in Camera or Record mode).

The next step will be to hit the Record and Play buttons on the VCR or camera. Then, play the movie you want to record in Windows Media Player. Switch to full-screen mode in Media Player so that you don't see the program window on the recorded tape.

Converting Video Formats

If you already have video on your hard disk that's in a format that Movie Maker doesn't support, you'll have to convert that video to WMV, MPEG, AVI, or some other supported format before you can import it. Likewise, movies you create in Movie Maker will be stored in WMV or AVI format. Note that your exported movie will be in AVI format only if you choose the DV-AVI (NTSC) format when saving your movie file.

There is nothing built into Windows XP that can convert video files from one format to another. There are, however, quite a few products on the market that can handle the job. Different products have different capabilities. So, you may need to shop around to find a program that can do exactly the conversion you need. Here are some products to consider, and the Web pages you can pursue for more information:

✦ **AVI MPEG Video Converter:** www.video-converter.net

✦ **AVS Video Converter:** www.avsmedia.com

✦ **Blaze Media Pro:** www.blazemp.com

✦ **FX Video Converter:** www.jhepple.com

✦ **Magic Video Batch Converter:** www.video-tool.com

✦ **SVCD Video Converter:** http://svcd.ws/video-converter.htm

Converting Audio and Music Files

When you rip a CD in Windows Media Player 10, you can choose between WMA or MP3 formats. If you buy Microsoft Plus! Digital Media Additional, you'll get the Plus! Audio Converter. With that program you can convert any .wma, .mp3, or .wav file to .wma, .mp3, or .wav format.

If you need to convert audio files to or from other formats such as Ogg, Mp4, AIFF, AU, MIDI, Real Audio (.ra, .ram, .rm), you'll need a more potent audio converter program. There are many such products on the market, so you'll need to shop around to find one that can handle the file types you need to work with. Here are some products and Web sites to look into:

✦ **Audio Converter/Audio Grabber:** www.e-soft.co.uk

✦ **Audio Converter:** www.mp3towav.org/

✦ **dBpowerAMP Music Converter:** www.dbpoweramp.com/

✦ **IntelliScore:** www.intelliscore.net/

✦ **Lead Capture and Convert:** www.leadtools.com/utilities/CaptureAndConvert

✦ **River Past Audio Converter:** www.riverpast.com/

Wrap Up

When it comes to working with the many different multimedia file formats in the world, Windows XP doesn't offer a whole lot. However, just because a feature isn't built into Windows XP doesn't mean that you can't do it. There are thousands of programs and hardware devices on the market that can do just about anything. This chapter has presented some of the requirements and examples, as summarized below:

✦ To capture video from a VCR or analog video camera, you need a video capture device to connect the camera to the computer.

✦ To capture music from LPs or cassette tape, you need a sound card with a Line In jack and appropriate software.

✦ To copy movies to DVD, you need a DVD burner and software that can write to blank DVD disks in that burner.

✦ To copy movie to VHS or 8mm tape, you'll need a "two-way" video capture device that can send audio and video out of the computer to the analog device.

✦ To convert existing music and video files to other formats, look for programs specifically written to convert audio and video files.

✦   ✦   ✦

Troubleshooting Multimedia

Troubleshooting Pictures and Photos

Most problems I see in the "pictures and photos" category stem from people who don't know how to work their digital cameras. So, if you fall into that category, remember that the only place to learn about your specific camera is from the instructions that came with that camera. Here, I can only focus on problems that concern Windows, not every make and model of digital camera ever created.

No Copy option when right-clicking a picture in a Web page

Not all Web browsers offer a copy option on the shortcut menu. Try browsing to the same page using Internet Explorer. Optionally, you can right-click a picture and choose Save Picture As to store the picture in your My Pictures folder, or any other folder of your choosing.

Cannot copy thumbnail from My Pictures to open document

Thumbnails represent closed documents and cannot be copy and pasted into an open document. You'll either need to insert the picture into the open document using whatever commands that program supports. Or open (double-click) the picture, right-click the open picture, and choose Copy, and then paste the picture into an open document.

Get Pictures from Scanner or Camera option not available under Picture Tasks

The *Get Pictures from Scanner and Camera* option under Picture Tasks is only available in your My Pictures and Shared Pictures folder, subfolders of those folders, and folders to which you've applied the Pictures template.

Make sure that the camera or scanner is properly connected to the computer and turned on. It may take a few seconds for the option to appear after you open the folder and make the connection.

If there's still no sign of the option, the camera or scanner might not be 100 percent compatible with Windows XP, especially if it's an older product. Try installing the most current drivers for the device (see Chapter 53) or visit the camera or scanner manufacturer's Web site for more information. Also, make sure that you understand how to use the device, as described in the documentation that came with that device.

Troubleshooting Windows Media Player

Multimedia is a combination of computer hardware (your graphics card, CD or DVD drives, and the like) as well as software (Windows Movie Maker and the specific song or movie with which you're having a problem). It's not always easy to tease out exactly where a problem lies. The following sections cover solutions to some of the more common Windows Movie Maker maladies.

Message "Invalid Function" when trying to burn a CD

Follow the steps below to verify that your CD-R or CD-RW is able and ready to burn CDs:

1. Open your **My Computer** folder.

2. Right-click the icon that represents your CD or DVD drive and choose **Properties**.

3. Click the **Recording** tab.

4. Select (check) **Enable Recording** on this drive.

5. Click **OK**.

Some other program opens when you open an icon or insert a CD

If the problem arises when you double-click the icon for a song or video file, follow these steps:

1. Open Windows Media Player normally, and choose **Tools** ⇨ **Options** from its menu.

2. Click the **File Types** tab in the Options dialog box.

3. Click the **Select All** button or choose the file types for which you want to make Media Player the default player, and then click **OK**.

Tip   Media Player can't play all types of media files. It can play only the file types listed on the File Types tab.

If some program other than Media Player opens when you put an audio CD in your CD drive, make Windows Media Player the default program for Music CD and Music Files, as discussed under "Setting Defaults for CDs and DVDs" in Chapter 15.

Video plays but no audio

If you're playing a .avi file, you may need the DivX codec to see the video. That codec won't download automatically. You have to get it from www.divx.com. If the problem occurs with all videos you play, check your volume controls as discussed under "Controlling sound volume" in Chapter 38.

Cannot see captions when playing a CD or DVD

Verify that the CD or DVD you're playing offers captions or subtitles (not all do). In Windows Media Player, choose Play ➪ Captions and Subtitles ➪ On if Available from Media Player's menu. Even if you've already done so, you may need to do so again after the computer goes into Stand By or Hibernate mode.

If the problem persists, choose Tools ➪ Options from Media Player's menu. Then, click the Security tab, select (check) *Show local captions when present*, and click OK.

Media Player can't find my MP3 player

Verify that the MP3 player if properly connected to the computer and turned on. If the player is brand new, wait a few minutes for Windows Media Player to detect the device. If nothing happens within several minutes, read the instructions that came with the device. You may need to install the original drivers and then update those drivers.

Once you've installed the drivers that came with the device, there may still be several minutes delay while Media Player checks the Windows Update site for new drivers. Make sure that you go online, and stay online, for several minutes after connecting the device so that Media Player can check for updated drivers.

You might also want to check the player manufacturer's Web site for information on using the device with Windows Media Player 10. Not all devices are 100 percent compatible with Media Player.

Song titles don't appear after inserting a CD

Song titles only appear in the Rip window if 1) You're online when you insert the CD and 2) the CD media information is stored in the online CDDB. See "Finding media information online" in Chapter 38 for more information.

Song won't play and ! appears in front of song title

The song you are trying to play is not longer available at the location specified in the File Path column. Most likely you've either moved or deleted the file. If you've moved or reorganized your media files, you can follow the steps given here to rebuild your media library to accurately reflect content currently available on your hard drive:

1. Open Windows Media Player, and click the **Library** button in the Features taskbar.

2. Choose **Tools ➪ Options** from Media Player's menu.

3. Click the **Library** tab, and clear the check mark (if any) next to *Delete files from computer when deleted from library* checkbox.

4. Click **OK**.

5. Click on **All Music** at the top of the contents pane. All song titles will be listed down that right pane.

6. Click the first-listed song title once to select it, then press **Ctrl+A** or **Shift+End** to select all song titles.

7. Right-click any selected song title, and choose **Delete**.

Caution   If you mess up on Step 8, you will permanently delete *all* the listed song titles from your computer. You don't want to be careless here!

8. Choose **Delete from library only**, and then click **OK**.

9. Wait until all song titles disappear from the contents pane (the right pane).

Once you've emptied out the library, you can rebuild it from your entire hard drive or just certain folders. Ideally, you'll want to put all the content that you want to play in Media Player into specific folders so that you don't end up with every single sound file in your library when you search for media files. Anyway, the next step is to search for media files as follows:

1. Choose **Tools ➪ Search for Media Files** from Media Player's menu bar.

2. Choose the hard drive(s) and folder(s) you want to search from the Search On and Look In options.

3. Choose **New files and all existing files in library (slow)**.

4. Under the Advanced search options, choose **Add files previously deleted from library**.

5. Click **Search** and wait for the search to complete, and then click the **Close** button.

Your media library should be completely up to date. Click the + sign next to All Music, if necessary, and any category name under All Music to verify the results. Similarly, click the + sign next to Contributing Artist, and then click any artist's name to verify that all songs by that artist are shown.

Error message appears with 0xC00 or other number

There are lots of these, more than I could even begin to fit into a single chapter. Currently most are listed in the Windows Media Player 9 FAQ at:

www.microsoft.com/windows/windowsmedia/9series/player/playererrors.aspx

By the time you read this, there may be a separate page for Media Player 10, though the existing list will likely be of use. The message numbers are listed without the leading 0x characters.

All other Windows Media Player issues

For all other Windows Media Player problems, see the following Web sites:

www.microsoft.com/windows/windowsmedia

www.microsoft.com/windows/windowsmedia/mp10/faq.aspx

www.microsoft.com/windows/windowsmedia/knowledgecenter

www.microsoft.com/windows/windowsmedia/mp10

www.microsoft.com/windows/windowsmedia/mp10/troubleshooting.aspx

www.msmvps.com/chrisl

www.microsoft.com/windows/windowsmedia/knowledgecenter/MediaAdvice.aspx

Tip   The Media Advice page below is specifically geared to capturing content from vinyl LPs, cassette tapes, and other sources.

Troubleshooting Windows Movie Maker

The most common Movie Maker problems stem from not quite understanding how to use the program. When I look at the questions posted in the message boards, I see that most don't require any troubleshooting. Rather, the problem stems from not knowing how to use Windows Movie Maker. For example, the whole concept of clips as "scenes" seems to elude many people, and many fail to notice the *Create clips when Wizard finished* option in the Video Capture Wizard (see Figure 40-9 in Chapter 40). Just about everyone seems to overlook the *Create clips for video files* option that appears in the Import File dialog box after you choose File ➪ Import into Collections from Movie Maker's menu bar.

There's also much confusion between what is a movie project file (.MSWMM) and what is a finished movie (.wmv or .avi file). As discussed under "Saving your project" in Chapter 40, the .MSWMM file is for storing a movie "work in progress," and never represents a finished movie to watch or copy to a CD or DVD. You need to complete the steps under "Stage 4: Creating the Final Product" in Chapter 40, and be able to recognize the icons as displayed there, to discriminate between a movie project file and an actual finished movie.

Aside from the common confusions, there are some actual error messages that can arise. Those really do come under the heading of "troubleshooting," and many are covered in the sections that follow.

Message "Your system is currently set to 800x600 . . ."

This isn't an error message — more like a suggestion. Click OK to use Windows Media Player at the current resolution. Optionally, you can increase your screen resolution to 1024×768 as described under "Choosing a screen resolution and color depth" in Chapter 6.

Message "A video capture device was not detected . . ."

This message appears when you attempt to capture video from an external video camera or other external device, but the device is either not connected, or the capture device isn't recognized by Windows Movie Maker. If your intent was to use video content that's already on your hard disk, choose File ➪ Import into Collections (not the Capture option) to import the video.

See the item that follows if you're using an S-Video cable or bridge that connects to the computer through a USB port.

Cannot capture content using S-Video cable

Verify that the S-Video port on your computer can be used for both input and output. If the port came preinstalled on your computer, check the documentation that came with the computer or your computer manufacturer's Web site.

Cannot capture content from USB bridge

If Windows Movie Maker cannot detect a bridge that's connected to your USB port, try capturing video using the software that came with the bridge. If you can save that captured content in MPEG, AVI, or WMV format, you can then import the captured content from the files on your hard disk.

Also, check the bridge manufacturer's Web site or written documentation for information on compatibility with Windows Movie Maker 2.1. The Web site may offer an updated driver that allows the bridge to work with Movie Maker.

No audio when capturing content

Verify that the Audio Out cables on the camera or VCR are connected to the Audio In or Line In port(s) on your computer. This is necessary whether you're using Video Out or S-Video to connect the player to the computer.

In the Record dialog box, use the Change Device button to choose the appropriate port or device for Audio. For example, that would be Line In if the cable(s) from the camera are connected to the Line In port on your sound card.

Movie Maker closes when you drag a clip

This error is caused by a conflict with a DivX file on the computer. To fix it:

1. Click the **Start** button and chose **Search**.

2. Choose **All files and folders**.

3. Type `Divxaf.ax` as the filename to search for.

4. Choose **Local Hard Drives . . .** as the area to search.

5. Under **More advanced options** choose **Search system folders**, **Search hidden files and folders**, and **Search subfolders**.

6. Click the **Search** button.

7. When the search is complete, click **Yes, finished searching**.

8. If the Search Companion found the `Divxaf.ax` file, right-click that filename in the right pane and choose **Rename**.

9. Rename the file to **divxaf.old** and press Enter. If asked for confirmation about changing the extension, choose **Yes**.

The problem should be resolved. If not, close all open programs, restart the computer, and try again.

All other Movie Maker 2.1 issues

For other issues on using Windows Movie Maker, see the following Web sites:

www.microsoft.com/windowsxp/moviemaker

www.microsoft.com/windows/windowsmedia/knowledgecenter

www.microsoft.com/windowsxp/using/moviemaker/hardware/default.mspx

www.microsoft.com/windowsxp/expertzone/newsgroups/reader.mspx?dg=microsoft. public.windowsxp.moviemaker

✦   ✦   ✦

Installing and Removing Programs

Thousands of programs run with Windows XP, as a quick visit to www.WindowsMarketplace.com will verify. This part of the book is about using those other programs with Windows XP. Chapters 44 and 45 cover installing new programs, both from Internet downloads and from CDs.

Chapters 46 and 47 tackles issues of getting older programs to run, and getting into setting default programs for certain activities and restricting access to others. Chapter 48 talks about uninstalling programs.

Finally, Chapter 49 talks about Task Manager, the program you use to check all running processes and applications, and tells you how to deal with hung programs and the blue screen of death.

Downloading Programs

There are several ways to acquire new programs for your computer. One is to go to the store and buy the program. Another is to order a program online and have it sent to you by mail. The third option, downloading and installing the program on the spot, is what this chapter is all about.

First, a word of caution. Not everything on the Internet is "good." Many programs that you can get for free make their money by causing pop-up ads to fill your screen. Still other programs intentionally plant viruses and the like on your computer. So, don't be in a hurry to download everything and anything that's free.

Playing It Safe with Installations

When you install new hardware or software, there's always a slight risk that the product won't be 100 percent compatible with everything else that's in your computer. Unfortunately, you won't know if there's a problem until after you install the program. By then, the installation procedure has already made some sweeping changes to your system. To protect yourself from problems that new software might create, you should set a restore point just before you install a new program.

System Restore is a feature of Windows XP that makes it easy to return to a previous configuration when some new hardware or software installation makes things go nutty. System Restore is *not* a simple "undo" command, and should not be used to undo minor mishaps. You should only use System Restore as discussed in Chapter 55 in this book.

However, you can set a restore point at any time without worrying about the details of System Restore. Setting a restore point doesn't alter your computer configuration in any way. Returning to an earlier restore point is where you run some risk, especially if you don't understand what's really going on. So, I'm not saying that you have to go read Chapter 55 now before you continue on in this chapter. Here you'll only set a restore point, which is always a safe and simple thing to do.

So, let's say you've found some program on the Internet that you want to download and try. To play it safe, you want to set a restore point before you download and install that program. Here's how:

1. Click the **Start** button, and choose **All Programs** ➪ **Accessories** ➪ **System Tools** ➪ **System Restore**. The System Restore window shown in Figure 44-1 opens.

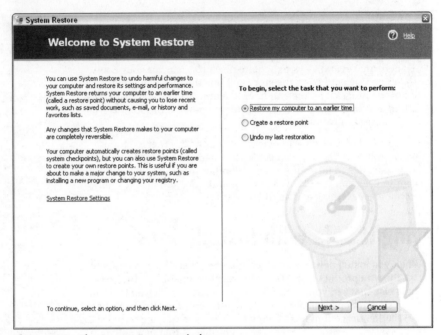

Figure 44-1: The System Restore window

2. Choose the second option, **Create a restore point**, and then click the **Next>** button.

3. Type a description, using your own wording, of this point (for example *Pre-ProgramX download*, where *ProgramX* is the name of the program you're about to download and install.

4. Click the **Create** button in the next page that appears, and then click **Close** on the next page.

That's all there is to it. Whether or not you'll ever need to revert to that restore point remains to be seen. If everything works correctly after the installation, you won't need to use the new restore point at all. If things get weird, however, you'll first want to uninstall the program, as described in Chapter 48. If things are still a little weird after you uninstall the program, you can revert to the restore point you just created, as explained in Chapter 55. (If things are still weird after you return to the previous restore point, you may have contracted some nasty adware or a virus and will need to refer to Chapters 28 and 29).

To Run or to Save?

Programs are different from documents in several ways. A document is just *data* that a program can use. Examples of documents include typed text, pictures, music, and video. Documents are stored in folders. To open a document, you double-click its icon. A document never opens on its own. It always opens in a program.

A program, on the other hand, contains *executable code*, instructions that tell the computer what to do. You don't start programs from folders. You start programs from the All Programs menu. But before you can start a program at all, you need to *install* the program. The installation procedure configures the program to run with your particular hardware, and also adds the program to your All Programs menu.

When you download a program, you'll generally be given the option to Save the program, or to Run (or Open) the program. The difference is:

✦ **Save:** Choosing Save copies the program's installation file to a folder on your hard disk, but doesn't install the program. You must install the program yourself before you can use the program.

✦ **Run** (or **Open**): Choosing Run or Open downloads and installs the program in one fell swoop. You don't need to go through an extra installation step.

Whether you choose Save or Run is entirely up to you. Obviously Run offers the convenience of not having to go through the extra installation step. Once the download is completed, you should be able to start the program from your All Programs menu.

The Save option, however, also offers some advantages. For one thing, you get a copy of the original installation file so that if you accidentally remove the program, you can always reinstall it right from the icon you downloaded. You might consider creating a folder named Downloaded Programs or something like that in your My Documents or Shared Documents folder. Then, Save all downloaded programs to that folder so that you always have a copy of the original installation program.

Tip It's not always easy to tell which downloaded file goes with which program, because the filenames can be somewhat arbitrary. Consider creating a subfolder, with a meaningful name, for each program you intend do download, and save each downloaded program in its own folder.

If your computer is part of a network, and you want to install the program on several computers, you can save the downloaded file to a shared folder. For example, create a folder named Common Downloads in Shared Documents, and put all your saved program files there. You should be able to get to that Common Downloads folder from any computer in your local network, making it easy to install the program on multiple computers.

Another advantage of choosing Save is that you can scan the downloaded file for viruses before installing the program. The virus won't be activated until you install the program. So, if you find a virus before you install the program, no problem. Just delete the infected file, and you're home free. No messy virus-removal ritual to go through.

Any time you download any program, Windows will show a generic warning message about the risks involved in doing so. The warning appears whether the program is safe or not. It's up to you to decide whether or not you trust the folks who are offering the program. While it's tough to come up with any kind of simple rule, some general things to consider are:

✦ Programs from legitimate software companies such as Microsoft, Adobe, Macromedia, and so forth are always safe. Legitimate software companies never distribute virus-infected files.

✦ Programs from services such as TUCOWS (`www.tucows.com`) are safe, especially if other people have given the program a thumbs-up rating.

✦ Free software that's offered out of the clear blue sky, from a pop-up ad or e-mail message is risky. There's a good chance you'll end up getting pop-up ads, or worse, if you install the program.

I have another general philosophy that maybe isn't terribly fair to all program providers. But it goes like this.

✦ If it's free, be suspicious.

✦ If it's cute, be even more suspicious.

✦ If it's free and cute, consider it lethal.

The preceding rules don't apply to free downloads from legitimate software companies. For example, Adobe Acrobat Reader is free, Microsoft Reader is free, and so are thousands of other programs. But, they're from legitimate software companies, and so are perfectly safe. The three rules above apply only to those situations in which the option to download or install something seems to pop up out of nowhere, when you weren't even looking to download or install a program.

Note   Depending on your browser and pop-up blocker settings, you may need to click the Information bar to allow the program to download. If you need help with the Information bar, see "Blocking Pop-Ups with Internet Explorer" in Chapter 29.

Downloading and Installing Programs

The Web is home to thousands of programs that you can download and install right on the spot. The exact procedure will vary a little from one program to the next. Typically, all the instructions you need will be available on the Web page that allows you to perform the download. You can print that page by choosing File ➪ Print from your Web browser's menu bar.

Tip   The Ultimate Collection of Windows Shareware at `www.tucows.com` is home to thousands of programs you can download and try out for free. One of the beauties of TUCOWS is that all programs are reviewed by people who've tried them out already. So you know any program that's been well rated is safe and works as it should.

If you don't see any installation instructions, but just a link to download the program, go ahead and click that link. Before Windows starts the download, you'll see some generic warnings about the risks you take whenever you download a program. The most common message in Windows XP with SP2 installed is the one shown in Figure 44-2.

Figure 44-2: The standard warning that appears when you download a program

Here's where you have to make a judgment call. If the dialog box seems to have popped up out of nowhere, then your best bet might be to choose Cancel. You don't want to download things at random. You only want to download things you need and trust.

Download and install

If you trust the source of the download, and you just want to install the program on the spot, click Run and follow the instructions on the screen. In some rare cases, you may have to restart the computer after you've finished the download. But you should be able to run the downloaded program from an icon on your All Programs menu.

Save now, install later

If you want to save a copy of the downloaded program to install later, click the Save button. You'll be taken to a Save As dialog box. In the Save As dialog box, navigate to the folder in which you want to place the downloaded installation file. Or, navigate to the parent folder (e.g., Downloaded Programs), click the Create New Folder button in the Save As dialog box, and create a new folder for the file you're about to download. Then click the Save button.

Note   If I lost you in the preceding paragraph, see Chapter 3, especially the section titled "Using the Save As dialog box." But even that section won't make much sense if you don't read the material that precedes that section in Chapter 3.

Caution   When you *save* a downloaded program, it's fine to use any folder you like. But when you *install* a program, you should always choose whatever folder the installation recommends. That will typically be a subfolder under `C:\Program Files`.

If you do Save, rather than Run, the download file, you'll have to install the program before you can run it. To do so, go to the folder in which you placed the downloaded file and double-click its icon. Most likely, you'll get another security warning like the example shown in Figure 44-3.

Remember, the warning is generic and not indicative of a problem or anything bad. It's just a reminder that you don't want to download and install things indiscriminately. If you feel that the program is something you really need, and you trust that its creator is a legitimate software company, then click the Run button to forge ahead.

Figure 44-3: Another security warning

The installation procedure will start. Just follow the on-screen instructions until the installation is complete. At that point, you should be able to start the program from the All Programs menu.

Remember, if the program turns out not to be what you'd hoped for, you'll need to uninstall it as explained in Chapter 48.

Wrap Up

Downloading and installing programs is a relatively easy business. Too easy, in some cases, because not everything you download is "good." Adware, spyware, viruses, and worms are lurking in many of the junky freebie downloads out there. When the option to download something is suddenly "in your face," and you had no intention of downloading anything, that's the time you want to be most suspicious. Some general things to consider when it comes to downloading and installing programs are:

✦ Setting a Restore Point before you download can make it easier to get things back to normal if the download proves malicious and does bad things to your computer.

✦ Whenever you download a program, you'll have the option to Run or Save the program.

✦ Choosing Run will download and install the program in one fell swoop. When the download is done, you should be able the start the program from the All Programs menu.

✦ Choosing Save will save the program's installation file whatever folder you specify on your hard disk. Open the downloaded program's icon to complete the installation.

✦   ✦   ✦

Installing and Upgrading Programs

Unlike documents, which you can freely copy to your hard disk and use on the spot, any new program you acquire needs to be installed before you can use it. The installation process configures the software to work with your particular hardware and software. The process also creates an icon or program group on your All Programs menu so that you can start the new program as you would any other.

You need to install a program only once, not each time you intend to use it. Once you've installed a program, you can put the disk from which you installed away for safe keeping. You'll need only the original installation disk to reinstall the program if you accidentally delete it from your hard disk or if some sort of hard disk crash damages the program on your hard disk.

Playing It Safe with Program Installations

Programs you buy in a store aren't likely to contain any malicious code such as viruses, worms, or adware. Those things tend to be spread by be freebie downloads from the Web and e-mail attachments. However, there's always an outside chance that the new program is incompatible with Windows XP or even just some hardware device on your computer. In those rare instances, you'll probably want to uninstall the program. You might also want to get your system files back to where they were before the installation.

Chapter 55 discusses system files and restore points in detail. For now, just be aware that many (but not all) programs will automatically set a restore point before they install. So if you forget to set a restore point before you install, you may still find a restore point ready and waiting in System Restore, should you need it. But you'll only use the restore point if you uninstall the program, and only after you've uninstalled the program.

Note　See "Playing It Safe with Installations" in Chapter 44 for step-by-step instructions for setting a restore point.

Fortunately, most of the time, program installations go smoothly and there's no need to uninstall or restore system files. Creating a restore point before installing a program is just a precaution.

Upgrading Programs

Many commercial programs are sold in regular and "upgrade" versions. The regular version is for people who have never bought the program before. The upgrade version, which costs less, is for people who have already purchased and installed a previous version of the program.

If you plan to buy the upgrade version of a program you already own, don't uninstall the current version first. The upgrade will check to make sure that you already have the previous version. If it doesn't find a qualifying earlier version, it will as you to insert the CD for that earlier version. You have to do one or the other: Either leave the earlier version installed or have the CD for that version handy when you start installing the upgrade.

> **Tip**   Upgrades to Windows components such as Media Player and Movie Maker are free, provided you do the upgrade online.

In almost all cases the new version will replace the old version. So, you won't end up with two versions of the same program. Any and all documents you created with that program (or any other program) will remain intact. When you install, upgrade, or even remove a program, that process has absolutely no effect on documents you've previously saved to your computer.

Installing from a CD or Floppy Disk

Programs sold through computer stores are usually delivered on CD-ROMs, although occasionally you'll still find programs delivered on floppy disks. Installation is usually pretty simple. With programs delivered on CD, the process usually goes like this:

1. Close all open program windows on your desktop by clicking their **Close** buttons or by right-clicking their taskbar buttons and choosing **Close**. You want to start from a clean Windows desktop.

2. Insert the CD into your computer's CD drive and wait a few seconds.

3. When the installation program appears on the screen, read and follow its instructions until the program is installed.

4. When the installation procedure is complete, remove the CD from your CD drive and store the disk in a safe place.

That really is all there is to it. You will be presented with some questions and options along the way. Exactly what you see varies from one program to the next. But some common items include the End User License Agreement (EULA), and choosing a folder in which to store the program, which I'll discuss in a moment.

If nothing happens within a minute of inserting the program CD into your CD drive, or if you're installing a program from a floppy disk, you may need to start the installation program manually. Here's how:

1. In My Computer, double-click the icon that represents the drive into which you inserted the disk.

2. Locate and double-click the icon named Setup or Setup.exe.

3. Read and follow the instructions presented in the installation program that opens.

4. When the installation is complete, remove the disk from its drive and put it away for safekeeping.

To start the new program, click the Start button and look around for its icon on the All Programs menu. Then, just click the icon that represents the new program.

Note   Some program disks will have a file named README on them. That file contains installation instructions or other pertinent information. To read the file, double-click its icon.

Common Installation Prompts

Every program is unique, and there's very little I can tell you that will apply to every program you purchase and install. About the only two things that most programs require are that you accept the End User License Agreement, and that you choose which folder you want to install the program in. The order in which you have to respond to prompts will vary as well. So, while I can't give you anything that applies to all programs, I can tell you what kinds of things you'll likely be faced with while installing a program.

The product key or serial number

Some programs require that you enter a product key or serial number, as in the example shown in Figure 45-1. All I can tell you here is that you must type the requested information exactly as given to you. Typing something that's "sorta like" the right serial number or product key won't work. Microsoft's product keys are usually on jewel box or folder packet that contains the CD.

```
┌─────────────────────────────────────────────────────────────────────┐
│ 🖳 Microsoft Office FrontPage 2003 Setup                    ⬚ ⬚ ☒ │
│ ┌─────────────────────────────────────────────────────────────────┐ │
│ │  Microsoft Office FrontPage 2003                        ▢▪▫      │ │
│ │                                                         ▫▫▫      │ │
│ │  Product Key                                                     │ │
│ ├─────────────────────────────────────────────────────────────────┤ │
│ │                                                                 │ │
│ │                                                                 │ │
│ │                                                                 │ │
│ │   In the boxes below, type your 25-character Product Key.  You will find this number │ │
│ │   on the sticker on the back of the CD case or on your Certificate of Authenticity. │ │
│ │                                                                 │ │
│ │   Product Key: [      ]-[      ]-[      ]-[      ]-[      ]      │ │
│ │                                                                 │ │
│ │                                                                 │ │
│ │                                                                 │ │
│ │                                                                 │ │
│ │                                                                 │ │
│ │   [ Help ]              < Back    Next >          [ Cancel ]    │ │
│ └─────────────────────────────────────────────────────────────────┘ │
└─────────────────────────────────────────────────────────────────────┘
```

Figure 45-1: Sample Product Key page

If you uninstall a program, whether intentionally or by accident, or if a disk crash causes you to lose the program, you'll need the product key (or serial number) to reinstall the program. So, you never want to lose that information. You'd do well to create a document that simply lists all your product names and product keys. Print a copy, and keep a copy on your hard disk. Keep the original too, so you have three copies of the key. Store these things so you'll be able to find them if you need them in the future.

Upgrade compliance

If you're installing an upgrade version of a program, the installation procedure will check to make sure that you own a product that qualifies you for the upgrade. You may see a prompt, like the example shown in Figure 45-2, telling you when this step is about to take place. If a qualifying earlier version of the program is installed on your computer, just click OK and that should be the end of that step in the process.

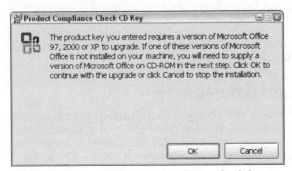

Figure 45-2: Sample product compliance check for an upgrade

If a qualifying earlier version of the program isn't installed on your system, clicking OK will lead to another product compliance message, like the example shown in Figure 45-3. This step in the procedure can be a bit challenging because CD drives tend to be slow. You have to be patient at this point.

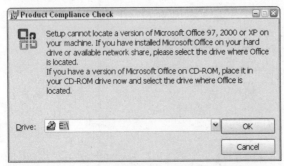

Figure 45-3: Need CD to verify upgrade compliance

First, you have to remove the CD that's currently in the drive and replace it with the CD for the qualifying product. Close the CD drive door, choose the drive's access letter (for example D: or E: for a CD drive) from the drop-down list, and wait. The "wait" part is important, because CD drives are slow compared to other types of drives. Then do the following:

✦ If a program for installing the *previous* version of the program pops up, close that (but don't close the Product Compliance dialog box).

✦ If nothing happens within about one minute, click the **OK** button.

Once you've gotten past the compliance check, you'll need to remove the CD that's currently in the drive, put the original CD that you're installing from back into the CD drive, and close the drive door. The installation procedure will carry on from there.

The End User License Agreement (EULA)

Just about every commercial program requires that you accept the End User License Agreement (EULA) as part of the installation process. The agreement is a bunch of legalese that basically says you have the right to install and use the program on one computer. You do not have the right to sell or give away copies, or even the right to install the program on two or more computers. Figure 45-4 shows an example of a EULA.

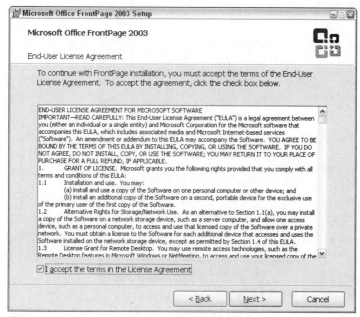

Figure 45-4: Sample End User License Agreement

The restriction on installing the program on only one computer is the biggest headache for most people. After all, if you own two or more computers, it's expensive to buy a copy of a program for each computer. Many people ignore that part of the EULA and just install the program on all their computers.

Microsoft, however, has made it impossible to install a program on more than one computer. Their product activation procedure, described in an upcoming section, "knows" when you've installed a program, and "can tell" when you're tying to install the same program on another computer.

The only legal way around the product activation problem, that I know of offhand, is to buy Microsoft's Academic Edition of a product (if one is offered for the program you're installing). While I can't speak to every product every created, nor products yet to be created, the Academic Editions I've purchased have all allowed me to install and activate the program on three computers.

Choosing a folder for the installed program

The installation procedure will often ask where you want to put the program, as in the example shown in Figure 45-5. There's really no reason to change the suggested folder. Most programs will install to `C:\Program Files` or perhaps some other folder. One thing's for sure, you *don't* want to put installed programs in document folders such as My Documents, Shared Documents, or anything else. If in doubt, just accept the suggested folder and move on.

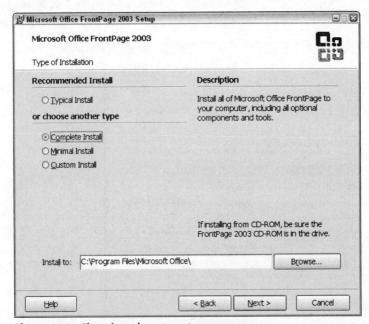

Figure 45-5: Choosing where to put a program

In some cases, like the example shown in Figure 45-5, you'll also be given some choices as to how much of the program you want to install. Given that hard disk space is cheap and plentiful these days, it probably makes sense to choose the Complete Install option. But, if you know for a fact that you're running low on disk space, you can choose a Minimal Install, Typical Install, or Custom Install.

Once you've answered all the questions posed by the program's installation procedure, and clicked the Finish button on the last page, you're done. You should remove the CD (or floppy) from the drive and store it away for safekeeping. That disk will be your one-and-only backup of the program. So don't lose it.

Note Most fire insurance policies don't cover computer software. If you have a fireproof safe, that would be a good place to store your original CDs as well as your product keys and serial numbers.

If the program requires restarting the computer, go ahead and restart it. When you get back to the Windows desktop, you may see a little notice telling you that the new program is available, as in the example shown in Figure 45-6. Options leading up to the new program's startup icon will likely be highlighted in orange. But even if you don't see a notice or highlights, you should be able to start the newly installed program from the All Programs menu.

Figure 45-6: Startup icon for the new program is on the All Programs menu.

Tip To alphabetize your All Programs menu, right-click any item on the menu and choose Sort by Name.

User accounts and programs

You won't need the original disk to run the program. On rare occasions, though, you might need the disk to set up the program in other user accounts. You don't need to *install* the program to multiple user accounts. Normally, every user account has access to every program that's currently installed. But once in a while you may need to use the CD just to get the program configured in other user accounts.

If you've set up multiple user accounts on your computer, you may want to take a moment to get the setup squared away. Put the CD back in the drive. When the installation program appears, just Cancel or Close it. Then, log into each user account and launch the program from the All Programs menu.

Installing and Removing Windows Components

Windows XP comes with a slew of freebie programs including games, wizards, and system tools. You'll find these on the Accessories menu (click the Start button and choose All Programs ⇨ Accessories). Some of the optional components are in program groups like Accessibility, Communications, Entertainment, and System Tools. Others are right on the Accessories menu, as in Figure 45-7.

Figure 45-7: Sample Accessories menu

You can install, and remove, optional Windows components at any time. If you installed XP yourself, you'll need your original Microsoft Windows XP CD for this. If Windows came preinstalled on your computer, you may or may not need the CD. It all depends on how your computer manufacturer set things up. If you're not sure, try leaving the CD out of the drive and installing the components without it — though, it wouldn't hurt to have the CD handy just in case.

When you first insert the Windows XP CD, its installation program will be launched. While you *could* get to Windows Components Wizard from that startup program, the steps below explain how to install and remove optional components right from the desktop. So, if you do get a prompt for installing Windows after inserting its CD, I suggest that you just Cancel or Close that program, but leave the CD in the drive.

The tool for installing and removing Windows components is called the Windows Components Wizard. You get to it via the Add or Remove Programs window. Here are the exact steps:

1. Click the **Start** button and choose **Control Panel**.

2. Click the Add or Remove Programs category, or open the Add or Remove Programs icon in Classic view.

3. In the left column of the window that opens, click on Add/Remove Windows Components. The Windows Components Wizard shown in Figure 45-8 opens.

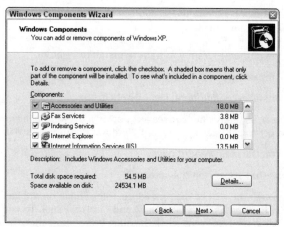

Figure 45-8: Sample Accessories menu

Caution

Clearing a check mark in the Windows Components Wizard removes the component from your hard disk. Don't clear a check mark unless you're certain you want to remove the component.

4. Some items in the list of components are actually groups. For example, many of the items on the Accessories menu are in the Accessories and Utilities group. Here are some general tips on where to look for common components:

- To get to general components such as Calculator and Paint, click **Accessories and Utilities**, and then click the **Details** button. Click **Accessories** in the next page that appears; then, click the **Details** button again. You'll see the components show in Figure 45-9.

- To get to games that come with Windows XP, click **Accessories and Utilities**; then, click the **Details** button. Click **Games** in the next page that appears; then, click the **Details** button again.

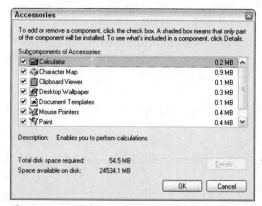

Figure 45-9: Subcomponents of the Accessories group

Tip

To see a description of a component, click the component's name (not the checkbox). You'll see its description under the components list.

5. When you see the name of the program you want to install or remove:

- To install a missing component, select (check) its checkbox.

- To remove and installed component, clear its checkbox.

6. You can select, and clear, as many checkboxes as you wish. If you're in a subcomponents list, click **OK** to get to get back to the main Windows Components Wizard page.

7. Click the **Next** button on the main Wizard page.

8. Follow the instructions that appear on the screen.

The Wizard will take you through the rest of the procedure. Click Finish on the last wizard page. Then, close the Add Or Remove Programs window and Control Panel. To verify that the components have been installed (or removed), click the Start button and choose Accessories. Then, take a look at the options and at the program groups available on the Accessories menu.

Wrap Up

Installing programs is usually an easy thing to do. The most common scenario these days involves inserting the program's installation CD into your CD drive, waiting a minute or so, and then following the on-screen instructions. Some general pointers we've covered in this chapter include:

✦ While most program installations go smoothly, it couldn't hurt to create a restore point just prior to installing a new program.

✦ If you plan to upgrade to a newer version of a program you own, don't uninstall the original first unless specifically instructed by the program manufacturer to do so.

✦ To install from a CD, insert the CD and wait a minute for the installation program to open. Then, follow the on-screen instructions.

✦ If an installation program doesn't start automatically, open the icon that represents the disk drive and double-click the Setup or Setup.exe icon on the disk.

✦ To install or remove optional Windows components, open Add or Remove Programs in Control Panel, and then click Add/Remove Windows Components from its buttons.

✦   ✦   ✦

Getting Older Programs to Run

As you probably know, you can run just about any program that's installed on your computer just by clicking its startup icon on the All Programs menu. But, there are always exceptions to the rule. Chief among the list of exceptions are old programs that were originally written to work with older versions of Windows. Or, even worse, programs that were written to run on DOS.

That's not to say Windows *can't* run old programs. Most of the time, it can run an older program as is, without any messing about or tweaking things at all on your part. So, before you assume that you have to do something to try to get an older program to run, try running the program normally. If it runs, you're done. If it won't run, then this is the chapter you need to (hopefully) get the program to run.

What Makes a Program "Old"

To understand what makes a program "old," you first need to understand the difference between 16-bit and 32-bit computing. The smallest unit of information that the computer works with is called a *bit*, short for binary digit. A bit can have one of two possible values, 0 or 1. We could say the bit can be "on" or "off," or "True" or "False," or whatever. But anyway you slice it a bit can only have one of two possible values.

The workhorse inside any computer is the *microprocessor*, or *processor* for short. It's a chip about the size of your thumbnail in which electrons, representing bits, zoom around at the speed of light (186,000 miles per second). The amount of work a processor can do in any given time depends heavily on how many bits it can work with at a time.

The earliest PCs were built around Intel's 16-bit 8086 and 80286 processors. Microsoft's operating system of the day was called DOS (pronounced *DAW*-sss), which stood for Disk Operating System. In the 1980s, Intel released the 32-bit 80386 processor, which in turn was followed by the 80486 and the Pentium and Celeron processors used in most computers today.

Despite the fact that processors had evolved to 32-bit processing power, the 16-bit DOS operating system hung around for years. DOS largely become "hidden" behind products like Windows 3.1, Windows 95, Windows 98, and Windows ME. But hidden or not, its 16-bit heritage never really allowed it to take full advantage of modern 32-bit processors.

Microsoft did, eventually, develop a 32-bit operating system. Initially it was marketed as Windows NT (for New Technology), and eventually it became Windows 2000. But those programs were marketed primarily to corporations. Casual computers tended to slog on through one 16-bit version of Windows to the next.

The year 2001 changed all that when Microsoft released Windows XP. Windows XP is a true 32-bit operating system that's marketed to both individuals and corporations. The release of Windows XP was the death knell for 16-bit computing. Microsoft has not created any 16-bit software since the release of Windows XP, nor will it ever create any 16-bit software in the future. I'm sure that the same can be said of virtually every software company in business today.

Ancient history, today, and the future

These days, 16-bit computing is ancient history, 32-bit is mainstream, and 64-bit computing is available, but pricey and still a bit "out there" on the technological bleeding edge. You might look at the numbers 16, 32, and 64 and thing "Big deal, how much difference could a few bits make?" You'd be mistaken there though, because each number is an exponent to the number 2.

The number of bits that the processor can handle at once defines the number of unique addresses that the processor can address directly (referred to as *addressable memory*). Simply stated, the more addressable memory, the more the computer can do within a given timeframe. When you realize that the numbers involved are exponents of 2, and you do the math, you can see that the differences between 16-, 32-, and 64-bit computing, in terms of addressable memory are truly astronomical, as summarized in Table 46-1.

Table 46-1: Processor Technology and Directly Addressable Memory

Technology	Meaning	Memory Addresses
16-bit	2^{16}	65,536
32-bit	2^{32}	4,294,967,296
64-bit	2^{64}	18,446,744,073,709,600,000

Note   A 64-bit processor can directly address about 18,000,000,000GB of RAM. Yes, that's 18 billion gigabytes, and a lot more than the 4-GB maximum of today's 32-bit processors! Current processors get over their limitations by indirectly addressing memory beyond their limitations. But that indirect addressing adds some processing overhead that slows things down a little.

So what does any of this have to do with getting older programs to run in Windows XP? Basically an "old program" is a 16-bit program, or a program that was written to run on

Windows 3.1, 95, 98, or ME. An *ancient* program would be some little game you run right from a floppy disk (though "ancient" isn't an official buzzword). Many such programs were written before there were such things as program windows occupying only a portion of the screen, even before there was any need to install a program to a hard disk!

Programs to avoid altogether

Before I go on, I should point out that the 16-bit business isn't the only thing that discriminates between "old" and current programs. There are some programs, particularly those that work directly with hardware, or directly with Windows system files, that you really shouldn't even try to force to run in Windows XP. These include:

✦ **Old disk utility programs:** Older disk utility programs such as Norton Utilities and various disk compression and partitioning tools should never be run on Windows XP. Many older CD-burning programs are likely to cause problems too. If you have such a program, you should really upgrade to the current XP-version of that program, or find a similar product that's designed to work with Windows XP.

✦ **Old backup programs:** If you have an older backup program, using it in compatibility mode could prove disastrous. Even if you're able to perform the backup, there's an outside chance you won't be able to restore from the backup is and when you need to. You should purchase and install the Windows XP-version of the program, or find a similar XP backup program.

✦ **Old "cleanup" utilities:** Any older program that purports to "keep your registry clean" or "fix your computer with one mouse click" should be avoided at all costs.

> **Note**
>
> Personally, I wouldn't even install the XP version of a "cleanup" or "instant fix" program, because as a programmer, I seriously doubt that these programs *can* do what they purport to do. But that's just my personal opinion. If you have such a program and you like it, you should upgrade to the XP-version of that program rather than use the existing version.

✦ **Old antivirus programs:** Virus detection and removal is dicey business, and needs to be handled with great care. Antivirus programs written for pre-XP versions of Windows should never be installed or run on a Windows XP computer.

Programs written for non-Windows operating system, such as programs written for the Macintosh, don't come under the heading of "old programs." Such programs are written for a completely different operating system, and there is no way to use the techniques described in this chapter to make such a program run on Windows XP.

About compatibility mode

To get an old program to work in XP, Windows runs the program in *compatibility mode*. That mode encases the program in a *virtual machine*, sort of an imaginary Windows 95, 98, or other version of Windows. The program "thinks" it's running in the older operating system, because everything looks and acts just as it did in that older operating system.

There is a catch to the whole compatibility issue though. And that is you need to *install* the program before you can run it in compatibility mode. Just getting the program installed can be a challenge in itself. So, let's deal with installation first.

Installing a Program That Won't Install

If you have an old program on a CD, you may see an error message like the example shown in Figure 46-1 shortly after you insert the CD into the drive or open the program's setup icon.

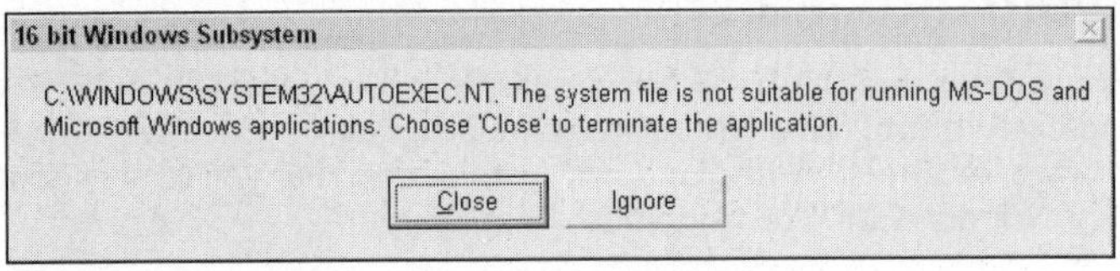

Figure 46-1: Can't install an older program from CD

The solution to this problem is a bit more complicated than using the Program Compatibility Wizard. You'll need to manually install the `Config.nt`, `Autoexec.nt`, and `Command.com` files from your original Windows XP CD. Make sure that you know the drive letter of your CD drive (for example, D: or E:). Then do the following:

1. Remove the CD that's in the drive and insert your original Windows XP CD.

2. When the installation program opens, click **Exit** to close it.

3. Click the **Start** button and choose **Run**.

4. Type `cmd`, and then click **OK**. A DOS command prompt window opens.

5. Type the following command, replacing *letter:* with the drive letter of your CD drive (e.g., D: or E:), and then press **Enter**:

   `expand letter:\i386\config.nt_ %systemroot%\system32\config.nt`

6. After the Expanding . . . message appears, type the following at the command prompt, again replacing *letter:* with your CD drive's letter:

   `expand letter:\i386\autoexec.nt_ %systemroot%\system32\autoexec.nt`

7. After the Expanding message appears, type this command and press **Enter**:

   `expand letter:\i386\command.co_ %systemroot%\system32\command.com`

8. Type `exit` and press **Enter** to exit the command prompt window.

9. Remove the Windows XP CD from the CD drive.

Now you can try installing the 16-bit program again. Insert the CD and wait for the installation program to start. If there is no installation program, open your My Computer folder, right-click the icon for your CD drive, and choose Open. Then, double-click the installation file (typically Install or Setup.exe) for the program.

The installation program should run now. If you're prompted for a folder in which to store the file, be aware that many older programs can't handle long file and folder names like Program Files. You may need to use whatever folder the installation program suggests. Though you can also use the short name for the Program Files folder, PROGRA~1, in the path to which you want to install the program.

Once you've installed the program, you should be able to run it from the All Programs menu. If the program won't run, at least you it's installed now. So you can use the Program Compatibility Wizard described next to run the program.

Using the Program Compatibility Wizard

The Program Compatibility Wizard provides a step-by-step means of configuring and testing a 16-bit program so that it will run in Windows XP. Before you bother with the wizard, try running the program without it. If the program runs, you're done. No need to use compatibility mode. But if the program crashes or displays an error message, then you need to close whatever is open and follow these steps:

1. Click the **Start** button, choose **All Programs** ➪ **Accessories** ➪ **Program Compatibility Wizard**.

2. Read the first wizard page, and then click **Next>**.

3. On the second wizard page, shown in Figure 46-2, choose whichever option best describes what you want to do:

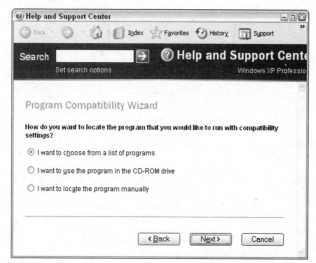

Figure 46-2: First selections in the Program Compatibility Wizard

- **I want to choose from a list of programs:** If the program is already installed and has an icon on the All Programs menu, choose this option.

- **I want to use the program in the CD-ROM drive:** If the program isn't installed and needs to be installed or run from a CD, choose this option.

- **I want to locate the program manually:** If the program isn't on the All Programs menu, but you know the path and filename of the program, choose this option.

4. Follow the instructions on the next wizard page. For example, if you chose the first option, scroll through the list of program names and click on the program you want to run in compatibility mode. Then click **Next>**.

5. When you get to the operating system page shown in Figure 46-3, choose the operating system that the program was written for, or the last operating system on which you were able to run the program. Then click **Next>**.

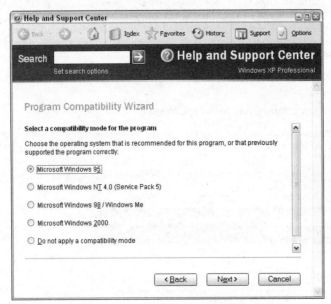

Figure 46-3: Choose an operating system for the program.

6. The next wizard page will ask about display settings, such as 256 colors, 640 × 480 screen resolution, and visual themes. If the program is an old game or educational program that fills the entire screen with simple graphics, choose all three options. If the program runs in a program window, you probably don't need to choose any of those options. Click **Next>**.

7. On the Test your compatibility settings page, click **Next>**. Then:

   • If the program starts, bring the Program Compatibility Wizard page back to the top of the stack (its taskbar button shows Help and Support), choose the Yes . . . option, and then click Next> and follow the wizard through to completion.

   • If the program fails to start, choose **No, try different compatibility settings**, and repeat the steps to try different options.

There's no guarantee that the Program Compatibility Wizard will make the program run. Some programs are so old, and so far removed from modern computing capabilities, that there's just no way to force them to run. In those cases, the only hope is to try to find a newer, more up-to-date version of the program.

Quick-and-Dirty Program Compatibility

The Program Compatibility Wizard provides an easy way to choose and test settings for program compatibility. But you can also force a program to run in compatibility mode right from the program's Properties dialog box. Here's how:

1. Click the **Start** button, choose **All Programs** and get to the startup icon that you'd normally click to run the program.

2. Right-click the program's startup icon, and choose **Properties**.

3. In the Properties dialog box that opens, click the **Compatibility** tab. You'll see the options shown in Figure 46-4.

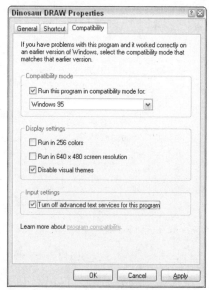

Figure 46-4: Compatibility tab of a program's Properties dialog box

4. Choose the operating system for which the program was written.

5. If the program is an old game or educational program, choose appropriate Display settings.

6. To turn off advanced text services such as speech recognition (which probably wouldn't work anyway), choose the option to turn off those features for the program.

7. Click **OK**.

The compatibility settings will "stick" to the program. So you can just start the program normally, from the All Programs menu, at any time. Though again, there's no guarantee that you'll be able to force all programs to run in Windows XP.

Wrap Up

Windows XP can run many older 16-bit programs without a hitch. But some older programs will refuse to install or refuse to run. There are several ways to deal with such problems:

✦ If you get an error message when trying to install a 16-bit program from CD, install the `Config.nt`, `Autoexec.nt`, and `Command.com` files from your original XP CD as described earlier in this chapter.

✦ If an installed program won't run on Windows XP, use the Program Compatibility Wizard to try, and test, possible compatibility settings to make it run.

✦ As an alternative to using the Program Compatibility Wizard, you can right-click the program's startup icon, choose Properties, and make your selections from the Compatibility tab in the Properties dialog box.

✦   ✦   ✦

Setting Program Access and Defaults

Service Pack 1 added a new option titled "Set Program Access Defaults" to Windows XP. This is an advanced tool for network administrators who need to enforce rules and limits for using specific Internet-related programs such as Web browsers, e-mail clients, and instant messaging.

For example, a company that wants to ensure that all employees use a specific e-mail client can set that client as the default e-mail client, and hide access to Outlook Express. If the company wants to keep people from yacking away all day using Windows Messenger, it can hide access to that program.

Setting Default Internet Programs

The Set Program Access and Defaults tool requires administrative privileges. Users with Limited accounts can't run the program. In a domain network, you must be a member of the Administrators group to run this program.

Note

To remove access to Microsoft Internet programs during an unattended setup, add a [Components] section to the `unattend.txt` file that contains `IEAccess=Off`, `OEAccess=Off`, `WMPOCM=Off`, and `WMAccess=Off`, each on a separate line. See `http://support.microsoft.com/default.aspx?scid=kb;en-us;328326&Product=winxp` for details.

The Set Program Access and Defaults tool is simple to use, but can be tough to find. You might find it on the right side of your Start menu. If so, then you just click the Start button, choose Set Program Access Defaults, and you're there. If you don't see Set Program Access and Defaults on your Start menu, here's how you get to it:

1. Click the **Start** button and choose **Control Panel**.

2. Open the **Add or Remove Programs** category (or icon, in Classic view).

3. Click on **Set Program Access and Defaults** in the left side of the Add or Remove Programs window.

Note   If you want to add or remove the Start menu Set Access to Program Defaults option, see "Personalizing Your Start Menu" in Chapter 6.

When first open, the program offers only the three mutually exclusive options shown in Figure 47-1. The Show/Hide button to the right of each option expands and contracts items beneath each option.

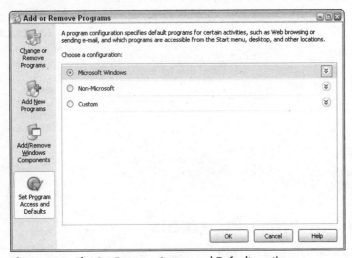

Figure 47-1: The Set Program Access and Defaults options

Each of the three options represents a general configuration. Whichever option you choose specifies the general configuration of the computer. We'll look at each configuration in the sections that follow. But be aware that what you see on your screen won't necessarily match what you see in this chapter. The options available to you at all times will depend on the programs currently installed on your computer.

Using the Microsoft Windows Configuration

If you want all users of this computer to use programs that came with Windows (or other Microsoft programs) as their defaults, choose Microsoft Windows. To expand that list, click its Show/Hide button. As you can see, when you choose this option you automatically enable access to all Microsoft Internet-related programs including Internet Explorer, Outlook Express (and Outlook), Windows Media Player, and Windows Messenger, the default IM program.

You don't have to use Outlook Express as the default e-mail client. If you use Outlook as your e-mail client, then you can chose Use my current Microsoft e-mail program, as in Figure 47-2, to make Outlook the default mail client.

The Virtual Machine for Java (also known as the *Java VM* and *Java 2 Runtime Environment*) is a program that runs *Java applets* — small programs used in some Web pages to display interactive content. Due to a legal dispute with Sun Microsystems, Microsoft's version of the Java Virtual Machine is no longer available for download. You can download the Java VM from http://Java.sun.com. The Microsoft Windows configuration option will use whatever Java Virtual Machine is currently installed.

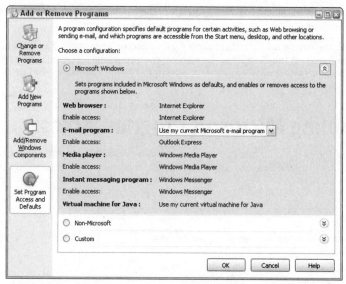

Figure 47-2: Choosing the Microsoft Windows configuration

Using the Non-Microsoft Configuration

If you choose the Non-Microsoft configuration, you remove access to Internet Explorer, Outlook Express, Windows Media Player, and Windows Messenger, as shown in Figure 47-3.

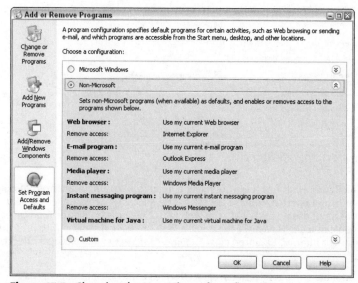

Figure 47-3: Choosing the Non-Microsoft configuration

If you have equivalent non-Microsoft programs, you'll be able to choose which programs you want to use for Web browsing, e-mail, multimedia, and instant messaging.

Removing access to those programs just hides their startup icons from users. The programs themselves remain installed on the computer. To remove the programs from the system altogether, use the Add/Remove Windows Components option in the left column of Add or Remove Programs.

Enabling/Disabling Microsoft Program Access

The Custom configuration is the only one that lets you enable or disable program access on a case-by-case basis. Expanding the Custom configuration list displays the options shown in Figure 47-4.

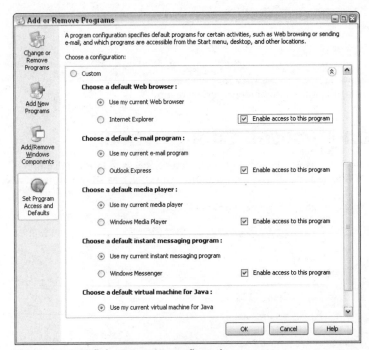

Figure 47-4: Defining a custom configuration

As you can see in the figure, each row lets you define a default program for an Internet-related service, and whether or not users even have access to the Microsoft program for that service. For example, if you want all users to navigate the Web with Netscape Navigator (and that program is installed), you can make Navigator the default Web browser. If you want to prevent users from browsing with Internet Explorer, clear the *Enable access to this program* checkbox for Internet Explorer.

When you've finished making your selections, click OK. There may be a brief delay as Windows reconfigures program access and defaults. You'll then be returned to the desktop.

Wrap Up

The Set Program Access and Defaults program is a simple tool for choosing default Internet-related programs. Organizations can use it to Internet access policies such as default Web browsers and e-mail clients. In summary:

✦ To get to the Set Program Access and Defaults options, open Add or Remove Programs in Control Panel, and then click that program icon in the left column.

✦ To give all users access to Internet Explorer, Outlook Express (or Outlook), Windows Messenger, and Windows Media Player, choose the Microsoft Windows configuration.

✦ To hide Internet Explorer, Outlook Express (or Outlook), Windows Messenger, and Windows Media Player choose the Non-Microsoft configuration.

✦ To pick and choose which programs users can and can't access, and default programs for Internet activities, choose the Custom configuration.

✦　　✦　　✦

Getting Rid of Programs

Getting rid of programs is called *removing* or *uninstalling* the program. The two terms mean the same thing: To remove all traces of the program from your hard disk, including the startup icon(s) on your All Programs menu. Simply deleting an icon from the All Programs menu will not remove the program. That just removes the icon, not the program.

All of the programs that are currently installed on your computer are listed in the Add or Remove Programs window, which you'll learn about in this chapter. As you'll see, that one window is "software central" for your PC. You can use it to get rid of just about anything — even junky toolbars and pop-up programs that you never intended to download in the first place.

Caution   There is no Recycle Bin or Undo for removed programs. Once you've removed a program, that party is over and there's no turning back. The only way to get the program back is to reinstall it.

Using the All Programs Menu to Uninstall

Before you go into the Add or Remove Programs window to remove a program, take a look at your All Programs menu, and click on the program group for the program you're considering removing. You just might see a Rremove or Uninstall option right there, as in the examples shown in Figure 48-1.

If the program you intend to remove offers such an option, by all means click on that option. Then, just follow the instructions that appear on the screen. If you do that, there won't be any need to go through the Add or Remove Programs window discussed in the sections that follow.

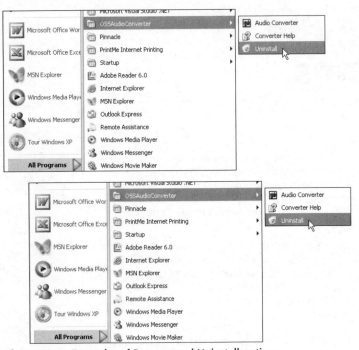

Figure 48-1: Examples of Remove and Uninstall options

Using Add or Remove Programs

If there is not Remove or Uninstall option to get rid of a program on your All Programs menus, you should be able to find the program in your Add or Remove Programs window. To get to that:

1. Click the **Start** button and choose **Control Panel**.

2. Open the **Add or Remove Programs** category or icon.

3. Be patient for a moment while Windows takes inventory of all your installed programs.

When Add or Remove Programs is ready to go, you'll see a list of all the application programs that are currently installed on your computer. The list will also contain things that don't quite qualify as Start menu programs like toolbars, hotfixes, and perhaps some ad-generating programs. Figure 48-2 shows an example.

Note   Optional programs that come with Windows XP can be installed or removed via Add/Remove Windows Components. See Chapter 44 for details.

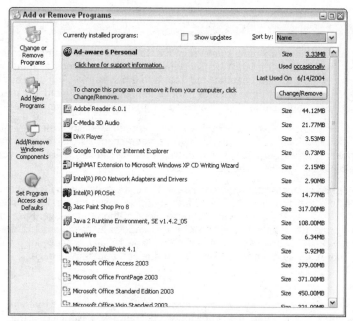

Figure 48-2: Sample Add or Remove Programs window

Above the list of currently installed programs, you'll see two options:

✦ **Show updates:** If selected, this option displays optional updates that you've installed since first acquiring a program. Each update is indented under the original program listing. For example, in Figure 48-3 the Windows Updates items and two items beneath it are visible only when I choose the Show Updates checkbox.

✦ **Sort by:** Lets you arrange programs by Name, Size, Frequency of Use, or Date Last Used.

Figure 48-3: Windows updates items in the currently installed programs list

Within the list you can get more information, and options, about any installed program just by clicking its name. That program's row will expand and be highlighted. I can't say with any certainly exactly what you'll see when you click on an item in the list. It varies from one program to the next. But at the very least you should see a Remove or Change/Remove button for the item.

What's a Hotfix?

You might find several Hotfix items in Add or Remove Programs. These are small security patches that Microsoft puts on their Windows Update Web site whenever someone finds a "hole" in some program that allows hackers to gain unauthorized access to the system. As irritating as all those Hotfix entries might be, you really don't want to remove them. Doing so would just reexpose the vulnerability, and likely cause some of your installed programs to stop working correctly.

Each Service Pack you download contains all the hotfixes that were released since the previous Service Pack. So when you download a Service Pack, there's a good chance all, or most, of the Hotfix entries will disappear on their own. That's only because the individual hotfixes that you downloaded have been replaced by fixes in the Service Pack.

Hotfix information is published in Microsoft's Knowledge Base. The code starting with KB or Q that appears in a Hotfix refers to a specific article. To quickly find an article based on that ID number, go to `http://support.microsoft.com` and choose Search the Knowledge Base or `Knowledge Base Article ID Number Search`. Choose Windows XP as the product, then enter the article ID in the Search For box. (Omit the leading letter "Q," if any, because Microsoft doesn't use the "Q" any more). Click Go, and you'll be taken to the appropriate Web page.

If the selected item shows a *Click here for support information* link, you can click that link for more information as in the Support Info dialog box shown in Figure 48-4. Notice that the Support Info box contains a couple of links of its own. You can click the Publisher link to find out who publishes the program. Click the Support Information link for that program's technical support Web page. When you've finished with the Support Info box, click its Close button.

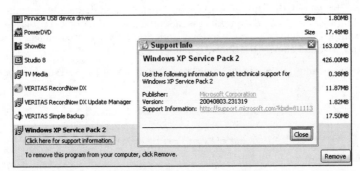

Figure 48-4: Sample Support Information dialog box

Caution   As mentioned near the top of this chapter, there is no Undo or Recycle Bin for remove programs. So, don't remove a program unless you know what it is and know you can live without it. Or you know how to reinstall it should you change your mind later.

To remove a program, click its Remove or Change Remove button, and follow the on-screen instructions. Some programs may require that you restart the computer to complete the removal. If that's the case, close and save any work in progress, close all open program windows, then restart the computer by clicking the Start button and choosing Turn Off Computer ➪ Turn Off.

Getting Rid of Notification Area Icons

Program icons that appear in the Notification area aren't all from applications listed in Add or Remove Programs. Some come from simple dialog box settings. Some are caused by settings within some program. Usually it's not so much a matter of uninstalling the entire program as it is just a matter of preventing the program from auto-starting and running in the background.

Unfortunately, there is no one-rule-fits-all when it comes to dealing with Notification area icons. Each icon plays by its own rules, and finding out what's really going on takes some exploration.

A good first step might be to stop hiding Notification area icons, so you can see them all. To do that, right-click the Start button and choose Properties. Click the Taskbar tab, clear the *Hide inactive icons* check mark, and click OK. When you've finished here, you can repeat the steps but choose (check) the *Hide inactive icons* option to put inactive icons back into hiding.

The next step is to find out just what the icon you're concerned with represents. There are three ways to gather that information, and you may have to try all three on any given icon to see what you get. The three methods are:

✦ Point to the icon to see its ToolTip.

✦ Right-click the icon to see what kinds of options are on its shortcut menu.

✦ Double-click the icon to see what opens (if anything).

As a general example, Figure 48-5 shows the results of pointing to, and right-clicking, the Windows Messenger icon.

Figure 48-5: Pointing to, and right-clicking, a Notification area icon

If double-clicking the notification area icon opens a program or dialog box, you need to look around for settings that control the items behavior. In most programs you'll choose Tools ➪ Options from the program's menu bar. In some programs, you might have to choose File ➪ Preferences. Again, there's no rule here that applies to everything. If all else fails you may have to search the program's Help.

Getting back to the Windows Messenger example, once that's open and you choose Tools ➪ Options from its menu bar. In the Options dialog box that opens, click the Preferences tab. The first two options on the tab, shown in Figure 48-6, determine how Windows Messenger behaves:

Figure 48-6: Options for Windows Messenger

Run Windows Messenger when Windows starts: If you clear this option, then Windows Messenger won't start automatically with Windows. Hence, its icon won't automatically appear in the Notification area every time you start your computer.

Allow Windows Messenger to run in the background: Programs that run in the background display their icons in the Notification area (as opposed to an open program window and taskbar button). Clearing this option will prevent Windows Messenger from appearing in the Notification area even after you intentionally open and close the program.

Not all programs will have the same options as Windows Messenger. But still, you need to gather as much information about as possible about the Notification area icon before you can do much of anything with it.

You may discover that the program is auto-starting because of an icon in the Startup folder for your user account or all user accounts. If that's the case, it's a simple matter of finding and deleting that Startup folder icon. If worse comes to worse, you may have to try to find the program's name in the Services snap-in and prevent the program from auto-starting there.

Note   See "Starting Programs Automatically" and "Auto-Starting from the Services Snap-In" in Chapter 8 for more information on the above-mentioned topics.

Of course, if the Notification area icon represents a program you don't want on your system at all, then it would make sense to remove the program altogether. You'll probably have to close the program before you can remove it though. Closing the program may be as simple as right-clicking its Notification Area icon and choosing Close or Exit. Again, there's no specific rule I can tell you. But once you've closed the program, you should be able to remove it via Add or Remove Programs, providing that the program is listed in that window.

Wrap Up

Deleting a program's icon from the All Programs menu isn't enough. To get rid of a program once and for all, and to reclaim the disk space it's using, you need to *remove* or *uninstall* the program. A quick review of what's involved:

✦ Some programs you can remove just by choosing Uninstall or Remove from the program's group on the All Programs menu.

✦ To see a list of all installed programs, including some toolbars, service packs, and other removable items, open Add or Remove Programs in Control Panel.

✦ To get more information about a program listed in Add or Remove Programs, click the program's name, and then click the support link (if available) in the selected row.

✦ To remove a program, click its name in Add Or Remove Programs, then click the Remove or Change Remove button.

✦ Notification area icons represent programs that are running in the background. It's not always necessary to remove the program entirely just to get it to stop showing up automatically in the Notification area.

✦   ✦   ✦

Managing Application Programs and Processes

T he term *application program* refers to most programs you start
from the Start menu. These programs all tend to run within a program window and show a button in the taskbar when open. In addition
to application programs, there are many *processes* running in the background. Processes don't have program windows or taskbar buttons.

Task Manager is a program built into Windows XP for viewing and
managing running application programs and processes. You can use
it to seek out performance bottlenecks, close hung programs without
restarting the system, and more.

Getting to Know Task Manager

Every running program and process is generally referred to as a *task*.
As its name implies, Task Manager is a program that lets you view
and manage those running programs. There are two ways to start
Task Manager:

✦ Press **Ctrl+Alt+Del**.

✦ Right-click the clock (or an empty portion of the taskbar), and
choose **Task Manager**.

Tip   If a program is hung (frozen), right-clicking the taskbar might not
work. But pressing Ctrl+Alt+Del will bring up Task Manager even
when a hung program is preventing normal taskbar access.

As shown in Figure 49-1, Task Manager has the same features as most
application programs, a title bar and menu bar at the top, a status bar
along the bottom. It also has tabs and buttons along the bottom, like
a dialog box. But it behaves more like a program window because it
has its own taskbar button, and you can size the window by dragging
any corner or edge.

Figure 49-1: Task Manager in its normal view.

Double-click here

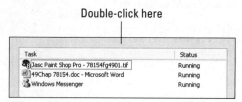

Figure 49-2: Show hidden menu bar and tabs.

Choosing Task Manager Views

There are several ways to view and use Task Manager. On the Options menu in the menu bar, you have the following options:

 ✦ **Always On Top:** Choosing this option ensures that Task Manager is always on the top of the stack when it's open, so no other program windows can cover it.

 ✦ **Minimize On Use:** If selected, this option just minimizes Task Manager whenever you choose the Switch To option to switch to another running program.

 ✦ **Hide When Minimized:** Normally when you minimize Task Manager, only its taskbar button remains visible. Choosing this option will also hide the taskbar button when you minimize Task Manager.

Whenever Task Manager is open, you'll see a small green square in the Notification area. Pointing to that icon displays the current CPU (processor) usage, as shown in Figure 49-3. When Task Manager is minimized, you can double-click that little square to bring Task Manager back onto the desktop.

Figure 49-3: Task Manager notification icon

On the View menu in Task Manager, you have the following choices:

✦ **Refresh Now:** Causes Task Manager to refresh all of its data immediately, regardless of the Update Speed setting.

✦ **Update Speed:** Task Manager needs to use some computer resources to keep itself up to date with what's happening in the system at the moment. The Update Speed option lets you choose how often Task Manager updates itself as follows:

- **High:** Updates Task Manager twice per second.
- **Normal:** Updates Task Manager every two seconds.
- **Low:** Updates Task Manager every four seconds.
- **Paused:** Updates Task Manager only when you choose View ➪ Refresh Now.

✦ **Icons:** The Large Icons, Small Icons, and Details View options on the View menu work in much the same way they do in Windows Explorer. Throughout this chapter I'll show Task Manager in Details View.

Not Responding? Task Manager to the Rescue

One of Task Manager's most useful roles is that of dealing with problems that cause programs, or your whole computer to *hang* (to "freeze up," so that the mouse and keyboard don't work normally). Even when you can't get the mouse or keyboard to work normally, you can usually force Task Manager to open by pressing Ctrl+Alt+Del.

Closing frozen programs

Once Task Manager is open, click on the Applications tab. If a particular program is hung, its Status column will read Not Responding rather than Running. To close the hung program, click its name in the Task column, and then click the End Task button. Task Manager will try to close the program normally, so that if you were working on a document at the time, you may be able to save any changes. (So, don't expect the program to close immediately).

Tip   You can right-click any program name in Task list for shortcuts to common actions.

If Task Manager can't close the program normally, it will still force the program to close. If you were working on a document in that program, you'll lose any work you did since you last saved the document. (A good reason to save your work often when creating or editing documents). Once the hung program is closed, everything else should work normally.

Switching and starting tasks

If the system is hung in such a way that you can't use the Start menu or taskbar normally, and you want to work with open program windows individually, Task Manager provides some ways to accomplish that.

To bring a running program to the top of the stack of windows on the screen, and make it the active window, click its name in the list of running tasks, and then click the Switch To button. If you were working on a document in that program, you can save your work, then exit the program normally.

If you need to bring up some diagnostic program or debugger, and you know the startup command for that program, click the New Task button. The Create New Task dialog box, shown in Figure 49-4, opens. Type the startup command for the program (or the complete path to the program if necessary), and then click OK.

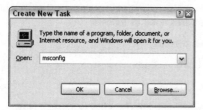

Figure 49-4: Create New Task dialog box

The Windows menu shown in Figure 49-5, offers many of the same window-arranging options you see when you right-click the clock. You can click any program name in the Tasks column (on the Applications tab) and choose Bring to Front to bring a buried program window to the top of the stack. This is handy when a hung program is hogging up the entire screen, and you need to see something, perhaps to save some work in progress, behind that hung program window.

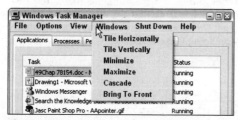

Figure 49-5: Window options in Task Manager

Restarting a hung computer

If the entire system is hung, and you can't get back to normal operation by ending Not Responding Tasks, and have no other recourse, you can reboot the system by choosing Shut Down ➪ Restart from Task Manager's menu bar, as shown in Figure 49-6.

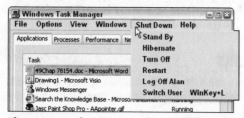

Figure 49-6: Shut Down options in Task Manager

Most likely, you'll want to choose the Restart option just to clear everything out of memory and get off to a clean start. You can, however, shut down the system, log out of your user account, or perform any other task on the Shut Down menu.

Send Error Report?

Often when a program hangs and you end its task, you'll see a message asking if you want to send an error report to Microsoft. This is not the kind of thing where someone will respond and tell you how to fix the error. I mention this because I got an e-mail from an irate user who had sent in an error report, and waited quite a while for the problem to fix itself. She finally got tired of waiting, assuming that the people at the other end were "out of the office."

There are no people at the other end of the error report, and there is no office for them to be out of. The error report is simply stored in a database along with millions of others. Microsoft programmers use that information to identify and find solutions to frequent problems. But they don't do that the minute you send in an error report.

Once in a blue moon you might get some feedback after you send an error report, but it won't be a person who contacts you. It will more likely be in the form of a Web page that tells you the source of the problem, and where you might look for a fix. But usually, you get no feedback at all after you send in an error report.

Monitoring Performance with Task Manager

In addition to helping you deal with hung programs, Task Manager lets you see which activities in your system are using computer resources. In this context, resource usage is about things that are currently open (which is all Task Manager ever shows). When you're talking about things that are open (or running), you're talking about two pieces of computer hardware, the CPU and memory.

Your computer's CPU (central processing unit) if the workhorse of your computer. In fact, the CPU *is* the computer. Just about everything else is just a peripheral device that feeds data to the processor. Also called the microprocessor or processor, it's a chip that's smaller than your thumbnail in which electrons travel at about 670 million miles per hour to perform billions of instructions per second. (Those numbers are accurate, not exaggerations).

Most PC microprocessors are manufactured by two companies, Intel and AMD. Intel makes the Celeron, Pentium, Pentium M, Xeon, and Itanium processors. AMD makes the Sempron and Athlon processors. The speed of a CPU is the number of instructions it can perform per second, usually expressed in gigahertz (GHz). For example, a 3-GHz computer can process three billion instructions per second.

Memory (also called random access memory, or RAM) is a group of chips that store information that the CPU operates on. Memory stores only what's currently open (and therefore visible in Task Manager).

Tip Your hard disk has nothing to do with memory. Memory contains only what you're using right now. Your hard disk is more like a filing cabinet—a place to store programs and documents you with want to open and use in the future. To see examples of CPUs, RAM chips, and hard drives, go to www.tigerdirect.com and click on CPUs(Processors), Memory, or Hard Drives in the left column.

The CPU and memory combined are the real workhorses of your PC. The faster the CPU, and the more memory available, the faster your PC runs. The reason why the *amount*, rather than *speed*, of RAM counts so much is because when RAM is full, Windows has to use a special area of the hard disk, called a *paging file*, to handle the overflow. The hard disk has moving parts, and therefore can't get data to and from the CPU as quickly as RAM can.

Physical Memory versus Virtual Memory

The term *physical memory* refers to the actual amount of RAM, on computer chips, installed in your computer. When you right-click the My Computer and choose Properties, the number to the left of the words "... of RAM" indicate the amount of physical memory installed on the motherboard inside your computer.

When things are busy in RAM, Windows moves some lesser-used items out a special section of the hard disk called a *paging file*. The paging file looks and acts like RAM (to the CPU), even though it's actually space on your hard disk. Every computer has some hard disk space set aside for this paging file. (More on that topic in Chapter 56, "Performance Tuning Your System").

A *page fault* is when the CPU "expects" to find something in RAM, but has to fetch it from virtual memory instead. Though, the term *fault* is a bit harsh here, since a certain amount of memory paging is normal and to be expected. Other terms used in this context include *Nonpaged memory* for physical memory and *Paged memory* for virtual memory.

Exactly how fast your computer runs at any given moment depends on the resources available to it at that moment. For example, if you have half a dozen programs running all doing very busy things, they are eating up CPU resources. If you start another program, that program may run slower than usual, because the other running programs are consuming CPU resources.

Likewise, everything you open stores something in RAM. If RAM is nearly full, and you start another program which needs more memory than what's currently left in RAM, Windows has to start sloughing some of what's currently in RAM off to the hard disk to make room. It takes time to do that, so everything slows down.

The status bar along the bottom of Task Manager's program window gives you a bird's eye view of how much stuff is going on in your system, and how much of your available resources are being used by all that stuff. Going from left to right along the status bar you see:

✦ **Processes:** Shows the total number of processes currently running on the system.

✦ **CPU Usage:** Shows what percentage of CPU capability is currently being used by the above processes.

✦ **Commit Charge:** Shows *total commit charge/total available memory* where total commit charge is the amount of memory currently being used by all the processes. The *total commit charge* is the amount of memory currently taken up by (committed to) all the currently running processes, and *total available memory* is the total amount of physical and virtual memory available in your system.

Tip

The two Commit Charge numbers form a fraction that indicates current memory usage. For example, if you do the division on values like 240/2463, you end up with 0.0974, or 9.74 percent, meaning all running processes are currently using a little less than 10 percent of available memory.

Managing Processes with Task Manager

Whereas application programs run in program windows and are listed on the Applications tab in Task Manager, processes have no program window. We say that processes run in the background, because they don't show anything in particular on the screen. Furthermore, processes tend to have a lower priority than application programs. This means that when you're actively using some program, a process won't take away resources and slow you down.

Your running application programs are actually processes. You can see which process correlates with a given program by right-clicking that program's name on the Applications tab and choosing Go To Process. To see all currently running processes, click the Processes tab in Task Manager. Each process is referred to by *its image name* (in most cases, the name of the program's main executable file), as in the example shown in Figure 49-7.

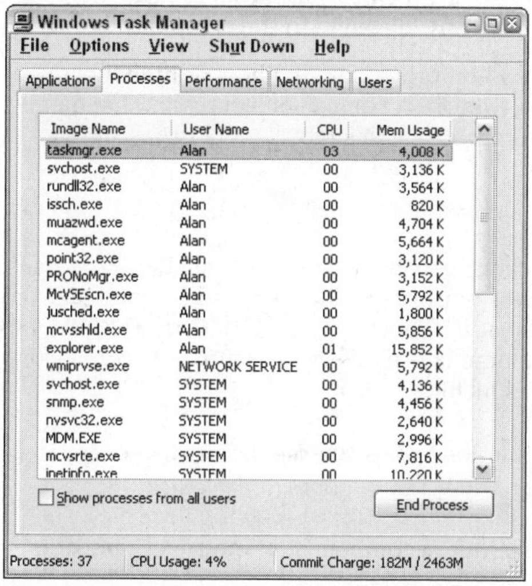

Figure 49-7: Processes tab in Task Manager

The Processes tab shows its information in columns. You can size columns in the usual manner (by dragging the bar at the right side of the column heading). You can sort items by clicking any column heading. For example, you can click the Mem Usage column to sort processes by the amount of memory each one takes up, in ascending order (smallest to largest) or descending order (largest to smallest). Here's what each column shows:

✦ **Image Name:** The name of the process. In most cases, this matches the name of the file in which the process is stored when not open.

✦ **User Name:** The user account in which the process is running. System, Local, Network services and are available to all users, and are necessary just to keep the computer running.

✦ **CPU:** The percent of CPU resources that the process is currently using.

✦ **Mem Usage:** The amount of memory the process needs to do its job.

Memory usage is probably the main cause of slow-running computers. The more stuff you cram into RAM, the more Windows has to use the paging file, and hence the slower everything goes. You can see which processes are hogging up the most RAM just by clicking the Mem Usage column heading until the largest numbers are at the top of the list.

Tip Amazingly, if you just minimize (not close) a program that's open on the desktop, its Mem Usage number will drop significantly. Even though the program is still in RAM, just getting its visible doodads off the desktop will reduce the amount of memory it consumes. That's a good thing to know if your computer is light on RAM and you need to conserve memory!

Hidden processes

Normally, the Processes tab only shows processes running in the user account to which you're currently logged. Choosing *Show processes from all users* shows the true number of running processes, from all users who are currently logged in to the computer.

Likewise, Task Manager might not show old 16-bit processes. To show or hide those processes, choose Options ➪ Show 16-bit Tasks from Task Manager's menu bar. That menu option is available only when you're viewing the Processes tab.

Common processes

You can end any running process by right-clicking its name and choosing End Process. (Or by clicking its name and clicking the End Process button). But doing so isn't a good idea unless you know exactly what service you're terminating. Some processes (mostly SYSTEM, LOCAL SERVICE, and NETWORK SERVICE) are commonplace, and even essential to normal computer functioning. Examples of common processes include:

Tip The process names that start with "Mc" in the figures you see in this chapter are all from McAfee security programs (www.mcafee.com).

✦ **alg.exe:** Application Layer Gateway service, a component of Internet Connection Sharing on networks

✦ **cidaemon.exe:** Windows catalog indexing service used for fast file searches

✦ **cisvc.exe:** Windows indexing service helper files

✦ **csrss.exe:** Client/Server Runtime service: Manages most graphical components on the screen and essential to proper computer functioning

✦ **explorer.exe:** The main component of Windows Explorer, but also required just to keep open windows visible on the screen

✦ **iexplore.exe:** Microsoft Internet Explorer

✦ **inetinfo.exe:** Internet Information Services (IIS) helper program and a core component of Windows XP

✦ **issch.exe:** InstallShield update service

✦ **jusched.exe:** Sun Java virtual machine update scheduler

✦ **lsass.exe:** Local Security Authority Service, a critical local security service required for normal functioning

Caution

There's a known virus that shows as lsass.exe in Task Manager. Do not confuse that with the real lsass.exe, and don't end the lsass.exe. If you think a process might be a virus or adware, search Google for its image name before you assume the worst and end the process.

✦ **mdm.exe:** Machine Debug Manager, provides script debugging in Internet Explorer

✦ **point32.exe:** Microsoft Intellimouse Monitor, provided with some Microsoft mice

✦ **pronomgr.exe:** Intel PRO Ethernet Adapter Manager, provided with some Intel networking devices

✦ **rundll32.exe:** Executes 32-bit dynamic link libraries, essential to normal computer functioning

✦ **services.exe:** Services Manager for Windows, required process

✦ **smss.exe:** Microsoft Session Manager SubSystem, a component of Windows XP

✦ **snmp.exe:** Microsoft Simple Network Management Protocol, part of Windows networking

✦ **spoolsv.exe:** Microsoft Printer Spooling Service, required for printing

✦ **svchost.exe:** Microsoft Service Host Process, an important component of Windows required for normal computer operation

✦ **System:** Microsoft Windows System database file, stores registry HKEY_LOCAL_MACHINE data; required for normal computer operation.

✦ **System Idle Process:** Represents the unused percentage of CPU resources

✦ **taskmgr.exe:** Task Manager

✦ **wdfmgr.exe:** Windows Driver Foundation, a video-licensing component of Windows Media Player 10

✦ **winlogon.exe:** Windows Logon Process, required for logging in to, and out of, user accounts

Where processes get their start

Processes that don't represent application programs you intentionally started from the All Programs menu start for many different reasons and from many different places.

✦ **Startup folders and options:** The Startup folders for All Users and individual user accounts start some programs. Controls in program Options dialog boxes and Preferences dialog boxes also cause some programs to start automatically. (See Chapter 8 for more information).

✦ **Registry:** The \Software\Microsoft\Windows\CurrentVersion\Run keys under HKEY_LOCAL_MACHINE and HKEY_CURRENT_USER start some processes. Both are favorite hiding places of viruses and adware. Also the RunOnce keys in the same locations (see Chapter 29).

✦ **Scheduled Tasks:** The Schedule Tasks folder in Control Panel runs some programs that are configured to run are regular time intervals. If Control Panel opens in Category view, click Performance and Maintenance to get to the icon for Scheduled Tasks.

✦ **Win.ini:** Though a hangover from the 16-bit days of yesteryear, the win.ini file used to launch processes in older versions of Windows can still exist and launch processes in Windows XP.

Note In a domain network, Group Policy and Logon Scripts can also launch processes.

Choosing columns in processes

The four column names that appear in Task Manager by default don't tell the whole story. When you're viewing the Processes tab in Task Manager, you can choose View ➪ Select Columns to choose other columns to view. Each column shows some detail of the process, mostly related to resource consumption. A programmer might use this information to fine-tune a program she's writing. Beyond that it's hard to think of anything terribly practical to be gained from this information. But here's a quick summary of what the other, optional columns show:

✦ **Base Priority:** The priority assigned to the process. When the CPU is busy, low-priority processes have to wait for normal and high-priority processes to be completed. To change a process's priority, right-click its name and choose Set Priority.

Caution Don't experiment with priorities, and never set a process's priority to Realtime without good reason. Doing so can really foul up your PC's performance.

✦ **CPU Time:** Total number of seconds of CPU time this process has used since starting. The number will be doubled for dual-processor systems, quadrupled for systems with four processors.

✦ **CPU Usage:** The amount of processor time, as a percent of the whole, this process has used since first started (the CPU column).

✦ **GDI Objects:** The number of Graphics Device Interface objects used by this process, since starting, to display content on the screen.

✦ **Handle Count:** The number of objects to which the process currently has handles.

✦ **I/O Other:** Nondisk input/output calls made by the object since it started. Excludes file, network, and device operations.

✦ **I/O Other Bytes:** The number of bytes transferred to devices since the process started. Excludes file, network, and device operations.

✦ **I/O Reads:** The number of file, network, and device Read input/output operations since the process started.

✦ **I/O Read Bytes:** The number of bytes transferred by Read file, network, and device input/output operations.

✦ **I/O Writes:** The number of file, network, and device Write input/output operations since the process started.

✦ **I/O Write Bytes:** The number of bytes transferred by Write file, network, and device input/output operations.

✦ **Memory Usage:** The amount of memory blocks used by the process (also called the process's *working set*) since starting.

✦ **Memory Usage Delta:** The change in memory usage since the last Task Manager update.

✦ **Non-paged Pool:** The amount of physical RAM used by the process since starting.

✦ **Page Faults:** The number of times the process has read data from virtual memory since starting.

✦ **Page Faults Delta:** The change in the number of page faults since the last Task Manager update.

✦ **Paged Pool:** The amount of system-allocated virtual memory that's been committed to the process by the operating system.

✦ **Peak Memory Usage:** The largest amount of physical memory used by the process since it started.

✦ **PID (Process Identifier):** A number assigned to the process at startup. The operating system access all processes by their numbers, not their names.

✦ **Session ID:** The Terminal Session ID that owns the process. Always zero unless Terminal Services are in use on the network.

✦ **Thread Count:** The number of threads running in a process.

Tip

A thread is a tiny sequence of instructions that the CPU must carry out to perform some task. Some programs divide tasks into separate threads that can be executed in parallel (simultaneously), to speed execution.

✦ **User Name:** The user, user account, or service that started the process.

✦ **USER Objects:** The number of objects from Window Manager used by the object, including program windows, cursors, icons, and other objects.

✦ **Virtual Memory Size:** The amount of virtual memory currently committed to the process.

Much or the information available from the extra columns on the Processes tab is summarized on the Performance tab.

Monitoring Performance with Task Manager

The Performance tab in Task Manager, shown in Figure 49-8, provides both graphical and numeric summaries of CPU and memory resource usage. To watch resource usage, leave Task Manager open and "always on top" as you run programs and use your computer in the usual ways. Here's what the Performance tab tells you about your resource use:

Tip

Double-click any chart to expand it to a larger size or to restore it to its previous size. The CPU Usage History will be divided into two panes if you're using an Intel processor with Hyper-Threading (HT) technology. If your system has multiple processors, each processor will also have its own pane under CPU Usage History.

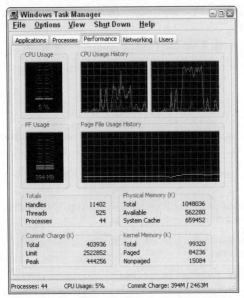

Figure 49-8: Performance tab in Task Manager

✦ **CPU Usage:** Indicates how much of the CPU's capability you're using at the moment.

✦ **CPU Usage History:** Shows CPU usage over time. Choosing View ➪ Show Kernel Times adds a second red line to the chart, which shows the amount of CPU resources used by kernel operations (core operating system processes).

✦ **PF Usage:** Paging file usage; the amount of data being paged to virtual memory.

✦ **Page File Usage History:** The amount of virtual memory usage over time.

✦ **Totals:** The number of handles, threads, and processes running at the time.

✦ **Physical Memory (K):** The total amount of physical memory in the system, the amount that's currently Available, and the amount used by the System Cache which maps to data stored in files. Each measurement is expressed in kilobytes.

✦ **Commit Charge (K):** The total amount of physical and virtual memory committed to programs and the operating system. The Limit is the sum of physical and virtual memory allocated to the system. The Peak is the largest amount of total memory used in the current session.

✦ **Kernel Memory (K):** The total memory used by the operating system kernel and device drivers; also shown as the amount of Paged (virtual) and Non-paged (physical) memory.

The Performance charts are useful for identifying major *performance bottlenecks*. For example, if the CPU Usage and History charts run high, you're CPU is working very hard. Unfortunately, the only real solution to that is to install a faster CPU, which generally means a whole new motherboard.

Note The performance statistics in Figure 49-8 are from a PC with a 3.0-GHz Pentium 4 CPU and 1 GB (1,024 MB) of RAM. To make the CPU Usage History line reach the heights shown, I simultaneously saved a movie file in Movie Maker, played a song in Media Player, checked my e-mail, and just did whatever I else could think of to keep the machine as busy as possible for a few seconds.

The most common performance bottleneck is limited physical memory. For example, 128 MB of RAM is "light" for Windows XP and modern programs. Running lots of programs with limited memory forces the system to use lots of virtual memory, which in turn slows things down. Increasing the amount of virtual memory, (as discussed in Chapter 56) can help. The best solution is to add more RAM (physical memory) to the system, but that's not always an easy thing to do.

Networking and Users Tabs

The Networking and Users tabs in Task Manager display information about your network and user accounts. The Networking tab, shown in Figure 49-9, shows network traffic, or the amount of network bandwidth used. If you have multiple network interface cards installed on the computer, each is displayed in its own chart.

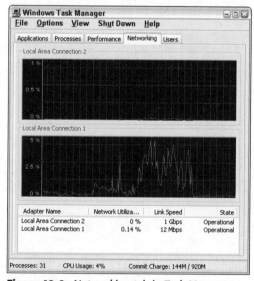

Figure 49-9: Networking tab in Task Manager

The charts are scaled, so don't be alarmed if they run high on the chart. For example, in Figure 49-9 the top of the chart represents only 5 percent of available network bandwidth. So, even the high points on that chart are using very little of the available bandwidth.

The Users tab shows the names of people currently logged in to the computer. That tab is only relevant on computers that are members of a workgroup where Fast User Switching is enabled. You can use the tab to log out other users.

Wrap Up

Task Manager is a handy tool for terminating hung programs (programs that are not responding), and for monitoring computer resource usage. Task Manager also provides detailed information that's of interest only to programmers and network administers. The main things to know about Task Manager are:

✦ To open Task Manager, press **Ctrl+Alt+Del** or right-click the time and choose **Task Manager**.

✦ The Applications tab shows the names of all running application programs. To end a program that's not responding, right-click its name and choose End Task.

✦ To see which process an application relates to, right-click the application name and choose Go To Process.

✦ The Processes tab shows all running processes, including application programs, background programs like antivirus software, and operating system processes.

✦ The Performance tab presents a bird's eye view of overall CPU and memory usage during the current computer session.

✦　　✦　　✦

Troubleshooting Software Problems

Troubleshooting Installation and Removal

There are lots of things that can cause problems with installing and removing programs. Many of those things have more to do with the program at hand than with Windows XP. There's no way to cover everything that might go wrong. Sometimes it's a simple matter of cleaning the CD with a little soap and water. The sections that follow provide some more technical approaches you might try.

Program will not install

Last time I checked, Windows Marketplace listed 88,567 compatible programs. There will probably be more by the time you read this. That probably leaves a few hundred thousand incompatible products still floating about on or floppies and CDs.

If you're having problems installing a program, check to see if it's compatible with Windows XP. If it's no longer compatible, there may be a newer version that is compatible. A quick way to check for compatibility is as follows:

1. Go to www.WindowsMarketplace.com, and click the **Software** button near the top of the page.

2. In the left column, scroll down to the **By manufacturer** heading.

3. If the program manufacturer's name isn't listed under the heading, click **More. . . .**

4. Click on the manufacturer's name to review their current products.

Check the version of the copy you're trying to install. If it's older than the compatible version, that may be your problem right there. You may need to get the newer version.

Optionally, you can check the program manufacturer's Web site to see if they have patches or recommendations on installing the program.

Tip   If you're currently logged in to a Limited account and have an Administrator account as well, log out of the Limited account (don't use the Switch User option). Log in to your administrator account, and try installing the program from that account.

Nonexistent program stuck in Add or Remove Programs

Some older programs install, but then don't uninstall properly when you want to get rid of them. So, you're left with an icon in Add or Remove Programs that represents the program. But when you click the icon, you can't get rid of the program. The fix involves a minor registry hack, but the usual caution applies. So, here goes:

Caution   Editing the registry can cause serious problems that can prevent your computer from starting and be very difficult to fix. Never experiment with registry settings; never try to resolve some problem by taking wild guesses in the registry. See Chapter 58 for more information.

To get to the list of programs in Add or Remove Programs, follow these steps:

1. Click the **Start** button and choose **Run**, or press ⊞+R to open the Run dialog box.

2. Type `regedit` and press Enter.

3. Drill down to the following registry key:

   `HKEY_LOCAL_MACHINE\SOFTWARE\Microsoft\Windows\CurrentVersion\Uninstall`

4. Make sure that you click on Uninstall so that is name is highlighted and the key name in the status bar matches the key in Step 3 (the status bar path will be preceded by `My Computer\`).

5. To play it safe, choose **File ⇨ Export** from the menu bar, and save the selected branch to any filename, such as `uninstall.reg`, and click **Save**.

6. Click the + sign next to **Uninstall** to expand the list. All installed program names will be listed. Note that not all names relate directly to names in the Add or Remove Programs window, so be careful here.

7. Click whichever program name best matches the name of the program you're trying to remove from the Add or Remove Programs window. After you click on a program name, look to the **DisplayName** setting in the right pane. You must find the key whose DisplayName exactly matches the icon you're trying to remove from Add or Remove Programs.

8. When you've found the correct key, right-click the key's name in the left pane and choose **Delete**.

Caution   Do not delete any items just because you don't recognize the name. Doing so will only create problems, not solve them.

9. Choose **Yes** when asked for confirmation.

10. Choose **File ⇨ Exit** from the Registry Editor menu bar.

Open your Add or Remove Programs window and verify that you've removed the correct item. Then:

✦ If you were successful, and Add or Remove Programs is now correct, delete the back up file you created in Step 5.

✦ If you were unsuccessful, double-click the backup file you created in Step 5 to reinstall the original keys. Then, try again by repeating the preceding steps and trying once again to find the appropriate key and DisplayName.

Troubleshooting Programs

Because there are so many programs available for Windows, there are no troubleshooting magic bullets that will solve all problems. Every program is unique and every problem is unique.

One of the most common mistakes people make is to not learn to use a program. They guess and hack their way through it, and when things don't work the way they guessed they would work, they think there's something wrong with the program, when in fact, the problem is that the person using the program has no clue how to use the program correctly. Troubleshooting can't fix ignorance; only learning can fix that.

You must eventually understand that every program has its own built in Help for a reason — it's because every program is unique. The only way to get information about a specific program is from the Help that came with that program, or from the support Web site for that program. The Help menu, which is always the last item on the menu bar, provides all the help options available to you.

The whole concept of troubleshooting only applies when you *do* know how to do something, but even things don't work the way the documentation from which you learned said they should work. (I realize that this is obvious to most readers. But you should see some of the e-mail I get).

Anyway, the big trick is to not just try one resource and then give up. There is no book, Web page, person, place, or thing that has all the answers to all questions, nor the solutions to all problems. Sometimes you really have to dig around for a solution. Start with the narrowest, most simple solution and work your way out frm there, as follows:

Try the Help that's available from the program's menu bar.

Then try the program manufacturer's Web site. With Microsoft products you may want to try searching `http://search.microsoft.com`, `http://support.microsoft.com`, or `http://office.microsoft.com` for Office products. At the program manufacturer's Web site, look around for other support options such as FAQs (Frequently Asked Questions), Troubleshooting, and Discussion Groups or Newsgroups.

For Microsoft products, you'll also want to go to `http://support.microsoft.com` and click on the Product Support Centers link for links to support for specific products. The Microsoft Public Newsgroups link on that same page will take you to areas for specific products where you can post questions and get answers.

Don't forget, too, that you can search the entire planet using a search engine like Google. Though, when you're searching the entire planet you want to use as many exact, descriptive words as possible in your search. Otherwise you'll get links to more pages than you could visit in a lifetime. Include the product name, version number, and specific words that describe what you're looking for.

Tip   To find out what version of a program you're using, choose Help ➪ About . . . from that program's menu bar.

Don't bother trying to form a question like "What is . . . ?" or "How do I . . . ?" because there are no human beings at the other side of the search — just 30 million or so computers. For example, if you're looking for help with Outlook Express version 6 backups, get all of the appropriate words into your search as in `Backup Outlook Express 6`. Be as specific as you can possibly be. The more specific you are when typing your search words, the better your results will be.

Researching Application Errors

Many software errors will provide hexadecimal memory locations in their error messages, as in the example shown in Figure 50-1. Sometimes searching for the number won't do any good. The title bar may provide some clues as to exactly what caused the problem. For example in the figure you can see that Acrobat IEHelper in Internet Explorer (`iexplore.exe`) generated an Application Error. The sentence after the hex addresses also contains some useful information, in the form of the exact application error that occurred.

Figure 50-1: Error message title bar is the most useful here.

Searching for a combination of the program name and keywords from the error message text can sometimes provide clues. You may want to start with a narrow search, such as `http://support.microsoft.com` to avoid getting too many hits. If that doesn't work, you can broaden the search to all of Microsoft.com (`http://search.microsoft.com`). If all else fails, you can search all five billion (or so) pages in Google's index at `www.google.com`.

But the key thing, in all searches, is to get the most unique words from the message into your search string. For example, if searching for the hexadecimal memory addresses from the error message don't pan out, you could try a combination of other words. Perhaps search for `Acrobat IEHelper memory could not be "read".` would be a good way to search form more information on the error that occurred in Figure 50-1.

Furthermore, the title bar in this example tells us that the Acrobat IEHelper in Internet Explorer caused the problem. If the problem were persistent, disabling that helper in Internet Explorer could make the problem go away. (Open Internet Explorer, and choose Tools ➪ Manage Add-ons to disable helper objects, browser extensions, and some toolbars). So, there is more information than you might think in even the most obscure error messages.

Getting rid of some of these things can take some doing. If the thing keeps coming back, scouring the registry for the item's name can help you find where the item is located. Deleting all references to the item from the registry, performing a clean boot, and then deleting the folder in which the item is contained could work, but this is risky business unless you *really* know what you're doing.

Caution   A clean boot is *not* the same as a clean install. See Chapter 54 for instructions on performing a clean boot.

Ideally, you'll want to try to dig up as much information about the error as you can via the Web. In this example, where the name Acrobat appears in the Application Error message, searching Adobe's Web site couldn't hurt, since they're the ones who make the Acrobat products.

✦   ✦   ✦

Installing, Using, and Troubleshooting Hardware

If you're into high-tech gadgets, you're in hog heaven with Windows XP SP2. Just when you thought they had thought up a gadget to do everything imaginable, something new comes along. Part IX is all about using those gadgets with your PC.

Chapter 51 covers all the devices you just plug into your computer and start using, which basically covers USB, IEEE 1394 (a.k.a. FireWire and iLink), PC Cards, and hot new wireless Bluetooth devices that are a breeze to plug in and use.

Chapter 52 gets into the more traditional internal and external devices that attach with cables and often require a bit of software installation. Change 53 covers everything you need to know about hardware drivers, which you often need to update to get your gadget to work with Windows XP SP2.

Installing Hot-Pluggable Devices

There are thousands of hardware devices you can purchase and add to your PC. If you just want to see some examples, go to www.WindowsMarketplace.com and take a look at all the gizmos listed under the hardware heading. Or go to any online computer store like www.CompUSA.com or www.TigerDirect.com and have a look around.

Many devices are *hot-pluggable*, meaning that you don't have to go through any elaborate installation procedure to connect them to your computer. You may have to install a driver first; it depends on the hardware you're using. But beyond that, it's just a matter of connecting the device to the computer with a cable and turning on the device.

This chapter will look at the major categories of hot-pluggable devices, including USB, IEEE 1394, PC Cards, and Bluetooth devices. Here, you'll learn the differences between them and, more importantly, how to install and use them.

Using USB Devices

USB (Universal Serial Bus) is the most common type of hot-pluggable devices. USB is used by many digital cameras, microphones, external disk drives, and many other types of devices. Like most technologies, USB has evolved over the years, and there are currently three versions of USB on the market.

The main differences among USB standards versions have to do with speed. USB 1.0 and 1.1 have two speeds: Low speed (1.5 Mbps) used by mice and keyboards, and Full Speed (12 Mbps), more often used by digital cameras and disk drives. USB 2.0 added a third, High Speed, data rate, which can transfer data at the much faster rate of 480 Mbps.

Finding out which type of USB connectors you have in your own computer is surprisingly difficult. If you bought your computer prebuilt, you may have to look at the specs that came with the computer. Or, find the spec sheet for the computer online at the computer manufacturer's Web site. But, there is one place on your system where you might be able to get a clue directly. Here are the steps:

1. Right-click your **My Computer** icon, and choose **Properties**.

2. In the System Properties dialog box that opens, click the **Hardware** tab.

3. Click the **Device Manager** button.

4. Scroll down to, and click on the + sign next to Universal Serial Bus controllers. If you have USB 2.0, you'll see an *Enhanced* controller listed among the device names, such as the Standard Enhanced PCI to USB Host Controller name in Figure 51-1. (The word "enhanced" in this context means USB 2.0).

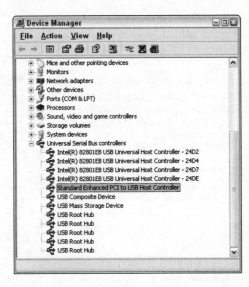

Figure 51-1: USB category expanded in Device Manager

5. Click the **Close** (**X**) button in the upper-right corner of the Device Manager window.

6. Click the **Cancel** button in the System Properties dialog box.

USB 2.0 is downwardly compatible with USB 1.1 and 1.0. Which means that you can use a USB 2.0 device in a computer with USB 1.*x* USB ports. However, the device will transfer at the 12 Mbps speed rather than the 480 Mbps speed available only in USB 2.0.

There are three different USB plug shapes, named Type A, Type B, and Mini-USB or On-the-Go (OTG). The computer has female Type A ports, into which you plug the male Type A plug on the cable. The device might have Type A, B, or a mini-port. Figure 51-2 shows the symbol for USB and the general shape of USB ports on the computer. Examples of Type A, B, and mini-ports are shown to the right of those.

The plugs are all keyed so that they only fit one way. Try pushing the plug gently into the port, and it if won't fit, flip the plug over and try again.

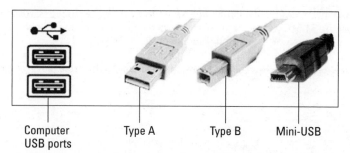

| Computer | Type A | Type B | Mini-USB |
| USB ports | | | |

Figure 51-2: USB symbol, ports, and plug types

Installing a USB device

The general rule of thumb on installing any and all hardware devices is to read the instructions that came with the device first. Some USB devices, especially devices used for networking, require that you install some drivers *before* you plug in the device for the first time. Failure to do so is likely to lead to many hours of hair-pulling frustration. But even if you do have to install drivers first, you only have to do that once, not each time you plug in the device. The rest is easy:

1. Leave the computer turned on and running.

2. Plug one end of the cable into the computer.

3. Plug the other end of the cable into the device.

4. Turn on the device and watch the screen.

When you see a notification like the one shown in Figure 51-3, your device is ready to use.

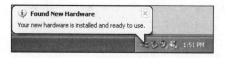

Figure 51-3: USB device installed and ready to go

Removing a USB Device

Some USB devices, such as cameras, disk drives, and network hardware, transfer data to and from the computer. Before removing such a device, it's a good idea to *close* all programs to make sure that you don't lose any data. If you have such a device connected to your computer, you'll see a Safely Remove Hardware icon in your notification area, like the example shown in Figure 51-4.

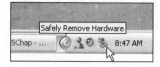

Figure 51-4: Pointing to the Safely Remove Hardware notification area

Before you remove the device, double-click that icon to get to the Safely Remove Hardware dialog box shown in Figure 51-5. Click the name of the device you want to remove, click the Stop button, and then click Close. You can then disconnect the device.

 Tip You can unplug the device from the cable and leave the other end of the cable plugged into the computer.

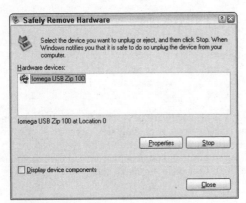

Figure 51-5: Safely Remove Hardware dialog box

Installing IEEE 1394 Devices

IEEE 1394 (often called 1394 for short) is a high-speed (400-Mbps) standard typically used to connect digital video cameras and high-speed disk drives to computer. The symbol and plug shape for an IEEE 1394 port is shown in Figure 51-6. IEEE 1394 also goes by the names FireWire and iLink.

Figure 51-6: IEEE 1394 symbol and port

Installing a 1394 device should be easy:

1. Leave the computer running, turn the device off (if it has an on/off switch).

2. Connect one end of the 1394 cable to the computer and the other end to the device.

3. Turn on the device and wait.

What happens next depends on the device. If it's a video camera, you'll most likely be taken directly to Windows Movie Maker or a dialog box asking what you want to do. If it's a disk drive, it should show up as an icon in your My Computer folder.

To disconnect a 1394 device, follow the same procedure as for USB devices. First, see if the Safely Remove Hardware notification icon is available. If so, double-click it. If you see the device name in the Safely Remove Hardware dialog box, click that name and click the Stop button. Then, click the Close button in the dialog box and disconnect the device.

Tip   If your computer doesn't have an IEEE 1394 port, you can add one inexpensively. Go to any store that sells computer hardware, or an online store like www.tigerdirect.com, and search for 1394 adapter.

PC Cards and Cardbus

PC Cards and Cardbus cards (also called PCMCIA devices) are commonly used on notebook computers. The device is usually a little larger and thicker than a credit card. Figure 51-7 shows an example of a PC Card wireless network adapter.

As always, be sure to read the instructions that came with the device before you install the device. You may need to preinstall some drivers. Then, leave the computer running and slide the card into the slot. You may have to push firmly to get it to fit in snugly.

Before remove the device, check for the Safely Remove Hardware icon in the notification icon. Double-click that icon and, if you see the name of the device listed in the dialog box, click its name, and then click Stop. Click the Close button in the dialog box, and then remove the device.

Figure 51-7: Sample PC Card

The World of Bluetooth

As I write this chapter late in 2004, Bluetooth is still a relatively new technology that provides wireless communications among computers, printers, mobile phones, PDAs, digital cameras, and other electronic devices. You can connect as many as eight devices together with Bluetooth. For example, you could link together a few desktop PCs, a notebook, PDA, digital camera, MP3 player, digital video camera, and mobile phone all linked together wirelessly. They could all share a high-speed Internet connection, shared data, and use a single printer.

Bluetooth transfers data at 732 Kbps (about three-quarters of 1 Mbps, which is slower than 802.11b (11Mbps) and 802.11g (54Mbps). So, if you're thinking if setting up a permanent wireless network between computers, you may want to stick with the 802.11 standards described in Part XI of this book. But when it comes to connecting noncomputer Bluetooth devices, or wirelessly connecting a printer, or occasionally transferring files between computers, Bluetooth can't be beat.

There are three types of Bluetooth devices, classified by the range across which devices can communicate:

✦ **Class 1:** Transmit and receive data to 330 feet (100m).

✦ **Class 2:** Transmit and receive data up to 66 feet (20m).

✦ **Class 3:** Transmit and receive data up to 33 feet (10m).

Some Bluetooth buzzwords and concepts that you'll encounter in this section as well as in the instructions that come with Bluetooth devices are:

✦ **Discovery:** A Bluetooth device finds other Bluetooth devices to which it can connect through a process called discovery. To prevent Bluetooth devices from connecting at random, discovery is usually turned off on a Bluetooth device.

✦ **Discoverable:** A discoverable (or *visible*) Bluetooth is device is one that has discovery turned on, so other Bluetooth devices within range can "see" and connect to the device.

✦ **Pairing:** Once two or more Bluetooth devices have discovered one another and been paired (connected), you can turn off their discovery features. The devices will forever be able to connect to one another, and unauthorized foreign devices will not be able to discover and hack into the paired devices.

✦ **Encryption:** A process by which data transferred is encoded to make it unreadable to any unauthorized device that picks up a signal from the device. Bluetooth offers powerful 128-bit data encryption to secure the content of all transferred data.

✦ **Passkey:** Similar to a password, only devices that share a passkey can communicate with one another. This is yet another means of preventing unauthorized access to data transmitted across Bluetooth radio waves.

A noncomputer gadget like a phone or PDA that supports Bluetooth is called a *Bluetooth device*. A standard desktop PC or laptop computer usually isn't a Bluetooth device. But as a rule, it's easy to turn your PC or laptop into a Bluetooth device. You just plug a Bluetooth USB adapter — a tiny device about the size of your thumb — into any available USB port and presto, your computer is a Bluetooth device. Making your computer into a Bluetooth doesn't limit it in anyway. It just extends the capabilities of your computer so that you can do things like:

✦ Connect a Bluetooth mouse or keyboard

✦ Use the Add Printer Wizard to use a Bluetooth printer wirelessly

✦ Use a Bluetooth-enabled phone or dial-up device as a modem

✦ Transfer files between Bluetooth-ready computers or devices by using Bluetooth

✦ Join an ad hoc personal area network (PAN) of Bluetooth-connected devices. (an ad hoc network is an "informal" network, where devices connect and disconnect on an as-needed basis, without the need for a central hub or base station).

Bluetooth devices use radio signals to communicate wirelessly. When you install a Bluetooth adapter on your PC or laptop, you also install *radio drivers*. Windows XP SP2 comes with many radio drivers preinstalled.

Note   For a complete list of installed radio drivers, see Microsoft Knowledge Base Article 883259 at `http://support.microsoft.com/default.aspx?scid=kb;en-us;883259&Product=winxp#001`. **If a built-in radio driver doesn't work with your device, install the drivers that came with the device per the device manufacturer's instructions.**

If you plan to share a single Internet account among several computers or Bluetooth devices, you should install your first Bluetooth USB adapter in the computer that connects directly to the modem or router. That will give other Bluetooth devices that you add later easy Access to the Internet through that computer's Internet connection.

Once you've installed a Bluetooth adapter, you'll see a new icon named Bluetooth Devices in Control Panel's Classic View, as in Figure 51-8. From Control Panel's Category view, click on Network and Internet Connections or Printers and Other Hardware to get to the Bluetooth Devices icon. You might also notice a Bluetooth icon in the Notification area, as is also shown near the mouse pointer in Figure 51-8.

Figure 51-8: New icons on a PC that's configured as a Bluetooth device

The Bluetooth Devices dialog box will be your central point for installing Bluetooth. To open that dialog box, double-click the Bluetooth Devices Notification area icon, or open the icon in Control Panel. Initially, the Devices tab in the dialog box will be empty. But as you install devices and join devices to a Bluetooth PAN, you'll see the names of those devices listed on that tab.

The Options tab in the Bluetooth Devices dialog box, shown in Figure 51-9, provides general options for controlling discovery and the ability to install Bluetooth devices. If you don't see a Bluetooth Devices icon in your notification area, make sure to choose the *Show the Bluetooth icon in the notification area* checkbox.

The shortcut icon that appears when you right-click the Notification area, also shown in Figure 51-9, provides options for adding a Bluetooth device, sending and receiving files, and joining a PAN.

There are many different types of Bluetooth devices on the market. Most have some means of making the device discoverable (visible) to other devices. Whether or not you have to make your PC discoverable to install a device depends on the type of installation you're about to perform. As always, you need to read the documentation that came with your device for specifics. But if you do need to make your computer discoverable, it's simple a matter of choosing the "Turn discovery on" option, visible in Figure 51-9.

On the shortcut menu for the Bluetooth Devices notification icon, the Add a Bluetooth device option opens the Add a Bluetooth Device Wizard, which takes you step by step though the process of adding a device. The sections that follow discuss general techniques for adding Bluetooth devices, many of which will involve the Add a Bluetooth Device Wizard.

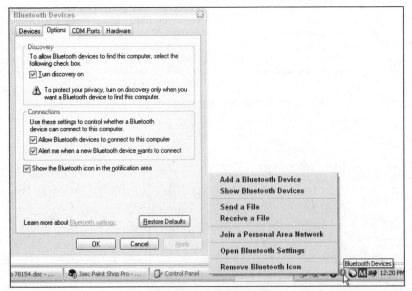

Figure 51-9: Options tab of the Bluetooth Devices dialog and Notification area shortcut menu.

Installing a Bluetooth printer

To install a Bluetooth printer, follow the printer manufacturer's instructions for turning on the printer and enabling its ability to connect to a computer. Then, on your PC:

1. Click the **Start** button, and choose **Printers and Faxes**. Or, click **Start** and choose **Control Panel**. If Control Panel opens in Category View, click **Printers and Other Hardware**. Open the **Printers and Faxes** icon.

2. Under Printer Tasks in the Explorer bar, click on **Add a printer**.

3. Click **Next** on the first Wizard page, and then choose **A Bluetooth printer** on the second wizard page.

4. Click **Next**, and follow the remaining Wizard instructions until you can click the **Finish** button to complete the job.

Once it is installed, you should be able to print from any Bluetooth device according to the instructions that came with that device. To print a document from your computer, follow the usual procedure (choose File ➪ Print from the program's menu bar), and choose the Bluetooth printer from the Printer Name options in the Print dialog box.

Install a Bluetooth keyboard or mouse

To install Bluetooth keyboard or mouse, you must first connect the device by cable, or use a cable connected mouse or keyboard to provide the initial connectivity. Also, you must know how to make your mouse or keyboard discoverable (visible). If you're not sure how to get started, refer to the instructions that came with the mouse or keyboard.

If you're installing a keyboard, check its documentation to see if the keyboard supports the use of a passkey. And if so, find out if it already has a preassigned passkey, or if you can use a passkey of your own choosing. Then, to perform the installation, follow these steps:

1. Right-click the Bluetooth Device Notification area icon and choose **Add a Bluetooth Device**. Or open the Bluetooth Devices dialog box from Control Panel or its notification icon, and click the **Add** button at the bottom of the Devices tab.

2. Choose **My device is set up and ready to be found** and, then click **Next**.

3. Click on the discovered device's name, and then click **Next**.

4. If you're adding a keyboard, do one of the following as appropriate for your device:

   • To have Windows create a safe, random passkey, click **Choose a passkey for me**.

   • If your device has a predefined passkey, choose **Use the passkey found in the documentation**, then type the passkey.

   • If you want to create your own custom passkey, click **Let me choose my own passkey**, then type a passkey.

   • If the device doesn't support the use of passkeys, choose **Don't use a passkey**.

5. Click **Next**, the follow the remaining instructions presented by the wizard.

Install a Bluetooth mobile phone

Some Bluetooth mobile phones can connect to a computer to synchronize phone books and transfer files. Some (but not all) mobile phones can also act as modems to connect to the

Internet. Make sure that you read the documentation that came with the phone so that you understand how to make the phone discoverable, how to name the phone (if necessary), basic information on setting up a passkey, and whether or not you can use the phone as a modem.

If your mobile phone can act as a modem, you'll need a dial-up Internet account to connect to the Internet. Most likely this will be a mobile service provider. You'll need to know your user name, password, carrier code or phone number, and other basic account information prior to setting up your Internet account. Only your Internet service provider (or mobile service provider) can give you that information.

The exact procedure for installing a Bluetooth phone will vary from one phone to the next. But to get started, make sure that discovery and the ability to add new devices is enabled on your PC. Then, follow these steps:

1. Right-click the Bluetooth Device Notification area icon and choose **Add a Bluetooth Device**. Or, open the Bluetooth Devices dialog box from Control Panel or its notification icon, and click the **Add** button at the bottom of the Devices tab.

2. Follow the instructions presented by the wizard, and as specified by the mobile phone manufacturer.

If the phone you installed in the preceding steps can act as a modem, you can then proceed with the following steps to set up a Bluetooth connection to the Internet:

1. Open your Network Connections folder using whichever of the following techniques is most convenient and works with your current PC configuration:

   • Click the **Start** button, and choose **Network Connections** (if available).

   • Or, click the **Start** button, and choose **My Network Places**. Then, click **View network connections** under Network Tasks in the Explorer bar.

   • Or, click the **Start** button and choose **Control Panel**. If Control Panel opens in Category View, click Network and Internet Connections. Open the **Network Connections** icon.

2. Under Network Tasks in the Explorer bar, click **Create a new connection**.

3. In the New Connection Wizard, follow the steps for connecting to the Internet using a dial-up connection. When you get to the Phone Number to Dial page, make sure that you include the carrier code (which is often *99#) or the phone number provided by your ISP.

4. Follow any remaining wizard instructions until you get to the Finish button, and then click **Finish**.

Once the phone is installed, you should be able to get online by opening the connection icon in your Network Connections folder. From the Properties dialog box for that connection, you may be able to show an icon for the phone in your Notification area. If that's the case, you can just double-click the Notification area icon when you want to connect. When you want to disconnect from the Internet, right-click that notification icon and choose Disconnect.

Tip To add a Network Connections option to the right side of your Start menu, right-click the Start button and choose Properties. Click the Customize button, click the Advanced tab, and choose Link to Network Connections Folder from the Start Menu Items list. See "Personalizing Your Start Menu" in Chapter 6 for a more detailed discussion.

Connect a Bluetooth Pocket PC

To connect a Bluetooth Pocket PC to your computer, make sure that you know the handheld PC well enough to make it discoverable (visible), and (if necessary) to give the handheld a name. Complete the necessary steps, and then follow these steps on your PC:

1. Right-click the Bluetooth Device Notification area icon, and choose **Add a Bluetooth Device**. Or, open the Bluetooth Devices dialog box from Control Panel or its notification icon, and click the **Add** button at the bottom of the Devices tab.

2. Follow the instructions in the Add Bluetooth Device Wizard to install your Pocket PC. When you get to the Finish page of the Wizard, jot down the incoming COM port number (also called the serial port number), because you'll need to know that number later.

After you've completed the wizard, install on your PC the ActiveSync software that came with your Pocket PC. Connect the Pocket PC or Pocket PC cradle to a USB port on your computer. If your Pocket PC has a cradle, put the phone in the cradle. Then, follow these steps on your desktop (or laptop) computer:

1. If the Get Connected Wizard doesn't appear automatically when you connect your Pocket PC, click the **Start** button and choose **All Programs** ⇨ **Microsoft ActiveSync**.

2. Choose **File** ⇨ **Get Connected**.

3. Choose **File** menu ⇨ **Connection Settings**.

4. Select the **Allow serial cable or infrared connection to this COM port** checkbox, and then select the COM port. (If one port does not work, try the other one).

5. Disconnect the USB cable from the computer.

6. On your Pocket PC, turn on the **Bluetooth wireless technology**.

From this point on, the Pocket PC is paired with your computer. You should be able to follow the instructions that came with your Pocket PC to synchronize that device with your PC.

Install a Bluetooth Palm PC

To connect a Bluetooth Palm PC to your computer, make sure that you know the handheld PC well enough to make it discoverable (visible) and (if necessary) to give the handheld a name. Complete the necessary steps, and then follow these steps on your PC:

1. Right-click the Bluetooth Device Notification area icon, and choose **Add a Bluetooth Device**. Or open the Bluetooth Devices dialog box from Control Panel or its notification icon, and click the **Add** button at the bottom of the Devices tab.

2. Follow the instructions presented by the Add Bluetooth Device Wizard.

3. If you see COM (serial) port numbers on the Finish page of the wizard, write them down, because you'll need those numbers later.

Note If the Finish page in the wizard doesn't list COM ports (or serial ports), don't worry about it. That just means your Palm PC doesn't use, or require, a COM port.

Now you can install, on your PC, the HotSync software, and any other software, that came with your Palm PC. (Unless, of course, you've already installed that software). But whether or not you've already installed the software, at some point you'll be asked to provide COM port, or serial port, numbers. Be sure to use the number provided on the Finish page of the Add Bluetooth Device Wizard as described in Step 4 above. To use your synchronization software, follow the instructions that came with your Palm PC.

Joining a Bluetooth Personal Area Network

A Bluetooth personal area network (PAN) is a short-range wireless network used to connect devices together wirelessly. It's commonly used to connect a laptop to a desktop PC, though can be used to connect other types of Bluetooth devices. As a rule, there's not much to joining Bluetooth devices to a Bluetooth network. Most of the action takes place automatically behind the scenes.

To understand the basic procedure, let's assume you already have a desktop computer with a functional Internet connection. You've already installed a Bluetooth USB adapter on that computer, so it's now a Bluetooth device. On that desktop computer, you can open the Bluetooth Settings dialog box, click the Options tab, and make sure that *Turn discovery on* and *Allow Bluetooth devices to connect to this computer* options are selected.

On a laptop computer, plug in a second Bluetooth USB adapter. You want to connect the laptop to the desktop in a personal area network. To do so, starting from the laptop computer, follow these steps:

1. Right-click the Bluetooth Devices Notification area icon and choose **Join a Personal Area Network**. A list of Bluetooth devices appears, as in Figure 51-10.

Figure 51-10: Bluetooth devices you can join in a PAN

2. Click the name of the computer to which you want to connect, and click the **Connect** button.

3. Choose a passkey method from the next wizard screen (the Choose a passkey for me option is sufficient), and then click Next.

4. You'll be given a passkey as in the upper-left corner of Figure 51-11. On the other computer, you'll be asked to type in that same passkey, as in the lower-right corner of that same figure. Type in the passkey exactly as shown in the first computer, and click **Next**.

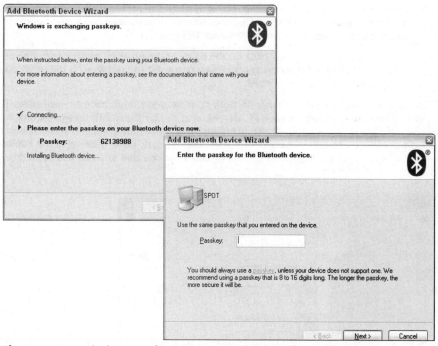

Figure 51-11: Assigning a passkey to two computers in a Bluetooth network

5. Follow any remaining instructions in the Wizards on both computers until you get to the Finish page, and then click the **Finish** button in each wizard.

Once the connection is established, you should have Internet access on both computers. You can share printers and folders, and move and copy files between computers using the techniques described in Chapters 62 and 63.

Note, however, that if you made the Bluetooth connection to only one computer in an existing LAN, you'll have access only to the shared resources on the Bluetooth-enabled computer, not all the computers in the LAN.

Troubleshooting a Bluetooth Network Connection

If you can't get any connectivity at all using Bluetooth, try the following remedy:

1. Go to the computer that's directly connected to the Internet via a modem or router.

2. Open your Network Connections folder using whichever of the following techniques is most convenient and works with your current PC configuration:

   • Click the **Start** button, and choose **Network Connections** (if available).

   • Or, click the **Start** button and choose **My Network Places**. Then, click **View network connections** under Network Tasks in the Explorer bar.

   • Or, click the **Start** button and choose **Control Panel**. If Control Panel opens in Category View, click Network and Internet Connections. Open the **Network Connections** icon.

3. In the Network Connections folder, scroll down to the personal area network group and look for the **Bluetooth Network Connection** icon. If it shows a red X, right-click that icon and choose **View Bluetooth Network Devices**.

4. In the dialog box that opens, click on the name of the other computer, and then click the **Connect** button. If you get another passkey, enter the passkey on the other computer as instructed by the wizard.

By the time you complete the wizards on both screens, you should have a connection. The Network Connections folder on each PC should have similar Bluetooth network icons, without the red X, as in the example shown in Figure 51-12. Note that when you select (point to, or click on, the Bluetooth network connector icon, the Network Tasks heading in the Explorer bar will shown numerous Bluetooth-related network options that you can use to further troubleshoot the connection.

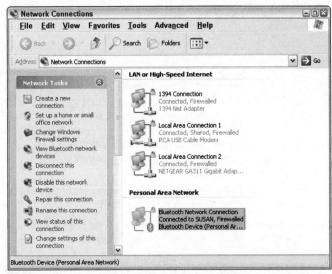

Figure 51-12: Bluetooth network icon in Network Connections folder

Sharing an Internet connection

If you still can't get Internet connectivity from the laptop computer, go to the computer that's connected to the modem or router once again. Open its Network Connections folder and find the icon that represents the Internet connection. (In the example shown in Figure 51-12, that's the RCA USB Cable Modem, but yours would reflect the name of your modem or router). Right-click that Internet connection icon and choose Properties.

In the Properties dialog box for the Internet connection, click the Advanced tab, and choose *Allow other network users to connect through this computer's Internet connection* as in Figure 5-13.

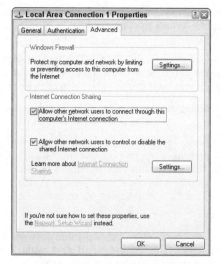

Figure 51-13: Internet connection sharing enabled

Also, click the top Settings button under Windows Firewall. In the Windows Firewall dialog box that opens, make sure that On (recommended) is selected, and that *Don't allow exceptions* is *not* selected. Click the Advanced tab in the Windows Firewall dialog box and make sure Bluetooth Network Connection is selected (checked) in the list of Network Connection Settings. Then click OK.

Transferring files between Bluetooth devices

When you connect two computers in a Bluetooth network, you can move and copy multiple files between computers using the techniques described under *Transferring Files between Computers* in Chapter 63. That's the quickest and easiest way to do it, providing that you know how to select files and use drag-and-drop techniques described in Chapter 14.

You can also use the Send a File and Receive a File options on the Bluetooth Devices shortcut menu as an alternative. However, you can't move files that way, and you can only copy one file at a time. So, this method usually is best for transferring files to a noncomputer Bluetooth device. But still, if you want to transfer one file between computers using this method, here are the steps:

1. On the computer to which you plan to send a file, right-click the **Bluetooth Devices** icon in the Notification area and choose **Receive a file**. The Bluetooth File Transfer Wizard opens and waits for you to send a file from the other computer.

2. On the computer that contains the file you want to copy, right-click the Bluetooth Devices notification icon and choose **Send a file**.

3. In the wizard that opens, click the **Browse** button, choose the computer (or device) to which you want to send the file, and then click **OK**.

4. If the two devices are already paired using a passkey, the passkey options will be disabled, and you can ignore those options. Just click **Next**.

5. Click the **Browse** button on the next wizard page, and navigate to the folder that contains the file you want to send. Then, click the icon of the file you want to send, and click the **Open** button. Then click **Next**.

6. On the receiving computer, the wizard asks what you want to name the file and where you want to put it. Type a filename for the file you're about to receive, and use the **Browse** button to choose the folder in which you want put the file. Then click **Next**.

7. When the transfer is complete, click the **Finish** button in the last wizard page on both computers.

Remember, there are many different Bluetooth devices on the market. If none of the techniques described here help you make the connection between two computers in a personal area network, be sure to refer to the instructions that came with your Bluetooth device.

Wrap Up

This chapter has been about installing and using various modern hot-pluggable devices. A hot-pluggable device is basically one you can connect to the computer and start using, without shutting down the computer or rebooting the system. Technologies covered in this chapter are:

✦ To install most USB devices, you simply plug the device into the computer, turn on the device (if it has an on/off switch), and wait for the notification message that tells you the device is installed and ready to use.

✦ Some USB devices, particularly networking devices, will require that you install some drivers first. So, always read the instructions that came with a device before you connect it.

✦ To safely remove a USB device that supports file transfers, double-click the Safely Remove Hardware icon in the Notification area, click on the name of the device, click Stop, and then click Close.

✦ To install an IEEE 1394 device, simple connect the device to a 1394 port on your computer, and then turn the device on and wait for options to appear on your screen.

✦ To install a PC Card, just slide the card into the PC Card slot on your computer and wait for a notification message that tells you the device is ready to use.

✦ Bluetooth is a relatively new technology that allows you connect cell phones, PDAs, mice, keyboards, and other Bluetooth devices.

✦ To turn a computer into a Bluetooth device, simple connect a Bluetooth USB adapter to a USB port on the computer.

✦ To connect a Bluetooth device to a computer, activate Discovery on the device, bring it within range of the computer, right-click the Bluetooth Devices icon in the Notification area, and choose Add a Bluetooth Device.

✦ To create a personal area network between two or more computers, add a Bluetooth USB adapter to each computer. Then, right-click the Bluetooth devices notification area icon and choose Join A Personal Network.

✦ Regardless of what type of device you intend to connect to your computer, always read the instructions that came with the device first.

✦   ✦   ✦

Installing Other Hardware

In This Chapter

External devices and internal devices

Things to do before you install any new hardware

Installing more RAM

Installing a second hard drive

◆ ◆ ◆ ◆

There are tons of cool gadgets you can add to your PC. The official buzzword for a gadget is a *hardware device*, or just *device* for short. Many modern devices are hot-pluggable, meaning that you just plug the thing into your computer and start using. Those kinds of gadgets were discussed in Chapter 51.

Then, there are other kinds of gadgets that aren't so easy to install. The number one rule for installing gadgets is this: Read and follow the instructions that came with the device. In view of that, it might seem strange for me to even write a chapter on this topic. There are, however, some general things that apply to hardware installations, and those are the things that this chapter is all about.

Internet and External Hardware Devices

Even though there are literally thousands of PC hardware devices on the market, they can all be categorized as either internal or external devices. External devices connect to the computer by a cable and a port of the computer. Internal gadgets connect directly to the computer motherboard inside the system case.

External ports

External ports are plugs that cables plug into. Different computers have different ports on them, so I can't tell you exactly what ports you have, or where they're located. But Figure 52-1 shows some common ports that you're likely to find on just about any computer, and the type of device that generally plugs into each port.

Note   There are so many different devices that plug into USB ports, it wouldn't make sense to even give an example of the type of device that plugs into that type of port. This chapter doesn't really apply to USB devices. See Chapter 51 for information on USB devices.

Internal ports

To install an internal device, you have to open the case and plug the device into a port on the motherboard (also called the *mainboard*). Some of those ports are referred to as *expansion slots*, or just *slots* because if they're rectangular shape. The motherboard is a circuit board that provides the wiring between all the hardware devices that make up the system, including the CPU, memory (RAM), internal disk drives, and everything else. Figure 53-2 provides a general idea of what different types of internal slots and ports look like.

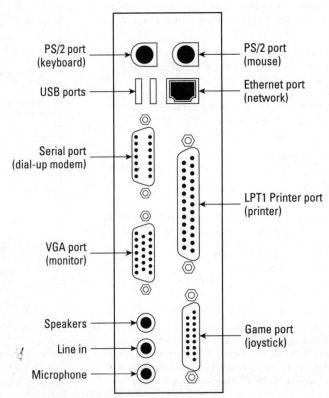

Figure 52-1: Sample external computer ports

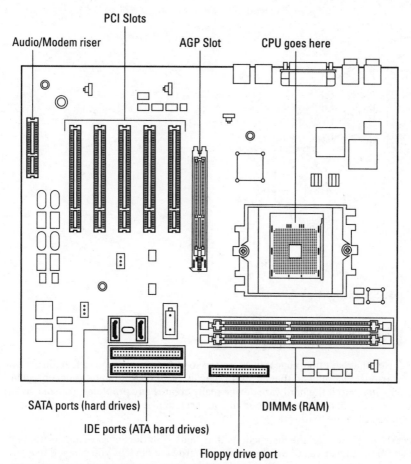

Figure 52-2: Sizes and shapes of internal ports and slots

Many internal hardware devices are PCI Cards, which slide into a PCI slot. The slots are positioned so that one end of the card lines up perfectly with the back of the computer, exposing an external plug. The AGP (Accelerated Graphics Port) port is used for a graphics card. As with the PCI cards, when you slide an AGP card into the slot, the back of the card exposes a plug on the back of the computer. Figure 52-3 shows an example of an AGP graphics card. When installed, the port on the back of the card exposes its plug at the back of the computer so that you can plug a monitor into the card.

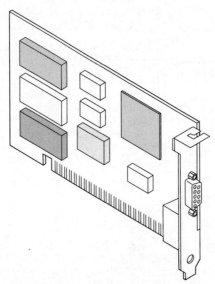

Figure 52-3: Sample AGP graphics card

Before You Install Anything . . .

For any device that isn't hot-pluggable, there are some steps you need to take before you even get started. I recommend that as Step 1, you create a restore point as described in Chapter 55. That way, if the hardware device really creates any problems, you can always uninstall it, remove it, and even get your all your system files back to the way they were before you installed the hardware.

The second thing is to read the instructions that came with the device. There is not one-rule-fits-all fact that applies to all of the thousands of hardware devices you can add to a PC. You should install the device exactly as told to in the instructions provided by the manufacturer of the device. Winging it is likely to lead to many hours of hair-pulling frustration.

Third, shut down the computer, turn off the power, and unplug the power cord. Unplugging the power cord is especially important when you plan to open the system case, as you don't want any electricity to even be available to the system when you're in the guts of the machine. Ideally, you should wear an antistatic wrist strap so that you don't generate any static electricity sparks. One little spark like that could turn the motherboard to trash, and void the warranty to boot.

Tip   You can buy an antistatic wrist strap at computer hardware stores, including online stores such as TigerDirect (www.tigerdirect.com), CompUSA (www.compusa.com), CDW (www.cdw.com), and Cyberguys (www.cyberguys.com).

When installing an internal device in a PCI or AGP slot, push firmly on the card to make sure you really get it in there. Don't force it and break it. But push real good so that it's in the slot evenly and as deep as it will go. Even a slightly crooked card may malfunction. Put the case cover back together again, plug in the power cord, and then turn on the PC.

For an external device, make sure that you get the plug in good and snug, both at the computer end and at the device end. If the external device needs power, plug it into the wall and turn it on. You definitely want to turn the device on before you start the computer. When you're ready to go, turn on the computer.

If the device plug-and-play (as virtually all modern devices are), the rest should be easy. The computer should boot up normally, but you won't necessarily get to the desktop right away. Instead, Windows should detect the new device, and go through an installation procedure to get the device working. You'll get some feedback on the screen as that's happening, in the form of notification area messages. When the notification messages stop and the desktop looks normal, the device should be ready to use.

Installing More Memory (RAM)

Installing more RAM isn't exactly like installing other devices, because you're not likely to get any feedback at all on the Windows desktop when you're done. RAM is such an integral part of the computer that it doesn't really get "installed." The processor just detects it as soon as you turn on the power. The only place you'd even see that you have more RAM is on the General tab of the System Properties dialog box.

The big trick to adding more RAM is finding the right type of memory. You need to match the type and speed of your existing RAM chip, and you need an available DIMM slot on the motherboard. Also, every motherboard has a limit as to the maximum speed and type of memory it can handle. When you build a PC you know exactly what's involved. But when you buy a prebuilt PC, it's not always easy to find out what you need to know.

Your best bet is to go to the computer manufacturer's Web site and find the main Web page for your exact model of computer. You can often find out exactly what type and speed RAM chip is currently installed using that method. PNY (a company that sells RAM chips) has a Memory Configurator link on their home page (www.pny.com). When you click that link, it asks some basic questions about your system and then tells you which RAM chips will work with that system.

> **Tip** The PNY site also has a How To Install link, which might help you get the feel for what you'll be doing when you purchase more RAM. Remember, you have to look inside the computer and see if you even have an available slot for adding more RAM first.

Even so, installing more RAM isn't really something for the technologically timid to undertake. Even the slightest mistake could prevent the computer from starting at all. If the speed of the new chip doesn't exactly match the speed of the existing chip, the computer will start but you're likely to end up with endless error messages when you try to do just about anything.

> **Caution** People will tell you that you can mix RAM chip speeds. Rather than argue the issue, let me just say this. If you want your computer to work, don't mix RAM chip speeds.

Upgrading the CPU

Every motherboard has a certain maximum CPU speed it can handle. You won't know what that is unless you can get the specs on your exact motherboard. Rather than try to upgrade just the CPU, you'd probably be better of upgrading the motherboard, CPU, and RAM while you're at it. That way you can speed up everything, but still use your existing hard drive, CD/DVD drive, mouse, keyboard, monitor, and everything else.

A barebones kit might be the best way to go. With a barebones kit you can get a motherboard, CPU, RAM, and power supply already assembled in a new case. You then transfer your existing hard drive, CD drive, mouse, keyboard, monitor, and everything else to that new case. So you get the benefits of a newer, faster computer without the expense of buying an entirely new PC.

Installing a Second Hard Drive

If you need more hard disk space, installing a second hard drive is the only way to go. Hard disk space is cheap, and it's a lot easier to just toss another 100-GB or 200-GB drive in there than it is to try to pinch a few more bytes out of a single drive by compressing files and moving things out to removable disks.

Most computer motherboards have two IDE ports, each of which can handle two drives. One of those drives (the one at the end of the cable) is the *master drive*. The second drive, which connects to a plug in the center of the cable, is a *slave drive*, as illustrated in Figure 52-4. On a prebuilt computer, the hard drive is typically the master and the CD/DVD drive is the slave. If you have a second IDE port on the motherboard, you can add two more IDE drives to the system.

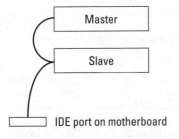

Figure 52-4: An IDE port with two drives connected

Some newer motherboards also have a couple of SATA (Serial ATA) ports. You can connect a single SATA hard drive to each of those, bringing the number up to a total of six drives.

But before you do anything, you need to get to your system BIOS and make sure that all the ports are enabled and set to autodetect new drives. I can't tell you exactly how to do that or what to look for because it varies. But typically you tap the F2 or Del key a few times right after starting the computer to bring up the BIOS setup screen. Then, you look around for IDE options and make sure that both IDE ports are enabled and set to autodetect new drives.

In Windows Device Manager (discussed in Chapter 53), you want to make sure that all the items under the IDE ATA/ATAPI controllers category are enabled as well. If any of those items is marked with a red X, right-click it and choose Enable.

There's more. The IDE ports will have a maximum speed capability ranging from 33 MBps to 133 MBps. That information you can only get from the motherboard specs, or the details specs that came with your PC, or from the manufacturer's Web site. As I write this, SATA drives are available in only one speed, 150 MBps.

Caution   Remember, you never want to open the system case or install any internal hardware until you've shut down the computer and remove the power plug.

Finally, you need to open up the PC and see what's available. For example, if only one of your IDE ports is in use, then you can add either one or two more drives to that port. If you're going to add one more drive, you need to configure the jumpers on the back of the drive to the Master setting, and connect the drive to the end cable. If there's already a drive at the end of a cable, you can set the jumpers on the back of the drive to the Slave setting, and connect the drive to the middle cable. (These facts hold true whether you're adding a second hard drive, or a CD/DVD drive).

All the instructions for physically adding the drive to the system will (hopefully) come with the drive. So, you'll want to refer to those. Sometimes, if you buy a drive real cheap, they'll just drop ship it to you. You get the drive in a box with no paperwork, instructions, cables, or anything else. Just the drive. The manufacturer assumes that you know what you're doing, or you can find the installation instructions for the drive on their Web site.

Anyway, Windows is completely out of the picture until the drive is physically installed in the computer and is connected to a power cable within the computer and connected to an IDE port or SATA port on the motherboard.

Checking the new drive

After you've physically added the new drive and started the computer, you can use Device Manager to make sure that Windows recognizes the drive. To do so:

1. Right-click your **My Computer** icon, and choose **Properties**.

2. In the System Properties dialog box that opens, click the **Hardware** tab.

3. Click the **Device Manager** button.

4. Expand the **Disk drives** category. You should see the model number of the second hard drive you just added as in Figure 52-5. There, the WDC drive is a SATA drive I just installed as an example to use in this chapter.

5. Close Device Manager and the System Properties dialog box.

Even though Windows recognized the drive, you can't use it yet. Getting the drive physically installed in the computer is only half the battle. You still have to partition and format the drive, as discussed in the next sections.

Figure 52-5: The second drive under Disk Drives is new.

Basic and dynamic disks

Before we get into making the new drive functional, there are some buzzwords and options to consider. First of all, in Windows XP Professional Edition, any hard disk can be configured as either a *basic disk* or a *dynamic disk*. (In Home Edition, a basic disk is your only choice).

A basic disk is what you probably already have in your computer. You can divide the disk into *primary partitions* and *extended partitions*. An extended partition can be divided into multiple *logical drives*. These are by far the easiest to set up and use, and generally are the preferred disk type on PCs.

A dynamic disk can be divided into volumes, and can be spanned across several drives. For example, you could span a dynamic disk to a second disk, and have the two drives appear as a single folder in Windows. You can also create striped sets, where multiple drives are combined into a single drive. Data is written and read across the disks in equal-sized chunks, which can improve performance on disk-intensive operations, such as those on a database or Web server that handles large amounts of traffic.

Note   Since this is a book about Windows XP, not Windows Server, I'll take the liberty of assuming that you don't want to go to the extra trouble of using multiple dynamic disks. If you're interested in learning more about that, go to `http://support.microsoft.com` and search for `basic dynamic disk`.

Primary and extended partitions

You can divide a basic disk into multiple *partitions*. Each partition looks like a separate drive from in Windows. For example, let's say you're adding a 200-GB hard disk to your system. You could split it into two partitions of any size. In My Computer, each partition would have its own icon and own drive letter, as though there were two separate hard disk rather than one.

You can divide the disk into a maximum of four primary partitions, or three primary partitions and one extended partition. Or, you could have one primary partition and one extended partition. The difference is that a primary partition can be used as a *system partition*, meaning you can install an operating system on it and boot the computer from it. Your current drive C:, from which your computer boots, is a primary partition.

An extended partition can't be a boot disk and can't contain an operating system. However, you can divide an extended partition into multiple logical drives, where each logical drive has its own drive letter and icon in My Computer, and looks like an entirely separate drive.

When you're adding a second hard drive to a system, probably the smartest thing to do is just treat the whole disk as one primary partition and one drive. This is so because when you start creating partitions, you automatically set limits on how much stuff each partition can hold. And it's hard to predict, in advance, how big a partition might need to be.

On the other hard, if you just create one large partition, you can then create folders for different types of files. There is no limit on how much stuff a folder can hold. You can just keep adding files to folders however you see fit, until you've filled the entire disk.

As I go through the steps for partitioning a drive here, I'm going to be adding a second 200-GB hard drive to my own system. It will be a basic disk with one partition, so it will be a new drive F:, with a capacity of 200 GB. I'll use this drive to store large files like all my video files and music files. I'll create one folder for music, and another for videos. Because they're just folders on a single partition, neither folder will have a capacity limit on it.

Partitioning and formatting the disk

Caution   Repartitioning and/or reformatting a disk that already contains files will result in the *permanent* loss of all files on that disk. You should not attempt to repartition or reformat an existing disk unless you fully understand the consequences, and are fully prepared to recover any lost files.

Next, you need to use the Disk Management tool in Administrative Tools to partition and format the drive. To get to the disk management tool:

1. Click the **Start** button and choose **Control Panel**.

2. If Control Panel opens in Category View, click on **Switch to Classic View** under Control Panel in the Explorer bar.

3. Open the **Administrative Tools** icon.

4. Open the **Computer Management** icon.

Tip   You can also start the Computer Management tool by clicking Start and choosing Run, or by pressing ⊞+R, typing `compmgmt.msc`, and then clicking OK.

5. Expand the **Storage** category, if necessary, and then click the **Disk Management** option.

The first time you click that option a wizard may pop up. But before I get to that, let's take a look at what the Disk Management tool shows. (This is all taking place in Windows XP {Professional). In Figure 52-6 the top half of the main pane shows the two partitions of the first drive I installed, named C: and DISK1_VOL2 (D:). In the lower half of that main pane, the row labeled Disk 0 represents that same disk drive. Each rectangle shows the relative size of the two partitions, C: and D:, on that disk.

The new drive, which I just installed, appears next to Disk 1 in that lower pane. The "No" sign, and the diagonal lines through the large rectangle, indicate that the drive is recognized, but has not yet been initialized, partitioned, or formatted.

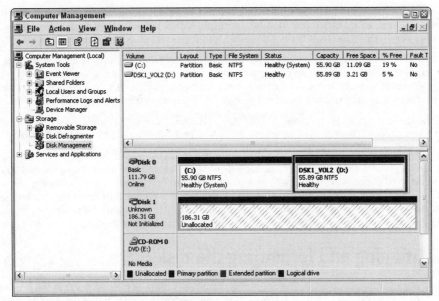

Figure 52-6: The Disk Management tool

Getting that new drive working requires going through that wizard that opened when you first opened the Disk Management tool. If it's too late for that, or if the Wizard never opened, close Computer Management, reopen it, and click Disk Management again. The wizard provides all the instructions you really need. When you initialize the new disk, you'll want to make it a Basic disk. You can also "convert" the disk (which seems odd at this point in the wizard). But by the time you're done, the "No" sign will be gone and the disk will be initialized.

Note   Don't be alarmed if the capacity of the drive shrinks as you go along. Initializing, partitioning, and formatting, by themselves, use up some of the available disk space. Also, the term "online" under each drive name means "known to Windows" in this context and has nothing to do with the Internet.

Now comes the final stage when you actually partition and format the disk. Once again, in my example here I'm just making it one large partition, because my main goal here is to get more storage space for large music and video files. In this case, there's just no real advantage to dividing the large drive into multiple smaller drives. To get started with partitioning and formatting:

1. Right-click within the unallocated space of the new drive, as shown in Figure 52-7, and choose **New Partition**.

2. On the first page of the New Partition Wizard that opens, click **Next>**.

3. The next page asks if you want to create a Primary or Extended partition. If this is the first partition, choose **Primary,** and then click Next. (If you choose Extended, the wizard will end and you'll need to create logical drives before you can proceed with formatting the disk).

4. The next wizard page asks what size you want to make the partition, and suggests the full capacity of the disk. In my case, where this is a second drive, I would just click **Next>** to use the suggested size, equal to the capacity of the disk. You can choose a smaller size if you intend to divide the disk into multiple partitions.

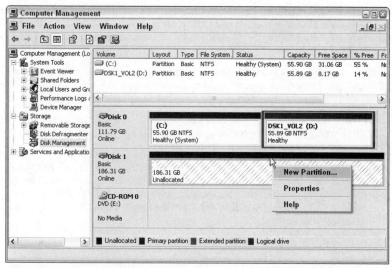

Figure 52-7: About to partition a new disk drive

5. The next wizard page asks you to assign a drive letter to the drive. It suggest the next available drive letter, which is a good choice. Click **Next>**.

6. The next wizard page, shown in Figure 52-8, asks how you want to format and label the disk. Your options are as follows:

   • **Do not format this partition:** If you choose this option, you'll have to format the partition later. I suggest that you not choose this option.

   • **File system:** Your choices here are NTFS or FAT32. In Windows XP, **NTFS** is the only way to go.

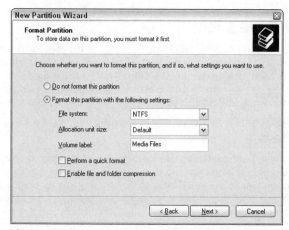

Figure 52-8: Formatting page of the New Partition Wizard

- **Allocation unit size:** This defines the cluster size. Larger clusters mean faster performance but more wasted space. The **Default** option automatically chooses the best allocation unit size given the type and capacity of the disk, so that would be your best choice.

- **Volume label:** This is the name that appears with the drive's icon in My Computer. You can enter any name you want up to 12 characters in length (including spaces). You can also change that name at any time in the future.

- **Perform a quick format:** If you choose this option, formatting will go quickly, but the drive won't be checked for errors. Better to leave this option unselected.

- **Enable file and folder compression:** Only available if you chose NTFS as the file system, this option automatically compresses all files and folders and the drive. This conserves disk space, but you pay for it in time, because it takes longer to open and save files when they're always compressed. You can still compress individual files and folders if you leave this option unselected. So, I suggest you leave this unselected.

7. Click **Next>** after making your selections.

8. The last wizard page summarizes your selections. Click **Finish**.

Now you get to wait for the disk to be formatted. This could take a long, long time. You can continue to use your computer while that's going on. Or, you can just let the computer run and go out to lunch or something. It's up to you. But you'll have to be patient.

If you set up the drive as one large partition, you're done when the Formatting . . . indicator reaches 100%. You can close the Computer Management tool and Control Panel, and go to the section titled "Viewing the new drive's icon."

If you are partitioning the disk into smaller units, you can repeat Steps 1 to 8 for each partition. Just make sure that you right-click an unpartitioned portion of the disk in Step 1. If you create an extended partition, the wizard will end as soon as you do. You'll then need to right-click the extended partition, choose New Logical Drive, and follow the instructions presented by the wizard.

Viewing the new drive's icon

When you've finished formatting the disk (or partitions and logical drives), the drive will be shown along with others in My Computer. To verify that, click the Start button and choose My Computer. In Figure 52-9, the hard disk drive named Media Files (F:) is the hard drive I just added while going through the steps. Point to that icon to see how much actual disk space you have left after all the formatting and partitioning.

If you did divide the disk into multiple partitions or logical drives, you'll see a separate icon for each partition and logical drive.

Keep in mind that Windows won't automatically use the new drive for anything. For example, data won't "spill over" to the second hard drive when the first drive is full. If you want to move any files or folders to the new drive, you'll have to do so using any technique described in Chapter 14. If you've previously set programs, such as Media Player, to save files to drive C: or whatever, and now want it to save to the new drive, you'll need to reconfigure each program.

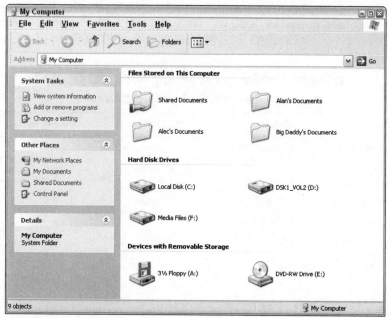

Figure 52-9: My Computer folder after adding new hard drive F:

Tip   If you have any problems at all with the drive, be sure to read the next chapter on Device Manager and downloading drivers.

Other hard drive operations

In this section, I'll cover some general issues concerning hard disks. All of these operations pose some risk of data loss, and should only be attempted by people who understand the risks and are confident they have backups of all important data.

Converting a FAT disk to NTFS

Windows offers three different file systems for formatting a hard drive. The earliest file system, FAT (File Allocation Table) was used in DOS, and the earliest versions of Windows. FAT32 was introduced with Windows 95. NTFS (New Technology File System) was introduced in Windows NT 4.0, largely to support user access control required in domain networking.

When you divide a hard drive into multiple volumes, you can format each independently of the other. (A volume is any partition or logical drive that has its own drive letter and icon in My Computer). NTFS is the preferred file system for Windows XP. There's no reason to use FAT32 or FAT unless you have multiple operating systems installed and can choose one or the other at startup. For example, if you can boot to either Windows 98 or XP, the Windows 98 operating system will not be able to access files on a local NTFS volume.

Note   On a network, a Windows 98 computer can access files on an NTFS volume from a remote computer in the network.

Each file system imposes minimum and maximum volume sizes, and a maximum file size. Keep in mind that these file systems apply only the hard drives, not to floppies or laser media like CD or DVD. Table 52-1 summarizes the differences among the file systems.

Table 52-1: Differences among NTFS, FAT32, and FAT File Systems for Hard Drives

	NTFS	FAT32	FAT
Locally accessible to	Windows 2000, XP, 2003	Windows 95 and later	DOS and all Windows versions
Minimum volume size	10 MB	512 MB	1 MB
Maximum volume size	> 2 TB*	32 GB	4 GB
Maximum file size	Entire volume	4 GB	2 GB
Supports domain networks	Yes	No	No

* Terabyte, a trillion bytes or 1,024 GB.

Caution   Changing the file system on a drive poses some risk of data loss, and should only be attempted by people who understand the risks and are prepared to recover from any loss of data.

You can convert a FAT or FAT32 file system to NTFS, but it's not possible to go in the other direction. That is, you can always upgrade to NTFS, but you cannot downgrade. Be sure to close all open documents and program windows prior to starting the conversion. To convert a FAT or FAT32 volume to NTFS, use the following syntax with the `convert` command:

```
convert drive: /fs:ntfs
```

where *drive* is the letter of the hard drive you want to convert. Advanced users can enter `convert /?` at the command prompt, or search Windows Help and Support, for more advanced options such as `/cvtarea`, which places all NTFS metadata in a contiguous place-holder file. To enter the command:

1. Close all open documents and program windows.

2. Click the **Start** button, and choose **All Programs** ➪ **Accessories** ➪ **Command Prompt**.

3. Type the command using the syntax shown. For example, to convert hard disk drive D: from FAT or FAT32 to NTFS, type `convert d: /fs:ntfs`.

4. Press **Enter**, and follow the instructions on the screen.

If you're converting your system drive (C:) you'll need to restart the computer to start the conversion. Don't use the computer during the conversion process.

Changing a volume label

A *volume label* is the name of a volume as it appears in your My Computer folder. A volume with no volume label shows as *Local Disk*, like drive C: back in Figure 52-10. In that same figure, *DSK1_VOL2* is the volume label for drive D:, *Media Files* is the volume label for drive F:.

Even though you're limited to a 12-character volume label when creating a new partition in the Disk Management tool, the volume label of an NTFS partition can actually be up to 32 characters in length, can contain spaces and punctuation, and can use any mixture of upper-case and lowercase letters. In FAT and FAT32 partitions, the label is limited to 11 characters, and cannot contain any of the following characters:

```
* ? / \ | . , ; : + = [ ] < > "
```

FAT volumes always store and display labels in uppercase letters, even if you type in lower-case letters.

To change the volume label of a hard drive:

1. Open **My Computer**, and right-click the icon of the hard drive you want to relabel.

2. On the General tab of the Properties dialog box that opens, type a new label into the first text box.

3. Click **OK**.

Tip   Optionally, you can just right-click the hard drive's icon, choose Rename, type the new name, and press Enter.

The top half of Figure 52-10 shows the top of the Properties sheet for my hard drive D:, where I've changed the original volume label DSK1_VOL2 (still visible in the title bar) to Documents. The lower half of that same figure shows how the drive icon looks in my My Computer folder after making the change.

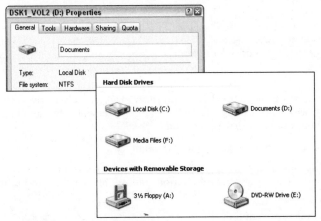

Figure 52-10: Changed drive D: volume label from DSK1_VOL2 to Documents

Changing a drive letter

Drive letters A, B, and C are reserved for floppy disk drives and your hard drive, and cannot be changed. Beyond those first three letters, you can assign drive letters as you see fit. Just be aware that when you do, Windows will *not* update your settings and programs to the change. All settings you've made concerning locations of files in all programs will be fouled up, and will need to be corrected on a case-by-case basis.

No two drives can have the same drive letter. If you need to swap two drive letters (for example change drive E: to drive F: and change drive F: to drive E:), you'll need to temporarily leave one of the drives without a letter. The Disk Management tool, which you need to make this change, will allow you to do that though. Here's how it works:

Caution   Changing drive letters is an operation that's best left to experienced users who understand the consequences and can solve, on their own, the problems that are likely to follow.

1. Start the **Computer Management** tool, as described earlier in this chapter.

2. Click on **Disk Management** under the Storage category.

3. Right-click the drive letter or graphical representation of the drive whose letter you want to change, and choose **Change Drive Letter and Paths**. For example, in Figure 52-11 I'm about to change the drive letter of my DVD drive, E:

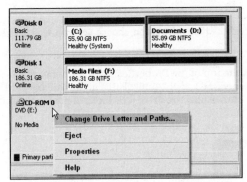

Figure 52-11: About to remove drive letter from drive E: (a DVD drive)

4. If you need to temporarily remove the drive letter to swap with another drive letter, click **Remove**. Otherwise, click **Change**. Heed the warning—newbies shouldn't attempt this operation—choose the new drive letter, and click **OK**.

5. Repeat Steps 2 and 3 for each drive you want to reletter.

6. If you removed a drive letter to swap letters, right-click that drive and choose **Change Drive Letter and Paths** again. Click the **Add** button, choose the new drive letter, and then click **OK**.

7. Close the Computer Management tool.

When you open your My Computer folder, you'll see the new drive letter assignments. For example in Figure 52-12 I've relettered the Media Files drive from F: to E:, and relettered the DVD drive from F: to E:

Formatting a disk

Caution   Formatting a disk that already contains files will result in the *permanent* loss of all files on that disk. You should not attempt to format *any* existing disk unless you fully understand the consequences and are fully prepared to recover any lost files.

If you opted not to format a new disk during the portioning phase, you can easily format the disk at any time just by right-clicking the drive's icon in My Computer and choosing Format . . . But heed the caution at the start of this section.

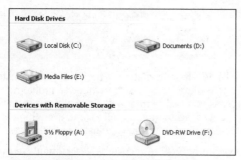

Figure 52-12: Swapped drive letters on drives E: and F:

You can format a floppy disk or any other magnetic medium the same way. If you have packet-writing software, such as DirectCD or DLA installed, you can format CD-RWs and DVD-RWs, and treat them like magnetic disks. That is, you can drag and drop files on a formatted CD-RW or DVD-RW.

But be aware that Windows has no such packet-writing of its own. If you can format CDs and DVDs, it's because of third-party packet writing software that's installed on your computer. Windows XP has nothing to do with that capability.

There is no need to format a CD or DVD if you intend to use it as an audio CD to play in stereos or as a DVD to watch on television.

Changing a basic disk to a dynamic disk (and vice versa)

You can use the Disk Management tool in Computer Management to convert a basic disk to a dynamic disk and vice versa. There are rules and consequences, of course, as summarized here:

✦ Do not convert a disk that contains both Windows XP and Windows 2000, or a disk that contains multiple installations of either operating system.

✦ When you convert a basic disk to a dynamic disk, each existing partition and logical drive is converted to a simple volume on the dynamic disk.

✦ Before you convert a dynamic disk to a basic disk, you must delete all existing volumes on the dynamic disk. You will permanently lose all data on those volumes in the process.

✦ You must have at least 1 MB of free space on any master boot record (MBR) disk that you want to convert. Windows 2000 and XP allocate that space automatically; other operating systems do not.

Note   For additional information on converting between basic and dynamic disk types, search http://support.microsoft.com for covert basic dynamic xp.

To perform either type of conversion, open the Disk Management tool described earlier in this chapter. Then:

✦ To convert a basic disk to a dynamic disk, right-click the gray area to the left of the graphical representation of the disk in the lower page and choose **Convert to Dynamic Disk**.

✦ To convert a dynamic disk to a basic disk, right-click each volume and choose **Delete Volume**. After you've deleted all the volumes, right-click the gray area to the left of the graphical disk representation and choose **Convert to basic disk**.

Urban Myth: Reformat Your Hard Drive and Reinstall Windows

If some tech support person on the phone tells you to reformat your hard disk and reinstall Windows, what he/she *really* means is they don't know how to solve whatever problem you called them about. Understand that in the process you will permanently lose all your installed programs, all your saved documents, e-mail messages, account information, and everything else that's "in your computer." You computer will not even start until you've reinstalled Windows.

Even after you've reinstalled Windows, there will be no way to recover any documents, e-mail messages, or anything else that was in your computer before you performed the clean install. You'll be at exactly the same place you were the first time you started your computer after purchasing it. Any programs other than Windows that were available before you reinstalled will be lost until you reinstall them from their original CDs.

Reformatting your hard disk and reinstalling Windows is only a last resort when the actual solution to a problem is not known. If you're in a situation where you have no choice but to reformat and reinstall Windows, then you need to do a clean install as discussed in Appendix B.

Wrap Up

This chapter has been about installing new hardware. As you've seen in this chapter and the previous chapter, the exact steps for installing hardware vary greatly. At the "easy" extreme you have simple hot-pluggable devices you plug into a USB or 1394 port while the computer is on, and wait for the Notification area to tell you when the device is ready. At the other extreme, adding more RAM requires knowing the details of your motherboard, and installing a hard disk requires substantial knowledge. To summarize the main points in this chapter:

✦ External hardware devices attach to the computer through a cable and a port on the outside of the computer.

✦ Internal devices attach to ports or slots inside the computer on the motherboard.

✦ Never open your computer case or attempt to change anything inside the computer while the computer's power is on.

✦ When installing a new hardware device, always follow the device manufacturer's instructions to a tee.

✦ When installing a device that isn't hot-pluggable, shut down the computer, connect the device to the computer, turn the device on, and then turn the computer on last.

✦ Installing more RAM requires substantial knowledge of the capabilities of your computer's motherboard and any RAM chips that are already installed.

✦ Reformatting a disk that already contains files results in the permanent loss of all files on that disk.

✦ ✦ ✦

Managing Drivers and Devices

Most hardware devices that connect to your computer rely on a small program called a *device driver* (or *driver* for short) to communicate with Windows XP and your system. The driver is required because hardware manufacturers generally don't design hardware to work with a specific operating system. Rather, they design the hardware to perform a specific function, and then write different device drivers to make the device work with different operating systems.

Problems with device drivers can wreak all kinds of havoc, ranging from the device simply not working, or not working properly, to more serious errors that make the whole system crash. Often, the sudden random reboot or blue screen of death can be traced to an outdated device driver.

Choosing Device Driver Options

Before you start tinkering with device drivers, there are some general options you can set that will apply to all device drivers. To get to those options, do whichever of the following is most convenient:

◆ Right-click your **My Computer** icon, and choose **Properties**. Then, click the **Hardware** tab.

◆ Or, click the **Start** button, and choose **Control Panel**. If Control Panel opens in Category View, click on **Performance and Maintenance**. Open the **System** icon.

On the Hardware tab in System Properties, shown in Figure 53-1, provide the general options that apply to all device drivers

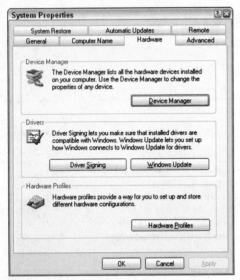

Figure 53-1: Hardware tab in the System Properties dialog box

Driver signing options

Driver signing is a means of identifying the party who is responsible for creating the device driver. In Windows XP, signed drivers are basically the drivers that have passed Windows Logo testing. Which, in turn, means that the device driver should work perfectly with Windows XP.

But, not all companies bother to have their device drivers tested and signed. Or, you may gain access to a new driver that works perfectly fine but hasn't gone through the testing the signing rigmarole. So, an unsigned driver isn't necessarily a bad thing. Clicking the Driver Signing button provides options for choosing how you want to handle unsigned device drivers, as follows:

✦ **Ignore - Install the software anyway and don't ask for my approval:** Unless you writing and testing your own device drivers, there's probably no good reason to select this option.

✦ **Warn - Prompt me each time to choose an action:** This is your best bet, because you'll be able to make a decision on a case-by-case basis. For example, if you're downloading the most recent version of a driver from the hardware manufacturer's Web site, then it's safe to assume that the driver will work, and you don't need to be concerned about signing.

✦ **Block - Never installed unsigned driver software:** This choice is more extreme than necessary, unless you share the computer with other people, and you don't want anyone else downloading and installing drivers.

✦ **Administrator option, Make this action the system default:** If you're an administrator, select this checkbox to apply the setting you chose earlier to all user accounts on the current computer.

Windows update options

Microsoft keeps copies of all it's tested and signed device drivers on the Windows Update Web site (`www.WindowsUpdate.com`). Clicking the Windows Update button on the Hardware tab provides three choices concerning if, and how, you Windows Update:

✦ **If my device needs a driver, go to Windows Update without asking me:** If you choose this option, Windows XP will attempt to download the signed driver for any new device you add that doesn't already have a signed driver.

✦ **Ask me to search Windows Update every time I connect a new device:** This choice is probably your best bet, because you'll know what's going on and will be able to make decisions on a case-by-case basis.

✦ **Never search Windows Update for drivers:** I can't think of any good reason to choose this option. Windows Update is a great resource for keeping up with device drivers.

Discovering Your Hardware and Drivers

In Windows XP, Device Manager is the place to go whenever you want to manage hardware devices and drivers. There are two ways to get to Device Manager:

✦ Get to the System Properties dialog box shown in Figure 53-1, and click the **Device Manager** button.

✦ Or, click the **Start** button, choose **Run**, type `devmgmt.msc`, and press **Enter** or click **OK**.

In Device Manager, hardware devices in your computer are organized into categories, as in the example shown in Figure 53-2. Click the + sign next to any category name to see devices within that category. Click the - sign next to any name to hide device names.

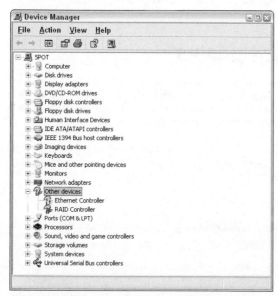

Figure 53-2: Device Manager in its standard view

Before I continue, I should point out that you do have some choices on how you view items in Device Manager. As in most programs, your options are on the View menu in Device Manager's menu bar. Unless you're some kind of hardware guru, I doubt you'll want to use any of the alternative views. But here's what the view options offer:

✦ **Devices by type:** This is the standard view shown in Figure 53-2.

✦ **Devices by connection:** Devices are organized by how they're connected to the computer, such as PCI Bus and USB Host Controller.

✦ **Resources by type:** List allocated resources by the type of device using each resource, such as Direct memory access (DMA), Input/Output (IO), Interrupt Request (IRQ), and Memory.

✦ **Resources by connection:** Same categorization as in the preceding item, but organized by connection type rather than device.

✦ **Show hidden devices:** If selected, this shows "ghosted" devices such as USB devices you connect and disconnect on the fly, but that aren't connected at the moment. This can also be useful for getting rid of device drivers for devices you've permanently removed from your system and have no intension or reconnecting.

Device Manager icons

Some categories and devices may show a question mark. The question mark, alone, generally means that there's an unknown device in the category. A specific device will show an exclamation point or X, indicating that the device has an "unknown" status, as described here:

✦ **X:** The device is disabled. To enable the device, right-click its icon and choose Enable.

✦ **!:** Indicates a problem with the device, such as a missing or faulty device driver.

Problem devices showing the exclamation point can usually be fixed by downloading a valid driver for the device.

Quick-and-Easy Driver Updates

Microsoft maintains many digitally signed device drivers at the Windows Update site. Using Windows Update is the quick-and-easy way to obtain current drivers for all your hardware devices. You don't even need to be in Device Manager for this approach. You can close Device Manager, and System Properties, and just follow these steps:

Note   Windows Update is a Web site, and Web sites are subject to change at any time. If the step-by-step instructions below don't work when you try this, follow the instructions on the Windows Update Web page that opens.

1. Close all open programs, and save any open documents.

2. Click the **Start** button, and choose **All Programs ⇨ Windows Update**. Or, open Internet Explorer and go to www.WindowsUpdate.com.

3. Click on **Custom Install**.

4. Click on the **Select optional hardware updates** option, and follow the on-screen instructions download any and all available drive updates.

5. Restart your computer (Click **Start** and choose **Turn Off Computer ⇨ Restart**).

Hopefully, then next time you go into Device Manager, all your drivers will be up to date and working perfectly. If not, there are extra steps you can take, as discussed next.

Getting Information about a Device

There are thousands of optional hardware devices for Windows XP, and finding drivers to them all isn't always easy. Some hardware manufacturers seem to make little or no effort to get their drivers "out there" where people can easily find them. But before you go looking, you need to gather up information about the device and current driver (if any). To get started with that, right-click the device's name in Device Manager. The Properties dialog box for the device will open, as in the example shown in Figure 53-3.

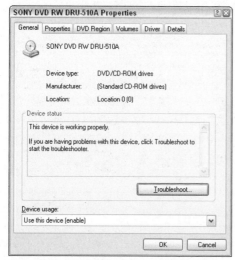

Figure 53-3: The General tab of a device's Properties dialog box

Tip   The Troubleshoot button in the Properties sheet provides a quick-and-easy way to troubleshoot a problem device.

The tabs and information that appear in the Properties dialog box for a device will vary from one device to the next. The example in Figure 53-3 is for a DVD burner, and it has more tabs than most. But right off the bat there's some important and useful information to know. Namely the make (Sony) and model (DRU-510A) of the device.

Tip   Once you know the make and model of a device, you can search the manufacturer's Web site for more information, and drivers, for the device. For example, to get info on the DVD drive in Figure 53-3 I'd go to www.Sony.com and search for DRU-510A. These days, you don't need to know anything about anything. You just need to know how to look and what to look for.

The Properties, DVD Region, and Volumes tabs for the DVD drive are unique to DVDs. You won't find those same tabs on other types of devices. But since I'm in the neighborhood, and you may have a DVD burner in your own system, and it may offer similar options, I'll describe these tabs. As you can see on the left side of Figure 53-4, the Properties tab offers options for player volume and digital audio playback. The DVD Region tab lets me choose a geographic region for DVDs. (That's a feature that's truly unique to DVD).

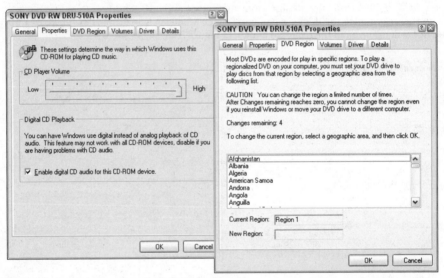

Figure 53-4: Unique properties of a DVD drive

Caution   The warnings on the sample DVD Region tab in Figure 53-4 apply to many DVD drives. Never change the DVD Region unless absolutely necessary. You don't want to use up your four (or whatever) changes, and be stuck with a drive that won't play DVDs from your own geographic region!

The Volumes tab in the sample appears in the Properties sheet for many disk drives. Though it's usually only relevant to a hard drive. When you click the Volumes tab, the property settings will likely be missing. Click the Populate button to fill in the blanks. Taking a slight detour from my DVD drive, Figure 53-5 shows volume information from my main hard drive (which Windows refers to a Drive 0).

Useful information I can gather from the Volumes tab includes the fact that my C: and D: drive are just two separate partitions (volumes) on one physical disk. The title bar tells me the model number of the drive, ST3120026AS, which is a nice specific string I could search for on the Web to get more information.

But getting back to device drivers, the Driver tab in the Properties dialog box is where you want to look for driver information.

Figure 53-5: Volumes tab for a hard disk drive

Getting the full scoop on a device driver

I've gotten sidetracked from drivers, so let's get back to that topic now. Remember that a driver is software that acts as an intermediary between the hardware device and the operating system. Some hardware devices have a single driver, some have multiple drivers. But regardless, the driver (or drivers) are the key factor in getting the device to work properly.

Using the wrong driver can result in anything from the device not working to the whole computer doing weird things like locking up, showing the blue screen of death, or causing the machine to reboot at random. In the case of my sound driver, I suspected that it was responsible for random reboots, an error message about recovering from "a serious error" after the reboot, and possibly another occasional error I got about a problem in lsass.exe sometimes when I shut down my computer.

Step 1 is to find out what driver you're currently using. To do that, click the Driver tab. Figure 53-6 shows an example where I'm viewing the driver tab for the sound chip on my computer's motherboard.

The Driver tab provides lots of useful information about the driver.

- ✦ **Driver Provider:** The company that created the driver. This gives you a company name to look up on the Web, where you're likely to find current drivers.

- ✦ **Driver Date:** This lets you know how old the driver is. The one in the example is two years old. I've been to Windows Update many times since then, so this one has never been updated by Windows Update.

- ✦ **Driver Version:** This is important because when looking around for drivers you'll want one that's newer (has a higher version number).

- ✦ **Digital Signer:** The driver in this example has no signature, and therefore I know it never passed Microsoft's Windows logo testing.

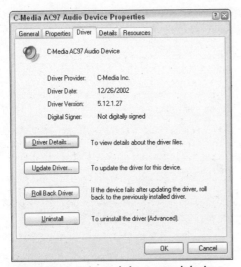

Figure 53-6: Driver tab for a sound device

Clicking the Driver Details button lists all the files that interact with the device. On a sound card, like the one in this example, that could be quite a few files because there are lots of different types of sound files. The Driver File Details dialog box show the exact location and filename of each driver file. When you click on path, the lower portion of the dialog box displays details of that specific driver. Paths that have a logo to the left are signed drivers. Those without a logo are unsigned. As you can see in Figure 53-7, my suspicious sound chip uses a mixture of signed and unsigned driver files.

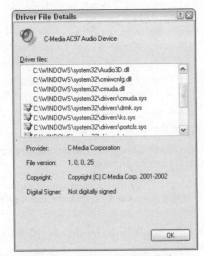

Figure 53-7: Driver File Details for a hardware device

Getting a List of All Drivers

At the command prompt, you can use the `DriverQuery` command to list, print, or save information about drivers. To get to the command prompt, click Start and choose All Programs ➪ Accessories ➪ Command Prompt. To see detailed information about the command, type `driverquery /?`, and press Enter. (You always need to press Enter after typing a line at the command prompt).

If you just type `driverquery` and press Enter, you'll see a list of driver names, types, and dates on the screen. Entering the command `driverquery /si` provides information about signed drivers. The command `driverquery /v` provides verbose (detailed) information about drivers.

To create a file of driver information that you can open and print using any word processing program, use the `/fo` switch with the option TABLE (which prints data in tabular form), CSV (which prints columns separated by commas, or LIST (which prints a list with only one column). Follow the `/fo` option and name with a greater-than character (>) and a filename. For example, the command below (when typed as one long line):

```
driverquery /fo table > C:\Documents and Settings\All
Users\Documents\drivers.txt
```

This creates a file named `drivers.txt` in your Shared Documents folder. You can then open your Shared Documents folder, right-click that file's icon, choose Open With, and then choose any word processor or editor (e.g., Microsoft Word, WordPad, Notepad) to open the file. Choose File > Print from that program's menu bar to print the list.

A second approach to getting signed drivers

For reasons I'm not altogether clear on, using Windows Update as described earlier in this chapter doesn't always get the most recent signed drivers for every device on your system. Sometimes, if you search for drivers for a specific device, you will find them that way. Here's how that works.

On the Driver tab for the device (Figure 53-6 in my example), click the Update Driver button. The Hardware Update Wizard opens. The first page asks if you want to search Windows Update for a driver. Choose Yes, This Time Only (or the second option — just don't choose No), and click Next. On the third page, just click Next.

If the wizard finds the updated drivers on Windows Update, it will download and install them. Just click Finish, and you're done. You can click the Driver Details button again to see your new driver files, all of which will have the Digitally Signed logo. Click the Finish button, close everything, and restart the computer to ensure that all the latest drivers are loaded.

If the wizard can't find updated drivers, you'll see a Cannot Continue the Hardware Update Wizard page. Not much to do there other than to click Finish. But all is not lost. You may be able to find newer drivers at the hardware manufacturer's Web site or through a service like Drivers Headquarters (www.drivershq.com). The latter isn't free. But if you're not comfortable with, or don't time for, searching the entire Web for device drivers, it can be a quick and easy way to keep your drivers up to date.

Hunting for device drivers

When all else fails, you can search the Web for updated drivers. Getting back to my suspicious sound card driver with random reboot capabilities, recall that I was using C-Media Inc.'s driver version 5.12.1.27, an unsigned driver released in December 2002 (almost two years ago as I write this book).

Taking a wild guess that C-Media's Web site is www.c-media.com takes me to a page covered with some sort of oriental writing I can't read. After locating and clicking the English link, I realize that I'm at the Web site for a magazine called C.Media. Bad guess on the URL. So, I search Google for C-Media audio driver to see what other resources I can find. After looking around through a few Web pages I find out C-Media's real URL is www.cmedia.com.tw. (So much for guessing about URLs).

Anyway, I was able to find a newer device driver at C-Media's site to download. When you find and download a driver and are given the Run/Open/Save options, always choose Save. You may want to create a folder for all your driver downloads. And even a subfolder for each specific driver download, because the filename of the download won't tell you much. For example, I'd put the downloaded driver for the C-Media device in a folder named something like C-Media May 04 Driver because the date on that driver was 5/24/04. If the file you download is a .zip file, you'll need to extract all the files before you install them.

> **Note**   For information on extracting files from a .zip file, see "Using Compressed Folders (Zip Files)" in Chapter 13.

In my example I did get a .zip file. After extracting all the files from it I see the filenames from the .zip file correspond to the filenames I saw in Driver Details, so I'll go ahead and install these drivers and hope for the best. To install new drivers, you use the Update Driver button on the Driver tab in the device's Properties dialog box.

Updating device drivers from files

To install drivers you've downloaded, get back to the Driver tab of the devices Properties dialog box (Figure 53-6, for my example). Click the Update Driver button, and the Hardware Update Wizard will appear. Figure 53-8 shows the first page of the wizard. There's no harm in searching Windows Update for drivers, even if you've already downloaded some drivers. So, choose any option you like and click Next.

The second wizard page, shown in Figure 53-9, asks where I want to search. In this case, I downloaded and extracted all the driver files to a specific folder on my hard drive, so I'd choose the second option *Install from a list or specific location (Advanced)*, and then click Next. (To install the drivers that came with a device, you'd insert the CD or floppy that came with that device and choose the first option, *Install the software automatically (Recommended)*.

On the third wizard page choose where you want to search. In my example, I know where I put the downloaded driver files, so I choose the second option and used the Browse button to browse to that folder. You would choose options relevant to wherever you put your updated drivers. Click Next, and wait.

Figure 53-8: First page of the Hardware Update Wizard

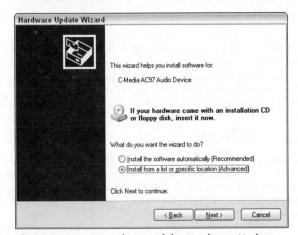

Figure 53-09: Second page of the Hardware Update Wizard

When the Wizard finishes, click the Finish button. Close up everything, and restart the computer (Click Start choose Turn Off Computer ⇨ Restart). Now you can go back the Device Manager and take a look at the Driver tab and Driver Details.

In the case of my C-Media driver, things definitely looked better after the driver update. As you can see at the left side of Figure 53-10, the driver date is now 4/21/04 and the version is 5.12.1.44, much newer than the original driver. On the right side of that same figure, you can see that all the drivers are signed, which is also good news. Hopefully my random reboots and other problems are over now.

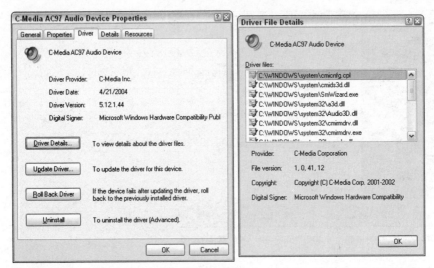

Figure 53-10: Looking good after driver updates

So, the moral of the story is that bad device drivers can cause all sorts of weird problems, even "big ones" like random reboots, the computer locking up, blue screen of death errors, and more. Realizing that every device has a driver and that there are ways to keep those drivers up to date can go a long way toward keeping your computer running in tip-top shape without the mysterious problems that bad drivers often cause.

Rolling back to previous drivers

There's always an outside chance that when you download and install new drivers for a devices, things will get worse rather than better. That's especially true if you can't find signed drivers and have to wing it on trying to find drivers that work. Should you ever find yourself in this situation, there's no need to panic. Just click the Roll Back Driver button on the Driver tab of the device's Properties dialog box.

Uninstalling drivers

There will be times when you need to uninstall the drivers for a device. For example, when Windows Update can't provide updated drivers and you have to dig around the Web, you'll sometimes see a warning about uninstalling the older drivers before installing the new ones. That's rare, but it happens. A more likely scenario is that you've permanently removed a device from your system. But when you choose View ➪ Show Hidden Devices, the drivers for that device show up as "ghosted" items.

Caution   Not all hidden drivers represent permanently removed hardware. Never delete any driver unless you know exactly what driver it is, why you're removing it, and what the consequences will be. Guessing here could be disastrous.

As an example, I had temporarily installed an ATI All-In-Wonder video card in the computer I'm using right now to capture some video from an analog digital camera. Normally that graphics card lives in a different computer. But I had to capture some enormous DV-AVI files, and the other computer didn't have the drive capacity to handle the files.

Anyway, when I was done with the video captures I uninstalled the ATI card from the current computer and put it back in its original computer. When I choose Show Hidden Devices on the current computer, I can see there are still a few drivers from the ATI card lurking around, as in Figure 53-11. (The drivers whose names start with the letters ATI in this example).

Figure 53-11: I don't need the ATI drivers listed here.

To uninstall a driver, right-click its name and choose Uninstall. Then choose OK. You'll be asked if you want to restart the computer. Choose No if you have to uninstall several drivers. Note that the drivers won't be removed from the list right away. So, don't keep right-clicking the same driver and choosing Uninstall over and over again, thinking that it will eventually disappear. It won't disappear until you reboot. When you've finished uninstalling drivers, *then* you can close everything up and restart the computer.

Enabling and Disabling Devices

You can enable and disable devices in Device Manager. The "disable" option sounds a little harsh. When you disable a device though, you're not harming it in any way. All you're really doing is telling Windows to pretend that the device isn't there, and to not waste any time or resources on making the device work. There are plenty of instances where doing so might make sense.

For example, back in Figure 53-2, under Other Devices, I have a disabled Ethernet controller and RAID controller. I disabled those on purpose because the Ethernet controller is a wireless one, which I don't use on that computer. I use a Gigabit Ethernet card that's connected by cable to a hub. So, there's no need for Windows to worry about the unused wireless controller. Likewise, I don't use the RAID capabilities of my motherboard because RAID is really a Windows Server thing, not a Windows XP thing.

If you have an Ethernet card in your computer, but you don't use it because you're not connected to a LAN, and you use a dial-up modem to connect to the Internet, you'll probably see the message *A network cable is unplugged* often, and maybe a little monitor icon with a red X through it in your Notification area. If you disabled your unused Ethernet controller, you wouldn't get the error message or red-X icon any more.

Going back to my sound chip driver example, I could have taken an altogether different approach. I could have just disabled that device and installed a sound card. In fact, I plan to do that because I happen to have a Sound Blaster Live card left over from an older machine, and I suspect that it will provide better quality sound and more capabilities than the on-board chip.

Note   In case you're wondering, I couldn't physically remove the C-Media audio device from my computer, because it's a chip on the motherboard that can't be physically removed. Not easily, anyway. But disabling the device basically does the same thing as physically removing it.

The only downside to disabling a device is forgetting that you did so. If you ever decide to use the device in the future and forget your disabled it, you'll drive yourself nuts trying to get it to work. (Been there, done that, not fun.). The device simply will not work until you reenable it. Anyway, disabling and enabling devices is a simple thing:

1. Get to **Device Manager** as described earlier in this chapter. Then,

   • Right-click the device you want to disable, and choose **Disable**.

   • Or, right-click the device you want to enable, and choose **Enable**.

Figure 53-12 shows a couple of examples.

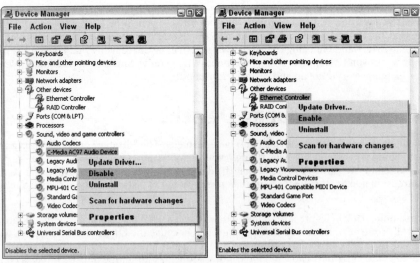

Figure 53-12: Disable/enable a device.

Permanently Removing Hardware Devices

Hot-pluggable devices such as USB, IEEE 1394, and Bluetooth devices don't really need to be installed or uninstalled. Those, you can plug in and remove on an as-needed basis without giving a second thought to Device Manager or anything else. More permanent internal devices, and devices that connect to other ports on your computer, really should be uninstalled through Device Manager before you physically remove the hardware. Especially if you have no intention of ever reinstalling the device again.

To uninstall a device through Device Manager, just right-click the device's name and choose Uninstall. Follow any instructions you see on the screen, but don't restart the computer. Instead, after you've finished in Device Manager, close everything, click the Start button, and choose Turn Off Computer ➪ Turn Off. When the computer shuts down, unplug the power cable at the back of the computer, and then remove the device.

If you ever forget to do that step before removing a device, and Windows shows error messages about the device not being found, you can still go through Device Manager and uninstall the (now nonexistent) device. Or, if you can't find the device in Device Manager, you may be able to find its drivers using Show Hidden Devices, and then uninstall those drivers.

Reinstalling Plug-and-Play Devices

The term "plug-and-play device" (PnP device) applies to just about every device on the market these days. It's not limited to hot-pluggable USB devices. Printers, modems, disk drives, and so forth are also plug-and-play devices. If you remove such a device for repair, or to use with a different computer, that's no problem. But when you reinstall it, you might find that it doesn't work anymore.

There's a solution to that problem. In Device Manager, right-click the heading under which the device is categorized. Or, if you're not sure, right-click the computer name at the top of the list, as in Figure 53-13, and choose Scan for Hardware Changes, and Windows will look around to see what's changed, and do whatever it takes to get the device working again.

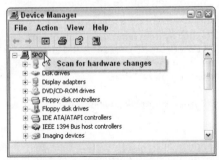

Figure 53-13: Disable/enable a device.

Another Way to Get Hardware Information

Most people who buy a PC really have no idea that the system is made up of so many different components. For example, when someone buys a PC from Dell, they think that it's all just one product made by Dell. Likewise for HP, IBM, Gateway, eMachines, Acer, Systemax,Wntergreen, and all the PCs out there. However, that's not the way it works.

People in the computer biz sometimes use the slang term *box* to refer to a PC. For example, a PC with Windows XP installed might be referred to as a *Windows box*. Computer geeks (and now people in the financial markets too) refer to companies like those mentioned above a *box makers*. That's because all those companies buy components from different manufacturers' and assemble them into boxes — computer systems.

For example, they my buy CPUs from Intel or AMD, hard drives from Seagate, Maxtor, or Western digital. They'll buy other components from other companies. But the point is, they don't make any of those components — they buy them in large quantities. Then, they assemble them into computers. Basically they do what computer ubergeeks do when we build our own computers. The box makers just do it on a larger scale, in assembly-line fashion. Then, they slap their own brand name and logo on the visible external parts and market the daylights out of them.

Note   Another term for box makers is OEM, for original equipment manufacturer. Though, that's a bit of a misnomer since they don't manufacturer the components, they buy them.

There's certainly nothing wrong with building and selling computers that way. That's the way everyone does it. Most people, especially when buying their first PC, don't even know what software is installed, or why, for months or even years after making their purchase.

The problem comes up when you're trying to fix some problem and people start asking you questions like "What sound card are you using?" or "What graphics card is installed?" If you didn't build the PC yourself, or didn't pay attention to all those mysterious specs before you bought the machine, chances are you won't have a clue as to how to answer such questions.

Device Manager will certainly fill you in on all the details. But there's a better, simpler way when you're just looking for the facts and don't want to mess with things. It's called System Information. To open it, you just click the Start button and choose All Programs ➪ Accessories ➪ System Tools ➪ System Information.

When System Information first opens, you'll see your System Summary. That covers some basic facts about the operating system installed (Windows XP), version, and so forth. Information about specific hardware components is in the Components category, which you can expand by clicking the + sign next to that category name.

Tip   Choose File ➪ Print from the menu bar in the System Information window to print the details of your computer system.

Admittedly, there's probably way more information in System Information than anyone really needs to know about their computer. But, when you click on a particular component type, such as CD-ROM, Sound Device, or Display, you can at least find out the make and model of the device that's in your system. And usually that's all you need to know to answer questions like "What sound card are you using?"

Figure 53-14 shows an example where I've clicked on Display under the Components category. The details in the right column show all kinds of information about the two graphics cards I have installed in my system including the Name, Adapter Type, Installed Drivers, Driver Version, current Resolution setting, and so forth.

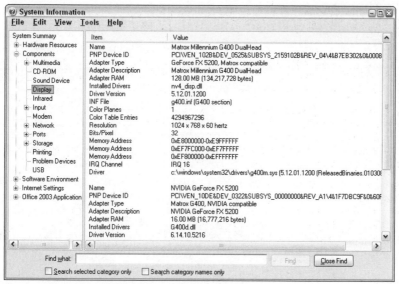

Figure 53-14: Sample System Information window

Now I'm not saying that anyone needs to know all these details about their computer. You can be a total whiz at using your computer without knowing all those details. But the point is, when you *need* information, you're not stuck with not knowing. You can open the System Information window and click around to find out just about anything you might need to know.

Wrap Up

This chapter has been an excursion into the mysterious world of device drivers. A device driver acts as the "communicator" between a hardware device and a specific operating system, such as Windows XP SP2. A bad device driver will not only cause a device to function poorly, it can cause more drastic problems like random reboots, hanging (freezing up) the entire system, the blue screen of death errors, and ". . . serious error" messages. To whit:

✦ Most devices use a device driver to communicate with your operating system.

✦ For general information about your installed devices and drivers, use the System Information window.

✦ To update all device drivers, visit the Windows Update Web site and use the Custom Install option to download any updated device drivers.

✦ If problems persist after updating drivers, you may need to focus on the specific device and its drivers, through Device Manager.

✦ Device Manager, as its name implies, is the place to go when you want to change, update, or remove a particular hardware device or driver.

✦　　✦　　✦

Troubleshooting Hardware Errors

First Aid for Troubleshooting Hardware

Whenever you have a hardware problem that's causing a device to misbehave or just not work at all, finding an updated driver will usually be your best bet. See Chapter 53, "Managing Drivers and Devices" for details on how that works. But even before you both with that, you might want to try running one of the built-in troubleshooters to see what's up. (The troubleshooter may just tell you to get a newer driver, but it's worth a try.)

There are a couple of ways to get to hardware troubleshooters. For starters, follow these steps:

1. Click the Start button and choose Help and Support.

2. Click on "Fixing a problem".

3. Under "Fixing a problem" in the left pane (Figure 54-1) click on "Hardware and system device problems", or click whichever option best describes the type of problem you're trying to resolve.

Note   If your computer manufacturer has removed "Fixing a Problem" from the Help and Support Center screen, you might try whatever solution their Help page offers. Or, search for one of the troubleshooter names shown in Figure 54-1 by name in Help and Support.

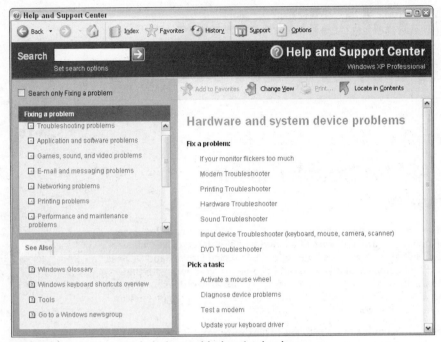

Figure 54-1: Windows XP help for troubleshooting hardware

After you've reached an appropriate troubleshooter or page in Help and Support, just click links or answer questions as they appear to work your way through possible solutions.

A second alternative is to run the troubleshooter right from the hardware device's Properties dialog box. Here's how:

1. Right-click your **My Computer** icon and choose **Properties**.

2. Click the **Hardware** tab.

3. Click the **Device Manager** button.

4. Right-click the name of the device that's causing problems and choose **Properites**.

5. If the General tab of the device Properties dialog box offers a **Troubleshoot** button, like the example in Figure 54-2, click that button and answer questions posed by the troubleshooter.

Figure 54-2: Example of a hardware device
Properties sheet

Dealing with Error Messages

Error messages come in all forms, from simple warning to the *stop errors* and "the blue screen of death" which causes the computer to stop dead in its tracks. The more serious errors are often accompanied by one of more of the following pieces of information:

✦ **An error number**: An Error number will often be a hexadecimal number in the format 0x00000*xxx* where the italicized numbers could be any numbers in the message.

✦ **Symbolic error name**: Symbolic error names are usually shown in all uppercase with underlines between words, like PAGE_FAULT_IN_NONPAGED_AREA.

✦ **Driver Details**: If a device driver caused the problem, you might see a file name with a .sys extension in the error message.

✦ **Troubleshooting info**: Some errors will have their own built-in troubleshooting advice, or a Help button. Use that information to learn more about what when wrong.

Whenever you get an error message that you can't solve just by reading the advice presented on the screen, go to http://support.microsoft.com and search for the error number, or the symbolic error name, the driver name, or some combination of words in the text or troubleshooting of the error message.

If searching Microsoft's support site doesn't do the trick you, consider searching the entire Internet using Google. You never know, someone out there in the world may have had the same problem, and posted the solution somewhere on the Internet.

Performing a Clean Boot

The biggest problem with hardware errors is that even a tiny error can have seemingly catastrophic results, like suddenly shutting down the system and making it difficult to get the system started again. Clean booting can also help with software problems that prevent the computer from starting normally or cause frequent errors.

Not for the technologically-challenged, this procedure is best left to more experienced users who can use it to diagnose the source of a problem that's preventing the computer from starting normally. The procedure for performing a clean boot is as follows:

Note A clean boot is not the same as a clean install. During a clean boot, you may temporarily lose some normal functionality. But once you perform a normal startup you should regain access to all your programs and documents, and full functionality.

1. Close all open programs and save and work in progress.

2. At the Window desktop, click the **Start** button and choose **Run**, or press ⊞+R.

3. Type msconfig and press Enter or click OK. The System Configuration Utility opens.

4. On the General tab, choose **Selective Startup** and clear all the checkboxes below it except for Load System Services and User Original BOOT.INI.

5. Click on the **Services** tab.

6. Select **Hide All Microsoft Services** then click the **Disable All** button.

7. Click **OK** then click restart to reboot.

If you're trying to locate the source of a problem, and the computer started properly in the current startup configuration, try choosing another option under Selective Startup. For example, choose Process System.INI, click OK, and restart the system. If the problem recurs, you know the source of the problem is in the system.ini file

To return to normal startup after diagnosis, open the System Configuration Utility. On the General tab, choose Normal Startup and click OK.

Using the Recovery Console

For more severe problems that require repairing an existing Windows XP installation, formatting drives, managing Windows system files and folders, repairing the Master Boot Record, or enabling or disabling services, you can boot from the Microsoft Windows XP CD to a recovery console. This method should only be used by hardware experts who can perform such tasks from a command prompt.

To boot from the Windows CD, first make sure that the CD is enabled as a boot device in the BIOS with a higher priority than any hard drives. Insert the Windows CD into the drive and restart the computer. Restart the computer and follow these steps:

1. During the POST, watch for the **Press any key to boot from CD** prompt, and tap a key.

2. After all files load from the CD, press **R** at the text menu to enter the recovery console.

3. When prompted for an operating system, type the number (**1** on a single OS system) and press Enter.

4. When prompted, enter the administrator password, or just press Enter if there is no password.

You'll be at a command prompt in the folder you specified in step 3. To see a list of available commands, enter **HELP** at the command prompt. For help with a command type the command name followed by /?.

The command set in the Recovery Console isn't the same ye olde DOS commands. So don't assume everything will work as it did in DOS. For example, in Recovery Console you can only get to the root folder (C:\) and system folders (C:\WINDOWS). For more information on troubleshooting via the Recovery Console, go to http://support.microsoft.com and search for XP Recovery Console. Or, take a look at each of the following pages:

http://support.microsoft.com/default.aspx?scid=kb;en-us;314058

http://support.microsoft.com/default.aspx?scid=kb;en-us;307654

http://support.microsoft.com/default.aspx?scid=kb;en-us;308402

http://support.microsoft.com/default.aspx?scid=kb;en-us;291980

http://support.microsoft.com/default.aspx?scid=kb;en-us;324465

http://support.microsoft.com/default.aspx?scid=kb;en-us;307545

Anyway, getting back to your computer and Recovery Console, when you've finished using the console, type **EXIT** and press Enter to restart the computer normally.

✦　　✦　　✦

Performance and Maintenance Issues

We all need to protect our investments and keep them running in tip-top shape. That's what Part X is all about. Chapter 55 starts off with an important discussion of the widely misunderstood System Restore feature. Chapter 56 covers performance and maintenance issues for keeping your computer running at its full potential.

Chapter 57 talks about power consumption, both from the perspective of conserving battery power on notebook computers and keeping your own electricity bills down. Chapter 58 gets into backing up and editing the Windows registry, where all the information about your entire system is stored.

Using System Restore the Right Way

System Restore is a handy feature of Windows XP that makes backup copies of your *system files*. Those system files include things like the Windows registry, programs that contain settings and performance-tuning options, and parts of Windows XP itself. System Restore does not back up, or affect your documents in any way. So, you don't have to worry about losing any work by using System Restore.

But System Restore is not a simple "undo," nor an excuse to try things our at random just to see what happens. To use System Restore correctly, you need to know how, and when, to set restore points. And also how to return your system to an earlier restore point. These are the topics of this chapter.

How System Restore Works

System Restore is basically a way to play it safe when making substantial changes to your PC. A substantial change would be installing a new program or installing a new piece of hardware. System Restore works by setting aside a small portion of your hard disk and using it to store backup copies of key *system files*. System files are files created, and used, by Windows and your computer. Examples include the registry, key executable files (.exe and .dll files), and system data files (.data, .inf, .ini files).

Caution The documents you download and create yourself aren't system files. Ditto for e-mail messages, names and addresses, account information and passwords. System Restore never backs up such items, and therefore can't be used to recover such items if you accidentally delete them.

When System Restore is active, Windows creates some restore points automatically. These are referred to as *system checkpoints*. Examples of when Windows automatically creates system checkpoints include:

✦ When you install certain System Restore–aware programs

✦ When you download and install an automatic update

+ When you install an unsigned device driver

+ When you restore backup data using the NT Backup program

+ When more than 24 hours have transpired since the last restore point was set

System Restore is activated automatically as soon as you install Windows XP. However, you can activate it, deactivate it, or change its behavior at any time as discussed in the next section.

Configuring System Restore

System Restore works only on system files on hard drives. Thus, you may only need to activate System Restore on your C: drive. Though if you have multiple hard drives, and the other drives have system files on them, you can configure System Restore to work with those as well. To configure System Restore, follow these steps:

Right-click a **My Computer** icon and choose **Properties**, or open the **System** icon in Control Panel.

Click the **System Restore** tab to see the options shown in Figure 55-1.

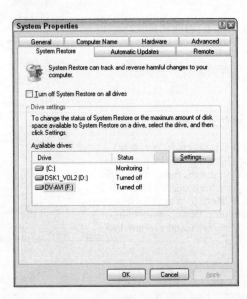

Figure 55-1: System Restore tab in System Properties

1. To activate or deactivate System Restore on all drives, choose **Turn off System Restore on all drives**. To enable System Restore for any drive, clear that checkbox.

2. To change System Restore settings for a specific drive, select (click on) the drive you want to configure, and then click the **Settings** button.

3. If you're configuring a hard drive other than C:, you can turn off System Restore on that one drive only. However, you cannot turn off System Restore on drive C: only.

4. Use the slider shown in Figure 55-2 to indicate what percentage of hard disk space you're willing to set aside for System Restore.

5. Click **OK** in each open dialog box.

Figure 55-2: System Restore Settings for a C: drive

When System Restore is active, it will automatically create system checkpoints for you. Optionally, you can create your own restore point just prior to making changes that affect the entire system.

Creating a Restore Point

Whenever you're about to make a change that affects system files, your best bet is to create a restore point before you do anything else. Changes that affect system files include:

✦ Installing new hardware

✦ Installing new software

✦ Replacing a device driver

You need to set the restore point *before* you make the change. That's because the purpose of the restore point is to make a backup copy of all your currently working system files before the newly installed item changes that. Setting a restore point is quick and easy. Here are the steps:

1. Click the **Start** button, and choose **All Programs** ⇨ **Accessories** ⇨ **System Tools** ⇨ **System Restore**. The System Restore window shown in Figure 55-3 opens.

Tip You can also get to System Restore via Help and Support in most Windows XP installations.

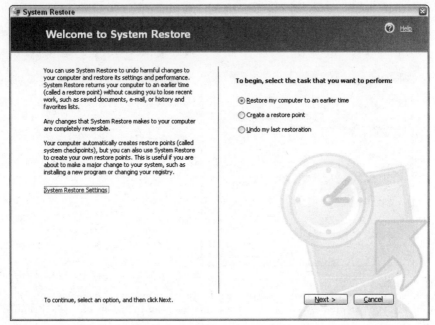

Figure 55-3: The System Restore window

2. Choose **Create a restore point**, and then click **Next**.

3. On the next page, type a plain-English description of why or when you're setting the restore point. For example *Pre-programX installation* or *Pre-Web cam installation* or whatever will help you identify the restore point later.

4. Click the **Create** button.

5. Click the **Close** button.

That's all there is to it. Now you can install your new hardware, software, or device driver as you normally would. If the new item works fine, you don't need to do anything about System Restore. As new restore points are created, older ones are removed automatically. So, there's no need to go in and manually remove the restore point.

However, of the system behaves badly after you've installed the new item, you'll probably want to return to the previous system files, as discussed next.

Restoring to an Earlier Time

Let's say that you've set your restore point and then installed your new hardware, software, or driver. Upon restarting the computer, you encounter all sorts of new problems that prevent the computer from running as well as it used to. If you want to get rid of the new item and get things back to normal, the first step *isn't* to return to the restore point you set. Rather, you want to uninstall the new item first. That is:

✦ If you installed a program, remove it via Add or Remove Programs.

✦ If you installed hardware, uninstall it via Device Manager. Then, turn off the computer and remove the new hardware device.

✦ If you installed a driver, roll back to the previous driver, if possible. If you can't, don't worry about it because System Restore will likely take care of the problem anyway.

Removing the item will remove all the files associated with that item. But the removal might not undo all changes that were made to system files during the installation. To get back to your previously working system files, you need to return your computer to an earlier time by following these steps:

1. Close all open documents and programs, saving any work in progress, to get to a clean desktop.

2. Click the **Start** button, and choose **All Programs** ⇨ **Accessories** ⇨ **System Tools** ⇨ **System Restore**. You're back to the System Restore window shown in Figure 55-3.

3. Choose **Restore my computer to an earlier time**, and then click **Next>**. You'll see a calendar as in the example shown in Figure 55-4.

Note

Each calendar date shown in boldface is associated with a restore point from which you can recover system files. As a rule, you only want to restore from the most recent restore point. But if doing so doesn't solve your problem, you may have to try restoring to an earlier restore point.

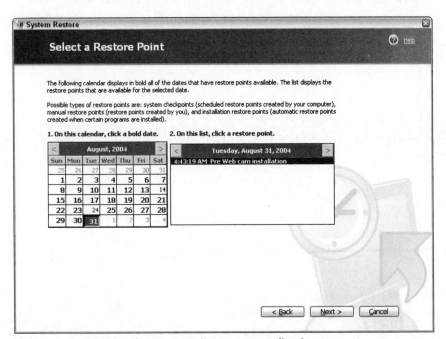

Figure 55-4: Returning the system to its stat at an earlier time

4. Click the date on which you created your restore point. If more than one restore point appears in the list to the right of the calendar, click on restore point you created just prior to installing your new hardware, software, or driver.

5. Click the **Next>** button and follow the rest of the wizard instructions all the way through.

Windows will reboot the system. But before it shuts down, it will restore all the system files from your selected restore point. When you get to the desktop, you'll see a confirmation of the restoration. You can close that window, and then go about using your computer normally.

Wrap Up

System Restore keeps track of your system files so that if things go seriously wrong, you can get things back to normal. Windows regularly makes its own restore points, called system checkpoints. But you can create your own restore points just prior to making a change to your computer system. In summary:

✦ To configure System Restore, right-click your My Computer icon and choose Properties, and then click the System Restore tab in the System Properties dialog box.

✦ To create a restore point, click the Start button, choose All Programs ➪ Accessories ➪ System Tools ➪ System Restore. Then, choose *Create a restore point* and follow the onscreen instructions.

✦ To restore your computer to its state at an earlier time, close all open documents and program files. Next, click the Start button, choose All Programs ➪ Accessories ➪ System Tools ➪ System Restore. Then, choose *Restore my computer to an earlier time* and follow the on-screen instructions.

✦   ✦   ✦

Performance-Tuning Your System

✦   ✦   ✦   ✦

In This Chapter

Getting information about your system

Maximizing CPU and memory resources

Maintaining your hard disk's performance

Defragmenting files for better performance

✦   ✦   ✦   ✦

Compared to most machines, a computer requires virtually no maintenance. That's because there are no moving parts to speak of. Just lots of little electrons whizzing around at the speed of light through microscopically small wires. The real workhorse of your computer is its central processing unit (CPU). It's a tiny chip that's smaller than your thumbnail, and there are several brands and models of them on the market, including Intel's Pentium and Celeron processors, and AMD's Athlon and Sempron processors.

The information on which the CPU does its work is stored in random access memory (RAM), often referred to as *memory*. The memory in your computer is just a few thumbnail-sized chips, and again there are no moving parts.

The hard disk determines how long it takes to open and save files. As you'll learn in this chapter, there are ways to control how Windows uses the CPU and memory. And there are things you can do to keep your hard disk running at tip-top speed.

Getting to Know Your System

A computer system is made up of many different components. The two main components that make up the actual "computer" are the CPU and RAM. The overall speed of your system is largely determined by the speed of your CPU, and the amount of RAM in your system. The speed of a CPU is measured in megahertz (MHz), or "millions of instructions per second," or gigahertz (GHz), billions of instructions per second.

The amount of RAM determines how much data the CPU can work with at any one time without accessing the much slower hard disk. RAM chips do come in various speeds. But the amount of RAM you have, more so than its speed, really determines the overall speed of your system. We generally measure RAM in megabytes (MB), and a megabyte is roughly a million bytes. A gigabyte (GB) is 1,024 megabytes. A byte, in turn, is the amount of space it takes to store a single character such as the letter "A." In short, the faster your CPU and the more RAM you have, the faster your computer can get things done, and the less time you have to wait.

Knowing your CPU and RAM

To see the brand name and speed of your processor, and the amount of RAM you have, right-click your My Computer icon and choose Properties. The General tab of the System Properties dialog box that opens shows that basic computer information as well as information about the version of Windows you're using, as in the example shown in Figure 56-1.

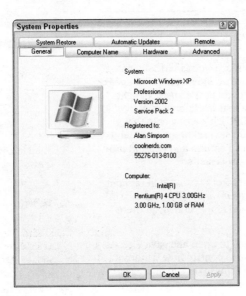

Figure 56-1: The General tab of the System Properties dialog box

Note How long it takes to download files from the Internet is determined strictly by the bandwidth (speed) of your Internet connection. This has nothing to do with the CPU or RAM. The only way to speed up Internet access is to get a faster Internet account. Putting a faster computer on a slow Internet account won't speed up your Internet access one iota.

Getting more detailed information about your PC

Even though your CPU and RAM do all the work, they alone don't make up an entire computer system. You need a lot more components to turn those two tiny gadgets into something a human being can use to get work done. For example, you need a hard disk to store an operating system (Windows), programs, and documents. You need a graphics card and monitor to see what's going on, and software to present information on the screen in a manner that makes sense to human beings. You need a mouse and keyboard to control the action, and so forth.

You can get more detailed information about all the components that make up your computer system from the System Information program. To open System Information, click the Start button and choose All Programs ➪ Accessories ➪ System Tools ➪ System Information. The System Information window, shown in Figure 56-2, opens.

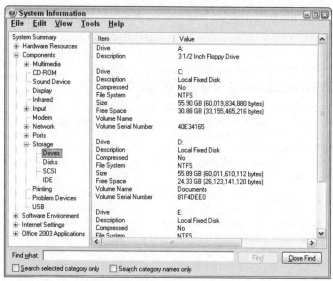

Figure 56-2: The System Information program window

The left column of System Information organizes your system information into expandable and collapsible categories. For example, clicking the + sign next to the Components category expands that category to display subcategories and the names of specific device types. When you click on specific type, such as Drives under the Storage category, the pane on the right shows information about the components installed in your computer system.

You don't actually do any work in the System Information program. Its job is to just present the facts about your particular computer's installed hardware and software. However, you can export a copy of the System Information data to a text file, which in turn you can open, format, or print using any word processing program or text editor. To export a copy of your system information to a file, just choose File ⇨ Export from System Information's menu bar.

You can also print your system information, either in whole or in part. To print all of your system information, first click System Summary at the top of the left column. To print just a category, first click a category name, such as Components. Then, choose File ⇨ Print from System Information's menu bar. In the Print dialog box that opens, choose All if you want to print everything, or choose Selection to print just the category you clicked on in the left column. To close System Information, click its Close (X) button.

Maximizing CPU and Memory Resources

Your operating system (Windows XP) takes care of managing the CPU and memory for you. It does this behind the scenes in such a way that a person could use a computer productively for his or her entire life without ever knowing the CPU and RAM exist. When you use an *application program* (which is basically any program you start from the Start menu), you control the action by choosing menu commands and so on.

In addition to the application programs you choose, RAM needs to maintain copies of certain *processes* that perform various day-to-day chores behind the scenes. Open application programs and processes both take up some space in RAM, and both require some CPU resources to do their jobs.

Priorities, foreground, and background

Your computer's CPU and RAM are very busy places. To keep the computer running at tip-top speed, and to ensure that the computer responds immediately to everything you do at your mouse and keyboard, Windows prioritizes tasks that need to be done. Your application programs always run in the *foreground*, which means that when you click an item with your mouse or do something at the keyboard, fulfilling that request gets top priority in terms of being sent to the CPU for execution.

Most processes, by comparison, run in the *background*. This means that they get a lower priority and have to momentarily step aside when you tell Windows or an application to do something. For example, printing a document is treated as a low-priority background process, and for a good reason. All printers are basically slow, mechanical devices anyway. So, by making printing a low-priority process, you can continue to use your computer and near normal speeds while the printer is slowly churning out its printed pages.

Controlling CPU priorities

By default, programs that you're using are given a higher priority than background processes. It's possible to reverse that by giving processes a higher priority than applications. Offhand, I can't think of any reason why a normal person would want to reverse the order. If you want to make sure that your applications are getting top priority, as they should be, follow these steps:

1. Right-click your My Computer icon, and choose Properties to open the System Properties dialog box.

Tip   The System icon in Control Panel also opens the System Properties dialog box. If Control Panel opens in Category View, click on Performance and Maintenance to get to the System icon.

2. Click the **Advanced** tab in the System Properties dialog box.

3. Under the **Performance** heading, click the **Settings** button. The Performance Options dialog box opens.

4. In the Performance Options dialog box (seen in Figure 56-3), click the **Advanced** tab.

The Processor Scheduling options determine whether your actions, or processes, get top priority when vying for CPU resources to do their jobs. If you choose Background services, your computer may not be as responsive as you'd like. So, you always want to choose Programs under Processor scheduling.

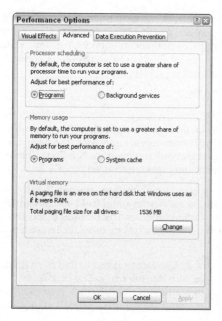

Figure 56-3: The Performance Options dialog box

Note   Choosing Background Services won't make your printer print any faster. There's really nothing you can do to speed printing, other than use the printer's Draft mode (if it has one). But even so, printers are just inherently slow mechanical devices. Not even a supercomputer can make a printer run any faster than the printer's mechanics allow.

Controlling memory priorities

Options under the Memory Usage heading determine whether programs, or the *system cache*, get the lion's share of RAM. The system cache stores copies of recently used information "closer to" the CPU than RAM does, and thus the CPU can get to that information more rapidly than it can get to information in RAM.

The whole idea of a system cache was invented when computer scientists who analyze computer performance discovered that the CPU spends much of its time repeating instructions that is has performed recently. They figured (correctly) if you kept recently executed instructions in the system cache, the CPU would be able to work more quickly. So, that's what the system cache does — it stores recently executed instructions so that when it has to repeat a set of instructions, it can get to them more quickly.

Computers that play a server role definitely repeat the same tasks over and over again. For example, a Web server just sits on the Internet (no human being involved) and fulfills requests for Web pages from the Internet. In that situation, where repetition is the norm, it makes sense to use a large system cache, even at the expense of eating up RAM that could be used by application programs.

On a PC, where you have a human being at the controls, things aren't quite so repetitive. There's no telling what a human user might do next. So, you want to keep the system cache to a reasonable size and leave plenty of RAM for programs and documents. So, the bottom line on the Memory Usage options, for a PC, is the choose Programs. Choose System Cache only on a server computer that requires minimal direct human interaction.

Managing virtual memory

In the olden days of DOS, a computer could only run one program at a time. Programs had to be written to fit in the available 64K (or whatever) of memory. Otherwise, the program wouldn't fit, wouldn't run, and would just end up displaying the message Not Enuf Memory on the screen (Yes, I know it's spelled "enough", but the message showed "enuf").

In the Windows world, you can load up and run as many programs as you want. But, if you tried to start a new program when you already had some running, and RAM was already full, or near full, you'd get a "Not Enuf Memory" error. Computer scientists realized you could avoid that error my using a small portion of the hard disk as extra memory, called *virtual memory*, to handle the overflow.

The CPU can't get information to and from the hard disk as fast as it can to and from RAM. That's because the hard disk is a mechanical device with moving parts. The disk spins around, and the drive head moves about the disk to read and write data. But even though the hard disk isn't quite as speedy as RAM, better to let things slow down a little than to just stop dead and announce "Not Enuf Memory."

All modern computers actually have two types of memory. There's the speedy *physical memory* (RAM) that's actually on the RAM chips installed on your computer's motherboard. And there's the slower virtual memory, stored on hard disk, used as a backup to handle anything that goes beyond the capacity of the physical memory. A system's total memory is the sum of its physical and virtual memory.

Tip   The amount of RAM shown on the General tab of the System Properties dialog box (see Figure 56-1) is the amount of physical RAM in your system.

The area on the hard disk that's used as virtual memory is often called a *paging file*, because information is swapped back and forth between physical and virtual memory in small chunks called pages. When you fill up both your physical memory and virtual memory, the computer doesn't just stop dead in its track and display "Not Enuf Memory." Rather, it displays a message in advance, warning that you're about to run out of virtual memory and suggesting that you make room for more.

Since the virtual memory is just a tiny paging file on the hard disk, you can easily add more just by increasing the size of the paging file. You don't have to buy or install anything. To the contrary, the only way to increase physical memory is to buy and install more RAM. As you may have guessed, the Change button under Virtual Memory in the Performance Options dialog box (shown in Figure 56-3) is the place you go to do that. When you click the Change button, you'll see the options shown in Figure 56-4.

Your main options in the Virtual Memory dialog box are:

✦ **Custom size:** You choose where you want to put your paging file(s), their initial size, and maximum size.

✦ **System managed size:** Tells Windows to create and size the paging file automatically for you.

✦ **No paging file:** Eliminates the paging file from a drive. Not recommended unless you're moving the paging file from one drive to another.

Figure 56-4: The Virtual Memory dialog box

If you have multiple hard drives, you can get the best performance by using the least busy drive for virtual memory. For example, if you have a D: drive on which you store documents, it may be better to use that, rather than the C: drive, because the C: drive is pretty busy with Windows and your installed programs.

If you have multiple *physical drives*, you can get a little performance boost by splitting the paging file across the two drives. A single drive that's partitioned into two or more partitions, to look like multiple drives, doesn't count. You don't want to divide the paging file across multiple partitions on a single drive, because that will have the reverse effect of slowing things down.

If you do opt for a custom size, you can work with any one hard drive at a time. The drives are listed by letter and label at the top of the dialog box. In the example shown, drives C and D are two partitions on a single physical hard drive. Drive E is a separate physical hard drive.

Tip The Computer Management tool discussed under "Partitioning and formatting the disk" in Chapter 52 lists hard drives by number. If you have a single physical hard drive, it will be Disk 0. If you have two physical hard drives, they'll be listed as Drive 0 and Drive 1, and so forth.

You need to set the paging file sizes individually. For example, to move the paging from drive C: to D:, first click on Drive C: at the top of the dialog box, choose No Paging File, and then click the Set button. Then, click Drive D:, choose Custom Size, set your sizes, and click Set.

The Total Paging File Size for All Drives section at the bottom of the dialog box shows the minimum allowable size, a recommended size, and the currently allocated size (the last measurement being the sum if all the Initial Size settings). The recommended size is usually about 1.5 times the amount of physical memory. The idea is to prevent you from loading up *way* more stuff than you have physical RAM to handle, which would definitely make your computer run in slow motion.

If your computer keeps showing messages about running out of virtual memory, you'll definitely want to increase the initial and maximum size of the paging file. A gigabyte (1,024 MB) is a nice round number. But of the computer runs slowly after you increase the amount of virtual memory, the best solution would be to add more physical RAM.

Note   The only way to increase physical memory is by adding more RAM chips to your system. See "Monitoring Performance with Task Manager" in Chapter 49 for the goods on assessing your need for more physical RAM. See "Installing more Memory (RAM)" in Chapter 52 for tips on adding more physical memory.

If you do change the Virtual Memory settings and click OK, you'll be asked if you want to restart your computer. If you have programs or documents open, you can choose No and close everything up first. But since the paging file isn't only created when you first start your computer, you'll eventually need to restart the computer to take advantage of your new settings.

Trading pretty for performance

All the fancy stuff you see on your screen while using Windows comes with a price. It takes CPU resources to show drop-shadows beneath 3-D objects, make objects fade into and out of view, and so forth. On an old system that has minimal CPU capabilities and memory, those little visual extras can bog the system down.

The Visual Effects tab of the Performance Options dialog box lets you choose how much performance you're willing to part with for a "pretty" interface. As you can see in Figure 56-5, the Visual Effects tab gives you for main options:

✦ **Let Windows choose what's best for my computer:** Choosing this option automatically chooses visual effects based on the capabilities of your computer.

✦ **Adjust for best appearance:** If selected, all "pretty" effects are used, even at the cost of slowing you down.

✦ **Adjust for best performance:** Choosing this option minimizes "pretty" effects to preserver overall speed and responsiveness.

✦ **Custom:** If you choose this option, you can then pick and choose any or all of the visual effects listed beneath the Custom option.

How you choose options is entirely up to you. If you have a powerful system, then the visual effects won't amount to a hill of beans. So, there's no need to back off on the visual effects. But if your computer isn't immediately responsive to operations that involve opening and closing menus, dragging, and other things you do on the screen, eliminating some visual effects should help make your computer more responsive.

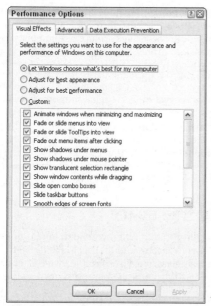

Figure 56-5: The Visual Effects tab of the Performance Options dialog box

Tip   If you leave the Performance tab of Task Manager open and visible on the screen while using your computer, you may be able to see how simply doing things on the screen with your mouse actually eats up some CPU time. See "Monitoring Performance with Task Manager" in Chapter 49 for details.

Maintaining Your Hard Disk

Your hard drive plays a relatively minor role in determining the overall speed of your computer. That's because the hard drive only comes into play what you're opening programs or documents, when you're saving documents, or when you're moving and copying files.

Internal hard drives vary in speed. Parallel ATA drives come in speeds of 33, 66, 100, and 133 Mbps (million bits per second). SATA (Serial ATA) drives, which represent a relatively new technology, are all at 150 Mbps as I write this chapter, but faster drives are expected to be available soon. SCSI (pronounced *skuzzy*) drives are available in speeds up to 360 Mbps. But they're expensive (about quadruple the cost of SATA), and generally used only in servers and computers dedicated to video editing.

Note   If you want to check current prices, or just see examples, go to www.tigerdirect.com and click on Hard drives in the left column. In case you're wondering, ATA stands for Advanced Technology Attachment and SCSI stands for Small Computer System Interface.

The type and speed of internal drive your system can handle, without adding and adapter card, is determined by the IDE ports on your computer's motherboard. Virtually all PC motherboards have two IDE ports, each of which can handle two drives. Your existing hard drive and DVD or CD drive take up two of those four possible drives. The speed of those ports isn't something you can determine from Windows. You have to know the exact make and model of your motherboard and look up the specs for that board to find out.

However, you can always add a *controller* card to your system and then add more drives of any type or speed that matches the controller. For example, you can buy an ULTRA ATA-133 card, a Serial ATA card, or a SCSI 360 controller card, plug it into a PCI slot on your motherboard, and then connect internal hard drives to the card. Assuming that you need more drives and/or faster drives. If you're not up for spending any money or tinkering with the guts of your computer, there are things you can do to ensure that your current drives runs at tiptop speed, as discussed in a moment. First, let's cover some hard drive basics.

Determining disk capacity and free space

Icons for all your disk drives are in your My Computer folder. When you open My Computer, you'll see hard drives listed under the Hard Disk Drives group heading, as in Figure 56-6. Though, any icon could represent a partition on a single drive. For example, drive C: and D: in the figure are each a partition in a single physical hard drive, while E: represents a second physical hard drive.

Figure 56-6: Icons for drives C:, D:, and E: All represent internal hard drives or partitions.

To see the total storage capacity of a drive, the amount of space you're currently using, and how much free space you have on that drive, right-click the drive's icon and choose Properties. The Used Space and Free Space are shown both in bytes and gigabytes (GB). The total capacity of the drive (or partition) is shown just above the pie chart that compares used space to free space. Figure 56-7 shows an example.

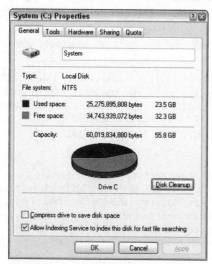

Figure 56-7: The General tab of a hard drive's Properties dialog box

For "exact number" lovers, the GB (gigabytes) number to the right of the bytes number is the number of bytes divided by (roughly) a billion. Though, if you do the math it's 1,073,741,824, which is the true number of bytes (2^{30}) in a gigabyte.

One gigabyte is roughly enough space to store 500,000 (half a million) typed, double-spaces pages of text. Or put another way, 1 GB equals about 1,000 floppy disks. If the amount of free space on your hard drive ever dips much below 1GB, you'll start seeing a notification icon that reads "You are running low on disk space."

Note

For you "exact number" folks, the "You are running low . . ." notification message kicks in when the free space drops below 800 MB, which is 8/10 of a gigabyte).

Recovering wasted hard disk space

At any given time, some of the space on your hard drive is being eaten up by *temporary files*. As the name implies, temporary files are not like the programs you install or documents you save. Programs and documents are "forever," in the sense that Windows never deletes them at random. The only time a program is deleted is when you use Add/Remove Programs in Control Panel to remove the program. Likewise, documents aren't deleted unless you intentionally delete them and also empty the Recycle Bin.

Urban Myth: Compression Is Always Good

Beginners really glom onto the term "compress" when they see it. When they see an option to compress some files, they just instinctively choose it, thinking it's a good thing with no downside. Not true. Compression is a trade-off between dirt-cheap hard disk space and your valuable time.

Every time you open a compressed file, it needs to be decompressed. And every time you save the file, it needs to be recompressed. That takes time, and slows you down. Furthermore, compression adds a layer of complexity to things. And any time you increase complexity, you also increase the likelihood of problems.

So, the bottom line on compression is: You should avoid it except in cases where it's absolutely necessary. For example, if you're low on disk space and have some enormous bitmap images (.bmp files) or uncompressed video (.avi files) that you rarely use, go ahead and compress those big files. (Or better yet, move them off to CDs or DVDs, or just add another hard drive!).

The files in your *Internet cache*, also called your *Temporary Internet Files* folder are a good example of temporary files. Every time you visit a Web page, all the text and pictures that make up that page are stored in your Internet cache. When you use the Back or Forward button to revisit a page you've viewed recently, your browser just pulls a copy of the page out of the Internet cache. That saves a lot of time when compared to how long it would take to redownload a page each time you clicked the Back or Forward button to revisit a recently viewed page.

Caution   Before you click the Disk Cleanup tool, be forewarned that the process could take several minutes, maybe longer. It's never *necessary* to use Disk Cleanup to get rid of temporary files. Because temporary files are, well, temporary and will eventually go away on their own.

The Windows Disk Cleanup tool, which you can start by clicking the Disk Cleanup button visible in Figure 56-7, lets you recover that wasted disk space at any time. You can also use it to compress old files to smaller size so that they take up less room.

Disk Cleanup takes some time to run. So it's not the kind of thing you want to do often. But even though it takes time, Disk Cleanup can reduce the amount of time it takes to do other full-disk operations. For example, if you intend to scan your entire hard disk for viruses, getting rid of temporary files before you start can reduce the amount of time it takes to do the scan. Likewise, if you intend to defragment your hard disk (as discussed in a moment), getting rid of temporary files first can speed up that lengthy operation, and also give you better, cleaner results than you'd get with the temporary files in place.

To clean up a hard disk, open your My Computer folder, right-click the icon of the hard drive you want to clean up, choose Properties, and click the Disk Cleanup button. Then, wait while Disk Cleanup checks the dates of all your files to see which ones you haven't used recently, and calculates how much space you'll recover if you compress those files.

When the calculations are done, you'll see the Disk Cleanup dialog box, similar to the example shown in Figure 56-8. The left column of the Files To Delete list shows categories of temporary files. When you click on a category name, the Description below the names explains the types of files in that category. Don't worry, all the categories represent temporary files that you can definitely live without. There won't ever be any important programs or documents you saved on your own in the list of temporary files.

Figure 56-8: The Disk Cleanup dialog box

The number to the right of each category name indicates how much disk space the files in that category are using, and how much you (might) gain if you delete them. I say "might" because there are some files, even temporary files, that can't be deleted. For example, you can't delete an open file. And no matter what, the Web Client/Publisher Temporary Files category never dips below about 36 KB. (Which, incidentally, is such a tiny amount of space as to be totally insignificant, because it takes a million kilobytes to make 1 gigabyte).

You choose which categories of files you want to delete by selecting (checking) their checkboxes. If you don't want to delete a category of files, clear the check mark for that category. The amount of disk space you'll recover by deleting all the selected categories appears under the list.

Near the bottom of the Files to Delete list, you'll see a *Compress old files* option. Unlike the other categories, that option doesn't represent temporary files that will be deleted. If you select that option, Disk Cleanup will compress (not delete) old files to reduce the amount of space they consume. If you don't select that option, Disk Cleanup won't compress (or delete) those files.

Once you've selected the items you want to delete, just click the OK button. You'll see an *Are you sure?* prompt. Click Yes and wait a while Disk Cleanup does its thing. as Windows does its cleaning. The dialog box will close automatically when the job is complete.

The More Options tab in the Disk Cleanup dialog box, shown in Figure 56-9, provides options for deleting still more files. Its options are self-explanatory. As discussed in Chapter 48, you can delete Windows Components and Installed Programs without using the Disk Cleanup tool.

The System Restore option will delete all but your most recent restore point. But that's not something you really want to do unless you're very desperate for hard disk space.

Figure 56-9: The More Options tab in Disk Cleanup

Scanning the disk for errors

Your hard disk spins at a walloping 7,200 to 10,000 RPM, and all the while the head that reads and writes data to the drive is zipping across its surface not more than a few molecules' distance away from its surface. With so much activity, it's not unusual for an occasional little hiccup to occur. These usually go by unnoticed. But they, too, can accumulate in the form of bad links and bad sectors. If enough of them accumulate, the speed at which you're able to move data to and from the disk can diminish.

If you scan your hard disk for errors two to four times a year (or whenever your hard disk seems to be running slowly), you can clean up the little blemishes and get the disk back to running at peak performance. Scanning can take a long time, and you can't use the computer while scanning. So, it's the kind of job you might want to do as a overnighter, or at least when you'll be away from the computer for an hour or two. Doing the scan is easy.

1. Open your **My Computer** folder, if it isn't already open.

2. Right-click the icon for your hard drive, and choose **Properties**.

3. In the Properties dialog box that opens, click the **Tools** tab.

4. Under **Error-checking**, click **Check Now**.

5. For maximum cleanup, select (check) both checkboxes.

6. Click the **Start** button.

7. If you see a message indicating that the disk check couldn't be performed because the program needs exclusive access to the disk, that's normal. Choose Yes to proceed.

8. Click **OK** in the dialog box.

9. Close all open programs, and save any unsaved work.

10. Click the **Start** button, and choose **Turn Off Computer ⇨ Restart**.

Your computer will be busy for a while, is going to take some time (maybe an hour or more). The screen will initially be blue when the computer restarts and will display the progress of the scan. When the scan is complete, Windows will boot up normally, and everything will be normal.

Defragmenting your hard drive

Whenever you delete a file, Windows makes the space it was using available to new files you save. If a file you're about to save is too big for one of the empty spaces available, Windows might divide up the file into several different old deleted files' old space. While this is not problem, it can get to a point where you have a lot of little chunks of files spread all over the disk.

When that happens, the drive head has to move around a lot to read and write files. You might even be able to hear the drive chattering when things get really *fragmented* (spread out). This puts some extra stress on the mechanics of the drive and also slows things down a bit.

To really get things back together and running smoothly, you can *defragment* (or *defrag* for short) the drive. When you do, Windows takes all the files that are split up into little chunks and brings them all together into single files again. It also moves most files to the beginning of the drive, where they're easiest to get to. The result is a drive that's no longer fragmented, doesn't chatter, and runs faster.

Defragmenting is one of those things you don't really have to do too often. Two or three times a year is probably sufficient. The process could take several hours, during which you won't be able to use the computer. So, it's another one of those "overnighter" jobs. Or at least one you'd want to start just prior to leaving for lunch.

Tip　For the ultimate in hard-drive performance tuning, do the maintenance tasks in the order described in this section. First, clean up the hard disk to get rid of any unnecessary temporary files. Next, do your error checking to fix any little blemishes. Then defragment what's left so that everything is perfectly arranged for quick and easy access by your computer.

To defragment a hard drive, starting at the desktop:

1. Open your **My Computer** folder.

2. Right-click the icon for your hard drive (C:), and choose **Properties**.

3. In the Properties dialog box that opens, click the **Tools** tab.

4. Click the **Defragment Now** button. The Disk Defragmenter program opens.

5. Click the **Analyze** button. The program will analyze your hard disk to see how much it's fragmented.

6. When the analysis is done, you'll see a message indicating whether or not the disk needs to be defragmented.

Tip   When it says you don't *need to* defragment, that doesn't mean that you can't or shouldn't. It just means the drive's not badly fragmented. But you can still defragment it.

7. To defrag the drive, click the **Defragment** button. Otherwise, you can click **Close** to skip it.

Defrag will defragment all the fragmented files and move some frequently used files to the beginning of the disk, where they can be accessed in the least time with the least effort. Some files won't be moved. That's normal. If Windows decides to leave them where they are, it's for good reason. You may hear a lot of disk chatter as defrag is doing its thing. That's because the drive head is moving things around to get everything into a better position.

While defrag is working, you'll see a graphical presentation of what's going on. When the job is done, you'll see fragmentation as it looked both before, and after, defragmentation. Figure 56-10 shows an example, though on your screen the information will be color-coded and make more sense.

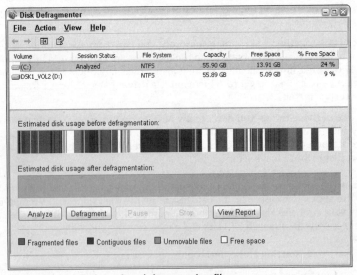

Figure 56-10: Defrag after defragmenting files

Not all files can be defragmented, so don't expect everything to be perfect when you've finished. But things will be better than they were. When defrag is finished, you can just close any open dialog boxes and the Disk Defragmenter program window.

Wrap Up

The components of your computer system that most determine how quickly things move along are its CPU and memory. (Internet access speed is determined solely by the bandwidth of your Internet connection, and isn't related to any of the topics discussed in this chapter). As an alternative to buying a faster computer, there are things you can do to make your current computer run faster, and keep it running at top speed. The main points in this chapter are:

✦ The System Information program provides detailed information about all the components that make up your computer system.

✦ To ensure that your computer is responsive to every your every mouse click and keyboard tap, Windows automatically prioritizes programs are foreground (high-priority) and background (low-priority) tasks.

✦ When your system runs our of physical memory (RAM), Windows automatically uses a portion of the hard disk as virtual memory to handle the overflow.

✦ If your computer is usually sluggish and unresponsive, consider turning off some of XP's visual effects.

✦ The speed of your hard disk determines how long it takes to open and save files.

✦ To keep your hard disk running at top speed, consider deleting temporary files, scanning for, and fixing, bad sectors, and defragmenting the drive a couple of times a year.

✦   ✦   ✦

Managing Your Power Options

Needless to say, it takes electrical power to run a computer. This is really obvious on a notebook or laptop computer that's running on batteries. If you're not careful to conserve battery power, you can easily run out of juice halfway to your destination on long flight or train trip.

This chapter is about managing power options. Not just for notebook computers, but for your electricity bill as well. Even for saving the planet. Environmental scientists claim that all the tens of millions of computer monitors that are lit up around the globe at any given moment are actually contributing to global warming!

Shutting Down Your Computer

Whenever you click the Start button and choose Turn Off Computer, you're given three or four options as to how you want to shut down:

+ **Hibernate** (or **Sleep**): Shuts down the computer in such as way as to ensure that when you restart the computer later, you're taken right back to where you left off rather than a clear Windows desktop.

+ **Stand By:** Same as above, but requires a little electricity to maintain the previous open program windows and documents. On many computers, simply moving the mouse or tapping a key brings the computer back up.

+ **Turn Off:** Turns off the computer so that it consumes zero electricity. The next time you start the computer, you're taken to a clear desktop.

+ **Restart:** Shuts down the computer and restarts at a clear desktop. This is often required after installing new hardware or to recover from serious errors that lock up the system.

+ **Cancel:** Cancels the shutdown procedure altogether and leaves you exactly where you were.

I suppose that most of those options are self-explanatory, though there's one pair of options that leaves most people scratching their heads. The question is if both Stand By and Hibernate bring the computer back to where you left it then next time you start the computer, what's the difference? Let's take a moment to talk about that.

Stand by versus hibernate

Stand By and Hibernate (called Sleep on some computers) are very similar shutdown options in that both allow you to restart your computer with whatever programs and documents were open still open and visible on the screen. The difference isn't in what they do, but rather how they do it.

First of all, realize that everything that's open on your desktop is actually stored in random access memory (RAM). Unlike a disk, which can retain information for years with zero electrical power, RAM is *volatile*. When RAM loses electricity, everything in RAM instantly disappears forever.

In order for your computer to come back to where you left off after you shut down, Windows needs some means of maintaining the contents of RAM while the computer is off. When you choose Stand By, Windows maintains the contents of RAM by using a small amount of electricity from a battery that's attached to your system motherboard.

In that regard, Stand By isn't totally reliable. If that battery goes dead, then the contents of RAM are lost. From a big-picture perspective, that's no big deal because you can still start the computer in the future. But you'll be taken to a clear desktop, rather than where you left off, the next time you start the computer. This is the same as if you'd chosen the Turn Off option rather than Stand By.

Hibernation works a little differently. Rather than maintain the contents of RAM electronically, Windows "takes a snapshot" of RAM's contents and stores it in a hidden file on the hard drive. Since the hard drive is a magnetic medium, it can hold information for years with absolutely zero electricity.

Whenever you start your computer, Windows automatically looks to see if that hidden hibernation file is on the hard disk. If it "sees" that file, it boots up normally, and then gets things back to where you left off by loading the snapshot back into RAM.

Note   Your computer is always disconnected from the Internet when you shut down, no matter which Turn Off option you choose.

Stand By is an available option on virtually all modern PCs. Hibernate isn't quite so ubiquitous, because it requires APM (Advanced Power Management) or ACPI (Advanced Configuration and Power Interface) hardware, and much more.

If hibernate is never an option . . .

There are many reasons why you might never see a Hibernate or Sleep option in your Turn Off options — so many that it would be a small miracle if you ever did see those options. The biggest catch is that *all* of your installed hardware needs to support hibernation. If Windows finds any device that it doesn't know how to handle after hibernation, the option to hibernate won't appear no matter what you do.

Your motherboard needs to support APM (Advanced Power Management) or ACPI (Advanced Configuration and Power Interface), and that capability needs to be enabled in the system BIOS. Exactly how you get to the BIOS option varies from one computer to the next. Typically, you need to press F2 or Del while the computer is starting, to get to the BIOS Setup program.

Even if APM or ACPI is available and enabled in the BIOS, and even if all your hardware supports hibernation, you still have to enable Hibernation in Windows. Here's how:

1. Click the **Start** button, and choose **Control Panel**.

2. If Control Panel opens in Category View, click on **Performance and Maintenance**.

3. Open the **Power Options** icon, and click the **Hibernate** tab (if one is available) in the Power Options Properties dialog box.

4. Choose the **Enable hibernation** checkbox, as shown in Figure 57-1.

5. Click **OK**.

Figure 57-1: The Hibernate tab of Power Options Properties

Remember, even if you select the Enable Hibernation option, there's no guarantee that you'll be given the Hibernate option when you shut down, because there are so many other requirements.

All in all, it's not terribly important because in the long run, it's too your advantage to save all your work and close all your open program windows before you turn off the computer. That way you know that everything is safely tucked away, and you can start with a nice, clear desktop the next time you fire up the computer.

Conserving Power

Most modern computers can shut themselves down after a period of inactivity. The computer itself doesn't use much electricity. The monitor is a bit of a power hog because it takes some juice to light up all those pixels on the screen. So, you also have the option of just shutting down the monitor. All the options for controlling power usage are located in the Power Options dialog box, which you can open from Control Panel per Steps 1 to 3 in the preceding set of steps.

Tip   You can also get to the Power Options dialog box from the Screen Saver tab of the Display Properties dialog box. Right-click the desktop and choose Properties, click the Screen Saver tab, and click the Power button.

Choosing a power scheme

The Power Schemes tab of the Power Options Properties dialog box, shown in Figure 57-2, offers some predefined power schemes. These range from Always On (nothing ever shuts down) to Max Battery (aggressive power saving to extend battery life on a notebook or laptop computer).

Figure 57-2: The Power Options tab of Power Options Properties

The idea here is to choose a power scheme from the drop-down list. Then, you can refine that scheme from the options below the drop-down list. Each time duration refers to a period of zero activity at the mouse or keyboard. For example, the settings shown in Figure 57-2 would turn off the monitor (only) if you let the computer sit idle for 20 minutes.

Needless to say, if you also chosen the Screen Saver in the Display Properties dialog box, the screen saver won't be visible once the power options turn off the monitor.

Turning off the hard disk just "spins down" the disk. The effect will be that the first time you launch a program after the hard disk has been turned off, it will take a little longer than usual for the program to open. That's because the disk needs to "spin up" to its normal speed before it can load the program into RAM. But once the disk reaches normal speed (which only takes a second or so), everything will be back to normal.

More power options

The Advanced tab in the Power Options Properties dialog box, shown in Figure 57-3, provides some additional power options, beyond those offered by the power schemes. They are:

✦ **Always show icon on the taskbar:** Relevant only on notebook computers, choosing this option displays a battery icon in the Notification area whenever you're running from the battery. The icon doubles as a power meter, showing how much batter power you have left. When the computer is plugged in, the icon shows as a standard power plug. You can double-click either icon to open the Power Options Properties dialog box.

✦ **Prompt for password when computer resumes from standby:** As stated, choosing this option prevents other people from using your computer when it resumes from Stand By mode.

✦ **When I press the power button . . . :** This option controls what happens when you turn off the computer from the main power switch.

✦ **When I press the sleep button . . . :** If your computer has a Sleep button near the main power button, this option controls what happens when you press that button.

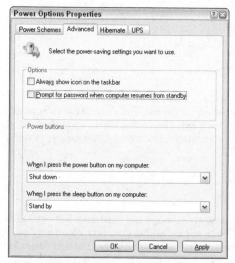

Figure 57-3: The Advanced tab of Power Options Properties

Using an Uninterruptible Power Supply

An uninterruptible power supply (UPS) is a useful device in areas where sudden power-outs are common. These devices can be noisy (and expensive). But, if you often lose work because of sudden blackouts, a UPS might be a worthwhile investment. You have to understand, though, that the computer won't keep working indefinitely after the power goes out. In most cases, you'll just get enough time to close everything up and shut down the computer after the power goes out.

To ensure that the UPS works with your computer, connect and turn on the UPS per the manufacturer's instructions. Then, open the Power Options Properties dialog box and click the UPS tab. Click the Select button (see Figure 57-4), and choose your UPS make and model, or "Generic" if your manufacturer name isn't listed.

Figure 57-4: The UPS tab of Power Options
Properties

If you chose Generic, click on Custom in the Select Model list, and choose the port to which
the UPS is connected from the On Port drop-down list. Then, click Next> and choose options
from the UPS Interface Configuration page per the instructions that came with your uninterruptible power supply.

Wrap Up

Computer power options exist mainly for two reasons: to get the maximum battery life from a
portable computer that's not plugged in to a wall socket and to conserve electricity on computers that are plugged in. The computer itself doesn't use much juice. Though the monitor
does suck it up and also generates heat. The main topics discussed in this chapter are:

✦ When you turn off your computer, choosing Stand By, Sleep, or Hibernate brings the
desktop back to wherever you left it when you shut down.

✦ The Power Options icon in Control Panel provides options for controlling how your
computer uses electricity during idle times where the computer is on, but there's been
no mouse or keyboard activity.

✦ The Max Battery power scheme in Power Options uses aggressive power conservation
to maximize notebook battery life.

✦ Turning off the monitor after a period of inactivity is a good way to reduce power consumption and prevent unnecessary heat from being generated by the monitor.

✦ A UPS kicks in whenever there's a sudden power outage, giving you a little extra time to
close and save everything and shut down your computer normally.

✦   ✦   ✦

Editing the Windows Registry

As you know, there are countless dialog boxes from which you can choose options to customize objects in Windows and other programs. For example, you use the Display Properties dialog box to customize your display (screen). You use Taskbar and Start Menu Properties to customize the Start menu and taskbar. All those settings you choose are stored in a database called the registry.

In this chapter you'll learn how the registry works, and techniques for editing the registry. Be forewarned that the registry stores its information in a way that's quick and efficient for Windows to access. But there's no attempt to make that information easily accessible to humans. There's really no reason for a person to go digging around the registry, except when a manual change to the registry is the only solution to some pesky problem.

What Is the Registry?

When you first turn on your computer, you have to wait a while for the system to boot up and the Windows desktop to appear. While you're waiting, Windows is gathering up lots of information about the hardware and software in your system and is storing that information in a centralized database called the registry.

Windows, and all your programs, use the information in the registry to carry out the tasks you demand of them. During any given session at the computer, your software will reach into the registry to get some piece of information many thousands of times. The information in the registry is organized and stored in such a way that's quick and efficient for the software to access. For example, numeric values are stored in hexadecimal, a numbering system that's quick and easy for computers to process, but not at all obvious to most human beings.

Human beings rarely, if ever, need to work with the registry directly. When you're choosing options from dialog boxes, or barking orders at some program through its menus, you are working with registry data in a roundabout way. You don't have to sit there and type in hex numbers and other weird codes to get the computer to work. You can just point, click, double-click, drag, and so forth to tell the software what to do. The software, in turn, takes care of all the messy details of gathering registry data and executing commands behind the scenes.

About the only time that average human computer user needs to work directly with the registry is when there's some problem that can't be solved through any other means. One thing is for sure. The registry is not a place to play around in, experiment with things, or try to resolve problems through sheer guesswork. When it comes to working in the registry, there is absolutely zero margin for error. Even a minor typographical error in the registry can have far-reaching negative consequences, to the point where you can't even start your computer anymore!

A working example

Let's take a moment to see how you interact with the registry without even knowing the registry exists. A simple example would be when you right-click a document icon and choose Open With, a list of installed programs that can open that type of document appears, as in the example shown in Figure 58-1.

When you right-click a picture's icon and choose Open With, you may get a different set of programs to choose from on your Open With menu. That's because you may have different programs on your system that are capable of opening that type of picture. So, how does Windows "know" what programs are installed on your computer, and exactly what types of files each of those programs can open? Easy, it gets that information from the registry.

How does the registry "know" what programs are installed and what kinds of documents each program can open? On its own, it doesn't. That's why you have to install a program before you can use it. When you install a program, the installation procedure *registers* the program with Windows by loading the registry with all the "facts" about itself, including all the types of files it can open.

Figure 58-1: Sample Open With menu for a document type

Every document type has a default program associated with it. The default program is the one that opens when you open a document by double-clicking (or clicking) its icon. Windows "knows" which program to use as the default because that bit of information is stored in the registry as well.

If you want to change the default program for a particular document type, you don't need to go into the registry and mess with hexadecimal numbers. Instead, you can just choose the Choose Program option from the bottom of the Open With menu to get to the Open With dialog box. Or, you can open the Folder Options dialog box and click the File Types tab. There, you can scroll through document types and make changes as you see fit without going through the registry.

Note See "Changing file associations" in Chapter 12 for more information on the Open With and Folder Options dialog boxes.

Any changes you make in the Open With or Folder Options dialog box are stored in the registry. Windows takes care of all the messy details required to ensure that your selection is stored in the right place and in the right format within the registry. And that's why you rarely need to work with registry data directly. Of course, the Open With and File Types examples are just examples. The registry contains thousands of additional facts about your specific hardware and software.

How registry data is organized

Windows and all your programs need to get information from the registry often. To keep things running at top speed, it's important that every request for information placed on the registry be handled quickly and efficiently. As with organizing your own files into folders, a hierarchical arrangement that organizes information from the general to the specific provides the best means of ensuring quick access to data.

But all the registry data is stored in one large file, so the concept of folders and files doesn't apply to the registry directly. Only the hierarchical arrangement is similar. Rather than folders, the registry uses *keys* and *subkeys* to organize data. Just as a folder can contain subfolders, a key can contain subkeys.

The registry doesn't store files or documents. Rather, it stores simple *values* — some number or code that has "meaning" to the software. The meaning of a particular value isn't at all obvious to a human being. Rather, the software that uses those values is just written in such as way as to do different things, depending on the value that happens to be stored in a subkey.

Standard root keys and subkeys

We'll get into the specifics of editing the registry in a moment. But first, Figure 58-2 shows an example of the registry editor as it might look when you first open it. The names listed down the left column are keys. Specifically, we refer to them as the *standard root keys*, because they're at the top (root) of the hierarchy, and each contains subkeys. Each standard root key stores a particular type of information, as summarized in Table 58-1. Note that most keys have a standard abbreviation, like `HKCU for HKEY_CURRENT_USER`.

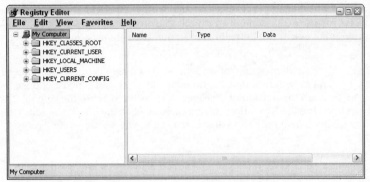

Figure 58-2: Standard root keys at left in the Registry Editor

Table 58-1: Standard Root Keys

Key Name	Abbreviation	Description
HKEY_CLASSES_ROOT	HKCR	Stores information about document types and extensions, registered programs that can open each file type, the default program for each file type, and options that appear when you right-click an icon.
HKEY_CURRENT_USER	HKCU	Stores information about the person who is currently using the computer, based on which user account that person is logged in to, and settings that particular user chose within his or her account.
HKEY_LOCAL_MACHINE	HKLM	Stores information about all the hardware that's available to the computer, including devices that might not be plugged in at the moment.
HKEY_USERS	HKU	Stores information about all users, based on user accounts you've defined via control panel.
HKEY_CURRENT_CONFIG	<none>	Similar to HKEY_LOCAL_MACHINE, this key stores information about hardware available to the computer. However, this key limits its storage to hardware that's connected and functioning currently.

When you click on the + sign next to a standard root key, it expands to display its subkeys. Some of the subkeys may have subkeys of their own. In that case, the subkey itself will have a + sign next to it, which you can click to see another level of subkeys. For example, in Figure 58-3 I've expanded the HKEY_CLASSES_ROOT key to reveal its subkeys. Each subkey represents a particular file type in that case. I've also expanded the subkey under the .aif file type's entry.

You'll often see a reference to a specific subkey expressed as a path, in much the way that you might see a file's location and name expressed as a path. For example, the path to a file might be expressed as C:\Documents and Settings\Alan\My Documents\My Pictures\ Summit01.jpg. The path tells Windows exactly where to find the file: "Go to drive C:, drill down through the folder named Documents and Settings, Alan, My Documents, and My Pictures, and there you'll find a file named Summit01.jpg".

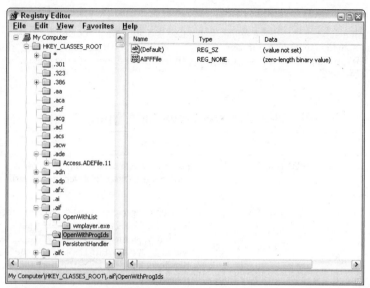

Figure 58-3: The HKEY_CLASSES_ROOT and .aif keys expanded

A registry path is the same idea, and even uses backslashes to separate the key and subkey names. For example, the highlighted subkey in Figure 58-3 is at HKEY_CLASSES_ROOT\ .aif\OpenWithProgIDs. The path to color schemes available to the current user is HKEY_ CURRENT_USER\ Control Panel\Appearance\Schemes. Following that path down through the keys, and clicking on Schemes reveals the values currently stored for that subkey, as shown in Figure 58-4. The values in the Data column for that key are mostly binary numbers.

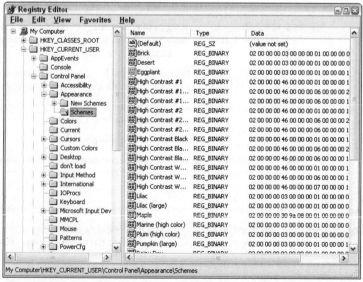

Figure 58-4: The HKEY_CURRENT_USER\Control Panel\Appearance\ Schemes subkey selected

Key values

The data stored in a subkey is called a *value*. The value is a specific piece of information that can be stored as a **string** (text) or a **number**. Though the terms "string" and "number" don't tell the whole story, because those types can be further broken down into the specific *data types* listed in Table 58-2.

Table 58-2: Registry Value Data Types

Name	Data type	Description
Binary Value	REG_BINARY	Raw binary data used mostly by hardware components. Often displayed in hexadecimal format.
DWORD Value	REG_DWORD	A 32-bit integer, often used to store parameters for device drivers and services. Subtypes include Related types such as DWORD_LITTLE_ENDIAN and REG_DWORD_BIG_ENDIAN with the least significant bit at the lowest/highest address, respectively.
Expandable String Value	REG_EXPAND_SZ	A variable-length string often used to store data for application programs and services.
Multi-String Value	REG_MULTI_SZ	A string that actually consists of multiple substrings separated by spaces, commas, or other special characters.
String Value	REG_SZ	A simple fixed-length text string.
Binary Value	REG_RESOURCE_LIST	A series of nested arrays (lists) often used by hardware and device drivers. Usually displayed in hexadecimal.
Binary Value	REG_RESOURCE_REQUIREMENTS_LIST	A series of nested arrays (lists) containing a device driver's hardware resources, displayed in hexadecimal.
Binary Value	REG_FULL_RESOURCE_DESCRIPTOR	A series of nested list of actual hardware device capabilities, usually displayed in hexadecimal.
None	REG_NONE	Data with no particular type that's displayed as a Binary Value in hexadecimal.
Link	REG_LINK	A string naming a symbolic link.
QWORD	Value REG_QWORD	A 64-bit number displayed as a binary value.

Registry hives

The standard root keys you see listed in the left column of the Registry Editor are stored in backup files referred to as *registry hives* or just *hives* for short. But there isn't a one-to-one correspondence between the root keys and the hives. Rather, the hives are organized more by security requirements, software requirements, and so forth. The registry hives and backup files that support each one are summarized in Table 58-3.

Table 58-3: Registry Hives and Supporting Backup Files

Registry Hive	Supporting Files
HKEY_LOCAL_MACHINE\SAM	Sam, Sam.log, Sam.sav
HKEY_LOCAL_MACHINE\Security	Security, Security.log, Security.sav
HKEY_LOCAL_MACHINE\Software	Software, Software.log, Software.sav
HKEY_LOCAL_MACHINE\System	System, System.alt, System.log, System.sav
HKEY_CURRENT_CONFIG	System, System.alt, System.log, System.sav, Ntuser.dat, Ntuser.dat.log
HKEY_USERS\DEFAULT	Default, Default.log, Default.sav

Note The registry hive supporting files are not standard documents, but rather system files that store data in machine-readable (not human-readable) form. Many supporting files don't even have filename extensions. Then, don't need extensions because it wouldn't make sense to open such a file in a normal application program like Microsoft Word or Excel.

Numbering Systems

Admittedly, I've already given you much more information about the registry than you'd probably ever need to know. About the only time you want to mess with the registry is when you've found the solution to some problem, and that solution requires a *registry hack* (a manual modification to the registry). In that case, the solution will always tell exactly what value to put in what key. So, you don't have to figure out how to convert some decimal value, such as 16 to a hexadecimal value (10) or binary (10000). But, for the techno-curious, here's a quick overview of how the numbering systems work.

In our day-to-day work we use decimal *base ten* numbers. The "base ten" part tells us that there are 10 unique characters for expressing all numbers, 0 to 9. After you go from zero to nine, you run out of characters and have to start using two characters to express numbers, 10, 11, 12, and so forth. Eventually, you get to 99, at which point you've exhausted all possible unique pairs of the characters 0 to 9, so you have to go to three digits, 100, 101, 102, and so forth, up to 999.

Other numbering systems use a different number of characters for expressing numbers. For example, hexadecimal is base 16, meaning that it has 16 unique characters, 0 through 9 plus A, B, C, D, E, and F. Counting from zero to 20 in hexadecimal goes like this: 0, 1, 2, 3, 4, 5, 6, 7, 8, 9, A, B, C, D, E, F, 10, 11, 12, 13, 14. The binary system is base 2 because it offers only two unique characters, 0 and 1. Counting from 0 to 5 in binary goes 0, 1, 10, 11, 100, 101. The octal base 8 system uses the unique characters 0 to 7 to express numbers.

I think it's safe to say that the alternative numbering systems aren't terribly important in day-to-day life. And it's a good thing, because if everybody didn't agree to use decimal, numbers would be a very confusing thing. For example, Table 58-4 shows the numbers 1 to 16, and some higher numbers, in decimal, hexadecimal, octal, binary, and exponential formats.

Table 58-4: Examples of Numbering Systems

Decimal	Hex	Octal	Binary	Exponent
0	0	0	0	
1	1	1	1	
2	2	2	10	2^1
3	3	3	11	
4	4	4	100	2^2
5	5	5	101	
6	6	6	110	
7	7	7	111	
8	8	10	1000	2^3
9	9	11	1001	
10	A	12	1010	
11	B	13	1011	
12	C	14	1100	
13	D	15	1101	
14	E	16	1110	
15	F	17	1111	
16	10	20	10000	2^4
32	20	40	100000	2^5
64	40	100	1000000	2^6
128	80	200	10000000	2^7
256	100	400	100000000	2^8
512	200	1000	1000000000	2^9
1024	400	2000	10000000000	2^{10}

After you get to 16 and start doubling each number, you encounter numbers that appear often in the computer world, 32, 64, 128, 256, 512, and 1,024. Those numbers appear frequently because they're powers of two, and everything a computer does centers around two digits, 0 and 1. That's because every little switch in the processor, and every little tiny dot of data on a disk can have only one of two possible values, "on" (1) or "off" (0). As a human being, you work with text, pictures, sound, and video. But the computer itself doesn't "see" or "know" anything about text, pictures, human beings, or anything else. It's just a machine that juggles "on" (1) and "off" (0) values.

Even the abbreviations K (kilo, M (mega), and G (giga) are powers of two. We say that K equals about a thousand, M about a million, and G about a trillion. But in truth K is 210 or 1,024, M is 220 or 1,048,576, and G is 230 or 1,073,741,824.

Unless you get into some serious programming or writing device drivers, it's very unlikely that you'll ever need to mess with hex or binary numbers directly. But just so you know, there is an easy way to convert numbers in Windows. Click the Start button and choose All Programs ➪ Accessories ➪ Calculator. From Calculator's menu bar choose View ➪ Scientific to see the larger scientific calculator shown in Figure 58-5.

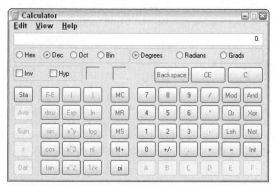

Figure 58-5: Windows Calculator in Scientific View

With Calculator in Scientific View, you first need to tell it which system you'll be converting the number *from*. For example, if you want to convert decimal 255 to some other numbering system, click on Dec.

Next, enter your number by typing it, or by clicking the appropriate calculator buttons. Finally, click the option that represents the numbering system you want to convert *to*. For example to convert that decimal 255 to hexadecimal, click on Hex. You'll see FF because FF is the value 255 expressed in hexadecimal.

When you start by clicking Hex, Oct, or Bin to convert a value *from* one of those numbering systems, you'll see the options Qword (64 bits), Dword (32 bits), Word (6 bits), and Byte (b bits) to the right. Choosing one of those options puts an upper limit on how large a number you can enter, as summarized in Table 58-5. The limitation is caused by the number of bits (binary digits, or "ones and zeroes" in simple terms) that each data type stores.

Table 58-5: Maximum Values for Types of Data

Type	Bits	Max number (Hex)	Max number (Decimal)
Byte	8	FF	255
Word	16	FFFF	65,535
Dword	32	FFFFFFFF	4,294,967,295
Qword	64	FFFFFFFFFFFFFFFF	18,446,744,073,709,551,615

Tip   Microsoft Excel can convert values among the decimal, octal, hexadecimal, and binary systems. You first need to load the Analysis ToolPak by choosing Tools ➪ Add-Ins from Excel's menu bar. Then, you can search Excel's help for conversion functions such as DEC2HEX(), HEX2DEC(), DEC2BIN(), BIN2DEC(), and so forth.

Well, I think that's about enough "theory" in terms of how things work. From a practical standpoint, most people only need to know how to make an occasional change to the registry to fix some problem. One important rule, though, is that before you do *anything* to the registry, you should make a quick backup copy of its current contents.

Tip   Modern computers are based upon a 32-bit processing model, which basically provides for 4,294,967,295 bits of directly addressable memory. As 64-bit processors enter the mainstream, you'll see much more powerful computing capabilities just because of the walloping 18,446,744,073,709,551,615 bits of addressable memory the 64-bit model provides.

Backing Up the Registry

Every time you start your computer Windows automatically creates the registry based on the hardware and software available to it. Then, it makes a backup copy of that registry. When you plan to manually change the registry, you should also make a backup copy of the registry just before you make your change. Because when it comes to editing the registry, there is no margin for error and even a tiny typographical error can have far-reaching, unpleasant consequences.

Tip   The System Restore feature described in Chapter 55 also makes periodic backup copies of the registry.

The easiest way to make a quick backup copy of your Registry is as follows:

1. Click the **Start** button and choose **Run** or press ⊞+R.

Note   If you don't have a Run option on your Start menu or a ⊞ on your keyboard, don't fret. Just right-click the Start button and choose Properties. Then click on Customize ➪ the Advanced tab, and choose (check) Run Command from the list of Start menu items. Then, click OK in each open dialog box.

2. In the Run dialog box type regedit and, then press **Enter** or click **OK**. The Registry Editor opens.

3. Choose **File** ➪ **Export** from the menu bar in the Registry Editor.

4. Choose a folder, and enter a filename of your own choosing.

5. To export the entire registry, choose **All** under the Export range heading.

6. Click the **Save** button.

That's it. In the event of a disaster, you can choose **File** ➪ **Import** from the Registry Editor's menu bar to restore all the entries you copied in the preceding step.

Using the Registry Editor

The first two steps you followed to backup the registry are the steps you follow whenever you need to make a change to the registry. There is no menu command for opening the Registry Editor, because there's nothing "simple" about the registry itself. Microsoft intentionally made it a little difficult to get to so that people wouldn't open it up and rummage about just to see what happens.

When you do open the Registry Editor, you'll most likely see the five standard root keys shown back in Figure 58-2. As in any expandable list, you can click the + sign next to any key name to see subkeys within that key. Click the - sign to put the subkeys back into hiding.

When you select a Registry key, the status bar shows the full path to this subkey. If you can't see the status bar at the bottom of your Registry Editor, choose View ➪ Status Bar from its menu bar.

Once you're in the Registry Editor, you can make any changes you want. Though once again, with feeling, I remind you:

Caution   Adding, changing, and deleting registry values is serious business and should never be taken lightly. Never experiment or play around with registry data. Always back up your registry just before you make any changes.

Creating and renaming keys

To create a new subkey, right-click the key that will act as the parent to the subkey and choose New ➪ Key from the shortcut menu. The Registry Editor creates a new key named New Key #*x* where *x* is a number. Type in a new name for the key and press Enter. If you make a mistake, right-click the key name, choose Rename, and try again.

Each new key will automatically have a placeholder named (Default) to store a value. But no specific value will be entered into the placeholder, so you'll just see (value not set).

Deleting a key

To delete a subkey, right-click its name and choose Delete. You'll see a message asking for confirmation. Be aware that when you delete a key, you also delete its data and all subkeys beneath it. So, make sure you deleted the right key before you choose Yes when asked for confirmation on deleting the key.

Viewing key values

When you select a key, the Registry Editor displays a list of values in the right pane. Notice the columns labeled Name and Data. A key can have any number of values, although most keys have none. The Registry Editor always displays one key, named (Default) which, in truth, is "nothing." Which is to say, the name (Default) really means something like "this value name intentionally left blank."

Modifying a value

You can change any value in the Registry. First you need to get to the appropriate subkey. For example, let's say that you've found the solution to some problem via Microsoft's Web site. Part of that solution involves changing the following subkey:

```
HKEY_LOCAL_MACHINE\SOFTWARE\Microsoft\Windows NT\CurrentVersion\Win
logon\SpecialAccounts\UserList
```

The first step is to get to the subkey by expanding the HKEY_LOCAL_MACHINE, SOFTWARE, Microsoft, Windows NT, CurrentVersion, Winlogon, and SpecialAccounts keys. Then, click on UserList, as shown in Figure 58-6. Notice the full path down in the status bar and the various values in the main pane to the right.

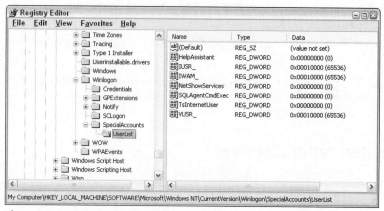

Figure 58-6: HKLM\SOFTWARE\Microsoft\Windows NT\CurrentVersion\ Winlogon\SpecialAccounts\UserList selected

If you just need to change an existing value in the right pane, just double-click that value. A dialog box will open allowing you to make a change, as in the example shown in Figure 58-7.

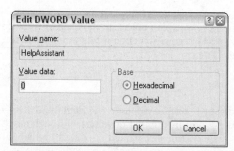

Figure 58-7: Dialog box to edit a Dword value

The Value data box contains the value you can edit. After you make your change, just click OK. That's it. You can then close the Registry Editor.

Whether or not you see any change on the screen depends on the subkey you changed. Many registry hacks will have no effect until you close the Registry Editor, close all open program windows, and restart the computer.

Adding a new value

Most changes you make to the registry will involve changing existing values. But once in a while you might be instructed to add a new value. For example, suppose that you need to create a new Dword value under that `HKLM\SOFTWARE\Microsoft\Windows NT\CurrentVersion\ Winlogon\SpecialAccounts\UserList` subkey. First make sure the correct subkey is still selected (highlighted). Then, right-click the subkey name and choose New as in Figure 58-8. Or choose Edit ➪ New from the menu bar, and then click on the value type you need to create.

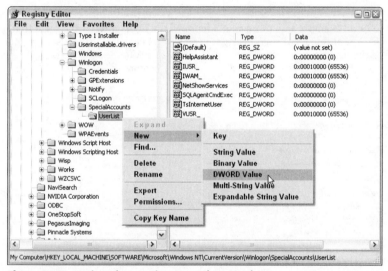

Figure 58-8: Options for creating a new key or value

The new entry in the main pane to the right will be named New Value #1. You'll need to rename that according to the instructions you're reading from the Web site. If you miss the opportunity to do so right after creating the value, just right-click the New Value #1 name, choose Rename, and type in the correct name. Then, to give the new name a value, double-click that new name. Fill in the blanks in the dialog box that opens, according you the instructions, then click OK.

> **Caution** There is no Undo in the Registry Editor. All the more reason to be very careful while make changes.

The main trick here is to follow, to a tee, the instructions that tell you how to modify the registry. When you've finished making your changes, close the Registry Editor by clicking the Close (X) button in its upper-right corner. Or, choose File ➪ Exit from the Registry Editor's menu bar.

Cleaning Up Add or Remove Programs

Unless you're a professional programmer, there won't be many situations in which you want to go into the registry and make a change without specific instructions from some Web page or book. There is, however, one pesky problem that most of us are faced with from time to time when a direct registry hack is the only solution. That situation occurs when you have a program listed in Add or Remove Programs that you want to get rid if, but can't. When you click on the program's Remove or Change/Remove button, you get an error message saying the program has already been removed (or some such thing).

Caution   Use this method *only* to remove programs you can't get rid of using the Remove or Change/Remove button.

Figure 58-9 shows an example and, quite coincidentally, the highlighted program in that figure really is "stuck" in Add/Remove Programs right now. When I click its Change/Remove button, I get a message that reads `Error loading C:\PRGRAM~1\MyWay\SrchAstt\1.bin\ mysrchas.dll. The specific module could not be found`.

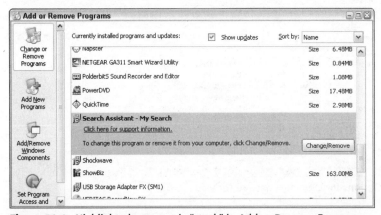

Figure 58-9: Highlighted program is "stuck" in Add or Remove Programs.

To get rid of the unwanted item, close the Add or Remove Programs window and Control Panel. Run the regedit program, and use File ⇨ Export to make a quick backup of the registry, just to play it safe.

The uninstall information about programs in Add or Remove Programs is stored in the registry under `HKEY_LOCAL_MACHINE\SOFTWARE\Microsoft\ Windows\CurrentVersion\ Uninstall`. When you get to that key and click the + sign next to Unisntall, you'll see many subkeys beneath it. Locate the name of the program you're trying to get rid of and click on its name. For example, in Figure 58-10, I found the appropriate subkey for the MySearch program from Figure 58-9.

Tip   As an alternative to drilling down through folders in the Registry Editor, you can choose Edit ⇨ Find from its menu bar. But be careful. Several keys and values might contain the text you searched for. So, you may have to choose Edit ⇨ Find Next or press F3 a few times to get to the exact subkey you're looking for.

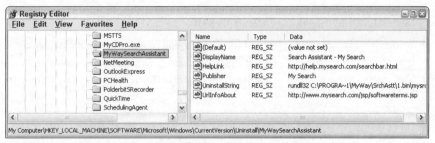

Figure 58-10: MyWaySearchAssistant found under Uninstall key

Before you forge ahead, take a close look at the text in the DisplayName, Publisher, UninstallString, and/or QuietUninstallString (if any) key in the right pane to make sure that you have the correct program. Then, just right-click the subkey name in the left column, as in Figure 58-11, and choose Delete. Click Yes when asked for confirmation. Then, close the Registry Editor.

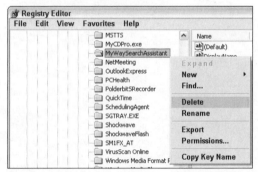

Figure 58-11: About to delete MyWaySearchAssistant's registry key

To verify the deletion, open Control Panel and Add Or Remove Programs again. The item should be gone. If not, restart the computer and check again. Good little registry hack when you need it!

Wrap Up

The registry is the central repository of all the information Windows and other programs need to know about your particular hardware and software. The information in it is organized and stored for efficient use by software. Which means it's not particularly "user-friendly" toward humans. Normally, you wouldn't want to mess directly with the registry. But occasionally you'll come across a problem that can't be fixed any other way. Important points about the registry are:

✦ The program for changing the contents of your registry is named Registry Editor, often called regedit for short.

✦ To open the Registry Editor, click the Start button and choose Run. Type `regedit` into the textbox, and then press Enter or click OK.

✦ Before you change the contents of the registry edit, make a quick backup by choosing File ➪ Export from the Registry Editor menu bar.

✦ The path to a registry key is displayed as the series for folder you must expand to get to that subkey, as in `HKEY_LOCAL_MACHINE\SOFTWARE\Microsoft\ Windows\ CurrentVersion\Uninstall`.

✦ Don't expect all registry changes to have an immediate effect. Some changes won't take effect until the next time you start your computer.

✦   ✦   ✦

Troubleshooting Performance Problems

Troubleshooting System Restore Problems

Most System Restore error messages display instructions for resolving the problem. Pay careful attention to the wording of the message, because some of the suggestions may refer to specific error messages.

Missing earlier restore points

Two factors determine how much data System Restore will store. The Disk Space Usage option in the Settings dialog box sets the maximum amount of space that System Restore will use. By default, each restore point is automatically deleted after 90 days. If you start running low on disk space, System Restore automatically starts deleting previous restore points. Disabling System Restore always deletes all existing restore points.

When available hard disk space falls below 200 MB, System Restore is suspended until available hard disk space climbs above that amount. On a single drive that's partitioned into multiple logical drives, running out of space on any one partition will cause System Restore to be suspended on all partitions.

Restoring from a command prompt

If a problem prevents you from booting to the Windows desktop, you can boot to a Safe Mode command prompt (press F8 after restarting and before the desktop opens). When prompted to log in, choose an account that has administrative privileges. Enter the following command at the command prompt:

```
%systemroot%\system32\restore\rstrui.exe
```

Follow the instructions on the screen to restore your computer to its state at an earlier time.

Viruses and System Restore

Viruses that affect system files will also affect restore points. Therefore, anytime you scan for, locate, and delete viruses, consider deleting all existing restore points and creating a new one from your current system files. To quickly and easily remove all existing restore points, follow these steps:

1. Right-click your **My Computer** icon, and choose **Properties**.

2. In the System Properties dialog box, click the **System Restore** tab.

3. Select (check) **Turn off System Restore on all drives**.

4. Click **OK**.

Wait a while for all restore points to be deleted. Then, repeat the steps but clear, rather than select, the *Turn off System Restore on all drives* checkbox and click OK. Finally, you may want to manually create a restore point with a descriptive name, as discussed in Chapter 55, once you've reenabled System Restore.

Troubleshooting Performance Problems

This section covers basic troubleshooting in terms of using Task Manager to monitor performance. You need to remember, though, that the speed of the hardware dictates the speed of the software, not vice versa. If you suddenly find your computer running much more slowly than usual, your best resource for help is likely to be your computer manufacturer. After all, they're the ones who built the computer. So, they should know best what kinds of things might cause that hardware to slow down unexpectedly.

Can't open Task Manager

If a computer administrator has disabled Task Manager in your user account, you'll see the message *Task Manager has been disabled by your administrator* when you try to start Task Manager. If you are an administrator, and the restriction wasn't intentional, you can reactivate Task Manager through the registry. Here's how:

Caution As always, editing the registry is risky business and must be handled with the utmost care. Never experiment with the registry settings. Back up the registry, as described in Chapter 58, before making any changes.

1. Click the **Start** button, and choose **Run**, or press ⊞+R.

2. In the left column, navigate to the following key:

```
HKEY_CURRENT_USER\Software\Microsoft\Windows\CurrentVersion\Policies\
System
```

Note The key is only available on systems where Task Manager has been disabled through Group Policy.

3. In the right pane, double-click **DisableTaskMgr,** and set its data value to 0.

4. Exit the Registry Editor.

Processor appears twice in System Information and Performance tab

If your microprocessor uses Intel Hyper-Threading (HT) technology, the processor name will be listed twice in System Information. The CPU Usage History Chart in Task Manager will be split into two panes, as it would be on a computer running multiple processors. (See Figure 59-1.) This is perfectly normal and is the way it should be when Hyper-Threading is working properly, so there is no error to correct here.

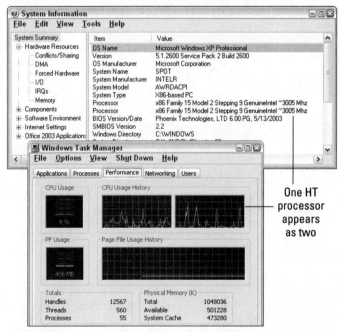

Figure 59-1: Intel HT processor doubled in System Information and Task Manager

CPU usage chart consistently runs high

If your CPU Usage chart consistently runs at a high percentage, you may be running two or more firewalls. Most likely, you'll need to disable and remove any third-party firewalls. Or disable the built-in Windows Firewall.

This problem has also been reported with Visioneer USB Scanners. See Knowledge Base article 303777 for a registry fix (http://support.microsoft.com/default.aspx?scid=kb; en-us;303777&Product=winxp).

Also, scan your system for viruses, adware, and other malware, and remove all that you can find to eliminate their resource consumption.

Troubleshooting Shutdown Errors

If you often receive an error message on shutting down your computer, particularly one that refers to LSASS (Local Security Authority Subsystem Service), your computer may be infected by the Sasser worm or one if its variants. To scan for and delete the worm, close all open program windows and browse to www.microsoft.com/security/incident/sasser.mspx. Scroll down to, and click on, the Check My PC for Infection button, and follow the on-screen instructions.

Variants of the Sasser worm can cause similar problems. If the above steps don't resolve the shutdown problem, browse to www.microsoft.com/security and check for recent incidents and worm removal tools.

✦   ✦   ✦

Home and Small-Business Networking

Contrary to popular belief, you don't need to be a network guru to connect two or more computers together. Doing so provides many advantages. All the computers can access the Internet through a single Internet account. All the computers can print to a single printer or multiple printers. And you can easily move and copy files from one computer to the other using simple drag-and-drop methods.

Chapter 60 starts off with the types of hardware available, and how you go about setting up that hardware. Chapter 61 talks about getting the computers to talk to each other using the Network Setup Wizard or new Wireless Network Setup Wizard.

As you'll learn in Chapter 62, sharing things among computers is a breeze. And using all those shared resources, as discussed in Chapter 63, couldn't be easier.

Creating Your Own Network

If you have two or more computers, you may already be using what's known as a *sneaker network*. For example, to get files from one computer to another, you copy files to a floppy of CD. Then, you walk over to the other computer and copy the files from the disk to that computer. Wouldn't it be nice if you could just drag icons from one computer to the other without having to use a floppy or CD?

What if you have several computers, but only one printer, one Internet connection, one DVD burner? Wouldn't it be nice if all the computers could use that one printer, that one Internet connection, and that one burner? All of these things are possible if you connect the computers to one another in a *local area network* (LAN).

What Is a LAN?

A *local area network* (sometimes referred to as a *LAN*, a *workgroup*, or just a *network*) is a small group of computers within a single building or household that can communicate with one another and share *resources*. A resource is anything useful to the computer. For example:

+ All computers in the LAN can use a single printer.

+ All computers in the LAN can connect to the Internet through a single modem and Internet account.

+ All computers in the LAN can access shared files and folders on any other computer in the LAN.

In addition, you can move and copy files and folders among computers using exactly the same techniques you use to move and copy files among folders on a single computer. Though, it's not entirely necessary to move or copy a document that you want to work on, because if a document is in a shared folder, you can open and edit it from any computer in the network. This is good, because you only have one copy of the document, and you don't have to worry about having multiple, slightly different copies of the same document all over the place to confuse matters.

Planning a LAN

To create a LAN, you need a plan and special hardware to make that plan work. For one thing, each computer will need a device known as a *network interface card* (NIC) or *Ethernet card*. Those you can purchase and install yourself. However, many PCs come with an Ethernet card already installed. In that case, you'll have an RJ-45 port on the back of the computer. It looks a lot like the plug for a telephone, just a little bigger. You just plug one side of an Ethernet cable into that port, the other side of the cable into a network hub or cable.

Then again, Ethernet cables aren't the only way to connect multiple computers in a LAN. In recent years, engineers have invented many new ways to connect computers using existing phone lines and power lines within the house. Better yet, you can connect computers without any cables at all by using wireless networking hardware. Exactly what you need, in terms of hardware, depends on what you want to do. The rest of this chapter describes your options.

Connecting Two Computers in a Traditional LAN

If you have two computers, and don't plan on getting more any time soon, you can install an Ethernet card (NIC) in each computer. Then, you just need a single Ethernet *crossover* cable to connect the two computers. The cable must be a crossover, as shown in Figure 60-1, or the connection won't work.

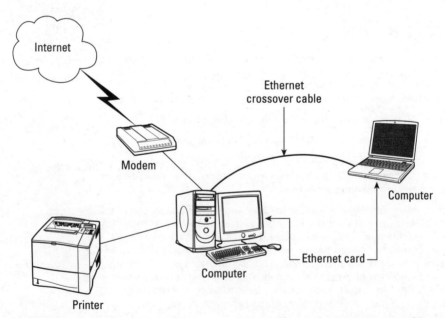

Figure 60-1: Example of connecting two computers with an Ethernet crossover cable and two NICs

Ethernet with Three or More Computers

If you have three or more computers to connect, and they're all in the same room and close to one another, you can use a traditional Ethernet hub and Ethernet cables to connect the computers. You'll need exactly one NIC and one traditional Ethernet cable (no crossover cables!) for each computer in the LAN. Figure 60-2 shows an example of four computers connected in a traditional LAN. Notice how each computer connects to the hub only — there are no cables that run directly from once computer to another computer.

By the way, even though the printer in Figure 60-2 is connected to the same computer as the modem, that's just an example. The printer can be connected to any computer. In fact, you could have several printers connected to several computers. All computers will be able to use all printers, no matter which computer that printer is (or those printers are) connected to.

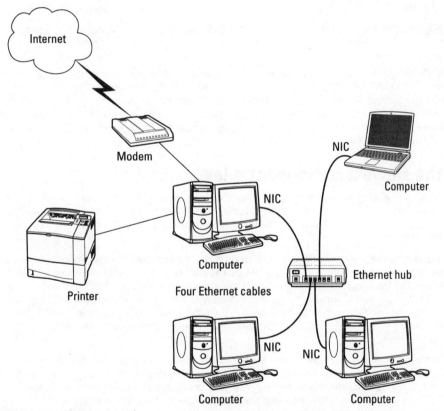

Figure 60-2: Example of four computers connected in a traditional Ethernet LAN

Traditional Ethernet speeds

When it comes time to purchase network interfaces cards, cables, and a hub, you'll need to decide on the speed you want. As with everything else in the computer industry, network speed costs money. However, in the case of networks, the costs differences are minor, while the speed differences are huge. The three possible speeds for Ethernet LANs are listed in Table 60-1.

Table 60-1: Common Ethernet Network Component Speeds

Name	Transfer Rate (speed)	Bits per second	Cable
10Base-T	10 Mbps	10 million	Category 3 or better
100Base-T	100 Mbps	100 million	Category 5 or better
Gigabit Ethernet	1 Gbps	1,000 million (billion)	Category 5 or better

If it's difficult to relate the numbers to actual transfer rates, consider a dial-up modem, which tops out at 50 Kbps. That's 50,000 bits per second. A 100Base-T network moves 100,000,000 bits per second. That's 2,000 times faster or, in other words, you only have to wait 1/2,000 as long to the same file to transfer across a 100Base-T connection. So, a file that takes 33 minutes (2,000 seconds) to transfer over a dial-up modem takes 1 second to transfer over a 100Base-T network.

The slowest component rules

When purchasing hardware, it's important to understand that the slowest component always rules. For example, if you get Gigabit Ethernet cards, but connect them to a 100Base-T hub, the LAN will run at 100 MBps. The faster Gigabit NICs can't force the slower hub to move any faster.

It makes sense is you envision the electrons going through the wire as cars on a freeway. Let's say lots of cars are zooming down a 10-lane freeway. But there's some road construction where the freeway narrows to one lane. Cars are going to pile up behind that point, because the 1-lane portion is slowing things down. Where the one lane reopens back to 10 lanes, cars will still be trickling out of the *bottleneck* — the single lane — one at a time. The 10 lanes at the other side of the bottleneck can't "suck the cars through" the bottleneck any faster than one car at a time.

Likewise, if your computers are connected together with a Gigabit LAN, but all share a single dial-up connection to the Internet, your Internet connection is still 50 Kbps. Your fast LAN can't force the data from your ISP to get to your computer any faster than 50 Kbps. Furthermore, if two people are using the 50-KBps dial-up connection at the same time, they have to share the available bandwidth. Meaning that each user gets only 25 Kbps. Though, if only one person is online, she gets the full 50 Kbps because she's not sharing any bandwidth when nobody else is online.

Connect with Wiring You Already Have

If you want to connect multiple computers in separate rooms and don't want to run cables all over the place, you can use the wires already there. You can either use phone jacks (provided that those phone jacks are all connected to the same phone number). Or you can use power outlets. These are actually two different technologies, the first called *phoneline networking* and the other called *powerline networking*. You have to get hardware designed for one or the other — don't try to mix and match.

For example, you can put a powerline NIC in each computer and connect each computer to a traditional power plug (the same plugs you use for lamps). You'll also need one hub specifically designed for powerline networks. If you prefer to use phone lines instead of power lines, you'll need a *phoneline NIC* for each computer in the LAN. You also need one hub specifically designed for phoneline networks. Figure 60-3 shows an example. The computers in the lower part of the figure would likely be in a different room from the computer shown in the top of that figure.

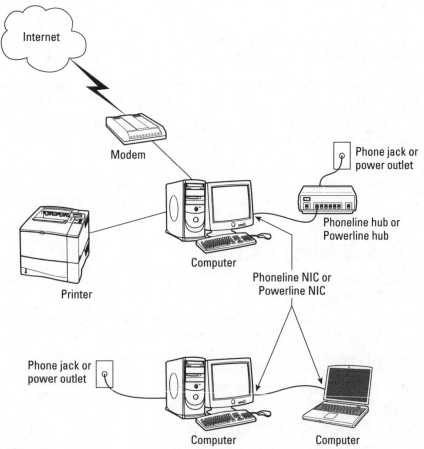

Figure 60-3: Example of three computers connected in a phoneline or powerline LAN

Tip   The network interface card (NIC) used in a phoneline network is often referred to as a *home phoneline network adapter*, abbreviated HPNA.

The advantage to using a phoneline or powerline LAN is that you don't have to run cables all over the house. The only disadvantage is that these LANs can't match the speed of some of the higher-end Ethernet connections. Table 60-2 shows the speeds of current phoneline and powerline networking hardware.

Table 60-2: Phoneline and Powerline Network Speeds

Name	Transfer Rate (speed)	Bits per Second	Standard
Phoneline 1 M	1 Mbps	1 million	HomePNA 1.0
Phoneline 10 M	10 Mbps	10 million	HomePNA 2.0
Powerline	14 Mbps	14 million	HomePlug 1.0.1

Note   As I write this, powerline netoworking is still a relatively new technology. Powerline networking hardware may be available in higher speeds by the time you read this.

If you go with a 10 or 14 Mbps phoneline or powerline network, you're still doing pretty well. Especially if you're mainly using your network to share an Internet connection and printer and don't need to transfer huge files across computers often. In that case, those speeds won't seem terribly slow. For example, there's isn't a printer on the planet that can print 10 or 14 million bits per second. So, your printer will run at top speed no matter which computer you print from.

Likewise, if you have a fast Internet connection, such as a standard Comcast.net Internet account, your bandwidth is about 2 Mbps (2,000 Kbps). Data coming in from the Internet at that speed isn't going to be slowed down one iota on a network running at 10 Mbps or 14 Mbps.

Creating a Wireless LAN

Wireless networking reigns supreme when it comes to convenience and ease of use. As the name implies, with wireless networks you don't have to run any cables. Plus, no computer is tied down to any one cable. For example, you can use your notebook computer in any room in the house, or even out on the patio, and still have Internet access without being tied to a cable. Wireless networking is definitely the wave of the future.

To set up a wireless LAN, you need a wireless NIC for each computer. You also need one Wireless Access Point (WAP) that connects to one computer, as illustrated in Figure 60-4.

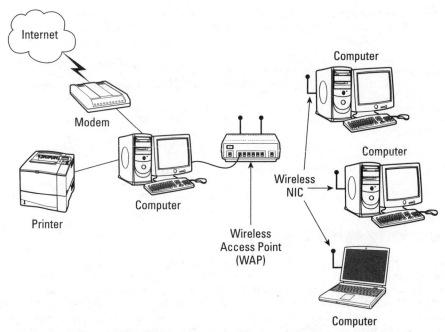

Figure 60-4: Example of four computers connected in a wireless LAN

The big advantage of wireless networking is, of course, the lack of cables. This is especially handy on a notebook computer, because the computer isn't tethered to one location by a cable. Granted, you can't stray too far from the wireless access point. Maybe 100 or 150 feet from the wireless access point, indoors. Not quite as far outdoors. But that's probably enough that you can access the Internet from your bed and patio.

Also, many universities and other locations offer public Internet access from any computer that has a 802.11b or 802.11g (Centrino) wireless network interface card installed. So, if you create your home wireless network using either of those standards, you'll also be able to use public Wi-Fi Internet access where it's available.

Tip   What Intel calls their Centrino technology is the same as the 802.11g specification described in this chapter. In other words, "Centrino" is just another name for 802.11g. The Centrino/802.11g standards are rapidly gaining ground as *the* wireless network standard to use.

The only disadvantages to wireless networking, as compared to wired networks, are speed and reliability. As I write this chapter, the fastest wireless networks run at about 54 Mbps. That's still pretty darn fast. It's just not as fast as the 100 Mbps or 1 Gbps speeds of traditional Ethernet cables. The reliability problem isn't a problem with the technology, per se. Rather, it has to do with the rare little "blind spot" here and there where the computer just won't connect to the network.

Wireless networks are built around three different standards. The 802.11g standard is the newest, and is rapidly gaining in popularity. Table 60-3 summarizes the main differences between the three standards. The Public Access column refers to Internet Wi-Fi hotspots such as those found at some airports, hotels, and other places. 802.11g is the preferred standard for Wi-Fi hotspots.

Table 60-3: Wireless Networking Standards and Speeds

Standard	Speed	Range	Public Access
802.11b	11 Mbps	100–150 feet	Yes
802.11a	54 Mbps	25–75 feet	No
802.11g	54 Mbps	100–150 feet	Yes

Networking with a Router

In each of the preceding examples, I've pictured one computer as already having an Internet connection through a modem. That could be either a dial-up modem or a broadband modem that connects through cable or DSL. The similarity among all those examples though is this: Only one computer in the network is physically connected to the modem by a cable. Or, in the case of an internal modem, the modem exists inside the case of only one computer. For our purposes, we'll say a modem is a communications device that's connected to only one computer.

As an alternative to using a modem connected to one computer, and a separate hub to connect the computers in a LAN, you can use a device known as a *router*, also called a *residential gateway*. A router is like a modem to which you can simultaneously connect two or more computers. In other words, the router plays two roles: It's both the modem that provides access to the "outside world" (namely, the Internet) and it's also the hub connects all the computers together.

Routers are typically used with broadband connections like DSL and cable. For that reason, they're often referred to as broadband routers. But no matter what you call it, it's going to have several plugs. One plug connects to the Internet via a phone line or cable TV cable. You connect computers to the other plugs using standard Ethernet cables, as in the example shown in Figure 60-5.

I just told a little white lie. It's possible to connect multiple computers to a router without using any cables at all. You just have to get a wireless router. On that kind of router, there's only one actual cable — the one that connects the router to the Internet through a phone line or cable line. Multiple computers still connect to the router. But they do so through wireless NIC cards rather than through cables, as in Figure 60-6.

Tip   If you order a new broadband Internet account, you can often get your ISP to send somebody out to the house and set up the whole kit and caboodle for you.

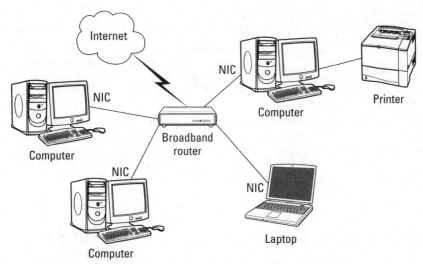

Figure 60-5: Example of four computers connected to each other and the Internet through a router

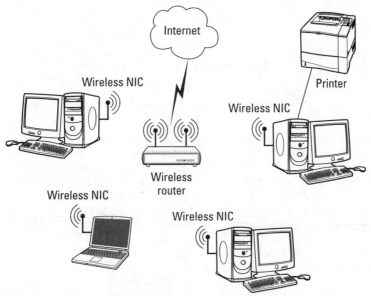

Figure 60-6: Four computers connected through a wireless router

Mixed-Mode Networking

There's no rule that says all the computers in a network need to connect the same way. For example, at my desk here I have a few computers connected to one another using a Gigabit Ethernet hub, gigabit NICs, and Cat 6 cables. In addition to my computers, I have a phoneline bridge connected to that hub. My kids' computers, from the other side of the house, connect to that bridge through phonelines.

I also have a wireless access point connected to that Ethernet bridge, and a notebook computer with a wireless NIC that connects to that access point. It's all one little network sharing a single Internet connection, printers, and files. Some computers connect by Ethernet net cable, some by phoneline, and one connects wirelessly. It's what you'd call a *mixed-mode* network. Figure 60-7 illustrates the idea.

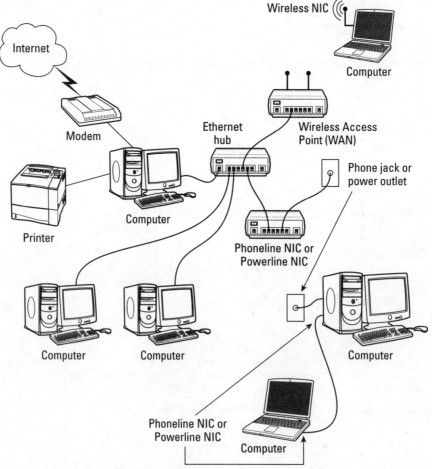

Figure 60-7: Example of a mixed-mode LAN

When it comes to networking, the possibilities are endless. All of the examples presented so far are just examples and aren't intended to show limitations. For example, you can have as many computers as you want in a LAN. You're not limited to three or four computers. You're basically limited to the number of Ethernet slots in your network hub or router.

Though, even the number of plugs on the hub isn't much of a limitation. With most products you can plug an entire hub into one port of another hub. You can keep adding hubs and computers to the network for as business growth requires.

Acquiring and Installing Network Hardware

Now that you know what you need to network two or more computers, you need to purchase and install networking hardware. There's little I can do to help you with that, except give you a couple quick pointers:

✦ If you're not too keen on opening the computer case and installing things inside the computer, consider getting hardware that connects to the computer via USB ports. Typically you just plug the devices in, and you're done.

✦ If you'll be adding a notebook to the network, you'll probably want a PC Card NIC (not to be confused with a PCI card, which goes in a motherboard slot inside the computer).

If you're new to all of this and just want to see what some of this stuff looks like, here are some Web sites you can visit. They're all network hardware manufacturers, not retailers:

✦ D-Link: www.d-link.com

✦ Gigafast: www.gigafast.com

✦ LinkSys: www.linksys.com

✦ Netgear: www.netgear.com

✦ SMC Networks: www.smc.com

✦ TrendNET: www.trendnet.com

✦ U.S. Robotics: www.usr.com

In terms of actually purchasing the products, you can find these products at any store that sells computer supplies, including many of the large office supply chains such as Staples and OfficeMax. Of course, you can buy the devices online at any Web site that sells computer stuff. Shopping jaunts include Web sites such as www.amazon.com, www.cdw.com, www.cyberguys.com, www.networkwarehouse.com, www.officemax.com, www.staples.com, www.tigerdirect.com, www.walmart.com, just to name a few.

Once you've acquired the hardware, you need to install it. I can't help you much there either. You'll have to follow the manufacturer's instructions on that one, because there is no one-rule-fits-all when it comes to installing hardware. As a general rule of thumb, you'll probably want to:

✦ Get the hub or router (if any) set up first.

✦ Install the network interface cards second.

✦ Connect all the cables last.

Once all the hardware is connected and installed, you're ready to set up the network. That part isn't so complicated because a wizard will walk you through each step. We'll get to that in the next chapter. As far as this chapter goes, it's time to . . .

Wrap Up

A local area network (LAN) consists of two or more computers that can communicate with one another through networking hardware. Multiple computers in a network can share a single Internet account, share printers, and share files and folders. Moving and copying files between networked computers is a simple matter of dragging and dropping. No fumbling around with floppies, CDs, or other removable disks required. Main points to remember when it comes to buying network hardware:

✦ The first step to creating a LAN is to purchase the computer networking hardware.

✦ Each computer in the network needs a network interface card (NIC) installed.

✦ Ethernet LANs provide the fastest speeds, but require running special Ethernet cables.

✦ Phoneline and powerline networks let you use wiring that's already in your house to connect computers.

✦ Wireless networking provides complete freedom from cables and wires.

✦ USB networking devices are easy to install and don't require opening the computer case.

✦ On a notebook computer you can use a PC Card NIC (not to be confused with PCI card) to connect to the network.

✦ After you acquire your network hardware, you have to set it all up per the manufacturer's instructions. Once you've finished that step, you're ready to run the Network Setup Wizard to get all that hardware working.

✦   ✦   ✦

Setting Up Your Network

Once you've purchased and installed networking hardware, as described in Chapter 60, you're ready to set up your network. Windows XP SP2 provides two wizards to simplify the job, the Network Setup Wizard for wired networks, and the Wireless Network Setup Wizard for wireless networks based on 802.11 specifications.

This chapter describes how to use the Wizards for different types of hardware setups. Remember, you should always follow the instructions that came with your networking hardware first. After all, those instructions are written for the exact products you've purchased. Use this chapter as a supplement to make sure that you're using the latest Windows XP SP2 versions of the network setup wizards.

Before You Begin

Before you begin, make sure that you've set up all your network hardware as instructed by the hardware manufacturer. If you'll be adding any non-Windows XP computers to the network, you'll need a blank floppy disk. The Network Setup Wizard will tell you when to insert the disk. If the Non-Windows XP computer you plan to add doesn't have a floppy disk drive, you can skip the floppy and add that computer to the network using your original Windows XP CD.

Caution   Read and follow the network hardware manufacturer's instructions to a tee before you run the Network Setup Wizard. If there's any conflict between what they say, and what's stated in this chapter, do as the manufacturer's instructions say. Failure to do so will lead to many hours of hair-pulling frustration!

Close any open programs and documents before you start the Network Setup Wizard. How you start the wizard, and what you choose along the way, depends on your network hardware. Here's what to look, depending on your network configuration:

+ If you have an Ethernet, phoneline, or powerline network (not a wireless network), and your modem is inside of, or connected to, one computer in the network, you'll use Internet Connection Sharing (ICS) to share a single Internet account. See the section titled "Setting Up a Wired Network with an ICS Host."

✦ If you have a router or residential gateway that all computers in your network connect to, you will *not* use Internet Connection Sharing. Each computer will have its own direct access to your Internet account via the router. See the section titled "Setting Up a Wired Network with a Router."

✦ If you have a wireless network, see the section titled "Setting Up a Wireless Network" later in this chapter.

✦ If you want to set up a Bluetooth Personal Area Network, see "The World of Bluetooth" in Chapter 51.

If you're setting up a mixed mode network, set up only the wired network first. If you have two or more wired networks, set up whichever network will provide the Internet connection first. For example, if you have several computers connected to a router that provides Internet access, set up that network first. If you have a modem connected to one computer in the network, set up that computer first. Then, set up other computers in that network that connect by the same means; Ethernet, phoneline, or powerline.

Setting Up a Wired Network with an ICS Host

The method for setting up a network described here applies only for a network that's connected by cables (not a wireless network). It also only applies if you're using a modem to connect to the Internet. If you're using a router, see the section titled "Setting up a Wired Network with a Router." If you're setting up a wireless network, see the sections on setting up a wireless network.

The scenario where these instructions do apply is illustrated in Figure 61-1. Only one computer in the network is connected to the Internet. That computer might have an internal modem that connects directly to a phone or cable jack on the wall. Or, it might have a external modem that connects to that one computer and a wall jack. That same computer uses a separate plug and cable to connect to the network hub.

In such a network, the computer that connects to the wall jack (or modem and wall jack) is the only computer that can access the Internet on its own. We call that computer the *Internet Connection Sharing Host*, or ICS Host for short. You must know, beforehand, which computer has that Internet connection. If you don't, and try to guess your way through it, your network won't work. To play it safe, you should sit down at the computer, and make sure you can get online. Leave that computer online as you go through the Network Setup Wizard described next.

Setting Up the ICS host

With all your hardware in place, and your ICS host online, you're ready to start the Network Setup Wizard. Here's how:

1. Click the **Start** button, and choose **Control Panel**.

2. If Control Panel opens in Category view, click the **Network and Internet Connections** icon.

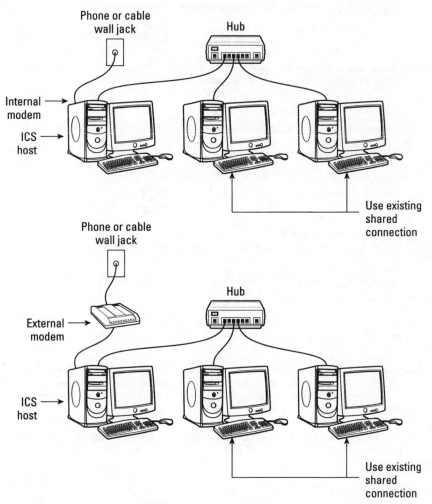

Figure 61-1: Example of networks with an ICS host

3. Open the **Network Setup Wizard** icon.

4. Read the first Wizard page, click **Next>**, read the second Wizard page, and click **Next>**.

5. On the third Wizard page, shown in Figure 61-2, choose the first option, **This computer connects directly to the Internet. The other computers on my network connect to the Internet through this computer.** Then click **Next>**.

6. On the next wizard page, highlight the item that represents your Internet connection. Most likely you'll see "modem" as part of that name, as in Figure 61-3. Click **Next>**.

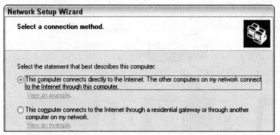

Figure 61-2: Select a Connection Wizard page.

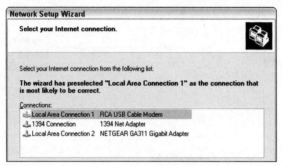

Figure 61-3: Select your Internet Connection Wizard page.

7. If you have multiple network connections (or an IEEE 1394 port), the next wizard page asks which one provides the connection to your local network. Choose the name that matches the brand name of your network interface card, as in the example shown in Figure 61-4, and then click **Next>**.

Tip

A *private connection* is a network connection between any two computers within your own network.

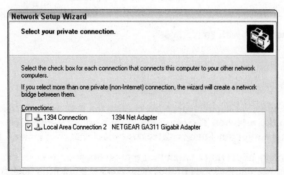

Figure 61-4: Select your private connection Wizard page.

Caution

If your computer already has a name that was provided by your ISP, do not change the Computer Name option in the next step.

8. The next wizard page asks for a computer description and name. Both names will appear in icons in My Network Places, so keep them short. You can use spaces in the description, but do not include any spaces in the name. Figure 61-5 shows an example. Click **Next>** after entering a description and name.

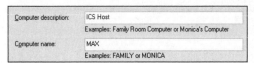

Figure 61-5: Computer name and description Wizard page

9. The next page asks that you name the workgroup. The default name is MSHOME and there's no reason to change that. If you do change it, do not include any spaces in the name you provide. Click **Next>**.

10. The next wizard page asks about file and printer sharing. Choose the first option, **Turn on file and printer sharing**, as shown in Figure 61-6. Choosing the second option will firewall the connections between computers, and you don't want that. **Click Next>**.

Cross-Reference

See Chapter 26 for more information on Windows Firewall. The sharing referred to in this wizard page is strictly for sharing between computers within your own network, not sharing on the Internet.

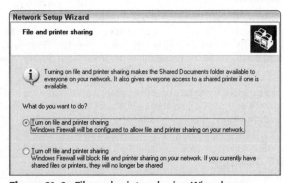

Figure 61-6: File and printer sharing Wizard page

11. The next page will review your selections. Click **Next>** and wait for the wizard to configure the computer.

12. When you get to the page shown in Figure 61-7, you have four choices. The first three apply only if you'll be adding non-XP computers to the network, such as a Windows 98 computer. If you won't be adding any non-XP computer, choose the last option, **Just finish the Wizard**.

Note

If you intend to add non-XP computers to your network, see "Adding Non-Windows XP Computers to your Network" later in this chapter.

Figure 61-7: Almost done

13. When you get to the last wizard page, click the **Finish** button.

That's it for the computer that's connected directly to the Internet. You'll need to run the Network Setup Wizard on every computer in your network, as discussed next.

Setting up other computers

You need to run the Network Setup Wizard on each of the remaining computers in your network. You'll use the Network Setup Wizard on those computers. But the way you answer the questions will be slightly different. I'll explain how those answers will be different in a moment. But first, make sure that you are still online, or can get online, from the ICS host. You want a live Internet connection as you set up other computers in the network.

You must run the Network Setup Wizard on the computer you plan to add to the network next. So, go to the next computer and repeat the steps above on that computer. Just me careful how you answer the wizard questions, because some of your answers will be different, as in the sections that follow.

Selecting a connection method

When you're setting up a computer other than the ICS host, and you get to the Select a Connection Method page in the Network Setup Wizard, make sure that you choose the second option, This computer connects to the Internet through a residential gateway or through another computer on my network, as shown in Figure 61-8.

Computer name and description

When you get to the wizard page that asks for a computer name and description, make sure you give each computer a unique name. Remember, the name should be one word (no spaces), like the examples shown in the wizard, FAMILY or MONIC.

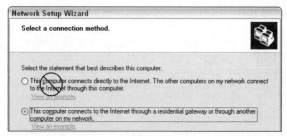

Figure 61-8: Choose the second option on all computers except the ICS host.

Workgroup name

On the wizard page that asks for the workgroup name, make sure that you use the same name for every computer. Choosing the suggested name, MSHOME, is your best bet, because it's the default and you don't have to worry about misspelling it on one of the computers in your network.

File and printer sharing

Choose *Turn on file and printer sharing* on every computer in your network. Turning off file and printer sharing on any computer will make that computer inaccessible to other computers within your network.

Completion

When you've completed the Wizard, choose *Just finish the wizard . . .* , and then click the Next> button. There's no need to create another Network Setup Disk, even if there are other non-XP computers in the network. Click Finish on the last wizard page. If you used a floppy disk or CD to start the Network Setup Wizard on this computer, remove that disk from its drive now.

Remember, you need to run the Network Setup Wizard on every computer in your network. When you've finished, you should be able to get online from every computer in the network. You should now be able to go straight to Chapter 63 to view shared resources on your network. If you feel that not all resources are available, see Chapter 62.

Setting Up a Wired Network with a Router

If your computer connects to the Internet trough a residential gateway or router, there won't be an Internet Connection Sharing host. With a residential gateway, you'll likely have an Ethernet hub to which all computers, and the gateway, attach. The gateway, in turn, connects to a cable or DSL modem which in turn connects to a phone jack or cable jack on the wall, as shown in Figure 61-9.

A router behaves in much the same was as a residential gateway, but everything is combined in a single unit. In fact, the router will look like a modem. But the big difference is that you can connect several computers — not just one computer — to the router. Figure 61-10 shows an example.

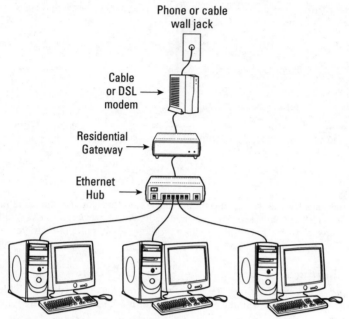

Figure 61-9: Sample residential gateway network

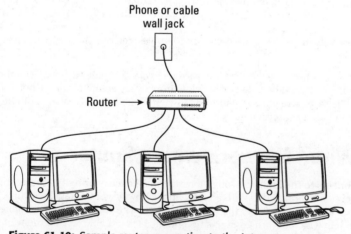

Figure 61-10: Sample router connection to the Internet

 Caution Before you run the Network Setup Wizard, make sure that you read and follow all the instructions that came with your router. Only use the Network Setup Wizard if your router manufacturer tells you to.

With a router or residential gateway, your first step will usually be to get online from one computer. You'll need to refer to instructions that came with your router, as well as your ISP's instructions, to do that. Make sure that you're online at that computer, and stay online until you've run the Network Setup Wizard. Then, follow these steps to start the wizard:

1. Click the **Start** button, and choose **Control Panel**.

2. If Control Panel opens in Category View, click the **Network and Internet Connections** icon.

3. Open the **Network Setup Wizard** icon.

4. Read the first wizard page, click **Next>**, read the second wizard page, and click **Next>**.

5. On the third wizard page, shown in Figure 61-11, choose the second option, **This computer connects to the Internet trough a residential gateway or through another computer on my network,** and then click **Next>**.

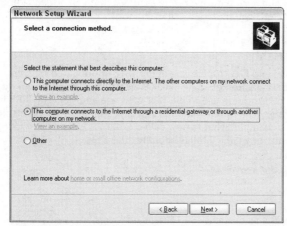

Figure 61-11: Choose second option for all computers in a router/gateway network.

6. Follow the remaining wizard instructions based on the guidelines below:

   • When you get to the page that asks for a computer description and name, make sure that you give each computer a unique name and description. Do not use blank spaces in the computer name.

   • When asked for a workgroup name, make sure that you make each computer a member of the same workgroup (for example, MSHOME).

   • If you're given the option to turn file and printer sharing on or off, choose the **Turn On** option.

7. When asked if you want to create a Network Setup Disk, you can choose **Just finish the Wizard . . .**, unless you intend to add Non-Windows XP computers to the network.

Note   If you intend to add non-Windows XP computers to your network, see "Adding Non-XP Computers to your Network" later in this chapter.

When you get to the last Wizard page, click Finish. You need to go to each computer in your network and repeat the preceding steps. Make sure that you vary only the computer name and description from one computer to the next. All other Network Setup Wizard options should be the same on every computer in your network.

After you've run the Network Setup Wizard on every computer in your network, head to Chapter 63, where you'll learn how to view, and use, shared network resources.

Setting Up a Wireless Network

There's something about the term "wireless" that makes it seem as though it must be easier than "wired." In truth, wireless networking is quite a bit more complicated terminology-wise. There are lots of buzzwords and acronyms everyone assumes that you already know. So, before we get into this topic, let's get all of that out of the way.

The 802.11 standard

The International of Electrical and Electronics Engineers, Inc., abbreviated IEEE and pronounced *EYE-triple-E* is an organization of some 360,000 electrical engineers who develop many of the standards that PC products use to interact with one another. The IEEE isn't big on giving fancy names to things. They prefer numbers (which somehow seems fitting). Names often get tacked on later. For example, what is now called Ethernet is actually IEEE 802.3. What Apple calls FireWire and Sony calls iLink is actually IEEE 1394.

Note   The home page for IEEE is at www.ieee.net.

Note   See Chapter 60 for specifics on different 802.11 standard flavors.

IEEE created the 802.11 standard for most wireless networking today. Several revisions to the original specification have been proposed, with 802.11a, 802.11b, and 802.11g being the three that actually have made it to market as I write this chapter. Most likely you'll be using 802.11b or 802.11g, because they're the standards to which most of the recently released wireless networking products adhere. And that's about all you really need to know about 802.11 right now.

Access Point, SSID, WEP, and WPA

Wireless networking requires some kind of *wireless access point*, also called a *base station*. The base station is the central unit with which all computers in the network communicate. It's the same idea as a hub in Ethernet networking. It's just that there are no wires connecting computers to the access point. Instead, each computer has a wireless network interface card (NIC), as illustrated in Figure 61-12.

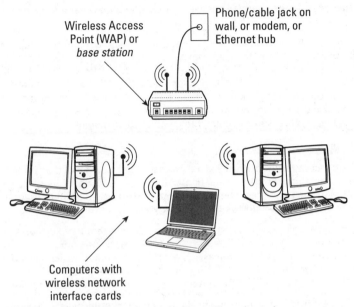

Wireless Access
Point (WAP) or
base station

Phone/cable jack on
wall, or modem, or
Ethernet hub

Computers with
wireless network
interface cards

Figure 61-12: Wireless communications all go through an access point or base station.

The access point in a wireless network plays the same role as the hub in a wired network, in that all traffic goes to the access point first, and is passed on to the appropriate destination from there. The problem is, with wireless networks, you have radio waves, which aren't confined to the inside of a wire. Radio waves go all over the place, just like when you throw a rock in water and make waves that spread out in a circle.

The radio waves can be a problem when you have multiple wireless networks that are close to each other. For example, let's say that a company has several departments, and each department has its own, separate wireless network. If the departments are fairly close to each other in the same building, then it's possible that network messages from one department might get picked up by another department's wireless access point, which in turn might send the message off to a computer in its own network rather than to the correct recipient.

To avoid that problem, you need some means of discriminating among multiple wireless access points. For example, you need some means of setting rules like "these six computers in the marketing department communicate only with each other through access point *X*, while these 12 computers in Accounting communicate with each other, only, through access point *Z*." The way you do that in today's wireless networking is through things like networks names, SSID, WEP, and WPA.

About SSIDs

Every wireless network has a unique name called a *service set identifier* (SSID) or just a *wireless network name* for simplicity. The access point in the network holds the SSID, and broadcasts it out at regular intervals. When you start a wireless network computer, it scans the airwaves for SSID. When you set up a wireless network access point (by reading the manufacturer's instructions, of course), you assign an SSID to your access point.

The name you assign doesn't have to be anything fancy. But it should be unique enough to avoid conflict with any close neighbors who also have wireless networks. The SSID doesn't provide any real network security. After all, the access point broadcasts the SSID out some distance from the access point. So if some hackers happened to be driving by with a notebook computer, they might be able to pick up the name or your wireless LAN from the car. Then they could join your network and receive data being sent by computers in your network. WEP and WPA are encryption tools designed to avoid such intrusions.

About WEP and WPA

Open System Wired Equivalent Protocol (WEP) is a wireless security protocol that protects wireless network data from falling into the wrong hands. Before any information leaves your computer, it's encrypted using a WEP key. The key is a simple string of characters that you can generate automatically, or have Windows generate for you.

Wi-Fi Protected Access (WPA) is a newer and stronger encryption system that supports modern EAP security devices such as smart cards, certificate, token cards, one-time passwords, and biometric devices. Eventually, IEEE will release a new 802.11i standard which will offer the type of security currently found only in WPA. If your wireless networking hardware supports both WEP and WPA, you should go with WPA because that's the wave of the future.

Configuring WEP and WPA keys was a real problem for nontechnical home users. To simplify matters, Windows XP SP2 has a new Wireless Network Setup Wizard that takes you though the steps of creating an SSID and encryption keys. Ideally, you'll want to use a small USB flash drive (also called *a jump drive* or *thumb drive*) that you can carry from one computer to the next while setting up the network. The Wireless Network Setup Wizard will automatically use the security data on the drive to correctly configure each computer in the network.

Installing the wireless networking hardware

The most critical step in setting up a wireless network is installing the hardware devices. It's imperative that you follow the instructions that came with the device to a tee, as guessing almost never works. In particular, it's important to note that even devices that plug into a hot-pluggable port like USB devices or a PC Card need you to install drives *before* you install the hardware device. That's unusual for hot-pluggable devices, and most people just assume that they can plug in the device and go. But it just doesn't work that way with wireless networking devices.

Finding available networks

The main trick to wireless networking is setting up the base station (access point). Typically, you do this by choosing one computer to operate the access point, and you configure the access point from that computer. There you give the network its name (SSID) and choose your encryption method. The access point then begins transmitting that name at regular intervals.

On any computer that's to join the LAN, you install a wireless network adapter. On a notebook computer, it's likely to be a PC Card that you slide into the PCMCIA slot on the computer. On a desktop computer, you can install an internal wireless network adapter, connect one to a USB port, or even slide one into a Compact Flash slot.

Once you've installed the network adapter, you can check for available networks by following these steps:

1. Open your **Network Connections** folder from Control Panel or My Network Places.

Tip   See Chapter 6 for tips on adding My Network Places and Network Connections icons to your Start menu and desktop.

2. Select the icon that represents your wireless network connection.

3. Click on **View available wireless networks** under Network Tasks in the Explorer bar.

You'll see a list of available networks, as in the example shown in Figure 61-13. Your own network's name should appear in the list. For example, in the Figure I have access to an unsecured wireless network with the name (SSID) linksys. (My wireless network, which I only use for one computer, is rather old. I'm not recommending that you use unsecured wireless networking. I just haven't yet gotten around to upgrading to updating to 802.11g and encrypting my network.)

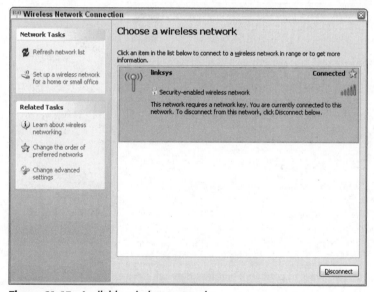

Figure 61-13: Available wireless networks

Connecting to a Wireless LAN

To connect a computer to your wireless LAN, make sure you're within range of a wireless access point. Then follow these steps:

1. Click the **Start** button and choose **All Programs** ➪ Accessories ➪ Communications ➪ Wireless Network Setup Wizard.

Tip

To create a desktop shortcut to the Wireless Network Setup Wizard, right-click its icon on the Communications submenu and choose Send To ➪ Desktop (create shortcut).

2. Read the first wizard page, and click **Next>**.

3. Assuming that you've already set up your access point as per the manufacturer's instructions, choose **Add new computers or devices to the '*ssid*' network**, where *ssid* is the name you've assigned to your wireless network. Then click **Next>**.

4. The next wizard page (see Figure 61-14) gives you two methods of setting up the network.

   • **Use a USB flash drive (recommended):** If you have a USB flash drive (also called a *thumb drive* or *jump drive*), and your access point supports the use of such drives, choose this option.

   • **Set up a network manually:** If you don't have a flash drive, choose this option. You'll later be given the option to print data needed to set up other devices.

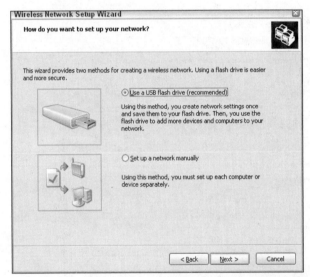

Figure 61-14: Two ways to configure wireless network devices

5. Click **Next>**, follow the remaining wizard instructions, and then click **Finish**.

Once you're connected, you'll see a notification like the example at the top of Figure 61-15. You can check the status of your connection at any time just by pointing to that icon, as in the center of that same figure. Right-clicking the notification icon provides handy shortcuts to Network Connections and other wireless network features.

About the Notification Icon

If you don't see an icon for your wireless network connection, check to make sure it's not just hidden by clicking the < button at the left side of the notification area. If you see it in the hidden icons, right-click the clock, choose Customize Notifications, and set the Wireless Network Connection icon to Always Show or Hide When Inactive. Then, click OK in each open dialog box.

If the icon isn't visible at all on the notification area, open your Network Connections folder, right-click the Wireless Network Connection icon and choose Properties. At the bottom the dialog box that open choose *Show icon in notification area when connected*. You may also want to choose the option beneath that one to see notifications or limited or no connectivity. Click OK, and close the Network Connections folder.

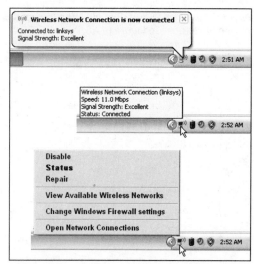

Figure 61-15: Wireless network notification and notification icon

Fixing limited connectivity

One potential point of confusion with wireless networking is the difference between weak signal strength and limited connectivity. When you see a "caution" sign (yellow triangle with exclamation point) on the wireless adapter's notification area, that's an indication of limited connectivity causes by encryption problems rather than signal strength. Simply pointing to the icon shows the signal's strength.

When you have limited connectivity, but good signal strength, the problem is more likely one of an invalid network address or an encryption problem. There are a couple of ways to approach the problem. Follow these steps:

1. Right-click the Wireless Network Connection icon in the Notification area, and choose **Open Network Connections**.

2. In Network Connections, right-click the Wireless Network Connection icon and choose **Properties**.

3. Click the **Support** tab, and then click **Repair**. Wait for the repair to complete.

Note   If you can't find a Support tab or Repair option, right-click the wireless network icon in the Notification area and choose Repair.

4. If the problem persists, repeat Step 2 and click on the **Wireless Networks** tab.

5. Click on the network name under Preferred Networks, and then click the **Properties** button beneath the list. You'll see options like those in Figure 61-16.

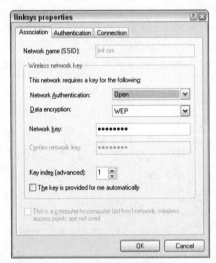

Figure 61-16: Wireless network notification and notification icon

6. Make sure the Data Encryption option is set to the appropriate encryption type for your network, or Disabled for an unsecured network.

7. If you chose WEP or WPA in the step above, reenter the appropriate encryption key for your network just below that option.

Note   If all else fails, run the Wireless Network Setup Wizard again to establish a new encryption type and key for the entire network.

8. Click **OK**.

When you're connected, you should see the wireless network notification icon without any warning signs. When you point to that icon, you should see a ToolTip that shows your status as Connected and other information about your wireless LAN. You may proceed to Chapter 62 to share network resources, or Chapter 63 to view existing shared resources.

Adding Non-Windows XP Computers to Your Wired Network.

As mentioned above in this chapter, the Network Setup Wizard gives you the opportunity to create a Network Setup Disk for adding non-XP computers to your LAN. How you add such a computer to your LAN depends on whether or not that computer has a floppy disk drive.

Adding a non-XP computer with a floppy drive

To add a non-XP computer to your network, make sure the computer is physically connected to the network via hardware. Turn the computer on as you normally would. Then follow these steps:

1. Insert the Network Setup floppy disk you created using the Network Setup Wizard into the floppy drive of the non-XP computer.

2. Open your My Computer folder on that computer, and then open the icon for the floppy drive, A:.

3. Double-click the **netsetup.exe** icon on the floppy disk.

4. Follow the instructions provided by the wizard.

Adding a non-XP computer without a floppy drive

If the non-XP computer you're trying to add to the network has no floppy disk drive, start that computer as you normally would. Then, follow these steps:

1. Put your original Windows XP CD into the computer's CD drive and wait for the installation options to appear

2. Choose **Perform additional tasks**.

3. Choose **Set up home or small office networking**.

4. Follow the instructions presented by the wizard.

Regardless of whether you use the floppy disk or CD, the Wizard will ask the same kinds of questions as it did on the XP computer. Remember that if you connect to the Internet through a router or residential gateway, you always choose the *This computer connects directly to the Internet . . .* option. You only choose the option to use a shared Internet connection if one of the computers in the network is acting as an ICS Host.

When you've finished, you're ready to move on to Chapters 62 and 63 where you'll learn to share resources, and use those shared resources from any computer in the network.

Wrap Up

Setting up a network requires purchasing and installing networking hardware, then running a network setup wizard and answering questions as appropriate to your hardware and situation. To summarize:

✦ Use the Network Setup Wizard, which is available from Control Panel in Classic View, to set up a wired network.

✦ If only one computer in your network connects to the Internet through a modem, that computer will act as the ICS host. Run the Network Setup Wizard on that computer first.

✦ If there's an ICS host in your computer, only that computer connects directly to the Internet. All other computers use its shared Internet connection to get online.

✦ If you network has a router or residential gateway, choose *This computer connects directly to the Internet . . .* on each computer that you add to the network.

✦ Modern wireless networking hardware is based on 802.11b and 802.11g specifications. Use the Wireless Network Setup Wizard, available in Control Panel, set up that type of network.

✦   ✦   ✦

Sharing Resources on a LAN

A local area network (LAN) consists of two or more computers
connected through some sort of networking hardware. In a local
area network, you can use *shared resources* from other computers in
much the same way as you use local resources on your own computer.
In fact, the way you do things in a LAN is almost identical to the way
you do things on a single computer.

For example, everything you learned about printing documents on
your own computer earlier in this book works just as well for printing
on a network printer. Opening a document on some other computer
in a network is no different from opening a document on your own
computer.

In this chapter, I'll briefly discuss options for using shared resources
on a network mainly to help you ensure that you're your shared
resources are, indeed, shared. Chapter 3 will discuss the topic of
using shared resources in more depth.

Some Networking Buzzwords

Like everything else computerish, networking has its own set of
buzzwords. All the buzzwords you learned in earlier chapters still
apply. But there are some new words to learn, as defined here:

- ♦ **Resource:** Anything useful, including a folder, a printer, or
  other device.

- ♦ **Shared:** A resource accessible to all users on a computer and
  to all computers within a network. A shared folder is often
  referred to as a *share* or *network share*.

- ♦ **Local computer:** The computer at which you're currently
  sitting.

- ♦ **Local resource:** A folder, printer, or other useful thing on the
  local computer or directly connected to the local computer
  by a cable. For example, if there's a printer connected to your
  computer by a cable, it's a local resource (or more specifically,
  a *local printer*).

✦ **Remote computer:** Any computer in the network other than the one at which you're currently sitting.

✦ **Remote resource:** A folder, printer, or other useful thing on some computer other than the local computer. For example, a printer connected to someone else's computer on the network is a remote resource (or more specifically, a *remote printer*).

Figure 62-1 shows an example of how the terms *local* and *remote* are always used in reference to the computer at which you're currently sitting.

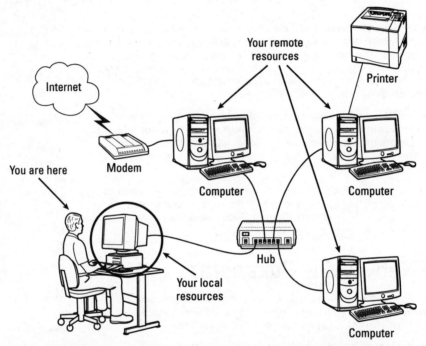

Figure 62-1: Examples of local and remote resources, from your perspective

Windows Firewall and Shared Network Resources

By default, Windows Firewall won't prevent you from sharing resources on a local area network. After all, you're not likely to encounter any malicious code or files within your own network. The bad stuff comes from the Internet. You firewall only needs to protect your network from Internet resources only, not from your own network.

If you have any trouble at all sharing printers, files, or folders, make sure you understand how Windows Firewall works. See Chapter 26, "26. Blocking Hackers with Windows Firewall" for the full scoop on configuring Windows Firewall. The key to firewall success is making sure the File and Printer Sharing exception, shown in Figure 26-4 of Chapter 26, is selected (checked) on all computers in your local network.

Using a Shared Printer

On a network, anybody can use a shared printer connected to any computer in the network. Printing to a shared printer is no different from printing to a local printer. The steps are the same:

1. While viewing the document you want to print, do whichever of the following is most convenient for you:

   • Choose **File** ⇨ **Print** from the program's menu bar.

   • Press **Ctrl+P**.

   • In some cases, you can just right-click the text you want to print and choose Print.

2. Click the name of the printer you want to use, or choose its name from the Printer drop-down list, as in the examples shown in Figure 62-2.

3. Click the **Print** button in the dialog box to start printing

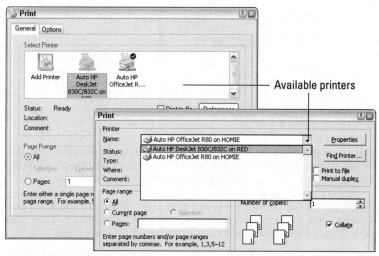

Figure 62-2: Multiple printers available in sample Print dialog boxes

If the document fails to print, the computer or printer you're trying to use may be turned off. You'll need to make sure both of those devices are turned on before you can use the printer.

If a printer on the network doesn't show up in your Print dialog box, either the printer isn't shared, or your computer doesn't know that the shared printer is available. Both problems are easily fixed, as described in the next sections.

Sharing a printer

Printers in a local area network will usually be connected to one of the computers in that network. To ensure that the printer is shared, so everybody in the network can use it, follow these steps:

Tip   With the right hardware, you can connect a printer directly to a LAN without going through a computer. With that type of arrangement, you need only to make sure that the printer is turned on.

1. Go to the computer to which the printer is connected by cable. If either is turned off, turn on the printer first and the computer second.

2. Click the **Start** button, and choose **Printers and Faxes**. Or, if that option isn't available, click the Start button, and choose Control Panel. Click Printers and Faxes (if you see that option); then, open the Printers and Faxes icon.

3. Click the icon that represents the printer you want to share.

4. Click **Share this printer** under Printer Tasks in the Explorer bar. Or, right-click the printer's icon, chose Properties, and click the Sharing tab in the dialog box that opens.

5. Choose **Share this printer**; then, type a name for the printer as in the example shown in Figure 62-3. Click **OK** in the dialog box.

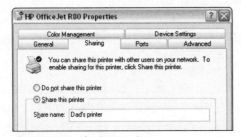

Figure 62-3: Sharing a printer

The printer's icon will show the little sharing hand. The printer should show up automatically in all network computers' Print dialog boxes. In case the printer doesn't show up on a particular computer, the next section will explain how to make it show up.

Tip   To add a Printers and Faxes option to your Start menu, right-click the Start button and choose Properties. Click the Customize button; then, click the Advanced tab in the dialog box that opens. Select (check) Printers and Faxes in the list of Start Menu Items. Click OK.

Adding a shared printer to your computer

If you know that a printer on the network is shared, but you still can't access the printer from your computer, add the printer to your Printers and Faxes folder manually. Here's how:

1. Make sure that the printer, and the computer to which it's attached, are turned on and shared.

2. Sit at the computer that cannot access the shared printer.

3. Click the **Start** button, and choose **Printers and Faxes**. Or, click the Start button, and choose Control Panel. Click **Printers and Faxes** (if you see that option); then, open the **Printers and Faxes** icon.

Advanced Sharing Security

In this chapter I'm assuming that you're using simple file sharing, which is the only kind that works on a home or small office network. More advanced sharing and security options are only available on domain networks that use centralized administration on a Windows Server domain controller. Windows XP can't *provide* advanced sharing capabilities, it can only make those options available on XP Professional computers that are configured as domain networking clients.

If your Sharing and Security tabs don't look like the examples presented in this chapter, you've most likely disabled simple file sharing in the Folder Options dialog box. To get in sync with the dialog boxes you see in this chapter, turn the recommended simple file sharing back on. Choose Tools ⇨ Folder Options form the menu bar in My Documents or any other folder. In the Folder options dialog box that opens, click the View tab, and then scroll to the bottom of the Advanced Settings list. Choose (check) the *Use simple file sharing (Recommended)* option, and then click OK.

4. Under Printer Tasks in the Explorer bar, click **Add a Printer**. The Add Printer Wizard opens. Click **Next** on the first wizard page.

5. Choose *A network printer or a printer attached to another computer*; then, click **Next**.

6. Choose **Browse for a printer**. Click **Next**.

7. Scroll through the list of available printers until you find the one you want. Click the printer's name. Click **Next**.

8. Follow any additional instructions that appear on the screen; then, click **Finish** on the last wizard page.

An icon for the printer will appear in your Printers and Faxes folder. If you want to make that printer your default (which means, it's the printer used automatically if you don't specify a different printer), right-click the printer's icon and choose Set as Default Printer. The default printer's icon will display a white check mark in a black circle.

Close the Printers and Faxes window. You should be able to access the printer from any program's Print dialog box as described under Using a Shared Printer, earlier in this chapter.

Using Shared Documents and Folders

Every Windows XP computer in a network has a Shared Documents folder. The subfolders and documents in the Shared Documents folder are available to everyone in the network. Files and subfolders in your My Documents folder are private, meaning they're invisible to other computers in the network and can't be accessed from the network.

If you want to share some of the documents currently in your My Documents folder (or any subfolder within My Documents), you can just move or copy those documents to an appropriate Shared . . . folder on your local computer. For example, moving songs from your My Music folder to your Shared Music folder will instantly make all those songs available to every computer in the network. You can use any of the techniques described in Chapter 20 to move and copy files between folders on your My . . . folders and your Shared . . . folders.

If you move a document to a shared folder, there will still be only one copy of the document on the entire network. So, if some other user on the network changes the document, you're stuck with the changes.

If you want other users to be able to play around with the document, but not change your original, *copy* (don't *move*) the document to the shared folder instead. The copy in your My Documents folder will remain invisible to other users, so they can't even see it, let alone change it. Whatever havoc other users wreak on the shared copy of the document won't affect the copy in your My Documents folder at all.

Using My Network Places

All of the shared folders and documents in a network are neatly bundled together in a single folder named My Network Places. To get to all shared folders and documents on the network, open your My Network Places folder. There are two quick and easy ways to do that, as illustrated in Figure 62-4 and described here:

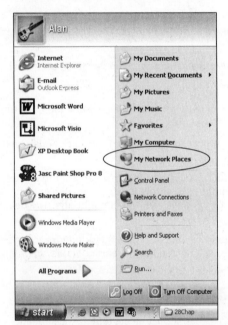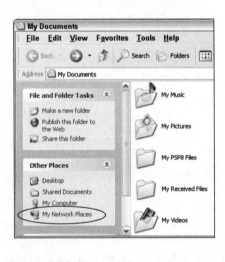

Figure 62-4: Two quick routes to your My Network Places folders

✦ Click the **Start** button and choose **My Network Places**.

✦ Or open your **My Documents** folder. (Click the **Start** button, and choose **My Documents**.) Then click **My Network Places** under Other Places in the Explorer bar.

If you don't see My Network Places on your Start menu, and want to add it, follow these steps:

1. Right-click the **Start** button, and choose **Properties**.

2. Make sure **Start Menu** (not Classic Start Menu) is selected. Then, click the **Customize** button next to Start Menu.

3. In the Customize Start Menu dialog box that opens, click the **Advanced** tab.

4. In the list of Start Menu Items that appears, scroll down to and select (check) **My Network Places**.

5. Click **OK** in both open dialog boxes.

From now on, whenever you click the Start button, the Start menu will display all the items you selected in the Start Menu Items list. Now let's get back to networking.

Opening shared documents and folders

To open, edit, or print a document on a remote computer, it's not necessary to copy that file to your computer first. You can just open it from its current location by following these steps:

1. From your own computer, open **My Network Places**. The folder containing icons for all shared resources to which you have access opens, as in the example shown in Figure 62-5.

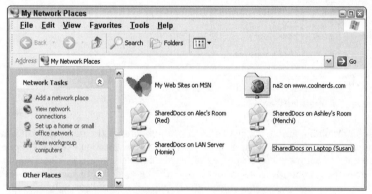

Figure 62-5: A sample My Network Places folder

 Tip   If My Network Places doesn't show everything you were expecting it to show, choose View ➪ Refresh from its menu bar. It may take a few seconds for all icons to appear.

2. Double-click the icon that represents the folder that contains the document you want to open. If necessary, navigate through subfolders until you find the document you want.

 Tip   In My Network Places, icons that look like folders represent shared folders on the local area network. Other icons might represent sites on the Internet to which you can upload files.

3. Double-click the icon for the document you want to open. Or, right-click the document's icon and choose **Open With** and the program you want to use.

The document should open normally on your computer — no differently from a document stored on your own computer's hard disk. If the document won't open because you don't have an appropriate program installed on your computer, see the "What about Sharing Programs?" sidebar that follows.

If you can't even find the shared document you're searching for, there are several possible causes:

✦ The computer on which the shared resource resides is turned off. You'll need to start that computer normally to access its shared resources.

✦ The resource you're trying to access isn't shared. You'll need to go to the computer on which the document resides and move it to a shared folder or share the folder in which the document is currently stored.

✦ The folder you need to access is already shared, but needs to be added to your local computer's My Network Places folder manually.

Solutions to the latter two problems are described in Chapter 64. But first, there's the possibility that when you double-click a shared folder's icon, the folder won't even open. Instead, you'll see an error message like the one in Figure 62-6.

Figure 62-6: Error message that could appear when you double-click a shared folder's icon

The most common and simple cause of such a problem is that the computer on which the shared folder resides is either turned off or disconnected from the network. Or, perhaps the person using that computer has stopped sharing the folder. If you check and eliminate all those possibilities, the Windows Firewall may be blocking access to the share. Make sure that the File and Printer Sharing exception is enabled on both computers' network connections as discussed under "Configuring Windows Firewall" in Chapter 26.

What about Sharing Programs?

While you can share folders and documents freely on a LAN, there's no way to share programs. You can only run programs currently installed on your computer and accessible from your All Programs menu. If you try to open a document on another computer, but don't have the appropriate program for that document type, you can't open the document.

Don't' bother trying to copy an installed program from one computer to another — it won't work. Only programs that you specifically install on your own computer will run on your computer.

The only solution will be to install the necessary program on your own computer. If the program you need is a freebie, like Adobe Acrobat Reader, you can download and install the program in the usual manner. (For Acrobat Reader, go to www.adobe.com and click Get Acrobat Reader.

Sharing folders

All documents within a shared folder—including documents within subfolders of that shared folder—are accessible to all users of the network. If you're using an older version of Windows that doesn't have a Shared Documents folder, you can create a folder and share it. Or, you can just share the folder as it stands. While the exact techniques and dialog boxes for sharing folders vary slightly from one version of Windows to the next, the general procedure described as follows will usually do the trick:

1. On your local computer, open **My Documents**, and navigate to the parent of the folder you want to share, so you can see the icon that represents the folder you want to share.

2. Right-click the icon of the folder you wish to share, and choose **Sharing and Security**.

Tip   In some versions of Windows, you may have to right-click the icon, choose Properties, and look for the Sharing options within the dialog box that opens. If in doubt, search that version of Windows' Help for *share*.

3. On the Sharing tab of the dialog box that opens, choose **Share this folder on the network**, as shown in Figure 62-7.

Figure 62-7: Sharing a folder and letting other people change its documents

4. Optionally, do either or both of the following:

   • Give this folder a unique name, which will appear only in My Network Places. On your own computer, the folder will retain its original name.

   • If you want other users to be able open and change the documents in the folder, select the **Allow network users to change my files** option. If you want only others users to open and view—but not change—documents in the folder, clear that checkbox.

5. Click **OK** in the dialog box.

Once shared, the folder's icon will display the sharing hand. To unshare the folder at any time in the future—so network users can't get to it anymore—repeat the preceding steps and click the Share this folder on the network checkbox.

Helping shared resources appear automatically

The folder should show up in My Network Places on all computers throughout the network automatically. If it doesn't show up on one of the computer in your LAN, the option to automatically search for shared resources might be disabled on that specific computer.

To check that setting, and enable it, choose Tools ⇨ Folder Options from the menu bar in My Network Places. In the Folder Options dialog that opens, click the View tab. Choose (check) the *Automatically search for network folders and printers* in the list of advanced settings, and then click OK.

Adding a shared folder to your My Network Places folder

Normally, your My Network Places folder will keep itself up to date, always showing shared folders from all computers in the network. Once in a while, you might need to give it a little slap upside the head, by choosing View ⇨ Refresh from its menu bar, to make it go out and check again. But if you know for certain that there's some shared folder out there in the network that isn't showing up, you can manually add that folder by performing the following steps:

1. On your local computer, open your **My Network Places** folder.

2. Under Network Tasks in the Explorer bar, click **Add a network place**. The first page of the Add Network Place Wizard opens. Click its **Next** button.

3. In the next wizard page, click **Choose another network location**; then, click **Next>**.

4. Click the **Browse** button on the next wizard page.

5. In the Browse For Folder dialog box that opens, expand the **Entire Network** and **Microsoft Windows Network** names by clicking the + signs.

6. Expand the name that represents your workgroup (typically MSHOME or Workgroup).

7. Click the + sign next to the name of the computer on which the shared folder is located. Shared folders on that computer are listed below the computer name, as in the example shown in Figure 62-8.

8. Click the name of the folder for which you need an icon; then, click **OK** in the Browser for Folders button. Click the **Next** button.

9. A suggested name for the icon appears. You can change that name, if you like, to something more meaningful. (The name change will be applied to your My Network Places folder only). Then click **Next>**.

10. On the last wizard page, select or clear the checkbox, depending on whether or not you want to open the folder immediately; then, click the **Finish** button.

An icon for the shared folder will be visible in your My Network Places folder from now on, so you can just double-click that icon at any time in the future to open the folder and view its current content.

Figure 62-8: Adding a link to a shared folder named Conference Photos on a computer named Spot

Tip You're free to rename icons in your My Network Places folder as you see fit (right-click any icon, and choose Rename). The new names won't have any effect on names outside of your folder.

Sharing a Disk Drive

Windows XP will allow you to share a disk drive, but will warn youthat doing so poses some risks. The warning is a bit misleading though, because it really only applies to sharing your entire C: drive, or at most an entire hard drive. The fact of the matter is, if you want to share a floppy, Zip, CD, DVD, or thumb drive or a Smart Card, you don't have much choice other than to share the entire drive. The only other option would be a share a specific file or folder on a specific disk. But that wouldn't allow you to freely copy data to and from whatever disk happens to be in the drive at the moment.

The steps to sharing a disk drive are the same as for sharing a folder. Though you'll need to start from the My Computer folder, because that's where icons for disk drives appear. Here are the steps:

1. Go to the computer that has the disk drive you want to share.

2. Click the **Start** button, and choose **My Computer**.

3. Right-click the icon of the drive you want to share, and choose **Sharing and Security**. You won't see the usual options, but rather a warning about sharing drives. Click the link below that warning.

4. Choose **Share this folder** on the network (yes, the option reads "share this *folder...*" even though you're actually sharing a drive).

5. You will probably want to change the share name as well, because the drive letter won't be very descriptive. A short name like *Zip Drive* or *Floppy Drive* is sufficient.

6. If you want to copy files to a disk in the shared drive, choose **Allow network users to change my files**.

7. Click **OK**.

The drive's icon will show the sharing hand. Figure 62-9 shows an example where I've shared a floppy, CD-RW, Zip, and thumb drive (drive F:), as well as a slot for a memory stick (drive G:). I named the shares Floppy Drive, CD-RW Drive, Zip Drive, Thumb Drive, and Memory Stick, respectively.

Figure 62-9: Examples of shared drives with removable media

When you open My Network Places on a different computer in the network, the icon for each shared drive will look like shared folder icon. Figure 62-10 shows an example where you can see the icons from the shared drives in the My Network Places folder on a separate computer on the same network.

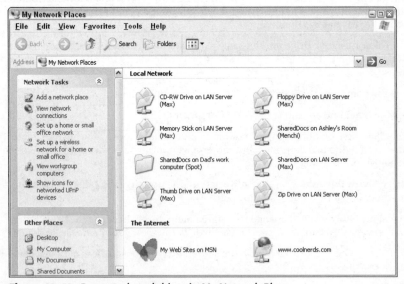

Figure 62-10: Remote shared drives in My Network Places

You can use the shared drive just as you would a local drive. Of course, the drive must contain a disk or memory card (except in the case of a thumb drive, which is basically a self-contained storage device that plugs into a USB port). Of course, CD and DVD drives are always exceptions to the rule, just by virtue of the fact that they're laser media. Chapter 63 will get into the specifics of how all that works in detail.

Wrap Up

On a network, you can share a printer, folder, file, or disk drive with other computers in the network. This allows users on other computers on the network to use the shared resource as though it were connected to their own computer. The way you share a resource is fairly simple— right-click the item's icon, choose Sharing and Security, and choose the option to share the resource. Here's a quick review of the specifics:

✦ To share the printer that's connected to the computer at which you're currently sitting, open your Printers and Faxes folder. Then, right-click the printer's icon and choose Sharing and Security.

✦ To share a folder or file from a hard drive on the current computer, navigate to the folder or file's icon, right-click that icon, and choose Sharing and Security.

✦ To share a disk drive or memory card slot that's on the computer at which you're sitting, open its My Computer folder. Right-click the icon that represents the drive you want to share, and choose Sharing and Security.

✦ In the Sharing and Security options, choose (check) the Share . . . checkbox to share the item. Clear that checkbox to stop sharing the item.

✦ The Share Name you give to an item need not match the actual name of the device. For example, you need not name a shared floppy drive just **A** as will be suggested in the dialog box. You can enter a more descriptive name such as Floppy Drive.

✦ To view shared resources on your local network, open its My Network Places folder.

✦   ✦   ✦

Using Shared Network Resources

C hapters 60 through 62 covered all the basics of setting up a LAN,
sharing resources on a local network, and access those shared
resources through your My Network Places folder. This chapter
assumes that you've already done all of that, and know how to get to,
and use, your My Network Places folder.

In this chapter, we'll delve a little deeper into using shared network
resources, focusing on things like opening and saving documents
from remote resources, moving and copying files between networked
computers, accessing remote Internet resources, and using UpPN
devices.

Opening Remote Documents

One of the advantages to having a network is that you can put documents in shared folders and open them from any computer in the network. For example, you might put all your important work documents
in a shared folder on your main work computer. If you also have a
portable computer you can use outside on sunny days (or in bed on
lazy days), you can work directly with those documents from the
remote computer.

The process is really no different from opening a document on a
local computer. You could, for instance, just navigate to the folder,
via My Network Places, in which the document is stored. Double-click
(or click) the document you want to edit, and the document will open
on the remote computer. (Providing that the remote computer has
the appropriate program installed for working with that type of
document).

Optionally, you can go through the program's Open dialog box to get
to the document. Here's how:

1. Open the program you want to use, and choose **File** ➪ **Open**
   from its menu bar.

2. In the Open dialog box, click on **My Network Places** (if available) at the left side of the Open dialog box. Or, choose My
   Network Places from the Look In drop-down list. The main pane
   of the Open dialog box contains the same icons as the local
   computer's My Network Places folder, as shown in Figure 63-1.

Figure 63-1: My Network Places in an Open dialog box

3. Open the folder for (or a parent folder to) the document. If you have to open a parent folder, just navigate down through the subfolders until you get to the document's icon.

4. Click or double-click the document's icon.

Once the document is open, you can edit it or print it however you like. When you save the document, your changes will be saved at the original location. If you want to save a local copy of the document to work with, choose File ➪ Save As from the program's menu bar, navigate to a local folder such as My Documents, and save your copy there.

Opening a read-only copy

If you try to open a document that someone already has open on another computer, you'll see a message telling you what your options are. Those options will vary from one program to the next. In Microsoft Word 2003, I got the message shown in Figure 63-2.

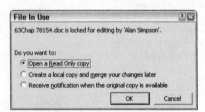

Figure 63-2: Someone else already has this document open.

You can always open a read-only copy of the document on the local computer. Then, you can choose File ➪ Save As from the program's menu bar to save a new, separate copy of the document. Once you've done that, your copy of the document will no longer be read-only, so you can edit it all you want. The only problem is, your changes won't be made to the original copy of the document.

Using merge features of Office programs

Some programs, like Microsoft Word, provide the second option, *Create a local copy and merge your documents later*, to handle the situation where another user on the network already has the document open. If you choose that second option, Word will open an editable copy of the document. If the other user closes her copy of the document while you still have yours open, you'll see the message shown in Figure 63-3. At that point, you can click the Merge to merge your changes to the original copy of the document and continue work on the document.

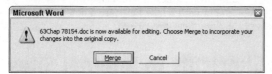

Figure 63-3: Using the Create a local copy and merge your documents later option

If the other person doesn't close his or her copy of the document before you save your copy, you'll be taken to the Save As dialog box. Word will suggest saving the file to the original folder with the original filename followed by the words *–for merge*. Later, when both copies of the document are closed, you can go to the computer on which the original copy of the document is stored and open the original document from there. Then, in Word, original location open Word choose Tools ⇨ Merge Documents from the menu bar, and follow the instructions to merge in changes from the *–for merge* copy of the document.

The third alternative, *Receive notification when the original copy is available* will also allow you to edit a copy of the document. You'd choose this option if you were reasonably sure that the other person was going to close their copy of the document before you're done. (For example, if you are the "other person," who left the document open and can just walk over to the other computer and close the document).

When you choose this option, and the other user closes their open copy of the document, you'll see the message shown in Figure 63-4. At that point, you can just click the Read-Write button to make your open copy of the document the only open copy, so that all your changes are made to the original document when you save the document.

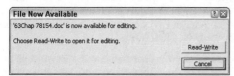

Figure 63-4: Using the Receive notification when the original copy is available option

Admittedly, I've digressed from "pure Windows" here by getting into Word options for simultaneously opening documents. Different programs will handle the situation differently. For example, I did the same little experiment with a digital photo and Paint Shop Pro. Paint Shop Pro just opened the second copy of the document as a Read-Write file with no warning whatsoever. I was able to edit, and save, both open copies of the document. Paint Shop Pro used a very simple technique to handle the situation. The most recently saved changes to the document are the ones that "stick."

In Microsoft Access, you can create a *project* and save it to a shared folder. You can also create *pages*, which are basically Access forms written in Hypertext Markup Language (HTML). Up to five people on five separate computers can then simultaneously edit data in the database through Internet Explorer and the pages.

In summary, when it comes to dealing with multiple copies of the same document open on multiple computers in a network, it's really up to the program you're using at the moment, not Windows, as to how this gets handled. Your best bet would be to check the Help or documentation that came with that program. Or, just experiment with it for a while until you get the hang of how the program is going to handle the situation. You can always choose File ⇨ Save As to save your open copy of the document with a new filename. Then decide what you want to do later, when all open copies of the document are closed.

Creating My Network Shortcuts to Internet Sites

If you have your own Web site, or permission to upload to an FTP site, or really anything on the Internet to which you can upload files, you can add a shortcut icon to that location to your My Network Places folder. Doing so will allow you to upload files to that location using the same techniques you use to save a file to your own computer.

You'll need to know the URL (address) to which you can download. Chances are you'll need a user name and password as well. The people who provide own the site to which you'll be uploading will provide that information when you set up your account. They might also provide upload instructions. But as long as you know the URL, your user name, and password, you should be able to use the technique described here in addition to whatever method they provide.

To create a shortcut to the Internet location, follow these steps:

1. Open your **My Network Places** folder.

2. Under Network Tasks in the Explorer bar, click **Add a network place**.

3. Click **Next>** on the first Wizard page.

4. If you don't see an icon for the remote site already, click on **Choose another network location**, and then click **Next>**.

5. Type the complete URL of the remote site. For example, if it's a Web site you own, include the `http://`. For instance in Figure 63-5 I'm about to create a shortcut to my `www.coolnerds.com` site. If the shortcut is to an FTP site for which you have upload permissions, use the `ftp://` prefix on the URL. Click **Next>**.

6. In the Connect To dialog box that opens, enter your user name and password as provided by the service as in Figure 63-6. If you're the only person who uses this computer, choose Remember by password so that you don't have to enter it every time you save to the site. Then click **OK**.

Tip   Don't bother trying to post stuff to my Web site by guessing my password from Figure 63-6. That's not my real user name, nor the correct password length.

7. The next wizard page will suggest the URL (without the `http://` or `ftp://` prefix) as the name of the shortcut icon. You can replace that with any name you like, because it's used only as the label for the icon. Click **Next>**.

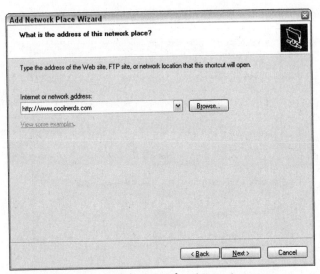

Figure 63-5: Providing the URL of an Internet resource

Figure 63-6: Enter your user name and password

8. On the last wizard page, you can select (check) the checkbox if you want to see the remote folder immediately. Or clear the checkbox if you don't want to see that right now. Then click **Finish**.

Tip The other nonfolder icons in Figure 63-7 are just custom icons I selected using the technique described in under "Choosing a Custom Icon for Folders" in Chapter 13.

When you double-click the icon for the remote site, it will open in Windows Explorer, looking much the same as any local folder on your own hard disk. You may not have quite as many options to choose from in the Explorer bar. Figure 63-8 show an example where I've opened the folder where all the files for my www.coolnerds.com site are stored.

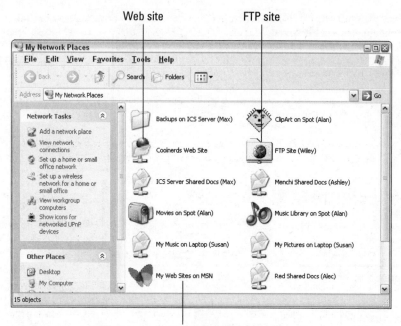

Figure 63-7: Internet site icons in My Network Places.

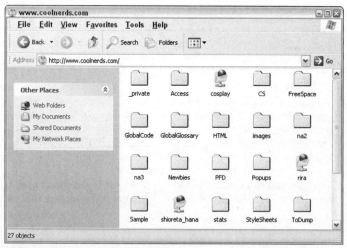

Figure 63-8: My www.coolnerds.com site as a folder in Windows Explorer

You can treat the folder as you would any other. For example, you can create a new folder, or rename or delete existing files and folders by right-clicking, just as you would in any folder on your C: drive. You can move and copy files to/from the site using any technique described in Chapter 14. Things will be slower than on your own computer, because the remote resource could be thousands of miles away. But the techniques should all be the same.

Tip   You can rename any icon, at any time, in My Network Places just as you would any other icon. Just right-click the icon, and choose Rename.

If things don't work as described here, your best resource for getting answers would be the people who provided the site. They're the only ones who know the details of that site.

Saving to a Remote Computer

Any time you save a new document—whether it's one you've created yourself, or something you're downloading—you'll get some kind of Save As dialog box. It may be titled File Download or something like that. But it will have a Save In drop-down list so that you can choose where you want to save the document.

As with the Open dialog box, you can choose My Network Places from the Save In drop-down list to get to all of the icons in your My Network Places folder, then navigate to wherever you want to save the file from there. It doesn't matter if it's a shared folder on your own network or a remove Web or FTP site—it's all the same at this point.

Downloading Programs to a Network

If you regularly download programs to install on multiple computers, consider creating a folder named Common Downloads (or something like that) within your Shared Documents folder. After you save a downloaded program file to that folder, you'll be able to install it on all the computers in the network. You have to install it one each computer individually still. But it beats downloading it on every computer, especially if you're sharing a not-so-speedy Internet connection.

I'll go through the procedure here using an example of a file I'm downloading from Tucows.com. In this example, I've already created a folder named Common Downloads in the Shared Documents folder on my main work computer (Spot). Start the download as you normally would. You'll probably have to jump through all the usual security hoops (choose Download File from the Information Bar in Internet Explorer, as at the top of Figure 63-9. Then, perhaps reclick the link that got you to that point in the Web page).

When you get to the Save/Run options, as shown at the bottom of Figure 63-10 (or Save/Open options), choose Save. (If you choose Open or Run, the program will install to the local computer only.) When the Save As (or File Download) dialog box opens, choose My Network Places from the Save In drop-down list or button icon (if available), as in Figure 63-10. If the filename of the downloaded program doesn't adequately describe the file, click the Create New Folder button, give the folder a more descriptive name, and choose that folder as the Save In location. Then, click the Save button to download the file.

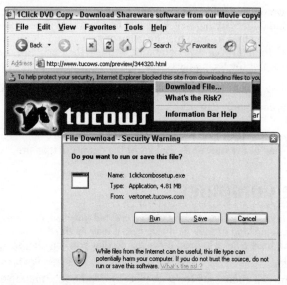

Figure 63-9: About to download and save a program

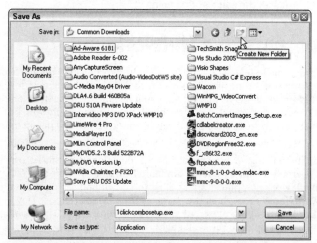

Figure 63-10: Saving a downloaded program file to the Common Downloads folder

In most cases, you should be able to install the program right from that Common Downloads folder to any computer in your network. Go to any computer and open My Network Places. Navigate to the Common Downloads folder, and the subfolder (if any) in which you placed the downloaded program file. For example, in Figure 63-11 I've navigated to the folder in which I downloaded the program I chose in Figures 63-9 and 63-10.

Figure 63-11: Icon for downloaded program file on remote computer

Once you see the icon for the downloaded program file, double-click it. The installation process should begin, so you can just follow the on-screen instructions to complete the installation. In the unlikely event that it doesn't work, you can try copying the downloaded program file to the local computer first, then open the icon from there. Or, if all else fails, go back to the original Web site from the local computer, start the download, and then choose Run or Open, when prompted, to install the program on the local computer.

Transferring Files between Computers

Moving and copying files on a LAN is virtually identical to doing so on a single computer. You can use any of the techniques described in Chapter 14 select, move, or copy files from any folder on your own computer to any shared folder or from any shared folder to any folder on your own computer. You can also use those same techniques to move and copy files between shared folders on any two remote computers on the network.

For example, let's say you're sitting at a computer named Spot, and you have a bunch of fonts on that computer that you're like to copy to another computer in the network, so you can use the same fonts on that computer. On Spot, you open your Fonts folder (you can do so from the Classic View in Control Panel. Or, from Windows Explorer get to your `C:\Windows\Fonts` folder, or `C:\Winnt\Fonts folder`).

Next, open your My Network Places folder and navigate to some shared folder on the computer to which you want to copy the fonts. (In this example, I opened the Shared Documents folder on a computer named Max. I then right-clicked within that blank folder, chose New Folder, named the new folder Copied Fonts, and opened that folder). Then, size and position for the two folders so that you can see a good portion of each, as in Figure 63-12.

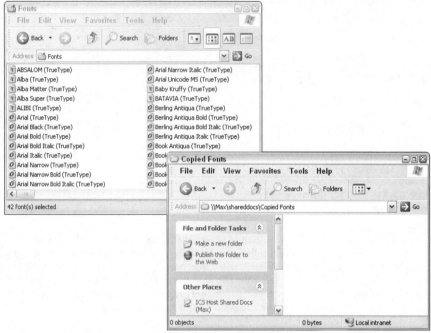

Figure 63-12: Local Fonts folder (top) and remote Copied Fonts folder (bottom)

With both folders open, as in the figure, you can select the files you want to copy in the top window using any technique you like, as discussed under "Selecting Files and Folders" in Chapter 14. To copy (rather than move) the items to the remove folder, right-drag any selected icon to the remove folder, and then choose Copy Here after you release the mouse button. (If you drag using the left mouse button, the files will be moved, rather than copied).

Universal Naming Convention (UNC)

If you have the Address bar open in Windows Explorer, and the *Display the full path in the Address bar* setting turned on, you'll see the path to the remote resource expressed in Universal Naming Convention (UNC) format. That format uses the syntax:

`\\machineName\folderpath`

where *machineName* is the name of the remote computer, and *folderpath* is the name of shared folder on that computer, followed by any subfolders with that folder. For example, while it may be too small to see in the figure, the Address bar in the lower-right corner of Figure 63-12 shows `\\Max\shareddocs\Copied Fonts`. That tells you that the main window is showing the contents of a folder named Copied Fonts in the Shared Documents folder on a computer named Max.

If you don't choose *Display the full path in the Address bar*, you'll see only the folder name (Copied Fonts in this example) in the Address bar. To set that Display full path . . . option, choose Tools ➪ Folder Options from any folder's menu bar, and click the View tab in the Folder Options dialog box. To show or hide the Address bar, choose View ➪ Toolbars ➪ Address Bar. See the "Folder Options View tab" section in Chapter 12 for more information.

That's all there is to it. As I said, it's no different from moving and copying files between folders and drives on your own computer, except that you have to use My Network Places to open the remote folder.

Mapping Drive Letters to Shared Folders

Some programs and networks require that you assign a drive letter to remote resources. You can assign any unused drive letter from E: to Z: to a resource. For example, if you already have drives E: and F: then you can assign drive letters G: through Z: to any shared resource. To map a drive letter to a shared folder:

1. Go to the computer on which you need to assign a drive letter, and open its **My Network Places** folder.

2. Choose **Tools** ⇨ **Map Network Drive** from Explorer's menu bar. The Map Network Drive dialog box opens.

3. Click the **Browse** button to open the Browse for Folder dialog box.

4. In the Browser for Folder dialog box, click the name of the shared resource to which you want to map a drive letter, so its name is selected (highlighted). For example, in Figure 63-13 I'm about to map the drive letter Y: to the shared ClipArt folder on a computer named Spot. Click **OK** after making your selections.

5. Click the **Finish** button.

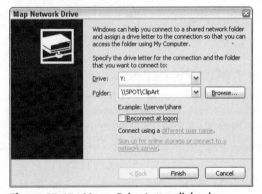

Figure 63-13: Map a Drive Letter dialog box

The remote resource will open. You can close that folder, and also close My Network Places. Since you've mapped a drive letter to the remote resource, it will appear in your My Computer folder under the Network Drives heading. Figure 63-14 shows an example where I've mapped two resources, where Y: refers to the ClipArt folder on the computer named Sport, and Z: refers to the folder named Copied Fonts on the computer named Max.

From that point on, you can access the folder either by going through My Network Places, as usual. Or, you can just open My Computer and open the resource's icon under Network Drives.

Tip   If your My Computer folders isn't arranged like the example in Figure 63-14, use the menu bar in My Computer to choose View ⇨ Arrange Icons By ⇨ Type. If headings don't appear, choose View ⇨ Arrange Icons By ⇨ Show in Groups.

Figure 63-14: Drives Y: and Z: are actually folders.

About network drives

Once you've mapped a drive letter to a shared resource, the resource becomes a *network drive*. But that's just a terminology thing. You haven't changed the shared resource, or what you can do with the resource, in any way, shape, or form. And the "drive" need not be a disk drive at all. It can be a folder. The term "network drive" just refers to the fact that the shared resource "looks like" a drive, by virtue of the fact that it has a drive letter and icon in My Computer.

Disconnecting from a network drive

In My Computer, you can disconnect from any network drive by right-clicking the drive's icon and choose Disconnect. If you originally chose Reconnect at logon, and now want to stop doing that, choose Tools ➪ Map Network Drive from the menu bar in My Computer. from the Drive drop-down list, choose the existing drive letter name. Then, choose a different shared folder from the Folder drop-down list or Browse button. Clear the Reconnect at logon checkbox, and then click Finish.

A message will ask if you want replace the existing drive letter assignment with the new one. Choose Yes. You can then disconnect from the drive by right-clicking its icon and choosing Disconnect. The network drive icon won't appear in My Computer automatically in the future either.

Installing copied fonts

As an example of where you'd actually need to use a drive letter, recall that earlier in this chapter, under "Transferring Files between Computers," I copied some fonts from the Fonts folder on one computer the a folder named Copied Fonts in the Shared Documents on the computer named Max. Simply copying the fonts isn't sufficient. You also need to install the fonts.

On the Max computer, this would require clicking the Start button and choosing Control Panel. If Control Panel opens in Category View, switch to Classic View, and then open the Fonts icon. Choose File ⇨ Install New Font from the menu bar in the Fonts folder. The Add Fonts dialog box opens.

The Folders list in the Add Fonts dialog box doesn't provide access to all your folders. So, if you can't find the folder from which you want to install icons there, you need to click the Network button and map a drive letter to the appropriate folder. For example, at the left side of Figure 63-15 I've use the Browse button to navigate to the Copied Fonts subfolder in the Shared Documents folder on the computer named Max. After clicking OK, the Map Network Drive dialog box, shown at right in that same figure, shows how I've mapped the drive letter Z: to \\Max\SharedDocs\Copied Fonts (though part of that UNC name is cut off in the figure). Because this is a one-time deal where I'm going to install some fonts, there's no need to select Reconnect at logon in this case.

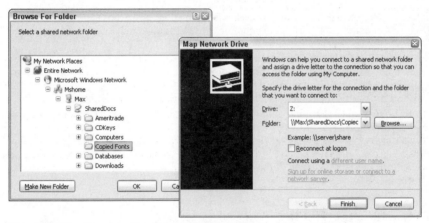

Figure 63-15: Mapping drive letter Z: to \\Max\Shared Docs\Copied Fonts

After clicking Finish in the Map Network Drive, the List Of Fonts in the Add Fonts dialog box shows the names of all the fonts I copied to the folder. Installing the fonts at that point is just a matter of clicking the Select All button, making sure that *Copy fonts to Fonts folder* is selected, clicking OK, and then click Close.

Note   For more information on installing fonts, see "Managing Fonts" in Chapter 22.

You can then close the Fonts folder. When you open a program that supports fonts and view your available fonts, you should see all the fonts you installed. In this case, there'd be no need to keep the Copied Fonts folder, because all of its fonts have been installed. So, I could delete that folder from the Shared Documents folder on Max.

Accessing UPnP Devices

Universal Plug-and-Play (UPnP) is a brand-new technology standard designed to simplify network connectivity, including connections to the Internet. The idea is that you connect the device to a network, and it configures itself to be visible and accessible to all computers in that network. Or, in the case of the Internet, the device would instantly be visible to the company that created the device.

The long-range goal of UPnP centers around the use of home automation devices. For example, you would buy a new refrigerator and connect it to the Internet. (Sounds weird, I know). When there's a problem with the refrigerator, the manufacturer gets a signal, or you call them on the phone and tell them about the problem. They can then analyze the refrigerator from their location, and perhaps fix it if it's the sort of problem that can be fixed electronically.

Other examples would be UPnP-enabled Web cams placed around the house for security or baby monitoring. You could connect a UPnP answering machine, PC, disk drive, VCR, or just about any other gadget to the Internet. You can then access all those devices from anywhere in the world where you can get Internet access. For example, Mom could take a look around the house through the Web cams. You could check your phone messages, copy files to or from your PC or UPnP drive, or program the VCR to record a TV show.

Note   If you're interested in staying up on developments in WPnP, take a look at `www.upnp.org` and `www.microsoft.com/technet/prodtechnol/winxppro/evaluate/upnpxp.mspx`.

As I write this chapter late in 2004, actual devices that support UPnP are few and far between. There are some external disk drives that support the standard. So, I can't really show you an example. But, when you open your My Network Places folder, you'll see that Windows XP SP2 is ready to support the technology as devices become available (see Figure 63-16)

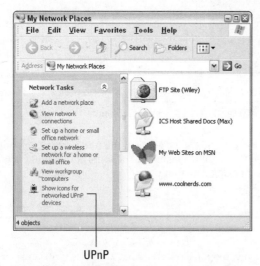

UPnP

Figure 63-16: My Network Places is ready to support UPnP devices

Clicking on *Show icons for network UPnP devices*" will install a bunch of drivers and other software required for UPnP support. Unless you already have some UPnP devices attached to your network, however, you won't actually see any new icons.

I suppose that it's somehow fitting that I end this book on that note—talking about a new technology for which there are virtually no devices yet. I figure I've typed about a million words by now. It's time for me to shut up and send this pup off to the printing presses. It's interesting to note, though, that even after a million words, there are still more things to come in the rapidly evolving world of high tech.

I hope the book has served you well. It's too bad that a million words aren't enough words to cover *everything* there is to know about Windows XP. I've tried to cover just about everything in sufficient depth to make the reading worthwhile. But you'll no doubt come across situations that I wasn't able to get to here.

You can always write to me from my Web site. (Best not to send an e-mail directly because my spam filter can't discriminate between junk mail and legitimate e-mails from readers). Just stop by www.coolnerds.com at any time. Thanks for reading, and I wish you all the best in mastering the seemingly endless capabilities of Windows XP SP2.

Wrap Up

In this chapter, we've looked at some fancy things you can do with a local network and your My Network Places folders. Here's a quick summary:

✦ To open a remote document from within a program, choose File ➪ Open from the program's menu bar, as usual. Then, choose My Network Places from the Look In drop-down list in the Open dialog box.

✦ To save a document to a remove computer, choose File ➪ Save (or File ➪ Save As), and choose My Network Places from the Save In drop-down list.

✦ To create a My Network Places icon to an Internet site, choose *Add a network place* under Network Tasks in the My Network Places Explorer bar.

✦ To move or copy files between computers in a network, use My Network Places to open the source and/or destination folders. Then, use the standard techniques described in Chapter 14 to select, move, or copy the files.

✦ If you ever buy a UPnP device and connect it to your network, you'll be able to access that device through My Network Places, providing you click that *Show icons for networked UPnP devices* link in the Explorer bar.

✦　　✦　　✦

Troubleshooting Network Problems

Troubleshooting a Wired Network

If network problems arise after you've installed all the hardware and run the appropriate Wizards for a wired network, your first step in finding a solution should be to run the Home and Office Networking Troubleshooter. Here are the steps:

1. Click the **Start** button, and choose **Help and Support**.

2. Click Fixing a Problem.

Note　If your Help and Support Center doesn't offer the Fixing a Problem option, search for network troubleshooter and click on Home and Small Office Networking Troubleshooter under Suggested Topics.

3. On each page that appears next, click the problem you're having, and then click **Next>** at the bottom of the page.

Hopefully, the troubleshooter will solve the problem for you.

Troubleshooting a Wireless Network

When problems arise with a wireless network or the Wireless Network Setup Wizard, the most likely cause will be a conflict between the hardware manufacturer's configuration software and the Wireless Zero Configuration service built into Windows XP Service Pack 2. For details and troubleshooting steps, see the following Web pages:

```
http://support.microsoft.com/default.aspx?scid=kb;
en-us;871122&Product=windowsxpsp2
```

```
http://support.microsoft.com/default.aspx?scid=kb;
en-us;870702&Product=windowsxpsp2
```

The Most Common Network Problem

Prior to Service Pack 2, the most common problem that prevented computers in a local network from communicating with one another was putting up a firewall between the two computers. You had to disable the firewall on some network connections to get the computers to communicate.

In Service Pack 2, it's "normal" to have a firewall on every icon in your Network Connections folder. But, you have to make sure File and Printer Sharing is selected on the Exceptions tab of each network connection folder.

To do that, you right-click an icon in Network Connections and choose Properties, and then click the Advanced tab in the Properties dialog box. Then, click the Settings button under Windows Firewall, leave the firewall On, click the Exceptions tab, select (check) File and Printer Sharing, and click OK in each open dialog box.

Troubleshooting a Bluetooth network

If you've set up a Bluetooth personal area network, first try the simple troubleshooting approach described in Chapter 51. When you're connecting two PCs, it's confusing to think in terms of one device discovering the other, and one device connecting to the other. Sometimes you just have to keep turn on discovery on both machine and keep trying the Connect button until the two computers finally get in sync.

If your Bluetooth network or devices were working prior to installing Service Pack 2 and have since then lost connectivity, you may need to change some settings or make some changes in the registry. For details, see the following Web page:

```
http://support.microsoft.com/default.aspx?scid=kb;en-us;883258&Product=
windowsxpsp2
```

✦   ✦   ✦

Upgrading to Windows XP

If you purchased your PC with Windows XP already installed, you need to hang a U-turn. There's nothing in the Appendix for you. Go straight to the introduction, or Chapter 1, at the start of this book, and forget all about this appendix.

If you purchased an upgrade version of Windows XP to replace your current version of Windows, and you haven't yet installed that upgrade, this is the place to be. To tell you the truth, you really don't have to read this entire appendix to install your upgrade. You really just have to do this:

1. Insert the CD that came with your Windows XP Upgrade into your computer's CD drive and wait a few seconds.

2. Follow the instructions that appear on the screen to install XP by upgrading your current version of Windows.

When the installation is complete, remove the new CD from your CD-ROM drive, put it someplace safe, and ignore the rest of this appendix. If these two steps don't quite get the job done, please read on.

Windows XP System Requirements

Windows XP requires a bit more hardware horsepower than the old 16-bit versions like Windows 98 and ME. The more hardware capability you have, the better XP will run. The absolute minimum hardware requirements are as follows:

+ 128 MB of RAM (though 256 MB is more like it)

+ A 233-megahertz (MHz) Pentium/Celeron or equivalent microprocessor

+ A 2-GB or larger hard disk with at least 650MB free space available

+ A VGA or better monitor

+ A keyboard

+ A mouse or similar pointing device

+ A CD-ROM or DVD drive

Preinstallation Housekeeping

If you've been using your PC for a while with an earlier version of Windows, you'll want to do some things before you begin your upgrade:

✦ If your computer has any time-out features, such as the power-down features found on some portable PCs, disable those features now.

✦ If you have an antivirus program handy, run it now to check for, and delete, dormant viruses that may still be lurking on your hard disk.

✦ Disable your antivirus software after you've run the check. Leave it disabled until after you've completed the upgrade.

✦ Make sure that any external devices (printers, modems, external disk drives, and so on) are connected and turned on so that Windows XP can detect them during installation.

✦ If at all possible, back up the entire hard disk at this point. At the very least, jot down all the information you need to connect to your Internet account. Back up all your documents, e-mail messages, names and addresses, and anything else you'll need after you complete the upgrade.

I realize that few people outside the corporate world have a means of backing up their entire hard disk. But you should be able to at least back up documents, e-mail messages, names and addresses, and so forth.

Note   See Chapter 18 for some general pointers on backing up documents.

Installing Windows XP

To upgrade an existing version of Windows, start your computer normally. You'd do well to restart the computer and get to a clean desktop with no open program windows or dialog boxes. Then, put the Windows XP CD in your CD-ROM drive and wait for the Welcome screen to open. If nothing appears on the screen within a minute or so, follow these steps:

1. Open My Computer on your desktop.

2. Open the icon for your CD-ROM drive. If the Welcome screen opens, skip the next step.

3. Click (or double-click) the Setup (or setup.exe) file on the CD.

By now, you should definitely see on your screen some options for Installing Windows XP. To get things rolling:

1. Choose the **Install Microsoft Windows XP** option.

2. When the Welcome to Windows Setup Wizard opens, choose **Upgrade (Recommended)** from the Installation Type drop-down list, and then click Next.

The installation procedure will begin. You might notice that the screen goes blank once in a while during the installation. Don't be alarmed; that's normal. If the screen goes blank for a long time, try moving the mouse around a bit to bring it back. From here on out, you can just follow the instructions on the screen.

Installation options

The exact procedure from this point on will vary a bit, depending on whether you're installing the Professional Edition or Home (Personal) Edition. Also, the specific hardware that's connected to your computer will affect the information that the setup procedure requests. Each request is largely self-explanatory, but here's a summary of the items you're likely to encounter along the way.

✦ **Regional and Language Options:** Choose your preferred location and keyboard layout.

✦ **Name and Organization:** Type your complete name and business name (if any).

✦ **Product Key:** Type the product key. You should be able to find it on the sleeve in which the Windows XP CD-ROM was delivered.

✦ **Computer name and Administrator Password:** (Professional Edition) Enter any name you wish to identify this computer, and enter a password. You'll need to enter the password twice to verify that you typed it as intended the first time.

✦ **Modem Dialing Information:** If you computer has a modem, choose the country you're in and enter the area code you're in now. If you're in an office that requires dialing some number to access an outside line, enter that number. If your system uses the older "pulse" dialing tone, as opposed to touch tone, choose Pulse dialing.

✦ **Date and Time Settings:** Set the date and current time; choose your time zone, and decide whether or not you want Windows to automatically adjust the time for daylight savings changes.

✦ **Network Settings:** Unless you're a network administrator who needs to customize networking capabilities on this computer, choose Typical Settings.

✦ **Workgroup or Computer Domain:** A workgroup is a collection of computers connected together in a local area network (LAN). If you've already set up a network and want this computer to be a member of an existing workgroup, choose No and enter the name of the workgroup to which this computer will belong. If this is a standalone computer, or you haven't set up a network yet, you can just select the suggested name, MSHOME or WORKGROUP. If this computer will be a member of a corporate domain, choose Yes and enter the name of the domain to which this computer will belong.

The Setup Wizard

When the installation is complete, the computer will reboot one more time, and you'll be taken to a final setup wizard. You'll be asked how you want to connect to the Internet:

✦ **DSL or Cable Modem:** Select this option if this computer is directly connected to a cable modem or DSL modem that provides access to the Internet.

✦ **Local Area Network:** Select this option if this computer is a member of a LAN and some other computer on the network shares its Internet connection with other LAN members.

✦ **Telephone Modem:** Select this option if this computer has an internal modem or is directly connected to an external modem, that provides Internet access through a standard (non-DSL) telephone line.

If you don't have an Internet connection at the moment but plan to get one, just choose whichever option best describes how you think you will connect. Don't worry, there's no big commitment here. You can make whatever kind of connection you want in the future.

If you connect through a LAN or broadband device (for example, cable or DSL), you'll be asked about IP (Internet Protocol) and DNS (Domain Name Service) addresses. The settings you enter must match the settings provided by your Internet service provider (ISP). Many ISPs automatically assign IP and DNS settings. So, if in doubt, you can select the options to obtain that information automatically.

Product activation

The wizard then asks that you activate your copy of Windows. If you have an Internet connection already, on a modem that's connected to a phone line, you can choose Yes . . . and activate now. Otherwise, select No to activate the connection later.

Getting online

If your computer has a modem, you'll be given the option to set up your existing account information, as provided by your ISP, or set up a new account from scratch. You'll want to keep your current ISP, unless you've previously set up an account with another.

Sharing the computer

If more than one person will be using the computer, you can choose to give each person his or her own user account. Doing so will allow each person to have a private My Documents folder, desktop, Internet favorites, e-mail address, and so forth.

If you're not so sure about the user account business, you can skip it for now. You can create user accounts at any time by referring to Chapter 7 in this book.

Getting Service Pack 2

When you've finished the final setup phase, click the Finish button. Whether or not you get all the Service Pack 2 features as part of your installation depends on the version you installed. To get those features you'll need to visit the Windows Update site at www.WindowsUpdate.com and Express download the service pack.

Note   See Chapter 1 for general information on Service Pack 2. See Chapter 27 for information on automatic updates.

Reenabling old startup programs

If you upgrade from an earlier version of Windows, you may discover that some of the programs that used to start automatically on your computer don't do so after you've installed Windows XP. You can follow these steps to get those programs to start automatically again in the future:

1. Click the **Start** button, choose **Run**, and type **msconfig**, and then click **OK**.

2. In the System Configuration Utility that opens, click the **Startup** tab.

3. To enable all previous auto-start programs, click the **Enable All** button. Optionally, select (check) only those programs you want to auto-start.

4. Click **OK**.

5. Click the Start button, and choose **Turn Off Computer** ➪ **Restart**.

> **Note** If you don't see a Run option on the right side of your Start menu, see "Personalizing Your Start Menu" in Chapter 6 to add that option.

Windows XP should restart with the programs from your previous version of Windows open and running.

✦   ✦   ✦

Installing XP on a New System

If you've just built a new computer from scratch, or if you've replaced your old drive C: with a new hard drive, you won't be able to upgrade to Windows XP. In fact, you probably won't be able to boot the computer at all, because the hard drive won't contain an operating system from which you can boot the system. You'll have to do a *clean install.*

You can also opt to do a clean install even if you already have a version of Windows installed on the hard drive. However, you must realize that doing so is *very* serious business. When you do a clean install you wipe out everything on your hard disk. And I do mean *everything*—all programs, documents, settings, Internet account information—everything. And there's no getting *any* of that stuff back. Just to make sure nobody misses this important fact, let me say it with a big caution icon:

Caution　The procedures described in this chapter are for advanced users only. You should know your hardware, your system's BIOS setup, all your Internet account information, how to export, backup, and restore messages, contacts, Favorites and the like, and how to find technical information about your hardware components on your own, before attempting any of the techniques described in this chapters. Don't confuse a "clean install" with a "clean boot" (the latter is described under "Performing a clean boot" in Chapter 54).

Gearing Up for a Clean Install

Most experts prefer to do a clean install when they upgrade to a new version of Windows, largely because it gets everything off to a clean start. Besides, it's a great excuse for upgrading to a bigger and faster hard drive. You can use your original hard drive as a second hard disk, and easily transfer documents from that drive to the new drive after you've installed Windows XP on the new drive. However, you'll still need to reinstall all of your programs and redo all your settings after you complete the installation.

Caution　If you upgrade a significant amount of hardware, especially the motherboard and processor, Microsoft Products Activation (MPA) may prevent you from reinstalling programs that you activated on the old hardware. Contact Microsoft about reactivating MPA via `http://support.microsoft.com` before you upgrade your hardware.

Back up all your Data

If you intend to keep your existing C: as the C: drive after the clean install, it's important that you understand that you will permanently lose everything on that drive during the clean install. Therefore you should:

✦ Write down all of your Internet Connection data so you can reestablish your account after the clean install.

✦ Backup or export all your e-mail messages, names and addresses, Favorites, and anything else you'll want after the clean install, so that you can recover them after the clean install. Remember, whatever you don't save will be lost forever. No ifs, ands, or buts about it.

✦ Back up all of your documents, because each and everyone one of them will be wiped out along with Windows and all your programs.

Caution A clean install permanently erases everything on your hard drive, which is basically everything that's "in your computer." Users who do not fully understand the ramifications of this should not attempt to do a clean install of Windows XP or any other operating system. Nobody on the planet can help you get back that which you've lost if you fail to heed this advice.

If Windows XP is currently installed on the C: drive you intend to reuse, you can use the Files and Settings Transfer Wizard to back up all your documents and settings. Ideally, you want to back up the data to another computer in the network. The wizard allows you to back up to floppies or to another computer using Direct Cable Connection. However, floppies are out of the question for backing up much of anything, and getting Direct Cable Connection to work at all is like pulling teeth from an angry alligator. Not fun, and not likely to be a successful undertaking.

Note See Chapter 18 for some general pointers on backing up documents, settings, messages, and contacts.

Given that hard drives are so inexpensive these days, it almost seems a shame *not* to start the clean install from a new hard drive. You don't have to worry about losing any data from the old drive is you clean-install XP to a new drive.

Make sure that you can boot from a CD

By far the easiest way to do a clean install on a new drive is to boot from the Windows XP CD. You'll want to make sure that you *can* do this before you do anything inside the computer. Most CDs aren't bootable, so you'll need to insert the Windows CD into the drive and restart the computer. Watch for the *Press any key to boot from CD* countdown, and tap the spacebar before the countdown runs out.

If you see the message *Setup is inspecting your hardware configuration*, then you know you can boot from a CD. Press Ctrl+Alt+Del to reboot before setup actually starts, and remove the CD from the drive while the system is rebooting. Then, shut down the PC altogether.

If you can't boot the system from the Windows CD, you'll need to adjust your BIOS settings. Again, this isn't something I can tell you how to do specifically, because it depends on your system's BIOS. But the usual scenario is to press F2 or Del as the computer is starting up to get to your BIOS setup. Once you get into the BIOS settings, make sure that booting from the CD drive is enabled, and that the CD drive has a higher priority that the hard drive.

After you change the BIOS settings, put the Windows CD back in the CD drive, save your BIOS settings, and exit so that the computer reboots again. If you got it right, you should see the *Setup is inspecting your hardware configuration* message again on restart, indicating that you've successfully booted form the CD. Cancel that startup as well, by pressing Ctrl+Alt+Del, and remove the CD from the drive before the computer gets another chance to boot from the CD.

Installing a new C: drive

If you're upgrading your C: drive along with your version of Windows, Step 1 is to hide existing hard drives from the system altogether so that the new drive appears, to the BIOS, to be the only hard drive in the system. Simply disconnecting the power and interface plugs from the backs of the drives will do the trick.

Caution   Never do anything inside your system case while the computer is turned on, or even plugged into a power outlet. Wear an antistatic wrist strap to prevent static discharge from wiping out components and the warranties that go with them!

The next step involves getting the new drive installed to the point where it's at least recognized by the BIOS. I can't tell you how to do that because the procedure varies from one drive manufacturer to the next. You must follow the instructions that came with the drive, or the instructions on the drive manufacturer's Web site, to get to the point where the system recognizes that drive at startup.

Chances are the drive manufacturer's instructions will include steps to partition and format the drive. You should probably do so, even if you intend to repartition and reformat the drive during the Windows XP clean installation. You still won't be able to boot from the drive. But at least the drive will be recognized as C: during the Windows installation.

Doing the clean install

When you feel confident that you'll be able to get back everything you want from your hard drive, you're ready to start the clean install. Put the Windows CD in the CD drive and shut down the computer. Then, restart the computer, and boot from the CD. The setup program will run in a text-only mode. Watch the highlighted bar along the bottom of the screen for opportunities to install specialized drivers. If you're installing to a standard IDE drive, you shouldn't need to install any special drivers.

Note   I clean-installed XP Professional on a brand new SATA (Serial ATA) drive with no significant problems. I didn't need to install any special drivers to pull this off. However, I was using a motherboard with built-in SATA ports. I can't say with any certainty that the same would be true for a PCI SATA adapter.

Formatting partitions

Before the actual installation procedure begins, you'll be give the opportunity to partition the drive and to format partitions. You can delete existing partitions, create new partitions within the available space, and size each partition. Note that whichever partition you specify as the primary partition will be the boot partition, drive C:.

You'll also be given the following options for formatting each partition:

✦ Format the partition by using the NTFS file system (Quick)

✦ Format the partition by using the FAT file system (Quick)

✦ Format the partition by using the NTFS file system

✦ Format the partition by using the FAT file system

✦ Leave the current file system intact (no changes)

Unless you have some compelling reason to use FAT, such as dual-booting with Windows 98 (Heaven forbid), you should format all partitions using NTFS. The "Quick" options are definitely much quicker than the "regular" formatting options. However, a Quick option will not scan the volume for bad sectors. Fixing bad sectors before you install Windows is really your best bet—hough you can scan a drive for bad sectors at any time using the Check Now button on the Tools tab of the drive's Properties dialog box.

Note See Chapter 56 for more information on the Check Now button. Optionally, if you're familiar with the command prompt you can use the `chkdsk /r` command. However, the scan will take just as long whether you do it during the clean install, after the install, using the Check Now button, or the chkdsk button.

The rest of the installation

Once you get past the partitioning and formatting options, and the installation procedure has installed enough files on the hard drive to boot from the hard drive, Windows will reboot the system. At that point, you'll be taken to the more traditional graphical installation procedure described in Appendix A. I'll take the liberty of assuming that, since you were able to follow along in this chapter, the few remaining prompts and questions posed by the installation procedure will be self-explanatory for you.

Professional Edition Features

The main differences between Windows XP Home Edition and Professional Edition center around corporate domain networks. In fact, it may have been more accurate for Microsoft to call the latter Windows XP Corporate Edition. This Appendix briefly lists features that are unique to Windows XP Professional Edition.

Internet Information Services (IIS)

Internet Information Services (IIS) allows Windows XP Professional to act as a personal Web server or a server on a local intranet. The version of IIS that comes with XP Professional is limited to 10 simultaneous user connections. So, you wouldn't use it publish a Web site to the Internet. You need the full-blown version of IIS found in Windows Server products for that kind of publishing.

Most people use XP Professional IIS to build and test a Web site prior to moving the site to a "real" Web server. By a "real" Web server I mean one that has a URL and is accessible to anybody with an Internet connection. Few people actually build their own Web servers though. Most just rent space from a Web presence provider (WPP) such as WinSave (`www.winsave.com`), and upload pages from their own computer to the server.

If you installed Windows XP yourself, IIS may, or may not, already be installed. If it's already installed, you should be able to type the URL `http://localhost` into Internet Explorer, press Enter, and actually get a page rather than an error message. If IIS isn't installed, you'll likely need your original Microsoft Windows XP Professional Edition CD to install it. And you'll need to follow these steps to install IIS:

1. Click the **Start** button, and choose **Control Panel**.

2. Open the **Add or Remove Programs** category or icon.

3. Click on **Add/Remove Windows Components** in the left column.

4. Choose (check) **Internet Information Services (IIS)** as in Figure C-1.

5. Optionally, click the Details button, and specify subcomponents you need.

Figure C-1: IIS option selected in the Windows Components Wizard

6. Click **Next>**, and follow the on-screen instructions.

7. Click **Finish**.

8. Close the Add or Remove Programs window, and Control Panel.

For information on functional chances to IIS in Windows XP Service Pack 2 see www.microsoft.com/technet/prodtechnol/winxppro/maintain/sp2brows.mspx.

Domain Networking

The domain networking features of Windows XP center around corporate domain networks. A domain is a local network with a Windows XP Server computer playing the role of a *domain controller*. The domain controller provides a centralized location for managing access to resources on the corporate network. Key features of Windows XP Professional Edition that allow it to act as a client on a domain network include:

Network Administrators who need access to the Access Control Lists can disable the *Use simplified file sharing* option in the Folder Options dialog box (see Chapter 12). Doing so reveals access control options on file and folder Properties sheets familiar to professional network administrators (see Figure C-2).

Tip

To join a Professional XP Edition computer to a domain, right-click My Computer and choose Properties. Click the Computer Name tab, and then click the Network ID button.

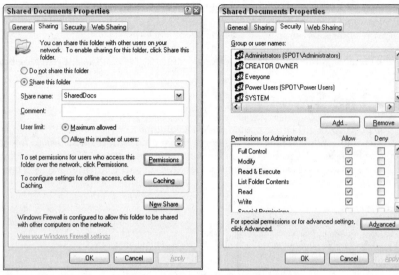

Figure C-2: Windows XP Professional Edition access control

Remote Desktop Connection

Remote Desktop allows you to operate your Windows XP Professional PC remotely across a dial-up connection, local area network, or virtual private network (VPN) connection. Options for enabling and configuring Remote Desktop are all on the Remote tab in the System Properties dialog box (see Figure C-3). You can open System Properties from Control Panel or by right-clicking your My Computer icon and choosing Properties.

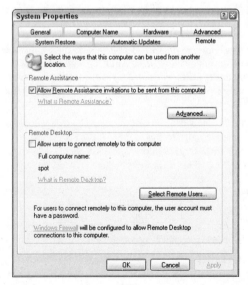

Figure C-3: Remote tab in System Properties dialog box

The local computer accessing the Remote Desktop computer can be running Windows XP Home or Professional Edition, Windows 2000, NT 4.0, or ME, 98, 98 Second Edition, or 95. To configure a Windows XP Home Edition as the client, click the Start button and choose All Programs ⇨ Accessories ⇨ Communications ⇨ Remote Desktop Connection. If only a portion of the dialog box opens, click the Options>> button to reveal the entire dialog box.

Encrypting File System (EFS)

The Encrypting File System (EFS), available on NTFS volumes in Windows XP Professional Edition, encodes information in files and folders to prevent unauthorized access to the contents. To apply EFS, select the icon(s) of the files or folders you want to encrypt and choose Properties. Then, click the Advanced button to open the Advanced Attributes dialog box shown in Figure C-4.

Figure C-4: Advanced Attributes dialog box

Note   You can either compress or encrypt an object, but not both. In XP Home Edition, the Encrypt option is disabled.

To encrypt the selected object(s), choose the *Encrypt contents to secure data* checkbox and click OK. If you're encrypting a folder that already contains files, you'll be asked for confirmation. You'll also be given the option to apply encryption to the folder, subfolders, and files. If you choose No, encryption will be applied only to new files you add to the folder. If you choose Yes, all items within the folder will also be encrypted.

Universal Shortcut Keys

Most of the shortcut keys listed in this Appendix are universal in the sense that they work the same in all programs. Some items, however, are unique to specific programs. Keep in mind that whenever you view a menu on a program's menu bar, items that support shortcut keys will show the appropriate key to the right of the item, as in the example shown in Figure D-1 — for example, Ctrl+Z for Undo, Ctrl+X for Cut, Del for Clear Contents, and so forth.

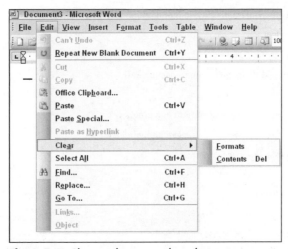

Figure D-1: Shortcut keys on a drop-down menu

A disabled (dimmed) menu command will also show a dimmed shortcut key. But that just means the menu command isn't relevant at the moment. The shortcut key will work whenever the situation allows it. For example, Cut and Copy on the Microsoft Word Edit menu in the figure are enabled only after you select text or a picture in the document. Once you select an item, you can use either the menu or the shortcut key to copy or cut the selected item.

Keyboard shortcuts that use ⊞ work only on keyboards that have that key, such as the Microsoft Natural Keyboard.

General Keyboard Shortcuts

Key	Description
←	Open the next menu to the left, or close a submenu
→	Open the next menu to the right, or open a submenu
↓	Move down to next menu item
↑	Move up to previous menu item
ALT+ENTER	View selected item's properties
ALT+ESC	Cycle through open programs
ALT+F4	Close the active window
ALT+SPACEBAR	Open the system menu for the active window
ALT+TAB	Switch between the open program windows
ALT+*letter*	Display menu or choose menu option showing underlined *letter*
CTRL+A	Select all
CTRL+C	Copy to clipboard
CTRL+*drag*	Copy the dragged item to destination
CTRL+ESC	Open the Start menu
CTRL+F4	Close the active document in a program
CTRL+SHIFT+*drag*	Create a shortcut to dragged item at destination
CTRL+V	Paste clipboard contents
CTRL+X	Cut to clipboard
CTRL+Z	Undo last action
DEL	Delete selected item(s)
ENTER	Choose highlighted menu item
ESC	Cancel the current task or close menu without selecting
F10 key	Open menu bar in the active program
F2 key	Rename the selected item(s)
F3	Search for a file or a folder
F4 key	Display the Address bar list in Windows Explorer
F5 key	Refresh the active window
F6 key	Cycle through open items in a program window or the desktop
SHIFT while inserting CD	Prevent the CD from auto-playing or auto-starting
SHIFT+DEL	Permanently delete selected item(s) without placing in Recycle Bin
SHIFT+F10	Display the shortcut menu for the selected item

Text Navigation and Editing Shortcuts

Key	Description
↓	Move cursor down one line
←	Move cursor left one character
→	Move cursor right one character
↑	Move cursor up one line
BACKSPACE	Delete character to left of cursor
CTRL+↓	Move cursor to start of next paragraph
CTRL+↑	Move cursor to start of previous paragraph
CTRL+←	Move cursor to start of previous word
CTRL+→	Move cursor start of next word
CTRL+A	Select all
CTRL+C	Copy to clipboard
CTRL+*drag*	Copy the selected text to destination
CTRL+SHIFT+↓	Select to end of paragraph
CTRL+SHIFT+→	Select to end of word
CTRL+SHIFT+←	Select to beginning of word
CTRL+SHIFT+↑	Select to beginning of paragraph
CTRL+SHIFT+END	Select to end of document
CTRL+SHIFT+HOME	Select to top of document
CTRL+V	Paste clipboard contents to cursor position
CTRL+X	Cut to clipboard
CTRL+Z	Undo last action
DEL	Delete selected text or character at cursor
ESC	Cancel the current task
SHIFT+↑	Select to character in line above
SHIFT+↓	Select to character in line below
SHIFT+←	Select character to left
SHIFT+→	Select character to right
SHIFT+Click	Select from cursor to here
SHIFT+END	Select to end of line
SHIFT+HOME	Select to beginning of line
SHIFT+PAGE DOWN	Select text down one screen
SHIFT+PAGE UP	Select text up one screen

Accessibility Keyboard Shortcuts

Key	Description
⊞ +U	Open Utility Manager
LEFT ALT+LEFT SHIFT+NUM LOCK	Switch the MouseKeys either on or off
LEFT ALT+LEFT SHIFT+PRINT SCREEN	Switch High Contrast either on or off
NUM LOCK for five seconds	Switch the ToggleKeys either on or off
RIGHT SHIFT for eight seconds	Switch FilterKeys either on or off
SHIFT five times	Switch the StickyKeys either on or off

Dialog Box Keyboard Shortcuts

Key	Description
ALT+ *letter*	Choose option with underlined *letter*
Arrow keys	Select a button if the active option is a group of option buttons
BACKSPACE	Open a folder one level up if a folder is selected in the Save As or Open dialog box
CTRL+SHIFT+TAB	Go to previous tab
CTRL+TAB	Go to next tab
ENTER	Same as clicking OK
ESC	Same as clicking Cancel
F1 key	Help
F4 key	Display the items in the active list
SHIFT+TAB	Move to previous option
SPACEBAR	Select or clear the checkbox
TAB	Move to next option

Windows Explorer Keyboard Shortcuts

Key	Description
- on numeric keypad	Collapse the selected folder
* on numeric keypad	Display all of the subfolders under selected folder
←	Select or collapse parent folder
→	Expand current folder or move to next subfolder
+ on numeric keypad	Display the contents of the selected folder
END	Display the bottom of the active window
HOME	Display the top of the active window
SHIFT+Double-Click	Open selected folder in new instance

Microsoft Internet Explorer Shortcuts

Key	Description
CTRL+B	Open the Organize Favorites dialog box
CTRL+E	Open the Search bar
CTRL+F	Start the Find utility
CTRL+H	Open the History bar
CTRL+I	Open the Favorites bar
CTRL+L	Open the Open dialog box
CTRL+N	Start another instance of the browser with the same Web address
CTRL+O	Open the Open dialog box
CTRL+P	Open the Print dialog box
CTRL+R	Refresh the current Web page
CTRL+W	Close the current window

Microsoft Natural Keyboard Shortcuts

Key	Description
⊞	Display or hide the Start menu
⊞+ L	Lock the keyboard
⊞+BREAK	Display the System Properties dialog box
⊞+D	Display the desktop
⊞+E	Open My Computer
⊞+F	Search for a file or a folder
⊞+F1	Display Windows Help
⊞+M	Minimize all of the windows
⊞+R	Open the Run dialog box
⊞+SHIFT+M	Restore the minimized windows
⊞+U	Open Utility Manager
CTRL+⊞+F	Search for computers

Speech Recognition/Language Shortcuts

Key	Description
⊞+C	Correct a dictated word
⊞+H	Turn handwriting on/off
⊞+T	Switch between Dictation and Voice Command
⊞+V	Turn microphone on/off
ALT+~	Turn Japanese keyboard on/off
CTRL+SHIFT or left ALT+SHIFT	Switch between keyboard layouts
CTRL+SPACEBAR	Turn Chinese keyboard on/off
Right ALT	Turn Korean keyboard on/off

Character Map Shortcut Keys

Key	Description
↑	Move up one row
↓	Move down one row
←	Move to the left or to the end of the previous line
→	Move to the right or to the beginning of the next line
CTRL+END	Move to the last character
CTRL+HOME	Move to the first character
END	Move to the end of the line
HOME	Move to the beginning of the line
PAGE DOWN	Move down one screen at a time
PAGE UP	Move up one screen at a time
SPACEBAR	Switch between Enlarged and Normal mode

✦　　✦　　✦

Index

SYMBOLS & NUMERICS

Continued

Continued

Continued

Q

quality
  for burning CDs, 740
  buying CDs and, 327
  for copying songs to portable players, 745
  of pictures, 683–684
  printer settings, 415–416, 422
  for ripping music CDs, 717–718
  video capture settings, 787–789
  video size and file size comparisons for 1-minute
    movie, 821
question mark (?)
  for help with DOS commands (/?), 319
  for unknown devices in Device Manager, 938
Quick Launch toolbar
  adding shortcut icons, 355–356
  defined, 15
  illustrated, 14
  Show Desktop button, 26, 102–103, 348
  showing or hiding buttons, 32, 102–103
  showing or hiding the toolbar, 31–32, 102, 125, 127
  starting programs from, 23
quitting. See closing
quotation marks (") for phrase queries, 381

R

radio broadcasts online, 748
radio drivers for Bluetooth devices, 907
RAID controller, disabling, 947
RAM (random access memory). See memory
raster fonts, 435
Reader for e-books (Microsoft), 207–208, 242
reading e-mail (Outlook Express), 589–591, 606
README files, 851
read-only files, 316–317, 333, 1058
Really Simple Syndication (RSS) feed or Reader, 653
rebooting your computer
  clean boot, 956
  hung computer, 884
  normal process, 39, 985
rebuilding the media library (Windows Media Player),
    837–838
rec newsgroups, 650. See also newsgroups
recovering. See restoring; Undo command
RecoverMyFiles program, 309
Recovery Console, 532, 956–957
Recycle Bin
  emptying (deleting files permanently), 309
  Norton Protected, 100–101
  overview, 20–21, 307–308
  restoring accidentally deleted files, 308

refresh rates
  for monitors, 117
  for Web pages, 573–574
regedit command, 1000
registering with .NET Passport, 614–615
registry
  adding a new value, 1003
  backing up, 1000
  backing up before making changes, 1001
  cleaning up Add or Remove Programs, 896,
    1004–1005
  creating a subkey, 1001
  deleting a subkey, 1003
  enabling Task Manager, 1008
  hives, 996–997
  key values, 996
  modifying key values, 1002–1003
  need for working with, 991–992
  numbering systems, 997–1000
  organization of, 993–997
  overview, 991–993, 1005–1006
  preventing Welcome screen, 239
  renaming a subkey, 1001
  restoring Search Results folder, 404–405
  standard root keys and subkeys, 993–995
  using the Registry Editor, 1001–1003
  viewing key values, 1001
  working example, 992–993
Registry Editor
  adding a new value, 1003
  backing up before making changes, 1001
  backing up the registry, 1000
  creating a subkey, 1001
  deleting a subkey, 1003
  modifying key values, 1002–1003
  opening, 1000
  overview, 1001
  renaming a subkey, 1001
  viewing key values, 1001
reinstalling plug-and-play devices, 949
reinstalling Windows XP, avoiding, 934
relational operators for searches, 383
Remote Assistance (Windows Messenger)
  ending a session, 632
  overview, 630–631
  starting a session, 631
  unblocking, 482, 630
  won't start after installing SP2, 673–674
Remote Desktop, 1087–1088
Removable Disk Properties dialog box
  Quality tab, 745
  Synchronize tab, 744–745

Continued

Continued

Continued

Continued

Continued